ENCYCLOPEDIA OF
AMERICAN
CULTURAL &
INTELLECTUAL
HISTORY

ADVISORY BOARD

ENCYCLOPEDIA OF
AMERICAN
CULTURAL &
INTELLECTUAL
HISTORY

VOLUME III

MARY KUPIEC CAYTON · PETER W. WILLIAMS
EDITORS

Charles Scribner's Sons
an imprint of the Gale Group
New York • Detroit • San Francisco • London • Boston • Woodbridge, CT

Charles Scribner's Sons
1633 Broadway
New York, New York 10019

1 3 5 7 9 11 13 15 17 19 20 18 16 14 12 10 8 6 4 2

Printed in the United States of America

The paper used in this publication meets the requirements of ANSI/NISO Z39.48–1992 (Permanence of Paper).

Library of Congress Cataloging-in-Publication Data

Encyclopedia of American cultural and intellectual history / Mary Kupiec Cayton, Peter W. Williams, editors.
 p. cm.
 Includes bibliographical references and index.
 ISBN 0-684-80561-8 (set : alk. paper) — ISBN 0-684-80558-8 (v. 1 : alk. paper) — ISBN 0-684-80559-6 (v. 2 : alk. paper) — ISBN 0-684-80560-X (v. 3 : alk. paper)
 1. United States—Civilization—Encyclopedias.   2. United States—Intellectual life—Encyclopedias.   I. Cayton, Mary Kupiec.   II. Williams, Peter W.

E169.1 .E624 2001
973′.03—dc21

2001020005

CONTENTS OF THIS VOLUME

CONTENTS OF OTHER VOLUMES

Part 10 Geography and Cultural Centers

BROAD GEOGRAPHICAL CONSTRUCTS

MAJOR CULTURAL REGIONS

URBAN CLUSTERS AND OTHER CULTURAL UNITS

Part 11 Nature, Human Nature, and the Supernatural

Part 12 The Political Order

ALPHABETICAL TABLE OF CONTENTS

Essay titles have been simplified to make a useful overview.
See index in volume 3 for a full analytical breakdown.

ENCYCLOPEDIA OF
AMERICAN
CULTURAL &
INTELLECTUAL
HISTORY

Part 13

THE ECONOMIC ORDER

SUCCESS

Susan Schulten

The meaning of success is intertwined with that of America itself and is as charged as ideas of "independence," "freedom," or "equality." One can understand why this is so by asking how ministers, philosophers, reformers, businessmen, and writers defined and redefined success in American life. The very decision to include "success" in this encyclopedia is significant. Here we find an entry for "success" but none for "failure," indicating that American history is replete with models, discussions, and invocations of the former, but is relatively silent on the latter. Furthermore, its inclusion under the heading "Economic Order" suggests that—at least in the American context—the word has come to be understood primarily in economic terms, despite frequent protestations to the contrary.

THE PURITAN CONTEXT

Sailing across the Atlantic on the *Arbella*, John Winthrop delivered to his fellow Puritans a vision of their future in the lay sermon, "A Modell of Christian Charity" (1630). For Winthrop, economic differences between men reflected God's will and design and were not to be taken as moral indicators: "noe man is made more honourable then another or more wealth etc., out of any perticuler or singuler respect to himselfe but for the glory of his Creator and the Common good of the Creature, Man" (Miller and Johnson, vol. 1, pp. 195–196). Furthermore, to find oneself blessed with abundance was to be charged with the duties that this blessing carried. Success was a gift from God and was to be exercised in turn to glorify him.

Similarly, Cotton Mather asked the faithful to remember that the "Hand of God" operated in economic gains as well as losses and to consider "a Wise, and a just God as the First Cause of all" (Grob and Beck, p. 67). Losses were signs that all was not right, even taken as signals to repent. Mather insisted that "All that we have, is but a Loan from the Great God unto us," and that any material gains were to be used in pious ways, such as paying taxes, lending for the development of other trades, relieving the indigent, and forgiving debts (p. 68). Mather's understanding of success in worldly pursuits was complex. He stressed that every Puritan was directed to serve Christ and save his own soul, but he also acknowledged the importance of finding a useful occupation in this life. As Mather wrote, each man is given two oars, the calling to serve God and the calling to find a useful occupation, and both are needed to row toward heaven. For the Puritans, man was not called to the contemplative or monastic existence, but rather to an active life that engaged directly with work in order to serve God. Men were to follow their occupations with industry, diligence, discretion, honesty, contentment, and piety.

Mather's words have drawn speculation among modern scholars about the relationship between Puritanism and capitalism, which together have gone a long way toward shaping American understandings of success. In the early twentieth century, Max Weber asked how the "lust for gain," which had long been considered antisocial and immoral in western Christianity, came to be so quickly approved by Puritan culture. The answer, he argued, came in the Protestant revolutions, which braced the new parvenus of the economic order for their battle against feudal structures. The pursuit of wealth was made a duty, which in turn gave work in the words of historian R. H. Tawney, "a halo of sanctification."

Weber suggested, if not a causal relationship between Protestantism and capitalism, at least an affinity in the style of life that each brought. The idea of the Puritan occupational "calling"—also the product of the Protestant Reformation—nicely coincided with the demands of an incipient capitalist order, which demanded a diligent, conscientious, and routinized approach to work. Mather's own words bear this relationship out:

as a man is *Impious* towards God, if he be without a *Calling*, so he is *Unrighteous* towards his *Family*, toward his *Neighbourhood*, toward the *Commonwealth*, if he follow no *Calling* among them. . . . Ordinarily no man does *Nothing*: If men have *nothing* to do, they'l soon do *Too much*; do what they *ought not*" (Rischin, p. 24).

Yet if this sounds like a modern prescription for success, it should be remembered that Mather and the Puritans were highly critical of unrestrained economic pursuits and worried incessantly that worldly occupational callings might eclipse the community's greater goal, the glorification of God. Worldly "success" could never be considered a transparent reflection of God's grace or salvation.

EIGHTEENTH-CENTURY DEVELOPMENTS

To Weber, the "calling" helped transform economic self-interest from a vice into a virtue, a way to demonstrate spiritual as well as economic strength. Whether this thesis accurately represents seventeenth-century Puritans is debatable. Indeed, Weber's "work ethic" has been endlessly challenged and reformulated over the course of the twentieth century. Weber extended his analysis into the eighteenth century by focusing on Benjamin Franklin, a figure who has become almost an axiomatic illustration of individual success in America. Franklin, unlike Mather, matured in the more humanized world of the Enlightenment, which freed him from both fear and awe of God. This important distinction meant that Franklin inherited the ascetic ideals of the Puritans—industry, frugality, self-discipline—but exercised them in a more secular framework. Franklin was relatively unconcerned with the problem of sin and divine will, but retained the preoccupation with leading a moral life.

Franklin spent a good deal of time thinking and writing about success in this regard, and these writings have done much to establish his reputation as the quintessential self-made man. Through his *Autobiography* (1789) we learn that Franklin was born the fifteenth of seventeen children in Boston. When his prospects seemed limited to working as a printing apprentice to his older brother, Franklin "escaped" to Philadelphia to remake his life. His rapid rise in his adopted city of Philadelphia, first as a printer and then as a journalist, spread his name through the city and the colonies. By his own account, Franklin was entirely "on his own" in the world, and used that position to speak to other young men about their own efforts to lead virtuous lives.

In the *Autobiography*, Franklin established his understanding of morality. As he explained it, moral perfection depended upon the inculcation of good habits, not just lofty hopes. To this end, Franklin tried to inculcate a method of moral virtue, which to him was precisely the goal of success. As he explained it, "it was therefore every one's Interest to be virtuous, who wish'd to be happy even in this World" (p. 158). He laid the groundwork for this "art of virtue" by enumerating those which seemed to him the basis for all others: temperance, silence, order, resolution, frugality, industry, sincerity, justice, moderation, cleanliness, tranquility, chastity, and humility. Franklin claimed to approach each of these virtues separately as a recipe for self-improvement, embodied by his involvement in civic life. As a founding member of the Junto Club, for instance, Franklin and his contemporaries discussed ways of earning wealth and securing business success. But the Junto was also a forum for civic engagement and individual moral development, and through it the members engaged in politics, served the community, and discussed the problems of virtue. Service to others and one's own advancement were in Franklin's mind absolutely inseparable.

Franklin's name was made familiar to the colonists through his annual *Poor Richard's Almanac* (1732–1757), which remained influential for decades after it ceased publication. "The Way to Wealth," published as the preface to the final edition of the *Almanac*, was a guide to success for young men that extolled the ascetic virtues of work, savings, and self-discipline while railing against pride, laziness, poverty, and debt. Reprinted hundreds of times and translated into dozens of languages, "The Way to Wealth" along with his "The Art of Virtue" have become seminal texts in the history of American concepts of success. To Weber, these two texts exemplified the spirit of bourgeois capitalism: both stressed work and savings, which for him signified the importance of self-denial for future gain, a precondition to the development of capitalism. Franklin is all the more important for secularizing what had previously been a pietistic ideal, which liberated later generations to set aside the weight of divine judgment and focus on this worldly gain. Diligence in one's calling, frugality, and piety all became less a means to glorify God and, increasingly, manifestations of one's earthly success and worth.

Franklin has also been celebrated as a uniquely American success figure for his relatively humble origins. John G. Cawelti highlights the importance of this dimension of Franklin's character by comparing him to George Washington. The latter was

4

to contemporaries a man beyond men, while Franklin represented a more common, public, and accessible figure, one who tried his hand at a number of enterprises, succeeding at some and failing at others. Franklin was to be judged not on his appearance or his lineage, the former inelegant and the latter unimpressive, but rather on his achievements and character. The ordered hierarchy of the eighteenth century was—perhaps presaged by Franklin's own self-image—beginning to give way to a new, more fluid ideal of success in the nineteenth.

THE SELF-MADE MAN IN THE NINETEENTH CENTURY

Economic and political changes in the Early Republic—the decline of property qualifications for suffrage, the dismantling of established churches, and the decline of primogeniture and entail—all created a more fluid and less hierarchical social structure. As Alexis de Tocqueville observed, the republican emphasis on independence began to resemble a concern for individualism, reflected in the new ideal of the "self-made man." The term originated in a speech of Henry Clay on the Senate floor that defended his "American system" of internal improvements, the protective tariff, and the central bank. In an emergent market economy, this ideal of a self-made man implied the hope of social mobility. This has become one of the most enduring characteristics of American success: the idea that, regardless of origin, one has the opportunity to rise through the ranks. It is implicit in the lives of Franklin, Clay, Abraham Lincoln, and in later apostles of success in the industrial era such as P. T. Barnum, James Russell Lowell, Horatio Alger, and Andrew Carnegie.

And yet this celebration of mobility stands in utter contrast to the expansion of slavery, as well as less institutionalized forms of racial and ethnic discrimination. As a system of forced labor, slavery effectively placed African Americans squarely outside of the emerging work ethic, whether it be Weber's Protestant work ethic or Benjamin Franklin's more secularized maxims. The very fact of slavery defined blacks as unsuccessful: for them, no degree of self-discipline or hard work could possibly produce social mobility. The "self-made" African American was a legal, political, and social impossibility.

In fact, the idea of the self-made man, premised on the fact of mobility, by its very nature downplays the importance of class distinctions by suggesting that they are not rigid and can be overcome. And yet, as Michael Katz has observed, mobility only occurs when there is an unequal distribution of resources, therefore creating chances for people to both rise and fall, to both win and lose. The losing side of this story has been recovered recently by Scott Sandage, whose cultural history of failure in the nineteenth century goes a long way toward refining our understanding of success.

Sandage asks how Americans understood failure in economic, legal, and cultural terms. Like many who have focused on the history of success, Sandage agrees that the nineteenth century was pivotal. The market revolution heightened the possibilities for dramatic, catastrophic financial loss in America. The Panic of 1819, for instance, made bankruptcy a public issue for the first time in history. Furthermore, the rise of contracts in the nineteenth century meant that every man was responsible for the fortune that befell him, making mobility more a function of individual will and responsibility. By contrast, Franklin, Jefferson, and their eighteenth-century contemporaries might have explained an individual's success and failure by reference to a complex of factors, including inborn qualities, intellectual and moral cultivation, and the needs or values of society.

As Sandage explains, capitalism demanded that debts be forgiven and regulated in the interest of continuing economic activity. The subsequent development of bankruptcy legislation (to forgive economic failure) and credit agencies (to predict economic failure) changed the legal, but not the moral, context of failure. In fact, institutions such as these not only left the moral dilemma of failure unsolved, but actually intensified its moral weight by evaluating, recording, and judging individuals' economic behavior. In Sandage's words,

> Americans began to think and worry about failure not only because more of them were going bust in an expanding and perilous market, but also because the institutions of nineteenth-century capitalism created so many new opportunities for judging people by writing down stories about their lives—and for investing those life stories with new rewards and new punishments ("Deadbeats," p. 26).

Phrased in the reverse, Sandage writes that the "articulation of a distinct idea of moral obligation made both contract theory and the legal discharge of debts possible" (p. 113).

This individualization of success was also furthered by some of the more popular and accessible essays of Ralph Waldo Emerson. Part of Emerson's tremendous appeal was his ability to unite the material and spiritual aspects of American life into some kind of larger, if tenuous, whole. Success, self-improvement, and cultural development all came together in Emerson's attempt to demonstrate that the transcendent and the practical were by no means mutually exclusive. In "Wealth" (1860), Emerson lays out as his scope the ability of men to progress in life, not just to subsist, and to follow their calling, arguing that "society can never prosper, but must always be bankrupt, until every man does that which he was created to do" (p. 1003). It is the application of industry, ingenuity, and perseverance to one's earthly calling that Emerson sees as so promising, and which recalls the earlier aphorisms of Franklin. But Emerson goes further than Franklin, extolling wealth for what it enables men to do. As he explains, "To be rich is to have a ticket of admission to the masterworks and chief men of each race" (p. 994). Instead of worrying about the tension between material progress and otherworldly devotion, Emerson finds it easier to reconcile the two:

> Success consists in close appliance to the laws of the world, and, since those laws are intellectual and moral, an intellectual and moral obedience. Political Economy is as good a book wherein to read the life of man, and the ascendency of laws over all private and hostile influences, as any Bible which has come down to us. (p. 997)

Here Emerson describes the harmonious design of life. In this context, success was an undeniable goal and meant simply discovering what was self-evident in the natural world. Based on this and other writings, Michael T. Gilmore makes Emerson a transitional figure in the nineteenth century, one who began with something of a traditional Jacksonian suspicion of the market as a threat to individualism but who concluded that wealth was a precondition to autonomy and individualism. In this regard, Emerson fits his age rather well: in 1853 *Harper's New Monthly Magazine* reported that success was, by most Americans, equated with economic achievement.

SUCCESS IN THE ERA OF INDUSTRIALIZATION

The growing identification of success with individual economic achievement did not, however, erode its moral dimension. Generations of nineteenth-century schoolchildren reared on the ubiquitous McGuffey's Readers learned the close relationship between character and success. Written by Ohio schoolmaster William Holmes McGuffey, these schoolbooks sold 122 million copies, not just during their original run from 1836 to 1857, but well into the early twentieth century. McGuffey's Readers enshrined the wisdom of hard knocks for generations to come by teaching that "if at first you don't succeed, try try again," and "where there is a will, there is a way."

While McGuffey ministered to the young, an outpouring of manuals guided older generations on the possibilities of success in the industrial era. This genre was heavily influenced by the work of English writer Samuel Smiles, whose *Self Help* (1859), *Character* (1871), *Thrift* (1875), and *Duty* (1880) sold over one million copies in the United States. The work of Smiles and his American counterparts encouraged young men to make the most of opportunities where they could be found; in an effort to be accessible to all, these authors emphasized the virtue of succeeding without higher education. For the most part ignoring the fundamental changes in the structure of the market, they reaffirmed the simple virtues of honesty, frugality, industry, and self-reliance. Ironically, however, most of these manuals were written by precisely those men who had benefited from higher education rather than from the economic growth of the late century—men such as ministers, journalists, and university graduates.

These success manuals generally described the economic world as a realm of intense competition, but rarely discussed problems of inequality. Instead, they continued to invoke mobility, and replaced class divisions with a moral differentiation between success and failure. Judy Hilkey has investigated these manuals for what they reveal not just about ideas of success, but also about gender. References to character, willpower, and manhood gradually gendered success as a masculine quality; by the same token, failure became feminized, and the fear of failure could be discussed as the fear of a loss of manhood. As she argues, the Gilded Age manuals framed character and manhood not just as means to success, but as success itself.

Perhaps the most extreme variation on this theme of success as virtue came from Russell H. Conwell, a Baptist minister, philanthropist, and founder of Temple University in Philadelphia. In 1861 Conwell first proclaimed what would become his legendary message, that "to make money honestly is to preach the gospel" (pp. 20–21). He challenged his audience, "Introduce me to the people who own their homes around this great city, those beautiful homes with gardens and flowers, those magnificent homes so lovely in their art, and I will introduce you to the very best people in character as well as in enterprise" (pp. 21–22). Gone was the modesty and humility of the McGuffey maxims and the tenuous formulations of the Puritans. In Conwell's mind, the rich had become by definition honest and good—wealth had become character—and the poor personally deficient. As he insisted, "there is not a poor person in the United States who was not made poor by his own shortcomings, or by the shortcomings of someone else" (p. 23). Here the work ethic was stripped to its barest form: it was the Christian duty to get rich. Conwell's message of the "Gospel of Success" was so popular that by 1915 he had delivered it over 6,000 times.

If Conwell made clear the goal of success, others charted the path. At the end of the century Elbert Hubbard designed an inspirational tract that enjoyed almost as much popularity as Conwell's sermon. *A Message to Garcia* (1899) told of the valiant delivery of a crucial military message to the Cuban insurgent leader García Íñiguez by an American military officer. The lesson of this story was one of initiative and obedience to instruction, which Hubbard extrapolated to the late-century world of wage work. Excoriating the "slipshod assistance, foolish inattention, dowdy indifference, and half-hearted work" (p. 17) that seemed ever more common among American workers, Hubbard urged his audience to reach higher than the minimum standard of competence in order to achieve excellence. His disgust with "moral stupidity, this infirmity of the will" (p. 19) bled into the realm of politics as he decried the "maudlin sympathy expressed for the 'downtrodden denizens of the sweat-shop'" (p. 20). The true victim in the Gilded Age was the employer, "who grows old before his time in a vain attempt to get frowsy ne'er-do-wells to do intelligent work" (p. 20). More than anything else, "it is the survival of the fittest," Hubbard reminded, that would determine success (p. 20).

It is no coincidence that Hubbard's Manichaean view of America developed in the era of industrialization and reflected not just the nation's new economic landscape but its shifting social profile as well. Nineteenth-century industrialization pulled waves of immigrants from all over the world—especially southern and eastern Europe—to America. These new ethnic minorities quite often lived apart from established white society, both by choice and economic circumstances. Their arrivals to American cities fed the ranks of unskilled and semiskilled labor, which highlighted the differences between native and foreign born. Perhaps this ethnic dimension exacerbated the stridency of Hubbard's language, and fueled his insistent reaffirmations of the simple paths to success even in the face of complex economic and social changes.

Less stringent in his formulation was Phineas T. Barnum, who became one of the most admired Americans of the century with his booming entertainment business. His autobiography, *Struggles and Triumphs* (1874), revealed for American young men the "commandments for success." Some were tried and true maxims, such as perseverance, determination, self-denial, and discipline. But significant as well is Barnum's insistence that one avoid debt, except in the case of merchants, for whom it was a necessity, and for the purchase of land. Also, Barnum emphasized innovation and manipulation, especially in the world of business. Perhaps Barnum himself said it best: "There's a sucker born every minute."

Barnum's own maxims complicate the assumption that the Gilded Age was dominated only by outworn appeals to industry in an age where it no longer mattered. Take for example the misunderstandings and assumptions surrounding the legendary stories of Horatio Alger. Alger published over one hundred exceptionally popular stories of young men struggling to make it in the world. Today, these stories have become shorthand for the mythic ideal of the self-made man in an era of industrialization. But the "rags to riches" tag that has accompanied Alger's name is in part undeserved. As many historians have pointed out, Alger's heroes are not simply parables for the rigid market demands of the industrial era. For one, his heroes are less hardworking than lucky. Perseverance and work figure less prominently into the plot lines than chance encounters, perhaps a reflection of the declining relationship between the work ethic and material progress. Furthermore, Alger's heroes rarely achieve alone and unaided; instead, patronage, aid, friendship, and nurturance play a strong role in their rise toward respectability. And despite the assumption to the contrary, these are not generally tales of the rise from rags to riches; his characters do not win extravagant fortunes as much as they secure white-collar positions. In fact it is usually the villains, such as the unscrupulous, wealthy bankers, who use cutthroat means to advance.

Michael Zuckerman has substantially revised the meaning of these stories. Alger's heroes are not by any stretch of the imagination the prudent calculators so necessary for the advancement of capitalist enterprise. Instead, they are "almost always impetuously improvident" in their financial dealings, frequently spending beyond their means in order to achieve some of the trappings of middle-class respectability or comfort. In their work, Alger's heroes find neither purpose nor personal fulfillment, and they seem almost uninterested in the future, hardly the persevering and forward-looking foot soldiers of capitalism. If they provide a formula for success, it is more one of "knight errantry" than industry or self-discipline. And if there is a moral to the stories, it is that the stronger can, and ought, to care for the weaker; these hardly match the "survival of the fittest" assumptions made about the Gilded Age. Instead of celebrating radical individualism, Alger's heroes generally abandon their autonomy willingly in exchange for a more stable set of social and economic relations, where nurturance, not self-sufficiency, is guaranteed.

Along with Horatio Alger, Andrew Carnegie has been invoked as the classic success story of the nineteenth century. Son to a father whose skills as a weaver had been made obsolete by mechanization, Carnegie knew firsthand the sting of failure in his native Scotland. His family emigrated to the United States when he was twelve. He rose quickly in his work as a telegrapher, and then won the favor and attention of his superiors when working at the Pennsylvania Railroad. By his thirties he was reaping substantial profits as an investor. His decision to invest in new steel production processes made him immensely wealthy, while his business techniques—cost cutting, low wages and salaries, frequent technological advancements, and aggressive competition—earned him the lion's share of the American steel industry. Unlike other contemporary "robber barons," though, Carnegie considered himself a public figure and a trustee of the nation's moral and material wealth. His frequent writings won him the admiration and attention of many Americans, especially his comments on success, wealth, and social justice. Carnegie celebrated those who began with little and moved up; he decried the evils of inheritance. In Carnegie we find older strains of caution, such as advising against drink and financial speculation, combined with appeals to naked ambition.

As Daniel T. Rodgers has pointed out, the transition in the rhetoric of industrialization produced more than a few ironies for the ideal of success. In service of the work ethic, Americans built a world in which some of its earlier values—such as frugality and industry—were no longer at home. The very success of industrialization meant that the work ethic no longer led to success. And with factories producing ever-larger quantities of consumer products, the asceticism of the Protestant ethic—work and save, delay self-gratification—necessarily gave way to a newer ideal that made room for its opposites: leisure, play, and consumption.

MODERN SUCCESS AND THE TRANSITION FROM CHARACTER TO PERSONALITY

This transition from an economy geared toward production to one based on consumption drove the emergence of advertising at the turn of the twentieth century. Some scholars have argued that it also created a new concept of the self, and thereby of success. While the nineteenth century has been described as a culture of character, where character development was the goal, by the early twentieth century the self was framed less in terms of self-sacrifice than self-realization. Warren I. Susman and Daniel T. Rodgers have both identified the career of success writer Orison Swett Marden as representative of this transition. Marden wrote *Pushing to the Front; or, Success under Difficulties* (1894) as his first guide to achieving success, and followed it with fifty others. Even the title of his 1899 guide, *Character: The Grandest Thing in the World,* suggests its emphasis on one's inner qualities. In 1897 Marden founded *Success* magazine, which advocated virtues familiar to earlier generations: punctuality, honesty, and hard work. But by 1910 he began to turn toward a new recipe for success, that of mental power. In his later writings, Marden conceived of success as depending upon banishing not the circumstances but the very idea of poverty. His *Masterful Personality* (1921) abandoned the focus on character, paid increasing attention to the cues of others, and stressed the importance of manners, proper clothes, and good conversation.

This transition has been interpreted as a sign that the nineteenth-century ethic of production was gradually giving way to one of consumption. Susman uses Bruce Barton as another representative figure in this transition. Barton, a U.S. representative who also founded one of the most important advertising agencies of the twentieth century, was known to Americans through his frequent essays and occasional self-help books. To Susman, Barton is pivotal for easing the transition between an earlier ethic of success, premised on a producer ethic, to one stressing consumption, leisure, and personality. By the early twentieth century, advertising had come to play an increasingly critical role in smoothing capitalist cycles and stabilizing the economy by strengthening consumer demand. Barton saw the role of advertising in even more epic terms: "Advertising is the power which keeps business out in the open, which compels it to set up for itself public ideals of quality and service and to measure up to those ideals" (p. 128). Advertising, in fact, had become central to the American way of life.

8

In the mid-eighteenth century, Franklin advised young men to "Imitate Jesus." Nearly two centuries later, Barton's *The Man Nobody Knows* (1925) remade Jesus from a paragon of self-sacrifice into a man who sanctified the new order of modern business, a vigorous and masculine leader, a sociable companion, and "the most popular dinner guest in Jerusalem" whose savvy turned a group of twelve into an organization that conquered the world. This is the idea of success that we live with at the start of the twenty-first century. It was entrenched substantially by the rise of mass media, and the attendant culture of celebrity, where appearances could be as important as any countervailing "facts" or truths. The proliferation of motivational speakers and the explosion of self-help literature all suggest that success continues to incorporate the emphasis on personal adjustment and mental health with material advancement.

The cottage industry of success seminars also attests to the enduring appeal of the American dream. Jennifer L. Hochschild has divided this dream of success into four basic tenets: the belief that success is open to all, that it is attainable by all, that it is under our control, and that it retains an element of virtue. Yet despite the consensus regarding the dream itself, there persists a deep division between whites and blacks regarding its relevance: whites believe that success is in a very real way open to all, while blacks see it working for others more than for themselves. Such a radical difference in perceptions, Hochschild warns, endangers the continuing legitimacy of success as any kind of real national ideal. As she puts it: "The right to aspire to success works as an ideological substitute for a guarantee of success only if it begins to approach it. When people recognize that chances for success are slim or getting slimmer, the whole tenor of the American dream changes dramatically for the worse" (p. 27).

THE IRONIES OF SUCCESS

Significantly, success in America—in its secular form—is implicitly understood to be something achievable by individuals, and is rarely discussed in communal or social terms. Furthermore, since the early nineteenth century success has been understood to take part—and to be most clearly valued when it has taken place—largely outside of social institutions. In fact, the concept of the self-made man is important not just for what it reveals about individualism but perhaps also for what it suggests about Americans' tendency to think of themselves as owing little to the community. In this form success is a function of one's individual will and control rather than a matter of fate. The term connotes deliberate effort, merit, and control, not luck or chance.

Perhaps this individualism explains why there has been such a strong moral dimension to both success and failure in American history. However, more often than not there seems to have been something of an uneasy relationship between success and virtue. John G. Cawelti posed this problem as a paradox when observing the ideals of the early nineteenth century: men were encouraged to pursue individual economic advancement, but were to do so without aspiring to be wealthy, or to rise dramatically through the social ranks. Men who did not work to improve their condition were corrupt and degraded, though at all times it was clear that the real purpose of industry was not wealth but moral merit. For Hochschild, success has been powerful precisely because of this moral ambiguity, for "it can be used to club the poor into accepting their lot, but it can also be used to make the rich squirm about their luxuries" (p. 250). The very brilliance of success lies in its elasticity, its capacity to contain so many variations and internal contradictions while continuing to represent something very real in American life.

See also **The Material Shape of Early American Life; Gender, Social Class, Race, and Material Life; The Athlete as Cultural Icon** *(volume 1);* **Working Class; Humanitarianism** *(volume 2); and other articles in this section.*

BIBLIOGRAPHY

Primary Works

Alger, Horatio. *Ragged Dick and Struggling Upward.* New York, 1985.

Barnum, Phineas T. *Struggles and Triumphs; or, Forty Years' Recollections of P. T. Barnum.* Buffalo, N.Y., 1874.

Barton, Bruce. *The Man Nobody Knows: A Discovery of the Real Jesus.* 1925. Reprint, Chicago, 2000.

Conwell, Russell. *Acres of Diamonds*. New York, 1985.

Emerson, Ralph Waldo. *Essays and Lectures*. New York, 1983.

Franklin, Benjamin. *The Autobiography of Benjamin Franklin*. Edited by Leonard Labaree. New Haven, Conn., 1964.

Grob, Gerald N., and Robert N. Beck, eds. *American Ideas: Source Readings in the Intellectual History of the United States*. New York, 1963.

Hubbard, Elbert. *A Message to Garcia: Being a Preachment*. East Aurora, N.Y., 1899.

Miller, Perry, and Thomas H. Johnson, eds. *The Puritans*. 2 vols. Rev. ed. New York, 1963.

Rischin, Moses, ed. *The American Gospel of Success: Individualism and Beyond*. Chicago, 1965.

Tocqueville, Alexis de. *Democracy in America*. Translated by Henry Reeve. New York, 1981.

Weber, Max. *The Protestant Ethic and the Spirit of Capitalism*. Translated by Talcott Parsons. New York, 1958.

Secondary Works

Banta, Martha. *Failure and Success in America: A Literary Debate*. Princeton, N.J., 1978.

Bercovitch, Sacvan. *The Rites of Assent: Transformations in the Symbolic Construction of America*. New York, 1993.

Cawelti, John G. *Apostles of the Self-Made Man*. Chicago, 1965.

Chudacoff, Howard P. "Success and Security: The Meaning of Social Mobility in America." *Reviews in American History* 10, no. 4 (1982): 101–112.

Conkin, Paul K. *Puritans and Pragmatists: Eight Eminent American Thinkers*. New York, 1968.

Gilmore, Michael T. "Emerson and the Persistence of the Commodity." In *American Romanticism and the Marketplace*. Edited by Michael T. Gilmore. Chicago, 1985.

Halttunen, Karen. *Confidence Men and Painted Women: A Study of Middle-Class Culture in America, 1830–1870*. New Haven, Conn., 1982.

Hilkey, Judy. *Character Is Capital: Success Manuals and Manhood in Gilded Age America*. Chapel Hill, N.C., 1997.

Hochschild, Jennifer L. *Facing Up to the American Dream: Race, Class, and the Soul of the Nation*. Princeton, N.J., 1995.

Rodgers, Daniel T. *The Work Ethic in Industrial America, 1850–1920*. Chicago, 1978.

Sandage, Scott. "Deadbeats, Drunkards, and Dreamers: A Cultural History of Failure in America, 1819–1893." Ph.D. diss., Rutgers University, 1995.

———. *Forgotten Men: Failure in American Culture, 1819–1893*. Cambridge, Mass., forthcoming.

Susman, Warren I. *Culture as History: The Transformation of American Society in the Twentieth Century*. New York, 1984.

Wyllie, Irvin G. *The Self-Made Man in America: The Myth of Rags to Riches*. New York, 1966.

Zuckerman, Michael. *Almost Chosen People: Oblique Biographies in the American Grain*. Berkeley, 1993.

TECHNOLOGY

Kathleen Franz

TECHNOLOGY AND REPUBLICAN VALUES, 1790–1860

Technology—defined in this essay as machines, systems, and knowledge, has been woven into the fabric of American intellectual and popular discourse since the late eighteenth century. Americans' cultural and intellectual responses to technology, since that time, have been articulated in debates surrounding the introduction of new technologies, from early industrialization to the computer age. The material forms and cultural meanings of technologies, whether the factory system or the automobile, have been the products of complex cultural negotiations. In general, Americans have been eager to invent, to adopt new innovations as solutions to economic and social questions, and to claim that each new technology embodies democratic promise and economic progress. Yet, there has also been a sometimes faint but consistent current of cultural ambivalence that has accompanied the enthusiasm for technology in America.

The story of America's relationship to technology began in the late eighteenth century. As the new nation emerged from the political revolution, American entrepreneurs pursued a revolution in manufacturing technology that raised important questions about the place of technology in the economic as well as the intellectual and cultural life of the nation. At the onset of the first industrial revolution, they also formed new ideas about work, community, and their relationship as a nation to technology.

Transferring and adapting spinning technology and the factory system from Britain in the 1790s, the first industrial revolution drew together southern plantations and New England manufacturers. Textile production, reliant on New England mills and southern cotton, was one of the earliest industries adapted from a British model by Americans. Entrepreneurs, such as Samuel Slater of Rhode Island, built the first American woolen textile mills in New England with the backing of investors eager to profit from new modes of production.

Mills, and later factories, flourished in America for material and cultural reasons. Unlike Britain, the United States had vast natural resources, including an abundance of land and wood, which aided the development of small mills, machines, and eventually large factories. A growing population of free immigrants and farmers as well as African slaves provided the skills and labor needed for industrial development in America. Finally, the new nation and its government were less bound by tradition and more ready for change than Europe. Economic and social freedom, as many historians have noted, fueled rapid technological change, the patent system, and industrial development in America.

The new factories concentrated labor and regulated the use of space and time in new ways that seemed, to some Americans, to violate the principles of individual autonomy fought for in the American Revolution. The introduction of new forms of technology, such as water-powered machinery, made it useful to gather large numbers of machines and workers in one place. Before this, farmers and artisans had used technology on their individual farms or in small mills. Beginning in the 1820s, entrepreneurs set up buildings to bring together workers, machines, raw materials, and power sources. For the workers, this was a disturbing change; they no longer had much control over where or how quickly they worked. Some of the workers in the new factories came from farms, but many were artisans who had worked in small shops. Work life in the artisan's shop was marked by camaraderie and featured an irregular timing, two things that could not continue in a factory where clocks, overseers, and the machinery itself dictated the place and the pace of work.

The first industrial revolution gave rise to new machines and manufacturing processes and fostered changes in the intellectual and cultural life of the nation. Political and intellectual leaders, as well as manufacturers and workers, debated the rewards and problems of industrialization. Most notably Alexander Hamilton and Thomas Jefferson debated the economic and the cultural meanings of the growing factories and their impact on American democratic principles and everyday life in the new Republic. Arguments for and against factory production encompassed both material and ideological concerns.

Industrialization struck at the heart of American political ideas; some argued that industrialization would ensure the economic and political independence of the new nation by cutting the number of imports and foreign debts. Manufacturing would keep the United States a free nation. Alexander Hamilton, the secretary of the treasury under President George Washington, promoted the cultivation of industry and new technologies in America. Hamilton believed that all work was virtuous and would give the poor occupations and keep them out of trouble. He also believed that homegrown industry would ensure the independence of the new nation. Hamilton encouraged government incentives for investment in new industries and contributed to the establishment of the Society for Encouraging Useful Manufacturers that transplanted British models for glass, textile, iron, and paper production in the United States. The federal government also encouraged innovation as well as industry by providing credit to entrepreneurs through a national bank and by establishing the patent system, which protected the rights of inventors and helped them profit by their ingenuity.

American ideas about technology have been marked not only by enthusiasm for new machines but a deep ambivalence about the changes brought by these new technologies. For Thomas Jefferson, the invention of new machines embodied the values of liberty and an individual striving for knowledge and a better life. However, Jefferson spoke out against the factory system, as an extension of feudalism. Although he saw in machines the ability to set men free, he feared that their application to manufacturing in the form of the British factory system would sacrifice the liberty of citizens to wage labor and create a permanent underclass in the new nation. Jefferson argued that American principles of liberty lay in the ability of a majority of citizens to be self-sufficient farmers and small landowners. In his *Notes on the State of Virginia* (1785), Jefferson warned, "Let us never see our citizens occupied at a work-bench, or twirling a distaff. . . . [F]or the general operations of manufacture, let our workshops remain in Europe" (pp. 157–158).

A variety of Americans saw British factories as negative examples of industrialization and some cautioned Americans about transplanting industrialization to the new nation. Opponents of the factory system argued that it would make slaves of citizens. The mill worker and teacher, Thomas Mann articulated these sentiments in a poem entitled "Picture of a Factory Village" published in 1833: "For liberty our fathers fought / Which with their blood, they dearly bought / The Factory system sets at naught. / A slave at morn, a slave at eve, / It doth my inmost feelings grieve; / The blood runs chilly from my heart, / To see fair Liberty depart" (p. 1).

As small mills grew into factories, Americans attempted to curb the harmful effects of industrialization through the application of republican political ideals to both labor and machinery alike. The first industrial laborers, comprised of the daughters of farmers who came to work in the textile mills in Lowell, Massachusetts, and male artisans, thought of themselves as "republicans," and claimed that they were the "true heirs" of the revolutionary principles of the American Revolution. For them, republicanism implied a respect for the dignity of the laborer's work and equal citizenship. It would be these workers who would lead the first labor strikes.

Early manufacturers incorporated republican values, expressed as simplicity, frugality, industry, and respect for authority, into their places of production. Some built their factory towns to encourage community ideals, if not always the preservation of individual liberty. For instance, the Boston merchant Francis Cabot Lowell, who visited British mills in the 1810s, founded the city of Lowell at the junction of the Concord and Merrimack Rivers north of Boston in the 1820s. Lowell wanted to design a new type of American industrial city without the poverty of British manufacturing towns. He decided to place his textile factories within a uniquely American setting to ward off the culturally corrupting effects of industrialization. Lowell hired young women from farms as laborers and housed them near to the factory in closely supervised and "respectable" boardinghouses, implementing strict rules that governed behavior at work and at leisure. In the same idealistic spirit, some of the first mill girls at Lowell contributed to a literary magazine entitled *The Lowell Offering*. Observers cited *The Lowell Offering* as an example of the high moral and artistic attainments of the uniquely American labor force. *The Lowell Offering* also became a marker of the golden age of Lowell, which lasted from the 1820s to the early 1840s. After 1840 a trend toward speeding up machines and "stretching out" workers, or using fewer laborers, prompted labor unrest and the eventual replacement of mill girls with Irish immigrants. Although the Lowell experiment did not last, Lowell's paternalism became a model adopted by late nineteenth-century manufacturers such as George Pullman in Pullman, Illinois.

Machine design and architecture became another expression of republican ideology. During the early national period, machines, and in particular steam engines, or motive sources, were designed to reflect national myths that connected America to the democratic virtues of ancient Greece. The addition of gothic arches and American eagles gave steam engines and printing presses religious and patriotic significance. These functional and decorative elements signified the honored status of these machines in American society. In 1799 the architect Benjamin Henry Latrobe designed a neoclassical water tower for the city of Philadelphia. With a domed roof and symmetrical, templelike exterior, Latrobe's Greek Revival design tried to reconcile the industrial technology of steam engines with the ideology of republicanism, fusing ideas of beauty with the American virtues of utility and ingenuity.

TECHNOLOGY AND IDEAS OF NATIONAL PROGRESS, 1860–1920

Architecture was not the only place where Americans attempted to reconcile the transformative power of the machine with the Jeffersonian pastoral ideal of beauty, peace, and simplicity. As historian Leo Marx has argued in his book *The Machine in the Garden*, American writers also attempted to solve the contradiction between a national passion for technological progress, which irrevocably changed the landscape, and the ideal of a rural nation. According to Marx, this contradiction has formed one of the unique characteristics of American intellectual and popular thought since the early nineteenth century.

By the 1840s, technology was widely linked to ideas of the social progress and the manifest destiny of the nation. As the premier technology of the mid-nineteenth century, the railroad embodied the promise of machine-driven progress. Between 1840 and 1860 thousands of miles of railroad track were laid across the United States. Railroads literally cut through the rural ideal, opening the land to commerce and development. Railroad companies rationalized business practices and the rhythms of daily life by creating vast transportation systems, forming corporations, consolidating business prac-

tices, and even dividing the country into national time zones. Objectively, the railroads contradicted the myth of a pastoral ideal. However they did not destroy a belief in pastoral simplicity, individuality, and untouched nature. Rather, as Leo Marx has argued, in this period the technological became sublime. Writers and poets, such as Daniel Webster and Walt Whitman, represented the new machines as noble devices that unified the nation, that improved nature by making it useful, and that insured the liberty of the individual by giving him access to the land. In this period, the natural landscape became a backdrop upon which American intellectuals could see the progress of a mechanical age.

On a popular level, as well, America became a technocracy, a culture that believed the development of new machines improved life and one that saw inventors, scientists, and, later, engineers as social benefactors and cultural heroes. The artist Christian Schussele illustrated the national respect for inventors in 1862 with a painting entitled *Men of Progress*. The painting, which includes inventors who had become successful businessmen, including, among others, Charles Goodyear (rubber), Samuel F. B. Morse (telegraph), and Elias Howe (sewing machine), personified invention and helped construct the myth that new machines sprung from the ingenuity of individuals. It also shaped other cultural notions: that inventions increased the wealth of the individual as well as the nation, and that technological innovation was the domain of whites and men. Many Americans would come to believe in this period that technological innovation determined the political, economic, and historical course of the nation.

With the growth of transportation networks and the rapid pace of industrialization, American universities began to offer specialized training in the mechanical arts, producing professional engineers and a new community of technical experts. Prior to the building of the Erie Canal in 1825 the majority of civil engineers in America had been trained at West Point, the only American institution with an engineering program at that time, or in British or French universities. Many others obtained on-the-job training in mills or educated themselves. The building of the canal and the subsequent development of railroads in the 1840s created a more urgent need for trained engineers. Slowly in the period between 1820 and 1860 some American universities added engineering programs to answer a definite need for trained professionals. Rensselaer Polytechnic Institute became the first private engineering school in 1829. Harvard and Yale followed in 1842

13

Men of Progress (1862) **by Christian Schussele.** Oil on canvas, 51⅜ × 76¾ in. *Left to right:* William Thomas Green Morton, James Bogardus, Samuel Colt, Cyrus Hall McCormick, Joseph Saxton, Charles Goodyear, Peter Cooper, Jordan Lawrence Mott, Joseph Henry, Eliphalet Nott, John Ericsson, Frederick Ellsworth Sickels, Samuel Finley Breese, Henry Burden, Richard March Hoe, Erastus Brigham Bigelow, Isaiah Jennings, Thomas Blanchard, Elias Howe. NATIONAL PORTRAIT GALLERY, SMITHSONIAN INSTITUTION/ART RESOURCE, NY

and 1847 respectively. The federal government provided the biggest boost to engineering education and technical training in 1862 with the passage of the Morrill Act. The Morrill Act granted federal aid to states for the support of colleges of agriculture and the mechanic arts. In the decade after the Morrill Act was passed the number of engineering schools at both private and public institutions increased substantially from six to seventy. By 1880 there were eighty-five schools including Cornell, MIT, Lehigh University in Bethlehem, Pennsylvania, and the Case School of Applied Science in Cleveland. Newly trained experts from these programs began to professionalize with the creation of engineering societies and organizations in the late-nineteenth century. These schools and societies helped build a new culture of technical professionals that would influence the development of technology in the United States throughout the twentieth century.

As a rural way of life seemed to give way to industrialization and urbanization on a grand scale some American writers challenged the notion that technology brought unfettered progress. In particular, Mark Twain and Henry Adams portrayed technology as uncontrollable and potentially destructive. In several works including *A Connecticut Yankee in King Arthur's Court* (1889), Twain reconsidered the recurrent theme of the machine and the pastoral garden and suggested that industrialization separated Americans from the ideal of the land and the past. In particular, *A Connecticut Yankee* explored the dangers of unchecked technological ingenuity and its impact on the land and a connection to the past. The novel's protagonist, Hank Morgan, an ingenious Yankee, is sent back to Arthurian England through a bump on the head. Once there he quickly became the "Boss" of King Arthur's court and began to industrialize the kingdom. In the end, however, Morgan's attempts to modernize sixth-century England serve to alienate him from the civilization he tried to help and eventually his new technologies destroy everything one could value in Arthurian England, including the peace, the land, and its people.

In 1907 Henry Adams in *The Education of Henry Adams* also explored the problems of industrialization through the twin symbols of the Dynamo, industralization, and the Virgin, preindustrial nature. Writing both an autobiography and a history of technological change in the United States, Adams reinforced the idea that industrialization separated Americans from the mythical idea of a rural nation and from the past. At the same time Adams reinforced the notion of technological determinism, that technology is an impersonal and uncontrollable force that shapes economic and human relations alike. Like Twain, Adams argued that technology threatened to destroy values central to pre-industrial America, including religion, beauty, and a pastoral landscape. Despite their critique they offered no alternative to industrialization, which they viewed as inescapable.

MASS PRODUCTION AND ENTHUSIASM FOR TECHNOLOGY, 1900–1940

At the beginning of the twentieth century, Americans witnessed another set of revolutionary changes in technology centered around mass production, scientific efficiency, and the proliferation of consumer technologies. The popular discourse surrounding the products of mass production cemented the relationship between technology and national progress. In the 1920s the central character in Sinclair Lewis's *Babbitt* (1922) inhabits a modern landscape of skyscrapers, factories, telegraph wires, glistening chrome, and electric razors. Wholly uncritical of technology, Babbitt thanks the "God of Progress" whenever he pulls on his BVDs or steps into his automobile. By the end of the 1920s, the cultural critic Waldo Frank declared that the machine in America had given rise to a cult of power based on technology. According to Frank, in an essay entitled "Gods and Cults of Power," the machine had become an instrument of corporate dominance and a "household idol."

Mass production encompassed a set of innovations in technology and business practice that centered around the moving assembly line. Henry Ford, often credited with inventing mass production through the implementation of the moving as-

sembly line at his Highland Park plant in 1913, combined mass production with mass consumption. Ford enacted his famous five-dollar day to dissuade workers from quitting what many considered dehumanizing work and to enable them to buy the product they produced, automobiles. The Model T became the archetype of Fordism, every black car was identical and affordable. Through standardization, vertical integration, and the moving assembly line, Ford realized a revolution in production and consumption; the assembly line reduced the cost of automobiles significantly and by 1920 about one in every fourteen Americans owned a car. However, the cost of owning an automobile still excluded many working-class whites, African Americans, and immigrants in urban areas.

Frederick Winslow Taylor, a mechanical engineer, led a contemporary movement for the application of scientific management techniques in the factory, known as Taylorism. Taylor wanted to solve labor problems, namely workers' efforts to slow the pace of work, through scientific problem solving. By attempting to measure and rationalize the process of work, he tried to make all sorts of labor, whether in the factory or the office, into a science. In 1911 he published *The Principles of Scientific Management* which made readers aware of "the great loss which the whole country is suffering through inefficiency in almost all our daily lives." He asserted that the "fundamental principles of scientific management are applicable to all kinds of human activities, from our simplest individual acts to the work of our great corporations" (p. 7).

Scientific management spawned many professional and popular practitioners and, as a cultural trend, spread from the factory and the office to the home. For instance, Frank and Lillian Gilbreth, the husband and wife team of efficiency experts inspired by Taylor, implemented the new technology of motion picture cameras to conduct micromotion studies of workers and improve time-motion studies. Lillian Gilbreth in particular expanded upon Taylor's work through application of psychology to management and by introducing the idea of efficiency to domestic tasks.

The growing movement of home economics in the 1910s and 1920s also emphasized the application of scientific management and new technology in the home and encouraged women to think of domestic work as an engineering problem and to save time through efficient planning and standardization of daily tasks. One home economist, Christine Frederick, whose advice columns appeared in mass-market magazines such as *Ladies Home Journal*, told housewives that "scientific management could, and must, solve housework problems as it had already solved other work problems." She advocated the standardization of household tasks, the redesign of the kitchen, and the cultivation of an "efficiency attitude" (*Household Engineering*, pp. 14, 15). Home economists not only worked on their own as independent writers, but many were employed by power and utility companies, manufacturers, and the federal government to introduce women consumers to new systems and machines. One of the primary missions of home economists was to convince women that these technologies would improve domestic work by saving labor and rendering the home safer, more sanitary, and more modern.

Standardization and efficiency captured the national imagination in the early decades of the twentieth century. Businessmen and popular writers alike promoted an ethos of mass production as socially and economically beneficial. Edward Filene, the Boston department store owner and author of various tracts on the social benefits of mass production, argued in his book entitled *Successful Living in this Machine Age* (1931) that mass production and mechanization would liberate the masses from the struggle for necessities. Henry Ford agreed and argued that the automobile and other technologies would solve the problems of modern life, which he defined as "congestion and inequality." In his weekly newspaper column in the *Dearborn Independent*, Ford declared the car would solve urban problems by allowing Americans to leave the city but, at the same time, take all the modern conveniences of city life with them to the suburbs. According to Ford, the car would revive pre-industrial values of community and rural living by facilitating the creation of suburbs and providing the American family with inexpensive vacations in "God's great open spaces."

Corporations invited Americans to admire, consume, and participate in the benefits of new technologies at pageants and at world's fairs. Fairs made apparent the "holy trinity" of the modern age: science, industry, and progress. For instance, during the Great Depression world's fairs constructed historical narratives that placed engineers and scientists at the center of American economic advancement. The organizing committee of the 1933 Century of Progress World's Fair in Chicago was made up of scientists from the National Research Council and industrialists such as the oil baron Rufus Dawes. These men sought to restore faith in engineers, scientists, and industrialists as national leaders at a moment when technology seemed to have failed to bring prosperity. The theme of the fair presented a cultural hierarchy based on scientific and technical knowledge: "Science discovers, genius invents, industry applies, and man adapts himself to, or is molded by, new things." The *Official Guidebook* to the 1933 Chicago World's Fair explained the didactic purpose of the exposition: to "help the American people to understand themselves, and to make clear to the coming generation the forces which have built this nation" (p. 11). The Big Three of automobile manufacturing did not let the public relations opportunities of the fair slip by. Ford, Chrysler, and General Motors in alliance with industrial designers and research scientists used the fairs of the 1930s to publicize their contributions to American life, and they argued that greater consumption of the automobile would end the economic depression. Ford and General Motors, in particular, created exhibits that placed industry and industrial designers as the leaders of technological and social change.

In the tradition of left social critique, novelists and artists contested the idea that scientific management and mass production, the engineering of work, had enhanced modern life. Writer Upton Sinclair portrayed Ford in *The Flivver King* (1937) as a new kind of dictator and the "most hated man" in Detroit. Aldous Huxley, in his science fiction novel, *Brave New World* (1932), painted a dark picture of a future world that had embraced Fordism and traded autonomy for the tyranny of standardization. Finally, Charlie Chaplin's *Modern Times* (1936) provides a vivid commentary on the mechanization of work. In the opening scenes of the film, workers are herded into the factory like cattle. Once at work, they labor at an ever-quickening pace under the constant supervision of the Big Boss and the probing instruments of efficiency experts. The uncontrollable and monotonous nature of assembly-line work drives Chaplin's character, the Little Tramp, to temporary insanity. Early in the film, the Little Tramp is depicted as caught, literally and metaphorically, in the giant gears of mechanization.

At a more popular level, however, American's cultural relationship to technology was marked by a great enthusiasm for new machines. Rather than seeing themselves as anonymous and powerless cogs in giant industrial and social mechanisms, the great majority of Americans embraced new technologies. Some even tinkered with the new machines, reshaping standardized consumer goods to fit their own needs and desires. In the 1920s, Herbert Hoover, "the Great Engineer," symbolized the social benefits of machine age rationality and the hegemony of technical experts, but he shared the spotlight with Tom Swift, a tinkerer who always stayed one step ahead of the engineers.

Popular advice literature on technology cultivated American's enthusiasm for new gadgets and helped them gain technical knowledge. Mass-market magazines such as *Popular Mechanics* (1902) and serial fiction such as *Tom Swift* (1910) encouraged Americans, particularly boys and men, to both understand new technologies and imagine themselves as participants in technological advancement. *Popular Mechanics* made technical problem solving and innovation accessible to readers with little or no technical training; its captions explained that this was technological advice "written so you can understand it." Popular technical literature marked an explosion of hobbyists, tinkerers, and amateur inventors who modified and improved upon the products of mass production. In the case of the radio, ham operators and home tinkerers adapted radio technology for home use and challenged corporate authority over both the device and the system of communication.

Popular technical advice literature in this period helped to reinforce cultural hierarchies based on race and gender. While seemingly inclusive and even potentially subversive in terms of encouraging technical knowledge among consumers, popular journals granted technical authority almost exclusively to men and boys, rather than women, and to whites rather than people of color. While black inventors had made significant contributions to the development of American technology from the seventeenth century, technical literature excluded African Americans as potential participants in technological progress. In fact, when popular journals did portray African Americans and other nonwhite groups journalists constructed these groups as primitive, and nontechnological. Popular journals, serial fiction, and instructional materials before World War II imagined the audience for technical advice as exclusively white and primarily male. Although some early serial fiction related to the automobile addressed girls, publishers did not see them as a viable audience for technological literature and the automobile and radio series for girls were short-lived. A wide cultural discourse that framed who could use technology in this period, actively discouraged girls from entering technical professions and from acquiring even the most basic knowledge of machinery.

POSTWAR PESSIMISM, 1945–1990

The explosion of the atomic bomb not only ended World War II but solidified the relationship between the federal government and scientific research. In the postwar period, Americans continued to search for technological solutions to all kinds of social problems, whether the Vietnam War, urban race riots, or the energy crisis. Yet this series of social and economic crises in the 1960s and 1970s prompted more Americans to question the place of technology in American life and its relationship to work, the environment, and corporate power over consumers. The result was a series of reform movements that can be referred to as "postmodern pessimism" about technology.

After World War II, federal and state authorities, along with corporations, continued the prewar trend of building national transportation and communication networks ostensibly in the interest of national security. In 1956 Congress passed the Federal-Aid Highway Act which would spend $50 billion to build a series of interstate highways. This act dovetailed with urban renewal efforts, also funded in part by the federal government, and cemented America's reliance on the automobile and the oil industry.

Cultural critics questioned the dominance of the automobile industry over public policy and critiqued America's technocratic approach to problem solving as oppressive forces that threatened the environment, the culture, and the individual. Lewis Mumford and the consumer advocate Ralph Nader condemned American reliance on the automobile and the social irresponsibility of automobile corporations. In his famous exposé of the automobile industry, *Unsafe at Any Speed* (1965), Nader disproved the idea that the automobile had liberated Americans from the problems of modern life. He charged auto manufacturers with disregard for consumer safety and argued that accidents cost the consumer billions of dollars and the manufacturers nothing. For Nader the social and political challenge of American life in the 1960s was "how to control the power of economic interests which ignore the harmful effects of their applied science and technology" (p. ix). In Mumford's estimation as well, more technology did not necessarily mean a better standard of living but a reliance on industry and technology to solve social problems.

Automation, deindustrialization, and environmental disasters in this period elicited more general pessimism among Americans about the social benefits of technology. The growth of highly automated factories, implementing newly developed computers and robotics to perform the labor of humans, fueled a general anxiety over the workerless factory and mass unemployment. Union leaders, in particular at the United Auto Workers and the United Farm Workers fought for policies that would limit the replacement of humans by machines. In addition, popular writers and filmmakers explored the dehumanizing effects of automation. They included Kurt Vonnegut's *Player Piano* (1952) and, later, Ira Levin's *Stepford Wives* (1972), which takes a satirical view of automation as a male solution to the challenges of second-wave feminism. In the end, unions maintained a place for workers in the new factories but did not prevent automation. And by the late 1970s and 1980s, American workers experienced massive deindustrialization as manufacturers moved outside the United States to find cheaper labor.

A variety of environmental crises in the postwar period, including Three Mile Island, Love Canal, use of the pesticide DDT in California, and the oil crisis illustrated for many the nation's dependence on technologies that often had negative side effects. Rachel Carson's *Silent Spring* explored the ecological problems of pesticides in 1962. The federal government enacted some initiatives to measure the impact of technology on the environment, such as the National Environmental Policy Act (1970). In California a much more radical agency, the Office of Appropriate Technology, started by the former California governor Jerry Brown, explored environmentally friendly alternatives to the combustion engine and coal-burning electrical plants, such as light rail, solar, and wind energy projects. Brown's program became part of a larger "appropriate technology" movement in the 1970s. Yet, even alternative sources of energy illustrated the entrenched relationship between well-established industries and government subsidy. The Department of Energy tended to grant funding to programs developed by the military-industrial complex rather than environmental action groups, such as a project for solar energy started by Boeing Aerospace Company, which combined space research with initiatives in solar power.

THE COMPUTER AGE, 1945–2000

As modern technocratic ideas seemed to fail, the postmodern technologies of the computer and the Internet emerged during the cold war era. The military-industrial complex contributed to the new set of technologies that would become, out of their flexibility, economically and culturally powerful as well as intellectually provocative. The first modern electronic computers, ENIAC, the Electrical Numerical Integrator and Computer (1943), and UNIVAC, the Universal Automatic Computer (1951), were the products of government-sponsored research during the war. Early computers, or "electronic brains," were powered by vacuum tubes, performed mathematical calculations, and had few applications. One of the first uses for computers outside the laboratory was crunching numbers for large institutions such as the U.S. Census Bureau and as office machines preparing payroll rosters and other paperwork. The development of transistors and subsequently microprocessors rendered the computer smaller and more useful in a variety of consumer technologies from cars to calculators.

The "information superhighway" of the 1990s also grew out of cold war military research. In 1969, the Pentagon helped institute ARPANET, or the Advanced Research Projects Agency, a network of super computers that linked elite science and technology institutions, such as MIT and Stanford. ARPANET provided a system for communicating and sharing scientific and mathematical data quickly. Linked to other computer networks in 1980, the Internet had two thousand users, mostly in universities. However, by the early 1990s, the number of users had grown to 15 million and numerous entrepreneurs and established corporations explored the commercial possibilities of the network.

The introduction of the personal computer and the Internet reinvigorated an older idea that new technologies held democratic and liberatory potential. Poststructuralist scholars, such as Andrew Ross, Constance Penley, and Donna Haraway, have considered not only the problems but the radical possibilities of information technology. In *Technoculture* (1991), Ross and Penley resisted the "tendency of fatalistic thought" in political and historical critique of technology and sought other kinds of stories that "do not fall into line with the tradition of left cultural despair and alarmism" (p. xii). Along with popular writers and early participants in the popularization of the Internet, these scholars saw the computer and the Internet as the site for fostering countercultural activity. Ross and Penley note that they "reject the postindustrial fantasy of technical sweetness and light. Nonetheless, we recognize that the kinds of liberatory fantasies that surround new technologies are a powerful and persuasive means of social agency" (p. xiv).

In the early 1990s, the World Wide Web, because it was both an anonymous and global form of communication, held the possibility for users to create new communities and re-create their identities online. The figures of the cyborg and the hacker became important cultural images. The cyborg, created from organic and cybernetic materials, as it existed in film, literature, and political discourse, represented both the oppressive potential of cyber-technology under the control of corporations, as in the films *Terminator I* and *II* and *Blade Runner,* and the potentially liberating qualities when co-opted by users, as in the work of the biologist Donna Haraway. The science fiction novels of William Gibson, such as *Neuromancer* (1984), imagine a new basis for cultural power in the intangible world of data and the cojoining of human and machine intelligence. The hacker became a postmodern hero, a social outsider who could upset the corporate elite through programming prowess. In this way, the hacker recalled the innovative and disruptive activities of ham radio operators in the 1920s.

As scholars interested in the cultural meanings of technology, Ross and Penley were not alone in considering the political potential of new technologies. In light of various social and intellectual movements of the postwar period, including new social history, feminism, and poststructuralism, historians of technology have questioned the dominant paradigm of technological progress, or what John Staudenmaier has defined as "progress talk." Many have argued for studying technology as socially constructed. Social construction of technology considers how specific historical forces, cultural desires, and social factors, such as race, gender, and region, have influenced the design and implementation of artifacts and systems. Social historians have fostered new perspectives on invention and innovation. Some have explored the process of innovation from the bottom up, examining the contributions of workers and shop-floor innovation. A few have begun to explore the contibutions of African American inventors and the relationship of technology to discourses of racial difference. Others, such as Susan Douglas, have acknowledged the role of consumers in shaping the design and use of new technologies.

Feminist scholars, in particular, have challenged progress talk by interrogating the gendered meanings of technology. In 1988 the historian Ruth Schwartz Cowan argued that consumer technologies did not save labor in the home but raised standards of cleanliness, among other factors, and created "more work for mother." Others have looked at women's access to engineering schools and the systems which have perpetuated technical knowledge and power. Ultimately, these scholars have contributed to the interpretation of technology as not only culturally constructed but as a form of cultural power.

See also **The Print Revolution; Industrialism and Its Critics; Anti-Modern Discontent between the Wars** *(volume 1);* **The Culture and Critics of the Suburb and the Corporation; Women and Family in the Suburban Age; The Design of the Familiar; The Discovery of the Environment; Working Class; The Natural World** *(volume 2);* **Technological Enclaves; The Internet and Electronic Communications; Television; Radio; Social Construction of Reality** *(in this volume); and other articles in this section.*

BIBLIOGRAPHY

Primary Sources

Official Guide Book of the Fair. Chicago, 1933.

Adams, Henry. *The Education of Henry Adams.* 1907. Edited by Ernest Samuels and Jayne N. Samuels. New York, 1990.

Carson, Rachel. *Silent Spring.* Boston, 1962.

Ford, Henry. *Being a Selection from Mr. Ford's Page in the Dearborn Independent.* Dearborn, Mich., 1926.

Frederick, Christine. *Household Engineering, Scientific Management in the Home.* Chicago, 1925.

Gibson, William. *Neuromancer.* New York, 1984.

Jefferson, Thomas. *Notes on the State of Virginia.* 1785. Reprint, New York, 1964. Page references in the text are from the reprint edition.

Levin, Ira. *The Stepford Wives.* Boston, 1972.

Lewis, Sinclair. *Babbitt.* New York, 1922.

Mann, Thomas. *Picture of a Factory Village.* Providence, R.I., 1833.

Mumford, Lewis. *The Highway and the City.* New York, 1963.

Nader, Ralph. *Unsafe at Any Speed: The Designed-in Dangers of the American Automobile.* New York, 1965.

Sinclair, Upton. *The Flivver King: A Story of Ford-America.* Gerard, Kans., 1937.

Taylor, Frederick Winslow. *The Principles of Scientific Management.* New York, 1911.

Twain, Mark. *A Connecticut Yankee in King Arthur's Court.* Reprint, New York, 1990.

Vonnegut, Kurt. *Player Piano.* New York, 1952.

Secondary Sources

Cowan, Ruth Schwartz. *More Work for Mother: The Ironies of Household Technology from the Open Hearth to the Microwave.* New York, 1983.

Douglas, Susan. *Inventing Amercan Broadcasting, 1899–1933.* Baltimore, 1987.

Hacker, Sally. *Pleasure, Power, and Technology: Some Tales of Gender, Engineering, and the Cooperative Workplace.* Boston, 1989.

Haraway, Donna J. *Simians, Cyborgs, and Women: The Reinvention of Nature.* New York, 1991.

Hindle, Brooke, and Steven Lubar. *Engines of Change: The American Industrial Revolution, 1790–1860.* Washington, D.C., 1986.

Hounshell, David. *From the American System to Mass Production, 1800–1932.* Baltimore, 1985.

Hughes, Thomas. *American Geniuses: A Century of Invention and Technological Enthusiasm, 1870–1970.* New York, 1989.

James, Portia P. *The Real McCoy: African-American Invention and Innovation, 1619–1930.* Washington, D.C., 1989.

Kasson, John. *Civilizing the Machine: Technology and Republican Values in America, 1776–1900.* New York, 1976.

Levy, Steven. *Hackers: Heroes of the Computer Revolution.* Garden City, N.Y., 1984.

Lubar, Steven. *InfoCulture: The Smithsonian Book of Information Age Inventions.* Boston, 1993.

MacKenzie, Donald A., and Judy Wajcman, eds. *The Social Shaping of Technology: How the Refrigerator Got Its Hum.* Philadelphia, 1985.

Marvin, Carolyn. *When Old Technologies Were New: Thinking About Electric Communication in the Late Nineteenth Century.* New York, 1988.

Marx, Leo. *The Machine in the Garden: Technology and the Pastoral Ideal in America.* New York, 2000.

Penley, Constance, and Andrew Ross, eds. *Technoculture.* Minneapolis, Minn., 1991.

Pursell, Carroll. *Machine in America: A Social History of Technology.* Baltimore, 1995.

Rydell, Robert. *World of Fairs: The Century of Progress Expositions.* Chicago, 1993.

Smith, Merritt Roe, and Leo Marx, eds. *Does Technology Drive History? The Dilemma of Technological Determinism.* Cambridge, Mass., 1994.

Staudenmaier, John M. *Technology's Storytellers: Reweaving the Human Fabric.* Cambridge, Mass., 1985.

Trescott, Martha Moore, ed. *Dynamos and Virgins Revisited: Women and Technological Change in History.* Metuchen, N.J., 1979.

POLITICAL ECONOMY

John Wenzler

Before the eighteenth century in Europe, the social process of production was so deeply embedded in cultural traditions, political struggles, and religious practices that economic theory was indistinguishable from moral philosophy. When pre-modern philosophers such as Aristotle or Thomas Aquinas discussed market exchange, they subordinated economic analysis to their moral goals. Generally, they sought to describe a system of "just prices" that would make market exchange consistent with an equitable social order. During the twentieth century, in contrast, intellectuals have become so accustomed to thinking of the market economy as an autonomous realm of nature that economic theory no longer seems to have any relationship to moral philosophy at all. Economics has become a "hard science," like physics, chemistry, or biology, studied by narrowly trained specialists with highly refined mathematical techniques. Although modern economists still believe that their conclusions have important normative implications, they insist that "positive economics" is an objective field of research no more amenable to the speculations of moral philosophers than theoretical physics.

"Political" economists of the eighteenth and nineteenth centuries pursued a more ambiguous form of social science that combined elements of positive economics with elements of Aristotle's moral philosophy. As the capitalist marketplace became the dominant means of organizing the process of production in Western Europe, these early economists applied the methodology of the natural sciences to society. Just as Galileo and Newton had discovered a few abstract principles beneath the diverse phenomena of the natural universe, they hoped to discover a few mechanical laws beneath the chaotic interactions of a market economy. Even as they began to think of the marketplace as an impersonal natural phenomenon, however, pre-twentieth-century political economists continued to assume that their speculations were deeply inter-

twined with the traditional questions of political and moral philosophy. Unlike twentieth-century economists, who combine economic theory with abstract mathematics, political economists combined economic theory with the study of philosophy and history. They believed that their new discipline could judge the moral legitimacy of capitalist society at the same time that it examined the objective laws of capitalist development.

Especially during the nineteenth century in Europe, political economy became an ideological battlefield in which intellectuals debated the relative merits of capitalism and socialism. The classical school of English economics, which dominated European economic thought until late in the nineteenth century, defended capitalism by arguing that political economy revealed the inevitable laws of nature. This version of political economy has been called the "dismal science" because it claimed that the poverty of the English working classes was the inescapable consequence of the "niggardliness of nature." The dismal scientists dismissed the socialists' desire to create a more humane society as an irrational dream. Socialist economists responded to these arguments by arguing that the evils of capitalism were neither natural nor inevitable. Karl Marx, the most influential socialist economist, employed the methodology of classical political economy to argue that capitalism was doomed to failure. According to Marx, capitalism was an unstable social system burdened by social contradictions and wracked by debilitating cycles of boom and bust. Whereas classical economists assumed that capitalism was inescapable, Marx argued that it was destined for the dustbin of history.

In the United States, nineteenth-century political economists developed a unique ideology of capitalism that differed from the dominant theories in Europe. The American version of political economy, which historians have called the "free labor ideology," combined the classical economists' belief that capitalism was based on natural law with the utopian hopes of the socialists. It expressed the conviction that the natural laws discovered by political economy corresponded to the designs of divine providence. American political economists promised that a capitalist society would achieve harmony, prosperity, and equality if only it could allow itself to be governed by the natural laws of the marketplace, without the artificial interference of human institutions. In the utopian market society imagined by American political economists, capitalist development would eliminate the poverty, misery, and class conflict that had plagued Europe for centuries. Economic growth would allow every worthy and hard-working citizen to achieve economic and moral self-reliance by becoming an independent producer, and free trade would create relative equality between men by preventing aristocrats from exploiting the labor of others and by allowing every worker to earn the entire fruits of his labor.

Although the free labor ideology was primarily an American interpretation of capitalism that reflected American social conditions, American economists built it out of intellectual material imported from England. In order to understand how the American economists translated England's "dismal science" into a utopian theory of capitalism, one must have some familiarity with the development of English political economy.

ENGLISH POLITICAL ECONOMY

Adam Smith's System Although English mercantilists and French physiocrats already had begun to develop economic ideas for over one hundred years before Adam Smith published *Wealth of Nations* in 1776, most historians still consider Smith the father of political economy. Smith was the first economist to describe the market economy as a comprehensive system of natural laws. He discovered several fundamental principles that seemed to govern the anarchic phenomena of a market society, and he gave a convincing explanation of how the marketplace transformed the quest for private profit into a means of producing social good. His system became the foundation for almost all economists in America and Europe throughout the nineteenth century, and it continues to influence twentieth-century economists. Three fundamental ideas developed by Smith became central to American economic thought throughout the nineteenth century.

(1) Smith argued that labor was the ultimate source of economic value and claimed that the true wealth of a nation ultimately was determined by the productivity of its labor. He distinguished between the exchange value and the use value of an economic commodity and argued that the exchange value was determined by the amount of labor invested in its production. Labor thus became the ultimate element or substance of nineteenth-century political economy. Just as Newtonian scientists assumed that the varied phenomena of the natural universe ultimately were composed of matter and mass, political economists assumed that all kinds of economic commodities ultimately were composed of labor value.

(2) Smith divided modern society into three fundamental economic classes: landlords, capitalists, and laborers. In a hypothetical "rude state of society," before landlords and capitalists had accumulated property, laborers kept all of the value produced by their labor. However, in modern civilized society laborers had to share their product with landlords who collected rent and capitalists who earned a profit on their business investments.

(3) Most important, Smith posited the existence of an "invisible hand" that governed economic development better than the conscious intentions of human agents. As long as the economy remained competitive, Smith argued that the profit motive would force capitalists to find the most efficient and productive uses for their resources. Unlike warfare, which led to chaos and destruction, a competitive marketplace transformed the natural selfishness of the human animal into an engine of social progress. Thus, most political economists came to believe that their science revealed unconscious laws that actually organized the process of production more efficiently than any laws consciously constructed by human governments.

The Dismal Science When he wrote the *Wealth of Nations* in the eighteenth century, Smith was cautiously optimistic about economic progress and the condition of the working class. He argued that English laborers enjoyed a better standard of living than did the kings of primitive tribes because the rise of capitalism had stimulated economic production. He believed that the economic condition of the working classes would continue to improve as long as the society continued to increase the productivity of its labor. By the beginning of the nineteenth century, however, there was little reason for optimism about the English working classes. Although the economy continued to become more productive, the industrial revolution had devastated the poor. In the first half of the nineteenth century, the stark contrast between the wealth of the English bourgeoisie and the poverty of the English laboring classes became an international scandal. Charles Dickens dramatized the disparity in his best-selling novels, and socialist revolutionaries pointed to the English working class as a revolutionary army waiting to explode.

Nineteenth-century political economists in England responded to this problem by transforming Smith's system of political economy into the dismal science. Although the dismal scientists continued to believe that the laissez-faire system was the most efficient means of organizing economic production, they increasingly emphasized the limitations that natural law imposed on human freedom. They portrayed natural law as an unavoidable constraint that invalidated the utopian schemes of socialist agitators. Thomas Malthus's famous *Essay on the Principles of Population* (1798) was the cornerstone of the dismal science. Malthus's essay asserted that natural law—not human sin or a flawed social system—made the working classes poor. Throughout history, according to Malthus, human populations always had increased faster than the supply of food. War, famine, and disease had been the natural means of regulating human populations. According to Malthus, any utopian scheme that hoped to lift the working classes out of poverty was doomed to failure. No matter how much wealth was redistributed from the rich to the poor, a rising population soon would reduce everyone to poverty.

David Ricardo combined Malthus's law of population with Smith's theories to develop the theory of distribution that dominated English economic theory until late in the nineteenth century. According to Ricardo, capitalists initiated the process of production, paid the other classes for their services, and kept the residual income as their profits. The rent that capitalists paid to landlords was a monopoly profit on the productivity of the soil. The "natural" rate of wages that capitalists paid to laborers equaled the minimum amount necessary for the laborers to maintain themselves and their families. If the supply of labor increased so that wages fell below the subsistence level, Ricardo assumed that Malthusian checks on population would reduce the number of workers until the supply of labor equaled demand. If the accumulation of capital or the increasing productivity of labor pushed wages above the subsistence level, Malthus's law of population proved that the supply of labor would increase until wages fell back to their "natural" level.

There were several pessimistic conclusions built into the theories of Malthus and Ricardo. Not only did they believe that wages naturally tended to fall to the minimum subsistence level, but they also suggested that the economic interests of the different classes conflicted with each other. When wages or rents increased, the profits earned by capitalists automatically fell. Furthermore, they argued that any attempt by the government to alleviate the suffering caused by the economic system would be counterproductive. For example, they vigorously attacked the English poor laws, which attempted to improve the lives of workers by providing them with unemployment relief. Although the poor laws made sense from the perspective of traditional moral philosophy, Malthus and Ricardo argued that they had disastrous consequences from the perspective of political economy. By reducing the penalties that nature had imposed on overpopulation, the poor laws encouraged paupers to have babies almost without limits. Eventually, all of the excess productivity of the economy would be devoted to the maintenance of a huge population of unproductive and unnecessary laborers. Therefore, instead of improving the lot of the poor, as the moralists intended, the poor laws simply would reduce everyone to poverty. According to the English classical economists, the inevitable laws of nature prevented men from shaping society according to the moral desires of romantic critics or utopian reformers.

POLITICAL ECONOMY IN THE UNITED STATES

American Social Conditions   The dismal science was less convincing in the United States than in England because American capitalism seemed to have less dismal consequences for the working classes. Unlike England, the United States possessed an abundance of fertile farmland and lacked an entrenched landowning aristocracy. Many small farmers continued to own land throughout the nineteenth century and often prospered in the growing market economy by selling grain to Europe. Manufacturing businesses also tended to be smaller in the United States than in England. Although a few entrepreneurs built large textile factories in New England, most American laborers worked in shops with less than ten people until the 1880s or the 1890s. They also earned higher wages than did English workers due to the relative scarcity of labor in the United States. Consequently, economic inequality and class distinctions seemed to be less severe in the United States than in Europe. Most nineteenth-century Americans believed that all men eventually would have the opportunity to participate in the

THE LABOR THEORY OF VALUE

It is plain, that if a man expend labor in the creation of a value, this labor gives him a right to the exclusive possession of that value; that is, supposing the original elements belonged to no one else. Now, as almost all the qualities which gratify human desire, can exist only by the exertion of this labor, it follows, that all such objects must have already become the exclusive possession of some human being. Hence, he who wishes to possess such objects, must either himself expend the labor necessary for producing them, or else he must procure them by voluntary concession, from some one who has already expended it. But he who has expended labor upon a substance, will never voluntarily surrender it up, either for nothing, or for that which he can obtain without labor. . . . Hence, every man who desires the means of happiness, must labor to obtain them.

Source: Wayland, p. 19.

growing market economy as independent producers. Although this belief ignored the economic aspirations of women, Native Americans, and blacks, most white males did have better economic opportunities in the United States than in Europe.

The political differences between the United States and England reinforced the economic differences. Not only did the average American man have a better chance to achieve economic independence than did the average English man, he also had more political liberty. The United States, where almost all white males could vote regardless of their wealth, was much more democratic than England until late in the nineteenth century. Nineteenth-century Americans constantly congratulated themselves on creating a democratic republic that had liberated them from the hierarchical, aristocratic society of Europe. In this democratic society, poor Americans were less likely to support revolutionary radicals than were poor Europeans because Americans believed that they could influence the government through the conventional political process. At the same time, political and intellectual leaders in the United States were forced to develop economic arguments that would appeal to the economic hopes of the lower classes. Unlike English political econ-

omists, who often ridiculed the economic aspirations of their disenfranchised working classes, American political economists tried to convince workers to support the existing economic system.

Most of the American economists in this period were public intellectuals who embedded their economic ideas in popular moral beliefs rather than academic experts who specialized in abstract theory. Henry C. Carey, probably the most original American economist of the early nineteenth century, was a publisher who had made an independent fortune before he began to write his *Principles of Political Economy*. Daniel Raymond, another influential theorist, was an unsuccessful lawyer who worked on his economics while waiting for clients in his office. Journalists and newspaper writers such a Jacob Cardozo and Horace Greeley also participated vigorously in economic debate. Within the universities, moral philosophers rather than highly trained experts taught economic theory until late in the nineteenth century. Francis Wayland, the president of Brown University, whose *Elements of Political Economy* became the most popular textbook of the nineteenth century, also wrote *The Elements of Moral Science*. According to Wayland, "the principles of Political Economy are so closely analogous to those of Moral Philosophy, that almost every question in the one, may be argued on grounds belonging to the other" (*The Elements of Political Economy*, p. iv). By combining economic ideas with moral philosophy, these theorists developed a popular moral defense of the American economy that twentieth century historians have called the "Free Labor Ideology."

Free Labor Ideology   Unlike the dismal scientist in England, the American political economists emphasized the generosity rather than the niggardliness of nature. Whereas the English economists had argued that a niggardly natural universe doomed most people to poverty, American economists argued that a bountiful natural universe could make everyone rich. Henry C. Carey perfectly articulated this belief when he claimed that:

the prosperity of nations and the happiness of the individuals composing them, are in the ratio in which the laws of nature have been allowed to govern their operations, and that the poverty, misery, and distress that exist are invariably to be traced to the interference of man with those laws, and that they exist in the ratio of that interference. (*Principles of Political Economy*, vol. 1, p. xvi)

Unlike Smith, who had seen laissez-faire primarily as a practical political policy, Carey and most other American economists saw the workings of providence in the invisible hand of economic law. They assumed that the system of laissez-faire was God's law and believed that the natural mechanisms of the market economy automatically would create a heaven on earth. They attributed the misery of the English working class to neither the niggardliness of nature nor the flaws of capitalism but to the continuing influence of artificial aristocratic institutions. In the New World, where American citizens had liberated themselves from the shackles of feudal oppression, poverty and social conflict soon would fade into memory.

Implicit in the American political economists' faith in natural law was the idea that Smith's labor theory of value expressed the fundamental moral principle at the heart of a capitalist economy. In a just society, according to the American political economists, every worker would get to keep all of the exchange value produced by his own labor. British political economists did not necessarily share this moral belief. They usually interpreted the labor theory of value as an objective means of determining the exchange value of commodities rather than a normative means of determining a just distribution of wealth. In their opinion, it was natural and beneficial that landlords and capitalists accumulated some of the wealth produced by labor. This arrangement benefited society because the profits earned by capitalists encouraged them to employ capital in the most productive way, and the rents collected by landlords gave them the freedom to cultivate the refinements of art and culture.

From the perspective of a nineteenth-century American, however, an amoral interpretation of the labor theory of value was incomprehensible. Whereas the English economists often saw labor as a degrading necessity imposed on an unfortunate class, American economists believed labor conferred moral dignity on the worker at the same time that it produced economic value. The notion that labor was the only morally legitimate means of earning an income was so pervasive in nineteenth-century culture that even slave owners tended to justify their income as the "fruits of their labor." In a society that attributed so much moral significance to labor, American political economists usually interpreted the labor theory of value as a moral contract between the individual worker and nature. As long as government allowed natural laws of exchange to work without interference, the labor theory of value guaranteed that every individual would earn exactly what he had produced. Only the artificial manipulations of aristocrats or monopolists

could disrupt the natural moral justice produced by a system of free market exchange.

American economists also argued that capitalist development tended to eliminate class distinctions. In England, the idea of a classless capitalist society never occurred to Smith, Malthus, or Ricardo. They assumed that the class divisions that they perceived in modern England were an inevitable consequence of social progress. It was only in Smith's "rude state of nature," when everyone had been poor, that there had been relative equality between men. According to the American economists, however, the English class structure was an unnatural vestige of feudalism. The European upper classes had accumulated their property through force and fraud, and they maintained their power only through their control of governmental institutions. In a perfectly natural market economy, American economists believed that class differences would dissolve.

Therefore, although they accepted Smith's distinction between capitalists, landlords, and laborers, American economists insisted that the interests of all of these classes were completely harmonious. Whereas Ricardo had argued that profits fell when wages rose, American economists argued that everyone would get richer at the same time in an increasingly productive society. They also argued that the social classes already had begun to melt together in the United States. In America, the difference between land and capital was much less important than in England because Americans had eliminated primogeniture laws that restricted the trade in land. American economists also believed that the divide between capitalists and laborers was disappearing in the United States. Because they assumed that laborers earned all of the value that they produced, American political economists believed that wages had to rise when the economy became more productive. Eventually, rising wages would allow almost everyone to become a laborer and a capitalist at the same time. No one would be rich enough to live off the labor of others, but no one would be so poor that he could not achieve economic independence at some point in his life.

This system of economic belief became a powerful defense of the American economy throughout the nineteenth century because it combined an appealing, quasi-religious faith in the laws of nature with a reasonably accurate description of early-nineteenth-century American society. However, the free labor ideology was burdened with a tragic flaw that ultimately doomed it to failure. It was dismally poor at predicting the future. Having observed that a little bit of capitalism had created some equality and independence, American political economists decided that more capitalism automatically would bring more liberty and equality. Contrary to their expectations, however, economic inequality increased throughout the nineteenth century. Factories constantly got larger and more expensive. Fewer and fewer workers managed to achieve economic independence, and an increasing number of independent producers lost their businesses. Although most contemporary historians believe that this concentration of wealth was the consequence of capitalist development itself, nineteenth-century American economists had trouble seeing it that way. In their minds, economic inequality and class conflict simply could not arise from the natural laws of the marketplace. Until the free labor ideology finally broke under the weight of its contradictions late in the nineteenth century, they constantly blamed their failed predictions on the interference of corrupt and aristocratic external forces.

Free Trade Versus Protectionism   Many of the anxieties caused by the inability of the American economy to fulfill the utopian expectations of American economists were channeled into debates about economic policy. In almost any policy debate, each side would describe its own proposals as a means of restoring natural law to the American economy while accusing its opponents of being aristocrats who would corrupt the economy for their private gain. Until the Civil War, two fundamentally different approaches to economic policy, "free trade" and "protectionism," competed for control of the government. Free traders, who were usually associated with the Democratic Party, small farmers, and southern planters, desired a minimal state that did almost nothing except protect the rights of property. They opposed high tariff rates, high taxes, centralized banks, and government investment of any kind. Protectionists, who were usually associated with Whigs, Republicans, and northern manufacturers, wanted the state to take a more active role in promoting industrial development. They favored high tariffs, a centralized banking system, and governmental investment in a transportation system that would connect western farmers with eastern manufacturers.

It was not difficult for free traders to employ the free labor ideology to support their position because they relied on the idea that laissez-faire corresponded to the natural laws of God. They argued that protectionists sought to interfere with the laws of the international marketplace only because they wanted to use the power of the government to rob independent producers of the fruits of their labor. According to the free traders, high tariffs allowed industrial monopolists to take income out of the pockets of honest producers, and central banks allowed powerful men to manipulate the money supply in order to acquire unearned income. Free traders also distrusted the protectionists' desire to stimulate manufacturing because they saw the United States as an agricultural society peopled primarily by independent farmers. They feared that too much industrial development would transform American citizens into helpless proletarians who would suffer the dismal fate of English laborers. Consequently, free traders usually favored territorial expansion rather than industrial development as the best means of promoting economic progress. They argued that the new land acquired in the Louisiana Purchase and the Mexican-American War would allow the United States to expand for years as an agricultural republic without encountering the problems that Malthus had traced to declining soil fertility. They were vague about what would happen when the United States ran out of empty farmland, but they believed that the nation could live in harmony with nature for a long time before facing that problem.

Protectionist economists had to work harder to connect their policy to the free labor ideology because it sounded paradoxical to argue that high tariffs corresponded with the natural laws of the marketplace. They made their case most convincingly by focusing on the evils of English capitalism. Whereas the free traders argued that industrial development would make the United States like England, protectionists argued that free trade would force Americans to suffer the fate of Englishmen. According to the protectionists, England suffered from poverty and class conflict because it had pursued an unnatural path of development. Powerful landlords and "loomlords" had hijacked the wealth created by economic progress and had undermined the utopian potential of economic development. When the United States engaged in free trade with such a powerful and pernicious economy, it was forced to follow the same corrupt pattern of development. Independent American producers were destroyed by competition with the cheap commodities and the "pauper labor" of England. Eventually, they exhausted their lands, lost their resources, and found themselves dominated by the same industrial monopolists that dominated the English working class. The only way for the United States to avoid this fate, according to the protectionists, was to "protect" itself from English imports. If America were to build an economic wall between itself and England, it could follow the natural process of development in which economic progress coincided with increasing social harmony and economic justice.

This analysis forced the protectionists to articulate more thorough arguments against the Malthusian assumptions of the dismal science than did the free traders. Whereas free traders suggested that the United States could avoid the penalties of overpopulation through territorial expansion, the protectionists believed that Malthus was simply wrong about the consequences of a growing population. They argued that technological progress and the increasing division of labor allowed the per capita productivity of agriculture to increase much faster than the population increased. Thus, the poverty of the English working class was due to the rapacity of the English ruling class rather than a decreasing supply of food. Much like the European socialists, the protectionists argued that classical economics simply allowed English rulers to avoid blame for poverty by attributing the evils of their society to the laws of nature. Of course, the protectionists did not combine this analysis with the revolutionary proposals of the socialists, and they failed to explain why American capitalists would not accumulate the same power as English industrialists when American industry became capital intensive. Nevertheless, the protectionist argument allowed American economists to believe that the United States could create a modern industrial society consistent with the moral values of the free labor ideology.

Free Labor and Slavery   The anxiety caused by the failures of the free labor ideology also was channeled into the debate about slavery. From the perspective of the twentieth century, of course, the continuing existence of slavery in the Southern states seems to be the most glaring contradiction of the free labor ideology. It is hard to understand how nineteenth-century Americans could have reconciled the moral belief that laborers deserved the entire fruits of their labor with a social system in which so many laborers had no property rights at all. However, the pervasive racism of nineteenth-century society allowed most Americans to ignore this contradiction in the early part of the century. Although there always were critics who attacked the evils of slavery, most Americans did not think that blacks (or women or Indians) had the same moral rights as white laborers. Furthermore, during the late eighteenth and early nineteenth century, many Americans believed that slavery was a dying institution that would disappear as the economy became more productive. Some economists argued that the gradual elimination of slavery would be one of the moral benefits of capitalist development.

During the 1840s and 1850s, however, it became harder for Northerners to ignore the contradiction between slavery and the ideals of free labor for a couple of reasons. First, it began to seem less likely that slavery would die a natural death because the growth of textile manufacturing in England rejuvenated slavery as an economic institution. Many planters in the Cotton Belt, who earned large fortunes by selling cotton to English manufacturers, did not intend to lose the slave labor that generated their wealth. Second, it also was becoming more obvious to some in the North that the predictions of the free labor ideology were failing to materialize. There was a small but growing working class in Northern cities during this period, and class conflict was increasing. The economic panics of 1837 and 1857 caused a great deal of economic suffering among the working class and cast doubt on the virtue and harmony of the free market system. Although most Americans continued to live on small farms as independent producers, the economy seemed to be moving in the wrong direction. Instead of creating harmony and independence, the economic development seemed to be creating conflict and anxiety.

There were a couple of intellectual responses to these economic developments. In the South, some apologists for slavery abandoned the free labor ideology to formulate a more vigorous defense of the "peculiar institution." They began to argue that all societies, even societies that claimed to honor free labor, were divided into a working class and a leisure class. Then, they pointed to the misery of the working classes in England and New England to suggest that slavery actually treated its laborers better than the system of free labor. Northern intellectuals responded to these charges by blaming slavery for the problems suffered by the North. They argued that the troubles suffered by Northern society were not due to the inherent inadequacy of the free labor system but to the corrupt influence of the slave system within the United States. Just as protectionists had argued that competition with the pauper labor of England impoverished Northern workers, northern politicians began to claim that competition with Southern slave labor enslaved Northerners.

Abraham Lincoln's famous assertion that the nation "cannot endure permanently half slave and half free" expressed this economic belief. If the United States continued to allow slavery to exist within its economy, many northerners believed that all workers would become virtually enslaved to Southern aristocrats and the "slave power."

When combined with the explicitly moral arguments of the abolitionists, these economic arguments helped to legitimize the Civil War in the North. In part, at least, the war attempted to preserve and protect the social vision articulated by American political economists. The elimination of the "slave power" would remove imperfections from the American market economy and allow the nation to achieve the utopian social order that the economists had imagined.

Decline of Free Labor Ideology   The Civil War did eliminate slavery, but it failed to realize the rest of the promises of the free labor ideology. During the last three decades of the nineteenth century, it became impossible to believe that industrial development would have drastically different consequences in the United States than in England. In this period, the United States became a country of large factories, giant corporations, robber barons, and captains of industry. Wealth and ownership increasingly concentrated in the hands of a few capitalists, who organized trusts and monopolies that dominated the national marketplace. At the same time, national organizations of labor began to raise the class-consciousness of workers and gave them the power to organize strikes and boycotts. Between 1877 and 1900, class conflict became particularly intense and bloody as workers and owners fought for control of the workplace. In such a bloody era of conflict and inequality, the vision of a classless capitalist society of independent entrepreneurs began to seem like a nostalgic dream rather than the natural end of capitalist development.

Several popular economic writers did try to preserve the ideals of the free labor ideology in the Gilded Age by transforming it into a radical call for social change. Henry George, whose *Progress and Poverty* (1879) became the best-selling economics text ever written by an American, claimed that a fundamental flaw in the American laws of property had undermined the promises of the free labor ideology. According to George, it was immoral for an individual to possess land as private property because land was the gift of God to humanity. Therefore, land rent was an illegitimate form of income

that generated economic inequality and distorted the entire economic system. If the government were to collect all rent through a single tax, George argued, the natural harmony of the economy would be restored. Other radical writers proposed similar remedies that promised to destroy the power of industrial capitalists and to achieve the utopian goals of the antebellum political economists. Their ideas resonated with large numbers of Americans and generated a powerful political protest during the last decade of the nineteenth century. Through the Populist Party of the early 1890s and William Jennings Bryan's Democratic campaign of 1896, political leaders inspired by the ideas of radical political economists threatened to take control of the entire political system.

By the beginning of the twentieth century, however, the power and influence of corporate capitalists had overwhelmed the radicals. In this century, economic thought and economic policy has been dominated by the goals and assumptions of corporate managers. Most economic thinkers have abandoned "political economy" for "economics." They have retreated from the idea that economic theory can judge the moral legitimacy of capitalism, and they focus on the analysis of capitalism as an objective system. Much like corporate executives, professional economists see themselves as technocrats who focus on amoral questions of efficiency rather than ideologically charged problems of justice and equity.

However, it is difficult to say whether the ideals of the free labor ideology will be banished permanently to history. Despite the retreat of professional economists from the moral values of nineteenth-century political economists, these values retain a surprisingly powerful hold on the popular imagination. Although modern economics has shaped the policies pursued by political and business leaders, it has never achieved the widespread popularity enjoyed by nineteenth-century economists. The same technical jargon and alienating mathematical prose that has allowed specialists to monopolize modern economic discourse has prevented them from articulating a powerful popular ideology. As long as economic leaders keep the economy running smoothly, this contrast between elite theory and popular opinion is relatively insignificant. During periods of social stress and conflict, however, the appealing moral vision articulated by nineteenth-century American economists still may influence American society in unexpected ways.

See also **Liberalism and Republicanism; Federalists and Antifederalists; Jacksonian Ideology; Whig Ideology; Agrarianism and the Agrarian Ideal in Early America; Slavery and Race; Gender, Social Class, Race, and Material Life; Industrialism and Its Critics** *(volume 1);* **The Culture and Critics of the Suburb and the Corporation; Women and Family in the Suburban Age; Working Class** *(volume 2);* **Class; Marxist Approaches; Weberian Approaches** *(in this volume); and other articles in this section.*

BIBLIOGRAPHY

Appleby, Joyce O. *Capitalism and a New Social Order: The Republican Vision of the 1790s.* New York, 1984.

Blaug, Mark. *Economic Theory in Retrospect.* London, 1997.

Boritt, G. S. *Lincoln and the Economics of the American Dream.* Memphis, Tenn., 1978.

Cardozo, Jacob N. *Notes on Political Economy.* 1826. Reprint, New York, 1960.

Carey, Henry C. *Principles of Political Economy.* Philadelphia, 1837.

——. *The Past, the Present, and the Future.* Philadelphia, 1848.

Conkin, Paul. *Prophets of Prosperity: America's First Political Economists.* Bloomington, Ind., 1980.

Dorfman, Joseph. *The Economic Mind in American Civilization.* 5 vols. New York, 1946–1959.

Foner, Eric. *Free Soil, Free Labor, Free Men: The Ideology of the Republican Party before the Civil War.* New York, 1970.

George, Henry. *Progress and Poverty.* 1879. Reprint, New York, 1971.

Heilbroner, Robert L. *The Worldly Philosophers: The Lives, Times, and Ideas of the Great Economic Thinkers.* New York, 1979.

Hunt, E. K. *History of Economic Thought: A Critical Perspective.* New York, 1992.

Huston, James L. *Securing the Fruits of Labor: The American Concept of Wealth Distribution, 1765–1900.* Baton Rouge, La., 1998.

Lloyd, Henry Demarest. *The Lords of Industry.* 1910. Reprint, New York, 1973.

Malthus, Thomas. *An Essay on the Principle of Population.* 1798. Reprint, London, 1926.

Mill, John Stuart. *Principles of Political Economy.* 1848. Reprint, New York, 1909.

North, Douglass C. *The Economic Growth of the United States, 1790–1860.* Englewood Cliffs, N.J., 1961.

Polanyi, Karl. *The Great Transformation.* 1944. Reprint, Boston, 1985.

Raymond, Daniel. *The Elements of Political Economy.* Baltimore, 1823.

Ricardo, David. *Principles of Political Economy.* 1817. Reprint, London, 1943.

——. *The Works and Correspondence of David Ricardo.* Vol. 1, *On the Principles of Political Economy and Taxation.* Edited by Piero Sraffa. Cambridge, U.K., 1951.

Ross, Dorothy. *The Origins of American Social Science.* Cambridge, U.K., and New York, 1991.

Schumpeter, Joseph A. *History of Economic Analysis.* Edited by Elizabeth Boody Schumpeter. New York, 1954.

Sellers, Charles G. *The Market Revolution: Jacksonian America, 1815–1846.* New York, 1991.

Smith, Adam. *An Inquiry into the Nature and Causes of the Wealth of Nations.* 1776. Reprint, New York, 1937.

Teilhac, Ernest. *Pioneers of American Economic Thought in the Nineteenth Century.* Translated by E. A. Johnson. New York, 1936.

Thomas, John L. *Alternative America: Henry George, Edward Bellamy, Henry Demarest Lloyd, and the Adversary Tradition.* Cambridge, Mass., 1983.

Wayland, Francis. *The Elements of Political Economy.* 1837. Reprint, Boston, 1852.

CONSUMERISM

Pamela Walker Laird

Americans celebrate the founding of their nation with the Fourth of July, but they celebrate the founding of their culture with a feast, Thanksgiving. In 1621 both Native Americans and the English residents of Plymouth Colony had long-standing traditions of harvest feasting and games. For the next two centuries, irregularly proclaimed official thanksgivings combined with traditional harvest celebrations on regional, and sometimes national, levels. In 1827 a determined campaign began to establish a permanent national holiday. This came to fruition in 1863, when, in the "midst of a civil war of unequaled magnitude and severity," President Abraham Lincoln proclaimed a "day of thanksgiving and praise." Lincoln solemnly hoped that the growing abundance from "the blessings of fruitful fields" and "the fields of peaceful industry" would "heal the wounds of the nation." Only decades later, in the 1890s, did the Plymouth Pilgrims become the central icon of this national celebration. Then, in the 1920s and 1930s, Thanksgiving took on, for most Americans, its contemporary form: a day of feasts and games—the latter now watched, not played—that serves as the ritual prelude to a season of frenzied stimulation, consumption, and social gatherings that ends with ringing in the new year.

BALANCING SPIRITUALITY AND MATERIALISM

Whether or not the Pilgrims balanced feasting and games with solemnity to their satisfaction, Americans have ever since worried about such balances, fearing declension from idealism. Yet Puritans and their cultural descendants have interpreted worldly success as a sign of providential favor or, later, of personal merit. These beliefs combined with abundant resources to produce a society in which most people prize materialistic progress even while many, sometimes the same, people decry a continuing fall

from grace. Within this broad context, goods and services have become increasingly purchased rather than homemade. Personal and family identities have hinged more upon purchase decisions, and agents farther and farther from consumers have come to influence the meanings of goods and activities. Moreover, Americans have come to see "need" as limitless and infinitely malleable. Through four centuries the meanings of goods and activities have changed right along with the changing relations between producers, marketers, and consumers.

Many different belief systems have competed for cultural authority over the centuries and across the country. For instance, not all the participants at the 1621 Thanksgiving were either Native American or Puritan. Most of the English on the *Mayflower* were unambiguously seeking material improvement, much like the Virginia settlers who developed a market-oriented tobacco agriculture. New England Puritans even argued among themselves, caught between theologians' admonishments and the attractions of "frivolous" goods. Sumptuary laws that defined who could wear such items as silver and gold buckles and buttons, or even silk scarves, linked social class and gender with the meanings of purchased goods. Not surprisingly, these laws peaked in the 1650s, just as New Englanders began to prosper enough to acquire decorative items and to expand their notions of what they needed. The 1690s saw dramatic increases in household inventories, and some scholars even attribute the virulence of the Salem witchcraft trials (1692–1693) to tensions between material and spiritual ambitions.

Predispositions to a Consumer Culture Despite conflicts between them, almost all of the European migrants to the New World brought with them sets of beliefs that clearly distinguished them from the Native Americans and that predisposed them to develop a consumer culture. For instance, European customs allowed land to be bought and sold outright while Native American customs did not. Thus, Europeans commodified land, as they did grain, cattle, and even people at that time, and exchanged them all in the marketplace. European migrants relied on market exchanges, including barter, and were rarely self-sufficient. People who did not participate in the market, who did not work hard to produce goods for exchange, and who did not try to enhance their material assets were generally considered morally as well as practically indolent or unwise. At the other extreme in the 1600s, many Virginian English defied laws that required planting grains and grew only tobacco; sometimes they even starved for lack of food, such was the lure of market ambition.

European customs also prized a permanent dwelling surrounded by a fence or wall to demarcate clearly and protect property and gardens from neighbors' livestock and other threats. Owners' ties to a place and its constructed environment combined with a growing acceptance of expanding needs and the rise of new aspirations to gentility and physical comfort in the eighteenth century. Rising trade with Europe and more exotic lands had begun increasing the varieties and quantities of goods available to the American colonies. Continuing a trend that began with the Crusades, people saw spices and teas, then teacups, sugar products, new textiles, and beddings, and sought to add them to their lifestyles. Falling prices and heightened availability fueled the consumer market as consumer demand, in turn, motivated ever more entrepreneurs to increase availability.

Meanings of Objects Simply seeing a new product does not suffice to make it desirable; meanings generate desires. The dynamics of cost and accessibility ensured that when new items entered the preindustrial marketplace, they entered through the experiences, lives, and homes of the elite. Even when costs decreased, the burnish of status adhered to goods as they moved into the mainstream. Yet neither emulation of higher classes nor distancing from lower classes sufficed to drive consumption. As Americans continued their struggle with tensions between inner and outer graces, they still sought signs of the former through the latter. So it was that gentility rose in their esteem and came to encompass politeness and refinement. Expressing these inner graces, in turn, required accoutrements, such as spoons, bowls, and knives, then forks and plates, to allow genteel people to avoid touching food directly. Respectability's requirements expanded to include soap, linen shirts, tables and

chairs, and a home with bedrooms separated from work, receiving, and dining areas. The middling and upper classes began to perceive some bodily functions, as well as direct contact with food and strangers, to be awkward and unseemly as privacy and delicacy rose in their esteem. Consequently, they came to seek out material goods that helped them to regulate and minimize such contacts. Unprecedented varieties of goods combined with increasingly homogeneous tastes by the 1760s and 1770s to help bond colonial consumers into boycotters of imports, then revolutionaries when Britain's mercantilism threatened the colonies' materialist expectations and ambitions.

George Washington understood that consumables had public meanings, for he purposefully took his presidential oath in a suit of American-made broadcloth. Although this cloth was not as fine as the imports that he could afford, his choice lent prestige to domestic manufacturers, just as the spread eagle on his buttons denoted national pride. Washington proclaimed a day of national thanksgiving, intended as a day of prayer to foster national survival, not consumption, but political battles soon raged about the new nation's material and economic goals. Alexander Hamilton and Thomas Jefferson each represented opposing factions, one arguing that the United States should strive for heightened industry and merchandising, the other that its citizens should seek virtue by avoiding engagement in the market. Debates about tariffs—taxes on imports that comprised most U.S. revenues into the twentieth century—likewise rocked federal politics: How much and what did citizens need to consume? From where should they make those purchases? How much profit should be possible, and to whom?

INDUSTRIAL EXPANSION AND MARKETING

By the 1820s Americans' options for participating in a marketplace of goods were expanding ever faster. Imports plus domestic processing and manufacturing increased the varieties of foodstuffs, beverages, textiles, fineries, and household items. For decades to come, however, most of the expanding choices of goods fit into categories people already understood—fancier, perhaps, but not unknown. Merchants and peddlers distributed the growing abundance; the former's advertising helped newspapers and then other printed media to grow, accelerating a trend that continues, as marketers have always subsidized advances in communication technologies in order to maximize their reach and appeal. The earliest published advertisements resembled today's classified ads. Rarely did products have brand names and rarely did advertisers try to persuade buyers. Both merchandisers and consumers generally assumed that demand exceeded supply and that people pretty much knew what they wanted from their own experiences. The exceptions to this rule proved it: neither the purveyors of medicinal and alcoholic products nor entertainers could assume demand. Competing fiercely with each other and with other claims on discretionary spending, they created early attempts at persuasive advertisement. So that people would remember who made which claims, these promoters pioneered the use of trademarks on consumer-sized packaging. By the middle of the nineteenth century, more and more producers took on the marketing strategies that they observed successfully promoting medicines, alcohol, and entertainments.

Desires for comfort and refinement had already expanded American material ambitions in the eighteenth century. Rather than serving as attainable goals, however, these ambitions sped up a reciprocal dynamic through which expanding desires encouraged entrepreneurs to add to the temptations. The growing realization that wants—indeed, needs—could continue to expand indefinitely fueled the nineteenth century's explosion of innovation. The changing meanings that people in a consumer culture attach to objects, and the ways in which those meanings reflect purchasers' identities, cause fashions to change and desires to mutate. This potential to change meanings (and therefore desires) provides entrepreneurs with their chance at fortune. In his classic 1942 analysis *The Economic Effects of Advertising,* Neil H. Borden explained that "Enterprise led to the building of factories, but their building and operation depended upon the entrepreneurs' seeing an opportunity to dispose of their outputs" (p. 27). The remarkably expanding abundance of Victorian gadgetry, foods, and fashions attests to the power of this cycle.

Gendered Consumption
Americans have increasingly purchased rather than made what they consumed. This participation in the marketplace required either cash or products such as cash crops that could be exchanged for goods and services. Whether or not the women in a family earned money, Americans increasingly expected all men to do so. So the social burden of "providing" for families fell on men, regardless of the contribution of

women. Unlike traditional workplaces on family farms or in artisans' shops, men earned these new livelihoods in mines, factories, and office buildings, making it impossible for families and neighbors to judge their diligence. Because diligence and worldly success still measured a man's moral character, a family's ability to consume—to build a house, to decorate it and its inhabitants—became important symbols, visible to all, of a man's personal merit and worth. Andrew Jackson Downing, the foremost authority on home design in the mid-nineteenth century, wrote that "Much of the character of everyman may be read in his house." As the tensions of the new social and economic orders rose, mainstream culture divided by gender into what came to be called separate spheres. Yet success in either sphere required cooperation in both. A woman could not nurture her family in a proper household unless she could acquire the expanding list of necessities for respectability. Likewise, a man required not only room and board but also the spiritual and social support of what Christopher Lasch called a "haven in a heartless world" in his 1977 book of that title. This version of cultural progress required, it seemed, a man to earn each family's livelihood and a woman to nurture its bodies and spirits. A bountiful, beautiful home and family bore witness to the success of such endeavors.

Popular culture widely advocated this symbiosis between men and women through pulpits, newspapers, magazines, books, and advertisements. Clarence Cook's influential 1877 book, *The House Beautiful,* expressed the standard belief: "When a man dwells in love, he can . . . retire home to his sanctuary and refectory, and his gardens of sweetness and chaste refinements" (p. 12). These refinements had long appeared to many as the link between home and nation, between private and public progress. Sarah Josepha Hale's decades-long campaign for a national thanksgiving holiday sought to strengthen national unity through a universal recognition of a refined and bountiful home life. As a popular writer and the editor of *Godey's Lady's Book,* Hale lobbied for a spiritual and patriotic holiday that rejoiced in the growing abundance of agriculture and industry. While many other New Englanders wanted to minimize the materialist components of Thanksgiving, its popularity elsewhere grew with what some thought were "abuses"—what Charles Francis Adams labeled in 1831 "the demolition of edibles." Hale encouraged indulgence in the pleasures of domestic consumption for this holiday, publishing Thanksgiving recipes and menus that already insisted on roasted turkey and pumpkin pie as "indispensable." She did not approve, however, of the public games some enjoyed.

Marketing and Consuming Material Progress

Participating in material progress became an important motivation for consumption by the middle 1800s, justified by popular beliefs that linked material and social improvement together and, in turn, linked both to hard work. A biblical saying that appeared frequently in nineteenth-century literature asserted, "Seest thou a man diligent in his business? He shall stand before kings." Because technical innovations provided the most visible signs of progress, they became—as the tools and products of progress—its most widely shared symbols. Advances in both continuous-process machinery and specialized batch production, as well as in distribution of information, goods, and people, reduced the costs and increased the variety of consumer goods. Demonstrating knowledge of and ability to purchase and use new devices and products came to measure people's modernity. For instance, almost everyone knew about electricity from public applications, such as the telegraph and arc lights, but few people could actually use it at home. Excitement about this technological wonder encouraged entrepreneurs to market everything from patent medicines to string beans to straight (nonelectric) razors with the word "electric" in their trade names and lightning bolts on their packages. The popularity of such products showed people's eagerness to participate in the new era, using products of new technologies marked with symbols and promises of other technologies. Locomotives, steamboats, and factories topped with billowing clouds of smoke filled advertisements and labels of everything from insurance to tobacco to ladies' corsets to vegetables. Even people who objected to the political economy of the time, such as Edward Bellamy, author of the enormously popular utopian novel *Looking Backward, 2000–1887* (1888), and Henry George, the well-known author of *Progress and Poverty* (1879), never questioned the merits of industrialization. Their concerns lay with the distribution of the benefits of industrial labors, profits, and goods. *Looking Backward,* in fact, imaginatively describes public palaces of consumption in which all citizens have both financial and physical access to more goods and services than they care to purchase.

Not all observers approved of this growing, if ill-distributed, abundance; many were concerned about its impact on idealism. Thorstein Veblen published *The Theory of the Leisure Class: An Economic Study of Institutions* in 1899 to object to the pride that successful Americans took in what he called conspicuous consumption. Current fashions for women and children, with all their frills and flounces, boasted of affluence. He rejected attempts to justify such consumption because of the strenuous labors that it required of men in the business world and women at home, or the educating and nurturing that success allegedly made possible. Manufacturers and merchants still promoted their wares in lavish ads that raised standards for consumption. Proper Victorians' leisure was expected to provide evidence of their prosperity through care of children, art, and elegance. Accordingly, prairie families proudly displayed their pianos or reed organs in front of their sod houses for itinerant photographers to include in family portraits.

Industrializing and Commercializing Time

American traditions of valuing time go back to Puritan roots and found popular expression later in Benjamin Franklin's writings. Industrialization rewarded time-thrift more than ever, and Americans have constantly sought ways to regiment labor. Industrialists often advertised their products as means of increasing the productivity of home labor, displaying clocks to measure their products' contributions to efficiency. Ads for laundry soaps and machines often insisted that women complete their washing by nine o'clock in the morning. Victorian Americans worried about fulfilling expanding cultural expectations, and what the physician George M. Beard had labeled by 1880 "neurasthenia" became a constant concern. For relief, entrepreneurs proffered alarm clocks, patent medicines, soaps, stimulants, "easy chairs," and commercialized leisure.

Leisure time and activities took on new meanings with commercialization. Americans consumed novel entertainments made available through new communication technologies, which in turn encouraged consumption of other commercialized goods and activities. In this context, magazines grew in circulation and cultural prominence as leisure reading that fostered spending. In 1903 the *Ladies' Home Journal* became the first magazine to reach a circulation of one million, because its publisher, Cyrus K. Curtis, had long since realized that the way to profit in publishing was to provide advertisers with a well-regarded, popular medium for their messages. Likewise, by the 1910s people began to pay to watch moving pictures, which presented other consumables, from automobiles to lipstick to cigarettes, in seductive lights. The first commercial radio stations in 1920 began to give people reasons to purchase receivers, but soon broadcasters sought advertising revenues to pay for programming. National networks made it possible for millions of Americans to enjoy the same shows, hear the same advertisements, and learn about the same products; with film and magazines, they standardized and commercialized a national culture. Sports events, sponsored by advertisers and reported over commercial media, increasingly acquired national audiences. From boxing and baseball to music and drama, local and amateur events gradually faded in prominence as spectators' access to professional performances grew. Stars from all these entertainments—especially film, broadcasting, and sports—completed the commercial circle, exploiting their celebrity by endorsing products. Such stars, teams, or other symbols from entertainment have since adorned or been embodied in commodities through licensing, which promoted $62 billion in retail sales in 1993. Mickey Mouse, Roy Rogers, Ninja Turtles, and Michael Jordan have been some of the most notable licensed figures, intimately linking entertainment and consumption. By the 1980s chain restaurants began to conduct licensing promotions, making this linkage quite literal.

WORK, DEBT, AND ANXIETY

By the end of World War I, Americans' use of packaged foods, ready-made clothing, electrical devices, mountains of print media, and, more slowly, automobiles, was changing living styles and priorities. Although the 1920s "roared" more for urban middle and upper classes than for most Americans, few could not indulge in some expanding desires—perhaps chocolates or Sundays at an amusement park. In their 1929 study of life in the United States, *Middletown: A Study in Contemporary American Culture*, Robert S. Lynd and Helen Merrill Lynd asked "Why Do They Work So Hard?" The Lynds concluded that through moving pictures, the commercial press, advertisements, and broadcasting, popular culture disseminated expectations and meanings that raised people's desires for consumer goods and entertainments, which raised their expenses. To a remarkable degree, Americans of the 1920s took on new heights of personal debt in order to purchase consumer goods. Radios and automobiles topped the lists of favored durable goods, but layaway plans and other novel forms of debt encouraged people to overcome traditional prejudices against personal debt other than for mortgages and food. Debt made heightened levels of consumption possible and, in combination with the expanding presence of a commercialized popular culture, still explains much of why Americans work so hard.

Why did the enticements succeed? The impacts of consumer products on personal identity intensified in the 1920s as never before. During World War I advertising professionals had created campaigns that insisted, in the name of patriotism, that true Americans could be identified according to how well they complied with the demands of the messages. Taking these skills into commerce, advertisers challenged consumers' self-esteem, insisting that refined ladies, strong men, and loving parents could be identified according to how well they responded to the messages of advertisements. Parents, therefore, threatened their own self-esteem and their children's futures if they denied them Lincoln Logs, Erector sets, or bicycles. Ads for etiquette and grammar books both raised anxieties and offered surcease to the many migrants into cities from rural America and other nations, as well as to everyone moving into the rapidly growing modern office workplace. Thus Sherwin Cody's admonishment debuted in 1919 and ran for decades, "Do You Make These Mistakes in English?" Only fifteen minutes a day could transform anyone's speech and writing from "lifeless, monotonous, humdrum" to that which signified the "person of breeding and education!" Personal transformation dominated the new appeals.

After discoveries of bacteriological infection became well known in the late nineteenth century, cleanliness became a near obsession in America. It came to symbolize respectability and responsibility. Reformers and paper manufacturers promoted a variety of disposable paper products, beginning by targeting public drinking cups; others then advocated paper towels out of concern about spreading germs in schools. Marketers learned to connect the use of disposable products to consumers' self-identities, arguing that only incompetent parents risked their children's health and their families' stature by not supplying endless paper cups, towels, tissues, and so on. Kleenex started marketing its disposable tissues in 1924, but sales soared only after 1930, when the company recognized the power of the germ theory approach. Warnings about the "germ-soaked handkerchief" doubled sales in short order. Playing on guilt and fears of offending others, mothers were cautioned in 1931, for instance, "Don't let your child menace a schoolroom." Such appeals successfully increased the frequency of purchases for home use as well—countless paper towels for every cloth towel that had served before.

The invisibility of germs empowered these appeals; the unaided eye could not judge risk. The ever vigilant increasingly relied on trusted products. Advertisements likewise taught consumers about other "offenses" unknowable to their victims. In the 1920s Listerine mouthwash alerted Americans to the social perils of "halitosis" about which "even your closest friends won't tell you." Such challenges to one's self-estimation have flourished ever since. A 1988 headline in *Self* magazine for Sure deodorant insinuates "Just because your blouse is dry doesn't mean that you smell good." The ever-present danger, the copy warns, is "a false sense of security." Insecurity about one's worth and presentation to the world, coupled with the promise of transformation, have been potent goads to consumption.

Holidays and Government in Service of Commerce

In 1920 Ellis Gimbel set the pace for the 1920s and its celebration of consumption by organizing a Thanksgiving Day parade for his department store. Four years later, Hudson's of Detroit and Macy's of New York topped Gimbel's spectacle, their more extravagant parades elaborating on the appearance of Santa Claus and festivities to begin holiday shopping. Although many people protested department stores' intense commercialization of both Thanksgiving and Christmas, by the late 1920s every store that could muster the resources opened Santa's workshops or Christmas villages for children's delight and parents' expense. So strongly did Thanksgiving become linked with holiday shopping that in 1939, during the Great Depression, President Franklin D. Roosevelt yielded to retailers' pressures to adjust its date. In 1941 Congress legislated this change to ensure a full four weeks of holiday shopping, sanctioning the commercial function that Thanksgiving had acquired by the 1880s.

President Roosevelt's decision to alter Thanksgiving's date typified the New Deal's priority on consumption. Roosevelt believed that consumers' activities in the marketplace paralleled in importance their citizenship in the polity. The New Deal moved mass consumption to the center of policy making, raising citizens' purchasing abilities and safety and so raising employment through consumption. Roosevelt and his policy makers understood that the consumer demand during the depression did not come from lack of desire but from lack of ability to consume. In addition to improving consumer protections, New Deal programs electrified rural areas and improved transportation to them. New Deal advocates were convinced that modernizing required access to the marketplace and the capacity to consume. The Federal Housing Administration, established in 1934, made purchasing houses easier. World War II military spending provided employment, but necessary policies curtailed consumption by rationing important materials such as sugar and rubber. As soon as the war ended, policy makers returned to raising consumption. The Employment Act of 1946, for example, declared that "it is the continuing policy and responsibility of the federal government to use all practicable means . . . to foster and promote free competitive enterprise and the general welfare, to promote maximum employment, production, and purchasing power."

Entitled to Consume?

The Great Depression and World War II presented Americans with many hardships, including drastic reductions in the ability to consume goods. However, dramatic expansions in radio broadcasting and motion pictures provided countless hours of pleasure and escapism that did help the years pass, all the while presenting audiences with appealing commercialized messages. The nation's recovery was driven by powerful materialist ambitions, legitimized by the former privations. The resulting sense of entitlement helped Americans set aside what remained of traditional concerns about materialism's possible negative consequences. Economic access to consumables, including housing and automobiles, grew for a larger proportion of the population than ever before, although still excluding large segments. The 1950s, as a result, became legendary as a decade of consumer gratification, even though the legend exceeds the reality.

Suburbanization, highways, and popular culture—transmitted through television, film, and magazines—dominated many Americans' experiences of the 1950s and 1960s. Motivation research added new tools to marketers' skills, such as focus groups, in-depth interviews, and observing children at play, along with many other techniques. Marketers devised ever more sophisticated messages to tighten the connection between consumption and personal identity at ever younger ages. Children had been directly targeted first in the 1930s, and the intensity since has only grown. Film, television programming, and magazine articles reinforced such messages and had an enormous impact on defining feminine and masculine models for both adults and children. For instance, even though many women earned money, mainstream stereotypes hearkened back to an exaggerated version of the separate spheres. Television programs such as *Father Knows*

CONSUMER PROTECTION

Before consumers make marketplace decisions, they try to judge the safety and quality of goods and services. Their success depends on the information they have. With industrialization and urbanization, individual consumers' abilities to study and judge each product and service has lessened. It had been easier for a purchaser to judge, for example, the quality of meat ground on request by someone known for years than to judge the quality of a sausage processed miles away by strangers. Individual consumers cannot gather all the information they need, for instance, to judge foods for poison or disease or toys for danger. Consumer protection policies in the United States began in order to gather and publicize information and have evolved by placing consumers' collective authority as citizens into regulatory agencies to set and enforce standards.

In 1883 Harvey W. Wiley became chief chemist in the U.S. Department of Agriculture and intensified the investigation of the content of foods. In the following decades public support grew for federal regulations, spurred on by deaths and illnesses. Wiley and other reformers wrote widely about dangerous ingredients in foods, about medicines that contained alcohol, cocaine, and opium, and about unsanitary conditions in product preparation. Samuel Hopkins Adams wrote "The Great American Fraud," a series in *Collier's* in 1905 and 1906. He documented deaths and illnesses caused by over-the-counter medications called patent medicines, as well as the promotional deceit that took its "toll of blood."

Upton Sinclair's 1906 novel *The Jungle* provided a powerful prod to reform, describing horrible conditions in the meat-packing industry. As part of Progressive Era reform, Congress passed two food and drug acts that year: the Meat Inspection Act and the Food and Drugs Act. Heavy lobbying weakened the final acts, so, for instance, they required the federal government to pay for meat inspection, did not require dating of canned meats, provided few resources for testing drugs, and made enforcement cumbersome. Even so, these acts supported information collection and modest enforcement of consumer protections. It was not until the New Deal, with its emphasis on encouraging and enabling consumer demand, that stronger legislation—the Food, Drug, and Cosmetic Act—was passed in 1938 in response to deadly "wonder" drugs on the market.

Nongovernmental sources of information developed as well, helping Americans make decisions as consumers and citizens. The Consumers' Union formed in 1936 from Consumers' Research, Inc., which had operated since 1929 to test and rate products. Ralph Nader became a leader in informing consumers with his book on automobile safety, *Unsafe at Any Speed* (1965). The National Traffic and Motor Vehicle Safety Act of 1966 resulted, establishing safety standards for motor vehicles. By informing Americans, Nader and his group of investigators vastly increased the safety of many products. Peggy Charron started Action for Children's Television in 1969 because of widespread concerns about extended commercials disguised as programs for young audiences.

Many different consumer activities came under protections, such as the Fair Packaging and Labeling Act of 1966 (Truth in Packaging and Labeling Act) and the Consumer Credit Protection Act of 1968 (Truth in Lending Act). A 1970s report estimated the cost of product-related accidents at $5.5 billion annually. Legislation in 1971 and 1972 set up the Consumer Product Safety Commission to assess

CONTINUED NEXT PAGE

risks and enforce standards, with mixed success. In the 1990s the rapidly expanding interest in minimally adulterated foods led to pressures to enact federal standards for defining "organic" and "natural" foods. To eliminate an inconsistent, state-by-state certification system and implement the 1990 Organic Foods Production Act, the U.S. Department of Agriculture proposed rules for federal organic certification in December 1997. Heated debates on these rules continued into the twenty-first century.

The mercantilist rule of caveat emptor (buyer beware) risked public health and safety in the modern world. How strongly the public insists upon protections depends on its levels of concern. Hence, the pressures tend to be cyclic: when protections weaken, people fall ill or are injured; then, concerns and protections rise, as outbreaks of illness from meat infected with *E. coli* bacteria in the 1990s demonstrated. Casualties or illnesses from products or services continue to prompt consumers to act as citizens to make the marketplace safe and fair.

Ralph Nader before the Senate Commerce Subcommittee, 1966. Nader filed an invasion of privacy suit against General Motors, claiming the company harassed him following the publication of his 1965 book *Unsafe at Any Speed*. Nader won the case and with the settlement money started the Center for the Study of Responsive Law in Washington, D.C. © BETTMANN/ CORBIS

Best portrayed women as delighted and delightful consumers of countless cleaning and fashion products and men as the strong providers of the incomes for purchasing appliances, houses, decorations, entertainments, and automobiles.

By the late 1960s both men and women expressed increasing dissatisfaction with commercialized stereotypes requiring gray flannel suits or wasp-waist dresses. Awareness of the contrived nature of popular media spread into the general culture. Books like Vance Packard's *Hidden Persuaders* (1957) and *The Status Seekers* (1959) told millions that their habits and tastes were the objects of deliberate manipulations. These assertions, along with a growing dissatisfaction about tightly structured and gendered roles, led many to reject mainstream ambitions. Yet, ironically, the same visual symbols with which some people adorned themselves, their abodes, and their vehicles in protest of commercial culture became commercialized—some say co-opted—in the service of selling. Tie-dyed shirts and "love beads" entered mainstream fashion so successfully because a wide range of people, including businesspeople, sought relief from earlier constraints. Sources of commercial popular culture learned to offer fabricated and standardized goods and entertainments in the name of rebellion, individualism, and authenticity. Many firms creatively used commercial techniques to define themselves as noncommercial alternatives to their competition.

Nonetheless, in the 1960s and 1970s environmental and health concerns provoked a small percentage of Americans to reject the dominant sense of consumerist entitlement. In the only truly novel consumer trend since the deprivation of the 1930s and 1940s, increasing numbers of people, although by no means a majority, began to reinvent old concerns about the risks of overusing and poisoning natural resources, of overstressing personal time and energy, and of adulterating foods. Ecological disasters gave credence to a new wave of writers, such as Frances Moore Lappé in *Diet for a Small Planet* (1971) and E. F. Schumacher in *Small Is Beautiful* (1973), who urged the reduction of consumption and waste. In 1981 Duane Elgin published *Voluntary Simplicity: Toward a Way of Life that Is Outwardly Simple, Inwardly Rich.* These authors led small but growing numbers in arguing that less expenditure does not entail impoverishment or disgrace. Instead, they offered a new source of self-definition, based on cultural reappraisals and innovative frugality, that saved money, time at earning money, and natural resources. Although by 1991 the United States per capita consumption of energy had reached 320 gigajoules per capita, compared to a world average of 60, the movement to reduce consumption, recycle waste products, and develop alternative energy sources entered the mainstream. Consumption levels had not lowered by the turn of the millennium, but recycling materials and seeking out "organic" or "green" foods (those grown and processed without inorganic fertilizers or pesticides, added hormones, or genetically altered organisms) had grown dramatically. By the late 1990s grocery chains specializing in organic foods had built a national presence, and older, conventional chains were increasingly stocking organic foods.

As environmental and health concerns gained wider acceptance, some marketers countered the philosophical substance of green marketing by offering consumers ways to identify with its goals without changing their levels of desires. So-called green-washing ensued, as oil companies placed full color ads with lovely scenery where federal regulations required correcting ecological damage; paper goods with only 10 percent reused materials proclaimed themselves as recycled; and producers labeled their foods as "natural," although that term has no legal or practical standing. Such green-washing offers painless, if sometimes expensive, ways to identify with the appearance but not the substance of the environmental movement, the first secular redirection with the potential to counter four centuries of increasingly commercial sources of personal identification and gratification.

See also **The Material Shape of Early American Life; Gender, Social Class, Race, and Material Life** *(volume 1);* **Women and Family in the Suburban Age; The Design of the Familiar; The Culture of Self-Improvement** *(volume 2);* **Class; Marxist Approaches; Weberian Approaches** *(in this volume); and other articles in this section.*

BIBLIOGRAPHY

Bellamy, Edward. *Looking Backward, 2000–1887.* 1888. Reprint, Boston, 1995.

Benson, Susan Porter. *Counter Cultures: Saleswomen, Managers, and Customers in American Department Stores, 1890–1940.* Urbana, Ill., 1986.

Berry, Christopher J. *The Idea of Luxury: A Conceptual and Historical Investigation.* New York, 1994.

Blaszczyk, Regina Lee. *Imagining Consumers: Design and Innovation from Wedgwood to Corning.* Baltimore, 2000.

Borden, Neil H. *The Economic Effects of Advertising.* Chicago, 1942. (Page numbers in the text are taken from the 1947 edition.)

Bronner, Simon J., ed. *Consuming Visions: Accumulation and Display of Goods in America, 1880–1920.* New York, 1989.

Bushman, Richard L. *The Refinement of America: Persons, Houses, Cities.* New York, 1992.

Butsch, Richard. *For Fun and Profit: The Transformation of Leisure into Consumption.* Philadelphia, 1990.

Cronon, William. *Changes in the Land: Indians, Colonists, and the Ecology of New England.* New York, 1983.

Elgin, Duane. *Voluntary Simplicity: Toward a Way of Life that Is Outwardly Simple, Inwardly Rich.* 1981. Rev. ed., New York, 1993.

Ewen, Stuart. *Captains of Consciousness: Advertising and the Social Roots of the Consumer Culture.* New York, 1976.

Frank, Thomas C. *The Conquest of Cool: Business Culture, Counterculture, and the Rise of Hip Consumerism.* Chicago, 1997.

Garvey, Ellen Gruber. *The Adman in the Parlor: Magazines and the Gendering of Consumer Culture, 1880s to 1910s.* New York, 1996.

George, Henry. *Progress and Poverty.* 1879. Reprint, New York, 1971.

Glickman, Lawrence B. *A Living Wage: American Workers and the Making of Consumer Society.* Ithaca, N.Y., 1997.

Horowitz, Daniel. *The Morality of Spending: Attitudes toward the Consumer Society in America, 1875–1940.* Baltimore, 1985.

Horowitz, Roger, and Arwen Mohun, eds. *His and Hers: Gender, Consumption, and Technology.* Charlottesville, Va., 1998.

Kasson, John F. *Amusing the Million: Coney Island at the Turn of the Century.* New York, 1978.

Laird, Pamela Walker. *Advertising Progress: American Business and the Rise of Consumer Marketing.* Baltimore, 1998.

———. "Progress in Separate Spheres: Selling Nineteenth-Century Technologies." *Knowledge and Society* 10 (1996): 19–49.

Lappé, Frances Moore. *Diet for a Small Planet.* New York, 1971.

Leach, William. *Land of Desire: Merchants, Power, and the Rise of a New American Culture.* New York, 1993.

Lears, T. J. Jackson. *Fables of Abundance: A Cultural History of Advertising in America.* New York, 1994.

Lears, T. J. Jackson, and Richard Wightman Fox. *The Culture of Consumption: Critical Essays in American History, 1880–1980.* New York, 1983.

Marchand, Roland. *Advertising the American Dream: Making Way for Modernity, 1920–1940.* Berkeley, Calif., 1985.

McCracken, Grant. *Culture and Consumption: New Approaches to the Symbolic Character of Consumer Goods and Activities.* Bloomington, Ind., 1988.

McKendrick, Neil, John Brewer, and J. H. Plumb. *The Birth of a Consumer Society: The Commercialization of Eighteenth-Century England.* Bloomington, Ind., 1982.

Miller, Daniel, ed. *Material Cultures: Why Some Things Matter.* Chicago, 1998.

Ohmann, Richard. *Selling Culture: Magazines, Markets, and Class at the Turn of the Century.* London, 1996.

Olney, Martha L. *Buy Now, Pay Later: Advertising, Credit, and Consumer Durables in the 1920s.* Chapel Hill, N.C., 1991.

Packard, Vance. *Hidden Persuaders.* New York, 1957.

——. *The Status Seekers: An Exploration of Class Behavior in America.* New York, 1959.

Pope, Daniel. *The Making of Modern Advertising.* New York, 1983.

Potter, David M. *People of Plenty: Economic Abundance and the American Character.* Chicago, 1954.

Restad, Penne L. *Christmas in America: A History.* New York, 1995.

Schivelbusch, Wolfgang. *Tastes of Paradise: A Social History of Spices, Stimulants, and Intoxicants.* New York, 1992.

Schumacher, E. F. *Small Is Beautiful: Economics As If People Mattered.* Translated by David Jacobson. New York, 1973.

Scranton, Philip. *Endless Novelty: Specialty Production and American Industrialization, 1865–1925.* Princeton, N.J., 1997.

Spears, Timothy B. *One Hundred Years on the Road: The Traveling Salesman in American Culture.* New Haven, Conn., 1995.

Stage, Sarah. *Female Complaints: Lydia Pinkham and the Business of Women's Medicine.* New York, 1979.

Strasser, Susan. *Satisfaction Guaranteed: The Making of the American Mass Market.* New York, 1989.

Strasser, Susan, Charles McGovern, and Matthias Judt, eds. *Getting and Spending: European and American Consumer Societies in the Twentieth Century.* New York, 1998.

Tedlow, Richard S. *New and Improved: The Story of Mass Marketing in America.* New York, 1990.

Veblen, Thorstein. *The Theory of the Leisure Class: An Economic Study of Institutions.* 1899. Reprint, New York, 1967.

Watkins, Julian Lewis. *The One Hundred Greatest Advertisements: Who Wrote Them and What They Did.* New York, 1959.

Xenos, Nicholas. *Scarcity and Modernity.* London, 1989.

Young, James Harvey. *The Toadstool Millionaires: A Social History of Patent Medicines in America before Federal Regulation.* Princeton, N.J., 1961.

WELFARE

Gwendolyn Mink

In twentieth-century parlance, "welfare" refers to income assistance to poor families with minor children. Although its roots trace from sixteenth-century English poor laws through nineteenth-century U.S. local relief practices, what we call "welfare" was actually a twentieth-century policy innovation designed for poor families without employable fathers. Part of a reform agenda to safeguard children by mitigating poverty, welfare policy drew its logic from prevailing Anglo American gender and family ideologies. Known initially as "mothers' aid" or "mothers' pensions," welfare offered a stipend to families without breadwinners so that mothers could pursue the work of providing care for their children.

This focus on children and child-raising distinguished welfare from ordinary relief. Unlike welfare, relief developed to mitigate labor market failures, attenuating destitution for those whose wages fell below subsistence levels or who did not find work in the labor market. During the early nineteenth century, "indoor" relief through county almshouses was the preferred method of helping the destitute, although churches also played an important role in attenuating some of the effects of destitution. Many of the almshouse poor were disabled or medically indigent. Over the course of the nineteenth century, publicly funded "outdoor" relief—payments to the individual poor rather than institutional housing for them—became the favored method of dealing with indigency.

At the same time, debates arose over whether assistance to the poor should be publicly provided or whether it should be provided by private charities. Some critics of public aid argued that it was too easily abused by corrupt politicians shopping for votes. During the late nineteenth century the most concerted opposition to public provision maintained that publicly provided relief was a kind of moral hazard. According to this view, public assistance rewarded indigency, rather than shaming it and curing it through moral discipline.

Still, even if recipients were insufficiently grateful for and humiliated by public relief, it did enforce labor discipline and aided employers by assuring the availability of workers willing to accept very low wages. Relief assistance was meager so as to not discourage wage earning, following the rule that "the willingly dependent upon alms should not live so comfortably with them as the humblest independent labourer without them" (New York Association for Improving the Condition of the Poor, *First Annual Report,* 1845, in Coll, p. 27).

Both public and private relief agencies were committed to assisting some of the poor, namely, those whose industry and frugality showed they were not "willing dependents" or malingerers. But most of the able-bodied poor were believed to be morally responsible for their own poverty. Hence, advocates of late-nineteenth-century "scientific" charity argued for the systematic surveillance and disciplining of the poor as a condition of receiving relief. According to the reformer Josephine Shaw Lowell, one of the great theorists and leaders of the Charity Organization Society, "relief should be surrounded by circumstances that shall . . . repel every one, not in extremity, from accepting it . . . because human nature is so constituted that no man can receive as a gift what he should earn by his own labor without a moral deterioration" (pp. 66–67).

The subjects of relief and charity were people generally deemed capable of earning a living in the labor market. Such persons might need relief because their wages were too low to survive on them, or they might need relief because of economic depression or other "unavoidable causes" of unemployment. Either way, relief was a temporary measure and was not intended as an alternative to participation in the labor market.

In contrast, welfare was designed to keep (primarily) widowed mothers out of the labor market so that they could devote themselves to raising their children. Despite this difference, many of the negative assumptions about the poor that powered the politics and policies of relief also powered the politics and policies of welfare, both in its origins and to the present day. A core assumption has been the idea that the poor fall easily into immorality and improvidence. It followed that welfare should be administered according to stringent eligibility criteria and that recipients' home lives should be monitored to ensure that assistance went only to the morally deserving.

Mothers' pensions were enacted by state governments during the 1910s and were implemented by localities. Promoted by the National Congress of Mothers as well as by upper-middle-class women reformers such as Jane Addams, Florence Kelley, and the sisters Grace and Edith Abbott, mothers' pensions offered an alternative to warehousing half-orphans in institutions. Based on the idea that the mother-care of children was the best form of care, mothers' pensions provided mothers (and sometimes fathers) in families without breadwinners the support they deserved for raising children in their own homes.

Pensions were provided for needy mothers; but not all needy mothers received benefits. Various rules conditioned income support on the moral worthiness and cultural assimilation of poor single mothers. In many northern and eastern cities, European immigrant mothers without breadwinning husbands often surrendered cultural autonomy and family privacy in exchange for economic support. Welfare agencies also differentiated among mothers, tracking some into the labor market for some or all of their income. Across the country, but especially in the South and West, women of color were customarily regarded as workers, rather than mothers, and thus were denied benefits.

Although state policies varied, most shared common purposes and assumptions. In principle, mothers' pensions honored the caregiving work of mothers but in practice discriminated among types of mothers. Pensions provided economic support to the "best" mother-workers, while regulating the dietary, kinship, and other cultural conditions under which such mothers did their jobs. On the one hand, mothers' pension policies recognized that many solo caregivers could not both provide care for children and earn an income to support them. Pensions made it possible for mothers to continue their caregiving work by providing a surrogate for a husband's income. On the other hand, pension policies recognized value in mothers' caregiving work only for those mothers who met certain cultural and moral standards, such as pious widows who seemed Americanizable. Thus, from its incep-

tion, welfare policy determined differences among mothers, pinning a mother's worthiness on her conformity to an Anglo American gendered cultural ideal.

Early initiatives yielded two enduring legacies. One was that while all mothers, in theory, performed socially valuable work, only some mothers deserved social support for it. The other was that even mothers who deserved social support had to earn it by submitting to social controls which ranged from the prohibition on male boarders, to instructions on what kind of food to buy, to regulation of wage-earning. In the 1930s the New Deal version of mothers' pensions—the Aid to Dependent Children (ADC) program—inherited these legacies.

Created by the Social Security Act of 1935, ADC (later renamed Aid to Families with Dependent Children, or AFDC) nationalized mothers' pension policies by providing for joint federal-state funding of welfare benefits and by requiring states to hew to certain administrative rules in exchange for federal dollars. Although the welfare measure—Title IV of the Social Security Act—abjured moral criteria, basing eligibility for benefits on need alone, it gave states the opportunity to impose moral criteria by delegating to them administration and management. States took old rules from mothers' pension programs—rules against nonmarital motherhood and heterosexual cohabitation, for example—and folded them into the new federal policy. By the 1940s states formalized new rules based on old practices, rules such as the "employable mother" rule that permitted welfare agencies to designate some mothers capable of work outside the home and accordingly ineligible for welfare benefits.

The welfare system set up in the 1930s was hardly an ideal system. On one hand, not all mothers who needed welfare were permitted to receive it. On the other hand, many recipients were subjected to surveillance by welfare agencies that were concerned that some mothers might not deserve their benefits. Still, at the end of the 1930s the prevailing image of recipients was that they did deserve their benefits. Welfare was not a controversial program.

Amendments to the Social Security Act in 1939 undermined the popularity of welfare. Under the amendments, single mothers who had been in durable marriages to better-paid men were placed in a different kind of welfare program, called survivors' insurance. This was a program for widows with minor children. Benefits under the program were national, regular, automatic—and far more generous than under welfare. Thus, anyone who could qualify for income support under the new program was likely to move out of welfare. White single mothers were more likely to qualify than mothers of color, because their dead husbands were more likely to have been in better-paid, industrial sector jobs that were socially insured.

Welfare then became a program for mothers who were divorced, had never married, or had been married to poor men who died. When the pitiful but blameless white widow left welfare for survivors' insurance, the stigma of welfare began to congeal. Still, it didn't fully congeal until welfare became associated with rights and with women of color.

Over the course of the 1960s, the administrations of Presidents John F. Kennedy and Lyndon B. Johnson and the Supreme Court identified constitutional barriers to the moral regulation of mothers enrolled in welfare and to the exclusion of other mothers from welfare on moral grounds. In 1968 the Supreme Court ruled in a pivotal case, *King v. Smith,* that poor single mothers and their children are entitled to participate in the welfare system on the terms specified in the federal law. This meant that the states could not add on moral or cultural eligibility requirements to the basic federal requirement of economic need.

During the 1940s, 1950s, and early 1960s, millions of mothers and children were kept off the welfare rolls by various discriminatory mechanisms such as "illegitimacy" prohibitions and "man in the house" rules. Often these rules were proxies for racial exclusion from welfare eligibility. When the Supreme Court struck down some of these rules beginning in 1968, millions of mothers and their children became eligible for welfare.

By 1968 a vigilant welfare rights movement had mobilized many of these mothers to claim the benefits the federal law said were their due. The movement included the scholar-activists Frances Fox Piven and Richard A. Cloward, who in 1971 published their pathbreaking *Regulating the Poor: The Functions of Public Welfare,* which showed how welfare served many economic, political, and social needs and interests—except for those of its recipients. Propelled by the energy and insights of thousands of welfare mothers, the movement brought considerable pressure to bear on the local governments that administered welfare policy and on the courts that heard constitutional claims.

Especially after the Supreme Court began to uphold some welfare rights claims, the number of welfare participants soared. Although the welfare

participation rates of white women soared, attention quickly fastened on the increasing numbers (but not percentages) of women of color enrolled in welfare.

The increased visibility of women of color among welfare recipients fueled concerns that women of color were "overrepresented" in the welfare program. Newsmagazine depictions of the poor reinforced these concerns. Between 1960 and 1963, when about 25 to 30 percent of the poor in America was black, about a third of newsmagazine photos of the poor were of African Americans. In 1967–1968, the percentage of blacks among the poor remained fairly stable, but close to 70 percent of newsmagazine pictures of the poor were of African Americans. This percentage was even higher in 1972–73. These sorts of media practices helped turn "welfare" into a code word for black.

In fact, the participation of women of color in the welfare program has been proportionately much higher than their presence in the general population. From the 1960s to the year 2000, for example, 35 to 40 percent of welfare participants have been African American. Latina and Asian American participation increased over this period (Latina participation was 22 percent in 2000)—as the Latino and Asian American populations as a whole have increased. About two-thirds of recipients in 2000 were African American, Asian American, Latina, and Native American. This racial distribution of welfare is the logical consequence of the racial distribution of poverty. Women of color have been and still are poorer than everyone else. They earn 36 cents less than the white male dollar and 10 cents less than the white woman's dollar.

The demographic shift in the welfare rolls began in the wake of the 1939 amendments to the Social Security Act and quickened as the gradual emigration of African Americans from the South took hold. Eruptions of largely racial reactions to welfare enrollments in such northern localities as Newburgh, New York, primed the racialization of welfare politics in general. But the racial politics of welfare did not fully congeal until welfare—and poor women of color—became associated with rights. Then, what gained currency was the idea that mothers who receive welfare—like able-bodied men who receive relief—are morally deficient. Such women not only did not deserve welfare, it was believed, they did not deserve rights, as well.

According to some policymakers, welfare "rights" were incentives to immoral behavior. Invoking myths of fecund and sexual black "welfare breeders" who scam the system, they argued that, at their core, welfare rights were the currency of black illegitimacy. While this kind of rhetoric was common in conservative circles, during the 1960s moderates and even some liberals took on this point of view. President Johnson, for example, often credited for expanding welfare as part of his War on Poverty, called for limits on payments to nonmarital children and complained, on White House tapes played on the CNN Morning News, that welfare mothers "sit around and breed instead of going out to work." The popularity of this attitude produced a clamor to temper rights with moral regulation.

At the local level, moral regulation took various forms, including home visits and supervised shopping or spending. Caseworkers searched closets for signs of another adult income—that is, for signs of a man. They also told mothers how to spend their money, sometimes even barring them from getting special grants unless they agreed to spend the grants as caseworkers decreed. At the federal level, moral regulation took the form of paternity establishment, child support rules, and work requirements. Put into place the moment welfare acquired a black face, these moral levers formed the centerpiece of welfare reform for three decades. All injured or erased the constitutional rights of poor single mothers.

Throughout the 1960s some of the most ardent criticism of welfare came from liberals and progressives who opposed both its stinginess and its humiliating intrusions into the lives of recipients. Such critics wanted to reform welfare by raising benefits and by strengthening recipients' rights. What is called "welfare reform," however, was undeniably the inspiration of conservative politicians. From the 1960s into the 1980s it drew its energy from white southern Democrats like Governor George Wallace of Alabama, Republican President Richard Nixon and the so-called silent majority, and Republican President Ronald Reagan, who invented the image of the "welfare queen" in 1976, while governor of California, and rode her to the White House in 1980.

During the late 1960s and 1970s many antiwelfare politicians staked themselves to the analysis provided and arguments precipitated by the assistant secretary of labor Daniel Patrick Moynihan's *The Negro Family: The Case for National Action*. The Moynihan Report, as it became known, was published in 1965 and offered a racialized explanation for poverty among African Americans. Claiming that "a tangle of pathology" follows from the "matriarchal" black family structure, the report provided a language and a framework for the backlash

against welfare. At a time when wage work was not yet hailed as the preferred solution to maternal poverty, the report incited moralizing about "black illegitimacy" and focused attention on male-headed, marital families as the alternative to welfare in African American communities.

Antiwelfare politicians of the 1980s had an additional racial playbook to draw from. In 1984 Charles Murray published *Losing Ground: American Social Policy, 1950–1980*. The book armed antiwelfare forces with data that seemed to prove their racist assumptions and claims. It also invigorated calls for a return to the intensive regulation of welfare recipients' lives, because, as Murray put it, "sticks and carrots work." In particular, Murray characterized welfare as a moral hazard, goading policymakers to devise ever more stringent punishments for "illegitimacy."

While the war against welfare since the 1960s has been couched most often in terms of the racial misbehavior of recipients, it also has been a war about gender, not simply because most adult recipients are women, but because arguments for welfare reform have simultaneously been arguments about the gender role of poor single mothers. If welfare had been invented to enable single mothers to meet their historic gender assignment—caregiving for children—by the late 1960s welfare had fallen into disrepute because recipients were meeting that assignment. One reason for the plunge into disrepute was that the wrong women were supported as mothers. These were women who were not married, whose children often were not born in marriages, and who were black. In many quarters, unmarried mothers were considered undeserving because their marital status proved their immorality. In these quarters and others, black mothers were not considered mothers at all. For three centuries African American women had been regarded as breeders by slaveowners, as nurturers of slaveowners' children, and as workers in other people's homes, fields, and factories. Even when they were married, they did not share white women's domestic sentence—at least not in their own homes. Moreover, they were invisible as their own children's mothers.

In 1972 the welfare rights leader Johnnie Tillmon summarized the double standard that applied to welfare recipients' motherhood. In the first issue of *Ms.* magazine, she wrote:

In this country, we believe in something called the "work ethic." . . . But the work ethic itself is a double standard. It applies to men, and to women on welfare. It doesn't apply to all women. If you're a society lady from Scarsdale and you spend all your time sitting on your prosperity paring your nails, well that's okay. Women aren't supposed to work. They're supposed to be married. ("Welfare Is a Women's Issue," p. 112)

The view that welfare mothers were "lazy parasites" and "pigs at the trough," as Governor Reagan put it, was the flip side of the view that the solution to recipients' need for welfare was work in the labor market. As these harsh stereotypes of recipients intensified, so did plans to move recipients into the labor market. Beginning in the 1960s various work incentives and welfare work programs proliferated. Although early "workfare" did not compel mothers to work outside the home, by the time Reagan entered the White House in 1981 outside work had taken root as the alternative to single mothers' "dependency." The only mothers for whom the labor market solution did not apply were those who married. Mothers who did not enter male-headed families were no longer viewed as impacted caregivers but, rather, as improvident workers.

The marital moralism of conservatives, along with a more generally racialized welfare politics, spelled doom for welfare as an income support system for caregivers. But, in some ways, it was post–World War II feminism that put the nail in welfare's coffin. During the early twentieth century, "maternalist" feminists—women who advocated government support and guidance for poor mothers—were the force behind welfare innovation. Theirs was a feminism that did not contest women's gender assignment. Rather, it called for material and political improvements in women's status and fortunes within an existing gender order. It was a feminism that was entirely comfortable with a policy designed for women as mothers and designed, no less, to enhance their ability to be mothers.

By the 1960s feminism clearly had changed. Although it had multiplied into many iterations and mobilizations, several common themes emerged. Two of these themes were of particular relevance to welfare politics. The first was the feminist quest for wider labor market opportunities for women. The second was the quest to end the lopsided sexual division of labor in families.

The feminist focus on women's labor market opportunities pivots on a kind of feminist work ethic. The ethic holds that work outside the home will liberate women from domesticity and from dependency on men. Because women's gender role as mothers has been used for so long to justify women's exclusion from the labor market or their inequality in it, many feminists have conflated re-

pudiating the gender role with winning alternatives. Hence, most feminists have not rushed to defend poor single mothers' right to income support as caregivers. Moreover, most feminists have argued that welfare mothers would improve their lot by moving into the labor market. A feminist labor market, unlike a conservative one, would acknowledge workers' caregiving conflicts. But according to the feminist work ethic, such conflicts should be resolved by providing for surrogate care (for example, subsidized child care) and for job-protected occasional departures from the workplace (such as parental leave). The presumption of the feminist work ethic is that women—even single mothers—ought to work outside the home. Hence, most feminists supported calls to reform welfare to encourage, even to require, work outside the home.

The feminist focus on men's unrequited responsibilities to families also reinforced the general thrust of late twentieth century welfare reform. Feminists have championed vigorous child support enforcement as part of an agenda for gender justice. Through their vigilant efforts on behalf of divorced and deserted mothers, they brought "deadbeat dads" into the national limelight. Although feminists and conservatives do not share the same goals for women in families, the feminist call to "make fathers pay" resonates with conservative appeals to restore the father-headed family. Both emphasize the financial dependency of mothers on individual men. To be sure, feminists want to force fathers to meet their financial obligations to families as a matter of equity, while conservatives want literally to return fathers to families that mothers have formed as a matter of patriarchal "family values." However orthogonal these perspectives, in welfare policy and politics they have worked synchronously to promote paternal responsibility as a key solution to single-mother poverty. As a result, poor single mothers who do not want to associate with biological fathers find themselves subject to additional coercion by government and potentially by the men upon whom feminists and conservatives say they should depend.

Reflecting stunning changes in the roles and ambitions of women over the course of the twentieth century as well as the centuries-old racialized politics of gender, by the beginning of the twenty-first century the idea that had spawned welfare had been wholly repudiated. In 1996 the federal government repealed welfare and with it any government responsibility for providing economic support to poor single mothers so that they could meet their caregiving obligations. Welfare—AFDC—has been replaced by Temporary Assistance for Needy Families (TANF), which not only rescinds government's assurance of income support for poor single-mother families but also mandates the moral regulation of mothers, compels association with biological fathers, requires increasing hours of work outside the home as a condition of welfare participation, and compels full-time work outside the home as the consequence of stringent time limits.

These various TANF program requirements frustrate recipients' basic civil rights, such as vocational freedom, sexual privacy, and reproductive choice, as well as the right to decide how to be and raise a family. Based on the hoary idea that poverty is a sign of individual moral failing and forwarding the claim that the characteristics of poor families cause social problems, the TANF system returns poor mothers and their children to the harsh regimes of poor relief and scientific charity. Hardly recognizable as "welfare," the TANF system tells poor single women that if they choose motherhood, they surrender equal citizenship.

See also **Reform Institutions; Patterns of Reform and Revolt** *(volume 1);* **The Culture of Self-Improvement; Resurgent Conservatism; Working Class; Humanitarianism; Social Reform; Socialism and Radical Thought** *(volume 2);* **Foundations and Philanthropy; Marxist Approaches; Weberian Approaches** *(in this volume); and other articles in this section.*

BIBLIOGRAPHY

Coll, Blanche D. *Perspectives in Welfare: A History.* Washington, D.C., 1969.

Gilens, Martin. *Why Americans Hate Welfare: Race, Media, and the Politics of Antipoverty Policy.* Chicago, 1999.

Goodwin, Joanne L. *Gender and the Politics of Welfare Reform: Mothers' Pensions in Chicago, 1911–1929.* Chicago, 1997.

Lowell, Josephine Shaw. *Public Relief and Public Change.* New York, 1884.

Mink, Gwendolyn. *The Wages of Motherhood: Inequality in the Welfare State, 1917–1942.* Ithaca, N.Y., 1995.

——. *Welfare's End.* Ithaca, N.Y., 1998.

Murray, Charles. *Losing Ground: American Social Policy, 1950–1980.* New York, 1984.

Piven, Frances Fox, and Richard A. Cloward. *Regulating the Poor: The Functions of Public Welfare.* New York, 1971.

Polanyi, Karl. *The Great Transformation: The Political and Economic Origins of Our Time.* New York, 1944.

Quadagno, Jill S. *The Color of Welfare: How Racism Undermined the War on Poverty.* New York, 1994.

Tillmon, Johnnie. "Welfare Is a Women's Issue." *Ms.* 1, no. 1 (spring 1972).

TWENTIETH-CENTURY ECONOMIC THOUGHT

John Wenzler

In nineteenth-century Europe, political economy often was described as the "dismal science" because English economists such as David Ricardo, Thomas Malthus, and John Stuart Mill believed that nature was "niggardly." They argued that agriculture constantly faced diminishing returns and assumed that laborers always were doomed to receive subsistence wages. In nineteenth-century America, however, political economy could well have been called the "optimistic science." Most American political economists believed that nature was generous and assumed that economic development would produce a society of universal abundance and harmony. They articulated a popular moral apology for America's free market economy based on the labor theory of value. They assumed that the labor invested in a commodity determined its exchange value and that all workers had a natural right to possess the value created by their efforts. Like President Abraham Lincoln, most nineteenth-century American economists believed that securing "each labourer the whole product of his labour, or as nearly as possible, [was] a most worthy object of any good government" (Boritt, *Lincoln and the Economics of the American Dream*, p. xxiv). In their opinion, the United States had achieved this goal better than any other nation because the American Revolution had liberated its citizens from the oppression of European aristocrats. They predicted that continuing economic development would allow every deserving American to achieve economic and moral self-reliance by becoming an independent producer.

During the last two decades of the nineteenth century, however, the predictions made by this popular version of political economy failed to come true. Instead of creating a classless society of self-reliant entrepreneurs, the industrial development of the Gilded Age widened the gap between the rich and the poor. The large investments required for modern capital equipment forced many small producers to become proletarians, while a few captains

of industry amassed immense fortunes. Furthermore, industrial development failed to produce the universal prosperity anticipated by American political economists. Despite rapid increases in labor productivity, between 1873 and 1896 the economy suffered through several severe depressions, which intensified conflicts between workers and their employers. In response to these disappointments, popular radicals such as Henry George, William "Coin" Harvey, and Henry Demarest Lloyd began to employ the moral ideals of nineteenth-century political economy to attack rather than to defend American institutions. They argued that wealthy industrialists had become a new class of aristocrats who appropriated the wealth created by American laborers. In the 1890s powerful political movements composed of workers, farmers, and small businessmen organized around these ideas and threatened to transform the American economy so that it really would achieve the moral promises implicit in the labor theory of value.

The neoclassical version of economic theory that dominated American economic discourse during the twentieth century emerged as a response to this threat. Several academic economists, including John Bates Clark and Irving Fisher, sought to make economics more compatible with modern capitalism by replacing the labor theory of value with the marginal utility theory of value. The new theory of value shifted attention from the physical process of production to the process of exchange and consumption. By doing so, it allowed economists to defend the American economy not as a means of giving every worker exactly what he had produced but as the most efficient system of satisfying consumer demand. Although few Americans would become self-reliant producers in an industrial economy dominated by large corporations, the new version of economics demonstrated that they still achieved "sovereignty" as consumers. At the same time, marginal theory insulated economic discourse from popular moral criticism by introducing increasingly sophisticated mathematical techniques into economic theory. The increasing complexity of neoclassical economics intimidated nonspecialists and allowed professional economists to see themselves as objective social scientists rather than moral ideologues. Whereas most nineteenth-century theorists had explicitly combined political economy with moral philosophy, twentieth-century economists considered themselves technical advisers who looked for the most efficient means of achieving the ends established by society.

For most of the twentieth century, this strategy was remarkably successful. In American universities, neoclassical theorists dominated most economics departments. They accumulated a vast amount of empirical data about the economy and built an imposing structure of theory on the fundamental assumptions of marginalism (modified to some extent by Keynesian ideas). Neoclassical economists also acquired more practical influence in government and in business enterprise than any other group of twentieth-century intellectuals. The president of the United States has met with the Council of Economic Advisers since its formation in 1946, the Federal Reserve System has been guided by economic experts since its creation in 1913, and corporations routinely hire professional economic advisers. As neoclassical economics acquired power, the American economy enjoyed relatively stable economic growth (except, of course, during the Great Depression), and the expertise of economists often was seen as essential to its success. Perhaps the most telling sign of the prestige achieved by neoclassical economic theory was the decision of the Nobel Prize Committee in 1969 to award a Nobel Prize specifically in economic science, an honor granted to no other social science.

The accomplishments of neoclassical economists have not impressed everyone, however. Throughout the twentieth century, institutional economists, Marxists, and other social critics vigorously attacked the fundamental assumptions of neoclassical theory. These critics argued that modern economists severely narrowed the scope of economic thought by focusing on timeless conditions of static equilibrium. They claimed that the elegant mathematical models employed by modern economists could not account for technical change, institutional values, or class conflict. Furthermore, many critics rejected the assertion that neoclassical theory had transformed economics into a value-free social science. In their opinion, neoclassical theory still serves as a powerful form of ideology because it prevents people from imagining alternative social institutions and values. It makes capitalism seem natural and inevitable, because it assumes that the selfish, calculating habits of thought inculcated by the capitalist marketplace are inherent in human nature. Although critical economists did not stimulate the widespread popular protests characteristic of the late nineteenth century, they maintained a healthy skepticism about neoclassical theory among the American public. Hence, a complete survey of twentieth-century economic thought must look at both neoclassical theory and its critics.

MARGINAL UTILITY AND MARGINAL PRODUCTIVITY

Three European economists, William Stanley Jevons, Léon Walras, and Carl von Menger, simultaneously published versions of the marginal utility theory of value early in the 1870s. Their new approach to value began to dominate economic discourse in the early twentieth century when Alfred Marshall's *Principles of Economics,* published in 1890, became the standard economics text in the English-speaking world. In the United States, Clark independently formulated a marginal utility theory in the 1880s and developed the marginal productivity theory of distribution in the 1890s. He and Fisher articulated the version of marginalism still employed by most academic economists in America. To understand the assumptions that motivated neoclassical analysis throughout the twentieth century, it is most helpful to study the ideas of these early marginalists. Although late-twentieth-century economists built elaborate mathematical models on the foundations established by the pioneers, they did not alter their underlying social vision.

The fundamental innovation of the marginal utility school was to argue that the use value of a commodity determined its exchange value. Most nineteenth-century economists, following Adam Smith, argued that this was impossible. Smith noted that useful substances such as water had very little value, whereas nearly useless commodities such as diamonds had a great deal of value. Consequently, he decided that the cost of production rather than the utility of a commodity determined its exchange value. The marginalists avoided Smith's conclusion by arguing that the "marginal" or final utility of a commodity determined its value. First, they claimed that the usefulness of any product decreased as consumers acquired more of it. Then they argued that the utility of the last or marginal unit of a commodity in the marketplace determined the exchange value for all units of that commodity. Hence, water had little value because it usually was so abundant that its marginal utility was negligible, whereas diamonds were so scarce that their marginal utility was extremely high to those who valued diamonds.

This new theory of value shifted economists' attention from the physical process of production to the process of market exchange. Because nineteenth-century economists traced exchange value to the costs of production, they conceived of value as a quasi-physical substance that workers put into a product while they were making it. When people bought and sold finished goods in the marketplace, nineteenth-century economists supposed that they merely exchanged objects that already contained equal amounts of value. Because the marginal utility theorists traced value to the psychological satisfaction of consumers, however, they believed that the process of exchange could produce new value. For example, A trades his used car to B for a used boat because the boat will give him more pleasure than did the car. Consequently, the exchange between A and B increases the amount of psychological utility enjoyed by the society without producing any new objects. In general, the marginal economists believed that free market exchange maximized the utility that a community would derive from any given supply of goods by distributing each commodity to the individual who would get the most satisfaction from it. This process of efficiently "allocating" a preexisting supply of commodities, which was an afterthought for the classical economists, became the chief virtue of capitalism for neoclassical economists.

The marginal theory of production similarly focused on the problem of allocating a preexisting supply of productive resources. Clark formulated his theory by making the process of production analogous to the process of exchange as it was envisioned by marginal utility theorists. The best way to illustrate Clark's theory is to envision a simple graph that Clark often employed in his analysis. In this graph (Fig. 1), the economist assumes that new workers are being added to an economy with a constant supply of capital. The first workers hired produce the most because they use the best tools available. Each new worker that is hired produces slightly less than the workers hired before him/her because he/she is using less efficient tools. The marginal productivity of labor equals the productivity of the last worker that is hired. If worker B were the last worker hired, B′ would equal the marginal productivity of labor. If worker M were the last worker hired, M′ would equal the marginal productivity of

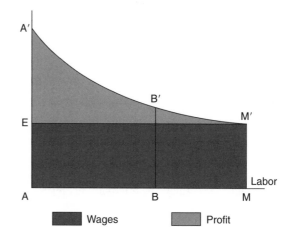

Figure 1.

labor. According to Clark, the marginal productivity of labor determined wages because capitalists would lose money if they paid higher wages. If the government or a union were to force capitalists to pay a minimum wage (say B′) that exceeded the marginal productivity of labor, capitalists simply would lay off workers until wages again equaled marginal productivity. Clark started by conceiving labor and capital as factors (or inputs) of production owned by workers and capitalists. Then he argued that both factors were subject to diminishing returns as they became more abundant. Each new unit of labor hired by a capitalist with a constant supply of capital equipment, according to Clark, added less new value to the final product than had previously hired units of labor. Similarly, each new unit of capital employed by an entrepreneur with a constant supply of labor added less value to the final product. The marginal productivity of labor equaled the productivity of the last unit of labor available in the marketplace and marginal productivity of capital equaled the productivity of the last unit of capital. Just as the marginal utility of water determined the value of all units of water, Clark argued that the marginal productivity of labor and capital determined the earnings of all workers and capitalists.

Clark worked prior to World War I, an era when American radicals and populists still seemed to pose a significant threat to the social order, and he believed that the marginal theory of productivity refuted the claim that capitalism exploited laborers. It proved that "the distribution of the income of society is controlled by a natural law and that this law, if it worked without friction, would give to each agent of production the amount of wealth which that agent creates" (*The Distribution of Wealth*,

1899, p. v). In Clark's mind, this meant that everyone would get exactly what he had "earned" in a perfectly frictionless capitalist economy. Later in the twentieth century, however, radical threats to the social order were less powerful, and most professional economists have distanced themselves from Clark's "naïve productivity ethics."

Instead of focusing on the principle of equity implicit in the theory of marginal productivity, they emphasized its vision of efficiency. According to modern economists, rewarding factors in accordance with marginal productivity achieves efficiency in resource allocation (Blaug, *Economic Theory in Retrospect*, p. 428). When labor unions or monopoly capitalists charge more than the marginal productivity of their respective factors of production, therefore, modern economists argue that they distort the process of allocating resources and reduce the productivity of the economy as a whole.

WELFARE ECONOMICS

The modern theory of welfare economics explicitly states the ideal of efficiency implicit in marginal analysis. The Italian economist Vilfredo Pareto developed the central propositions of welfare economics early in the twentieth century because he recognized that earlier formulations of marginal utility theory seemed to justify the redistribution of wealth. If one assumes, for example, that the utility of any commodity, including money, decreases as people acquire more of it, one can argue that rich people get less marginal utility from their money than do poor people. This means that the government could increase social welfare by redistributing wealth, because poor people would gain more utility than rich people lost. Taken to its extreme, this argument implies that a perfectly egalitarian distribution of wealth would maximize the collective utility enjoyed by society. Pareto, who thought that it would be unwise to make scientific arguments in favor of soaking the rich, sought to avoid this line of argument by claiming that it was impossible to calculate the total utility of society by adding up the subjective satisfactions experienced by each individual. According to Pareto, no objective standard of measurement could compare one person's private experience of utility with that of another because internal psychological experiences were incommensurate. Hence, decisions about the best distribution of social wealth involved interpersonal comparisons of utility that transcended the scope of objective economic science.

Nevertheless, Pareto believed that economists still could not make some judgments about the collective welfare of a society as scientists rather than moralists. He argued that an economist definitely could decide that economic state B′ produces more welfare than economic state B if at least one person prefers B′ to B, and no one prefers B to B′. In this case, modern economists say that B′ represents a "Pareto improvement" over B. An economy has achieved a "Pareto optimum" if it is impossible to make any more Pareto improvements to it.

Of course, most economists acknowledge that real economies never achieve the perfect competition envisioned by their theories. To prove that an economy is Pareto efficient, theorists must employ abstract mathematical models built on several heroic simplifications. The following list indicates only a few of the assumptions employed in these models:

1. The economy must be completely static, which means that consumer tastes and technological knowledge do not change.
2. All production and exchange must occur simultaneously.
3. Economic agents must make rational choices based on the desire to maximize their private sense of welfare. Their decisions must not be overly influenced by envy of the rich or sympathy for the poor.
4. Consumers must have perfect knowledge of all prices in the present and the future.
5. "Externalities," utilities or disutilities (such as pollution) that do not have a market price, must not exist.
6. All producers must be "price-takers," who lack monopoly power in their markets.

Because the modern economy is dominated by large corporations with a great deal of market power, critics argue that such assumptions are so unrealistic that neoclassical theory is pointless and irrelevant. Yet neoclassical economists assume that the theory gets at the heart of social reality beneath the "friction" that disturbs everyday life. Just as Newtonian physicists discovered the force of gravity beneath all varied phenomena of the physical world, neoclassical theory discovers individual consumer tastes and the process of market exchange beneath the various institutions of the social world.

Furthermore, the gap between theory and reality in neoclassical thought justifies the authority that twentieth-century economists have achieved as advisers and technocrats. Modern economists believe that if politicians pay attention to their economic advisers, governmental interference can reduce economic friction so that the real world acts more like the perfect world of neoclassical theory. Consequently, most neoclassical economists are willing to accept a much larger role for the government than did nineteenth-century laissez-faire economists. Even the pre-Keynesian neoclassical economists, who frequently have been portrayed as staunch proponents of laissez-faire, supported progressive politicians in their attempts to manage the corporate economy. Clark enthusiastically endorsed President Woodrow Wilson's progressive reforms and claimed that "the extreme laissez-faire policy once dominant in literature and thought now finds few persons bold enough to advocate it or foolish enough to believe it" (*Social Justice without Socialism*, pp. 4–5). For Clark and most other twentieth-century economists, the economic harmony produced by Adam Smith's invisible hand became a normative ideal to be emulated through policy, rather than an automatic natural reality. Although they often disagree about what or how much the government should do, orthodox economists are united by their theoretical vision of efficiency.

KEYNESIAN ECONOMICS

Although external critics have attacked this vision throughout the twentieth century, neoclassical economists themselves began to doubt it only during the Great Depression of the 1930s. Conventional economic thought had few explanations for the massive unemployment that plagued the industrial world in the depression, and conventional remedies seemed powerless to end it. Ultimately, the growing doubt and confusion about the viability of capitalism led many economists to embrace the intellectual reforms proposed by John Maynard Keynes's *The General Theory of Employment, Interest, and Money* in 1936. Keynes's analysis, although it was radical and innovative, attracted professional economists primarily because it seemed to explain depressions without destroying the foundations of neoclassical theory. At a time when socialist and fascist solutions to the depression were becoming increasingly popular, Keynes offered a means of escape that would least disrupt the virtues of market exchange.

Keynes called his book *The General Theory* because he believed that existing theory applied "to a special case only and not to the general case, the situation which it assumes being a limiting point of the possible positions of equilibrium" (p. 3). According to Keynes, neoclassical theory assumed the

John Maynard Keynes in His Bloomsbury Study, 1940. Keynes was a member of the Bloomsbury group, a London circle of artists and writers that included Virginia Woolf, Clive Bell, and Lytton Strachey. © HULTON-DEUTSCH COLLECTION/CORBIS

existence of a full-employment economy and offered an adequate analysis of it. If all of the workers and capital equipment in an economy were employed, Keynes agreed with the marginalists that the marketplace would allocate these resources in the most efficient way. As seemed evident in the 1930s, however, Keynes claimed the economy also could reach a position of equilibrium with an unemployment rate of 20 or 30 percent. In this case, society might be using all of its employed resources in the best possible way, but it would be wasting much of its productive potential. Just as Albert Einstein's general theory of relativity explained physical environments in which the assumptions of Newtonian mechanics did not apply, Keynes promised to explain economic states in which the neoclassical assumption of full employment did not apply.

Keynes built his theory of unemployment equilibrium on the idea that consumption often lagged behind production in a modern industrial economy. As an economy expanded its productive capacity, the incomes of individuals within the economy increased. As their incomes increased, however, most people in advanced capitalist societies spent a declining proportion of their income on consumption. In Keynes's terminology, an individual's marginal propensity to save increased and his marginal propensity to consume decreased as he got richer. Consequently, the aggregate demand for consumption goods within the economy failed to expand as fast as the industrial capacity to produce them. Eventually, firms were forced to lay off some of their work force because they no longer could sell their entire product when they produced at full capacity. Once workers lost their jobs, according to Keynes, there was no automatic mechanism within the economy to force it back toward full employment. People with money did not demand increased production because they were able to buy and save everything that they wanted at current levels of production. Unemployed people obviously did have unfulfilled demands that the economy's excess capacity could satisfy, but they had no money to make their demands effective.

Although market forces were incapable of rescuing the economy from an unemployment rut, Keynes argued that wise legislators could do so without too much trouble. The government had a couple of powerful tools for increasing aggregate demand. First, it could decrease interest rates by increasing the supply of money. This would stimulate production and employment by encouraging businesses to invest. Second, it could increase consumption and investment directly through deficit spending. No matter how the government spent its money—on welfare, public works projects, or military adventures—Keynes argued that it would increase aggregate demand if it spent more money than it received in taxes. Deficit spending created a ripple effect throughout the economy that Keynesian economists call the multiplier effect. The demand created by government spending would stimulate businessmen to hire new workers, then the income of these new workers would increase the demand for consumption goods, encouraging businessmen to hire other new workers, and so on. As long as the economy was producing at less than its full-employment capacity, deficit spending would greatly increase employment without causing inflation. If capitalist politicians employed these tools for managing aggregate demand intelligently, Keynes believed that they could maintain full employment without drastically altering the free enterprise system.

Because Keynes's argument indicated that government intervention ultimately could reproduce a full-employment equilibrium, most economists had little trouble integrating Keynesian analysis with neoclassical theory. John R. Hicks, Alvin H. Hansen, and Paul A. Samuelson, three of the most influential twentieth-century economists, developed a neoclassical synthesis that explicitly combined Keynes with the classics. Although a few radical economists who believed that Keynes had destroyed the premises of neoclassical economics dismissed this synthesis as "bastard Keynesianism," most American economists readily adopted it. Samuelson's *Economics,* the dominant undergraduate text of the mid-twentieth century, was divided into two parts, "Macroeconomics" and "Microeconomics." Macroeconomics described Keynes's theory and explained its implications for fiscal and monetary policy. Microeconomics explained the neoclassical theories of Clark, Walras, and Marshall with few alterations or amendments. According to Samuelson, this approach made sense because Keynesian policies validated neoclassical ideas:

> Under the managed microeconomics of the mixed economy, many of the old classical principles of microeconomics will again apply; but now they apply because our macroeconomics has validated their premise of adequate demand—not because the world is lucky enough to have them apply automatically and at all times.

In many ways, Samuelson saw Keynesian demand management as an extension of the governmental policies advocated by pre-Keynesian progressives. For Samuelson as for Clark, the perfectly competitive world of neoclassical theory served as a normative ideal that economic policy tried to realize. Fiscal and monetary policy simply became two more tools that economic advisers could employ to make the real economy conform to the theoretical ideal.

During the 1950s and 1960s, when the American economy was doing especially well, many mainstream economists believed that Samuelson's synthesis had solved the worst economic problems faced by capitalist society. During the 1970s and 1980s, however, Keynesian policies became less popular with politicians as economic growth stagnated and inflation increased. At the same time, academic economists began to question the theoretical assumptions of Keynesian theory. They argued that Keynes's analysis of unemployment was inadequate and developed several alternative theories, including monetarism, rational expectations theory, and real business cycle theory that sought to explain the effectiveness of Keynesian policies.

Monetarism, which was popularized by Milton Friedman, argued that the government could influence the economy only by altering the supply of money in circulation. As long as the government increased the money supply at a steady rate of 3 percent per year, there would be no inflation and the economy would be efficient. Friedman also argued that there was a natural rate of unemployment that the government could do nothing to eliminate. Rational expectations theory, which was developed by Robert Lucas, argued that the government policy always would fail to manage the economy when people could anticipate the actions of the government. For example, if people knew that government would increase public spending every time that unemployment began to increase, they would decrease their private spending and thereby cancel the effects of government policy. Thus, rational expectations theory suggested that Keynesian policies lost their effectiveness after people had become accustomed to them. Real business cycle theory, which emerged out of rational expectations theory, attributed fluctuations in employment and output to unexpected technological changes rather than to the conscious policies of the government. According to real business cycle theorists, involuntary unemployment does not exist. They argued that unemployed workers simply make a rational choice in favor of leisure when their marginal productivity is low due to technological changes.

None of these "new classical" theories represents a radical departure for neoclassical economics. Instead, they seek to return to the world of the pre-Keynesian theory by arguing that neoclassical premises really do not need to be "validated" by Keynes's ideas. Essentially, they deny the possibility of Keynes's unemployment equilibrium and thereby argue that Keynesian analysis is pointless. The new classical theorists effectively express the conservative and libertarian mood of the late twentieth century by arguing that the economy requires even less governmental control than most pre-Keynesian theorists desired. Nevertheless, they continue to share Samuelson's and Clark's underlying vision of economic efficiency. Like most twentieth-century American economists, Friedman, Lucas, and other new classical theorists continue to assume that the free market system is the most efficient means of allocating resources to satisfy the private psychological demands of individual consumers.

CRITICS OF NEOCLASSICAL THEORY

The few economic theorists that have challenged this neoclassical vision have been inspired primarily by the work of Karl Marx and Thorstein Veblen. Unlike Keynes, who shared many of the premises and the values of neoclassical theorists, Marx and Veblen built their theories on completely different assumptions about human nature and the social relationships characteristic of capitalism. Marx, of course, inspired several generations of economists who continued to criticize capitalist institutions. Veblen inspired a looser group of American "institutionalists" who also criticized the foundations of neoclassical theory. Few of these theorists obtained positions within economic departments, but they had a great deal of influence outside them. Radical theories often appeal to intellectuals who are not economists yet who seek a deeper understanding of the economic system, and these theories influenced American social critics, especially during periods of social stress such as the 1930s or the 1960s.

Marxism Marxist economists believe that neoclassical theory cannot explain the American economy because it ignores the underlying social structure of capitalism. According to the Marxists, different kinds of societies, such as slave societies in which laborers are owned as property or communist societies in which the community jointly owns the means of production, require different kinds of economic analysis. An accurate theory of the American economy has to begin with the social fact that laborers must work for wages while capitalists own the means of production as private property. Marxists believe that the relationship between workers and employers in the process of production generates conflict between them and shapes their economic transactions in the marketplace. But neoclassical theory has no way of comprehending these class relationships, because it reduces all phenomena to the process of exchange between putatively equal individual agents.

Because neoclassical theory ignores class analysis, Marxists also argue that it distorts the goals that motivate capitalist production. Whereas neoclassical theorists assume that consumers are sovereign in modern capitalism because consumer demand determines the allocation of social resources, Marxists argue that capital is the real sovereign because the quest for profit determines the use of social resources. According to Marxists, most capitalists—who already have more commodities than they ever could use—are motivated by the desire to accumulate capital rather than the desire to increase their consumption. For a capitalist, the process of exchange seems pointless if he merely produces and exchanges use values without increasing his accumulation of money. However, by identifying exchange value (or money) with use value, neoclassical theory describes capitalism as if it were merely a system for exchanging use values—as if the quest for accumulation were irrelevant. In fact, exchange makes no sense from the perspective of a capitalist in neoclassical theory because economics assumes that profit does not exist in a perfectly competitive economy. Consequently, Marxists claim that equilibrium theory explains away capitalist reality and replaces it with a myth of consumer sovereignty.

Beyond their criticisms of orthodox economics, American Marxists have had trouble formulating a unified analysis of twentieth-century capitalism. Many still believed that the labor theory of value is essential to economic analysis, but others, influenced by Piero Sraffa's *The Production of Commodities by Means of Commodities* (1975), abandoned it. Some tried to combine Marxist ideas with the ideas of radical Keynesian theorists such as Joan Robinson. Some argued that neoclassical welfare theory, although it is false as a theory of capitalism, could be employed by socialist planners to maximize productive efficiency. Others rejected centralized planning and sought to develop versions of market socialism. The diversity and conflict of opinion among socialists is largely a consequence of their political weakness. Although Marxist theory has offered a powerful analysis of the flaws of capitalism, the failure of most socialist experiments in the twentieth century has caused doubt and confusion among Marxist theorists.

Institutionalist Critics Veblen, who worked at the University of Chicago and Stanford University early in the twentieth century, developed the most penetrating criticism of neoclassical theory articulated by an American economist. Veblen turned the neoclassical interpretation of consumption and competition on its head. Neoclassical economists believed that consumption was the absolute goal of economic endeavor and assumed that people competed with each other because the goods that they wanted to consume were limited in supply. Veblen argued, in contrast, that competition and accumulation were the culturally determined end of capitalism. People acquired respect and prestige in modern society through their market exploits, through their ability to conquer others in the battle to accumulate property. Hence, Veblen believed that most consumption was conspicuous consumption, not an end in itself but a means of advertising one's success in the game of accumulation. Whereas the neoclassical theorists argued that a market system

forced wealthy capitalists to employ their social resources in the most efficient way, Veblen argued that it encouraged them to waste their property in vainglorious displays of honor.

Veblen also rejected the neoclassical assumption that labor was a painful disutility imposed on human existence by the desire to acquire consumer goods. Arguing that "man is an agent . . . seeking in every act the accomplishment of some concrete, objective, impersonal end," Veblen claimed that human beings possessed a native "instinct of workmanship" (*The Theory of the Leisure Class,* p. 15). This instinct meant that, beyond a basic level of subsistence that had been far surpassed by modern industrial society, work tended to provide more human fulfillment than consumption. According to Veblen, the disdain for productive labor evident in capitalist society was based on acquired cultural attitudes rather than natural human inclinations. Modern people had learned to despise labor because the necessity of labor had become a sign of social inferiority imposed on losers in the battle to acquire power and property.

Whereas Marxists focused on the difference between capitalists and laborers, Veblen focused on the difference between businessmen and engineers. Businessmen were motivated primarily by the desire to achieve honor and prestige through accumulation, and they tended to waste social resources in their quest to acquire and display wealth. Engineers, in contrast, were motivated primarily by the instinct of workmanship. They had little interest in conspicuous consumption and took pleasure in achieving the generic ends of society through the most efficient means. Although he did not think that it was likely, Veblen envisioned a future society organized by engineers rather than businessmen that would validate the instinct of workmanship and eliminate conspicuous consumption. In this vision Veblen employed the neoclassical ideal of efficiency to attack American capitalism. According to Veblen, society would achieve the rational efficiency that neoclassical theorists falsely attributed to capitalism only in an alternative social order that had eliminated the price system.

Most of the institutionalists who followed Veblen were liberal reformers who did not share his radical social vision. From their perspective, the most important aspect of Veblen's analysis was his rejection of methodological individualism. They shared his belief that the marginal analysis of consumer choice was superficial because it did not shed light on the social institutions that governed human values. This approach to economics liberated the institutionalists from the constraints of neoclassical theory, but it did not provide them with a unified theory of their own. The first generation of institutionalists often focused on chronological and empirical studies of economic variables because they did not trust any form of theoretical analysis. Wesley Clair Mitchell developed detailed empirical studies of the business cycle. John R. Commons produced historical studies of labor organizations and legal institutions.

The influence of this first group of institutionalists waned after World War II, but Veblen's work continued to serve as an inspiration for intellectuals dissatisfied with neoclassical theory. John Kenneth Galbraith, one of the best-known American economists of the 1960s and the 1970s, was deeply influenced by Veblen. Galbraith argued that the notion of consumer sovereignty had become ridiculous in the mid-twentieth century because corporations managed and controlled consumer demand for their own purposes. In the late twentieth century, institutionalism seemed to experience an organized revival among economists unhappy with both tra-

ditional theory and the Marxist alternatives. Several biographies and critical works about Veblen were published in the 1990s, and a new journal, the *Journal of Economic Issues,* became the official organ for this second wave of institutionalists.

Unlike economists, historians are not in the business of predictions, but it seems safe to say that neoclassical theory will not disappear in the twenty-first century as fast as the labor theory of value disappeared in the twentieth. Despite the efforts of the institutionalists and other radicals, most economists seemed to be more confident than ever about the fundamental propositions of neoclassical theory. Inspired by the increasingly global reach of capitalism in the post–cold war era, neoclassical economists also began to expand their reach, exporting their intellectual capital into other fields and disciplines. Gary S. Becker, winner of the Nobel Prize in economics in 1992, argued that the logic of neoclassical theory can be applied to everything from family choice to drug addiction. Capitalism is notoriously unstable, of course; the mood of optimism within economics at the beginning of the twenty-first century may crash, but it seems unlikely.

See also **Industrialism and Its Critics; Radical Alternatives** *(volume 1);* **The Culture and Critics of the Suburb and the Corporation; Women and Family in the Suburban Age; Working Class** *(volume 2);* **Class; Foundations and Philanthropy; Marxist Approaches; Weberian Approaches** *(in this volume); and other articles in this section.*

BIBLIOGRAPHY

General Histories

Blaug, Mark. *Economic Theory in Retrospect.* 4th ed. New York and London, 1985.

Boritt, G. S. *Lincoln and the Economics of the American Dream.* Memphis, Tenn., 1978.

Breit, William, and Roger L. Ransom. *The Academic Scribblers.* Chicago, 1982.

Heilbroner, Robert L. *The Worldly Philosophers: The Lives, Times, and Ideas of the Great Economic Thinkers.* 5th ed. New York, 1980.

Heilbroner, Robert L., and William Milberg. *The Crisis of Vision in Modern Economic Thought.* New York, 1995.

Hunt, E. K. *History of Economic Thought: A Critical Perspective.* New York, 1992.

Huston, James L. *Securing the Fruits of Labor: The American Concept of Wealth Distribution, 1765–1900.* Baton Rouge, La., 1998.

Schumpeter, Joseph A. *History of Economic Analysis.* Edited by Elizabeth Boody Schumpeter. New York, 1954.

Neoclassical Economics

Black, R., D. Collison, A. W. Coats, and Craufurd D. W. Goodwin. *The Marginal Revolution in Economics.* Durham, N.C., 1973.

Clark, John Bates. *The Distribution of Wealth: A Theory of Wages, Interest, and Profits.* New York, 1956. Originally published in 1899.

————. *Social Justice without Socialism.* Boston, 1914.

Ferguson, C. E. *Microeconomic Theory.* Homewood, Ill., 1969.

Marshall, Alfred. *Principles of Economics.* London and New York, 1961. Originally published in 1890.

Pareto, Vilfredo. *Manual of Political Economy.* Translated by Ann S. Schwier. Edited by Ann S. Schwier and Alfred N. Page. New York, 1971.

Stigler, George. *Production and Distribution Theories, the Formative Period.* New York, 1941.

Keynesian Economics

Hicks, John R. "Mr. Keynes and the Classics: A Suggested Interpretation." *Econometrica* 5 (April 1937): 147–159.

Keynes, John Maynard. *The General Theory of Employment, Interest, and Money.* New York, 1964. Originally published in 1936.

Krugman, Paul. *The Age of Diminished Expectations: U.S. Economic Policy in the 1990s.* Cambridge, Mass., 1994.

Samuelson, Paul A. *Economics.* 8th ed. New York, 1970.

Marxist Economics

Baran, Paul A., and Paul M. Sweezy. *Monopoly Capital: An Essay on the American Economic and Social Order.* New York, 1966.

Dobb, Maurice. *Theories of Value and Distribution since Adam Smith.* Cambridge, U.K., 1973.

Henwood, Doug. *Wall Street: How It Works and for Whom.* New York, 1997.

Mandel, Ernest. *An Introduction to Marxist Economic Theory.* New York, 1973.

Sraffa, Piero. *The Production of Commodities by Means of Commodities: Prelude to a Critique of Economic Theory.* Cambridge, U.K., 1975.

Steedman, Ian. *Marx after Sraffa.* London, 1977.

Institutional Economics

Galbraith, John Kenneth. *Economics and the Public Purpose.* Boston, 1973.

Veblen, Thorstein. *The Theory of the Leisure Class: An Economic Study of Institutions.* 1899. Reprint, New York, 1967.

————. *The Theory of Business Enterprise.* New York, 1904. Reprint, New Brunswick, N.J., 1978.

New Classical Economics

Becker, Gary Stanley. *Human Capital: A Theoretical and Empirical Analysis, with Special Reference to Education.* New York, 1975.

Begg, David K. H. *The Rational Expectations Revolution in Macroeconomics: Theories and Evidence.* Baltimore, 1982.

Friedman, Milton. *Capitalism and Freedom.* Chicago, 1962.

Snowdon, Brian, Howard Vane, and Peter Wynarczyk. *A Modern Guide to Macroeconomics: An Introduction to Competing Schools of Thought.* Brookfield, Vt., 1994.

Part 14

THE SOCIAL ORDER AND SOCIAL IDENTITY

INDIVIDUALISM AND THE SELF

Wilfred M. McClay

"Individualism" and "self": it is hard to imagine what present-day discourse would sound like without these two nouns. All the more reason, then, to keep in mind that "individualism" is actually a relatively new addition to the lexicon of Western intellectual and religious history—and the concept of the "self," particularly in its reified, psychological sense, even more so. That is not to deny that both words have long and distinguished pedigrees, informed by rich antecedents and fertile anticipations. They did not acquire their power overnight. Indeed, belief in the profound dignity and infinite worth of the individual person has always been a distinguishing mark, and a principal mainstay, of what is imprecisely called Western civilization.

PREMODERN ANTECEDENTS

Elements of the concept of transcendent individual worth can be detected as far back as classical antiquity, particularly in the Greek discovery of "philosophy" as a distinctive form of free rational inquiry, and in the Greco-Roman stress upon the need for virtuous individual citizens to sustain a healthy republican political order. Other elements appeared later, particularly in the intensely self-directed and self-oriented moral discipline of Hellenistic-era Epicureanism and Stoicism. And perhaps even more important, the traditions and institutions arising out of biblical monotheism placed heavy emphasis upon the infinite value, personal agency, and moral accountability of the individual person. That emphasis reached a pinnacle of sorts in Western Christianity, which brilliantly incorporated the divergent legacies of Athens and Jerusalem into a single universalized faith, one that enabled every individual man and woman, irrespective of tribe or nation, language or culture, to come into a full and saving relationship with God.

Nearly all the most influential figures in Western Christianity, whatever their differences on contested questions of faith or morals, served to reinforce this belief in the central importance of the individual human person. The *Confessions* of St. Augustine (c. 400) bespoke the importance of the individual precisely through the gripping tale of individual conversion it rendered. In 1486 the Italian scholar Pico della Mirandola offered an effusive *De hominis dignitata oratio* (Oration on the dignity of man) as a ringing assertion of the individual human being's profound moral freedom. To be sure, Protestant reformers, particularly those of Calvinist hue, took a far dimmer view of unredeemed human nature, and a far more robust view of the doctrine of Original Sin. And yet, with their belief in the priesthood of all believers, which radically de-emphasized the efficacy of the institutional church, and their insistence that salvation was to be gained only through an uncoerced individual confession of faith in Jesus Christ as the redeemer of a sinful world, the advocates of a reformed Christian faith intensified the emphasis upon the conscience and choices of the individual believer. That such changes lent support to the key economic developments of the age, particularly as reflected in the rise of commerce and capitalist enterprise, only made it all the more likely to succeed.

None of these expressions of belief, explicit and implicit, in the individual amounted to anything approaching what modern individualism connotes, however, and it is important to grasp why. Such freedom as the premodern individual enjoyed, particularly since the advent of Christianity, was always constrained either by belief in the existence of an objective moral order, which could not be violated with impunity by Antinomian rebels and enthusiasts, or by belief in the inherent frailty of human nature, which indicated that virtue could not be produced in social isolation. Although nearly all influential Western thinkers before the dawn of modernity had conceded the signal importance of the individual, none employed the term "individualism" to express that belief.

"INDIVIDUALISM" IN EUROPE AND AMERICA

Instead, "individualism," like many useful terms, began life as a term of critique, even opprobrium. It first appeared in French, and in the discourse of one of the most fierce opponents of the French Revolution and modernity. The nineteenth-century French archconservative Joseph de Maistre devised the label of "individualism" to describe much of what he found horrifying about the Revolution: its overturning of established social hierarchies and dissolution of traditional social bonds, in favor of an atomizing and leveling doctrine of individual natural rights, which freed each individual to be his or her own moral arbiter. Maistre's "individualism" was not an affirmation of dignity, but a nightmare of egotism and moral anarchy run riot.

A few years later, the French writer Alexis de Tocqueville, in his classic two-volume study *Democracy in America* (1835 and 1840), also employed the term "individualism" in a manner that was subtler, if no less critical. Individualism was, he argued, a characteristic pathology of "democratic" societies, that is, societies which lacked any legally recognized distinctions of rank and station among their members. Although the American nation was but a few decades into its history, Tocqueville already found individualism to be one of its defining characteristics—and therefore, he thought, a characteristic of all modernity, since America represented the avant garde of modern history, the first "great republic."

But Tocqueville's complaint was different from Maistre's. Egotism, he thought, was an emotional disorder, a "passionate and exaggerated" self-love, of a sort one could find throughout human history. But individualism was a self-conscious social philosophy, "a mature and calm feeling, which disposes each member of the community to sever himself from the mass of his fellow-creatures: and to draw apart with his family and friends: so that . . . he willingly leaves society at large to itself." For Tocqueville, individualism is not merely a self-indulgent form of social atomism, but something new, a conscious and calculated withdrawal from the responsibilities of citizenship and public life. For Tocqueville, who was, unlike Maistre, a qualified friend of democracy, there was no greater threat to the new order than this tendency toward privatism.

So "individualism" began its life as a term of abuse. Now and then, particularly when it is employed by social critics, one will see indications that it has not entirely lost this sense. And yet the critical view of these two French critics seems strikingly at odds with the self-conception of most Americans, who after all had no experience of feudal, aristocratic, monarchical, and other premodern political institutions, and who are likely to see individualism, in one form or another, as a wholly positive thing, the key ingredient in what it means to be American. Such a view is, of course, a bit too simple. It presumes that American history is nothing more than the story of an unfolding liberal tradition, a tale that can be encapsulated in the classic expression of individual natural rights embodied in the Declaration of Independence. Such a view ignores the profound influence of religious, republican, radical communitarian, socialist, feminist, and other nonliberal elements in the national saga, including the most illiberal institution of all, chattel slavery. What national commitment to individualistic values Americans now possess has certainly evolved over time, and there have always been countercurrents challenging the mainstream.

Nor, for that matter, is it always easy to know what is meant by the term "individualism." In the twenty-first century, it is used, albeit legitimately, in a bewildering variety of ways. It may refer to the self-interested disposition of mind that Tocqueville described, or to the passionate egotism Maistre deplored, or to the self-reliant frontiersman or self-made small proprietor praised in American popular lore. "Individualism" may be taken to refer to an understanding of the proper relationship between the individual and society or state, wherein the liberty and dignity of the former is to be protected against the aggrandizing or social-conformist pressures of the latter. More radically, it may point toward a philosophy of the state or society, in which all political and social groups are viewed as mere aggregations of otherwise self-sufficient individuals, whose social bonds are entirely governed by consensual contract. Even more radically, it may point toward the increasingly popular view that, to the maximum degree possible, the individual should be regarded as an entirely morally autonomous creature—accountable to no person and no putative "higher law," armed with a quiver of imprescriptible rights, protected by a zone of inviolable privacy, and left free to "grow" and "develop" as the promptings of the Romantic "self" dictate. All these meanings of "individualism" have in common a presumption of the inherent worth of the individual person, but they may diverge in dramatic ways.

And yet, caveats aside, there can be little doubt that the dominant American tradition of the twenty-first century has become one of endorsing the highest possible degree of individual liberty and self-development in political, religious, social, and economic affairs. American history is a record of the defeat or erosion of most competing ideas. Whether the realities of American political, social, and economic life actually reflect such an advanced level of individualism on the level of behavior is, of course, another question, to which this essay shall turn in a moment. But it seems clear that the highly pejorative connotation that "individualism" had at the time of its origins never took deep hold in Anglo-American discourse.

If anything, the language of individual rights, and the tendency to regard individual men and women as self-contained, contract-making, utility-maximizing, and values-creating actors, who accept only those duties and obligations they elect to accept, had grown steadily more powerful and pervasive in the latter part of the twentieth century. The recourse to individual rights, whether expressed as legal rights, voting rights, expressive rights, reproductive rights, sexual rights, membership rights, or consumer rights, became the near-invincible trump card in most debates regarding public policy, and it was only in the rarest instances (such as the provision of preferential treatment for members of groups that had been subjected to past legal or social discrimination) that this trump was effectively challenged. The fundamental commitment to what the suffragist Elizabeth Cady Stanton called the "individuality of each human soul" had never been stronger than in the last decades of the twentieth century.

CORPORATIST AND COMMUNITARIAN COUNTERCURRENTS

Again, it is important to remember that this has not always been the state of affairs in America. Much of the best late twentieth-century scholarship in colonial and early national history demonstrates just this contention. The political scientist Barry Alan Shain's book *The Myth of American Individualism* (1994) argues powerfully that it was not Enlightened liberalism, but a very constrained form of communitarian Reformed Protestantism, that best represented the dominant social and political outlook of early America. The political theorist Michael Sandel, one of the most influential communitarian critics of rights-based liberalism, argued in the 1990s that until the twentieth century America's public philosophy was based on the "republican" assumption that the polity had a formative, prescriptive, "soulcraft" function to perform in matters

of the economy, the family, church-state relations, personal morality, free speech, constitutional law, privacy, productive labor, and consumption. That assumption, observed Sandel, was so completely undone by the individualistic liberalism of the late twentieth century that most Americans forgot it was ever there.

In the end it was the expansive, mid-nineteenth-century voices of men like Ralph Waldo Emerson and Walt Whitman, Romantic American nationalists and prophets of the unconstrained self, that generally had the better end of the debate, sounding the liberatory yawp that has resounded over the rooftops and resonated through the streets of the American imagination, even down to the present day. It was Emerson who declared famously that a society is a "conspiracy against the manhood of every one of its members," and that "nothing is at last sacred but the integrity of your own mind." And it was Whitman who declared that "the Great Idea" was "the idea of perfect and free individuals," and that "nothing, not God, is greater to one than one's-self is." And although both men would live long enough to be disillusioned by the crass economic opportunism and material acquisitiveness that seemed to take hold of American society in the post–Civil War years, one could hardly deny that such driving, self-interested ambition was a logical corollary to the spirit of unrestrained self-development. So, too, was the unforgettable image of Mark Twain's Huckleberry Finn, the semi-noble, semi-savage boy "lighting out for the territory," rather than face any more of the pinched and morally questionable rigors of "sivilization."

As the example of Huckleberry Finn suggests, American thought and expression has always been rich with figures of heroic individuality—and correspondingly poor in convincing and binding representations of community or social obligation. Whether one considers the accounts of colonial religious controversies, such as those involving the rebels Roger Williams and Anne Hutchinson, or in the moral fables of popular culture, such as those offered by the movies *One Flew Over the Cuckoo's Nest* (1975) and *Dead Poets Society* (1989), Americans seem almost invariably to be asked to side with the put-upon individual, invariably cast as an unjustly thwarted soul yearning to breathe free, and instructed to hiss at the figures of social or political authority, whose efforts to sustain order establish them instead as enemies of humanity itself.

There have, however, been a few notable efforts over the years to present a counterexample to this celebration of individuality. The immense human suffering and dislocation wrought by postbellum industrialization led to a rash of utopian novels, perhaps best exemplified by Edward Bellamy's fabulously best-selling 1888 fantasy *Looking Backward 2000–1887,* an effort to imagine a perfected post-industrial Boston, reconstituted as a socialist cooperative commonwealth in the year 2000. Bellamy openly reviled individualism, proposing in its place a post-Christian "religion of solidarity," which would radically deemphasize the self, and instead emphasize social bonds over individual liberty (and traditional Christian theological doctrine). The popularity of Bellamy's book showed that there was a market hungry for such ideas, and many of the most "progressive" forces of the day, whether one thinks of the cooperation-minded Knights of Labor, the theological advocates of a modernist "social gospel," or Progressive reformers such as the *New Republic* founder Herbert David Croly, the social worker Jane Addams, and the philosopher John Dewey, unreservedly admired and emulated its spirit.

The Progressive movement itself advanced, at least in some of its manifestations, a new corporate ideal, which sought to downplay individualism and instead to defend and preserve "the public interest," in the face of industrial capital's depredations. In the hands of a sophisticated thinker like Dewey, and some of his followers, a case was made that the values of community and individuality, far from being in opposition, are mutually supporting and mutually sustaining, particularly in an age dominated by large industrial combinations, immense asymmetries of wealth and power, and vast impersonal networks of communication. It was pointless, in their view, to attempt to restore the small-scale community of days past. The forces of economic and social modernity had rendered such community, with its personal bonds and face-to-face business transactions, obsolete. The task ahead was the creation of something new, which Dewey called the "Great Community," a systematically reconstituted social order that, it was hoped, would adapt the best features of the old community forms to the inexorable realities of the new economy and society.

TOTALITARIANISM AND THE RISE OF NEO-INDIVIDUALISM

In retrospect, the new corporate ideal seems never to have had a fighting chance. Historians have patiently documented a thousand ways in which American life in the twentieth century had in fact become more corporate, more organized, more standardized. But Americans' self-conception did not followed suit. Perhaps doing so would have cut too much against the American grain. To be sure, the privations of the Great Depression gave the values of community and solidarity a temporary boost in American social thought, as the historian Richard Pells has convincingly argued. But even President Franklin Roosevelt's New Deal, riven as it was by pragmatic accommodations and intellectual inconsistencies, paid such values little more than lip service.

The decisive blow, however, was administered by the rise of the totalitarian regimes of Europe, whose terrifying success in suppressing the individual for the sake of the collectivity threw all corporate ideals into doubt and disrepute, from which they have yet to recover. The concerns generated thereby decisively shaped both the liberalism and conservatism of the postwar years. Libertarians like the economists Ludwig von Mises and Friedrich von Hayek, liberals like the sociologist David Riesman, the literary critic Lionel Trilling, and the theologian Reinhold Niebuhr, even conservatives like the historian-sociologist Robert Nisbet and the social critic Russell Kirk—all paid their disrespects to the Leviathan state, and thereby called into question the efficacy of any modern corporate ideal. Instead, the social and political thought of postwar America seemed to be dedicated to a different ideal: the guardianship of the self.

There were examples galore of this neo-individualist turn. Riesman's *The Lonely Crowd* (1950) warned against the conformism of "other-direction" in the American personality, and William H. Whyte's *The Organization Man* (1956) deplored the predominance of a "social ethic" in America's white-collar classes. Ayn Rand's fierce pop-Nietzschean novels celebrated the autonomy of the individual creative genius, and reviled the dullness of hoi polloi. Neo-Freudian psychology concerned itself with the problems of the ego, and leading psychological theorists such as Carl Jung and Erik Erikson focused obsessively on the problem of individuation. Even the emergence of a New Left movement in the early 1960s, which purported to rebel against the complacency of its liberal forebears, did little to alter this trend, since the movement's communitarian tendencies were no match for its commitment to a radical, near-anarchic standard of behavioral and expressive liberty, in speech, dress, sexuality, drug use, and so on. As such, it provides a textbook illustration of the difficulty entailed in pursuing the politics of progressive reform while remaining programmatically suspicious of any and all sources of authority and value outside the self.

This difficulty represents a serious obstacle not only to radicalism, but to the reform aspirations of both liberalism and conservatism in contemporary times, since each of these ideological camps contains within itself anarcho-libertarian elements that, while undeniably popular, militate against the establishment and sustenance of communal values, and thereby undermine the very idea of a stable public interest. For conservatives, the principal such obstacle stems from an ideological commitment to economic liberty; for liberals, it arises out of an equally rigid commitment to moral and expressive liberty. In crucial ways, both ideological camps have in common an unwillingness to accept the need for an authority, a tradition, an institutional nexus that is capable of superseding individual liberty in the name of social cohesion and the public interest.

THE SELF AS MORAL CENTER

In the age of modernity and postmodernity, then, the self has become the chief source of moral value. The term "self," which has had an amorphous history, has nevertheless evolved into something crucially different from the term "soul." In general, it is used as a psychological term, largely stripped of metaphysical implications. The self is understood as the seat of personal identity, source of mental cohesiveness and psychological integrity—the vanishing point, as it were, where all lines of psychological energy converge in the life of a "healthy" and "integrated" individual. The word "soul" maintains a link to the transcendent realm, and is suggestive of an imperishable essence distinct from the bodily state, while the self is strictly immanent, secular, worldly, transitory, adaptive, pragmatic. "Soul" is a word that rarely crosses the lips of modern thinkers, unless they employ it in a deliberately rhetorical or fanciful way. Souls are judged by the vanished god of faith; selves by the all-too-present god of health. By way of compensation, though, there remains a lingering ambiguity about self—some residue of the romantic "authentic" self always lurking in the corners of psychotherapeutic discourse, promising that the recovery and expression of that "authentic" self brings psychological health and well-being.

There are complications inherent in such a strictly psychological approach to the self. As the communitarian thinker Charles Taylor argued in his magisterial study *Sources of the Self* (1989), personal integrity inevitably rests on a moral foundation, on a set of prerational moral presuppositions. In other words, a moral disposition toward one's world, and a prior assent to certain moral criteria, are the preconditions of there being any psychological order and consistency at all in a human personality. If Taylor was right in his analysis, then health is built upon morality, rather than the reverse. And yet that is not always the way modern Americans talk about the self. Therapies for survivors of childhood abuse, for example, are openly geared toward the construction of new life narratives, ones that serve to overturn the disabling effects of the abused individuals' life experiences. Great care is taken to employ a cool pastel language of "narrativity," in order to give an aura of moral neutrality to the process. But in fact, far from being morally neutral, such processes are in fact meant to reallocate moral praise and blame in the client's world, in entirely new and "healthier" ways. Most often, they do this by re-describing the client as a "victim" and the abuser as a moral transgressor. The language of therapy only pretends to banish the lingering concept of moral responsibility.

But the question arises, Does it not matter tremendously whether or not these new narratives are *true,* or can be sincerely believed to be true? Can such therapies succeed if they are self-consciously regarded as nothing more than the construction of empowering narratives? Can morality be effective if it is denied the support of some warrant of truth? Here is a juncture at which the difference between a modernist and postmodernist approach to the self can be discerned. A modernist like Freud would have insisted that it is the *truth* about oneself that sets one free. A postmodernist would respond that there are multiple truths, and one of the key elements in the achievement of psychological health is the ability to navigate between and among the elements of this multiplicity.

There is no escape, then, from difficult epistemological choices, even in the antiphilosophical precincts of psychology, let alone the less buffered realm of public affairs. One possible solution to the general dilemma of truth discernment has been sought by scholars such as Richard Rorty, who are promoting the revival of the philosophy known as pragmatism. They tout pragmatism as a method that can arrive at consensual and provisional "truths" that will serve the purposes of the hour without falling into the pit of nihilism on the one hand, or committing the error of reintroducing "objective truth" on the other. This suggestion has proved fruitful in the academic realm, a realm to which pragmatism would seem to be particularly well suited, since it legitimates the kind of continuous discussion and rethinking that characterize academic life at its most engaging. American academics approve of pragmatism, because pragmatism is good for their business. How successful such methods can be in actual political and social operation, however, remains to be seen, since they seem to amount, in practice, to little more than a mechanism for producing arbitrary pronouncements, propounded by elites but dressed up in the language of majoritarianism—or majoritarian pronouncements that are dressed up to appear as if they are principled and disinterested dicta. The provisionality of pragmatism, the very feature that makes it so attractive in academic settings, makes it peculiarly unsuited for public life, a realm that needs the legitimating effects of broad values and large principles to produce a workable consensus for governing. What looks like "redescription" in the lecture hall looks a whole lot like "dissembling" in the public square.

POSTMODERN FRAGMENTATION OF THE SELF

An even bigger problem with a subjectivist moral order is the inherent instability of the self. One of the most powerful themes of postmodernism is its assertion that the modern self cannot bear the weight placed upon it by fragmented modern life, and that in fact the multiplicity of the world *requires* people to operate on the basis of multiple selves. Just as in atomic physics, where the unsplittable entity (the Greek *atomos*) turned out to have a multitude of subparticles in its makeup, so, too, the self has proved to be a complicated and vulnerable entity, as vulnerable as the idea of truth itself. The French philosopher René Descartes inaugurated modernity with the assertion that the "I" is the most fundamental building block in the individual's apprehension of reality, the still point in a moving world. Now it appears that the self, far from being foundational, is the most protean and variable thing of all. In the postmodern view, the search for "individual integrity" and "authenticity" is outmoded. The postmodern self is not a unitary identity, but an ever-shifting ensemble of social roles, a venue in which the ego functions less as a commander in chief than as a skilled air-traffic controller.

It is hard to know how to respond to this description, or to the phenomenon it describes. Ought one celebrate it, in the manner of writers such as Robert Jay Lifton, Walter Truett Anderson, and Sherry Turkle, who found exciting elements in the postmodern liberation from unitary personality? Or is one obliged to deplore it, in the manner of the social critic Christopher Lasch, as an effort to "redescribe" mental illness as a new form of mental health? Or should one merely treat it neutrally, as an provisional account of a new set of psychosocial conditions, to be analyzed and somehow coped with? Whatever one's answer to those questions, it seems clear that the modernist ideal of the individual, the ideal that underwrites modern and postmodern conceptions of the self, has been rendered far more confused and unsteady than ever before.

THE PROBLEM OF EQUALITY AND THE RECOVERY OF CITIZENSHIP

One element in the ideal of equality that has been made especially problematic is its bedrock assumption of the fundamental and interchangeable equality of all selves. This axiom has been challenged in a number of ways. For example, the last three decades of the twentieth century saw major legal and jurisprudential struggles over the ways that the doctrine of equality should be applied to questions of group identity. These struggles were manifested in debates over race, affirmative action, multiculturalism, and the like; but nowhere had the problem become more complex than in the area of gender. As the scholar Elizabeth Fox-Genovese argued in *Feminism without Illusions* (1991), it is no easy matter to determine the extent to which irreducible biological asymmetries—particularly women's ability to bear children—should influence legal and political structures. Is women's equality best honored by obliterating all distinctions of sex, across the board, treating men and women interchangeably? Or is it best honored by building certain recognitions of female difference into the law? Surely the sensible, if evasive, answer is: it depends. Fox-Genovese attempted to answer the point by distinguishing between the imposition of a mechanical equality, which would be undesirable for most women, and a more amorphous standard of "equity," which would take difference into account.

To be sure, Fox-Genovese's notion of "equity" might be exceedingly hard to define in practice, particularly given the propensity of the law to be an exceptionally blunt instrument. But she pointed toward an understanding of individual dignity that, if achieved, would be strikingly different from doctrinaire egalitarian individualism. In many respects, it would resemble a recovery and adaptation of the Judeo-Christian understanding of the individual person as deriving dignity from his or her intrinsic being, rather than from the greater or lesser degree of freestanding autonomy—what is sometimes called "quality of life"—that he or she can demonstrate. Such a view would stand in the longer Western tradition of individualism, affirming the diversity of legitimate human roles and ranks in society. At the same time, it would stand in direct competition to the increasingly influential view that the dignity and standing of any individual life is dependent upon the competency of the individual in question. Whether and how such debates will be resolved in the future is hard to discern. Historians and sociologists can anticipate, too, that their growing knowledge of the biogenetic bases for human psychology and behavior in years to come will have a profound, and equally unpredictable, effect upon their view of the individual, and have their own influence on the outcome.

What seems clear, however, is the need to rescue the idea of individual dignity from its captivity in the realms of individual psychology and postmodernist subjectivity, and return it to the public realm, where it may be able to find a firmer footing and deeper roots. This would mean reaffirming the core meaning of individualism: its insistence upon the transcendent value of the person. But it would also embrace the core insight of communitarianism: the recognition that the self is made in culture, and the richest forms of individuality are achieved in the company of others. And it would build upon Tocqueville's further insight that it is in the school of public life, and in the embrace and exercise of the title of "citizen," that the selves of men and women become most meaningfully equal, individuated, and free—not in those fleeting, and often illusive, moments when they escape the company of others, and retreat into a zone of privacy, subjectivity, and endlessly reconstructed narratives of the "self."

Equality and individuality—and freedom—are inherent in the very idea of citizenship. Indeed, citizenship is an artificial construct meant to encompass, and correct for, the imperfections and inequalities inherent in the endowments of nature and the accidents of culture. In addition, it grounds itself in something that the social-scientific view of human nature has sorely neglected: the human ability to initiate, to deliberate, to act, and in so doing to transform the very conditions of action. The study of politics takes seriously the human capacity to be a cause, and not merely an effect. More than anything else, Tocqueville feared that their tendency toward individualism would inhibit Americans' willingness to act in public ways. Accordingly, the most fruitful response to the present-day disintegration of the self may be a movement away from the characteristic preoccupations of modern sociology and psychology, and toward a fresh reconsideration of the political side of our nature, in all its complexity, contingency, and promise. The Western Christian tradition has always taught that the fractured soul can only be healed by being poured into relationship with the things outside itself. In the twenty-first century, that insight has much to commend it.

See also **Philosophy from Puritanism to the Enlightenment; Moral Philosophy; Transcendentalism; Manhood** *(volume 1);* **The Culture of Self-Improvement; Artistic, Intellectual, and Political Refugees; Psychology, the Mind, and Personality** *(volume 2);* **Success; Biography** *(in this volume); and other articles in this section.*

BIBLIOGRAPHY

Primary Texts

Augustine. *The Confessions of St. Augustine.* New York, 1978.

Bellamy, Edward. *Looking Backward 2000–1887.* New York, 1989.

Croly, Herbert. *The Promise of American Life.* New York, 1909.

Dewey, John. *The Public and Its Problems.* New York, 1927.

Emerson, Ralph Waldo. *Essays: First and Second Series.* New York, 1990.

Hayek, Friedrich A. *The Road to Serfdom.* Chicago, 1949.

Rand, Ayn. *Atlas Shrugged.* New York, 1996.

——. *The Fountainhead.* New York, 1996.

Riesman, David, et al. *The Lonely Crowd: A Study of the Changing American Character.* New Haven, Conn., 1950.

Tocqueville, Alexis de. *Democracy in America.* Translated by Henry Reeve, with Francis Bowen and Phillips Bradley. New York, 1945.

Twain, Mark. *The Adventures of Huckleberry Finn.* Edited by John Seelye. New York, 1995.

Whyte, William Hollingsworth. *The Organization Man.* New York, 1956.

Historical and Theoretical Studies

Anderson, Walter Truett. *The Future of the Self: Inventing the Postmodern Person.* New York, 1998.

Coleman, Janet. *The Individual in Political Theory and Practice.* Oxford, 1996.

Davies, Joseph E. "Healing the Fragmented Self" and "Identity and Social Change: A Short Review." *The Hedgehog Review: Critical Reflections on Contemporary Culture* 1 (1999): 47–54.

Fox-Genovese, Elizabeth. *Feminism without Illusions: A Critique of Individualism.* Chapel Hill, N.C., 1991.

Gress, David. *From Plato to NATO: The Idea of the West and Its Opponents.* New York, 1998.

Harvey, David. *The Condition of Postmodernity: An Enquiry into the Origins of Cultural Change.* Cambridge, Mass., 1989.

Lear, Jonathan. *Aristotle: The Desire to Understand.* New York, 1988.

Lifton, Robert Jay. *The Protean Self: Human Resilience in an Age of Fragmentation.* New York, 1993.

Long, A. A. *Hellenistic Philosophy: Stoics, Epicureans, Sceptics.* 2d ed. Berkeley, Calif., 1986.

Lukes, Steven. *Individualism.* Oxford, 1973.

Lyotard, Jean-Francois. *The Postmodern Condition: A Report on Knowledge.* Translated by Brian Massumi. Minneapolis, Minn., 1984.

McClay, Wilfred. "The Judeo-Christian Tradition and the Liberal Tradition in the American Republic." In *Public Morality, Civic Virtue, and the Problem of Modern Liberalism,* edited by Gary Quinlivan, pp. 124–136. Grand Rapids, Mich., 1999.

Morris, Colin. *The Discovery of the Individual, 1050–1200.* Toronto, 1995.

Rieff, Philip. *The Triumph of the Therapeutic: Uses of Faith after Freud.* Chicago, 1987.

Shanahan, Daniel. *Toward a Genealogy of Individualism.* Amherst, Mass., 1992.

Taylor, Charles. *Sources of the Self: The Making of the Modern Identity.* Cambridge, Mass., 1989.

Turkle, Sherry. *Life on the Screen: Identity in the Age of the Internet.* New York, 1995.

American Individualism

Arieli, Yehoshua. *Individualism and Nationalism in American Ideology.* Cambridge, Mass., 1966.

Bellah, Robert N., et al. *Habits of the Heart: Individualism and Commitment in American Life.* Berkeley, Calif., 1985.

Blake, Casey Nelson. *Beloved Community: The Cultural Criticism of Randolph Bourne, Van Wyck Brooks, Waldo Frank, and Lewis Mumford.* Chapel Hill, N.C., 1990.

Cayton, Mary Kupiec. *Emerson's Emergence: Self and Society in the Transformation of New England, 1800–1845.* Chapel Hill, N.C., 1989.

Curry, Richard O., and Lawrence B. Goodheart, eds. *American Chameleon: Individualism in Trans-National Context.* Kent, Ohio, 1991.

Hewitt, John P. *Dilemmas of the American Self.* Philadelphia, 1989.

Lasch, Christopher. *The Culture of Narcissism: American Life in an Age of Diminishing Expectations.* New York, 1979.

Leinberger, Paul, and Bruce Tucker. *The New Individualists: The Generation after the Organization Man.* New York, 1991.

McClay, Wilfred M. *The Masterless: Self and Society in Modern America.* Chapel Hill, N.C., 1994.

Pells, Richard H. *Radical Visions and American Dreams: Culture and Social Thought in the Depression Years.* Urbana, Ill., 1998.

Rorty, Richard. *Achieving Our Country: Leftist Thought in Twentieth-Century America.* Cambridge, Mass., 1997.

Sandel, Michael J. *Democracy's Discontent: America in Search of a Public Philosophy.* Cambridge, Mass., 1996.

Shain, Barry Alan. *The Myth of American Individualism: The Protestant Origins of American Political Thought.* Princeton, N.J., 1994.

Westbrook, Robert B. *John Dewey and American Democracy.* Ithaca, N.Y., 1991.

FAMILY

Elisabeth Lasch-Quinn

Since the family would seem to be, at some fundamental level, necessary—at least for the biological reproduction of humankind—it is an interesting phenomenon of modern life that the family itself has come under intense questioning and debate. Even those who share an avowed commitment to defending or promoting the family hold very different, even competing, assumptions and ideals. People disagree on everything from how to define a "family" and whether the family can be said to be in "decline" to whether one can even speak of the family at all, given the remarkable diversity in family practices and ideals. When turning to the past, observers have also disagreed vehemently about what changes in family life have been the most significant, about how many Americans actually experienced noted trends, and even about whether a certain transformation ever happened at all.

While allowing for the limits of generalization and the existence of important exceptions and complexities, as well as the often subtle interplay between mainstream and minority (or individual) experiences, the richest scholarship has pinpointed sweeping, long-term transformations in the history of the American family that are crucial for understanding dominant mores both past and present. Some of the most important transformations include a drastic decline in the size of immediate families; a shift from the extended family to the nuclear family as the primary unit of familial experience; a gradual loss of the functions once performed by the family to outside institutions; the privatization of the family; the intrusion of professional experts into the family increasingly under the mantle of therapeutic assistance; growing equality among family members; the family's shift from a productive unit to one devoted primarily to consuming goods and services; the increased prevalence of marriage based on self-selection of partners rather than parental arrangement; and the decline in the prevalence of what might be called the classic family (mother and

father and their children), particularly since the 1960s. A sketch of the broad contours of change introduces some of the more important questions that have been raised regarding the American family. Brief forays into particular themes or phases in the history of the family take a look at the origins and ramifications of these overarching transformations with the aim of raising ideas for further study.

BROAD CONTOURS OF CHANGE

Over the course of American history, the size of the immediate family has seen a striking overall decrease. However, particular eras and social groups defy this generalization. For instance, from 1940 to 1957 the fertility rate rose 50 percent despite a downward trend for over a century, creating what became known as the "baby boom." And working-class families of various ethnic origins sometimes did not witness the same decline experienced by white, middle-class families. Acknowledging the limits of generalizing based only on averages, observers cannot fail to remark upon the shift from colonial times, when records show that white families had an average of seven to eight births, to roughly 1900 when the average number of children per family was around three or four. By the end of the twentieth century, the average number of children per family had divided in half again, down to one or two (see Mintz and Kellogg).

One of the most important changes in the family—and one of the most controversial—has involved the shift in emphasis on the extended family unit (a term that loosely includes the mother, the father, and their children, as well as other relatives such as grandparents, aunts, uncles, and cousins) to an emphasis on the nuclear family (variously defined as consisting of one or both parents, along with their children). According to most historians of the family, it is a widespread myth held by the public and by many scholars before the 1950s that members of extended families commonly resided in the same household before industrialization, after which households tended to include only nuclear families. Instead, most historians now say, households in Western societies have primarily consisted of nuclear families for several centuries. And, in fact, as the historian Tamara Hareven pointed out in her writings, at times the extended family came to live under one roof after industrial life had commenced, since low wages and the process of migration caused immigrant workers to share households with kin.

But while most scholars say that the shift from extended families to nuclear families living under one roof is largely a myth, they agree that the extended family used to be a much more central unit than it became by the twentieth century. While grandparents and the like might have lived in another household, there were often close bonds and reciprocal duties knitting the larger group together to a degree more rare at the start of the twenty-first century (although, how rare it really is remains a matter of some dispute among scholars).

The French historian Philippe Ariès drew a lively and compelling portrait of the pre-modern family as a place of tremendous sociability, a setting in which the division between the community and the family was nonexistent, where children and adults mixed freely. In this setting, he argued, children learned about the outside world much more completely and at an earlier age. They had multiple adults from whom to learn and on whom to model their behavior. Modern Western families, in contrast, in the process of becoming self-contained and private, recast childhood as a distinct and separate stage of life and focused much more self-consciously on children's upbringing even while prolonging it. This symbolized not only a new definition of childhood but also the rise of the concept of the family itself as a discrete entity. Richard Sennett later studied Ariès's and the sociologist Talcott Parsons's portraits of the family in the context of nineteenth-century Union Park, a Chicago neighborhood, and concluded that the isolated, privatized family created enormous problems within families, including loss of paternal authority and difficulty for adolescents in adjusting to the adult world.

Focusing on England, the British historian Lawrence Stone also pointed to a narrowing of the traditional sphere of the family. The family saw its domain gradually diminish from one that involved the extended kin network and others to one closed to all but the nuclear family at the same time that infant mortality rates fell, fertility dropped, and life expectancy rose. This shrinkage allowed individuals, Stone argued, to start making more of an emotional "investment" in the each of the other family members (p. 407). The result was a transition from a situation governed by "diffuse" emotional attachments in which the family was "a group of replaceable surrogates" (pp. 408–409) to one in which particular relationships strained under the weight of the new pressures on them to satisfy all that family members demanded of one another. These demands, in fact, grew to be out of proportion with what they could reasonably deliver. Though Stone certainly did not celebrate the pre-modern family, with its predilection to deference and authoritarianism, he thought the modern family was characterized by deep tensions owing to its trait of "explosive intimacy" (p. 423).

While other scholars have disagreed about aspects of these ideas (for instance, the portrait of weak bonds and parental remoteness when mortality rates were higher), they largely agree that at the same time that the family unit came to define itself as the immediate family in the West, the functions performed by the family changed, as did the family's relation to the larger community. As observed, among others, by Talcott Parsons in the 1950s, the family witnessed a gradual replacement of its functions over time. By the twentieth century the family had become mainly a source of emotional nurture and the "socialization" of children (the induction of children into social rules and norms). As advanced industrial society became more populous and complex, the whole spectrum of social experience became more fragmented and specialized. The advent of the factory inaugurated, for instance, the separation of the homeplace and the workplace, the breaking down of tasks into smaller, discrete parts, and the division of manual and mental labor. This pattern of specialization greatly affected social experience by isolating different sectors of daily reality. The family's loss of functions was part of this growing segmentation and specialization, both of which drove the formation of institutions of all types, from schools to social work. Where once the family was an arena for everything from recreation to production, education, and sociability, it now became a site specifically limited to emotional nurture and the rearing of children. Some have lamented this change while others, like Parsons, have seen the family's new single-minded devotion to emotional sustenance and socialization as crucial given the complexity of modern life.

The most vital function lost to the family was economic production, and this change in turn altered social relations drastically. As long as production was centered in the home, women and men tended to view work as a cooperative enterprise, even though there was a division of actual tasks by sex. Male and female tasks were complementary and crucial to production, even if they were not identical. During the nineteenth century, this cooperative, productive enterprise transformed into a much more sex-segregated structure as productive work came increasingly to be performed in factories or other enterprises separate from the actual household. As production moved out of the home, middle-class women largely lost their essential, direct role in economic production and men performed their productive work increasingly in the absence of women. In the middling classes, separation of labor according to sex was echoed by a separation of whole realms of experience, with women held responsible for that arena now considered private—the home and child rearing—and men held responsible for more public pursuits such as politics and earning a living. By the late twentieth century, it became clear that a variety of historical developments had brought a re-merging of these "separate spheres" as women entered the work force in climbing numbers. Likewise, a smaller but significant view has it that men should be responsible for more of the domestic tasks, including child rearing. So a move from cooperation in production to a separation of spheres and then to a re-merging of spheres is another tendency that marks the history of the family.

Another long-term change entailed a growing sense that family members were less part of an ordered hierarchy than equals. In *At Odds: Women and the Family in America from the Revolution to the Present* (1980), the historian Carl N. Degler showed how the idea of parental involvement in the arrangement of marriages waned by the nineteenth century. By the twentieth century, increasingly permissive and experimental child-rearing practices further displayed acquiescence to the erosion of parental authority. From the eighteenth to the twentieth century, movements for women's equality accompanied the fundamental change in women's economic role, further questioning the inherited order.

While defining itself increasingly as a nuclear unit and becoming more pared down both in size and in its range of functions, the family has generally become more private. By turning inward to focus primarily on the emotional well-being of its own members and the related job of rearing its own children, the family gradually tended to extricate itself in some arenas from the larger community and think of itself as defined in opposition to the rest of society instead of deeply embedded in or intertwined with it. As the public world of the marketplace, the political arena, and new forms of production such as the factory seemed to foster conditions that were less than ideal for the human spirit, many Americans, particularly of the middle classes, reconceived of the family as a private refuge set apart from the public tumult.

Ironically, at the same time that the family tried to set itself apart from the outside world, new sources of intrusion occurred in the form of what the scholars Jacques Donzelot and Christopher Lasch respectively called the "tutelary apparatus" and "the helping professions." Professional experts of all kinds eventually insinuated their way into family affairs, as schools, reform organizations, social work associations, the courts, government, and other institutions stepped in to fulfill any functions that did not seem adequately performed by families. The process of privatization itself, diminishing as it did the connections between the family and the community, lent itself to this kind of dependency. Thus, the privacy sought by families in response to the ways in which industrial realities degraded their members' lives ended up being subtly, but thoroughly, compromised. In the twentieth century, this involvement in the family—often invited by family members themselves—was increasingly explained or legitimated by the coalescence of a therapeutic mentality according to which the family's very raison d'être came to be seen as not only emotional succor but also self-fulfillment and happiness. Because so many of the traditional functions of the family that might have provided a more solid basis for such an effusion of good feelings were diminishing, and because the family had lost its ability to solve its own problems, this mentality made substantial inroads, furthering the family's dependence on outsiders.

Finally, in the late twentieth century, according to a number of indicators, such as the steep rise in the rates of divorce and the increased number of children born to single mothers, the classic family itself seemed to be on the wane. Beginning beforehand, but heightening in the 1960s, a noticeable set of changes occurred that altered family arrangements drastically, setting off a wave of controversy and debate about the past, present, and future of the family. Crucial developments in previous periods help set the stage for the state of the family as it exists in the early twenty-first century.

THE PURITAN FAMILY

The historians John Demos and Edmund Morgan described the family in colonial times as the cornerstone of society. According to firmly held religious beliefs, Puritans thought that the purpose of social life was to create a truly good community, a kind of ethical paradise on earth that would glorify God. The entire social, spiritual, and political world ultimately rested on the premise that in order to have a harmonious society one needed harmonious families. Such families were vital if the community were to serve as a shining example of virtue to the world. Harsh penalties for adultery and disobedience to parents were in place, not so much as real resorts, but as guides to behavior. Marriage was considered such a powerful good that sexual compatibility and satisfaction were deemed crucial. At a time when divorce was very rare, physical neglect of or willful separation from one's spouse was considered grounds for divorce, whether on the part of the husband or the wife. Despite Puritans' belief in a hierarchical social world, with women subordinate to men, it appears that the spousal relationship was one of reciprocal obligation, shared decision making, and mutual respect.

Puritans clearly held an ideal of family life as so closely related to the life of the community that the family was considered "a little commonwealth." The boundary between the family and the rest of society was clearly much more permeable than it became later, in part because of the ideological connection between the family and the community and in part because of the family's numerous functions, many of which constituted vital services to the community. Demos states that the family served as everything from the center of economic production and exchange to school, vocational institute, church, house of correction, welfare institution, hospital, orphanage, asylum, old folks' home, hospital, and poor house.

THE CULT OF DOMESTICITY

Democratic revolutions in England, France, and the United States, together with the Enlightenment and other major events, helped raise the whole question of social relations. Figures like John Stuart Mill and Mary Wollstonecraft in particular brought up the "woman question," raising fundamental questions about women's place in the home and beyond. This early feminist movement helped spur a reconsideration of the family that has lasted into the twenty-first century.

In the early nineteenth century, a full-blown "cult of domesticity" emerged as a possible answer to the question of women's position in the family and society. According to this set of ideas, the historian Barbara Welter writes, women were naturally endowed to reign in the domestic sphere, as "true womanhood" rested on the virtues of "purity, piety, submissiveness, and domesticity" (in Gordon, pp. 372–392). Men, conversely, moved in the public world of business and politics. To many scholars who drew on Welter, the bourgeois family of the Victorian era merely replicated long-term Western tendencies of patriarchal domination. Others implied that the cult of domesticity actually mitigated patriarchal authority.

Catharine Beecher, one of the greatest champions of women's domestic role, did not so much help to confine women in the kind of narrowly delimited sphere against which later feminists, like Charlotte Perkins Gilman, chafed. As illustrated in the historian Kathryn Kish Sklar's rich 1973 biography, Beecher's promotion of female domesticity actually expanded that realm to such a degree that some women managed to employ it as a way to legitimate their participation in realms well outside of the home. Ethical sensitivity was deemed a feminine trait cultivated in the serenity of home life, as uncorrupted as it was by the crassness of the public world, whose economic and political pursuits increasingly threatened to corrupt its male inhabitants. In their position as emissaries of domestic bliss or else as guardians of morality, women went on to gain considerable social influence.

While some observers argue that any division of labor as drastic as that represented by this "doctrine of separate spheres" signals continued female subordination, the elevation of feminine domesticity at the time was, in some measure, a protest against the rise of American aristocratic pretensions in the eighteenth century (see Lasch, *Women and the Common Life*, pp. 67–89). A cornerstone of such elite aspiration was the role of the aristocratic lady, whose ostentatious leisure and pursuit of fashion rendered her a badge of status to the family. The economist and social scientist Thorstein Veblen later wrote of this role as the ultimate embodiment of "conspicuous consumption," one of the most potent symbols of the distortions of social relations and identity by capitalism. Christopher Lasch showed that the cult of domesticity took root among feminists and antifeminists alike out of the desire to restore to middle-class women a useful position. It was not, in fact, always directly at odds with the more self-consciously egalitarian position. Actually, major female activists of the nineteenth century went on to call on women, citing their special moral temper forged in the domestic sphere, to advance justice and equality. For instance, Catharine's sister, Harriet Beecher Stowe, asked women to redeem the nation by calling for the abolition of slavery. In her famous 1852 novel, *Uncle Tom's Cabin,* women's well-honed moral sense tends to give them superior insight into the immoral practices of slavery.

THE RISE OF PROFESSIONAL EXPERTISE

The rise of new institutions of professional expertise, combined with the growth of the apparatus of government, severely compromised any egalitarian implications of the cult of domesticity, as well as of women's more direct agitation for equal rights, according to Lasch. In fact, a whole army of self-proclaimed experts on family life capitalized on women's search for power in the primary realm open to them—the family. Women turned to such outsiders to buttress their own growing voice within the family but ended up losing that voice to experts whose position was fortified by the rise of professional education and accreditation.

The privatization of the family had created the context for the intrusive "tutelary" institutions. Privatization was rooted in the removal of economic production from the family. The community as comprised of an interwoven fabric of families had become a more impersonal public world from which participants needed constant nightly escape and rejuvenation in the privacy of their own homes. This turning inward constituted a revolt of sorts against the increasingly competitive and materialistic realities of economic life, particularly the unabashed individuality that characterized market capitalism and early industrialism as well as the deskilling and degradation of work itself by large-scale industrial practices. Families walled themselves off from others, whom they generalized into predators and direct competitors, and the ideal household became defined in contrast to this outside world. Within the home, the virtues of order, kindness, and nurture replaced the selfish free-for-all of public life and repaired the damaged psyches of the men whose job it was to stand up to such brutal conditions. Responsibilities for soothing ministrations

fell to a good wife. Childhood came to be set aside as a distinct phase of life, which needed to be protected, whereas in Puritan times, children beyond the age of six had been seen basically as "little adults."

In *Haven in a Heartless World: The Family Besieged* (1977), Lasch argues that the "helping professions" seized on this model of the family as a special place of refuge to purvey the idea that their own ministrations were needed by women, the importance of whose role they rendered as colossal. In turn, many women were open to outside opinion for several reasons: the privatization of the family had increasingly cut them off from larger networks among kin and community members which had customarily imparted accumulated wisdom; experts seemed to be natural allies in women's quest for decision-making power vis-à-vis men, whose own power was reinforced by their real public power; women's lot was an increasingly lonely one and self-appointed advisors often posed as sympathetic listeners and a "friend" to the mother and wife. In addition, the new reduction in the functions of the family placed pressure on wives and mothers not only to feed, clothe, clean, and teach but also to foster the emotional well-being—and by the twentieth century, emotional fulfillment—of the other family members.

The expanding role of experts, many allied with the state, created a situation of dependency that was buttressed by the emergence of a therapeutic way of thinking. This ideology focused on individual self-fulfillment as the primary end of family life. Philip Rieff's *Triumph of the Therapeutic* (1966) asserts that the rise of this new therapeutic mentality was such a thoroughgoing change that it replaced an earlier way of thinking about human activity, one based on religion. It is difficult to underestimate the importance that emotional fulfillment took on over the course of the twentieth century.

CONSUMERISM

Professional experts were tied to the market in the sense that wholly new careers and needs were manufactured and services purchased and delivered, the existence of which had not been deemed necessary in the nineteenth century. But the marketplace intervened in family affairs in a much more obvious way with the rise of modern advertising in the 1920s. In *Captains of Consciousness* (1976), Stuart Ewen shows that advertisers capitalized on the push for women's equality in the early twentieth century as they recognized the incredible possibilities for lucrative sales among women. One of the obstacles facing modern mass production was resistance to mass marketing, since many Americans, both new and old, believed in savings and sacrifice. Individuals did not eagerly embrace the notion of parting with a sizeable portion of their earnings for items that they did not need. Industry rightly (it turned out) identified women as a potential market and launched a campaign not only to sell a variety of goods to women but also to sell the *idea* of consumption as a part of women's role in the family. Advertisements from the 1920s played on both inflated notions of domestic responsibility and women's agitation for social equality to make the case that consuming was an avenue both to relieving guilt and acquiring status. Freedom was redefined as the choice of consumer items and social power was recast as the ability to command attention through fashion.

This bargain proved fatal for the family. It did help erode men's power in relation to their wives and children, but now corporations stepped in to fill the void. The freedom gained by women, and eventually children, was merely the freedom to choose which goods and services to purchase. Self-determination actually declined as families lost their independence to the intrusions of the market, and this ultimately affected both men and women, exacting costs in terms of growing dependency, recriminations, and unresolved tensions in the family. Such tensions become painfully apparent, for instance, in extensive interviews conducted among people who lived through the Great Depression of the 1930s. Conducted by the oral historian Studs Terkel and published in his book *Hard Times,* these interviews suggest that, while some families drew together in hard times, it was common for both wives and children to turn angrily on husbands for not fulfilling their role as providers. Ewen shows how the corollary to the expansion of women's role as consumer was the paring down of male responsibility into nothing but wage earner. The consequences in terms of declining respect for (and self-respect among) men based on anything but money-making capacity seems borne out by the inability of many men to face their families once their source of income was lost. A marked rise in the number of men who deserted their families was the result.

The two world wars exacerbated consumerism, both by raising real wages and creating jobs and expanding manufacturing, and by contributing to a kind of escapist and cynical mentality chronicled in some of the fiction of the 1920s and afterward. F. Scott Fitzgerald's *The Great Gatsby* (1925) and Joseph Heller's *Something Happened* (1974) evoke a degree of self-absorption completely at odds with family and community feeling. After the deprivations of the Great Depression and World War II, the general prosperity of the 1950s and 1960s, coupled with a sudden increase in the birth rate, spurred further consumption. Governmental assistance, through the GI Bill and the construction of highways, underwrote the erection of whole suburban communities practically overnight.

THE DECLINE OF THE FAMILY

Despite simplified images of the family in popular culture at the time, and despite stereotypical images of the 1950s family ever since, it became clear that something was desperately wrong with the conditions that prevailed for families. Rising concerns about the angst of adolescent males, nostalgia for experiences resulting in the formation of masculine character, and preoccupation with transgressions such as "wife-swapping" and illicit sex in general, signified indirection. Books like Paul Goodman's *Growing Up Absurd* (1960) and Betty Friedan's *The Feminine Mystique* (1963) describe widespread dissatisfaction with modern life among both men and women of the era, particularly as a result of suburban isolation, lack of meaningful work, and loss of purpose. Friedan's book, for instance, struck such a chord among American women that it helped fuel the women's liberation movement and helped justify, if not hasten, the entry of increasing numbers of women into the work force. While Friedan emphasized women's need for meaningful activity and engagement in a world beyond the confines of the household, by that time quite narrowly delimited, other critics faulted the family itself. The 1960s witnessed a number of attacks on the family as exploitative of women and children, narrow-minded and authoritarian, gauche and capitalistic. Some critics, such as the radical feminist Kate Millett, went so far as to say that heterosexual sexuality itself was inherently degrading to women.

Perhaps the greatest pressure on stable family life was the growing stress on individual self-fulfillment, which became an increasingly noted influence on the family from the 1960s to the end of the twentieth century. Modes of therapy dedicated to the quest for individual fulfillment replaced character formation as the main personal enterprise of the self. The movement for sexual liberation, the human potential movement, the revolt of youth, the liberation of women, and the men's movement all had a strong emphasis on the freeing of the self from constraints on the pursuit of desire, individual "needs," and self-development. Barbara Ehrenreich's *The Hearts of Men* (1983) shows how this radical individualism translated, in the family context, to a growing male unwillingness to make long-term commitments and a female incapacity to keep husbands and fathers from succumbing to wanderlust. Beginning in the 1950s, a number of forces particularly targeted the staid middle-class formula of corporate job and marriage as the culprit for a variety of male woes, from boredom to heart attacks. New industries capitalized on men as a new consumer market, selling the clothing, magazines, and other accoutrements of the "playboy" image, including a lifestyle that celebrated being single. Popular psychology in the 1970s helped rationalize this behavior further, among women as well as men, with its insistence that it was unhealthy for an individual not to follow one's "growth curve." "Divorce, then, no longer signaled a 'failed marriage' but an accomplished growth opportunity, a 'passage' successfully navigated along the broad course of personal growth," Ehrenreich wrote (p. 97).

From the 1960s to the 1990s statistics reinforced the recognition that a major shift had occurred. As Steven Mintz and Susan Kellogg spell out in their survey of American family life, *Domestic Revolutions* (1988), everything from the divorce rate to the number of households consisting of just one member, the number of stepfamilies, the number of children born to single women, and incidents of teenage pregnancy all rose precipitously, providing clear evidence for those who noted a decline of the family in American life.

Such conditions, however, did not have a universally shocking effect. In fact, similar signs of family distress had invited attention in earlier periods, but usually in the context of groups not considered part of mainstream America. Desertions among the white immigrant poor were a source of concern in the Progressive Era, and the situation of the black family was similarly noted by the United States senator and sociologist Daniel Patrick Moynihan in his famous 1965 report on the black family, "The American Negro: The Case for National Action." The document cites high rates of illegitimacy, teen pregnancy, and separation or divorce. Moynihan's characterization of these indicators as evidence of the pathological state of the black family drew much ire, as it seemed to belong to a long American tradition of zeroing in on black deficiency and fostering stereotypical images of blacks as abnormally plagued by problems. In the context of the growing militancy of the civil rights movement, with its emphasis on black pride, this seemed to many like an unneeded assault. A whole school of thought claimed that the statistics reportedly showing a crisis in the black family merely indicated the "cultural differences" between black and white families. Black women more commonly served as the backbone of the family, with an extended network (mainly of other women) comprising the remainder of the family's support. In the late 1970s the black intellectual William Julius Wilson publicly questioned this portrait and insisted that the black family was in deep trouble. Wilson was also met with criticism, but his work clearly resonated for many others who realized that the problems formerly considered to pertain to the black population were clearly present in all sectors of the population.

The evidence of a more generalized trend toward family dissolution was a source of great controversy in the 1980s and 1990s. By every standard, the integrity, cohesion, strength, and independence of the classic American family was on the wane. In the 1980s the Republican Party seized on real anxieties present throughout the population when they brought into the political arena the notion of "family values." The motives underlying such a platform seemed to others concerned to be largely disingenuous, given that many politicians who pushed for the so-called traditional family embraced many of the very forces that undermined the family.

In opposition, some observers responded that any defense of the classic family, as composed of husband and wife and their children, involved a nostalgic reluctance to accept changes that could actually be construed as signs of progress. Advocates like Judith Stacey celebrated the idea of a flexible concept of the "postmodern family" that would take into account the much greater choice involved in the formation of households in the late twentieth century. Many pushed for a redefinition of "the family" to include single-parent households, same-sex partnerships, combinations of adults serving as parental or relative surrogates, extended kin networks, and other increasingly common replacements for incomplete nuclear families. These arrangements, which in many cases resulted from strained and troubled circumstances as compensation in the face of necessity, drew the praise of those who saw them as positive indicators of increased personal freedom.

In addition to these changes, it became increasingly common within two-parent families to find both parents working outside the home. This meant that day care—traditionally seen as a last-ditch resort of poor or working-class parents—became a fact of life for many middle-class families. Those who could afford to, usually those in the upper echelons of American society, solved this problem—which is now referred to as the "work-family balance"—by hiring full- or part-time nannies or hosting an au pair from overseas. Others sent their children, some no older than two years old, to "schools," perhaps bridling at the term "day care centers" which, critics argued, often merely warehoused children. The issue of balancing work and family, particularly if both parents worked outside the home, remained a major source of strain on contemporary families. Some families turned to "flextime" (altering the starting or ending times of the usual shift, for instance) as offered in some workplaces, family leave (the government allowance of several weeks away from a job for childbirth or child care), or nonsynchronous work schedules. Special commitment on the part of some parents to raising their own children, combined with special resources or the ability to cut back financially, sometimes resulted in creative alternatives usually involving sharing the burden of sacrifice. An underlying sense of the ultimate fragility of families might help explain the more common resort to day care, even among those who could afford a reduction in income.

Late-twentieth-century scholarship suggests that even where such malleable arrangements are possible, Americans often fail to implement them, suggesting the extent to which the factors cited have transformed conceptions of family life. In *The Overworked American* (1991), Juliet Schor asserts that a major reason for Americans' widely cited lack of free time is their inflated desire for material consumption which causes, for instance, both spouses to work even when it is not really necessary. The sociologist Arlie Hochschild reinforces this portrait in *The Time Bind* (1997), stating that, even where flexible time schedules exist, workers often fail to take advantage of them, actually preferring work life to home life. The atmosphere at work, these workers find, is one of orderliness, calm, and civilized collegiality versus the chaos that often reigns at home.

Turning the cult of domesticity on its head, some Americans at the start of the twenty-first century apparently see work as a sanctuary from the demands of home life. Perhaps this should not come as a surprise, since it is a logical consequence of the drastic changes endured by the family in recent and not-so-recent years. New pressures on the limited number of relationships in the immediate family and new dependence on outside experts to cope with everyday life have helped obscure the benefits of a loving family and erode basic habits such as cooperation, loving parental discipline, complementary work, trust, and sacrifice—habits that not only order and stabilize family life but also potentially make it a source of infinite pleasure.

Part of the twentieth-century revolt against tradition, patriarchal hierarchy, and inhibition took aim at the family as the locus of repression and inequality. The decision to remain single or to divorce has been increasingly championed by many since the 1950s as an act of personal liberation. But by the end of the twentieth century, stirrings of discontentment with this promise of liberation and consternation about its unintended consequences arose and not only among those who touted "family values" as a political slogan. In *The Unexpected Legacy of Divorce* (2000), the liberal family counselor and author Judith Wallerstein detailed the life stories of adults whom she had interviewed periodically since they were children in families undergoing divorce. What she found was that in divorcing families—undergoing mild difficulties that were no worse than those prevalent in many families that chose to stay together, the children's experiences were nothing short of traumatic.

The twenty-first-century American family seems to be at a crossroads. Having largely rejected a strictly hierarchical family organization resting on inequality between men and women or a segmented organization based on separate male and female preserves, Americans face vital questions. How will the family adapt to the unprecedented numbers of women in the work force? Who will care for young children and other dependent family members? How will the work both outside and inside of the home be shared? Which traditions are appropriate and adaptable to contemporary American desires and expectations? The inverse of this last question—which contemporary American desires and expectations are appropriate and adaptable to cherished traditions, such as family life itself—strikes some as the most important of all. How we answer this question, of course, will have everything to do with the future of the family.

See also **The Material Shape of Early American Life; Conflicting Ideals of Colonial Womanhood; Women in the Public Sphere, 1838–1877; Domesticity and Sentimentalism; Gender, Social Class, Race, and Material Life; Manhood** *(volume 1);* **Women and Family in the Suburban Age; Second-Wave Feminism; Women; Working Class** *(volume 2);* **Consumerism; Welfare** *(in this volume).*

BIBLIOGRAPHY

Ariès, Philippe. *Centuries of Childhood: A Social History of Family Life.* Translated by Robert Baldick. New York, 1962.

Beecher, Catharine E., and Harriet Beecher Stowe. *The American Woman's Home, or Principles of Domestic Science; Being a Guide to the Formation and Maintenance of Economical, Healthful, Beautiful, and Christian Homes.* New York, 1869.

Degler, Carl N. *At Odds: Women and the Family in America from the Revolution to the Present.* New York, 1980.

Demos, John. *A Little Commonwealth: Family Life in Plymouth Colony.* London, 1970.

——. *Past, Present, and Personal: The Family and the Life Course in American History.* New York, 1986.

Donzelot, Jacques. *The Policing of Families.* Translated by Robert Hurley. New York, 1979.

Ehrenreich, Barbara. *The Hearts of Men: American Dreams and the Flight from Commitment.* New York, 1983.

Ewen, Stuart. *Captains of Consciousness: Advertising and the Social Roots of Consumer Culture.* New York, 1976.

Friedan, Betty. *The Feminine Mystique.* New York, 1963.

Gordon, Michael, ed. *The American Family in Social-Historical Perspective.* 3d ed. New York, 1983.

Hareven, Tamara K. *Family Time and Industrial Time: The Relationship between the Family and Work in a New England Industrial Community.* New York, 1982.

——. "The History of the Family and the Complexity of Social Change." *American Historical Review* (February 1991): 95–124.

Hochschild, Arlie Russell. *The Time Bind: When Work Becomes Home and Home Becomes Work.* New York, 1997.

Lasch, Christopher. *Haven in a Heartless World: The Family Besieged.* New York, 1977.

——. *Women and the Common Life: Love, Marriage, and Feminism.* Edited by Elisabeth Lasch-Quinn. New York, 1997.

Mintz, Steven, and Susan Kellogg. *Domestic Revolutions: A Social History of American Family Life.* New York, 1988.

Rainwater, Lee, and William L. Yancey. *The Moynihan Report and the Politics of Controversy.* Cambridge, Mass., 1966. Includes Daniel Patrick Moynihan's original report, "The American Negro: The Case for National Action."

Schor, Juliet. *The Overworked American: The Unexpected Decline of Leisure.* New York, 1991.

Sennett, Richard. *Families against the City: Middle-Class Homes of Industrial Chicago, 1872–1890.* Cambridge, Mass., 1970.

Sklar, Kathryn Kish. *Catharine Beecher: A Study in American Domesticity.* New York, 1973.

Smith, Daniel Scott. "Recent Change and the Periodization of American Family History." *Journal of Family History* 20, no. 4 (1995): 329–346.

Stacey, Judith. *Brave New Families: Stories of Domestic Upheaval in Late Twentieth Century America.* New York, 1990.

Stack, Carol B. *All Our Kin: Strategies for Survival in a Black Community.* New York, 1975.

Stone, Lawrence. *The Family, Sex, and Marriage in England, 1500–1800.* New York, 1979.

Terkel, Studs. *Hard Times: An Oral History of the Great Depression.* New York, 1970.

Verenne, Herve. "Love and Liberty: The Contemporary American Family." In *A History of the Family,* vol. 2, *The Impact of Modernity.* Cambridge, Mass., 1996.

Wallerstein, Judith S., Julia M. Lewis, and Sandra Blakeslee. *The Unexpected Legacy of Divorce: A 25 Year Landmark Study.* New York, 2000.

Wilson, William Julius. *The Declining Significance of Race: Blacks and Changing American Institutions.* Chicago, 1978.

SEXUALITY

Susan E. Myers-Shirk

The history of sexuality is a relatively new area of study for historians, in part because earlier scholars assumed that factors such as genes or hormones determined sexual behavior and that, as a result, sex and sexuality really needed to be studied by biologists or medical doctors rather than historians. In the years after World War II, however, some scholars became convinced that the social and historical context, as much as biological factors, determined sexual behavior and experience. To understand the changing nature of sexuality, historians began to examine all of the behavior, symbols, and rituals associated with reproduction, eroticism, and sensuality and explored all kinds of topics including abortion, prostitution, medical discourse, and media representations of sexuality. Two conclusions emerged from that research. First, historians discovered that in every historical era, the constructed meaning of sexuality had important implications for social relations. Second, they observed that the predominant meaning of sexuality in the United States changed markedly from the colonial era to the twentieth century. Historians have disagreed about the precise nature of the change, but one argument suggests that Americans moved from a reproductive ideal to a pleasure ideal. That is, they moved from seeing sex primarily as a means for reproduction to seeing sex primarily as an avenue to pleasure. Historians also noted that as Americans moved toward a pleasure ideal, they began to see their sexuality (sexual behavior, desires, and experience) as a source of identity. This article examines the meaning of a social constructionist view of sexuality, explains how socially constructed sexual ideals have affected social relations, traces the changes in predominant sexual ideals from the colonial era to the present, and explores the reasons for change.

THE SOCIAL CONSTRUCTION OF SEXUALITY

One extended example can illustrate what it means to take a social constructionist view of sexuality.

Expectations with regard to white, middle-class women's sexual behavior changed dramatically from the late nineteenth to the early twentieth centuries. Much of the advice literature directed at middle-class Americans assumed a degree of female passionlessness. For example, when Eliza Duffey in her book *What Women Should Know* (1873) instructed her readers regarding women's passion, she reminded them that "'the passions of men are much stronger and more easily inflamed' than those of women" (D'Emilio and Freedmen, p. 70) This idea that women possessed less sexual drive than men was so powerful that some people could not even imagine same-sex relations between two women because they assumed that sex required an aggressor and that, in a relationship between two women, neither could fill that role. In the early twentieth century, new expectations regarding women and sexuality accompanied the emergence of a new ideal of womanhood. Much of the literature of this period, whether popular, medical, or academic, credited women with sexual desires and encouraged them to take a much more active and equal role in sexual relations. For instance, Theodore Van de Velde, in his book *Ideal Marriage* (1930), recommended a number of techniques including the "equestrian attitude" in which the woman sat astride the man. Of course, most of the literature also still sought to contain that sexuality within the boundaries of marriage with talk of the joys of companionate marriage and husbands' obligations to meet the sexual needs of their wives.

Most historians agree it was not women's biological needs that changed from one century to the next, but the social and cultural context in which their sexuality was interpreted. The idea that women were passionless emerged in the context of mid- to late-nineteenth-century developing capitalism, where middle-class families were concerned about controlling the size of their families and where middle-class women were establishing their dominance over domestic affairs as well as the emotional lives of their families. In contrast, the idea that women could and should enjoy sexual experience emerged as women were claiming equal rights in the social, political, and economic spheres.

SEXUALITY AND POWER

This social constructionist approach to the study of sexuality derived particularly from cultural anthropology, feminist scholarship, the work of an increasingly visible gay and lesbian community, and the writing of the French philosopher and historian Michel Foucault. Each of these argued that the meaning of sexuality was not simply constructed, but it was constructed with a purpose. The construction of sexuality, they contended, served to reinforce social and cultural hierarchy. In particular, Foucault's three-volume series on the history of sexuality helped to emphasize the idea that the construction of hierarchy is complex and not simply a matter of one group imposing its will on another.

Women's experience in the nineteenth century provides an excellent example of these complexities. Much of the nineteenth-century advice literature linked passionlessness with a cluster of related qualities that supposedly characterized women. Advice literature writers contrasted female sexual passiveness with male sexual aggressiveness and deemed women morally superior by virtue of that passiveness as well as their responsibility for bearing children and overseeing the virtue of both husband and children in the domestic sphere. Middle-class women in the middle and late nineteenth century found their access to public space and activities constrained by the assumption that their sexuality (that is, their ability to bear children) made the domestic sphere their "natural" sphere of influence and mothering their only skill. Many of these middle-class women, however, used the very same understanding of female sexuality to expand their access to public space.

The New York Female Moral Reform Society used its weekly publication the *Advocate of Moral Reform* to highlight the sexual depravity of men and to call women to take concerted action. They urged women not only to condemn licentious male behavior, but also to enter the city's almshouses, hospitals, and jails to lead prayer meetings and distribute tracts. Female moral reformers even argued that women should take a special responsibility for teaching their sons complete obedience to their mothers' wills in order to avoid moral ruin. These middle-class women believed that their moral superiority especially suited them for efforts at moral reform and they led the way in a whole host of activities ranging from antislavery to antiprostitution crusades.

Women's experience illustrates the extent to which sexuality served as a means for individuals to locate themselves and others in a social and cultural hierarchy and functioned both to limit and expand the control those individuals exercised over their own lives. While gender hierarchy is one of the most obvious examples of sexuality used as a tool of power, it is not the only one. For instance, in the late nineteenth and early twentieth centuries, Americans began to distinguish between same-sex and different-sex relations (homosexuality and heterosexuality) in a discussion that reinforced a sexual hierarchy and ultimately privileged heterosexuality.

As with the construction of gender hierarchies, the power dynamics were complex. In the late-nineteenth-century United States, gender and sexual hierarchies were intimately linked. Most of the early literature described what would eventually become known as homosexuality in terms of gender "inversion," in which the invert adopted the gender characteristics of the opposite sex as well as its object of desire. Hence, the male invert assumed feminine characteristics and desired men. Much of the medical and scientific discourse portrayed homosexuals as deviant, diseased, pathological, or abnormal because they challenged gender ideals. The German psychiatrist Richard von Krafft-Ebing in *Psychopathia Sexualis* (1886) viewed homosexuality as a modern disease of the nervous system that spawned a downward spiral of degeneracy and immorality. Some doctors, such as Havelock Ellis, who co-authored the first edition of his book *Sexual Inversion* (1897) with the British homosexual John Addington Symonds, resisted the idea that homosexuality was a vice, arguing instead that homosexuality resulted from a "congenital predisposition" and deserved tolerance and sympathy. His defense of homosexuality, however, did not elicit the support Ellis desired.

If much of the medical discourse was intended to explain, classify, and control the behavior of sexual inverts, it ended up serving other purposes. Gays and lesbians participated in shaping medical discourse and made use of it for their own ends. For one thing, homosexuals played a key role in defining homosexuality. Karl Heinrich Ulrichs offered one of the first scientific theories of homosexuality; Karoly Maria Benkert coined the word "homosexuality"; and Magnus Hirschfeld conceptualized homosexuality as a "benign variation" in sexual behavior. Each of these men was responding to the political situation in Europe and attempting to provide homosexuals with a defense against increasingly restrictive laws affecting homosexuals. Their contributions had important implications for the American discussion. Ultimately, some homosexuals used medical discourse to claim a distinctive identity.

Americans' understanding of sexuality shaped not only their gender and sexual hierarchies but also their racial and class hierarchies. The most obvious example of the way in which sexuality was used to reinforce hierarchies of race is the construction of black male sexuality in the post–Civil War era. White southerners, in particular, promoted the image of dangerous, black male sexuality, insisting that southern white women were in constant danger from the voracious black male sexual appetite. Black men were regularly accused of raping white women and ended up dead at the hands of white lynch mobs without the benefit of a trial. Frequently, the black men who were accused of rape had really done something else to challenge the social order of the Jim Crow South, but sexuality was the point at which the hierarchy was reinforced.

In the face of heavy penalties, African Americans challenged lynching at the same point. Under the leadership of the reformers Ida B. Wells and Mary Church Terrell, African Americans attempted to defy and reconstruct sexual stereotypes. Wells created an uproar and fueled an ultimately successful anti-lynching movement by arguing that white women seduced black men into consensual sex and that white male lust for black women lay at the root of lynching. She even suggested that the inability of white men to control their sexual aggressiveness made their manliness suspect.

Sexuality played a similar role in supporting class and ethnic hierarchies. In the late nineteenth century, middle-class reformers perceived working-class women's sexuality as dangerous and threatening and attempted to inculcate middle-class values of self-control and continence. White, middle-class attempts to link class and ethnic hierarchies become apparent in the extent to which middle-class reformers attributed prostitution to ethnic minorities and African Americans, even though, by the turn of the twentieth century, the majority of prostitutes were native born and white. Working-class women generally resisted middle-class mores and viewed their sexuality as an asset necessary to their survival. In the dance halls and saloons, which were once entirely the province of prostitutes, working-class girls spent their hard-earned wages on leisure pur-

suits that were closed to middle-class women. In general, however, most young women did not earn enough to support themselves and enjoy all that the growing commercial culture offered. In this context a system of "treating" emerged, in which young women offered young men companionship and sexual favors in return for dinner, gifts, or a visit to an amusement park. The very behavior that middle-class reformers censured, working-class girls used to extend their freedom and range of choices.

A similar dynamic occurred in the West and Southwest where white, middle-class Americans disapproved of and attempted to control much of what they discovered there. Thus, in the Southwest they censured Mexicans who did not adopt their ideals of female passionlessness. Among the Chinese in California, they condemned polygamy and attempted to convert them to monogamy. And among Native Americans, they discouraged premarital sexual relations as well as too much variety in marital sexual relations—insisting, in fact, that Native Americans adopt the so-called missionary position.

REPRODUCTION, IDENTITY, AND PLEASURE

These examples suggest the meaning of sexuality shaped social relations in such a way that gender, race, class, and sexual preference determined both Americans' place in the social hierarchy and their experience of sexuality. Despite their differences, however, Americans did share a common set of beliefs about sexuality, and it is possible to trace the changing nature of those beliefs from the colonial era to the twenty-first century. In general, colonial Americans placed a high premium on their ability to produce offspring, while twentieth-century Americans insisted on the right to limit offspring and highlighted pleasure as the purpose of sex. These two cultural ideals existed in a complex relationship. For instance, while twentieth-century Americans pursued an ideal of sexual pleasure, they still viewed sex as a means for reproduction. Likewise, while colonial Americans saw reproduction as their central social duty, they still derived pleasure from their sexuality. Understanding the relationship between reproduction and pleasure is complicated further by the emergence of yet another cultural ideal. In the mid- to late nineteenth century, at about the same time that Americans began to value pleasure more than reproduction, they also began to see sexuality as a means to understanding and naming themselves, as a marker of identity. Each of these ideals resulted in very different definitions of transgression and very different strategies for dealing with transgressors.

Colonial America and the Reproductive Ideal

In colonial society the reproductive ideal meant that female sexuality was defined in terms of women's ability to bear children while male sexuality was defined in terms of men's ability to father children (their virility). In this society, which viewed marital relations as the highest expression of sexuality, impotence was grounds for ending a marriage. Sexual behavior that worked against these goals was viewed as immoral or illegal. Colonial court and church records reveal harsh penalties for adultery, fornication, and sodomy. Sodomy in the colonial era referred to all nonprocreative sexual acts. Punishments ranged from fines and whippings to banishment or execution. Historians do not know much about whether the average colonial American upheld these values, but they do know that state and church imposed heavier penalties on colonists who lacked power and influence in the society. Women were more likely than men to be prosecuted for adultery, fornication, and bastardy. Lower-class men were more likely to be charged with rape than were men of standing in the community. Black men could be castrated for miscegenation while white men pursued black women with impunity.

Industrial America, Gender, and Sexual Identity

Nineteenth-century, middle-class Americans continued to share colonial assumptions about the importance of marital fidelity and procreation, but they also reconfigured the meaning of marital relations in a way that highlighted the importance of sexual pleasure. The correspondence and diaries of nineteenth-century Americans stressed the importance of sex as a means to emotional intimacy and as the physical expression of romantic love and the spiritual bond between husband and wife. The novelist Nathaniel Hawthorne wrote to his fiancée, Sophia Peabody, in highly romantic terms—"Dove come to my bosom"—even as he imagined her there in bed with him. The two postponed physical expression of their love until after marriage and, even then, continued to view sex in highly spiritual terms as "'a spiritual joy' and 'a wondrous instrument . . . for the purposes of the heart'" (D'Emilio and Freedman, p. 76).

Simultaneously, much of the medical and advice literature of the period stressed the importance of sexual self-control or "continence." Talk about continence probably originated to some extent in concerns about the growth of a private or domestic sphere over which the community exercised little direct influence. In the colonial era, church and community had played an active role in policing sexual behavior with individuals willingly reporting their neighbors' indiscretions. By the mid-nineteenth century, however, few such restraints still operated. Medical and advice literature writers intended the ethic of self-control that they promoted for both men and women to be internalized and to serve as a limit on sexual behavior in a way the community had once served. But talk of "continence" also benefited Americans who were concerned about limiting the size of their families. The marital birth rate had declined markedly by the end of the nineteenth century. Evidence suggests that continence was one of several methods, including contraception and abortion, to which Americans resorted to limit or end pregnancies. Taken together the celebration of romantic love and the rising availability and use of contraception promoted an ideal of sexual pleasure and diminished the importance of reproduction.

Much of the public talk about sex, however, stressed yet another set of priorities. Specifically, much of the advice literature of the time stressed the connections between sexuality and gender identity, clearly linking sex organs to certain gender traits. For instance, some doctors suggested that the role of the ovum in the process of reproduction was essentially passive, and that, as a result, women were naturally more passive or "passionless" and more capable of sexual control. In the late nineteenth century, some medical doctors suggested that there was such an intimate connection between sexual organs and gender characteristics that the young woman who engaged in intellectual pursuits risked damaging her uterus and acquiring masculine characteristics. In fact, the Harvard physician E. H. Clarke warned that too much time devoted to studying diminished women's reproductive capacity.

By the end of the nineteenth century, concerns about sustaining gender identity ultimately fueled efforts to sustain sexual identity. White middle-class discourse at the end of the nineteenth century was marked by concerns that modern civilization had weakened and "feminized" white men. White middle-class men responded by redefining the ideal of male sexuality. The new sexual ideal, which was in turn linked to a new gender ideal, emphasized the distance between masculinity and femininity by highlighting the importance of sexual aggressiveness, downplaying the virtues of restraint, and celebrating physical prowess and labor. It also stressed the importance of sexual object choice. As a consequence, middle-class discourse targeted the "gender invert" or "fairy," who possessed male sexual organs but adopted the characteristics and mannerisms associated with women. Previously, men who engaged in sexual relations with fairies were not seen as gender inverts as long as they possessed the gender characteristics appropriate to their sexual organs. As concerns about masculinity escalated, however, same-sex relations became less acceptable, and the choice of the opposite sex became increasingly important as a marker of masculinity.

Nineteenth-century definitions of sexual transgression were controlled to a large extent by the middle class and their attempts to regulate sexual behavior reflected their concerns about gender and sexual ideals. Drawing on religious, medical, and legal discourse, they sought to circumscribe, in particular, the behavior of racial and ethnic minorities and the working class. For instance, in the 1830s members of New York City's Female Moral Reform Society visited hospitals, jails, and brothels attempting to persuade the inmates to give up prostitution. In the 1870s and 1880s the social purity movement gained national attention as its members attempted to prevent prostitution by intervening in the lives of young women who appeared to be at risk. Social purity advocates also insisted upon a single standard of sexual purity for both men and women to prevent men from participating in sustaining prostitution. Social purity campaigners used the law to advance their agenda, calling, for instance, for Congress to raise the age-of-consent laws so that men who engaged in sexual relations with very young women could be held accountable. Some moral reformers also called for stricter obscenity laws, and their efforts culminated with the passage of the Comstock Law in 1873. Named for a Connecticut dry-goods salesman named Anthony Comstock who led the crusade to create stronger anti-obscenity laws, the law prohibited sending so-called obscene materials through the U.S. Postal Service. Finally, at the end of the nineteenth century the expanding social sciences played an increasingly important role in regulating sexuality and policing transgression. For instance, social workers in homes for unwed mothers attempted to reinforce middle-class sexual and gender ideals.

The Media and an Ethic of Sexual Pleasure

Questions of gender and sexual identity remained important to twentieth-century Americans' sexual experience, but pleasure figured ever more prominently. Growing access to birth control and an increasingly visible gay community reinforced the message that sex did not have to be connected to reproduction. The media promoted that message assiduously, helping to make images of sexuality generally and sexual pleasure specifically ever more visible.

Beginning in the 1920s information about contraception became more widely available to Americans. The activist Margaret Sanger led the way in campaigning against restrictions on disseminating information about birth control. Sanger focused in particular on the Comstock Law, which prohibited sending information about contraception through the mail. With the support of an organization she had founded, the American Birth Control League, Sanger wrote books, edited a journal, lectured widely, and lobbied Congress in an effort to change laws and attitudes. She succeeded. In 1936 the portion of the Comstock Law that regulated the distribution of contraceptive devices was overturned by a federal appeals court, allowing doctors to prescribe contraceptives. Evidence suggests that by the early 1950s, significant numbers of women who were looking for ways to limit pregnancy had adopted the use of the diaphragm, the method of contraception most often recommended by birth control activists. Oral contraceptives became available in 1960, precipitating an even greater contraceptive revolution in that decade. By the 1970s the birth control pill, diaphragms, and voluntary sterilization were available to most women regardless of race or class. Limiting the number of pregnancies had become not only acceptable, but expected. In fact, women of color and working-class women found themselves under pressure to submit to sterilization. In any case, the widespread acceptance and use of contraception suggested that the thoroughgoing connection between sex and reproduction that colonial Americans had taken for granted had all but vanished by the early 1970s.

The gay and lesbian community underlined the message of the contraceptive revolution by suggesting that sexuality was not, of necessity, linked to reproduction. But the community served another purpose by suggesting that it was possible to claim an identity that was predicated on one's erotic desires. Fueled by urban growth and world war, the gay and lesbian community became increasingly visible after World War II. Actually a visible gay community had begun to appear as early as the 1880s in some urban areas, particularly in the Red Light and Furnished Room districts (although the term "gay," did not come into common usage until the late 1930s and early 1940s). In fact, society's liminal spaces provided a place for homosexuals to find one another. Places such as transvestite clubs, waterfront areas, boardinghouses, and the YMCA permitted a way of life that small-town America would not tolerate. "Fairies," men who exhibited the gender characteristics usually associated with women, were the most visible, although not the only, members of these communities. In the 1920s, places such as New York City's Greenwich Village provided a space where homosexuals could congregate with relative impunity, but the social and cultural anxiety precipitated by the economic crisis of the 1930s led to a crackdown on the gay community.

World War II, however, provided the context for the resurgence of a visible gay community. Young men and women who left small town lives to fight in the war or go to the city to work in wartime industries discovered a life very different from the one they left behind. A more visible gay community, the Kinsey Report with its suggestion that there was more homosexual practice than Americans had imagined, and rampant cold war paranoia combined to create a very repressive atmosphere in the 1950s. Some Americans used federal, state, and local resources to police the activities of gays and lesbians, arguing that they represented a threat to democracy and freedom. Middle-class men and women risked losing their jobs or becoming the objects of violence if their sexual proclivities were revealed, forcing them to keep their lives a secret or to "stay in the closet." Some gays and lesbians, however, actively resisted the discrimination. Quietly organizing to challenge it, gay men formed the Mattachine Society and lesbians formed the Daughters of Bilitis. In the summer of 1969, the struggle for gay rights became much more visible when patrons at a Greenwich Village gay bar, the Stonewall Inn, resisted the nightly police raid and touched off rioting throughout the city. Stonewall provided the starting point for a highly visible gay liberation movement that received media attention and, for many gays and lesbians, made "coming out of the closet" a possibility.

The contraceptive revolution and the increased visibility of gays and lesbians underlined the declining power of the reproductive ideal. Concurrently, the mass media promoted an ethic of sexual pleasure and desire and made sexuality central to public discourse. Beginning in the 1920s advice literature gave specific advice to men about how to give their wives pleasure and promoted sexual pleasure for both partners as central to a successful marriage. Advertisers made use of sexual images to sell products ranging from Lysol to Listerine. Movies portrayed passion and desire frequently in stories that downplayed the importance of marriage and childbearing. True confession magazines, with their stories of illicit sexual relations, multiplied. In the 1950s Hugh Hefner began publication of his magazine *Playboy*, in which he intentionally challenged the ideal of marriage and presented women as objects of male sexual desire. In the wake of the 1960s sexual revolution, the "sex industry" expanded with pornography entering the mainstream with films such as *Deep Throat*. Television programs grew increasingly explicit. By the 1970s Americans no longer purchased marital advice manuals, they purchased, in significant numbers, sex manuals such as *Everything You Ever Wanted to Know about Sex, The Sensuous Man,* and *The Sensuous Woman.*

With the advent of a pleasure ideal, the question of transgression became increasingly complicated. Much of that which earlier Americans had considered immoral, illegal, or abnormal, twentieth-century Americans viewed as good and acceptable. In a society that celebrated the public expression of sexuality, the definition of obscenity had narrowed considerably and the boundaries of acceptable sexual behavior had expanded well beyond marriage and reproduction. The AIDS epidemic and more general fears about sexually transmitted diseases in the 1980s helped to draw the ethical lines for those who subscribed to the pleasure ideal. This was true not only for the gay and lesbian communities that felt the terrors of AIDS first, but for all Americans who were sexually active with multiple partners. Some conservative Americans used the epidemic to castigate the gay community, claiming the disease was divine retribution for homosexuality. But the disease also highlighted the responsibility gays and lesbians had to one another and they mobilized to care for those who had fallen to the illness. Transgression, then, was defined as failing to care for oneself or others, and its regulation proceeded primarily by what amounted to what nineteenth-century reformers would have called "moral suasion." Everyone from college students to the federal government launched campaigns to convince sexually active Americans to use protection and to be responsible to their partners.

MARKET, SCHOLARSHIP, AND EVERYDAY LIFE

A complex set of factors contributed to constructing the American definition and experience of sexuality.

In each era, however, three competing and integrally linked elements contributed to effecting the change—the market, medical and scholarly literature, and the everyday experience of individuals.

The market shaped sexuality in two ways. First, changes in the market directly affected what Americans believed about sexuality. Most obviously, the growth of industrial capitalism and the factory system in the nineteenth century allowed for the creation of separate spheres by reinforcing the distinction between home and work. Similarly, a growing market demand for slaves encouraged white slave owners to view their female slaves in terms of their ability to reproduce. In both world wars, the need for workers to meet wartime production demands opened the door for women's participation in industries previously closed to them based on the argument that their biological makeup left them ill suited for industrial work.

But the market also sold sex and sexuality, both figuratively, as in the case of movies and television or advertising where businesses used sexual images to sell products, and literally, as in the case of prostitution and the sex trades. Nineteenth-century prostitution centered in dance halls, massage parlors, and brothels and grew as the nation industrialized and urbanized. Titillating pictures and sensational literature such as *Maria Monk,* with its fictional and viciously anti-Catholic account of the licentious behavior of priests and nuns, were also available to the interested male client. The Civil War contributed to the expansion of prostitution by providing a readily available pool of customers as did westward expansion. For the most part, prostitution was a female enterprise with brothels under the control of the madame.

In the late nineteenth century, moral reform movements made some inroads into the business of prostitution. When doctors recommended regulating prostitution in the interest of public health, female moral reformers (among others) launched a vigorous campaign to eradicate prostitution. In particular, they focused on preventing young women from ever entering the business. Campaigns against prostitution during the Progressive Era attacked the problem at the local, state, and national level, but were only partially successful. While the 1920s saw the end of the brothels and Red Light districts, prostitution survived in the form of streetwalkers and call girls. Wartime almost guaranteed prostitutes' prosperity. In wartime Hawaii military officials ignored local and federal laws that outlawed prostitution and looked the other way while the madames made their fortunes. Ultimately, the market governed the success of prostitution.

Americans did not live entirely at the mercy of the market. Medical opinion and scholarly research also helped to shape the meaning of sexuality. From the late nineteenth century on, scholars produced a prodigious amount of literature on human sexuality. The Viennese psychoanalyst Sigmund Freud played a crucial a role in prompting much of that scholarship. A number of Freud's ideas enjoyed particularly long and successful careers in the United States. First, Americans embraced Freud's ideas about sexual pleasure and promptly misinterpreted them. Americans took Freud's ideas about sexual pleasure as grounds for sexual license. Freud's idea of the vaginal orgasm as the mark of mature female sexuality was equally popular. Finally, Freud's tendency to construct homosexuality as arrested development contributed to constructing homosexuality as abnormal and his ideas about the "proper" choice of sexual object contributed to constructing a heterosexual ideal.

Freud, however, was neither the final nor definitive voice on human sexuality. Sociologists, psychologists, anthropologists, biologists, and endocrinologists, to name a few, contributed to the ongoing debate about the nature of sexuality. They were particularly interested in determining which figured most prominently in shaping sexuality, biology or social context. Several important scholarly studies revealed the nature of American sexual experience and fueled public debate. In the late nineteenth century, the physician and college professor Clelia Mosher interviewed female patients about their sexual lives. In 1929 the professional social worker Katharine Bement Davis published an extraordinarily detailed account of the sex lives of 2,200 women based on lengthy questionnaires. In the late 1940s Alfred Kinsey published the first of his reports on human sexuality. Kinsey's discoveries about the frequency of marital infidelity and homosexuality startled most Americans and fueled a vigorous debate about the meaning of those findings. In the late 1960s the work of William Masters and Virginia Johnson circulated widely. Using both interviews and laboratory studies to reach their conclusions, Masters and Johnson were interested primarily in therapeutic applications for their research. The research of both Kinsey and Masters and Johnson undermined what later feminist scholars called "the myth of the vaginal orgasm."

As important as market forces and scholarly opinion may have been in shaping Americans' understanding of sexuality, the experience of individual

Americans repeatedly proved definitive. Recognizing the interplay between these forces helps to resolve what appear to be anomalies or contradictions. Once again, the ideal of passionlessness serves as a good illustration. Nineteenth-century advice manuals and medical literature promoted the related ideals of female passionlessness and continence and a cursory reading of these materials might lead the historian to conclude that nineteenth-century middle-class women were, indeed, passionless creatures. The private correspondence of these same middle-class women reveals something quite different. For instance, in the letters they exchanged, Victorians Robert Burdette and Clara Baker expressed their desire for one another quite explicitly, even as their public demeanor belied their passionate natures. Neither admitted, for instance, that they had consummated their relationship before they married, behavior strictly forbidden by nineteenth-century advice literature. A similar disjunction existed in the twentieth century where medical literature constructed homosexuality as pathological even as the gay and lesbian community became increasingly visible and the research of social scientists such as Alfred Kinsey revealed a much higher incidence of homosexuality than most Americans imagined. In other words, individual experience could and did shape cultural ideals as much as market and science.

CONCLUSION

In the 1990s the meaning of sexuality continued to be highly contested, with Americans disagreeing, sometimes vociferously, about the relationship between sexuality and reproduction, pleasure, and identity. Through the media, the legal system, and sometimes violence, Americans attempted to promote their particular view on issues as varied as abortion, homosexual marriage, and pornography. The result was a highly volatile social mix that continues into the twenty-first century. For example, some gays and lesbians can find positive role models in television and movies, enjoy the protection of the law in some places, and even be honest about their sexual preferences without fear of losing their jobs. Simultaneously, other Americans remain outspoken in their opposition to homosexuality, attempting to regulate the behavior of those they see as transgressors. They boycott companies that provide spousal benefits to gay couples. They legislate against gay marriage and refuse to extend the full protection of the law against hate crimes to gays and lesbians. They require gay military personnel to serve under a policy that leaves them vulnerable to harassment. Sometimes they even attack and murder young men and women because of their sexual preference.

This example reveals the extent to which sexuality continues to be a socially constructed instrument of power and suggests at least one avenue of further research open to historians. To understand the persistence of homophobia in the twenty-first century, historians might profitably explore further the constructed nature of heterosexuality, perhaps by examining the rituals and practices some Americans have relied on to reinforce the perception that heterosexuality is somehow "normal." To understand more generally the persistence of sexuality as a tool of power, historians might examine more extensively the role of the media in shaping sexual ideals. Finally, historians need to investigate further the implications of an ethnically diverse culture for the construction of sexual ideals, perhaps focusing more specifically on Hispanic and Asian Americans. Each of these approaches will help to illuminate the ways in which sexual ideals continue to shape American thought and culture.

See also **Conflicting Ideals of Colonial Womanhood; Women in the Public Sphere, 1838–1877; Domesticity and Sentimentalism; Gender, Social Class, Race, and Material Life; Gender and Political Activism; Manhood; The Behavioral and Social Sciences** (*volume 1*); **Women and Family in the Suburban Age; Second-Wave Feminism; Gays and Lesbians; Women** (*volume 2*); *and other articles in this section.*

BIBLIOGRAPHY

General Reading in the History of Sexuality

D'Emilio, John, and Estelle Freedman. *Intimate Matters: A History of Sexuality in America.* 2d ed. Chicago, 1997. This work provides a general overview of the topic beginning with colonial America and concluding with the AIDS crisis.

Fout, John C., and Maura Shaw Tantillo. *American Sexual Politics: Sex, Gender, and Race Since the Civil War.* Chicago, 1993. This collection of articles from the *Journal of the History of Sexuality* gives an excellent introduction to some of the basic issues in the history of sexuality from the mid-nineteenth to the late twentieth century.

Peiss, Kathy, and Christina Simmons, with Robert A. Padgug. *Passion and Power: Sexuality in History.* Philadelphia, 1989. This collection of works begins with the late eighteenth century and concludes with a good discussion of the AIDS crisis. Also provides an excellent introduction to the basic issues in the history of sexuality.

Smith, Merril D. *Sex and Sexuality in Early America.* New York, 1998. This is a collection of articles that focuses particularly on North America, including the Carribbean and Spanish America up to 1800.

Middle-Class Sexuality

Bederman, Gail. *Manliness and Civilization: A Cultural History of Gender and Race in the United States, 1880–1917.* Chicago, 1995. This work focuses in particular on middle-class male sexuality and masculinity and is especially important for its exploration of the importance of race to the construction of white, male sexuality.

Lystra, Karen. *Searching the Heart: Women, Men, and Romantic Love in Nineteenth-Century America.* New York, 1989. Lystra's work is important because she examines both male and female sexuality in Victorian America.

Smith-Rosenberg, Carroll. *Disorderly Conduct: Visions of Gender in Victorian America.* New York, 1985. This is the classic work on middle-class female sexuality and gender identity. Smith-Rosenberg's conclusions have shaped much of the subsequent scholarship.

Male Sexuality

Rotundo, E. Anthony. *American Manhood: Transformations in Masculinity from the Revolution to the Modern Era.* New York, 1993. Rotundo focuses primarily on the nineteenth century.

White, Kevin. *The First Sexual Revolution: The Emergence of Male Heterosexuality in Modern America.* New York, 1993. White picks up where Rotundo leaves off, addressing particularly male heterosexuality.

Sexuality and Working-Class Women

Kunzel, Regina G. *Fallen Women, Problem Girls: Unmarried Mothers and the Professionalization of Social Work, 1890–1945.* New Haven, Conn., 1993.

Meyerowitz, Joanne. *Women Adrift: Independent Wage Earners in Chicago, 1880–1930.* Chicago, 1988.

Odem, Mary. *Delinquent Daughters: Protecting Adolescent Female Sexuality in the United States, 1885–1920.* Chapel Hill, N.C., 1995.

Peiss, Kathy. *Cheap Amusements: Working Women and Leisure in Turn-of-the-Century New York.* Philadelphia, 1986.

Stansell, Christine. *City of Women: Sex and Class in New York, 1789–1860.* New York, 1986.

Gay and Lesbian Communities in the Twentieth Century

Berubé, Allan. *Coming Out under Fire: The History of Gay Men and Women in World War II.* New York, 1990.

Chauncey, George. *Gay New York: Gender, Urban Culture, and the Making of the Gay Male World, 1890–1940*. New York, 1994.

D'Emilio, John. *Sexual Politics, Sexual Communities: The Making of a Homosexual Minority in the United States, 1940–1970*. 2d ed. Chicago, 1998.

Duberman, Martin. *Stonewall*. New York, 1993.

Kennedy, Elizabeth Lapovsky, and Madeline D. Davis. *Boots of Leather, Slippers of Gold: The History of a Lesbian Community*. New York, 1993.

History of Prostitution

Bailey, Beth, and David Farber. *The First Strange Place: Race and Sex in World War II Hawaii*. Baltimore, 1992.

Cohen, Patricia Cline. *The Murder of Helen Jewett: The Life and Death of a Prostitute in Nineteenth-Century New York*. New York, 1998.

Gilfoyle, Timothy. *City of Eros: New York, Prostitution, and the Commercialization of Sex, 1790–1920*. New York, 1992.

Rosen, Ruth. *Lost Sisterhood: Prostitution in America, 1900–1918*. Baltimore, 1982.

Intellectual History of Sexuality

Hale, Nathan G., Jr. *Freud and the Americans: The Beginnings of Psychoanalysis in the United States, 1876–1917*. New York, 1976.

———. *The Rise and Crisis of Psychoanalysis in the United States, 1917–1985*. New York, 1995.

Katz, Jonathan Ned. *The Invention of Heterosexuality*. New York, 1995. Katz makes a convincing argument for the socially and culturally constructed nature of heterosexuality.

Robinson, Paul. *The Modernization of Sex: Havelock Ellis, Alfred Kinsey, William Masters, and Virginia Johnson*. New York, 1976.

Russett, Cynthia Eagle. *Sexual Science: The Victorian Construction of Womanhood*. New York, 1989.

Terry, Jennifer. *An American Obsession: Science, Medicine, and Homosexuality in Modern Society*. Chicago, 1999.

GENTILITY AND MANNERS

Daniel Wickberg

The history of manners is a complex field of study. It exists at the juncture between an anthropological concern with daily habits, gestures, and particular modes of social behavior, and an historical concern with changing ideas of the self, the body, and social order. Manners, politeness, and etiquette all refer to a symbolic and expressive domain of everyday life. The rules of conduct govern the most casual everyday interactions, as well as the most elaborate formal ceremonial occasions. Manners are at once one of the most necessary features of cultural life, making communication and interaction between people possible, and also one of the most invisible, because they are simply taken for granted. Beyond a merely antiquarian interest in the different habits of different people at different times, the study of the history of manners seeks to connect the ordinary, everyday realm of conventional behavior to the larger cultural and social changes occurring from the seventeenth century to the present.

Historians of manners have approached this issue in three ways. First, they have asked how changing standards of polite behavior are related to the formation of social classes, particularly the middle class. Second, they have tied the relationship between ideas of the self and its expression in external behavior to the emergence of an urban market society in the nineteenth century. Finally, they have seen a change in manners in terms of the shift from a rank-ordered hierarchical vision of social order to an egalitarian and republican one. The most crucial period in the history of manners has accordingly been that from the Revolutionary era to the Civil War. In addition, historians have attempted to understand changing standards of manners in the twentieth century in terms of an increasing "informalization," rather than, as popular commentators have sometimes suggested, a decline from a golden age of civility. The key to understanding the history of manners is to find in the prescriptive literature of conduct books and etiquette manuals a guide to understanding changing value systems, rather than simply changes in particular rules or practices.

THEORETICAL AND HISTORICAL PERSPECTIVES

The most prominent theoretical understanding of the history of manners is that associated with the Swiss sociologist Norbert Elias. In *The Civilizing Process* (1978), he endeavored to connect a centuries-long transformation in European manners to the rise and fall of society centered on the court, and the coming of an urban bourgeoisie. Elias's great innovation was to read the proliferating courtesy books and etiquette manuals of the early modern era in terms of what was increasingly absent from them. For instance, in the Middle Ages, readers were instructed not to spit on the table or into the basin in which they were washing their hands. By the eighteenth century it was no longer necessary to make this requirement explicit, but readers were now told that it was polite to spit into a handkerchief, and not on the floor, when in church and in the houses of the great. In twentieth-century manuals spitting is rarely even mentioned, for the book's compilers simply assumed that readers would know it is a disgusting habit that is not acceptable under any conditions. The pattern is the same for eating habits, table manners, toilet functions, and bed habits. Silence on a particular subject matter or behavior doesn't mean it is no longer forbidden. Rather, it means that it has fallen beneath what Elias called the rising "threshold of delicacy." According to Elias, the history of manners reveals a greater and greater internalization of rules, a greater and greater disgust with bodily and animal habits, and a rising bourgeois emphasis on self-control. Authority over bodily habits was no longer exercised by explicit orders, but by the internalized authority of feelings of disgust. Bourgeois society privatized and internalized all kinds of activities that were once part of the larger public life.

While Elias's theoretical perspective is illuminating and reveals a pattern in the prescriptive literature of conduct books over several centuries of European history, it is problematic for historians of manners for at least two reasons. *The Civilizing Process's* focus on bodily functions and comportment tends to ignore a great number of the concerns that are present in conduct books. Undoubtedly, conduct books have concerned themselves with the use of napkins, eating with the mouth open, blowing the nose, and other presentations of the body, as Elias suggested. But they also have concerned themselves with writing letters, the proper forms and subject of conversation, giving and receiving gifts, and forms of introduction and social calling. The internalization model does very little to explain the increasing prominence of these concerns in modern etiquette manuals, nor does it explain the systems of social deference and authority built into the idealized vision of social relations contained in them. Also Elias's book tends to abstract individual rules from the texts in which they are embedded, so as to compare them with earlier and later rules concerning the same behaviors. This procedure allowed Elias to see how specific prescriptions have changed over centuries, but at the cost of taking those prescriptions out of the historical and cultural contexts that make sense of them. The historian of manners assumes that a given conduct manual is not just an unrelated group of prescriptions that are packaged together, but that it forms some kind of system or whole that says something about the society in which it was produced. In general, historians find Elias's brand of classical sociology to be too wide ranging and abstract, and not empirically specific about the societies in which certain manners were prescribed and practiced.

An alternative perspective on the history of manners in the nineteenth and twentieth centuries is suggested by the work on the history of the emotions, the self, and bodily management associated with Peter Stearns. While Stearns is concerned less with the history of manners or etiquette per se, and more with changing standards and modes of self-control, his interpretations suggest a way of integrating the history of manners into the history of self-control. Stearns's focus has been on the shift from Victorian to twentieth-century patterns of emotional and bodily control. In general, he has seen this shift as a matter of what he calls emotional "de-intensification." While Victorians advocated firm restrictions on certain behaviors, they also reveled in intense emotions. Moderns, on the other hand, have appeared to be freer and more informal in their social lives, and in the course of the twentieth century moved away from the formal conventions that governed Victorian etiquette. In doing so, however, they placed more emphasis upon self-control rather than following prescribed rules, and accomplished this by disciplining the emotions. This model suggests that the formality of etiquette as a prescribed set of rules allowed for a greater emotional range and freedom of feeling in Victorian America, and the increasing informality of American life indicates not a greater range of self-expression and emotional freedom, but a more restricted one.

Yet another approach to understanding the history of manners might be characterized as "postmodern." Instead of seeing changes in the prescriptive literature, such as etiquette manuals, self-help books, and conduct-of-life texts, as indicating a shift in behavioral norms, as both Elias and Stearns did, the postmodern approach emphasizes the discursive and textual meanings of conduct literature. From this point of view, what the historian finds in the literature of manners is not a set of rules prescribing behavior, but a sensibility or way of thinking about the world, the self, and its relationship to society. The larger historical shift in these texts is one in which an ever-deeper, more interiorized self is actually being constructed in the elaboration of rules of behavior. Instead of concentrating on what kinds of behaviors are being prescribed, such an approach concentrates on the assumptions that make it possible to prescribe behavior in the way in which these texts do. This approach has the virtue of considering the primary sources for the history of manners—the prescriptive literature of conduct—as the subject matter of history, rather than as indicators of some changing standard of behavior that is held to lie outside the sources. It is hard to get around the fact that the vast majority of sources available to study the history of manners are prescriptive rather than merely descriptive. That is, they emphasize how people ought to behave, rather than describing how they do behave. Most historians, however, are wary of postmodern approaches, and would prefer to use the prescriptive literature as indicators of general norms and attitudes toward behavior.

THE RISE OF GENTILITY: THE EIGHTEENTH CENTURY

Up through the seventeenth century, European and British conduct literature revolved around aristocratic court society. It was a world of intrigue and scheming for position, finely graded social distinctions, and admission by birth. The codes of conduct that governed it were based on assumptions of landed wealth, titled nobility, and extensive leisure. Courtesy books of that era focused on refinement of manners as the highest courtly ideal, and what appeared from the outside to be rather minute and trivial distinctions of behavior assumed critical importance for the courtly insider. Although a concern for the feelings of others has always been one of the legitimating features of manners, different standards of politeness applied to those higher and lower in the rank of society—there was no general principle of politeness by which to treat all equally. The ethic of refinement emphasized the value of an extensive education in the artifice and conventions of courtesy. It was a discipline that stressed not the natural amiability of persons, but the acquisitions of habits that indicated good breeding.

Beginning in the seventeenth century, and expanding in colonial North America in the eighteenth, bourgeois merchants and men of capital began to aspire to the status of refinement evident in the courtly ideal. The ideal of gentility—a mode of life based on refinement and courtesy, supported by an achieved status of material well-being—became the norm for the colonial elite of the mid-eighteenth century. From the beginning, a kind of ambivalence was evident in the bourgeois imitation and acquisition of courtly refinement. Bourgeois norms of work, thrift, and plain living were very much at odds with the luxury, leisure, and ostentation of the ideal of refinement, but that older ideal occupied the position of highest status in a society that was still very much based on rank and deference. For the emerging great merchants, traders, and gentlemen farmers of New England and the middle colonies, and for the planters of the South, to make their claim to the status of social elite was to acquire the trappings of a social elite. And in the British colonies of the eighteenth century, that meant aspiring to the manners of the court, which were increasingly the manners of the English gentry. Gentility thus represented courtly and aristocratic refinement adapted to the needs of a commercially based elite. Its uneasy accommodation of work and leisure ethics, of artificial manners and "natural" politeness, gave it its characteristic form.

Probably the most important text for understanding eighteenth-century gentility is the infamous Earl of Chesterfield's *Letters to His Son* (1774), which went through innumerable American editions in the eighteenth and nineteenth centuries.

Chesterfield's views were not representative of those of the American gentry, and his book, in fact, raised a storm among the members of that class. For instance, Abigail Adams, the prolific letter writer and wife of John Adams, blamed Chesterfield for "inculcateing [sic] the most immoral, pernicious and Libertine principals into the mind of a youth," while instructing his son how "to wear the outward garb of virtue" (Schlesinger, *Learning How to Behave*, p. 12). While the American gentry and later the nineteenth-century middle class would look to Chesterfield for advice and instruction on numerous points of etiquette, they were leery of his cosmopolitan sophistication and apparent immorality. What precisely was so troubling about Chesterfield? The earl synthesized an older courtly ideal of refinement and good breeding with an understanding of manners as a realm of flattery and, to use the sociologist Erving Goffman's phrase, "impression management." "You will negotiate with very little success," Chesterfield said, "if you do not previously, by your manners, conciliate and engage the affections of those with whom you are to negotiate" (p. 271). What was immoral to Abigail Adams was that manners were motivated not by the natural kindness and concern of the well-bred actor, but by a desire to win approbation for social benefits. This points to one of the characteristic views associated with American gentility and with American manners in the centuries to come—the idea that manners and morals are intimately linked, and that one should be the expression of the other. Etiquette, from this point of view, is merely morality made practical. The culture of eighteenth-century gentility created a stage on which its characters were to perform, but also insisted that the play was not artifice, but an expression of the performer's moral nature.

Eighteenth-century gentility was also committed to the notion of manners as an expression of a rank-ordered society. Colonial conduct literature stressed the deference due those of superior rank more than any other relation of inferior to superior. The subordination of youth to elders, and of women to men, for instance, while certainly present in seventeenth- and eighteenth-century advice books, took a backseat to the demand that social rank be recognized and deferred to in all the details of social interaction. The fact that colonial society lacked the clear and unambiguous marks of rank evident in England perhaps made the need to reaffirm the hierarchical nature of the social order even more pressing. As sumptuary laws fell into disuse, and the fluidity of eighteenth-century society made the simple image of a fixed hierarchical social order less tenable, conduct manuals either repeated demands for deference that were increasingly inapplicable, especially after the American Revolution, or focused on gentility as an achieved status. One of the features of Chesterfield's Letters that made it attractive to a revolutionary-era audience, whatever the reservations many members of that audience might have had, was that it provided a set of guidelines to achieving status, rather than merely affirming the order of society based on birth. Chesterfield by no means advocated an egalitarian system of manners—his advice revolved, after all, around inferiors and superiors—but his *Letters* captured something of the fluidity of a society moving from a fixed hierarchical order to a more open system.

One of the legacies of colonial-era gentility is in its association of manners and refinement with elitism. If courtesy books were the property of a social elite, and refinement functioned as a kind of cultural passport to the world of that elite, manners themselves could appear as arbitrary behaviors designed simply to preserve social distinctions. Despite the attempt to root manners in morality and to see etiquette as primarily concerned with the feelings of others, the ideology of rank order and deferential behavior was deeply embedded in gentility. Manners themselves would come under sustained attack in the nineteenth and twentieth centuries from those who saw them as essentially antidemocratic. Those who would try to make manners consistent with a democratic ethos were fighting an uphill battle against the elitist legacy of gentility. They were not aided by defenders of manners such as the French writer and politician Alexis de Tocqueville, who claimed, "True dignity in manners consists in always taking one's proper station, neither too high nor too low, and this is as much within the reach of a peasant as of a prince. In democracies all stations appear doubtful; hence it is that the manners of democracies, though often full of arrogance, are commonly wanting in dignity" (p. 228).

REPUBLICAN MANNERS: THE NINETEENTH CENTURY

Given the association of manners with aristocratic immorality and elitism, it is interesting that the significance and cultural centrality of etiquette increased in the nineteenth century, and particularly in the decades between 1820 and the Civil War. The era of Jacksonian democracy and increasing political egalitarianism was certainly not as egalitarian in practice as historians once thought, even for white men, but its ideology and cultural orientation was. Building on the republican principles of self-government that emerged from the revolutionary era, and a Jeffersonian egalitarianism that spelled an end to the Federalist vision of a politics built on deference to "the best men," the cultural vision of the social order in northern society emphasized its open, fluid, and egalitarian nature. And yet, this era saw a greatly increased number of etiquette books published and marketed to a larger and larger public. Over one hundred new volumes were published between 1830 and 1860, and none of them were targeted at a social elite such as those previously aimed at the colonial gentry. Just as the colonial commercial elite had adapted courtly manners to their bourgeois status, so the expanding middle class of the antebellum North adapted gentility to the conditions of antebellum society. The genteel ideal of good breeding, refinement and distinction was synthesized with republican notions of virtue and the compulsive energies of evangelical religion to create a new middle-class cultural orientation. The antipathy toward manners as an arbitrary and affected system of social distinctions vied with the notion that manners and gentility could help create the conditions for a republican social order.

This period saw an enormous divergence in the role of manners in the North and the South, paralleling the increasing sectional division. Because republican manners and the ideal of gentility were instrumental in the formation of a northern middle class of merchants, industrialists and professionals in an increasingly urban, market-driven social order, they had less and less to do with the model of manners that appealed to the southern planter elite. The increased wealth and availability of goods essential to it supported the expansion of gentility in the North. Houses, furnishings, tableware, and clothing ranked among the necessary accoutrements of genteel manners. The prescribed behavior of etiquette books demanded a certain set of material implements, but the commercial and industrial revolution were making those material goods much more widely available in northern cities, towns, and villages. The small planter elite, on the other hand, sat atop a southern social order governed by agriculture. This elite was commercial in its orientation, but it adapted aristocratic notions of honor and leisure as emblematic of its manners and modes of living. As the antebellum middle class attempted to make manners into a sincere expression of the inner qualities of virtue and honesty that it valued, the southern planter elite stressed the outer qualities of the person and the dynamics of honor and shame. Where the northern middle class rejected the elaborate formalities of the duel, with its highly ritualized violence, as unworthy of a sober, honest, and industrious people, southerners seized on it as an important means to restore social order in a situation in which honor had been challenged. The South looked back to an older ethic and model of manners. It was in the new milieux of the northern middle class that an entirely new and original understanding of manners was being crafted. This novelty explains the endless outpouring of etiquette manuals during this period—the old texts would no longer do.

The new etiquette manuals of the antebellum era stressed etiquette as a problem in a mobile world of strangers. These texts were not simply guides to well-bred manners that anybody could achieve with some effort, but were guides to reading the character of others from their behavior. The aim of etiquette in the commercial and social milieu of the city was to provide some sense of stability and order in a context where change and the unknown were the order of the day. Antebellum guides to behavior repeatedly insisted on the transparency of manners—those who possessed the proper outward forms of breeding were held to possess an inner virtue. From this point of view, manners were not artificial conventions, but were the natural expressions of an inner quality—gentility. As the ideal of gentility was unmoored from its place in a rank-ordered society, it was redefined as an essential quality of persons, rather than a marker of rank status. Middle-class identity in nineteenth-century America increasingly relied on a sense of the essential features of the self that found expression in the idea of gentility. Good manners, proper dress, the proper social forms and conventions: all were held to be the outward manifestations of an underlying nature. Manners could serve as a guide to understanding the selves of strangers.

That this was not an entirely satisfactory solution to the problem of middle-class identity and the courtly heritage of refinement in a fluid market society of acquired goods and identities is evident in the antebellum concern with the figure of the confidence man. The image of the confidence man bespoke the fear and the contradiction that lay at the heart of the antebellum reinvention of gentility. The confidence man had acquired all the outward traits of gentility, but was in fact an imposter posing as one of the naturally virtuous. He acquired the forms of etiquette and good breeding to win the trust of his victims, only to use that trust in order to accomplish his nefarious ends. The sense that the outward forms of good manners could be easily put on and taken off pointed to a greater fear. Perhaps all of social life among strangers was a form of theater, a playing of roles, a series of masks. If the outward forms of gentility could be so convincingly mimicked, perhaps there was no such inherent quality; perhaps there was only the artifice of social performance. Fear of the confidence man thus pointed to the greater fear that all the members of society were confidence men.

One of the characteristic ways that nineteenth-century etiquette manuals sought to contain the problem of "the stranger" in the new social milieu of the middle class was to erect a strong boundary between the spheres of public and private life. This ideological restructuring was related to the creation of the "separate spheres" doctrine that drew a sharp distinction between women's and men's natures and the domestic and public arenas of action. But etiquette manuals stressed the differences in terms of behavior in public spaces, such as city streets, and the more contained spaces of social life, such as the middle-class parlor. Any behavior in public that called attention to oneself, or brought oneself into the vision or concern of strangers was strictly prohibited by etiquette advisors. Similar behaviors could be admissible among friends and social acquaintances in private. For instance, many nineteenth-century etiquette advisors warned readers that loud conversation or laughter in public should always be avoided. But the same advisors might also indicate that boisterous laughter was a sign of good-natured amiability and should not be checked by an undue sense of propriety, if among a private circle of acquaintances. The double standard was an attempt to maintain an ideal of natural self-expression in one realm, by creating an opposite realm of the public world of strangers. The latter realm was one in which the "true" feelings and expressions of the self had to be severely contained because of the uncertainty of the meaning of social interactions among strangers.

GENTILITY UNDER FIRE: THE TWENTIETH CENTURY

Given how committed the etiquette advisors and conduct manuals of the nineteenth century were to creating a system of manners that was both egalitarian and natural, it is ironic that in the twentieth century their legacy came under increased attack for being both elitist and artificial. This turnabout is due primarily to three factors. First, nineteenth-century manners became codified in manuals and governing conventions as the late-nineteenth-century class structure grew increasingly rigid; what had started out as a republican rejection of a rank-ordered system of manners now served to legitimate the class position of the late-nineteenth-century bourgeoisie. Second, twentieth-century thought and culture, for a number of reasons, was engaged in a widespread revolt against formalism in areas as diverse as law, literature, and popular culture. The rejection of the formalism of etiquette as a set of rules was part of this larger revolt. Third, at times American culture seems possessed by a sense of historical amnesia. It pays its debts to the generations that have gone before by forgetting the original impulse that drove those generations, and revolting against their legacy in almost the very same terms that those earlier generations revolted in creating that legacy. In this way, twentieth-century critics of gentility had been saying the same things as many of their nineteenth-century forebears: that people need a system of manners that is both more egalitarian and more natural than the prevailing system.

Perhaps the most prominent and explicit criticism of gentility in the first decades of the twentieth century came from those modernist intellectuals and critics who found in the Harvard philosopher George Santayana's phrase of 1911, "the genteel tradition," a sign of everything that was wrong with American culture. Santayana himself was primarily concerned with a specific philosophical or intellectual tradition, and not with manners per se, but the terms of his critique had an extension well beyond a narrow construction of them. "The American Will," said Santayana, "inhabits the sky-scraper; the American Intellect inhabits the colonial mansion. The one is the sphere of the American man; the other, at least predominantly, of the American woman. The one is all aggressive enterprise; the other is all genteel tradition" (*The Genteel Tradition,* p. 40). Gentility, from this perspective, was a kind of feminized and aesthetisized moralism, detached from the actual, "manly" practical features of life. The realm of manners, the Victorian drawing room, the polite conventions all seemed artificial, thin, and unreal to the young intellectuals who were drawn to Santayana's critique. The demand for more "realistic" art, pragmatic philosophy, and vital religion was coupled with a rejection of manners, understood as artifice that stood in the way of authentic experience and expression.

Instead of seeing manners and etiquette as necessary features of cultural life that actually make social interaction and communication possible, the dominant mode of thinking in the twentieth century was to reject manners as unnecessary formality. Beginning with the modernist revolt against Victorianism in the 1920s, the general middle-class orientation was toward less formality and greater casualness in the daily affairs of social life. The most prominent twentieth-century cultural sensibility was strongly anti-formalist, believing that the only possibility of communication and authentic interaction between people arises when they reject the artificiality of etiquette and express themselves in natural and spontaneous ways. The disappearance of formal modes of address and the extension of casual dress from the world of leisure to the world of work in the late twentieth century are the most obvious examples of the anti-formalist sensibility.

These changes represent not so much the decline or disappearance of etiquette in American life as what the Dutch scholar Cas Wouters called its "informalization." In fact, twentieth-century publishers continued to publish etiquette manuals and guides to behavior, including those of the famous writer Emily Post and, in postmodern fashion, those of Judith Martin, also known as Miss Manners. Martin positioned herself as one of the great lamenters of the decline of manners, but her pseudo-Victorian persona was pitched at those hip readers who didn't take manners too seriously. Contrary to those who, like Martin, saw a decline from an era when politeness was, if not universally practiced, universally recognized, the trend in the twentieth century was to make manners, consideration for others, and awareness of the feelings of others a primary feature of middle-class life. In fact, the twentieth century's prevailing belief had been that too much formality was actually inconsiderate, that to treat others with the rigid rules of etiquette was to be cold and aloof. The post-1960s etiquette, in particular, stressed a kind of therapeutic "sensitivity" to others, rather than an adherence to "irrelevant" rules about thank-you notes and salad forks.

By the end of the twentieth century, the ideal of interpersonal sensitivity had replaced gentility in middle-class circles. The latter indicates a kind of fixed personal identity tied to natural qualities of the self; the former indicates an openness and flexibility to the needs of others. In particular, issues of multiculturalism and racial interaction were formulated in terms of the ethic of sensitivity and the need to develop communication and interaction between all people, especially in bureaucratic contexts.

The cultural sensitivity training that took place in the 1990s corporate workplace and other bureaucratic offices was premised on the idea of respect for "difference." But like the informalization of manners that erases the lines between private and public life, this approach often has the effect of making people think about their cultural identities in bureaucratic and therapeutic terms. Nineteenth-century manners had the benefit of creating a public sphere of recognized behavior that served as a kind of protective shell for people. Even its theatricality, problematic for the genteel in so many ways, gave people recourse to what Erving Goffman described as a "backstage" area, where people could relax and let their hair down. The twentieth-century demand that people be themselves all the time, that they be sensitive to others, and casual and informal in their manners, created a world where the "backstage" became the "frontstage." Ironically, the rejection of manners as artificial led to a world in which all social life is a performance, albeit a deliberately casual one.

See also **Conflicting Ideals of Colonial Womanhood; American Romanticism; Domesticity and Sentimentalism; Gender, Social Class, Race, and Material Life; Manhood; The Behavioral and Social Sciences** *(volume 1);* **Women and Family in the Suburban Age; Women** *(volume 2); and other articles in this section.*

BIBLIOGRAPHY

Primary Sources

Chesterfield, Philip Dormer Stanhope, Earl of. *Letters to His Son.* Philadelphia, 1878.

Goffman, Erving. *The Presentation of Self in Everyday Life.* New York, 1959.

Santayana, George. *The Genteel Tradition: Nine Essays.* Edited by Douglas L. Wilson. Cambridge, Mass., 1967.

Tocqueville, Alexis de. *Democracy in America.* Vol. 2, edited by Phillips Bradley. New York, 1945.

Secondary Sources

Arditi, Jorge. *A Genealogy of Manners: Transformations of Social Relations in France and England from the Fourteenth to the Eighteenth Century.* Chicago, 1998.

Burke, Peter. *The Art of Conversation.* Ithaca, N.Y., 1993.

Bushman, Richard L. *The Refinement of America: Persons, Houses, Cities.* New York, 1993.

Elias, Norbert. *The History of Manners. The Civilizing Process.* Vol. 1, translated by Edmund Jephcott. New York, 1978.

Grier, Katherine C. *Culture and Comfort: People. Parlors, and Upholstery, 1850–1930.* Rochester, N.Y., 1988.

Halttunen, Karen. *Confidence Men and Painted Women: A Study of Middle-Class Culture in America, 1830–1870.* New Haven, Conn., 1982.

Hemphill, C. Dallett. *Bowing to Necessities: A History of Manners in America, 1620–1860.* New York, 1999.

Kasson, John F. *Rudeness and Civility: Manners in Nineteenth-Century Urban America.* New York, 1990.

Lasch-Quinn, Elisabeth. "How to Behave Sensitively: Prescriptions for Interracial Conduct from the 1960s to the 1990s." *Journal of Social History* 33, no. 2 (1999): 409–427.

Persons, Stow. *The Decline of American Gentility.* New York, 1973.

Schlesinger, Arthur M. *Learning How to Behave: A Historical Study of American Etiquette Books.* New York, 1946.

Shields, David S. *Civil Tongues and Polite Letters in British America.* Chapel Hill, N.C., 1997.

Stearns, Peter N. *Battleground of Desire: The Struggle for Self-Control in Modern America.* New York, 1999.

Tomsich, John. *A Genteel Endeavor: American Culture and Politics in the Gilded Age.* Stanford, Calif., 1971.

Wouters, Cas. "Etiquette Books and Emotion Management in the Twentieth Century: Part One—The Integration of Social Classes." *Journal of Social History* 29, no. 1 (fall 1995): 107–124.

———. "Etiquette Books and Emotion Management in the Twentieth Century: Part Two—The Integration of Social Classes." *Journal of Social History* 29, no. 2 (winter 1995): 325–339.

ETHNICITY: EARLY THEORIES

Werner Sollors

The word "ethnicity" was introduced in 1941–1942 by the sociologist William Lloyd Warner as a noun to serve as a parallel to "age" and "sex" in categorizing the inhabitants of Newburyport, Massachusetts, in his study *Yankee City Series* (1941–1959). His coinage (or more precisely, his revitalization of an obsolete English word denoting "heathen superstition" or "heathendom") revealed a tension at the core of the word. On the one hand, the parallel to age and sex suggested that all inhabitants of Yankee City, as he called Newburyport, had to have an ethnicity, so Yankees also had to be classified as an ethnic group in New England. On the other hand, Warner assigned ethnicity only to nondominant groups, thus imagining a social system in which the most powerful group was imagined not to be ethnic. This ambiguity, which goes back to the very etymology of "ethnic"—referring both to people in general and to people who are different or heathens—has remained active in many uses of the word "ethnicity." Still, on the whole it was a successful coinage, because different intellectual strands had come together that found an adequate expression in Warner's term.

DEFINING ETHNICITY

One of those intellectual strands was the sociological sense in which the ethnic group had become the subject of discussion, starting with the German social scientist Max Weber, who defined ethnic groups as

> those human groups that entertain a subjective belief in their common descent because of similarities of physical type or of customs or both, or because of memories of colonization and migration; this belief must be important for the propagation of group formation; conversely, it does not matter whether or not an objective blood relationship exists. (quoted in Sollors, *Theories of Ethnicity*, p. 56).

Written before World War I and published posthumously in 1922, Weber's foundational definition in *Economy and Society* emphasized the sense of commonality (*Gemeinsamkeit*, rendered as "ethnic membership" in the English translation) that does not constitute a group but that facilitates group formation. Weber offered a broad international perspective and discussed such ethnic groups as American blacks, Serbs and Croats, German-speaking Alsatians, and French Canadians. Weber's formulation was echoed by numerous scholars and adopted by Milton Gordon's widely influential *Assimilation in American Life* (1964).

Second, there was the psychological component, implied in Weber's focus on the "subjective belief." Here it was the Austrian psychoanalyst Sigmund Freud who made the crucial contribution, whereas the American psychoanalyst Erik H. Erikson offered the formulaic term that has been commonly adopted. In a 1926 B'nai Brith address, Freud wondered about his subjective sense of Jewishness—which seemed to exist independent of religious faith or ethnic pride. He viewed his subjective feeling of Jewishness as the result of what he called "the secret familiarity of identical psychological construction." When Erikson attempted to translate Freud's phrase in *Childhood and Society* (1950), Erikson offered the term "identity" as a shortened English formula for Freud's notion. It was a formula that took. Philip Gleason has shown how the use of the phrase "ethnic identity" was amazingly still absent from books like Oscar Handlin's *The Uprooted* (1951), whereas it proliferated soon thereafter (in Sollors, ed., *Theories of Ethnicity*). The term "identity" is so omnipresent today, in connection with words like "ethnic," "racial," and "national," that it seems hard to remember that it goes back only to 1950.

Third, there was the growing problem surrounding the term "race." For Weber, "racial" and "ethnic" were synonyms, and he believed that the question of whether conspicuous racial differences are based on biological heredity or on tradition is usually of no importance as far as their effect on mutual attraction or repulsion is concerned. Freud, however, had already directed his reflections against the growing racial underpinning of anti-Semitism. When racial anti-Semitism became the official state doctrine in National Socialist Germany in the 1930s, "race" became too problematic to serve as a neutral term for a scholarly understanding of group relations within society. "Race" became too closely associated with "racism," a term Nazi ideologues used as a positive term (analogous to other modern "isms," such as communism) before Magnus Hirschfeld turned "racism" into a pejorative word in his remarkable book *Racism* (1938).

There was also the heterogeneity of origins among the American population. In 1800 the United States population was approximately five million, including one million African Americans and an estimated half million diverse nations of Native Americans. Nearly 80 percent of the white population was descended from British colonists. In 1900 there were 76 million Americans, almost 9 million of them blacks and only 237,000 Indians. Eleven million were foreign-born, mostly from Europe. The number of foreign-born goes up to 25 million if one includes the children of foreign-born Americans. More than half a million of the 1900 population came from Russia, a million from Scandinavia, a million and a half from Ireland, and well over three million from Germany and Austria. The majority of the newcomers arrived during what is termed the "new immigration," the wave that peaked in the years from the 1880s to the 1920s. There were also about 23,000 Japanese and 85,000 Chinese immigrants, as well as many people of Spanish and some of French descent who had been incorporated into the United States by annexation and territorial expansion. In the course of the nineteenth century the United States grew from a British-dominated provincial country into a large, modern, polyethnic, and increasingly urban world power.

"Ethnicity" turned out to be the perfect noun for both the sociological sense of group membership and the sense of secret psychological construction, while offering a semantic substitute for the word "race" during and after World War II and helping to describe the important feature of the heterogeneous makeup of the twentieth-century U.S. population. "Ethnicity" was a neutral noun for reflections on the concepts of group membership and exclusion and, at the same time, described varieties of American origins and functioned like a shorter synonym for "ethnic identity." As such, it is used in examinations of a long series of older issues connected with American diversity and its social and psychological consequences. Its applications range from the relation of ethnicity to other group identities, from the significance of marginality and immigration to notions of insiders and outsiders, from pluralism and assimilation to generational succession, from the importance of culture to the role of ethnic boundaries, and from questions of ethnocentrism and its relationship to collective violence to the quest for democratic polyethnic and multicultural structures. ("Multicultural" is a term that also was introduced during World War II, in Edward F. Haskell's *Lance: A Novel about Multicultural Men,* published in 1941.)

At about the same time that Weber offered his pioneering definition of the ethnic group, the German sociologist and essayist Georg Simmel approached conceptual aspects of ethnicity that would have important consequences in American thought. Simmel described the individual as enmeshed in a web of group relations, including multiple group affiliations, and he focused especially on the figure of the "stranger" who is "near and far *at the same time*" (quoted in Sollors, ed., *Theories of Ethnicity,* p. 41). Simmel's stranger is "the person who comes today and stays tomorrow" without ever becoming completely part of the group within which he lives, and he viewed the European Jew as the exemplary stranger. This attention to the complications of overlapping and contradictory group membership and to the special role of an outsider who is also an insider gave rise to much conceptual attention and questions among sociologists and psychologists in subsequent decades. What is the sociological significance of the marginal figure whose group membership is problematic? How does ethnicity relate to other, simultaneously existing group affiliations? How important are insiders and outsiders?

In his influential essay "Human Migration and the Marginal Man" (1928) Robert E. Park, founder of the Chicago school of sociology, was inspired by Simmel to think of the importance of migration for human history, making mixed races the rule and not the exception, and the "marginal man" (Simmel's stranger writ large as the "divided self" of American immigrant and a mixed-race culture) as the ideal figure for the study of "the processes of civilization and of progress." Park saw the personality type who "lives in two worlds" and experiences "inner turmoil and intense self-consciousness" in American immigrant autobiographies as representative, in a heightened and more permanent fashion, of "periods of transition and crisis in the lives of most of us." The marginal man became a key figure for an understanding of modernity, urbanism, and cosmopolitanism. Countless studies of

American immigrant intellectuals, mixed-race individuals, and ethnic groups have followed this approach, which was further fleshed out in Park's own essays and in Everett V. Stonequist's *The Marginal Man: A Study in Personality and Culture Conflict* (1937).

The ethnopsychiatrist George Devereux took as his point of departure the question (that was related to Simmel's inquiry into group affiliations) of how ethnic identity can be related to other forms of identity. In "Ethnic Identity: Its Logical Functions and Dysfunctions" (1975), Devereux emphasized the contrastive and what he called the dissociative nature of ethnic behavior that was not actually prompted by any truly ethnic or cultural tradition but was informed by a contrastive strategy of opposition (in Sollors, ed., *Theories of Ethnicity*). Ethnicity, seen this way, "is logically and historically the product of the assertion that 'A is an X because he is not a Y' "—a proposition that made it remarkably easy to identify *X*ness and tended to make *X*s appear more homogeneous than they were. By the same token, the definition of *X*s as non-*Y*s exaggerated the differences between the *X*s and the *Y*s. Since the *X*s tended to think of themselves as human, they could therefore consider the *Y*s as somehow nonhuman. "*X* does not equal *Y*" was thus the fundamental ethnic formula.

Devereux located the fascist potential of ethnic movements in this reduction of complex authentic identity (we could say identity within Simmel's web of group affiliation) to contrastive one-dimensionality in the name of ethnicity: "If one is nothing but a Spartan, a capitalist, a proletarian, or a Buddhist, one is next door to being nothing and therefore even to not being at all." Ethnicity could easily become one variable that demanded that it overrule all other group affiliations with which it might be in conflict. Devereux saw the psychological danger of ethnicity as an all-or-nothing proposition. "An individual's absolute uniqueness is defined by an induplicable accumulation of imprecise determinations," he wrote. In this complex ensemble that constituted individual identity, ethnicity could turn out to be one feature that is superimposed—Devereux calls it "hypercathected"—over all other features of personality, including the important characteristic of shared membership in the human race. This was a strange logical operation, but it was undertaken only too often. This subordination of all nonethnic traits was actually a straitjacket that could produce catastrophic and disastrous actions—including ethnic cleansing and genocide.

Devereux's pointed critique focused on the dangers of ethnicity that would at crucial moments be put to the service of curtailing empathy along affiliational lines other than ethnic ones. However, other discussions about ethnicity also stressed the difficulty of understanding across lines of social and ethnic divisions. In 1900 the American psychologist and philosopher William James, in whose "divided self" in *The Varieties of Religious Experience* (1902) Park saw a model for the marginal man, also called attention to human blindness in such encounters, starting with his own attempt to imagine the difference that separated the worldview of a North Carolina mountaineer from James's own academic way of life. Such pioneering observations became widespread during the century, and the cultural relativist notion that only insiders fully understand a given group gained ground, so much so that this aspect of relativism may be considered a feature of American culture in the last decades of the twentieth century. (Simmel's stranger and Park's marginal man were still personifications of modern culture in general, precisely by virtue of their analytical relationship to social systems to which they do not fully belong.) The sociologist Robert K. Merton, who also took a point of departure from Simmel and Weber, argued in "Insiders and Outsiders: A Chapter in the Sociology of Knowledge" (1972) that the terms of this dichotomy had hardly been sufficiently examined. His essay, which surveys the insider and outsider doctrine, as well as examples of insiders as outsiders, remains the fullest conceptual contribution to the issue. His manifesto-like ending has perhaps not yet been as widely adopted as it deserves to be: "Insiders and Outsiders in the domain of knowledge, unite. You have nothing to lose but your claims. You have a world of understanding to win."

James had another, and perhaps the most significant, influence on conceptualizations of ethnicity in America. When he gave the Hibbert Lectures at Manchester College in 1909, which were published as *A Pluralistic Universe,* his former student Horace M. Kallen was in the audience. It was Kallen who coined the term "cultural pluralism" in order to find a formula for his vision of the United States as a possible model polyethnic republic, a federation of nationalities. Kallen's *Culture and Democracy in the United States* (1924) included the essay "Democracy versus the Melting-Pot" (1916). If assimilation (a word also used by Park in his description of the marginal man), Americanization, and the melting pot were the central metaphors for ethnic group transformation into a national mold, then

Kallen imagined ethnic identity to be unchangeable: "Men change their clothes, their politics, their wives, their religions, their philosophies, to a grater or lesser extent: they cannot change their grandfathers." His belief in ethnic stability was the basis of his vision of cultural pluralism as a mystical "multiplicity in unity, an orchestration of mankind," and he embellished that metaphor into a social parable: "As in an orchestra, every type of instrument has its specific tonality, founded in its substance and form; as every type has its appropriate theme and melody in the whole symphony, so in society each ethnic group is the natural instrument, its spirit and culture are its theme and melody, and the harmony and dissonances and discords of them all make the symphony of civilization."

The essayist and critic Randolph S. Bourne was inspired by Kallen's opposition to the melting pot and in his essay "Trans-National America" (1916) saw the cultural opportunity of creating a cosmopolitan American civilization that thrives on the linguistic and cultural richness that ethnic variety brings to a country in which each citizen could also remain connected with another culture. Whereas Kallen still viewed English as the backbone of the different accents and dialects in his model of pluralist harmony, Bourne opposed the English orientation in American culture and the requirement that newcomers shed their cultural, religious, or linguistic pasts. Yet Bourne did not think that immigrants could remain fixed to their pasts, for he saw that crucial features of their ethnic orientation were American-made. Instead, Bourne advocated the new idea of dual citizenship, both for immigrants who came to the United States and for the increasing number of internationally oriented individuals who, like American expatriates in France, had been born in one country but lived in another. In Bourne's hands the contemplation of Americanness in its relation to ethnicity (a word not yet available to him) led to a reconsideration of the nationalist premises of citizenship. Bourne argued memorably: "We are all foreign-born or the descendants of foreign-born, and if distinctions are to be made between us they should rightly be made on some other ground than indigenousness." Bourne's essay had a long afterlife, as it was often reprinted and discussed from the time he first published it into the era of multiculturalism.

GENERATIONS

The investigation of the dialectic of an assimilative national identity and of ethnic pluralism led to some important reflections on the significance of generations in this process. Were the numerically significant children and grandchildren of Simmel's strangers, Park's marginal men, Kallen's musical types and grandfathers, and Bourne's transnational dual citizens undergoing processes of assimilation that could be divided into stages or that should be visualized as a straight line? Or were they undergoing alternating phases of assimilation and ethnic revival?

The Hungarian-born sociologist Karl Mannheim, in his pathbreaking essay "The Problem of Generations" (1928), called attention to generations in a general way. Criticizing positivistic notions of measurable and quantifiable generations as well as romantic-mystical concepts of generations as based on "felt experience," Mannheim proposed instead to focus on the "social location" of presumptive members of a generation. Contemporaries living in countries remote from each other, for example, might not share such a community of location. Social and historical forces alone transformed a group of contemporaries from a "generation as potentiality" into a "generation as actuality," "where a concrete bond is created" among them. Imagining a society in which "one generation lived on forever and none followed to replace it," Mannheim described our world by contrast as one "developed by individuals who come into contact anew with the accumulated heritage." Mannheim called this phenomenon "fresh contact" and made a comparison with the experience of social mobility: "Fresh contacts play an important part in the life of the individual when he is forced by events to leave his own social group and enter a new one—when, for example, an adolescent leaves home, or a peasant the countryside for the town, or when an emigrant changes his home, or a social climber his social status or class."

The best known modern formulation of generational succession among American immigrants was developed by the historian Marcus Lee Hansen in the address, "The Problem of the Third Generation Immigrant" (1938). According to Hansen, the typical member of the second generation favored assimilation, whereas the third generation often tried to reverse rather than continue that process. Hansen formulated this notion so memorably— "what the son wishes to forget the grandson wishes to remember"—that Will Herberg, in his widely ready study *Protestant, Catholic, Jew: An Essay in American Religious Sociology* (1955), referred to this formula as "Hansen's law." Hansen's notion of immigrant generations was widely adopted after Oscar

Handlin reprinted and endorsed Hansen's essay in *Commentary* in 1952.

The sociologist Vladmir C. Nahirny and Joshua A. Fishman, the author of several works on Yiddish, extended Hansen's concept when they argued in "American Immigrant Groups: Ethnic Identification and the Problem of Generations" (1965) that the first generation's attachment was to a specific place in the old world, an attachment the second generation could not possibly share. "While estranged from their parental heritage, the sons, nevertheless, remained more conscious of their ethnic identity than were their immigrant fathers." The German-born sociologist Herbert J. Gans suggested that "Hansen's Law applies only to academics and intellectuals." In the foreword to Neil C. Sandberg's *Ethnic Identity and Assimilation* (1974), Gans points out that this study of Polish-American immigrants in California "does not provide any evidence that the rest of the third generation is more interested in its ethnic origins than the first or second" (p. xiii). Gans instead thought that the model of straight-line assimilation was more convincing and that each subsequent generation was more assimilated than the previous one.

ASSIMILATION

This was a position that the writer Charles W. Chesnutt took in 1900 in order to describe "The Future American." Chesnutt focused on the color line and predicted that a consequence of the Spanish-American War in 1898 would be that it would "enhance the relative importance of the non-Caucasian elements of the population, and largely increase the flow of dark blood toward the white race, until the time shall come when distinctions of color shall lose their importance, which will be but the prelude to a complete facial fusion." Chesnutt thought that the gradual arrival of a more homogeneous American type would make for more harmonious social progress; and he viewed amalgamation as an improvement over white and black traits. While Chesnutt's concept of assimilation was based on intermarriage and race mixing, the Swiss psychiatrist Carl Gustav Jung, in the American character essay "Your Negroid and Indian Behavior" (1932), moved the discussion from "blood" to the "spirit of the place" when he observed that "sometimes a foreign country gets under the skin of those born in it" and that this "external assimilation of man to the peculiarities of a country" was what made white Americans walk like Indians and laugh like blacks. Reversing

the more common way of imagining assimilation as conformity to dominant groups, Jung thought that Americans only confirmed the old rule that the "conqueror overcomes the old inhabitant in body, and succumbs to his spirit."

The poet and novelist Jean Toomer turned the discussion of assimilation in yet another direction when he noted in his essay "Race Problems and Modern Society" (1929) that the rapidly ongoing process of assimilation could paradoxically enhance the creation of more difference: Toomer noticed that the "sociological types, the types which are arising among Negroes, such as the business man, the politician, the college student, the writer, the propagandist, the movie enthusiast, the bootlegger, the taxi driver, etc. . . . are more and more approaching the corresponding white types." This would signal that a process of assimilation leading toward ultimate fusion was at work. "But, just as certain as it is that this increasing correspondence of types makes the drawing of distinction supposedly based on skin color or blood composition appear more and more ridiculous, so it is true that the lines are being drawn with more force between the colored and white groups." For Toomer, assimilation could thus take place at the same time as differentiation. This direction of thinking implied that what was often viewed as ethnic persistence could also be a reinvention of ethnic differences under assimilative conditions.

Assimilation could be more than a cooperative step toward fusion. Devereux coined the term "antagonistic acculturation," according to which, in an ethnic confrontation, means and ends may be adopted from the opponent. X, defined in contrast with Y, becomes somewhat like Y in the confrontation. In the important essay "Symbolic Ethnicity: The Future of Ethnic Groups and Cultures in America" (1979), Gans called attention to the ways in which modern ethnic identification works by external symbols rather than by continuous activities that make demands upon people who define themselves as "ethnic," so that a gentle ethnic diversification could take place in an assimilative framework.

These observations were important for approaches that looked at ethnic processes and conflicts not only as residues of primordial differences but as new constructions and inventions. Three widely received books supported this direction of inquiry: Peter L. Berger and Thomas Luckmann, *The Social Construction of Reality: A Treatise in the Sociology of Knowledge* (1966); Eric Hobsbawm and Terence Ranger, eds., *Invention of Tradition* (1983); and Benedict Anderson, *Imagined Communities:*

Reflections on the Origins and Spread of Nationalism (1983). The constructivist turn opened up the whole interrelationship of ethnicity and culture to new inquiries, as the focus shifted from the issue of how ethnic culture was preserved, or succumbed to assimilation, to the question of how ethnic groups emerged.

NEW APPROACHES TO ETHNICITY

In his landmark *Ethnic Groups and Boundaries* (1969), Fredrik Barth signaled the core issues of the new approach to ethnicity. Previous scholars tended to think about ethnicity "in terms of different peoples, with different histories and cultures, coming together and accommodating themselves to each other." Instead, Barth suggested, we should "ask ourselves what is needed to make ethnic distinctions *emerge* in an area." With a statement that runs against the grain of much thinking about ethnicity, Barth argued that

> when one traces the history of an ethnic group through time, one is *not* simultaneously, in the same sense, tracing the history of "a culture": the elements of the present culture of that ethnic group have not sprung from the particular set that constituted the group's culture at a previous time, whereas the group has a continual organizational existence with boundaries (criteria of membership) that despite modifications have marked off a continuing unit. (p. 38)

Barth saw the essence of ethnicity in mental, cultural, social, and not necessarily territorial boundary-constructing processes that functioned as cultural markers between groups. For Barth, it was "the ethnic *boundary* that defines the group, not the cultural stuff that it encloses." Barth directed attention to processes of boundary maintenance and argued that "members of all ethnic groups in a poly-ethnic society" could "act to maintain dichotomies and differences."

Stephen Steinberg's *The Ethnic Myth: Race, Ethnicity, and Class in America* (1981) makes a comprehensive case for questioning and demystifying ethnicity. Steinberg felt that the "tendency in modern social thought [had] been to treat ethnicity as a given and to explore its consequences." By contrast, Steinberg set out to explore the "historical and structural foundations" of ethnicity (p. x) and to expose the "ultimate ethnic myth," "the belief that the cultural symbols of the past can provide more than a comfortable illusion to shield us from present-day discontents" (p. 262). Half a century after Warner brought the term "ethnicity" into circulation and ninety years after Weber's definition of ethnic groups, David A. Hollinger went further than Steinberg and advocated "postethnicity." In his book *Postethnic America: Beyond Multiculturalism* 1995) Hollinger wrote, "Postethnicity reacts not against commitment but against prescribed affiliations on the basis of descent" (p. 117). He restated Simmel's case for a web of group affiliations, criticized Kallen's backward-looking pluralism as well as monolithic notions of assimilation, and ended with a hope that "being an American amid a multiplicity of affiliations need not be dangerously threatening to diversity" (p. 163). If Hollinger's manifesto is indicative of the direction of future thinking on that matter, then the history of ethnicity and identity may yet turn out to be a history that had its peak in the second part of the twentieth century.

See also **The Behavioral and Social Sciences** *(volume 1);* **Anthropology and Cultural Relativism** *(volume 2);* **Cultural Studies; Social Construction of Reality** *(in this volume); and other articles in this section.*

BIBLIOGRAPHY

Anderson, Benedict. *Imagined Communities: Reflections on the Origins and Spread of Nationalism.* London, 1983.

Barth, Fredrik, ed. *Ethnic Groups and Boundaries: The Social Organization of Culture Difference.* London, 1969.

Berger, Peter L., and Thomas Luckmann. *The Social Construction of Reality: A Treatise in the Sociology of Knowledge.* London, 1966.

Bourne, Randolph S. "Trans-National America" (1916). Reprinted in Werner Sollors, ed., *Theories of Ethnicity,* New York, 1996, pp. 93–108.

Chesnutt, Charles W. "The Future American" (1900). Reprinted in Werner Sollors, ed., *Theories of Ethnicity,* New York, 1996, pp. 17–32.

Dennis, Lawrence. *The Coming American Fascism.* New York, 1936.

Devereux, George. "Ethnic Identity: Its Logical Functions and Dysfunctions" (1975). Reprinted in Werner Sollors, ed., *Theories of Ethnicity,* New York, 1996, pp. 385–414.

Erikson, Erik H. *Childhood and Society.* New York, 1950.

——. *Identity: Youth and Crisis.* New York, 1968.

Francis, E. K. *Interethnic Relations: An Essay in Sociological Theory.* New York, 1976

Gans, Herbert J. "Symbolic Ethnicity: The Future of Ethnic Groups and Cultures in America" (1979). Reprinted in Werner Sollors, ed., *Theories of Ethnicity,* New York, 1996, pp. 425–429.

Glazer, Nathan, and Daniel P. Moynihan, eds. *Ethnicity: Theory and Experience.* Cambridge, Mass., 1975.

Gordon, Milton. *Assimilation in American Life: The Role of Race, Religion, and National Origins.* New York, 1964.

Handlin, Oscar. *The Uprooted: The Epic Story of the Great Migrations that Made the American People.* Boston, 1951.

Hansen, Marcus Lee. *The Problem of the Third Generation Immigrant.* Rock Island, Ill., 1938.

Herberg, Will. *Protestant, Catholic, Jew: An Essay in American Religious Sociology.* New York, 1955.

Higham, John. *Send These to Me: Jews and Other Immigrants in Urban America.* New York, 1975.

Hirschfeld, Magnus. *Racism.* London, 1938. Translation by Eden and Cedar Paul. London, 1938.

Hobsbawm, Eric, and Terence Ranger, eds. *Invention of Tradition.* New York, 1983.

Hollinger, David A. *Postethnic America: Beyond Multiculturalism.* New York, 1995.

James, William. *A Pluralistic Universe.* New York, 1909.

——. *The Varieties of Religious Experience: A Study in Human Nature.* New York, 1902.

Jung, Carl Gustav. "Your Negroid and Indian Behavior" (1932). Reprinted in Werner Sollors, ed., *Theories of Ethnicity,* New York, 1996, pp. 191–201.

Kallen, Horace M. *Culture and Democracy in the United States: Studies in the Group Psychology of the American Peoples.* New York, 1924.

——. "Democracy versus the Melting-Pot" (1916). Reprinted in Werner Sollors, ed., *Theories of Ethnicity,* New York, 1996, pp. 67–92.

Kivisto, Peter, and Dag Blanck, eds. *American Immigrants and Their Generations: Studies and Commentaries on the Hansen Thesis after Fifty Years.* Urbana, Ill., 1990.

Mannheim, Karl. "The Problem of Generations" (1928). Reprinted in Werner Sollors, ed., *Theories of Ethnicity,* New York, 1996, pp. 109–155.

Merton, Robert K. "Insiders and Outsiders: A Chapter in the Sociology of Knowledge" (1972). Reprinted in Werner Sollors, ed., *Theories of Ethnicity,* New York, 1996, pp. 324–369.

Miles, Robert. *Racism.* New York, 1989.

Nahirny, Vladimir C., and Joshua A. Fishman. "American Immigrant Groups: Ethnic Identification and the Problem of Generations" (1965). Reprinted in Werner Sollors, ed., *Theories of Ethnicity,* New York, 1996, pp. 266–281.

Park, Robert Ezra. "Human Migration and the Marginal Man" (1928). Reprinted in Werner Sollors, ed., *Theories of Ethnicity,* New York, 1996, pp. 156–157.

——. *Race and Culture: 1913–1944.* Glencoe, Ill., 1950.

Sandberg, Neil C. *Ethnic Identity and Assimilation: The Polish-American Community.* New York, 1974.

Shuffelton, Frank, ed. *A Mixed Race: Ethnicity in Early America.* New York, 1993.

Sollors, Werner, ed. *Theories of Ethnicity: A Classical Reader.* New York, 1996.

Steinberg, Stephen. *The Ethnic Myth: Race, Ethnicity, and Class in America.* New York, 1981.

Stonequist, Everett V. *The Marginal Man: A Study in Personality and Culture Conflict.* New York, 1937.

Thernstrom, Stephan, ed. *The Harvard Encyclopedia of American Ethnic Groups.* Cambridge, Mass., 1980.

Todorov, Tzvetan. *On Human Diversity. Nationalism, Racism, and Exoticism in French Thought.* Translated by Catherine Porter. Cambridge, Mass., 1993.

Toomer, Jean. "Race Problems and Modern Society" (1929). Reprinted in Werner Sollors, ed., *Theories of Ethnicity,* New York, 1996, pp. 168–190.

Warner, W. Lloyd. *Yankee City Series: An Anthropological Study of a Modern New England Community,* 5 vols. New Haven, Conn., 1941–1959.

Weber, Max. *Economy and Society: An Outline of Interpretive Sociology.* Edited by Guenther Roth and Claus Wittich. Translated by Ephraim Fischoff et al. New York, 1968.

ETHNICITY AND RACE

Henry Yu

The term "ethnicity" gained widespread currency only in the mid- to late twentieth century. Ethnic consciousness, for instance, became the label for the process by which an individual or community came to understand themselves as separate or different from others. Ethnicity has also commonly referred to the actual group consciousness expressed by excluded or subordinated groups. By extension, ethnicity could describe the language, religion, social rituals, and other patterns of behavior that were defined as the content of a group's ethnic culture. Ethnic culture also came to define the set of material objects uniquely utilized by a particular ethnic group, so that ethnic goods became synonymous with the people who were members of that group or who practiced that culture.

Ethnicity as a category of experience was the historical product of mass migrations in the late nineteenth and early twentieth centuries to the United States. As an intellectual concept and a mode of social analysis, however, ethnicity was shaped by early-twentieth-century reformulations of social theory, in particular the rise of the concept of culture as a way of understanding social life. The spread of theories emphasizing differences in cultural consciousness (as distinct from descriptions of social differences based upon theories about biological race) was coincidental with a political shift among many American intellectuals between the 1920s and the 1940s toward what might be termed antiracism. Ethnicity as a social theory repudiated attempts to use the physical body to explain differences between people. Ethnic theory, as a branch of cultural theory, was an argument against claims that social conflicts were fixed because they resulted from immutable physical differences. For instance, in explaining how European immigrants with distinct social practices (such as language and religion) interacted in the United States, ethnic theory both described the creation of social conflict and prescribed ways of overcoming such differences. Such prescriptions were then applied to the problems of racial discrimination against African Americans, Asian Americans, and other people defined as nonwhite. However, at the same time that ethnicity as a theory offered hope for transcending race-based social hierarchies in American society, it also reformulated and reinforced a distinction between white and black in the United States, further exacerbating a false distinction between race as a physical trait and ethnicity as a cultural phenomenon.

PERIODIZATION OF INTELLECTUAL THEORIES ABOUT ETHNICITY

Ethnicity as both a lived experience and an intellectual concept has been profoundly shaped by the immigration history of the United States, which can be divided roughly into the period of open immigration before 1924, the era of immigration exclusion between 1924 and 1965, and the return to a more open immigration policy since 1965. The four decades of federal immigration exclusion between 1924 and 1965 were the aberration in U.S. history. At every other time, significant new migration to the nation has been the rule. Global labor migration and population displacement due to industrialization and colonization led to massive U.S. immigration in the late nineteenth and early twentieth centuries. An estimated thirty-five million new immigrants came to the United States in the century before immigration was curtailed in 1924, with the majority of them in the decades surrounding the turn of the century. By the 1920s American social scientists (some of whom were themselves either immigrants or children of immigrants) had created a body of theories defining "race" and "culture" that had grown out of this world of mass movement.

After the 1924 Johnson Act created restrictive national quotas that practically ended immigration from everywhere except northern and western Europe, a politically charged debate about the desirability of immigration slowly began to fade.

Nativism, a xenophobic popular movement that united a coalition of earlier migrants to the United States against more contemporary immigrants, had created a category of so-called "native" or "old stock" Americans. Characteristics such as Protestant Christianity were meant to distinguish these "natives" from recent Catholic immigrants (Italian in this period much more than earlier migrations from Ireland), from Orthodox Christians from southern and eastern Europe, and from Jewish émigrés fleeing eastern Europe and Russia. Language was also used as a defining characteristic in the differentiation of "old stock" from "new," since few of the recent immigrants spoke English as a first language. By midcentury, nativism had been blunted by decades of immigration exclusion. In the 1970s and 1980s, after the United States was re-opened to immigration, it was clear that the new groups of migrants and refugees were again from very different geographic origins than earlier waves; their visual appearance tied them to Asia, Latin America, Africa, and the Caribbean.

Theories about ethnicity served throughout the twentieth century as both a description and prescription for social life in the United States. In the period before 1924, questions about whether recent immigrants could be incorporated into the nation were answered with the theory of cultural assimilation. In the era of immigration exclusion between 1924 and 1965, theoretical claims about the parallel between race and ethnicity were an attempt to address an intellectual and social crisis concerning race relations. By the 1940s and 1950s, the transformation into "white ethnics" of people earlier considered racially inferior was at its height. Liberal social thinkers hoped that this process of cultural assimilation, considered a success with European immigrants, could be extended to seemingly nonwhite racial groups such as "Negroes" and "Orientals." Since the resumption of mass immigration in 1965, theories about ethnicity have been dominated by either the development and application of earlier theories about ethnicity (focusing in particular on its transitory nature), or theories about racial formation that challenge the primacy of ethnicity as a universal process and which often assert the intractable nature of racially defined social hierarchies. The problem of tying together race and ethnicity as unified social processes came to a crisis during this period, and debates over how to define ethnicity and ethnic consciousness continued to the end of the twentieth century.

At every stage, the increasing power of twentieth-century social science in defining, justifying, and implementing public policy, including educational curricula, carried these theories and debates into the realm of everyday American social life. Social scientists began to assert the need for scientific control of public policy during the era of Progressive reform between roughly 1890 and 1920, and they achieved their height of influence and funding at midcentury. Even with a decline in the power of social scientists to define public policy at the end of the twentieth century, the importance of social theorists in defining and justifying policy remained high.

THE RISE OF CULTURAL THEORY AS THE FOUNDATION FOR ETHNICITY

The genealogy of ethnicity as a concept can be traced to theories in the 1920s about the phenomenon of cultural consciousness. Although the term ethnicity was not commonly used before the 1940s, the categories of social phenomena that it purported to name had already been created as analytical concepts. A spate of social-scientific studies of immigration conducted in the first three decades of the twentieth century provided the theoretical foundation for the concept of ethnicity. Among the most significant of these studies were those by sociologists William I. Thomas and Robert E. Park and their associates at the University of Chicago. Thomas and his Polish colleague Florian Znaniecki wrote perhaps the most significant study of immigration of the period, their five-volume *The Polish Peasant in Europe and America* (1918–1920). Charting the changes that migration to the United States had wrought in individuals and communities, Thomas and Park went on to write another study, *Old World Traits Transplanted* (1921), which surveyed a myriad of European immigrant groups. Both Park and Thomas were at the forefront of an attempt among sociologists and anthropologists to advance a new theory about social interaction that was based upon the concept of culture. In opposition to earlier theories about the importance of racial or biological characteristics in determining human behavior, cultural theories emphasized the centrality of consciousness, of the mental attitudes and forms of self-understanding that people communicated through writing, speech, and other media.

The centrality of the formation of group consciousness became a key to later definitions of both race and ethnicity, de-emphasizing the analytical importance of physical ancestry. For instance, in many immigrant studies, social scientists noted that migrants coming to the United States did not have a strong sense of community or group consciousness until they had lived in their adopted country for a significant period. A large factor in the formation of group consciousness was a common exclusion from the host society. Ironically, so-called nativists enhanced the group consciousness of immigrants. By lumping together all Italians or all Armenians, for example, as a group to be kept out, the nativists helped reinforce a sense of solidarity within disparate groups that might not have felt much fellowship in their homeland. People whose self-identities were originally tied closely to their village or region began to feel stronger affinities to all of those in the United States who were purportedly of the same national origin. Of course, this sense of commonality in the United States was not merely a response to nativism. National independence movements back in their native lands, newly formed networks of trade and sociality, the formation of geographic and linguistic enclaves, media such as immigrant newspapers, and even a nostalgic sense of longing for the home country, also drew people together and created institutions and social practices unique to the United States. Thus, social scientists emphasized how arrival in their new country modified or completely changed the social practices of migrants. The importance of ancestry was de-emphasized in favor of processes of group formation in the United States.

One of the most important theories that Park and Thomas popularized concerned what they labeled cultural assimilation, the process by which two groups in contact communicated with each other and came to share common experiences, memories, and histories. Applied specifically to immigrants in the United States, the theory of assimilation promised that any migrant, no matter how different from other Americans in language, religion, or other social practices at the moment of landing, could learn to assimilate the cultural norms of other Americans. A progressive, inclusive vision of the United States, the assimilation theory became the foundation for later arguments about the nature of ethnic consciousness.

ETHNICITY VERSUS RACE

The conceptual split that defined race as a set of physical traits and culture as a form of consciousness is crucial for understanding later confusion about the difference between race and ethnicity. Race before the rise of the theory of culture was a much broader category, referring to a person's ancestral stock and including all traits, physical and behavioral, associated with membership in that race. To be of the Irish race in the nineteenth century, for instance, meant that one's ancestors hailed from Ireland, even if the individual had never been to Ireland. Descriptions of Irish racial characteristics encompassed social practices as well as physical features, and little analytical importance was attributed to the differentiation between behavioral and physical traits. The spread of a theory of culture, however, created two mutually exclusive categories that were analytically separate, with cultural traits utterly divorced from the workings of the physical body.

When anthropologists such as Franz Boas of Columbia University and sociologists and anthropologists from the University of Chicago began to teach students in the early twentieth century that cultural characteristics were the most interesting social phenomena for study, they at the same time spread the idea that any attention to physical characteristics was intellectually inappropriate. Arguing against eugenics programs that sterilized men and women deemed unfit for reproduction, and attacking justifications for racial hierarchy based upon biology, social scientists used the theory of culture as a weapon against racial thinking. In particular, sociologists such as Robert E. Park shifted the definition of race away from actual physical characteristics to the awareness of these physical traits, and thus made race a matter of consciousness. Thinking that a group of people was racially different and thus should be treated badly was a matter of prejudicial thought and attitude, and antiracism came to be defined as the elimination of such attitudes.

This shift of race from the physical to an awareness of the physical was crucial in creating a new category of analysis, what Park labeled racial or cultural consciousness. If a collection of individuals was seen to be different, and the individuals therefore came to understand themselves as different, then they could develop a group consciousness of themselves as a separate race or culture. The creation of the concept of cultural consciousness made possible the later definition of such categories as ethnic consciousness, self identity, and group identity. When W. Lloyd Warner, a prominent social scientist trained at Harvard and working at the University of Chicago, wrote a five-volume study called the Yankee City series between 1941 and 1959, he helped popularize the term ethnicity and enshrine it as a category of social experience, but the intellectual shifts that created ethnicity as an analytical category had been put in place decades earlier. In a similar manner to ethnicity, identity (another term not used by social scientists in the 1920s) was essentially a concept popularized in the 1950s by social psychologists such as Erik Erikson, but which commonly served as a label for the same processes by which self and group consciousness were formed.

The analytical power of cultural theories based upon consciousness resulted from their ability to tie together seemingly disparate phenomena under the same rubric. For instance, an emphasis upon consciousness of physical traits rather than the traits themselves explained racial passing, as with the passing as white of light-skinned children of people otherwise defined as black. At the same time, cultural theory also described the formation of group consciousness as immigrants formed ethnic communities, whereby migrants who might not have considered themselves alike before their arrival in the United States came to see each other as compatriots, both because they were lumped together by others and because of a newfound sense of being from the same place.

The subsuming of race under the broader category of ethnicity was a significant attempt to offer a solution to racial conflict. For instance, individuals whose skin color was dark enough for them to be considered nonwhite might be thought of as a different race, and thus treated as different. A group of "colored" people might then be formed, with its members coming to have a consciousness of themselves as a separate community, with lives very different from those who were considered white. The possibility for a self-consciously "black culture" meant that such a racial culture was just one variety of a larger spectrum of cultures, each of them defined by the act of self-consciousness (both on the part of individuals who considered themselves members of a group, and of the group as a whole considering itself a separate community). As a matter of consciousness, the racial culture of African Americans was no different in kind than the ethnic culture of Polish Americans, and purely cultural processes of assimilation could eliminate the differences between white and nonwhite.

Robert E. Park was the primary theorist of this attempt to solve what was labeled the "Negro Problem" with the seemingly successful model of culturally assimilated European immigrants. Interestingly, the bridge for Park was Asian migrants on the West Coast. As a nonwhite racial group, Asian Americans were commonly understood as an "Oriental Problem," just as African Americans were seen to be a "Negro Problem." As immigrants, however, Asian Americans could provide an analytical example that tied racial difference to the predominantly white European migration that cultural assimilation theory analyzed. In a large-scale research program of the 1920s and 1930s, Park and other sociologists from the University of Chicago attempted to prove that Chinese American and Japanese American immigrants were just as successful as European immigrants in assimilating the culture of older-stock Americans. The reward for such a project was to tie race and ethnicity under the same rubric of cultural theory. Earlier definitions of race had counted a myriad of groups as racially different, from Irish to Jewish to Negro. Cultural theory redefined race to mean only those groups that could not merely change behavior to lose themselves within a newly expanding category of white. African Americans and Asian Americans were thus the two most prominent groups that were now being defined as racially different in a new way.

Antiracist theories often used ethnicity as an alternative term to escape the biological emphases of racial hierarchy. In *Man's Most Dangerous Myth: The Fallacy of Race* (1945), one of the most significant antiracist books published in the twentieth century, anthropologist Ashley Montagu argued that race as a category of analysis should be dropped as a dangerous invention, and that "ethnic group" was a more neutral term. Ethnicity became synonymous with cultural difference, and any theory dependent upon physical characteristics was dismissed as racist. Similarly, the attempt by anthropologists such as Ruth Benedict to array all societies as a spectrum of different cultures aided in the flattening of all human distinction into a matter of cultural or ethnic difference. In her book, *Patterns of Culture* (1934), Benedict advanced a model of cultural relativism that attacked the use of physical differences between bodies as a basis for analyzing human societies. The possibilities for the elimination of racial prejudice (defined specifically as the expression of conscious attitudes about a group of people considered racially different, even if the actual existence of physical race was an illusion) depended upon a very specific definition of race as a form of consciousness. Race was a myth because it had no basis in biology, yet race as a consciousness about the importance of a set of physical attributes could still exist. But because consciousness of race was claimed to be merely one form of ethnic consciousness, race and ethnicity were concepts both distinct and indistinct from each other.

There were chronic difficulties with the distinction between race and ethnicity. W. Lloyd Warner's categorization in the 1940s of the varieties of ethnic groups, a development of earlier sociological studies of immigrants, embodied the paradox inherent in this phenomenological conception of race and ethnicity. In the third volume of the Yankee City series, *The Social Systems of American Ethnic Groups* (1945), Warner and Leo Srole argued, in a section called "The American Ethnic Group," for a difference between ethnicity and race. The host society that viewed racial and ethnic groups as different accepted some ethnic groups more easily than others. Class differences tended to fragment ethnic groups, and the class mobility of some members of ethnic groups was the major determinant of acceptance within the host society. Most difficult to accept, however, were those groups seen to be racially different. At the same time that Warner and Srole argued that group conflict was a matter of ethnic identification (in the sense that the host society viewed a group as different, and the group viewed itself as different), they also assumed that there was some characteristic that set apart ethnic groups that were racially defined. Indeed, the consciousness of biological differences that theoretically made a group only seem racially different was commonly analyzed as if the biological differences really did exist.

Like many theorists of ethnicity, Warner and Srole were caught by the limitations of cultural theory. Ethnicity as a matter of culture offered hope for the cultural assimilation of all ethnic groups, but even if an awareness of racial difference was a matter of consciousness and therefore could be overcome through the processes of cultural change and exchange, the racial formations built around the color hierarchy in the United States seemed intractable. If ethnicity was limited to cultural traits rather than what seemed to be obvious physical differences, then race and ethnicity would have to be separate phenomena analytically. Ethnicity was a category in practice limited to those who could visually pass as white. Clarifying this distinction between ethnicity as white and race as nonwhite, Warner and Srole concluded at the end of *The Social Systems of American Ethnic Groups* that the "future of American ethnic groups seems to be limited; it is likely that they will be quickly absorbed. When this happens one of the great epochs of American history will have ended and another, that of race, will begin." (p. 295).

ETHNICITY AND THE EXPANSION OF THE CATEGORY OF WHITE

The sense that a great epoch of ethnicity was about to end at midcentury was a product of a crucial social transformation in the decades following immigration exclusion. The twentieth-century alchemy of race, as described recently by historian Matthew Frye Jacobson, lay in how European immigrants, defined at the beginning of the century as racially different, came to be seen as white ethnics by the end of the century. The crucial period was the two decades following the 1924 exclusion acts. Along with the intellectual transformation wrought by cultural theory, popular writers such as Louis Adamic, who was himself of recent immigrant ancestry, pushed for an overcoming of the nativist divide between old and new Americans. In books such as *From Many Lands* (1940) and *A Nation of Nations* (1945), Adamic reconceived the United States as a land of immigrants, subsuming what had earlier been major dividing lines such as religion and language by arguing that they were mere differences of ethnic culture. In the journal *Common Ground*, published in the 1940s by the Common Council of American Unity (which Adamic helped found), he stated what many liberal intellectuals were calling for at the time: "We need to work toward a synthesis of the old stock and the new immigrant America" (*Common Ground*, autumn 1940, p. 66). Organizations such as the National Council of Christians and Jews, founded in 1928, were creating support for the unification of Protestants, Catholics, Orthodox Christians, and Jews into a so-called Judeo-Christian tradition, and arguments for the end of religious discrimination were becoming widespread, perhaps most visibly in 1950s Hollywood motion pictures such as *The Ten Commandments* (1956) and *Ben-Hur* (1959).

The focus upon the assimilation of religious differences, powerfully propelled by wartime propaganda against the genocidal science of Nazism, helped lessen anti-Semitism and anti-Catholicism in the 1940s. By the end of the 1950s class mobility, fueled by the postwar GI Bill and federal subsidies of suburban housing, had made Adamic's dream of an amalgamation of new and old seem viable. The effects of such programs of social engineering, however, were predominantly focused upon male Americans able to pass as white. Immigrants who had been treated in the period between 1890 and 1920 as racially different (Slavs, Jews, and southern Europeans such as Italians, Greeks, and Armenians) were now transformed into white ethnics, mere varieties of the so-called Caucasoid race. The continuing problem of race and color that W. Lloyd Warner described was left firmly upon those who remained nonwhite, specifically persons labeled as being in the Negroid or Mongoloid race. In fact, the lingering significance of color was one of the by-products of the successful amalgamation of "new stock" European immigrants into Caucasian whiteness. Just as dividing lines over religion, which had seemed intractable a generation before, were now reduced to mere denominational differences, all culturally defined elements of difference had disappeared into a generic whiteness marked only superficially by vestiges of ethnic culture.

The creation of the concept of a Caucasian race expanded the category of white and extended the social and legal privileges of white supremacy to a host of immigrant families that had theretofore been excluded. Ironically, the civil rights movement of the 1950s helped reinforce this process of ethnic transformation. Jewish American intellectuals of the 1930s and 1940s—such as social scientist Louis Wirth, a German Jewish immigrant teaching at the University of Chicago and a member of the National Council of Christians and Jews—had been at the forefront of political coalitions with African Americans seeking civil rights. The two groups faced discrimination and exclusion at work and were impacted by the legal segregation of housing, public facilities, and social institutions. This had drawn Jewish Americans and black Americans together to fight for civil rights. However, paralleling the larger transformation of white ethnics, Jewish Americans by the end of the civil rights era in the 1970s had become solidly white, even if anti-Semitism remained in vestigial and virulent forms.

In many ways, the political and social process of civil rights helped reinforce the lumping together of formerly nonwhite ethnic groups into the larger pantheon of whiteness. The ways in which some of the popular rhetoric of civil rights struggle helped transform white ethnicity were clear in the impact of Gunnar Myrdal's landmark study, *An American Dilemma* (1944). It was commissioned by the Carnegie Corporation Foundation as a comprehensive survey of American race relations, and was heavily dependent upon research conducted into the "Negro Problem" by intellectuals associated with Robert E. Park at the University of Chicago, in particular by prominent African American sociologists and writers such as Charles S. Johnson, E. Franklin Frazier, Horace R. Cayton, and St. Clair Drake.

Myrdal's study argued that the racial problems of the United States were caused not by the existence of minority races, but by the prejudice and discrimination of white Americans. Labeling white supremacy as the dilemma that undermined the "American creed" of equality, democracy, and justice, Myrdal's description of race relations helped galvanize popular support for civil rights. However, since arguments about the problem of race drew attention to the ways that white supremacy structured almost every moment of the daily lives of nonwhites, one of the results was that the intellectual conception of a singular white America was further solidified. Ironically, the civil rights movement for blacks ended up helping to amalgamate into this new conception of ethnic whiteness immigrant groups that previously had been the targets of racial nativism.

ETHNICITY AS THE HISTORICAL PRODUCT OF MIGRATION

A key to the strategy for theoretically transforming ethnicity into a universal process was the redefinition of all Americans as migrants. Ironically, this redefinition occurred during the exclusion period between 1924 and 1965, when legal immigration to the United States was sharply curtailed. Becoming popular in the 1940s and 1950s with the writings of historians Marcus Lee Hansen and Oscar and Mary Handlin, the epic narrative of American history as a story of migrants made every individual currently in the nation the historical product of the same universal cycle of departure and arrival. Ultimately a triumphant tale of progress, the difficulties suffered by immigrants in any given historical period were relegated to an initial period of adjustment to a new world. Handlin himself directed a number of graduate student dissertations at Harvard that expanded on this theme, and by the 1960s a significant number of historians around the nation had focused on immigration as the central theme of U.S. history. As in the social scientific studies on immigrants decades earlier, these histories of immigration took European migration as the model, in particular what was labeled the "great migrations" of the late nineteenth century. Even if not all migrants had experienced similar adjustments, the epic story professed universal application. Each migrant group created its own ethnic culture, distinct yet the product of the same general process of incorporation into the greater body of American society.

114

This depiction of the United States as a nation of immigrants has powerfully shaped scholarly and popular conceptions of American history. Even when scholars have attempted to move beyond its Eurocentric focus by comprehensively including non-Europeans into their studies, as in *Ethnicity in the United States* (1974) by Andrew Greeley, they have only partially succeeded in extending to universal applicability the experience of immigration. Were Native Indians the first immigrants, having crossed the Bering Strait thirty thousand years before in the same manner that the Mayflower crossed the Atlantic? Even more difficult to assimilate has been the forced migration of enslaved captives from Africa, sold against their will into a life of labor in the New World. Even counternarratives of U.S. history that have focused upon non-European migration have often served to replicate the grand narrative of coming to America, as in historian Ronald Takaki's popular history of Asian American migration, *Strangers from a Different Shore* (1990).

THE EMBRACE OF ETHNICITY

Despite formidable intellectual problems in expanding the application of migration as a universal process, ethnicity as a description and as a prescription for social life in the United States has continued to be widespread. Indeed, the acceptance and eventual celebration of ethnic difference was one of the most significant developments during the twentieth century. Coincidental with the increasing awareness of migration at the beginning of the century, the rise of a cosmopolitan appreciation of exotic difference was associated with intellectuals such as Randolph Bourne and Horace Kallen. Writing in the days before World War I, a number of the New York intelligentsia embraced the rich diversity of the city, forecasting that the eclectic mix of migrants from Europe, Asia, and the American South was the future of U.S. society. Bourne's vision of a "transnational America" and Kallen's description of "cultural pluralism" argued against the xenophobia of nativists, replacing it with toleration and acceptance of the different.

The racially exotic were defined as valuable and positive contributions to American society. The consumption of the music and art of the Harlem Renaissance that flourished in the 1920s, along with periodic fads for Oriental art and so-called primitive tribal objects, reflected an elite white embrace of the exotic. As historian T. J. Jackson Lears has argued in *No Place of Grace* (1981), American elites

since the beginning of the industrial age in the late nineteenth century had searched the mystical, mythic Orient and the simplicity of primitive savagery for answers to a growing sense of spiritual vacuum. Both Orientalism and primitivism were outgrowths of a desire for the "different" that would answer questions about an eroding self. Chinese and Japanese watercolors and vases were tastefully collected alongside African tribal carvings. In New York City in particular, the travel of elite intellectuals into the exotic spaces of Harlem uptown and Chinatown and Little Italy downtown were the spatial embodiment of their desire to sample and experience the exotic. Their extolling of such exoticism in theories about the cosmopolitan self laid the groundwork for two major developments concerning ethnicity. The first was the theoretical foundation for the eventual commercialization of ethnic difference; the second was the creation of a new definition of elite, enlightened whiteness.

As ethnic identity has proliferated through the twentieth century, it has also increasingly become commodified as a commercial product. Beginning with the fascination with exotic art forms expressed in modernism, but also embodied in the hunger for ethnic food and objects, a tasteful appreciation of the exotically different that began with cosmopolitan elites became part of an educational program to combat racism and ignorance that began in the 1920s but only came to fruition in the 1960s. Education was being touted as the answer to racial problems in the later decade. At the same time, ethnic music and other forms of exotic art and entertainment were offered, at first as alternatives to the mass productions of popular culture; by the 1990s, however, they had become important commodities distributed and consumed in the marketplace.

Interestingly, the rise and spread of a cosmopolitan embrace of exotic difference helped expand the boundaries of whiteness. One of the ways in which those formerly excluded as racially or ethnically suspect could become good whites was by embracing cosmopolitan ideas. Those who continued to express racist opinions became subsumed under the newly enlarged rubric of white racists (a category that strangely whitened former ethnics at the same time that it tarred them as ignorant, unenlightened bigots of the lower classes). The embrace of cosmopolitan ideals during the exclusion period was a way of becoming an elite, enlightened white. Whether it was black music or Chinese food, an appreciation of exotic difference served as one of the pathways to a higher class status. The successful spread of the idea that while ignorance of other cultures was a lower class phenomenon, expertise about exotic cultures was a mark of elite status, was accomplished through the educational system starting in the 1940s. Occurring at precisely the moment that higher education expanded to include working-class white ethnics, these lessons in the enlightened appreciation of cultural difference equated aspirations for class mobility with antiracism.

The process by which ethnicity has been defined as a valuable object links its creation as a scholarly object of interest to its transformation into a commercial object with value. When Stephan Thernstrom completed the *Harvard Encyclopedia of Ethnic Groups* (1980), a project begun by immigration historian Oscar Handlin, the comprehensive tome epitomized the academic genre that collected and organized information about a vast array of ethnic cultures. Written for a learned audience from the point of view of the scholarly collector of knowledge concerning exotic cultural groups, the encyclopedia surveyed the rituals, religious beliefs, traditional costumes, and everyday social life of ethnic groups. Ethnicity was an object to be collected and consumed by enlightened readers. In the same way, cosmopolitan patterns of consumption created the ideal of a tasteful, enlightened consumer able to appreciate an array of objects marked by ethnic differences.

The commercialization of ethnicity also allowed those defined as being different to turn their exotic identification into an object with value. In music, for instance, styles such as rhythm and blues, rock and roll, soul, rap, and hip-hop were marketed by an association with their black origins. By the 1970s the commercialization of ethnicity also extended to those ethnics formerly the target of xenophobia but now comfortably white. White ethnics could continue to express cosmopolitan appreciation for the exoticism of nonwhites, but they could now also embrace signs of their own ethnicity without fear of exclusion from the privileges of whiteness. White ethnicity was securely different from nonwhite racial ethnicity, and white ethnics drew upon a history of being victims of discrimination in ways that both attenuated their own enjoyment of the privileges of being white and consciously paralleled the historical suffering of nonwhites.

Near the end of the twentieth century, objects associated with ethnicity enjoyed a popular boom as commercial goods. Ethnic objects that had assumed the status of collectible art (such as African tribal masks and Native American totem poles), items of everyday use (such as Chinese woks and chopsticks or Scottish tartan kilts), and performances of identity that could be consumed (ethnic music and dance) were all packaged as desirable objects of consumption. As the marketing of ethnicity has expanded, however, the seemingly universal embrace of ethnic culture has obscured the lingering legacies of social structures in determining social difference and hierarchy.

ARGUMENTS AGAINST ETHNICITY AS A CULTURAL PHENOMENON

In the 1960s theories such as sociologist Milton Gordon's "structural assimilation" moved social analyses away from their emphasis upon cultural assimilation and group identity. The work of Gordon and others addressed the inability of many Americans identified with ethnic and racial ancestry, no matter how culturally assimilated they behaved, to achieve entrance into exclusive social institutions (for instance, country clubs or positions of power in corporate boardrooms). Gordon explained the tendency of organizations to reproduce themselves socially and to embrace as new members only those already socially tied to existing members. Social structures operated in ways that cultural theories describing ethnic identity could not adequately explain. Even if an outsider looked and behaved the same as someone already a part of an institution, the seeming "progress" of cultural assimilation did not align at all times with what Gordon now described as "social assimilation," the actual inclusion of new and diverse members in existing institutions.

Since Gordon's explication of social assimilation in the early 1960s, the state of thinking about processes of identity formation have been dominated either by the development and refinement of earlier theories about ethnicity as a process dominated by cultural consciousness and assimilation (as in, for instance, the works of Herbert Gans and Nathan Glazer), or by theories about racial formation that challenge the primacy of ethnicity as a universal process (for instance, work on racial formation by Michael Omi and Howard Winant). Emphases such as Gordon's upon the actual diversification of social institutions provided intellectual justification for many women and racial minorities to insist that public policy legally challenge organizations not taking positive steps to include members previously excluded.

116

POST-1965 CHALLENGES TO ETHNIC THEORY

As the demography of the United States changed with new, post-1965 immigration, understandings of immigration changed as well. During the four decades after immigration exclusion, migration to many Americans consisted of the memories of parents or grandparents. Assimilation theory and vast social programs had succeeded in creating a heterogeneous white ethnicity that promised to erase most markers of cultural difference, in particular among American-born children. Remembrance of an ethnic past seemed to be a choice for many. The application of ethnic theory to black-white race relations was intellectually promising, although many questioned its potential. However, because a large proportion of post-1965 migrants came from Asia, Latin America, Africa, and the Caribbean, and because of social changes wrought by the civil rights movement, debates over race came to dominate discussions of ethnicity. In particular, questions about the intractability of racial subordination in both historical and contemporary settings became the crux of disagreement.

At the core of debates over ethnicity has been the question of the applicability of assimilation as a process that extends to Americans identified as non-white. In 1975, for instance, Nathan Glazer argued that America had an ever-increasing capacity to absorb successive waves of ethnic groups, and that the same process that had seemingly allowed every immigrant group to become American (after an obligatory period of subordination and discrimination) would continue to serve as an adequate social process of inclusion. His study, a development of earlier assimilation theories claiming that ethnicity was the same for "blacks and Orientals, Jews and Catholics, Indians and Mexican Americans," served also as an argument against the need for legal interventions such as affirmative action. (See Ronald Takaki, *From Different Shores,* 1987, for a collection containing various arguments, including Glazer's, about affirmative action as one of the solutions for problems of race and ethnicity.)

Among Glazer's examples was that of Chinese Americans. Vilified to the extent of becoming in 1882 the first group of American migrants to be excluded on the basis of race, they nevertheless, according to Glazer, had over time become acceptable as Americans. The use of Asian Americans (commonly referred to as "Orientals" before the 1970s) as an ethnic success story had begun during the 1950s, as social scientists criticized the internment during World War II of 120,000 Japanese Americans (two-thirds of whom were native-born American citizens) by asserting their hyperassimilated quality and successful citizenry. By the 1960s, as civil unrest spread among African Americans dissatisfied with second-class status, this "model minority" theory was increasingly used as an argument against political interventions to solve racial inequity. The seemingly natural social process of ethnicity, some said, should be enough to transform society. As with Park's theories about cultural assimilation in the 1920s, Asian migrants played a crucial role in attempts to overcome the problem of a visually nonwhite identity in theories about ethnicity.

By the 1980s many social theorists were addressing the fear that the theoretical and social experiment to subsume all differences into ethnicity, and thus defuse race, might fail. Sociologist Thomas Sowell admitted in *Ethnic America* (1981) that the "road to pluralism and cosmopolitanism has been long and rocky," but reaffirmed the relentless progress of ethnic assimilation. "Ethnic groups themselves have changed in ways that made their acceptance easier," Sowell argued, and if there were various obstructions to the integration of racially marked ethnic groups, they could be overcome (p. 9). Sociologist Nathan Glazer blamed the potential for failure on the continuing subordination of and consequent unrest among blacks. In the early 1980s Glazer wrote that the "ethnic analogy" seemed to be losing ground among "black youth." He expressed his fear that this would lead to a slippery slope by which other racialized groups (Mexican American, Puerto Rican, American Indian, and what he labeled "relatively prosperous Oriental communities") might lose faith in the assimilation process of ethnic America. Even the "white ethnic groups," Glazer prophesized, might begin to "reflect on their experiences and position in American society and perhaps to decide that they too are subject to insupportable deprivation and that the American ethnic system has failed" (*Ethnic Dilemmas,* p. 92). Glazer reasserted the overall promise of ethnic assimilation, however, so long as a group did not try to maintain too separate an identity or demand formal political solutions such as affirmative action.

The importance of Asian Americans as a key to arguments such as Glazer's also exposed the limitations of ethnic theory. First and foremost was a misapprehension of the periodization of migration. Connecting early migrants who had survived the virulent anti-Asian discrimination of the late nineteenth and first half of the twentieth century with completely different groups of Asian American migrants arriving after 1965 was analytically suspect. The highly educated migrants from Taiwan, Hong Kong, the Philippines, India, and Pakistan who arrived after 1965 were not forced to overcome the discriminatory anti-Asian legislation and violence of early migrant groups. Similarly, the first wave of refugees from Vietnam after the end of American intervention in Southeast Asia in 1975 contained highly educated, upper-class professional and political elites whose family backgrounds helped them succeed in the United States. Other migrant groups from Asia, such as Hmong refugees from Cambodia and many Pacific Islander groups, were absent from the claims of an Asian model minority because their statistics for economic and educational attainment did not support such arguments. The common erasure of differences between the historical experience of Asian migrants before and after 1965, and between different classes of migrants within national groups, was crucial to portrayals of Asian Americans as a successful ethnic group. The monolithic portrayal of Asians generalized, just as all definitions of ethnic culture did, a singular cultural experience when there were varying experiences. Significant numbers of Asian American migrants and refugees did not do well and continued to struggle in the United States. The perception that Asians as a group had bootstrapped themselves to success in the United States belied a complex mix of reasons for the educational and economic achievements of certain Asian Americans. Racial distinctiveness, continuing structures of racial subordination, and a lingering sense of Asians as somehow foreign (no matter how long and for how many generations they have lived in the United States) continue to mark Americans of Asian ancestry in ways that white ethnics are not.

CONCLUSION

The central place of whiteness in the history of ethnicity has had long-term consequences. Ethnic theory derived its popular appeal from the combination of two elements. On the one hand was the description of how European immigrants were transformed into white ethnics during the mid-twentieth century; on the other hand was the hope that this social process would also work for Americans subordinated as nonwhite. The extension of what Nathan Glazer called the "ethnic analogy" to the problems of racial hierarchy, however, has often

foundered intellectually because of a widespread belief that ethnicity was somehow voluntary, an act of individual volition. This mistake was the direct result of the way ethnicity was modeled upon the extension of whiteness to those who could erase signs of their foreign origins. A definition of ethnicity as a matter of choice has been implied in many analyses of American social life. Historians such as David Hollinger and Arthur Schlesinger Jr., who echoed in the 1990s earlier theories that an overly separate ethnic identity was detrimental to American society, relied on the conception of ethnic culture as somehow being a choice. Both argued that cosmopolitan perspectives provided answers to overt ethnicity, shifting the burden of social dysfunction away from institutional structures that reinforced racial inequities, and toward those "ethnic" individuals and groups whom they asserted had chosen to remain separate.

The ideal of ethnicity as a choice was based upon the historical amalgamation of European immigrants into a common whiteness; the process seemed a forgetting of past ancestry. (It did not matter whether one was of Jewish, Irish, or Italian descent.) However, consciousness of race based upon physical characteristics that suggest a nonwhite ancestry remains widespread in practice, even if in the science of biology racial categories have been found to be fallacious. At the beginning of the twenty-first century, the ever-increasing number of migrants from Mexico and Latin America encapsulate best the complicated ways in which ethnicity operates both as a process of racial formation and as a market phenomenon. Beginning in the 1920s and 1930s, Mexican immigration was increasingly seen on the West Coast as a problem. Racialization of Spanish-speaking immigrants, however, has always been complicated. Since migrants from the rest of the Americas embody the complex global admixtures of Native, European, African, and Asian ancestry that have also marked North American history, attempts to encapsulate such migrants into a single category have reflected the same difficulties that all racialization incurs. Although these migrants are stratified by distinctions in skin color, class status, and country of origin, there have nevertheless been marked attempts to envision a unified ethnic Hispanic America. Such attempts have utilized the concept of ethnicity as a marketing tool, in particular an awareness of the Spanish language as a distinct cultural unifier. But beyond entertainment and other forms of ethnic objectification that have defined the seeming wholism of other forms of ethnicity in the market, it remains to be seen how ethnic consciousness will develop. In particular, issues of racial differentiation remain operative. Within the vast spectrum of Spanish-speaking migrants to the United States, some will find it relatively easy to pass as white, whereas for others linguistic differences will be less salient than a visual identification of them as having nonwhite ancestry.

The ideal that enlightened, educated individuals can will themselves to transcend their own consciousness of race or ethnicity remains widespread. Yet, most social theorists of ethnicity since the days of W. Lloyd Warner have struggled to explain the ubiquitous social effects of racial hierarchies in American society. Even as the boundaries that historically defined who was of which race shifted and changed through time and between places, beliefs in the existence of boundaries based upon physical features, and the social consequences of such racial beliefs have stubbornly remained. As new immigration continues to change the demography of the United States, both popular conceptions and scholarly theories about ethnicity and race will be profoundly shaped by the constant presence of recently arrived immigrants, and ideas about ethnicity formed in the aberrational period of immigration exclusion will be left in the dustbin of history.

See also **Multiculturalism in Theory and Practice; Working Class; Anthropology and Cultural Relativism** *(volume 2);* **Cultural Studies** *(in this volume); and other articles in this section.*

BIBLIOGRAPHY

Adamic, Louis. *From Many Lands.* New York, 1940.

——. *A Nation of Nations.* New York, 1945.

Bell, David A. "The Triumph of Asian-Americans." *The New Republic,* 15 and 22 July 1985, 24–31.

Benedict, Ruth. *Patterns of Culture.* Boston, 1934.

Brodkin, Karen. *How Jews Became White Folks and What That Says about America.* New Brunswick, N.J., 1998.

Daniels, Roger. *Coming to America: A History of Immigration and Ethnicity in American Life.* New York, 1990.

Glazer, Nathan. *Affirmative Discrimination: Ethnic Inequality and Public Policy.* New York, 1975.

——. *Ethnic Dilemmas, 1964–1982.* Cambridge, Mass., 1983.

Glazer, Nathan, and Daniel Patrick Moynihan. *Beyond the Melting Pot: The Negroes, Puerto Ricans, Jews, Italians, and Irish of New York City.* Cambridge, Mass., 1963.

Greeley, Andrew. *Ethnicity in the United States: A Preliminary Reconnaissance.* New York, 1974.

Handlin, Oscar. *The Uprooted: The Epic Story of the Great Migrations That Made the American People.* Boston, 1951.

——. *Immigration As a Factor in American History.* Englewood Cliffs, N.J., 1959.

Hansen, Marcus Lee. *The Atlantic Migration, 1607–1860: A History of the Continuing Settlement of the United States.* Cambridge, Mass., 1940.

Hollinger, David. *Postethnic America: Beyond Multiculturalism.* New York, 1995.

Jacobson, Matthew Frye. *Whiteness of a Different Color: European Immigrants and the Alchemy of Race.* Cambridge, Mass., 1998.

Lay, Larry. *The Big Tomorrow: Hollywood and the Politics of the American Way.* Chicago, 2000.

Lears, T. J. Jackson. *No Place of Grace: Antimodernism and the Transformation of American Culture, 1880–1920.* New York, 1981.

Montagu, Ashley. *Man's Most Dangerous Myth: The Fallacy of Race.* New York, 1945.

Myrdal, Gunnar. *An American Dilemma: The Negro Problem and American Democracy.* New York, 1944.

Novak, Michael. *The Rise of the Unmeltable Ethnics.* New York, 1972.

Omi, Michael, and Howard Winant. *Racial Formation in the United States: From the 1960s to the 1980s.* New York, 1986.

Park, Robert Ezra. *Race and Culture: The Collected Papers of Robert Ezra Park.* Edited by Everett C. Hughes, et al. Glencoe, Ill., 1950.

Peterson, William. *Japanese-Americans: Oppression and Success.* New York, 1971.

Schlesinger, Arthur, Jr. *The Disuniting of America.* New York, 1992.

Sollors, Werner. *Beyond Ethnicity: Consent and Descent in American Culture.* New York, 1986.

Sowell, Thomas. *Ethnic America: A History.* New York, 1981.

Takaki, Ronald. *Strangers from a Different Shore: A History of Asian Americans.* Boston, 1990.

Takaki, Ronald, ed. *From Different Shores: Perspectives on Race and Ethnicity in America.* New York, 1987.

Thernstrom, Stephan. *Harvard Encyclopedia of American Ethnic Groups.* Cambridge, Mass., 1980.

Thomas, William I., and Florian Znanieki. *The Polish Peasant in Europe and America.* 5 vols. Boston, 1918–1920.

Warner, W. Lloyd, and Leo Srole. *The Social Systems of American Ethnic Groups.* New Haven, Conn., 1945.

Warner, W. Lloyd, et al. *Yankee City.* Abridged ed. New Haven, Conn., 1963.

Yu, Henry. *Thinking Orientals: Migration, Contact, and Exoticism in Modern America.* New York, 2001.

RACE

Mia Bay

"Race and races are American history," Matthew Frye Jacobson has written. "To write about race is to exclude virtually nothing" (*Whiteness of a Different Color*, p. 11). As Jacobson indicates, ideas about race have figured prominently in American politics and culture from the beginning of European settlement onward. Yet the nature of these ideas has not remained stable over time. A conception of human differences used to divide up the world's peoples, race has held a wide variety of social, legal, political, and scientific meanings in the course of American history.

In recent years Americans have begun to understand race as a social and ideological construction rather than as a natural phenomenon. But throughout the nineteenth century, and for much of the twentieth century, most Americans understood race as an objective scientific classification of human variation. Furthermore, prior to the advent of biological conception of mankind that shaped such classifications, race meant something different still: early uses of the word "race," which first appeared in European languages in the late Middle Ages, invoked concepts such as kinship, lineage, and blood ties.

The changing meanings attached to the idea of race underscore the fact that race is a concept that can only be understood historically. Accordingly, the relatively recent rejection of biological conceptions of race does not allow us to abandon race as an outmoded scientific fallacy. On the contrary, the modern-day understandings of race as a cultural creation—rather than as an accurate description of the reality and complexities of human variation—have challenged scholars to map the historical construction of racial categories. Such efforts have been particularly central to American history, where ideas about race loom large in a national history shaped by slavery, segregation, and continuing racial divisions and inequities. Indeed, a brief review of the story of the settlement of British North America and the formation of the United States can illustrate both the development of racial ideology and the various meanings of race.

Central to the story is the fact that the settlement of the New World and the development of racial ideology were linked from the outset. The idea of race took shape during the era of Western economic expansion that led European traders to Africa and the Far East and fueled European exploration of the New World. Encountering new and distinctive populations in these areas, European travelers used the concept of race to describe and categorize these groups. In doing so they referred not to biological or cultural conceptions of race, which both lay in the future, but rather to one based on lineage. Possibly derived from animal husbandry, early European uses of the word "race" centered on descent, breeding, and bloodlines: races were people of the same "stock." This lineage-based conception of race reflected the social realities of early modern Europe, where an individual's political power, class status, and economic entitlements were determined largely by descent.

However, this idea of race slowly altered as it was applied to non-European groups within the context of European colonization. The concept of lineage helped organize new schemes of racial organization that took shape in European colonies by virtue of its articulation of a system of inherited entitlements and privileges. But within the context of colonialism, lineage-based conceptions of race eventually gave way to new ones that put far less emphasis on family ties. In time, skin color and other physical characteristics, rather than lineage, became the mark of a given people's common substance.

THE ORIGINS DEBATE

How and when skin color and physical characteristics became the basis for racial organization remains one of the major questions in the history of racial thought. While scholars tend to agree that race is a modern phenomenon, the question of when color prejudice originated is by no means settled. Conceivably, distinctions made on the basis of color differences could have predated any notion of racial groupings. People could have had other reasons to be ill-disposed toward human beings whose complexions differed greatly from their own.

In particular, historians have long speculated about whether antiblack sentiment preceded the rise of racial slavery or arose as a consequence of that development. On the European side such questions are complicated by a history of interactions between European and African peoples that dates back to antiquity. Not all of these interactions were marked by European hostility toward the latter. Indeed, classicists seem to agree that the xenophobic Greeks held Africans in no greater disdain than any other foreign peoples.

Antiblack prejudices may well have emerged as early as the ninth century among the Muslims who then ruled the Iberian Peninsula. Within the context of the Muslim slave trade, European slaves were worth more than their African counterparts because they could command Christian ransoms or be exchanged for Muslim captives. By contrast, African slaves were valued primarily for their labor and employed in the most menial occupations. As a consequence, their skin color became associated with a low social status.

The extent to which such prejudices spread to the Christian world, however, is difficult to assess, since Christian Europeans saw both the Muslims and their black slaves as dark-skinned infidels. Certainly, early European images of Africans were by no means uniformly negative. Fourteenth- and fifteenth-century European representations of Africans include flattering depictions of African kings and rulers, as well as a recurring image of a black man as one of the New Testament's Three Wise Men—portrayed in fifteenth-century European art as a pious and wealthy African. However, this period also saw images of Africans as evil infidels—devils, executioners, and tormentors of Christ.

Given this mixture of evidence on how Christian Europeans saw Africans, the relationship between antiblack imagery and the development of racial slavery remains a matter of debate. Looking at slavery in a North American context, especially, historians have asked, Which came first, slavery or color prejudice? Attempts to answer this question have most often focused on colonial Virginia.

The first mainland British colony to adopt slavery, Virginia has long provided fascinating terrain for historians interested in the origins of slavery and racial prejudice. The colony imported its first slaves in 1619, when Jamestown colonists purchased twenty Africans brought in on a Dutch trading vessel. But Virginia did not enact slave laws until the 1660s and 1670s. Moreover, the status of the colony's early African residents is hard to determine. It is by no means clear that the colony's African residents were enslaved prior to the codification of slavery. On the contrary, starting with Oscar and Mary Handlin in the 1950s (for example, "Origins of the Southern Labor System"), some historians have argued that these Africans initially retained their liberty in a society where bondage had no legal or traditional standing—since slavery no longer existed in the colonists' homeland. Rather than being enslaved, early Afro-Virginians were servants and held the same status as English laborers who traveled to the colony under indentures. Like indentured servants, African bondsmen were bound to service but not for life and shared most of the same rights and responsibilities as other Virginians.

According to the Handlins' interpretation of Virginia history, racial slavery did not emerge in the colony until the 1660s and 1670s, as the status of black servants declined in relation to that of whites. In the face of a growing labor shortage, white Virginians began to hold black servants for life, while at the same time offering English laborers shorter and shorter indentures to attract these voluntary migrants to Virginia. Blacks became slaves, and their low condition was soon associated with their color, which also offered white Virginians an easy means of distinguishing between their free and unfree populations. Seen in this light, Africans fell victim to racial slavery because they provided colonies such as Virginia with a convenient source of labor and proved more vulnerable to European exploitation than the colonists' own countrymen. But they did not encounter racial prejudice from the outset; rather, racial prejudice developed as a consequence of slavery.

The Handlins' thesis has been opposed by a variety of commentators who insist that English biases against blacks predate both the codification of Virginia's slave laws and the colony's settlement. Starting with Carl Degler, who published his rebuttal to the Handlins in 1959, the Handlins' critics have insisted that Afro-Virginians ranked lower than white servants from the start. Their terms of service were longer; they were subject to legal punishments different from those for whites; and they were treated differently along gender lines (for example, black women were taxed as potential field workers, while white women were not). Moreover, the Handlins' critics have added, pejorative attitudes toward blacks preceded the codification of slavery in Virginia. Even during their earliest years in Virginia, blacks were identified by color rather than by name on Virginia censuses, whereas white servants were listed by name.

Arguments for the early emergence of color prejudice in Virginia have generally been supported by studies of sixteenth-century English attitudes toward Africans. Published in 1968, Winthrop Jordan's *White over Black: American Attitudes toward the Negro, 1550–1812* posits that English prejudices against Africans predated the settlement of Virginia. An "emotionally partisan color," black held negative connotations in English culture as early as the Elizabethan era, Jordan argues. Laden with a tradition that linked the color black to filth and evil, sixteenth-century British travelers to Africa viewed blacks with suspicion from the outset. In recent years Jordan's conclusions have received considerable reinforcement from scholars who have reviewed Elizabethan performance and print culture and found its portrayals of Africans to be largely derogatory. Still, the meaning of African characters imagined by the English is far from transparent. Denounced by his enemies as "the devil," "an old black ram," and "a lascivious Moor," Shakespeare's Othello is an articulate, complex, and largely heroic character who proves wholly undeserving of these epithets.

In any case, attempts to map out the relationship between slavery and racial prejudice in colonial Virginia cannot fully explain the slave system that emerged there. Early English prejudices toward blacks may have facilitated the development of racial slavery, but they did not necessitate it. Virginia's colonists explored a variety of labor options and initially preferred to employ indentured servants rather than buy slaves. Over the long run, slavery prevailed not because it allowed the colonists to exercise their color prejudices, but because it offered economic and political advantages that indentured servitude could not match.

Virginia's conversion to servitude was fueled by the emergence of Britain as a major slave trader in the late seventeenth century. As British slave trade expanded, it offered colonial buyers a virtually limitless supply of affordably priced African slaves at a time when English servants were increasingly expensive and in short supply. During the same period the cost advantages of buying slaves also improved in other ways. Whereas early-seventeenth-century Virginia was a death trap, where many laborers succumbed to disease within a few years of arrival, by the late seventeenth century morbidity rates had fallen. As the life span of the colony's immigrants increased, so too did the return on Africans purchased for life.

Meanwhile, the use of enslaved African laborers also proved to have social advantages. Once purchased, black laborers proved less troublesome than English servants. They could be enslaved for life precisely because they could not claim the rights of Englishmen—as did English servants when their masters attempted to treat them like slaves. Better yet, as slaves for life they posed less challenge to the colony's social order than did white servants, who at the end of their terms became landless freemen—a "giddy multitude" who then challenged the political power of the colony's elite.

FROM SLAVERY TO RACE

Whatever their preconceptions about Africans, white colonists in North America soon learned to see them as their inferiors. From the late seventeenth century onward, English settlers encountered Africans as a mostly enslaved, propertyless people who were ever more distinct from whites under colonial law and custom. Also distinct under law were American Indians, another group of people who were physically distinct from the English. Still, color was far from the sole impetus for setting these two groups apart, for like the Africans, American Indians differed from the English in far more than complexion. Both groups were additionally distinguished from the colonists by religion, nationality, culture, and geographical origins. Ultimately, it was not one but all of these differences, whose relative importance fluctuated over time, that shaped the English colonists' growing willingness to set these groups apart. Over time, however, the social and political distinctions the colonists imposed on blacks and Indians obscured the complexity of their original differences, creating a society divided along color lines. And these color lines, in turn, slowly came to be understood as racial distinctions.

The initial importance of color per se to the colonists' willingness to enslave Africans is called into question by their early attempts to enslave Indian captives. The English had no traditional distaste for the Indian's color or physiognomy; indeed the existence of these indigenous peoples was unknown to Europeans prior to the discovery of the New World. Moreover, English travelers' accounts of the Indians, such as Sir Thomas Hariot's *A Briefe and*

True Report of the New Found Land of Virginia (1590), painted a largely favorable portrait of America's native populations. Yet, favorable preconceptions did not prevent early English settlers in both Virginia and New England from enslaving members of local Indian tribes. On the contrary, Indian slavery was curtailed and ultimately ruled out by a variety of practical obstacles. Central among these was that the Woodlands tribes encountered by early English settlers were unaccustomed to settled agricultural labor and not easily made into useful slaves. Moreover, as natives of the region they could easily escape. And worse, their enslavement tended to trigger attacks on English settlements.

While Indians remained free, their liberty was qualified. Whether adjudicated as tribes or as individuals, Indians were never fully incorporated into the colonists' body politic. Classified under colonial law as nominal foreigners, Indian tribes had tenuous dominion over their own lands, which English explorers and settlers claimed on behalf of their sovereigns. In practice, English claims on Indian land meant that, with the advance of Anglo-American settlement, tribes that did not sell or cede their land to the colonists were subject to wars of extermination, or, as became more common in the nineteenth century, forced removal. Meanwhile, both individual Indians and members of tribes that lived within the bounds of English settlement were subject to a wide variety of special laws and legal exemptions promulgated for their governance.

Both subject to different laws from those of the English colonists, Indians and Africans were often coupled in colonial statutes that restricted the rights of the non-English. For instance, a law passed by the Virginia Assembly in 1670 declared that "noe negro or Indian though baptised and ejoyned their own Freedome shall be capable of the purchase of christians, yet not debarred from the buying of any of their own nation" (Jordan, p. 94). As can be seen in the assembly's language, blacks and Indians were initially distinguished from Englishmen by virtue of religion and nationality rather than physical or racial distinctions. Likewise, early on, the colonists most frequently distinguished themselves from the other two groups by use of the term "Christian"—although they also sometimes described themselves as English.

However, the colonists' distinctions between Christians and heathens were soon complicated by the mutability of such religious distinctions. Blacks and Indians could convert to Christianity, and when they did they undermined and confused such distinctions, requiring colonial lawmakers to add ever more detailed specifications about the various groups they regulated. In particular, lawmakers found it necessary to emphasize that slaves who converted to Christianity did not automatically become free. Moreover, they also had to distinguish Indians and slaves both from each other and from other foreign nationals. Their difficulties can be seen in the torturous language of a 1705 Virginia statute:

> That all servants imported and brought into this country, by sea or land, who were not christians in their native country, (except Turks and Moors in amity with her majesty, and others than can make proof of their being free in England, or any other christian country, before they were shipped, in order to transportation hither) shall be accounted and be slaves, and as such be here bought and sold not withstanding a conversion to christianity afterwards. (Jordan, p. 94)

In the face of such complications, it is not surprising that the colonists ultimately abandoned heathenism as the distinguishing feature of blacks and Indians in their midst.

Nonetheless, the evolution of the racial categories into the taxonomy that ultimately replaced their initial distinctions between heathens and Christians should not be oversimplified. Before they could divide their population into races, the colonists first had to invent a racial category for themselves. They arrived in the New World identifying themselves as English Christians; only in the late seventeenth century did they begin to refer to themselves as "white."

The identifying trait of a new racial category, "whiteness" was the product of the political and social needs of a rapidly expanding colonial society whose growth was fueled by both slaveholding and frontier settlement. Within this context, the rights of citizenship quite logically adhered only to individuals who could be relied upon to help put down slave rebellions and fight in Indian wars: "white" men, in other words. Accordingly, over the course of the eighteenth century a wide variety of rights conferring full citizenship on white men were written into law. White men were entitled to vote, hold office, indenture other whites, and serve in the militia, whereas blacks and Indians were usually denied such prerogatives.

Crafted under British rule, colonial equations between color and citizenship survived the American Revolution. Indeed, although the Revolution inspired a wave of antislavery sentiment that ultimately led to the emancipation of northern slaves, the laws of the Republic inscribed a uniform set of white rights on both the "free" states of the North and the slave states of the South. In 1792, for example, the nation's new Congress reaffirmed that its military protection would be left in the hands of white men. That year, "an Act more effectually to provide for the National Defense by establishing a Uniform Militia throughout the United States" (Jacobson, p. 25) limited participation in new militias to "each and every free able-bodied white male citizen of the respective states." Similarly, the naturalization law of 1790 offered citizenship to "all free white persons" who met its residency requirements. And finally, without even using the word "white," the Constitution affirmed the whiteness of "the People" whose rights it outlined. Exempt from taxes, Indians were outside the polity, as were blacks, who were recognized in the Constitution only as the property of others. Neither group was explicitly represented in the system of government laid out in the Constitution. Nor would they routinely qualify for the rights and responsibilities the Constitution conferred on white Americans—such as the right to bear arms and the freedom to serve in the militia.

In short, the Republic codified the patterns of prejudice and discrimination against nonwhites that took shape during the colonial era. Moreover, it did so at a time when white Americans were increasingly inclined to see such patterns as natural, rather than man-made. Arguably, republicanism and racial ideology grew up together, with racial ideology supplying white Americans with a means for explaining how slavery could flourish in a republic whose founding fathers claimed liberty as a natural right. Race offered a rationale for denying some people the liberties deemed natural to others.

SCIENTIFIC RACISM

Explicit racial rationales for slavery and discrimination appear surprisingly late in American history. Comparing the races in the late eighteenth century, Thomas Jefferson was among the earliest American thinkers to make a formal argument for black inferiority. However, his discussion of blacks in *Notes on the State of Virginia* (1785) made no attempt to justify their enslavement. Rather, Jefferson suggested only that blacks compared unfavorably with whites in their physical appearance, and more important, with regard to endowments such as reason and imagination. He credited blacks with musical gifts and powers of memory equal to those of the white race but concluded with a tentative brief on behalf of black inferiority: "I advance . . . as a suspicion only, that the blacks, whether originally a distinct race, or made distinct by circumstance, are inferior to the whites in the endowments both of body and soul" (p. 262). Only in the nineteenth century, however, did suspicions such as Jefferson's flower into scientific theories that both ranked the races and provided ample justification for slavery and discrimination. Although not always employed in support of a proslavery agenda, the racist theories that proliferated in nineteenth-century American science presented blacks and other people of color as innately and permanently inferior to Caucasians—a status that would seem to license their oppression.

By no means monolithic or uniform over time, white American racial theories were shaped by both the ideological needs of a racially divided democracy and a long series of developments in European thought. Leaving their ideological functions aside for the moment, the specific ideas at work in nineteenth-century U.S. racial thought are best understood in reference to questions that had preoccupied European thinkers for some time.

One consequence of the age of exploration was a new European interest in the history and families of man. Confronted with new peoples and new regions, European thinkers began to classify mankind by their geographical origins and physical differences. For instance, the great Swedish naturalist Carolus Linnaeus included man among the many species whose varieties he classified in his *Systema naturae* (1735). He divided human beings into four varieties: *Homo europeaus, Homo asiaticus, Homo afer,* and *Homo americanus.* With such classifications came new questions about how distinct different kinds of people were, and how their distinctions originated. In considering these questions, eighteenth-century European naturalists generally concluded that the differences among men were shaped by the influence of environmental factors. Subscribers to the Scriptural account of creation, they believed that all human beings descended from Adam and Eve. Accordingly, they saw the races as members of the same human family, and their physical variations as the product of different climates and habitats. Such theories necessitated no ranking among the races. Indeed, German naturalist Johann Friedrich Blumenbach mocked the possibility of any objective method of ranking men. "If toads could speak," he noted, they would no doubt class themselves "the loveliest creatures on God's earth." In the long run, however, environmentalist classifications of human subspecies did lend themselves to racial rankings. A new system of classifying humankind on the basis of color and other physical characteristics, environmentalism presented race as a fundamental and important human distinction. From there, it was but a short step to racial hierarchies.

In the United States a hierarchical ordering of the races would prevail over the course of the nineteenth century. Abandoning any environmentalist conception of human differences, white Americans would come to view themselves as innately and permanently superior to nonwhites. The shift commenced in the early nineteenth century, when American thinkers began to explore Jefferson's speculation that blacks might be "originally a distinct race." Informed by Enlightenment-era challenges to the literal meaning of the Bible, they revisited the traditional scriptural account of human origins. Whereas the Bible shows mankind originating in one creation (monogenesis) American scientists began to suggest that the different races might be the product of multiple creations (polygenesis).

The most prominent American exponent of polygenesis was Samuel Morton of Philadelphia, a renowned physician and geologist. A Quaker with no evident interest in slavery, Morton spent the last few decades of his career amassing evidence for the separate origins of the races. After measuring and comparing collections of skulls from both America and ancient Egypt, he concluded that blacks and Indians were quantifiably inferior to the Caucasian ideal by virtue of having smaller crania—a conclusion that we now know relied on systematic errors in his measurements. With reference to his Egyptian skulls, Morton further argued that the distinctions dated so far back into antiquity as to preclude the possibility of a common origin.

Proponents of what came to be known as the American school of ethnology, Morton and other U.S. converts to polygenesis never entirely succeeded in persuading their fellow Americans that Christian monogenesis must be overturned. Any such conclusion would have contravened the Bible, which not only portrays a single creation but also instructs that God "hath made of one blood all nations of men for to dwell on all the face of the earth" (Acts 17:26). Still, the American school's findings proved influential. Proslavery and antiblack thinkers did not have to embrace the idea of a separate creation to make use of the American school's ethnological evidence for black inferiority. On the contrary, Morton's charts ranking the races by skull size were more widely respected and reproduced than his ideas about polygenesis.

Indeed, Morton's statistical charts outlived his theoretical arguments, supplying evidence of black inferiority to late-nineteenth-century scientists who subscribed to neither monogenesis nor polygenesis. Informed by the work of English naturalist Charles Darwin, these scientists rejected Scriptural accounts of creation in favor of evolution. But they did not abandon the American school of ethnology's system of racial rankings. On the contrary, they cast the Caucasian race as the supreme outcome of the evolutionary process outlined by Darwin: the most mature expression of human development. American interpretations of Darwinism were aided by the work of Herbert Spencer, a British thinker who transposed the evolutionary laws that Darwin drew from the physical world to the social world. Social Darwinism cast nonwhites as "further back" in their evolutionary development than whites.

First popularized during Reconstruction, social Darwinism proved as well suited to postemancipation white supremacy as polygenesis had been to the defense of slavery. Polygenesis had offered proslavery theorists the perfect rationale for slavery: products of a separate and inferior creation, blacks could never equal other men, and therefore might be justly enslaved by their betters. Likewise, social Darwinism offered a convenient justification for continued white domination over the newly freed slaves, who were judged members of the least-developed of the races. When African Americans were seen in this light, the citizenship and voting rights bestowed on them during Reconstruction represented a dangerous experiment that might prove beyond the current capacities of their race. Moreover, the African American disenfranchisement and segregation that followed Reconstruction could be interpreted as prudent from a Darwinian point of view. Some races were not ready to live on equal terms with others.

Also counted among the less-developed races were Native Americans, who in the late nineteenth century were widely seen to be losing the evolutionary struggle. Pushed west by forced removal during the Jacksonian era, when the Five Civilized Tribes were marched from the Southeast to what is now Oklahoma, decimated by a long series of frontier wars, and increasingly confined to reservations, Indians were a vanishing presence in American life. Although largely a consequence of federal policies directed against them, the displacement and rapid decline of America's Indian populations was attributed to inborn racial failings rather than white hostility. The Indians were incapable of adapting to civilization, racial theorists predicted, and would vanish entirely unless confined to reservations or forced to take up white ways.

Other races that also ranked behind whites on the evolutionary scale included Asians, Mexicans, and a wide variety of groups considered unequivocally white today. Considered most racially distinct were the Asians, who were widely seen as unassimilable. Almost from the founding of the United States, Asians were effectively barred from citizenship by the U.S. naturalization law of 1790, which limited naturalization to "free white persons." Moreover, the Chinese were subject to further racial restriction in 1882, when the first Chinese Exclusion Act went into effect. Designed to put an end to the migration of Chinese laborers to the Pacific Coast, this act, which was reinforced by subsequent legislation, barred the Chinese from entering the country and reinforced existing prohibitions against Chinese naturalization by specifying that the Chinese already in the United States were ineligible for citizenship. In the early twentieth century similar measures were passed to terminate Japanese immigration.

Racial restrictions on citizenship were more complicated for other "inferior" races. Although frequently not considered white, Mexicans were eligible for citizenship by virtue of a series of treaties conferring citizenship on Spaniards and Mexicans in the wake of U.S. expansion into Florida and the Southwest—they were naturalized along with their land. Still more problematic were European immigrants whose whiteness was considered questionable by native-born Americans, who deemed themselves Anglo-Saxons.

Starting in the mid-nineteenth century successive waves of emigration from Ireland, Italy, Poland, and Russia brought newcomers widely considered "inferior stock." These Irish, Slavic, Mediterranean, and Jewish immigrants qualified as white under U.S. immigration law. But during the late nineteenth and early twentieth centuries, many Americans saw the new immigrants as a challenge to the racial purity of their nation's white population. Southern Europeans were so dark, wrote a Chicago law professor in 1894, that "they can be termed 'white' not in the ordinary sense, but only in contrast with the African negro." Moreover, the same could be said of "the Semites, the Balkan People, the Greeks, the Italians, and the Hispano-Portuguese of Europe."

The professor's perception of racial difference among free white persons reflected the social effects of the shifting patterns of European immigration that repeopled nineteenth-century America. The new immigrants were more numerous than previous arrivals, were more likely to be Catholic or Jewish than their predominantly Protestant prede-cessors, and frequently spoke languages other than English. Confronted with these often impoverished foreigners, members of the traditional American elite scrambled to distance themselves from the newcomers by stressing their Anglo-Saxon heritage. Such claims also served to mediate political and economic conflicts between the new immigrants and native-born Americans in the familiar language of race.

From 1869 onward American nativists were able to reinforce their anti-immigrant hostility with a new racial theory propounded by Darwin's cousin Francis Galton. In a book entitled *Hereditary Genius* (1869), Galton proposed that not only could the races be ranked but the people within them could also be divided into higher and lower grades. Coining the word "eugenics," he suggested that the transmission of the best racial qualities not be left to chance. Social engineering could be used to improve the racial stock of a given population. Among other things, eugenics fueled nativist arguments for immigration barriers designed to check the flow of undesirable newcomers from places such as eastern and southern Europe. Stricter immigration laws were needed from a "eugenic standpoint," argued the Immigration Restriction League in 1910. "We should see to it that the breeding of the human race in this country receives the attention which it so surely deserves." Current immigration laws were too lax. "A considerable proportion of the immigrants now coming . . . are from races and countries . . . which have not progressed, but have been backward, downtrodden, and relatively useless for centuries." The eugenicist influence on American social thought was enshrined in the Johnson Act of 1924, which imposed a formula of quotas on immigrants from the various European countries. Designed to ensure that future immigrants would be racially compatible with American ideals, the Johnson Act set aside the greatest number of slots for immigrants of northern and western European descent.

In many ways, the early twentieth century marked a new high in the consolidation of racist ideology in the United States. This period not only saw the passage of the new immigration law but also featured the national resurgence of the Ku Klux Klan and the entrenchment of racial segregation in the South. On the academic front, racism was reinforced by new forms of scientific data that seemed to provide incontrovertible support for inegalitarian assessments of human differences. Most notable in this regard were the results of mass mental testing of U.S. soldiers at the beginning of World War I. Early versions of the IQ test, the crude measures used by the army ranked draftees of English descent above all others, and seemed to provide scientific evidence for the intellectual inferiority of a wide variety of non–Anglo-Saxon races.

THE RETREAT FROM RACISM

Yet racial determinism was not as unassailable as the army's test results seemed to suggest. On the contrary, the early twentieth century also saw the emergence of new questions about the role of biology in human affairs—questions that would ultimately challenge the legitimacy of race as scientific concept. These questions came out of anthropology and were first raised by Franz Boas, a German Jewish immigrant. The founder of modern cultural anthropology, Boas launched his critique of established ideas about race in the 1890s by arguing that science had established no fixed equation between race and intellect. Over the next several decades he and his followers broadened this critique by assembling an impressive body of evidence to disprove the existence of any significant innate differences between the peoples of the world. Boas's studies of immigrant children, for example, showed that physical characteristics frequently regarded as racial, such as head size and shape, could change drastically from one generation to the next. By underscoring the mutability of human physical characteristics, Boas reintroduced the importance of environmental influences, such as climate and nutrition, as the major determinants of many physical traits. Moreover, he also posited culture as an alternative to race in explaining human differences.

The work of Boas and his followers in no way put an end to scientific attempts to discover measurable differences between the races. Such attempts continue to this day. However, the work of Boas and his followers did put racial determinists on the defensive, requiring them to provide data for their broad and poorly documented assertions—data that have proved hard to find. Meanwhile, through the mid-twentieth century the concept of race was also challenged by developments in biology. In particular, scientists in the field of population genetics concluded that there is greater variation among people within the geographic gene pools associated with the racial classifications Negroid, Mongoloid, and Caucasian than there is across these groups. Likewise, genes for anything other than the superficial physical features associated with these—such

as eye and skin colors—have not been proved to cluster along racial lines. As a result, biologists have largely rejected any traditional notion of racial differences in favor of dividing humanity into loosely configured breeding populations, which are distinguished from each other primarily by the relative frequency of hereditary traits found in all human populations.

As the concept of race slowly lost its scientific authority over the course of the twentieth century, a variety of historical developments helped undermine racism in American social and political life. Beginning in the 1930s the hardships of the Great Depression—and racially discriminatory allocation of its New Deal remedies—helped mobilize minority groups to press for equal civic status through the courts. Such struggles continued throughout the twentieth century, reaching their fullest expression during the civil rights movement of the 1960s. Over time, such grassroots movements have forced government intervention to protect nonwhite Americans from legalized and extralegal discrimination.

Meanwhile, world events have also put pressure on American policymakers to end racial discrimination at home. Most notable in this regard are the genocidal excesses of the Nazis during World War II, which gave racism a bad name the world over. Likewise, the political exigencies of the cold war that took shape after World War II also helped reshape American race relations. Embroiled in ideological war against Communism in the Soviet Union and elsewhere, America sought the support of newly independent countries in the "third world." These newly independent countries were populated by a variety of peoples of color, including Africans, making American policymakers increasingly sensitive to charges of racial discrimination at home.

The long-term effects of twentieth-century alterations in American racial thinking and policy remain to be seen. The second half of the century saw the abolition of de jure racial discrimination at home as well as racial restrictions on foreign immigration, in addition to the continuing erosion of scientific racism. Yet race and racial divisions remain exceedingly important in contemporary American life. Americans continue to be divided along racial lines by many economic indicators, cultural practices, residential patterns, and educational outcomes. Moreover, race continues to hold meaning for individual Americans whose debates over the future of their multiracial nation are inscribed with racial theories drawn from its past.

See also **Africa and America; Race as a Cultural Category; Slavery and Race; Gender, Social Class, Race, and Material Life; Racialism and Racial Uplift; The Behavioral and Social Sciences** *(volume 1);* **Race, Rights, and Reform; Whites and the Construction of Whiteness; Anthropology and Cultural Relativism** *(volume 2);* **The Social Sciences** *(in this volume).*

BIBLIOGRAPHY

Barkan, Elazar. *The Retreat of Scientific Racism: Changing Concepts of Race in Britain and the United States between the World Wars.* Cambridge, U.K., and New York, 1992.

Berkhofer, Robert F., Jr. *The White Man's Indian: Images of the American Indian from Columbus to the Present.* New York, 1978.

Degler, Carl. "Slavery and the Genesis of American Race Prejudice." *Comparative Studies in Society and History* 2 (1959): 49–66.

Fields, Barbara. "Slavery, Race, and Ideology in the Unites States of America." *New Left Review* 181 (1990).

Constructing Race: Differentiating Peoples in the Early Modern World. Special issue of the *William and Mary Quarterly* 54, no. 1 (January 1997).

Fredrickson, George M. *The Black Image in the White Mind: The Debate on Afro-American Character and Destiny, 1817–1914.* New York, 1971.

Gould, Stephen J. *The Mismeasure of Man.* New York, 1981.

Hakluyt, Richard. *Principal Navigation, Voiages, Traffiques, and Discoveries of the English Nation.* London, 1598–1600. Reprint, Baltimore, 1972.

Haller, John S. *Outcasts from Evolution: Scientific Attitudes of Racial Inferiority.* Urbana, Ill., 1971.

Handlin, Oscar, and Mary F. Handlin. "Origins of the Southern Labor System." *William and Mary Quarterly* 7 (1950): 199–222.

Hannaford, Ivan. *Race: The History of an Idea in the West.* Washington, D.C., 1996.

Haney-López, Ian F. *White by Law: The Legal Construction of Race.* New York, 1996.

Hariot, Sir Thomas. *A Briefe and True Report of the New Found Land of Virginia.* 1590. Reprint, New York, 1972.

Jacobson, Matthew Frye. *Whiteness of a Different Color: European Immigrants and the Alchemy of Race.* Cambridge, Mass., 1998.

Jefferson, Thomas. *Notes on the State of Virginia.* 1785. In *The Life and Selected Writings of Thomas Jefferson,* edited by Adrienne Koch and William Peden. New York, 1944.

Jordan, Winthrop D. *White over Black: American Attitudes toward the Negro, 1550–1812.* Chapel Hill, N.C., 1968.

Morgan, Edmund S. *American Slavery, American Freedom: The Ordeal of Colonial Virginia.* New York, 1975.

Pieterse, Jan Nederveen. *White on Black: Images of Africa and Blacks in Popular Culture.* New Haven, Conn., 1992.

Roediger, David. *The Wages of Whiteness: Race and the Making of the American Working Class.* New York, 1991.

Saxton, Alexander. *The Rise and Fall of the White Republic: Class Politics and Mass Culture in Nineteenth-Century America.* London and New York, 1990.

129

Stanton, William. *The Leopard's Spots: Scientific Attitudes towards Race in America, 1815–1959.* Chicago, 1960.

Stocking, George. *Race, Culture, and Evolution: Essays in the History of Anthropology.* New York, 1968.

Smedley, Audrey. *Race in North America: Origin and Evolution of a Worldview.* Boulder, Colo., 1999.

Takaki, Ronald T. *Iron Cages: Race and Culture in Nineteenth-Century America.* New York, 1979.

Vaughan, Alden T. *Roots of American Racism: Essays on the Colonial Experience.* New York, 1995.

Wolpoff, Milford, and Rachel Caspari. *Race and Human Evolution: A Fatal Attraction.* New York, 1997.

CLASS

Fred Pfeil

To speak of social class in America is to confront a constitutive paradox. Virtually throughout its history, but certainly from the middle of the nineteenth century on, the United States has been deeply marked by the division of its citizens into distinct social classes. Yet at the same time, nothing has been more characteristic of mainstream U.S. ideology—and any number of would-be counter-hegemonic ideologies as well—than the view that the pressures and effects of social class on identity, culture, economics, and politics in the United States are, on the whole, fairly slight. As George H. W. Bush, when he was a candidate for the Republican nomination for president, put it in the winter of 1987–1988, class is really only "for European democracies or something—it isn't for the United States of America. We are not going to be divided by class" (quoted in DeMott, *The Imperial Middle,* pp. 9–10).

Such stout assertions may mock themselves when uttered by a privileged scion of America's ruling elite. Yet most social historians and cultural analysts of American life agree that certain desires and beliefs about class, with few exceptions, have been legion throughout American history. First, there is the desire not to become a class-divided society or to believe that the United States is one. Perhaps even more frequently, there was the desire to believe that although there are class divisions in America, they are relatively bridgeable, especially when compared to the chasmic separations of race, gender, and sexuality, by themselves or in combination, and are far less decisive in their unjust and abusive effects. What are the roots of such a widespread reluctance to grant class its shaping power and concede its formative role in American life? What are the major class divisions in American life, and what has been their shaping role? In addition, when and under what conditions have those divisions and their decisive effects on our political, economic, and cultural life become starkly clear as such, and how has

it been that such moments of clearsightedness have since become forgotten and obscured?

DEFINITIONS

To reply sensibly to such questions, we begin by demarcating the various senses of "class" in play, both conceptually and in actual history. First, there is "class" in its most objective sense, denoting, in classical Marxist usage, one's location within and relationship to the mode of economic production: those who own and effectively control the means of production, and therefore the economic surpluses in goods and profits that the system generates, versus those who have only their skilled or unskilled labor to offer for sale. Or, in another equally objective but more mainstream usage, "class" is defined by some combination of the type of work one does, the amount of remuneration one receives for that work, and the amount or percentage of national wealth one has at one's command. Under a scheme derived from this usage, for example, Dennis L. Gilbert divides the population of the late-twentieth-century United States into six classes: (1) the underclass, which is either wholly unemployed or working at part-time menial jobs, makes up 12 percent of the population, and receives an average income of $10,000 a year; (2) the working poor, 13 percent of the population and earning $20,000; (3) the working class, 30 percent of the population and earning $30,000; (4) the middle class, another 30 percent of the population but earning about $45,000 a year; (5) the upper middle class, 14 percent of the population and earning $80,000; and (6) 1 percent of the American population—investors, heirs, and executives—who in 1997 received an average of $1.5 million per year (*The American Class Structure,* p. 18).

Whichever more or less empirical definition we accept, it is not hard to see how this sense of class as an objective relation or condition also gives rise to definitions and manifestations of class at the level of distinct cultural practices and identities. These conceptions of class for itself, that is, as a formative conditioning element in one's subjective experience and in the forms of common life one shares with others in the same general economic circumstances, may be imagined along a kind of spectrum. At one end are the most seemingly instinctive notions of what is comfortable and familiar on the one hand, and unfamiliar, uncomfortable, or simply impossibly distant on the other. These are entirely learned but largely preconscious "structures of feeling," as the British cultural critic Raymond Williams called them, that lead some people to prefer *The Simpsons* to *Masterpiece Theatre* for their television viewing, or, conversely, to imagine the New York subway system as a network of unspeakable dangers and unthinkable propinquities that no one in his or her right mind would enter. At the other end of the spectrum is class consciousness in its most restricted sense, that is, as a conscious and explicit sense of one's shared interests and perspectives with others in the same economic location and over and against those at other locations and with interests that are opposed to one's own. Between these two poles, both conceptually and in reality, is stretched the whole canvas of "class culture."

With these three definitions or registers of class in mind, we can specify in just what sense and to what degree class seems not to exist or to count for much in American society at any given historical moment. Clearly, real objective differences in economic circumstances have always been present in American life, beginning with those between the merchants and planters who shaped and signed the U.S. Constitution and those artisans and yeomen who, unlike slaves and women, were also endowed as full citizens of the new Republic. But in part precisely thanks to that same enfranchisement, the resulting sense of democratic equality impeded the development of class consciousness within the emerging working class as much as it shaped it, even as the objective disparities between workers and owners increased and sharpened from the Jacksonian Era up to the Civil War, as the United States moved from mercantile capitalism into the early stages of the industrial capitalism for which the Civil War would clear the way. As Sean Wilentz and others have shown, those caught up in this turbulent transition created vibrant class cultures for themselves, from workingmen's guilds to festivals, parades, and entertainments. They also frequently invoked the rhetoric of democratic egalitarianism and the vision of the "producers' republic" in pursuit of their rights to fair treatment in the workplace and full inclusion in political and civic life. But this ideology of producerism, as Mike Davis has written, "mapped class relations along an axis of 'producers' versus 'parasitic money power'"—these latter viewed in unholy tandem, with unemployed or underemployed slackers and wastrels below—"and conflated all strata of workers and most capitalists into a single industrial bloc" (*Prisoners of the American Dream*, p. 14).

By the middle of the nineteenth century, while increasingly distinct working-class, middle-class, and ruling-class cultures organized the social landscape, especially in the major cities of the United States, class consciousness, especially on the part of the emergent working class, remained stuck in this mud. Both then and at the end of the twentieth century the same productivist ideology lent itself to altogether less savory dialects, as when wielded by skillful demagogues who do not scruple to recast the vision in openly bigoted and racist terms. After all, while the enemy above may be too far away to see, and therefore oppose, except as an abstraction, the enemies below are, often as not, living all too closely nearby. So the stout figure of the nativist white working man may be opposed not so much to the parasitically profiteering capitalist above, but to the dirty, dishonest, untrustworthy foreign immigrant below—the drunken Irish "mick," beast-like "Polack," treacherous "Chink," or dirty "spic"—and always to the spectral figure of the permanently unequal and undeserving "black," whether free or slave, employed or unemployed, on public assistance or in jail.

The resulting notion of the working class in the United States as being rightfully open only to those deemed "white"—a notion quite skillfully deployed by late-twentieth-century politicians from Richard Nixon to Ronald Reagan and George Bush—is thus of longstanding and lasting effect. Nor have those effects been limited to white workers alone, given that the same notion, when put into practice in (for example) exclusionary hiring practices and racist union policies, virtually guarantees that nonwhite workers will, quite understandably, come to identify primarily with the racial label by which so much of their reality both on and off the job is forcibly defined. Likewise, both recent and long-term history clearly demonstrate that those white workers still beguiled by the siren songs of racism will be that much more susceptible to invitations issued from other, higher class quarters, to view their interests as one and the same as those of upper-class whites, in this fantasyland of opportunity in which no undeserving person is ever left behind.

CONFLICT

If some such version of this free and fair "producer republic," complete with its backdrop of liberal individualism and, as options in the foreground, its panoply of infinitely accessorizable racist dialects, is the primary hegemonic vision through which notions of class have been both occulted and perversely expressed, it must also be said that it has not always been uniformly successful in blocking class consciousness and class struggle from below throughout American history. In the outbreak of the first great wave of railroad strikes in the 1870s through the bloody Homestead Strike in 1892 and the agonizing Pullman Strike of 1894, a new level of militant class consciousness was discernible in response to the industrialization and mechanization of an economy undergoing its first full-scale depression, as well as to the rapacity of the robber barons, the oligopolistic concentration of primary industries, and the appearance of the industrial trusts. Such seismic upheavals brought factory laborers together with small farmers, "native" workers with newly arrived immigrants, and for a time and in various regional pockets black workers and farmers with whites; in various accents and to various degrees, they provided the seedbed from which a host of explicitly anticapitalist discourses, visions, newspapers, books, and political institutions could spread across the land. A second such upsurge, arguably a somewhat weaker echo of the first, took place around the first decade of the twentieth century, including the heroic efforts of the syndicalist Industrial Workers of the World (also known as "Wobblies") in the mines and logging camps of the West, and climaxing with the strong organizing drive to unionize the new wave of immigrants, most of them from southern and eastern Europe, in the giant enterprises of the steel oligopoly. A third upsurge occurred in response to the Depression of the 1930s, which lasted into the mid-1940s and was arguably centered around the formation and expansion of the unions of the Congress of Industrial Organizations (CIO).

What made such outbreaks of militant and class consciousness and class struggle from below possible, and what brought each of them to a halt? The answer to each question suggests the limits of the power of the hegemonic racist-productivist ideology. At times of economic dislocation and depression in particular and more generally in the midst of the shift from relatively decentralized production and industrial capitalism to monopoly capitalism and mass production, that ideology was unable to cover over or explain away the growing disparities in the conditions of life between millions of increasingly massified workers on the one hand and a plutocratic elite on the other: the Henry Fricks, John D. Rockefellers, J. P. Morgans, and Henry Fords. And at these historic moments not even the most racist subdialects of that ideology were dependably able to keep the working class sufficiently unconscious of itself and therefore in check.

So, when a hegemonic ideology fails to do its work in a nominally democratic society, that is, keeping the subalterns from disidentifying with the privileged and allying with each other instead, it is time to refurbish the ideology and to call in the troops. This, in effect, was what was done to combat and close down the first two of these upsurges in class struggle; nor, for that matter, were the two sides of this dual response in many respects more than analytically distinct. In the General Strike of 1877, those railway workers still hearkening back to the vision of the producer republic as warrant for their protest and proof of their legitimacy as American citizens were shocked out of their ideology to find themselves confronted by the armed might of the federal government. But those on the line in the Pullman Strike of 1894—two years after the Homestead steelworkers strike and the National Guard had long since been formed to contain such "urban disorders"—had ceased to harbor or depend on such illusions of republican citizenship to stay the state's hand. But the ideological flip side of such repression must also be given credit for its share of the work, for the old republican productivism was now given some new vicious twists.

From the 1880s through the early 1920s, the distorted doctrines of Social Darwinism supplied the pseudo-scientific warrant for an increase in nativist racist attacks, both verbal and physical, against new immigrants from southern and eastern Europe and the socialist and anarchist doctrines they supposedly brought with them and, of course, against African Americans, who were lynched in record numbers at that time. Likewise, the proud sense of republican citizenship that both informed and deluded working-class sensibilities, particularly in the run-up to the Spanish-American War in 1898 and in its aftermath, was often channeled into an overtly imperialist and jingoist national pride.

The end result of this potent new combination of state violence and reactionary ideology was the tidal wave of repression that rolled over the United States at the close of World War I and that, in 1919–1924, brought a halt to a forty-year period of more or less continuous and open class struggle. Nativist workers joined forces with reactionary small business leaders through local chapters of the American Legion and other civic and social organizations to root out the "reds" (Communists) and "Wobblies" in their midst. Some of these latter were castrated; with the assistance of the federal government and its newly repressive edicts and laws, some were deported to the lands from which they had come; and others, such as blacks in the South and Midwest, were simply and summarily lynched. It was not until the Depression of the 1930s took hold that anything like mass working-class consciousness emerged again, and, even then, it would appear less as a revival than a rebirth.

THE PROFESSIONAL-MANAGERIAL CLASS

It would be wrong to vault ahead from this protracted moment of what Alan Trachtenberg has aptly called "the incorporation of America" to the class conflicts of the Great Depression without noting the emergence onto the political, cultural, and economic scene of a third collective actor that was neither working class nor capitalist, protagonist nor antagonist, but was precisely the liaison and broker of relations between the two: the professional-managerial class, or PMC. By 1880, according to Richard Ohmann, the most sensitive biographer of this class's early life, "the PMC did not exist as a recognizable or conscious formation"; by 1910, however, it had not only expanded its ranks and proliferated its professions but had evolved its own self-consciousness as the cultural intermediary between high and low culture and as mediators of the increasingly vexed relationship between capital and the laboring classes, thanks to its "vision of progress through expertise and planning" in production and politics (*Selling Culture,* pp. 119, 156). The PMC's taste in products was for brand-name nationally advertised goods; in magazines, *McClure's* and the *Saturday Evening Post;* in politics, progressive reform and uplift; and in social space, the suburban neighborhood, with its houses and yards, entirely distinct from both the urban landscape's fraught opposition between the mansions of Park and Fifth Avenues and the tenement neighborhoods of the Lower East Side. Yet if the PMC's position between labor and capital allowed it to play a decisive role in banking the fires of overt class conflict, the sweet rain of its

mediating efforts hardly fell equally on labor and capital alike. Ohmann wrote a graceful but unflinching summary of the balance sheet:

> The PMC both assisted and rationalized capital's reassertion of dominance around the turn of this century. It did so through foundational work in the culture industry . . . as well as by exercising managerial skill in corporations, bringing applied science and engineering to bear on production, doing the legal work required for mergers, and so on. Other PMC activities looked and felt more like opposition to the untrammeled workings of big business: social work, urban reform, muckraking, the regulatory legislation of the 1900s. Yet in none of these projects did the anti-union, anti-populist PMC support working class self-organization; indeed, in retrospect, all of them tended to strengthen the rule of capital by making it less abrasive and coercive, more reasonable, more "natural," more hegemonic. (*Selling Culture,* pp. 344–345)

As the buffer between the two primary classes, and in the final analysis itself the hireling of capital, however unique its privileges and great its comparative autonomy, the PMC would play a decisive role throughout the century in reproducing the relations of production through its positions in management, education, and culture and the media, and in determining the limits both of respectable mainstream "good taste" and socioeconomic and political "common sense." The PMC played an important role in dissent as well. At moments of economic or political crisis, such as in the 1930s or from the mid- to late 1960s and much of the 1970s, by which time its size and social power were greater than ever, large sectors of its ranks identified more with those below than those above them and thus dragged the center of gravity in national politics in a weakly social-democratic direction for a time. Thus, from the late 1930s through the aftermath of World War II, and in the later 1970s as well, the countervailing effort by capital from above to defuse potential threats to its rule had to win over key sectors of two classes. Such efforts to disarticulate potentially oppositional formations of the working class, disaffiliate the PMC from any effective coalitions with any members or sectors of that class (for example, African Americans or the poor), and to rearticulate sectors of both subordinate classes into coalition with itself under the terms of a rejuvenated hegemony would necessarily call for new, more sophisticated blends of suasion and coercion than those cruder cocktails of force and ideology employed at the turn of the century.

Partly for this reason, and partly given the depth and breadth of both the objective economic crisis of the depression and what Michael Denning in *The*

Cultural Front (1996) has aptly called "the laboring of American culture" that working-class and PMC Americans wrought in response to it, the restoration of a secure capitalist-PMC hegemony in culture and politics took years of steady effort. Although World War II spurred both new corporate-capitalist growth and consolidation and a far more intimate relationship between corporations and the national state, such "laboring" was only brought to a gradual halt in the years after the war, thanks to the convergence of three factors: one politico-ideological, one political-economic, and the third, we might say, economic-cultural. The first was cold war anti-communism, promoted by the state in the years after World War II with the fervent support of the most reactionary sectors of the small business community and of the working class itself, by the leaders of the outsized defense industries of a military-industrial complex largely created by the war and requiring at least the threat of war for its continued expansion and good health, and with at least the more passive consent of the rest of big business. The second was the passage of the Taft-Hartley Act in 1947 and related legislation, which simultaneously institutionalized and neutralized a labor movement already being purged of its most obstreperously radical elements, by outlawing its most potent forms of concerted collective action (for example, sympathy strikes) and prohibiting it from bargaining over such key issues as investment strategy or managerial control over the labor process itself. The third factor was in no small part a consequence or at least beneficiary of the preceding two. It was the triumphant expansion and consolidation across the field of class relations, from the lower edges of the working class to the highest echelons of the white-collar "upper-middle-class" PMC of consumer society itself: that is, of a profoundly depoliticized mode of life centered around the unfinished construction of so many pseudo-individualized, anti-collective selves—the "herd of independent minds," as Harold Rosenberg once wrote—via the purchase, public display, and privatized consumption of a seemingly infinite array of commodities—from the color and make of one's car to the shape and size of one's suburban home.

The synergistic effect of these developments throughout the 1950s and a good part of the 1960s was not only an erosion of working-class consciousness but at least to some extent of working-class cultures as well. As consumerist lifestyles became increasingly affordable in a variety of shapes and sizes, widely publicized surveys revealed that larger and larger majorities of white Americans declared themselves simply and smugly "middle class." Such workers, now homogenized from ethnic specificity into a uniform whiteness, fled the urban neighborhoods and cultures into which they had been born, abandoning the cities to minority populations of the underemployed and unemployed. Meanwhile, the most progressive sectors of a purged and largely self-policing PMC intelligentsia no longer bothered its head about issues of poverty and economic justice but instead agonized over how to contain the contagion of mass conformity and its even more insidious offspring, a premasticated "middlebrow" culture trying to pass itself off as real critical thought or genuine art. Likewise, an "end of ideology" was declared, at least on the domestic front, as all social or economic issues seemed to be only so many technical problems, capable of being resolved once the right combination of technocratic PMC expertise could be brought to bear on them—after which the answers could be tendered to the appropriate economic or political agencies and elites for implementation. Such was the mainstream ideology of the time—and such, willy-nilly, was at least to some extent the social reality of the time, given the power of a dominant ideology to realize itself in and as the actual way of the world.

MODERN CONFLICTS

Small wonder, then, that the next widespread wave of revolt against dominant institutions and ideologies of American life would be focused on issues and identities that had little, directly at least, to do with class. Class nonetheless had much to do with both where those rebels and those who opposed them came from, and how the revolts and counter-revolutions they provoked worked themselves out. The great upheavals of the 1960s and 1970s received their initial impetus from the southern civil rights movement that began in the mid-1950s, spear-headed and fueled in its subsequent development by a potent coalition within the African American community of seasoned elders—many of them wise heirs to the institutions and organizing lessons of the 1930s and 1940s, from A. Philip Randolph's Brotherhood of Sleeping Car Porters to the Highlander Folk School in Tennessee; black college students who aspired to at least the lower levels of a vastly expanded postwar PMC; and a vibrantly resistant community of black workers and farmers, from the well established to the poorest and most oppressed. Some vision of a similar or equivalent cross-generational, cross-class alliance became the dream-ideal of all subsequent would-be revolutionaries of the 1960s and 1970s, from the Students for a Democratic Society to the movement against the war in Vietnam, from second-wave feminism to the Black Panthers. In most, if not all, cases such a dream fell far short of realization, in no small part thanks to the deep class divisions it dreamed of overcoming, between the largest generation to date of college-bound PMC trainees from the postwar "baby boom" straining against its leash for "liberation" on the one hand to a deeply incorporated and internally disarticulated working class on the other.

During the Republican administrations of presidents Nixon and Reagan, though by no means through the Republican Party alone, those forces seeking to reestablish then deepen their ideological, political, and economic power have skillfully exploited and enlarged these divisions between the complicit resentment of the working class and the privileged self-indulgent self-righteousness of the baby-boom PMC. Thus, there was Nixon's "silent majority" of (implicitly and indicatively white) working-class support in the late 1960s and early 1970s and the image of hard-hatted flag-waving workers storming gatherings of flag-burning, long-haired kids. Thus, too, the brilliant divide-and-conquer strategies of the Reagan years, strategies devised in the course of a long and quite conscious ideological counteroffensive on the part of wide sectors of capital, dating from 1978 on. In the course of the 1980s, particularly following Nixon's disgrace and resignation in 1974, it appeared at least possible that from the resulting "excess of democracy" (in the words of one highly feted elite Harvard-based government policy adviser) some version of a progressive alliance between PMC and working-class perspectives and interests might eventually emerge to bid for hegemony after all.

The election of Ronald Reagan in 1980 and its aftereffects, which decisively resolved a economic-political deadlock that had expressed itself as a seemingly chronic and mysterious "stagflation," were prepared for by a host of new conservative research centers and think tanks, by new funding arms and recruitment techniques designed to roll back this threat from below, as well as by a flood of funds from corporate political action committees (PACs), which went for Republican challenger Reagan over incumbent Jimmy Carter by the staggering ratio of five hundred to one. Politically and economically, the class strategy of the new Republican conservatives was devised to deepen and exploit the existing split both within and between PMC and

working-class interests and views by appealing ideologically to the most socially conservative, national-chauvinist, and outright racist elements of the white working class, while simultaneously pursuing a program of economic deregulation and preferential tax breaks by which many in the PMC stood to profit substantially—albeit nowhere near as well as financiers and CEOs, corporations, banks, and insurance companies with whose interests the PMC was thus increasingly identified.

The administrations of William Jefferson Clinton (1993–2001) did little to resist, transform, or mitigate the reign of capital it inherited. Indeed, in certain respects, most notably in Clinton's championing of welfare reform policies with disastrous effects on the underemployed and unemployed, especially poor single mothers, the administrations had actually increased both the ideological and the actual economic chasms that separate the working class and poor from the upper middle class and the outright rich. A glance at some of the chapter titles from the Economic Policy Institute's biennial survey *The State of Working America, 1994–1995* conveys a general impression of the result: "Family Income: Slow and Unequal Growth"; "Taxes: Despite Recent Progressive Changes, a Further Cause of Worsening Inequality"; "Wealth: Enriching the Wealthy, Creating Financial Insecurity for the Majority"; "Poverty: High Rates Unresponsive to Economic Expansion"; and "International Comparisons: The United States Is Falling Behind in Productivity and Wage Growth." Likewise, with more than two million of its citizens in prison, the United States became both per capita and in absolute numbers the most incarceration-minded of all the developed countries, as well as the country with the highest ratio of average CEO earnings per year to those of the average worker—well over three hundred to one.

Despite the ever-more obvious and insistent pressure of such yawning inequalities at the beginning of the twenty-first century, an extraordinary number of Americans continued to discount or ignore the determining presence of class in American history, which disbelief paradoxically enables the most blatant class-based politics to be practiced from above on those most afflicted with it from below. This overview of the weight and effect of social class in American life has ignored an extraordinarily rich literature on class-centered subjectivities and the milieux of the past and present, for example, the ruling-class mores explored by Thorstein Veblen at the beginning of the twentieth century, the ruling-class mindsets depicted by Nelson Aldrich, or the painful feelings of guilt and worthlessness Richard Sennett and Jonathan Cobb found among those trapped within a working class that was fed daily doses of American individualist self-reliance. This overview has also shied away from serious engagement with the complex interactions of other factors, especially those of race, gender, and sexuality, with those of class.

See also **Gender, Social Class, Race, and Material Life** *(volume 1)*; **Working Class** *(volume 2)*; **Success; Marxist Approaches** *(in this volume); and other articles in this section.*

BIBLIOGRAPHY

Aldrich, Nelson W., Jr. *Old Money: The Mythology of America's Upper Class.* New York, 1989.

American Social History Project. *Who Built America: Working People and the Nation's Economy, Politics, Culture and Society,* 2nd ed., 2 vols. New York, 2000.

Bledstein, Burton J. *The Culture of Professionalism: The Middle Class and the Development of Higher Education in America.* New York, 1976.

Blumin, Stuart M. *The Emergence of the Middle Class: Social Experience in the American City, 1760–1900.* New York, 1989.

Bowles, Samuel, and Herbert Gintis. *Schooling in Capitalist America: Education and the Contradictions of Economic Life.* New York, 1976.

Brenner, Johanna. *Women and the Politics of Class.* New York, 2000.

Coontz, Stephanie. *The Social Origins of Private Life: A History of American Families, 1600–1900.* London and New York, 1988.

Cox, Oliver Cromwell. *Race: A Study in Social Dynamics.* New York, 2000. Reprint of *Caste, Class and Race,* 1948.

Davis, Angela Y. *Women, Race, and Class.* New York, 1981.

Davis, Mike. *Prisoners of the American Dream: Politics and Economy in the History of the U.S. Working Class.* London and New York, 1986.

DeMott, Benjamin. *The Imperial Middle: Why Americans Can't Think Straight About Class.* New York, 1990.

Denning, Michael. *Mechanic Accents: Dime Novels and Working-Class Culture in America.* London and New York, 1987.

———. *The Cultural Front: The Laboring of American Culture in the Twentieth Century.* London and New York, 1996.

Ehrenreich, Barbara. *Fear of Falling: The Inner Life of the Middle Class.* New York, 1989.

Gilbert, Dennis L. *The American Class Structure: In an Age of Growing Inequality,* 5th ed. Belmont, Calif., 1998.

Gutman, Herbert G. *Work, Culture, and Society in Industrializing America: Essays in America's Working-Class and Social History.* New York, 1976.

Halttunen, Karen. *Confidence Men and Painted Women: A Study of Middle-Class Culture in America, 1830–1870.* New Haven, Conn., 1982.

Josephson, Matthew. *The Robber Barons: The Great American Capitalists.* New York, 1934.

———. *The Politicos, 1865–1896.* New York, 1938.

Levine, Lawrence W. *Highbrow/Lowbrow: The Emergence of Cultural Hierarchy in America.* Cambridge, Mass., 1988.

Marable, Manning. *How Capitalism Underdeveloped Black America: Problems in Race, Political Economy, and Society.* Boston, 1983.

Mills, C. Wright. *White Collar: The American Middle Class.* New York, 1951.

Ohmann, Richard. *Selling Culture: Magazines, Markets, and Class at the Turn of the Century.* London and New York, 1996.

Roediger, David. *The Wages of Whiteness: Race and the Making of the American Working Class.* London and New York, 1991.

Rubin, Lillian B. *Families on the Fault Line: America's Working Class Speaks about the Family, the Economy, Race, and Ethnicity.* New York, 1994.

Ryan, Mary P. *The Cradle of the Middle Class: The Family in Oneida County, New York, 1790–1865.* New York, 1981.

Sennett, Richard, and Jonathan Cobb. *The Hidden Injuries of Class.* New York, 1973.

Trachtenberg, Alan. *The Incorporation of America: Culture and Society in the Gilded Age.* New York, 1982.

Vannesman, Reeve, and Lynn Weber Cannon. *The American Perception of Class.* Philadelphia, 1987.

Veblen, Thorstein. *The Theory of the Leisure Class.* New York, 1899.

Wilentz, Sean. *Chants Democratic: New York City and the Rise of the American Working Class, 1788–1850.* New York, 1984.

Wilson, William Julius. *When Work Disappears: The World of the New Urban Poor.* New York, 1996.

Part 15

THE PURSUIT AND EXCHANGE
OF KNOWLEDGE

Part 15, *continued*

THE SCIENTIFIC IDEAL

Daniel P. Thurs
Ronald L. Numbers

Although the European settlement of North America coincided with the so-called scientific revolution, colonial Americans paid little attention to science. Instead, they busied themselves subduing the land and carving a society out of a "howling wilderness." The handful of colonial Americans who systematically studied nature rarely described their activities as "science," a term that had long referred to organized knowledge generally, whether about God, morals, or nature. Instead, scientifically inclined Americans talked of doing "philosophy" or cultivating specific fields such as astronomy or botany. In the late 1760s, when Benjamin Franklin's Philadelphia friends founded the American Philosophical Society, the nation's oldest surviving scientific society, they established sections devoted to commerce, architecture, and agriculture as well as to natural philosophy, natural history, and medicine. Students of nature regarded themselves as philosophers or men of science. Neither the term nor the concept of "scientist" existed. Except for a handful of college professors, itinerant lecturers, and subsidized collectors, no Americans earned a living doing natural philosophy (e.g., physics and astronomy) or natural history (e.g., geology, botany, and zoology), the two primary divisions of the scientific enterprise. Yet by the mid-eighteenth century the number was growing. As Franklin phrased it, the "Drudgery of Settling new Colonies" was "now pretty well over," giving "Virtuosi or ingenious Men residing in the several Colonies" the leisure to cultivate useful knowledge (Carter, "*One Grand Pursuit*," p. 12).

Because of Sir Isaac Newton's immense influence, astronomy and physics enjoyed the greatest prestige of any of the sciences during the eighteenth century. According to the historian Brooke Hindle, "the simplicity and perfection of Sir Isaac Newton's laws of motion" became "the ideal of the age and influenced every field from physics to religion" (*The Pursuit of Science*, p. 381). Cotton Mather, a prominent minister-naturalist in Boston, honored New-ton as "the Perpetual Dictator of the learned World in the Principles of Natural Philosophy." "Be sure," wrote the Reverend Mr. Mather, "the Experimental Philosophy is that, in which alone your Mind can be at all established" (Miller, *The New England Mind,* pp. 437, 440). Despite the small number of Americans engaged in scientific work, the intellectual impact of natural philosophy was relatively great. On the eve of the Revolution, David Rittenhouse of Philadelphia observed that astronomy "has a much greater influence on our knowledge in general, and perhaps on our manners too, than is commonly imagined. Though but few men are its particular votaries, yet the light it affords is universally diffused amongst us; and it is difficult for us to divest ourselves of its influence so far, as to frame any competent idea of what would be our situation without it" (Hindle, *David Rittenhouse,* p. 119).

The more that natural philosophy explained about comets, earthquakes, and planetary motion, the less colonial Americans invoked the direct agency of God. Samuel Johnson, an Anglican divine in eighteenth-century New England, complained that "it is a fashionable sort of philosophy (a science falsely so-called) to conceive that God governs the world only by a general providence according to certain fixed laws of nature which he hath established without ever interposing himself with regard to particular cases and persons" (Hornberger, "Samuel Johnson," p. 391). In response to such fears, Cotton Mather sought in *The Christian Philosopher* (1721) to "demonstrate, that *Philosophy* is no *Enemy,* but a mighty and wondrous *Incentive to Religion.*" Most colonial intellectuals seem to have agreed with Mather.

THE EARLY REPUBLIC

Well into the nineteenth century, "science" remained an amorphous term. The 1806 edition of *Webster's Dictionary* still identified science as "knowledge, deep learning, skill, art." But increasingly the term came to be associated with the natural sciences, both physical and biological, and by the 1830s the term "science" was replacing "philosophy." In 1834 the British philosopher William Whewell coined the word "scientist." The American astronomer Benjamin A. Gould independently reinvented it fifteen years later, but the term did not gain currency until the latter part of the nineteenth century.

Scientifically literate Americans typically associated science with a fact-centered, inductive methodology, which they linked to the seventeenth-century English philosopher Francis Bacon. As the prestige of science grew in the nineteenth century, the so-called Baconian method came to influence not only science but other activities, including theology. As one Presbyterian theologian explained in 1832, "We avow our belief that the theologian should proceed in his investigation precisely as the chemist or the botanist proceeds," reasoning from particular facts to general laws (Bozeman, *Protestants in an Age of Science*, p. 151). Christian thinkers became so enamored of science that they began reinterpreting the Bible in the light of its findings. Naturalists such as Yale's Benjamin Silliman, Amherst's Edward Hitchcock, and Princeton's Arnold Guyot proposed popular readings of the first chapters of Genesis that accommodated the accumulating paleontological evidence of the antiquity of life on earth and the diminishing evidence of a geologically significant flood at the time of Noah.

Between the American Revolution and the Civil War, the number of persons earning a living by doing science swelled from a couple of dozen (at most) to an estimated fifteen hundred or more, many of whom found employment with government agencies such as the U.S. Coast Survey, the largest and most powerful scientific institution in antebellum American, or in the growing number of public and private colleges. By the 1850s the best American colleges were sometimes hiring as many as four or five science professors. Scientific leadership shifted from a diffuse group of men such as Franklin and Mather, who had cultivated science as a leisure-time activity, to a group of career-oriented practitioners.

The acceptance of an authoritarian and autonomous scientific elite in a self-consciously democratic culture was not easily attained, especially since scientists believed that society should foot the bill for their ambitious plans. They attempted to reconcile their overtly elitist aims with the democratic values of American society by stressing their commitment to free inquiry and their willingness

(in theory, at least) to embrace any person of talent, regardless of class. Men of science also promised to produce useful knowledge, not only applicable to agriculture, commerce, and manufacturing, but to ethics and religion. The study of nature, many claimed, amply revealed God's power, wisdom, and goodness.

The dissemination of science, like American culture generally, became increasingly democratic in the early decades of the nineteenth century. After about 1815 local scientific societies flourished, scientific lectures attracted large crowds, and scientific reports filled the pages of local newspapers, a cornerstone of American democracy. During the 1840s and 1850s the popularization of science grew as men of science sought to capitalize on their growing appeal by lecturing and writing for profit. Some leading men of science, such as Alexander Dallas Bache, superintendent of the Coast Survey, feared that popularizing science would not only divert attention from research but encourage charlatanism, which he associated with those who lacked appropriate training, character, and knowledge. Indeed, some of the most successful popularizers were phrenologists, who assessed a person's character by "reading" the contours of the head; health reformers, who drew on physiology to promote dietary and sexual changes; and the notorious author of *Vestiges of the Natural History of Creation* (1844), at first anonymous but later identified as the Scottish publisher Robert Chambers, who sketched the history of the world from a primordial cloud of gas to the advent of humans. All of these popularizers presented themselves as representatives of science, but the leaders of American science denounced them as "charlatans" and their teachings as "humbuggery."

FROM THE CIVIL WAR TO WORLD WAR I

In the years after the American Civil War, the meaning of "science" grew increasingly narrow and rigid. As the Princeton theologian Charles Hodge perceptively noted in 1874, the very word science was "becoming more and more restricted to the knowledge of a particular class of facts, and of their relations, namely, the facts of nature or of the external world." To his dismay, such science required purely naturalistic explanations. Phrases such as "science tells us" or "science demands" surfaced routinely in books and articles. Before long, science came to represent "another name for truth," as Daniel Coit Gilman of the Johns Hopkins University put it (Roberts and Turner, *The Sacred and the Secular University,* p. 64). About the same time that "pseudoscience" came into common use, replacing more general terms such as humbuggery to distinguish what science was not. Mary Baker Eddy might boldly call her metaphysical musings Christian Science, but to critics they represented a blatant manifestation of pseudoscience.

The intense public debate over evolution, prompted by the publication of Charles Darwin's *On the Origin of Species* (1859), highlighted the changing conceptions and authority of science. The overwhelming attraction of evolution, especially within the scientific community, was—as one layman bluntly phrased it—that there was "literally nothing deserving the name of Science to put in its place" (Numbers, *Darwinism Comes to America,* p. 47). The young geologist William North Rice made much the same point. "The great strength of the Darwinian theory," he wrote in 1867, "lies in its coincidence with the general spirit and tendency of science. It is the aim of science to narrow the domain of the supernatural, by bringing all phenomena within the scope of natural laws and secondary causes" (ibid., p. 48).

The acceptance of the Darwinian hypothesis both reflected and facilitated a change in attitude toward the appropriate methods of science, especially with regard to theorizing and the use of "working hypotheses," which Baconian inductivists had shunned. The astronomer Percival Lowell, at the center of a turn-of-the-century debate over canals on Mars, articulated a vision of science in which "mere" gatherers of facts were to be guided by a higher class of scientific thinkers. Although no consensus on scientific method existed, references to "*the* scientific method" began appearing. "I make bold to say," declared astronomer Simon Newcomb in a widely disseminated statement in 1880, "that the greatest want of the day, from a purely practical point of view, is the more general introduction of the scientific method and the scientific spirit into the discussion of those political and social problems which we encounter on our road to a higher plane of public well being" (Moyer, *A Scientist's Voice,* p. 91). By scientific method he apparently meant rejecting metaphysical "speculations" and testing of propositions by "experience."

Between the Civil War and World War I, the number of persons earning a living in science-related occupations, not including medicine and engineering, increased from about fifteen hundred in 1860 to over fourteen thousand in 1900, about four hundred of whom actively engaged in original research. Various government agencies, led by the U.S. Department of Agriculture, provided many of the new jobs; but especially after 1900, the year in which General Electric created the first industrial research laboratory, scientists increasingly found employment in industry. Medical schools, which had previously ignored research, slowly began cultivating it and promoting "scientific medicine." Engineering schools provided training in "applied science." Basic researchers tended to concentrate in the new American universities as original research came to play an increasingly important role in hiring and promoting science faculty. Science also found support in charitable institutions, including, most prominently the Rockefeller Institute for Medical Research, founded in New York City in 1901, and the Carnegie Institution of Washington, founded in the District of Columbia in 1902.

The rhetoric of elite scientists continued to clash with the language of democracy, especially when they began advocating the pursuit of "pure science," unrelated to utilitarian goals. They wanted support from society without offering any reciprocity in the form of social control or even the promise of short-term benefits. However, the leaders of American science recognized that their professional interests required at least the promise of vague returns in the future. Thus, they took the stance, as expressed by the historian George H. Daniels, that "utility is not to be a test of scientific work, but all knowledge will ultimately prove useful" ("The Pure-Science Ideal," p. 1705).

In return for status and autonomy, scientists also promised to live exemplary lives. "The more detached from their fellow citizens that scientists became," notes David A. Hollinger, "the more necessary did it become for the Victorian moralists—including those who were scientists—to trust that scientists were subject to an ethical code intrinsic to their practice" ("Inquiry and Uplift," p. 147). As humble, incorruptible seekers of truth, scientists assumed the role of latter-day saints living in a climate of moral decay, and science itself took on the trappings of a quasi-religious vocation. Ministers, being committed to dogma rather than to truth, began to suffer by comparison. Among educated Americans, observed Harvard's president Charles W. Eliot in the 1880s, the scientific method of inquiry had come to set a new standard for sincerity and truth to which "Protestant theologians and ministers must rise . . . if they would continue to command the respect of mankind."

Much of the public's enthusiasm for science derived from its conflation of science with inventions, a habit some scientists found annoying. In 1883, for example, the Johns Hopkins physicist Henry Rowland protested the common practice of calling "telegraphs, electric lights, and such conveniences by the name of science." Rowland and his high-minded colleagues did not deny that scientific knowledge had produced many useful devices, but they wanted science to be valued—and supported—for its own sake.

The cultural authority of science soared as the news media reported one breakthrough after another. Medical developments, long slighted by the popular press, now became occasions for celebrating the miracles of science; from the rabies vaccine in the mid-1880s to diphtheria antitoxin and X rays in the mid-1890s. After the rediscovery of the Moravian monk Gregor Mendel's pioneering work on genetics, biologists proved their social worth by helping to breed better crops, animals, and even humans, which gave rise to the eugenics movement. Paeans to scientific and technological progress reached utopian heights in the early 1900s, following the development of the flying machine, the holy grail of inventors. The developing genre of science fiction often depicted a future created by science and technology.

The popularization of science flourished in the 1870s and 1880s as publishers flooded the market with books carrying such titles as *Half-Hours with Famous Scientists* and magazines, such as the *North American Review* and *Harper's,* that revealed the thoughts of successful scientists. Beginning in 1872, *Popular Science Monthly* offered men of science a new outlet for educating the masses. About this time the phrase "popular science" became a commonplace, distinguishing the science consumed by ordinary Americans from real science, which required no modifying adjective. Toward the close of the century, depictions of the places and practices of science grew increasingly remote from the common experience of most Americans. Photographs of scientific laboratories began to appear in magazines such as *Harper's* in the 1890s, and the idea of the laboratory as a distinct and special location gained prominence as World War I approached.

FROM WORLD WAR I THROUGH WORLD WAR II

If American scientists needed additional demonstrations of their social worth to solidify their professional authority, they received them in dramatic fashion in the two world wars. By giving scientists— especially chemists and psychologists, who tested new recruits by the thousands—a chance to prove their usefulness to the military and to industry, World War I helped to elevate science to the status of a valuable national resource. The successes of wartime science also led to increased philanthropic support for basic research, which usually flowed into the coffers of a handful of major research universities. World War II, in which physicists contributed both radar and the atomic bomb to the Allied victory, raised scientists to even greater professional heights. The number of scientists soared as jobs proliferated. The production of Ph.D.s in the natural sciences rose from fewer than three hundred in 1916 to more than three thousand annually in the 1950s. Careers in science became a means to achieve upward social mobility, particularly for lower- and middle-class white Protestant males.

The power of science and scientists to transform the world occupied a central place in popular images of science. World fairs during the interwar years displayed the many ways science could improve daily life. Advertisers invoked the name of science to sell products from appliances to nostrums. Science-fiction writers told of new worlds created by science. The much-vaunted scientific method played an important role in this powerful vision of science, but the details of this method often remained mysterious, especially in the pages of popular magazines, where the phrase frequently appeared.

Yet for all of the success scientists had in securing jobs and winning acclaim during the early years of the twentieth century, science grew increasingly distant from the general public as it became more and more complex and remote from ordinary experience. With the important exception of eugenics, the popularization of science slumped during the second decade of the century and even *Popular Science Monthly* began losing money. After World War I, however, the tide began to turn as journalists replaced scientists as the agents of popularization. The founding in 1919 of Science Service, a source for syndicated news stories about science, heralded this shift. By the early 1930s professional science writers were outpublishing scientists in popular magazines.

The growth of the mass media gave scientists and their work unprecedented publicity. For example, press coverage of the empirical confirmation of Albert Einstein's general theory of relativity in 1919 and his visit to the United States two years later catapulted him to a level of celebrity virtually unheard of for scientists of previous generations. The content of his ideas contributed little to his iconic status, because Einstein's enduring fame rested in part on the incomprehensibility of his science to all but a handful of fellow physicists.

In some guises—chemical warfare, animal vivisection, human experimentation—science appeared not only incomprehensible but menacing. The public debate over human evolution in the 1920s also endangered the reputation of science in some quarters. But even evangelical Christians who deplored the alleged consequences of teaching evolution professed loyalty to science. "It is not 'science' that orthodox Christians oppose," a fundamentalist editor insisted defensively. "No! no! a thousand times, No! They are opposed only to the theory of evolution, which has not yet been proved, and therefore is not to be called by the sacred name of *science*." The Depression years witnessed a mild backlash against science, as articles critical of scientists for their fondness of obscure language and narrow topics reached a peak, but scientists' practical contributions during World War II rescued them from public criticism.

THE ATOMIC AGE

In the years after World War II, the atomic bomb dominated images of science in America. The new weapon immediately entered popular culture as the topic of jokes and songs and lent its name to motels and cocktails. The bomb also graphically demonstrated the material power of science. Although an undercurrent of anxiety occasionally surfaced among the general public after the late 1940s, public opinion polls revealed that most Americans continued to view science as a very good thing. They even respected nuclear physicists, though not as much as scientists generally.

Images of the lone researcher persisted, but increasingly magazines, newspapers, and movies depicted science as a large-scale, organized, impersonal activity. After the public found out about the wartime Manhattan Project, which had produced the atomic bomb, secret government research projects became a staple of novels, movies, and television shows. In films such as *Forbidden Planet* (1956), science appeared as a threat to human existence. Popular images of science often linked it to the military. The hypothetical science of such science-fiction writers as Isaac Asimov and E. E. "Doc" Smith often focused on making war and building empires.

Postwar optimism about science continued into the 1960s, especially in response to the stunning successes of the space program. But then optimism began to wane. The outspoken opposition of the scientific establishment to such widely held views as creationism (believed by nearly half of all Americans and tolerated by millions more), together with suspicions of scientists' complicity in many of society's ills, had begun by the late 1960s to erode public confidence in the morality of science. Rachel Carson's *Silent Spring* (1962) warned of the environmental danger of science and its products, especially DDT. Concern over nuclear waste in the 1970s and 1980s exposed other harmful effects of science. In the 1990s public anxiety became focused on genetic engineering.

Scientists had won immense sums of money for their research and gained virtual autonomy over their own affairs, in exchange for an implicit promise to maintain impartiality and probity and to punish those who failed to do so. Nonetheless, when problems arose, the scientific community frequently chose to deny or minimize them, thus appearing to violate the public's trust. Scientists frequently claimed credit for making the world a better place through science, but shunned responsibility for unwelcome applications of science. When charged with contributing to the death of humans and the destruction of the environment, they carefully distinguished between the production of scientific knowledge and its subsequent uses.

Advocates of alternative science, such as ufologists, parapsychologists, and creationists, often criticized "established science," which they characterized as authoritarian, overspecialized, and closed-minded. Like the phrenologists of the nineteenth century, they sought to make science more open and participatory, an activity in which even the untutored might participate. But as in earlier periods, even the severest critics of elite science commonly professed love of what they regarded as true science. "No one condemns 'science' or 'scientists'—only anti-Christian and evolutionary philosophies of science, biases toward which often cause misinterpretation of scientific 'facts,'" declared one of the country's leading creationists.

Defenders of science as objective truth, concerned by what they perceived to be a surge of irrationality, fought back. In 1976, for example, the Committee for the Scientific Investigation of the Paranormal (CSICOP), which included such scientific luminaries as Carl Sagan, launched an offensive against the various manifestations of "pseudoscience." When some sociologists and historians of science began portraying science as socially constructed knowledge, reflective of the politics and values of the investigators, representatives of the scientific establishment dismissed the revisionist academics as left-wing advocates of what has been condemned as "higher superstition." Meanwhile, ordinary Americans may not have understood—or enjoyed—science, but they continued to respect it and to believe that scientists actually discovered, rather than invented, knowledge of nature.

See also **Science and Religion; The Struggle over Evolution; The Behavioral and Social Sciences** *(volume 1);* **The Ideal of Spontaneity; The Natural World; Psychology, the Mind, and Personality; Anthropology and Cultural Relativism** *(volume 2);* **Technology; The History of Ideas** *(in this volume); and other articles in this section.*

BIBLIOGRAPHY

General Works

Burnham, John C. *How Superstition Won and Science Lost: Popularizing Science and Health in the United States.* New Brunswick, N.J., 1987.

Dupree, A. Hunter. *Science in the Federal Government: A History of Policies and Activities to 1940.* Cambridge, Mass., 1957.

Gieryn, Thomas F. *Cultural Boundaries of Science: Credibility on the Line.* Chicago, 1999.

Hofstadter, Richard, and Walter P. Metzger. *The Development of Academic Freedom in the United States.* New York, 1955.

Kevles, Daniel J. "American Science." In *The Professions in American History,* edited by Nathan O. Hatch. Notre Dame, Ind., 1988.

———. *The Physicists: The History of a Scientific Community in Modern America.* New York, 1978.

Kohlstedt, Sally Gregory, and Margaret W. Rossiter, eds. *Historical Writing on American Science: Perspectives and Prospects.* 1985. Reprint, Baltimore, 1986.

Pauly, Philip J. *Biologists and the Promise of American Life: From Meriwether Lewis to Alfred Kinsey.* Princeton, N.J., 2000.

Numbers, Ronald L. "Science As a Profession." In *Encyclopedia of American Social History,* edited by Mary Kupiec Cayton, Elliott J. Gorn, and Peter W. Williams. Vol. 3, pp. 2285–2295. New York, 1993.

Numbers, Ronald L., and John Harley Warner. "The Maturation of American Medical Science." In *Scientific Colonialism: A Cross-Cultural Comparison,* edited by Nathan Reingold and Marc Rothenberg. Washington, D.C., 1987.

Reingold, Nathan, *Science, American Style.* New Brunswick, N.J., 1991.

Rosenberg, Charles E. *No Other Gods: On Science and American Social Thought.* Baltimore, 1976.

Ross, Dorothy. *Origins of American Social Science.* Cambridge, U.K., 1991.

Warner, John Harley. "The History of Science and the Sciences of Medicine." *Osiris,* 2d series, 10 (1995): 164–193.

Colonial America

Carter, Edward C., II. *"One Grand Pursuit": A Brief History of the American Philosophical Society's First 250 Years, 1743–1993.* Philadelphia, 1993.

Cohen, I. Bernard. *Franklin and Newton: An Inquiry into Speculative Newtonian Experimental Science and Franklin's Work in Electricity as an Example Thereof.* Philadelphia, 1956.

Fortune, Brandon Brame, with Deborah J. Warner. *Franklin and His Friends: Portraying the Man of Science in Eighteenth-Century America.* Washington, D.C., 1999.

Hindle, Brooke. *David Rittenhouse.* Princeton, N.J., 1964.

———. *The Pursuit of Science in Revolutionary America, 1735–1789.* Chapel Hill, N.C., 1956.

Hornberger, Theodore. "Samuel Johnson of Yale and King's College: A Note on the Relation of Science and Religion in Provincial America." *New England Quarterly* 8, no. 3 (1935): 378–397.

———. *Scientific Thought in the American Colleges, 1638–1800.* Austin, Tex., 1946.

Mather, Cotton. *The Christian Philosopher.* Edited by Winton U. Solberg. Urbana, Ill., 1994.

Miller, Perry. *The New England Mind: From Colony to Province.* Cambridge, Mass., 1953.

Stearns, Raymond Phineas. *Science in the British Colonies of America.* Urbana, Ill., 1970.

The Early Republic

Bozeman, Theodore Dwight. *Protestants in an Age of Science: The Baconian Ideal and Antebellum American Religious Thought.* Chapel Hill, N.C., 1977.

Brigham, David R. *Public Culture in the Early Republic: Peale's Museum and Its Audience.* Washington, D.C., 1995.

Daniels, George H. *American Science in the Age of Jackson.* New York, 1968.

Greene, John C. *American Science in the Age of Jefferson.* Ames, Iowa, 1984.

Kohlstedt, Sally Gregory. *The Formation of the American Scientific Community: The American Association for the Advancement of Science, 1848–60.* Urbana, Ill., 1976.

Lucier, Paul. "Commercial Interests and Scientific Disinterestedness: Consulting Geologists in Antebellum America." *Isis* 86, no. 2 (1995): 245–267.

McCandless, Peter. "Mesmerism and Phrenology in Antebellum Charleston: 'Enough of the Marvelous.'" *Journal of Southern History* 58, no. 2 (1992): 199–230.

Numbers, Ronald L. "Charles Hodge and the Beauties and Deformities of Science." In *Charles Hodge Revisited: A Critical Appraisal of His Life and Work,* edited by James H. Moorhead and John W. Stewart. Grand Rapids, Mich., in press.

Numbers, Ronald L. *Creation by Natural Law: Laplace's Nebular Hypothesis in American Thought.* Seattle, Wash., 1977.

Ross, Sydney. "Scientist: The Story of a Word." *Annals of Science* 18, no. 2 (1962): 65–85.

Rossiter, Margaret W. "Benjamin Silliman and the Lowell Institute: The Popularization of Science in Nineteenth-Century America." *New England Quarterly* 44, no. 4 (1971): 602–626.

Slotten, Hugh Richard. *Patronage, Practice, and the Culture of American Science: Alexander Dallas Bache and the U.S. Coast Survey.* Cambridge, U.K., 1994.

Zochert, Donald. "Science and the Common Man in Ante-Bellum America." *Isis* 65, no. 229 (1974): 448–473.

From the Civil War to World War I

Bruce, Robert V. *The Launching of Modern American Science, 1846–1876.* New York, 1987.

Daniels, George H. "The Pure-Science Ideal and Democratic Culture." *Science* 156, no. 3783 (1967): 1699–1705.

Hansen, Bert. "New Images of a New Medicine: Visual Evidence for the Widespread Popularity of Therapeutic Discoveries in America after 1885." *Bulletin of the History of Medicine* 73, no. 4 (1999): 629–678.

Hollinger, David A. "Inquiry and Uplift: Late-Nineteenth-Century American Academics and the Moral Efficacy of Scientific Practice." In *The Authority of Experts: Studies in History and Theory,* edited by Thomas L. Haskell. Bloomington, Ind., 1984.

Kevles, Daniel J. *In the Name of Eugenics: Genetics and the Uses of Human Heredity.* New York, 1985.

Kline, Ronald. "Construing 'Technology' as 'Applied Science': Public Rhetoric of Scientists and Engineers in the United States, 1880–1945." *Isis* 86, no. 2 (1995): 194–221.

Moore, R. Laurence. *In Search of White Crows: Spiritualism, Parapsychology, and American Culture.* New York, 1977.

Moyer, Albert E. *A Scientist's Voice in American Culture: Simon Newcomb and the Rhetoric of Scientific Method.* Berkeley, Calif., 1992.

Numbers, Ronald L. *Darwinism Comes to America.* Cambridge, Mass., 1998.

Roberts, Jon H., and James Turner. *The Sacred and the Secular University.* Princeton, N.J., 2000.

Rothstein, William G. *American Physicians in the Nineteenth Century: From Sects to Science.* Baltimore, 1972.

Schoepflin, Rennie B. "The Christian Science Tradition." In *Caring and Curing: Health and Medicine in the Western Religious Traditions,* edited by Ronald L. Numbers and Darrel W. Amundsen. New York, 1986.

Warner, John Harley. "Ideals of Science and Their Discontents in Late Nineteenth-Century American Medicine." *Isis* 82, no. 313 (1991): 454–478.

From World War I through World War II

Apple, Rima D. *Mothers and Medicine: A Social History of Infant Feeding, 1890–1950.* Madison, Wisc., 1987.

Carson, John. "Army Alpha, Army Brass, and the Search for Army Intelligence." *Isis* 84, no. 2 (1993): 278–309.

Hollinger, David A. *Science, Jews, and Secular Culture: Studies in Mid-Twentieth-Century American Intellectual History.* Princeton, N.J., 1996.

LaFollette, Marcel C. *Making Science Our Own: Public Images of Science, 1910–1955.* Chicago, 1990.

Lederer, Susan E. *Subjected to Science: Human Experimentation in America before the Second World War.* Baltimore, 1995.

Marchand, Roland. *Advertising the American Dream: Making Way for Modernity, 1920–1940.* Berkeley, Calif., 1985.

Rydell, Robert W. *World of Fairs: The Century-of-Progress Expositions.* Chicago, 1993.

Servos, John W. *Physical Chemistry from Ostwald to Pauling: The Making of a Science in America.* Princeton, N.J., 1990.

Tobey, Ronald C. *The American Ideology of National Science, 1919–1930.* Pittsburgh, Pa., 1971.

The Atomic Age

Boyer, Paul S. *By the Bomb's Early Light: American Thought and Culture at the Dawn of the Atomic Age.* New York, 1985.

Leslie, Stuart W. *The Cold War and American Science: The Military-Industrial-Academic Complex at MIT and Stanford.* New York, 1993.

Lewenstein, Bruce V. "Was There Really a Popular Science 'Boom'?" *Science, Technology, and Human Values* 12, no. 2 (1987): 29–41.

Numbers, Ronald L. *The Creationists.* New York, 1992.

Wang, Jessica. *American Science in an Age of Anxiety: Scientists, Anticommunism, and the Cold War.* Chapel Hill, N.C., 1999.

THE HUMANITIES

Naomi F. Collins

The humanities begin the twenty-first century without a common view of their definition, origins, meaning, and value. This lack of consensus emerges from a period of intellectual ferment, social turbulence, and dramatic change in the last third of the twentieth century. New theoretical constructs, expanded participation of minorities and women in civic and campus life, the impact of technologies, and the forces of globalization and ethno-cultural mobility and diversity have all brought the humanities, fields that address questions at the core of the human condition, into the center of the battlefield of debate and search for consensus about core personal, civic, and social values.

New skepticism about methodology and substance has challenged long-held assumptions about the meaning and coherence of the humanities themselves. As a result, clarity, comfort, and confidence in the meaning, content, and value of the humanities have been called into question. Yet this very ferment has created even greater demand for answers to the very questions the humanities have traditionally addressed. Thus, the humanities sit at the beginning of the twenty-first century on the unsettled and unsettling terrain of social and demographic change.

DEFINING THE HUMANITIES: MEANINGS, ORIGINS, AND USES OF THE TERM

The term "humanities" is difficult to define in part because it is used in at least two different ways: (1) to denote specific branches of learning or academic disciplines that explore human experience and values, past and present; and (2) to describe ways of thinking about the human condition. Because the humanities as academic disciplines, or, as "a body of knowledge and insight" and "program for education," may be more easily addressed than the humanities as "ways of thinking," or "an underlying attitude toward life," the former is where this essay begins (ACLS *Report,* 1964, p. 1).

As one way to view the world, the humanities have their own methods, approaches, and content. There is, however, no single view about the origin of the term "humanities." Scholars commonly say that the humanities are of ancient Roman origin, and that modern use of the term derives from Renaissance thinkers to whom the term "humanism" denoted the study of rediscovered ancient Greek and Latin texts (texts on all subjects, not simply on what we now view as the humanities). Scholars have also said, however, that "humanism" was actually a nineteenth-century term, applied retrospectively to the Renaissance.

Scholars view humanistic studies, based in the reading and interpretation of texts, not only to include the cultivation of academic knowledge but to foster the development of character, refined sensibilities, and civic virtue. Although it is not clear whether, historically, classical education actually succeeded in these goals, the ideal has remained embedded in the concept of humanistic study. The *Oxford English Dictionary* and *Webster's* (unabridged) both recognize the role of ancient classics, defining the humanities, respectively, as "learning or literature concerned with human culture, especially the ancient Latin and Greek classics" and as "branches of polite learning regarded as primarily conducive to culture; especially ancient classics and belles-lettres."

The establishment of formal academic disciplines that scholars call the humanities began in the late nineteenth century when the prestige of Renaissance humanistic study was married to the rigor of German scholarship. The goals of humanities disciplines, like the German scholarship they emulated, became scientific objectivity—systems, specialization, and the search for facts—with the aim of adding to a body of human knowledge and texts, while keeping the pursuit and the products "value free." The modern use of the word "humanities," as one of three divisions of knowledge (the other two, science and arts), was a twentieth-century development, not yet graced by consensus on categories and content. Definitions based on disciplinary specialties are used in twenty-first-century language not only for academic but administrative purposes. Governments and higher education institutions, in order to set boundaries for funding, budgets, courses, and buildings, have established recognizable definitions. For these purposes, the humanities are generally considered to include literature, philosophy, religion, and all historical fields.

CLASSIFYING HUMANITIES

Since texts are basic to the humanities, the ways in which libraries (and media) categorize works affect one's access to them. With a term as elusive and evolving as the humanities, classification is not easy. Library of Congress computerized bibliographic searches under "the humanities," for example, reveal works under a broad range of call numbers, but without offering definitions. The old Library of Congress card catalogue offers a two-card entry typed unevenly on a manual typewriter:

> "Humanities." "The studies or branches of learning, collectively, which deal with man and his affairs as contrasted (historically) with (1) nature (natural sciences) and (2) the divine (theology and religion). Corresponds, in general, with 'geisteswissenschaften,' 'humanistic studies,' and 'polite learning,' etc. Includes art and letters, classical studies, the social sciences, history, philosophy, etc. To be used only for works treating of so many of these studies that it is not practicable to make subject entries for each of the [sic] (e.g., art, literature, language and languages, classical education, social sciences, history, philosophy, etc.)."

Search engines on the Internet may in the long term provide new ways to organize and access information on the humanities; but are (as of the year 2000) a work in progress.

The humanities are difficult to discuss because they explore questions at the core of human concerns, probing personal convictions, stirring sensitivities and complacency, confronting cherished values, and challenging certainty. They treat questions that lack easy or conclusive answers. The humanities are also abstract, dealing with ideas rather than techniques, and can appear ambiguous, opaque, and lofty simultaneously. Furthermore, talking about the term "humanities" depends on language, on words and their meanings; and language itself is not precise, but symbolic, representational, and connotative. Sometimes the term "humanities" is confused with terms like "humane" and "humanitarian." And sometimes the humanities are described by what they are not; juxtaposed, for example, to the arts, the sciences, the social sciences, or divinity.

DISCIPLINES, METHODOLOGY, AND SCHOLARSHIP

Each academic discipline of the humanities offers a different approach, body of works, and understanding of the human condition. History, by conveying a sense of the past, provides perspectives and contexts in which to view the present and consider the future. Philosophy helps people think clearly, systematically, and logically; frame questions and construct arguments about complex issues; form ways to judge and evaluate complicated matters; and to separate questions that can be answered from those that cannot. It teaches those who study it to analyze an argument, and avoid the pitfalls of bogus logic.

Language communicates and connects people in ways that are not only precise and informative, but imaginative and evocative. Literature and the arts provide aesthetic experiences that enrich lives and, by reaching beyond limitations of time and place, connect its students to the range of human experience and emotion, and increase one's understanding of cultures and the human condition.

The victory of specialization in academic disciplines has set apparent boundaries within the world of knowledge. Yet there is no universal acceptance on parsing disciplines: some scholars include history under the humanities, others consider humanities a social science; some tilt the humanities toward literary studies and arts, some toward historical and social fields. According to the classicist John H. D'Arms, shifts in "ways of mapping the intellectual territory that falls under the rubric of the humanities" now include "emerging interdisciplinary" fields, such as "cultural, ethnic, and gender studies; literature and law" (in Kernan, *What Happened to the Humanities?*, p. 33). Clearly, the introduction and rapid growth of "interdisciplinary," "cross-disciplinary," and "multidisciplinary" studies affect older definitions, boundaries, classification, and approaches to thinking about, studying, and teaching the humanities. They also challenge traditional administrative delineation of university departments and budgets.

Methodology—approaches to inquiry, understanding, and expression that shape the humanities—has traditionally united humanities disciplines.

152

Whether the humanities are seen to reveal eternal values and truths, or provide historical and temporal contexts for understanding, both approaches share a methodology of interpretation through analysis and critical thinking, systematic logic, and reasoned argument. And they employ language as their medium.

The Rockefeller Commission's *Report: The Humanities in American Life* affirms that the humanities "presume particular methods of expression and inquiry—language, dialogue, reflection, imagination, and metaphor." The historian Gertrude Himmelfarb noted that in the humanities "the method is the message," and feared "postmodernist" questioning of the concept of a discipline or methodology would challenge the core defining feature of the humanities themselves. In any case, it is difficult to imagine the humanities without an explicit or implicit use of methodology, even in arguments refuting the centrality of reasoning, or questioning the value of discipline or methods.

As academic disciplines, the humanities derive from, and rest on, a base of research and scholarship. Although research content and topics change, shaped by changing views on what questions to ask, new sources of information emerge to address new questions, and new ways evolve to examine existing sources. Nonetheless, broad understandings prevail in how scholars should approach and present material.

Underlying the profession of the humanities are: habits of rigorous analysis; critical evaluation and interpretation of sources and texts; reasoned argument; accuracy and integrity of exposition; respect for complexity (and avoidance of oversimplification); recognition of limits (and restraint from overstated conclusions beyond what research warrants); originality (shunning plagiarism and appropriated concepts); systematic, not haphazard, approaches to material and explication; withstanding the test of peer review; and other written and unwritten codes of ethics and practice, and rules of scholarship unique to each field.

Furthermore, the evolving body of scholarship in each discipline serves as the foundation not only for facts or discoveries, but for new theoretical approaches to methodology and interpretation of the field, new contexts, prisms, or lenses for viewing, for example, the interpretation of the past, the reading of texts, and the framing of arguments. Research and scholarship underpin all professional, academic, and public discourse and education in the humanities; and are intended to advance not only each field, but also knowledge itself.

A PROGRAM OF EDUCATION

The humanities as academic disciplines and a body of knowledge, based in research and scholarship, are also "a program of education." They are part of the liberal arts, studies and approaches that "liberate" the mind rather than impart technical or vocational skills. Traditionally viewed by academics as a body of knowledge about human and natural life, the liberal arts, or arts and sciences, include not only the humanities and the arts, but also the natural, physical, and social sciences. University degrees still reflect this broad meaning in their names, the bachelor's degree and master of arts. The degree of doctor of philosophy, or Ph.D., likely reflects the "philosophic" or theoretical approaches to the disciplines that the advanced degree requires. Underlying the study of all liberal arts is training in rationality and introspection, following the Greek philosopher Socrates's precept that the unexamined life is not worth living.

The humanities as a "program of education" have rarely been free of controversy and self-scrutiny. By 1905, the Harvard professor of history Charles Homer Haskins told the American Historical Association that "the most difficult question which now confronts the college teacher in history . . . seems to be the first year college course." Contemporaneously, the Harvard president Charles William Eliot aroused fear of curricular chaos when he introduced the concept of electives, with the intention of "enlarging the circle of the liberal arts."

The introduction of electives, decline in traditional classical curricula, growth of specialization, and founding of professional associations (including the Modern Language Association in 1883 and the American Historical Association in 1884) stimulated the development of new curricula. By 1919–1920, courses in contemporary or Western civilization, introduced at Columbia University and spread elsewhere, revived the late-seventeenth-century "battle of the books." These courses, representing hopes for shared historic and civic understanding, also served larger social purposes: assimilation of immigrants into the American "melting pot" and augmenting United States commitment to involvement with Europe through bolstering European-focused civic culture. But World War I also introduced non-Western cultures to Americans through battles surrounding colonial empires. Domestically, the flourishing creativity of African American arts in the Harlem Renaissance drew the attention of a much larger audience worldwide to the diversity of the United States.

Late-nineteenth- and early-twentieth-century sciences and social sciences provided the humanities new tools and approaches to human motivation and social dynamics, and supported secular intellectual perspectives. The interpretations of Max Planck, Albert Einstein, and Werner Heisenberg in the sciences, Franz Boas in anthropology, and Sigmund Freud in analytic psychology, as well as a growing Marxist school in political economy, introduced concepts of the relativity and uncertainty of truth and values, the hidden world of individual motivation, and deterministic forces of political economy. Things not being what they seem, questions about the nature and interpretation of knowledge, and skepticism about ascertaining objective meaning raised gigantic intellectual questions that in the twenty-first century still roil the humanities. Simultaneously, new technological inventions, especially radio and film, that affected and created mass audiences, and popular and commercial culture, shifted the meaning of "culture."

The 1920s and 1930s also witnessed the growth and spread of ideologies. Theoretical systems and applied practices of communism in the former Soviet Union, national socialism in Germany, and fascism in Italy stimulated highly charged discourse and new formulations in the humanities. Socialism, Marxism, and other related nineteenth-century political philosophies shaped humanities' theory and studies into the twenty-first century. With World War II, optimism about human perfectibility, progress, and betterment diminished as awareness grew of state-sanctioned mass murder performed in the name of ideology and theory. Faith, and loss of faith, in ideology, forms a leitmotif of twentieth-century humanities.

American intellectual life after World War II was fashioned in part by a growing recognition of (and sometime discomfort over) United States hegemony in a global context, and of cultural diversity and pluralism worldwide as Europe lost its centrality and third world nations entered Western consciousness. Meanwhile, the growing cold war and arms race competition with the former Soviet Union spurred an education race. With the Soviet launching of the first *Sputnik* in 1957, specialization and electives (especially in sciences and math) captured more attention than humanities and liberal arts.

Government support for veterans' education (the GI Bill) broadened access to education overall, swelling university enrollments. Historic migration of African Americans from the rural South to the urban North increased and shaped urbanization.

Course content and curricula were challenged by large classes, diverse student bodies, and new global contexts. In the humanities, emphasis shifted to the "problems" approach, for example, "problems in democracy," requiring critical analysis and the use of (excerpted) sources over textbooks. And, intellectually, the humanities were influenced by new definitions of culture: from the anthropologists, values, mores, and practices of a people (including Ruth Benedict's *Patterns of Culture* [1934] and Franz Boas's earlier works); and from what would become cultural studies, a new focus on the culture of nonelites, invalidating taste as a criterion of cultural distinction.

The Vietnam War and its aftermath in the 1960s and 1970s stimulated major changes in public and university life. These assisted the breakup of traditional Western and contemporary civilization curricula and the consensus in the humanities. Questioning the United States government's role in the war led to questioning all power and authority, including that of established texts and interpretations of Western civilization, with concomitant demand for greater student involvement in shaping curricula. These forces, combined with trends in ethnic identification, shifting demographics, larger global vision, and expanded inclusion and expression of women, minorities, gays, people with disabilities, and others, form a prelude to the "culture wars" of the last thirty years of the twentieth century.

HUMANITIES AS WAYS OF THINKING

If the humanities are both a body of learning (parsed into disciplines) and ways of thinking, and methodology is a common denominator, then talking about what the humanities "mean" or "are about" yields varied responses. In general terms, people speak of the humanities as ways to think about what it means to be human; about what human beings have said, done, thought, and created; and as ways of interpreting human experience and making sense of life.

Sometimes people identify a dual function for the studies: both a value to the individual and a role in society. The humanities "have both a personal and civic dimension . . . take the long perspective . . . deal with ends as well as means . . . [and] cultivate critical intelligence," noted the historian Merrill D. Peterson in his 1987 *Humanities and the American Promise*. "The goal of the humanities," he added, "is to heighten consciousness." The American Council of Learned Societies' *Report of the Commission on the Humanities* observes, after conceding "how difficult it is for any committee to discuss the humanities," that "the humanities mirror our own image and our image of the world. Through the humanities we reflect on the fundamental question: what does it mean to be human?" The Columbia University professor Charles Frankel, whose vision was central to the founding of the National Endowment for the Humanities, remarked on the contradictions inherent in the humanities: "The humanities are a curious combination of involvement and detachment; of the search for scientific objectivity and irrepressible personal idiosyncrasy; of piety toward the past and the critique of the past; of private passion and public commitment" (Agresto, *The Humanist as Citizen*, p. 6).

Private Value and Public Role   These ways of talking about the humanities and their meaning reflect a basic dualism between what people view as the humanities' private value and their public role—their individual and social dimensions and their personal and civic application. This bifurcation is central to a discussion surrounding the humanities and their relation to public life. Although most writers acknowledge both roles for the humanities, in stressing one over the other they shape the outcome of their argument about the use or value of the humanities.

This dichotomy has historic roots and political implications, sometimes complicated by claims on either or both sides that the other is partisan or political. The continuing discourse and discord generated by this theoretical, historical, and philosophical dialectic has itself shaped the humanities, and it underlies and fuels issues surrounding what has come to be called the "culture wars" or the "politicization" of the humanities.

Civic Role for the Humanities   For all the differences surrounding public and private "uses" of the humanities, there is an area of broad consensus about roles for the humanities in public life: civic and educational. Writers with a range of views agree that the humanities play a major role in creating an informed, enlightened, and reasoning citizenry in a democracy; and in conveying through education the content and methods of cultural understanding.

It is this area of consensus—education for citizenship—that elicits public support of the humanities. The United States Congress, when it created the National Endowment for the Humanities (NEH) in 1965, echoed themes sounded by the

drafter of the Declaration of Independence Thomas Jefferson in his vision for the United States that civic participation in a democracy requires a deeply informed and educated citizenry, and that in a democracy, humanism is itself a civic ideal. According to legislation establishing NEH:

> A high civilization must not limit its efforts to science and technology alone, but must give full value and support to the other great branches of man's scholarly and cultural activity in order to achieve a better understanding of the past, a better analysis of the present, and a better view of the future. . . . democracy demands wisdom and vision in its citizens, and that it must therefore foster and support a form of education designed to make men masters of their technology and not its unthinking servant. . . . [Therefore] it is necessary and appropriate for the Federal Government to help create and sustain not only a climate encouraging freedom of thought, imagination, and inquiry, but also the material conditions facilitating the release of this creative talent. (Declaration of Findings and Purposes, 20 U.S.C. 951, Sec. 2)

The continued existence of the NEH, a 1985 *Report* of the American Council of Learned Societies affirms, "says a resounding yes to the question whether humanistic learning and scholarship is important to American culture and to the American people."

For purposes of the 1965 legislation and creation of the NEH the definition given by Congress of the humanities was based in both disciplines and application:

> The term "humanities" includes, but is not limited to, the study of language, modern and classical; linguistics; literature; history; jurisprudence; philosophy; archaeology; comparative religion; ethics; the history, criticism and theory of the arts; those aspects of the social sciences which have humanistic content and employ humanistic methods; and the study and application of the humanities to the human environment with particular attention to reflecting our diverse heritage, traditions, and history and to the relevance of the humanities to the current conditions of national life.

The relationship of the humanities to government is complex and controversial, but significant in the United States for the lack of a Ministry of Culture, and/or national policy in the arts and humanities, that characterize most other countries.

The Humanities in Public Life   Outside universities, the humanities actively influence public life, strengthening citizenship and enriching peoples' lives. The humanities engage citizens in discussions of literature at public libraries; in re-creations of history at museums; and in debating civic, ethical, and community issues at public fora nationwide. The humanities inform videotapes on public television, dramatizations at historic places, interpretations at archaeological sites, and explorations of music and theater performance. Public engagement with humanities disciplines and ways of thinking play a key role in what the educator and University of Chicago president Robert M. Hutchins called "the learning society," and what has come to be seen as "lifelong learning" and "continuing education."

THE CULTURE WARS: CURRICULUM, CANON, CULTURE, AND "CORRECTNESS"

Within academe, yet linked to public debate on political and social issues, controversy has marked humanities discourse from the late 1960s through the 1990s in what commentators dubbed "the culture wars." The term derives from the German word *Kulturkampf*, the battle over culture, used to describe the German chancellor Otto von Bismarck's efforts in late-nineteenth-century Germany.

In the United States, debate stemming from a panoply of social issues and built on new theoretical bases of (primarily European) deconstructionist philosophies, has manifested itself in some institutions as struggles over the nature and content of humanities curricula. Departments dispute whether humanities education and curricula ought to be (or remain) rooted in a body of shared texts reinterpreted over time; or whether cultural content needs to be extended beyond traditional texts (some say "dominant" tradition), to incorporate the diverse heritage and expression of people of different genders, social classes, and ethnic and other groups. The key issues implicit in the debate include: Who is, or should be, empowered to select content and shape curriculum (or "the canon" or body of works read and discussed)? What aspects of culture and whose culture should be reflected in the curriculum?

Challenges to traditional humanities theories and curricula, as well as classification of people for admissions, hiring, and promoting by group affiliation (ethnic, race, gender, sexual preference) have since 1990 come to be called, by opponents, "political correctness." Attempts to characterize the debate are fraught with potential bias, as formulations themselves shape the argument. But for twenty-first-century purposes (and recognizing the oversimplification), opposing positions may be characterized as: on one side, acknowledging and incorporating cultural diversity and new perspectives into the humanities through new content and methods, and questioning assumptions underlying traditional rationalism, universalism, and hierarchy of assigned merit; and on the other side, concern that these changes, and their premises, threaten cultural and curricular cohesion, a core of common knowledge, the rigor of the disciplines and standards of institutions, and a shared civic and civil identity in the United States. While one side embraces pluralism and a broadening base of those empowered to define and interpret culture, the other fears particularism and polarization of self-identifying categories of citizens. Some public officials, journalists, and academics assert that power within universities has been assumed by a radical Left that, in the name of cultural sensitivity, silences speech (through speech codes and intimidation). Others contend that, in attacking universities, conservatives seek to discredit theories that support broadened participation in governance and academic fields by previously unempowered groups, especially minorities and women.

Because humanities fields articulate cultural discourse, they become weapons and casualties of battle. Combat for control of humanities curricula and theory are seen by some as part of a greater struggle for control of the nature, purpose, and content of American education. The division in higher education between traditional canon and inclusive curriculum parallels that between "elite" and "popular" culture, or a highbrow/lowbrow split in culture. Academic and public debates mirror one another in arguing the validity and worth of particular forms of cultural expression; the criteria for judging cultural inclusion and exclusion; and the significance of a hierarchy of culture.

With social changes, new interest has arisen in histories and cultural expressions of previously less-documented groups (women, immigrants, minority groups), requiring the identification, validation, and use of new sources. Government records, published books, archived letters, and official documents essential to political and military history are not the best sources for illuminating history "from the bottom up." Private materials, diaries, inventories, material artifacts, and unstudied forms of cultural expression (popular song, crafts, photography, recreation, and entertainment), have enlarged the scope of humanities subjects, and added inter-, multi-, and cross-disciplinary fields to university catalogues. Other scholars question the validity of these approaches, the legitimacy of these materials, and the rigor and standards in these new studies.

Thus, debates over curriculum, canon, culture, and "correctness" reflect larger civic and social issues about which there is no clear consensus. Furthermore, escalating accusations of "politicization" on both sides incite escalated rhetoric, which in turn increases polarity through dramatically delineated extremes, without common language. These debates are linked to profound questions about methodology and whether texts can or should be interpreted; the nature of (or possibility of finding) meaning in texts; and prospects for achieving disinterestedness or objectivity. These issues and concepts (expressed through rubrics, including "postmodernism," "deconstruction," and "poststructuralism"—terms without uniform definition) have implications not only for the content and curriculum of the humanities, but also for ways of approaching and knowing the humanities themselves.

After some three decades' debate (from the late 1960s), late-twentieth-century literature claims the end of the culture wars, and asks who won. It appears that both "liberals" and "conservatives" (using these terms advisedly) agree on one thing: that curricula in many institutions have expanded to encompass groups not previously included, and to explore topics not previously addressed. Whether this change is profound and sustainable, and new works have "displaced" traditional texts, is less clear. Media coverage, often reported by those outside academic disciplines and institutions, highlights disproportionately conferences and topics with the most dramatic discourse. As the humanities evolve through changing times, and, in the process, resolve opposing extremes and balance polarities in an ongoing academic and civic debate dating back to ancient times, the topics of culture wars and political correctness are being relegated to the past.

With traditional liberals and conservatives both believing they have lost the wars, American humanities are at an intellectual turning point—the expansion of canon and methodology less than hoped by liberals; more than desired by traditionalists. As a possible corollary, there has been a decline in study, research, and financial support in the humanities.

ROLES FOR THE HUMANITIES TODAY AND IN THE FUTURE

Perhaps as great a challenge to humanities education as the battles over theory are those over teaching the humanities in new media. "Distance education"—teaching and learning transmitted electronically (via Internet, video, and emerging technologies), rather than in shared space and time—raises new questions about conveying and comprehending fields based in participatory, reasoned discourse, in a new context of solo study and asynchronous setting. Other new forces—privatization pressures on institutions, a thinning line in the media between education and entertainment, and between authentic and fictionalized presentation, challenges to government support for culture, and discord dividing academic departments—will also shape the future of the humanities.

As current trends have led some people to doubt the value of the humanities, and to question their future, responsible citizens and scholars must ask, Of what significance will the humanities be in the twenty-first century?

The disarray in humanities studies at the beginning of the twenty-first century reflects a central paradox. The very forces that brought decline to study, research, and support for the disciplines; cast doubt on content, methodology, and "knowability" at the core of humanities thinking; and disrupted consensus about the meaning and use of the humanities have also validated the centrality of the humanities to discussion of core issues of personal values and civic change.

Even as the humanities have become unsettled, reflecting and affecting personal choices and social challenges, one's sense of oneself and the meaning of community and one's personal values and civic life, they continue to explore and explain those questions most central to human lives, politics, beliefs, histories, cultural expressions, values, and ideals. This suggests at least three major areas in which the humanities will have continued value and use.

First, in support of democracy as a political and social concept and practice, the argument inherited and elaborated by the nation's early leaders Thomas Jefferson and James Madison still holds: that is, that democracy demands an educated and reasoning citizenry to inform choice of leaders and representatives, to tackle complex social and political issues and decisions, to maintain civic and civil values, and to participate actively at all levels of governance to ensure that power remains with the people as a whole. And as public participation broadens within and across societies, education in the humanities and liberal arts becomes more, not less, central to shaping and maintaining social and political discourse.

Second, as the impact of technology more deeply permeates each person's life, and more broadly affects all parts of the globe and deeper levels of society within each, the role of the humanities

157

will become more, not less, crucial. Insofar as technology addresses and affects human needs and quality of life issues, it requires more, not less, participation of citizens making informed and reasoned choices about the nature and use of technology—ethical choices surrounding life and death issues; economic and social decisions setting priorities and allocating resources; civic issues concerning equity and access—all in an arena of competing priorities. Addressing the choices and dilemmas that technology poses, but does not resolve, provides another significant role for humanities education, methodology, and ways of thinking.

Third, as traditional nation-states shift focus to greater economic and commercial trade interests in the new "globalized" world of business, finance, and popular culture, and traditional political borders assume different roles, centers of political and economic power arise locally and regionally. The traditional walls that separated people—spatial barriers in distances that could not easily be breached, political barriers in national attitudes, and physical barriers in stone and mortar fortifications, like the Berlin Wall—have given way to cultural barriers separating people over ethnic and tribal identification; linguistic, sectarian, historical, and cultural differences in perception and behavior. In both benign and hostile manifestations, ethnic banding requires more, not less, understanding of the clash of historical, religious, linguistic, and cultural ideas, fields for which the humanities best prepare people.

Implicit in these roles for the humanities are two basic premises. First, that human beings are blessed and burdened with the power of choice; and these choices, including the choice not to act, shape personal lives and communities. Thoughtful, reasoned decisions draw on knowledge, values, and ways of thinking, the foundations of which reside in the humanities. And second, as the world witnesses accelerating but discontinuous change, with choppy and unpredictable leaps and lurches in civic life, citizens are best prepared by a grounding in the branches of inquiry and knowledge dedicated to providing context and understanding of critical issues faced by individuals, nations, and cultures.

In sum, an important terrain for academic and public humanities will be in addressing civic issues in emerging, expanding, and rejuvenating democracies worldwide; shaping technological possibilities with human choices; and mediating cultural clashes within and among populations molded by historic hatreds or mixed by massive migrations. As the humanities continue to articulate cultural discourse, they will sit perpetually on the unsettled and unsettling terrain of social and demographic change. And they remain destined for controversy as they challenge the certainties of traditional values, revealed faith, and scientific law. But with or without the humanities, human beings will continue to confront vital and vexing questions, which the humanities help address. The issue will not be whether Americans confront these questions, but whether they are equipped to address them well, through reasoned, thoughtful, and productive discourse based in the humanities as branches of learning and as ways of thinking about the human condition.

See also **Philosophy from Puritanism to the Enlightment; Moral Philosophy; Southern Intellectual Life; The Behavioral and Social Sciences** *(volume 1);* **New Philosophical Directions; Psychology, the Mind, and Personality** *(volume 2);* **The History of Ideas; Hermeneutics and American Historiography; Cultural Studies; Social Construction of Reality** *(in this volume); and other articles in this section.*

BIBLIOGRAPHY

General

Agresto, John, and Peter Riesenberg. *The Humanist as Citizen.* Chapel Hill, N.C., 1981. Published as a memorial to Charles Frankel; includes twelve-page bibliography of his works.

Allardyce, Gilbert. "The Rise and Fall of the Western Civilization Course." *The American Historical Review* 87, no. 3 (June 1982): 695–725.

American Council of Learned Societies, et al. *A Report to the Congress of the United States on the State of the Humanities.* New York, 1985.

———. *Report of the Commission on the Humanities.* New York, 1964.

Arthurs, Alberta. "The Humanities in the 1990s." In *Higher Learning in America, 1980–2000.* Edited by Arthur Levine, 259–272. Baltimore, 1993.

Association of American Colleges. *Liberal Learning and the Arts and Sciences Major.* Washington, D.C., 1991. Includes useful chapter on interdisciplinary studies. See chapter 4, pp. 61–76.

Bender, Thomas. *Intellect and Public Life: Essays on the Social History of Academic Intellectuals in the United States.* Baltimore, 1993.

Callahan, Daniel, Arthur L. Caplan, and Bruce Jennings, eds. *Applying the Humanities.* New York and London, 1985. Companion piece to Hastings Center Report.

Carnochan, W. B. *The Battleground of Curriculum: Liberal Education and American Experience.* Stanford, Calif., 1993.

Collins, Naomi F. *Culture's New Frontier: Staking a Common Ground.* Occasional Paper, no. 15. 1990. (ERIC ED 357 979.) New York, American Council of Learned Societies, 1990.

——. "Technological Challenges/Human Choices." Speech delivered to Commission of National Research Council, National Academy of Sciences, 1993.

——. *Unlocking the Secrets of Time: Maryland's Hidden Heritage.* Baltimore, 1991. Conference conceived by author on interpreting history through new materials.

Commission on the Humanities. *Report: The Humanities in American Life.* Berkeley, Los Angeles, London, 1980. [The Rockefeller Commission Report.]

Daedalus. "The Future of the Humanities." 98, no. 3 (Summer 1969); and "Theory in Humanistic Study." 99, no. 2 (spring 1970). Two special issues devoted to the humanities.

Hollinger, David A., and Charles Capper, eds. *The American Intellectual Tradition.* 3rd ed. New York and Oxford, 1997. A two-volume sourcebook of readings with introductions.

House Committee on Education and Labor. (1970); Senate Committee on Labor and Public Welfare. (1973); Senate Committee on Labor and Human Resources, Subcommittee on Education. (1979); House Committee on Education. Field Hearings on the Reauthorization of the National Foundation on the Arts and Humanities. (1980); House Committee on National Foundation of the Arts and Humanities, Reauthorization of the National Foundation for the Arts and Humanities. (1980); House Committee on Education and the National Foundation on the Arts and Humanities, Hearing on Reauthorization of the National Foundation on the Arts and Humanities. (1984); House Committee on Education and National Foundation on the Arts and Humanities, Reauthorization of Foundation on the National Foundation on the Arts and Humanities. (1986)

Hutchins, Robert M. *The Learning Society.* New York, 1968.

Kammen, Michael. "Culture and State in America." *The Journal of American History* 83 (December 1996): 791–814. Includes notes for further reading.

Katz, Stanley N. "Influences on Public Policies in the United States." In *The Arts and Public Policy in the United States,* edited by W. McNeil Lowry, pp. 23–37. Englewood Cliffs, N.J., 1984.

National Endowment for the Humanities. "An Introduction to the National Endowment for the Humanities." Washington, D.C. (January 1989).

——. "NEH and State Programs." Washington, D.C. (n.d.).

National Foundation on the Arts and Humanities Act of 1965, 89 Congr., 1 sess., P.L. 89–209. Declaration of Findings and Purposes, 20 U.S.C. 951, Sec. 2.

Peterson, Merrill D. *The Humanities and the American Promise.* Colloquium on the Humanities and the American People. 1987.

Stimpson, Catharine R. "A Welcome Treaty: The Humanities in Everyday Life." In *Where the Meanings Are,* edited by Catharine Stimpson, pp. 165–178. New York, 1988.

Tolo, Kenneth W., ed. *Government and the Humanities: Toward a National Cultural Policy.* 1979.

U.S. House Committee on Education and Labor. White House Conference on the Humanities. Washington, D.C., 1979.

Works Speaking to Humanities Issues and Debates

Bennett, William. "The Humanities, the Universities, and Public Policy." *The Humanist as Citizen* (1981): 188–201.

——. "The Shattered Humanities." *American Association of Higher Education Bulletin* 35, no. 6 (February 1983): 3.

Berman, Paul, ed. *Debating P.C.: The Controversy Over Political Correctness on College Campuses.* New York, 1992.

Bloom, Allan. *The Closing of the American Mind: How Higher Education Has Failed Democracy and Impoverished the Souls of Today's Students.* New York, 1987.

Cheney, Lynne V. *Humanities in America: A Report to the President, the Congress, and the American People.* Washington, D.C., 1988.

——. *Tyrannical Machines: A Report on Educational Practices Gone Wrong and Our Best Hopes for Setting Them Right.* Washington, D.C., 1990.

Duignan, Peter. *Political Correctness: A Critique.* Stanford, Calif., 1995.

Feldstein, Richard. *Political Correctness: A Response from the Cultural Left.* Minneapolis, Minn., 1997.

Gitlin, Todd. "Have the Culture Wars Ended?" *The Chronicle of Higher Education* 44, no. 26 (March 6, 1998): B 4–5.

Graff, Gerald. *Beyond the Culture Wars: How Teaching the Conflicts Can Revitalize American Education.* New York, 1992.

Hirsch, E. D., Jr. *Cultural Literacy: What Every American Needs To Know.* Boston, 1987.

Kernan, Alvin, ed. *What's Happened to the Humanities?* Princeton, N.J., 1997.

Levine, Lawrence W. *Highbrow/Lowbrow: The Emergence of Cultural Hierarchy in America.* Cambridge, Mass., 1988.

——. *The Opening of the American Mind: Canons, Culture, and History.* Boston, 1997.

Newfield, Christopher, and Ronald Strickland, eds. *After Political Correctness: The Humanities and Society in the 1990s.* Boulder, Colo., 1995.

Novick, Peter. *That Noble Dream: The "Objectivity Question" and the American Historical Profession.* New York, 1988.

Nussbaum, Martha C. *Cultivating Humanity: A Classical Defense of Reform in Liberal Education.* Cambridge, Mass., 1997.

Stearns, Peter N. *Meaning over Memory: Recasting the Teaching of Culture and History.* Chapel Hill, N.C., 1993.

Stimpson, Catharine R. "A Call for Cultural Democracy." Address presented at the National Conference of State Humanities Councils, December 11, 1988. Federation of State Humanities Councils, publication no. 8–89. Washington, D.C., 1989.

———. "A Call for Cultural Democracy" reviewed, summarized, and quoted in "The Necessities of Aunt Chloe." *Humanities Discourse* 3, no. 1 (January/February 1989): 14–15.

Williams, Mary E. *Culture Wars: Opposing Viewpoints.* San Diego, Calif., 1999. Book contains excerpts of readings from popular journals, written for the most part by sociologists, political leaders, and journalists. The bibliography lists books (unrelated to the essays) on the "culture wars."

THE SOCIAL SCIENCES

Hamilton Cravens

The social sciences in America owe their origins to the American Revolution, for the Imperial Crisis (1763–1776) and the Revolution made it essential for Americans to become producers as well as consumers of social speculation and knowledge. The ideology of the Revolution was taken from the English and American Enlightenments, but the events of 1763–1789 forced Americans to think about government, society, the economy, and the relationship of the past, the present, and the future. From this basis Americans from a variety of social classes elaborated and articulated the social disciplines in historical and institutional contexts throughout the early to late nineteenth century. The political system continued to serve as the institutional nexus for social sciences discourse for almost a century. In the late 1830s and early 1840s, in common with like-minded Europeans, Americans worked out an intellectual strategy for social investigation and interpretation. They formulated a concept of the social group and the meaning of the individual's membership in a social group, thus abandoning older notions of an atomistic society populated by autonomous individuals.

With the advent of research universities in the late nineteenth and early twentieth centuries, the character of the social disciplines changed. No longer was it the intelligent and honorable citizen of high moral character who wrote and taught and participated in the work of the social science disciplines in the United States. Now came the academic social scientist, with new notions of expertise, scientific authority, truth, and objectivity. Now the discourses of the social sciences had two loci—in government and in higher learning.

SOCIAL SCIENCE IN A REVOLUTIONARY ERA

When the American patriots went to war with their imperial British masters, it was with a musket in one hand and a potential state constitution in the other. Both the study of politics and the dismal science of economics received quite an intellectual workout in the quarter century following the musket fire at the Battles of Lexington and Concord (1775). In 1776 Thomas Paine, an English immigrant to America, published *Common Sense,* the thesis of which was that British imperial rule had become intolerable and had to be overthrown. But Paine's deeper assumptions entered into the rapidly crystallizing American political discourse. His larger—and more radical—assumption was that government was artificial and society was natural, and that the best government was that which was the smallest. If the state could melt away and leave good republican citizens to live their lives and conduct their public and private business according to the moral precepts of civic virtue, then all would be as it should. Paine boldly outlined his other assumption in *The Rights of Man,* part 2 (1792), arguing that sovereignty was indivisible. It should be invested in a unicameral legislature, from whose representatives would come the executive leaders as well. Paine disputed the tripartite division of sovereignty among the legislative, executive, and judicial branches of government that was allegedly so much a part of British government and that had been installed in the state constitutions and in the new U.S. Constitution (1788). Much of the federal constitution was presaged in the state constitutions of the Revolutionary War era, which called for a republican form of government with no established church, titled aristocracy, permanent military, or governmental monopoly. The state constitutions also called for periodic elections, a bicameral legislature, an executive branch, and a court system, and they guaranteed some civil liberties and the right to own property.

The U.S. Constitution provided the structure for a limited federal government that would perform but a handful of functions beyond the creation of an apparently indivisible national union. The federal

163

government's main duties were to provide for interstate commerce, a common defense and foreign policy, and a republican form of government for all present and future states, from the Atlantic to the Pacific.

In the years before 1800, however, other components of the revolutionary settlement crystallized, chief of which was citizenship. Education mattered here, for it would train future citizens to be literate voters and competent heads of households, able to wrest a living and support a family. Education plans proposed during this period included Thomas Jefferson's proposal for state education as governor of Virginia in 1779, the professor, physician, and patriot Benjamin Rush's model for his polyglot Philadelphia population in 1798, and the clergyman and educator Timothy Dwight's proposition for coeducation during the same period. In the Revolution's aftermath, slavery became a southern institution. Northern states banned or prevented the practice within their borders but permitted the segregation of African Americans into a status below that of white aliens. Jefferson and a succession of presidents and other public officials made certain that the indigenous peoples of North America could never become citizens. Public figures in the new republic also debated the virtues of laissez-faire capitalism and the role of the state in the economy. On one side of the debate were those who agreed with the relatively moderate views of Adam Smith, author of *Wealth of Nations* (1776). Smith's views were expounded by the brilliant Alexander Hamilton. On the other side were Jefferson and his political followers, who held more extreme views and struggled valiantly to keep government action to a minimum.

By the time of George Washington's inauguration as president of the United States in 1789, the growing political and economic systems of the fledgling country had created an institutional and conceptual framework for the elaboration of several social sciences. These included law, constitutional and political theory, political economy, education as both pedagogy and training for citizenship, the comparative anthropology of the white, black, and red races, and even agriculture, which was celebrated by Jefferson and many others as the basis of the good life. The Revolution's heritage defined white women as mothers of the new republic. They were the preservers of morality, culture, and private life, whereas white men were the breadwinners and the voting citizens, who dealt in the spheres of work and public life. Thus had the new political system rejected much of the European past, even the British past, and for more than a century laid the foundation of innovation in social and political institutions and in the development of the social sciences. The creation of multiple religious denominations owing to the separation of church and state, along with the passing of control of government from the Federalists to the Jeffersonians, completed the development of a civic republic with freedom of thought and republican stability.

SOCIAL SCIENCE IN THE AGE OF CIVIC INDIVIDUALISM

In 1795 the inventor Oliver Evans and Thomas Ellicott, a millwright, published an important book, *The Young Mill-Wright and Miller's Guide.* In its pages they published what appeared at first blush to be a very practical guide to water-milling practices. Yet they did not write about practices in the past or present so much as about what might take place in the future. They wrote about activities not yet typical in their young country, about large and complicated milling operations—such as milling flour—which contrasted with the small-scale milling that characterized the American scene. Here was a new idea, of a world without limits, of a future of prosperity guaranteed by the promise of technology. The world of mercantilism, the world of limits, was cast aside, and the idea of progress—a major assumption of post-Enlightenment social science and liberal politics—was born.

The individual was the key to American society and culture in the early nineteenth century. Americans wanted a free society in which civilized individuals could pursue commerce and trade via the laissez-faire principles of the radical and highly individualistic Scottish philosopher and economist James Mill, not through Adam Smith's more moderate (and more mercantilist) doctrines. Competition was welcome, but monopoly was not. There was no justification for special privilege in American society and culture, because America had such abundant resources. All civilized individuals could pursue commerce and trade without interference from government. The corporation was radically restructured, so that it no longer served a mercantilist monopoly. States permitted corporate charters to do one task or a few closely related ones, so that they would not throttle opportunity elsewhere. Business enterprise flourished in these circumstances.

In politics radical individualists such as the Locofocos, a New York Democratic group organized in 1835, represented the urban artisan or mechanic in the Northeast, whereas radical individualists in the countryside supported the independent yeoman farmer, thus creating a specific discourse for a particular program in political economy. Political economy was becoming a body of customs and an intellectual discourse with theories, assumptions, rules of proof, and a growing body of knowledge that fused the material with the spiritual aspects of the world. Dr. Jacob Bigelow, a lecturer at Harvard, coined the term "technology" in his book *The Elements of Technology* (1829). He insisted that the application of science to the useful arts made modern civilization superior to that of the ancients—that technology assisted enterprise in bringing about human progress. Most Americans began to equate moral and economic progress and celebrated the heroic individual who invented technology—the material sign of moral progress.

Education also blossomed in the early 1800s. In the North and the West the district school spread. It constituted the smallest governing unit in American politics. Each district had at least one ungraded school, which was in session during the winter months, after harvest and before seed planting. The teachers were men, symbols of knowledge and authority—and individual autonomy. Their pedagogy, or teaching methods, borrowed from the age's focus on individualism. Pupils often ranged in age from seven to seventeen. The teacher gave them daily assignments from a particular book that they were to learn by rote memorization, because it was through mastery of language that individuals became intelligent. As pupils learned one text, they were given another, until the sum of the important knowledge of the world had been thus imparted, all in a few winter seasons. Mechanics' institutes and agricultural societies met the need for more education, especially for the virtuous yeomanry, whether independent, self-employed mechanics (that is, artisans and shopowners) or those who tilled the soil. The mechanics' institutes and the agricultural societies aimed to teach young men practical knowledge for self-improvement and commercial or economic success. They competed for prizes that would advance knowledge, especially technical knowledge. Academies offered instruction in subjects too advanced for the district school and too elementary for the college or university. Before the 1830s only young men, not young women, could attend. A distinguished academy was the Albany Academy in New York's capital city. It numbered among its faculty some of the nation's leading scientists and scholars, including no less a rising star than the natural philosopher Joseph Henry. From

such institutions and pedagogic principles emerged the social science of education. And education was a blueprint of society. White males could take advantage of education as much as they wished, including higher education, where the institutional action was in the rise of the denominational college. White females had fewer opportunities than white males, and nonwhites had few, if any, opportunities for education.

A body of political doctrine and constitutional law was developed in the early decades of the 1800s as well. Americans grounded their political and constitutional theory upon a unique notion of constitutional federalism in which there was a sharply defined and limited national government (the reverse of the European pattern), with most of the power remaining at the lowest possible level, whether the states or the localities. John Taylor of Caroline, a politician and agriculturist, published tracts on agricultural reform as well as broadsides in which he attacked centralizing tendencies in political and economic life from a more radical perspective than had Thomas Jefferson. The jurists Joseph Story of Massachusetts and James Kent of New York codified constitutional and common law and achieved a reconciliation of American law and British common law precedents, which Andrew Jackson and his supporters attacked and finally began to overthrow after Jackson's election to the White House.

DEMOCRATIC CULTURE AND THE INVENTION OF THE GROUP IN SOCIAL SCIENCE

Between the late 1830s and the 1870s many Americans began to act and think as if the most important fact about people was their membership in a particular social group—for example, a gender, racial, ethnic, or religious group, or a social or occupational class. Americans thought of their culture as a happy, homogeneous social unit made up of many distinct groups whose value resided precisely in how close they were to some imagined norm or standard of being "American." The new democratic culture of the mid-nineteenth century took for granted a common national identity that was based on a certain moral worth. In that sense it was a parallel cultural transformation to the nationalistic-cum-folkish movements then sweeping Europe and Latin America. As Americans abandoned identification with the Old World, they thought of themselves as a people who shared the same values, manners, and hopes. Conformity, not individualism, mattered now. This notion had obvious consequences for social thought and social science. Two developments in the human sciences help us grasp the cultural transformation from the age of the individual to that of the group: (1) the redefinition of a species as an aggregate of individuals with many traits in common, rather than an atomistic assemblage whose similarities came from adaptation of individuals to a common environment; and (2) the development of statistics, or the dynamics of group coherence and behavior. Both took shape in the late 1830s and early 1840s.

With the advent of the group as a social and political concept came a corresponding crystallization of the social science disciplines. The group-individual nexus provided a theoretical framework from which to develop systematic knowledge about categorizing groups and their traits. This new conceptual structure allowed social scientists to move beyond the old-time Baconian thinking, in which there were no norms save God's design. With the new thinking, the data of society and of nature were simply data, shorn of theological or moral value. The group, not the individual, stood at the center of society and culture. Thus, the laissez-faire market economy functioned according to the actions of various groups—farmers, bankers, investors, manufacturers, mechanics, and so on. When President Andrew Jackson vetoed the renewal of the charter of the Bank of the United States in 1832, he insisted that the bank allowed a class of rich and powerful men to enjoy the benefits of governmental protection, and that "the humble members of society— the farmers, mechanics, and laborers" (Sellers, p. 325) were unfairly treated. And so it went. The effect of the Supreme Court's *Charles River Bridge* decision of 1837 was to permit corporations to rewrite their charters to engage in multiple business activities. Writers of books of "political economy," as economics was known, could insist that their field was a science, because the laws of economics were drawn from nature. Political economy, now configured as a natural science of the behavior of groups, was no longer merely a political discourse but a social science as well.

Starting in the 1830s there was a dramatic shift in the way white Americans perceived persons of color in America, especially African Americans. They began to consider blacks to be Americans of African ancestry, a people whose history and destiny were linked to the United States, not to Africa. This idea was evident in the shift from colonization to emancipation as the solution to the problem of slavery in American culture.

In *Crania Americana,* published in 1839, Dr. Samuel G. Morton discussed a study in which he measured the cranial capacities of the skulls of more than twenty different "races," most Native American, and derived an average cranial capacity. Assuming that the larger the brain, the smarter its owner, Morton constructed a racial hierarchy, with whites on top, thus deploying the new concept of the group or species and the new statistics simultaneously. Morton and other colleagues and supporters, including the Mobile, Alabama, physician Josiah Knott and the naturalist Louis Agassiz of Harvard, constituted the so-called American school of physical anthropology, whose influence spread across the Atlantic and persisted into the early twentieth century. This new racial (and racist) anthropology provided whatever scientific justification was needed in mid-nineteenth-century America for the segregation of the white and nonwhite races. Hence, the emphasis in social science was on the physical traits and characteristics of the various groups in the population, whether the science was phrenology, hydropathy, religious communitarianism, or even the treatment of the insane, otherwise known as moral therapy. If people could be cured through the ministrations and special knowledge of these social sciences, it was through the reformation of habits. In other words, a common material experience was what made people a group and was the key to the causes of their ideas and conduct.

Education became a social science discipline as well, cut out of the whole cloth of experience with public education in the new republic. Starting in the 1830s, various interest groups agitated for the expansion of public education at public expense. They insisted that a democratic and egalitarian society demanded public education to render well-informed voters and well-trained workers in the market economy. No longer was the district school an appropriate remedy. Society was composed of groups—Catholics, Protestants, immigrants, the native born, the rich, the poor, the middle class, and many others—and it was essential to integrate them all into a common American cultural and political identity. Hence, the grammar school of the democratic era sought to impose that identity on girls as well as boys to make them all democratic citizens, enamored of the promises of American civilization. In the grammar school a common pedagogy emerged in which pupils were taught to recite the lessons of the "three R's" (reading, writing, and arithmetic), and whatever else was offered, according to the principles of American nationalism and a vague Protestant morality. In the classroom, the teacher's authority was absolute. Pupils recited their lessons as a group and memorized texts. Conformity of behavior and unity of mind and purpose were the real goals. Schools were manufacturing citizens. The underlying scientific assumption of this patriotic pedagogy was that behavior and attitudes could be made and reformed through the teaching of the right habits—of conformity. Alexis de Tocqueville and other aristocratic commentators on mid-century American democracy had a point when they insisted that democracy might well stifle individuality for the sake of equality.

SYSTEMATIC SOCIAL SCIENCE IN THE AGE OF EXPERTISE

Between 1870 and 1920 American social science took on key elements of its recognizably modern institutional and intellectual character. Social scientists found a new institutional home in the emerging private and public research universities. Correspondingly, they adopted—not without contention and struggle—the coda of expertise, common to the new era of hierarchy and system. Knowledge of the world and of society was constantly expanding. It was no longer possible for one to know everything, although Americans (and Europeans) had been able to convince themselves they could as late as the 1830s. Specialization, or "expertise," was the watchword of the age. Such expertise, to be valid, had to be objective, unbiased, and patterned after the rigor of the most exact of the physical sciences. Science had made great strides in a few decades. Chemistry, physics, biology, and medicine had all changed the lives of many people, and their advances proved the worth of the scientific method. Each discipline of knowledge had its own methods, ideas, and information. Some disciplines were more valuable than others, just as some peoples or nations or races could be arranged in a systematic hierarchy of worth.

In the 1870s an important shift in determining social status began to take place. Since the 1790s character, reputation, or morality determined social status—talent was the consequence of virtue, in Thomas Jefferson's felicitous words. But starting in the 1870s Americans reversed that equation: skill, talent, ability, and intelligence (or lack thereof) determined one's character, morality, or reputation. This principle was clearly evident in the new for-

mulations of social science in the five decades following the end of the Civil War in 1865.

Evolutionary science had a major influence on the social sciences during this era. From the discipline of philosophy arose naturalistic psychology. Its practitioners declared their intellectual affiliations with the experimental natural scientists and insisted that they wished to understand the traits of the mind. They sought to explain human nature and conduct by invoking human social instincts, starting with the Darwinian insight that instincts were survival mechanisms in the struggle for existence. Countless psychologists in America repeated this doctrine in lectures, textbooks, and articles—without subjecting the doctrine to experimental verification. Other psychologists anxious to measure the differences in intelligence among individuals and various racial and ethnic groups discovered the French psychologist Alfred Binet's standardized intelligence test. They changed its orientation and structure to help classify groups in the American population that differed from the white Anglo-Saxon Protestant (WASP) middle class upon which the American versions of the Binet were standardized or normed. The most extensive example of this sort of work was the U.S. Army mental tests, conducted by overeager mental testers in uniform during World War I. The army merely wished for help in sorting out officer material, whereas the psychologists wanted a national IQ test for all "races." The army tests showed, or seemed to show, that various races performed less well than the WASP middle class—that, in short, there was a natural and inevitable hierarchy of racial intelligence. The new psychology showed that the meaning of group membership for the individual had changed since the mid-nineteenth century. No longer were Americans a common people with a common heritage. Every group was distinct from every other group, and some were superior to others. Nor could an individual change through a modification of habits, as had been argued during the democratic era.

Psychology's applied branch, education, embraced and generated similar theories and attitudes. During these decades the great mass of students were segregated into schools deemed fitting for their innate characteristics. The advent of emancipation (1863) brought slaves the kind of racially segregated schools in the South that free blacks had in the North before the Civil War. Neighborhood determined to a large extent where a child attended elementary or grammar school, and, often, high school. The increasing ethnic, class, and racial segregation of the nation's cities, towns, and even villages in these five decades sorted pupils accordingly. In urban high schools the children of the poor, whether native born or immigrant, found themselves in curricula designed to put them into the workforce without benefit of the college education that more and more middle- and upper-class pupils were receiving. Although public schools through high school were coeducational, boys and girls studied gender-segregated curricula—no cooking classes for boys and no woodshop (or, tellingly, calculus) for girls. Some of the nation's most prestigious private colleges and universities remained open to men or women only throughout the era. Land grant colleges became racially segregated, while their curricula for whites was determined by gender. For instance, men were allowed to study basic chemistry, but women were shunted off into food and nutrition. In medical education reforms after 1910, admission was restricted to the scientifically gifted. This practice also reduced the number of women and nonwhites in medical schools dramatically by the period's end. And within educational institutions at all levels, hierarchy ruled.

Political science and constitutional law, or the study of government in action, underwent changes apposite to the era's ruling assumptions. In *The Common Law* (1881), the American jurist Oliver Wendell Holmes Jr. insisted that the social and psychological forces behind the law should be understood so that one could predict, with scientific precision, what the courts would decide in particular cases at hand. His perspective gained ground among constitutional lawyers, judges, scholars, and activists, especially after 1900, as federal and state courts threw out or weakened social legislation important to many reformers. In his famous work *An Economic Interpretation of the Constitution* (1913), the American historian Charles A. Beard, by arguing that politicians and investors created and ratified the Constitution to serve the interests of the elite class to which they belonged, suggested the historical relativity of the law and its vulnerability to the vicissitudes of social and economic interest group pressures, thus undermining absolutist reverence for an unchanging constitution. At several leading state universities, especially at the University of Wisconsin, professors in political science and economics helped advise governors and legislators on laws that would change governmental favoritism for particular groups in the body politic. Many states changed their constitutions during these years; they considered more than fifteen hundred constitutional amendments and adopted 60 percent

of them. Professors worked hand in glove with politicians. These constitutional changes were intended to strengthen the executive over the legislative branch; centralize administration by adopting civil service and executive, not legislative, public budgets; and increase popular control over government, chiefly by weakening the power of the parties through the direct primary, the initiative, and other such devices and inventing similarly hierarchical reforms of municipal government. Most political scientists welcomed these changes and worked toward their adoption. Perhaps the most important text in the field was Arthur F. Bentley's *The Process of Government* (1908), in which Bentley argued for the group basis of politics. Members of interest groups, in his view, always had similar attitudes on the issues because of their history and social attributes. The groups exerted pressure on government, and the outcome was always the result of that pressure. Law, like the political process itself, was not the result of abstract and disinterested deliberations, but an attempt to systematize and rationalize interest group relations. Politics and law were historical events, struggles among interests, nothing more, nothing less.

Between 1870 and 1920 social science found an institutional home in higher education. Social scientists depicted reality as three-dimensional and spoke in reductionist terms, emphasizing how and why the various parts—or groups—fit into the larger whole. They succeeded in presenting their work as that of neutral, detached, and rigorous experts—academic professionals—whatever their activities as interested political activists might have been.

THE RISE OF HOLISTIC BEHAVIORAL SCIENCE

The academic revolution had run its first phase by the 1920s. Social scientists were becoming entrenched in colleges and universities, where there was still more teaching than research. This would be the case until the 1950s, when government contracts and grants would reshape scientific and intellectual life in ways that the budgets of institutions of higher learning and the new foundations of the age, such as the Carnegie, Rockefeller, and Ford Foundations, could not. A new conception of the nature of social and natural reality crystallized during these years. It was a holistic or organic network, a system of systems, consisting of many distinct yet interrelated parts. This was a vision that often led to interdisciplinary work. Individuals still could not change their group identity, but all groups somehow fit into the larger whole, or the national population. In the interwar years, social scientists took up a behavioral perspective of the phenomena they studied. They were interested in the description and, whenever possible, the experimental or statistical measurement of human behavior. No longer were mere static (and normative) descriptions of traits of group members sufficient. The dynamics of systems of systems in constant movement were now what mattered.

Probably the most improved social science in this era was sociology, which had barely been a social science at all and had no commonly agreed upon methods, assumptions, or research results. The basis of a discipline had yet to be established. Sociology's main achievement up to then was the great success with which its practitioners insinuated themselves in colleges and universities, persuading trustees, presidents, administrators, and even colleagues of their bona fides even though all their discipline had to offer intellectually was, at most, potential. Crucial were developments at the University of Chicago, where members of the "Chicago school" worked on group relations, especially the relations of immigrants and African Americans to the majority white culture. These sociologists maintained that human nature could be acquired only through interaction with other persons, the consequence of living in groups. No one could exist in society as an individual. No individual could change his or her group membership for another; thus, once an African American, always an African American, and so on. The Chicago school's leading lights insisted that in all modern societies, there was incessant group conflict and competition, but with ultimate assimilation, at least in the American case. In *The Ghetto* (1928), Louis Wirth examined the history of Chicago's Jews by going back to their early history in Roman times; their history as a dispersed people in medieval Europe; their adaptation in western and eastern Europe as somewhat different peoples—the one urban and cosmopolitan, the other rural and traditional; and their migration to America, in particular, to Chicago. Once the Jews settled in Chicago, the ghetto became so large that members began to assimilate into the majority culture, thus completing the process of integration into the mainstream of American life. Wirth's African American colleagues, including E. Franklin Frazier, author of *The Negro in America* (1949), did not have

so rosy a view of the majoriy culture's receptivity to the prospect of assimilation of outsiders—especially blacks, but also Jews and other ethnic groups.

Economists fared well in the interwar years, with professional and political triumphs aplenty as they studied the movement of the economy. Wesley Clair Mitchell of Columbia University and his students pioneered in statistical studies of the business cycle. True to the age's holistic and interactionist paradigm of natural and social reality, they argued that the business cycle resulted from the interdependence of prices of many goods in the economy. Unlike the classical laissez-faire economists, Mitchell insisted that the market was not the result of rational calculations, but instead of irrational habits, instincts, fear, and other emotions, thus borrowing from both his mentor, Thorstein Veblen, and his idol, the philosopher and educator John Dewey. In 1919 Mitchell and a handful of colleagues founded the National Bureau of Economic Research as a fact-finding institution that would provide objective interdisciplinary research to all interested economic parties in the hope of resolving economic conflicts with the unifying findings of professional social science. Yet it was Alvin Hansen of the University of Wisconsin and later Harvard University who imported the most important bundle of economic theory of the age, Keynesian economics (developed by the English economist John Maynard Keynes), to the United States. Keynes's general theory posited an interdependent economy of many distinct yet interrelated elements. It was not until 1946, with the enactment of the Full Employment Act, that the U.S. government committed itself, however timidly, to the principles of Keynesian economics. Its commitment, however, stemmed more from concern about a return of the Great Depression than from interest in the fine points of economic theory.

A final example of interwar behavioral science was community health, an explicitly interdisciplinary outgrowth of the public health movement, whose champions, such as Charles-Edward Amory Winslow of Yale University's School of Public Health, insisted that the key to proper and effective community health was to have experts in medicine, social work, disease prevention, delinquency prevention, and the like attack the multiple problems of physical, social, educational, and moral health in any community. The graduates of such programs became school nurses, child guidance counselors, epidemiologists, teachers of health and nutrition, and workers in public health positions in government, education, and industry.

SOCIAL SCIENCE AND THE END OF EXPERTISE

Since about 1950 Americans from many walks of life have acted and spoken as if there is no longer any unified or authoritative expertise. The late-nineteenth- and early-twentieth-century faith in the neutral and scientific expert yielded to an interwar-era notion of multiple fields of expertises, especially between business and government, appropriate for an era in which the interrelatedness of many different things—of oil and water, so to speak—was taken for granted. And such had given way to an individuation of expertise, that any individual could judge truth from falsity, and right from wrong. In a post–World War II society and world in which people increasingly witnessed the breakdown of tradition and authority in such widely scattered fields of activity as food, fashion, sex, the monopoly of economic, social, and cultural elites, music, art, and education, it was to be expected that expertise would come under attack, and from all quarters imaginable—and some not imaginable.

Beginning in the 1950s psychology and psychiatry were considerably transformed. An important breakthrough of the interwar era had been the articulation of group dynamics and group theory, especially at the University of Iowa's Child Welfare Research Station, with Kurt Lewin and his students, and a few years later by Gordon Allport at Harvard. Here group behavior was subjected to experimental testing and verification. Thus in *The Nature of Prejudice* (1954) Allport addressed the problem from all possible angles, always with the effect of group dynamics on all members. Starting in the 1950s, with the fitful elaboration of game theory in mathematics and later in the social sciences, behavior scientists looked again at the individual, not the group, as a basis of their science. And the new approach was symbolized on a semipopular level by William H. Whyte's witty, erudite *The Organization Man* (1956), in which the white, middle class recruit to the corporate world is given lessons in institutional survival—hardly the desperate circumstances of the nonwhite residents of urban ghettoes. The larger social message here was that the organization—the system, crudely put—was oppressing the individual, a thesis that became the leitmotif of much of American politics and various socio-political movements in the 1960s and beyond.

Advocates of compensatory education for young nonwhite children claimed, with considerable accuracy, that such was needed to bring their charges up to the norms of middle-class white children. The emphasis on redistributionist social justice for individual victims of society became a major theme of American political discourse and, to some considerable extent, of psychological science. Professionals in child development in the early 1960s conducted a baker's dozen of unrelated longitudinal projects on inconstancy of the IQ among preschool children. They reported that children in that age category experienced shifts of one standard deviation or more up or down from prior examinations, thus suggesting the plasticity of intelligence in response to environmental stimuli and pressures among very young children. The federal government's response to this work, compensatory preschool education for poor children (especially those who were nonwhite) developed into Head Start, a federal program that, at its peak at the century's end, funded no more than 40 percent of the eligible children for no more than one of the three recommended years of such training. Correspondingly most social psychology in the post–World War II era shifted to individual psychology, and group psychology, defined as the study of group-caused behavior, went into decline. The individual, not the group, seemed to be, for many psychologists, the point of departure for their science.

The mental health field also changed dramatically. Increasingly it became infeasible for psychiatrists, trained in medical schools, to provide therapy for the growing numbers of Americans demanding it. As clinical psychologists came to enter the field, they began to take up the slack for those who could not afford long-term psychiatric sessions or who did not need such therapy. And there was a paradigm shift in notions about mental health. The Freudian revolution of the 1940s was overthrown in the 1980s by a new paradigm in which basic biological and even chemical mechanisms were identified as fundamental causes of mental disorders, and the old-time distinction between neuroses and psychoses disintegrated. Psychiatrists now mainly administered drugs to their patients, and psychologists did therapy in discussion with clients on a short-term basis. Hence, in the mental disciplines there was an adjustment in the concept of expertise. It seemed as if anyone who could persuade others of his or her expertise in mental health could get a hearing, and the basis of therapy shifted from the patient's psychosocial environment and early life to the patient's biology and current situation.

Although it would be a fallacy to reduce the social and behavioral sciences' history to one or two "essential truths"—for that would be to commit the fallacy of essentialism, that their history was constituted of essentially this truth or that—we can draw at least two important conclusions about the social disciplines from what we have reviewed above. First and foremost, the social sciences have been always about us, about our society, our politics, our economy, our way of life, and the larger social world in which we and our contemporaries live, and only secondarily have they been academic disciplines encased in universities and colleges. Second, it would appear that both the underlying notions of social thought in the larger society, and those of more formal social and behavior science theory, depend to a considerable extent on the relationship of the individual to the group or, more simply put, on the changing meaning of group identity for the individual. It may be noted that the meaning of group identity for the individual has changed in various eras of American history, from the individualism of the Revolutionary and Early National Eras, to the differing notions of group identity for the individual in the cultural epochs 1830–1870, 1870–1920, and 1920–1950, not to mention the resurgent individualism of the period since the 1950s.

See also **The Behavioral and Social Sciences** *(volume 1);* **The Culture and Critics of the Suburb and the Corporation; Working Class; Anthropology and Cultural Relativism** *(volume 2);* **Ethnicity: Early Theories; Ethnicity and Race; Class; Social Construction of Reality; Weberian Approaches** *(in this volume).*

BIBLIOGRAPHY

Primary Sources

Allport, Gordon W. *The Nature of Prejudice.* Cambridge, Mass., 1954.

American Psychiatric Association. *Diagnostic and Statistical Manual of Mental Disorders.* 4th ed. Washington, D.C., 1994.

Beard, Charles A. *An Economic Interpretation of the Constitution of the United States.* New York, 1913.

Bentley, Arthur F. *The Process of Government; A Study of Social Pressures.* 1908. Reprint with an introduction by H. T. Davis, Evanston, Ill., 1949.

Bigelow, Jacob. *Elements of Technology: Taken Chiefly from a Course of Lectures Delivered at Cambridge on the Application of the Sciences to the Useful Arts.* Boston, 1829.

Evans, Oliver, and Thomas Ellicott. *The Young Mill-Wright's and Miller's Guide.* 1795. Reprint, Octoraro, Pa., 1807.

Frazier, E. Franklin. *The Negro in the United States.* Chicago, 1949.

Holmes, Oliver Wendell, Jr. *The Common Law.* 1888. Reprint, Boston, 1938.

Mitchell, Wesley Clair. *Business Cycles: The Problem and Its Setting.* New York, 1927.

Morton, Samuel G. *Crania Americana; or, A Comparative View of the Skulls of Various Aboriginal Nations of North and South America. To Which Is Prefixed an Essay on the Variety of the Human Species.* Philadelphia and London, 1839.

Paine, Thomas. *Common Sense.* 1776. Reprint, edited and with an introduction by Isaac Kramnick, Harmondsworth, England, and New York, 1982.

———. *Rights of Man: Being an Answer to Mr. Burke's Attack on the French Revolution. Part 2. Rights of Man: Combining Principle and Practice.* 1791–1792. Reprint, New York, 1892.

Smith, Adam. *An Inquiry into the Nature and Causes of the Wealth of Nations.* 6th ed. 3 vols. London, 1791.

Whyte, William H., Jr. *The Organization Man.* New York, 1956.

Winslow, Charles-Edward Amory. *The Conquest of Epidemic Disease. A Chapter in the History of Ideas.* 1943. Reprint, Madison, Wisc., 1980.

Wirth, Louis. *The Ghetto.* Chicago, 1928.

Secondary Accounts

Bay, Mia. *The White Image in the Black Mind: African American Ideas about White People, 1830–1925.* New York, 2000.

Cravens, Hamilton. *Before Head Start: The Iowa Station and America's Children.* Chapel Hill, N.C., 1993.

———. "The Social Sciences." In *Historical Writing on American Science. Perspectives and Prospects,* edited by Sally G. Kohlstedt and Margaret W. Rossiter, pp. 183–207. 1985. Reprint, Baltimore, 1986.

———. *The Triumph of Evolution: The Heredity-Environment Controversy, 1900–1941.* 1978. Reprint, Baltimore, 1988.

Curti, Merle. *Human Nature in American Thought: A History.* Madison, Wisc., 1980.

Danziger, Kurt. *Constructing the Subject: Historical Origins of Psychological Research.* New York, 1990.

Dorfman, Joseph. *The Economic Mind in American Civilization.* 5 vols. New York, 1946–1959.

Frana, Philip L. "Coordinating the Experts and the Masses: The Professions of Health and the Creation of Modern American Public Health, 1915–1940." Ph.D. diss., Iowa State University, 1999.

Fredrickson, George. *The Black Image in the White Mind: The Debate on Afro-American Character and Destiny, 1817–1914.* New York, 1971.

Furner, Mary O. *Advocacy and Objectivity: A Crisis in the Professionalization of American Social Science, 1865–1905.* Lexington, Ky., 1975.

Grob, Gerald N. *Mental Illness and American Society, 1875–1940.* Princeton, N.J., 1983.

Higham, John. *Strangers in the Land: Patterns of American Nativism, 1860–1925.* New Brunswick, N.J., 1955.

Karpf, Faye Berger. *American Social Psychology: Its Origins, Development, and European Background.* New York, 1932.

Marcus, Alan I. *A Plague of Strangers: Social Groups and the Origins of City Services in Cincinnati, 1819–1870.* Columbus, Ohio, 1991.

Marcus, Alan I., and Howard P. Segal. *Technology in America: A Brief History.* 2d ed. Fort Worth, Tex., 1999.

National Bureau of Economic Research. *Retrospect and Prospect, 1920–1936.* New York, 1936.

Persons, Stow. *American Minds: A History of Ideas.* New York, 1958.

Sellers, Charles. *The Market Revolution: Jacksonian America, 1815–1846.* New York, 1991.

Shapiro, Henry D. *Appalachia on Our Mind: The Southern Mountains and Mountaineers in the American Consciousness, 1870–1920.* Chapel Hill, N.C., 1978.

Stocking, George W., Jr., ed. *Race, Culture, and Evolution: Essays in the History of Anthropology.* New York, 1968.

Welter, Rush. *Popular Education and Democratic Thought in America.* New York, 1958.

THE VISUAL ARTS

R. F. Bogardus

PROLOGUE:
ART AND THE AMERICAN MIND

The Puritans did not hate visual art, Neil Harris tells us in *The Artist in American Society* (1966); they just doubted its usefulness, questioned its spiritual value, and thought it a wasteful extravagance—when they thought about it at all. The seventeenth-century English, after all, were a people of words, not images. England was the land of Shakespeare and Milton: no great painter would appear there until the next century. The colonists took their aesthetic apathy to America, and their difficult encounters with the wilderness reinforced their unconcern with the fine arts.

This attitude meshed with the republican ideology of the eighteenth century and the utilitarian capitalist view replacing it in the nineteenth: reason, simplicity, usefulness, and moral clarity were virtues; extravagance and sensuality were vices. These contradictory sets of values, though, birthed an enduring aesthetic dialog. As Robert Hughes argues ("American Visions," p. 23), much American art reflects the "virtues": John Singleton Copley's empirically direct, detailed portraits; the Shakers' simple, finely proportioned architectural and furniture design; John James Audubon's rigorous illustrations in *Birds of America* (1827–1838); the Lancaster Amish quiltmakers' simple shapes and sober colors; and Donald Judd's rectilinear sculptures made from industrial materials. Yet the "vices" are also present in works by equally impressive artists: Benjamin West's rebellious, often mysterious canvases; Thomas Cole's grand allegorical landscapes; Albert Pinkham Ryder's eerie dreamscapes; Georgia O'Keeffe's colorful, sensuous images; Jackson Pollock's densely dripped, existential fields of paint; Walter De Maria's awesome collaborations with landscape itself; and Frank O. Gehry's elegant, voluptuous public architecture.

ART IN THE COLONIES AND
THE NEW REPUBLIC

The English tradition influenced the early development of America's visual arts. Spanish and French visual artifacts were too far removed geographically from population centers of the English colonists to be noticed. Native Americans, too, were geographically separate from the colonists; besides, their visual cultures could not be seriously regarded by the colonists, who saw them as lesser beings. Africans, though in close proximity, were invisible; except for music and dance, their cultural practices were repressed or ignored. Of course, the art productions of non-English groups possessed richness, beauty, and value, but they would have no impact until their "discovery" in the twentieth century. Living along the eastern seaboard, Americans looked across the ocean for cultural guidance and westward for opportunity. Based on European models, the American art tradition evolved initially in such port cities as Newport, Boston, Philadelphia, New York, Baltimore, and Charleston. As new urban centers emerged in the West, they looked eastward for models, but by then the East included the Atlantic seaboard.

The fine arts were, of course, introduced into American culture slowly, since ways had to be devised to integrate artists and the idea of art into society. Except as craft, no distinct cultural sphere existed for either. Until after 1800 there were few significant artists and only a handful of institutions to nurture and speak for them. There was also a dearth of patronage. Portraiture predominated but was considered a craft that recorded loved ones or persons of importance. Many painters were anonymous, though capable artists such as Pieter Vanderlyn, John Smibert, and Robert Feke were kept busy. Termed limners, or depicters of likenesses, and varying widely in ability and achievement, they served the need for likenesses.

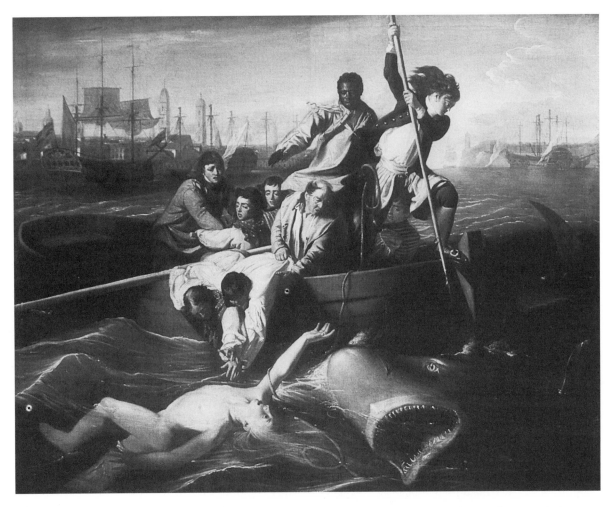

Watson and the Shark (1778) **by John Singleton Copley.** Audacious in its depiction of the ordinary subject, Copley's scene, with its terrifying drama of men and nature, also foreshadows the Romantic movement that would soon emerge in Western literature and painting. © BURNSTEIN COLLECTION/CORBIS

By the late eighteenth century, the situation began to change. Benjamin West, John Singleton Copley, John Trumbull, Gilbert Stuart, and Charles Willson Peale emerged as America's first significant painters, but they had to travel to Europe to find instruction, institutional support, and community. Because there were no art schools in America, artists were self-taught, learning their craft from art-book engravings, English mezzotints, art histories, and the instruction of older painters. Still, they honed their skills and found support before crossing the ocean. Indeed, it was with the help of a patron that West went to Italy in 1759 and then on to England in 1763 to study at the British Royal Academy. With the appearance of William Hogarth, Sir Joshua Reynolds, the Academy, and a more sophisticated group of patrons, England had begun developing a serious visual culture, and expatriate American painters

profited from it. West in particular thrived, becoming historical painter to George III in 1772 and, subsequently, president of the Academy. He did not leave America entirely, though. He painted New-World subjects such as *The Death of General Wolfe* (1770), a radical departure in history painting that featured a contemporary historical event and presented the figures in modern dress instead of classical garb. Copley followed West to Europe. Already an accomplished artist, he first went to Italy in 1774 and then to London for study. The Royal Academy softened and generalized his "photographic" style but did not completely blunt his audacity. His *Watson and the Shark* (1778), like West's current-history pictures, was also a grand-style, modern-dress painting, except that the incident depicted was historically insignificant, merely a personal occurrence in a friend's life.

174

"The Revolution proved a godsend to art . . . created a History," argues Neil Harris. Artists were asked to "record the features of the patriots for posterity," for Americans wanted "visible assurances of unity and harmony" (pp. 15, 16–17). Portraits of revolutionary heroes and pictures of historical moments like the signing of the Declaration of Independence were needed, though only Trumbull, Stuart, and Peale returned to America to take up this task. Trumbull, acting on the advice of West, sought to become America's preeminent history painter. His *Death of General Montgomery in the Attack on Quebec* (1788) was modeled on West's *The Death of General Wolfe.* Early in his career, he tried to interest the federal government in purchasing his work for public spaces, but his ambition would not be realized until 1817, when a wary Congress commissioned four large panels memorializing the Revolution's events and heroes. The paintings have hung in the Capitol rotunda since 1824. Gilbert Stuart's ambition was narrower. He became the foremost portraitist of the Republic's leaders, particularly George Washington, whom he painted again and again. Peale stayed in Philadelphia, painting and promoting art by opening the first art museum in 1782 and helping to found the Pennsylvania Academy, chartered in 1806.

Sculpture, too, began to thrive. The earliest able sculptor was William Rush, a Philadelphia woodcarver who made beautiful American eagles, figureheads, and a masterful *George Washington* (1814). Another was Horatio Greenough, who unlike Rush was a trained neoclassicist. His giant marble *George Washington* (1832–1836) was an instant sensation because of its size and the partial nudity of the toga-clad hero seated on a throne. Another neoclassicist, Hiram Powers, carved *The Greek Slave* (1843), but this nude was less sensational because it presented flesh as an abstract ideal through the beauty, purity, and coldness of white marble. Their colleague Thomas Crawford, on the other hand, produced uncontroversial bronzes such as a figure symbolizing freedom that was placed on Washington's Capitol dome.

Late-eighteenth- and early-nineteenth-century artists sought to create saleable works. Their success depended upon their skills and stylistic approach. Americans, of course, were partial to the republican ideals of simplicity, clarity, balance, and order. Style had to embody those values and reflect a distrust of luxury, since extravagance was believed to undermine citizenship and destroy democracy; John Adams and Thomas Jefferson certainly thought so, even if Benjamin Franklin disagreed. Art had to affirm American values and national identity clearly, hence realism in painting and neoclassicism in sculpture and architecture became official styles.

Since artists were so dependent on the market for their livelihood, most lived precariously and frugally, often traveling to find customers. Their works toured, too. In an effort to gain recognition, artists such as the painter Samuel F. B. Morse sent their work around the country to attract paying audiences. Sometimes, as in the case of Powers's *The Greek Slave,* they were successful. Its tour made his reputation. But for most, the effort had disappointing results. Besides pursuing a living, artists sought to raise their social status. Their efforts, however, were thwarted by the atmosphere of backbiting competitiveness that is natural when individuals work in a limited market and are engaged in what is generally regarded as dubious social purpose.

In such a world, supporting institutions were slow to develop. When they first appeared, their success was short-lived or, at best, mixed. The earliest art schools were little more than finishing schools: for example, Alexander Marie Quenay's New York City Academy, founded in 1784, advertised that it taught dancing, drawing, French, and the "culture of the polite arts." Painters frequently gave private instruction in their studios, but no school of consequence appeared until well after 1800. By then, a number of art-supply shops had opened in several cities, doubling as art galleries showing and selling art. Art-auction houses appeared, too. In Harris's estimation, such places were "the most effective art institutions of their era," but they reinforced the idea of art as a market commodity and impeded the formation of community and group consciousness. Efforts at building community were impeded by the democratic ideology that distrusted the old-style aristocratic patronage epitomized by European royal academies, the only alternative to the market. In 1795 Peale organized the Columbianum, a group of Philadelphia artisans and architects, but it soon became defunct. Other organizations fared better—the Pennsylvania Academy, for example. The New York Academy of the Fine Arts emerged in 1802, becoming the American Academy of the Arts in 1808. Philadelphia's Society of Artists of the United States appeared in 1810. Finances were always a problem, but organizations like New York City's National Academy of Design, established in 1826, and the Pennsylvania Academy solved it by holding large exhibitions that attracted paying audiences. Their presence provided "a point for artistic concentration" and "new customers." Facing the pressures of the market, artists fought to control their own finances and standards, and the academies sought to aid them. Such organizations were attacked for their elitism, pretentiousness, and presumed tendency to promote mannerism (expressive, exotic art). Still, artists persisted.

Their efforts were both helped and hindered by growing private patronage. Americans of means bought art for investment and for home decoration, both dubious kinds of support. Yet a small group of individuals, including New York City's Philip Hone and Luman Reed, Baltimore's Robert Gilmor, and Cincinnati's Nicholas Longworth, purchased works to encourage artists. Such patrons, however, often challenged artists on questions of taste. Gilmor and Thomas Cole had an ongoing debate. Gilmor disliked mannerism, preferring literalism instead. Cole loved idealization and defended the expressive imagination. Many artists, such as John Vanderlyn and Washington Allston, agreed with Cole. The post-Revolutionary generation wanted to do more than make realistic portraits and record history. Allston, Cole, William Sidney Mount, and John Frederick Kensett painted pictures as various in topic and sentiment as *Diana in the Chase* (1805), *The Oxbow* (1836), *Eel Spearing at Setauket* (1845), and *Lake George* (1869). Each depicted nature in his work. Nature, after all, was the great American fact, the locus of empire—the future. After 1830, it became the great American subject, too.

Employment opportunities for artists existed mostly in eastern cities with their developing arts institutions and audiences. As early-nineteenth-century publishing centers, Boston, New York, and Philadelphia needed artists to illustrate books, magazines, and newspapers. Banknote engravers and advertising artists were also required. Cities, moreover, hosted art journals, such as *The Crayon* and the *Cosmopolitan Art Journal,* and art clubs such as New York City's The Century and The Sketch Club. Western cities also created literary and arts organizations, and art lecturers toured widely.

Growing interest in the fine arts was stimulated by James Herring's creation of an art lottery in 1838 at the Apollo Gallery in New York City. Initially he exhibited artists, charged admission, and sold catalogues. But soon he invited people to pay an annual subscription of five dollars, entitling each subscriber to an engraving of a painting and a numbered ticket. At every year's end, winning ticket holders received genuine American paintings. By 1844 membership numbered two thousand. Renamed the American Art-Union, it offered works by America's best artists, including Cole. By 1849 there were over sixteen thousand subscribers, but

Kindred Spirits (1849) by Asher B. Durand. The painter Thomas Cole and the poet William Cullen Bryant commune with each other in God's placid temple of the Catskills. A contemporary of Cole, Durand portrays nature as a spiritually restorative phenomenon rather than an awesome one. His sublimity is that of the Transcendentalists. © FRANCIS G. MAYER/CORBIS

the Union's bright future was cut short by a lawsuit challenging its legality. In 1852 the New York State Supreme Court held that the art lottery was invalid. Though its final 1853 sale was not a success, the number of art dealers had increased considerably during the 1840s, partly in response to the popular interest the Union generated.

Once thought romantic, impractical, even dangerous, artists began to exemplify, in Harris's words, "the virtues of industry and material success which dominated the business community." Shortly before the Civil War they were acquiring respect and prosperity, and were also beginning to be recruited into the growing efforts to improve American morals, manners, and tastes. Protestant ministers such as Edward Everett Hale urged that leisure had potentially healthy uses and that art could be a positive leisure activity. Though artists benefited from this broad change in attitude and situation, "the arts remained tied 'to the aid of necessity,'" Harris argues—albeit a social rather than political one.

ART AND THE GILDED AGE

Vast new accumulations of American private wealth contributed to improving the social and cultural status of artists after 1860. Taste became the symbol of both moral order and social position—a refuge from, and antidote to, industrial chaos and the dangers of materialism. A new pattern of collecting emerged; it stressed the purchase of European masters, although established Americans were supported, too. Collectors included J. P. Morgan, Henry Marquand, Henry Clay Frick, and Isabella Stewart Gardner. The accumulations of such wealthy patrons eventually found their way into public museums that, along with opera houses and symphony orchestra halls, were built in most major cities. New York's Metropolitan Museum of Art and Boston's Museum of Fine Arts were founded in 1870, the Philadelphia Museum of Art in 1876, and Chicago's Art Institute in 1879. Elite patrons were busy sanctifying and segregating the fine arts by placing them in palatial buildings, limiting access to their enjoyment, and giving them the aura of refinement, difficulty, and respectability. The new spaces and strictly enforced viewer etiquette discouraged appreciation by the general public, so the average American remained indifferent or hostile toward fine art.

Arguments continued over aesthetics and the artist's role. Was the empirical or expressionist method appropriate? Should art be morally edifying or visually satisfying? James Jackson Jarves, an important critic and collector, thought that individual genius and unique expression were crucial; art was an end in itself. His views were vigorously attacked by the Society for Advancement for Truth in Art (1863), whose members—followers of John Ruskin—disseminated their ideas in a journal, *The New Path*. For them, art was not a manifestation of the artist's conception but was in nature itself. Art was based on direct experience; seeing led to knowing. This aesthetic was exemplified by the landscapes of Frederick E. Church, Albert Bierstadt, and Thomas Moran. Church was a meticulous renderer of detail, Bierstadt was atmospheric, and Moran was colorful, but all recorded nature as grandiose fact. But other seemingly literal artists suggest the difficulty of labels. Fool-the-eye painters William Harnett and his student, John F. Peto, created collage-like still lifes that combined realism and sensuousness. Harnett's *After the Hunt* (1885) and Peto's *Reminiscences of 1865* (1897) go beyond nostalgia to symbolize something deeper: death. Winslow Homer, who worked as an illustrator for *Harper's Weekly* before

and during the Civil War, wished to satisfy the eye. Clear shapes, patterns, light, and luminous atmosphere dominate paintings such as *The Morning Bell* (c. 1866). Albert Pinkham Ryder and expatriates Mary Cassatt and John Singer Sargent also painted distinctive perceptions: Ryder's expressionist; Cassatt's and Sargent's, impressionist.

Art became more professionalized, its study more formalized. Art schools acquired prestige, becoming more competitive as standards were imposed and selection processes were instituted. More Americans wished to study art, and art schools arose in cities such as Boston, Chicago, St. Louis, San Francisco, and Providence. However, Europe still held special significance for art education. In addition to Paris and Düsseldorf, there was Munich, which gradually surpassed Düsseldorf in importance. Paris's École des Beaux-Arts, however, was still the art school that drew the most aspiring Americans. Among its accomplished pupils were the sculptors Augustus Saint-Gaudens and Daniel Chester French and the painter Thomas Eakins. Saint-Gaudens's public sculptures include the small but powerfully modeled relief *Robert Gould Shaw and the Fifty-Fourth Regiment Memorial* (1900). French is famous for his giant, seated *Abraham Lincoln* (1918–1922) inside Washington's Lincoln Memorial. Eakins, a student of anatomy, was a realist painter who used photographic studies to guide his portraits and figurative compositions. He also taught at the Pennsylvania Academy, helping to make it one of the best art schools in America and a place that welcomed women and blacks to the study of art. Henry O. Tanner, the first significant African American painter, was his student. As a painter, Eakins displayed brilliant compositional skill and psychological depth, but his realism was too blunt for some. *The Gross Clinic* (1875), a masterful, bloody record of a surgical lesson, was refused a place in the art exhibition at the Philadelphia Centennial Exposition of 1876. Instead, it hung in the Medical Department's display.

The conflict over aesthetics was also manifested at the National Academy of Design in 1874 and 1875, when its salon juries rejected works by young painters such as Ryder. In 1877, perhaps to make amends, works by the new generation were accepted; the gesture, however, angered the old guard, which vowed to prevent it from happening again. In retaliation, young artists formed the Society of American Artists in 1878 and held an exhibition in open rebellion against the Academy. Yet by the time that Chicago's Columbian Exposition of 1893 was being planned, the rebels had become academic

Gloucester Harbor (1873) by Winslow Homer. © FRANCIS G. MAYER/CORBIS

gatekeepers. École-des-Beaux-Arts aesthetics dictated the design of Chicago's "White City." Merging beaux-arts architecture, sculpture, and mural painting, the planners and artists hid the fair's modern steel structure and packaged its material contents in Renaissance clothing: art idealized industrial civilization and its materialism.

MODERNITY, MODERNISM, AND ART

In academic circles, Taylor writes, "a poster was a poster and a salon painting was a painting, reaching for higher values" (p. 153). But that distinction could not last. An assault on academic idealism occurred, coming from disparate phenomena, individuals, ideas, and events that radically altered the intellectual and cultural landscapes of Europe and America. The overarching factor was modernity. New technologies, new science, capitalism, industrialization, and urbanization were in place by the 1893 Exposition, disrupting traditional modes of life and thought by changing the patterns, rhythms, and grounds of existence.

A consequence of no small importance was the aesthetic revolution that occurred first in Europe. One manifestation of this, William Morris's arts and crafts movement, began in the 1880s as a reaction to industrialization. It sought to integrate arts, crafts, decoration, and architecture, elevating artisanship to the level of fine art and sanctifying handcraft and design values derived from nature. With an emphasis on patterns, color, and shape, it caught on quickly in the United States, influencing successful product ventures such as Newcomb pottery and Stickley furniture as well as changing art education. An early proponent was the painter and influential instructor Arthur Wesley Dow. First at Pratt and then at Columbia Teachers College, Dow taught art students such as Georgia O'Keeffe to organize line and shape in two-dimensional space, relate light and dark shapes, and use color. He published his views in *Composition* (1899), an often reprinted book. The Prang Educational Company, an art supplies manufacturer, also promoted this aesthetic. In 1887 the company began free distribution of an art teacher's guide to help stimulate sales. The "stylized" approach also caught on in commercial-art circles, practiced by illustrators such as Kenyon Cox. Magazine and sheet-music covers, illustrations for articles and advertisements, and poster art increasingly featured modern design in what, like Chicago's Columbian Exposition, was a blending (and blurring) of the realms of industry and art.

Another challenge to Academic school of thought's idealism came from painter and teacher Robert Henri and his coterie of former newspaper artists George Luks, William Glackens, John Sloan, and Everett Shinn. In 1907, when three of his friends' paintings were rejected by the jury of the National Academy of Design, Henri withdrew his own works and helped put on the "Exhibition of Paintings" show at New York City's Macbeth Gallery in 1908. These artists painted modern street life and ordinary people with a gritty, energetic realism, so they were variously called "the revolutionary black gang," "Apostles of Ugliness," and "Ashcans." Theirs was largely a rebellion in content and rendering: the results were antithetical to the Academic painters' "ingratiating prettiness" (Taylor, p. 169). Also, scorning the Academy's practice of placing important works at eye level and lesser works above and below, they hung all the paintings at eye level, democratically. The show was well attended, made money, and helped change American exhibiting practices.

Modernist art, emerging in Europe during the mid-nineteenth century, was among the earliest rebellions against Academic taste. The impressionism of Édouard Manet and others evolved into a post-impressionist phase pioneered by artists such as Vincent van Gogh and Paul Cézanne. The next generation of innovators included Henri Matisse, Wassily Kandinsky, and Pablo Picasso. The term "modern" had been used since the 1890s to identify art that rejected Western visual traditions. As practiced by Europe's new masters, the new art was a direct response to modernity—sometimes positive, at other times negative—and a rallying cry for the experimental. Expressionism, fauvism, and cubism were in place by 1907. By then, expatriate Americans such as the Steins—Michael, his wife, Sarah, and his sister and brother, Gertrude and Leo—were collecting modernist works. Young American painters studying abroad, such as Alfred H. Maurer, Marsden Hartley, and Max Weber, also saw the moderns and began absorbing their influence.

The modernists' first American exhibitor was Alfred Stieglitz. Stieglitz promoted photography as fine art, founding the Photo-Secession Group of art photographers in 1902, editing the handmade art journal *Camera Work* (1903–1917), and running a succession of galleries that began with 291, the Little Galleries of the Photo-Secession. The 291 gallery had exhibited photographs since its opening in 1904, but in 1908 Stieglitz also began showing European modernist painters and sculptors as well as American practitioners of the new art. He also exhibited African carvings and pictures by children and the insane, a mix that pushed the definition of art. Stieglitz, of course, spoke mainly to a small New York City arts community. The general public learned about the new art from newspapers, which by 1910 were giving it considerable coverage. "Futurism became a favorite word in the American press," notes Taylor, "used to describe any iconoclastic activity that was not at once understandable" (p. 163).

Into this sensationalized atmosphere was thrust New York City's Armory Show of 1913. Conceived by the Association of American Painters and Sculptors as a vehicle to show American Independents, it evolved into an overview of the development of modern art. The Association head, Arthur B. Davies, sent his co-organizer, painter Walt Kuhn, to Europe to gather pictures. Kuhn selected a sampling of Europeans, from Jean-Auguste-Dominique Ingres and Eugène Delacroix to van Gogh, Cézanne, Matisse, Kandinsky, and Picasso. Also chosen were Americans such as Ryder, the Ashcans, and Max Weber. There were gaps in this compilation—the Barbizon painters, for example, were not represented—but the exhibition was amazing in its breadth and included a showstopper, *Nude Descending a Staircase, No. 2* (1912), by Marcel Duchamp. An estimated sixteen hundred works were displayed, and part of the exhibit traveled to Chicago and Boston. The exhibit was controversial. Newspapers attacked it with inventive humor and righteous outrage, but about three hundred thousand people paid twenty-five cents a head to see it in three cities, the audience including artists, art teachers and students, and collectors. Over 450 of the works shown were sold and many new galleries opened in response. Collector John Quinn bought modernist works, as did Walter Arensberg, Henry Clay Frick, Andrew Mellon, and Katherine Drier. The show had an impact on artists, too, as illustrated by the early career of Stuart Davis. Beginning as an Ashcan realist, he experimented with modernist styles immediately after seeing the show and had become a cubist by 1921.

Davis's evolution hints at the complicated, paradoxical path of modernity's influence on fine art during the twentieth century. By 1900 mass media and advertising had emerged in response to the im-

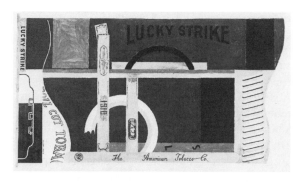

Lucky Strike (1921) by Stuart Davis. Oil on canvas, 33¼ × 18 in. Davis's paintings capture the dynamic sense of the modern American urban scene, weaving their sharply defined, irregular shapes, vibrant colors, jagged rhythms, and chaotic energies into single, complexly ordered, gorgeous images. THE MUSEUM OF MODERN ART, NEW YORK. GIFT OF THE AMERICAN TOBACCO COMPANY, INC. PHOTOGRAPH © 2000 THE MUSEUM OF MODERN ART, NEW YORK

peratives of capitalism and materialism. These industries absorbed qualities of the new formalist art. Mass magazines, for example, mingled pictures and words in a discontinuous fashion, and commercial artists moved toward abstraction by their emphasis upon color and form rather than mimesis. In turn, media and advertising art influenced new generations of painters and sculptors. Consumerism, popular culture, machines, and new urban patterns and rhythms were pervasive and marked art works after 1913. Davis's first cubist works were a series of paintings, each titled *Lucky Strike* (1921), based on that cigarette's package design.

The modern city—with its elevated trains, automobiles, and skyscrapers—was an influence too. These modern innovations provided the subject matter and formal models for much American modernist art. Weber's *Rush Hour, New York* (1915) and *Morton Schamberg's Telephone* (1916) were cubist responses to modernity. Charles Demuth's *My Egypt* (1927), a depiction of a grain elevator, Charles Sheeler's *Church Street El* (1920), a picture of an elevated train's tracks, and Louis Lozowick's *Pittsburgh*, an image of clustered skyscrapers, express the simplified, fragmented geometry of American architecture and machines. The boundaries of fine arts practice were also being stretched by new techniques, such as photography, film montage, Duchamp readymades, and assembled sculpture utilizing industrial materials. Artists often worked in more than one medium. Man Ray painted and made objects, photographs, and films. Schamberg painted and constructed sculpture. Sheeler was a

photographer as well as a painter who based his paintings on his photographs.

Art institutions thrived during the decades after the Armory Show, and they, too, reflected the changes taking place. The Art Students' League (1875) remained an important school. The Whitney Studio Club was established by Gertrude Vanderbilt Whitney in 1918 as a gathering place and exhibition outlet for artists; it was institutionalized as the Whitney Museum of American Art in 1930. The Société Anonyme was formed in 1920 by Dreier, Duchamp, and Ray and showed modern art. Modernism had become such a force by the mid-1920s that some of its practitioners were finally invited to exhibit at the National Academy's 1927 Salon. As if to underscore the impact of modernism, the Museum of Modern Art (MOMA) was established in 1929. It was organized into departments of painting, sculpture, architecture, decorative arts, folk art, photography, and film. After only a decade of activity, MOMA would mount a major exhibition, *The Art of Our Time* (1939), that defined the new art. Before that could take place, however, a terrible social upheaval occurred, sidetracking modern art and burying aesthetics in politics.

ART AND THE AMERICAN EARTHQUAKE

Realism did not disappear during the 1910s and 1920s. The Ashcans continued to paint and exhibit. Younger painters such as Charles Burchfield, Edward Hopper, and O. Louis Guglielmi created realist depictions of the everyday social world—with a surrealist edge. "Few major figurative painters persisted in simply recording a scene.... Representation no longer meant simply looking," notes Taylor (p. 205). After the stock market crash of 1929, however, realism took on new importance. It fit both conservative cultural agendas and radical political ones. In 1931 realist painters Thomas Hart Benton, Grant Wood, and John Steuart Curry were praised by the conservative critic Thomas Craven. He called them regionalists because they painted rural and small town scenes in search of America's native roots. Other artists received inspiration from history and social causes. African American painter Aaron Douglas created *Aspects of Negro Life* (1934), a mural housed at the Countee Cullen Branch of the New York Public Library. The Russian Jewish immigrant Ben Shahn painted a series, *The Execution of Sacco and Vanzetti* (1931–1932), protesting their trial as a travesty of justice. An exhibit, *The Social Viewpoint in Art*, was mounted in 1933 by the

Baptism in Kansas (1928) **by John Steuart Curry.** Curry painted idealized American scenes depicting the frontier experience as the shaper of American character. Self-reliance and community emerge within the context of struggle. © GEOFFREY CLEMENTS/CORBIS

New York branch of the John Reed Club—a Communist organization of writers and artists—and social realism was born. Besides Shahn, its adherents included William Gropper and Philip Evergood.

Economic depression also led to patronization of the arts by the federal government. In 1933 and 1934 the Public Works of Art Project was sponsored by the Treasury Department for the purpose of hiring unemployed artists to create murals for public buildings. In 1934, the Treasury Department instituted a longer-term program, with works of art to be selected by competition. The Federal Art Project, a branch of the Works Progress Administration founded in 1935, employed artists to create easel and mural paintings, teach art classes, and staff community centers. These programs helped sustain artists such as the youthful African American

painter Jacob Lawrence and novice midwesterner Jackson Pollock during tough times.

Abstract art was being eclipsed by realism by the early thirties. Modernists such as Davis and Lozowick were political radicals, yet their artistic methods were questioned by a Communist-led left that espoused the production of proletarian art—socialist realism—as well as by aesthetic conservatives. In 1933 the Artists' Union was born, functioning as a trade union. Its organ, *Art Front,* began publication in 1934 and lasted three years. In its pages, Davis debated aesthetics with Benton and Curry, who considered abstraction politically irresponsible. The unrepentant Davis retorted that it was the essence of free expression and thus antifascist. The American Artists' Congress, a popular-front organization, appeared in 1936. At its meetings, discussions were vigorous, but gradually the Congress was taken over by the American Communist Party with its Stalinist line, so the best artists had withdrawn by 1940.

In 1937, twenty-two abstract artists formed American Abstract Artists in order to promote modern art. The founders included painters Balcomb Greene, his wife Gertrude Greene, Burgoyne Diller, George L. K. Morris, Arshile Gorky, Willem de Kooning, and Lee Krasner. David Smith, who would become America's preeminent sculptor, was also involved. This resurgence of activity by modernists was stimulated by a number of events. Many had traveled through Europe in the 1920s and early 1930s and seen the latest aesthetic developments. Also, works by European moderns—particularly non-representational biomorphic surrealists (who borrowed amoeba-like shapes from biology in their art) such as Joan Miró and Max Ernst—had been exhibited in America during these decades. But most important, Europe's most talented intellectuals, writers, and artists began leaving Europe in the 1930s because of Nazism. Individuals such as Piet Mondrian, Joseph Albers, and László Moholy-Nagy moved to the United States to work and teach, creating an intellectually charged atmosphere.

HOT WAR, COLD WAR, AND ART

World War II had a more discernible impact on visual art than did World War I. America was involved earlier and longer, made a greater commitment and sacrifice, and exited a world power with a thriving economy. Artists who lived through the depression and the wars became marked by signal events like the Holocaust and Hiroshima. Facing a world of horrible, irrational forces, they sought a visual language to express their sense of dislocation, doubt, and anxiety. In 1939 the young critic Clement Greenberg argued in the *Partisan Review* for the separation of art from mass politics; each art medium, he wrote, had to explore its inherent characteristics. Geometric abstraction was inadequate while surrealism's antirationalism, irregular forms, and automatism method held promise—points made at MOMA's Picasso retrospective in 1939, where the surrealist, antifascist protest painting *Guernica* (1937) was shown. European surrealist artists had settled in New York City and exhibited. In 1942 art patron Peggy Guggenheim opened a gallery, Art of This Century, featuring surrealism. Immigrant painters Hans Hofmann and Roberto Matta taught the importance of connecting with the unconscious mind, espousing automatism as

a method of reaching it. Their ideas influenced de Kooning, Gorky, Pollock, Mark Rothko, and Adolph Gottlieb. Painters were now seeking something elemental and looking to the primitive for inspiration—to archaic myth, primordial symbols and calligraphic figures, Jungian psychology, and Native American art.

Together they founded a radical stylistic movement by the late 1940s, abstract expressionism. It took two directions, the gestural method and color-field painting. Pollock and de Kooning were gestural painters: their art expressed the random flow of motion that produced it, reflecting energy, process, and performance. Rothko was a color-field artist. In his paintings, shapes dissolve and fields of sensual, diaphanous colors disappear into each other, suggesting the immateriality of consciousness itself—its transcendence of the physical. The movement also included several sculptors, the most important of whom was David Smith.

The abstract expressionists began exhibiting in the early 1940s: Pollock had his first one-man show at Guggenheim's Art of This Century gallery in 1943. They eventually contributed to the hegemony of American art during the cold war period and made New York City the world capital of art, but not without a struggle for acceptance. During the postwar years several exhibitions of American paintings toured Europe. The first, *Advancing American Art,* was a survey of American painting since the 1920s. It was put together by the State Department in 1946 and included only two abstract expressionists, Baziotes and Gottlieb. However, Gorky, Pollock, and de Kooning were shown at the 1950 Venice Biennale and the 1952 exhibit, *American Vanguard Art for Paris,* also included abstract expressionists. By 1958, when MOMA toured its show *New American Painting,* Europeans had acknowledged the greatness of the new school.

At home their critical reception was initially mixed. The 11 October 1948 issue of *Life,* Henry Luce's popular photo-story magazine, contained a feature story, "A *Life* Roundtable on Modern Art," that sought to explain modernism to readers. It included a two-page spread, "Young American Extremists," that highlighted abstract expressionists and pronounced their efforts baffling, interesting, and promising. In its 8 August 1949 issue, *Life* gave Jackson Pollock a four-page spread, "Jackson Pollock: Is He the Greatest Living Painter in the United States?"

The average American, however, preferred the realistic, anecdotal paintings of Andrew Wyeth and Norman Rockwell. Moreover, conservative artists

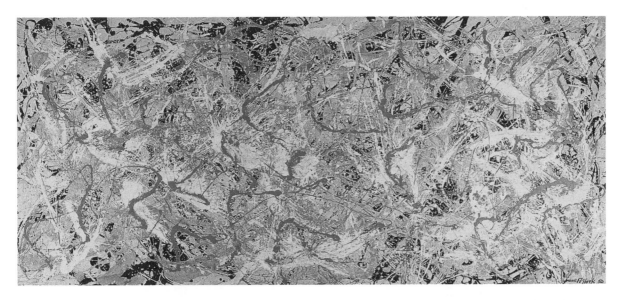

Number 27 (1950) by Jackson Pollock. Pollock's heroic, grandly gestured paintings capture the Romantic sublime; his landscape, however, was the unconscious mind. © FRANCIS G. MAYER/CORBIS

and their organizations, such as the Allied Artists Professional League, resented the attention given abstract painters. They attacked the *Advancing American Art* exhibit and were abetted by popular newspapers and magazines, such as the Hearst paper, the *New York Journal-American,* which called the exhibition a "Red Art Show." Conservative politicians assailed government spending on art created by presumed subversives.

Yet abstract art, particularly abstract expressionism, prevailed in the 1950s. Collectors and museums bought works by the New York painters. The number of art galleries featuring abstraction increased from about thirty in 1950 to around three hundred in 1960. Collectors emerged among newly rich, urban professionals and business entrepreneurs. In cities such as New York, it became fashionable to collect modern art. Success came to a group of alienated, heroic, anti-materialistic avant-gardists and soon abstract expressionists began receiving high prices for their work.

Meanwhile, they had a major impact on the next generation of artists. Helen Frankenthaler, Joan Mitchell, Morris Louis, and Richard Diebenkorn emulated them. But others—Robert Rauschenberg, Jasper Johns, and Claes Oldenberg, among them— used their talent to tear down the wall between art and life that the abstract expressionists had built. Rauschenberg's combine paintings, a spontaneous mixture of painted surface, collage, and cast-off objects, mocked the abstract expressionists' heroic stance. Johns's painterly, ironic images were sensual,

mysterious, and cerebral. Oldenberg's early action-painted plaster sculptures of popular common objects like pies and cakes were irreverent and inscrutable. Another response was minimalism, a return to the geometric abstraction that appeared in the late 1950s. Borrowing from Alexander Calder and David Smith, whose large welded steel objects explored space as well as mass, minimalists used industrial materials such as steel, lead, glass, and plastic in their works. Donald Judd, Richard Serra, and Sol Lewitt were minimalist sculptors; Ellsworth Kelly, Frank Stella, and Agnes Martin were minimalist painters. Others, termed conceptualists, utilized both the human-made and natural environments as ingredients in their art. Walter De Maria's *The Lightning Field* (1977) brilliantly illustrated this wedding. His four hundred stainless-steel poles aligned in a grid pattern on a New Mexico field drew lightning during storms, creating a spectacular effect and restoring the grandeur of that old American subject, nature.

The 1950s were not only years of prosperity and optimism but also of cold war, featuring the Iron Curtain, Korea, Senator Joseph McCarthy and the anti-Communist scare, the bomb, diplomatic brinksmanship, and conformity as the price of prosperity. America had become a media- and consumer-driven society. Mass magazines, movies, radio, and television were ubiquitous and global in their reach. Advertising proliferated images and messages of consuming fantasies. By 1960, however, cracks had begun to appear in the glittering surface.

The civil rights movement, the Beat generation writers, Elvis Presley and rock 'n' roll, and finally Vietnam rudely thrust themselves into Americans' consciousness, through media.

Artists—even the abstract expressionist de Kooning, in his painting *Marilyn Monroe* (1954)—had long borrowed from popular culture, media, and consumer goods. But a new wrinkle occurred. Image, brand name, celebrity—product identities created by media and advertising—began to provide art with its style as well as its subject. Pop art was introduced at *The New Realists* show, held at the Sidney Janis Gallery in 1962. Andy Warhol, Roy Lichtenstein, James Rosenquist, and Claes Oldenburg were among those exhibited. Their hard-edged, machine-like art seemed both ironic and celebratory. It packaged banality instead of heroism. Warhol's garishly colored oil, *Twenty-Five Colored Marilyns* (1962), is a multiple portrayal of film star Marilyn Monroe, executed with a silk screen made from a publicity photo. The Janis show was a success, receiving favorable publicity in the glossy press; drawing young, rich collectors; and finding museum advocates. A new generation of dealers emerged to cash in on pop's market potential. Warhol himself became an industry, he opened up a production studio, the Factory, in 1963, and founded a celebrity magazine, *Interview*, a year later.

A shift in the artist's status and place in society had occurred. Avant-garde art became indistinguishable from its subjects, popular culture and media; it was chic, and the hot artists were celebrities. Critics such as Hilton Kramer thought them glib and corrosive in their uncritical embrace of popular culture. But the best works did engage hard questions: Oldenburg's giant sculpture *Lipstick on Caterpillar Tracks* (1969), for instance, acidly joined anti–Vietnam War protest, wit, and art.

POSTMODERNISM, IDENTITY POLITICS, AND ART

The production of art after the 1960s reflected a blossoming or a mannerist disappointment, depending on who is asked. In "Anti Form" (*Artforum*, April 1968), sculptor Robert Morris called for experimentation with new materials, exploration of irregular or protean shapes or immateriality, and the conception of art works that would never be built. Morris, Richard Serra, Eva Hesse, and others made art of lead, rope, latex, fiberglass, dirt, mirrors, and words. They used new media, blended disparate media, blurred and destroyed boundaries.

Art works were pastiche efforts through which artists expressed all the "isms": artistic, social, and political, past and present. Sexism, racism, and homophobia became targets. Feminism, multiculturalism, and open sexuality were celebrated. More women, African Americans, and Hispanics found success—for example, Jennifer Bartlett, who made grid-like works that mingle abstraction with personal and figurative allusions; and Jean-Michel Basquiat, who created primitive, grafitti-like paintings. Many older artists continued to produce brilliant work: Philip Guston, Romare Bearden, and Alice Neel, for instance. Fine arts departments proliferated at American colleges and universities. Teaching became a way for artists to make a living and still have enough time to create.

The federal government resumed sponsorship of the arts when Congress established the National Endowment for the Arts in 1965. The NEA supported individual artists, exhibitions, programs, and performances. Of course, it frequently came under attack by the left and right, and during the 1980s it was seriously threatened by controversies. One surrounded a sculpture by Serra, *Tilted Arc* (1981), purchased with NEA funds and sited in front of a federal building in New York. The arts community praised the work, but the building's employees and the general public hated it. Protests led to its removal in 1985. Another involved two exhibitions funded by the NEA. Awards for the Visual Arts was a long-standing program. Its 1988 catalogue, containing *Piss Christ* (1987), a photograph by Andres Serrano of a plastic crucifix in urine, was seen by the Reverend Donald Wildmon, the leader of the Mississippi-based American Family Association. Outraged, Wildmon contacted Senator Jesse Helms, a North Carolina Republican. Helms attacked this and another NEA-sponsored exhibit, *Robert Mapplethorpe: The Perfect Moment* (1988–1989). Mapplethorpe's photographs were hard-edged and homoerotic. (The photographer died of AIDS during the show's tour.) Helms and his compatriots wanted to close down the NEA. Instead, its funding was cut.

Despite public hostility, the market for old and new art expanded after 1960, becoming inflated during the Reagan years and dipping precipitously by 1990. Arts institutions flourished. New museums—the Walker Art Center in Minneapolis, the Museum of Contemporary Art and the Getty Center in Los Angeles, and Frank Gehry's tour de force, the Guggenheim Museum in Bilbao, Spain—were all completed after 1970. Yet American art was adrift in a postmodern sea. Robert Hughes sums it up:

F-111 (1964–1965) by James Rosenquist. Oil on canvas with aluminum, 10 x 86 ft. Scenes of materialism, destruction, and fantasy are joined in this huge painting. Linking them is a state-of-the-art fighter-bomber. THE MUSEUM OF MODERN ART, NEW YORK. PURCHASE. PHOTOGRAPH © 2000 THE MUSEUM OF MODERN ART, NEW YORK

The energies of cultural periods don't last forever. The Italian Renaissance came to an end. . . . And one would need to be an extreme optimist—some would say, a willfully blind one as well—to think that the big energies of American Modernism are still with us. Which is not to say that there are not plenty of gifted and interesting visual artists in America, doing valuable work at the end of the 20th century. But cultures do decay and run out of steam; and the visual culture of late American Modernism, once so strong, buoyant and inventive . . . may be no exception to that fact. (p. 88)

See also **The Fine Arts in Colonial America; The Arts in the Republican Era; Realism in Art and Literature; The Popular Arts; The Artist and the Intellectual in the New Deal** *(volume 1);* **Postmodernism and the Arts** *(volume 2);* **Artistic, Intellectual, and Political Refugees; Architecture; Film; Painting; Sculpture; Public Murals** *(in this volume); and other articles in this section.*

BIBLIOGRAPHY

Ashton, Dore. *The New York School: A Cultural Reckoning.* New York, 1973.

Brown, Milton W. *American Painting from the Armory Show to the Depression.* Princeton, N.J., 1955.

Crane, Diana. *The Transformation of the Avant-Garde: The New York Art World, 1940–1985.* Chicago, 1987.

Egbert, Donald Drew. *Socialism and American Art in the Light of European Utopianism, Marxism, and Anarchism.* 1952. Reprint, Princeton, N.J., 1967.

Guilbaut, Serge. *How New York Stole the Idea of Modern Art: Abstract Expressionism, Freedom, and the Cold War.* Chicago, 1983.

Harris, Neil. *The Artist in American Society: The Formative Years, 1790–1860.* New York, 1996.

Haskell, Barbara. *The American Century: Art and Culture, 1900–1950.* 2d. ed. New York, 1999.

Hughes, Robert. *American Visions: The Epic History of Art in America.* New York, 1997.

———. "American Visions." In *Time* (special issue, spring 1997).

Littleton, Taylor D., and Maltby Sykes. *Advancing American Art: Painting, Politics, and Cultural Confrontation at Mid-Century.* Tuscaloosa, Ala., 1989.

Novak, Barbara. *American Painting of the Nineteenth Century: Realism, Idealism, and the American Experience.* New York, 1969.

———. *Nature and Culture: American Landscape and Painting, 1825–1875.* New York, 1980.

Phillips, Lisa. *The American Century: Art and Culture, 1950–2000.* New York, 1999.

Rose, Barbara. *American Art since 1900.* Rev. ed. New York, 1975.

Taylor, Joshua C. *The Fine Arts In America.* Chicago, 1979.

Tomkins, Calvin. *The Bride and the Bachelors: Five Masters of the Avant-Garde.* Rev. ed. New York, 1968.

Varnedoe, Kirk, and Adam Gopnik. *High and Low: Modern Art and Popular Culture.* New York, 1990.

EDUCATION

William J. Reese

Faith in the efficacy and salutary influence of education is a hallmark of American culture. Evidence of this faith has abounded through the centuries, long before schools became a central feature of everyday life. "Knowledge is power," claimed many writers before the American Revolution. Ignorance and freedom are incompatible, the Founding Father Thomas Jefferson insisted, in promoting education and learning in the early American republic. By the middle of the nineteenth century, Americans spent more money on education than any Western nation. Private academies, seminaries, institutes, a fledgling public school system, numerous colleges, technical schools, and other places of learning dotted the land. The twentieth century similarly witnessed an enormous expansion of formal educational opportunities, from kindergarten through graduate school, testifying to a widespread belief in the power of education. That faith has been nearly universal despite considerable debate about the aims and purposes of education.

Over the course of American history, citizens have expected education to address a host of economic, political, and social concerns. Colonial Americans emphasized the religious foundations and moral aims of education, though an increased number of people in the eighteenth century advocated a more utilitarian form of instruction. In the early national period and nineteenth century, education for citizenship, social cohesion, and moral training were frequently championed, as formal schooling became a more important aspect of learning. The twentieth century continued to emphasize the importance of education and especially schooling in American culture, but increasingly stressed their relationship to economic growth and development.

THE COLONIAL PERIOD

By the time of the American Revolution, leading citizens in different regions offered competing no-

tions about the value and potential of education. Many claimed that education and literacy encouraged godly living while others emphasized their material benefits. Education was often touted for its positive contributions to community life. Literacy rates for white men, and increasingly for white women, were among the highest in the Western world. To learn to read—whether at home or at school, or through the efforts of parents, teachers, or tutors—had become increasingly commonplace. In a world with an expanding print culture, education served multiple purposes and seemed to be a benefit to society.

The spread of literacy and emphasis on the importance of schooling among some colonists owed much to the Protestant Reformation. The first white settlers in New England, especially the Puritans, emphasized the importance of learning to read to gain direct access to God's word through the Bible. Schools at all levels in the colonies frequently reflected the influence of Protestantism. Harvard College was established in 1636, the first of nine colonial colleges, all of which were controlled by church and state. Harvard promoted the discovery of truth—revealed religious truth, that is. In 1647 the Puritans in the Massachusetts Bay Colony characteristically passed a law to promote learning and to counter the influence of that Old Deluder, Satan. The law mandated the creation of reading and writing schools in towns with fifty families and college-preparatory Latin grammar schools in larger communities. Enforcement of the law was lax. But Protestant denominations throughout the colonies commonly endorsed education to help transmit religious and moral values to ease the path to eternal salvation.

Throughout the seventeenth and eighteenth centuries, numerous colonial leaders—ministers, governors, magistrates, and college presidents—viewed religious training as the foundation of education. So said missionaries trying to convert the heathen and slave and the village schoolmaster teaching young scholars the alphabet. Reading materials were heavily religious and didactic. The most widely used school text, the *New England Primer,* taught Calvinist notions about creation and human nature. As children progressed from A to Z, they were simultaneously taught orthodox religion: from "In Adam's fall, we sinned all" to "Zaccheus he did climb the tree, our Lord to see." Ministers routinely served as teachers, professors, and college presidents. Like the universities in Reformation Europe, Harvard, Yale, and the other colonial colleges aimed to prepare a learned ministry as well as other professionals to serve church and state. The classical curriculum helped steep young men in the wisdom of the ancients while they imbibed the larger truths of Protestantism. Colonial educators at this level thus intended to create pious, godly, learned individuals. What was taught was not necessarily what was learned. Rebellion within student ranks on the college level, usually interpreted as a sign of heresy and sedition, was common enough, and in the 1670s Governor William Berkeley of Virginia worried that schools would lead to social disorder. Southern leaders would long emphasize the instability that access to learning would produce among freedman and slave.

The secular goals of education grew increasingly prominent in the eighteenth century. The spread of free trade and markets undermined mercantilism but strengthened emerging utilitarian ideals. Private venture schools, taught by independent teachers without clerical backgrounds, opened in many towns and cities along the eastern seaboard. They offered courses in navigation, advanced arithmetic, cartography, modern languages, and other useful subjects. While the elementary schools founded by church and state in various colonies taught rudimentary subjects and the colleges offered a traditional classical curriculum, these private schools reflected a newly emerging strain of educational thought in early America. The benefits of learning in the marketplace became increasingly evident.

The life and educational views of Benjamin Franklin epitomized this rising faith in a useful education. Scientist, inventor, man of letters, diplomat, and entrepreneur, he well articulated the values of the middling classes of the northern colonies. Born into a Puritan family in Boston, Franklin attended the famed Boston Latin grammar school, feeder to Harvard; his quick exit dashed his father's hope that his bookish son would train for the ministry. Making his fortune as a printer, publisher, and writer in Philadelphia, the creator of *Poor Richard's Almanac* rejected sectarian religion and embraced the sturdy

virtues of hard work, punctuality, striving, and achievement. Franklin affirmed the Enlightenment emphasis upon reason, science, and faith in human ability and criticized the teaching of the dead tongues and the metaphysics of the higher learning. Latin and the classics had their place in life for the few, he admitted. For the majority of citizens, however, a more practical education was superior. In the 1740s Franklin proposed the establishment of an English academy in Philadelphia that would teach modern, nonclassical subjects. He explained that a classical education did not prepare most young men for business or the professions very effectively. "As to their STUDIES," he wrote, "it would be well if they could be taught *every Thing* that is useful, and *every Thing* that is ornamental: But Art is long, and their Time is short. It is therefore propos'd that they learn those Things that are likely to be *most useful* and *most ornamental.* Regard being had to the several Professions for which they are intended." Franklin's school opened, the forerunner to the University of Pennsylvania, but to his chagrin it emphasized the traditional classical curriculum.

On the eve of the American Revolution, therefore, education was already a contested intellectual and cultural activity. Many citizens continued to emphasize the close ties between education and Protestant Christianity. This was challenged by the growing secularization of society, especially evident in the seaboard cities, where trade, commerce, and the professions opened widening avenues to individual advancement and social prominence. Literacy rates among whites, especially males, were impressively high, and reading had expanded intellectual vistas to those who read not only the Bible but also newspapers, magazines, and political broadsides, all of which proliferated in the eighteenth century. Education was not synonymous with schooling, but leaders of the new nation increasingly suggested so in the coming decades.

THE EARLY NATIONAL PERIOD TO THE EARLY TWENTIETH CENTURY

Between the decades separating the victory at Yorktown and the dawn of the twentieth century, education assumed heightened importance. The creation of a new nation, the rise of a more urban, commercial, and industrialized society, the growth of more religious and ethnic diversity due to immigration, and the desire to reconstruct race and social relations generally after the Civil War strengthened the role of education and especially schooling in local communities. By 1900 education and schooling had become more synonymous, as public schools, colleges and research universities, and various other educational institutions grew more prominent.

New ideas about education and schooling emerged late in the eighteenth century, none more important than attempts to define the place of learning in the new nation and government's role in its promotion. A variety of schools, for example, had existed in colonial America, most of them neither public nor private in a modern sense. At different times, northern elementary and grammar schools were funded by a mix of public taxes, charitable donations, and tuition. Academies, often controlled by a private board of self-perpetuating trustees, typically charged tuition, though the schools sometimes received donations of land and cash grants from legislatures. Colleges, funded by church and state, often benefited from private bequests. There was no system of education anywhere in America, no clear demarcation between public and private spheres, and growing debate about how government might promote learning. Through provisions within the famous land grants of 1785 and 1787, the federal government had modestly encouraged the creation of schools on the frontier. But education's role in the republic remained hotly contested at the birth of the new nation.

Many of the Founding Fathers as well as prominent clerics and civic leaders agreed that education and schooling had to assume heightened responsibilities in society. Themselves suspicious of centralized authority, many political leaders nevertheless favored the establishment of a national university, based in the nation's capital, a project that died aborning. Benjamin Rush—the famed Philadelphia physician, patriot, and child of the Enlightenment—called for the creation of a system of free schools to ensure that youth became "republican machines," citizens prepared to live in a land of laws, not men. Only then would republicanism triumph. Noah Webster, a Connecticut Federalist, similarly championed a system of tax-supported schools to unify the nation. Schools would teach a uniform language, grammar, and spelling. Webster's blue-backed spellers, dictionaries, and readers ultimately became best-sellers. Other prominent publicists, men as well as women, argued that girls needed enhanced educational opportunities, partly to ensure the cultivation of better republican wives and mothers. Enlightenment views on human improvement led some citizens to theorize that women were fully educable and should even attend higher schools. Clearly, new educational ideals were in the air.

No individual offered more original thoughts on education in his generation than Thomas Jefferson. The author of the Declaration of Independence, the nation's third president, scientist, diplomat, and founder of the University of Virginia, Jefferson contributed several radical notions about education and schooling. He spoke eloquently of the necessity of education as a foundation for citizenship. Ignorance was the enemy of a free people, whose republican sentiments would flourish with the diffusion of knowledge. In *Notes on the State of Virginia* (1787), Jefferson called for state-financed elementary education for all white boys and girls, provision for some talented boys to attend grammar schools, and the encouragement of the most talented among them to enroll at the state university, William and Mary. Thus did the Sage of Monticello, an aristocrat and slaveholder, link democratic and egalitarian aspirations to the fate of the schools. The Virginia legislature failed to endorse his plan, which was visionary in its day. Jefferson's belief that talent existed in all social groups, including the poor, and that state-sponsored schools should help educate more children, remained controversial but ultimately attracted considerable popular support. America's schools would identify and reward talent, making a fluid social system a reality, in contrast with the class systems of Europe.

Social and economic changes in the nineteenth century profoundly shaped educational thought. As capitalist markets spread throughout the North in the antebellum period and the slave power was defeated in 1865, a new economic system was born. Immigration from the German states, Ireland, and Scandinavia produced greater religious and cultural diversity, and American industry grew phenomenally late in the century despite recurrent panics and economic depressions. Most importantly, northern reformers began by the 1830s to build a system of tax-supported public schools, a process that continued in fits and starts in the South during Reconstruction in the 1870s. Education had long served different causes: religious salvation, moral training, economic advance, and, in the new nation, citizenship. These claims on educational institutions did not disappear in the nineteenth century, when old ideals were refashioned and new goals put forward as public schools, colleges, and then research universities became more familiar aspects of American culture.

The diffusion of knowledge continued to take many forms: through rising rates of school atten-

JEFFERSON

Every government degenerates when trusted to the rulers of the people alone. The people themselves therefore are its only safe depositories. And to render even them safe, their minds must be improved to a certain degree.

Source: Jefferson, *Notes on the State of Virginia,* 1787.

dance, increased accessibility to newspapers and books as printing costs declined after the 1820s, and lyceums, political debates, and other means of learning. But the prime impetus for a sharpened national focus on education resulted from the movement for free public schools. The idea of a common school—where in theory all children could have access to the same curriculum, the same teachers, in the same schools—seemed a godsend to many northern citizens by the 1830s, when class conflict, ethnic and religious divisions, and sectional controversies were rife. Schools became the great hope in building stronger communities and curing a host of social ills.

Horace Mann was the nation's leading champion of the public school systems emerging in the free states. Lacking the wit or bonhomie of Franklin and the intellectual curiosity of Jefferson, Mann was nevertheless a tireless advocate of education. Born to Calvinist parents on a farm in Massachusetts, Mann grew to adulthood in an age of railroads, immigration, and cities. Like Franklin, he worried about the acculturation of immigrants in a predominantly British culture, and similarly applauded hard work, obedience, and achievement in the classroom. Like Jefferson, Mann insisted on the importance of state-sponsored, free public education, which increasingly became a reality for most white children in the North during his lifetime. He supported more education for women, typically endorsing coeducation. And Mann underscored the idea that the safety and perpetuation of the republic depended upon a universal system of free schools that would provide opportunity, especially to the talented children of the poor. In an often quoted statement, the nation's leading school reformer wrote in 1848 that public schools were "the great equalizer of the conditions of men—the balance

wheel of the social machinery." Like many educators of his day, Mann stressed the importance of schools for moral education, not social mobility. Few jobs, except for some of the professions, required much formal education, and schools were encouraged to teach nondenominational Protestant values over explicitly vocational subjects. The common schools by the 1820s taught the traditional three R's plus a smattering of geography, history, and grammar. They aimed to bind a nation through the reading of Webster's spellers and readers, and through the inspiration provided by the moral tales in the ubiquitous McGuffey's *Readers,* the leading textbooks of the century.

Catholics famously protested against the so-called nondenominational character of the public schools, which to them was simply a cover for anti-Catholicism. Mann urged teachers to begin each school day by reading without comment from the Bible—the King James version—which infuriated Catholics. Textbooks, often written by native-born, Protestant ministers, commonly contained garden-variety slurs on immigrants and "papists." Archbishop Thomas Hughes of New York City caused a national furor in the 1840s by demanding a share of public taxes to help each religious group establish its own schools. Mann and the public school leadership insisted upon drawing ever sharper lines between the public and private sectors. For the rest

MANN

Without undervaluing any other human agency, it may be safely affirmed that the Common School . . . may become the most effective and benignant of all the forces of civilization. Two reasons sustain this position. In the first place, there is a universality in its operation, which can be affirmed of no other institution whatever. If administered in the spirit of justice and conciliation, all the rising generation may be brought within the circle of its reformatory and elevating influences. And, in the second place, the materials upon which it operates are so pliant and ductile as to be susceptible of assuming a greater variety of forms than any other earthly work of the Creator.

Source: Mann, *Twelfth Annual Report,* 1849.

of the century, the main emphasis of the schools remained moral education of a strictly nondenominational Protestant (though nonsectarian) character. Believing that education and religion were inseparable, Catholics and a handful of Protestants (including a large number of Lutherans) frequently withdrew their children from the public schools and constructed alternative parochial systems.

College leaders shared Mann's emphasis on moral training. The moral purposes of the higher learning remained strong throughout the century, even in the emerging state universities. The classical curriculum promised to train the mind, but professors often emphasized the moral lessons embedded in the favored writings of antiquity. Chapel remained mandatory at many schools, whether at denominational colleges or public institutions, which increasingly admitted women after the Civil War. Tensions between secular and religious values accelerated later in the century as Darwinian science grew popular, and as original research, not teaching, became the predominant activity in the nation's universities. Harvard and other prestigious colleges became universities, where the search for truth through original study, research, and laboratory experiments was increasingly divorced from the concerns of sectarian religion. The moral atmosphere of the higher learning remained everywhere evident, however, even though support for useful, practical subjects intensified. Many of the academic leaders in the new social sciences—economics, sociology, history, and political science—were often reared in pious Protestant homes, were deeply religious, and advocated social justice and a more equitable society.

Education's role in the promotion of social justice faced its severest test not in the colleges, but in the public schools, especially in the period immediately following the Civil War. Since the time of the Revolution, political leaders had pondered the precise role of the federal government in education. The Morrill Act (1862) had recently provided federal support for education in the agricultural and mechanical arts at state universities. But the states, not the federal government, had established common schools, which were controlled by local districts and largely funded by property taxes. What role should the federal government play to ensure that four million former slaves, most of them illiterate, gained access to public schools? Debates in Washington, within state legislatures, and in local communities centered on the capacity of African Americans to learn, society's moral obligations to the freedmen's families, and the place of schools in the social order. Radical Republicans in Congress demanded schools for African Americans and military support to ensure southern compliance. Some, like Thaddeus Stevens of Pennsylvania, endorsed integrated schools though stopped short of advocating social equality between the races. The white southern majority, led by a resurgent Democratic Party in the early 1870s, opposed the construction of many black schools, which were often maintained by the former slaves and aided by white northern philanthropists and teachers. As southerners continually reminded northern radicals, public schools north of Mason Dixon were often racially segregated. Jim Crow triumphed in the South in education and every other sphere in the 1880s and 1890s, a policy upheld in a landmark ruling by the U.S. Supreme Court, *Plessy v. Ferguson* (1896).

By the turn of the twentieth century, African American leaders responded to these developments with competing views on the place of education in American life. Born into slavery, Booker T. Washington was catapulted into national prominence in the 1890s and became the most influential black leader of his generation. His autobiography, *Up from Slavery* (1901), urged African Americans to set aside demands for suffrage and civil rights, which whites violently resisted, and focus instead on education, especially vocational and industrial education. There was nothing more pathetic, he claimed, than to see poor blacks with rags on their backs studying "big books" and "many high-sounding subjects." Like Franklin, he applauded the time-tested virtues of Poor Richard. Learning a trade as well as honesty, industry, and thrift—albeit in a segregated society—might lead to greater economic advancement. Unlike most black colleges, which continued to teach an academic, often classical curriculum, Washington's famed Tuskegee Institute emphasized teacher education, trade training, and, especially, hard work, reflecting the utilitarian orientation becoming more prominent in higher education.

Initially favorable toward Washington's self-help philosophy in the 1890s, W. E. B. Du Bois soon became his great rival. Du Bois became one of the greatest American intellectuals of the twentieth century. Unwilling to sacrifice civil liberties and political participation, Du Bois demanded full recognition of a "dignified manhood" and the rights of citizenship. In *The Souls of Black Folk* (1903), he attacked an educational vision based solely on industrial and vocational education. There was more to life than "bread winning," he argued. "We shall hardly induce black men to believe that if their stomachs be full, it matters little about their brains." In contrast to segregationists and white southerners who doubted the capacity of blacks to learn, Du Bois emphasized the need for integrated schools, increased spending on education, and, much like Jefferson, more public support for the higher education of the "Talented Tenth," the very few who would become leaders in the arts, business, and professions in the coming generation.

While schools were legally segregated by race in the South and often by custom in the North, coeducation was the most common practice in the public schools for all races. In the antebellum period, American Protestant school leaders emphasized that the schools should imitate the family and educate everyone together. In addition to cutting expenses, the policy was consciously pursued as an alternative to European and Catholic school traditions, which traditionally separated the sexes. By the time of the Civil War, boys and girls who attended the typical public school—a one-room building in the countryside—sat in the same classroom and studied the same basic subjects. While most citizens, and teachers, assumed that girls, upon reaching adulthood, would usually marry and become mothers, the curriculum of public schools was largely oriented around moral training and academics and not toward future vocations. For disciplinary or other purposes, teachers often separated boys and girls, and younger and older pupils, onto separate benches or sections of the classroom. Some urban schools segregated boys and girls into separate buildings, but even in those cities coeducation was becoming more common by the early twentieth century.

Girls became the majority of high school pupils in the nineteenth century, and most also attended coeducational institutions. The first public school opened in Boston in 1821 and was restricted to boys. By midcentury, separate high schools for white boys and girls appeared in the larger towns and cities in the Northeast and sometimes in the urban South. But once again, coeducation became increasingly common as villages, towns, and cities built high schools in the second half of the nineteenth century. Local school records consistently show that girls, who had meager access to high-paying jobs in the workplace, attended high school more frequently than boys, received better grades, and were more likely to graduate than boys. High schools often provided enough academic training to prepare young women to become elementary or grammar-level teachers, a common occupation for those who attended or graduated from high school.

The job market for women remained restricted, however.

By the early 1900s many of society's basic concerns centered on the function and purpose of education, especially its expanding public schools. Civic leaders since the postrevolutionary era wanted schools to help unify the nation. Antebellum reformers further demanded the teaching of traditional values such as the work ethic, punctuality, and achievement in a system that nevertheless emphasized moral training above intellectual accomplishments. Increasingly, institutions of higher learning attempted to train people more directly for the workplace. Gender differences were pronounced: men entered the higher status professions and business, women less prestigious occupations such as teaching. As the new century dawned, ideas about education reflected the challenges of life in an urban and industrial age.

THE TWENTIETH CENTURY

In the twentieth century, education remained a significant and controversial issue in American culture. Schools became increasingly important. By the 1950s high schools had become mass institutions, and colleges, universities, and other forms of higher education would boom in subsequent decades. Educational thought remained vibrant and diverse. The secular, utilitarian purposes of education, while often contested, became more prevalent over the course of the century on all levels of schooling. Progressive notions of child-centered education vied for prominence, arrayed against traditional subject matter and conventional pedagogy. Countless citizens debated the precise relationship between education and citizenship, the economy, race relations, and social justice as the nation became more multiethnic and multiracial. By the early twenty-first century, as America became a postmodern nation transformed by technological innovation and the global economy, the place of the schools in society seemed more important than ever.

In the early 1900s the nation's civic and educational leaders remained convinced that education, especially schooling, was the key to social progress. In the wake of the industrial revolution, however, reformers sought to emulate science to stimulate factory-like productivity in the nation's schools. In the first half of the twentieth century, schools were increasingly consolidated, school boards were reduced in size, superintendents and other experts gained influence over educational policy, and teachers increasingly attended normal schools and teacher training colleges to enhance their professional skills. Except during the Great Depression, when declining fertility rates reduced elementary school enrollments, school attendance skyrocketed, especially during the baby boom between 1946 and 1964, which produced 76 million new citizens. The key word in educational thought during most of the century was efficiency: how to maximize school expenditures, adapt the curriculum to the child (or vice versa), and best link educational training to jobs. By the 1960s a well-known television commercial made the main purpose of schooling explicit: "To get a good job, get a good education."

At the turn of the century, Edward Lee Thorndike, one of the founding fathers of educational psychology, pioneered in applying the insights of experimental science and behaviorism to the schools. Thorndike's research demolished the traditional view within education that the mastery of difficult subjects such as Latin or mathematics trained the mind and made learning other subjects easier. Like a growing legion of educational researchers, Thorndike applauded scientific methods of testing, evaluation, and data gathering in the schools. His famous dictum was widely quoted: "Whatever exists, exists in a quantity and can be measured." By the 1920s administrators commonly adopted the use of intelligence tests and achievement tests in the schools. This was a pedagogical revolution. Like Thorndike, the creators of these tests were impressed with human differences, not similarities, and emphasized the hereditarian over environmental determinants of intelligence. Educators used standardized test scores to place children in particular courses of study, spelling doom for the nineteenth-century ideal of a common education for everyone. In the elementary grades, ability grouping (often based on reading proficiency) became common; in high schools, pupils were tracked into academic (college preparatory) or nonacademic (vocational) or less academic (general) tracks. That education should promote individual and social efficiency became a mantra in public school circles.

Throughout the twentieth century, this preoccupation with human difference dominated educational thought. Educational psychologists before the 1920s generally believed that the children of native-born Protestants were the most intelligent; they regarded the children of immigrants, from central and southern Europe especially, and then African Americans and Native Americans, as several rungs below them on the evolutionary ladder. A new generation of psychologists and social critics in

THORNDIKE

The variations from the ordinary, common, or typical man range continuously to such extreme conditions as appear in the idiot and the genius, or Nero and Lincoln. But the great majority cluster somewhat closely around the "average man.". . . The differences that characterize men of the same time, country, and social status are largely original, determined directly by the germs from which the individual develops, and so indirectly by the ancestry from which he springs. . . . All the sciences and arts of controlling human nature must accept the original variety of human nature as a condition for thought and action. . . . Specialization of schools is needed not only to fit pupils for special professions, trades, and the like, but also to fit the schools to original differences in the pupils. Specialization of instruction for different pupils within one class is needed as well as specialization of the curriculum for different classes.

Source: Thorndike, *Individuality,* 1911.

the 1920s contested these deterministic, eugenics-based views which were further discredited in the 1930s due to the rise of fascist ideologies, the efficiency of death camps, and the declining reputation of capitalism. But the claim that many children could not benefit from academic instruction remained entrenched, lowering expectations for everyone except for those in the college preparatory track. The revival of the economy after 1945 and the onset of the cold war revived respect for corporate values and stimulated government and private investment in technology and science, strengthening the education of the college bound.

While education for efficiency was a dominant theme in the early twentieth century, John Dewey and other critics had a different educational vision. In a series of philosophical works including most prominently *Democracy and Education* (1916), Dewey became associated in the popular mind with "progressive education," though he eschewed the label and wrote very damning indictments of child-centered instruction. Dewey endorsed a scientific approach to education but criticized the testing movement, narrow vocational movements, and

John Dewey (1859–1952). Among Dewey's earlier books on education were *The School and Society* (1899) and *The Child and the Curriculum* (1902). © BETTMANN/CORBIS

similar attempts to pigeonhole the child into a predetermined curriculum and course of study, fatal to individual growth and to democracy. Influenced by the German philosopher Georg Wilhelm Friedrich Hegel and the English naturalist Charles Darwin, he recognized the contingent nature of life, especially evolution and change. He emphasized that learning environments should be continually reassessed in the best interests of the child. To Dewey, democracy was not a set of abstract propositions but best found expression in social relationships, including interactions at school, which should expand a child's intellectual world and human potential. Narrow industrial training that channeled the young into unskilled, dead-end factory jobs (which disappeared even for many adults during the depression) undermined individual opportunity and social progress.

"Progressive education," whose advocates were often inspired by Dewey's writings, assumed many forms in the twentieth century. Dewey criticized most forms of child-centered education, whose "sugar coated" qualities denied the need for adult authority. This form of progressivism drew upon diverse Romantic traditions, especially the writings of Jean-Jacques Rousseau, Johann Pestalozzi, and

Friedrich Froebel. Romantics generally emphasized the goodness of the child, favored more "natural" teaching methods that elevated life and experience over books, and accused schools of excessive discipline. In the 1920s a number of self-styled progressives opened private schools, usually for the upper middle classes, that had a more experimental curriculum and flexible teaching methods. These notions had some appeal among reform-minded public school educators, who hoped that the atmosphere and methods of the kindergarten, the perfect expression of child-centered education, could spread throughout the system. But the popularity of vocationalism for the many and traditional academic subjects for especially the college bound meant that child-centered methods never became the norm in most schools.

Without question, however, Dewey and other outspoken critics of testing and classroom rigidities often tempered the power of those who reduced education to test curves and educational outputs. Elementary school classrooms remained structured around ability grouping, separating pupils by academic achievement and presumed potential. But the atmosphere of many elementary classrooms softened over the course of the twentieth century. The adoption of diverse teaching methods, group and cooperative learning, field trips, and smaller class sizes brought genuine change to the classroom. And "progressive education" served a very important political function. Throughout the century, conservatives and traditionalists routinely blamed John Dewey and "progressive education" for any curriculum, behavior, or tendency in the schools they disliked. Whether in the 1920s, 1950s, or 1990s, they blamed progressive education for low academic standards, classroom violence, and permissiveness. Those who periodically called for "back to the basics" in the classroom were especially convinced that Dewey and the progressives had undermined schools that once educated everyone to a high academic and moral standard.

In periods of political conservatism such as the 1950s and 1980s, educational critics emphasized declining academic and moral standards in the schools. President Dwight D. Eisenhower pointed the finger directly at John Dewey. Others feared that schools, like the larger society, had grown too secular. In the 1960s, the teaching of evolution and the constitutional ban on school prayer convinced many Christian fundamentalists and other conservatives that liberalism in general and progressive education in particular were to blame. Nondenominational Christian day schools began to proliferate,

A NATION AT RISK

Our nation is at risk. Our once unchallenged pre-eminence in commerce, industry, science, and technological innovation is being overtaken by competitors throughout the world. . . . [T]he educational foundations of our society are presently being eroded by a rising tide of mediocrity that threatens our very future as a Nation and a people. . . . If an unfriendly foreign power had attempted to impose on America the mediocre educational performance that exists today, we might have viewed it as an act of war. As it stands, we have allowed this to happen to ourselves. We have even squandered the gains in student achievement made in the wake of the Sputnik challenge. . . . We have, in effect, been committing an act of unthinking, unilateral educational disarmament. Our society and its educational institutions seem to have lost sight of the basic purposes of schooling and the disciplined effort needed to attain them.

Source: National Commission on Excellence in Education, *A Nation at Risk,* 1983.

also spurred by the problems associated with racial integration, and by the 1970s the secular press applauded Catholic schools for teaching sound ethics and the basics. Leading conservatives nevertheless emphasized the tight fit between rigorous schools and a sound economy. That was the theme in the most famous educational document of the late twentieth century, *A Nation at Risk* (1983). Sponsored by the Reagan administration, the report blamed the schools for a weak economy and demanded more academic requirements and higher standards and test scores. The report was silent on childhood poverty, multiculturalism, the inclusion of children with handicaps or disabilities in the regular classroom, or race relations, the burning social issues of the period. In *Brown v. Board of Education* (1954), the U.S. Supreme Court had ruled segregated schools unconstitutional, but racial separation, especially in large urban areas, remained common at the end of the century.

While racial segregation was the dominant civil rights issue of the twentieth century, women's rights certainly gained increasing prominence. A backlash against coeducation early in the century led by

G. Stanley Hall, a renowned psychologist, bore little fruit, but the rising popularity of vocational education led to more classes for women in typing, commercial subjects, and home economics. At the same time, women were often overall academically superior students, attended school more regularly, caused fewer disciplinary problems, and graduated at higher rates than boys. Their attendance at normal (teacher training) schools, coeducational public and private universities, and other institutions of higher learning soared over the course of the twentieth century. By the early 1970s even the most elite private colleges and universities had also opened their doors to women, including professional schools beyond the traditional trio of education, nursing, and social work. By 2000 the majority of pupils attending colleges and universities were women, a remarkable social change whose influence upon the nature of the economy and larger society will continue to reverberate in the coming decades. Access to education had not brought full civil rights and equality but, for those able to extend their schooling beyond high school, the promise of greater choice in career and lifestyle.

Native Americans similarly fought for more access to educational institutions and social justice over the course of the twentieth century. The focus of some missionary activities since the colonial period, Native peoples whose children attended white-sponsored and controlled schools faced the daunting challenge of cultural and economic survival. The federal government established a number of off-reservation boarding schools in the late nineteenth and early twentieth centuries, and numerous other schools were established in the coming decades: reservation-based day schools, nearby public schools, and a variety of contract schools. The disastrous policy of terminating reservations in the 1950s, which was later reversed, led to an influx of Native peoples to the cities, which meant greater reliance upon urban public schools that were entering a period of educational decline. But Native Americans, whose great diversity makes generalizations about their educational experiences difficult, fought for more self-determination and control over their own schools and even successfully pressed for the establishment of their own institutions of higher learning.

Without question, the ever-increasing ties between schools and the economy was the most important educational trend in the twentieth century. The public schools became less the province of child centeredness and more the center of vocational education. The same trends were evident in higher education, whose credentials were increasingly necessary for access to the best jobs. By the 1960s, the ties between religion and education at the most elite private and all public universities had been completely severed. Humanities enrollments began to decline, as the traditional liberal arts gave way to majors in the professional schools, sciences, and especially business late in the century. During the cold war, the federal government invested in areas deemed essential to economic growth and national security, especially mathematics, science, and technology. The collapse of the Soviet threat, the revival of the economy in the 1990s, and the relative affluence of American society further deepened society's consumer and materialist orientation. Market solutions to every social ill became popular, including the radical notion of expending public monies on private schools, the majority of which were sponsored by religious groups.

While educational thought and debate at the dawn of the twenty-first century occasionally focused on moral questions and concerns about poverty, ethnicity, and race, most centered on how schools could better promote individual mobility and the economy. Citizens concerned with standardized scores in the educational marketplace rarely spoke of the intrinsic joys of reading or learning. As in the past, many citizens expected the schools to perform multiple functions—from teaching English to immigrants to ensuring high test results on academic subjects. There are few things that Americans believe cannot be solved by education. Fundamentally, however, citizens largely expect education to be useful and to lead to well-paying jobs and to the greatest good for the greatest number. Like test scores, that is something that presumably exists in a quantity and can be measured.

See also **Education in Early America; The Classical Vision; Southern Intellectual Life; Urban Cultural Institutions** *(volume 1);* **The Professional Ideal; The Struggle for the Academy** *(volume 2); and other articles in this section.*

BIBLIOGRAPHY

Altenbaugh, Richard J. *Historical Dictionary of American Education.* Westport, Conn., 1999.

Anderson, James D. *The Education of Blacks in the South, 1860–1915.* Chapel Hill, N.C., 1988.

Beatty, Barbara. *Preschool Education in America: The Culture of Young Children from the Colonial Era to the Present.* New Haven, Conn., 1995.

Brown, Richard D. *The Strength of a People: The Idea of an Informed Citizenry in America, 1670–1870.* Chapel Hill, N.C., 1996.

Cremin, Lawrence A. *The Transformation of the Schools: Progressivism in American Education, 1876–1957.* New York, 1961.

Curti, Merle. *The Social Ideas of American Educators.* Paterson, N.J., 1959.

Franklin, Barry M. *From "Backwardness" to "At Risk": Childhood Learning Difficulties and the Contradictions of Reform.* Albany, N.Y., 1994.

Harlan, Louis R. *Booker T. Washington: The Making of a Black Leader, 1865–1901.* New York, 1972.

Jefferson, Thomas. *Notes on the State of Virginia.* London, 1787.

Kaestle, Carl F. *Pillars of the Republic: Common Schools and American Society, 1780–1865.* New York, 1983.

Kliebard, Herbert M. *The Struggle for the American Curriculum, 1893–1958.* New York, 1986.

Lucas, Christopher J. *American Higher Education: A History.* New York, 1994.

Mann, Horace. *Twelfth Annual Report of the Board of Education, Together with the Twelfth Annual Report of the Secretary of the Board.* Boston, 1849.

McClellan, B. Edward. *Moral Education in America.* New York, 1999.

Mirel, Jeffrey. *The Rise and Fall of an Urban School System: Detroit, 1907–1981.* Ann Arbor, Mich., 1993.

National Commission on Excellence in Education. *A Nation at Risk.* Cambridge, Mass., 1984.

Ravitch, Diane. *The Troubled Crusade: American Education, 1945–1980.* New York, 1978.

Reese, William J. *The Origins of the American High School.* New Haven, Conn., 1995.

Spring, Joel H. *The Sorting Machine Revisited: National Educational Policy since 1945.* New York, 1989.

Thorndike, Edward L. *Individuality.* Boston, 1911.

Tyack, David B. *The One Best System: A History of American Urban Education.* Cambridge, Mass., 1974.

Urban, Wayne, and Jennings Wagoner Jr. *American Education: A History.* New York, 1996.

Wollons, Roberta Lyn, ed. *Kindergartens and Cultures.* New Haven, Conn., 2000.

Zilversmit, Arthur. *Changing Schools: Progressive Education Theory and Practice, 1920–1960.* Chicago, 1993.

LAW AND THE AMERICAN MIND

James R. Hackney Jr.

The historical development of law in the United States is a complex and multifaceted tale. Tracing the development of a single important element of United States law as it relates to overarching cultural and intellectual themes will provide the reader with a clearer understanding of the development of American legal theory.

A major issue in American law and one that clearly reflects broader intellectual trends is accident, or tort, law, specifically liability of manufacturers of consumer products (commonly referred to as products liability law). Product liability law plays a major role in the American economy, dictating the allocation of loss to the consumer or the manufacturer when an accident occurs while a product is being used. How the law determines this allocation has a large impact on whether accident losses are covered as a tax on business or as an economic hardship on consumers. As such, this is a subject of great political significance and debate.

It is impossible to understand how products liability law developed without taking into account the general intellectual trends that influence legal institutions (courts and the legal academy). As with the more general intellectual trends, discontinuities, rather than uninterrupted construction, mark the law's development. Three discontinuous episodes—the classical period, the legal realist movement, and the age of analysis—constitute the cartography of American legal theory that shaped products liability law.

CLASSICAL ROOTS

Post–Revolutionary War legal theory in the United States was rooted in a culture with distinct beliefs and commitments. Legal scholars often refer to this era as the classical period. The legal intellectual community (judges and scholars) was wedded politically to a laissez-faire doctrine and methodologically to a formalist approach.

Formalism is abstract, conceptual, and deductive in nature. It divorces reason from experience, relying solely on rationality. Classical adherents believed that these were preordained principles. One such principle was the belief in individual freedom. This led to the laissez-faire bias against government intervention.

Nowhere was this formalist methodology more evident than in the rise of the legal treatise. The legal treatise was not the invention of American legal theorists; William Blackstone in his famous *Commentaries on the Laws of England* (1766–1769) had established the tradition in England. The allure of treatises in America was that they gave a veneer of objectivity to the common law, an important move at a time when the common law was coming under assault as being political.

The basic claim inherent in the treatises was that legal reasoning was scientific. Judges could deduce the outcome of a case from enduring principles. The "commentaries" of early-nineteenth-century legal theorists crystallized in James Kent's *Commentaries on American Law* (1826–1830), in which he systematically laid out the principles of American law. Careful examination of what classical theorists took as the founding of principles of American law reveals that they simply represented the status quo—either in the form of legal precedent handed down from England or principles derived from laissez-faire ideology. For classical theorists, it was simply a given that government should not interfere with the "natural" social order. This was particularly the case in the economic arena. So it should come as little surprise that laissez-faire ideology would constitute one of the bedrock principles. As early as the founding of the Republic, political theorists had argued for—and indeed structured—government on the basis of individual property rights.

Nowhere is this stance more evident than in James Madison's *Federalist* 10 (1787), in which he warns against the possibility of conflict between the factions. It is a principal justification for a republican, as opposed to democratic, governmental system. Madison argued that "the most common and durable source of factions, has been the various and unequal distribution of property." These factions fell along class lines: "A landed interest, a manufacturing interest, a mercantile interest, . . . with many lesser interests, grow up of necessity in civilized nations, and divide them into different classes, actuated by different sentiments and views." Out of necessity the government would be called upon to mediate conflicts that arose between factions: "The regulation of these various and interfering interests forms the principal task of modern Legislation."

However, Madison warned against the "rage for . . . equal division of property" as well as other "wicked project[s]." The protections against this wickedness in the antebellum period and continuing though the Civil War would come from the courts under the guise of scientific objectivity. Throughout the antebellum era courts decided a series of cases limiting government intervention, in the form of minimum wage, the right to strike, and employment law. Employers and employees were viewed as individual actors who had freely agreed to contractual arrangements. The first principle, or natural law, was individual freedom. From the principle of individual freedom, classical theorists deduced that all contracts, including employment contracts, were voluntarily entered into. Economic disparities were not relevant. Classical theorists did not think in terms of groups. Those who did not thrive economically were simply, as individuals, not as well equipped as those who succeeded. No thought was given to the prospect that economic relationships were socially constituted and frequently coerced.

This laissez-faire ideology, masked under the guise of objectivity, is epitomized in the U.S. Supreme Court opinion in *Lochner v. New York* (1905). *Lochner* involved the constitutionality of a New York state regulation limiting the number of hours bakers could work in a week. The regulation was passed under the guise of the state's police powers—governing the safety, health, morals, and general welfare of the public. However, the Court held that the legislation was an unwarranted intrusion upon the employers' and employees' freedom to contract. The Court's focus was on the liberty interests of the parties to enter into an agreement. The Court held that bakery workers did not need the state's protection because "there is no contention that bakers as a class are not equal in intelligence and capacity to men in other trades or manual occupations." With the *Lochner* case, the Court effectively continued the antebellum tradition of minimal state interference in business enterprise, arguing that upholding the New York regulation would effectively place the state in a position of "supervisor, or *pater familias,* over every act of the individual."

Classical thought thus helped sustain the existing distribution of wealth, protecting the powerful. It also provided a measure of certainty regarding legal "principles." The benchmarks for classicists were certainty and objective truth.

The quest for legal science, as manifest in the treatise movement, would become a fixture in modern legal theory. However, conceptions of science changed and were contested over time. For example, the classical theorists disdained the burgeoning social sciences because their approach ran against the grain of formalist practice, giving greater weight to experience and observation than to "scientific" theory. For modern theorists, however, the social sciences, particularly economic theory, would play a major role in legal theory.

THE REALIST ANECDOTE

While classical theory dominated eighteenth- and early-nineteenth-century thought, its premises were severely shaken as Charles Darwin's theory of evolution began to take hold in the American mind. During the classical period intellectuals could rest assured that at least certain bedrock principles were available from on high. Darwinism, the new scientific paradigm, marked a break from this view because the theory of evolution, juxtaposed to creationism, implied that there was no preordained path for human development. In fact, human progress owed more to chance than to destiny. The certainty associated with classical theory was eclipsed by the historical and relativist ethos that marks the realist period.

This new scientific ethos was reflected philosophically in American pragmatism, whose beginnings are commonly identified with the Metaphysical Club. This turn-of-the-century "club" included among its members Charles Sanders Peirce, William James, Chauncey Wright, Nicholas St. John Green, and Oliver Wendell Holmes, all of whom were Harvard University affiliates. They met periodically to present papers and critique one another's ideas. It would be an understatement to say that this group was eclectic. Its members' interests were as colorful as varied. However, they did articulate certain shared themes that marked their times and that stand in stark contrast to classical theory, the central ideal being the contingent nature of truth. This theme owed much to Darwin's *Origin of Species* (1859), and it influenced a host of fields, including legal theory.

Oliver Wendell Holmes, a legal theorist and later U.S. Supreme Court justice, was the first to systematically introduce pragmatist concepts into American legal theory. In a direct assault on classical theory, Holmes set forth this pragmatist formulation in *The Common Law* (1881):

> What has been said will explain the failure of all theories that consider the law only from its formal side, whether they attempt to deduce the *corpus* from *a priori* postulates, or fall into the humbler error of supposing the *science* of the law to reside in the *elegantia juris,* or logical cohesion of part with part. The truth is, that the law is always approaching, and never reaching, consistency. (emphasis added; p. 36)

In other words, the law is contingent—its contours and precepts dependent on time, place, and context. The law was not located in the ether waiting to be discovered. Indeed, judges exercised a policy function, basing their decisions upon "what is expedient for the community concerned." Expedience could not be measured by any particular a priori principles, including laissez-faire ideology. In the *Lochner* case, it was Holmes, who in dissenting from the majority's opinion argued, "This case is decided upon an economic theory which a large part of the country does not entertain." Moreover, "a Constitution is not intended to embody a particular economic theory, whether of paternalism . . . or of *laissez faire.*" Common law judges are obligated to render judgment based on the social-historical context of the particular dispute at issue, not from any particular set of "fundamental principles."

Holmes viewed the historical development of accident law as exemplifying this approach. Before *The Common Law* there was no systematic approach to conceptualizing accident law. Holmes's endeavor was essential in answering one of the key policy questions raised in accident law: whether those who caused harm, irrespective of fault, would compensate accident victims. Doctrinally, a system that required that fault be proved was labeled negligence. If fault was not required, the regime was "strict liability" (enhancing the likelihood of victim compensation).

Holmes recognized that the choice between negligence and strict liability had major policy implications. In pre-industrial America, the choice seemed relatively straightforward. Negligence was favored over strict liability because "the public gen-

Oliver Wendell Holmes Jr. (1841–1935). Holmes served as a justice of the Massachusetts Supreme Judicial Court (1888–1902) and the U.S. Supreme Court (1902–1932). © Bettmann/corbis

erally profits from individual activity" (p. 95). This worldview fit very nicely with a society composed principally of dispersed, individual actors and small business enterprises and that was entranced with laissez-fair ideology. However, with the rise of industrialism at the turn of the century, Holmes and other American intellectuals reassessed the merits of strict liability. The re-evaluation was consistent with a view that legal rules are historically contingent.

Holmes reconfirmed the need for policy-based legal rules: "For the rational study of the law . . . the man of the future is the man of statistics and the master of economics" ("Path of the Law," p. 469). With industrialization on the horizon, the merits of strict liability had to be revisited. Specifically, in the context of employer liability for harms to employees, Holmes noted, "If any one thinks it can be settled deductively . . . he is theoretically wrong" (p. 467). To determine the merits of strict liability, one must take into account the societal shift from "isolated, ungeneralized wrongs" to a milieu in which most harms involve "certain well-known businesses." Industrialization and its effects would have a profound influence on how products liability was viewed.

Law and legal theory were swept up not only in the pragmatism of the time but also in the period's progressivism in a stark contrast to their laissez-faire roots. The turn-of-the-century symbiosis between pragmatism and progressivism is reflected in John Dewey's philosophy. Dewey constructed his philosophy, in part, upon ideas initially put forth by members of the Metaphysical Club, particularly Charles Sanders Peirce and William James. He believed that philosophy should facilitate critical inquiry and promote social reform. His philosophy blended well with progressivism and its emphasis on social improvement through governmental action. Critical inquiry required a "heightened consciousness of deficiencies and corruptions in the scheme and distribution of values that obtains at any period" (*Experience and Nature*, p. 73). Uncovering those deficiencies required that would-be social reformers collect evidence concerning society's various ills.

With the spread of corporate power in America, the corporation naturally became a focal point. Between 1860 and 1900 investment in American industrial plants increased from $1 billion to $12 billion, and employment increased from 1.3 million employees to 5.5 million. Correspondingly, there were a large number of workplace injuries. In the railroad industry, each year one in every twenty-six laborers was injured, and one in every three hundred was killed. Additionally, manufacturing output was reaching a larger consuming public and, correspondingly, was responsible for an increasing number of product-related injuries (West, *American Evasion of Philosophy*, p. 79). Dewey expressed the general concerns of progressives when he bemoaned the "socially unnecessary deaths, illnesses, accidents and incapacitations that come from the bad economic conditions under which so much of modern industry is carried on" (Dewey, "Elements of Social Reorganization," p. 749).

Progressive economists, particularly institutionalist, also criticized corporate power. Institutionalist economists included such figures as Thorstein Veblen, John R. Commons, Wesley Clair Mitchell, Robert Hale, and Henry Seager. Institutionalists emphasized the vagaries of finance capitalism and argued that big business was more focused on profit than product, and that cost considerations overshadowed concerns over employee and consumer safety.

Thorstein Veblen was a particularly harsh critic. He set forth his views in the seminal work *The The-*ory of Business Enterprise* (1904). He accused business of being more concerned with profit than product. The classical justification for a laissez-faire approach—that business owners deserved the profits they reaped due to their contributions to society—no longer held true. Modern business focused on mass marketing and sales, not production. This dictated a changed relationship with consumers:

> In the older days, when handicraft was the rule of the industrial system, the personal contact between the producer and his consumer was close and lasting. Under these circumstances the factor of personal esteem and disesteem had a considerable play in controlling the purveyors of goods and services. (pp. 51–52)

Consumers were now pitted against manufacturers. Progressives expressed a similar view on the relationship between employees and corporations.

Legal academics, particularly legal realists, adopted many of these perspectives on corporate power. For legal realists, the policy concern was setting up a legal regime that would curtail corporate power and benefit accident victims. Tort law scholars focused on employee injuries and consumer accidents, arguing respectively for workers' compensation policies (guaranteeing that workers injured during the course of employment would receive compensation) and strict products liability (ensuring that consumers injured by products would be compensated).

The spearhead for the workers' compensation movement was the American Association for Labor Legislation (AALL). It was founded in 1906 as an offshoot of the American Economics Association, which was heavily influenced by institutional economists. The AALL based its arguments for workers' compensation on the grounds that, in cases involving a worker and a corporation, the corporation should bear the loss of injury. This view was motivated by sentiment against corporate power. It was also influenced by another Progressive Era tenet: social insurance.

Progressives believed that social insurance policies should be established to avoid the economic dislocation associated with life's misfortunes. This had implications for a range of public policy issues, including workers' compensation, unemployment insurance, health care, and accident compensation. In keeping with the belief that policy should be dictated by empirical realities, progressives gathered statistical evidence in each of these areas. Researchers investigated industrial accidents and "measured" the human suffering. Their studies had a journalistic flavor. Statistics were augmented with narratives chronicling the effects of accidents on peoples' lives. The purpose was to spur on a revolution in social consciousness. Much as Dewey believed that philosophy without a connection to social justice was barren, progressive activists for workers' rights believed in marshaling facts for a larger purpose. The same belief informed the work of legal theorists.

Legal theorists continued their break with formalist jurisprudence initiated by Holmes. A touchstone of this break, and connected with the rise of legal realism, was the sociological jurisprudence movement. Adherents of sociological jurisprudence, including Benjamin Cardozo (another prominent legal theorist and later U.S. Supreme Court justice), shared an affinity with legal realists in wanting to examine the law in social and historical context. The connection between sociological jurisprudence and pragmatism is found in Cardozo's admonition that "the juristic philosophy of the common law is at bottom the philosophy of pragmatism" (*Judicial Process*, p. 102). A pragmatist perspective on legal rules required judges to recognize that principles were not "floating in the air" just waiting to be revealed. The law was the product of policy choices. In examining a legal case, the judge should look at its context. Legal certainties were ephemeral and the law was in flux, a product of the times.

Nowhere was this relativistic view more prominent than in products liability law. Under classical jurisprudence, parties to a products liability dispute would be individuated and abstracted from their social context. For example, a classical jurist would look at the manufacturer of a product and the victim as "A" and "B" ("seller" and "purchaser"). From there, à la *Lochner*, he would apply deductive reasoning from the primary principle, freedom of contract, thus determining whether liability was warranted. No attention was given to power dynamics in the relationship, and distributive consequences (the effects on the relative wealth of victims and manufacturers as groups) were accepted as "natural."

Cardozo, sitting as a judge on the highest court in New York State, chipped away at classical abstractions. The landmark opinion was *MacPherson v. Buick Motor Co.* (1916) and it illustrates how taking a realist view of the world radically changes jurisprudential perspective. The case involved a consumer who had been injured in an automobile manufactured by Buick but sold by a dealer. In defending itself, Buick argued that since the car had been purchased from the dealer there was no con-

tract between Buick and the victim, and therefore no liability. This is quintessential classical reasoning. Buick was obviously right that face-to-face negotiations had never occurred between it and the consumer. If one were to take an abstracted, individualized worldview, no relationship existed between Buick and the injured party.

Examining the social context yielded a more complex connection. Cardozo recognized that consumers and manufacturers were not operating in a vacuum but within a complicated network of social-power relationships. Given the nature of these relationships, an analysis based solely on contract would be partial.

Manufacturers, although they did not contract directly with consumers, were responsible for putting products into the stream of commerce. They also exercised power over dealers. Moreover, if the policy objective of legal rulings was preventing accidents from occurring in the first place, who better to assume responsibility than the manufacturer? If manufacturers were held liable to consumers for harms caused by their products, they would have an incentive to make those products safer. Manufacturers could also further the social insurance goal by passing on increased liability costs to all those who purchased products, thus sparing individual victims.

This set of considerations would have been political anathema to classical theorists because redistributive policies disturbed the ("natural") status quo. In addition, while contextual and temporal analyses were unsettling to classicists, they were vital for legal realists, as shown by Cardozo, echoing Veblen, in his *MacPherson* opinion:

> Precedents drawn from the days of travel by stagecoach do not fit the conditions of travel to-day. The principle that the danger must be imminent does not change, but the things subject to the principle do change. They are whatever the needs of life in a developing civilization require them to be. (p. 1053)

Once again, legal certainty was not a priority.

The same focus on social context and temporality influenced the adoption of strict products liability. California Supreme Court Justice Jesse Traynor was the principal architect of strict products liability. In a series of opinions from 1944 through 1962 he laid out the argument for the doctrine, beginning with historical context:

> As handicrafts have been replaced by mass production with its great markets and transportation facilities, the close relationship between producer and consumer of a product has been altered. . . . The manufacturer's obligation to the consumer must

keep pace with the changing relationship between them. (*Escola v. Coca Cola Bottling Co. of Fresno*, p. 443)

Unlike their forerunners in the classical era, realists believed that group affiliation (consumer versus manufacturer) had particular relevance and that the average consumer "no longer ha[d] the means or skill enough to investigate for himself the soundness of a product." Concern over consumers was not limited to the information gaps in an increasingly technological society. Realists focused on the human toll due to industrial accidents. Traynor emphasized this point in *Escola*, noting that "the cost of an injury and the loss of time or health may be an overwhelming misfortune to the person injured."

Through the 1960s, legal theory, as laid out in academia and judicial opinions, reflected the combination of philosophical pragmatism and progressivism articulated by Dewey. Post-1960s legal theory would continue to be linked to larger American intellectual and political movements. This relationship can be seen clearly by looking at the forces that led to "the age of analysis" and how they influenced legal theory.

THE AGE OF ANALYSIS

After World War II both progressivism and philosophical pragmatism came under heavy assault, owing in large part to contemporary geopolitics. The emergence of the Soviet Union crystallized political opinion regarding progressivism. Conservatives, most notably F. A. Hayek in *The Road to Serfdom* (1944), argued that societies adopting progressive policies would inevitably become totalitarian. This argument had particular force in a political culture where the specter of Soviet Communism and Nazi atrocities was dominant.

Not only did the fear of totalitarianism affect the perception of progressive policies, it also influenced views on philosophical pragmatism (as well as legal realism and institutional economics as offshoots of philosophical pragmatism). In a culture thirsting for certainty, at least respecting the "rightness" of democratic capitalism, critics claimed that philosophical pragmatism's relativism fell short. If everything depended on context, then it was impossible to claim that any political system was favored. The uncomfortable position in which this placed academics was nowhere more evident than in Mortimer Adler's 1940 declaration at a gathering of over five hundred intellectuals that "we have more to fear

from our professors than from Hitler" (in Purcell, *The Crisis of Democratic Theory*, p. 218).

While the merits of these attacks were weak, they did put those associated with philosophical pragmatism on the defensive. This created intellectual space for the "analytic turn"—a historical movement that began in the 1940s and culminated in the 1970s, marked by the ascendancy of analytic philosophy (logical positivism, logical empiricism, and linguistic philosophy). Although analytic philosophy, particularly logical positivism, had some affinity with pragmatism, the differences are more noteworthy. Most significant, analytic philosophy rejected the focus on historical consciousness and context that marked philosophical pragmatism. There was a departure from the socially engaged philosophy urged by Dewey. In its stead, emphasis was placed on formalism and logical erudition.

A key text in analytic philosophy, A. J. Ayer's *Language, Truth, and Logic* (1936), illustrates the flavor of the argument. Ayer divided all propositions into two categories, empirical and analytic. Empirical propositions could be verified through observation. Analytic propositions were tautologous, such as those found in mathematics. For example, the analytic proposition $2 + 2 = 4$ is necessarily true. Nevertheless, it has absolutely no relationship to real-world phenomena. One can compare it to the empirical statement that there are four cups on the table; this statement is not necessarily true, but is verifiable through observation.

To understand the role of analytic philosophy in shaping the post–World War II intellectual climate, one should note the types of arguments that were not included. Ayer and others believed that ethical statements could not be dealt with scientifically. These types of statements Ayer deemed unanalyzable and mere "pseudo concepts" in *Language, Truth, and Logic*, adding that the "presence of an ethical symbol in a proposition adds nothing to its factual content." Ayer illustrated the point: If I were to say, "You acted wrongly in stealing that money," it could be reduced to, "You stole that money," because the ethical admonition adds nothing to the statement (pp. 107–108). Of course, this would also render statements such as "poverty is unjust" as "unanalyzable." The drift away from ethical concerns marked a sharp contrast to the considerations at the forefront of philosophical pragmatism.

This general philosophical shift filtered down into the social sciences, including economics and legal theory. Whereas economics had been heavily influenced by institutional economics in the realist era, with the analytic turn it was displaced by a new "classical" economics. This neoclassical economics had distinct methodological and political consequences for American legal theory.

Neoclassical economics is highly abstract and based on a few key assumptions, including a laissez-faire philosophy reminiscent of the classical era. These features made neoclassical economics an extremely attractive intellectual discipline in post–World War II America. The neoclassical economists' assumptions are simple: (1) humans have preferences as to outcomes; (2) we attempt to have our preferences met given constraints; (3) decision-making information is readily available; and (4) if we all act in our own self-interests, society will be better off.

Neoclassical theory has the virtue of being axiomatic, or self-evident. If you take the first three assumptions to be true, the fourth (which is the policy conclusion) is necessarily true. In this sense, it resembles the type of analytic statement admired by Ayer. But neoclassical economists are not making abstract statements about the world, although much of their work is couched in mathematics. They are making statements about how markets operate. However, there is no claim that the statements are empirically verifiable. For some, such as the great American neoclassical economist Frank Knight, there is no need for empirical verification, because the truths of the assumptions are intuitive. However, for those not so given to leaps of faith (particularly logical positivists), some form of empiricism is necessary.

Neoclassical economists, following the prompt of the Nobel laureate Milton Friedman, attempt to evade the dictates of analytic philosophy by asserting that neoclassical economics should be judged by the success of its predictions. If it does well at predicting economic phenomena, which seems to be the case, then the truth of its assumptions is irrelevant.

While neoclassical economics does not meet the criteria laid out by analytic philosophy, it comes closer to doing so than institutional economics. The methodology behind institutional economics was primarily inductive. Thus, unlike the deductive analysis of neoclassical economics, it failed the analytic test. It also did not qualify as an empirical science. Neoclassical economists used the two drawbacks to discredit institutional economics as unscientific.

Institutional economics was also infused with ethical imperatives that are antithetical in the analytic era. Institutional economists endeavored to champion the cause of the poor and others who suffered as a result of industrialism. Neoclassical economists criticized this aspect of institutionalism as mixing politics with science. Just as A. J. Ayer believed that statements about ethics lay outside the realm of philosophy, neoclassical economists asserted that ideals concerning what constitutes the just society were outside the bounds of economic science. This criticism ensured the downfall of institutional economics. A similar fate awaited legal realism, the intellectual cousin of institutional economics. In place of legal realism, today law and economics (an offshoot of neoclassical economics) plays the dominant role in American legal theory.

One of the first incursions of law and economics into legal theory came about in tort law. Legal theorists, beginning with the 1991 Nobel laureate Ronald Coase, began thinking about tort law issues from an economic point of view in the 1960s. They took the same assumptions used by neoclassical economists and applied them to situations involving legal disputes. A classic example is the case of pollution. Polluting on someone else's property was always considered to be a tort, and there was some general agreement that one who did so should be held strictly liable. Ronald Coase, utilizing neoclassical economics, made the observation that even if the polluter was not held liable, if the parties were allowed to reach a bargain regarding pollution, the best outcome (from a societal perspective) would be reached.

Richard Posner and Guido Calabresi, both former law professors who later ascended the judicial bench, would later expand on Coase's analysis. One of the central areas of debate was whether or not, and in what context, tort law should be based on strict liability or negligence. In resolving this fundamental policy issue, law and economics is now the dominant paradigm, supplanting legal realist arguments. Posner was prescient in noting the shift. He referred to legal realism as the "branch of legal scholarship that emphasizes facts rather than logic." In arguing for its displacement, he stated, "one displaces a scholarly approach not by showing that it has limitations but only by producing a better approach" ("The Costs of Accidents," pp. 637–638).

This displacement would mean a wholesale reevaluation of strict products liability law. Indeed, on the basis of law and economics analysis there has been legal reform aimed at shifting the basis for products liability from strict liability to negligence. While this might seem to be a relatively narrow doctrinal shift, of concern primarily to lawyers, it has huge policy implications. As mentioned earlier, how

205

one fashions liability rules determines victims' compensation and businesses' financial obligations.

Aside from the policy implications, the debate surrounding products liability reflected the general shift in American legal theory. The discussion moved to abstract concerns over "efficiency," "perfect information," and individual "rational actors." These abstractions hark back, although in a very different form, to the classical era.

CRITICAL LEGAL THEORY

There has been a powerful reaction to the new "classicism" in modern legal theory. Beginning in the 1970s a group of scholars adopting the rubric "critical legal studies" to denote the work began asserting the claim that the law is predominantly a political, as opposed to scientific, endeavor. These scholars, including such theorists as Duncan Kennedy, Morton Horwitz, Roberto Unger, and Mark Tushnet, echoed the legal realist critique of classical theory. However, they were very much influenced by Continental thinkers such as Max Weber, Karl Marx, Jürgen Habermas, and Michel Foucault—to name only a few.

Critical legal studies reflects the postmodern turn in Western thought and, like much postmodern theory, questions the very notion of objectivity. This turn also manifested itself in American academic philosophy with the rise of neopragmatism. Neopragmatism, particularly of the type articulated by Richard Rorty, has a strong affinity to the pragmatism of the early 1900s (including a commitment to social engagement) and has many adherents in the legal academy.

Critical legal studies theorists believe that the law is an inherently political enterprise. Their primary focus is on the legal system's class bias, which they claim favors the wealthy. For example, in the field of torts Morton Horwitz has argued that the rise in negligence in American law constituted an industrial subsidy designed to favor business interests. This reflects the general critical legal studies argument that the fundamental issue left unconfronted by "depoliticized" law is the distribution of wealth in society, the very issue James Madison warned against raising.

The basic critique made by critical legal studies scholars, while initially focusing on class analysis, has implications for a host of unaddressed issues in American law and legal theory. For instance, critical race theorists, such as Derek Bell, Richard Delgado and Patricia Williams, might raise issues of racial subordination, and feminist theorists, Catharine MacKinnon and Martha Minow, might raise issues of gender inequality.

CONCLUSION

America began as a country deeply rooted in classical theory—formalist and biased against government intervention. The rise of pragmatism called into question these classical tenets, the world was not as simple as the classicist had assumed. In order to understand and remedy social ills one had to undertake contextual analysis and at times champion government intervention. Analytic philosophy in many ways marks a return to our classical roots. Postmodernism represents a revolt against this neoclassicism. As one might expect, changes in American law and legal theory reflect these transformations in "the American mind." In this regard, law and legal theory are quintessential examples of the pursuit and exchange of knowledge.

See also **Law (Colonial)** *(volume 1);* **The Professional Ideal; Constitutional Thought** *(volume 2); and other articles in this section.*

BIBLIOGRAPHY

General Works

Duxbury, Neil. *Patterns of American Jurisprudence.* Oxford, U.K. and New York, 1995.

Horwitz, Morton J. *The Transformation of American Law: 1780–1860.* Cambridge, Mass., 1977.

———. *The Transformation of American Law, 1870–1960: The Crisis of Legal Orthodoxy.* New York, 1992.

White, G. Edward. *Tort Law in America: An Intellectual History.* New York, 1980.

Classical Legal Thought

Blackstone, William. *Commentaries on the Laws of England.* Oxford, U.K., 1766–1769.

Gillman, Howard. *The Constitution Besieged: The Rise and Demise of Lochner Era Police Powers Jurisprudence.* Durham, N.C., 1993.

Kennedy, Duncan M. "Toward an Historical Understanding of Legal Consciousness: The Case of Classical Legal Thought in America, 1850–1940." *Research in Law and Sociology* 3 (1980): 3.

Kent, James. *Commentaries on American Law.* New York, 1826–1830.

Madison, James. *Federalist* 10. *New York Packet,* November 23, 1787.

Wiecek, William M. *The Lost World of Classical Legal Thought: Law and Ideology in America, 1886–1937.* New York, 1998.

Lochner v. New York, 198 US 45 (1905).

Pragmatism

Croce, Paul J. *Science and Religion in the Era of William James: Eclipse of Certainty, 1820–1880.* Chapel Hill, N.C., 1995.

Darwin, Charles. *The Origin of Species.* London, 1869.

Dewey, John. "Elements of Social Reorganization." In *Characters and Events: Popular Essays in Social and Political Philosophy,* edited by Joseph Ratner (1929).

———. *Experience and Nature.* Chicago and London, 1925.

Summers, Robert S. *Instrumentalism and American Legal Theory.* Ithaca, N.Y., 1982.

West, Cornel. *The American Evasion of Philosophy: A Genealogy of Pragmatism.* Madison, Wisc., 1989.

Wiener, Philip. *Evolution and the Founders of Pragmatism.* Cambridge, Mass., 1949.

Legal Realism

Escola v. Coca Cola Bottling Co. of Fresno, 150 P2d 436 (Calif. 1944).

MacPherson v. Buick Motor Co., 217 NY 382 (1916), 111 NE 1050.

Cardozo, Benjamin N. *The Nature of the Judicial Process.* New Haven, Conn., 1921.

Hackney, James R. "The Intellectual Origins of American Strict Products Liability: A Case Study in American Pragmatic Instrumentalism." *American Journal of Legal History* 39, no. 4 (1995): 443.

Holmes, Oliver Wendell. *The Common Law.* Boston, 1881.

———. "The Path of the Law." *Harvard Law Review* 10, no. 8 (1897): 457.

Purcell, Edward, Jr. *The Crisis of Democratic Theory: Scientific Naturalism and the Problem of Value.* Lexington, Ky., 1973.

Institutional Economics

Commons, John R. *Institutional Economics: Its Place in Political Economy.* Madison, Wisc., 1959.

Dorfman, Joseph. *The Economic Mind in the American Civilization: 1918–1933.* New York, 1959.

Veblen, Thorstein. *The Theory of Business Enterprise.* New York, 1904.

Analytic Philosophy

Ayer, A. J. *Language, Truth, and Logic.* London, 1936.

Coffa, J. Alberto. *The Semantic Tradition from Kant to Carnap: To the Vienna Station.* Cambridge, Mass., and New York, 1991.

Gross, Barry R. *Analytic Philosophy: An Historical Introduction.* New York, 1970.

Janik, Alan, and Stephen Toulmin. *Wittgenstein's Vienna.* London, 1973.

Neoclassical Economics

Calabresi, Guido. *The Costs of Accidents: A Legal and Economic Analysis.* New Haven, Conn., 1970.

Coase, Ronald H. "The Problem of Social Cost." *Journal of Law and Economics* 3, no. 1 (1960): 1.

Hackney, James R. "Law and Neoclassical Economics: Science, Politics, and the Reconfiguration of American Tort Law Theory." *Law and History Review* 15, no. 2 (1997): 275.

Hayek, F. A. *The Road to Serfdom.* London, 1944.

Knight, Frank H. *Risk, Uncertainty, and Profit.* Boston, 1924.

Posner, Richard A. "The Costs of Accidents—Book Review." *University of Chicago Law Review* 37 (1970): 636.

———. *Economic Analysis of Law.* Boston, 1972.

Critical Legal Studies

Kennedy, Duncan. *A Critique of Adjudication: Fin de Siècle.* Cambridge, Mass., 1997.

Unger, Roberto. *The Critical Legal Studies Movement.* Cambridge, Mass., 1986.

Critical Race Theory

Bell, Derrick. *And We Are Not Saved: The Elusive Quest for Racial Justice.* New York, 1987.

Crenshaw, Kimberle, Neil Gotanda, Gary Peller, and Kendall Thomas, eds. *Critical Race Theory: The Key Writings That Formed the Movement.* New York, 1995.

Delgado, Richard. *The Rodrigo Chronicles: Conversations about America and Race.* New York, 1995.

Delgado, Richard, ed. *Critical Race Theory: The Cutting Edge.* New York, 1995.

Hackney, James. "Derrick Bell's Re-Sounding: W. E. B. Du Bois, Modernism, and Critical Race Scholarship." *Law and Social Inquiry* 23 (1998): 141.

Williams, Patricia. *The Alchemy of Race and Rights.* Cambridge, Mass., 1991.

Feminist Theory

MacKinnon, Catharine A. *Feminism Unmodified: Discourses on Life and Law.* Cambridge, Mass., 1987.

Minow, Martha. *Making All the Difference: Inclusion, Exclusion and American Law.* Ithaca, N.Y., 1990.

MEDICINE

Joel D. Howell

Americans have witnessed striking changes in medical ideas, in the ways that medical knowledge has been created, and in the organizational structures in which medical care has been delivered. Although throughout the early years of the Republic most knowledge was created abroad, the story of William Beaumont and Alexis St. Martin provides a fascinating tale of medical science, quite literally, in the wilderness. Ideas about medicine changed, as did the institutions in which people learned how to be a physician. The past century has given us an increasing emphasis on hospitals and technology, albeit with new tensions around how medical knowledge is to be applied. This essay will sketch some highlights and themes that will help illuminate broad changes over the past three centuries; the bibliography provides suggestions for additional reading.

Settlers in colonial America lived their lives and cared for their medical needs in worlds confined largely by the community in which they lived. A handful of European-trained physicians worked in the larger port cities, such as Philadelphia, Charleston, and Boston. But most people lived in small towns, in places far from trained medical personnel. Transportation on muddy roads and ice-bound rivers was difficult in the best of times. Community members thus needed to rely upon each other for medical care. Basic knowledge was often carried about in popular handbooks on health care, such as *Gunn's Domestic Medicine* (1830), which included practical advice on what to do for epilepsy, a dislocated kneecap, or inflammation of the eyes.

Medical theories in the eighteenth and nineteenth centuries did not usually assign illness a specific cause. There was no identifiable microorganism—no bacteria or virus—to guide treatment. Instead, treatment was designed specifically for each person. The healer's role was to select from the range of possibilities the proper drug in the proper dose to treat a specific individual. Each person's temperament would play a key role not only in making a diagnosis but also in guiding the hand of the healer. Thus, medical practice required getting to know the patient. Was John easily angered? Or was he somewhat slow and quiet? Did Mary have a history of acting strangely? As the medical historian Charles E. Rosenberg noted in his essay "The Therapeutic Revolution," "It was assumed that both the action of drugs and reaction of patients varied with season and geography." Thus, a physician from afar, no matter how well trained, was of necessity less competent than a physician who knew the patient and the region well. Because physicians treated patients in the home, they tended to be familiar with a family's specific living conditions. Seeing the patient at home served to reinforce the centrality of a local and specific understanding of disease. This epistemology made hospitals seem irrelevant to most medical care, for disease in a hospital might have little resemblance to disease in the community.

In the absence of state licensing laws, during most of the nineteenth century people could seek medical advice from practitioners who based their therapy on a range of different belief systems. Some systems were based on the idea that minute dilutions of substances could produce beneficial effects, while others were grounded in the healing powers of herbs or of water. These systems were often marketed directly to the ordinary citizen. Many treatments, such as the use of ferns, depended on the local availability of therapeutic agents and thus served (again) to emphasize the local nature of health care and to encourage healers to see patients as part of their local environment.

Along with the diversity of therapeutic ideals came the relatively modest status accorded the medical profession. The ideas and abilities of physicians were not taken to be so very different from the ideas of any well-educated citizen of the republic. Science in general, including medical science, was held in far lower esteem than it is in the twenty-first century. As *Gunn's Domestic Medicine* put it, "For the common and useful purposes of mankind, the refined fripperies and hair-drawn theories of mere science, are of no use whatever; indeed they have never had much other effect, than to excite a stupid admiration of men who pretended to know more than the mass of mankind" (p. 98). Patient and physician were expected to share not only knowledge about treatments but also the measurement of the results. Meaningful therapies were thought to produce actions readily perceived by patient and physician alike. Unlike the twenty-first century's instrumentally mediated blood pressure measurements or laboratory-based blood counts, the results of these therapies were measured in terms of sweating, bleeding, vomiting, or copious production from the bowels—results that all could see.

BEAUMONT, ST. MARTIN, AND NINETEENTH-CENTURY MEDICAL SCIENCE

Most knowledge of medical science in nineteenth-century America came from abroad. One of the most striking exceptions to this generalization began on a lovely June day in 1822 on Mackinac Island, where the cold, deep waters of Lake Michigan and Lake Huron unite. The tiny, isolated island was a rendezvous point for Native Americans and fur trappers. William Beaumont was the only physician on the island; Alexis St. Martin was a Canadian trapper working for the American Fur Company. The story of William Beaumont and Alexis St. Martin is important not only for what Beaumont discovered and St. Martin endured but also because it demonstrates some of the realities of nineteenth-century American science and medicine.

Initially a village schoolmaster in upstate New York, William Beaumont had spent his spare time reading medical books. He apprenticed to a physician in 1809, a typical educational pathway. An apprentice would carry instruments, help with chores, and follow the supervisor on his visits. The education thus received would be as good as the practitioner with whom the student studied. In two years Beaumont had completed his training.

In 1812 Beaumont found himself the U.S. Army physician on Mackinac Island, where, on 22 June 1822, a carelessly loaded musket went off into the side of Alexis St. Martin. The shot perforated his stomach, through which St. Martin's breakfast was pouring when Beaumont arrived. Beaumont did what little he could and left with the words, "The man cannot live thirty-six hours." St. Martin's very

bad prognosis soon became worse. He developed a violent pneumonia with a high fever, a grave situation even in the twenty-first century. Beaumont treated St. Martin in the usual manner, by bleeding him twelve to fourteen ounces and by giving him a cathartic to make his bowels move (a common treatment for many ailments), which had no effect, as it merely came out the hole in St. Martin's stomach. The wound became "very fetid."

Amazingly, St. Martin recovered. Moreover, he did so with a large hole remaining, extending from his skin all the way into the cavity of his stomach, through which fluid could be removed and into which food could be placed. Beaumont plugged the hole with a piece of beef, and when he removed the beef, its end was "as smooth and even as if it had been cut with a knife." Beaumont sent a report to Joseph Lovell, surgeon general of the United States, stating that one could "look directly into the cavity of the stomach, observe its motion, and almost see the process of digestion."

It was unclear to nineteenth-century observers just how food is digested. Some believed that the stomach contained acid; others wondered, if so, why did the acid not dissolve the stomach itself? In Europe the debate raged. The Academy of Sciences in Paris sponsored a contest on the topic. Beaumont did not have access to any of this literature, but he did have direct access to a human stomach. And so at noon on 1 August 1825, Beaumont unplugged St. Martin's stomach and put in a variety of foods, including raw, salted lean beef; raw, salted fat pork; raw, lean fresh beef; and raw cabbage. Every hour Beaumont pulled the food out to see what was happening. What happened is that St. Martin became rather ill. Beaumont treated him with a cathartic, this time dropped directly into the stomach, and St. Martin improved. From 1825 to 1833 Beaumont experimented on St. Martin at several army posts—Fort Mackinac, Niagara, Crawford, and St. Louis. Beaumont systematically put various foods into and out of St. Martin. He also took out gastric juices and investigated digestion outside of the body.

The experiments hardly went smoothly. In 1826 St. Martin returned to Canada, married, fathered two children, and eventually came back to Beaumont, but became increasingly impatient with the discomfort and inconvenience of constantly having food pulled in and out of his stomach on a string. Beaumont and St. Martin signed a contract stating that for one year St. Martin would "serve, abide, and continue" with Beaumont as a subject in medical experiments, for which Beaumont would pay room and board and $150. A subsequent contract paid him an additional $400, and finally, Beaumont arranged a paid position in the U.S. Army for St. Martin.

Beaumont spent about a year in Washington, D.C., reading about digestion in the libraries, making up for his years at the frontier, and preparing the book that would outline his findings. While in Washington, Beaumont tried to convince the U.S. Congress to support his research. He asked for funds for past and future work, conveniently forgetting that St. Martin had been for more than a year a sergeant in the army and that Beaumont himself had been an army employee while doing his research. All in all, he asked for more than $8,000, equivalent to over $110,000 today. Beaumont's request highlighted the question of whether Congress should support research. One member of Congress opined that the only way the House could constitutionally support Beaumont would be for each member to buy one or more copies of his book. Beaumont was turned down.

Beaumont published his findings in 1833. He argued that all types of food are digested in the same basic manner. He listed the basis for his arguments, almost two hundred experiments, and as was the custom of the time, the dates and times of each experiment, often with the weather noted as well. He compared the digestion time in the stomach (faster) and in vials (more slowly). Beaumont advised that people usually eat more food than necessary. He also described psychic influences on gastric secretion and digestion, arguing that gentle exercise facilitates digestion. Beaumont's book was widely read and discussed in the United States and abroad.

What ever became of Alexis St. Martin? St. Martin, the "man with a hole in his stomach," was demonstrated around the country and even aroused the interest of the famed circus promoter P. T. Barnum. When St. Martin died in the spring of 1880, the noted Canadian physician William Osler tried unsuccessfully to purchase the right to do an autopsy and put the stomach on display. To ensure that the spectacle of St. Martin would end with his death, his family chose to leave his body outside during hot weather long enough to let decomposition set in; they also buried the body deeper than was usually the case.

Beaumont was a pioneer scientist: the first American physiologist. He was also perhaps the first to do major human experiments in the United States. How should we consider the ethics of Beaumont's relationship with St. Martin? There can be no doubt that the experiments caused St. Martin considerable pain. In April 1854, the London *Athenaeum* commented that Beaumont, in his haste to create knowledge, forgot that he was operating on a "living, irritable human stomach." Perhaps in order to counter such criticism, Beaumont took every opportunity to point out the excellent state of St. Martin's health. Beaumont also referred to him often as a "boy"; despite the fact that Beaumont was not even a decade older than St. Martin, he doubtless wanted to emphasize the social distance between them. Beaumont was one of the earliest basic scientists to get federal support, albeit indirectly, to do research. For generations to come, people would have to pursue scientific experiments only while holding other full-time jobs. Not until the twentieth century would there be opportunities for American physicians and scientists to create new knowledge as part of their primary jobs as medical professionals.

MICROORGANISMS AND SPECIFIC CAUSE

If a single event marked the end of nineteenth-century ideas about medical knowledge, it would probably be the German physician Robert Koch's 1882 discovery of the organism responsible for tuberculosis. The news of this discovery spread like wildfire around the world. If the cause of tuberculosis, the "white plague," the scourge of countless millions of human beings, had at long last been uncovered, surely a cure would not be far behind. Indeed, Koch soon claimed he had discovered a cure, "tuberculin," although scientists eventually realized that it did not work. A more lasting result of Koch's work is what has come to be known as Koch's postulates, a set of four criteria by which one can judge whether a specific disease is caused by a specific organism. Presented in various forms at various times, the essence of these four postulates is that (1) every time a disease is present, one can isolate the responsible organism; (2) the organism can be isolated and maintained in pure form outside of the body (a process requiring technology new for the second half of the nineteenth century); (3) the organism must produce the same disease when presented to a new experimental animal; and (4) the initial organism can be recovered from this newly infected animal.

Koch's 1882 discovery opened the floodgates for the discovery of pathogenic microorganisms. Within a few years investigators had isolated the organisms responsible for cholera, diphtheria, tetanus, and many other diseases. Each discovery held out the hope that for each disease a specific treatment could be found. The medical model of disease causation and treatment shifted toward an increasingly reductionist model of specific cause for specific disease, a model that has at the start of the twenty-first century come to invoke the human genome. This disease model also put expert medical knowledge into forms progressively less accessible to the general public. At the turn of the nineteenth century, a patient might reasonably expect to be able to see and understand the primary evidence that lay at the basis for her physician's advice; by the turn of the twentieth century this was much less likely to be possible. For example, a layperson could not usually interpret visual findings through a microscope.

Interestingly, the number of deaths from tuberculosis had been declining for some time before Koch's discovery and continued to do so even before effective antimicrobial treatment was developed. This pattern demonstrates that most of the decline was due not to specific treatment for a specific disease but to general public health measures. Other diseases, such as diphtheria, declined in ways that reflected new knowledge of the specific disease-causing agent.

REVOLUTION IN MEDICAL EDUCATION

In the United States, the first medical school opened at the College of Philadelphia in 1765. It was designed for people like William Beaumont, who had already served an apprenticeship; soon other medical schools followed the same model. Thus, there was no clinical instruction; rather, the course of study was a four-month series of lectures. Students heard the same lectures for two years; the education was not graded. Under this educational model, the creation of new knowledge was not part of the faculty's job. During the nineteenth century many states began to require an M.D. (doctor of medicine) degree to practice medicine, and there was a proliferation of medical schools—often small, poorly equipped, with no laboratories, few books, and perhaps only part of a human skeleton to study. Entrance requirements were minimal. Medicine was a mediocre profession; good students went into law or the church, not medicine.

Near the end of the nineteenth century, some elite physicians started to see Germany as an exemplar of medical science; about fifteen thousand Americans studied in Germany between 1870 and the start of World War I in 1914. There they saw German successes, such as their advances in microbiology, including Koch's discovery of the tubercle bacillus. They acquired both attitudes and role models. They saw the full-time teacher, the professor, supported by the government both to teach and to create new knowledge. They saw the value of learning by doing, of laboratory work, and of the importance of scientific research. They saw what could result when investigators were able to focus on the creation of new knowledge as an essential part of their careers, rather than simply doing research as a sideline to their primary task.

These Americans returned to an America with a new university system and enough industry and capital to support educational changes. The transformation of medical education started in the 1870s and 1880s at a few universities, most notably Harvard, the University of Pennsylvania, the University of Michigan, and Washington University. The changes started with increased entrance requirements—first a high school diploma, later a college degree—and a graded and lengthened curriculum. Reformers emphasized that medical knowledge changes and thus requires laboratory instruction and up-to-date libraries. A perceived need for clinical instruction led to the invention of university hospitals at the University of Michigan in 1869 and at the University of Pennsylvania in 1874. Johns Hopkins, the first university to combine all major aspects of these educational transformations, opened in 1893. The medical school required a college degree for admission and offered a four-year graded curriculum, taught by full-time, nationally recruited faculty. Residency training was offered in a brand-new hospital, and hospital positions were linked with the medical school. The general reforms spread to many other schools. Many smaller schools simply did not have the financial resources to make the necessary changes and closed their doors between 1895 and 1910.

Abraham Flexner's 1910 report has come to be seen as a milestone in the history of medical education. Not a physician like his famous brother, Simon, Abraham Flexner was teaching Greek in a Louisville, Kentucky, high school when he was approached by the Carnegie Foundation to survey medical schools. When Flexner asked permission to visit medical schools in the United States and Canada, their leaders gave him relatively easy access, doubtless anticipating that his visit might be the prelude to additional funds. It was not. In his report, Flexner delivered blistering muckraking attacks on many medical schools, particularly those he deemed grossly inadequate or dishonest. For example, about one Kansas school he stated, "The dissecting room is indescribably filthy; it contained, in addition to necessary tables, a single, badly hacked cadaver, and was simultaneously used as a chicken yard." About another school he noted some dissembling: "The catalogue states that 'clinics are held weekly at the Kansas City, Missouri, General Hospital,' but the statement is denied by the superintendent of the hospital."

What was the result of the report? Flexner did not transform American medical education, nor was he responsible for the dramatic decrease in the number of schools. In 1906 there were 162 schools; by 1910 that number had fallen to 131 schools, a reduction that cannot have been due to a report not yet made public. The report did have enormous influence on the public, making the reform of medical education a broad-based cause célèbre, and also on foundations, particularly the Rockefeller Foundation, which gave $91 million to medical education by 1936 in an active attempt to shape it into the type of model idealized by Flexner.

FEMALE PHYSICIANS

Although women have long played key roles in health-care delivery, published medical knowledge and elite medical practice were almost exclusively male bastions throughout the early years of the nineteenth century. During the second half of the century, increasing numbers of women chose to become physicians. Women who chose to enter the medical profession were torn between wanting to create new scientific knowledge and wanting to continue in the sympathetic, caring mode believed to make women innately skilled at caregiving, as described in the aptly titled book by Regina Morantz-Sanchez, *Sympathy and Science* (1985).

In 1849 Elizabeth Blackwell became the first woman physician to graduate from medical school in the United States. She was an effective and articulate spokesperson for the role of women in medicine. Blackwell came of age in an era when physicians were increasingly explaining disease in terms of specific microorganisms. But she rejected laboratory medicine, in part because it emphasized specific microbes as important for patient care and in so doing tended to draw attention away from the social connectedness of patients. She was also concerned about the practice of vivisection, animal experimentation done to create new knowledge. She was not so much concerned about the plight of the animals as she was with the idea that vivisection

Elizabeth Blackwell (1821–1910). In 1857, Blackwell founded the New York Infirmary for Indigent Women and Children, which provided free medical care to the city's poor. The Infirmary lasted for 139 years and then merged with the New York University Medical Center in 1996. © BETTMANN/CORBIS

would continue the tendency (started by microbiologists) to detach physicians from patients. She feared that physicians might come to see their patients as mere "clinical material" rather than as people connected to a larger social and community structure. Blackwell feared that laboratory medicine would lead physicians to treat the body as a machine and to turn "real patients into objects."

Women were first admitted to a major American medical school at the University of Michigan in 1870, albeit not on equal terms with their male counterparts. In 1893 women were admitted on an equal basis with men at Johns Hopkins School of Medicine. The number of women in American medical schools remained low throughout most of the twentieth century, but near the end of the century, the number of women medical students began to increase rapidly and was nearing 50 percent by the turn of the twenty-first century. However, women have not advanced equally in all areas of medicine; they continue to be overrepresented in specialties such as pediatrics and obstetrics and gynecology. The effects of increasing gender diversity on medical practice and medical knowledge remain to be seen.

INVENTION OF THE MODERN HOSPITAL

Although Americans consider hospitals as the defining image of modern medicine, this has not always been so. Most nineteenth-century physicians in the United States spent their entire careers without setting foot in (or even seeing) the few hospitals in existence, all located in the larger cities. Even in these cities, anyone who could afford it received medical care at home. The nineteenth-century hospital was a moral institution for dependent people. Hospitals were small, simple affairs, usually run by a single lay superintendent who knew everybody by name and asserted parental authority over all decisions, including whether to admit patients and how to treat them. Many early hospitals were simply refurbished residences. Everybody lived in the house—physicians still refer to being "in the house" or to "house officers." The hospital's finances resembled those of a house; expenses were primarily for food and for heat, not very different from an orphanage of similar size. Money played only a minor role in the operation of the enterprise; budgets were low, house officers were paid in room and board, attending physicians were paid in prestige, patients were there (and stayed there for months) precisely because they could pay. And the hospital was almost devoid of technology. If the hospital was extremely progressive, it might have a thermometer. It would almost certainly not have a microscope, although the instrument was by then several centuries old. Many of the reasons modern hospitals use technology stem from the idea that medicine is scientific, a peculiar idea indeed to the typical nineteenth-century American.

In 1873 there were 120 hospitals in the United States with a total of about 50,000 beds. By 1909 there were 4,359, with around 421,000 beds. Beyond increased numbers, by 1920 the hospital had become a totally new institution, one that would seem familiar by twenty-first-century standards. Hospital training was understood to be an integral part of medical education. People who were seriously ill went to the hospital, no matter what their financial standing. The hospital had many different departments and a complex administrative structure. Physicians were assumed to hold expert knowledge about medical care and thus made almost all of the medical decisions. House officers and attending physicians were paid in cash, not only in room and board. Money played an important role, and dozens of people tracked the flow of dollars using complex accounting procedures. The very structure of the hospital became itself a new technology, with the addition of middle management, standardized forms and procedures, and a self-conscious attempt to make the whole enterprise as efficient as possible. In general, machines and technology played a central role throughout the institution.

TWENTIETH-CENTURY MEDICAL TECHNOLOGY AND SCIENCE

Often, people placed new, big, bulky, specialized, capital-intensive medical technology in hospitals. Perhaps the single most important example of medical technology is the X-ray machine, partly responsible not only for creating the new hospital but for profoundly altering conceptions of medical care. Invented late in 1895, the machine finally made it possible for all to see deep within the human body. Although people had viewed the insides of human beings prior to this time—during surgery, for example—the X-ray image was fundamentally new. Surgical visions that were accessible only to a privileged few now became available to many. Because the X-ray was a black-and-white, two-dimensional image, it could easily be reproduced without significant loss of fidelity. It also happened to be invented at a time when new technology was making it possible to reproduce images easily in magazines and newspapers. A glance at almost any popular publication from 1896 reveals many X-ray images.

Moreover, because it was not particularly difficult or expensive to make an X-ray machine, soon after its invention the device was widely applied in the medical and nonmedical world alike. The X-ray quickly became a part of popular culture. Machines were set up in public places. Many persisted in shoe shops until several decades into the 1900s, and wealthy New York women had their pictures taken to give to friends. Within the medical world, adopting X-rays into routine practice took several decades. Medical structures had to change to accommodate the concept of a special technology routinely used for patient care. Eventually the X-ray came to be primarily based within medicine, although it continued to serve as an inspiration for artists and writers.

Other scientific advances in modern medicine aroused excitement. The identification of the microorganisms responsible for many human diseases led to the hope that a "magic bullet" might prevent or cure these newly recognized causes of human death and disease. But arguably the ultimate medical miracle of the early years of the twentieth century was not for the cure of an infectious disease but for the treatment of a metabolic one—the 1921 discovery of insulin, which was first used early the next year to treat diabetes. Children who had previously wasted away before the eyes of their parents could suddenly be transformed into what at first seemed to be the picture of health; but all too soon the difficulties of long-term insulin treatment became apparent, as diabetes was transformed from an acute into a chronic disease. This general phenomenon—that of a "cure" for an acute disease serving instead to transform it into a chronic disease—continued throughout the twentieth century, most notably exemplified in the treatment of patients with acquired immune deficiency syndrome (AIDS).

Twentieth-century ideas about genetics followed the rediscovery of Mendel's laws, basic laws of heredity based on the breeding of garden peas by the nineteenth-century Austrian monk Gregor Mendel. These concepts helped achieve a new understanding of how characteristics such as blood groups or eye color were passed on from generation to generation. Also, the study of genetics was used to justify racial and religious prejudice and bigotry. Many leading scientists and physicians advocated "judicious breeding" to improve the human race. Such racist ideas were reinforced by the idea that different races are biologically distinct, a view that formed the basis for what was termed "scientific racism" in the early years of the twentieth century.

On the basis of these views, a group of scientists from the U.S. Public Health Service set out in the 1930s to study the natural history of syphilis in Macon County, Alabama. Those who designed this study, based in the town that later gave the study its commonly used name—the Tuskegee syphilis study—assumed that syphilis would have a different clinical course in African Americans than in Caucasians. Some four hundred African American men with syphilis were "selected" to join the study. They were not told the truth about the study's purposes, nor were they permitted to obtain treatment for syphilis. Over the following decades—through the discovery of penicillin (and its introduction into routine use as a treatment of many diseases, including syphilis), through the civil rights movement, and even through a 1969 meeting specifically called

to address the study—the Public Health Service continued the experiment. Finally, it was halted in 1972, when the study and its unethical methods were exposed in the *Washington Star*. By the time President Bill Clinton apologized for this egregious trampling on the rights of the men in 1997, only eight had survived to hear his words.

During the twentieth century allopathic medicine—practiced by physicians with an M.D.—came to emphasize the natural sciences and to standardize both laboratory observations and patient depictions. Other alternative medical systems took different paths. Some alternative sects, such as osteopathy, started with a radical stance but, over the course of the century, came to closely resemble allopathic medicine. Others, like chiropracty and homeopathy, have tended to maintain a distinctive therapeutic stance. Alternative medical practitioners felt their sects maintained more contact with their patients' specific social and cultural circumstances than sects focused more closely on the natural sciences. This viewpoint may account for some of the popularity of complementary and alternative medicine in the twenty-first century.

The late twentieth century witnessed a remarkable rise in the concept of autonomy, with patients claiming the right to make informed decisions about their treatment plans. No longer was it acceptable for physicians to withhold information from patients, even if they believed that doing so was in the patient's best interests. The classic book *Our Bodies, Our Selves* (first published in 1971) helped mark an effort among women to assert control over their own bodies in the midst of a medical profession widely viewed as misogynistic. New technology played a role here as well, with the invention of the birth control pill allowing women to easily self-regulate their own fertility. Some feminist scholars questioned whether the concept of autonomy was the best way for women to thrive in the twentieth-century medical care system and have suggested that autonomy tends to perpetuate existing power inequities.

Finally, the late twentieth century witnessed a new way of organizing medical care. Rather than a single physician seeing patients in her or his solo office, medical care came to be far more structured, organized into multispecialty group practices, health maintenance organizations, and other forms of managed care. Created both to improve care and reduce costs, these new systems of care will doubtless continue to change in the twenty-first century, with results that remain unclear.

See also **Science and Religion** *(volume 1);* **The Professional Ideal** *(volume 2); and other articles in this section.*

BIBLIOGRAPHY

Beaumont, William. *Experiments and Observations on the Gastric Juice, and the Physiology of Digestion.* Plattsburgh, N.Y., 1833.

Bliss, Michael. *The Discovery of Insulin.* Chicago, 1982.

Boston Women's Health Book Collective. *Our Bodies, Ourselves: A Book by and for Women.* 1971. Reprint, New York, 1973.

Brandt, Allan M. *No Magic Bullet: A Social History of Venereal Disease in the United States since 1880.* New York, 1985.

Duffin, Jacalyn. *History of Medicine: A Scandalously Short Introduction.* Toronto, 1999.

Flexner, Abraham. *Medical Education in the United States and Canada: A Report to the Carnegie Foundation for the Advancement of Teaching.* New York, 1910.

Gunn, John C. *Gunn's Domestic Medicine, or Home Book of Health.* 1830. Reprint, Knoxville, Tenn., 1986.

Horsmann, Reginald. *Frontier Doctor: William Beaumont, America's First Great Medical Scientist.* Columbia, Mo., 1996.

Howell, Joel D. *Technology in the Hospital: Transforming Patient Care in the Early Twentieth Century.* Baltimore, 1995.

Jones, James H. *Bad Blood: The Tuskegee Syphilis Experiment.* New York, 1981.

Kevles, Daniel J. *In the Name of Eugenics: Genetics and the Uses of Human Heredity.* New York, 1985.

King, Lester. *Medical Thinking: A Historical Preface.* Princeton, N.J., 1982.

Ludmerer, Kenneth M. *Learning to Heal: The Development of American Medical Education.* New York, 1985.

———. *A Time to Heal: American Medical Education from the Turn of the Century to the Era of Managed Care.* New York, 1999.

Morantz-Sanchez, Regina. *Sympathy and Science: Women Physicians in American Medicine.* New York, 1985.

Rosenberg, Charles E. *The Cholera Years; The United States in 1832, 1849, and 1866.* Chicago, 1962.

———. "The Therapeutic Revolution." In *The Therapeutic Revolution: Essays in the Social History of American Medicine,* edited by Morris J. Vogel and Charles E. Rosenberg, pp. 3–25. Philadelphia, 1979.

DISCIPLINES AND THEIR INSTITUTIONALIZATION

David R. Shumway

The "academic discipline" as it is defined by historians has emerged only recently, no earlier than in the late eighteenth century in Germany and in the late nineteenth century in the United States. In the English language, the word "discipline" was used in the English poet Geoffrey Chaucer's time to refer to branches of knowledge, especially to medicine, law, and theology, the "higher faculties" of the new university. The persistence of the term "discipline" has masked the historical specificity of the organization and production of knowledge. The branches of knowledge themselves, as well as what "knowledge" means, have changed radically since the word was first introduced into the English language. The disciplinary regime of knowledge production is distinguished from its predecessors by many features, including its particular divisions, the institutions that support them, the organization of practitioners, and the importance of boundary work.

DIVISIONS

The division of knowledge into the seven liberal arts was hegemonic before the thirteenth century and was perpetuated in the structure of the curricula of the late medieval universities. In spite of this traditional conception, a new scholastic division of knowledge, dominated by dialectic and philosophy rather than logic, grammar, and rhetoric, emerged in these universities and lasted into the seventeenth century. The beginning of the scientific revolution in that century represents a shift that would ultimately lead to the modern disciplines. The newly founded scientific societies, the Royal Society (1660) and the Académie des Sciences (1666), devoted themselves to the study of all nature, which included not only the old category of physics (or natural philosophy), but mathematics as well. The new science continued to be called "natural philosophy," but, in distinguishing knowledge of nature from other

kinds of knowledge, it established the possibility for future specialization. From the mid-seventeenth century to the end of the eighteenth, the sciences twenty-first-century scholars differentiate as physics, chemistry, and biology emerged as branches of natural philosophy. Modern disciplines, however, came into being only with the breakup of natural philosophy into independent natural sciences at the end of the eighteenth century. Moral philosophy broke up somewhat later into the social sciences. "The humanities" is a twentieth-century term of convenience for those disciplines that were excluded by the natural and social sciences. While modern philosophy was defined by what was removed from it in the creation of the sciences, the other modern humanities emerged first in the form of classical philology, which produced history, the modern languages, and even art history as descendants.

KNOWLEDGE

If disciplinarity were merely reflected in new divisions of knowledge, it would be interesting but perhaps not very significant. But these new divisions are distinctive in much more than their names. One of the most salient differences involves the very character of the knowledge being divided. Before the modern discipline, knowledge was regarded primarily as something that needed to be preserved and inculcated. Knowledge was supposed to be contained in a relatively small body of texts. The assumption was that the most significant knowledge was already available, having been recorded in "literature," understood not as belles lettres but as learning. This conception of knowledge remained dominant in nineteenth-century American colleges, where the classical curriculum was in part intended to give students access to this learning by teaching them the languages in which much of it was written. The emphasis on rhetoric was intended to enable students to communicate such wisdom effectively.

Nothing that happened in the college was designed to discover or produce knowledge.

Disciplinarity has as it raison d'être the production of new knowledge. Here again, historians can trace the roots of this project to the new science of the seventeenth century. The investigation of the new domain of nature was approached by a new method—not scholastic disputation but "experimental philosophy." Experiments were acts of knowledge production or "discovery." But until disciplinarity became dominant, knowledge in general was not regarded as something to be produced. Under the scientific ethos of disciplinarity, the scope of possible knowledge is regarded as infinite but the knowledge humans actually possess is limited. Under such circumstances, the quest for knowledge comes to replace the dissemination of knowledge as the chief goal of higher education.

What the old college and new university shared, however, was that they both existed in societies where knowledge itself was highly valued. Disciplines developed in a world where knowledge was thought to be scarce. While the disciplinary model did not depend on the assumption that all knowledge is of equal value, its raison d'être was the belief that all knowledge has some value. Moreover, it was assumed that all knowledge is amenable to discovery via the methods of science. Thus, the disciplines that constitute the modern humanities were constituted to bring about scientific knowledge of culture. The modern language disciplines, for example, were never primarily devoted to literary appreciation. Originally, they were sciences, devoted to producing knowledge about the language, works, and authors that constituted literature. Knowledge produced by the humanities was valued because: (1) it was assumed not to be epistemologically distinct from knowledge of any other sort; and (2) the objects humanists studied were themselves regarded as highly valuable, in part paradoxically because the older conception that knowledge is contained within literature and other works of art continued to carry cultural weight.

PEDAGOGY

In nineteenth-century America, "discipline" was less strongly associated with the branches of knowledge than with habits that study produced in individuals. The value of study was often touted by analogy with the rigor of bodily exercise, and the preparatory and undergraduate curriculum, dominated by the classical languages, was justified on the grounds that it provided mental "discipline." In learning classical languages, students had to memorize large quantities of information, a process that was thought to train their minds for many other applications. The mind was presumed to be improved, like the body, by strenuous exercise, and the memorization entailed in learning dead languages was thought to be the most strenuous mental exercise. The mission of the college was to produce strong minds in students.

This public rhetoric of mental discipline represents merely the tip the disciplinary iceberg, however, for nineteenth-century schools were among the most important sites for the development of the ensemble of strategies and techniques that the French philosopher Michel Foucault called "discipline." These are based on simple instruments: "Hierarchical observation, normalizing judgment and their combination in a procedure that is specific to it, the examination" (*Discipline and Punish*, p. 170). While the formal examination had long had a place in education, pedagogy in the nineteenth century tended toward perpetual examination. Recitation was perhaps the most common classroom activity. The use of grades, especially the arithmetical "mark," became common for the first time. As the scholar Keith W. Hoskin has argued, the mark differs from earlier approaches, such as ordinal evaluation, in that it promotes not emulation but competition for "a *currency* that denotes self-worth. Marks put an objective value on performance" (p. 273).

Moreover, the specific spaces that define twenty-first-century education also came into being in the period from 1750 to 1800. The most broadly important of these, the classroom, typifies the disciplinary arrangement of space as Foucault described it. Everything and everyone had a precise place: pupils were classified by level of attainment in reading and arithmetic; each one had a number used to mark his or her coat nail, slate, and desk; the desks in their schoolroom were arranged geometrically so that the monitors could easily survey and assess the students; and the school day was apportioned periodically often by the ringing of bells to mark the commencement of every task. If the classroom had the widest impact, the other new spaces, the seminar and the laboratory, were more directly related to the emergence of the disciplines. Both were spaces in which knowledge was not merely transmitted but actually produced. As Hoskin has shown, these three pedagogical spaces make possible both the emergence of the disciplinary form of knowledge and the general spread of discipline as a form of power.

THE RESEARCH UNIVERSITY

The modern disciplines were nurtured by new institutions including the research university in Germany and the higher educational institutions known as *grandes écoles in* France. In late-nineteenth-century America, the research university emerged on the German model. These universities, whether newly founded, like Johns Hopkins, or transformed colleges, like Harvard, reflected disciplinarity in both their curriculum and in their administrative structure. In the college, all students took more or less the same course of study, a model that reflected the presumed unity of knowledge. Undergraduate education in research universities featured an elective curriculum designed to allow students to specialize—or major—in one of the new disciplines. Specialization flourished unimpeded in graduate education, which prior to the research university had barely existed in the United States. The new Ph.D. degree became the basic credential for the disciplinary practitioner. On the other hand, specialization in a single discipline was controversial at the undergraduate level. The influential notion of the liberal arts education emerged in reaction to the elective curriculum and the perceived narrowness of a course of study restricted to a single discipline. Thus, historians should view the liberal arts curriculum as neither a direct descendent of the nineteenth-century college nor as antidisciplinary. The liberal arts are precisely a collection of disciplines.

The departmental organization of the university followed from and helped to foster the rise of the disciplines, and it reflects a major change in the way institutions were administered. The old college had been run autocratically by its president, who could and did hire and fire faculty at will. Not only was academic freedom restricted in practice, it wasn't even a significant ideal. Since most colleges were sectarian, it should not be surprising that the faculty were expected to share the president's and the sect's beliefs. The research university was in principle nonsectarian since it was founded on the notion that beliefs need to be subject to the scrutiny of science. Moreover, the rise of disciplines as informal interinstitutional associations created a check on the power of the president. The administration of the university thus became decentralized, with the faculty assuming a great deal of power within departments. Tenure and its guarantee of academic freedom did not come without significant struggle, but it was a policy consistent with the form and ideology of the research university.

ORGANIZATION

The relative autonomy the new departments had did not leave them free to pursue any course. Rather their authority was shared nationally and sometimes internationally with the other practitioners of the discipline. As one historian of research universities observed, "A discipline is, above all, a community based on inquiry and centered on competent investigators. It consists of individuals who associated in order to facilitate intercommunication and to establish some degree of authority over the standards of that inquiry" (Geiger, p. 29). What is perhaps most distinctive about modern disciplines is their peculiar form of organization, reflected in but not identical with the disciplinary associations (often called "professional associations or "learned societies") they created. Disciplinary associations have historical roots in the first scientific institutions, the Royal Society and the Académie des Sciences. These seventeenth-century societies initiated the development of some key mechanisms necessary for the disciplinary organization of knowledge. An example is the use of publication as the primary means of authorizing new knowledge. Originally conceived to witness the discovery of new knowledge in experiments, the Royal Society soon began to represent them in *Philosophical Transactions.* The journal became the means whereby the results of experiments and observations performed or recorded in private were presented to the public. As a result, the academic journal's role as a gatekeeper emerged because the integrity of scientific information obtained in private now became questionable and needed authorization.

The early societies, however, were neither professional nor disciplinary organizations. New organizations were required to produce in the early nineteenth century what scholars have called a " 'second' scientific revolution" in which the generalized learned society was replaced by more specialized associations that established professional standards for particular disciplines. In the United States the major disciplinary associations, such as the Modern Language Association and the American Economic Association, were founded mainly in the 1880s and 1890s, and the emergence of such associations was largely complete by 1905. The existence of research universities enabled the development of these specialized organizations by providing steady employment and financial security to practitioners and by encouraging them to identify with others of their specialty. The new specialized organizations increased the power and influence of the disciplines by joining scholars who were geographically dispersed and serving as arenas where interinstitutional leadership could emerge. The journals they sponsored furnished the means by which scholars' work could be evaluated relative to the discipline, and even the fact of publication in these journals indicated a positive evaluation. This apparatus provided the mechanism of evaluation that was necessary if disciplines were to exercise authority over their own ranks.

Just as civil regulation established the cognitive exclusiveness of lawyers and physicians in their respective domains, the university enabled disciplinary practitioners to achieve cognitive exclusiveness over their regions of the academic world. These practitioners relied not on licensing but on credentialing; they controlled the apparatus for training future practitioners and admitting them to their ranks. A discipline establishes its own standard form of training which becomes a prerequisite for admission into the discipline, and it determines what forms of examination are to be administered to demonstrate the trainees' competence. A discipline is thus a professional form, claiming control of a certain kind of work based on the cognitive exclusiveness of its knowledge. On the basis of such systems examination, academic disciplines are able to create formal restrictions on the discourse produced in their name and on who has the right to speak it.

DISCIPLINED SUBJECTS AND DISCIPLINARY IDENTITY

The organization of academic disciplines as informal but self-regulating networks of practitioners permitted Foucauldian discipline to be applied to faculty. Power shifted from a center in the college president to be dispersed among the various disciplines with their national associations supporting and shaping individual departments. The development of specialized academic journals made for the anonymous surveillance and judgment of practitioners, since the discipline, rather than individuals, was perceived to be the source of such judgments. Such judgments do not rest on the authority of individuals but on the authority vested in an anonymous system of methods, of propositions considered to be true, of rules, definitions, techniques, and tools that may in principle be taken over by anyone who has been trained in them.

The training of disciples in modern academic disciplines involves a process similar to the one used with children in nineteenth-century schools, although it perhaps involves more subtle methods of control. In order to attain his or her terminal degree, the modern disciple is repeatedly ranked and evaluated on the basis of norms. Ranking and normalizing judgments are usually rendered with the aid of various examinations. Undergraduate and graduate education obviously are replete with examinations, which do not end with the dissertation defense. The "reviews" to which most faculty are regularly subjected are also forms of examination. The price of failing a retention or tenure "review" is the loss of one's job. More important, however, is the publication process on which the results of this other procedure usually hinge. The "refereeing" of manuscripts not only limits what can be said to the confines of a discipline, but also serves as the principal means of rewarding or punishing researchers and serves as the basis for subsequent rewards or punishments. In this light, modern academic disciplines are revealed to be regulated and regulating elements of a larger disciplinary regime.

Discipline in this sense is a distinct form of power that trains both body and soul, and, by systematically observing and distinguishing its subjects, makes individuals. Disciplines do not merely train or impose limitations on individuals. The distinctions and rankings produced by disciplinary technologies individualize their subjects, as do the dossiers that disciplinary institutions keep of their inmates. Modern academic disciplines, founded on such disciplinary technologies, doubtless contribute to individualization in this sense. But disciplined individuals also identify with the institution that disciplines them, thus making the disciplines sources of identity, just as nationalism, gender, or class can be such sources. The discipline dominates the disciple, but the disciple derives a sense of recognition from the discipline. The discipline depends on its disciples, since it will die if it is not practiced; the disciple, having internalized the discipline, can retain his or her identity only by practicing it. A practitioner masters a discipline even as it masters the practitioner. The power of disciplines to create identity partially explains their endurance and their resistance to change.

DISCIPLINARY OBJECTS

An academic discipline is not defined only by those who practice it, or its techniques of control, or by it rules of exclusion. All academic disciplines constitute their own objects of investigation which are not identical with the objects the layperson uses or experiences in everyday life. The object that disciplinary inquiry addresses is not available independently of disciplinary language and practice. At one level, this means that physical entities—air or money or texts—are understood differently by practitioners in different disciplines. In a larger sense, each discipline constitutes an idealized object that is the domain of its investigation. A discipline's object has only the properties and attributes that fit the discipline's assumptions, methods, practices, and tools. The object constituted by the discipline embodies the assumptions of the discipline, without those assumptions being made available for reflection. The disciplinary object appears to members of a discipline engaged in their normal practice as entirely natural and independent. This state of affairs enables production, but it inhibits the skepticism that the sciences claim as their own internal check.

MACHINES FOR THE PRODUCTION OF DISCOURSE

If disciplines both limit and structure what may be said in their name, it makes sense to assume that they typically produce a unified body of knowledge even if the disciplines are historical artifacts not divided into essential categories. But, in fact, disciplinary practice is characterized not by harmonious agreement, but by continual disagreement within the limits the discipline defines for itself. Thus, while disciplinary practitioners typically share a set of assumptions, methods, and practices, the knowledge they produce tends toward dispersion rather than unity. The criterion of unity functions *socially,* for it is one of the chief means by which a discipline asserts control over its domain. Disciplines are not organized in order to solve real-world problems or to achieve consensus, but rather for the purpose of producing more knowledge about their objects. In spite of its exclusions, disciplinarity did not have the effect of reducing the overall quantity of discourse on a subject. On the contrary, while the demand for evaluation encouraged the repetition of previously successful work, it also required the continual production of such work. Thus, disciplinarity requires the production of increasing amounts of similar work. As a result, disciplines can be conceived as machines for the production of statements. According to Foucault, "for a discipline to exist, there must be the possibility of formulating—and of doing so ad infinitum—fresh propositions" (*The Archaeology of Knowledge,* p. 224). Thus, disciplines are structured by problems or questions that are in some way self-reproducing. Since new statements must differ appropriately from previous ones, disciplines tend to produce an increasing quantity of narrowly diverging statements.

BOUNDARY WORK

In the interest of maintaining cognitive exclusiveness—the control of a certain domain of knowledge and the work it is believed to enable—disciplines regularly engage in "boundary work." Boundary work is the production of arguments and strategies to justify, maintain, and construct the divisions of knowledge to achieve, according to the scholar Thomas F. Gieryn, "an apparent differentiation of goals, methods, capabilities, and substantive expertise" ("Boundary Work," p. 783). The importance of the disciplines is revealed in the fact that members of disciplinary communities routinely engage in this differentiating activity. The commonly used geographical metaphors such as "territories," "fields," and "frontiers" reveal the degree to which disciplines are understood as bounded spaces. Boundary work is performed for various purposes. When the point is to establish or protect a discipline, boundaries mark it as a territory to be possessed by its owners, not appropriated by others, and they indicate the relations it may have with other disciplines. But these same boundaries may be redefined if the discipline is attempting to expand into new territory. When the point is to regulate disciplinary practitioners, boundary work determines which methods and theories are included, which should be excluded, and which may be imported. Boundaries may be established within the domain of a discipline to distinguish work that is "central" from work that is peripheral. In contemporary economics, neoclassical theory is central and other theories—Marxian, Austrian—are effectively marginalized even though they are not completely divorced from the discipline. Even within their centers, disciplines typically are divided into subdisciplines or fields that may defend their boundaries against other subdivisions. English and American literary studies, according to the Modern Language

Association in their *Redrawing the Boundaries* (1992), can be divided into twenty-one subdivisions, none of which are treated as peripheral.

Some disciplines have relatively rigid internal and external boundaries, while others have ones that are more permeable. Those with rigid boundaries are immune from competition from other disciplines, while those with boundaries that are more permeable may be subject to "invasion." Physics, for example, has been well protected from other disciplines, but physicists were leaders in creating the molecular revolution in biology. In this case, physics did not "annex" biology, but the physicists' methods and assumptions came to replace those traditionally held by biology. While the domains of the natural sciences are strongly protected from assault by nonacademics, the social sciences and humanities often must defend their boundaries against journalists, amateurs, and even common sense.

NONDISCIPLINARY KNOWLEDGES

As this final point suggests, not all forms of knowledge production are disciplinary. Folklore and street smarts are the work of different subjects under very different conditions; they are produced and passed on by collectives gathered for such occasions as quilting parties and gang meetings. These might be what Foucault called "subjugated knowledges," which he believed contained elements of truth ignored by official knowledge. Print technology helped the development of disciplinary knowledge, but Internet technology may work against it. The World Wide Web makes it easier for disciplinary knowledge to be shared among practitioners and disseminated to the public, but it also has the capacity to level distinctions among knowledges. Much of the information on that "superhighway" is not disciplinary in origin. Here, for better or worse, subjugated knowledges—ranging from alternative medicine to Holocaust denial—compete on equal terms with disciplinary knowledge. Even some aspects of academic practice seem to be largely outside of disciplinarity. As Keith Hoskin observed, education is widely regarded as lacking disciplinary status even though educational practices are foundational to the disciplines. It has been argued that in spite of a great deal of research on the teaching of writing, most teachers in that field still depend on lore to inform their pedagogy.

There is authoritative knowledge that is not disciplinary. Newspapers, magazines, radio, and television provide news that is widely believed even as it is also assumed to be biased. Knowledge of current events, then, is almost wholly nondisciplinary, yet it is powerfully authorized by the reputations of the large corporations and the personalities they employ. Journalists routinely draw on disciplinary knowledge and its producers, yet they use this knowledge in different ways depending on how much symbolic capital the discipline holds. The natural sciences are typically treated as disciplines deserving of respectful treatment and a genuine attempt to understand and translate specialized language into a vernacular rendering. The humanities, on the other hand, are as likely to be regarded as competitors as they are to be sources of authority on which to report. Literary journalists may cede certain kinds of knowledge to literary scholars, but the former claim the right to make their own judgments of taste and interpretation.

It is often assumed that interdisciplinarity represents an alternative to the disciplines. Like the older liberal arts ideal, however, interdisciplinarity is better understood as an aspect of the disciplinary world. Julie Klein has presented the wide variety of activities that academics consider to be interdisciplinary, including educational movements, colleges, undergraduate programs, area studies, research centers, think tanks, temporary teams, and study groups. Like disciplinary activities, they depend on the usual apparatus of publications, conferences, and societies. While it is clear that the concept of interdisciplinarity continues to carry with it the hope of overcoming specialization, it is not clear that it very often—if ever—succeeds in doing so. Moreover, while some interdisciplinary enterprises were indeed started in opposition to the perceived distortion of some disciplinary narrowness—American studies, for example—many other such enterprises entirely lack such motivation. Some scholars engage in them because disciplinary knowledge does not allow them to solve real-life problems. Some of what appears to be interdisciplinary is better described by the scholars Mattei Dogan and Robert Pahre's conception of "hybridization," in which new specializations are created on the margins of existing disciplines by combining fragments they have sloughed off.

Interdisciplinarity, then, cannot be considered a likely source for a postdisciplinary form of knowledge production. If there is to be postdisciplinarity, it seems unlikely to be undisciplined. The greatest challenge to the disciplines in the twenty-first century comes from the increasing dependence of universities on corporations for financial support. Instead of merely providing philanthropic grants, these corporations increasingly contract with universities to produce the sort of knowledge they need to make profits. This could turn universities away from relatively independent disciplines and their self-constituted domains to new enterprises identified with salable products. In this world, knowledge itself will have lost its value, and thus the motive for maintaining machines for the production of discourse will also disappear. Profits will then determine what knowledge is worth producing, most likely driving vast areas of human experience out of the university.

See also **Science and Religion; The Behavioral and Social Sciences** *(volume 1);* **Poststructuralism and Postmodernism; The Struggle for the Academy; Psychology, the Mind, and Personality** *(volume 2);* **The History of Ideas; Biography; Cultural Studies** *(in this volume); and other articles in this section.*

BIBLIOGRAPHY

Abbott, Andrew. *The System of the Professions.* Chicago, 1989.

Amariglio, Jack, Stephen Resnick, and Richard D. Wolff. In *Knowledges: Historical and Critical Studies in Disciplinarity,* edited by Ellen Messer-Davidow et al., pp. 125–149. Charlottesville, Va., 1993.

Bazerman, Charles. *Shaping Written Knowledge: The Genre and Activity of the Experimental Article in Science.* Madison, Wisc., 1988.

Becher, Tony. *Academic Tribes and Territories: Intellectual Enquiry and the Cultures of Disciplines.* Milton Keynes, U.K., 1989.

Dogan, Mattei, and Robert Pahre. *Creative Marginality: Innovation at the Intersections of Social Sciences.* Boulder, Colo., 1990.

Foucault, Michel. 1972. "The Discourse on Language." Translated by Rupert Swyer. In *The Archaeology of Knowledge,* translated by A. M. Sheridan Smith, pp. 215–237. New York, 1972.

———. *Discipline and Punish: The Birth of the Prison.* Translated by Alan Sheridan. New York, 1978.

———. *Power/Knowledge: Selected Interviews and other Writings, 1972–1977.* Edited by Colin Gordon. Translated by Leo Marshall Gordon, John Mepham, and Kate Soper. New York, 1980.

Geiger, Roger. *To Advance Knowledge: The Growth of the American Research Universities, 1900–1940.* New York, 1986.

Gieryn, Thomas F. "Boundary-Work and the Demarcation of Science from Non-Science: Strains and Interests in Professional Ideologies of Scientists." *American Sociological Review* 48, no. 8 (1983): 781–795.

Greenblatt, Stephen, and Giles Gunn, eds. *Redrawing the Boundaries: The Transformation of English and American Literary Studies.* New York, 1992.

Hahn, Roger. *The Anatomy of a Scientific Institution: The Paris Academy of Sciences, 1666–1803.* Berkeley, Calif., 1971.

Hoskin, Keith W. "Education and the Genesis of Disciplinarity: the Unexpected Reversal." In *Knowledges,* edited by Ellen Messer-Davidow et al., pp. 271–304. Charlottesville, Va., 1993.

Keller, Evelyn Fox. "Fractured Images of Science, Language, and Power: A Postmodern Optic or Just Bad Eyesight?" In *Knowledges,* edited by Ellen Messer-Davidow et al., pp. 54–69. Charlottesville, Va., 1993.

Klein, Julie Thompson. *Interdisciplinarity: History, Theory, Practice.* Detroit, Mich., 1990.

Larson, Magali Sarfatti. *The Rise of Professionalism: A Sociological Analysis.* Berkeley, Calif., 1977.

Messer-Davidow, Ellen, David R. Shumway, and David J. Sylvan, eds. *Knowledges: Historical and Critical Studies in Disciplinarity.* Charlottesville, Va., 1993.

North, Steven. *The Making of Knowledge in Composition.* Upper Montclair, N.J., 1987.

Shumway, David. "Disciplinarity, Corporatization, and the Crisis: A Distopian Narrative." *Journal of the Midwest Modern Language Association* 32 (winter/spring 1999): 2–18.

Shumway, David R., and Ellen Messer-Davidow. "Disciplinarity: An Introduction." *Poetics Today* 12 (1991): 201–225.

Veysey, Laurence R. *The Emergence of the American University.* Chicago, 1965.

THE ROLE OF THE INTELLECTUAL

Neil Jumonville

STAGE ONE: THE HISTORY BEFORE 1894

At the beginning of the twenty-first century, what historians call an intellectual role had already been performed for centuries—and maybe millennia—before the name "intellectual" was attached to it in the late nineteenth century. These early intellectuals were critics, teachers, or priests, and they worked with symbols to explain cultural values and duties. Largely this role was the province of the church, but it was also performed by bards, prophets, and royal cabinets.

Initially, the term "intellect" meant nearly the same thing as the word "intelligence." The word surfaced into occasional use in Middle English in the thirteenth century, created from the Latin *intellectus,* meaning to understand or perceive. In this sense it was used as a noun by Chaucer in 1386, Shakespeare in 1588, and Milton in 1667. Throughout this same period the word "intellectual" was used as an adjective meaning to belong to the understanding. But the term "intellectual," as a noun referring to the identity of a person (that is, an intellectual), was not used until the nineteenth century when English writers such as Lord Byron and John Ruskin did so. Yet even then it carried only the suggestion that a person was notably intelligent.

The more recent usage of the word, to signify an individual or a group with a special social function, dates from late-nineteenth-century France where the Dreyfus Affair formed how people currently employ the term. So, while it is useful for historians to speak of early American intellectuals, readers should remember that these individuals at the time would have been called writers, thinkers, speakers, philosophers, or ministers.

Because American ideas before the Revolution were predominately religious, intellectuals were usually connected to the church. In the seventeenth century, for example, American Puritans such as John Winthrop performed an intellectual role, since he was a political leader, a religious thinker, and an individual who articulated a cultural vision for the Massachusetts Bay Colony. During the early eighteenth century, however, secular politics and culture began to inch more firmly into the colonial consciousness, and, as a result, the discussion of ideas slowly detached itself from the dominance of the church.

Benjamin Franklin operated as one of the earliest American secular intellectuals when he wrote essays of political satire and criticism under the pseudonym Silence Dogood for his brother James Franklin's *New-England Courant* in the 1720s. Franklin and other American writers of this period patterned themselves after British literary reviewers such as Joseph Addison.

Franklin's example is important, because one of the common ways to perform as an intellectual has been to write in periodicals, and perhaps especially to review the work of others. Because magazine and newspaper journalism is aimed at the general public, and, because periodicals are issued frequently, the emphasis of their articles is often on matters of immediate political or social concern. Essays and reviews in periodicals are effective ways of debating public matters at hand. This practice is often called "criticism," or "cultural criticism," and the writer is often called simply a "critic." People who worked in this reviewing tradition—or who wrote short essays on cultural and political and social matters—were often called men or women of letters, and they worked in the "letters tradition."

Beginning in the early nineteenth century, the kind of essays and cultural criticism associated with intellectual culture slowly began to flourish in the United States. In Boston in 1815, the *North American Review,* the first important journal of ideas, began in America under the editorship of William Tudor. Based on the sort of English journal that employed reviews of books and matters of culture, it commented on political, religious, and social matters. Although it often clipped pieces from England that it ran in its own pages, the *North American*

Review defended America from British cultural attacks, and tried to encourage the growth of American culture. In 1833 in New York, the *Knickerbocker Magazine* was founded to serve as a cultural outlet for reviews and essays, and among its group of critics and essayists was Washington Irving, who began to contribute drama criticism and satirical essays under the pseudonym Jonathan Oldstyle. The Boston Transcendentalists—Ralph Waldo Emerson, Elizabeth Palmer Peabody, Orestes Brownson, and others—founded the *Dial* in 1840, with Margaret Fuller as editor, as a vehicle for the essays and opinions of the group.

Intellectual or critical culture began in the early nineteenth century because of several factors. The circulation of journals was prompted partly by an expanding affluence and the American nationalism that was brewing early in the century. And demographic factors, the growth of cities such as New York and Boston, made the financing and distribution of journals more possible.

African American speakers and writers such as David Walker and Frederick Douglass joined the growing intellectual exchange soon after it began. In the late 1820s, Walker contributed articles to *Freedom's Journal*, a black New York newspaper, and in 1829 his militant *Appeal to the Colored Citizens of the World* was published, created a furor in the South, and led to his early death. Douglass not only became a recognized anti-slavery speaker, but also published the weekly paper *The North Star* beginning in 1847 in Rochester, New York.

In the last half of the nineteenth century, figures such as Henry James and William Dean Howells functioned as prominent critics. James, after the Civil War, published criticism regularly for the rest of the century, and became a model of the novelist as essayist. In 1891 he wrote an essay entitled "Criticism," in which, as the self-conscious leader of American commentary, he instructed others how to operate as literary intellectuals. So James wrote not only criticism itself, but essays on criticism.

It was at this point, in the late nineteenth century, that the term "intellectual" came to have its current meaning. With the establishment of a definition, inevitably that definition became challenged, and the dispute over the meaning and role of the definition lasted throughout the twentieth century—and now occupies an important place in the field of intellectual history itself.

Part of that dispute focused on whether an intellectual was a "professional" and earned his or her living by shaping and interpreting ideas—or whether an intellectual was one who thinks in a particular way and therefore could be a common citizen or worker instead of a member of a professional elite.

Defining the Intellectual Role Roles for what scholars call an intellectual existed in most societies long before the term was applied to those individuals. In 1894 Alfred Dreyfus, a Jewish military officer of France, was convicted of espionage for Germany and was sentenced to life in prison. Although evidence of his innocence quickly surfaced, military leaders believed that to set him free would hurt the image and authority of the army. Gradually, defenders of Dreyfus surfaced in the French press and were joined by some of France's prominent writers. On 13 January 1898, Émile Zola published his famous open letter "J'accuse" ("I accuse") in the French newspaper *L'Aurore*. Soon after that a petition demanding a new trial for Dreyfus was signed by figures such as Anatole France, Marcel Proust, André Gide, Claude Monet, and Jules Renard. In August 1898, several authorities admitted framing Dreyfus, and he was later pardoned.

Shortly afterward the conservative writer Maurice Barrès used the term "intellectual" as an epithet against the defenders of Dreyfus. Intellectuals, Barrès warned, were unpatriotic, disloyal, and uprooted from national ties. The Dreyfusards accepted Barrès's insult as a compliment. As one of them wrote defiantly, "Let us use this word since it has received high consecration." In the United States in 1899, the pragmatic philosopher William James, who supported the Dreyfusards, wrote in a letter, "We 'intellectuals' in America must all work to keep our precious birthright of individualism, and freedom from these institutions" of the church, army, and aristocracy (Hofstadter, p. 39). James and others helped begin the use of the term in the United States early in the twentieth century.

Because the Dreyfus struggle featured a sharp conflict between thinkers with different attachments to society, it immediately suggested a role for the intellectual. Aligned against Dreyfus were established individuals of substance, conservative lawyers, doctors, and medical students, who defended traditional authority. Standing with Dreyfus were liberal arts professors and humanities students, many of them from lower backgrounds who had ambitions to join the middle class and who were less attached to established society. The Dreyfusards were thinkers who insisted on elevating a national argument about a miscarriage of justice into an international debate about basic principles. The battle lines were not drawn by narrow political interests and, instead, as the sociologist Lewis A. Coser noted, the struggle forged "new alliances among men who had little in common before the Affair brought them together (*Men of Ideas*, p. 218).

After this point, the word "intellectual," used as a noun to refer to a particular kind of person, became a more frequently used term with a more specific historical meaning, a meaning that no longer meant only intelligent.

The historian Richard Hofstadter later summarized the most noticeable distinctions between the intelligent and the intellectual. Intelligence is narrower, more immediate, and predictable; it is especially useful for technical and administrative problems because intelligence calculates and arranges; and its practicality is easy to see in the thinking of scientists and engineers. In contrast, the operation of the intellect is critical, evaluative, creative, imaginative, and theoretical; it ponders large meanings and systems; and the presence of the intellect is noticeable in literary critics and philosophers. It was in this redefinition after the Dreyfus Affair that intellectuals became a distinctly different category with a different role than is found in the broader category of thinker. That is, intellectuals became a distinct subcategory of thinkers.

STAGE TWO: THE PERIOD OF AMERICAN IDEOLOGY, 1930–1970

Until the 1930s, conditions had not prompted much discussion of the intellectual role in the United States. But, beginning in about 1930, several new features of American life converged to initiate a sustained consideration of the intellectual function that lasted for forty years. One of those features was the onset of the Great Depression and the ensuing national discussion about ways to escape the economic and cultural crisis. Allied to this was the threat abroad from Marxism, fascism, and other ideologies, and the appearance of those ideas on American shores. At nearly the same time, President Franklin Roosevelt began to employ thinkers as advisors, many of them from academia, to help craft the New Deal. Further, within a decade the American university system began to grow quickly under pressure from defense needs and the post–World War II GI Bill. In addition, at this point the field of sociology, whose members would lead the analysis of the intellectual function, expanded and seemed more important than ever. Also, newer media forms such as movies, radio, and television meant that more cultural and political critics could be employed. And, finally, the expansion of corporate and postindustrial employment underlined a need for experts and strategists. Consequently, the years from 1930 to 1970 witnessed the most intense consideration of the intellectual role.

During these four decades, the descriptive (which were also prescriptive) explanations of the intellectual function grouped themselves into three main categories: occupational roles; sacred and religious roles; and political roles.

Occupational Roles and Professional Communities The first of these groupings suggests that intellectuals are identified by their occupational roles or are members of professionally validated communities of thinkers. The functionalist sociologist Talcott Parsons was the most prominent proponent of this view. An intellectual, Parsons explained in his essay "The Intellectual," puts cultural concerns (such as symbolic meaning) above social concerns (such as the administration of economic or political units). The oldest and most important of these cultural occupations are "the priest, the teacher, and the specialist in 'law'" (p. 7).

The intellectual occupation, according to Parsons, has long roots that reach into the deep history of humankind. It originated with mystics and holy people who performed religious acts, rites of passage, therapeutic functions, and magic. Later this role was peopled by the philosophers of Greece and the prophets and scriptural writers of the Middle East and Asia. Later still these functions were taken up by the Dominican and Franciscan orders of an increasingly philosophical Christianity, and the cultural specialists who lived by the patronage of princes. "Indeed the ancestors of the modern university, in Paris, England, and Italy," Parsons reported, "were essentially offshoots of the monasteries" (pp. 10–11).

The position of cultural gatekeeper is another occupational role of the intellectual. "Gatekeepers of ideas," as Coser called them, decide which individuals and issues have the standing to be heard. Usually, according to the sociologist J. P. Nettl, one needs to be a member of "a culturally validated profession," someone "accepted as qualified" to speak on cultural questions (pp. 81–82). And, as the sociologist Edward Shils explained, "These communities are not mere figures of speech. Their common standards are continually being applied by each member in his own work and in the institutions which assess and select works and persons for appreciation or condemnation." Academics and others encounter these groups continually. "The

EDWARD SHILS:
"THE INTELLECTUALS AND THE POWERS"

Intellectual work arose from religious preoccupations. In the early history of the human race, it tended, in its concern with the ultimate or at least with what lies beyond the immediate concrete experience, to think with religious symbols. It continues to share with genuine religious experience the fascination with the sacred or the ultimate ground of thought and experience, and the aspiration to enter into intimate contact with it. In secular intellectual work, this involves the search for the truth, for the principles embedded in events and actions or for the establishment of a relationship between the self and the essential, whether the relationship be cognitive, appreciative, or expressive. The deeper religious attitude, the striving for contact and communion with the symbols of the ultimate powers which dominate human life, has a very intimate affinity with the profoundest scientific orientations, which seek to discern the most general and comprehensive laws of universal and human existence. Differently disciplined, both the religious and the scientific dispositions at their most creative, have in common the striving for contact with the most decisive and significant symbols and the realities underlying those symbols. It is therefore no stretching of the term to say that science and philosophy, even when they are not religious in a conventional sense, are as concerned with the sacred as religion itself. In consequence of this, in our enumeration of the traditions under which intellectual pursuits are carried on, we should say that the tradition of awesome respect and of serious striving for contact with the sacred, is perhaps the first, the most comprehensive and the most important of all the traditions of the intellectuals.

Source: Philip Rieff, ed., *On Intellectuals*, p. 41.

editors of learned scientific, scholarly, and literary journals, the readers of publishing houses, the reviewers of scientific, scholarly, and literary works, and the appointments committees which pass judgments on the candidates for posts in universities or scientific research institutes," Shils noted, "are the central institutions of these communities" (p. 38).

So it was the professors in intellectual disciplines in the university, particularly in the humanities and social sciences, and the gatekeeper editors and manuscript referees, who Parsons, Coser, and Shils thought best personified the occupational role of the intellectual.

Symbols and the Sacred Some observers, however, believed that the occupational definition was insufficient—because it identified intellectuals by what they did and where they worked instead of by what and how they thought. If explanations focused instead on the kinds of ideas intellectuals used, and the kinds of uses for which those ideas were crafted, then it would be easier to distinguish intellectuals from the intelligent.

Thus the second category of the definition of the intellectual includes the ability to create and interpret symbols, myths, and values. Edward Shils provided the best explanation of this rather religious orientation of intellectual work. An "unusual sensitivity to the sacred" marks intellectuals, who also possess "an uncommon reflectiveness about the nature of their universe, and the rules which govern their society." Like their monastic forebears, intellectuals also create and interpret symbols, which is a moral undertaking. These individuals, Shils explained in anthropological language, seek "frequent communion with symbols which are more general than the immediate concrete situations of everyday life, and remote in their reference to both time and space." The interaction with these symbols and "this interior need to penetrate beyond the screen of immediate concrete experience marks the existence of the intellectuals in every society" (pp. 25–26).

Similarly, the sociologist Charles Kadushin emphasized that intellectuals have a responsibility to analyze and promote "value concepts," which he defined as "those kinds of symbols which express some moral apprehension of experience and action." Freedom of speech, natural rights, and justice are examples of value concepts, and intellectuals "are creatively expert in finding the relationship of one value concept to another and in tracing the use and application of these concepts in a society's tradition" (p. 6). Some of the ways that symbols can be expressed imaginatively by intellectuals are through painting, fiction, criticism, poetry, and other artistic endeavors.

The religious and the anthropological meet again in the intellectuals' creation and interpretation of myths. The literary critic Malcolm Cowley once noted that writers are those who create the myths of the tribe. Scholars might say the same for intellectuals generally. They create the meanings and myths that bond the culture together. "As a poet," Gary Snyder explained in 1961, "I hold the most archaic values on earth. They go back to the late Paleolithic: the fertility of the soil, the magic of animals . . . the common work of the tribe" (Kherdian, p. 52). Cowley and Snyder both spoke of myths and tribes. With the passing of formal religion from a central place in American culture in the twentieth century, literature, broadly conceived, moved in to take religion's place in the interpretation of experience. Some of those who operate as intellectuals, then, are writing contemporary scriptures—constructing the American fund of meaning, values, symbols, and myths.

Yet for all of the emphasis on intellectuals' responsibility for culture more than society, political culture was prominently represented in the areas that mid-century intellectuals assigned themselves. In 1927 the French writer Julien Benda scolded intellectuals for becoming involved in political passions. In *La trahison des clercs* (The betrayal of the intellectuals, 1955) Benda claimed that the aim of intellectuals should be "metaphysical speculation" instead of "practical aims," and he urged them to avoid politics and to realize that they are "not of this world" (Coser, p. vii). Benda had hardly finished giving his advice before ideological conflict began its sweep around the globe in the 1930s and 1940s.

Beginning in the 1930s, in America as elsewhere, one of the main roles for intellectuals was to construct appropriate ideologies either to defend or to justify attacks on power. As Parsons put it in 1968, "Ideology has become the primary instrument of the modern secular intellectual classes in their bid to be considered generally important" (p. 22). Others agreed. "In the main," Hofstadter reported, "intellectuals affect the public mind when they act in one of two capacities: as experts or as ideologues" (p. 35).

Dissenters, Activists, and Generalists The third and final grouping of the mid-twentieth-century definition of the intellectual role orbits around intellectuals' political orientations and their audiences. Like the second group of criteria, the third focuses on the kinds of ideas people use.

During the entire period from 1930 to 1970, America had only a weak and sporadic tradition of intellectual conservatism. Nearly the entire intellectual community, that is, inhabited the political spectrum from the center to the Left. As Fred J. Evans has shown, only 27 percent of American faculty members in the early 1970s thought of themselves as conservative, and, if one were to judge from intellectual magazines and journals, the effect of conservative opinions probably was even smaller (p. 997). So a disproportionate amount of the discussion about intellectuals and ideology in this period emanated from leftist groups.

And why did a capitalist culture shelter a primarily leftist intellectual community? As early as 1942, Joseph Schumpeter tried to answer that question by pointing out, "Unlike any other type of society, capitalism inevitably and by the very logic of its civilization creates, educates, and subsidizes a vested interest in social unrest." Intellectuals, he noted, are not a class like laborers, but come from all parts of society, and "a great part of their activities consist in fighting each other and in forming the spearheads of class interests not their own." (Here one might think of university professors in the last quarter of the twentieth century.) Schumpeter observed that "from the criticism of a text to the criticism of a society, the way is shorter than it seems." Ironically, the middle class and business interests defend these intellectual critics who criticize them, because the bourgeoisie knows that "the freedom it disapproves cannot be crushed without also crushing the freedom it approves." As a result, capitalism cannot control its intellectuals effectively. In return, these critics cannot help chipping away at the liberal order that protects and subsidizes them because the intellectual community "lives on criticism and its whole position depends on criticism that stings" (pp. 146–151).

An example of a leftist group that discussed intellectuals and ideology is the school of New York Intellectuals, those figures who revolved around the *Partisan Review, Commentary,* and similar publications, most notably Sidney Hook, Daniel Bell, Lewis Coser, and Irving Howe. More than any other group in American history, the New York Intellectuals wrestled very publicly for decades, among themselves and with others, about the proper definition and role for intellectuals. While in college during the Great Depression, as Marxists or democratic socialists, members of the group felt that intellectuals had to remain outside mainstream society and adopt a dissenting stance. They were schooled in ideology and theory, and were committed to fighting dangerous ideology (such as Stalinist communism) with what they considered better ideology (such as Trotskyist socialism).

Disillusioned in the 1940s, however, the New York Intellectuals and much of the American intellectual community abandoned ideology for liberalism and pragmatism—because of the ruin large messianic ideological systems had caused. Now they believed that the proper intellectual should be anti-absolutist, tentative, and unbeholden. Intellectuals should oppose a priori ideologies and utopias.

Yet it was uncomfortable for the New York Intellectuals to embrace the United States, which they once had denounced. They worried about whether they had sold out, and, in the midst of their discomfort, they argued about whether some level of nonconformity was still an essential part of the intellectual role. Did a person automatically have to be a dissenter, or could one be an affirmer of mainstream culture and still qualify as an intellectual? Irving Howe, a *Dissent* editor, advised that to serve as a countervailing presence to mainstream society and its power, intellectuals should take a perpetual position of critical opposition. But Sidney Hook, who responded that unthinking nonconformity is no more intelligent than unthinking conformity, believed that affirming a culture that one supported was the intelligent and intellectual thing to do. This same disagreement surfaced in the symposium "Our Country and Our Culture," in *Partisan Review* in 1952, at a time when the questions of appropriate levels of dissent and affirmation were at their most combustible. In the symposium, Norman Mailer encouraged a continuing outsider status and argued that "the writer does not need to be integrated into his society," while only two pages later the theologian Reinhold Niebuhr warned, "This type of social criticism does not have quite the relevance which it once possessed" (pp. 299, 301).

One of the most important reasons that writers and thinkers, many of whom had been members of the political Left, supported the capitalist West after World War II, is that they felt this was where the dissent important to the intellectual role was tolerated. In the West, an unpopular opinion was not likely to earn a person a bullet in the back of the head by the secret police.

If the level of social and cultural criticism began to moderate in the 1950s, still there remained a conviction in the intellectual community at large that a critical and skeptical detachment was a necessary part of the intellectual role. Talcott Parsons saw this detached function as partly that of the prophet "who by definition stands outside the main social structure and always in important respects in opposition to it" (p. 7). Edward Shils pointed out that "it is practically given" that intellectuals will oppose their society, and also oppose those entrenched intellectuals who preceded them. In fact, as he said, "The function of modern intellectuals in furnishing the doctrine of revolutionary movements is to be considered as one of their most important accomplishments" (pp. 30, 33). J. P. Nettl, throughout his work, emphasized, "The actual definition of an intellectual must accordingly include not only a certain type of thinking but also a relationship to sociostructural dissent" (p. 81). Lewis Coser, one of the founders and editors of *Dissent*, described intellectuals as "those who 'think otherwise,' the disturbers of intellectual peace." Without their challenge to "the established routines and the traditions of the eternal yesterday . . . our culture would soon be a dead culture" (p. x). Perhaps Harold Rosenberg put it most concisely: an intellectual is one who turns answers into questions.

After 1970, when a strong intellectual conservatism arrived in the United States, it could no longer be assumed that intellectuals hailed exclusively from the Left. In the last decades of the twentieth century, figures as diverse as William Kristol, Patrick J. Buchanan, and Rush Limbaugh demonstrated that a dissenter could be an outsider from the Right as legitimately as from the Left.

As is evident, there is no single agreed-upon description of the intellectual role that emerged from the debates between 1930 and 1970. Instead, there is a collection of suggestions and definitions from which individuals can construct a role tailored to their goals and to their most valued philosophical and political principles. So an intellectual might choose to address culture, work with myths and symbols, serve as a gatekeeper, operate as a social or cultural critic as an outsider, or deal with political values, ultimate meanings, or sacred assumptions.

These roles and functions do not have to be the province of the elite, nor are they reserved for those whose occupations are considered intellectual. Much of being an intellectual is in the way one thinks, not in the position one fills. A truck driver in her conversations might create or criticize myths or sacred values. A fry cook in his spare time might act as an unattached outsider whose criticism of society turns answers into questions. On a highway overpass near a housing project, a teenage graffiti artist might create new images and symbols that challenge accepted convictions. Further, an individual need not act as an intellectual twenty-four hours a day in order to perform a significant intellectual function.

STAGE THREE: CULTURAL HISTORY AND THE FALL OF THE INTELLECTUAL AFTER 1970

In the 1950s and 1960s in the United States a massive social and cultural revolution occurred, the effects of which still influence twenty-first-century America directly. The civil rights movement, the women's movement, the New Left, and the counterculture all produced a desire in the intellectual and academic communities for social and cultural democracy and egalitarianism. Compared especially to the Old Left of the preceding generation, the uprising in the 1960s was hostile to many of the values and hierarchies of middle-class society and many of the convictions of liberalism. The reformist passions of the 1960s, led by the baby boomer generation, employed anthropological insights, structuralism and then poststructuralism, gender and cultural theory, social history, and a collection of other approaches in order to challenge racial and gender roles, traditional cultural and middle-class standards, the authority of the dominant culture, and elite concepts of culture.

As a result, by the 1970s there was already a push within the field of history to find ways to locate and analyze the ideas of the voiceless and excluded. Critics accused traditional intellectual history, justifiably, of having focused on the ideas of elites, the dominant culture, and such cryptic concepts as national character, identity, and mind. By the time of the Wingspread Conference in Racine, Wisconsin, in 1977, where intellectual historians gathered to analyze their situation, John Higham found intellectual history so unpopular that he had trouble or-

ganizing and funding the event, and at the conference Alan Lawson heard one of the organizers comment that the field "seems as dated as narrow ties" ("Symposium on Intellectual History," p. 35). Within a short time, cultural history and culture studies moved past intellectual history as the chosen approach for most young scholars to talk about ideas.

Cultural history drew from a variety of sources, including the work of cultural critics and philosophers such as Stuart Hall, Raymond Williams, Michel Foucault, and Jürgen Habermas, to name only a few of the most obvious influences. Cultural historians learned to distrust intentions, study the producers and receivers of culture, and think in terms of widespread mentalities. Not least of their teachers was the Italian politician and founder of the Italian Communist Party Antonio Gramsci, from whom cultural historians learned that "in any physical work," even of peasants or laborers, there is "creative intellectual activity." Therefore, each individual is, as Gramsci explained, a philosopher, "an artist, a man of taste, he participates in a particular conception of the world, has a conscious line of moral conduct, and therefore contributes to sustain a conception of the world or to modify it, that is, to bring into being new modes of thought" (pp. 8–9).

After considering the advice of Gramsci and others, cultural historians focused on analyzing large collections of ordinary people, particularly women and people of color when their examples were available, and to use as many newly discovered or fugitive sources as possible. Employing this method, cultural historians have enriched the historical record considerably, and have added important insights about little-known outlooks.

One topic to which they have added little, however, is the role of the intellectual. Likely, that is because it has not been their ambition. Simply, most scholars interested in the voiceless have gravitated to the fields of social or cultural history, so the role of the intellectual was not thought to be their assignment. Moreover, for a cultural historian, producers of ideas often are anonymous, and, even when they are not, these producers are not called intellectuals nor said to carry out an intellectual function. Consequently, readers are left in the dark about what relation exists between the creative process of the intellectual and that of the newer concept of the cultural producer. The function and role of the intellectual had been ignored, that is, when instead it could have been a useful referent. The last quarter of the twentieth century placed the concept of the intellectual in the closet, out of view, because of what the academician Ross Posnock called "the embarrassed status of the modern intellectual in postmodern culture." As the critic and historian Michael Roth noted about his students, even though they were interested in ideas, they "were never very comfortable with the title 'intellectual history.' Most of them did not want to be associated with intellectuals" ("Symposium on Intellectual History," pp. 18, 39).

In 1996 a "Symposium on Intellectual History in the Age of Cultural Studies" was published in the *Intellectual History Newsletter*. Although it was a forum for intellectual historians and cultural historians to discuss the relevance and future of intellectual history, there was almost no attempt whatever by any of the participants (whether intellectual or cultural historians) to define the twentieth-century use of the term "intellectual" or to decide whether an intellectual role still existed. It is difficult to imagine a clearer indication of the reduced scholarly interest in the intellectual.

Still, since the late 1970s there has been some intelligent and important work published on the intellectual role. David A. Hollinger has encouraged historians to look at the discourse of intellectuals within their relevant communities, and a benefit is that one can maintain a focus on a specific group, and the analysis is less likely to produce hazy and grand conclusions. Similarly, Thomas Bender has written on professional organizations and communities of intellectuals, and Thomas Haskell has analyzed communities of experts.

There has also been a welcomed interest in the intellectual roles of women and African Americans and the special obstacles they have faced over the centuries. The feminist scholar Linda Kerber has shown how, despite the limitations that confined them, early-nineteenth-century women played an important function as cultural thinkers in their role as republican mothers by raising children and constructing the moral values of families. Similarly, Gerda Lerner has pointed to nineteenth-century women authors and thinkers who succeeded, despite the reality that "women intellectuals" lacked social spaces, institutions, and female audiences and mentors ("affinitive clusters") that could properly nurture their intellectual roles.

Black writers such as W. E. B. Du Bois, James Baldwin, Richard Wright, Harold Cruse, and Nathan Huggins have pointed out that black intellectuals faced many of the same dilemmas and insecurities as whites, but also had to confront a separate collection of issues because of race. The irony, of course, is that the very marginality of blacks in American culture made them especially representative of major traits of the intellectual identity. That is, intellectuals are often encouraged to step outside of mainstream society, at least temporarily, in order to experience enough critical detachment to evaluate it. But with respect to critical detachment, the black intellectual is ahead of the game, since, as Du Bois maintained, the black individual is forced to deal with a double soul from the beginning—as a black and as an American. Whereas a white intellectual might have to throw him- or herself out of society in order to gain the proper detachment, blacks have lived their entire lives in a forced exile within American culture.

Since the 1980s, Cornel West has been the African American figure who has written the most articulately and prominently about the role of the black intellectual. The "dilemma of the black intellectual," West complains, is that he or she is caught between a hostile American society and uninterested black society. Because "there is a deep distrust and suspicion of the black community toward black intellectuals," the latter remains marginal to both the white and black communities. Yet, unwilling only to complain, West points out the special opportunities for an "organic" intellectual tradition that could grow out of "the black Christian tradition of preaching and the black musical tradition of performance." Then, if blacks were allowed the same entry as whites into universities and journals, and if the black community would support its own intellectuals, a healthy black intellectual community might result (pp. 302–305).

Since the mid-1980s, there has been a growing interest in the fate of the public intellectual in American life. Those historians who have been interested in the role of the public intellectual have taken care to separate the function of the intellectual from that of the scholar.

According to this view, scholars are normally specialists who keep to a single academic discipline. They are professionals who write peer-refereed books or articles for professional journals, and their work is aimed at those with a similar background. When acting as historians, they turn to the past and take to the archives to get as close as possible to the truth of a conflict, idea, or claim. Scholars usually are employed in a university or another institution, and often attempt an Olympian neutrality and objectivity—because they are required by their profession to maintain a detached neutrality, like a judge in a courtroom.

CORNEL WEST:
"THE DILEMMA OF THE BLACK INTELLECTUAL"

The way in which one becomes a black intellectual is highly problematic. This is so because the traditional roads others travel to become intellectuals in American society have only recently been opened—and remain quite difficult. . . .

Ironically, the present-day academy and contemporary literate subcultures present more obstacles for young black intellectuals than those in decades past. This is so for three basic reasons. First, the attitudes of white scholars in the academy are quite different than those in the past. It is much more difficult for black students, especially graduate students, to be taken seriously as *potential scholars and intellectuals,* owing to the managerial ethos of our universities and colleges (in which less time is spent with students) and to the vulgar (racist!) perceptions fueled by affirmative-action programs, which pollute many black student–white professor relations.

Second, literate subcultures are less open to blacks now than they were three or four decades ago. . . . Needless to say, black presence in leading liberal journals like the *New York Review of Books* and the *New York Times Book Review* is negligible—nearly nonexistent. . . .

Third, the general politicization of American intellectual life (in the academy and outside), along with the rightward ideological drift, constitutes a hostile climate for the making of black intellectuals. . . . This hostile climate requires that black intellectuals fall back upon their own resources—institutions, journals and periodicals—which, in turn, reinforces the de facto racially separatist practices of American intellectual life.

The tragedy of black intellectual activity is that the black institutional support for such activity is in shambles. The quantity and quality of black intellectual exchange is at its worst since the Civil War. There is no major black academic journal, no major black intellectual magazine, no major black periodical of highbrow journalism, not even a major black newspaper of national scope. In short, the black infrastructure for intellectual discourse and dialogue is nearly nonexistent. This tragedy is, in part, the price for integration—which has yielded mere marginal black groups within the professional disciplines of a fragmented academic community. But this tragedy also has to do with the refusal of black intellectuals to establish and sustain their own institutional mechanisms of criticism and self-criticism, organized in such a way that people of whatever color would be able to contribute to them.

Source: *The Cornel West Reader,* pp. 303–304.

The role of public intellectuals is said by these historians to be significantly different from that of scholars. Intellectuals, in this account, are those who become involved as partisans in contemporary social and cultural issues, like a lawyer in a courtroom. They are activists and support causes, in the tradition of the Dreyfusards. Public intellectuals are sometimes freelancers who do not work for a university or institution, or, if they do, find time away from their institutional assignments to do freelance work. Instead of writing for peer-reviewed journals, intellectuals often are essayists, columnists, reviewers, or cultural critics for general circulation magazines or newspapers. The essay and the periodical are their vehicles because debating contemporary issues requires that ideas be printed and exchanged quickly.

Public intellectuals, as opposed to scholars, include a subjective and normative element to their work. Believing that the wide public is the audience, an intellectual sometimes serves a national or regional congregation as a sort of secular preacher. Seeking a broad relevance, intellectuals are interdisciplinary generalists rather than specialists, and tend to popularize their specific specialties for the educated person. Most are found in the media, humanities, or social sciences, but even a scientist can function as a public intellectual. The paleontologist Stephen Jay Gould, for example, operates as an intellectual when he addresses the general twenty-first-century reader and brings his knowledge of paleontology and evolution to the relevant cultural and political debates of the day.

The roles of scholar and public intellectual are not mutually exclusive, so a person can function as a scholar on Mondays and Wednesdays, and as an intellectual on Tuesdays and Thursdays—so long as the two sets of assumptions don't mix together in the same task and undermine the different requirements of each role. The historian Henry Steele Commager and Reinhold Niebuhr are examples of individuals who operated both as scholars and as public intellectuals, taking care to separate their roles for different projects. The intellectual as a public figure fits well with Commager's description of the difference, in the Enlightenment, between *philosophes* (intellectuals) and philosophers (scholars). The role of the intellectual, as opposed to the scholar, is to engage in the civic discussion among all of those who make up, in the words of the historian Allan Nevins, that "one democratic public—the public to which Emerson and Lincoln spoke."

Russell Jacoby's *The Last Intellectuals* (1987) is a good analysis of the role of the public intellectual, a civic function that has seemed near extinction. Jacoby places most of the blame for the decline of the public intellectual on the university system. Academia employs most potential intellectuals, but turns them into scholars instead—with narrow interests, no need for an audience, and more concern for promotion than for influencing public debate on important issues. Neil Jumonville's *Henry Steele Commager* (1999) is a work that considers the proper public role for intellectuals and scholars, particularly historians, in civic debate. In many of the writings collected in *The Cornel West Reader* (1999), West has written intelligently about the role of the public intellectual, and, at the same time, has been willing to adopt and carry out the function of a public intellectual himself.

At the dawn of the twenty-first century, the historical profession is not especially interested in intellectuals or the intellectual role. In the future it is possible that academic fashions will change and there will be a renewed interest in intellectuals to complement the discipline's interest in cultural history. But, even if not, historians need to realize that many people who are not elites think in ways that are intellectual, at least part of the time. That is, even some of the voiceless of history, about whom historians are justifiably interested at the beginning of the twenty-first century, employ intellectual modes of thought some of the time. Because of this, it is necessary and beneficial, as fashions and generations change, to continue to define and redefine the term "intellectual thought," and to reassess what the American society expects out of those who perform intellectual roles.

See also **Rhetoric and Belles Lettres; Popular Intellectual Movements: 1833–1877; Southern Intellectual Life; The Artist and the Intellectual in the New Deal** *(volume 1);* **The Professional Ideal; Intellectuals and Ideology in Government; The Struggle for the Academy; Artistic, Intellectual, and Political Refugees** *(volume 2);* **Biography; History, the Past, and Historicism** *(volume 3); and other articles in this section.*

BIBLIOGRAPHY

Books

Benda, Julien. *The Betrayal of the Intellectuals.* Translated by Richard Aldington. Boston, 1955.

Bender, Thomas. *Intellect and Public Life: Essays on the Social History of Academic Intellectuals in the United States.* Baltimore, 1993.

Commager, Henry A. Steele. *The Empire of Reason: How Europe Imagined and America Realized the Enlightenment.* New York, 1977.

Coser, Lewis A. *Men of Ideas: A Sociologist's View.* New York, 1965.

Cowley, Malcolm. *And I Worked at the Writer's Trade: Chapters of Literary History, 1918–1978.* New York, 1978.

Gramsci, Antonio. *Selections from the Prison Notebooks of Antonio Gramsci.* Edited by Quintin Hoare and Geoffrey Nowell Smith. New York, 1971.

Haskell, Thomas L. *The Authority of Experts: Studies in History and Theory.* Bloomington, Ind., 1984.

Hofstadter, Richard. *Anti-Intellectualism in American Life.* New York, 1963.

Jacoby, Russell. *The Last Intellectuals.* New York, 1987.

Jumonville, Neil. *Critical Crossings: The New York Intellectuals in Postwar America.* Berkeley, Calif., 1991.

———. *Henry Steele Commager: Midcentury Liberalism and the History of the Present.* Chapel Hill, N.C., 1999.

Kadushin, Charles. *The American Intellectual Elite.* Boston, 1974.

Kerber, Linda K. *Women of the Republic: Intellect and Ideology in Revolutionary America.* Chapel Hill, N.C., 1980.

———. *Toward an Intellectual History of Women: Essays.* Chapel Hill, N.C., 1997.

Kherdian, David. *Six Poets of the San Francisco Renaissance: Portraits and Checklists.* Fresno, Calif., 1967.

LaCapra, Dominick. *Rethinking Intellectual History: Texts, Contexts, Language.* Ithaca, N.Y., 1983.

Lerner, Gerda. *The Creation of Feminist Consciousness.* New York, 1993.

Nevins, Allan. *Allan Nevins on History.* Edited by Ray Allen Billington. New York, 1975.

Posnock, Ross. *Color and Culture: Black Writers and the Making of the Modern Intellectual.* Cambridge, Mass., 1998.

Rieff, Philip, ed. *On Intellectuals.* New York, 1969.

Schumpeter, Joseph A. *Capitalism, Socialism, and Democracy.* 3d ed. New York, 1975.

West, Cornel. *The Cornel West Reader.* New York, 1999.

Edited Collections

Higham, John, and Paul K. Conkin, eds. *New Directions in American Intellectual History.* Baltimore, 1979.

de Huszar, George B., ed. *The Intellectuals.* Glencoe, Ill., 1960.

Articles in Books or Periodicals

Evans, Fred J. "Toward a Theory of Academic Liberalism." *Journal of Politics* 42 (1980).

Hansen, G. Eric. "Intellect and Power: Some Notes on the Intellectual as a Political Type." *Journal of Politics* 31, no. 2 (1969).

Hollinger, David A. "Historians and the Discourse of Intellectuals." In *In the American Province,* edited by David A. Hollinger, pp. 130–151. Bloomington, Ind., 1985.

Nettl, J. P. "Ideas, Intellectuals, and Structures of Dissent." In *On Intellectuals,* edited by Philip Rieff, pp. 53–122. New York, 1969.

Parsons, Talcott. "'The Intellectual': A Social Role Category." In *On Intellectuals,* edited by Philip Rieff, pp. 3–24. New York, 1969.

Shils, Edward. "The Intellectuals and the Powers." In *On Intellectuals,* edited by Philip Rieff, pp. 25–48. New York, 1969.

Symposia

"Our Country and Our Culture: A Symposium." *Partisan Review* 19, no. 3 (1952).

"Symposium on Intellectual History in the Age of Cultural Studies." *Intellectual History Newsletter* 18 (1996).

AUTHORSHIP, INTELLECTUAL PROPERTY, AND COPYRIGHT

Scott E. Casper

In the past several decades, scholars in literature, history, and print culture have attempted to historicize the definition of "authorship." When and how did the modern definition of an author, as the imaginative creator of literary work, emerge? How has authorship as an intellectual and literary pursuit been related to the profession or career of authors? How have individual writers constructed the notion of authorship in their own contexts (or, to use the sociologist Pierre Bourdieu's term, their own "literary fields")? How have the legal systems of intellectual property and copyright contributed to the rise of "the author" as an artistic or economic entity? In the American context, how was the definition of authorship connected to the development of republican ideology after the Revolution, to the rise of a capitalist literary market in the nineteenth century, and to the emergence of celebrity culture in the twentieth? Even as literary historians probe these issues, poststructuralist theorists have interrogated the very concept of "the author" as an autonomous subject.

The word "author" derives from Latin *auctor,* a medieval term denoting the writers who developed the rules of the disciplines in the trivium and the quadrivium. Their cultural authority derived from providing the cosmological terms through which subsequent scholars explained ordinary events. Several recent scholars have argued, however, that the modern definition of authorship emerged with the overthrow of the *auctores'* authority between the Renaissance and the eighteenth century. Donald E. Pease has suggested that the European encounter with non-European societies—and explorers' attempts to write about cultures that did not fit the cosmologies that the *auctores* described—produced the "author" as a figure who introduced the unfamiliar to European readers, and who thus stood at odds with accepted cultural principles. Other scholars, notably Martha Woodmansee and Mark Rose, have argued that modern authorship emerged in conjunction with the rise of legally defined "literary property" in the eighteenth century: copyright laws created the "author" as a proprietor of his work. Another definition, associated with the Romantic movement of the early nineteenth century, suggested that the essence of authorship lay in individual, creative inspiration, not in mediation of divine authority, presentation of observed fact, or legal property rights.

Beyond delineating the development of authorship as a cultural, legal, and economic category of endeavor, this essay seeks to present different modes of authorship that have existed in American history. Authorial pursuits have included formulaic work and imaginative creation, in media that include magazines and newspapers as well as books. It is too simple either to accept the Romantic definition of "the author" as the genius whose cultural expression transcends or challenges its immediate context, or to consider authorship as purely an economic relation between the writer, the process of publication, and the reader.

AUTHORSHIP IN COLONIAL AMERICA

Among the new "authors" of the sixteenth and seventeenth century, who described unfamiliar places for European readers, were the early chroniclers of North America. Some, such as Thomas Harriot, wrote explicitly for publication, to promote North American colonization. Others, such as George Percy, kept diaries of their experience that others subsequently abridged for published compilations, including Samuel Purchas's *Purchas His Pilgrimes* (1625). The early Virginia leader John Smith understood the fundamentally English context for such authorial efforts. In the prospectus for his *General History of Virginia, New England, and the Summer Isles* (1624), Smith referred to two possible sources of support for the work: potential patrons from the nobility and gentry, and the booksellers of London. These, along with organizations (such as colonization companies, religious communities, or later the Royal Society), were the entities upon whom authors depended. Because the seventeenth-century Chesapeake boasted no local patrons, no printing presses or booksellers before 1680, and a scant reading public, authors necessarily relied upon English support. A writer such as Smith, whose ambitious, illustrated work needed financial backing and who hoped to make money from its sale, immediately subjected himself to suspicion. Were the sights and events he depicted—and claimed to have witnessed with his own eyes—true? Indeed, the suspicion that attached to commercial publication led some English authors, including the poet John Donne, to confine themselves to scribal publication: circulating their works in handwritten form.

In seventeenth-century New England, authorship was conditioned by "the power of the Protestant vernacular tradition," in which the purpose of writing was "to replicate the transformative power of the Word." In this tradition, authors emphasized in self-effacing prefaces that they wrote to serve God, and renounced any desire for financial gain or literary fame. Several additional factors also shaped early New England authorship. The clergy regulated the output of the Boston and Cambridge presses, and booksellers helped determine "what was printed and how texts were transmitted." Writers often had little control over how their texts appeared in print: the vernacular tradition militated against a notion of "literary property," and the logistics of printing worked against an author's opportunity to review copy, especially if a work was sent to England for publication. Women were expected to refrain from public expression, a presumption revealed in learned men's prefaces to Anne Bradstreet's poetry and Mary Rowlandson's captivity narrative. Finally, learned men such as the Congregational minister Cotton Mather—whose works were published in London because the local presses could not afford to print them and because these men's intellectual world was transatlantic—felt the "pressure of alternative conceptions of writing and authorship," especially cosmopolitan models at odds with Puritan plain style. A civic tradition of authorship in early New England, "grounded in the tenets of classical republicanism and Christian humanism," built upon the Puritans' own reformist tendencies (Rice, p. 18). This tradition found more of a voice among New England's dissenters, who—given the orthodox clergy's effective censorship—had their works published elsewhere: in London,

especially before the Licensing Act of 1662, or in Philadelphia and New York after the establishment of presses there late in the seventeenth century.

Other modes of authorship flourished in the eighteenth century, notably those associated with an emerging "public sphere" in England and America. As delineated by the German philosopher-sociologist Jürgen Habermas and extended to the American context by Michael Warner, this public sphere was comprised of a constellation of sites—coffeehouses, salons, gentlemen's clubs such as the Tuesday Club of Annapolis—in which "a public independent of state control and capable of criticizing state power" could emerge (Shields, *Civil Tongues and Polite Letters in British America*, p. xv). In many of these sites, members eschewed print publication but circulated poetry, essays, and other genres scribally among themselves, thus reinforcing their sense of community. More familiar to scholars of eighteenth-century America are the printed words in newspapers, which from the 1720s on borrowed genteel forms from cosmopolitan English belles lettres and from the polite discourse of clubs and coffeehouses. Anonymous or pseudonymous newspaper authorship differed from the use of cognomens within private society, where particular names were associated with specific members of a coterie. In print, authorship could be more disguised: authors such as the statesman-inventor-printer Benjamin Franklin shifted pseudonymous identities. Pseudonymity also served the creation of a republican public sphere, to the extent that republican "virtue comes to be defined by the negation of other traits of personhood, in particular as rational and disinterested concern for the public good" (Warner, *The Letters of the Republic*, p. 42).

Whether within a belletristic community in which scribal publications were intrinsically ephemeral, or within a republican framework that linked authorship with the public weal, the very notion of literary property might seem incongruous. The former associated literary productions with their creators, but hardly required those creators to seek legal "ownership" of works circulated only among an intimate coterie. The latter might challenge an author's right to own his work at the expense of the broader public. However, soon after the American Revolution, a different republican argument, that authorial protection would encourage the development of American letters, helped to justify the emergence of American copyright law—alongside a liberal ideology of property that militated for literary property on different grounds.

FORGING AMERICAN COPYRIGHT

The earliest form of copyright laws—*privilegii,* or exclusive rights for printers to print or sell classes of books for specified terms—appeared in Renaissance Venice between 1469 and 1517. Here and elsewhere in Europe, most versions of copyright were agreements among or licenses to publishers, not protection for authors. England was no exception. In the sixteenth century, the Crown granted printers licenses to publish particular works, usually for a specified term. In 1557, Queen Mary chartered the Stationers' Company, an association that all printers were required to join; along with royal supervision, censorship, and licensing, the Stationers received a virtual monopoly on printing in England. The Stationers' Register recorded which rights belonged to each publisher, although clandestine presses actively published unlicensed works. The Licensing Act of 1662, which remained intermittently in force until 1694, required that books be licensed by the Stationers' Company before printing.

Authors' legal rights were generally implicit at best. The earliest English copyright to an author, a seven-year protection, occurred in 1530. Authors could sell publishers the rights to copy their manuscripts, but this sale abrogated control over their work. A 1637 proclamation, and provisions in laws of the 1640s and 1650s, implied a common law ownership right that might include authors. The Licensing Act, which forbade the printing of books without their owners' consent, suggested that "owners" might include authors as well as printers and publishers.

The first comprehensive English copyright act, and the first to recognize authors' rights explicitly, was the 1710 Statute of Anne. Under this law, authors of previously published books for which the copying privilege was unassigned would "have the sole Right and Liberty of printing such Book and Books" for twenty-one years, and authors of future books (or their assignees) would hold a fourteen-year copyright, with the possibility of a fourteen-year renewal. In order for the property right to be enforceable, the proprietor—author or publisher—had to register the book with the Stationers' Company and place nine copies in various libraries. The Statute of Anne raised another fundamental question: were authors' rights thereby *limited* to the term of the copyright, or did authors hold a permanent literary property in their works? In other words, did the statute copyright law override authors' presumedly perpetual common law right? In

Donaldson v. Becket (1774), the King's Bench overturned its decision in *Millar v. Taylor* (1769), and limited authors' copyrights to those specified in the Statute of Anne.

Among England's North American colonies, only Massachusetts offered authors a form of copyright protection. In 1672, at the order of the General Court, the bookseller John Usher hired the printer Samuel Green to print a revised edition of the colony's laws. Usher persuaded the General Court to pass legislation forbidding any other printer to reprint the work without his consent. Not until after the Revolution would American legislatures address the issues of copyright and literary property. James N. Green's essay, "English Books and Printing in the Age of Franklin," describes a skirmish between the political pamphleteer Thomas Paine and Robert Bell, the first printer of *Common Sense* (1776), which reveals the difficulties authors faced in the absence of American copyright law. Bell took all the risks: he paid the printing expenses, and only his name appeared on the title page, courting charges of treason. Printer and author were to split any profits. Paine's agents disputed Bell's accounts, and they argued over who had the right to print subsequent editions. In the end, Paine's inability to secure authorial rights enabled numerous printers to issue editions of America's first best-seller—and provided an example that proponents of copyright laws would use in the 1780s.

In 1782, the lexicographer Noah Webster, seeking to protect his American grammar book in the face of similar piracy, began campaigning for general copyright legislation. Webster's native Connecticut had already secured another author a copyright for his collection of psalmody, and in January 1783 the state legislature passed "an act for the encouragement of literature and genius," the first general copyright law in America. Based largely on the Statute of Anne, Connecticut's law provided the author of a yet-unpublished book, pamphlet, map, or chart with a fourteen-year "liberty of printing, publishing, and vending" it within the state, to be renewed for an additional fourteen years if the author were still alive. Licensing regulations also applied: the work must be registered with the secretary of state, the act could not shield an author from punishment for libel or defamation, and authors who resided in other states could receive protection only if their own states passed similar laws. The U.S. Congress recommended that each state enact similar legislation, and by the end of the Confederation period every state except Delaware had done so.

The 1787 United States Constitution assigned Congress the power "to promote the progress of science and useful arts, by securing for limited times to authors and inventors the exclusive right to their respective writings and discoveries." This clause became the basis for the 1790 Copyright Act, which drew upon Great Britain's Statute of Anne and the recent state laws: the fourteen-year term, renewable for another fourteen years; registration of works (by depositing copies with the clerk of the district court where the author lived, and with the U.S. secretary of state). The 1831 Copyright Act extended the initial term to twenty-eight years. Through the nineteenth century, revisions of the copyright law extended the range of works that could receive protection: prints (1802), musical compositions (1831), performances of dramatic compositions (1856), photographs and negatives (1865), paintings, drawings, chromos, statuaries, and models or designs "intended to be perfected as works of the fine arts" (1870).

Scholars have debated the meaning of copyright in the American context. William Charvat's classic statement valorized the 1790 act: "no literary profession was possible until law had given products of the mind the status of *property*" (*The Profession of Authorship in America,* p. 6). In contrast, Grantland S. Rice has argued that the preeminent tradition of authorship in America before 1790 was neither professional nor market driven, but "political and belletristic." Hence the copyright law did not unleash a latent profession of authorship, but rather helped redefine authorship within an economic rather than a political framework. Meredith L. McGill has suggested that, far from the heroic liberator of authorial imagination, nineteenth-century American copyright law was concerned with "the circumscription of individual rights and not with their extension" (*American Literary History* 9, p. 22–24). In *Wheaton v. Peters* (1834), the Supreme Court established a republican doctrine of copyright that built upon the premise of the 1790 act: that the central purpose of copyright was to promote the useful arts, not to protect the author. In denying a common law right of literary property, *Wheaton* confirmed that "*perpetual* private ownership and control over printed texts was unacceptable in a culture that regarded the free circulation of texts as the sign and guarantor of liberty" (pp. 22–24). Moreover, the 1790 act and subsequent modifications limited the author's rights as much as it created them: authors had to comply with numerous procedural regulations in order to assert copyright (and that only for

limited terms), implying that literary property existed only as a legal, not a natural, right.

One feature of the U.S. Copyright Act, drawn from ten of the early state laws but not present in the Statute of Anne, provoked a century of controversy: only American citizens or residents could receive copyright protection. In the absence of international copyright, publishers could produce editions of foreign works without paying royalties to their authors. In practice, an informal system known as "courtesy of the trade" emerged, in which a foreign book belonged to the American publisher who first announced its acquisition through newspaper advertisement, who first produced it, or who purchased the right to publish it from its author or original publisher. Nineteenth-century authors and some modern scholars have argued that the lack of international copyright retarded American authorship, because publishing popular European works without royalty considerations was cheaper and less risky than supporting unfamiliar American authors. The drive for international copyright persisted through the nineteenth century; ultimately an international agreement led to passage of the Chace Act in 1891.

FORGING AMERICAN AUTHORSHIP

Authorship as a profession faced several obstacles before 1820. Belletristic writing seemed a less-than-useful trade in a republican society. Textbook writers such as Webster could easily justify their productions (and most copyrights secured in the first decades were for similarly useful or didactic works), but imaginative writers took pains to explain how their work served the new nation. The state of publishing made a steady authorial living nearly impossible, for American writers unlike their British counterparts generally had to bear the financial risks of publication in a market without extensive and reliable national distribution or well-developed promotional techniques. A few authors of the 1780s and 1790s—Joel Barlow, Joseph Dennie, Susanna Rowson, Charles Brockden Brown—were willing to be considered "writers by occupation" rather than amateurs who derived their income elsewhere, but none of them actually made a living as authors.

How, then, did a profession of authorship emerge after 1820? Changes in the literary market enhanced authors' prospects. The rise of publishers such as John Wiley (James Fenimore Cooper's longtime publisher), Harper and Brothers, and Ticknor and Fields shifted the financial risks, as well as the process of coordinating publication, from author to publisher. New technologies, especially stereotyping, facilitated the production of multiple editions of popular works, even as the stereotype plates became a form of capital that—if owned by the publisher—diminished the author's financial control. Trade journals, publishers' advertisements in local newspapers nationwide, and railroads all helped create regional and national networks of marketing and distribution and broadened the reach of authors' works. An expanding reading public at once underpinned and profited from these developments in publishing and distribution. At the same time, the proliferation of magazines and annual gift books in the 1830s and 1840s provided outlets for men and women to get into print. Buoyed by the examples of James Fenimore Cooper, Washington Irving, and Catharine Sedgwick in the 1820s, writers could now envision making a living in print, if they worked within the commercial marketplace and catered to its reading public.

Changes in material conditions cannot fully explain the emergence of literary careers, however. As early as 13 March 1821, the Bowdoin College student Nathaniel Hawthorne wrote to his mother about potential careers. After discounting the ministry, law, and medicine, he asked, "What do you think of my becoming an Author, and relying for support upon my pen? . . . How proud you would feel to see my works praised by reviewers, as equal to the proudest productions of the scribbling sons of John Bull" (Newbury, *Figuring Authorship in Antebellum America*, p. 1). Hawthorne was *imagining* authorship in particular ways: not as anonymous participation in a public sphere or literary hackwork, but as a career with nationalistic undertones, as a labor of original production, and as a vehicle for respect outside the established professions. Such an imaginative leap had several sources. The Romantic celebration of authors as prophetic, imaginative voices had crossed the Atlantic. Moreover, English Romantic writers had become literary celebrities, their activities chronicled in print and their homes the sites of pilgrimages. The call for an "American literature" had also been a recurring trope for decades, and by the second quarter of the nineteenth century critics were calling for a literature that reflected the nation's distinctiveness. The nation's first generation of commercially successful novelists—Cooper, Irving, Sedgwick—all wrote about American subjects, perceiving their role as, in Cooper's words, "the task of making American Manners and American scenes interesting to an

American audience" (Layman, *The Professions of Authorship*, p. 109).

Scholars of nineteenth-century American literature have examined the diverse ways in which writers constructed the notion of "authorship" itself, particularly in relation to other social and cultural transformations. Antebellum figurations of authorship often used other forms of labor as analogues or counterpoints. In an era when industrial labor was eroding workers' control over the processes and economics of production—and when the literary market threatened to make authorship into yet another commercial trade—the Romantic figure of the solitary genius could stand for a different, more autonomous vision of authorship. Conversely, invocations of "industrially rationalized labor or trade to describe their own work" might mark authors' embrace of the literary market. White, middle-class women, among the most prolific magazine contributors and the best-selling novelists, often couched their work in terms of domestic responsibility, broadly conceived: providing economic support for their families or spiritual nourishment for their readers. Scholars disagree about how women authors imagined themselves: whether they experienced psychological tensions in stepping onto the "public stage"; to what extent their fictions of self-abnegating female protagonists can be read as autobiographical; how their negotiations with publishers fit into a paternalistic model or exhibited more assertiveness. By 1870, however, Virginia Penny could argue in *How Women Can Make Money* that writing fiction was a particularly lucrative source of income for women, who needed no excuse for venturing into public in print and who could derive satisfaction from their literary endeavors and fame.

LITERARY PROFESSIONALS AND FICTION FACTORIES

Virginia Penny's emphasis on pecuniary reward distinguished an emergent class of professional authors, "who wrote for and managed to live from the literary marketplace only in the most distant sense to which the word *literary* can be stretched" (Weber, *Hired Pens*, p. 2). In his 1893 essay "The Man of Letters as a Man of Business," William Dean Howells summarized the change: "it is only since the war that literature has become a business with us." Before the war, Howells claimed, American authors had lived on independent wealth, editorial work, or political patronage. "But many authors live now, and live prettily enough, by the sale of the serial publication of their writings to the magazines.... the prosperity of the magazines has given a whole class existence which, as a class, was wholly unknown among us before the war. It is not only the famous or fully recognized authors who live in this way, but the much larger number of clever people who are as yet known chiefly to the editors, and who may never make themselves a public, but who do well a kind of acceptable work."

After 1840 and especially after the Civil War, the proliferation of magazines indeed encouraged a kind of American Grub Street. In the 1840s, Edgar Allan Poe and Nathaniel Parker Willis were among the most famous magazinists—Poe with ambivalence about the relationship between his literary hackwork and his artistic fiction and poetry, Willis with more unalloyed enthusiasm for the periodical market and the celebrity it brought. Although the major antebellum magazines, such as *Godey's Lady's Book* and *Graham's,* did not pay every contributor, they did compensate writers with familiar names, ranging from literary stars such as Cooper to lesser-known figures such as Elizabeth F. Ellet. By the 1850s, authorship could be a path to celebrity. Books such as *Homes of American Authors* (G. P. Putnam and Co., 1853) offered readers glimpses inside famous writers' parlors and studies. Popular authors such as Fanny Fern (Sara Payson Willis Parton's pseudonym) became virtual brand names, whose publishers promoted their new works on the basis of previous ones' commercial success. (At the turn of the twentieth century, the acclaimed novelist Mark Twain would seek to copyright his own name.) Robert Bonner's *New York Ledger* contracted famous English and American writers as regular contributors, literally banking on their names to build one of America's best-selling periodicals. After the war, the lecture circuit became another lucrative source of authors' income, presenting them to the public on the stage as well as the page.

Journalism also offered avenues to professional writing careers, especially as several changes in the 1880s and 1890s made reporting into a viable professional identity. Emphasizing current events and personalities, a new breed of magazines, exemplified by *Cosmopolitan* and *McClure's,* supplanted genteel monthlies such as *Harper's New Monthly* and *Scribner's* in popular circulation. Newspapers also fostered a culture of reportage, in contrast to their earlier identity as partisan organs. An emerging periodical literature of fact, analogous to realism and naturalism in fiction, rewarded authors who could observe the world, understand manners and customs, and mimic speech. Some authors, such as Jack London and Stephen Crane, bridged the worlds of periodical reportage and literary fiction. Others, most famously muckrakers such as David Graham Phillips and Lincoln Steffens, became celebrities for their journalistic exposés. In this new literary culture, the image of the author as original genius gave way to an idea of authors as realist reporters, whose success lay in "ritualized routines, careful sounding of the market, and hard work" rather than inspiration (Wilson, *The Labor of Words,* p. 3). This construction of authorship occurred in the context of a culture of professionalism, in which expertise replaced genteel amateurism in fields ranging from the sciences to social work. It also privileged the masculine, part of the larger literary movement away from ostensibly feminized Victorian literature and values.

A different form of literary professionalism developed in the realm of book publishing, especially cheap fiction. The first wave of American cheap books occurred in the 1840s, as the costs of manufacturing paper fell. Several publishing houses of the 1840s and 1850s specialized in cheap, sensational paperbacks; their successors were the two great dime-novel companies, Beadle and Adams and Street and Smith. Before the Civil War, a few authors, such as George Lippard, E. D. E. N. Southworth, and Ned Buntline (the pseudonym of E. Z. C. Judson), became literary stars through their sensational fiction. After the war, Beadle and Adams bought some stories from well-known writers, and a few authors (such as Horatio Alger Jr.) made personal reputations though cheap fiction. But dime-novel companies worked primarily as fiction factories. Scores of writers produced novels within days and were paid by the story, without royalties. Thus the profits accrued to, and the pen names—transferred from one writer to another—belonged to, the publishers. In the production of dime novels, then, the very concept of "authorship" is obscured. Beginning in the 1880s and peaking during the Great Depression, pulp magazines operated along similar lines: their experienced writers received two cents a word, new hands half as much. Some famous authors, such as Upton Sinclair and Mary Roberts Rinehart, had their start in the pulps; other writers toiled unknown in the magazines for decades.

THE TWENTIETH CENTURY AND BEYOND

Unlike the writers-for-hire who built careers in journalism and fiction factories, self-consciously literary writers in the twentieth century found themselves in an "economically classless" position, "neither professionals nor proletarians" in a period when other workers within the literary marketplace became increasingly organized. From early in the century, some publishers reversed the traditional creative process by generating their own ideas for books and finding proven authors to write them, rather than simply waiting for authors to propose or submit manuscripts. At the same time, major publishing firms grew more departmentalized and hierarchical. Authors were now more likely to deal with editors within a firm than with one of the publishing partners (as mid-nineteenth-century authors had dealt with James T. Fields or Fletcher Harper). Literary agents also emerged as key players in the market, increasingly valuable to authors as publication and subsidiary rights grew more complex.

In the wake of these publishing shifts, authors' sense of their own profession and of the status of their work changed. Against the increasingly commercial literary market in which magazine and book publishers sought to satisfy particular niches or readerships, a modernist authorial reaction reemphasized the author's autonomy and creativity. Authors' attempts to organize in their own interests have represented another tack. Authors had formed leagues to promote international copyright in the nineteenth century; thereafter, the Association of American Authors (1892) lasted for ten years, replaced by the Authors League of America. Among the more ambitious endeavors was James M. Cain's effort to create the American Authors' Authority in 1946–1947. Cain wanted an association that would organize literary property, not personnel: the AAA would represent authors "in contract negotiations and in court." The idea foundered on its final requirement, that "members sign over all their copyrights to the AAA." More successful have been associations such as PEN, which "keep authors in contact with one another and provide financial and contractual advice," but are not unions (West, pp. 14–15). Authorial labor organization has worked best in fields of writing that resemble shops or industries: newspaper reporters and Hollywood scriptwriters.

Screenwriting, in fact, challenged its early practitioners' sense of the author's role. In the 1920s and 1930s, movie studios actively recruited authors affiliated with New York's literary community, and nearly 140 writers went to Hollywood between 1927 and 1938. These writers complained bitterly about the movie industry, in great measure because it challenged their sense of "creative autonomy, personal independence, legal control and ownership of their work, and fair compensation" (Fine, *Hollywood and the Profession of Authorship*, p. 14). Many of these authors had worked with relatively small, personal publishers in New York; now they felt like cogs in the large wheels of the studios. Ironically, the publishing industry itself has increasingly resembled those Hollywood studios ever since World War II: small companies merged into large publishing houses, and eventually into the media conglomerates of the late twentieth century.

The twentieth century also witnessed new ideas of literary property, connected especially to the proliferation of subsidiary possibilities. The nineteenth-century legacy of literary property was ambiguous at best. Copyright law and court interpretation limited authors' rights as much as protected them: in 1853, for example, the Supreme Court ruled that Harriet Beecher Stowe's copyright in *Uncle Tom's Cabin* could prevent neither an unauthorized translation nor the use of her characters by other writers. Some authors, however, profited from early versions of subsidiaries: Longfellow and Howells continuously revised their works into new editions and formats, each tailored to different markets. Since 1920, subsidiary possibilities have grown exponentially: book clubs, paperback reprints, adaptations for radio, stage, screen, and television, and translation rights. Authors and their agents attend carefully to their publishing contracts—which in the nineteenth century often assumed a standard form—in order to protect subsidiary rights, which have eclipsed the first-run hardcover as a source of income. Two major revisions of the copyright code occurred during the century: the Copyright Act of 1909 extended the term of copyright to a twenty-eight-year initial period and a renewal of the same length; the 1976 act, which substantially modified its 1909 predecessor, extended the term to the life of the author plus fifty years.

Since the 1960s, literary theorists and critics have complicated the meanings of "the author" and "authorship." One approach, summarized in this essay and exemplified by the works of the scholars Mark Rose, Martha Woodmansee, Richard Brodhead, and others, historicizes these terms and emphasizes their construction within particular contexts. Another approach, exemplified in Roland Barthes's "The Death of the Author" (1968) and Michel Foucault's "What Is an Author?" (1969), questions the existence of "the author" as a category. Barthes contrasted two terms: "the Author," who bore "the same relation of antecedence to his work as a father to his child," and the "modern scriptor," who is "born simultaneously with the text, is in no way equipped with a being preceding or exceeding the writing, is not the subject with the book as predicate." Barthes privileged the reader (for whom "every text is eternally written *here* and *now*") over the author or the critic, whose classic function was to "decipher" the author's meaning. For Barthes, "a text is made of multiple writings . . . but there is one place where this multiplicity is focused and that place is the reader, not, as was hitherto said, the author" (pp. 145–148). Foucault sought to redefine authorship in terms of the "author function" rather than the Romantic genius. The author's name enables classification and differentiation of texts, and it confers particular status on texts. Historically, the author function has rendered discourses into "objects of appropriation," originally for penal purposes (punishing the identifiable authors of transgressive texts) and later in the name of property rights. Its meaning, moreover, is not fixed but emerges through "the operations that we force texts to undergo, the connections that we make, the traits that we establish as pertinent, the continuities that we recognize, or the exclusions that we practice." The notion of "the author," Foucault concluded, was a regulatory one: if we live in "an inexhaustible world of significations," the concept of "the author" provides a way to limit the indeterminate meaning and circulation of texts (pp. 108–110, 119).

If poststructuralist theory suggested the possibility for linguistic play beyond the constraints of "the author," the information age challenges those boundaries structurally and technologically. Traditional copyright laws, and the concept of the individual proprietary author that underlies them, have generally failed to take account of the collaborative nature of thought and writing, in which texts are rarely the product of autonomous individuals. This failure has become increasingly apparent as collaboration has become the norm in most fields. Moreover, much of today's authorship occurs within corporate structures: like the dime-novel publishers of a century ago, the company not the author owns the rights to the text. For every "name" author like Stephen King, dozens of other writers work in obscurity—not simply as authors of lesser-selling books, but as anonymous employees. Above all, numerous characteristics of electronic communication obscure authorship in the traditional sense: the frequent indeterminacy of authorship on the World Wide Web; the loss of authorial control once a work is placed in the electronic realm; hypertext, in which the reader makes the links between textual elements; the possibility that anyone with access can become his or her own author, bypassing the traditional practices of publishing and copyright. These changes in the twenty-first century reinforce the need to consider authorship, literary property, and copyright in historical perspective.

See also **Artistic, Intellectual, and Political Refugees** *(volume 2);* **Books; Journalism; Rhetoric; Fiction** *(in this volume); and other articles in this section.*

BIBLIOGRAPHY

Amory, Hugh, and David D. Hall, eds., *A History of the Book in America: Volume One, The Colonial Book in the Atlantic World.* Cambridge, Mass., 2000.

Barnes, James J. *Authors, Publishers, and Politicians: The Quest for an Anglo-American Copyright Agreement, 1815–1854.* Columbus, Ohio, 1974.

Barthes, Roland. "The Death of the Author." 1968. In *Image, Music, Text,* translated by Stephen Heath, pp. 142–148. New York, 1977.

Bourdieu, Pierre. "Flaubert's Point of View." *Critical Inquiry* 14 (spring 1988): 539–562.

Brodhead, Richard H. *Cultures of Letters: Scenes of Reading and Writing in Nineteenth-Century America.* Chicago and London, 1993.

Bugbee, Bruce W. *Genesis of American Patent and Copyright Law.* Washington, D.C., 1967.

Charvat, William. *The Profession of Authorship in America, 1800–1870.* New York, 1992.

Coultrap-McQuin, Susan. *Doing Literary Business: American Women Writers in the Nineteenth Century.* Chapel Hill, N.C., and London, 1990.

Denning, Michael. *Mechanic Accents: Dime Novels and Working-Class Culture in America.* London, 1987.

Fine, Richard. *Hollywood and the Profession of Authorship, 1928–1940.* Ann Arbor, Mich., 1985.

Foucault, Michel. "What Is an Author?" 1969. In *The Foucault Reader,* edited by Paul Rabinow, pp. 101–120. New York, 1984.

Green, James N. "English Books and Printing in the Age of Franklin." In *A History of the Book in America: Volume One, The Colonial Book in the Atlantic World,* edited by Hugh Amory and David D. Hall, pp. 248–298. Cambridge, Mass., 2000.

Greenspan, Ezra. "Pioneering American Authorship: James Fenimore Cooper in the 1820s." In *The Professions of Authorship: Essays in Honor of Matthew J. Bruccoli,* edited by Richard Layman and Joel Myerson, pp. 106–120. Columbia, S.C., 1996.

Halbert, Debora J. *Intellectual Property in the Information Age: The Politics of Expanding Ownership Rights.* Westport, Conn., and London, 1999.

Hall, David D. *Cultures of Print: Essays in the History of the Book.* Amherst, Mass., 1996.

——. "Readers and Writers in Early New England." In *A History of the Book in America: Volume One, The Colonial Book in the Atlantic World,* edited by Hugh Amory and David D. Hall, pp. 117–151. Cambridge, Mass., 2000.

Howells, William Dean. "The Man of Letters as a Man of Business." *Scribner's Magazine* 14 (1893): 429–445.

Kelley, Mary. *Private Woman, Public Stage: Literary Domesticity in Nineteenth-Century America.* New York, 1984.

Layman, Richard, and Joel Myerson, eds. *The Professions of Authorship: Essays in Honor of Matthew J. Bruccoli.* Columbia, S.C., 1996.

McGill, Meredith L. "The Matter of the Text: Commerce, Print Culture, and the Authority of the State in American Copyright Law." *American Literary History* 9, no. 1 (spring 1997): 21–59.

Newbury, Michael. *Figuring Authorship in Antebellum America.* Stanford, Calif., 1997.

Patterson, Lyman Ray. *Copyright in Historical Perspective.* Nashville, Tenn., 1968.

Pease, Donald E. "Author." In *Critical Terms for Literary Study,* edited by Frank Lentricchia and Thomas McLaughlin, pp. 105–117. Chicago and London, 1990.

Rice, Grantland S. *The Transformation of Authorship in America.* Chicago and London, 1997.

Rose, Mark. *Authors and Owners: The Invention of Copyright.* Cambridge, Mass., and London, 1993.

Shields, David S. *Civil Tongues and Polite Letters in British America.* Chapel Hill, N.C., and London, 1997.

Warner, Michael. *The Letters of the Republic: Publication and the Public Sphere in Eighteenth-Century America.* Cambridge, Mass., 1990.

Weber, Ronald. *Hired Pens: Professional Writers in America's Golden Age of Print.* Athens, Ohio, 1997.

West, James L. W., III. *American Authors and the Literary Marketplace since 1900.* Philadelphia, 1988.

Wilson, Christopher P. *The Labor of Words: Literary Professionalism in the Progressive Era.* Athens, Ga., 1985.

Wittenberg, Philip. *The Protection of Literary Property.* Rev. ed. Boston, 1978.

Woodmansee, Martha, and Peter Jaszi, eds. *The Construction of Authorship: Textual Appropriation in Law and Literature.* Durham, N.C., and London, 1994.

ELITE VS. POPULAR CULTURES

Kathryn J. Oberdeck

Though cultural elites existed in the New World regions that would become the United States prior to the American Revolution, the emergence of an "elite culture" distinct from and hostile to a "popular culture" was a product of the late eighteenth and the nineteenth centuries. Colonial cultural elites had been, first of all, religious leaders who participated in a transatlantic culture of theology. But clerical participants in this culture were expected to speak in ways meaningful to the lay audience who listened to and read their sermons. That audience participated in broader folk cultures of magic and wonder that complemented more often than they competed with religious authority.

Throughout the eighteenth century, lay cultural elites began to develop styles of gentility and refinement expressed through luxury household goods and an increasing participation in a widening secular world of letters. This "refinement" produced incipient elite social strata whose members might spurn the pretentious efforts to mimic their style on the part of those at a "lower" station. Still, even these emerging cultural distinctions did not imply irreconcilable cultural tastes that divided social groups. Rather, in accordance with the broader eighteenth-century ethos of classical republicanism, which assumed a hierarchical culture of shared values, the styles and tastes of cultural elites were supposed to represent values respected by all social orders. Only when this republican vision of cultural hierarchy began to fragment around the growing commercialization of culture did distinctive levels of culture associated with irreconcilable tastes and values begin to develop.

The meeting of commerce and culture in the late eighteenth and early nineteenth centuries had paradoxical consequences that provoked the identification of separate spheres of "elite" and "popular" culture. On the one hand, growing markets in such cultural accoutrements as books, newspapers, art, and household decorations meant a democra-

tization of cultural refinement. New groups gained access to the trappings of gentility, breaking down republican hierarchies into wider, more egalitarian publics. On the other hand, once the solvent of the market had eaten away at the religious and aristocratic values that had informed the authority of earlier cultural elites, "culture" acquired values and authorities of its own. Experts in these values began to erect new hierarchies that distinguished "authentic" culture from debased and popular forms often criticized for being too saturated with the ethos of the market. The defenders of the "popular," in turn, shot back with attacks on newly minted elites who insulted the tastes of commercial entertainment audiences.

Such antagonism between proponents of elite as opposed to popular cultural forms changed shape over the course of the nineteenth and twentieth centuries. Nineteenth-century elites who were at pains to distinguish their cultural preferences from the tastes of newly emerging popular audiences tended to police and protect the boundaries of their cultural enclaves. In the second half of the century, however, a new group of cultural experts began campaigns to protect popular audiences from what they regarded as the exploitative practices of commercial entertainment entrepreneurs. Less devoted to the boundaries of high culture than previous cultural elites, these reformers saw their genteel cultural heritage as a source of improvement for popular audiences, and sometimes even sought to revise genteel traditions that they were beginning to experience as stale. Their critique of the exploitative nature of popular culture was further developed by twentieth-century critics of "mass culture," though by midcentury many of these began to combine their concern for the cultural well-being of the masses with a renewed sense of protectiveness toward their own threatened cultural values. At other times cultural professionals crossed or at least questioned the lines between elite and popular cultures. By the late twentieth century, "postmodern" cultural theories and practices began to erase such lines altogether. These contests took place within various specific cultural forms and institutions over the course of the prior two centuries.

DEFINING THE POPULAR IN THE NINETEENTH CENTURY

Museums and Print Culture Changing institutions of museum and print culture provided important examples of the kinds of emergent popular fare against which early-nineteenth-century cultural elites mobilized. Museums of the late nineteenth and early twentieth centuries mixed emerging genres of fine art—particularly history and portrait paintings focused on the heroics of the American Revolution—with natural history exhibits that provided specimens of the grandeur of North American nature to make up for the ancient classics that the new nation lacked. Those conceiving these museums intended this fare to be refined and uplifting, in the spirit of an emerging high culture. But even museum managers like Charles Willson Peale of Philadelphia, who sought to use such collections to educate and enlighten his patrons, were willing to indulge some entertaining spectacles to attract patrons. To advertise the new Mammoth room in his museum, Peale sent his handyman parading through the streets dressed in American Indian garb, riding a white horse and preceded by a trumpet. Peale's "lecture room" incorporated further compromises between enlightening and entertaining culture. Peale himself regarded the lecture room as a facility for learned discussions of science and art, but sought to attract audiences with more exciting performances such as Signor Hellene, a one-man band who played the viola, Turkish cymbals, tenor drum, Pandean pipes, and Chinese bells simultaneously.

Peale's combinations of high and popular cultural fare derived from both principle and necessity. Dedicated to a democratic spread of refined and learned culture, he wanted both to enlighten and amuse. In the absence of public sponsorship for his enterprise, however, Peale increasingly resorted to popularly pleasing exhibits and acts in order to generate revenue. With Jeffersonian Democratic-Republicans loathe to expand the federal government, Peale accepted that republican cultural aims needed to rely on a popular market to succeed. However, he also rued the excesses to which such commercialism led. When his son, Rubens, who administered the museum after 1810, discarded edu-

cational exhibits in favor of curiosities and expanded the entertainment fare in the lecture hall, the elder Peale pleaded for some restraint. However, Rubens's innovations proved prescient, heralding the more candidly commercial museum enterprises of P. T. Barnum.

Barnum's celebrated museums in New York City, along with the national tours of high and popular cultural celebrities that he sponsored to spread his fame, defined a new stratum of popular entertainment from which many guardians of an emerging high culture recoiled. The exhibits and performances that Barnum staged were frankly entrepreneurial, offering curiosities and cultural celebrities to wide audiences in the interests of profit. To draw such audiences, Barnum resorted to shameless fabrications in advertising and promotions for his museum as well as for touring artists such as the Swedish opera singer Jenny Lind, the diminutive Tom Thumb, and the "feejee mermaid" manufactured from the body of a fish attached to the head and hands of a monkey. This "humbuggery" was decried by self-proclaimed cultural experts who found it antithetical to the enlightening purposes of culture.

But, as the historian Neil Harris has observed, Barnum's frauds and puffery had a certain democratic morality of their own. Many among the young nation's populace believed themselves possessed of the reason and sense to understand virtually any topic or idea. They relished the opportunity to try to catch a hoax in action or measure their knowledge against the purported facts presented in Barnum's exhibits and advertising. Opportunities to question self-styled cultural and scientific experts also appealed to audiences who distrusted hierarchical authority. As one advertisement, touting trumped-up controversy among so-called experts over the authenticity of the "feejee mermaid," put it, "Who is to decide, when doctors disagree?" The implication that ordinary citizens could decide matters of truth and beauty as adequately as highly trained experts directly challenged republican notions of culture and taste. Rather than uplifting popular audiences to a higher standard of refinement held by a few, Barnum's aesthetic promised to turn truth and beauty into consequences of democratic debate—or mob rule, from the perspective of elites.

Cultural elites objected to Barnum's exhibits in part because they associated his promotional methods with trends in print culture represented by burgeoning cheap daily and weekly papers as well as by an emergent industry of dime novels. Here, too,

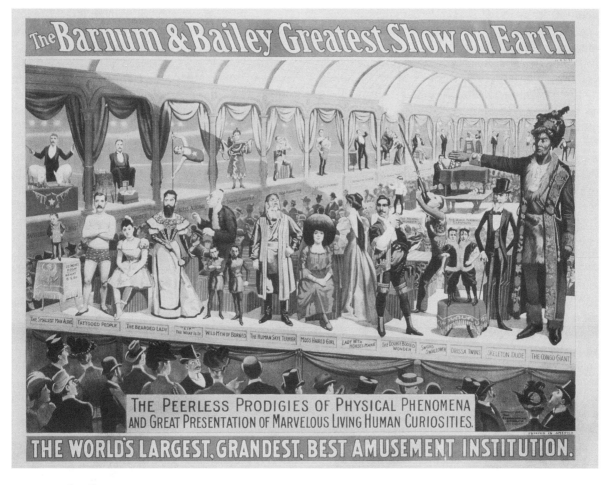

Barnum and Bailey Poster, c. 1898. © CORBIS

new commercial venues of knowledge and entertainment promised to democratize information. Self-consciously differentiating themselves from the six-penny subscription papers that had dominated the market previously, penny dailies promised wide-ranging access to information unrestricted by wealth or social position. In contrast to the commercial and "aristocratic" news in the six-penny journals, the new cheaper dailies emphasized crime stories that lent themselves to the "sensational" narratives that cultural elites snobbishly decried. Such stories, however, also exposed the unjust workings of legal institutions that operated in the interests of the wealthy and prestigious. The themes of the cheap papers found reinforcement in cheap fiction that focused on immoral secrets hidden within elite homes and institutions. As fascination with such exposure led to infiltration of their own entertainments and functions, increasingly self-conscious elites began to assert the boundaries of their social rank more forcefully. Constructing new institutions

of high cultural art and performance throughout the second half of the nineteenth century, these elites began to define the contours of an "elite culture" protected from the prying eyes and questionable tastes of popular audiences.

Still, throughout the nineteenth century the lines between elite and popular museum and print cultures were never completely clear. Museums established as temples of solemn instruction in the arts still advertised themselves as institutions of popular uplift. Only gradually did curators restrict themselves to "pure" and "original" art unsullied by the mechanics of reproducibility increasingly associated with the popular arts. Weekly illustrated papers aimed at the very emergent middle class that P. T. Barnum served. They treated the penny dailies' crime news as a kind of fearsome city "mystery" but also played to middle-class readers' fascination with neighborhoods and populations from which they distanced themselves publicly. Nor, on the other hand, did the cheap dailies remain resolutely

249

democratic; by the end of the century their increasing dependence on advertising revenue from growing corporations made them less sympathetic to the causes of newly militant workers. Other erstwhile defenders of democratic culture also repositioned themselves in America's developing cultural hierarchy; by late in the century, P. T. Barnum had recast himself as a protector of refined culture. In short, the distinction of elite from popular culture was more a process than an accomplished partition. Although the process had made an early appearance in museums and print, it became most palpable in the theater.

Elite and Popular Theater   It was in part because many Americans experienced the theater of the 1830s and 1840s as an arena of the diverse offerings and audiences that the development of distinct elite and popular cultures became especially apparent there. During these decades, aristocrats and workingmen went to the same theater to watch a full-length play whose acts were interspersed with specialties such as songs, jugglers, acrobats, and blackface actors. Theaters themselves were arranged to accommodate this multifarious audience. Appropriately priced seats placed the upper class in the boxes on the second tier. The rowdier element, along with prostitutes and African Americans who were not permitted to sit elsewhere, sat in the third tier and the upper gallery. Middling classes of tradesmen, small proprietors, and their families occupied the pit facing the orchestra. All of these audience sectors expected to be active participants in the evening's festivities, whether by jeering or cheering performers, pelting actors and spectators with missiles from the gallery, or using the evening as an opportunity to display their own finery and wealth.

Theatrical forms and audiences of the 1850s and after separated into distinct theaters along the class lines that had previously distinguished parts of the audience *within* early-nineteenth-century theaters. This separation was punctuated by riots over what theater should be. These violent events highlighted the distinctive character of elite and popular performances and their audiences. The most explosive and important of these riots occurred in 1849 outside the Astor Place Opera House in New York City.

The hostilities at the Astor Place Opera House were sparked by the appearance at the theater of the British tragedian William Charles Macready, who for years had been engaged in a sharp rivalry with the American actor Edwin Forrest, the darling of American working-class audiences. Macready's appearance at the Astor Place Opera House in May

1849 inspired posters giving vent to the class prejudices of Forrest's fans with messages reading "WORKING MEN, SHALL AMERICANS OR ENGLISH RULE IN THIS CITY?" (Grimsted, *Melodrama Unveiled*, p. 71). Long chided as an effete pet of nobles who was fawned upon by an untrustworthy American aristocracy, Macready found his first Astor Place performances disrupted by noise and barraged by chairs thrown from the gallery, the theatrical turf of Forrest's democratic legions. Ready to return to England, Macready was persuaded to continue on with his scheduled New York performances of *Macbeth* by a committee of prominent New Yorkers, including Washington Irving and Herman Melville, who disdained to have the theater ruled by ruffians. A large crowd gathered outside the theater for Macready's next performances. Aroused by news of arrests inside the building, the crowd outside began to throw stones, drawing the militia and the unprecedented use of armed force to quell, with a number of fatalities, the hostilities of an American theater crowd.

In the years following the Astor Place riot, the elite attended symphonies, operas, and "legitimate" theatrical performances into which the previously popular Shakespeare was absorbed. Here dressy audiences marked performances as enactments of elite cultural consolidation. This involved the construction of new organizational models to demarcate a "high" culture separate from popular fare, as the sociologist Paul DiMaggio has observed. Especially from the 1870s on, such organization took the form of elite-sponsored institutions like the Museum of Fine Arts and Symphony Orchestra in Boston, which provided master artworks, classical music, opera, and serious theater to select audiences. Springing up in many cities, these organizations were privately funded, controlled by elite boards of trustees, and modeled on the corporate form increasingly prevalent in business and industry. They often began with a mission of education aimed beyond the social boundaries of the elites that founded them. Many museums of the late nineteenth century, for example, assembled plaster reproductions of great statuary from around the world for the edification of their patrons. But they found themselves competing with a growing industry of mechanically reproduced art designed for mass audiences. In response, many such institutions abandoned reproductions (or, in the case of music, combinations of classical masterworks and more popular band repertoires) in order to devote themselves to "pure" cultural products that they aimed to protect from popular corruption.

On the "popular" side of the new divide in theatrical culture, variety acts were collected into specifically popular theatrical forms. The first form of popular theatrical entertainment to organize these variety specialties into a unified performance was the blackface minstrel show. Enacted by northern, white showmen, the minstrel show borrowed such features of African American culture as animal tales with instructive themes of weaker animals using guile and wit to outsmart the stronger animals threatening their lives. As blackface performers knew, stories and songs in which shrewd slaves used their masters' presumptions of power and superiority as objects of ridicule had particular resonance for white northern working-class audiences. The theatrical wars these audiences had fought against urban cultural aristocrats betrayed the workers' own uncertainty about the security of their status in a rapidly shifting, increasingly industrial world.

While alive to the hostility and aggression implicit in Afro-American songs and tales, however, minstrel actors did not wholly take sides with the African Americans from whom they borrowed material. Along with white masters, they also caricatured both southern and northern blacks, offering uncertain white audiences a group to whom they could feel superior. In the process, they mocked the rising class of urban professionals that pretended to a higher culture, while perpetrating racist slurs against the black characters that minstrel actors claimed to be impersonating. When a white man in blackface got up on a stage and started a lecture with the sentence, "Transcendentalism is dat spiritual cognoscence ob pscyhological irrefragibility" (Toll, *Blacking Up,* p. 70), he made fun not only of the pretensions of cultural elites, but also of the intelligence and capabilities of black people themselves. Such examples remind us that not only "elite" culture but the popular performances that challenged it drew important boundaries around the audiences and communities to which it spoke.

In the 1870s and 1880s, the minstrel show began to face competition from newer forms of popular performance that recombined the specialty acts of nineteenth-century theater in appealing ways. Immigrant groups that made up a growing proportion of the American working class—first Irish and Germans, later Italians and Jews—increasingly became the mainstays of popular ethnic characterization on American stages. A good example is the comic theater of Edward Harrigan and Tony Hart, who emerged from minstrelsy to develop their own full-length musicals in the 1870s and 1880s.

Harrigan and Hart's musicals poked fun at the Irish, German, and black guard companies that regularly marched around the Lower East Side of Manhattan bound for target practice or simply turning out to puff the name of a local politician, from whom they had exacted tribute in the form of uniforms and prizes. By making institutions that immigrants erected the subject for dramatic adventure, Harrigan and Hart granted the institutions themselves a special kind of comic dignity. Their sketches and plays ennobled a number of immigrant community activities, including boat rides, picnics, balls, political campaigns, and the regular marching of the guard companies as the subject for theatrical sketches for years to come. In the midst of these entertainments, Harrigan's song lyrics, set to the rousing or sentimental tunes composed by his father-in-law, David Braham, celebrated the ethnic neighborhood itself. In these cases, caricature grew into characterization, giving popular audiences fantasy pictures of themselves.

The vogue of Harrigan and Hart's theater waned in the late 1880s, but characterizations of immigrants such as the two had developed continued to dominate the variety and vaudeville theaters that succeeded them. Variety shows gathered blackface and ethnic caricatures into a format made up of several distinct acts. The venues for such shows included saloons that allowed for drinking and boisterous repartee along with dime museums that perpetuated P. T. Barnum's commercialism and eclecticism without his commitment to moral uplift and propriety. Performances in these venues often advertised salacious themes and images offensive to the tastes of both elite and middle-class audiences. Maintaining many of the ethnic caricatures and characterizations that typified minstrelsy and Harrigan and Hart, variety performers also spoke to increasingly stark divisions between their popular audiences and the exclusive audiences for elite cultural fare. For example, the variety performer Tony Pastor's song "The Upper and Lower Ten Thousand" pointed to the luxurious diets of the rich and the tendency of courts to overlook their financial indiscretions, while the poor went without dinner or ended up in jail for stealing a small amount for a meal. Variety shows in concert saloons and dime museums, as well as the female burlesque in vogue during the 1860s and 1870s, also poked fun at upper-class emphasis on feminine docility and propriety. They offered a morally ambiguous environment that often exploited female patrons and performers as sexual objects while also allowing

251

actresses more scope for verbal expression than they found in more staid venues.

By the late nineteenth century, several aspirant variety managers and other impresarios began to seek a rapprochement between their popular fare and the more refined audiences that shunned them. The result was a tremendously successful theatrical form called vaudeville, which attracted broad-ranging audiences from the mid-1880s into the 1920s. Vaudeville retained the succession of specialty acts that had characterized the variety show, but moved this form to new theatrical environments that mimicked (sometimes in caricature) the characteristics of elite theatrical fare. Often opulently decorated and provided with lush comforts and amenities, vaudeville theaters encouraged and often enforced a more discreet and dignified audience demeanor than variety halls expected. This shift of variety acts to vaudeville has prompted some cultural historians of the 1980s and early 1990s to see the new form as a triumph of elite refinement over popular rambunctiousness. As a mass audience drawn from multiple classes was reassembled in vaudeville theaters, these historians suggest, they were obliged to adopt the manners of the elite and bourgeois and thereby forfeit the underlying critique of elite culture their previous cultural pastimes had implied.

However, several cultural histories of the later 1990s argue that the day-to-day fare and tone of many vaudeville theaters revealed a more complicated cultural negotiation. Though vaudeville impresarios offered comfortable interiors of baroque ornamentation to the masses, they also provided theatrical fare appealing to a variety of audience tastes. "Gold brick" acts were brought from the high cultural worlds of opera, classical music, and "legitimate drama" to add a tone of solemnity and cultural improvement to many vaudeville programs. But these "refined" acts were accompanied by comic turns and musical numbers that poked fun at pretensions to cultural superiority or improvement. As in previous forms of theatrical performance that used ethnic caricatures to raise questions about social elites and authorities, vaudeville sketches made fun of local dignitaries and celebrated the popular leisure pastimes of working-class and ethnic communities. And while vaudeville managers made much of the "family" atmosphere of their theaters in order to attract women and children, female vaudeville performers often styled their own acts in more ribald terms that questioned or criticized middle-class codes of feminine propriety and sentimentality. In sum, far from fostering a clear triumph of one stratum of "taste" over another, vaudeville shows provided commentaries on debates over the terms of cultural hierarchy that had emerged out of the partition of elite and popular culture earlier in the century.

Vaudeville also became an arena for the introduction of novel popular cultural forms and themes that would provoke new critiques of popular culture in the twentieth century. It was in vaudeville theaters that many audiences first encountered the movies. In years to come, film developed into a popular performance form in its own right, playing first of all in neighborhood storefront nickelodeons to working-class audiences interested in humorous or sympathetic treatments of some of their own struggles with elite pretensions and prejudices, among other issues. New cultural experts would worry over these working-class pastimes and lobby for more wholesome cinematic fare. They would worry, too, over the values implied by new cultural hierarchies that an increasingly corporate vaudeville industry promoted. As the vaudeville industry became nationally organized into circuits that could underwrite tours for lavish acts, themes of luxury and fashion began to compete with the ideals of high-cultural refinement that had previously occupied the summit of the cultural hierarchy depicted in vaudeville shows. Critics anxious to use culture to convey proper morals to popular audiences worried over this new twist in the commercialism of popular culture, as the tone of much Progressive Era cultural criticism demonstrated.

CULTURAL CRITICISM FROM THE PROGRESSIVE ERA TO THE DEPRESSION

Unlike their earlier counterparts, who tended to disdain popular audiences even while trying to "uplift" their tastes, cultural reformers of the Progressive Era expressed greater sympathy for the mass audiences flocking to vaudeville and film. Though this new generation of elites also wanted to improve popular culture and its devotees, they were less censorious and exclusive than previous advocates of high culture. Some even saw in popular culture a vitality absent from the increasingly arcane venues for elite culture. Though most Progressive Era cultural critics thought that this vitality was exploited by commercial popular entertainments and needed alternative institutions to flourish, some in the 1910s and 1920s even praised existing popular arts themselves. This position continued to provoke considerable debate among the growing ranks of cultural critics in the 1920s and 1930s, but also gained new prominence with the rediscovery and celebration of American "folk" culture during the Great Depression.

American settlement-house pioneer Jane Addams provides a good example of the first-generation of Progressive Era cultural reform. Though Addams disdained as unwholesome and exploitative the commercial entertainments available to urban dwellers, and especially to working-class youths, she nevertheless sympathized with the desires that led audiences to such venues. According to Addams, young people sought in five-cent movies and dance halls the same hope that there was more to life than grim workaday realities that inspired the creative traditions associated with "high" culture. The goal of cultural reform, from this perspective, was not so much to "improve" audiences but to provide cultural experiences that would fulfill their already burgeoning artistic sense and channel it in creative and moral directions. Productions of Greek tragedies, Shakespeare, and religious plays in settlement-house dramatic clubs engaged the same longings that drove young people to popular amusements but satisfied those longings more substantially, Addams believed. Even urban sports such as baseball leagues provided a more meaningful and participatory outlet for the desire to be part of the excitement of urban life than more passive shows or morally dangerous dance halls. Focusing primarily on the growing population of immigrant youths crowding America's industrial cities, Addams sought to bring them in contact with what she regarded as the best of her own high-cultural tradition in order to satisfy artistic capacities they already had.

A younger generation of Progressive cultural critics revised the aims that Addams espoused. Though equally critical of popular amusements like film, comic strips, and cheap fiction as degrading cultural fare, these younger reformers also questioned the appropriateness of the high-cultural traditions that Addams favored for the vibrant American culture they hoped to construct. In an article advocating a "trans-national" American culture, Randolph Bourne argued in 1916 that efforts to assimilate immigrants to Anglo-Saxon traditions of high culture were inadequate. What both native-born Americans and immigrants required instead was the intermingling of English-inspired American high culture with the cultural heritage of the immigrant groups who had transformed America in the previous twenty years, especially southern Europeans and Russian Jews. Bourne did not see pop-

ular culture as offering a fertile ground for such intermingling, however. Immigrants who embraced popular culture exchanged their own traditions for cultural "license," becoming the "flotsam and jetsam of American life, the downward undertow of our civilization with its leering cheapness and falseness of taste and spiritual outlook, the absence of mind and sincere feeling which we see in our slovenly towns, our vapid moving pictures, our popular novels" (Bourne, *Radical Will,* p. 255). Bourne believed that his vision of a revitalized American tradition would happen instead among educated native-born and immigrant youths at American colleges.

Bourne's contemporary and associate, Van Wyck Brooks, took a different approach to the reconciling of American elite culture and twentieth-century conditions. Though he had little more use than Bourne for the forms of popular culture he saw around him, Brooks traced the absence of a meaningful community of culture to a longstanding division between "highbrow" and "lowbrow" in American life. Limited to choices between arcane intellectual traditions and prosaic practical (and often commercial) realities, Brooks thought, Americans failed to fashion cultural forms that could speak to everyday life. However, Brooks saw little hope for such forms in the popular culture around him. His vision of cultural revitalization, like Bourne's, called for critics like himself to construct a "middle plane between vaporous idealism and self-interested practicality" (Blake, *Beloved Community,* p. 119).

Of course, popular commercial entertainments continued to flourish in spite of the consensus of two generations of Progressive reformers that they did not serve the cultural longings of twentieth-century Americans. As many scholars of the 1980s and 1990s argued, popular audiences at the turn of the twentieth century found in dance halls, vaudeville theaters, and cheap movies more diversity of meaning and debate of ideals than reformers saw. Often these venues were welcome respites from the authority of employers and parents, providing a ground upon which young people could construct their own cultural tastes. Though more liberating for some than others (especially young women who found themselves trading sexual favors for entertainment pleasures they could not otherwise afford), they nevertheless represented a zone of self-definition that few reformers and cultural critics appreciated.

One who stood out in this regard in the 1920s was Gilbert Seldes. Seldes took aim at the distinction between highbrow and lowbrow to argue that both traditions of art were vital and meaningful. What critics should decry, he believed, were the bogus arts that appealed to low emotions and jeopardized both great art and what Seldes called the "lively arts." In his pioneering volume, *The Seven Lively Arts* (1924), Seldes praised the brilliance of slapstick film stars like Charlie Chaplin, popular songwriters such as Irving Berlin, comic performers like Fanny Brice, vaudeville artists like Joe Cook, and cartoon strips such as George Herriman's Krazy Kat. He found in these popular cultural forms meaningful connections to "average American life" and distinctive expressions of American experience that devotees of high culture ignored at their peril. Though Seldes regarded himself as a highbrow, he saw in the lively arts a kind of technical mastery in presenting humor and humanity that all audiences should learn to appreciate.

Scholars from the social sciences also tried to respect different levels of culture in the 1920s, but with somewhat less success than Seldes. Inspired by the example of anthropologist Franz Boas and his students, many social scientists turned away from traditional hierarchies of "civilization" and "savagery" to try to understand the cultures of various societies and social groups on their own terms. Social scientific scholars studying American culture followed suit. They went into various American communities as participant observers intending to record dispassionately the lives and tastes they found.

These scholars' own cultural preferences, however, often colored their analyses. One of the most famous of these studies, Robert and Helen Lynd's *Middletown* (1929), a study of working-class and middle-class families in Muncie, Indiana, during the 1920s, offers a good example. Claiming to emulate anthropologists, the Lynds aimed for "a degree of detachment indispensable for clearer vision" of their own society (p. 5). But their study portrayed the cultural changes brought about by the use of radio, movies, automobiles, and other modern leisure conveniences through a lens that made these appear more impersonal and anomic than the community-oriented folkways of the late nineteenth century that they used as a point of comparison. The Lynds thereby reproduced the invidious comparison implicit in many anthropological accounts that drew on "primitive" cultures to pass judgment on the materialism and superficiality of popular American culture.

Still, social scientists provided a language and perspective for more sympathetic assessments of American popular culture in the 1930s. New Deal arts and culture programs mobilized an army of cultural workers to record and preserve the "folk" culture of various American regions. Themselves the children and grandchildren of turn-of-the-twentieth-century working-class immigrants, many of these cultural workers had tastes that had been shaped by commercial entertainment, and their record of American cultural tastes reflected this background. At the same time, these New Deal enthusiasms also spread to commercial entertainment, which began to feature such previously ignored folk traditions as folk songs, blues, and jazz. Though later generations would come to criticize as phony this popularization of the "folk" traditions prized by scholars, the depression era saw a broad critical appreciation of folk and popular traditions as wholesome American cultural fare.

But not all depression-era cultural critics joined in this sympathy. Especially at the beginning of the 1930s, many Communist-inspired critics bemoaned even more sternly than Progressive Era critics the crass commercialism of popular culture in the United States. Other left-leaning émigré intellectuals in New York City celebrated the virtues of avantgarde modernism over the banalities of popular fare. These arguments anticipated the criticism of "mass culture" during the 1940s and 1950s.

FROM MASS CULTURE TO POSTMODERNISM

The depression era's critical enthusiasm for folkways of American popular culture quickly waned. From the late 1930s on, American cultural critics took aim with a vengeance at what they newly defined as "mass culture." In the process, they codified criteria of "genuine" elite culture that succeeding generations would call into question. Beginning in the 1960s, critics and audiences increasingly saw the divisions between elite and popular culture as contrived conventions. As both theorists and practitioners of what came to be known as "postmodernism" challenged earlier cultural categories, they left cultural audiences and scholars alike with the problem of how to understand and use categories like "highbrow" and "lowbrow," "elite" and "popular."

Many cultural critics joined the 1940s and 1950s chorus that attacked the inanities of mass culture. But two essays stand out for their influential definition of the issues at hand. Clement Greenberg's "Avant-Garde and Kitsch," originally published in *Partisan Review* in 1939, wielded the affection that many left-wing émigré intellectuals felt for avant-garde modernism as a cudgel to flail popular culture for its failings. Greenberg asserted that the avant-garde, while increasingly remote from the cultural tastes of even wealthy and cultivated art patrons, was "the only living culture we now have." All other culture was either "academicism"—an overreliance on "old masters" for aesthetic value—or "kitsch." Kitsch comprised all of popular culture and much of mechanically reproduced high culture, too. It was formulaic, mass-produced culture for masses that had no aesthetic sensibilities and were unlikely to acquire them. As such, it threatened to kill all living culture.

Dwight Macdonald expanded on and refined Greenberg's ideas in an essay on "The Theory of Popular Culture," originally published in 1944 in Macdonald's journal, *Politics,* and revised increasingly pessimistically in 1953 and 1960. Macdonald at first saw popular culture as composed of commercial products foisted by cultural entrepreneurs on popular audiences who were, increasingly, deprived of more participatory "folk" traditions. As Macdonald revised his essay, he expressed growing reservations as to whether popular audiences could be redeemed from the corruption of commercialized culture—an early hope that Greenberg had intended to dispel in "Avant-garde and Kitsch." Macdonald, too, began to see mass cultural audiences as hopelessly passive creatures of a mammoth culture industry whose control and manipulation paralleled that of the totalitarian states, which he and other critics had seen as the architects of kitsch in the 1930s. By 1960 he, too, offered modernist high culture as the dim beacon of authentic cultural light in a dark night of formulaic conformity. This argument echoed in cultural criticism the wider concerns about increasingly passive "organization" men and women that academic social scientists were voicing about American life.

Questions remained, however, as to how removed the advocates of modernism were themselves from this conformity, and how formulaic the culture they criticized really was. Greenberg and Macdonald belonged to a last generation of "public intellectuals" or critics writing for a general audience outside academia. Like other intellectual pursuits, high-cultural criticism was being absorbed by ever-growing universities. Here, the vast bureaucratic organizational structures that seemed to the critics to deaden popular culture also routinized intellectual life. Meanwhile, as more late-twentieth-century scholars of midcentury popular cultural forms such as television suggest, the popular culture

of the era was more ironic and self-reflective about its own formulas and themes than elite critics suggested. For example, though many 1950s situation comedies reinforced prevailing standards of suburban domestic life, others suggested something of the variety of domestic experience across class and ethnic divisions, as in the case of the urban, working-class *Honeymooners* and the immigrant *Mama.* Moreover, some show-business versions of the family sitcom such as *I Love Lucy* poked fun at the material culture and the stereotyped gender roles of 1950s family life.

In the 1960s a new generation of activists and artists responded to these developments in both high and popular culture by beginning to blur the boundaries between them. The left-liberal tradition that had nourished much of mid-twentieth-century cultural criticism was revised by a new generation of student activists. Like their predecessors, they criticized the culture industry for producing passivity and unquestioning conformity, but they also turned on the universities where they were supposedly educated in the more robust values of modernist art and criticized them for the same qualities. Meanwhile, architects began to disregard the unity of past academic styles and also to eschew modernist formalism in favor of a pastiche of styles drawn from multiple eras and even from such vernacular sources as Las Vegas and the strip mall. Artists also combined creative technique with everyday popular cultural sources, muddying the boundary between modernist high art and kitsch that previous generations of critics had tried to reinforce.

The result, first in the arts, then in cultural criticism, was the phenomenon called "postmodernism." In place of the modernists' efforts to use popular culture "to bring into sharp relief the line between art and life," according to one commentator, postmodern art and culture "labors under no illusions: we are all deliberately playing, pretending here—get the point?" (Gitlin, "Postmodernism," pp. 349–350). Moreover, the pretense was accompanied by an emotional blankness—not the anxiety of the modern but an ironic sense that all cultural-political possibilities have been tried and found wanting. In particular, the effort to divide high and popular culture was called into question. In criticism this had a liberating effect for some. The skill and art of the popular might be placed alongside the creative technique of high art as the topic for scholarly commentary and cultural education. Others recognized the shift to the postmodern but maintained a critical distance. They identified postmodern culture with a morally questionable new global economy that equated all values, aesthetics, and cultures, robbing them of all distinctive substance in the process.

There remains the question of how useful the critical categories of elite and popular remain for cultural historians in the postmodern age. However questionable and blurred these categories may have become in our own time, and however conventional and constructed we now understand them to have been in the past, they constituted an important language in which audiences and critics understood the social relations implied in distinctions between different cultural forms. By continuing to study them, historians do more than uncover outmoded cultural debates of merely antiquarian interest. They help us to explore the ways in which culture and its differences have afforded ways of talking about vital issues of sameness and distinction within American history. In the process, they challenge us to understand how new cultural forms imply complex relations involving control and exploitation as well as anxiety and hope.

See also **The Fine Arts in Colonial America; The Arts in the Republican Era; Popular Intellectual Movements, 1833–1877; Urban Cultural Institutions; The Popular Arts** *(volume 1);* **Multiculturalism in Theory and Practice** *(volume 2);* **Ethnicity: Early Theories; Ethnicity and Race; Class** *(in this volume); and other articles in this section.*

BIBLIOGRAPHY

Adams, Bluford. *E Pluribus Barnum: The Great Showman and the Making of U.S. Popular Culture.* Minneapolis, Minn., 1997.

Addams, Jane. *The Spirit of Youth and the City Streets.* New York, 1909.

Allen, Robert C. *Horrible Prettiness: Burlesque and American Culture.* Chapel Hill, N.C., 1991.

Blake, Casey Nelson. *Beloved Community: The Cultural Criticism of Randolph Bourne, Van Wyck Brooks, Waldo Frank, and Lewis Mumford.* Chapel Hill, N.C., 1990.

Bourne, Randolph. *The Radical Will: Selected Writings, 1911–1918.* Edited by Olaf Hansen. New York, 1977.

Bushman, Richard L. *The Refinement of America: Persons, Houses, Cities.* New York, 1993.

Denning, Michael. *The Cultural Front: The Laboring of American Culture in the Twentieth Century.* New York, 1996.

Gitlin, Todd. "Postmodernism: Roots and Politics." In *Cultural Politics in Contemporary America.* Edited by Ian Angus and Sut Jhally. New York, 1989.

Gorman, Paul R. *Left Intellectuals and Popular Culture in Twentieth-Century America.* Chapel Hill, N.C., 1996.

Grimsted, David. *Melodrama Unveiled: American Theater and Culture, 1800–1850.* Berkeley, Calif., 1968.

Harris, Neil. *Humbug: The Art of P. T. Barnum.* Boston, 1973.

Huyssen, Andreas. *After the Great Divide: Modernism, Mass Culture, Postmodernism.* Bloomington, Ind., 1986.

Jacoby, Russell. *The Last Intellectuals: American Culture in the Age of Academe.* New York, 1987.

Jameson, Fredric. *Postmodernism; or, The Cultural Logic of Late Capitalism.* Durham, N.C., 1991.

Kammen, Michael G. *The Lively Arts: Gilbert Seldes and the Transformation of Cultural Criticism in the United States.* New York, 1997.

Kasson, John F. *Rudeness and Civility: Manners in Nineteenth-Century Urban America.* New York, 1990.

Kibler, M. Alison. *Rank Ladies: Gender and Cultural Hierarchy in American Vaudeville.* Chapel Hill, N.C., 1999.

Levine, Lawrence. *Highbrow/Lowbrow: The Emergence of Cultural Hierarchy in America.* Cambridge, Mass., 1988.

Lipsitz, George. *Time Passages: Collective Memory and American Popular Culture.* Minneapolis, Minn., 1990.

Lott, Eric. *Love and Theft: Blackface Minstrelsy and the American Working Class.* New York, 1993.

Lynd, Robert S., and Helen Merrell Lynd. *Middletown: A Study in Contemporary American Culture.* New York, 1929.

May, Lary. *Screening Out the Past: The Birth of Mass Culture and the Motion Picture Industry.* Chicago, 1980.

Mukerji, Chandra, and Michael Schudson, eds. *Rethinking Popular Culture: Contemporary Perspectives in Cultural Studies.* Berkeley, Calif., 1991.

Oberdeck, Kathryn J. *The Evangelist and the Impresario: Religion, Entertainment, and Cultural Politics in America, 1884–1914.* Baltimore, 1999.

Peiss, Kathy. *Cheap Amusements: Working Women and Leisure in Turn-of-the-Century New York.* Philadelphia, 1986.

"The Port Huron Statement." In *The New Left: A Documentary History.* Edited by Massimo Teodori. London, 1970.

Schiller, Dan. *Objectivity and the News: The Public and the Rise of Commercial Journalism.* Philadelphia, 1981.

Snyder, Robert W. *The Voice of the City: Vaudeville and Popular Culture in New York.* New York, 1989.

Spigel, Lynn. *Make Room for TV: Television and the Family Ideal in Postwar America.* Chicago, 1992.

Toll, Robert. *Blacking Up: The Minstrel Show in Nineteenth-Century America.* Oxford, 1974.

CULTURE FOR MASS AUDIENCES

D. L. Le Mahieu

Culture for mass audiences in the twentieth century relied upon the marketplace as the decisive arbiter of success, thus circumventing the traditional authority of cultivated elites. In "mass culture," a term that eludes precise definition but usually encompasses most forms of widely distributed information and entertainment, economic factors superseded aesthetic judgment as the primary standard of merit. The culture industry regarded its products more as profitable commodities than embodiments of artistic virtue. Those who marketed mass culture might claim to be guardians of American values, but fundamentally they acted as businessmen pursuing their self-interest in a competitive marketplace.

Yet during the twentieth century the questions of who controlled the marketplace and the cultural implications of such control generated intense controversy. To some, the consumer exercised ultimate sovereignty in an open market. The economic success of the commercialized mass media, for example, hinged upon its ability to entertain a diverse public. Television networks gave the public what it desired, and American capitalism, for all its sins, satisfied the general population. To others, control of entertainment conglomerates such as Time-Warner carried with it enormous power to determine agendas and manipulate audiences. Proprietors exercised sovereignty over the market and imposed their views on the public in a one-way fashion. To still others, neither producer nor consumer reigned supreme. Mass culture evolved through a complex interactive process. Many groups shared responsibility for its content.

SUPPLY AND DEMAND FOR MASS CULTURE

Despite intensive empirical study, much remains uncertain about the structure of demand for mass culture, particularly as it existed in the early twen-tieth century. Sufficient statistical data became available only in the 1930s, and much of this material lacked sophistication. Even if good evidence existed for earlier decades, however, knowledge of the age, sex, class, region, and occupation of the audience for newspapers, films, and music would reveal only part of the story. Participation in a cultural activity could not be equated confidently with acquiescence to its values. Even a sophisticated questionnaire might not excavate the deeper reasons for individual tastes, which often related intimately to notions of personal identity. The "masses" consisted of individuals whose distinctiveness statistical aggregates easily obscured.

Although the evidence explaining demand for mass culture is elusive, evidence regarding supply has been abundant and less intractable. Culture for a mass audience was produced by a relatively limited number of institutions that prospered by practicing economies of scale. The greatest costs were incurred in creating the first copy of a newspaper, master print of a film, or videotape of a television program. For this reason, large companies such as the major film studios of the 1930s exercised a number of advantages over their smaller, more independent competitors. Because they could afford the latest, most efficient technology, larger firms could create a technically superior product at less cost per unit. Bigger companies also enjoyed a more sophisticated division of labor, thus increasing both efficiency and quality. Moreover, they raised more money and diversified their financial risk.

Throughout the twentieth century the political implications of the concentration of power within the culture industries remained a contentious topic. To commentators on the Left—an extraordinarily diverse group—the trend toward monopoly ownership rendered nonsensical any unqualified claims to consumer sovereignty. Some orthodox Marxists equated economic control of the mass media with cultural authority over its audience. These observers replaced the doctrine of consumer sovereignty, where demand generated supply, with the opposing orthodoxy of producer sovereignty, where supply created demand.

IDENTIFYING THE DOMINATORS: CONSUMERS OR PRODUCERS?

Others among the New Left strongly criticized this "economic reductionism." Borrowing their analytic categories from the socialist theoretician Antonio Gramsci and others, they maintained that elites sustained their cultural hegemony, or persuasive power, over society in complex ways, including tolerance of opposing political philosophies and a pious but essentially hollow commitment to liberal-democratic principles. Though in this view producers still remained ultimately sovereign, the general public consented to its own domination and thereby bore some responsibility for its cultural plight.

The arguments of the New Left embodied an important corrective to the naive doctrine of consumer sovereignty. The growing concentration of ownership of the mass media in the twentieth century unquestionably carried with it power to help set cultural agendas, shape tastes, and mold political opinions. Owners of American newspapers, such as "Colonel" McCormick of the *Chicago Tribune,* beginning in 1914, routinely used their newspapers to disseminate their partisan views. There were also, of course, more subtle ways of promoting favored causes or relegating opposing views to the political margins. Clearly, ownership of a major branch of communications carried with it the power to generate favorable publicity for self-serving causes and, often less overtly, for the interests of the dominant social order.

At the same time, significant economic and cultural restraints limited this power. Owners often faced intense competition from within their own medium and from other media. Thomas Edison's attempt to monopolize the American motion picture industry early in the twentieth century was broken, in part, by independents who refused to be excluded from a lucrative market. When these independents themselves gained control of the industry, their dominance, like that of the Motion Picture Patents Company earlier, proved short-lived. Moreover, the economies of scale that gave large enterprises an advantage over their smaller competitors existed in part because the public was often unpredictable in its tastes. In the film, television, and recording industries, owners needed to create their products in quantity, since a remarkably high percentage of movies, television programs, and popular recordings failed to generate a profit. For every hit recording, scores languished unsold. For every successful film, others attracted disappointing audiences. Though film producers often overstated their dependence on the changing tastes of the paying customer, few could portend what films would prove successful. The fickleness of demand limited the powers of supply. Even a complete monopoly could not assure profitable sales of a discretionary cultural item that few wanted to purchase. The doctrine of producer sovereignty, like that of consumer sovereignty, simplified the relationship between producer and consumer.

FEEDBACK AND IDENTIFICATION WITH THE AUDIENCE

Scholars from a variety of disciplines have proposed models that describe the relationship between mass communicators and their audiences in liberal-democratic societies. These models range greatly in complexity. The simplest claimed that messages proceed directly from the media to the public—a variation of the notion of producer sovereignty. The more complicated theories argued in favor of a complex interrelationship between communicators and the audience. These models rejected the view that any single group or factor determined the nature of mass communication. Though the models differed substantially, they shared the notion that mass communication always involves some degree of "feedback." This inelegant and now pervasive term refers, of course, to the way in which a system regulates itself in response to changing conditions. In the study of mass media, the term usually encompassed opinion polls, market surveys, letters, and other means of discovering audience reaction. The communicator employed this information to modify his product in response to changing public demands.

The feedback mechanism of sales and box office receipts was only one means whereby consumers helped shape the content of commercial culture. A more important and less obvious bond between producer and consumer occurred whenever either, or both, identified with the other. On the one hand, producers shaped their products in expectation of audience response. Communicators routinely accommodated their self-serving messages to correspond to public expectations. Newspaper editors instinctively anticipated the views of their intended audience and adjusted their journalism accordingly. The networks created television programs that identified with their targeted public. On the other hand, audiences also pursued their cultural self-interest in the marketplace. The economic power of the culture industry remained in part contingent upon the approval of the audience it sought to inform and amuse. Far from dictating the cultural preferences of their public, producers needed to accommodate themselves to the tastes of a diverse audience.

Many within the mass media privately expressed contempt for the general public. Hollywood insiders, in particular, experienced the greed and cynicism which permeated the "democratic art." It might therefore seem naive to argue that media bosses identified strongly with their public. Yet it is crucial to distinguish between private opinions and professional roles. As private individuals, journalists, screenwriters, composers, and other fabricators of mass culture might indeed have been cynical about their craft and contemptuous of the public. As professional communicators, however, these same people could not afford to alienate their audience. The creators of the media needed the goodwill of the public to survive. They needed to engage their audience. Private attitudes could not be allowed to cloud professional responsibilities.

Consumers also played a complex role in the process of mass communication. As audience members in a cinema, for example, they willingly suspended disbelief in order to be entertained. They accepted fantasies which, as private individuals, they rejected in their daily lives. Men and women who recognized life to be tragic often demanded happy endings as audience members. Individuals who knew evil could prevail in actual circumstances often demanded moral order to be restored in films and television programs. Professional communicators responded to these desires. Although they understood only superficially the actual individuals who constituted their targeted public, they knew a great deal about the expectations of audiences. In mass culture, it could be argued, the key relationship was often that between the "communicator" and the "audience member," not between the two private individuals who happened to be filling those roles.

FORMULAS FOR TARGETING A MASS AUDIENCE

By identifying pragmatically with their public, and then measuring success by actual sales, culture for a mass audience evolved through a process of trial and error. In general, the culture industry played it safe. It adopted techniques that proved successful over time. Early in the twentieth century, for example, film producers borrowed from the literary formulas of nineteenth-century popular culture and adapted them to a new medium. The Western film drew from a popular literary tradition that began with James Fenimore Cooper and included the dime novels of the late nineteenth century. Hollywood producers relied upon a dependable audience for the simple adventure stories of the early Western films. When it sought a larger audience, however, Hollywood needed to alter the formula to anticipate the demands of a more diverse public. Once a new variation became successful, imitators quickly exhausted the market until yet another departure invigorated old themes and stereotypical characters. This preference for refurbishing established formulas rather than experimenting with new genres exasperated critics, but Hollywood claimed it could not afford radical innovation.

The "human interest story" also engaged a mass audience by borrowing liberally from nineteenth-century traditions. Easy to recognize but hard to define, the human interest story gained prominence in the American "penny press" that emerged in the 1830s. The *New York Sun* (1833), *New York Evening Transcript* (1833), and *New York Herald* (1835) rapidly increased their circulations by filling their pages with reports of crime, animal stories, anecdotes about bizarre occurrences, and other entertaining bits of information. In the Yellow Press of the late nineteenth century, Joseph Pulitzer and William Randolph Hearst specialized in exposing corruption among the rich and powerful. Their newspapers became self-proclaimed champions of populist causes.

Human interest stories engaged their audience on a number of levels. First, by extending the definition of news beyond its customary preoccupations with politics and business, such stories underscored the significance of commonplace events. Though the general population could become intensely involved with such issues as peace and war, politics remained the preserve of a relatively small group, often remote from the daily life of most citizens. Then too, although economic news might retain its objective importance, a vast majority of people lacked the disposable income to be concerned with fluctuating business fortunes. Human interest stories permitted newspapers to reflect a broader mosaic of American society. News no longer concentrated exclusively on the public lives of powerful elites. The everyday life of the common man acquired more importance. Human interest stories engaged their audience because they allowed a large public to read about a world they recognized.

Second, human interest stories dignified common existence by transforming it into a form of literature. On any given day, journalists detailed events from which they created "stories." These stories often imitated the narrative conventions of popular literature. Newspapers became filled with mysteries of unsolved robberies, adventure stories of heroic aviators, and romances about devotion, sacrifice, and love. Journalists often portrayed the protagonists of these dramas stereotypically. Narratives that involved sudden changes in wealth and status proved especially attractive.

Human interest stories engaged their readers because they drew upon the emotions of private life. Journalists presented recognizable people undergoing difficult experiences that required no special expertise to grasp. It was not difficult to understand why a mother grieved over the loss of a son, or how an impoverished bank teller brought himself to ruin by embezzling funds. Nor was it difficult to comprehend the triumph of the first flight over the Atlantic or the grim irony of a zookeeper trapping himself in a cage of wild animals. "The fundamental element of human interest," Helen McGill Hughes wrote in her pioneering study of the subject, "is a curiosity to know what it is like to undergo those common personal crises and visitations of good and bad luck . . . suffered by persons who are shown to have essentially one's own nature. In the end, human interest approaches the interest every man has in himself." When critics accused the journalists of triviality, they underestimated how even minor incidents aroused important human emotions. A small girl trapped in an abandoned well in 1987 gained the sympathy of an entire nation. Human interest stories invited vicarious participation in distant events. They provided endless variations on the constant themes of human existence.

THE EXPANSION OF THE CULTURE INDUSTRY

The human interest story, like the use of formulaic plots in the cinema, were both examples of cultural conservatism engendered by a preoccupation with commercial success. At the same time, however, the mass media developed more novel means of anticipating and responding to the demands of a large public. Daily newspapers learned to target their audience by gender. To interest their male readership,

editors expanded their coverage of sports, devoting a whole new section to college and professional athletics. At about the same time, newspaper proprietors began to recognize the purchasing power of women, who often controlled the budgets of family households. Newspapers and display advertising became intricately linked, and the fortunes of modern display advertising rose with those of the popular daily press. By providing stories and features specifically directed toward females, the popular daily press gave women a voice in a medium previously dominated by men. This recognition meant that the notion of "news" underwent yet another redefinition. Like the human interest story, the woman's page undermined the orthodox view that only politics and business mattered. For different reasons, both broadened the scope of inquiry to include the everyday lives of average individuals. Then too, the woman's page contributed to the increasing social homogenization of the modern era. The attention that the popular daily press devoted to fashion, for example, meant that a larger portion of the community might participate in an area of social life previously restricted by income and class. The notion of fashion itself became less elitist. Finally, and perhaps most important, the woman's page succeeded because it spoke to the perceived needs of a large section of the population. It offered practical guidance and romantic diversion. It sought to mold fashions, while at the same time reflecting the tastes of its diverse audience. The woman's page did not deliver revolutionary prescriptions for the emergence of women from their subordinate position in American society. What the woman's page did provide was a forum, a platform, a place, where the self-esteem of women might be enhanced.

Perhaps most important, the rapidly expanding culture industry in the early twentieth century discovered a seminal paradox of mass communication. As new technologies helped create audiences of phenomenal size, the most effective strategy of communication was personal, intimate, and subjective. The mass media often created strong bonds between a communicator and millions of individual consumers. In daily newspapers, late-twentieth-century columnists such as Anna Quindlen of the *New York Times* and Bob Greene of the *Chicago Tribune* approached readers as if they were valued acquaintances. Writers brought the public into their confidence, often revealing details about themselves or others usually confided only among close friends. In cinema, movie moguls discovered that certain actors and actresses engendered intense loyalty among the general public. For example, John

Wayne remained a popular film star among audiences from the 1930s through the 1970s. As late as 1995, he was still ranked first in a poll that asked a thousand Americans "Who is your favorite star?" His film persona, though sharply controversial during the Vietnam War, helped shape a generation of American men. Stars transcended the fictional roles that initially defined them and became international celebrities. In cinema, the press, and eventually television, audiences often showed as much interest in the messenger as they did in the message. The fame of movie stars dwarfed in scope and intensity that of their predecessors in other arts during the nineteenth century. The reputation of actors and actresses from the nineteenth-century theater, for example, rarely extended beyond national boundaries. The cinema, with its capacity to record a performance on film, replicated it endlessly and distributed it around the world, creating a much more potent form of celebrity. Movie stars helped redefine the meaning of fame. A star's audience identified closely with the patiently crafted figure on the screen. It was the persona they appreciated. They expressed great curiosity, but remained apart, save in their fantasies, from the person of wealth and fame. The emotional identification that existed between a creator of commercial culture and a member of the public created a new elite of heroes, whose success distanced them from their audience. Though mass communication often succeeded best when it emphasized the subjective and the personal, such intimacy remained a compelling, convenient fiction.

Unlike the elites who formed the subjects of earlier gossip columns, movie stars exercised no real political power over their admirers. They were a status group separate from the traditional hierarchies of American life. Perhaps in this absence of threatening authority lay their accessibility and appeal. Then too, movie stars often emerged from the humblest of backgrounds, exhibiting an upward mobility that movie publicists never ceased to emphasize. For most people, it was easier to imagine becoming a movie star than a captain of industry. Yet realistic ambitions may not have been the key to a star's appeal. Stars embodied fantasies of youth, sex, beauty, wealth, and fame. They lived in fabulous houses, commanded huge salaries, and spent enormous sums entertaining themselves. Young and beautiful, they attracted publicity when they worked, played, married, divorced, and died.

As personalities whose business involved calling attention to themselves, movie stars faced a problem not shared by most other celebrities. It was as fictional characters on the screen that they first attracted wide attention. Fame often depended upon a screen persona that may not have corresponded to their actual personalities. This potential conflict between their screen roles and their authentic character aroused intense curiosity. Audiences felt especially betrayed when the disparity between the persona and the actual person became too great. Scandal ruined the career of the jovial Fatty Arbuckle in the early 1920s, and Ingrid Bergman's career suffered in the late 1940s when her personal romantic entanglements clashed with her virtuous screen persona. Gossip about the stars in newspapers, magazines, and television programs represented an ongoing but highly mediated attempt to expose the relationship between an individual and, quite literally, an image.

MEASURES OF THE CULTURAL STANDARD

When for their own economic benefit the culture industry identified with the preferences of its audience, it created an enormously popular and increasingly pervasive standard of cultural judgment. Culture for a mass audience was at once both materialist and egalitarian. It was materialist because the profit motive lay at its heart. The producers of commercial culture were in the business of providing entertainment and information. As businessmen, they tried to minimize their risk. Both the film and newspaper industries sought to concentrate their power and to practice economies of scale. Both faced competition not only from within their own industries, but from other media as well. Commercial culture served the self-interest of its producers, but it also served the self-determined interests of the audience who supported it with their pocketbooks. For shrewd business reasons, the culture industry could not afford to alienate its intended public. It could not afford to treat them like subordinates or "masses."

American intellectuals responded to mass culture with a wide range of emotions, prejudices, and opinions. Initially many reacted with studied indifference. The newer forms of communication, so pervasive among the lower classes, often took time to penetrate refined sensibilities. To some, the cinema in the early twentieth century, for example, was not only silent but invisible. Others, more alert to the potential dangers of these new technologies, responded with hostility to the leveling tendencies of a culture based upon market forces. These critics, pessimists drawn from both sides of the political spectrum, believed in the fundamental incompatibility of equality and excellence. Still others, while deeply suspicious of commercialism, welcomed the newer media as future liberators of a poorly educated public. Astonished by the capacity of mass media to reach an enormous public, they sought to uplift tastes. Among all these groups, attitudes often changed over time. Cynics occasionally came to acknowledge the aesthetic possibilities of a technically improving medium, while enthusiasts became disillusioned with audiences recalcitrant to the pleasures of self-improvement. Moreover, many intellectuals held contradictory or unconsciously ambivalent views about mass culture.

For all the differences among them, however, the cultivated elites shared a fundamental allegiance to the notion of cultural hierarchy. Arguments about the nature and intricate ordering of this hierarchy preoccupied discourse, both formal and informal, heated and urbane, in a number of disciplines, but few intellectuals challenged the centrality of such a concept. Standards existed and needed to be maintained. These standards, often asserted to be objective realities, were believed to serve as impersonal measures for evaluating the quality of a single performance, collected works, or individuals themselves. Like artistic creation, aesthetic judgment demanded a combination of talent, training, discrimination, and taste. Since these qualities were not universally shared, those who possessed them, such as critics and creators, constituted an elite, though the precise composition of this elite remained another contentious topic. Sometimes, as with an avant-garde, it was self-declared, while in other cases it became identified by more formal, institutionalized mechanisms.

This notion of cultural hierarchy embodied within it a spatial metaphor of crucial significance for understanding one of the fundamental differences between commercial and elite culture. Elite culture conceptualized, and then usually treated as concrete, hierarchies in which, according to the metaphor, vertical distance separated high and low. These vertical distances could not be measured in any literal sense, of course, but they did help serve figuratively to distinguish one cultural product from another. Critics measured the value of a work by its distance, either near or far, from implicit cultural standards. They sought to separate themselves, both in their imaginations and practical life, from anything that compromised or rejected those standards. Culture for a mass audience sought to max-

imize its audience by collapsing cultural distances. Elite culture measured itself by the distances it constantly reaffirmed.

In the 1950s and 1960s, Marshall McLuhan challenged the derisive attitude of most intellectuals to mass communications. Borrowing from his Canadian colleague Harold Innis and others, McLuhan argued that the introduction of any new technology of communication vitally altered the configuration of sense data whereby humans come to know each other and the outside world. To McLuhan, the printing press radically transformed Western thought and society. Johannes Gutenberg initiated a technology that converted words into detached, uniform, infinitely repeatable images that demanded a trained visual sense for interpretation. By forcing knowledge into the linear and sequential segments of words on a page, the printing press changed communication into a solitary, private experience. The rise of mass media in the twentieth century, however, re-created an environment of communications not unlike that of primitive societies. To McLuhan, the capacity to transmit sight and sound electronically restored the ability of audiences to grasp messages as a whole, and not from a linear, fixed point of view. The mass media resurrected the sensual richness of oral communication. Still, the notion that the introduction of new technologies of communication helped transform human consciousness often met with serious reservations. Critics such as Elizabeth Eisenstein recoiled from the reductive arguments of technological determinism. They pointed out that innovative techniques prospered only in certain social contexts, and they questioned any model that elevated inanimate objects into primary agents of historical change. Such caution avoided mechanistic historical interpretations in which a separate entity called "technology" acted independently upon another phenomenon, "culture." More sophisticated analyses emphasized the continuities and adaptations between generations of technology.

In the late twentieth century, the culture of postmodernism represented an even more decisive liquidation of traditional cultural hierarchies. A pervasive term that proves difficult to define precisely, postmodernism embodied, in part, an embrace of mass culture. Generations of intellectuals born after World War II found the mass media and especially television less threatening than their predecessors warned. A new generation celebrated what their elders scorned. Ironic and self-reflexive, postmodernist theory provoked a reaction among neoconservatives who reasserted the traditional hierarchies, in part because the complex discourses of "cultural studies" involved numbing obscurities and mystifications. Still, if postmodernism represented a more thorough integration of American intellectuals into mass media, culture for a mass audience existed within a context of great social diversity as a shared experience that vaulted boundaries without eliminating them. In the twentieth century, youth carved out its own culture separate from that of its elders. Generational affiliation sometimes superseded social allegiance as a decisive constituent of taste. And of course there were always members of the general public whose cultural tastes and social allegiances confounded fallible sociological catego-

ries. Class, region, generation, and personal idiosyncrasy each contributed to a complex national mosaic. Culture for a mass audience might be experienced differently by a wide variety of groups around the globe and yet still retain its value as mutually acknowledged frame of reference. Such unity within the diversity of an increasingly integrated global economic system could not be translated into agreement on divisive issues. Mass culture often appealed to values and emotions that transcended the controversies of the moment. As its technologies evolved, creating new opportunities for collective experience, culture for mass audience never satisfied everyone but within a pluralistic system it linked individuals of widely divergent backgrounds.

See also **Urban Cultural Institutions; The Popular Arts; The Athlete as Cultural Icon** *(volume 1);* **The Culture of Self-Improvement; The World According to Hollywood; Popular Culture in the Public Arena** *(volume 2);* **Books; Journalism; Film; Photography; Television; Radio; Advertising; Public Murals; Music** *(in this volume); and other articles in this section.*

BIBLIOGRAPHY

Abercrombie, Nicholas, Stephen Hill, and Bryan S. Turner. *The Dominant Ideology Thesis.* London, 1980.

Baughman, James L. *The Republic of Mass Culture: Journalism, Filmmaking, and Broadcasting in America since 1941.* Baltimore, 1992.

Cawelti, John G. *Adventure, Mystery, and Romance: Formula Stories as Art and Popular Culture.* Chicago, 1976.

Cross, Gary. *Time and Money: The Making of Consumer Culture.* London, 1993.

Czitrom, Daniel J. *Media and the American Mind: From Morse to McLuhan.* Chapel Hill, N.C., 1982.

Dyer, Richard. *Stars.* London, 1979.

Grossberg, Lawrence, Cary Nelson, and Paula A. Treichler, eds. *Cultural Studies.* New York, 1992.

Hughes, Helen MacGill. *News and the Human Interest Story.* Chicago, 1940.

Jameson, Fredric. *Postmodernism; or, The Cultural Logic of Late Capitalism.* Durham, N.C., 1991.

Lears, Jackson. *Fables of Abundance: A Cultural History of Advertising in America.* New York, 1994.

McLuhan, Marshall. *Understanding Media: The Extensions of Man.* New York, 1964.

Mannheim, Karl. *Essays on the Sociology of Culture.* London, 1956.

Marchand, Roland. *Advertising the American Dream: Making Way for Modernity, 1920–1940.* Berkeley, Calif., 1985.

Schudson, Michael. *Discovering the News: A Social History of American Newspapers.* New York, 1978.

Shils, Edward. *The Intellectuals and the Powers, and Other Essays.* Chicago, 1972.

Sklar, Robert. *Movie-Made America: A Cultural History of American Movies.* New York, 1975.

Vogel, Harold L. *Entertainment Industry Economics: A Guide for Financial Analysis.* 2d ed. Cambridge, U.K., and New York, 1990.

Williams, Raymond. *Keywords: A Vocabulary of Culture and Society.* New York: 1976.

Wills, Gary. *John Wayne's America: The Politics of Celebrity.* New York, 1997.

THE AMERICAN UNIVERSITY

Roger L. Geiger

The university is, above all, a place for the creation, cultivation, and dissemination of knowledge. It has always, implicitly or explicitly, made a special claim of autonomy in order that those tasks could be fulfilled in an unfettered and undistorted manner. Well before the United States had universities in the modern sense, its institutions of higher learning paid obeisance to this ideal.

Thus, universities are chiefly concerned with knowledge—in its myriad forms and uses. While all of this activity might in theory pertain to the intellectual life of the nation, intellectual history perforce prospects a smaller territory. Surveying the compass of university knowledge, four ideal-typical functions stand out: (1) curricular knowledge—what is taught to students in the classroom—is intended to foster cognitive skills, knowledge of the world, and/or general intellectual development; (2) specialized academic knowledge aims to contribute to the knowledge base of an academic subject and is directed initially at current and apprentice experts who alone comprehend the field (as with scientific research); (3) professional knowledge may be equally specialized and esoteric, but ultimately, however indirectly, it pertains to the realm of practice; and (4) university knowledge has an interface with ideas that matter in some respect to the rest of society. Here, universities—and their collegiate predecessors—become relevant to intellectual history.

Such an interface can cover a variety of interactions. Ideas developed in universities, for example, may initiate important currents of thought among the public. Ideas originating outside the university may tempt academic mediators to ponder implications for academic and popular understanding. And university knowledge is often reactive, offering theoretical explanations for natural or social phenomena. An intellectual history of the university ideally would ascertain the independent impact of universities, other things being equal, on American intellectual life. Since no such history has yet been written, this essay attempts a reconnaissance to identify the materials that might illuminate the interplay of universities and ideas.

BEFORE UNIVERSITIES

During the 1600s and 1700s, higher education was inescapably linked with religion. The Puritans who settled Massachusetts Bay Colony in the 1630s, "dreading to leave an illiterate Ministry to the Churches, when our present Ministers shall lie in the Dust," founded a college "to advance *Learning* and perpetuate it to Posterity" (emphasis in original). Harvard College was chartered in 1636 and, after one aborted start, began teaching regularly in 1640. Like the Oxbridge colleges it hoped to emulate, it sought to convey liberal learning. Most of its liberally educated graduates subsequently studied for the ministry. Its library, consisting largely of theological volumes, served many of those aspiring clerics, but the college itself made little contribution to the doctrines of Calvinism. Rather, a group of far more influential magistrates and ministers assured doctrinal conformity as overseers of the college itself. In the course of the seventeenth century Harvard actually diminished in intellectual stature, ultimately being unable to secure a full-time president.

The fortunes of the college were reversed, according to the historian Samuel Eliot Morison, during the presidency of John Leverett (1708–1724). As Puritan Calvinism fragmented, Leverett placed Harvard solidly within the liberal tradition. Leverett's policies were reinforced by the creation of a professorship in divinity bestowed upon the college by the English Baptist Thomas Hollis in 1721. The occupants of this chair were in the forefront of a more rational and tolerant interpretation of Christianity. A second Hollis professorship in mathematics and natural philosophy in 1726 provided for another resident intellectual. Harvard at this juncture was already an institution of appreciable learning, even while Virginia's College of William and Mary (founded in 1693) and Connecticut's Yale College (founded in 1701) were in a rudimentary state.

The American colonies were essentially provincial outposts of European, mainly English, culture. For the first half of the eighteenth century, the colleges were deeply invested in the culture of Calvinism. In the 1740s, the Great Awakening of evangelical fervor, which largely emanated from England and Scotland, caused the greatest intellectual upheaval of this era. Yale took the lead in repulsing this threat to the unity of learning and orthodox piety.

By midcentury, the colleges were just beginning to assimilate the most momentous intellectual movement of the era—the Enlightenment. An Enlightenment preference for nonsectarian institutions played an important role in the founding of new colleges in New York (1754) and Philadelphia (1755). William Livingston's campaign against a purely Anglican institution made King's College more ecumenical, and William Smith's pamphlet describing a secular, utopian College of Mirania won him an appointment to the nonsectarian College and Academy of Philadelphia.

Nevertheless, the quintessential American intellectual was the self-educated Benjamin Franklin, who as a young man had nothing but scorn for the colleges. In New England, the most learned individuals still pursued careers in the pulpit. Only after long service as ministers did those like Samuel Johnson uneasily assume the presidency of the new King's College (1754–1763) or Jonathan Edwards reluctantly accept a (fatal) call to the College of New Jersey (1757–1758) or Ezra Stiles allow himself to be persuaded to lead Yale (1778–1795). Outside of New England, the colleges relied chiefly upon immigrants educated in England or Scotland. This was true for William and Mary, Philadelphia, King's College after Johnson's appointment, and the College of New Jersey (now Princeton University).

The College of New Jersey made a singular contribution to the intellectual life of the colonies by bringing the Presbyterian minister John Witherspoon from Scotland to be its president (1768–1794). His inaugural address, "The Unity of Piety and Science," signaled the nexus of Enlightenment rationalism and evangelical religion, conjoined in the "common sense moral philosophy" Witherspoon brought over from Scotland. More than any other college, the College of New Jersey embodied what the historian Henry May called the Moderate Enlightenment in America. Witherspoon not only expanded the teaching of science in the college, but he instilled the values underlying the cause of American independence. The only clergyman to sign the Declaration of Independence, his college trained a generation of political leaders for the new nation.

On the eve of the American Revolution, the College of New Jersey set a standard for assimilating the new learning that other colleges soon followed. The intellectual synthesis of reason, revelation, and moral earnestness harmonized with the dominant notions of philosophy, religion, and politics held by gentlemen of this era. The new ideas were no small cause of what Ezra Stiles called "college enthusiasm" throughout the colonies. They also shaped the beliefs of the Founding Fathers.

THE UNIVERSITY IMPULSE

The years from the American Revolution to early in the nineteenth century were the zenith of the American Enlightenment and the nadir of organized religion. Both developments had implications for the colleges. Despite their status as inherently Christian institutions, they became decidedly more secular in outlook and nondenominational in spirit. Nonministers even presided over several campuses. In curricular offerings, both rhetoric and experiment followed familiar Enlightenment themes: incorporation of more science, some effort to include the practical and the professional, the teaching of modern languages, including English, and civic education to shape the citizens of the new republic. All told, these impulses led Americans to envision a new form for higher education—the republican university.

Such universities were conceived as essentially public institutions. The Colleges of Philadelphia and William and Mary were taken over by their respective states at the start of the American Revolution. Harvard was reconstituted as a university in the Massachusetts constitution of 1780 and added a medical school as well. Columbia (previously King's College) was resuscitated as a part of the University of the State of New York. And North Carolina, Georgia, Maryland, and Vermont incorporated universities into the structure of the state. Columbia actually came closest to the republican ideal when a state grant allowed it to appoint professors in four new subjects (law, chemistry, Hebrew, and French). Their lectures, however, were not integrated with the required curriculum. Ignored by students, they were dropped by the college when the funds ran out.

As with many Enlightenment projects, aspirations far exceeded realistic possibilities for republican universities. By the first decade of the nineteenth century, they appeared to have failed miserably. These years, in fact, witnessed perhaps the most difficult ordeal of American higher education. In a relatively impoverished new nation, few could afford prolonged schooling, especially away from home. The states, for their part, lacked currency to support universities, and democratic politicians endeavored to keep what little funds were available from these "aristocratic" institutions. The state of preparatory schooling was more woeful than the colleges, causing many students to arrive quite young or ill prepared. The colleges could afford few professors, and even fewer individuals possessed the requisite learning for such positions. Growing student unruliness further discouraged intellectual life; when colleges attempted to tighten discipline, students often rioted. The Reverend Samuel Miller accurately described this sorry state in *Brief Retrospect of the Eighteenth Century* (1803): the colleges were "filled with *children*" and plagued with "defective plans and means of instruction" (emphasis in original). Due to "inadequate funds," "professors are few in number" and could convey "but very superficial knowledge."

In this parlous condition, the colleges found themselves bracketed by conflicting ideological tempests. Enlightenment thought appeared to have been appropriated by revolutionaries in France and radical sympathizers in America—like the political pamphleteer Thomas Paine, whose *Age of Reason* (1794) included a scathing attack on the Bible. At the other extreme, the emotional evangelicalism of the Second Great Awakening again seemed to imperil the moderate Calvinism of Presbyterian and Congregational colleges. The best available defense on both these fronts lay with the common sense philosophy. Refined since Witherspoon's day, it rationalized the natural order revealed by science, the moral order perceived by the human conscience, and the theological order upheld by Calvinism. Entrenched in the colleges and taught to every senior as moral philosophy, these shallow doctrines were appropriately labeled by Henry May as the final, didactic phase of the Enlightenment in America.

The displacement of the expansive republican outlook by an inward focus on pedagogy was accomplished most completely by president Timothy Dwight at Yale (1795–1817). From the chaotic state of the postrevolutionary curriculum Dwight fashioned a credible classical course, and he imposed order on boisterous students as well. His direct heirs immortalized this system in the famous *Yale Report* of 1828 as providing "the *discipline* and the *furniture* of the mind." But while this report epitomized the curricular focus of early-nineteenth-century colleges, the institution that produced it was at the same time a leader in science and theology. The former was represented in America's first regular scientific journal, Benjamin Silliman's *American Journal of Science;* the latter was ensconced in the Yale Divinity School.

Perhaps the most remarkable academic advance in the bleak first quarter of the nineteenth century was the founding of schools or seminaries of theology, both linked with and independent from colleges. The first of these schools were formed in repudiation of the colleges. Orthodox Calvinists of eastern Massachusetts reacted to the entrenched liberalism of Harvard by launching the Andover Theological Seminary in 1807. Presbyterians then countered the apparent waning of piety at the College of New Jersey by establishing the Princeton Theological Seminary (1812), next to but not part of the college. Soon, Yale and Harvard opened their own theological departments (1819 and 1822). By 1825 more than twenty theological seminaries had been founded. Although they formalized the former practice of postgraduate ministerial training, the seminaries greatly advanced this tradition. Scholars have called them the first graduate schools. In fact, at least for their professors, they permitted the kind of serious intellectual activity that was virtually precluded in the colleges. For students, however, they were chiefly a place to acquire professional skills. They prepared thousands of students for the pulpit in an atmosphere at once serious and scholarly. In addition, most antebellum professors outside of science studied at least some time in a seminary.

During the first quarter of the nineteenth century only one American university explicitly aspired to be a fount of intellectual life. The "university at Cambridge," as Harvard then called itself, did not make this effort alone, but rather as part of a larger movement within Greater Boston society. When the Hollis professorship of divinity and the university presidency were both captured by Unitarians, Harvard became aligned with a liberal group of area ministers and professionals. Dedicated to advancing "literature" in Boston and the new republic, they published a journal, the *Monthly Anthology,* and were instrumental in establishing the Boston Athenaeum in 1807. When one of their number, John Thornton Kirkland, became president of Harvard in 1810, the university was irrevocably associated

Andover Theological Seminary. Though formed in response to liberalism at Harvard, Andover merged with Harvard's Divinity School in 1908, a partnership that would last until 1931. In 1965 Andover merged with Newton Baptist Institute to become the Andover Newton Theological School. LIBRARY OF CONGRESS

with the Boston Brahmins—a class that combined mercantile wealth and intellectual accomplishment.

Kirkland envisioned the university as "the most efficacious means to . . . support . . . a few men of genius in the pursuit of letters." In 1820 private gifts permitted Harvard to employ ten professors, far surpassing any other American college. Kirkland also sponsored European studies for four young men to prepare them for this role. Upon their return, however, all became demoralized by the burdens of college pedagogy. Only George Ticknor endured (until 1835) as a professor and scholar of European literature. The university was not yet able to institutionalize the pursuit of letters, but with its wealth and patronage it did in fact nurture a few men of genius who were both academics and intellectuals. Charles Eliot Norton perhaps epitomized this type. Harvard's first professor of Fine Arts, Norton also edited the *North American Review* and founded the American schools of classical studies in Rome and Athens. Harvard served as an intellectual center for the Boston Brahmins well before it be-

came an effective center for advanced academic training.

Intellectual leadership of a different sort emerged from South Carolina College during the presidency of Thomas Cooper (1820–1834). An expatriate Englishman of wide learning but dogmatic views, Cooper legitimized the convictions of the state's dominant planter class. An extreme partisan of state's rights, he helped to foment the nullification controversy from 1832 to 1833, which foreshadowed secession of the states from the Union. Cooper surrounded himself with teachers of similar views. Thus, his strident doctrines were well instilled into graduates of South Carolina College, who carried them throughout the Deep South.

It is difficult to identify a similar intellectual impact for the multitude of colleges that dotted the Midwest. Oberlin may come closest. An evangelical community, it spawned a college (1833) and theological seminary (1835), and put into practice radical notions of opening education to women and African Americans. The famous evangelist Charles

Grandison Finney was long associated with the college as pastor, professor, and president, but Oberlin seems largely to have served as a base for his national evangelical efforts.

Somewhat later, the president Henry Tappan (1852–1863) sought to make the University of Michigan into a center of advanced learning. His effort achieved considerable internal progress, raising the institution to be the foremost public university outside of the South. But this accomplishment inspired more resentment than intellectual resonance among citizens of the state. Tappan was ultimately fired by hostile regents in what amounted to a coup.

The colleges of the mid-nineteenth century were on the cutting edge of few intellectual currents. Perhaps only in the serious study of the classics, especially Greek, did they offer a unique contribution. Seminal minds of this era were more likely to eschew the stultifying collegiate regime. The Transcendentalist Ralph Waldo Emerson, for example, considered both colleges and the theological schools to be inimical to the "American scholar." The leading American scientists were only intermittently connected with higher education. The emergence of "scientific schools" at Yale and Harvard tipped the balance slightly, offering a peripheral place for a limited amount of scientific investigation and teaching. Far from the avant-garde, the colleges were actually near the mainstream of American intellectual life.

Higher education in the middle decades of the nineteenth century still purveyed the worldview of moderate, evangelical Protestantism that was shared by the majority of educated Americans. A direct descendent of the common sense moral philosophy, it perceived unity among the realms of mind, nature, and spirit. As the most widely used text for the senior course in moral philosophy stated, "The truths of revealed religion harmonize perfectly with those of natural religion" (emphasis in original). These truths were not merely academic; they were repeatedly presented to adult audiences through sermons, lectures, pamphlets, and other popular writings of college faculty. They also required interpretation and emendations to account for new and perplexing facts about the natural world. Nowhere was this task pursued more systematically than at Yale, where the "New Haven scholars" combined rigorous scholarship with the conviction that greater knowledge would illuminate divine truth. Their endeavor, according to the scholar Louise L. Stevenson, reveals that the defenders of the collegiate order were neither reactionaries nor obscur-

antists. Rather, they were intellectual craftsmen of considerable skill who were, in effect, finishing the upper stories of a building whose foundation had already begun to crumble.

TOWARD THE MODERN AMERICAN UNIVERSITY

During the last third of the nineteenth century the moral and religious underpinnings of American higher education rapidly collapsed. In an academic revolution of unprecedented scope, the rise of the academic disciplines transformed the knowledge base of higher education. This revolution was accompanied by an extended debate about the appropriate nature and structure of this new constellation of ideas and tasks.

The unified worldview of the common sense philosophy and natural theology found itself increasingly on the defensive not only against inconvenient geological discoveries but also against the new biblical criticism based on philology and archaeology. However, the English naturalist Charles Darwin's *Origin of Species* (1859) symbolically and substantively forced the issue. Academic opinion was divided among scientific supporters of evolution, those who rejected it on biblical grounds, and large numbers of academics who still sought an increasingly elusive reconciliation. A consensus of sorts eventually emerged: science and religion each in its own sphere represented separate pathways to different forms of truth. But religious truth in this scheme could hardly be represented by the many dogmas of the different denominations. Rather, it ought to be found in a nonsectarian, scientific approach to religion. Such an approach, however, offered little succor to the faithful and appeared quite irrelevant to those seeking scientific truth. By the end of the century, as the education historian Julie A. Reuben has explained, no moral or religious foundation remained as an underpinning of academic knowledge. This intellectual development was but one facet of the larger academic revolution.

American acquaintance with German science, mostly in humanistic fields, dated from early in the nineteenth century. By midcentury the achievements of German science were drawing American students to German universities and spawning wistful dreams of emulation. American science was hampered by an association in the popular mind with utilitarian ends and by the curricular and pedagogical constriction of the classical college course. The Morrill Act of 1862, which provided land grants to the states to support colleges teaching agriculture and the mechanic arts, touched off a national debate on the most effective means to teach and discover "useful knowledge." The educator Daniel Coit Gilman promoted the fledgling land-grant colleges as "national schools of science," much like his own scientific school at Yale. But politics and the utilitarian sentiments oriented almost all these institutions, at least initially, toward agriculture and the mechanic arts. In the following decade Gilman received another chance to realize his ideal. As founding president of the Johns Hopkins University (1875–1901), he consciously set out to create an American institution dedicated solely to the advancement of academic knowledge.

Although it had a small undergraduate college, Johns Hopkins was explicitly devoted to graduate education and faculty scholarship. Both of these contributions accelerated the inchoate academic revolution. Ph.D.s graduated by Hopkins quickly carried this spirit to other universities. They and the Hopkins faculty also took the lead in organizing the academic disciplines. From 1880 to 1905 all of the major disciplines established professional societies and national journals. The foremost scholars and scientists were rewarded with senior appointments at major universities, and they in turn enforced rigorous standards for knowledge in their fields. A mutually reinforcing system emerged among institutions—later called research universities—disciplines, and academic research.

This academic revolution had numerous dimensions. Academic scholarship was greatly enlarged by the faculty appointments of Charles W. Eliot (1869–1909) at Harvard; by the audacious ambition of William Rainey Harper (1891–1906) in recruiting faculty to the new University of Chicago; and by the expansion of Columbia College into a large university under Seth Low (1890–1901). Other major universities, public and private, were swept along: either they would try to emulate the leaders in building disciplinary knowledge or be relegated to the status of follower. Eliot at Harvard was the first to bring the new curriculum to undergraduates by permitting the free election of courses. Students could now enroll in courses of their own choosing, and, more momentous for the growth of disciplines, professors had the opportunity to teach their subjects on an advanced level. The academic revolution extended to professional subjects as well. Harvard and Johns Hopkins pioneered the joining of science, research, and medical education, and this inexorable process propelled other professional schools down this same path.

The scholar Laurence Veysey acutely depicted how bureaucracy and rhetoric papered over the compromises and contradictions built into the modern American university. At its center was the implacable drive to advance knowledge through systematic, rational inquiry. But this research imperative generated tension with other university tasks almost in proportion to its emphasis. Humanists soon perceived that historical or philological scholarship was no substitute for the spirit of art and literature. They groped to define a liberal culture as an alternative. For scholarly faculty, curricular knowledge—what was taught to undergraduates—was less challenging than findings shared with doctoral students or research colleagues. Thus, while instructing undergraduates remained the chief task of the university, it was not the chief interest of the faculty. Professional education frequently encountered a similar disjunction between education for praxis and faculty preoccupation with theory. However, the university excelled, above all, in specialized knowledge produced by and for experts in their academic fields. But even contemporaries wondered about the relevance of such knowledge for society at large.

PARADOXES OF THE MODERN UNIVERSITY

In the twentieth century American universities emerged as a system for producing and transmitting specialized knowledge and an inexhaustible reservoir of expertise. They have been dogged, however, in the fulfillment of these roles by three generic concerns. What among this profusion of knowledge has value for the general education of young people? How can such largely theoretical knowledge be of use to society? And what should be the relationship of academic experts to the intellectual life of the nation?

The academic revolution required no less than a reinvention of the notion of liberal education. Alexander Meiklejohn, president of Amherst College (1912–1923), was among the first to propose that such a course of study encompass philosophy, natural and social sciences, history, and literature—in other words a general distillation of key areas of disciplinary knowledge. Following World War I, Columbia established a course for all students in contemporary civilization. This approach was popularized after World War II. For roughly fifty years universities sought to teach students their cultural heritage through a selective rendering of the history of Western civilization. This approach succumbed by the 1970s to a combination of curricular laissez-faire, anti-Western sentiment, and the sponsorship of "diversity." But, although universities were loath to admit it, the reigning concept of diversity was more nebulous and ideological than the Western culture it sought to replace. Academic culture, in contrast, possessed far greater resilience.

Between the wars, a number of educators concluded that radical measures were required to achieve a liberal education. In the most notorious of these attempts, Meiklejohn himself created the Experimental College at the University of Wisconsin from 1927 to 1932, and the University of Chicago president Robert Maynard Hutchins (1929–1951) advocated a curriculum based on the study of the Great Books. Such efforts to secede from the disciplinary curriculum were in fact testimony to its hegemony. More easily implemented were approaches that adapted disciplinary knowledge to the needs of beginning students, like that proposed by Harvard's *General Education in a Free Society* (1945). Such strategies inevitably gravitated back toward departmental offerings. In the absence of any consensus about what students ought to learn, disciplinary knowledge remained more authoritative than courses, no matter how well conceived, aimed at conveying an ineffable general education.

The notion that universities and their faculties should make useful contributions to the society and economy has waxed and waned. Proponents and opponents have always existed, but the specifics of their argument change with the times. World War I and its aftermath gave a great stimulus to the belief that universities and industry ought to work together. Cooperative efforts ensued in subjects like chemistry and engineering, blessed by foundation largesse and foundation-assisted mediators like the National Research Council. Foundations played a larger role in the social sciences where millions of Rockefeller dollars were disbursed ostensibly to develop a knowledge base for addressing social problems. Although the original purpose was largely lost, these resources greatly enhanced the elaboration of academic social science. By the end of the 1920s, though, a drift away from utility was clearly in the air. The medical school muckraker Abraham Flexner criticized universities for being service stations to society, Hutchins accused them of materialism, and the great foundations now preferred that academic science be pure.

World War II permanently altered the role of academic knowledge. University scientists were naturally mobilized for the war, but peace brought no surcease to the vital projects on which they worked. The cold war then assured that the federal government would be an enduring, interested patron of academic research. This system was little challenged until the late 1960s, when a revulsion toward all links with the government, the military, and industry too swept across campuses. In its wake, an ivory tower mentality pervaded universities. These attitudes were challenged at the end of the 1970s. Universities were called upon to develop and share technology for industry, and the paradigm of biotechnology seemed to demonstrate that there could be no epistemological distinction between academic and commercially valuable knowledge. By the 1990s ideas had become intellectual property. Universities were fully committed to serving the economy, and they expected to profit from doing so.

In the matter of intellectual contributions, the role of the modern university has been more ambiguous. Since the academic revolution there has existed a perceptible breach between the academic role of generating certifiable knowledge for experts and the intellectual role of offering critical interpretations of ideas for society at large. Many of the celebrated violations of academic freedom in that era involved professors who crossed this gap to advocate unpopular political views. Still, some individuals succeeded in both making eminent contributions to their disciplines and communicating with the American public as intellectuals. Thomas Bender featured a number of them in *New York Intellect* (1987), but also noted a detectable tension between these two roles. After midcentury, the tensions may have grown greater. A second academic revolution in the 1950s and 1960s, described by Christopher Jencks and David Riesman in *The Academic Revolution* (1968), intensified academic specialization and the self-absorption of disciplines.

Even while this second revolution was taking place, the historian Richard Hofstadter perceived a somewhat different problem. Postwar intellectuals had at least in part become a new "clerisy," working directly with the powers that governed American society and sharing their basic outlook. For Hofstadter such conformity blunts the sense of alienation that animates an intellectual's critical edge. This was particularly true for scholars, who "ha[d] no real choice" but to work in accredited institutions. Hofstadter's concerns reflected a growing apprehension toward academic careerism in the cold war economy and what would soon be condemned as the "military-industrial-university complex." But he may have underestimated the potential for criticism. The university-based New Left soon shattered the very complacency that Hofstadter decried.

The American student rebellion that stretched from the mid-1960s to the early 1970s was the most far-reaching internal convulsion in the history of American universities. Insofar as it had a doctrine, it paid lip service to the 1962 "Port Huron Statement" of Students for a Democratic Society (SDS). Identifying the university as a key institution and "participatory democracy" as a basic strategy, SDS sought to mobilize students in order to change American society. Intellectually, however, the student movement soon degenerated into slogans and cant. Overwhelmingly negative in its goals, it eventually turned to blatantly anti-intellectual slogans to manipulate students. Although SDS came to an ignominious end, the student rebellion was in the forefront of a transformation of American values. Universities, in particular, became self-appointed guardians for a somewhat tendentious commitment to egalitarianism and social justice.

In its aftermath, large numbers of those who had experienced the student movement subsequently entered academic life. New Left scholars established a Marxist presence in every relevant discipline, and feminist scholars created a similar genre for women's studies. However, the intellectual historian Russell Jacoby saw this work vitiated by academicization. He described the writings of the academic Left as "largely technical, unreadable, and—except by specialists—unread." The university conquered the leftist intellectuals rather than the other way around. This particular outcome was symptomatic of a larger development. Both Jacoby and, more thoughtfully, Thomas Bender feared that the overweening contemporary university threatened to co-opt or to suffocate independent intellectuals. The late-twentieth-century university not only had annexed all matter of intellectual activity into its capacious maw, but it had then transmogrified intellectuals and their subject matter into theoretical, self-referential academic studies.

Whatever truth may lie in such foreboding, it is overshadowed by the larger role of the American university in contemporary society. Of the four foci of university knowledge the outset of this essay presents, there can be no doubt that the dominant development of the twentieth century was the hypertrophy of specialized academic knowledge. Thus, the twenty-first-century university system is an engine for the perpetual generation and transmission of such expertise. If academic knowledge is basically esoteric and arcane, so too is the comprehension of complex and specialized subject matter. Producing such knowledge in fact is the chief role of universities in the national ecology of knowledge. But they have no monopoly. One half of basic research in the United States is performed in nonuniversity settings; and other forms of serious inquiry are undertaken by writers, journalists, and professionals in a wide variety of circumstance. However, the synergies of research, teaching, and service have allowed universities over the long run to accumulate and sustain vast amounts of specialized expertise more efficiently than any single-purpose institution.

Herein lies the resolution to the central issue of this essay. University-generated knowledge has had a substantial independent effect on contemporary intellectual life precisely through university dominance of specialized academic fields. The primary work of discovering, refining, and certifying new knowledge is indubitably the province of small groups of academic experts, but the findings of academic scholarship nevertheless inform public understanding in myriad ways. The intellectual history of the modern university cannot be captured in a few large ideas, but rather touches virtually all realms of knowledge affecting modern life—at the dawn of the twenty-first century more so than ever before.

See also **Education in Early America; The Classical Vision** (volume 1); **The Professional Ideal; The Struggle for the Academy** (volume 2); **Cultural Studies; History and the Study of the Past** (in this volume); and other articles in this section.

BIBLIOGRAPHY

Bender, Thomas. *Intellect and Public Life: Essays on the Social History of Academic Intellectuals in the United States*. Baltimore, 1993.

———. *New York Intellect: A History of Intellectual Life in New York City, from 1750 to the Beginnings of Our Own Time*. New York, 1987.

Field, Peter S. *The Crisis of the Standing Order: Clerical Intellectuals and Cultural Authority in Massachusetts, 1780–1833*. Amherst, Mass., 1998.

Geiger, Roger L. *Research and Relevant Knowledge: American Research Universities since World War II.* New York, 1993.

———. *To Advance Knowledge: The Growth of American Research Universities, 1900–1940.* New York, 1986.

Geiger, Roger L., ed. *The American College in the Nineteenth Century.* Nashville, Tenn., 2000.

Graff, Gerald. *Professing Literature: An Institutional History.* Chicago, 1987.

Graubard, Steven, ed. *American Academic Culture in Transformation: Fifty Years, Four Disciplines. Daedalus* (special issue, winter 1997).

Guralnick, Stanley A. *Science and the Ante-bellum College.* Philadelphia, 1975.

Hawkins, Hugh. *Between Harvard and America: The Educational Leadership of Charles W. Eliot.* New York, 1972.

———. *Pioneer: A History of the Johns Hopkins University, 1874–1889.* Ithaca, N.Y., 1960.

Hofstadter, Richard. *Academic Freedom in the Age of the College.* 1955. With an introduction by Roger L. Geiger. Reprint, New Brunswick, N.J., 1996.

———. *Anti-intellectualism in American Life.* New York, 1963.

Hofstadter, Richard, and Wilson Smith, eds. *American Higher Education, A Documentary History.* 2 vols. Chicago, 1961.

Humphrey, David C. *From King's College to Columbia, 1746–1800.* New York, 1976.

Jacoby, Russell. *The Last Intellectuals: American Culture in the Age of Academe.* New York, 1987.

Jencks, Christopher, and David Riesman. *The Academic Revolution.* Chicago, 1968.

McCaughey, Robert A. "The Transformation of American Academic Life: Harvard University, 1821–1893." *Perspectives in American History* 8 (1974): 239–332.

May, Henry F. *The Enlightenment in America.* New York, 1976.

Miller, Samuel. *A Brief Retrospect of the Eighteenth Century: A Sketch of the Revolutions and Improvements in Science, Arts, and Literature during That Period.* 2 vols. 1803.

Morgan, Edmund S. *The Gentle Puritan: A Life of Ezra Stiles, 1727–1795.* Chapel Hill, N.C., 1962.

Morison, Samuel Eliot. *Three Centuries of Harvard, 1636–1936.* Cambridge, Mass., 1936.

Noll, Mark A. *Princeton and the Republic, 1768–1822: The Search for a Christian Enlightenment in the Era of Samuel Stanhope Smith.* Princeton, N.J., 1989.

Oleson, Alexandra, and John Voss, eds. *The Organization of Knowledge in Modern America, 1860–1920.* Baltimore, 1979.

Reuben, Julie A. *The Making of the Modern University: Intellectual Transformation and the Marginalization of Morality.* Chicago, 1996.

Robson, David W. *Educating Republicans: The College in the Era of the American Revolution, 1750–1800.* Westport, Conn., 1985.

Sloan, Douglas. *The Scottish Enlightenment and the American College Ideal.* New York, 1971.

275

Stevenson, Louise L. *Scholarly Means to Evangelical Ends: The New Haven Scholars and the Transformation of Higher Learning in America, 1830–1890.* Baltimore, 1986.

Storr, Richard. *The Beginnings of Graduate Education in America.* Chicago, 1953.

Turner, James. *The Liberal Education of Charles Eliot Norton.* Baltimore, 1999.

Veysey, Laurence R. *The Emergence of the American University.* Chicago, 1965.

Winterer, Caroline. "The Humanist Revolution in America, 1820–1860." *History of Higher Education Annual* 18 (1998): 111–130.

FOUNDATIONS AND PHILANTHROPY

Judith Sealander

"A foundation," the journalist Dwight Macdonald once declared, is a "large body of money completely surrounded by people who want some." That mordant description fit his target, the Ford Foundation, in 1956. In fact, it was true for any year between 1901 and 1999. But it raises a question. Why was the incorporated charitable foundation a twentieth-century phenomenon uniquely embraced by Americans? The answer requires asking several others. What factors spurred the creation of foundations in the early twentieth century? How have they been structured? What motivated their donors? Finally, in what ways have they brokered and promoted certain ideas?

Foundations have been powerful players in the politics of knowledge, but have also been widely misunderstood. As private institutions with records and agendas beyond public control, their image has been a Manichaean one. They were doing "God's work," giving money that promoted hundreds of good ideas—from new thinking about the nature of the human body to novel ideas about the structure of a community's "soul." They were the sinister agents of private wealth whose benevolence masked the fright of rich men who knew that in the twentieth century they not only had to control a society's physical resources but also its worldview. They had to convince everybody else that they deserved "hegemony," that the ideas promoted by a ruling elite were common sense, nothing remarkable, not to be debated.

Neither one of these portraits is correct. In the early twentieth century only about one hundred American foundations existed. By the 1990s, tens of thousands had incorporated. However, in any decade of the twentieth century, most existed primarily as legal buffers that sheltered their donors. Only a relatively small percentage of foundations wanted to promote new ways of thinking. However, they had an influence out of proportion to their numbers, and their wraith focused attention on their agendas. That, however, did not make foundations

shadowy puppeteers. It simply gave them one of many strings attached to the flexible creature of ever-changing American culture. Understanding the impact of foundation philanthropy, however, requires a review of its history.

THE EMERGENCE OF THE CHARITABLE FOUNDATION

Wealth and people eager to have some of it have characterized human societies for thousands of years. But charitable foundations as vehicles used to distribute wealth have not. They were a creation of the twentieth century, and far more popular among the American rich than in any other country. Why?

Americans had always depended on a combination of voluntary and government organizations. They scorned the state-sanctioned and funded churches, centralized educational systems, and government-owned museums of Europe. Dramatically repudiating that tradition, the First Amendment of the United States Constitution formally separated church and state. Moreover, it stipulated that all citizens could meet when they wished, say what they wanted, and form associations as they pleased.

Throughout the nineteenth century Americans exercised these rights with a vengeance. They pursued lucre relentlessly; they also created a society with thousands of nonprofit organizations—from churches to workmen's burial societies. However, these associations were not charitable foundations. The latter's invention required an unprecedented burst of economic growth between 1870 and 1900, a redefinition of the legal rights of corporations, and the professionalization of charity work.

Between the Civil War and the beginning of a new century, America's victorious North and Midwest boomed. A country with 21 million people in 1850 strained to accommodate over 75 million people fifty years later. Large cities grew huge; transportation networks became national, industries global. As the United States grew, so did the number of its very rich. A country of farmers and regional businesses with fewer than one hundred millionaires in the 1870s was one with an estimated forty thousand millionaires by 1916, with each of those dollars worth an estimated fifteen dollars by the end of the twentieth century.

Great wealth alone did not spur the establishment of foundations. The corporation itself was an invention of the nineteenth century. Its guarantee of limited liability provided a safety net to investors, but until the 1880s states were still leery of the new economic institutions. Most demanded that their attorneys general oversee their operations and examine their objectives. In fact, few state governments had the resources to do that effectively, but most demanded that a corporate charter state the nature of the business enterprise in detail. The idea that a charter could be issued to a corporation that did not intend to make a profit had to wait for a relaxation of legal attitudes. Even through the 1930s, many municipal governments and state legislatures responded queasily to requests to incorporate philanthropies.

Finally, the charitable foundation was a twentieth-century development because so too was the professionalization of charity. In the 1870s and 1880s millions of new immigrants crowded America's cities, overwhelming traditional efforts by earnest, church-based "friendly visitors" to dispense aid to the sick, poor, or homeless. Especially along the nation's East Coast, the New York Charity Organization Society, established in 1882, sought to address social problems collectively by coordinating the work of a city's benevolent groups. Hoping to do good was not enough. Charity demanded organization.

large. The vast majority acted as vehicles that shielded donors from direct appeals for help. Once they acquired reputations for generosity, most creators of foundations discovered that the business of giving away money was exhausting, even frightening, work. They found themselves trailed on the street by people with sad stories. Strangers hounded them on trains, in airports, at church. Even when they hired additional support staff, the thousands of begging letters that arrived were overwhelming. How could they determine which appeals were bogus? How could they decide which cause was the most deserving? John D. Rockefeller Sr. spoke for many other rich people who wanted to improve their communities or society when he complained that giving away his money was far more difficult than making it.

All American charitable foundations ever had in common was a shared legal status and an obligation to control and disperse money. Most were local and contributed to causes favored by their patrons. Overwhelmingly, these were specific, sometimes even eccentric, and had always been: particular schools or colleges, a favored hospital, a beloved opera company, homes for retired music teachers, a pipe organ for a concert hall. Only a tiny fraction of American foundations ever had larger purposes. Even in the 1990s fewer than two hundred had annual grant budgets greater than $10 million. If they thought about foundations at all, most Americans assumed they bore the names of the country's superrich: Rockefeller, Carnegie, Ford, Gates, Packard, Kellogg. In fact, far more commonly, they did not. Moreover, foundations were a small part of a larger nonprofit universe: the "third sector," a label initially promoted by John D. Rockefeller III.

AN OVERVIEW OF AMERICAN FOUNDATIONS

In 1901, John D. Rockefeller Sr. endowed the Rockefeller Institute for Medical Research. It, like all charitable foundations to follow, utilized a corporate model and had a board of trustees, a stated purpose, and a government charter. By 1935, about 150 other foundations existed. This small congregation exploded after World War II—growing especially rapidly in the last three decades of the twentieth century—to, by the late 1990s, over 42,000 incorporated charitable foundations.

Although in the 1990s the United States' two biggest foundations were West Coast institutions, most still clustered in the East. And very few were

THE STRUCTURE OF FOUNDATIONS

There have been two types of American foundations: private foundations and community foundations. Both have historic origins in the period between 1900 and 1916. For most of the twentieth century private foundations have been the insular creations of wealthy individuals or families; that is, vehicles for the distribution of gifts. Overwhelmingly, the beneficiaries have been close at hand—local schools, health-care institutions, arts companies. The minority of foundations not bearing a family name have always betrayed that orientation with the second most popular title, the name of their city.

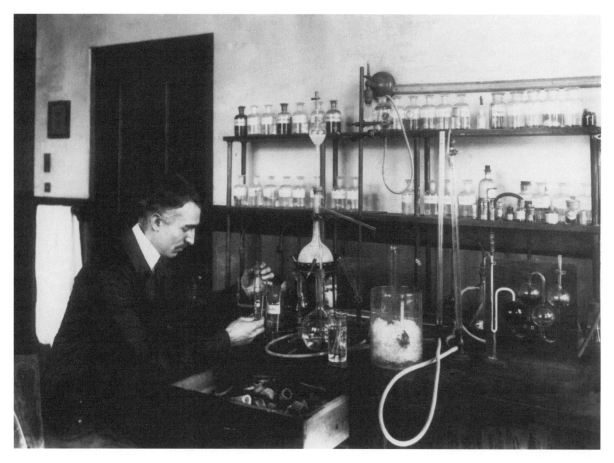

George W. Heimrod at the Rockefeller Institute for Medical Research, 1908. In 1965, the Institute expanded its mission to include education and was renamed Rockefeller University. COURTESY OF THE ROCKEFELLER UNIVERSITY ARCHIVES

The trustees of foundations have usually been insiders. Legally, the board of a foundation, as is the case with any corporation, conducts all its business. Naturally, founders wanted people on whom they could rely. Historically a foundation trustee was a wealthy white man in his fifties or sixties—an officer in a donor's company, a long-time family lawyer, a business partner, a beloved relative. He was Protestant, Republican, and a graduate of an elite Ivy League school. With rare exceptions, he served without pay, an indication of a genuine desire to do good. Nonetheless, most boards had highly conflicted relationships with the sources of their foundation's money. Foundations linked with the automobile industry did not promote research on exhaust pollution. Those linked to petroleum did not study alternative fuels. Those sponsored by tobacco companies did not fund investigations into connections between nicotine and cancer. Foundation philanthropy, moreover, could never be entirely separated from corporate self-promotion. To patronize improvements in society, however defined, was usually good public relations.

This insulated, interconnected world began to change a bit in the 1970s, prodded by the Tax Reform Act of 1969. In 1961 Representative Wright Patman of Texas launched an eight-year crusade against American foundations. Since solid Republicans interested in endowing their local hospitals ran the vast majority, his charge that foundation philanthropy supported "left wing" un-American causes was wildly exaggerated. Nonetheless, the idea that if foundations were to continue to enjoy tax-exempt status they had to submit themselves to greater public scrutiny took hold. The Tax Reform Act of 1969 gave the federal government the right to restrict cash contributions and deductions for gifts in trust, established a 4 percent annual excise tax on net investment income, and demanded greater financial disclosure of all foundation assets.

Before 1970, only a handful of foundations made their annual reports available to the public.

Fewer than one-third had any paid professional staff. Even in that minority, the staff generally mimicked the board; most were well-educated white males. The faces of women or minorities were rare sights, seen only at board meetings or behind office desks. In 1970, one critic counted board members of the fifty largest American foundations and discovered only three African American trustees.

But in the next three decades, foundations began to diversify and professionalize. By the end of the twentieth century, a majority of foundations had at least one paid professional staff member to help with grants administration and program planning. In a stunning turnaround, significant numbers of these people were women or people of color. By the end of the 1990s, in fact, the proportion of both exceeded those reached in other professions.

Moreover, the process of grant-giving had changed. For most of the century, foundations had given away money quite informally. Trustees and donors relied on word of mouth to assess the worthiness of recipients. In 1967 the Rockefeller Foundation staffer Warren Weaver recalled that he and his colleagues thought it was "simply criminal to overburden scholars and scientists with unnecessary formal paperwork. It is a great delight to a foundation officer when someone writes in and asks for 'blanks,' how requests must be made, how many copies he must submit, to be able to tell him there are no blanks." This system, even at one of America's largest foundations, meant that personal connections were paramount. By the 1990s, under the pressure of government regulation, "project" grants demanded not just the dreaded multiple copies, but detailed proposals and budgets.

Community foundations, the smaller, quiet siblings of the better-known, if often misunderstood, private foundations, had always required more comprehensive disclosure systems. Beginning with the establishment of the Cleveland Foundation in 1914, community foundation endowments came from a variety of sources, including the donations of thousands of ordinary citizens. Board members had always included public officials as well as citizens chosen by groups like local chambers of commerce. Though most private foundations, through preference, served only their cities or regions, community foundations had to do so. The Dayton Foundation, established in 1921, could not take up the problems of New York City, though Charles F. Kettering, a Dayton, Ohio, engineer, inventor of the automotive electric self-starter, and patron of the Charles F. Kettering Foundation, was free (at least theoretically) to do so. Through the 1980s community foundations controlled only about 10 percent of all monies distributed by foundations and, unlike private foundations, for whom New York City was still an informal capital, their home base was the American Midwest, especially Ohio, Indiana, and Minnesota.

In the 1980s and 1990s, community foundations were the fastest growing type of American foundation. As Americans once again debated proper private and public obligations, hundreds of cities and counties created new community chests, trusts, or foundations, many of them concerned with the same sorts of problems that had bedeviled the city leaders who created the Cleveland Foundation: poverty in the midst of plenty, urban education, public health, and child care.

WHAT MOTIVATED THE FOUNDERS OF FOUNDATIONS?

The social reformers who masterminded the Cleveland Foundation thought that the problems confronting their community urgently demanded solutions and that they had a moral obligation to try to find them. Though few of them commanded the resources of the families who created private foundations, they shared one trait. They were not typical, even among members of the privileged elite. Americans had always been a relatively stingy lot, a people who prided themselves on a generosity that they did not really display. Even the wealthiest among them generally relinquished their assets only when they had no choice about it, in wills or on deathbeds. That was true in the early twentieth century and at its end.

For a minority of truly charitable rich Americans, religious principle, civic conviction, and fear of social unrest spurred the creation of foundations. This was especially true in the first three decades of the twentieth century when they were largely free to spend their money entirely as they pleased, free from the need to create stratagems to shelter wealth from taxes. Before 1932, customs duties remained the primary source of federal revenues, while state and local taxes were not onerous. Most Americans paid no income taxes, and taxes on property were minimal.

Throughout the twentieth century, the most important foundations were the creations of self-made entrepreneurs with a keen eye for chances others missed. All created business corporations that made them vastly wealthy, often ones that controlled all aspects of a new product's creation and sale—be it oil, steel, or, in the case of Will K. Kellogg, packaged, ready-to-eat breakfast cereals.

The ability to recognize and seize possibilities was one shared by the creators of many early foundations. But in an era with tens of thousands of new millionaires, that valuable skill did not set them apart. Rather, unlike many of their counterparts, they felt a religious or ethical obligation to share their good fortune. Moreover, they worried that if problems were not addressed American society and democracy would suffer. In the early twentieth century, they knew that America's wealth and power had surged dramatically, but they also recognized that the prosperity was not evenly shared. Rural families in the South barely survived on cornmeal and weak molasses. In Kansas they ate too many meals of pancakes and gravy. Even in industrial regions, people suffered. They fought tuberculosis in airless city tenements and battled rats for the control of muddy streets in mining towns.

The nation ratified the Sixteenth Amendment, allowing the federal government to tax income, in 1913. However, it took the Great Depression, the New Deal, and the passage of the Personal Income Tax Act of 1935 to prompt what became permanent use of that authority. For the next sixty years, efforts to minimize taxes did play a role in both philanthropic giving and the creation of charitable foundations. Indeed, the 1935 legislation motivated Henry Ford, famously contemptuous of the virtues of charity, to create the Ford Foundation in 1936, as a way to shelter income for his heirs. Only after his death in 1947 did the foundation become more than a Michigan-based tax dodge.

Nonetheless, were tax avoidance paramount in the minds of those who gave charitably, even average citizens would have been more generous. Americans held onto what assets they had. The rich clung to wealth they did not consume. Everybody paid higher income and estate taxes for the privilege. Even when, in the 1980s and 1990s, the country enjoyed another enormous economic boom, that pattern did not change significantly.

By the late 1990s the top 1 percent of the population possessed almost 40 percent of the nation's wealth. At the end of the century, there were no fewer than 3.5 million American millionaires. The number of billionaires skyrocketed from 13 in 1982 to 170 in 1997, and analysts guessed that the fortune of the planet's richest man, the multibillionaire American computer software magnate Bill Gates, was increasing annually by more than $1 billion. Moreover, the largest intergenerational transfer of wealth in American history had begun, as the par-

ents of baby boomers died and passed the assets they had amassed, valued in the trillions of dollars, to their offspring.

Nonetheless, charitable giving remained constant. In the 1990s, as they had for decades, Americans gave less than 2 percent of personal income to charity. Only a few of the newly very rich did better. As had always been true, only a minority were philanthropic, and only a tiny percentage established charitable foundations. Like their predecessors, religious faith, civic concern, and worries about the future impelled their decisions. In important ways, the late twentieth, like the late nineteenth, century was also a "gilded" age. Gaps between the very rich, the middle class, and the poor, which had been shrinking since the 1930s, widened dramatically. Some of the nation's citizens went on a mansion-building and luxury-car-buying spree. Others discovered that food pantries they patronized ran out of everything but dried beans by the end of the month. Once again, a few among the extremely wealthy worried that such developments could strain the comity of a democratic society to the breaking point. And, once again, they tended to be self-made entrepreneurs who saw opportunities where others did not. Gates began his William H. Gates Foundation with a $17 billion endowment. In 1999, his announcement of the gift of another $1 billion made his foundation the largest, and potentially the most influential, in the world. Ted Turner, another man who made an immense fortune from an enterprise others had initially scorned—cable television—pledged $1 billion to the United Nations and the cause of international peace. But the nation's second richest man, the investment manager Warren Buffett, openly scorned philanthropic activity. That too was a tradition. In the early twentieth century, when John D. Rockefeller Sr. was the world's wealthiest individual and the creator of the country's biggest foundations, his partner and brother William Rockefeller, whom Standard Oil also made fabulously wealthy, gave little or nothing away.

WHAT DID FOUNDATION PHILANTHROPY ACCOMPLISH?

Community foundations always had to operate by consensus, since large boards with a variety of viewpoints spent their money. However, until the end of the twentieth century, they controlled only a small percentage of funds distributed by foundations. Private foundations were, especially during the lifetimes of their donors, often different. Certainly, a founder's wish, even if viewed as whimsical by others, frequently prevailed. When Woodrow Wilson, as president of Princeton University, not the United States, personally begged Andrew Carnegie for funds to refurbish campus buildings, the steel baron politely mulled the request. However, he decided that what Princeton really needed was an ornamental lake. The lake won.

So, any survey of foundation interests and accomplishments must acknowledge the often personal and usually local quality of the institution. Nonetheless, patterns emerged. Whether they were small or enormous, American foundations of the twentieth century overwhelmingly favored two causes as they sought to better their communities, the nation, or the world: American education and medical research. Especially in the latter area, foundation sponsorship spread new ideas. For a minority of foundations, especially the few with broadly stated general purposes and national missions, the promotion of new social sciences was also consistently important. In the early twentieth century a small group of foundations led the pursuit of the politics of knowledge. Overwhelmingly the many institutions founded by Andrew Carnegie and John D. Rockefeller Sr. and Jr. were the most important. Not until around 1930 did their many, quite independent, philanthropies begin to merge around the leadership of one major institution, in the former case, the Carnegie Corporation (also referred to in this essay as the Carnegie Foundation), in the latter, the Rockefeller Foundation. Carnegie and Rockefeller were the early twentieth century's two richest Americans and America's most influential philanthropists, but they had allies who were also interested in using their money to rethink society: significantly the Julius Rosenwald Fund, the Milbank Memorial Fund, the Twentieth Century Fund, the Commonwealth Fund, and the Russell Sage Foundation.

As the twentieth century ended, Bill Gates was the country's wealthiest individual and the patron of its biggest foundation. But the Gates Foundation was too young yet to have created a track record. The Rockefeller and Carnegie Foundations remained important, though no longer the nation's best endowed. In a country with many thousands of foundations, not just one hundred, larger numbers of foundations were interested in expanding knowledge, though proportionally they remained a small, if highly influential, minority among all foundations. At the end of the twentieth century, the

Ford Foundation had long since assumed a place as a prominent ideas broker, as had a collection of foundations that emerged after World War II. Among them were a prominent new group of nineteen foundations: the W. K. Kellogg Foundation; the Pew Memorial Trust; the David and Lucile Packard Foundation; the Andrew W. Mellon Foundation; the Lilly Endowment; the Robert Wood Johnson Foundation; the Danforth Foundation; the Bush Foundation; the John D. and Catherine MacArthur Foundation; the Moody Foundation; the Patricia Crail Brown Foundation; the Houston Endowment; the Sid Richardson Foundation of Texas; the Alfred P. Sloan Foundation; the Kettering Foundation; the Kresge Foundation; the Henry J. Kaiser Foundation; the Henry Luce Foundation; and the William T. Grant Foundation. Veterans, like the Milbank Memorial Fund and the Russell Sage Foundation, remained hardy survivors and, along with the Rockefeller and Carnegie philanthropies, began planning their centennials.

FOUNDATION PHILANTHROPY AND EDUCATION

Americans, more than other people, have embraced education as a solution for social and economic problems. So too did foundation philanthropy. Throughout the twentieth century, education received the bulk of foundation funds and commanded its greatest interest. Foundation support spurred improved professional standards and training programs, helped create world-class American universities, promoted innovation in public school classrooms, and, with less success, tried to better the educational opportunities of minorities, especially African Americans.

Until the late nineteenth century, no widely observed standards for entrance into most American professions existed. Indeed, many state legislatures banned licensing as undemocratic until just before the Civil War. Through the early twentieth century, some of that old bad odor still stuck to the idea that special training, rather than learning through apprenticeship, was necessary to prepare for particular occupations.

Foundation philanthropy, especially the actions taken by the few hundred foundations with very large assets, most importantly the Rockefeller, Carnegie, Ford, Mellon, and Kellogg Foundations, played an important role in upgrading and standardizing training for many professions, among them engineering, medicine, and the law. Moreover, foundations pushed the professionalization of entirely new fields like social work, demography, and applied psychology. Foundations championed the notion that professionalization was a social good, to immense consequence. By the late twentieth century America had become a country where formal credentials were indispensable, and tests, even retests, were ubiquitous. That was a foundation idea that changed culture, not just educational policy.

Most important, foundation intervention powerfully influenced American medical training. At the beginning of the century, American physicians lagged badly behind their European counterparts. The elite, with big-city practices and university reputations, generally studied in Germany or France. The average physician's income and skills were quite modest. The nation's hundreds of medical schools were proprietary, for-profit institutions owned by the faculty. Entrance requirements, when they existed at all, were minimal. Often a medical student lacked even a high school diploma. The vast majority of doctors did not belong to the American Medical Association (AMA), still an association of better-educated, younger, reform-minded physicians.

But by 1930, the AMA, with the considerable help of the Carnegie and Rockefeller Foundations, had transformed requirements for the practice of medicine in the United States. The Carnegie Foundation for the Advancement of Teaching "Bulletin No. 4" (1910), generally called the Flexner Report after its author the Kentucky educator Abraham Flexner, demanded that most of the hundreds of American medical schools be shuttered, and that the few remaining require four-year programs of study: two years of classwork combined with two years in hospital wards. Medical schools themselves should be part of larger universities, the report maintained, and should be in big cities where prospective doctors could see a wide variety of illnesses. Despite the rage of the proprietary schools, the Flexner Report triggered a professional coup. The former, always precariously financed, lost to Flexner's preferred model: the Johns Hopkins Medical School.

A pattern had been set that dominated professional education, and not just for physicians. Professions would require years of schooling. They would demand that candidates pass standardized, commonly accepted, often state-sanctioned tests. Professionals would become better educated, and, until the last three decades of the century, far more likely to be white and male. Only late in the century,

for example, did the percentages of women physicians and dentists in the country match and then exceed those of the early twentieth century. Minority membership in medicine, as well as many other professions, continued to be small.

Foundations promoted professionalization, not just in specific disciplines but through widespread support for the expansion and modification of college education in America. That, too, was a highly influential foundation idea. At the end of the nineteenth century, American colleges still emphasized a curriculum that had changed little since the seventeenth century: Greek, Latin, philosophy, and theology.

Throughout the United States, foundation philanthropy supported something else: the elective system, first developed at the Rockefeller-supported University of Chicago. Undergraduates generally spent two years studying a wide variety of required subjects: in the humanities and biological, physical, and social sciences. Then, for their final two years, they specialized in a "major." This system supplanted the old almost everywhere.

Especially after World War II, foundations became more interested in the problems of American public schools. Here they were less successful than they had been at promoting new models for professional and college education. The result of another investigation of education sponsored by the Carnegie Foundation for the Advancement of Teaching, the educator James B. Conant's *The American High School Today* (often called the Conant Report) damned American grade schools and high schools as places that paid their teachers far too little, emphasized too much rote memorization, and were resistant to new ideas. Since the report's publication in 1959, many foundations sponsored innovation in public school curriculums: adding teaching machines to classrooms in the 1960s, adding television to classrooms in the 1970s, and wiring grade-schoolers into the Internet in the 1980s and 1990s. The results were mixed. The Hollywood filmmaker George Lucas, the mastermind of the fabulously successful *Star Wars* films and the founder of the George Lucas Educational Foundation, which in the 1990s gave millions to promote the teaching of science in public elementary schools, hoped that school would not be as "boring and frustrating" for other kids as it had been for him. That remained to be seen at the end of the twentieth century. Public schools still struggled with large class sizes, shortages of properly trained science and math teachers, poor faculty salaries, and teacher burnout.

Bill Gates of Microsoft and Former President Nelson Mandela of South Africa. In July 2000, the Gates Foundation donated $90 million to fight HIV/AIDS with a focus on decreasing the rate of new infections in Africa. The Gates Foundation has an asset base of $21 billion. © REUTERS NEW MEDIA INC./CORBIS

Minority education also remained a terrific problem, as it had always been. Between 1917 and 1928 Julius Rosenwald, using the fortune he made from his Sears, Roebuck and Company's retail empire, spent over $18 million trying to provide educational equality for black grade-school children. His programs focused on southern states, where three out of four blacks still lived, and emphasized the construction of modern schoolhouses. By 1930, over half a million rural black kids studied in clean, well-built "Rosenwald" schools. But the Rosenwald Fund had wanted these schools to "shame" public educators into providing public money for equal facilities for all minority children. That did not happen in the 1930s. It had not happened by the end of the 1990s, when declining black graduation rates, especially for black males, and worries about a "digital" computer-literacy "divide" between whites and African Americans, encouraged Bill Gates to designate $1 billion for minority education.

FOUNDATION PHILANTHROPY AND MEDICINE

If success in all its initiatives in education awaited another century, foundation philanthropy's partnership with medicine between 1900 and 1999 was extraordinarily productive, both in areas of pure medical research and the promotion of public health. Both at the beginning and at the end of the century the country's richest men created foundations to support basic medical research. The Rockefeller Institute for Medical Research became a magnet for many of the world's most talented medical researchers. After 1965, as the Rockfeller University, it continued to produce Nobel Prize–winning discoveries. Its scientists contributed to hundreds of medical advances—from serums for meningitis and treatments for yellow fever to groundbreaking work on the functions of skin tissue. The Gates Foundation focused on vaccine research. Joining the work of these two colossuses were thousands of other medical research programs helped by foundation philanthropy.

Foundations also promoted public health work, often in partnership with government agencies too underfunded to do the job alone. In the early twentieth century the Rockefeller Sanitary Commission allied with public health departments in the South to fight hookworm and other fecal-borne diseases, while the Milbank Memorial Fund worked with New York State officials to control tuberculosis. In the post–World War II era, led by the Rockefeller, Grant, and Ford Foundations, philanthropies broadened their concerns about health even further—sponsoring sanitation campaigns throughout the world, as well as extending efforts to promote population planning and scientific agriculture as solutions to illness and poverty abroad.

FOUNDATION PHILANTHROPY AND THE ADVOCACY OF SOCIAL SCIENCE

The creed of educational modernization told scholars that rather than parse Latin, they should pursue the study of society. That, too, was a foundation idea with a large impact. In 1900, few academics even used the terms "sociology," "psychology," or "anthropology." They surely did not belong to separate departments, sponsor well-organized professional associations and journals, or get much notice. With foundation help, these professions were transformed and their insights promoted.

Foundation sponsorship of sociology provides an illustration paralleled by the rise to academic and general acceptance of other new social science disciplines. In the late nineteenth century something usually called "social science" sometimes replaced a moral philosophy course at a university. The professors of these courses, all philosophers, asked quasi-theological questions like, What was the ideal relationship between loyalty to family and state? By 1930, all that had changed. Sociologists at the University of Chicago and at the other elite schools that created the discipline were not debating the nature of a perfect society. They were too busy conducting interviews, making surveys, and producing charts and tables. They and their foundation patrons wanted practical applications, not theory. They wanted, and got, criminologists who invented juvenile courts, not abstract speculation.

They wanted, and got, "applied" psychology as well. With support from the Rockefeller-sponsored General Education Board, a first generation of American psychologists modified tests created by the French psychologist Alfred Binet to measure human intelligence, then used them on World War I draftees before discovering their true calling: the intelligence testing of American schoolchildren. It was a decision that would affect the lives of millions of children and permanently change the way Americans thought about ability and education. Decisions about their intelligence determined whether children would enter an academic, general, or vocational "track." Even when words created by the tests, like "idiot," "moron," and "imbecile" ceased to have psychological significance, they remained as invectives, and Americans constantly tried to be "normal."

Sponsorship of sociological "opportunity theory" provides another example of foundation philanthropy's enthusiasm for "practical" social science. Society, itself, opportunity theorists argued, creates criminal youth, by failing to provide them with a way to succeed. Therefore, programs like the Ford Foundation's "Grey Areas" initiative accepted the premise that schools, social welfare agencies, and other institutions in a community have to improve before juvenile delinquency can be solved.

Many social science ideas first promoted by philanthropy became mantras, embedded in government policy without much real proof of their validity. And many of the beneficiaries of foundation largesse proved rebellious—figuratively or literally. The middle-class mothers recruited by the Laura Spelman Rockefeller Memorial to learn about behaviorism often spent their time in classes exchanging recipes and their own independent insights on child rearing. Leaders in poor neighborhoods incorporated into the Ford Foundation's Grey Areas or Mobilization for Youth Health Services programs sometimes went beyond "opportunity theory" to rent strikes and school boycotts, angering their sponsors. Nonetheless, social science ideas changed twentieth-century American culture, and foundation philanthropy promoted many of them.

FOUNDATION PHILANTHROPY AND AMERICAN LIFE

What does this brief survey of foundation activities suggest? Above all it confirms an assessment voiced by the longtime Carnegie Corporation president Alan Pifer: "Foundations have a restricted capacity to lead change, but an unusual capacity to help it along." When ideas won broad public approval, like the promotion of research in pure science or the expansion of practical curriculums in American colleges, foundation initiatives became firmly established in the public mind and as public policy. Other foundation-supported ideas—like equal rights and educational opportunities for minorities or better pay for public school teachers, where widespread public support lagged behind rhetorical acceptance—were less successful.

Throughout the twentieth century critics had accused foundations of arrogantly creating empires that controlled the creation and exchange of knowledge. No question: foundations, indeed philanthropy writ large, was not democratic. Only at the end of the century did a very few activist foundations try to involve their grant recipients, much less the American public, in their decision making. But in a society where power was divided and public approval, in the end, was crucial, foundations were part of the process by which society operated, not its dictators.

Moreover, they were part of the process of organizing knowledge, not its hegemons. Indeed, as the century ended, many scholars began to rethink definitions of knowledge. It was not a phenomenon where individual ideas could be viewed as freestanding entities. Instead, information of any kind could only be discussed when centered by its social contexts. Ideas about the causes of heart attack or cancer, for instance, could really only be understood when discussed as originating in a scientific community dominated by whites whose research subjects were overwhelmingly male. Some of the most influential thinkers who spread this new view of the organization of knowledge had won grants from the Pew Memorial Trust, the Lilly Endowment, or the MacArthur Foundation.

An essay titled "Foundations and Philanthropy" should, finally, acknowledge that philanthropy in the late twentieth century changed in some dramatic ways. The dominance of East Coast foundations waned, as the nation's biggest foundations acquired West Coast addresses. More importantly, since 1940, an interesting national trend remained constant. Per capita, the very rich gave far less than did ordinary Americans. In the 1990s more than 80 percent of the more than $150 billion Americans contributed to charity came from the donations of middle-class families, and almost half of those gifts were made when members of congregations dropped money into plates passed in their own houses of worship. Major foundations certainly helped create and transfer knowledge in the twentieth century. But in America, the exchanges of information and values that philanthropic giving encouraged also included huge numbers of humbler venues: the pulpits of hundreds of thousands of local churches, synagogues, and mosques.

See also **Reform Institutions; Urban Cultural Institutions** *(volume 1);* **Humanitarianism; Social Reform** *(volume 2);* **Welfare; Public Murals; Monuments and Memorials** *(in this volume).*

BIBLIOGRAPHY

This essay relies heavily on manuscript and archival materials. The best archive in the country for the study of American foundations and philanthropy is the Rockefeller Archive Center in Tarrytown, New York. Housed there are many important record groups and personal papers that provide invaluable information on the varied Rockefeller philanthropies. Also at the Rockefeller Archive are records of the Russell Sage Foundation, the Commonwealth Fund, and dozens of other small personal and organizational collections that shed light on American philanthropy.

Yale University houses the Milbank Memorial Fund Archives as well as many records that explore the role of philanthropy in promoting medical research and public health. The Rosenwald Fund Papers are at the University of Chicago, as are many other collections important to a study of philanthropy. Columbia University is home to the voluminous records of the Carnegie philanthropies. The Ford Foundation Archives are housed within Foundation headquarters in New York City, but their access, even to bona fide scholars, is not unrestricted. As William McKersie and other scholars have noted, regrettably, the vast majority of community and small foundation records are difficult for researchers to see.

Using them often requires that a researcher enjoy personal connections to the foundation or a friendship with the donor's family.

The literature on American foundations and American philanthropy, however, became much richer in the 1980s and 1990s. For information on foundations in the early twentieth century see: Judith Sealander, *Private Wealth and Public Life: Foundation Philanthropy and the Reshaping of American Social Policy from the Progressive Era to the New Deal* (Baltimore, 1997); Olivier Zunz, *Why the American Century?* (Chicago, 1998); David Hammack and Stanton Wheeler, *Social Science in the Making: Essays on the Russell Sage Foundation* (New York, 1994); Kathleen D. McCarthy, *Noblesse Oblige: Charity and Cultural Philanthropy in Chicago, 1849–1929* (Chicago, 1982); and Estelle B. Freedman, *Maternal Justice: Miriam Van Waters and the Female Reform Tradition* (Chicago, 1996).

For books that examine foundations' impact, with a focus on their importance since 1935, see the classics: Dwight Macdonald, *The Ford Foundation: The Men and the Millions* (New York, 1956); and Waldemar A. Nielsen, *The Big Foundations* (New York, 1971).

For more scholarly studies see: Ellen Condliffe Lagemann, *The Politics of Knowledge: The Carnegie Corporation, Philanthropy, and Public Policy* (Middletown, Conn., 1983); John Ensor Harr and Peter J. Johnson, *The Rockefeller Century* (New York, 1988); Peter Dobkin Hall, *Inventing the Nonprofit Sector and Other Essays on Philanthropy, Voluntarism, and Nonprofit Organizations* (Baltimore, 1992); A. McGehee Harvey and Susan Abrams, *For the Welfare of Mankind: The Commonwealth Fund and American Medicine* (Baltimore, 1986); Robert E. Kohler, *Partners in Science: Foundations and National Scientists, 1900–1945* (Chicago, 1991); and Susan A. Ostrander, *Money for Change: Social Movement Philanthropy at the Haymarket People's Fund* (Philadelphia, 1996).

Two wonderful biographies of major American creators of foundations are: Ron Chernow, *Titan: The Life of John D. Rockefeller, Sr.* (New York, 1998); and Joseph Wall, *Andrew Carnegie* (New York, 1970), still the best book on the steel tycoon. *The Big Foundations* contains many lively sketches of foundation donors, but full-scale treatments of the lives of many post–World War II foundation figures await willing biographers.

For insider accounts and autobiographies see: Andrew Carnegie, *The Autobiography of Andrew Carnegie* (Garden City, N.J., 1909); Frederick Taylor Gates, *Chapters in My Life* (New York, 1977); Frederick P. Keppel, *The Foundation: Its Place in American Life* (New York, 1930); Abraham Flexner, *I Remember: The Autobiography of Abraham Flexner* (New York, 1940); Clyde V. Kiser, *The Milbank Memorial Fund, Its Leaders and Work, 1905–1974* (New York, 1975); Walter Guzzardi, *The Henry Luce Foundation* (Chapel Hill, N.C., 1986); Alan Pifer, *Philanthropy in an Age of Transition: The Essays of Alan Pifer* (Washington, D.C., 1984); John D. Rockefeller III, *The Second American Revolution: Some Personal Observations* (New York, 1973); and Warren Weaver, ed., *U.S. Philanthropic Foundations: Their History, Structure, Management, and Record* (New York, 1967).

Recent excellent collections of essays touching all aspects of foundation philanthropy include: Ellen Condliffe Lagemann, ed., *Philanthropic Foundations: New Scholarship, New Possibilities* (Bloomington, Ind., 1999); and Charles T. Clotfelter and Thomas Ehrlich, eds., *Philanthropy and the Nonprofit Sector in a Changing America* (Bloomington, Ind., 1999).

For discussions of American foundations' impact abroad see: Robert Arnove, ed., *Philanthropy and Cultural Imperialism: The Foundations at Home and Abroad* (Boston, 1980); and Marcos Cueto, ed., *Missionaries of Science: The Rockefeller Foundation and Latin America* (Bloomington, Ind., 1994).

LEARNED SOCIETIES AND PROFESSIONAL ASSOCIATIONS

Anne Ruggles Gere

Ask most people to delineate the differences between the American Philosophical Society and the American Philosophical Association and you will get looks of confusion and blank stares. Yet, juxtaposing these two groups shows a great deal about the shifting nature of learned societies in the United States. Comparison of the two organizations also demonstrates how changing conceptions and circulation of knowledge have both influenced and been influenced by learned societies across three centuries.

THE AMERICAN PHILOSOPHICAL SOCIETY

The American Philosophical Society (APS) was founded in 1743 by Benjamin Franklin to encourage investigations that would benefit the American colonies in "useful" areas such as agriculture, mining, and manufacturing. The APS lapsed after a few years and was revived as the "American Philosophical Society, Held at Philadelphia for Promoting Useful Knowledge" (APS) in 1766, in response to Britain's imposition of the Stamp Act in 1765. In 1769 it established six committees:

1. Geography, Mathematics, Natural Philosophy, and Astronomy
2. Medicine and Anatomy
3. Natural History and Chemistry
4. Trade and Commerce
5. Mechanics and Architecture
6. Husbandry and American Improvements

APS members included George Washington, John Adams, Alexander Hamilton, Thomas Paine, and Thomas Jefferson. The membership, always highly selective, met monthly to present papers and participate in symposia on a wide range of topics. The APS library was established when Franklin bequeathed his papers to the group, and its strongest collections were in areas such as Indian ethnohistory, linguistics, and western exploration.

As its array of committee topics suggests, the APS took a generalist approach to knowledge. In the eighteenth century, when this and other learned societies, like the Massachusetts Historical Society (1791), the American Academy of Arts and Sciences (1780), and the Connecticut Academy of Arts and Sciences (1799), were founded, members were assumed to have a broad range of interests and expertise. Practical and academic knowledges were intermingled so that "philosophical" included both agriculture and astronomy. A figure like Benjamin Franklin, whose accomplishments ranged from science to commerce to diplomacy, typified the conception of knowledge dominant at the time. It was not unreasonable to assume that one individual could contribute to the production and circulation of knowledge in several distinct areas. While a degree of specialized knowledge was assumed about each of the fields included in the committee list, areas such as geography, mathematics, natural philosophy, and astronomy could be put in a single category, and it was reasonable to assume that members of the APS could participate in discussions of all committee topics. The APS also manifested the localized circulation of knowledge in the eighteenth century. Although the APS identified itself as an "American" institution, its membership was drawn from the Philadelphia area, and the American Academy of Arts and Sciences was founded to provide residents of the Boston area with an organization similar to the APS. Groups located in different areas of the country could share knowledge through print, but as both the production and circulation of knowledge were much more localized than they are today, learned societies were constituted accordingly.

Eighteenth-century colleges and universities took a broad approach to knowledge, one that paralleled that of learned societies during the period. The eighteenth century's uniform curriculum emphasized the classics, and knowledge of Latin and Greek was the chief criterion for admission to higher education. Subjects studied in college included biblical languages like Greek, Hebrew, and Syriac; philosophy, which included logic, physics, ethics, and astronomy; rhetoric; and divinity. For most courses, Latin was the language of instruction. Students did not major in a particular subject but moved through the prescribed set of courses (Machlup, pp. 130–132). When more scientific courses, such as chemistry and geology, were introduced, an instructor's general intelligence and theological position were as important as specialized training. In 1801, for example, Timothy Dwight, president of Yale University, asked Benjamin Silliman, a 1796 graduate of Yale, to become a professor of chemistry and natural history. Silliman had no training in either field. What he did have was "a Yale background and a belief that God's divine plan was evident in the natural world" (Ellsworth, p. 46). While it is true that Silliman undertook a program of self-education that included listening to lectures and observing experiments in Philadelphia and Princeton, as well as visiting with geologists in Scotland, "chemistry and minerology as he studied and taught them did not show a history of the world in contradiction to that revealed in Scripture" (ibid., p. 99). Nor did he have recourse to books or systematic approaches to geology, since there were none. Silliman's route to the professorate typified the state of knowledge in most American universities as well as learned societies in the eighteenth and early nineteenth centuries. The prominence accorded to generalists no doubt inspired the French statesman Alexis de Tocqueville's oft-repeated remarks about the state of knowledge in America.

TOCQUEVILLE ON AMERICAN EDUCATION

It is not only the fortunes of men that are equal in America; even their acquirements partake in some degree of the same uniformity. I do not believe that there is a country in the world where, in proportion to the population, there are so few ignorant and at the same time so few learned individuals. Primary instruction is within the reach of everybody; superior instruction is scarcely to be obtained by any. . . . A middling standard is fixed in America for Human Knowledge.

Source: *Democracy in America* (1838).

THE AMERICAN PHILOSOPHICAL ASSOCIATION

As the nineteenth century progressed, and particularly after the Civil War, shifts in the organization, production, and circulation of knowledge led to a more national perspective on knowledge making and knowledge dissemination, and "ownership" of knowledge came to be seen in less egalitarian terms. As disciplines became more distinct from one another, it was assumed that access to a given field required specialized learning, and that not everyone could become equally conversant in multiple areas of investigation. The generalist who could, like a member of the eighteenth-century APS, move comfortably from discussions of agricultural methods to language variations among American Indian populations gave way to the specialist who focused on a specific area of science, such as chemistry.

Although controversies raged between traditionalist defenders of the prescribed classical curriculum and the reformist advocates for mathematics, physical sciences, vocational training, and modern languages, the reformers eventually won. At some universities, professional schools were part of the landscape from the beginning. When the University of Virginia was organized in 1824, for example, it included professional training in medicine and law, along with philosophy, languages, mathematics, and chemistry. By the 1860s higher education had moved toward an elective rather than a prescribed curriculum, and students could choose to specialize in disciplines like chemistry, philology, or economics.

The move to instruction in English came slowly, and some universities maintained parallel curricula, one in classical languages and one in English with an emphasis on science. One of the ways new disciplines could command a place in the "academy" of higher education was to demonstrate themselves to be intellectually rigorous. In the field of English, for example, scholars trained in German universities urged their colleagues to focus on systematic methods and "make English as hard as Greek" (March, p. 27).

During the last third of the nineteenth century, American higher education looked to the model of German universities as it shifted toward an emphasis on research, instituted the Ph.D., and established university presses. Johns Hopkins University (founded 1876) can be described as the first research university because it assigned greater importance to its graduate school than its undergraduate division. Increasing specialization of disciplinary knowledge accompanied these changes at universities, and learned societies followed suit. No longer the province of the generalist, the learning society became dominated by university professors who did research in highly specialized areas of study.

The American Philosophical Association (APA) took shape in this new intellectual environment. Unlike the APS, which brought together generalists from a broad range of backgrounds, the APA attracted a much more specialized membership. Founded in 1901 by a group of philosophers at Cornell University, the APA quickly attracted a national membership, affiliating itself with philosophers in the Midwest and on the Pacific Coast. The genesis of this learned society lay in the increasing divergence of interests between psychologists and philosophers, and the founding of the APA took place shortly after the American Psychological Association was organized. From its beginnings, the APA's membership has consisted almost exclusively of professors of philosophy in colleges and universities, and its publications have featured scholarly articles on topics in philosophy. Its close affiliation with higher education, its focus on a highly specialized area of knowledge, and its evolution into a national organization distinguish the APA from the APS, which fostered a more general and local type of knowledge.

Not only did the nature of learned societies change as higher education's approach to the organization, production, and dissemination of knowledge shifted, but the number of societies also increased dramatically, particularly toward the end of the nineteenth century. Many of these groups emerged as variants of an existing academic field, similar to the way philosophers and psychologists diverged to form distinct disciplines. Botanists, zoologists, biologists, and microbiologists all moved in separate directions from their common home in natural science, and each field established its own learned society. The APS was one of four learned societies founded in the eighteenth century, and by the time the APA took shape in 1901, it joined over fifty similar groups.

NINETEENTH-CENTURY PROFESSIONALISM IN THE ACADEMY

The increasingly specialized view of knowledge that took shape in the nineteenth century led to the emergence of professionalism among those who could lay claim to a specific area. As Magali Larson explained, the features of professionalism included,

in addition to specialized knowledge, institutionalized training, licensing, work autonomy, colleague "control," and a code of ethics (pp. x–xviii). These features varied across fields; the university professor did not undergo a process of licensure in the way that a medical doctor did, and the nature of institutionalized training for a lawyer, say, differed from that of an architect, both because of differences in the specialized knowledge of each and because of the variation in the nature of institutionalized training for each. Despite these differences, all professions depended upon an extended period of training that was nearly always provided by higher education. University professors thus took on responsibility for credentialing professionals in a variety of fields. In the process, members of the academy become more professionalized themselves.

One mark of the growing professionalism of university professors was the rate at which they established learned societies that lent their new fields additional authority. Between 1851 and 1899 learned societies for geography, social sciences, philology, chemistry, archaeology, modern languages, history, economics, physiology, mathematics, geology, zoology, psychology, botany, astronomy, physics, philosophy, and microbiology were formed. Taking as their chief end the production and distribution of knowledge within the given field, these societies provided a forum where those with common training and interests could share and critique one another's work. The membership of each of these new organizations came predominantly from college and university faculties, and in addition to the governmental structures of officers and annual meetings, these societies sponsored publications that helped to circulate their knowledge among others in the same discipline.

One effect of professionalization within the academy was the creation of a greater distance between amateurs and specialists in a given field. Unlike the eighteenth-century American Philosophical Society, whose members were expected to have a broad range of interests and expertise, discipline-based professionalism took a more narrow view of the production and circulation of knowledge. Specifically, the academic specialists discounted amateur institutions outside the academy, sometimes actively seeking to discredit them. English professors, for example, were careful to distinguish their scholarship from that of women's clubs, which engaged in similar literacy practices (Gere, pp. 208–247).

Even though they boasted national memberships, nineteenth-century learned societies were very small. The American Chemical Society (1876), for example, was founded by thirty-five men, and in 1880 less than the necessary quorum of fifteen attended its meetings. An impulse toward elevating their profession frequently led professors to include only the "better" candidates in their learned societies. Needless to say, few women, people of color, or instructors at less-than-prestigious institutions were welcomed into such organizations. Still, because they drew members from many states, organized themselves into representative systems of government, and could describe themselves as speaking for an entire profession, these learned societies wielded influence that transcended their numbers.

The growth of learned societies continued through much of the twentieth century, with another 112 groups taking shape by 1977. The American Association of Immunologists (1913), the American Meteorological Society (1919), the American Musicological Society (1934), the American Studies Association (1951), and the American Association for the Advancement of the Humanities (1977) were among these groups. With their increased numbers, learned societies began to face complicated identity questions. What would constitute the boundaries of their activity? Where did knowledge making end and advocacy begin? What role would they assume in relation to American culture?

As early as 1898, learned societies began to participate in discussions that extended beyond knowledge making in a given field. Gary Marotta, for example, has argued that the American Historical Association (1884) helped to shape post–Spanish American War debates about whether the United States should retain the Philippines. Imperialistically inclined members of the AHA endorsed empire; their peers in the American Economic Association urged the United States to create markets for domestic production; and the American Academy of Political and Social Sciences, arguing from the perspective of social Darwinism, supported an acquisitive foreign policy as necessary to the national interest. According to Marotta, "American scholarly societies were biased in an imperialist direction, identified closely with business interests and governmental policy, displayed more cupidity than circumspection, frequently eschewed moral concern for the main chance, and generally avoided dissenting opinions within their own ranks" (p. 232). By attempting to shape United States foreign policy, some members of learned societies like the AHA, AEA, and AAPSS moved beyond producing and disseminating knowledge into a posture of

advocacy. They moved from disinterest to intervention.

Of course, one can argue that professors in these learned societies were doing no more than they had been asked to do. Many people saw higher education's production and dissemination of knowledge as a resource that should serve the national interest. Daniel Coit Gilman, founding president of Johns Hopkins University, took this view, urging that professors offer their knowledge to those outside the university. In an 1898 speech at Princeton, Gilman argued that scholars should address the "perplexities which now involve our countrymen" with an eye to offering solutions based on their specialized knowledge (p. 201).

Although the essential purposes of learned societies remained what they had been since the eighteenth century—the discovery, preservation, and dissemination of knowledge—their role became less clear as professors become more professionalized and more willing to put their knowledge to use in support of particular agendas, such as retaining the Philippines. The late-nineteenth-century emergence and growth of professional associations further complicated the identities and purposes of learned societies.

THE EMERGENCE OF PROFESSIONAL ASSOCIATIONS

Professional schools were part of higher education from the eighteenth century forward. Indeed many colleges owed their origins to the early American need for professionally trained ministers and theologians. Harvard, for instance, was established because "a Puritan minister must be able to expound the Sacred Scripture from the original Hebrew and Greek, and be cognizant of what the Church Fathers, the Scholastic Philosophers, and the Reformers had written in Greek and Latin" (Morison, p. 3). Although professional schools of theology appeared first, they grew slowly, increasing from eighteen in 1801 to forty-seven in 1900. During the nineteenth century professional schools for lawyers grew from three to fifty and those for physicians grew from twelve to eighty-six (Bledstein, p. 84).

With this growth came increasing concern for quality, and standards for professional schools became more rigorous during the nineteenth century. The majority of law schools, for example, had moved to a three-year course by 1899, whereas only a small number required this amount of training in the middle of the century. This impulse toward

---

༄༅

DANIEL COIT GILMAN ON THE ROLE OF THE UNIVERSITY

[Universities] have the historical and geographical archives; they have trained investigators; they know the principles of human progress; they have the knowledge of constitutional law and historic jurisprudence. They are non-partisan. . . . What a service they might render by combining their forces and distributing their tasks to teach the world, in light of history, how it is that great nations have failed in the business of advancing civilisation and how other great nations have succeeded. . . . A word from the President or a request from the Secretary of State would set the universities at work. It would be better still, if Congress would authorise the appointment of a commission to be made up of the most learned, the most wise, the most experienced statesmen of the land, not now holding public office, and charge them to investigate for years to come, these problems. . . . What nobler work could a civilised nation undertake than to study its present in the light of the past, calmly, leisurely, and under conditions which ensure wise conclusions, full of instruction for mankind. A commission, made up of jurists, students of international law, economists and historians, could bring together, arrange, digest, and make known the conditions of success and the conditions of failure, and thus prepare the way for such legislation or for such Constitutional amendments as will enable the government of the United States to administer for the good of humanity its new responsibilities in the islands of the sea.

Source: *The Launching of a University* (1906).

---

academic rigor in institutional training helped strengthen the position of professionals in the United States. For professionalism to take hold in American culture, knowledge had to be seen as an unevenly distributed resource. Professionalism depends upon rendering large segments of the population powerless by claiming an authoritative knowledge presumed to be unavailable to those outside the given profession. Increasing the number and quality of professional schools, as higher education did during the last decades of the nineteenth century, aided this process significantly.

Specialized training gave professionals an opportunity to enter a full-time occupation that granted both authority and autonomy. Authority derived from what Bledstein describes as "powers existing beyond the reach or understanding of ordinary humans" (p. 94). Specialized knowledge could be exchanged for special status within American culture, thus creating a link between higher education and social mobility. The trappings of professional authority—including everything from the number of entries on a résumé to the practitioner's income—fostered professional autonomy by increasing feelings of dependence in the general public. A doctor's ability to purchase an expensive home contributed to his (and it was usually "his," not "her") professional autonomy just as his medical-school training did. This move by professionals to create patterns of dependence upon their specialized knowledge did a great deal to foster the upward social mobility and control over working conditions that came to characterize their lives.

Professional associations frequently served as the vehicle by which members of specific categories of professionals controlled both membership in and working conditions of a particular field. Emerging in great numbers during the middle and late nineteenth century, these organizations helped to bolster the authority and autonomy of architects, dentists, doctors, engineers, lawyers, and many others with specialized training. Although they shared with learned societies an interest in producing and disseminating knowledge, professional associations differed from those more scholarly organizations in their attention to issues of licensure, working conditions, and compensation. In seeking to control the terms by which individuals entered and functioned within a given field, professional associations addressed material as well as intellectual concerns.

Many professional associations originally formed for predominantly social reasons, but they quickly shifted toward controlling who could enter the profession and the nature of working conditions for all members. Attorneys may have joined the American Bar Association (1878) for the pleasures associated with joining their peers in Saratoga Springs during summer vacations, but they soon realized that their status and power depended upon controlling the number and quality of people who became lawyers. Accordingly, lawyers, like members of many other professional associations, developed state organizations that could exert pressure on legislatures that would pass many of the laws affecting their professions. Determining who could, for example, be certified to teach in a state's schools, practice law, or be licensed as a physician was and remains the decision of the state, so professional associations have continually sought to influence state regulations. Between 1890 and 1915 many professional associations developed into organizations with both national and state components. In some cases existing state associations merged to create national groups, and in others national organizations developed state affiliates. In 1920 the National Education Association reconfigured itself as a federation of state and local associations. At that time it concentrated on professionalizing members through publications and meetings, but later in the twentieth century it addressed the working conditions of teachers by unionizing its members.

Between 1890 and the 1920s professional associations became much more organized and vocational in their orientation. In part this resulted from the growing careerist nature of their members. The nineteenth-century doctor who might practice law for a period and also dabble in architecture gave way to a twentieth-century professional who would spend an entire career in a single profession. Members of professional associations realized that they needed to advocate on their own behalf or risk losing the substantial benefits of professionalism. Like the guilds who came before them, professional associations worked to include an ever larger percentage of professionals into their organizations and to integrate local and national levels into a more coherent whole.

Initially, professional associations had strong ties with government. A school superintendent might serve as president of the state education association, or members of a state affiliate of the American Medical Association (AMA) might determine who would serve on state licensing boards. As the twentieth century progressed, professional associations became more autonomous. Rather than being part of state government, they moved to influence it from the outside because professionals in a variety of fields were subject to state control. Public health laws shaped the practice of doctors; architects had to conform to the codes established by city and state engineers; and accountants were subject to state regulations.

Professional associations also became increasingly concerned with advocating for their constituents on the national level. The 1990s lobbying efforts of the AMA against managed health care systems represent a contemporary instance of the ways professional associations have long mounted campaigns that aim to influence national policy affecting the working conditions of their members. Such efforts would have effect only when the AMA could demonstrate that it represented a significant percentage of all practicing physicians. Corinne Lathrop Gilb shows, for example, that in 1912 only 50 percent of all doctors in the United States belonged to the AMA, but by 1960 that figure had risen to over 90 percent, thereby increasing the AMA's credibility (p. 119).

Another way professional associations augmented their ability to influence public policy and protect their own interests was to take a more inclusive approach to membership. At the time of their founding, most professional associations were composed of white Protestant men. African Americans were specifically excluded from professional associations in many states, and as a result, they formed their own. Since many national associations often refused to accredit African American state associations, blacks formed their own national associations as well. By the middle of the twentieth century, the National Medical Association of Negro Physicians, the National Dental Association, the National Bar Association, and the American Teachers Association all had substantial African American membership in many states. As the originally white-only professional associations opened membership to people of color, many professional associations of African Americans disbanded. The National Association of Colored Graduate Nurses, for example, was founded in 1908 and dissolved in 1951.

Women, who faced similar exclusion in many professional associations, followed the same pattern of establishing their own professional associations, both locally and nationally. Because they were excluded from the American Bar Association until 1918, female attorneys formed the National Association of Women Lawyers in 1899. Female journalists who were excluded from the National Press Club in Washington, D.C., formed their own association. Sometimes, no doubt as a last resort, women in predominantly male professions joined the auxiliaries designed for wives of professionals. The female professor, for example, would join the faculty wives' club. Catholics, whether from preference or from feelings of exclusion is not clear, also formed separate associations, such as the National Catholic Education Association (1904), the Catholic Library Association (1921), and the Catholic Hospital Association (1915).

The more inclusive membership policies of professional associations in the twentieth century not only increased membership but also led to changes in the nature of the knowledge produced and disseminated. For example, as it has become more gender balanced, the American Medical Association has given more attention to such health problems as heart disease among women. Legal responses to issues such as domestic violence have likewise changed as more women have joined the American Bar Association.

LEARNED SOCIETY OR PROFESSIONAL ASSOCIATION?

Like professional associations, learned societies attempted to attract a broader membership in the twentieth century. Along with greater inclusion in both learned societies and professional associations has come a blurring of the distinctions between the two. Several learned societies serve as national clearinghouses for connecting colleges and universities with those seeking professorial positions. The Modern Language Association (MLA; 1883) typifies this role. Each fall it solicits paid advertisements from colleges and universities that anticipate openings in English and foreign language departments. These advertisements are compiled in the *Job Information List,* to which graduate students and others seeking positions subscribe. Most institutions conduct interviews at the MLA's annual convention, and current dues-paying membership is required of those attending the convention. Although the MLA exerts no control over the quality and number of those who enter the profession, it provides a venue for

that entrance and accrues financial benefit from the process. In 1997, for example, subscriptions to the *Job Information List* yielded $354,835 (Franklin, p. 465).

Some learned societies and professional associations have merged, creating a single organization that serves both scholarly and professional interests. The American Association of Geographers (AAG) began in 1904 as a learned society to "serve as a clearing house for ideas among mature geographers" (Cohen, p. 4), thereby excluding young geographers. In 1937 those who were excluded formed the Young Geographers' Society (YGS) to help members find university positions; in 1943 it morphed into the American Society for Geographical Research; and in 1944 it became the American Society of Professional Geographers (ASPF). The AAG and the ASPF merged in 1948, thus uniting "the research selectivity of the learned society and the multi-purpose services of the professional association" (p. 4).

In recent years learned societies have struggled with issues of identity, trying to delineate the boundaries between themselves and professional associations. Writing in 1970, George Winchester Stone Jr. articulated a question that learned societies continue to confront: "Are scholarly, pedagogical, and professional concerns as interrelated as we have thought?" (p. 67).

Since Stone's question, the blurring between learned societies and professional associations has only increased. The MLA, for example, has adopted policies on teaching loads and class size, and it has addressed the declining percentage of tenure-track positions in the academy by convening a conference on part-time and adjunct faculty members. It has also planned a conference on the future of graduate education and worked with other humanities and language organizations to advocate for a variety of professional issues, including continued funding for the National Endowment of the Humanities and the National Endowment for the Arts (Franklin, p. 459). The MLA is not unusual in this regard; learned societies of anthropologists, economists, and historians have taken similar actions.

Ironically, the increase in professional concerns within the learned societies that draw most of their membership from higher education came at a time of radical change within the professorate. Between 1970 and 1997 the number of professors holding tenured or tenure-track positions decreased from 88 percent to 57 percent (Leatherman). This change has been incremental, with the number of part-

---

∽○∽

LEARNED SOCIETY VIS-À-VIS PROFESSIONAL ASSOCIATION

Nine times in its long history the MLA [Modern Language Association] has revised its Constitution to reflect broadening intellectual interests and professional responsibilities of its members. Its basic document now defines the purposes of the Association: "to promote study, criticism, and research in modern languages, and their literatures, and to further the common interests of teachers of these subjects."

All this we feel is to the good. The learned society in such a basic subject as modern languages and literatures accepts its responsibility for professionalism, and the pedagogical steps which lead to it. The question to be asked is whether in doing so have we confused our objectives in our spread of general tolerance and wide-spread activity. What has become of our concern for the traditional aspects of higher learning, and criticism and literary research? Are scholarly, pedagogical, and professional concerns as interrelated as we have thought. . . . For the MLA, though it has moved along professional and pedagogical lines "to further the common interests of teachers of modern languages," has not issued edicts as to teaching loads, or class sizes, or salary scales, or policies as to sabbatical leaves, or tenure—the AAUP [American Association of University Professors] is concerned about some of these issues, the NCTE [National Council of Teachers of English] about others. And this division of labor seems sound, for tenure affects not modern language teachers alone, nor does a sabbatical policy, nor a teaching load policy, nor a salary scale.

Source: George Winchester Stone Jr., "Learned Society or Professional Association?" (1970).

---

timers in the professorate increasing slightly each year. The two-tier faculty resulting from this division presents learned societies with an increasingly dissimilar set of professional concerns. One group has the luxury of focusing exclusively on the production and dissemination of knowledge, whereas the other must attend to working conditions that affect basic survival.

Furthermore, learned societies lack some of the crucial mechanisms that have traditionally enabled professional associations to control their membership and working conditions. Although members of learned societies who serve on Ph.D. committees at their individual universities determine who will and will not enter the profession, learned societies have no mechanism like state examinations to control the number who enter a given field. For the last three decades of the twentieth century, the production of Ph.D.s in most academic fields has exceeded demand, thus providing universities opportunities to treat a significant percentage of the faculty as casual labor.

Professional associations are not immune from difficulties either. Long-held ethics of noncompetition in, say, the American Bar Association, are being eroded by greed and blatant self-promotion. Changes in the legal rights of patients and in the insurance industry have transformed many physicians into petty bureaucrats who spend more hours filling out forms and seeking permission to carry out procedures than dealing with their patients, and the AMA has been able to do little to reverse this situation.

In the twenty-first century both learned societies and professional associations will continue to explore and participate in the production and circulation of knowledge. The terms of that production and circulation will, however, continue to change. There is growing internationalism in such organizations; the foreign membership in the American Mathematical Society, for example, grew from 22 percent in 1989 to 37 percent in 1999, and 70 percent of the articles published in *Physics Today* are written by foreigners (McMurtrie, p. A21). Some associations are forging new links with companies that produce tests for licensure (Basinger, p. A48). And it is still too soon to tell how the Internet, which has certainly fostered internationalism, will shape learned societies and professional associations. Only time will tell how these two social institutions will be configured at the end of another century and how they will relate to American culture.

See also **Education in Early America; Popular Intellectual Movements, 1833–1877; Urban Cultural Institutions** *(volume 1);* **The Professional Ideal; Intellectuals and Ideology in Government; The Struggle for the Academy** *(volume 2); and other articles in this section.*

BIBLIOGRAPHY

Basinger, Julianne. "Teacher-Accreditation Group and Testing Service Work on Licensure Exams." *Chronicle of Higher Education* 45 (24 October 1999): A48.

Bledstein, Burton J. *The Culture of Professionalism: The Middle Class and the Development of Higher Education in America.* New York, 1976.

Cohen, Saul B. "A Question of Boundaries: The Response of Learned Societies to Interdisciplinary Scholarship." In *Learned Societies and the Evolution of the Disciplines,* edited by Saul B. Cohen, David Bromwich, and George W. Stocking Jr. New York, 1988.

Ellsworth, Mary Ellen. *A History of the Connecticut Academy of Arts and Sciences, 1798–1999.* New Haven, Conn., 1999.

Franklin, Phyllis. "Report of the Executive Director." *PMLA* 112 (1998): 456–466.

Gere, Anne Ruggles. *Intimate Practices: Literacy and Cultural Work in U.S. Women's Clubs, 1880–1920.* Urbana, Ill., 1997.

Gilb, Corinne Lathrop. *Hidden Hierarchies: The Professions and Government.* New York, 1966.

Gilman, Daniel Coit. *The Launching of a University, and Other Papers: A Sheaf of Remembrances.* 1906. Reprint, New York, 1969.

Kiger, Joseph C., ed. *The Greenwood Encyclopedia of American Institutions: Research Institutions and Learned Societies.* Westport, Conn., 1982.

Larson, Magali Sarfatti. *The Rise of Professionalism: A Sociological Analysis.* Berkeley, Calif., 1977.

Leatherman, Courtney. "Part-Timers Continue to Replace Full-Timers on College Faculties." *Chronicle of Higher Education* 46 (28 January 2000): A16.

Machlup, Fritz. *Knowledge: Its Creation, Distribution, and Economic Significance.* Vol. 2, *The Branches of Learning.* Princeton, N.J., 1982.

March, Francis A. "Recollections of Language Teaching." [1893] Reprinted in *The Origins of Literary Studies in America: A Documentary Anthology,* edited by Gerald Graff and Michael Warner. New York, 1989.

Marotta, Gary. "The Academic Mind and the Rise of U.S. Imperialism: Historians and Economists as Publicists for Ideas of Colonial Expansion." *American Journal of Economics and Sociology* 42, no. 2 (April 1983): 217–234.

McMurtrie, Beth. "America's Scholarly Societies Raise Their Flags Abroad." *Chronicle of Higher Education* 46 (28 January 2000): 21.

Morison, Samuel Eliot. *Three Centuries of Harvard: 1636–1936.* Cambridge, Mass., 1936.

Stone, George Winchester, Jr. "Learned Society or Professional Association?" In *Confrontation and Learned Societies,* edited by John Voss and Paul L. Ward. New York, 1970.

Tocqueville, Alexis de. *Democracy in America.* 3rd ed. Translated by Henry Reeve. London, 1838.

GOVERNMENT

Donald T. Critchlow

The complexity of advanced industrial systems requires governments to acquire an enormous range of specialized knowledge and administrative expertise with which to order their affairs. Uniformity in demand, however, has not produced uniformity in the character and supply of knowledge for government purposes. There are significant variations, related to diverse cultural traditions, in the means of acquiring knowledge and applying methods of expertise. For example, central government bureaucracies in western Europe and Japan directly provide many more sources and opportunities for the development of policy expertise than do their counterparts in the United States, which in modern times rely heavily on private research organizations operating outside government bureaucracies for functional expertise. As the federal role in economic and social policy expanded in the post–World War II era, increased federal funding did not produce a commensurate increase in the size of government. Instead it strengthened the complicated network of relationships among the federal government, state and local governments, and private groups, including nonpartisan research institutes.

Indeed, federal employment increased less than one-fifth from 1955 to 1980, while federal spending rose from $22 billion to $167 billion, principally for payments to individuals for Social Security, health care, veterans' pensions, unemployment insurance, and public assistance. To implement these programs, following a characteristic pattern of devolution, the federal government operated indirectly, through intermediary organizations in state and local government, and in civil society. This reliance on private, nonpartisan research organizations imparts a unique quality to the acquisition and use of knowledge by the administrative state in contemporary America.

U.S. GOVERNMENT: FOUNDATIONS AND EARLY DEVELOPMENT

The vast size, complexity, and expense of this system of acquiring knowledge by government in the United States suggests the pluralistic nature of the American polity, deeply rooted in its republican distrust of centralized government. This distrust of centralized government found expression in the United States Constitution, drafted in Philadelphia in 1787. Its famous beginning, "We the people," asserts that the source of its authority rests in the people rather than state or centralized government. In *Rights of Man* (1791) the Anglo-American political writer Thomas Paine eloquently expressed this sentiment when he declared, "A constitution is a thing antecedent to government, and a government is only the creation of a constitution. The constitution of a country is not an act of its government, but of the people constituting a government." The Constitution assigns powers to various branches of government, but limits the power that any branch may have and allows each branch to check and balance the others. Moreover, the Constitution denies certain powers to the national government, reserving them for the states and the people.

Those who accepted the idea of a stronger central government with widening administrative powers naturally gravitated to the statesman Alexander Hamilton's Federalist program, which expressed the belief that the nation's future lay in high tariffs, internal improvements at the national expense, and a national bank as a bulwark of sound currency and credit. Opposition to Hamilton's system developed slowly, but finally coalesced around the Continental Congress delegate James Madison's opposition to the refunding of the debt and the national assumption of states' debts incurred during the American Revolution. This opposition to the Hamiltonian program assumed a more strident and ideological character with the government's effort to charter the Bank of the United States in December 1790. By 1792 this opposition congealed into a Republican "party," led by Madison and the principal author of the Declaration of Independence, Thomas Jefferson. What tied the diverse sectional and social elements together in a national Democratic-Republican Party was a common republican ideology that involved a deep hatred of bloated state power.

The election of Thomas Jefferson to the presidency in 1800 entailed the explicit rejection of the cherished Federalist conviction that government is the most effective mechanism of social integration. Under Jefferson, Democratic-Republicans set about to reduce the overawing and dangerous power of government. Democratic-Republicans believed that the abuse of political establishments had led to most of the evils afflicting humankind in the past. In adhering to the principles of republican ideology, Jeffersonians sought to separate the national government from intimate involvement in society. As a consequence, the federal government's role in accumulating social knowledge remained limited, although Jefferson approved several scientific, military, and commercial expeditions into the foreign-held trans-Mississipi West, most notably the Lewis and Clark expedition of 1804–1806 that brought back new scientific information about Native Americans, flora, and fauna of western North America. This knowledge served Jefferson's continental vision of an "empire of liberty" and American westward expansion. Moreover, Jefferson's library, consisting of approximately six thousand books, provided the basis for rebuilding the Library of Congress, which had been burned by the British during the War of 1812. At the beginning of the twenty-first century, the Library of Congress is one of the largest and most valuable research libraries in the world, with approximately 84 million items in its collections, including over 20 million books and pamphlets, and millions of charts, engravings, maps, motion pictures, musical compositions, photographs, and recordings. In addition, the library holds a 35-million-piece manuscript collection containing the papers of almost every president from George Washington to Calvin Coolidge. Its collection of Chinese, Japanese, and Russian materials is the largest in the world outside the Far East and Russia.

The 1824 election of John Quincy Adams to the presidency revived the Hamiltonian ideal of a strong central government with widening administrative powers. In his first message as president, Adams boldly called for far-reaching programs of national development led by the government in Washington. He asked for huge expenditures for internal improvements, poured scorn upon the idea of limited government, and declared that a strong national government ensured the most liberty. To strengthen the knowledge of the federal government, he called for the founding of a national university and other such agencies in the nation's capital. He proposed federal support for science and the arts.

Adams's program met with rage and ridicule. Thomas Jefferson angrily declared that liberty was not power, but rather the restraint of power. In the election of 1828, Adams suffered a crushing defeat at the hands of the popular war hero Andrew Jackson, who rallied the Democratic Party around a program of laissez-faire economics, state rights, and restoration of government to "the people." Jacksonian policy rested on a belief that government nonintervention guaranteed social fluidity and an expansion of limitless opportunity. Once in power, Jackson ardently defended the theory that most public offices required no special abilities or experience, thereby belying the notion of expertise in government and the establishment of a permanent class of civil servants. Jeffersonian-Jacksonian sentiments against centralized government, civil service, and specialized knowledge determined American political culture and the meaning of government knowledge well into the late nineteenth century.

Because of this considerable opposition to federal support for the development of scientific and technological knowledge, Congress approved of only those projects that showed military or commercial justification. In 1798, with war with France appearing imminent, the American inventor Eli Whitney received a contract for the delivery of four thousand muskets within eighteen months that he proposed could be mass-produced through interchangeable parts. While Whitney failed to perfect the manufacture of interchangeable parts and was thus unable to fulfill his contract, the federal War Department continued to maintain hope that this idea would be realized. From 1822 to 1826, John Harris Hall, at the National Armory at Harpers Ferry, Virginia, succeeded in mass-producing interchangeable weapons, one of the most important technological advances in the early nineteenth century. The War Department also played a vital role in the exploration and mapping of the continent. Moreover, the need for technically trained officers resulted in the founding of the West Point Academy. By the 1820s, West Point was the major source of engineers in the United States, who would be used to survey for canals, roads, and railroads.

During this same period, Joseph Lovell, the new surgeon general of the United States Army, instructed his personnel to collect weather data on the assumption that disease and weather were connected. The establishment of the Naval Observatory by Congress led to the storage and maintenance of nautical charts and chronometers. The head of the observatory in the 1840s, Matthew Fontaine Maury, compiled data from ship's logs to produce the first comprehensive guides to ocean currents and meteorological data.

PRIVATE SOCIAL KNOWLEDGE AND THE FEDERAL GOVERNMENT

In this environment of relatively weak centralized government, however, the craft of social investigation developed within a middle-class subculture of reformers, many of them women, who documented the plight of slaves, the poor, prisoners, and the insane. This capacity for social investigation focused on the abolition of slavery, temperance, and social reform. The affinity of antebellum social reform and feminism became evident in reports issued by American abolitionists who documented the conditions of slave life, as well as in reports on the care of prisoners, the indigent, and the insane. In the 1840s, the social reformer Dorothea Dix issued a series of groundbreaking reports to state legislatures calling for the humane care of the mentally ill. This tradition of empirical research into social problems conducted by private individuals associated with reform movements was extended into the late nineteenth century on account of the weakness of a federal government generally lacking the capacity for extensive or well-coordinated social investigation.

Government capacity for social knowledge developed more readily on the state level in the antebellum period. By the outbreak of the Civil War, state legislatures in the most populous states regularly received detailed narrative and statistical reports on dependency, crime, public health, labor conditions, and economic development. Most of these reports called for the need to regulate social conditions, hours and working conditions of labor, quality of goods offered for sale, and institutions for the poor and the indigent. These reports relied more on democratic and humanitarian sentiments associated with moral reform than they did on claims of science and disinterested expertise. Female reformers, as suggested by the role of Dorothea Dix,

played an especially important role in this early endeavor to bring social knowledge to state legislatures and the public. While denied the right to vote, American women exerted power in this realm of social investigation by addressing social issues and translating them to moral questions, where their credentials were deemed superior to those of men.

While the capacity for social knowledge grew in the antebellum period, the federal government revealed an institutional impoverishment that reflected a unique antistatist tradition in America, reinforced by sectionalist politics of the period. The major institution in Washington for the gathering and accumulation of scientific and social knowledge remained the Smithsonian Institution, which opened in 1846 at the instigation of a single individual, the English scientist James Smithson, for whom the institution was named. In the decades following the Civil War, the Smithsonian Institution became a center for people such as the economist Francis A. Walker, the educator John Eaton, the geologist-ethnologist John Wesley Powell, and the statistician Carroll D. Wright, who took leading roles in establishing a rudimentary infrastructure of social investigation in the nation's capital. These individuals served as conduits for a transition from moral reform to scientific reform. Most came from evangelical backgrounds, but they considered themselves men of science, even while they maintained, albeit in muted form, evangelical commitments to reform. These individuals became the guiding spirits for the development of federal agencies and government-sponsored institutions involved with generating knowledge and its application in the social, economic, and political affairs of the nation.

By the early twentieth century, a large resident class of scientific and professional civil servants had emerged in Washington. Especially important in the development of the government's capacity for disseminating social knowledge was the growth of the Department of Agriculture in the late nineteenth century, which provided farmers with information about the latest advances in agriculture. Moreover, the Morrill Act of 1862 mandated states to invest proceeds from the sales of large areas of federal land in the establishment of colleges of agriculture and the mechanical arts, thus leading to the founding of many land-grant colleges. These colleges, in turn, produced many remarkable advances in U.S. agriculture in the late nineteenth and twentieth centuries. In 1904, the Bureau of the Census reported that 3,919 civil servants fell into the classification of "professional, technical, and scientific" workers. Within this group, nearly 1,100 people were described as "special agents, experts, and commissioners," while another 300 or so were designated simply as "scientific experts and investigators."

Many of the early organizers in the Smithsonian Institution played a critical role in the establishment of the American Social Science Association (ASSA) in 1865. The ASSA sought to serve as a clearinghouse of social knowledge in order to promote reform in education, public health jurisprudence, finance, and social economy. Directly influenced by the achievements of the Sanitary Commission during the Civil War and modeled on the British National Association for the Promotion of Social Science, the ASSA attracted commercial elite groups interested in promoting sound fiscal and monetary policy; lawyers, doctors, ministers, and teachers who sought professional affirmation; and middle-class reformers who combined humanitarian moral reform with the new scientific spirit. The ASSA involved feminists such as Carolyn Heally Dall, a founding member of the ASSA who established a data bank of government philanthropic reports on poverty and dependency from several countries. The ASSA also enlisted public officials, including Carroll Wright, Francis Walker, and John Eaton, who called for the creation of state and federal agencies to gather and disseminate social knowledge for the new age of industrialism and the perceived crisis of laissez-faire capitalism.

Important to the ASSA was the involvement of liberal academic social scientists who brought to the organization their concerns with professionalization and objectivity of social science research in the name of reform. Influenced by German historicism, these academics called for a revision of liberal economic and social theory, necessary in their eyes, to foster state capacity on the state and federal levels. In this way, the ASSA and other professional organizations that arose in the late nineteenth century paved the way for a new liberalism, grounded in social empiricism.

These reformers called for new measures of efficiency and economy in voluntary charity organizations and in public administration. Behind this concern with efficiency and economy lay a deep conviction that the polity was threatened by the corruption of partisan political machines that served special economic interests. These political machines, run by local and state political bosses, consistently manipulated the mass of voters to maintain political power in flagrant disregard for any notion of public morality or efficiency and economy in government. Thus progressive reformers—the new social scientists, humanitarians, and certain elite

businessmen—called for new social knowledge to help restore political order and representative government to American society. Beneath the slogan "efficiency and economy"—the rallying cry of reformers—lay strong antimajoritarian values fused with antiparty perspectives.

This movement for efficiency found early expression in late-nineteenth-century charity endeavors. Concerned that relief was being wasted on the undeserving poor, new professionals were brought into charity organization to centralize recipient roles, provide vouchers for relief funds to be distributed to recipients, institute periodic checks on recipients, and implement budget systems within agencies to keep a close watch on funds. Essential to this reform was the gathering of data through statistical measures and new accounting procedures. In the process, professionals and experts, generally men, replaced older volunteer workers, often women, who had staffed these agencies. Behind this movement lay a sentiment expressed by the industrialist Andrew Carnegie, who declared, "One of the most serious obstacles to the improvement of our race is indiscriminate charity." Carnegie's infatuation with the new social sciences would lead him to create a number of new nonprofit philanthropic institutions concerned with the gathering of public knowledge.

At the vanguard of this movement for efficiency and economy in government were university-trained and highly specialized social scientists. In the latter half of the nineteenth century, the social sciences were radically transformed from disciplines based on deductive reasoning derived from natural law into those of inductive procedures founded on historical analysis and empirical research. This new methodology allowed social scientists to mask any preoccupation with political matters in the terminology of scholarly objectivity and empirical research. The transformation of political impulses into the quest for public knowledge and administrative solutions reflected the aspirations of a new professional class anxious to gain influence in a highly industrialized society through expertise. They sought reform by placing "the best people"—objective-minded experts—into government.

EFFICIENCY AND ECONOMY: PROFESSIONAL RESEARCH AND ADMINISTRATIVE GOVERNMENT

This movement to place administrative authority in the hands of a professional elite would have been doomed in all likelihood without the breakdown of party organization in the late nineteenth century. During this time the American electorate acquiesced in its loss of political control, as evidenced by the general decline in voter turnout following the election of 1896. A comparison between the election of 1896 and 1916 reveals that of the thirty-four nonsouthern states only eight experienced increased voter participation. The majority of industrial states lost 15 to 20 percent in voter turnout. Institutional reforms enacted during this time—the Australian ballot, antifusion laws, and personal registration laws—only hastened the decline of partisan identification and voter turnout. With the decline in party feeling, nonpartisan independence found new vitality.

The call for efficiency and economy in government, and the need to develop new public agencies for the gathering of public knowledge essential to the restoration of a representative government, began on the municipal level first in New York with the creation of the city's Bureau of Municipal Research in 1907, organized by social scientists and civic-minded philanthropists and businessmen. Municipal research bureaus would be established in Philadelphia; Rochester, New York; Cleveland, Akron, and Toledo, Ohio; and San Francisco. Central to these municipal research bureaus was the creation of executive budget systems that allowed a strong executive office, public officials, and the general electorate to have a means of discerning how public funds were being expended. Essential to the functioning of an executive budget was the creation of an agency staffed by nonpartisan experts who would prepare and analyze budgetary finances and expenditures.

This demand for an executive budget system reached the national level under the administration of President William Taft in 1910. When Taft assumed office in 1909, the federal budget stood at over one billion dollars and the federal debt had reached disturbing proportions, largely as an aftermath of the financial panic of 1907. In these circumstances, Taft was able to convince Congress to appropriate $100,000 for a commission on economy and efficiency in government. To staff the commission, Taft called on the best social scientists in the United States. After two years of painstaking work, the President's Commission on Economy and Efficiency came out with its 1912 report, *The Need for a National Budget*. Yet proposed in an election year, a recalcitrant Congress refused to enact an executive budget system that would have served to strengthen the executive branch of the government

at the expense of Congress. The failure of the Taft commission, however, did not dismay reformers. Instead they created the Institute for Government Research in 1916, a predecessor to the Brookings Institution. Only during the Harding administration would budget reform be enacted in the Budget and Accounting Act of 1921.

Taft's successor to the presidency, Woodrow Wilson, both in his first term and later in his second term as wartime president, reflected in many respects the deep ambivalence that middle-class Americans felt about the state during the first two decades of the twentieth century. The creation of the progressive regulatory state under Presidents Theodore Roosevelt and William Taft and in Wilson's first term established an array of new government agencies involved in conservation, consumer protection, corporate regulation, trade practices, and monetary and financial policies. Yet, Woodrow Wilson in his pioneering essay on public administration warned that the model of Prussian administration should be avoided in America. He declared that European bureaucratic practices would have to be adapted to fit the highly decentralized form of government in the United States. If the European model is to be employed in the United States, he told his fellow reformers, "We must Americanize it. . . . We must learn our constitutions by heart and we must get the bureaucratic fever out of its veins."

Wilson's ambivalence pervaded his response to World War I until American entry in April 1917. Both the federal government's defense and civilian departments failed to consider mobilization tasks before 1917. As a consequence, private planning preceded public planning. Financial and manufacturing firms such as J. P. Morgan and Du Pont Company, by receiving Allied war orders, were among the first to assess the financial, technical, and labor requirements of munitions production. At the same time, a number of professionals in the private sector established reputations as independent authorities on the special requirements of modern war.

War, however, compelled the enormous administrative expansion of the federal government in the short period between April 1917 and November 1918. In the course of this administrative expansion, government agencies appeared in haphazard fashion, drawing corporate and academic personnel into government management. This involvement led many to the belief that the capacity for public knowledge and for effective social action rested in the mobilization of private, public-spirited professional and business groups willing to work in cooperation with a state sympathetic to private voluntary activities. The war demonstrated for these individuals how a uniquely American combination of state-society relations could be forged.

Herbert Hoover put this insight into practice as secretary of commerce in the Harding and Coolidge administrations and later as president of the United States by using the techniques of private-public cooperation he had learned as a wartime administrator. Hoover sought to develop state voluntary cooperation in the collection of specialized data required for rational decision making in both the private and public sectors. For Hoover and others concerned with public knowledge, the war revealed just how essential government knowledge was for economic and social planning. Through the development of an administrative state, he sought to develop a new mechanism for collecting public knowledge without the coercive element of state power.

In keeping with his views about the credibility of privately financed researchers, Hoover arranged for the Rockefeller Foundation to fund a comprehensive survey of social changes in American life between 1900 to 1930. Staffed mainly by academics outside of government, the survey project was organized by the Research Committee on Social Trends, a committee of the nation's leading social scientists, chaired by the economist Wesley Mitchell and the political scientist Charles Merriam, with the research program administered by the sociologists William F. Ogburn and Howard W. Odum. The three-year study resulted in the massive, 1,600-page *Recent Social Trends in the United States: Report of the President's Research Committee on Social Trends* (1933). This study presented the full panoply of available knowledge for public purposes.

During the Great Depression, government agencies continued to use science as a technical tool. Most research, with the exception of the Department of Agriculture and its state experimental stations, was centered in agency laboratories. With the outbreak of war in Europe, however, federal involvement in research changed dramatically when President Franklin Roosevelt established the National Defense Research Committee (NRDC), under its chairman Vannevar Bush, to involve the scientific community in weapons research. Bush also headed the Office of Scientific Research and Development, established in 1941 by executive order to serve as a clearinghouse for the military branches, the NDRC, and the National Advisory Committee for Aeronautics. During World War II, the government developed new contractual devices to provide a legal framework for research and design relationships. Under these new contractual arrangements, the Los Alamos National Laboratory was established under an army contract with the University of California. Federal support for scientific research led to an array of new scientific and medical breakthroughs, including the first electronic computer, the Electronic Numerical Integrator and Computer (ENIAC), developed by John W. Mauchly and J. Presper Eckert from the University of Pennsylvania, and concurrent work by the mathematician John von Neumann for the internal memory of the computer; the development of the pesticide DDT; improved radar technology; and, perhaps most significantly, the atomic bomb, conducted through the Manhattan Project.

Federal funding for basic scientific research continued and grew profoundly in the postwar years. In 1946, the Atomic Energy Commission was formed to investigate the uses of atomic energy. The National Science Foundation (NSF), founded in 1950, provided federal funds for basic research in the general sciences, engineering, and social sciences. The National Institutes of Health (NIH) became the primary supporter of medical research and research in the life sciences. By 1958, the federal government had become the predominant source of academic research funding, contributing 55 percent of total research funds for that year; by 1968, the federal government was providing 70 percent of total funding. Government research funding continued to increase during the 1970s to support projects such as the Kitt Peak National Observatory and the National Center for Atmospheric Research, and to develop defense systems such as the Strategic Defense Initiative missile shield (or "Star Wars"). By 1998, federal government research expenditures to universities and colleges reached $12 billion, with 14 percent of this money going to the Johns Hopkins University, the Massachusetts Institute of Technology, Stanford University, and the University of Washington.

One of the most significant scientific projects undertaken by the government was the establishment of the National Aeronautics and Space Administration (NASA), following the launching of the Russian satellite *Sputnik* into orbit in October 1957. That same year, Congress passed the National Defense Education Act that provided federal scholarships, a federal student loan program, state grants for science and foreign language education, and research into the development of radio, television, motion picture, and related technologies for educational purposes. The federal government's involvement in the space program represented the government's commitment to scientific research. The operational budget of NASA doubled every year between 1959 and 1964, reaching a peak in 1966 with a budget of $5.9 million, almost 6 percent of the federal budget. The space program led to telecommunication satellites, advanced Doppler radar for meteorological forecasting, global positioning systems, and vastly improved digital mapping.

The federal government also played a major role in the development of the Internet and the World Wide Web. Along with the formation of NASA, the Department of Defense also created a new subagency, the Defense Advanced Research Projects Agency (DARPA), concerned with ballistic missile defense and nuclear test monitoring. In early 1962, DARPA established the Information Processing Techniques Office (IPTO) to explore computers and networking. In 1965, this office formally sponsored a study to look into the possibility of joining computers through a network for time sharing and data transfers. Lawrence Roberts, a scientist at the Massachusetts Institute of Technology, submitted in 1967 a preliminary network design dubbed ARPANET. Shortly afterward, DARPA awarded a small private corporation, Bolt Beranek and Newman, Inc. (BBN), a million-dollar contract to build the system physically. By late 1969, four computers had been linked into the first network joining the National Measurement Center at the University of California at Los Angeles, the Stanford Research Institute, the University of California at Santa Barbara, and the University of Utah. In 1972, Ray Tomlison at BBN wrote the first electronic messaging program, and Lawrence Roberts wrote the first e-mail managing software. In 1974, BBN opened the network to the public through Telenet. By 1984, there were more than 1,000 network hosts on ARPANET.

In 1986, the NSF replaced DARPA as the primary agency funding the network, and created its own network system. The following year, the NSF commissioned management of the network to a private corporation. By 1990 there were over 100,000 hosts. The Internet, as it is known by twenty-first-century terminology, provides a network connecting a multitude of smaller subnetworks, widely available to private individuals and public academic and research institutions. The Internet received its largest source of funding through the United States High-Performance Computing Act of 1991, sponsored by Senator Albert Gore. Additional federal support helped boost the number of Internet hosts to more than 56 million from 170 countries with more than 300 million websites.

GOVERNMENT AND THE IDEOLOGICAL ORIENTATION OF SOCIAL KNOWLEDGE

As federal research in scientific and technological research expanded in the post–World War II period, so did the government's involvement in the development of social knowledge. Yet, while state capacity for gathering social knowledge expanded radically during the Great Depression, the war, and the postwar period, the federal government continued to rely indirectly on intermediary organizations in state and local government, and in civil society for the accumulation of government knowledge. The commensurate increase in the size of the federal government led to the creation of fluid networks of policy specialists, who operated in and between government and the private sector, identifying policy issues, generating "solutions" to policy problems, and overseeing and evaluating the implementation and administration of policies within their specific areas of competence. Essential to these policy networks are private policy research institutes, "think tanks," a peculiarly American social invention. By the 1990s, there were an estimated 1,200 nongovernment think tanks of various descriptions, various focuses on social and economic issues, and various sources of funding at work in the United States. The Second World War, the postwar continuation of a large defense program, and the expansion of federal social programs were all important in the evolution of the American think tank. At the end of the Second World War, Americans made a political decision to have the government train, subsidize, and regularly consult a sizable population of civilian experts on such issues as defense, welfare, health, and economic stability. Of the major think tanks, only the Brookings Institution (1927) and the Carnegie Endowment for International Peace (1910) were founded before the war. The American Enterprise Institute for Public Policy Research was founded in 1943.

Although think tanks are ostensibly nonpartisan, in many instances they function as extensions of state power, coming into and falling out of influence with changes in governments and shifts in the ideological climate of America. In other cases, think tanks function more independently, questioning and monitoring state strategies and structures. For example, the Rand Corporation of the 1940s and 1950s was designed to strengthen the programs of the U.S. Air Force, whereas the Institute for Policy Studies (IPS) has been a major center of criticism of U.S. foreign policy and domestic social programs and policies in the areas of civil rights and poverty.

Often the ideological orientation of these think tanks reflected changes in historical context and political climate as well as dominant trends in high and popular culture, changes in voting behavior, and shifts in political leadership such as occurred between the cold war consensus of the 1950s and the crisis and breakup of centrist liberalism that accompanied the Vietnam War, the perceived failure of Johnson's Great Society, and the polymorphous counterculture in the 1960s. The founding of the Heritage Foundation in 1973 revealed a new ideological climate in the analysis of public knowledge. In general, think tanks reveal that there is space in the knowledge-policy continuum for very different orientations along the political spectrum, stretching from the democratic socialism of the Institute for Social and Policy Studies to the free-market conservatism of the Heritage Foundation and the libertarian orientation of the CATO Institute, founded in 1977.

Additionally, these private institutions served to supplement social research conducted by federal agencies and institutions. In the 1990s the number of personal and committee staff of Congress exceeded 11,000, with another 20,000 persons responding to the information needs of the legislature from the Congressional Budget Office, the Office of Technology Assessment, and the General Accounting Office. The executive branch commanded far greater numbers. By the 1990s, the scale of spending by the federal government was massive for the acquisition and application of public knowledge. Funding was routed through an estimated 180 bureaus and agencies. The research they sponsored or undertook themselves was often limited in range and strongly influenced by their interpretation, broad or narrow, of the mission itself. This research included a mixture of "in-house" research conducted by career civil servants, and a larger body of research conducted by outside parties via grants and contracts on a "for-profit" basis and some of it by university-based scholars on a "not-for-profit" basis. An estimated one-third of this research activity was supported by the federal government to meet its needs, while the remaining two-thirds was authorized for state and local government, school systems, policy forces, welfare agencies, and industrial and agricultural groups. In addition, a vast array of trade and professional organization and "public interest" groups conducted research in the areas of environmental policy, consumer affairs, civil rights, and foreign policy issues.

In the twenty-first century, the proliferation of government and private institutions involved in public knowledge research marshals expert against expert, testing the credibility of each and enriching the information environment in which policy discourse occurs and decisions are made. On highly technical issues, opposing experts often cancel each other. Yet the growth of public and private agencies involved in collecting public knowledge allows for a more democratized policy process, much closer, in a sense, to the Jeffersonian-Jacksonian vision of an open, competitive democracy. Still, two qualifications are in order: neither Jefferson nor Jackson envisioned a world of competing experts representing various interests and ideological positions; and this contemporary world of competing institutional research is not equally open to all comers. Access to financing is one limitation, access to those in power is another, and the two are not necessarily reciprocal.

The proliferation of expertise and the expansion of government knowledge that has arisen in response to the demand for more policy inquiry have not necessarily improved the information base on which political decisions are made. The emergence of more complicated patterns of political mobilization by a larger and more diverse array of interests and groups has necessarily politicized the nature of policy knowledge and thereby redefined the nonpartisan ideal espoused at the turn of the twentieth century. Competition for attention to research places heavy demands on the time and attention of legislators and policy makers, who are left ultimately, in a value-laden universe, to decide what information counts for them on the basis of their own values. A widespread acceptance of relativism, embodied institutionally in public and private research organizations, has irrevocably altered the process of social investigation and the uses of social knowledge.

See also **Liberalism and Republicanism; Federalists and Antifederalists; Jacksonian Ideology; Whig Ideology; Nationalism and Imperialism; The Artist and the Intellectual in the New Deal** *(volume 1);* **Intellectuals and Ideology in Government; The Struggle for the Academy; International Relations and Connections; Anti-Statism** *(volume 2); and other articles in this section.*

BIBLIOGRAPHY

Government Knowledge before 1945

Alchon, Guy. *The Invisible Hand of Planning: Capitalism, Social Science, and the State in the 1920s.* Princeton, N.J., 1985.

Brewer, John. *The Sinews of Power: War, Money, and the English State, 1688–1783.* Cambridge, Mass., 1990.

Brock, William R. *Investigation and Responsibility: Public Responsibility in the United States, 1865–1900.* Cambridge, Mass., 1984.

Bulmer, Martin, Kevin Bales, and Kathryn Kish Sklar, eds. *The Social Survey in Historical Perspective, 1880–1940.* Cambridge, Mass., 1991.

Cassedy, James H. *Demography in Early America: Beginnings of the Statistical Mind.* Cambridge, Mass., 1969.

Cohen, Patricia Cline. *A Calculating People: The Spread of Numeracy in Early America.* Chicago, 1982.

Critchlow, Donald T. *The Brookings Institution, 1916–1952: Expertise and the Public Interest in a Democratic Society.* DeKalb, Ill., 1985.

Daniels, George H. *American Science in the Age of Jackson.* New York, 1968.

Dupree, A. Hunter. *Science in the Federal Government: A History of Policies and Activities to 1940.* Cambridge, Mass., 1957.

Furner, Mary O. *Advocacy and Objectivity: A Crisis in the Professionalization of American Social Science, 1865–1905.* Lexington, Ky., 1975.

Furner, Mary O., and Barry Supple, eds. *The State and Economic Knowledge: The American and British Experiences.* Cambridge, Mass., 1990.

Haskell, Thomas. *The Emergence of Professional Social Science: The American Social Science Association and the Nineteenth-Century Crisis of Authority.* Urbana, Ill., 1977.

Karl, Barry. *Charles Merriam and the Study of Politics.* Chicago, 1974.

Leach, William. *True Love and Perfect Union: The Feminist Reform of Sex and Society.* New York, 1989.

Marshall, Helen E. *Dorothea Dix: Forgotten Samaritan.* New York, 1937.

Nelson, William E. *The Roots of American Bureaucracy, 1830–1900.* Cambridge, Mass., 1982.

Ross, Dorothy. *The Origins of American Social Science.* Cambridge, Mass., 1991.

Wilson, Woodrow. *The State: Elements of Historical and Practical Politics.* Boston, 1909.

Government Knowledge after 1945

Dixon, Paul. *Think Tanks.* New York, 1971.

Dupré, J. Stefan, and Sanford A. Lakoff. *Science and the Nation.* Englewood Cliffs, N.J., 1962.

Edwards, Lee. *The Power of Idea: The Heritage Foundation at 25 Years.* Ottawa, Ill., 1997.

Friedman, John S., ed. *First Harvest: An Institute for Policy Studies Reader, 1963–1983.* Washington, D.C., 1983.

Lacey, Michael J., and Mary O. Furner, eds. *The State and Social Investigation in Britain and the United States.* Cambridge, Mass., 1993.

National Research Council. *The Federal Investment in Knowledge of Social Problems.* Washington, D.C., 1978.

Peschek, Joseph G. *Policy-Planning Organizations: Elite Agendas and America's Rightward Turn.* Philadelphia, 1987.

Smith, James Allen. *The Idea Brokers: Think Tanks of the New Policy Elite.* New York, 1991.

ORGANIZED RELIGION

Robert Wuthnow

In most societies, organized religion plays a significant role in the production and dissemination of knowledge. Although religion is often regarded as the subjective beliefs and sentiments of individuals, it is also a massive complex of social organizations: congregations, special interest groups, lobbying organizations, seminaries, institutes, and publishing houses. These organizations generate vast quantities of information.

Scholarly studies of organized religion emphasize that knowledge is one of the main dimensions of religious commitment (along with religious belief, religious experience, participation in religious rituals, and ethical behavior). Knowledge provides adherents with a basis for shared beliefs and activities by giving them information about their tradition and by orienting them to the current practices and policies of their religious communities. For these reasons, all forms of organized religion include mechanisms for imparting religious knowledge to children that includes an elementary familiarity with the stories and events that constitute the core of the faith tradition, and these mechanisms are generally supplemented by efforts to instruct adults in how to train children and in more mature understandings of the same materials. All organized religions provide for more specialized knowledge to be communicated to persons who wish to become certified as members of the professional clergy. These clergy in turn become responsible for disseminating information to adherents about the relevance of beliefs and practices to their lives and to current events. Some of this information may be highly technical, such as that concerning appropriate ways of conducting weddings and funerals or the understanding of theological concepts. Organized religions also require knowledge of practical administrative matters to be produced and shared, such as how to conduct elections of religious officials or how to dispose of grievances that may be expressed toward the organization.

SOCIAL INFLUENCES

Sociologists generally emphasize the ways in which broad changes in society have influenced the capacity of organized religion to play a significant social role, including a role in the production of knowledge. Secularization is the process by which religion is said to have lost influence over activities in other spheres of social life. For example, in some societies religious leaders have also been political leaders, but in modern societies these are more likely to be separate roles. Thus, it was not uncommon for Egyptian pharaohs to be regarded as both the religious and political leaders, whereas in the twenty-first century world, church leaders are different from a country's political leader. Differentiation is the process by which institutions such as religion and politics come to be more clearly demarcated so that they can play more specialized social roles. Differentiation has resulted in organized religion playing less of a role in the overall production of knowledge. One example of this change would be the fact that in the 1600s and 1700s organized religion controlled most institutions of higher learning in the United States and influenced the content of research and teaching in these institutions, whereas twenty-first-century higher learning is more likely to be supported by public funds rather than by religion, and instruction is more likely to occur in organizations that guard their autonomy in relation to the influences of religious traditions. Institutions such as Dartmouth College in New Hampshire and Vanderbilt University in Tennessee (once associated with Congregational and Methodist churches, respectively) are secular.

Through the process of differentiation, organized religion has come to play less of a role in producing most forms of so-called secular knowledge. Scientific knowledge that in tribal or archaic contexts may have been the preserve of religious functionaries, such as priests or shamans, is generated by highly trained professionals who specialized in particular branches of the sciences. Political knowledge that may have been derived from sacred texts in the past is separated from these texts and derived more from specialized political theories and empirical studies. Medical and therapeutic knowledge is largely distinct from organized religion as well, although there are continuing efforts by theologians and religious ethicists to influence debates in these areas. Since the mid-1900s, for instance, the debate about genetic engineering shifted from one in which theologians dominated to one organized around presidential commissions at which secular bioethicists testify. The mass communications industry has also differentiated itself from organized religion.

Despite the fact that organized religion has become increasingly differentiated from other producers of knowledge and information, historical studies suggest that organized religion has played a significant role in furthering the development of knowledge in other spheres, such as scientific and medical knowledge, new understandings of government, and ideas about moral behavior. Many of these studies have focused on the distinctive contributions of Protestantism to these developments in western Europe and the United States. The twentieth-century German sociologist Max Weber argued that Protestantism contributed to the emergence of industrial capitalism in western Europe and the United States by popularizing ideas about the importance of serving God through worldly vocations and by encouraging believers to conduct their lives in a rational and disciplined fashion. Other studies have extended Weber's arguments by examining the role of Protestantism in the development of science in the seventeenth century, especially in England. These studies suggest that Protestantism encouraged scientific work by teaching that the universe followed orderly patterns and by emphasizing the possibility of glorifying God by discovering knowledge about these patterns. Other research has followed a similar logic, suggesting that Protestantism encouraged the growth of disciplined or bureaucratic procedures of government and that its emphasis on each individual believer's relationship to God was favorable to the growth of democracy. The American Great Awakening in the 1740s, for instance, is often credited with paving the way for the American Revolution.

These studies continue to be widely debated among historians and other scholars. Some critics suggest that the emphasis on rationality and discipline in early modern Protestantism was the decisive factor, rather than particular religious teachings, and these critics have suggested that similar consequences were evident in other places where religion encouraged rationality and discipline, such as in Japan during the Tokugawa period (1603 to 1867) or as a result of the Benedictine reforms in medieval Catholicism. A more extreme form of criticism suggests that religious teachings in early modern Europe were inconsequential in comparison with technological developments in warfare, navigation, weaving, and printing, or economic developments such as the growth in markets and the shift from an agrarian to an urban economy. More recent scholarship has revived interest in the distinctive role of organized religion, but has focused less on the exclusive contribution of religious teachings and more on the interplay of teachings and the ways in which religion was organized. For example, the tensions between local clergy and their superiors has been emphasized as a reason for the democratic tendencies that emerged in religious teachings and in views toward secular government in seventeenth-century England. Other work suggests that the rationality and personal discipline that appears to have had wide-ranging effects on political and economic behavior in early modern Europe may have largely been the result of a distinctive Protestant invention called the conventicle, which imposed a system of lay and clerical leadership in local congregations capable of monitoring the behavior of members and strongly oriented toward providing them with practical moral and theological understanding. The main conclusion to be drawn from such research is that organized religion contributed to the growth of rational systems of knowledge in the early modern era and that these systems of knowledge have become progressively differentiated from organized religion in the intervening centuries.

THE PRODUCTION OF RELIGIOUS KNOWLEDGE

Just as knowledge in general has become more highly specialized, the knowledge produced by organized religion has undergone a similar process of differentiation. Research on small tribal societies suggests that religious knowledge may be highly complex but is often produced and maintained by only one or a few specialists, such as a shaman or magician. In the larger societies in which the world's major religions emerged, religious knowledge was often internally differentiated between that produced by priests, whose role was to guard the purity of religious traditions and to uphold familiar forms of religious practice, and prophets, who were more likely to challenge conventional knowledge by claiming direct revelations from God. In modern societies, the various kinds of religious knowledge have become more highly differentiated.

Clergy who have direct contact with the adherents of organized religion remain among the most important purveyors of religious knowledge. By virtue of professional training, they are generally regarded by members as having more authoritative interpretations of sacred texts and traditions than members themselves. Most religious services in Christianity, Judaism, and Islam include opportunities for clergy to give sermons or other public addresses and to teach classes, while in traditions such as Buddhism and Hinduism these public occasions for influencing participants are likely to be supplemented by individual instruction or by the clergy serving as role models in such practices as meditation and prayer. Organized religions generally emphasize the importance of believers coming together for worship and instruction, and the congregational or small-group method of organizing believers has been particularly effective in providing clergy with ready-made audiences. Congregational life also provides for an increasingly differentiated variety of clergy roles to be fulfilled, ranging from specialists who focus on preaching, others who devote full attention to the instruction of children or teenagers or young adults, and others who serve as musicians, administrators, or ministers to the wider community. At some of the larger Protestant congregations in the United States, for example, as many as one hundred specialized clergy may be employed full time.

The role of local clergy is typically supplemented by culture producers who work in more centralized religious settings, such as national bureaus. These bureaus depend on a portion of the charitable donations received by local congregations being sent to national offices for the support of activities that cannot be performed effectively at the local level. Publishing has often been regarded as one of these activities. Centralized bureaus (such as that of the Methodist church in Nashville) employ writers, editors, and artists to produce books used for training clergy, study guides for those in charge of education in local congregations, and perhaps copies of official reports or statements that are to be shared by the membership of the organization. These bureaus also provide leadership for committees charged with studying particular theological or social issues and making recommendations to the governing bodies, and other staff positions are devoted to the internal record keeping that any complex organization requires. Many religious organizations maintain statistical bureaus or conduct periodic surveys of their memberships. For instance, the Presbyterian Church (U.S.A.) conducts surveys of its members several times a year.

Besides such bureaus, seminaries and religiously sponsored colleges and universities contribute significantly to the overall knowledge and information produced by organized religion. Seminary personnel generate specialized treatises on theology or on the responsibilities of members, teach and write about the role of religious faith in making moral and ethical decisions, and address issues of contemporary social concern. Seminaries are generally governed by the larger religious bodies that sponsor them and provide them with students, but seminaries are also sufficiently insulated from the demands of these bodies that they sometimes play an important role in generating new or alternative ideas. Religiously sponsored colleges and universities, while faced with increasing competition from public institutions of higher education, continue to attract sizable numbers of students. These organizations play a key role in efforts to integrate religious concerns with developments in the sciences and humanities.

The production of religious knowledge in the twentieth century to the present has increasingly come to depend on special purpose groups, such as missionary organizations, federations concerned with the translation and dissemination of sacred texts, ministries to college students, and quasi-political groups that also promote moral reform or bring religious perspectives to bear on public issues. These special purpose groups are sometimes supported by larger religious bodies, but they also appear increasingly to depend on the mass media for support. Television ministries, such as those of the Baptist minister Jerry Falwell or the Protestant evangelist Pat Robertson, are perhaps the clearest example. Through broadcasting, they reach audiences that cross the boundaries of organized religious bodies, and by direct financial appeals and special solicitations through mail or by telephone, they raise sufficient funds to pay the costs of broadcasting. Some of these ministries have also provided a base from which other special purpose groups emerged, such as campaigns to strengthen families or to address issues concerning abortion or race relations. The Moral Majority and the Christian Coalition are examples.

The effectiveness of these various methods of producing and disseminating religious information on the beliefs of members is a matter of debate. Most studies show that participants in religious congregations are more likely than nonparticipants to share some of the basic beliefs taught by those congregations, such as teachings about the existence of God or the value of prayer. Some research suggests that exposure to particular teachings, such as sermons about responsibilities toward the poor, prompts members to think more about these issues and in some cases to behave in keeping with these teachings. Yet research also suggests that knowledge of even the most basic teachings and doctrines is often less extensive than religious leaders would wish; for instance, surveys in the United States sometimes reveal relatively low levels of knowledge on such topics as the names of books of the Bible or familiarity with biblical figures. Research also suggests that religious teachings that contradict the lifestyles of members with respect to sexual behavior or financial activities have little impact on these lifestyles.

Twentieth-century scholarship on the cultural effects of organized religion has for these reasons focused increasingly on noncognitive influences, such as those associated with the social relationships that develop in religious communities or the religious objects and rituals to which children are exposed in their families. The idea of material culture emphasizes the role of tangible objects that may have special symbolic value, such as a family Bible, crucifix, home altar, or photograph of an ancestor. The material culture of congregations has also been emphasized, especially the architecture of religious buildings and the arrangement of meeting space or the inclusion of ceremonial and artistic artifacts. Research suggests that people often remember the material culture of religious organizations in which they participated as children throughout their lives and associate complex meanings with these objects.

Studies have also emphasized the idea of "lived religion." Lived religion connotes the daily rituals in which religious people may engage, such as praying or meditating; it also includes special occasions, such as holidays and birthdays or weddings and funerals that acquire significance because religious meanings are attached to food, gifts, and special dress; and lived religion sometimes refers to the implicit habits that become carriers of religious meaning, such as perfunctory petitions for divine blessings, casual conversations with co-workers about religious topics, or the friendships that people develop in their congregations.

GENERATING NEW IDEAS

In the study of religions, much attention has been given to questions about the conditions under which organized religion generates new ideas that may challenge traditions. These questions have been of interest because organized religion is often regarded as a protector of tradition, helping to legitimate loyalty to families or undergirding the authority of divinely appointed monarchs or the sanctity of ethnic customs. But organized religion has also been the source of reform movements, protests, revolutions, and violent social upheaval. In the United States, the impact of the Second Great Awakening in the 1830s and 1840s on the antislavery movement of the mid- to late 1800s is a frequently cited example.

One reason for organized religion becoming the source of new ideas is that a new group or class of people emerges in a society with interests that conflict with established groups. The growth of the middle class as a result of industrialization is one example. Where a sizable middle class emerged, organized religion typically experienced strains that resulted either in reforms occurring within established groups or new groups appearing. For example, in eighteenth-century England and the United States the growth of Methodism was fueled by the expansion of a middle class of industrial workers and shopkeepers whose interests were not well served by the Anglican hierarchy and who were attracted by the more individualistic teachings of Methodism. Other examples of new groups becoming carriers of new religious ideas include the emergence of warrior elites in some traditional societies, merchants in early modern settings, and scientists and intellectuals or members of the helping professions in more contemporary settings.

Twentieth-century scholarship challenged the adequacy of associating possibilities for new religious ideas simply with the rise of new status groups. Twenty-first-century thinking focuses more on the competition that exists among different expressions of organized religion, arguing that competition is one of the salient features of modern religion (whereas religion in traditional societies was more likely to be organized around a single system of beliefs) and suggesting that competition is a major source of continuing religious vitality and renewal. One line of thinking suggests that organized religion experiences an inevitable cycle of stagnation and renewal. The possibilities for new ideas to emerge are thus heightened by the appearance of new competitors. For example, new immigrant groups (such as Korean Americans or Hispanic Americans) may prompt new ideas within organized religious bodies that would otherwise have stagnated because the leaders of these bodies perceive the new groups as a threat to their continuing existence or borrow ideas from them. Another line of thinking suggests that competition among religious groups imposes a kind of rational decision-making process on the activities of potential adherents. As they think about their choices, prospective members attempt to maximize the reward they are likely to receive by joining one group or another. For instance, some groups may promise members eternal salvation, while others offer only the opportunity to make friends and serve their communities. By this argument, people would be more likely to join the group offering eternal salvation, because that reward matters a great deal and cannot be found in other settings, whereas the group offering friends and opportunities for service would face competition from secular organizations. This argument helps to explain the persistence and resurgence of fundamentalist groups.

A broader view of how organized religion may generate new ideas comes from linking arguments about competition with greater recognition of the heterogeneity of the social environment. This approach suggests that the appearance of new religious ideas can be understood by emphasizing at least three phases in their appearance. In the initial or production phase, social conditions permit a variety of new ideas to emerge and to compete with one another. Uncertainties that lead people to believe they can no longer depend on familiar social relationships are often a source of new purveyors of religious ideas emerging. For many younger Americans, the social unrest of the 1960s was such an experience. Generalized affluence may be a contributing factor, or new possibilities may be more likely because of a stalemate that prevents existing organizations from suppressing these possibilities (for example, a stalemate between leaders of organized religion and political leaders).

In the next phase of religious idea generation, a selection process occurs in which some of the new ideas generated in the previous phase gain adherents while others cease to be popular. The selection process may be likened to that governing the adaptation of natural species to their environment. Particular ideas may resonate more effectively in a particular social niche than in others, and these ideas may then receive the support of the wealthy and powerful, or find ways to control their members so that wealth or power is unnecessary. For instance, in the 1960s Zen Buddhism and transcendental meditation appealed to college students from upper-middle-class backgrounds, while smaller cults often attracted students from less advantaged families.

Finally, there is a phase of institutionalization in which new ideas and the organizations promoting them gain greater autonomy from their environment. In this phase the movement carrying the new ideas starts to be financially self-sufficient and leaders attend to the internal coherence of the ideas, such that their relevance in other settings can more readily be seen. Since the 1960s, for instance, New Age spirituality has been institutionalized through bookstores, retreat centers, and holistic health classes. Above all, this perspective indicates that social conditions influence the likelihood of organized religion generating new ideas, but does not regard these conditions as being reducible to a single factor. It suggests that religious ideas have internal coherence and become more or less attractive to people because of the social experiences to which people have been exposed.

In all such studies, a lingering question is whether the knowledge and information produced by organized religion is in some way distinctive from that generated in other institutions. The sharpest difference is that between knowledge derived from divine revelation and knowledge derived from human reason or intuition. Yet it is often unclear, in specific instances, whether this distinction necessarily sets religious knowledge apart. Much of the content of religion is typically defended with rational arguments, while knowledge in other spheres is often, as it is said, "taken on faith." While studies of religion continue to recognize conflicts between religious arguments and scientific or philosophical arguments about such topics as the origins of the universe, most contemporary research points to the similarities among religious and nonreligious forms of knowledge. These similarities emphasize the ways in which all knowledge is influenced by social experience and by discourse, and the complexity with which the meanings of statements are surrounded. The differentiating characteristics of religious discourse are thus that it often focuses on statements about the transcendent or ultimate dimensions of life, is explicitly rooted in the teachings of organized religion, and may be recognized as discourse about that which is ultimately beyond proof through logical argument or empirical evidence.

TWENTIETH-CENTURY DEVELOPMENTS

Since the 1950s one of the most significant developments in organized religion with respect to its role in cultural production is its declining ability to control information that is produced about religion itself. Whereas the early decades of the twentieth century saw religious books, training, speeches, and other messages about religion were virtually monopolized by religious organizations, the later decades saw these modes of communication shared with many other organizations, including the mass media, commercial publishing houses, television personalities and producers, filmmakers, therapists, colleges and universities, and retreat centers. Examples of religious information that was and is controlled by organized religion include statements by the Catholic Church that bear the papal imprimatur or books and pamphlets for catechetical instruction produced by a denomination such as the Lutheran or Methodist churches. Such information comprises less of the overall stock of information concerning religion than it did prior to the mid-twentieth century. In the twenty-first century, religious information competes with all of the following: stories about clergy carried by the news media (which may cast them in a negative light); lyrics of popular musicians that may include messages about God or spirituality; television programs and books that convey attractive images of angels; movies that reinterpret biblical themes; cable television coverage of physicians or therapists who present idiosyncratic views of the relationships between healing and spirituality; carefully orchestrated publicity events showing political candidates and elected officials in the presence of selected religious leaders; best-selling books with esoteric religious interpretations that gain popularity because of large marketing and publicity expenditures by commercial publishers; courses about world religions taught at colleges and universities where a negative or critical stance toward these religions is an implicit norm; and weekend retreats sponsored by entrepreneurs who draw participants interested in eclectic forms of spirituality.

The decline in organized religion's control over information about religion and spirituality is thought to have resulted in qualitative changes in how the public thinks about religion. Although opinion surveys show continuing confidence in clergy and organized religion, at least to a greater degree than toward the leaders of many other institutions, this confidence has eroded and is vulnerable to the effects of particularly well-publicized events (such as the 1988 scandal involving the well-known television preacher Jimmy Swaggart). Membership in organized religion and attendance at religious services may remain relatively stable, but participants often reveal in surveys and especially in qualitative interviews that their views about religion are influenced by other sources as well (for example, by art and music or by reading their horoscopes and visiting fortune-tellers).

Many observers have remarked on the public's increasing willingness to distinguish religion from spirituality: religion connotes organized structure and is thus regarded as being arbitrary, distant from genuine personal interests, and perhaps a mere carryover from the past, whereas spirituality is regarded as a more authentic expression of people's quest for the sacred. The distinction between religion and spirituality helps legitimate people's interest in information that comes from a wider variety of sources than from organized religion alone. By favoring spirituality over religion, they gain authority as decision makers to expose themselves to messages about religion and spirituality from many sources and to determine for themselves which of these messages to believe.

The resulting qualitative change in religious commitment is what has variously been called a more privatized faith, a seeker-oriented spirituality, or a new voluntarism in religion. These styles of spirituality reflect the broader market that has emerged for purveying information about religion. Because markets are dominated by competition, producers attempt to provide goods and services that maximize gratification and minimize cost for consumers. Many examples of a consumer-oriented style of spirituality are evident in contemporary culture: depictions of God that emphasize ease of access and intimacy or familiarity rather than relating to God through an arduous quest; emphasis on divine love and mercy to a greater extent than divine righteousness or wrath; stories about angels that picture them as nonjudgmental and caring or as beautiful women or handsome men with virulent sexual appetites; and how-to books or pamphlets that offer five or six easy steps to becoming spiritually enlightened.

The exception to religious information ceasing to be under the auspices of organized religion is fundamentalism. Whether it is Christian, Muslim, Jewish, or from some other tradition, fundamentalism emphasizes absolute truth that is knowable uniquely or exclusively by those who believe in the teachings of a particular leader or group. Fundamentalism is characterized by strong boundaries between its adherents and people in the wider world. These boundaries consist of explicit injunctions to avoid contact with the wider world, condemnations of worldly evil, and distinctive modes of dress or language that create barriers against outsiders. Fundamentalists also encourage adherents to receive information only from authorized sources. This information is likely to include special sacred texts that are thought to contain divine revelations given only to leaders or members of the group, interpretations of divine truth that have been authorized by charismatic leaders or appropriate forms of deliberation, stories about the group's history and its struggles that encourage in-group loyalty, and distinctive interpretations of events in the wider world that may give them apocalyptic meaning or imbue them with conspiratorial overtones. Fundamentalists generally maintain their own publishing houses and in recent decades have relied heavily on tape recordings and videotapes of sermons and rallies to control the information they provide their followers.

Because fundamentalism has flourished in many parts of the world at the same time that more secular or eclectic versions of spirituality have emerged, some scholars have suggested that a culture war exists that pits proponents of radically different worldviews against one another. The culture war is described as a battle between proponents of an orthodox worldview that respects absolute truths and fixed definitions of right and wrong and proponents of a progressive worldview that denies the possibility of knowing absolute truth and instead emphasizes the relativism of moral decisions depending on different circumstances. Critics of the culture wars argument suggest that there is little evidence that public opinion became more polarized in the late twentieth century or that it is rooted in worldviews that divide easily into these two kinds. Most observers nevertheless acknowledge that special interest groups have tried to influence public opinion by presenting extreme positions that resemble these differences in worldviews. As special interest groups gain media attention, they in turn influence the kinds of information that are available to the public. Much of the information about religion (and by religious leaders) that has captured media attention in recent years has thus been characterized by rhetorical extremes, by catchy slogans, and by adversarial language, rather than by moderate or rational tones that aim to promote dialogue.

Because of the dominant influence that special interest groups and the mass media appear to exercise in public discussions, renewed efforts have been made to understand the ways in which organized religion may contribute positively to public debates about collective values. Increasing attention has been paid to the idea of social capital—the social networks and norms that promote cooperative behavior. Participation in organized religion generally increases social capital, both among adherents themselves and by linking them to their neighbors and to other organizations in their communities (such as membership in Rotary, Kiwanis, or the League of Women Voters). Through these networks, information is produced and disseminated informally; for example, when people discuss zoning laws in their communities or when information spreads about the needs of an elderly person as a result of a prayer chain among the members of a religious congregation. Such information appears to play a positive role in mobilizing people to engage in volunteer efforts and to take part in community organizations. Through their actions, these volunteers often display humanitarian values, such as caring and compassion, meaning that organized religion indirectly reinforces information about these kinds of values through the social networks it encourages.

Apart from social networks, organized religion also contributes to public debates about collective values by providing meeting space for such debates and by helping members develop civic skills. These skills include specific abilities, such as the confidence to express one's views in public or to lead a committee meeting, and more general characteristics, such as a willingness to trust others and respect their views. The democratic procedures on which participatory government depends are an important aspect of the knowledge that organized religion contributes. People learn the procedures for electing officers and for managing a business meeting when they participate in such activities in their congregations. These are transferable skills that can be used for mobilizing community action or expressing opinions to elected officials. At a larger level, organized religion includes many forms of internal governance (in many cases called judicatories), such as presbyteries, councils, synods, and assemblies, that follow procedures similar to those used in government and business.

Organized religion exists in an uneasy relationship with secular authority. Because it claims to be guided by revealed truth that may transcend particular societies, organized religion has been a source of dissenting movements in many societies and of separatist groups in others (the Adventists in nineteenth-century New York are an example). These movements and groups have variously been a source of utopian or revolutionary ideology that played a role in overturning established regimes or promoting significant social reforms. It is for this reason that governments often attempt to suppress or regulate the information that religious groups produce.

On balance, since the 1950s there appears to have been a resurgence of conflict between organized religion and government. Some of this resurgence in the late twentieth century can be explained by the collapse of the Soviet Union and the end of the cold war. These developments opened the way for traditional religions that were associated with local and ethnic groups to play a greater role in public life. As concerns about national security eroded in other societies, more room for local religious groups to express their views also appeared. Part of the knowledge that religious groups were able to bring to public discussions was information about the local traditions and customs that truly motivated people. Decentralized views of government that emphasize grassroots participation in local civic associations have reinforced the idea that organized religion should play an increasing role in public life.

See also **Puritanism as a Cultural and Intellectual Force; Anglo-American Religious Traditions; The New England Theology from Edwards to Bushnell; The Transformation of American Religion, 1776–1838; The Black Church: Invisible and Visible; Evangelical Thought; Science and Religion; The Rise of Biblical Criticism and Challenges to Religious Authority; The Struggle over Evolution; Religious Liberalism, Fundamentalism, and Neo-Orthodoxy** *(volume 1);* **Jews; Roman Catholics** *(volume 2);* **Hermeneutics and American Historiography** *(in this volume).*

BIBLIOGRAPHY

Bellah, Robert N. *Beyond Belief: Essays on Religion in a Post-Traditional World.* New York, 1970.

Berger, Peter L. *The Sacred Canopy: Elements of a Sociological Theory of Religion.* Garden City, N.Y., 1969.

Casanova, José. *Public Religions in the Modern World.* Chicago, 1994.

Dumont, Louis. *Homo Hierarchicus: The Caste System and Its Implications.* Chicago, 1970.

Durkheim, Émile. *The Elementary Forms of the Religious Life.* New York, 1965.

Gager, John G. *Kingdom and Community: The Social World of Early Christianity.* Englewood Cliffs, N.J., 1975.

Geertz, Clifford. *The Interpretation of Cultures: Selected Essays.* New York, 1973.

Hunter, James Davison. *Culture Wars: The Struggle to Define America.* New York, 1991.

Marx, Karl, and Friedrich Engels. *On Religion.* New York, 1964.

Ozment, Steven E. *The Reformation in the Cities: The Appeal of Protestantism to Sixteenth-Century Germany and Switzerland.* New Haven, Conn., 1975.

Weber, Max. *The Protestant Ethic and the Spirit of Capitalism.* New York, 1958.

———. *The Sociology of Religion.* Boston, 1963.

Wuthnow, Robert. *Meaning and Moral Order: Explorations in Cultural Analysis.* Berkeley and Los Angeles, 1987.

———. *Producing the Sacred: An Essay on Public Religion.* Urbana, Ill., 1994.

LITERARY REVIEWS AND "LITTLE MAGAZINES"

Robert S. Fogarty

Literary magazines form a significant part of America's intellectual and creative history and have, particularly in the twentieth century, been seen as the crucible of creative writing, avant-garde culture, and critical discourse. Personal relationships between editor and audience and editor and writer have been crucial to this literary culture. There has always been an assumed community of values, opinions, and interests evoked by a particular magazine that when coupled with an editor's determination to shape taste has led to the creation of an eclectic tradition which has produced "little magazines," "magazines of opinion," or "literary magazines." There have been thousands of literary magazines (often with flamboyant names) representing every strand of literary, political, and aesthetic opinion. Variety rather than uniformity has characterized this subculture.

ORIGINS

With the publication of *Poetry* beginning in October 1912, the "little magazine" got its modern start. This magazine of verse was edited in Chicago by Harriet Monroe with the financial backing of Hobart Chatfield-Taylor and one hundred other patrons who agreed to give fifty dollars for a five-year subscription. It was dedicated to the idea that commercial magazines (*Harper's,* the *Atlantic Monthly,* and *Scribner's,* for example) failed to print daring, new poetry and that—on the eve of the 1913 Armory Show in New York City—the international literary world needed a magazine that reflected the latest and best voices. During the latter part of the nineteenth century, national mass circulation magazines, fueled by a growing population, new advertisers, and increased literacy, supplanted the older belles lettres journals represented by the *Dial* and the *North American Review.* Magazines appealed to an emerging middle-class audience, leaving the elite literary culture in search of outlets. *Poetry* was such an outlet.

Within the first year of *Poetry*'s publication, Ezra Pound, Rabindranath Tagore, Vachel Lindsay, and Amy Lowell appeared on its pages. It became the prototypical literary magazine and the site for an experimental and oppositional culture dedicated to unearthing and printing new writers. In the second issue, Monroe announced that "the Open Door will be the policy of this magazine—may the great poet we are looking for never find it shut, or half-shut, against his ample genius. To this end the editors hope to keep it free of entangling alliances with any single class or school" (November 1912, p. 64). By embracing an "open door" policy, the magazine took a stand against "coterie" publishing and against the idea that the magazine should represent a "clique" attached to a manifesto.

Poetry spawned a whole generation of magazines—some, paradoxically, cliquish and urban based, and others located on rural college campuses. There were other journals, called "personal" magazines, driven by the passions of an editor rather than the need to promote a particular genre or literary cause. These personal magazines were best exemplified by Margaret Anderson's *Little Review* (1914), which followed her enthusiasms (feminism, dadaism, symbolism) and her devotion to criticism of books, music, art, drama, and "life." In 1917 Ezra Pound became the foreign editor of the magazine and it was through his efforts that James Joyce's *Ulysses* (1922) ran in installments in the magazine. Subsequently, four issues were seized and burned by the U.S. Post Office.

The *Little Review* was one of the few American outlets for experimental work by American writers such as T. S. Eliot, Sherwood Anderson, and Djuna Barnes. In its final issue in 1929 the magazine said it had been a "trial-track for racers. We hoped to find artists who could run with the great artists of the past or men who could make new records. . . . We have given space in the *Little Review* to 23 new systems of art (all now dead), representing 19 countries" (in Jane Heap, "Lost: A Renaissance." 11:56

[May 1929]). *Broom* (1921) was started in Rome as an "international magazine of the arts published by Americans in Italy" and moved to New York in 1923 under Malcolm Cowley and Matthew Josephson's sponsorship. It was a "vanguard" magazine committed to American and European experimentalism and to a flamboyant editorial style.

There were other "vanguard" magazines. The *Liberator* (1918), edited by Max Eastman, Robert Minor, Claude McKay, and Floyd Dell, sought a politically conscious audience and attacked capitalism. The *New Masses* (1926), under the leadership of Michael Gold, pursued both social and literary goals and became an important vehicle during the Great Depression for writers with a social rather than an aesthetic message. Social realism held sway in the *New Masses* (subsidized by the Communist Party), *Modern Quarterly,* and *Left Front.* Critical essays in such magazines attacked 1920s aesthetes like Pound and Eliot and hammered at writers like Sherwood Anderson for failing to connect their work to larger struggles. In 1934 William Phillips and Philip Rahv established the *Partisan Review* as an organ of the John Reed Club in New York City. It had a distinguished history. In its first issue it published a section from James T. Farrell's *Studs Lonigan Trilogy* (1932–1935) and a glowing review of Jack Conroy's *The Disinherited* (1933). Shortly thereafter it announced an independent editorial policy and broke with the Communist Party. Its subsequent stance, according to Frederick Hoffman, "emphasized the 'Trotskyist' position—world revolution, opposition to nationalism, and definite disapproval of Stalinist policies" (*The Little Magazine,* p. 168). Dwight Macdonald, Mary McCarthy, F. W. Dupee, and George Morris were key figures in putting the "second" *Partisan Review* together.

Writing about the spirit that motivated the magazine in December 1937, William Phillips said that it was an "unusual combination of modernism, a radical sensibility, critical intelligence, and a variety of talents that had not been siphoned off by the larger and the commercial publications." During the 1940s and 1950s it published every major American writer and critic and a host of Continental figures such as Jean Genet and Simone de Beauvoir. In the 1950s the magazine became more culturally conservative and in the following decade it was critical of the emerging New Left. Throughout its history the *Partisan Review* emphasized both its interest in contemporary European literature and its political opposition to Stalinist authoritarianism. It was a major force in the development of American critical and political thought and often attempted to find a way between traditional literary values and sectarian political battles.

UNIVERSITY AND REGIONAL MAGAZINES

Despite the political and economic tone of the 1930s, a number of new magazines, many launched on college campuses, stressed a commitment to both literary values and academic criticism. *Prairie Schooner* (1927) at the University of Nebraska, *Kenyon Review* (1939) at Kenyon College, the *Southwest Review* (1924) at Southern Methodist University, and the *Antioch Review* (1941) at Antioch College were all shaped by the depression years and the political and economic issues of the day, including regionalism and economic change. *Prairie Schooner,* under the longtime editorship of Lowry Wimberly, was a magazine published from the "land between the mountains" and emphasized its midwestern and regional roots for most of its history.

The cause of literary regionalism was particularly strong in the South, where literary magazines became vehicles for the expression of southern values, taste, and sensibility. The *Sewanee Review* (1892) was founded at the University of the South in Tennessee to promote a humane and civilized literary culture. Essays on such varied subjects as Thomas Hardy, modern Spanish fiction, Chinese missionaries, and the old South filled the initial issue. During its first fifty years *Sewanee* was regional in emphasis. That regional quality took on national significance in the 1940s under the editorship of Andrew Lytle and then Allen Tate, both proponents of regionalism and the New Criticism. T. S. Eliot praised the magazine in 1945, saying: "I wish we had in England a periodical occupying a position analogous to *Sewanee Review,* with issues fundamental for the future of civilization" (Janssen, *Kenyon Review,* p. 37). After the civil rights movement of the 1960s, *Sewanee* maintained a dialogue in its pages between tradition and literature, adding more fiction and poetry to its pages yet maintaining its distance from contemporary culture. It has remained a "Southern" magazine.

With the founding of the *Southern Review* in Louisiana in 1935, an older tradition of belles lettres was revived. The first quarterly to carry the title *Southern Review* was published at Charleston in 1828 and championed an autonomous literary culture within antebellum southern society. Subsequent versions of the *Southern Review* were always concerned with the interplay of literature and southern tradition. During the early twentieth century there were several literary magazines (most started at universities) in the South, with the *South Atlantic Quarterly* launched at Trinity College (later Duke University) in 1902; the *Texas Review* in 1915 at the University of Texas, which in 1924 shifted to Southern Methodist and was renamed the *Southwest Review;* and the *Virginia Quarterly Review* in 1925 at the University of Virginia. The *Double-Dealer* (1921) came to life in New Orleans, while the most prominent of them all was Nashville's *Fugitive* (1922), the vehicle for the literary school known as the Agrarian Movement.

John Crowe Ransom, Donald Davidson, Allen Tate, and Robert Penn Warren were all interested in exploring, in poetry and criticism, the relationship between literature and tradition—southern tradition, that is. Warren and Cleanth Brooks had both graduated from Vanderbilt, had been Rhodes scholars at Oxford, and were close to the Agrarian Movement. In 1935 the first number of the revived *Southern Review* appeared in order to present and interpret "Southern problems to a national audience" and interpret "national issues to the Southern scene" (*Reveille,* 16 April 1935). It had a short history and was revived again in 1965 under the editorship of Louis Simpson and Donald Stanford.

The *Kenyon Review* is synonymous with the career of John Crowe Ransom and the rise of the New Criticism. Ransom had come to Kenyon from Vanderbilt and was a leading proponent of the Southern Agrarians, but at Kenyon College in 1939 he launched a critical journal that frequently published the works of Allen Tate, Cleanth Brooks, William Empson, and I. A. Richards. Important poets such as Wallace Stevens and Marianne Moore appeared in the magazine regularly. Though it always had a small circulation (rarely above two thousand), it was tremendously influential in the literary and academic world. During Ransom's tenure as editor little fiction was published, and with his retirement in 1959 and the waning of New Critical theory, the magazine searched for an audience. It suspended publication in 1970 as part of a cost-cutting drive by a new president of Kenyon College, but resumed publication in 1979.

The *Antioch Review* was launched in 1941 by a group of Antioch faculty as a liberal political magazine. At first figures like Carey McWilliams, John Dewey, and Max Lerner published critical political and social pieces. After 1945 poetry, fiction, criticism, and social science essays gained a prominent place. A 1957 issue contained work by Clifford Geertz, James T. Farrell, Sylvia Plath, Bennett Berger, and Lewis Turco. Yet *Antioch* remained true to

its initial impulse to be a magazine for the mythical "general" reader with a wide interest in the world at large and the political activism of the late sixties. In the years before the hippie conclave at Woodstock, one might find a long translation of José Ortega y Gassett's "The Mission of the Librarian," poetry by Mark Strand and Denise Levertov, and work by the television writer Rod Serling. Joyce Carol Oates made her first appearance in 1966, William Trevor in 1967. In the last decades of the twentieth century, it published cultural commentary by figures like the sociologist David Riesman, the critics Gerald Early and Daniel Harris, and the fiction writers T. Coraghessan Boyle, Jorge Luis Borges, and Gordon Lish. It continued to emphasize poetry as part of its literary menu, publishing long pieces by Jorie Graham and William Merwin. The *Antioch Review* never became an academic journal nor a purely coterie magazine; it tried—like *Salmagundi* (1965)—to define its place somewhere between the larger literary culture represented by the *New Yorker* and the smaller avant-garde journals, like the *Unmuzzled Ox* (1971).

The interplay between university culture and literary culture allowed journals like *Kenyon, Antioch,* and *Gettysburg Review* (1988; at Gettysburg College) to play a role that supported and defined elite attitudes. Some critics have argued that after the 1970s the university culture became inimical to creative and independent work, even though creative writing programs flourished on campuses. Despite their base in academic culture, such magazines came to face the same problems as the commercial magazines and the same questions as mass circulation journals concerning new technologies and audience.

MAGAZINES FOUNDED AFTER 1945

After 1945 the independent literary magazines like the *Little Review* and the *Sewanee Review* had both a vigorous and troubled career. During the post–World War II era, there was an active magazine "scene" that promoted new literature, a culture of protest, and an aggressive experimentalism that mirrored the period's literary culture. Magazines with names like *Neon* (1965), *Kullchur* (1960), *Big Table* (1959), *Wormwood* (1959), *Trace* (1952), and the *Chicago Review* (1946) came and went, and magazines like the *Kenyon Review* and the *Antioch Review* went through economic crises that threatened their survival because institutional support was denied. Small magazines such as *Evergreen*

EVERGREEN

EVERGREEN REVIEW NO. 39 / FEBRUARY 1966 / ONE DOLLAR

JACK KEROUAC / HERBERT GOLD / SAMUEL BECKETT / ALAIN ROBBE-GRILLET
NAT HENTOFF / MAURICE GIRODIAS / BARBARELLA / PHOEBE ZEIT-GEIST

Evergreen Review. The publication was admired and influential during its short lifespan of ninety-six issues (1957–1973). This is issue no. 39 (February 1966). COURTESY OF ROBERT S. FOGARTY

(1957) and *Origin* (1951) published work by Beat writers that assaulted both the academy and the elite taste it represented.

The *Chicago Review* (1946) was founded by J. Radcliffe Squires and Carolyn Dillard, students at the University of Chicago, and was subsequently edited by students. In 1958, when it published a special issue on the Beats (including chapters from William Burroughs's *Naked Lunch,* 1959), charges of obscenity were made in the pages of the *Chicago Daily News* and literary censorship by the university ensued. With its regular editorial turnover, the *Chicago Review,* like the *Iowa Review* (1970) and the *Columbia Review* (1931), represented a kind of consistent pulse within an "aspiring" literary community. Such magazines were a handy barometer for changing cultural and literary taste.

Origin, founded in 1951 by Cid Corman, was clearly oppositional in tone and content and embraced the abstract expressionist world of Jackson Pollock and the experimental jazz music of Charlie Parker. Charles Olson and Robert Creeley were the major poetic voices trumpeted by Corman, who gave their work an audience interested in transla-

tion and language theory. A spin-off of *Origin* was the *Black Mountain Review* (1954) founded by Creeley and devoted to a larger set of international values and writers than Corman's *Origin.* Its name and beginnings came from a series of letters between Creeley and Olson about their desire to expand on the vision of the experimental Black Mountain College in North Carolina where both had taught. Its final issue in 1957 featured writing by Allen Ginsberg, Jack Kerouac, and William Burroughs and bridged the gap between the radical writers of the thirties and the emerging Beats.

The *Paris Review* (1953) was cofounded by Peter Matthiessen and Harold Humes in Paris and was edited by George Plimpton. It made its reputation by publishing distinctive contemporary fiction, poetry, and interviews with authors. The magazine was dedicated to experimental writing rather than the criticism stressed in many literary magazines. Poetry prospered at the *Paris Review* with the publication of Donald Hall, X. J. Kennedy, Tom Clark, and Jonathan Galassi, and in the 1960s it published short fiction by Philip Roth, Jack Kerouac, and Raymond Carver. It became an institution in part because it achieved name recognition with a wider public and because Plimpton courted publicity at every turn and became a celebrity. Though founded as an anti-institutional, anti-status quo journal, it came to represent the literary establishment.

LeRoi Jones and Hettie Cohen founded *Yugen* in New York City in 1958 and touted the magazine as a "new consciousness in arts and letters" on its masthead. In fact, it was an outlet for New York City Beat writers like Jones and Diane Di Prima and followed in the wake of the more important *Evergreen Review* (1957), edited by Barney Rosset and published by Grove Press. *Evergreen* championed the French writers Jean-Paul Sartre, Eugène Ionesco, and Alain Robbe-Grillet and, like Grove Press, challenged censorship regulations by running sexual material and then aggressively defending itself in the courts. In 1964 the district attorney of Nassau County in New York seized more than twenty thousand copies of the magazine, labeling it "obscene." In the same year the U.S. Supreme Court upheld Grove Press's publication—the first in the United States—of Henry Miller's *Tropic of Cancer* (1934). *Evergreen* was the most notorious literary magazine of the 1950s and its radical politics prefigured the anti-establishment tone of the 1960s anti–Vietnam War generation. Its scope was wider than that of *Yugen* and it was best remembered for the radical social stances it took. *Caterpillar* (1967) was founded by Clayton Eshleman in New York City to promote the work of certain Beat poets, including Diane Wakoski and Jerome Rothenberg, and to highlight the relationship between art, poetry, and culture. In the opening number it printed an essay on the painter Nancy Spero by the political painter Leon Golub, poems by Gilbert Sorrentino, and an extended piece by the neo-Freudian Norman O. Brown. Later, the publication moved to California.

As a number of older commercial magazines such as the *Saturday Review* (1924) began to lose readers, a burst of energy in the literary magazine world during the 1960s produced *Tri-Quarterly, Salmagundi,* and *Field,* all based on university campuses. *Tri-Quarterly* (1964), under the leadership of Charles Newman and with support from Northwestern University, emphasized special theme issues (Eastern Europe, Edward Dahlberg, science fiction) of some four hundred pages. Under Newman, Eliot Anderson, and Reginald Gibbons, *Tri-Quarterly* maintained high standards in their choice of fiction and essays and avoided identification with any prevailing literary dogmas.

Salmagundi (1965), sponsored by Skidmore College, favored cultural issues over mere literary ones and under Robert and Peggy Boyers it championed nonfiction prose and published distinguished cultural critics like Christopher Lasch, Gerald Graff, and George Steiner. Along with the *Hudson Review* (1948), *Salmagundi* emphasized the importance of criticism as a vital part in a creative mix that produced serious writing. Both magazines, along with the *Antioch Review,* argued for the importance of critical judgment and taste in a mass-consumer society. Though based at universities (*Hudson Review* was completely independent), these reviews avoided formal academic criticism (like that found in the *Publications of the Modern Language Association,* or *PMLA*) and published essays and fiction that went against the grain of both the academic culture and the larger society. *Field* (1969), supported by Oberlin College, was committed to contemporary poetry and poetics. The original editors, Stuart Friebert and David Young, had a strong interest in translation and the magazine was quick to introduce to its readers poetry from eastern Europe and South America. Every major American poet appeared in its pages and it was alert to changing tones and movements within the poetry world (the rise of confessional poetry and contemporary Irish poetry, for example), and it has provided a serious forum for discussing tendencies and issues. By concentrating on a single form, *Field* was able to sustain a critical audience. *Boundary 2* (1972), founded by faculty members at the State

University of New York at Binghamton, emphasized experimental fiction and poetry "in the Pound-Williams-Olson-Creeley line," and was one of the first academic journals to promote a "postmodern" view of contemporary writing while *Epoch* (1947), from Cornell University, was content simply to continue publishing short fiction in the James Joyce tradition.

Antaeus (1970) was the product of the political eclecticism of the 1970s and, under Daniel Halpern's direction, it published some of the finest mainstream writers from the international literary scene. With the financial support of food-family heir Drue Heinz, the magazine published important works in translation, including work rarely found in English translation in the period—such as Aztec, Nuer, Berber, and Vietnamese—and promoted modern European poetry.

The 1980s saw a burst of interest in the short story, a form that had been promoted and supported by the academic literary quarterlies and commercial magazines like the *New Yorker*. Writers like Raymond Carver, William Taylor, Cynthia Ozick, and T. Coraghessan Boyle gained popular audiences, and major publishing houses like Knopf published short-story collections. *The Quarterly* (1987), edited by Gordon Lish, championed realistic and expressive short fiction and poetry that was linguistically experimental and personal. Lish, Raymond Carver's editor and amanuensis, was among the first to publish young writers like Amy Hempel, Mark Richard, and Rick Bass. *The Quarterly* considered itself "the magazine of new American writing" and Lish courted controversy by publishing attacks on other magazines like *Grand Street* for their literary timidity, running provocative cartoons as one means of assault. The publication's handsome design set a new standard for magazines, where design had taken a back seat to content. *Grand Street* (1981) attempted to become a latter-day *Partisan Review* by publishing essays by European intellectuals and glossy photographs. It aimed at an avant-garde audience, but one that been nourished on postmodern and popular culture. Because it was able to pay its writers well, it attracted—as did the *New Yorker* under editor Tina Brown—"star" writers while the smaller literary magazines had to be content with gleaning talent from the "slush pile" (unsolicited submissions).

Reading the slush became an enormous task for all these magazines with the expansion of writing programs at universities from the 1970s onward. As always there were too few outlets, but new magazines came on the scene. Numerous creative writing programs sponsored magazines. Columbia University, the University of Alabama, and the University of Iowa offered their students an opportunity to edit and produce literary journals. This practice allowed for further experimentation and innovation, which influenced the older literary quarterlies and the commercial magazines.

Magazines came and went depending on their editorial vision and their ability to find a sponsor; few were able to survive in the twentieth century without institutional or patron support. The *Threepenny Review* (1980) was able to create a new literary voice on the West Coast under Wendy Lesser by drawing on the academic and literary talent of the Bay Area while *ZZZYVA* (1985), with Howard Junker's guidance, made itself hospitable to writers from California, the most populous state and the largest cultural region. With the development of multicultural studies and ethnic studies within the university, several magazines emerged in the 1980s to focus energy on the literature of women, blacks, and other minorities. *Callaloo: A Black South Jour-*

nal of Arts and Letters (1976) now at the University of Virginia, *Manoa: A Pacific Journal of International Writing* (1989), *Kalliope: A Journal of Women's Art* (1979), and the *James White Review* (1983) are representative journals addressing black, Asian Pacific, women's, and gay culture, respectively.

In summarizing the impact of such magazines Frederick Hoffman, a major historian of magazines, has written in *The Little Magazine*:

> Edited for a discriminating minority, they afforded writers a haven from the pressures of the marketplace. They opened their pages to authors who were too daring, too shocking, too recondite for the mass circulation magazines. They provided an outlet for fiction, poetry, and criticism which was of literary value but of little popular appeal. They encouraged literary experimentation, and they pleaded for social reform. Their influence, as their editors saw it, lay not in the numbers of persons they reached but in the kind. By speaking to a few persons in positions of influence, their editors believed, the magazines would more surely affect the course of events than if they spoke to the multitude. (p. 229)

See also **The Print Revolution; Rhetoric and Belles Lettres; The Rise of Biblical Criticism and Challenges to Religious Authority** *(volume 1);* **Artistic, Intellectual, and Political Refugees** *(volume 2);* **Books; Journalism; Periodicals; Fiction; Poetry** *(in this volume); and other articles in this section.*

BIBLIOGRAPHY

Anderson, Elliot, and Mary Kinzie, eds. *The Little Magazine in America: A Modern Documentary History.* Evanston, Ill., 1978.

Chielens, Edward E., ed. *American Literary Magazines: The Twentieth Century.* Westport, Conn., 1991.

Fogarty, Robert S., ed. *The Antioch Review, 1941–1991: The Survival of the Imagination.* Yellow Springs, Ohio, 1991.

Hoffman, Frederick, Charles Allen, and Carolyn F. Ulrich. *The Little Magazine: A History and a Bibliography.* 2d ed. Princeton, N.J., 1947.

Janssen, Marian. *The Kenyon Review, 1939–1970: A Critical History.* Baton Rouge, La., 1989.

———. *The Little Magazine and Contemporary Literature: A Symposium.* New York, 1966.

Peterson, Theodore. *Magazines in the Twentieth Century.* Urbana, Ill., 1964.

TEXTBOOKS

Michael W. Apple

The English sociologist and philosopher Herbert Spencer was more than a little insightful when he suggested in the nineteenth century that one of the most important educational questions a society needs to ask is "What knowledge is of most worth?" Behind this lies an even more contentious question, "Whose knowledge is of most worth?" From the vast universe of possible knowledge only some will be called legitimate to pass on to future generations. What counts as "official" knowledge, as knowledge that should be taught in schools, is the result of an extremely complex process of ideological, political, and economic decisions and conflicts. At the middle of these conflicts sits a particular artifact—the textbook. Whether historians and academics approve of it or not, it is the textbook that has been and is at the very center of the curriculum in the elementary and high schools of most nations.

Textbooks signify, through their content and their form, particular ways of selecting and organizing the vast universe of possible knowledge. They embody what the cultural analyst Raymond Williams called the "selective tradition," someone's vision of legitimate knowledge and culture, one that in the process of enfranchising one group's cultural capital often disenfranchises another's. Texts are really messages to and about the future. As part of a curriculum, they participate in no less than the organized knowledge system of a society. They participate in what a society has recognized as legitimate and truthful. They help set the canons of truthfulness and as such also help recreate a major reference for what knowledge, culture, belief, and morality really are. This has been true throughout their history as the dominant teaching tool in the United States.

EARLY HISTORY

The first American textbooks embodied one of the primary purposes of nineteenth-century public schools: to train citizens in "proper" character and principles. The textbook was seen as one of the most important ways of furthering the aims of moral development and correct conduct. Indeed, early schoolbook writers such as Noah Webster were clear in their advocacy of virtue. As Webster put it, one should use his book "to instil into [children's] minds, with the first rudiments of the language, some just ideas of religion, morals, and domestic economy." As early as 1789, Webster stated that his purpose in writing a schoolbook was clear: "To refine and establish our language, to facilitate the acquisition of grammatical knowledge and diffuse the principles of virtue and patriotism is the task I have labored to perform" (Elson, *Guardians of Tradition*, pp. 1–2).

Nearly all early textbooks saw their function not only as the teaching of literacy and numeracy, but the formation of a specifically American character. The first textbooks were spellers, readers, and arithmetics, to be followed later by geographies and histories. Often, they were organized around particular pedagogic principles—memorization, moral lessons, an urge to differentiate between European and American characteristics, and at times an organization that seems to be highly fragmented by twenty-first-century standards. The focus in the early textbooks on memorization as the dominant pedagogic device, with less attention to meaning, is striking. It points to the relationship over time between seeing literacy as what might be called a "moral technology of the soul," the contradictory vision of children as simultaneously passive and in need of control, and the perception that teachers were poorly trained and thus needed to be expressly guided by a reductive style of teaching that emphasized control and passivity. The connections among textbooks, visions of childhood, and views of teachers are powerful and constitute one of the continuing sources of tensions and changes in the history of textbooks.

Thus it would be a mistake to see texts as simply a delivery system of "facts and concepts." They have always been at once the results of political, economic, and cultural activities, battles, and compromises. They are conceived, designed, and written by real people with real interests. They are published within the political and economic constraints of markets, resources, and power. And what they mean and how they are used are dependent on the communities, and the teachers and students, that use them.

POLITICAL AND ECONOMIC CONCERNS

In general, the "cultural capital" of dominant groups has been considered the most legitimate knowledge. This knowledge, and one's ability to deal with it, has served as one part of the complex mechanisms in which the economic and cultural reproduction of class, race, and gender relations has been accomplished or it has served as part of the arena in which such reproduction is contested. Indeed, the textbook has been at the very heart of the ways in which official knowledge is contested. This is partly because the United States is unlike many nations with central ministries of education where conflicts over whose knowledge should be taught are usually focused on decisions by the national government itself. Instead, given the relatively decentralized models of educational governance in America, where no one centralized national body makes decisions on the curriculum, many more conflicts are centered on the artifacts—textbooks— that embody the accumulated decisions of many, relatively decentralized, bodies. Thus, conflicts over textbooks have a very long history in the United States and often serve as proxies for larger issues that would be more tightly focused on the national level in systems where decisions are made by a central ministry of education. For this very reason, textbooks historically have been at the center of economic and political dynamics and conflicts.

From an economic standpoint, the world of the book has not been cut off from the world of commerce. Books are not only cultural artifacts. They are economic commodities as well. Even though texts may be vehicles for ideas, they still have to be sold on a market. This is a market, however, that— especially in the national and international world of textbook publishing—is politically volatile.

Historically, there have been four structural conditions that have shaped publishing in the United States. First, the publishing industry sells its commodities in a market that has been and is fickle and uncertain. Second, although there has been considerable concentration of ownership and control over the past decades, the industry has a history of decentralization among a number of sectors whose operations and markets are not totally similar. Third, these operations have had a mixture of modern mass-production methods and a residue of older craftlike procedures, with textbooks falling under the former more and more over time. Finally, publishing has been perilously poised between the requirements of profit and commerce on the one hand and the responsibilities and obligations that it carries as one of the prime "guardians" of the symbolic culture of the nation on the other.

This tension has a long history. Textbook publishing cannot be divorced from the larger dynamics of book publishing in general. For example, in the nineteenth century the topics that European writers were dealing with had a distinct market advantage in the United States due to the oddities of United States copyright laws. During much of the nineteenth century, American copyright laws protected citizens or permanent residents of the United States but not foreign authors. This resulted in an odd situation in which British and other foreign books could be reprinted in the United States without royalties being paid to the authors, while American authors had to receive royalties. Thus, American publishers had very little inducement to publish U.S.-based work. Even given the pedagogic, moral, and nationalistic characteristics of the earliest textbooks, it was not unusual for a large portion of early United States schoolbooks to be unrevised versions of books originally published in England. As late as the middle of the nineteenth century, there were complaints about the dominance of reissued English textbooks in the grammars and readers being used in schools. This lead United States authors to find areas that were not covered by the works of foreign writers in order to find a market for their work. This larger set of dynamics then—market concerns, regulatory structures, writing with prospective audiences in mind, and so on—played a considerable role in the development of the standardized textbook as it developed over time.

In essence, two types of capital—symbolic and financial—differentiate between two orientations toward publishing. Those firms that are more commercial, that are oriented toward rapid turnover, quick obsolescence, and the minimization of risks, are following a strategy for the accumulation of financial capital. In contradistinction to this, those publishers whose goal is to maximize the accumulation of symbolic capital operate in such a way that immediate profit is less important. Higher risks may be taken and experimental content and form will find greater acceptance. Thus, these kinds of publishers have a longer time perspective. Both are interested in profit; but for the latter, long-term accumulation is more important. It is clear that the logic and interests of finance capital have tended to dominate textbook publishing throughout its history.

The concern of economics has led to a growing concentration of power in textbook publishing that has intensified even more since the 1960s. Politically speaking, there has been increased competition, but this has been among a smaller number of large firms. The increasingly competitive environment has also over time reduced the propensity to take risks. Instead, there has been a steady movement by publishers to expend most of their efforts on a smaller selection of carefully chosen and targeted "products." In some cases, this has led to the growth of what publishers have called "managed texts," textbooks for both "el-hi" (elementary-high school) and college-level courses that are based on outlines provided by well-known educators and academics and then in essence ghostwritten under stringent cost controls. This has exacerbated the movement toward publishing texts in which what will sell becomes more important at times than what is most important to know.

Textbooks, then, have been caught up in a complicated set of political and economic—not only educational—dynamics. Textbook publishing is often highly competitive. In the United States, where textbook production is a commercial enterprise situated within the vicissitudes of a capitalist market, decisions about the "bottom line" have long played a major role in determining what texts are published and for how long. Yet, this situation has not just been controlled by the "invisible hand" of the market. It has also been largely determined by the highly visible political hand of state textbook adoption policies.

THE REGULATORY STATE: CLASS AND RACE DYNAMICS

Nearly half of the states—most of them in the southern tier and in the Sun Belt—have textbook adoption committees that generally choose what texts are approved for purchase in that state. These statewide adoption bodies were formed in the latter half of the nineteenth century and the early decades of the twentieth century. Over time, the economics of profits and loss in this situation has made it nearly imperative that publishers devote a large portion of their efforts to guaranteeing a place on the list of approved books. Because of this, the texts made available to the entire nation, and the knowledge considered legitimate, have often been determined by what will sell in Texas, California, and other states with strong regulatory procedures.

For example, sales to California and Texas can account for 20 to 30 percent of the total sales of a textbook, and the simple fact of getting one's name on the list of approved material can make all the difference for a text's profitability. Because of this, the writing, editing, promotion, and overall strategy of book production have historically been aimed toward guaranteeing a place on the list of state-approved material. Since this is the case, the political and ideological climate of these primarily southern states has played a crucial role in the determination of the content and form of textbooks. This sometimes led to considerable controversy and scandal throughout the early twentieth century as publishers seeking to guarantee the adoption of their textbooks were accused of bribery, assisting state or city school officials' careers, or even attempting to tarnish the reputations of officials (or those of other textbook publishers). This, in turn, led to attempts to regulate even more closely the selection and selling of textbooks.

Because of this regulation, the development of standardized textbooks has historically been linked to the growth of an active role for state government in policing legitimate content and its production and distribution for schools. Given regional differences in class and race dynamics, it was in the South that state power to restrict and regulate official knowledge grew, especially in the latter half of the nineteenth century and the early years of the twentieth. "Reform from above" was a clear educational strategy in the South, rather than "reform from below," which had a longer history in the North. A tradition of state intervention and control was established rather early on in the development of school reforms in the South after the Civil War. This was a result of a compromise between an emergent urban-based white middle class, a landed planter class, and poor whites in both cities and rural areas, especially those poor white farmers who had participated in groups such as the Farmers' Alliances in the South.

The increasing power of the state in the regulation of textbooks was also due to regional ideological differences. Historically, for example, there was strong sentiment after the Civil War for textbooks to reflect the perspectives of either the North or the South. But in the South this became more readily integrated into "reform from above" strategies. Thus, in one instance, in Texas a popular arithmetic text was pressured to make certain that its arithmetic problems featured the victories of southern generals. At the same time, in 1867 advertisements for textbooks throughout the South claimed that a particular publishing house printed only those textbooks that were specifically prepared for southern schools, by southern authors, and therefore "free from matter offensive to southern people." That the definition of people here largely applied to whites of all classes rather than African Americans once again connects the processes of state regulation of content to both class and race dynamics.

TEXTBOOKS AND TEACHERS

There were other elements involved in the growth of such regulation of textbooks over time. The increasing geographical mobility of the population, the urge to lower the cost of textbooks by purchasing large numbers at one time, the perceived need to establish uniform standards, and the wish to have "disinterested" experts rather than ordinary people make decisions on what should be taught all had important effects. Yet, one of the most important reasons for regulation was the belief that teachers were often incompetent. In a phrase that resonated throughout many parts of the nation, "The poorer the teacher, the better the textbooks need to be." While many people had more positive views of teachers, the growth of both standardized textbooks and the processes of their regulation in the mid- to late nineteenth and early twentieth centuries is closely connected to the views state officials and powerful groups had of teachers at the time.

The relationship between teachers and textbooks is a complicated one, however. Textbooks often have been related to forms of bureaucratic regulation both of teachers' lives and those of students. The historian James Fraser wrote of one late-nineteenth-century teacher in Boston who related a story of what happened during an observation by the school principal in her first year of teaching. As the teacher proudly watched one of her children read aloud an assigned lesson from the text, the principal was less than pleased with the performance of the teacher and her pupil. In words taken from the teacher's diary:

The proper way to read in the public school in 1899 was to say, "page 35, chapter 4" and holding the book in the right hand, with the toes pointing at an angle of 45 degrees, the head held straight and high, the eyes looking directly ahead, the pupil would lift up his voice and struggle in loud, unnatural tones. Now, I had attended to the position of the toes, the right arm, and the nose, but had failed to enforce the mentioning of page and chapter. (Warren, *American Teachers*, p. 128)

Here the textbook participates in both bodily and ideological regulation. As in earlier periods, the textbook in this instance is part of a system of enforcing a sense of duty, morality, and cultural correctness. Yet, paradoxically, historically the standardized text often was struggled for as well as against by many teachers. Faced with large classes, difficult working conditions, insufficient training, and even more important, little time to prepare lessons for the vast array of students and subjects for which they were responsible, throughout the nineteenth and twentieth centuries teachers often looked upon textbooks as essential tools. For young women elementary school teachers, the text helped prevent exploitation and overwork. It solved a multitude of problems. It led not only to deskilling—a loss of one's power and ability to make decisions about what to teach—but to time to become more skilled as a teacher as well. Thus, there were demands for standardized texts by teachers even in the face of what the Boston schoolteacher experienced.

The struggle over texts was often linked to broader concerns about who should control the curriculum in schools. Throughout the history of public schooling in the United States, teachers, especially those most politically active, constantly sought to have a say in what they taught. This was seen as part of a larger fight for democratic rights. Margaret Haley, for instance, one of the leaders of the first teachers union formed in the late 1890s in Chicago, saw a great need for teachers to work against the tendency to make the teacher "a mere factory hand, whose duty it is to carry out mechanically and unquestioningly the ideas and orders of those clothed with authority of position." Teachers had to fight against de-skilling or, as she called it, "factoryizing" methods of control being sponsored by administrative and industrial leaders. Along with many other teachers, she was committed to reducing the immense power over teaching and texts that administrators possessed. Thus, in this instance teacher control over the choice of textbooks and how they were to be used was part of a more extensive movement to enhance the democratic rights of teachers on the job. Without greater emphasis on teacher voice, teachers would be the equivalent of factory workers whose every move was determined by management. The fact that by the 1920s the vast majority of teachers, especially in the elementary school, were women points to the underlying gender dynamics at work. Women teachers, like many other women workers, have had to struggle constantly for recognition of their professional skills. Standardizing the textbooks and regulating what is to be taught are part of the history of this dynamic, as well as the larger history of gendered labor in the United States.

POLITICAL CONFLICTS

These historical points about the contradictory relationships teachers have had with textbooks and the way such books depower and empower at different moments document something of importance. It is too easy to see a cultural practice or a book as totally carrying its politics around with it, as if it is "written on its brow for ever and a day." Rather, its political functioning depends on the network of social and ideological relations in which it participates. Text writing, reading, and use could be retrogressive or progressive (and sometimes some combination of both), depending on the social context. Textbooks could be fought against because they were seen to be part of a system of imposed moral regulation. They could be fought for both as providing essential assistance in the labor of teaching or as part of a larger strategy of democratization. Thus, what textbooks did, the social roles they played for different groups, was and is very complicated.

One thing has remained constant, however. Textbooks have always been a site of ideological contestation. In the 1930s, for instance, conservative groups mounted a campaign against one of the more progressive textbook series in use in the schools. Harold Rugg's social science series, "Man and His Changing Society," became the subject of a concerted attack by the National Association of Manufacturers, the American Legion, the Advertising Federation of America, and other groups. They charged that Rugg's books were socialist, anti-American, and antibusiness. The conservative campaign was more than a little successful in forcing school districts to withdraw the series from classrooms and libraries. So successful were they that sales fell from nearly 300,000 copies in 1938 to only approximately 20,000 in 1944.

During the cold war, in the 1960s, in a break with tradition the federal government itself sponsored the development of text material. This was part of an attempt to create a more rigorous "discipline-centered" curriculum in schools because of a fear that the Soviet Union was about to overtake the United States in science and technology. Even with large amounts of federal money, the results echoed earlier periods of criticism of the text. Much of it became mired in political and ideological conflicts amid claims that such curriculum development gave the federal government too much power, was too bureaucratic, and was too controlling of teachers. Of considerable importance as well was the controversy that some of this material stimulated among religious conservatives worried about the evolutionary emphasis of the best-known material.

These are not isolated examples. Throughout the twentieth century the textbook has been at the center of often intense conflicts over religious beliefs, politics, race, gender, and class relations. From the continuing controversies over the place of religion and evolution in the text to the ongoing battles over the politics of representation concerning gender, race, and sexuality, there have been few times in which there has not been a serious controversy over the textbook. At times, these conflicts serve as proxies for other things. For instance, few places in the United States are more well known in this regard than Kanawha County, West Virginia. The region has been at the center of religious battles over textbook content multiple times throughout the twentieth century. But in the 1970s it again became the scene of one of the most explosive controversies over what schools should teach, who should decide, and what beliefs should guide educational programs. What began as a protest by a small group of conservative parents, religious leaders, and businesspeople over the content and design of the standardized textbooks that had been approved for use in local schools, over time spread to include school boycotts, violence, and a wrenching ideological split in the community and region over the teaching of evolution, literacy, and other areas of the curriculum. The community became so polarized that schools were set on fire, with blame being placed on conservative religious activists.

There were a number of important contributing factors that heightened tensions in that region and that tell historians and educators much about the historical dynamics and complexities surrounding textbooks as arenas of struggle and as proxies for the working out of larger tensions. In the mid-1960s and 1970s, schools in rural areas of West Virginia had been consolidated. Class relations and relations between country and city were increasingly tense. The lack of participation of parents in text selection and in general educational decision making had led to growing alienation. Furthermore, the cultural history of the region, with its fierce independence, its fundamentalist religious traditions, and its history of economic depression, helped create the conditions for serious unrest. Finally, the textbook controversy became a cause célèbre for nationally organized right-wing groups who became increasingly active in offering moral, legal, financial, and organizational support to the local conservative activists. In this case, as in so many others over time, the conflicts over the textbook served as a focal point for more widespread cultural, political, and economic discontent.

This case and many like it echo the power of cultural and regional conflicts in education. Thus, some of the peculiarities of American political history come into play. Unlike many European nations, the United States educational system grew out of a federation of relatively independent states. Thus, the power of national control, and the pattern of state control over official knowledge, is dependent on this history. Regional differences do count. The Northeast does not have the exact same history as the Midwest, the South, or the West. Specific class and race structures and histories, and differences in the power of an interventionist state in the control over knowledge and the text, are important elements in understanding conflicts and compromises over textbooks.

While the process of state regulation of the textbook has included attempts to eliminate some of these conflicts and may have made it easier for publishers to know their markets, it has quite often led to uncertainty because of the political and cultural conflicts such a regulatory ambition has generated. For example, throughout the twentieth century religious and ideological conflicts over the absence or presence of various interpretations of the relationship between science and religion have been extremely powerful factors in textbook decisions. These conflicts have made it difficult for publishers to make what they consider "rational" decisions based on the accumulation of finance capital. Given the uncertainty of a market, publishers have historically been very cautious in making decisions based on political controversies in highly charged curriculum areas. An example is provided by the controversy over creationism versus evolutionism in California in the 1970s. A group of "scientific crea-

tionists," supported by political and ideological conservatives, sought to ensure that all social studies and science textbooks would give equal weight to creationist and evolutionary positions. Even when the California Board of Education recommended editorial qualifications that were aimed at meeting some of the objections of creationist textbook critics, the framework for text adoption—what is recommended to be said in the texts—was still not totally clear. Thus, textbook publishers resisted investing in major changes. They made minor qualifications and did not agree to provide substantive accounts of creationism in their texts. Unclear directives and the potential loss of sales in other states led publishers to hold the line against such material.

Textbooks have been at the center of controversies not only over religion, internal politics, and the relations between country and city; they have been sites of intense conflicts over race and gender and over international policy as well. Throughout the early decades of the twentieth century, science textbooks were often strongly influenced by theories of racial hierarchy and by the popular eugenics movement centered around "race betterment." Similar kinds of sentiments about the biological roots of gender hierarchies and relations were often equally apparent. Each of these led to serious debates and to challenges to alter the content.

It is not only that textbooks themselves have a history, however. They also interpret history through the narratives of progress they construct and the way they tell the story of America. This too has repeatedly led to significant controversy. For example, contentious issues concerning the representation of the role the United States has played in international affairs have surfaced repeatedly, with the Vietnam conflict and its interpretations being one of a long and continuing line of historical controversies. Similar arguments over the history of colonization, immigration, racial antagonisms, and gender relations have been an equal part of the conflicts over the historical "truths" that texts construct. Because of all this, competing definitions of legitimate content have not only had an impact on the history of textbooks but have played an important part in the formation of oppositional social movements in the United States surrounding class, gender, race, religion, and, increasingly, sexuality.

ALTERNATIVE TEXTS

Most analyses of textbooks have focused their attention on the books produced for use in public schools. However, these are not the only books to which one should pay attention. For instance, populist and leftist movements have a history of either providing education for adults or children in informal settings or of building alternative schools (usually after-school or weekend programs) that would expressly teach a counter-hegemonic curriculum. They quite often produced their own textbooks, reading materials, and songbooks. As Kenneth Teitelbaum has shown, such material played a crucial role in "schooling good rebels" in the socialist movement in the early years of the twentieth century. Much of this material was published informally or was provided at cost by party-affiliated publishers.

For example, a series of pamphlets was written during the period of 1910 to 1920 for use by teachers in "socialist Sunday schools." Material such as the lesson on "The World's Coal and Oil and Who Should Own Them" was typical:

> What is coal? What is oil? ... Who should own them? ... Could we do without them? ... Is it easy to get coal and oil? Who does the work? Who makes the money? Who owns the coal mines and oil wells? Who ought to own and control them? ... Would they cost less or more under socialism? Why? (Teitelbaum, *Schooling for Good Rebels*, p. 151)

Even commercially produced textbooks were not necessarily uniform across the public and private educational sector. One of the most popular textbook series provides a case in point. For example, for much of the inter- and postwar period of the twentieth century children in the United States were introduced to written literacy through what were known as the "Dick and Jane readers." These were among the most widely sold textbooks in the history of standardized texts. The series became the prototype of the industrial era, secular textbook, one that presented portrayals of a generic and idealized white, patriarchal, middle-class world to an increasingly diverse population. The series brought together a number of influences that emerged in the twentieth century to dominate the construction of textbooks, especially in literacy. It was the result of the combined influences of the corporate publishing sector, exponents of a supposedly neutral educational science, and state educational decision-making bodies. These combined interests led to uniform texts guided by psychological principles, and published under the aegis of profit-driven and increasingly dominant large corporations.

Yet these standardizing conditions were partly interrupted by religious tensions. The secular read-

ers were seen as inadequately grounded in religious values. This led to the development in the 1940s of the Catholic readers, a church-sanctioned version of the Dick and Jane literacy textbooks that were to be used in Catholic schools. These had similar idealizations of white, male-dominated, middle-class life, but contained much more overtly religious content.

In many ways, the religious "interruption" of the secular textbook was actually a continuation of earlier tendencies. From the very beginning, the modern Western tradition created textbooks for identifiably ideological and religious purposes. Secular passages stood side by side with scriptural ones and were almost always organized with a moral and political purpose in mind. In part, this is related to the fact that historically, unregulated access to literacy has often been seen as a potential threat to established political and religious order. Even if access to the text could not be totally controlled, regulation of the norms of literacy practices could provide some measure of control.

Thus, similar to the sentiments expressed by Noah Webster, early textbooks in the United States such as the nineteenth-century McGuffey's Readers—developed by the educator William McGuffey and perhaps the most famous of all reading textbooks in United States history—expressed clear orientations toward ethics, family, work, and religion. These orientations were not only clear, but they were just as clearly Protestant. Even earlier, the *New England Primer*, one of the first mass-produced textbooks in the nation, was expressly anti-Catholic and contained caricatures of the pope. For example, the primer displayed a picture parodying the pope and said, "Child, behold the Man of Sin, the Pope, worthy of thy utmost hatred." This tendency clearly was a contributing factor in mistrust that Catholic officials had of state-sponsored literacy instruction. For them, such educational programs and the textbooks that accompanied them were "Protestant proselytizing." Thus, once again one cannot divorce the history of textbooks from the religious conflicts that were a part of cultural and ideological politics of America's history. That religious mistrust continues to the twenty-first century is evident in the fundamentalist movements that have challenged the content and pedagogy of official textbooks as being "secular humanist" and as not being based on specific, largely phonics-based approaches to literacy. Such Protestant fundamentalist movements, ones rooted in irredentist readings of the Bible, themselves have a rich history in the United States since the millenarian movements of the mid- to late nineteenth century.

It is clear that textbooks were and continue to be complex artifacts. They have been at the center of educational practice for much of United States history. Yet they also have been arenas where the economic, political, and cultural tensions and dynamics of the larger society come together in the ongoing contest to decide what gets to be official knowledge. Understanding the textbook requires that scholars and laypeople alike understand the larger tensions of the American polity.

See also **Science and Religion; The Rise of Biblical Criticism and Challenges to Religious Authority** *(volume 1);* **Books; The History of Ideas; Hermeneutics and American Historiography; History and the Study of the Past** *(in this volume); and other articles in this section.*

BIBLIOGRAPHY

Apple, Michael W. *Teachers and Texts.* New York, 1988.

——. *Ideology and Curriculum.* 2d ed. New York, 1990.

——. *Official Knowledge.* 2d ed. New York, 2000.

Bourdieu, Pierre. *Distinction.* Cambridge, Mass., 1984.

Cornbleth, Catherine, and Dexter Waugh. *The Great Speckled Bird: Multicultural Politics and Education Policymaking.* New York, 1995.

Coser, Lewis A., Charles Kadushin, and Walter W. Powell. *Books: The Culture and Commerce of Publishing.* New York, 1982.

Delfattore, Joan. *What Johnny Shouldn't Read: Book Censorship in America.* New Haven, Conn., 1992.

Elson, Ruth Miller. *Guardians of Tradition, American Schoolbooks in the Nineteenth Century.* Lincoln, Nebr., 1964.

FitzGerald, Frances. *America Revised: History Schoolbooks in the Twentieth Century.* New York, 1979.

Fraser, James. "Agents of Democracy: Urban Elementary School Teachers and the Conditions of Teaching." In *American Teachers: Histories of a Profession at Work,* edited by Donald Warren, 118–156. New York, 1989.

Graff, Harvey J. *The Labyrinths of Literacy: Reflections of Literacy Past and Present.* Philadelphia, 1987.

Kaestle, Carl F., Helen Damon-Moore, Lawrence Stedman, Katherine Tinsley, and William Vance Trollinger Jr. *Literacy in the United States: Readers and Reading since 1880.* New Haven, Conn., 1991.

Loewen, James W. *Lies My Teacher Told Me: Everything Your American History Textbook Got Wrong.* New York, 1996.

Luke, Allan. *Literacy, Textbooks, and Ideology: Postwar Literacy Instruction and the Mythology of Dick and Jane.* Philadelphia, 1988.

——. "The Secular Word: Catholic Reconstructions of Dick and Jane." In *The Politics of the Textbook,* edited by Michael W. Apple and Linda Christian-Smith, 166–190. New York, 1991.

Mitchell, Theodore. *Political Education and the Southern Farmers' Alliance, 1887–1900.* Madison, Wisc., 1987.

Moffett, James. *Storm in the Mountains: A Case Study of Censorship, Conflict and Consciousness.* Carbondale, Ill., 1988.

Richardson, John. "Historical Sequences and the Origin of Common Schooling in the American States." In *Handbook of Theory and Research for the Sociology of Education,* edited by John Richardson, 35–63. New York, 1986.

Selden, Steven. *Inheriting Shame: The Story of Eugenics and Racism in America.* New York, 1999.

Teitelbaum, Kenneth. "Critical Lessons From Our Past: Curricula of Socialist Sunday Schools in the United States." In *The Politics of the Textbook,* edited by Michael W. Apple and Linda Christian-Smith, 135–165. New York, 1991.

——. *Schooling for Good Rebels.* New York, 1996.

Westerhoff, John H. *McGuffey and His Readers.* Nashville, Tenn., 1978.

Williams, Raymond. *The Long Revolution.* London, 1961.

Whipple, Guy Montrose, ed. *The Textbook in American Education.* Bloomington, Ill., 1931.

Zinn, Howard. *A People's History of the United States: 1492–Present.* Revised and updated. New York, 1995.

TECHNOLOGICAL ENCLAVES

James Spiller

On any late-twentieth-century night, millions of American televisions flickered with images of technological enclaves. News shows regularly covered the growing biotechnology industry, picturing goggled technicians sequencing human DNA or synthesizing genetically engineered wonder drugs. Commercials for computer chip manufacturers swept through spotless production facilities where space-suited workers handled finely etched silicon wafers. And network dramas, exploiting public fascination with technological catastrophe, focused on nuclear power plants at the brink of meltdown, space centers at the moment when launch vehicles exploded, or telecommunications command stations at the point of computer system failure. America's televisions, themselves products of and links in vast technological systems, were windows on many of its technological enclaves, the facilities where trained professionals pushed forward the frontiers of science and technology. With schools and popular science and technology museums offering more detailed information on these facilities, many Americans could identify university laboratories, government research centers, and industrial design and production plants as the places where scientists and engineers generated new scientific knowledge and applied it to innovative new technologies.

Owing to the fact that computers and biotechnology appeared to be economically promising and life transforming, private companies dominating these fields became common emblems of scientific and technological advance. Americans who came of age during or the few decades after the Second World War, however, may have identified government, university, and industry centers conducting nuclear and aerospace scientific research and technological development (R&D) as the premier high-tech enclaves of their age. Similarly, early-twentieth-century Americans may have looked at the relatively new research universities, foundations, and industrial R&D labs as quintessential technological en-

claves, places where scientists and engineers generated the chemicals, medicines, and electrical machinery that were then remaking the world. Each age has had its own technological enclaves, institutions of advanced technical education, innovation, and production. As long as state-of-the-art technology was based on scientific principles or research, those institutions also educated scientists, generated new knowledge, and applied that research.

Many colonial and nineteenth-century technological enclaves did not directly incorporate scientific principles or research, but they did share a number of characteristics with their twentieth-century counterparts. First, all of these institutions were collective and interconnected enterprises. Even Thomas Edison, celebrated as a "wizard" who single-handedly generated scores of important inventions, worked with skilled machinists and scientists, stocked his library with technical books and journals, drew on corporate capital, and depended on the federal government's technical standards and patent system. A second and related characteristic is that as interconnected enterprises, these institutions had very fluid, even indistinct boundaries. Edison's Menlo Park laboratory, for instance, was embedded in a network of other institutions—universities, journals, professional societies, corporations, and government agencies—that collectively comprised larger high-tech enclaves. Without the work done in those other institutions, Edison's team could not have left a legacy of thousands of patents. Although Americans cherish a history of private enterprise unfettered by government control, a third characteristic is that state and federal governments, particularly the military, have consistently been important patrons of technological innovation and related scientific research. Last, technological enclaves have never been organized solely by the demands of autonomous technologies. Those technologies and the institutions that produced them have all been historically contingent, influenced by the prevailing political, economic, and social currents of American society. America's technological enclaves embodied America's human complexity even as they symbolized straightforward technological progress.

COLONIAL AND EARLY NATIONAL ENCLAVES

As part of the mercantilist pattern of British colonialism, settlers of the future United States tended to extract for local consumption and export the New World's abundant natural resources. Aside from a limited number of shipyards, sugar refineries, and iron smelters, there were very few colonial enterprises that rivaled Britain's highly capitalized manufactories producing finished goods for use throughout its empire. Scattered across the thirteen colonies, however, were more humble centers of technical skill and sophistication, those workshops in which craftsmen such as blacksmiths and leather tanners repaired or fashioned goods that settlers did not import or provide for themselves. By investing in expensive tools and facilities and passing on specialized knowledge to apprentices, these craftsmen created a network of relatively high-tech enclaves providing services that largely self-sufficient settlers could not furnish themselves. An important element of this network were millwrights who, wielding the skills of carpenter, blacksmith, machinist, and surveyor, built the water-powered mills that turned local crops and timber into usable commodities. These technical complexes stood alone, but guidebooks such as Oliver Evans's *The Young Mill-Wright and Miller's Guide* (1795) and millwrights' apprentices who later built their own mills blurred the boundaries of these enclaves, situating them in a larger system of technical education and production. The growing number of colonial presses and newspapers in mid-eighteenth-century America were additional sites of specialized technical skill and production. But master printers such as Benjamin Franklin and their apprentices who pioneered what were then high-tech processes of printing and paper and ink production also provided important new media through which millwrights and other skilled craftsmen could disseminate their technical knowledge. Supplementing expensive European books and manuals, these domestic publications became influential conduits of technical education as more sophisticated machines and manufacturing processes were transferred from Europe to the infant United States.

Though it had a growing printing industry and legacy of technological enterprise, the newly independent nation still depended heavily on British and continental European education and publications, skilled technicians, and machinery. The tale of Samuel Slater, a young spinner who secreted away plans of British machinery and established America's first waterpowered textile mill in 1790, is a well-known version of a common story. The historian Norman Wilkinson helped illustrate the extent of America's technological indebtedness to Europe by showing how an early cluster of gunpowder, tanning, textile, and paper industries along Delaware's Brandywine Creek depended heavily on European skills and machinery. These industries, individually and collectively, were technological enclaves in their own rights, spinning out new products, trained personnel, and machinery for other technological endeavors. But if such enclaves include the original sources of personnel, training, and machine specifications, then a wider field of European inventors and factories were constituent parts of the Brandywine industrial phenomenon. While many Americans continued to rely on Britain and the continent for technical skills and equipment, the United States did excel in a few industrial niches. According to the scholar Nathan Rosenberg, owing to its abundance of wood relative to capital and labor, America became the worldwide leader in the design and use of woodworking machinery in the early nineteenth century. As long as wood was cheap and skilled labor scarce, Americans could afford to replace well-paid craftsmen with innovative, domestically made mechanical planners, jointers, and lathes. American mills and tool and furniture factories were among the world's most advanced woodworking industries until the 1850s.

Although antebellum America trailed several of its European contemporaries in scientific learning, technological sophistication, and industrial production, the young country was then building institutions and infrastructures that would make it home to a highly developed network of interdependent technological enclaves. During this period of early factory production, a number of urban educational institutions spread the gospel of scientific and technical literacy. Though most mechanical innovation was then based on practical experimentation rather than scientific principle, savants and scientific practitioners regularly identified science as the basis of new and useful technologies. According to the authors Sally Gregory Kohlstedt and George Daniels, newspapers, magazines, textbooks, early science museums, and speakers at public schools, colleges, and Lyceum lecture halls raised the scientific literacy of the educated public, exposed it to new

Thomas Edison in His Menlo Park Laboratory. Undated photograph. This laboratory was in use between 1876 and 1884. During these years, Edison perfected the incandescent lightbulb and invented the phonograph, the mimeograph machine, the electric fuse, and the multiplex telegraph.
© BETTMANN/CORBIS

technical apparatus and mechanical systems, and urged it to associate science with technological progress. Working men who required increasingly specialized skills and expensive tools to work in the growing urban manufacturing shops also learned about science and its application to machine design at the mechanic's associations and institutes that proliferated in American cities between the 1820s and the 1850s. The historian Edward Stevens has explained that through their technical libraries, classes on science, mathematics, and drafting, and exhibitions of mechanical models and diagrams, these educational institutions served an upwardly mobile generation of high-tech mechanics who wanted to design and build, rather than simply operate, the machines of the dawning industrial age. Often modeled after Philadelphia's Franklin Institute, established in 1824, these enclaves of scientific and technical training provided a relatively short-lived bridge between a period of craft-based production and an age in which college-trained scientists and engineers dominated industrial and technological innovation.

Commercial rivalry among eastern ports led state governments at this time to survey and finance turnpikes, canals, and railroads, some of the earliest large-scale technological endeavors in America. When New York began building the Erie Canal in 1817 so as to capture the lion's share of trade with the western agricultural frontier, it leveraged an unprecedented technological endeavor, a vast system of dams, locks, and bridges. The canal was essentially a 365-mile enclave of state-of-the-art technology, and it served as a practical training ground where budding civil engineers learned and applied basic surveying, mathematics, hydraulics, and earthen construction techniques. As the historian Terry Reynolds has noted, state-financed public works like the Erie Canal helped spawn other institutions of specialized scientific knowledge and technical skill. By accelerating transportation and communication among American towns and cities, these projects enabled a national network of professional societies and educational institutions and the diffusion of their specialized publications. Further, skilled veterans of efforts such as the Erie Canal worked on other high-tech projects like railroad lines and urban water and sewage works.

Government was a primary patron of these technological systems, financing city waterworks, granting valuable land for canals and railways, and providing scientific data in the form of geographic and geological surveys for projects. The federal government supplemented the growing cadre of technicians who received on-the-job training with many of America's first college-educated engineers, men who had studied engineering sciences at the United States Military Academy at West Point. Founded in 1802 and charged with providing the army's Corps of Engineers with native engineering talent, the Academy became America's first formal engineering school by adopting the French scholastic emphasis on mathematics and laboratory training. An important enclave of science education and training in high-tech production, West Point produced army engineers who designed transportation projects across the country and civilian specialists who started private consulting firms or taught in proliferating college science and engineering classes. Little more than ten years old in 1835, Rensselaer Polytechnique Institute (RPI) in Troy, New York, became the first of a half dozen collegiate institutions that started successful engineering programs before the Civil War. Like West Point, these colleges spawned a growing legion of researchers and engineers who designed, built, and staffed America's increasingly dense and mutually reinforcing network of colleges and technical institutes, transportation and communications systems, and factories.

American industry profited too from the fact that the federal government pioneered key technical innovations whose initial development costs placed them beyond the financial means of private, for-profit companies. The internationally vaunted "American system of manufacturing"—the mass production of uniform and interchangeable machine parts—though fully achieved only in the late nineteenth and early twentieth centuries, was originally developed in antebellum United States armories. The author Merritt Roe Smith has explained that owing to Washington's desire for military advantage, based on easily repaired weapons, and the army's ability to underwrite financially unprofitable projects, it financed the long and costly development of the precise jigs, gauges, machines, and manufacturing processes that enabled America's future industrial preeminence. Over the course of the next century, many of America's most productive manufacturing enterprises, those best admired as examples of its scientific and technological advance, adopted the system of uniform and interchangeable parts initiated at the armories. These government facilities, then, were important technological enclaves by virtue of their own technological sophistication and the fact that their skilled technicians moved to other industries, transplanting their pre-

cision equipment and specialized design and operating talents to other nascent enclaves.

Perhaps the most significant enclave to emerge before the Civil War centered on the steam railroad. Owing to their surveys, land and loan subsidies, and future regulatory actions, federal, state, and local governments had enormous influence on the birth and development of this technologically advanced transportation system. The knowledge and facilities needed to design, forge, and repair iron rails and steam engines demanded new theories and practices of precision manufacturing. The Franklin Institute and the federal government, alarmed over deadly steamship explosions, provided critical data for the production and maintenance of safe boilers and steam engines. College-trained engineers joined craftsmen and machinists in swelling railroad workshops and factories, the nation's largest and most advanced metalworking facilities. As the steel tentacles of this industry spread throughout the country, they became the fertile field for a rich new crop of interlocking technological enclaves. The railroads fed iron-boned cities with grain harvested by mechanical reapers and heated them with coal stripped by steam shovels. Many manufactories exploited a growing railroad-based national market by expanding operations, replacing craftsmen with specialized unskilled laborers, and adopting innovative labor-saving machines. And the telegraph, the first of the high-tech electrical devices to remake the world, spread symbiotically on the back of the railroad. Allowing railroad companies in the second half of the nineteenth century to make precise schedules, avoid train collisions, and standardize time across the entire United States, telegraphs, as the historian Paul Israel has argued, also pulled America into a new age of technological development. By virtue of their mechanical design and operation, telegraphs were often improved by traditional means of practical experimentation. But their electrical properties also required new methods of invention based on scientific theory and professional engineering know-how. In addition to its role in spawning new technologies and large-scale factories, railroads became important models for future high-tech enclaves by inventing the corporate machinery—including financial administration, accounting, and personnel and operations management—later adopted by industrial enterprises that were home to extensive technical training and innovation.

HIGH-TECH INDUSTRIAL ENCLAVES

In the period between the American Civil War and World War II, the United States underwent a series of related developments that made it a first-rate technological force in the world. Greased by the wheels of America's railways and patterned after their corporate structures, other highly capitalized industries used their economies of scale, pricing powers, and labor-saving machinery to dominate the extraction of minerals and fossil fuels, production of chemicals and electrical machinery, and national distribution of food and consumer manufactures. Many of these Gilded Age enterprises were America's most high-tech enclaves. They organized growing legions of specialized craftsmen and machine operators and used the power of steam and then electricity, near the turn of the twentieth century, to fashion technically complex new products, machinery, and manufacturing processes. These innovations were often made in the mine and on the shop floor by skilled mechanics or in corporate planning departments staffed by engineers educated at liberal arts colleges, West Point, RPI, or such new institutions as the Massachusetts Institute of Technology (MIT), chartered in 1861. Trained in multiplying enclaves of higher education, these engineers also formed specialized organizations, patterned after nascent scientific societies, that established professional standards of practice, codes of ethics, and continuing education through peer-reviewed journals. Founded in 1852, the American Society of Civil Engineers was the first of many national professional societies that soon organized mining, mechanical, electrical, and chemical engineers.

Though they were typically trained in United States colleges and guided professionally by these societies, most American scientists and engineers seeking graduate training at this time studied in European institutions. In 1876, however, with the establishment of the Johns Hopkins University, the United States had the first of what would soon be many research universities that not only educated college professors, government scientists, and industrial engineers, but generated new scientific knowledge and engineering techniques. Many of these institutions, endowed by captains of industry, developed curricula and research facilities that, the scholar David Noble has argued, funneled needed scientific practitioners and engineering managers into their benefactors' corporate enterprises. In addition to corporate schools and training programs and to public land-grant universities that, after the 1862 Morrill Act, developed facilities for agricultural and mechanical research and education, these research universities became critical extensions of industrial technological enclaves. They trained personnel and fostered new ideas that, transferred to those companies, enabled them to generate new technologies and products. Rising industrial competition and federal anti-trust regulation forced many high-tech companies to try to capture market share by conducting in-house research necessary to develop such technologies and products. Beginning in the electrical and chemical industries, these companies formed their own R&D laboratories, staffed by scientists and engineers with graduate university degrees, to conduct the applied research that would allow them to file patents and control technologies that gave them market advantage. R&D laboratories built by General Electric in 1900 and soon thereafter by the DuPont Company, Westinghouse Electric Corporation, Kodak, and AT&T, continued to draw personnel from research schools at the same time that they displaced universities as favored sources of scientific research and technological design. These industrial facilities were modeled partly after Thomas Edison's Menlo Park "invention factory," erected in 1876, in which his team of mechanics and scientists devised remarkable and profitable devices ranging from telephonic and phonographic equipment to incandescent lighting systems. Whereas the Wizard of Menlo Park accreted scientific analysis to traditional empirical methods of technological innovation, the hundreds of industrial R&D labs inspired by Edison's example embodied a new age of science-based technology. Staffed by scientists like Irving Langmuir, who won a Nobel Prize in 1932 for research he conducted at General Electric, these R&D facilities relied on scientific research rather than cut-and-dry experimentation to invent profitable new technologies.

In the first few decades of the twentieth century, then, industrial enterprises qualified as technological enclaves owing to their mechanized production lines and to the fact that their staff generated original research that, after securing patents, they often shared through professional journals and conferences and at technology exhibitions. Further, by adopting the techniques of scientific management formulated by the inventor and engineer Frederick Winslow Taylor and his disciples, many industrial firms not only used and made engineered objects, they became products of engineering. Writing in 1911 that "in the past, the man has been first; in the future the system must be first," Taylor counseled corporate managers to organize men and machines into a system of production as efficient as a well-oiled machine. Though his plans often met severe resistance on the shop floor, he argued that his techniques of increasing productivity by streamlining

337

the manufacturing process and minimizing the physical effort of manual laborers would ultimately benefit industrial workers and corporate managers. Though these techniques often exacerbated labor strife and undermined industrial efficiency, scientific managers, in effect, intensified the high-tech character of industrial enclaves by applying the logic of the machine to the human element of production. An insightful social critic, the actor Charlie Chaplin captured the humorless drudgery of these enclaves in the 1936 movie *Modern Times,* which comically depicts an industrial worker swallowed into the gears of his scientifically managed assembly line.

Though the federal government avoided labor strife by restricting the use of Taylor's methods in the industrial enterprises it contracted during the First World War, that global maelstrom made the government a major, albeit temporary, patron of R&D. In addition to its traditional role as oceanic and continental surveyor and mapmaker, the federal government became home to many technological enclaves in the half century before World War I. Its agricultural experiment stations in states throughout the country disseminated productive new seeds and counseled farmers to adopt new technologies and practices. By the early twentieth century, government engineering experiment stations and Bureaus of Standards, Census, and Mines provided research support, statistical data, and needed regulatory standards for America's expanding industrial economy. Recognizing the economic potential and security benefits of the new airplane, Washington chartered the National Advisory Committee for Aeronautics in 1915 to conduct R&D to advance this awesome new flying machine. These precedents, however, paled in comparison to the scale of federal support for technological development during the war. The government organized medical systems and psychological tests to evaluate and treat millions of soldiers. It swore in the venerated Thomas Edison as president of the Naval Consulting Board, a group of eminent inventors and engineers who evaluated potential new weapons and war-related devices. The National Research Council solicited scientists' advice on submarine detection, radio communication, aviation, explosive, and optical technologies. And as Hugh Slotten has noted, the wartime United States Chemical Warfare Service capitalized on America's patriotic chemists who invented masks and poison gas that were unleashed in European battlefields.

The wartime heyday of such prolific federal support for high-tech R&D quickly ended. The United States Navy opened its own lab in 1923, and President Herbert Hoover's Commerce Department sponsored a number of scientific and technical bureaus through much of the 1920s. Throwing money at nearly every niche of the depressed economy, President Franklin D. Roosevelt's New Deal agencies sponsored some industrial and university-based R&D, and the Tennessee Valley Authority (TVA) set a precedent for expensive, high-tech, and multiuse government public works programs. But industrial enterprises, research universities and institutes, and such philanthropic foundations as the Rockefeller Institute for Medical Research and the Carnegie Institution of Washington, remained America's most important technological enclaves by virtue of their extensive R&D expenditures during the interwar period. Further, the so-called American system of manufacturing, which came of age in this period and was characterized in part by mechanical assembly-line mass production, made many factories in the United States the most technically complex operations in the world. As the TVA demonstrated, however, the federal government was uniquely able to organize vast technocratic programs in response to public need and national crises. With the subsequent crisis of world war and then of a cold war, Washington became the primary estate of science and technology. It fed vast sums of public money into the government, corporate, and academic technological enclaves that helped the Allies win the Second World War and lift the United States to global superpower status.

THE GOVERNMENT-INDUSTRY-ACADEMIC COMPLEX

By the eve of World War II, the United States had long supported large-scale scientific endeavors and technological projects. The Japanese attack on Pearl Harbor and America's entry into a second global war, however, triggered a quantum leap in public support for R&D. Franklin Roosevelt's depression-era administrations had set an important precedent by vastly expanding federal expenditures. Pearl Harbor and the subsequent rapid pace of technology and weapons development convinced Washington that the United States had to make even greater expenditures, particularly for R&D, if it was to achieve military and economic security. Funneling billions of dollars annually into its own military and civilian R&D centers and, through a contract system first tested in the 1930s, into industrial enterprises and university laboratories, the federal government made the United States home to the world's most diverse and sophisticated network of technological enclaves.

A naturally rich continental nation, separated from the war's belligerents by two oceans, the United States became the global "arsenal of democracy" owing to its highly evolved system of industrial production and transportation. Retooling their factories for the war, American industrialists and their increasingly diverse workforces manufactured prodigious amounts of war-related matériel, from humble uniforms and field rations to sophisticated armaments and synthetic rubber. In old Frost Belt factories of the Northeast and new Sun Belt facilities of the South and West, assembly lines rendered Midwestern coal and ore into the thousands of tanks and ships, hundreds of thousands of airplanes and artillery pieces, and millions of guns and bombs that turned battlefields in Europe and Asia into enclaves of high-tech slaughter. Dubbed by England's prime minister Winston Churchill "a wizard war," World War II witnessed an unprecedented deployment of scientific and engineering expertise for the design and manufacture of novel weaponry. Mobilizing American scientists for a weapons race against Germany and Japan, the Office of Scientific Research and Development (OSRD) spent more than $1 billion during the war to develop such technologies as jet aircraft, rocket weapons, sonar devices, pesticides, and synthetic drugs. Much of this money flowed into industrial R&D labs, but even more went to university departments and centers such as MIT's Radiation Laboratory, which worked on radar, Harvard University's Radio Research Laboratory, which devised antiradar measures, and Johns Hopkins' Applied Physics Lab, which invented the proximity fuse.

America's most significant wartime scientific and technological undertaking was its development of the atomic bomb. Initiated by the OSRD in 1941 and taken over by the army less than two years later under the code-named "Manhattan Project," the program to build a fissionable atomic weapon secretly employed more than 120,000 people and cost more than $2 billion. In little more than three years, legions of scientists and technicians, working in industry, universities, and military installations in Tennessee, New Mexico, and Washington, transformed esoteric atomic theories into precisely engineered weapons that, when exploded over the Japanese cities of Hiroshima and Nagasaki in August 1945, instantly killed nearly 200,000 people. In the fearsome postwar age of bombers, rockets, and atomic weapons, Washington determined that it had

to maintain and even expand the interconnected complex of military-industrial-academic technological enclaves to secure its safety and global leadership. For example, rather than demobilizing wartime academic laboratories, the Department of Defense (DOD) financed such installations as the California Institute of Technology's Jet Propulsion Laboratory with long-term contracts. Similarly, the Atomic Energy Commission (AEC), upon its establishment in 1946, took over the Manhattan District's gas-diffusion facilities and plutonium-generating reactors and sponsored the University of California's Los Alamos National Laboratory.

The intensification of the cold war and its expensive arms race insured that the federal government, and especially the military, became a heavy underwriter of industrial R&D and academic science and engineering. The National Science Foundation (NSF), established in 1950 to be the federal government's primary sponsor of basic research, provided peer-reviewed grants to a limited number of exceptional scientists and academic institutions. But the NSF's budget never approached those of the DOD, the AEC, or, after its establishment in 1958, the National Aeronautics and Space Administration (NASA). While serving America's security interests, reclaiming its prestige after the Soviet Union's 1957 launch of *Sputnik*, and adapting missile technologies for the exploration and commercial utilization of outer space, NASA quickly became a major sponsor of university science and engineering programs and of electronics and aerospace enterprises. Arcing across California and the southern states, NASA research and development centers joined a new geographic crescent of American technological military and industrial enclaves. The billions of dollars that NASA, the DOD, and the AEC annually spent on R&D and high-tech equipment modernized this region's economy and changed the priorities of many of America's industrial enterprises and academic centers. Companies like General Electric and Westinghouse Electric pursued federal weapons and nuclear power contracts just as hard, if not more diligently, than they did their traditional consumer markets. The historian Stuart Leslie has rightly asserted that the benefit of rich government contracts enjoyed by American scientists came at the price of their "diminished capacity to comprehend and manipulate the world for other than military means" (*The Cold War and American Science*, p. 9). And Bruce Seely has argued that federal funding even affected the content of college classes. During the 1950s and 1960s, before Washington leaned heavily toward applied research, government grants generally went to academic departments pursuing fundamental research. According to Seely, to prepare students for graduate school and work in these federally financed laboratories, research universities increasingly emphasized theory in their science and engineering curricula.

Despite these legitimate criticisms, the fact remains that the seemingly inexhaustible money that government agencies like the DOD, the AEC, and NASA devoted to research for and development of extremely complex technologies enabled the three primary estates of science and engineering—government, industry, and academia—to be among the world's most innovative and sophisticated technological enclaves. Federal money boosted the American electronics industry, helping to finance the AT&T Bell Laboratory's 1948 invention of the transistor, the subsequent development of the microchip and computer software, and the Internet platform that suddenly seemed to transform commerce and information exchange at the end of the twentieth century. Although NASA's critics have accused it of giving the public only two practical technologies—Teflon nonstick pans and Tang orange drink—the space agency has helped change the world by working with industry and universities to develop new jet engines, synthetic materials, microelectronics, and communications, weather, and land-surveying satellites. And the National Institutes of Health sponsored biotechnology and human genome sequencing research that many late-twentieth-century Americans insisted would lead to technologies that would remake people in the twenty-first century, turning their bodies into enclaves of high-tech micromachines and genetically synthesized drugs.

The cold war coordination among universities, industries, and rich federal sponsors produced several of the most recognized, even iconic, geographic technological enclaves in the United States. Owing to its dominating influence on the computer hardware and software markets, Silicon Valley in central California is the best-known example of this type of enclave. Springing up around Stanford University in the 1950s and 1960s, this region's electronics and aerospace companies often enjoyed federal R&D support and were either started or supported by university faculty. Similar zones have coalesced around Austin, Texas; North Carolina's so-called "Research Triangle"; and Massachusetts's Route 128, near Boston's many research universities. Washington, D.C., though unusual for its dearth of research universities, became by many measures the largest geographic technological enclave in the

Intel Corporation. The first 106 Intel employees stand in front of the company's Mountain View, California, building in 1970. At front are co-founders Robert Noyce (1927–1990) and Gordon Moore (b. 1929). COURTESY OF THE INTEL CORPORATION

United States in the late 1990s as aerospace, biotechnology, computer, and telecommunications giants clustered around each other and their federal patrons and regulators.

Though these technological enclaves were fattened by federal largesse, they took off in the last two decades of the twentieth century as research universities and corporate enterprises established closer relations. After the passage of the 1980 congressional Bayh-Dole Act, which allows institutions of higher education to patent the results of federally funded research, universities sought revenue-generating R&D projects more aggressively. American industrial enterprises, pursuing new and competitive high-tech products, increased their financial outlays to these solicitous universities more than fivefold over this period. Many universities profited spectacularly, building gleaming new computer and biotech research centers and watching high-tech corporations break ground nearby. But this commercialization of higher education also raised the following unsettling questions about universities. Would they downgrade their commitment to the arts and humanities as they pursued high-tech R&D? More ominously, would these universities appease their corporate sponsors and protect their own patent prospects by restricting the free exchange of scientific knowledge and research that professionals had long insisted was essential to ongoing scientific and technological progress?

These unsettling questions barely registered on American investors and financial analysts who were seduced on the eve of the new millennium by the soaring stock value of high-tech firms. Computer, telecommunications, and biotechnology companies, in particular, registered phenomenal stock growth. The consequent leaps in stock market indexes may have represented the sound valuation of those American corporations that collectively devoted billions of dollars annually to in-house and university R&D and to acquiring start-up companies holding patents on niche technologies. But these leaps may have reflected Americans' fetishes for anything high-tech. Equipped with synthetic sweaters and super-strength composites, cell phones and desktop computers, and genetically engineered medications and food products, many well-to-do Americans understandably invested their retirement money in those interlocking technological enclaves that, for better or worse, were making incredible profits as they were remaking the world.

See also **Mercantilism; The Print Revolution; Expansion and Empire** *(volume 1);* **World War and Cold War** *(volume 2);* **Technology** *(in this volume); and other articles in this section.*

BIBLIOGRAPHY

Bruce, Robert V. *The Launching of Modern American Science, 1846–1876.* New York, 1987.

Cowan, Ruth Schwartz. *More Work for Mother: The Ironies of Household Technology from the Open Hearth to the Microwave.* New York, 1983.

Cutcliffe, Stephen H., and Terry S. Reynolds, eds. *Technology and American History: A Historical Anthology from Technology and Culture.* Chicago, 1997.

Dupree, A. Hunter. *Science in the Federal Government, A History of Policies and Activities to 1940.* Baltimore, 1986.

Hindle, Brooke. *The Pursuit of Science in Revolutionary America, 1735–1789.* Chapel Hill, N.C., 1956.

Hindle, Brooke, and Steven Lubar. *Engines of Change: The American Industrial Revolution, 1790–1860.* Washington, D.C., 1986.

Hounshell, David A. *From the American System to Mass Production, 1800–1932: The Development of Manufacturing Technology in the United States.* Baltimore, 1984.

Hughes, Thomas P. *American Genesis: A Century of Invention and Technological Enthusiasm, 1870–1970.* New York, 1989.

———. *Rescuing Prometheus.* New York, 1998.

Israel, Paul. *From Machine Shop to Industrial Laboratory: Telegraphy and the Changing Context of American Invention, 1830–1920.* Baltimore, 1992.

James, Portia P. *The Real McCoy: African-American Invention and Innovation, 1619–1930.* Washington, D.C., 1989.

Kevles, Daniel J. *The Physicists: The History of a Scientific Community in Modern America.* New York, 1978.

Kevles, Daniel J., and Leroy Hood. *The Code of Codes: Scientific and Social Issues in the Human Genome Project.* Cambridge, Mass., 1992.

Leslie, Stuart W. *The Cold War and American Science: The Military-Industrial-Academic Complex at MIT and Stanford.* New York, 1993.

McDougall, Walter A. *The Heavens and the Earth: A Political History of the Space Age.* New York, 1985.

McGaw, Judith A., ed. *Early American Technology: Making and Doing Things from the Colonial Era to 1850.* Chapel Hill, N.C., 1994.

Noble, David F. *America By Design: Science, Technology, and the Rise of Corporate Capitalism.* New York, 1977.

Reynolds, Terry S., ed. *The Engineer in America: A Historical Anthology from Technology and Culture.* Chicago, 1991.

Rhodes, Richard. *The Making of the Atomic Bomb.* New York, 1986.

Rossiter, Margaret W. *Women Scientists in America: Struggles and Strategies to 1940.* Baltimore, 1982.

———. *Women Scientists in America: Before Affirmative Action, 1940–1972.* Baltimore, 1995.

Smith, Bruce L. R. *American Science Policy since World War II.* Washington, D.C., 1990.

Smith, Merritt Roe. *Harpers Ferry Armory and the New Technology: The Challenge of Change.* Ithaca, N.Y., 1977.

Stapleton, Darwin H. *The Transfer of Early Industrial Technologies to America.* Philadelphia, 1987.

Stevens, Edward W. *The Grammar of the Machine: Technical Literacy and Early Industrial Expansion in the United States.* New Haven, Conn., 1995.

SALONS, COFFEEHOUSES, CONVENTICLES, AND TAVERNS

David S. Shields

Concurrent with the exploration and settlement of America, intellectual life in Europe underwent a transformation. The traditional sites of genteel and learned culture—the royal court, the church, and the college—lost their monopoly on the exchange of knowledge. New institutions emerged that became central to the creation of a cosmopolitan learned culture predicated on the freedom to inquire and to air opinions. The role of the printing press as an agent of this change has been well documented by historians. Less well documented and more complicated have been the contributions made by the host of communicative venues that emerged simultaneously in Europe and then became established in America: conventicles, salons, coffeehouses, societies of gentlemen, and tea tables. These institutions formed new modes of discourse—news, belles lettres, polite learning, scientific reportage. They encouraged a dialogic style of philosophical inquiry suited to conversational settings; they used wit (rather than shared interest or custom) as a means of forming communal identity (*sensus communis*); and they fixed liberty of expression as the desideratum of social communication.

The activities of these organizations increasingly stood in tension with the piety of the church, the gravity of the state, and the propriety of the college. Yet often the institutions mirrored what they stood against. Conventicles established a reformed order of worship that made them in effect an alternative church. Clubs often mocked the constitution and symbolism of states. Coffeehouses and academia set themselves up as "penny universities."

The influence of the college on the new institutions was singularly powerful in the earliest part of their development. For young men, there was something transformative about participation in a community of learning. Whether in the Italian universities during the burgeoning of humanist philosophy or Cambridge University during the Reformation, the intellectual vibrancy of life in those settings made the conversation of society at large seem rather lackluster. One finds during the sixteenth century an intense desire to reconstitute the collegiate community after graduation. In Europe the formation of "academia"—discussion circles or groups dedicated to the muses—gave rise to a constellation of extra-collegiate bodies concerned with cultivating the arts and sciences. In Holland and England the renovation of Christian practice wrought in the college halls spread into the countryside as young ministers formed associations— "classes" (sing.: "classis")—wherein they experimented with means of promoting godliness. These cultural developments spread to British America.

THE CONVENTICLE

The evolution of the classis into the conventicle and the conventicle into the prayer meeting proved particularly significant for the establishment of a Christian intellectual culture in the New World. In England, the classis expanded by 1600 to include recent graduates in other walks of life, yet drawn to the new Puritan practice. These private meetings of ministers and laypersons were termed "conventicles," and expanded to include women in their membership, thus breaking free of the collegiate model. Both the classis and the conventicle fell under legal proscription because the established church feared that they constituted a rival church. The fear was justified, for the conventicles were the seedbeds of religious independency. The Pilgrims were one fruit of this movement, the Massachusetts Bay Puritans who set up Congregationalism were another. Many of the leaders of the Puritan diaspora had belonged to conventicles in the southeast of England. John Winthrop, for instance, joined one in 1613 organized in Boxford. These founders of a Christian commonwealth in New England brought with them Christian practices pioneered in the English meetings, such as spiritual diary-writing, spontaneous communal prayer, "prophesying," and the singing of hymns. The conventicles remained the laboratory of Reformed Christianity, and much of the radical thought and innovative practice of Protestantism emerged in them. The Antinomian outbreak of the 1630s owed much to the preaching in the conventicle of the religious liberal Anne Hutchinson. Nearly every sect and heresy of the seventeenth century—the Gortonists, Fifth Monarchists, Familists—grew out of a private meeting.

In New England the conventicle operated in tension with the church congregation at large. Whereas the conduct of congregational worship tended to be inflexibly routine on Sunday, on the weekdays at the meeting, spiritual expression was given wide latitude. Whereas the membership of the town church tended to be fixed by neighborhood and church covenant, participation in a conventicle was voluntary and not constrained by locality or rite of admission. All ages, sexes, and classes attended Sunday worship; the conventicle's membership was limited to adult men and women, usually literate and invariably zealous. From 1600 to 1680, the conventicle operated as the driving engine of Puritanism on both sides of the Atlantic. As the seventeenth century drew to a close, the institution transmuted, turning into the prayer meeting, a body further segregated by age, sex, or profession.

The particularization of the membership of the prayer meeting by gender, age, vocation, and religious interest paralleled developments in European civil society. However, Protestant private meetings did not take place in a vacuum, isolated from other transformations in intellectual culture. Membership in a classis or conventicle did not preclude one's interest in or even participation in one of the humanist academies. John Winthrop Jr., the founding governor of Connecticut, participated in private religious meetings, experimented in alchemy, and was New England's first corresponding member to the Royal Society. That active champion of private religious society, the Reverend Increase Mather, in the 1680s also organized a natural philosophy discussion group. His son, Cotton Mather, who promoted the formation of prayer meetings in a dozen imprints, desired nothing more than election to the Royal Society. Harvard College itself would refashion its curriculum to accord with humanist learning. Christian denigration of learning—particularly "pagan fictions"—was a mark of parochialism restricted to few who attended Harvard, Yale, the College of William and Mary, and the College of New Jersey.

THE TAVERN

Conventicles met at the home of a member. Learned societies, academia, and humanist conversation circles might meet in a domestic setting, yet just as frequently convened at public houses. The tavern at the outset of the seventeenth century was unchallenged as the principal site of sociability in the English-speaking world. In rural places it was deemed necessary for the accommodation of strangers; in urban areas, essential for the conduct of business. In contrast to the lower-class alehouse and dramshop, the tavern possessed an aura of gentility. Besides its upper-class ethos, the polite society considered the tavern to be a "rational" institution, because each establishment posted house rules that regulated conduct on the premises. In the tavern, sociability became bound to gentility. In the eyes of some patrons, it became the essential institution of civil culture in the English-speaking world. At Jamestown, the Virginia Company's directors ordered that the tavern be erected before the church. The Puritan colonies acknowledged its utility by legislatively mandating its existence. Because of its service as a place of accommodation for the mobile population of merchants and traders, the tavern was the space, aside from the holds of ships, most intimately identified with England's, and later Great Britain's, commercial empire.

Several problems troubled the tavern as an outpost of imperial civilization. While the tavern in England and Holland tended to be a domestic institution that invited women on premises, in the hinterland of America it primarily served the male population of merchants and tradesmen. The conversation of the taverns consequently suffered from drunken crudity, an absorption with shoptalk, promiscuity of subject, and jest. The degeneracy of tavern conversation, while a problem in the metropolis, was a prevailing condition in the colonies. Early in the eighteenth century, champions of politeness arose in various cities (customs collector Henry Brooke in Philadelphia, Archibald Home in New York, the Reverend Edward Marsden in Charleston) to attempt a reform of tavern talk. Their success was limited, and invariably those who desired a more sober, genteel, and amusing intellectual commerce resorted to one of two other institutions—the club or the coffeehouse.

THE CLUB

The club first coalesced within the tavern. Out of the indiscriminate welter of the public, persons who discovered a shared interest, appetite, or ruling passion hired a private room and gathered together. Invariably a club formalized the fellowship, usually adopting a name, an emblem, a set of rules (often imitating features of house rules), and rites of club conduct. By the 1660s in London, the sense that clubs constituted a species of civil society gave rise to political experimentation. James Harrington's Rota Club set up as a miniature state where different methods of executive rule might be tried out. Throughout the eighteenth century a number of American clubs conceived of themselves as mock states that engaged in an ironic mirroring of imperial politics in their proceedings. The liberty of conversation entailed in club raillery would become recognized as an important element in the formation of public opinion. The third earl of Shaftesbury in *Sensus Communis* (1704) saw the total raillery of club discourse as the greatest insurance for honesty in the expression of opinion and as a means of testing and polishing, though before it entered the public sphere as opinion. It was, in effect, the great solvent of the civil fictions of the state and the dogmatism of churches.

If clubs were to be the political counterweight to church and state, their opposition would bring them under scrutiny by both powers. To evade repression the clubs made their proceedings secret, circulated misinformation about themselves, and effected a public image of frivolity, innocence, or benevolence. Often these devices disguised well-defined political programs. Indeed, the birth of factions and political parties can be seen as an outgrowth of club formation. London's King's Head Club provided the nucleus of the English Whig Party. Sir William Keith's Tiff Club and Gentleman's Club were the nucleus of Pennsylvania's anti-proprietary faction. Boston's Long Room Club organized patriot resistance in the American Revolution. Inevitably, however, the public ends of these groups led to their transformation. They ceased being private societies; they ceased depending upon an ethic of sociability; they foreclosed liberty of conversation to propound specific policies or political doctrines.

Throughout the eighteenth century, clubs repeatedly transmuted to factions. The creation of parties, however, required the surrender of the exclusivity and intimacy of membership that were the hallmarks of private sociability. When publicity and the management of public affairs became the sole ends of associations, they ceased being institutions of civil society and became political bodies. When the associations acknowledged this, as did the revolutionary committees of correspondence, they usually prospered in their public endeavors. When associations attempted to combine political action with the secrecy and exclusivity of private society—as did the Society of the Cincinnati in the 1780s or the Democratic-Republican clubs of the 1790s—they inspired intense public criticism and enjoyed limited effectiveness. Popular anxiety about the "antidemocratic" character of "secret societies" led to the formation of the anti-Masonic party of the early nineteenth century.

Not every club was driven by a public project. Indeed, a substantial number of clubs operated as retreats from public affairs and commerce. George Webb, whose poem "Batchelor's Hall" (1731) expressed the creed of these clubs, wrote that "Tir'd with the bus'ness of the noisy town, / The weary Batchelors their cares disown." The most interesting of these enclaves were groups that playfully mocked politics in business in their proceedings. The burlesque state trials of club officers who were entertained at the Tuesday Club or the Homony Club, the mock declarations of war on White Perch made by the Fort St. David's Fishing Company in Pennsylvania, the bestowal of titles, offices, and ranks by Charleston's Fancy Club, all evinced an aesthetic disinterestedness in public life. When political opponents and commercial rivals gathered together in this exercise of mockery, as they did in the Homony Club on the eve of the American Revolution, the club operated as an institution maintaining the solidarity of the ruling class. Its operation suggested that neither political principle, nor interest, nor moral passion was as strong as elite men's friendship or shared love of pleasure. The primacy of aesthetics over politics, friendship over duty, *sensus communis* over ideology, homosociality over heterosociality and domesticity proved controversial. Alternative visions and institutions of sociability emerged, rivaling the club in popularity and cultural influence.

THE COFFEEHOUSE

The coffeehouse replicated the homosociality of the tavern club, but embraced politics, business, and public matters rather than distancing its community from them. Indeed its absorption in these matters has led to its identification by scholars as one of the originating sites of the bourgeois public sphere. The sober stimulus of caffeine was ideally suited to commercial work, enhancing acuity of judgment rather than clouding it as alcohol did. First appearing in London during the latter years of the Commonwealth era, the coffeehouse became the temple of Restoration England's commercial imperium. Clustered around the exchange in London, the commercial coffeehouses became the clearinghouses of colonial commerce and sounding boards of imperial news. News was the distinctive discourse of the coffeehouse. In Ned Ward's theatrical portrait, *The Humours of a Coffee-House* (1707), readers can hear echoes of this compelling, novel sort of talk. Rumors of wars, tidings of battles, narratives of prodigies and novelties, fantasies about the possibilities of gain, political gossip, and current prices melded into a type of communication that sensationalized fact and confused actuality, probability, and possibility under the heat of acquisitive desire. Charles II's fear that the political speculation in the coffeehouse posed a threat to the project of Restoration led to an unsuccessful attempt at their repression. Thereafter, they remained a free zone of intelligence and opinion.

In British America the coffeehouse operated as an outpost of metropolitan commerce and thought. In port cities there was usually one coffeehouse linked to the exchange by name or clientele. Here ship captains, merchants, factors, the larger tradesmen, news writers, and provincial officials met and conducted business. Early in the eighteenth century, prior to the construction of state houses, the colonial and municipal governments often met in coffeehouses, which were the only public houses capacious enough to accommodate crowds. In Philadelphia, for instance, the London Coffeehouse housed most public business for two decades. Throughout the century coffeehouses were advertised as places of vendue, where stock from ships were displayed and sold. At the close of the century, insurance companies and stock exchanges formed on premises, as the New York Stock Exchange did at the Tontine Coffeehouse. While news, negotiation, and politics pervaded American coffeehouse discourse, there was less of the learned talk found in London. New York's coffeehouse managed a culture where wits could coin Latin epigrams about one another's chess play. Annapolis's coffeehouse hosted many learned discussions of the law. But the majority of the coffeehouses throughout the eighteenth century conformed to the portrait found in *The Philadelphiad:*

What various faces here we thronging view
From Nova-Zembla down to swart Peru,
Met for the mutual benefit of each,
To gather news or useless lore to teach.

(vol. 1, p. 61)

While the coffeehouse may have had its enemies among the governing class, its most strident critics were women, protesting the homosocial exclusivity of the institution. Until the arrival of the coffeehouse, work and trade took place primarily in one's household. Once trade and work were removed from the home, women were left with the task of domestic management, without the aid of their "helpmates." They resented this abandonment in no uncertain terms. Female screeds against coffee flooded the metropolis, claiming it to be an "emasculating" liquor. Women rallied around tea and established, in domestic settings, a female institution to counter the coffeehouse, the tea table.

THE TEA TABLE

By the 1690s the tea table had become a fixture of metropolitan life. It became established in the colonial metropolises in the first decades of the eighteenth century. The coffeehouse had its discourse of public affairs—news—and the tea table had its discourse of private affairs—gossip. A man or woman who violated the mores of a community risked the ruin of his or her reputation. Word would be sent out from the town matrons who monitored manners that someone had offended their sensibilities, and the perpetrator would suffer a social embargo. This discipline did not require force, the coercion of law, or any formal exercise of authority. Punishment was by a tacit covenant of social excommunication. One would be barred from the households of the gentility, frozen out of the marriage mart, and not invited to assemblies, card parties, or other heterosocial diversions in civil society. The power of the tea table lay in its rationalization of social discipline on behalf of a female interest. In cases where the law's masculine bias made women vulnerable to the abuse or drunkenness of a husband, the tea table organized public sentiment against malefactors. While the tea table, given the luxury status of tea early in the eighteenth century, began as an upper-class institution, its ambition was to consolidate a broader cultural power, organizing a woman's interest or sphere. To this end it marshaled fashion and domestic information in a campaign to capture the imaginations of country and common women. With trepidation male commentators analyzed the tea table, describing its methods:

If you visit the Tea-Table of some few Ladies, (to speak genteelly) you have good Manners, a civil sort of Impertinence, Remarks made with excelled Judgment upon the Fashions . . . or fine Lectures upon the Affairs of a House . . . and it is very well if you excape hearing a long Roll of your Neighbor's Faults. (Adams, *New England Weekly Journal*, 1727)

Its success was attested in letters and articles that flooded the colonial gazettes bemoaning the fact that "ever Custom taken up by Ladies of Quality, is presently follow'd by the Trulls and Gossips of the vulgar Herd" (*New England Courant*, 1724).

The tea table's discourse was primarily oral. It left relatively few literary artifacts in British America: schoolmistress Madam Sarah Kemble Knight's *Journal* (1704), a scattering of letters, and some controversial poems published in the provincial gazettes. Yet its cultural effects were registered widely in print. Its promulgation of fashion, particularly the wearing of hats, whalebone petticoats, and hoopskirts, was rebuked by ministers and moral critics of luxury. Its campaign to expand female presence in public places—such as the auditories of courtrooms and city streets and parks—was waged with success in the 1720s and 1730s. Its sentimentalization of morality, its consolidation of sensibility as a female disposition, and its embrace of consumerism all proved decisive developments in colonial civil society. Always controversial, the tea table provoked two sorts of criticisms among women: members of Christian prayer meetings admonished the tea table for its worldliness and lack of spirituality; learned women rebuked the tea table for its fascination with social trivia and its disinclination to cultivate sense. The latter group believed that nothing of enduring worth would emanate from the tea table unless it incorporated the conversation of learned men and bound sense to sensibility. These women developed the institution that would rival and eventually supplant the tea table as the most influential female institution in the polite world—the salon.

THE SALON

The salon was a heterosocial institution in which the conversation of the sexes occurred under the superintendence of a hostess. In the salon a young gentleman's or lady's manners were refined, tested by wit and intelligent exchange. In the salon musical performances took place, original poetry and prose were read aloud, and the latest books were discussed. Here learning was rendered polite by being made "conversible." Two old-world models operated. The French model made intellectual brilliance, female wit, and public controversy the chief activities. The English salon placed a premium on moral sentiment rather than wit, often had a projecting element, and had proportionately a larger number of women than its French counterpart. In British America heterosocial state salons—sponsored by the wives of governors—existed as early as the 1730s. For example, the matriarch of the Levy-Franks clan (a wealthy merchant family), Abigail Franks, described Lady Cosby's (the wife of New York's governor) "court" in New York. Franks's experiences offer the first recognizable glimpse of the British form: a male poet reads aloud his composition and suffers the criticism of several female auditors; the current political crisis is dissected over tea and biscuits; and the lady governor enforces a genteel tone. By the 1750s, literary salons, analogues to the English Bluestocking circles, formed in Charleston, Philadelphia, Princeton, Trenton, and Boston. Invariably poetry was the favored form of literary expression cultivated in these circles, and the *salonnières* who hosted the gatherings were among the most reputable women writers of the eighteenth century: Annis Boudinot Stockton, Elizabeth Graeme Fergusson, Abigail Streete Coxe, Hannah Simmons Dale, and Mercy Otis Warren.

The seriousness with which the salons sought to intermix learning, sense, and philosophy into the pleasantry of polite conversation can be seen in certain of their literary artifacts. Elizabeth Graeme's "A Pastoral Dialogue between Damon and Alexis," a neoclassical poem she wrote in 1755, captures the tone. It is a debate between reason and passion, stoicism and enthusiasm, a homosocial male and a heterosocial male about their relationships with women and society in general. The diction is decorously neoclassical, the form conversational, and the disagreement philosophical, yet the stakes of the debate are nothing less than the continuance of society, for unless the stoic, individualistic male can be bound by sympathy into the social contract, civil society remains at risk. The salons' politics of sympathy linked an ideal of companionate marriage to an image of public civility. The salons understood in this politics of sympathy that there were public roles for women: they would form and police manners; and they would ensure that fellow feeling would be tied to judgment.

Given this scheme of values there is little wonder that encouraging courtship became one of the important tasks of the salon. Often this end was disguised by a rhetoric of platonic friendship. Yet the possibility of love and partnership between intelligent and genteel young women with young men of property, talent, and sense was a promise held out by the first literary projector of the British American salon, Elizabeth Magawley. And it remained a central purpose of the greatest of American salons, First Lady Martha Washington's Friday Night "Drawing Room," at the end of the eighteenth century. Martha Washington's "Republican Court" made explicit the connection between companionate marriage and the harmony of civil society, using the partnership of talented women and men as a means of nation building. Washington believed that the most effective way of overcoming the regional parochialism of state representatives was to link them by marriage with persons from other regions. Sixteen such marriages took place during the first Washington administration. The most noteworthy of the Republican Court couplings was that between the statesman James Madison and Dolley Payne, who became a famous Washington hostess while her husband was secretary of state and president of the United States. Radical Republicans looking upon this attempt to consolidate a continental governmental class saw the importation of the Old World's aristocratic practice of dynastic marriage.

The Republican Court embodied all of the cultural ambitions of the salons and certain of the governmental functions of a court. It instituted a republican scheme of gentility, less lavish than those of European metropolises, yet preserving politeness, familiarity, and stylishness. Fashion, however, was muted. It promoted conversation among intelligent persons, including political discussion, for the enlightenment of its members. Yet it promoted a public project as well—the education of women. It fulfilled the governmental function of serving as a place of reception for foreign dignitaries and visitors of state. It was a zone where one could approach officials in their private capacity of citizens to discuss public business. Martha Washington turned the Republican Court over to First Lady Abigail Adams, who presided over its transfer to Washington, D.C. When Thomas Jefferson ascended to the presidency, he dismantled the national drawing room as an antidemocratic institution. Well-acquainted with the Parisian salons and their power, Jefferson feared the creation of a similar public sphere for women in the United States. A believer in the republican doctrine of female domesticity, he saw little merit in women's direct participation in public affairs. When Dolley Madison revived the women's public sphere in Washington,

she did so with an elaborate domestic symbolism surrounding it—a masquerade of privacy.

Jefferson personally debated the question of whether women should broker the creation and exchange of knowledge in salons with the woman who would become the most Parisian of *salonnières* on the American scene, Anne Willing Bingham. Brilliant, beautiful, and ambitious, Bingham had created a sensation in Paris in the early 1780s when she debuted in the French drawing rooms. The wife of the president of the Bank of the United States, and niece of Eliza Willing Powell (the Republican Court's female paragon and dedicatee of Benjamin Rush's *Thoughts on Female Education*), Bingham made her Philadelphia townhouse, Lansdowne, the center of both the haut monde and the American intellectual universe. She was unembarrassed about talking politics with legislators, diplomacy or philosophy with foreign diplomats, and the role of the sexes with intellectuals such as Comte de Volney or Susanna Rowson. Even Jefferson attended the salon, for to disdain it would have shown an inability to transcend personal opinion. Because the style of the exchange mattered as much as the content, Bingham's gatherings were anathematized by Republican levelers, such as the poet Charles Crawford, as the quintessence of aristocracy. There is some merit to that accusation, for Bingham was not interested in illuminating the masses, or even educating her sex (as Martha Washington, Abigail Adams, and Eliza Powell wished), but in creating that critical energy among the best minds and most avid spirits that produces a rarefied elevation of discourse. This sublime conversation was not for everyone. Yet for those few who were party to it, there was such depth of understanding, attunement of sentiment, pleasure of familiarity, that it became an end in itself. In the diaries of the principle figures of the 1790s, a visit to Anne Bingham's salon was invariably celebrated. An invitation stood as proof of achieved civility.

The pleasure of this Olympian sort of communication was an important concern during the seventeenth and eighteenth centuries. Sociability was an important, at times requisite, feature of learned converse. The historian Anne Goldgar has argued that gentlemanly comity and friendliness characterized the institutionalization of scientific conversation. The Royal Society, the American Philosophical Society, and various associations for useful knowledge invented ceremonies of reportage, and created a venue for public celebrity. The gentleman reporter—the "transactioneer" as was called by contemporaries—was so modish and distinct a creature at the outset of the eighteenth century that he was satirized on the stage. When the sociable and ceremonious components of learned association were downgraded, an organization was likely to fail. The botanist Alexander Garden, for instance, organized an experimental agricultural society in South Carolina in the 1750s that collapsed because of its seriousness. Garden, who had excited the great natural philosophers of Europe by shipping them the first specimens of electric eels and sirens, should have realized that curiosities, natural prodigies, and like matter were sufficiently amusing to bind the attention of a disparate and spatially dispersed community. The lesson was not lost on others. The Fort St. David's Fishing Company maintained a clubhouse of curios so famous that foreign visitors traveled miles out of their way to see it. Yet collecting Native American artifacts, gathering, preserving, and displaying the local flora and fauna, and festooning the walls with curiosities gleaned from members' global adventures were ancillary to the social ends of talking, fishing, and eating. Natural philosophy was a polite amusement as much as a branch of learning. Even the American Philosophical Society, for all its institutional gravitas, sought to make the act of reading members' correspondence, transactions, and reports as entertaining as possible for the membership.

The eighteenth century saw the emergence of an ideal of polite learning—learning easier, more eloquent, and more conversible than that promulgated in seminaries, schools, and the inns of court. While this phenomenon manifested itself in the broad scope of texts and expressions—in the stylish correspondence of transactioneers addressing scientific bodies, in the renovation of the ancient form of dialogue in philosophy to suit the new conversational spirit of the age, in the collection of the "table talk" of statesmen, wits, and thinkers—its most potent and characteristic manifestation was in the great projects of translation in which learned poets rendered ancient classics in vernacular verse, or university men brought the Greek and Roman tracts and histories into clear English prose. British America was home to numbers of polite gentlemen— ministers, schoolmasters, lawyers, physicians, and placemen—translating or paraphrasing the classics for the amusement of their coteries. Archibald Home, the secretary of New Jersey, entertained and instructed his circle in Trenton (Abigail Coxe, Richa Franks, Moses Franks, Joseph Warrell, and Robert Hunter Morris) with manuscript versions of Horace's *Epistles*. David French translated Anacreon and Ovid for his club of Pennsylvania friends (Joseph

Breintnall, Achilla Rose, and Robert Hall among them). Thomas Craddock renovated Virgil into "The Maryland Eclogues" to amuse his friends in the Baltimore and Annapolis clubs, including the famous Tuesday Club. This general interest in classical literature among those seeking improvement constituted a potential audience for printed versions of these performances. The British print market for belles lettres was built on the great translations, from John Dryden's Ovid and Virgil, to Alexander Pope's Homer. In British America, too, historians find works that inaugurate a "polite culture" in print. Richard Lewis's translation of "Musciplia" announced itself as the foundational event in the establishment of the republic of letters in Maryland. The subscriber list constituted the membership of the politely learned.

Though the printing press would come to mediate the communication of the learned and the polite over the course of the eighteenth century, it did so by assuming the mask of the venues it supplanted. Newspapers, when they aspired to be something more than the shipping news and register for advertisements, often invented a virtual club whose proceedings were recorded in the paper. The example of the Spectator Club loomed large over the world of provincial print. Newspapers and magazines often commented on manners and morals through the mask of a friendly society. From the Janus Club that dominated the pages of the *New England Courant* in the 1720s to the Drones, who enlivened the pages of the *New York Gazette* in the 1790s, the impersonality of print was overthrown by a masquerade that the isolated reader was somehow participating in the conversation of a conventicle, coffeehouse, club, or salon.

The consolidation of a national print culture during the nineteenth century in the United States did not cause the entire eclipse of early forms of intellectual association. Though the tavern suffered cultural demonization at the hands of the temperance movement and the coffeehouse lost its aura of cultural vitality, the salon and the club thrived. The salon became linked to the promotion of the fine arts, while the club became the ubiquitous institution of American culture, no longer restricted to the society of men. Virtually every social and intellectual initiative arising outside of the academy was nourished in some voluntary association or professional society. Conversation, debate, and colloquy retained their power to refine ideas even when the printing press became the primary means of their dissemination.

See also **Rhetoric and Belles Lettres; Popular Intellectual Movements, 1833–1877; Southern Intellectual Life; Urban Cultural Institutions** *(volume 1);* **Artistic, Intellectual, and Political Refugees** *(volume 2);* **Rhetoric** *(in this volume); and other articles in this section.*

BIBLIOGRAPHY

Adams, John. "Proteus Echo no. 29." *New England Weekly Journal,* no. 30 (October 23, 1727).

Amory, Hugh, and David D. Hall. *The Colonial Book in the Transatlantic World.* Vol. 1 of *The History of the Book in America.* New York and Cambridge, U.K., 1998.

Blecki, Catherine La Courreye, and Karin A. Wulf, *Milcah Martha Moore's Book.* University Park, Pa., 1997.

Collinson, Patrick. "The English Conventicle." In *Voluntary Religion,* edited by W. J. Sheils and Diana Wood, pp. 223–259. Oxford, 1986.

Conroy, David. *In Public Houses: Drink and the Revolution of Authority in Colonial Massachusetts.* Chapel Hill, N.C., 1996.

Ellis, Aytoun. *The Penny Universities: A History of the Coffeehouses.* London, 1966.

Goldgar, Anne. *Impolite Learning: Conduct and Community in the Republic of Letters, 1680–1750.* New Haven, Conn., 1995.

Graeme, Elizabeth. "A Pastoral Dialogue between Damon and Alexis." Philadelphia, 1775.

Griswold, Rufus Wilmot. *The Republican Court; or, American Society in the Days of Washington.* New York, 1855.

Klein, Lawrence E. *Shaftesbury and the Culture of Politeness: Moral Discourse and Cultural Politics in Early Eighteenth-Century England.* Cambridge, Mass., 1994.

Kowalski-Wallace, Beth. "Tea, Gender, and Domesticity in Eighteenth-Century England." In *Studies in Eighteenth-Century Culture,* pp. 131–145. East Lansing, Mich., 1994.

Mulford, Carla, ed. *Only for the Eye of a Friend: The Poems of Annis Boudinot Stockton.* Charlottesville, Va., 1995.

The Philadelphiad; or, New Pictures of the City. 2 vols. Philadelphia, 1784.

Shields, David. *Civil Tongues and Polite Letters in British America.* Chapel Hill, N.C., 1997.

LYCEUMS, CHAUTAUQUAS, AND INSTITUTES FOR USEFUL KNOWLEDGE

Andrew Chamberlin Rieser

"There are," wrote historian Clinton Grattan in 1955, "very, very few 'new' ideas in adult education" (*In Quest of Knowledge*, p. 89). Buried in this aphorism is a crucial insight into American cultural history. Self-culture—that is, adult self-betterment through learning—has often been regarded as a universal American trait, as if a straight line could be drawn from Benjamin Franklin to Bill Gates. Indeed, the self-culture habit was central to the American mythology of middle-class prosperity. However, closer inspection of the history of popular education, or "useful knowledge" in nineteenth-century parlance, reveals few fixed truths. From its inception, the concept was enmeshed in a dense matrix of material and ideological relations. Early national educators, for example, struggled to reconcile the spirit of progress with their deeply rooted paternalism. Later exemplars of useful knowledge encountered new tensions and conflicts, often between groups—including workers, clubwomen, ministers, and self-made millionaires—whose criteria for what made knowledge "useful" differed widely. The story of useful knowledge, therefore, is a tale of a seemingly stable concept given new meanings as it was buffeted by the winds of nation-building, industrialization, immigration, state formation, and civil rights.

This essay summarizes some of the institutional activities going under the banner of useful knowledge from 1700 to 1950. Special attention is given to two issues—citizenship and consumerism—addressed vitally in recent scholarship on the modern reorganization of knowledge, particularly that of T. J. Jackson Lears, Joseph F. Kett, and Joan Shelley Rubin. Citizenship training, initially a side benefit of useful knowledge, emerged as its organizing principle by the end of the nineteenth century. Meanwhile, publishers repackaged useful knowledge as an "authentic" form of self-realization and marketed it for sale in the consumer economy. Most historians agree that by the 1920s, the burden of popular enlightenment had largely shifted from private to bureaucratic and corporate control. The larger meanings of that pivotal development are in dispute, however, pointing to new directions of research and interpretation.

REPUBLICAN EDUCATION

Associations for mental self-improvement first took shape within the ranks of the commercial elite in the colonial port cities of Boston, New York, and Philadelphia. For the restless sons of mercantile wealth, belletristic clubs like the Society for Improving Themselves in Useful Knowledge, founded by New York lawyer William Livingston in the early 1740s, imparted a familiarity with au courant European philosophies—enough, at any rate, to stump their elders and display a stylish erudition. Many saw their own ambitions mirrored in the "Rising Glory" of America. In earlier scholarship on American adult education, Benjamin Franklin's Junto, a "club for mutual improvement" formed in Philadelphia in 1727, enjoyed a prominent place as a symbol of robust, upwardly mobile manhood on the eve of war and rebellion. Consistent with Franklin's reputation as a folklorist of "self-betterment," Junto's charter members included fellow printers, surveyors, and clerks. But like the various subscription libraries (of which there were fifty in New England by 1780), the Junto was predicated on the assumption of literacy, itself a privilege of wealth in colonial society.

Learned Societies The emergence of republican ideology brought the need for leadership training into sharp focus. A symbolic declaration of cultural independence came during the Stamp Act agitation of 1769, when members of Junto met to establish the American Philosophical Society (APS) with Franklin, then in London, as president. Similarly, nationalistic impulses lay behind Boston's American Academy of Arts and Sciences (AAAS), an institute formed in 1780 around a nucleus of Cambridge science professors and devoted to "knowledge of various kinds, and greatly useful to mankind." The AAAS's ambition to promote experimental research, however, went unfulfilled. Indeed, little of the knowledge it generated, mainly in the form of dry philosophical treatises, ever passed beyond its neoclassical porticos. At the dawn of the nineteenth century, fears of a demos unleashed, fueled by deep suspicions of the capacity of "brutish" men to display the republican virtues necessary for true democracy, set limits on the diffusion of useful knowledge.

For knowledge to be made useful to mankind, the argument went, it must respect the hierarchies of occupation, class, and rank essential to a well-ordered republic. For some, education served as a means by which prodigies from the lower classes were drafted into the society of gentlemen. In *Notes on the State of Virginia* (1785), Thomas Jefferson called for a system of general education by which "twenty of the best geniuses will be raked annually from the rubbish." Particularly in New England, a powerful culture of deference stifled arguments for a patriotic or utilitarian diffusion of knowledge. But in the first thirty years of the new century, expanding suffrage, evangelical revivals, and the decline of the Federalist Party would help undermine the deferential system upon which earlier formulations for the dissemination of useful knowledge rested. The new scientific societies, reading clubs, and library companies would provide a solid institutional foundation for the democratization of useful knowledge.

THE DEMOCRATIZATION OF USEFUL KNOWLEDGE

During the Jacksonian era, industrialization, religious revival, and reform placed self-education at the center of an envisioned "benevolent empire." Advocates of useful knowledge, including ministers, educators, and reformers, viewed themselves as beneficiaries of a democratizing force in Western civilization: the end of medieval Scholasticism and the rise of inductive reason as the new epistemological basis of knowledge. Indeed, the ongoing conquest of the frontier and technological advances in manufacturing, communication, and transportation struck many as triumphs of Baconian logic. But without an adult populace well educated in Christian and republican tenets, the empire would falter. A panoply of charities, many spurred by a revival of evangelical Protestantism, cemented the link between education, progress, and social order. During the Jacksonian era, even the more conservative benevolent groups, such as the American Bible Society (1816), American Sunday School Union (1824), and the American Tract Society (1824), wove secular instruction into their sacred publications. Few disagreed with Scotsman Thomas Dick's claim, in an 1833 book printed widely in the United States, that "superstitious notions engender vain fears and distorted views of the government of the Almighty" (*On the Improvement of Society,* p. 35).

Mechanics' Institutes The democratizing trend of useful knowledge is seen most dramatically in the rise of mechanics' institutes in the 1830s and 1840s. Outgrowths of a "softened" version of utilitarianism, newly amenable to the independent shop culture of laborers, mechanics' institutes endeavored to train men who had technical aspirations but no formal education. The first American mechanics' institute started as a benevolent extension of the APS. Formed in 1824 at the behest of the future railroad magnate Samuel Merrick and the University of Pennsylvania chemistry professor William H. Keating, the Franklin Institute featured a laboratory, lecture hall, museum, scientific journal, high school, courses in philosophy and science, and a school of architectural drafting. The success in Philadelphia spurred imitations throughout the Northeast and Midwest, most notably the Ohio Mechanics' Institute in Cincinnati (1828) and Cooper Union in New York (1859). Many took shape when mutual aid societies and apprentices associations appealed to civic-minded businessmen to sponsor a meetinghouse or library. By the 1840s Iowa boasted four institutes.

While Jefferson planned to rake geniuses from the rubbish, Merrick and Keating strove to promote enlightened leadership within the community of skilled workers. The institutes evolved from the proposition that mechanics should be respected as creative agents in the industrial process. In this regard, they gave hope to those struggling to avoid occupational obsolescence and preserve craft traditions in an age of industrialization. For immigrants with craft skills, particularly, the institute offered a portal into fuller assimilation with a masculine producer culture. German artisans brought to the institutes their own scientific culture and tradition of useful knowledge; in 1848, after all, Berlin had sixty lending libraries. By their very existence, moreover, the institutes leveled an implied critique against the scientific professionalism and formal technical culture arising on college campuses. The

The Franklin Institute, Philadelphia, Pennsylvania. The Franklin Institute was founded in 1824 to honor Benjamin Franklin and advance the usefulness of his inventions. © JOSEPH SOHM; CHROMOSOHM INC./CORBIS

Bigelow Mechanics' Institute in Massachusetts was not the only one to invoke the iconic power of the lone inventor. Once a tinkerer and by the 1840s a wealthy manufacturer of straps used by horse-drawn carriages, Erastus Bigelow sponsored this institute for local machinists and craftsmen in 1846.

The mechanics' institutes did not belong to mechanics. In Great Britain, workingmen tried hard, if unsuccessfully, to free the institutes from liberal politicians and management. Workingmen maintained a strong presence at the Franklin Institute's progenitor, the Glasgow Mechanics' Institute (1823). American institutes, however, adhered to the notion that workers and proprietors shared a common culture. Not surprisingly, many workingmen stayed away. In the marble steps, Ionic columns, and carpeted halls, some mechanics detected a strategy to lure them away from their union or workingmen's party. Others resented the expectation that their manners would be softened and refined by rubbing shoulders with members of higher classes. And as historian Joseph F. Kett has shown, the most talented lecturers would soon be drawn to the lyceums and common schools. Yale University's

Benjamin Silliman Sr. began lecturing to public audiences at a New Haven institute in 1831. By 1838, however, he had found a larger audience and honorarium for his lectures at the Lowell Institute (founded that year by the philanthropist John Amory Lowell) and before paying lyceum crowds. And in 1862, the Morrill Land-Grant Act ushered in an era of state-led technical education. Founded under the banner of liberal reform, mechanics' institutes on both sides of the Atlantic failed to attract their target audience and by midcentury were catering to the self-improvement impulses of urban middle classes.

The Lyceum By contrast, the lyceum was well calibrated to the needs of its target audience and soon captured a wide middle-class following. Josiah Holbrook, a Yale graduate and school keeper, organized the first lyceum in Millbury, Massachusetts, in November 1826. For a small subscription fee, adult members of the lyceum met in a dedicated building and participated in a course of lectures, demonstrations, and debates. By 1831 lyceums had spread into all of the New England states and New York; in the

353

1830s they spanned the Alleghenies and sprouted in Ohio, Kentucky, and Missouri; by the 1840s over three thousand lyceum organizations operated throughout the country. To the criticism of superficiality, defenders invoked the democratic mantra of useful knowledge. The lyceum stood for popular enlightenment; it spoke for the common man; and its instructors, while not always credentialed, enjoyed authority because of, not despite, their popular acclaim.

As the lyceum grew into the dominant medium of self-education, it absorbed the educational arms of numerous benevolent associations and mercantile libraries, inheriting their unrealized political expectations. Ostensibly secular and apolitical, the lyceums shared the evangelicals' distaste for freethinkers, atheists, radical feminists, and Catholics. Indeed, lyceumites used their sessions to agitate for public schools and a host of other social reforms led by Protestant evangelicals, including sabbatarianism, temperance, and abolition. At Berea, Ohio, from 1837 to 1842, Holbrook attempted to make the lyceum the basis of an experimental utopian community. His "Lycenia" venture failed; worse, it had attracted the admiration of some anti-Catholics, who viewed the lyceum as a means of counteracting "popish" influence. J. F. Hey, a lyceum leader in Carlisle, Pennsylvania, in 1836 agreed that "something must be done to illuminate the great mass of mind overspreading our land" ("Lyceums," p. 4). The rise of nativism after the lyceum vogue is not entirely coincidental. The public lecture, according to historian Donald M. Scott, consolidated "the collective cultural consciousness" by which the lyceums' white, northern, Anglo-Saxon audience "came to assert a claim that it was the real American public" ("The Popular Lecture," p. 809).

Other historians, focusing on the class dynamics of public lectures, have suggested that the first merging of culture and consumption can also be traced to the midcentury lyceum. At first, the lyceum relied on an artisanal style of cultural production. Managers wrote inquiries and made arrangements directly with the desired speakers. The rise of speakers bureaus in the 1840s, however, established economy of scale as the ruling principle of the lecture market. Addresses by local intelligentsia all but disappeared. The new standards of charisma and physical vigor tended to squelch women's voices, except for a few female celebrities like the reformer Mary A. Livermore. Bureau directors James Redpath and J. B. Pond franchised the most popular speakers, filling eastern wallets and making small fortunes for stars Ralph Waldo Emerson, Mark Twain, Henry Thoreau, Orestes Brownson, George William Curtis, Oliver Wendell Holmes, Theodore Parker, Henry Ward Beecher, Benjamin Silliman, and Wendell Phillips. Moreover, lyceum guests tended to fixate on the finery of setting and attire. As historian Mary Kupiec Cayton discovered, they often mistook Emerson's concept of "self-reliance," meant as a spiritual metaphor, as an argument for material acquisition. In this declension narrative of the lyceum, one detects many of the traits normally reserved for discussions of twentieth-century mass culture: the demise of local cultural autonomy, the logic of corporate efficiency, the shift from instruction to entertainment, and the cult of personality.

THE MODERNIZATION OF USEFUL KNOWLEDGE

The standardization of lyceum fare should not obscure the variety of local self-education efforts throughout the nineteenth century. New and old forms of nonprofessional culture-study, including farmers institutes, urban settlement houses, institutes for religious education, and literary clubs, continued to flourish among the growing ranks of the managerial middle class. Still motivated by the ideal of a "benevolent empire," these institutions availed themselves of modernity's advantages for the spread of knowledge: higher literacy, faster communications, and cheaper print. Diffusers of useful knowledge also enlisted the help of generous philanthropists, liberal Protestants, and nonsnobbish professors. But as useful knowledge was institutionalized and reoriented to the needs of the state, those who hoped to preserve an authentic ideal of self-culture from what they viewed as commercial, political, or ideological motives would be faced with new challenges.

Farmers Institutes and Unions Midwestern farmers, emboldened by their entrance into politics, formed a newly receptive audience for instruction in the vocational and political sciences. Logistical challenges and yeoman individualism delayed the formation of institutes for the spread of useful agricultural knowledge until the 1870s. Farmers institutes generally met for two days in the winter. Sponsored by country agricultural societies or Granges (fraternal associations of farmers), the retreats included a program of theater, music, and socials. In the 1880s and 1890s state appropriations incorporated the farmers institutes into a growing network of state agricultural schools, experimental laboratories, and extension centers. The Smith-Lever extension act of 1914 ushered in a new era of federal funding and control in vocational education.

This grassroots model of useful knowledge, with its blending of cultural transmission and political advocacy, also took root in labor circles. A series of failed strikes in the 1870s convinced labor leaders of the need for a better-educated union. If workers were to be uplifted, they would need to understand the intricacies of the wage system, the dangers of alcohol, and the importance of cooperation. The Knights of Labor and the National Labor Union encouraged workers to create their own newspapers, libraries, theater groups, and socialist Sunday schools. Not content with the preachy liberalism of middle-class reformers, unions created a sort of alternate university extension system, using faculty from workers' schools like Work People's College (1903) in Minnesota and Brookwood Labor College in New York (1921). Notable were the Socialist Lyceum Bureau (1911) and the Training School for Women Organizers (1914) in Chicago; the latter defied the union race barrier and taught leadership skills to black and white women workers.

YMCA, Bible Schools, and Sunday School Institutes

Religious leaders actively contributed to the modernization of useful knowledge. Victorious and riding a wave of self-righteousness, Northern evangelicals after the Civil War embarked on an ambitious program of religious education focusing on the industrial city. In the 1870s the Reverend Dwight Moody teamed with the retail magnate John Wanamaker to create a system of urban Bible institutes. Moody's schools worked closely with the Young Men's Christian Association (YMCA) and the Young Women's Christian Association (YWCA), settlement houses that offered lodging, education, and the certainties of religion to dislocated urban youths.

Religious educators were also inspired by the efficiency of the emerging public schools. Hoping to apply the advanced techniques of secular education to sacred instruction, Methodists, Presbyterians, Congregationalists, and Baptists met in the 1850s and 1860s to forge consensus on a universal curriculum and new standards for the training of Sunday School teachers. The adoption of the Uniform Lesson plan in 1869 spurred a wave of ecumenical Sunday School institutes. These modified camp meetings segregated revival-style proselytizing to specific times, reserving the bulk of the day for instruction in Bible history, languages, pedagogy, and even science. Prospective teachers learned modern pedagogical techniques, such as setting long lists to music, multimedia displays, and other mnemonic devices. One especially active evangelist for education, the Methodist minister (and future bishop) John Heyl Vincent, proposed an elaborate system of testing and certification. The system ensured that teachers of Scripture, like their secular counterparts, would benefit from the trappings, if not the authority, of professional accreditation.

The Chautauqua Assembly

The decision to locate Sunday School institutes at preexisting religious resorts signaled a new strategy for religious educators. For many, the new frontier of progress lay in the increasing time for leisure. In 1874 the Reverend John Heyl Vincent joined with the industrialist Lewis Miller to convert Fair Point, a sleepy camp meeting on the shores of Lake Chautauqua in western New York, into an ecumenical institute for training Sunday School teachers. Cleverly hiding its evangelical roots under an Indian place-name, Chautauqua grew into an "outdoor university" combining Bible study with courses in science, history, literature, and the arts. At one point, the intricate matrix of overlapping institutions at the lake included Chautauqua University, an accredited degree-granting college. Consistent with the "gospel of good cheer," Vincent and Miller embraced the summer vacation as a fact of modern life and turned it into an occasion for cultural and spiritual renewal. The casual vacationer, reasoned Vincent in 1886, provided "financial support" for the assembly's "more radical work." Moreover, Vincent believed, the indolent could be coaxed into enlightenment once inside the gates of the assembly. The "awakening which comes from great ideas" would "gradually improve their tastes and ideas" (Gould, *The Chautauqua Movement*, p. 30).

The formula worked. By the 1880s Chautauqua had evolved into the foremost institutional expression of the self-culture impulse. Its eight-week summer program gave visibility to social gospel–minded academics, politicians, preachers, prohibitionists, and reformers. Within twenty-five years of Chautauqua's founding, over one hundred towns, mainly in the Midwest, had held assemblies on grounds patterned on the original Chautauqua. Independent assemblies developed close ties with local boosters and railroad executives, who saw them as profitable (yet moral) tourist attractions. The nineteenth-century Chautauqua movement spawned thousands of such outposts of pious self-culture, managed by local elites and as yet largely free from bureaucratic or corporate control.

Women's Clubs   For middle-class women and men alike, the lyceums and Chautauquas raised expectations, imposed structure, and filled holes in their reading. But the incentives for self-education differed widely by gender. Indeed, the gap separating their respective motives for structured reading began to widen after 1850. If men found the public lecture and the literary society to be a diversion from work, some women yearned to overcome the barriers separating them from formal education. Dissatisfied with the role of passive consumer, many retreated to the safer confines of their parlors, transforming them into salons for all-women reading clubs like Sorosis, an exclusive New York club formed by the editor Jane Croly in 1868. While formed to study "culture for culture's sake," these organized crucibles of womanhood questioned masculine claims to intellectual authority. Important here is the rise of "maternalist" rhetoric, by which women extended their authority over the domestic sphere into the world of politics and policy. The General Federation of Women's Clubs, organized by Croly and others in 1890, absorbed a number of literary societies and Chautauqua reading circles as educational departments, while expanding its advocacy into areas of social reform and policy. And Frances Willard of the Woman's Christian Temperance Union (1874) initiated an ambitious program of education, including reading lists, educational retreats, and schools for the training of speakers.

Women's special interest in self-education accompanied a wider trend in the educational labor market: the emergence of teaching as a woman's vocation. Some used the knowledge they gleaned from literary clubs to improve their pedagogy, pass tests devised by the emerging teachers institutes, and improve their standing with their employers. According to psychologist Hugo Münsterberg, the symbolic diploma offered to graduates of the Chautauqua Literary and Scientific Circle (CLSC), a reading system and correspondence school introduced by John Heyl Vincent in 1878, was "highly prized among teachers" (*The Americans*, p. 384).

Widest in the 1880s and 1890s, the self-education gender gap closed quickly in the first quarter of the new century. Of the approximately 275,000 students who had enrolled in the CLSC reading course before 1914, four out of five were women. Criticized by some as superficial, the CLSC nevertheless provided safe spaces for "public ladies" to test the waters of greater involvement in general affairs without appearing unwomanly. African American, Jewish, and eastern European clubwomen embellished the traditional canon—laden with Shakespeare, Wordsworth, and Thackeray—with selections that reaffirmed their religious and cultural heritage. The self-culture model represented in the lyceum, literary society, and CLSC had sufficed for many public-minded women of the nineteenth century. However, as chances for formal education multiplied, the appeal of self-culture as a vocational strategy diminished. Younger feminists in the early years of the new century grew frustrated with Chautauqua's limitations. In pursuit of political reform, Chautauqua's daughters rarely followed in their mothers' footsteps.

University Extension   Although most historians trace the origins of the American university extension system to the University of Wisconsin's outreach courses of the 1880s, the early part of the movement bore the deep imprint of Chautauqua. In 1888 John Heyl Vincent called a meeting of the university extension partisans William Rainey Harper (on the Chautauqua staff), Herbert Baxter Adams, Richard T. Ely, and Frederick Starr. The committee proposed that Chautauqua promote a "revival" of education by becoming the umbrella organization for the "libraries, mechanics' institutes, lyceums, labor unions, guilds, young men's Christian associations, Chautauqua literary and scientific circles." The Chautauqua University Extension system, led by William Rainey Harper, would promote "good citizenship . . . by the organization of the most intelligent and progressive local forces" (Willoughby, *Report of the Commissioner of Education*, pp. 935–936). While the system proved too expensive for Chautauqua, John D. Rockefeller's deep pockets enabled Harper, as president of the University of Chicago from 1891 to 1906, to build one of the largest extension systems in the country.

University extension peaked in the 1890s. Thereafter, Chautauqua's intellectual authority rested increasingly on the listing shoulders of its academic partners. While Adams and Ely viewed Chautauqua as a means of extending their popular audience, not all scholars embraced Chautauqua. To sharpen the boundaries of the scholarly canon, some academics distanced themselves from Chautauqua's priggishness, flowery rituals, crowd-tested conventions, and—as some male academics saw it—feminine superficiality. In some cases, Chautauqua emerged as the vox populi against which academics defined their professional identity as objective social scientists. Many resented Chautauqua for invading academia's territory. More intractable still was the animus against radical scholars, especially

Chautauqua Literary and Scientific Circle Procession (1882). Recognition Day ceremonies borrowed elements from Masonic ritual and traditional collegiate graduations. Led by elders and accompanied by girls dressed in white, graduates would pass through the Golden Arch en route to the Hall of Philosophy, where they received their largely symbolic diplomas. COURTESY OF THE CHAUTAUQUA INSTITUTION ARCHIVES, CHAUTAUQUA, N.Y.

Ely, who used Chautauqua to further political arguments. The academics' reluctance foretold new challenges as Chautauquans strove to maintain leadership in the diffusion of useful knowledge.

Chautauqua Circuits After 1900 Chautauqua fell prey to a commercial trend not unlike that faced by the lyceum movement. In 1904 for-profit lyceum organizers, led by the Redpath agency of lyceum fame, introduced a network of mobile chautauquas, or circuits. The circuits used aggressive sales tactics, one-sided contracts, and a carefully orchestrated "tight booking" system to reduce costs. Competition from circuit chautauquas forced many in-dependent assemblies to hire lecture bureaus to handle their programming, relinquishing the podium to big-city companies and hastening the assemblies' decline. By anyone's measure, the educational emphasis shrank after 1904, freeing space for an array of dramatic impersonators, political debaters, and inspirational speakers like Russell Conwell. To modernists like Sinclair Lewis, the circuit chautauqua, with its "animal and bird educators" (that is, pet tricks), hucksters, William Jennings Bryan lectures, sentimental plays, and crude wartime patriotism, symbolized the shallowness of middle-class culture. Despite ridicule from the urban avant-garde, the circuits launched the careers of numerous performers and served as vital links to the outside world for some six thousand small towns. After a steep decline in the late 1920s, the last tent show folded in 1933.

What caused Chautauqua's decay? There is no doubt that by the mid-1920s the maturation of state universities, trade schools, museums, and libraries, along with the rise of commercial radio, movies, automobiles, book-of-the-month clubs, and an expanded consumer culture, had eroded Chautauqua's popularity in rural America. Also, Chautauqua's foundation in the poet (and school inspector) Matthew Arnold's pedagogy of "sweetness and light" relied on a Victorian model of bourgeois family relations—a complex of associations, values, and gender coercions under severe attack in the 1920s. However, a more debatable explanation of Chautauqua's decline came from the adult education historian Clinton Grattan in 1955. Chautauqua shrank, Grattan warrants, because "it failed to find a dynamic *secular* principle to sustain in an increasingly secular world a movement which was based upon a religious impulse and throve with the support of religious-minded people" (*In Quest of Knowledge,* p. 182).

Secularization theory recurs frequently in explanations of Chautauqua's decline, as it does in other theories of middle-class life at the turn of the century. But its application is often flawed. Chautauqua *did* find a dynamic secular principle to sustain it, albeit one simultaneously discovered by a number of better-situated institutions—liberalism. Educators at Chautauqua had for decades been advocating a progressive vision of informed civic debate, enlightened governance, and social welfare. The movement was most popular in the upper Midwest, where rural radicalism had pushed the Democratic Party closer to its twentieth-century liberal inheritance. Ideas about the need for proactive governance spread in "a moderating way," reflected the

New Dealer Rexford Tugwell, whose mother was an avid Chautauquan. "Even a mild sort of socialism was given a hearing in the literature going out to the Reading Circles" (*The Light of Other Days,* p. 61).

In other words, by the time of Chautauqua's decline after 1905, it had already detected the paradigm shift in self-education and had redefined its role as a training ground for the principles of citizenship in a liberal state. Between 1905 and 1925, the architects of Chautauqua unloaded the burden of education for a progressive society, sacrificing its leadership position to the new professionals of citizenship training: high school teachers, social workers, corporate Americanizers, municipal authorities, university extension schools, and adult educators. With underlying moral impulses directed elsewhere, the de-Christianized public space of the Chautauqua assembly dissolved into its component spheres of familial ownership and control—private consumer and career choices, private land, private suburbs, private golf links, private study, and private spiritual beliefs.

USEFUL KNOWLEDGE AND THE STATE

The mid-1920s saw a paradigm shift in the history of useful knowledge in the United States. Many of those in pursuit of "self-education," "self-improvement," or "culture-study" in the nineteenth century, especially women and rural non-elites, came to those activities with little schooling or prior experience with formal education. But compulsory attendance had dramatically increased high school attendance, and the rise of state universities, trade schools, and "normal" colleges (that is, institutes devoted to teacher training) had vastly expanded the availability of higher education. The proponents of useful knowledge adopted new approaches with revealing titles: "adult education" or "continuing education," phrases designed to encompass those who had already been educated but desired more. Meanwhile, the burden of promoting adult education passed from voluntary associations to bureaucratic organizations. The cultural value of self-culture had not diminished much, if at all; in fact, the demand for adult education remained powerful enough to attract the attention of the managers of charitable foundations, New York publishers, universities, and municipalities. To the new professionals, adult education, with its tangible rewards for the cause of participatory democracy,

tolerant debate, and informed citizenship, was too vital to be left to amateurs.

American Association of Adult Education The use of education as an instrument of Americanization dates back to the earliest years of useful knowledge and emerged as a central theme of the mechanics' institutes and the lyceum movement. The merging of adult education and welfare capitalism, however, made adult education vulnerable to managerial interpretations of public opinion. In the 1910s staffers at the Ford Motor Company's sociology department suggested a system of education be developed to teach an elite corps of "Five-Dollar Men" how to become better husbands, fathers, and workers. Ford was not alone in its concern. As the philanthropist Andrew Carnegie's interest in libraries waned in the 1910s, the Carnegie Corporation funded a series of studies on the effect of schools on immigrant assimilation. The tip of the adult education iceberg surfaced in 1924, when Carnegie's board of trustees asked Frederick Keppel to convene a panel of experts on adult education in America. The panel included Dorothy Canfield Fisher, two years later to be named a member of the Book-of-the-Month Club's board of judges, and Eduard Lindeman. From this conference sprang the American Association for Adult Education (AAAE) in 1926, a clearinghouse for the activities of labor groups, women's organizations, prison educators, and industrial schools.

In Eduard Lindeman, son of Norwegian immigrants, adult education found its philosopher. Spruced with quotations from Nietzsche, John Dewey, and George Santayana, *The Meaning of Adult Education,* published to coincide with the AAAE's founding in 1926, revealed the influence of the contemporary critics Walter Lippmann and Thorstein Veblen. But against their technocratic solution to the dilemmas of modernity, Lindeman offered a pure and authentic revival of self-education, a "modern quest for life's meaning," a "revolution of the mind" (pp. 11, 38). Here, Lindeman displayed an older, progressive faith in the capacity of ordinary men, even laborers facing a soul-crushing work regimen, to achieve spiritual renewal. "Labor will come into its own," wrote Lindeman, "when workers discover better motives for production and finer meanings for life" (p. 39). Adult education would empower human creativity to ignore Veblen's machine mentality and the ticking of Frederick Taylor's stopwatch. In his critique of specialization, his call for "smaller collective units" as an alternative to mass society, and his perhaps naive expectation that labor would prefer adult education over direct action—in these ways, Lindeman reached back to a modified version of Chautauqua for inspiration, offering adult education as a means of reestablishing core meanings in a modern age.

Black Education The great migration of southern African Americans into northern cities represented the first major test of Lindeman's "revolution of the mind." The lyceum and Chautauqua had long since established whiteness as the unmarked norm of adult education, with people of color marked as passive recipients of white benevolence. Pushed by liberal adult educators, older institutions of self-education began to confront their deep-seated racial assumptions. At least one halting attempt was made to sustain Chautauqua's leisure-education model: in 1923 George Vincent, son of a Chautauqua cofounder and then director of the Rockefeller Foundation (1913), secured funding for the black chautauqua of Gulfside, Mississippi, a place for "tired mothers" to "learn something of Home Economics" and where "YMCA and YWCA workers might hold staff conferences" (Mason, pp. 241–242). More often, adult educators sought ways to fulfill Booker T. Washington's call for an educational system geared to the needs of a black underclass; no "abstract knowledge," as Washington put it, but knowledge "harnessed to the things of real life" (quoted in Fultz, p. 93).

Black migration to a hostile urban environment dramatized the need for practical knowledge. Early efforts contrasted awkwardly with white strategies of adult education: the National Association of Colored Women, acknowledging the burdens of the job market for blacks without accepting them, stressed training for jobs in domestic service. The National Urban League and the YMCA created separate black branches in northern cities in the 1910s, offering vocational and cultural training. In 1928 the YWCA published a book of African American folk songs. Meanwhile, adult education efforts of the National Association for the Advancement of Colored People (1910) focused on leadership training. Mute on black education throughout the 1920s, the AAAE funded programs in Harlem and Atlanta in the 1930s. These, in concert with the free classes and workshops sponsored by the Emergency Educational Program (part of the Federal Emergency Relief Administration), linked black self-determination with managerial support from the emerging adult education profession. As a new service of the wel-

fare state, adult education had become newly responsive to the needs of non-elite women and African Americans.

CONCLUSION

Republican educators in the early national era viewed self-education as both a privilege of gentlemanly status and a symbol of cultural independence and vitality. In the 1830s religious awakening and reform spurred a revival of interest in popular education. The founders of the mechanics' institutes, while they missed their target audience, earnestly hoped to spread useful knowledge and train an enlightened leadership stratum within the working class. The middle-class yearning for self-improvement found expression through these institutes and through the lyceums. At first organized locally, by midcentury the lyceums were less educational than edifying; lecture bureaus treated them as delivery systems for lecture packages designed for mass consumption. Despite a continuing trend toward corporate standardization, disparate forms of independent self-culture flourished throughout the middle to late nineteenth century, including Bible institutes, farmers institutes, urban settlement houses, and Chautauqua assemblies and circles. By 1920, however, Chautauqua's embrace of citizenship training as a model of voluntary education—and its subsequent decline as other institutions emerged better situated to promote the new model—signaled a new approach to adult education.

In the 1920s and 1930s, rival bureaucratic regimes were managed by governments, and universities took up the cause of useful knowledge and used it to further particular institutional goals. Riding atop mass culture in the form of correspondence schools, educational radio, and Book-of-the-Month clubs, "middlebrow" culture helped legitimate the act of consumption by linking it to the timeless ideals of self-enlightenment. Meanwhile, through training programs designed to disseminate useful knowledge to an industrial polity, the liberal state gave compelling reasons for its existence.

Among intellectuals, however, the illusion that self-culture derived from nobler purposes than commerce, that it transcended the commonplace, turned eyes upward to matters of the spirit, and exemplified racial and national progress, had been largely debunked. Replacing it was a language of declension. The ephemeral gratification of consumer culture had so trivialized the pursuit of knowledge, the argument went, that a new commitment to the arts and humanities, insulated from profits and politics, was needed to preserve an absolute social good. Useful knowledge has a useable past, as the National Endowment for the Humanities (NEH) discovered in the 1990s when it found a familiar name to entitle its plan for a "national conversation" on pressing issues: Chautauqua. As more and more Americans look to corporate-dominated media such as the Internet for directed self-learning, the need for new models of democratic action, involved citizenship, and authentic human exchange—what educator Paulo Freire calls the "pedagogy of hope"—will grow more acute.

See also **Education in Early America; Rhetoric and Belles Lettres; Thought and Culture in the Free Black Community; Communitarianism; Popular Intellectual Movements, 1833–1877; Southern Intellectual Life** (*volume 1*); **Rhetoric** (*in this volume); and other articles in this section.*

BIBLIOGRAPHY

Learned Societies and Mechanics' Institutes

Dick, Thomas. *On the Improvement of Society by the Diffusion of Knowledge.* Glasgow, Scotland, and London, 1833. Went through four printings with Harper's Library in the United States.

Filla, Wilhelm. "Enlightenment in Austrian Popular Education: From Joseph II to the Early 1930s." In *Democracy and Adult Education: Ideological Changes and Educational Consequences,* edited by Jurij Jug and Franz Pöggeler. Frankfurt, Germany, and New York, 1996.

Oleson, Alexandra, and Sanborn C. Brown. *The Pursuit of Knowledge in the Early American Republic: American Scientific and Learned Societies from Colonial Times to the Civil War.* Baltimore, 1976.

Sinclair, Bruce. *Philadelphia's Philosopher Mechanics: A History of the Franklin Institute, 1824–1865.* Baltimore, 1974.

Story, Ronald. "Class and Culture in Boston: The Athenaeum, 1807–1960." *American Quarterly* 27, no. 2 (1975): 178–199.

Lyceums and the Public Lecture

Bode, Carl. *The American Lyceum: Town Meeting of the Mind.* New York, 1956.

Cayton, Mary Kupiec. "The Making of an American Prophet: Emerson, His Audiences, and the Rise of the Culture Industry." *American Historical Review* 92, no. 3 (1987): 597–620.

Hey, J. F. "Address on the Advantages and Importance of Lyceums." Carlisle, Pa., 1836.

Mead, C. David. *Yankee Eloquence in the Middle West: The Ohio Lyceum, 1850–1870.* East Lansing, Mich., 1951.

Scott, Donald M. "The Popular Lecture and the Creation of a Public in Mid-Nineteenth Century America." *Journal of American History* 66, no. 4 (1980): 791–809.

Women's Clubs and Reform

Blair, Karen J. *The Clubwoman as Feminist: True Womanhood Redefined, 1846–1914.* New York, 1980.

Gere, Anne Ruggles. *Intimate Practices: Literary and Cultural Work in U.S. Women's Clubs, 1880–1920.* Urbana, Ill., 1997.

Martin, Theodora Penny. *The Sound of Our Own Voices: Women's Study Clubs, 1860–1910.* Boston, 1987.

Mjagkij, Nina, and Margaret Spratt, eds. *Men and Women Adrift: The YMCA and the YWCA in the City.* New York, 1997.

Weisenfeld, Judith. *African American Women and Christian Activism: New York's Black YWCA, 1905–1945.* Cambridge, Mass., 1997.

Chautauqua Assemblies and Circles

Gould, Joseph E. *The Chautauqua Movement: An Episode in the Continuing American Revolution.* New York, 1961. This misnamed book traces William Rainey Harper's career as a pioneer in university extension.

Knicker, Charles Robert. "The Chautauqua Literary and Scientific Circle, 1878–1914: A Historical Interpretation of an Educational Piety in Industrial America." Ed.D. diss., Columbia University, 1969.

Moore, R. Laurence. *Selling God: American Religion in the Marketplace of Culture.* New York, 1994. See chapter 6, "Chautauqua and Its Protective Canopy: Religion, Entertainment, and Small-Town Protestants."

Morrison, Theodore. *Chautauqua: A Center for Education, Religion, and the Arts in America.* Chicago, 1974. A well-written narrative history of Chautauqua's leaders and major figures, honoring the institution's centennial.

Münsterberg, Hugo. *The Americans.* New York, 1905.

Noffsinger, John S. *Correspondence Schools, Lyceums, Chautauquas.* New York, 1926.

Rieser, Andrew C. "Canopy of Culture: Chautauqua and the Renegotiation of Middle-Class Authority, 1874–1919." Ph.D. diss., University of Wisconsin–Madison, 1999.

——. "Secularization Reconsidered: Chautauqua and the De-Christianization of Middle-Class Authority, 1880–1920." In *Middling Sorts: Essays in the History of the American Middle Class,* edited by Burton Bledstein and Robert Johnston. New York, 2000.

Trachtenberg, Alan. "'We Study the Word and Works of God': Chautauqua and the Sacralization of Culture in America." *Henry Ford and Greenfield Village Herald* 12, no. 2 (1985): 3–11. A brilliant deconstruction of CLSC symbolism, part of a volume of essays on the Chautauqua movement.

Tugwell, Rexford G. *The Light of Other Days.* Garden City, N.Y., 1962.

Vincent, John Heyl. *The Chautauqua Movement.* Boston, 1886. A passionate homily on the spiritual benefits of a Chautauqua.

Willoughby, W. W. *Report of the Commissioner of Education for the Year 1891–92.* Vol. 2. Washington, D.C., 1894.

Black Adult Education

Denton, Virginia. *Booker T. Washington and the Adult Education Movement.* Gainesville, Fla., 1993.

Fultz, Michael. "Education in the Black Monthly Periodical Press, 1900–1910." In *Education of the African American Adult: An Historical Overview.* Edited by Harvey G. Neufeldt and Leo McGee. New York, 1990. See articles by Michael Fultz, Lillian S. Williams, Cynthia Neverdon-Mortin, Felix James, and V. P. Franklin.

Mason, Henry J. "A Black Chautauqua." *Opportunity: Journal of Negro Life* 7 (1929): 241–242.

Savage, Barbara Dianne. *Broadcasting Freedom: Radio, War, and the Politics of Race, 1838–1948.* Chapel Hill, N.C., 1999.

Adult Education and the State

Altenbaugh, Richard J. *Education for Struggle: The American Labor Colleges of the 1920s and 1930s.* Philadelphia, 1990. Includes a useful summary of the educational efforts sponsored by unions.

Coben, Diana. *Radical Heroes: Gramsci, Freire, and the Politics of Adult Education.* New York, 1998.

Freire, Paulo. *Pedagogy of the Oppressed.* 1972. Translated by M. Bergman Ramos, New York, 1995.

Grattan, Clinton H. *In Quest of Knowledge: A Historical Perspective on Adult Education.* New York, 1955.

Kett, Joseph F. *The Pursuit of Knowledge under Difficulties: From Self-Improvement to Adult Education in America, 1750–1990.* Stanford, Calif., 1994. Likely to be the definitive book for some decades to come.

Knowles, Malcolm S. *A History of the Adult Education Movement in the United States.* Huntington, N.Y., 1977. A revision of his 1962 book.

Kornbluh, Joyce L., and Mary Frederickson. *Sisterhood and Solidarity: Workers' Education for Women, 1914–1984.* Philadelphia, 1984.

Lears, T. J. Jackson. *No Place of Grace: Antimodernism and the Transformation of American Culture, 1880–1920.* Chicago, 1981. Not on education, per se, but an argument with undeniable importance for historians of culture and education.

Lindeman, Eduard. *The Meaning of Adult Education.* New York, 1926.

Rubin, Joan Shelley. *The Making of Middlebrow Culture.* Chapel Hill, N.C., 1992.

———. "Self, Culture, and Self-Culture in Modern America: The Early History of the Book-of-the-Month Club." *Journal of American History* 71, no. 4 (1985): 782–806.

Stubblefield, Harold W. *Towards a History of Adult Education in America: The Search for a Unifying Principle.* London and New York, 1988.

ALMANACS AND EPHEMERAL LITERATURE

Molly A. McCarthy

The early American almanac is hard to categorize. Is it literature? A book of facts? A calendar? An artifact of popular religion? A diary? Perhaps it is all of the above. Because the almanac is such a difficult genre to place, many scholars have overlooked or simply dismissed it when surveying the publishing output in British North America and the early American Republic. It was not until 1878, when Moses Coit Tyler devoted several pages to the almanac in his survey of American literature, that anyone paid attention to the lowly annual. Even Tyler admitted it was the "very quack, clown, pack-horse, and pariah of modern literature," and yet the "most indispensable of books, which every man uses, and no man praises." Even today, the almanac gets little respect, except among book historians and bibliographers. Although it continues to struggle for scholarly recognition, American almanacs—from the earliest seventeenth-century to the late-twentieth-century versions—can tell us much about the people who read them and produced them. The material squeezed between the almanac's flimsy paper covers is a key source of popular thought and, as one historian put it, reveals the "collective mentality" of early American settlers, elites and commoners alike. Many readers recited passages aloud to family members and passed copies among friends; booksellers and publishers relied on the almanac for a steady stream of income. Thus, this survey of the consumption and production of the lowliest of literary productions provides a valuable window into the cultural world of early America.

ORIGINS

Before discussing almanacs in America, a look at the genre in England, where the almanac has even deeper roots, seems appropriate since the colonists inherited the genre from their homeland. In the traditional English almanac, publishers served up a mixture of information, both literary and utilitarian. Among the standard components was a calendar marking key dates for the Church of England, astrological predictions, and a symbol known as the "man of signs" that connected parts of the human anatomy with signs of the zodiac. Besides predictions and "red-letter days" (festivals traditionally marked in red), the calendars included daily tide tables, the times of local sunrise and sunset, and the moon's phases. In addition, almanac compilers sprinkled the remaining pages with literary verse, ballads, morality tales, humorous anecdotes, and occasionally political criticism. "Useful and entertaining" was one of the most prevalent phrases listed in the almanacs' often-lengthy subtitles.

THE PURITAN ALMANAC

Considering its utility, perhaps it is no surprise, then, that an almanac was the second publication to come off the first American printing press in Cambridge, Massachusetts, in 1639. Stripping the almanac of its astrological predictions and the "man of signs," Puritan compilers adapted the genre to match the mission and ideology of the early religious settlement. In the earliest extant version, dating to 1646, Samuel Danforth struck out all references to Christmas, Valentine's Day, and other remnants of the English church calendar and replaced the names of the months with neutral phrases, such as "First Month." Puritan ministers denounced the pursuit of astrology because, they argued, it implied that the stars and planets had more power than God's will. It wasn't long, however, before the astrological matter crept back into American almanacs as competitors challenged the Puritanized versions. An almanac published in 1690 by Harvard College, for instance, reported an astrological prediction of "Famine, great Sickness, Pestilent Diseases, and the Like" based on an interpretation of eclipses. Instead of titling their publications "almanacs," many of the late-seventeenth-century American compilers chose "ephemeris," a Greek word referring to an astronomical table or calendar.

Arguably the most widely read and circulated publication in colonial households after the Bible, the seventeenth-century American almanac—often no longer than 24 pages and no larger than 4.5 by 7.5 inches—represented an integral part of the colonial worldview. A great majority of colonists could read. Because of the scarcity of print, much of that reading was intensive: readers pored repeatedly over the same texts, such as the Bible, the primer, or the almanac. Thus, the almanac had an indelible impact on a print-starved populace. After all, the first American newspaper would not begin publication until 1704, and even then, the publisher of the *Boston News-Letter* merely reprinted dispatches from London. So, before the newspaper, the almanac filled the role of dispenser of local information. Compilers often included local court dates, lists of roads, coach fares, currency exchange rates, and other information unavailable elsewhere. Buyers frequently added to that indispensability by inserting diarylike notations on blank sheets interleaved in its pages. Samuel Sewall, the renowned Puritan diarist, was an almanac fanatic who regularly bound his almanacs, gave them as gifts, and interleaved his 1718 and 1719 copies of Thomas Paine's *Almanack* with blank pages littered with extensive notes. He often jotted down appointments or copied an eloquent biblical verse. Joshua Moody, a Puritan minister, is said to have "kept 30. years' Almanacks together with fayr paper between every year, setting down remarkable Providences" (Hall, *Worlds of Wonder*, p. 82).

The almanac was also a timepiece of sorts in this pre-pocket-watch era. Justifying the publication of his first Pennsylvania almanac in 1686, William Bradford observed after a recent journey through the province and neighboring Maryland that "the People . . . scarcely knew how the Time passed, or that they hardly knew the day of Rest, or Lords Day, when it was, for want of a Diary, or Day Book, which we call an Almanack." Compilers added to the calendar's utility by incorporating weather forecasts or prognostications, based on astrological events. Nathaniel Ames, a physician and innkeeper at Dedham, Massachusetts, liked to poke fun at these prognostications in his best-selling almanacs. Here are some of his predictions for 1749:

January 1.

> About the beginning of the year expect plenty of rain or snow. Warm and clears off cold again.

May 22.

> Some materials about this time are hatched for the clergy to debate on.

December 7–10.

> Ladies, take heed,
> Lay down your fans,
> And handle well
> Your warming-pans.

December 15–18.

> This cold, uncomfortable weather
> Makes Jack and Gill lie close together.

December 20–22.

> The lawyers' tongues—they never freeze,
> If warmed with honest clients' fees.

Many early American almanacs appeared to have one foot in the past and another in the future. For, while almanac writers continued to disseminate the Old World views on astrology and prognostications, some compilers—especially the Harvard-educated ones—began to publish mini-essays on newer topics, such as Copernicus's sun-centered theory of planetary motion. In his 1697 almanac, John Clapp ruminated for ten pages on the new Copernican system. B. A. Philo-Astro did it in twelve pages. Ames advised his readers to rely not on their senses but on science: "To the naked Eye, the Aether, appears like a solid Arch, the Stars like the Heads of brass Nails, the Sun flat and about as big as a Chease, but our reason informs us better." Like the Bradfords of New York, many almanac compilers prided themselves on publishing almanacs "for the Information of the unlearned, that they may know the general Opinion of the Learned World." Some almanac makers chose a more light-hearted approach to the promotion of new scientific theories—the benefits of the telescope or features of the solar system. For his 1723 *Ephemeris*, Jacob Taylor transmitted the new scientific views in verse:

> 'Twas once a crime to say this Earth turns round,
> Not one that doubts it now on Earth is found.

EIGHTEENTH CENTURY

By the eighteenth century, the American almanac was at the height of its popularity. No longer did the colonists have to rely exclusively on imports to satisfy most of their reading material. Printers, publishers, booksellers—often one and the same person—sprouted in every metropolitan area. In 1700, Boston alone counted nineteen booksellers and

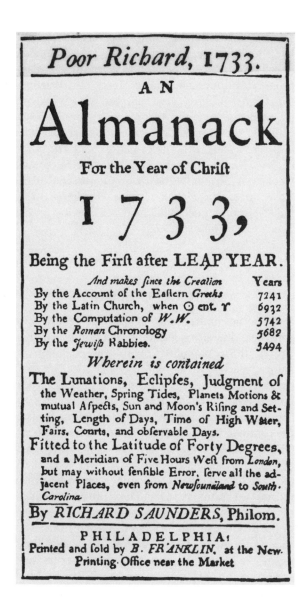

Poor Richard's Almanac, **1733.** Playful in style, Franklin's almanac contained poems, aphorisms, tables of astronomical data, calendars, advertisements, and other bits of practical information. © BETTMANN/CORBIS

In his autobiography, Franklin claimed to have sold an average of ten thousand annually of his *Poor Richard* series, first published in 1732. In New England, Nathaniel Ames was champion, with sales averaging upward of fifty thousand a year for his *Astronomical Diary, or Almanack,* published from 1726 until his death in 1764. Ames's material was so sought after that he often had to contend with pirated editions published in New London, Portsmouth, and New Haven.

What made Ames's almanacs so popular? If we could ask him, he would probably respond that his weather predictions were more accurate, his verse more poetic, his anecdotes more entertaining than others'. The reasons for his success are hard to recover at this distance in time. However, we do know Ames was never afraid to write what he thought. He reveled in satirical commentary, a feature very popular with readers. In 1743, Ames took on the preachers of the Great Awakening: "Many illiterate Pedlars in Divinity take up their Hoes, & go to Planting." The next year, he aimed at its followers: "There is not a more melancholy object, than a Man who has his Head turn'd with Religious Enthusiasm." Of government officials, he wrote: "The Public Good Men oft pretend / While private Interest is their End." As moral reformer, he cautioned against indulging in tobacco, snuff, or punch. According to Ames, snuff may mark a gentleman, but "excessive Use of it produces Apoplexies and Disorders arising from the Obstructions of the Animal Spirits."

BROADSIDES, PAMPHLETS, AND OTHER STREET LITERATURE

Ames's wit, though, did not alone account for the number of almanacs he sold. The rise in printing outlets was good for Ames and almanac sales in general. At the same time, it spawned a growth in the number and variety of street literature of the sort England had boasted nearly a century earlier. Once consigned to issuing government- and church-sponsored material such as statutes or election sermons, colonial printers began to respond to market demand for ballads, broadsides, elegies, pamphlets, and other kinds of ephemeral literature. Franklin's output illustrates how central ephemeral literature became to the profitability of any eighteenth-century printing enterprise. In addition to putting out a newspaper, Franklin published 432 known books, pamphlets, and broadsides over the course of his twenty-year career in printing. And Franklin did not just print his own almanac;

seven printers. Philadelphia and New York were further behind, with William and Andrew Bradford serving as the sole printers until competition arrived in the 1720s. The South was last in developing publishing; Virginia didn't open its first printing office until 1730. Readers could soon choose from over fifty different almanacs. By 1800, that number climbed to 125. This proliferation of print hatched a healthy competition among almanac compilers. In fact, some almanac makers, such as Benjamin Franklin and Titan Leeds, played out fictional rivalries in the pages of their almanacs to drum up business. These tactics worked for many publishers.

he also put out John Jerman's *American Almanack* and another compiled by Thomas Godfrey. In 1731, Franklin issued Godfrey's almanac as a broadsheet. What copies he did not sell locally he sent to Boston or along a southern route toward Charleston. Franklin bragged that he "reap'd considerable profit" from his almanac sales.

Broadsides, too, could be as ubiquitous and as profitable as the almanac in the eighteenth-century world of print. As large as a poster or as small as a handbill, the single-sheet broadside took many forms. They could be serious or silly in their content or serve a singularly commercial purpose. Booksellers often issued catalogues in broadside or pamphlet form, conveying to their customers the latest imports or local publications in their voluminous stock. Beginning in 1720, many newspapers published broadside poems known as "Carriers' Addresses," hawked by newsboys on New Year's Day. The poems summed up the year's local, regional, and national events in entertaining verse. In addition to the commercial end of the broadside market, local governments frequently used the format to distribute essential information to constituents in the form of maps, acts, proclamations, or announcements. Broadsides remained popular into the nineteenth and twentieth centuries for a variety of purposes, such as campaign literature or wartime posters. The Broadsides Collection of the John Hay Library at Brown University, housing more than forty thousand items ranging from eighteenth-century government proclamations to the Beat poems of the twentieth century, illustrates the wide variety of this ubiquitous form of American street literature.

Pamphlets (loosely stitched booklets of twenty to eighty pages that generally sold for a shilling or two) rivaled the number of broadsides coming off American presses in the eighteenth century. Mentioned most often in relation to the writings of the American Revolution, pamphlets were not necessarily political in content. Like the broadside, they could serve a variety of purposes. Booksellers and other merchants issued pamphlets to advertise their wares. Ministers, reaching beyond their local flock, published moving sermons. Indian captivity narratives could also take this form. Yet perhaps the most famous pamphlet from this period takes us back to the subject of the colonies' break with England—Thomas Paine's *Common Sense*. In preparation for his Pulitzer Prize–winning study of the ideological origins of the American Revolution, the historian Bernard Bailyn tallied more than four hundred pamphlets—political treatises, historical

essays, sermons, poems, and correspondence—related to the American struggle for independence. The titles of a few illustrate the sheer variety of approaches authors could take: Mercy Otis Warren's *The Group: A Farce . . .* (1775); James Otis's *Rights of the British Colonies Asserted and Proved* (1764), *Essay on the Constitutional Power of Great-Britain over the Colonies in America* (1774), and *The Battle of Brooklyn: A Farce in Two Acts* (1776); Samuel Cooke's *A Sermon Preached at Cambridge, in the Audience of His Honor Thomas Hutchinson, Esq.* (1770); and Samuel Williams's *A Discourse on the Love of Our Country* (1775).

ALMANACS IN THE AMERICAN REVOLUTION

Despite the volume and significance of this vast ephemeral literature, David D. Hall doubts whether any of those pamphlets, with the exception of Paine's, reached the common reader. The less educated, however, did not miss out. They got their politics elsewhere. Traditionally, most historians assumed that almanac makers avoided politics for fear the controversial content might hurt sales. More recent work, however, has revealed that in the latter half of the eighteenth century almanac compilers did take on politics more readily, albeit with a humorous or satirical bent. They often embedded their lessons in proverbs or aphorisms. In the midst of the debate over import taxes, Nathaniel Ames Jr. added a few pointed phrases to the usual predictions in his 1765 almanac calendar: "It is better to wear a homespun coat, than to lose our LIBERTY" and "It's time to think of raising Hemp & Flax, if we've a Mind to save a Tax." When the hated Stamp Act was repealed, many almanac writers celebrated the colonies' escape from "slavery." As armed conflict approached, Benjamin West, like many of his counterparts, included patriotic songs in his almanacs, such as "The Liberty Song," which included a chorus exclaiming,

> In Freedom we're born and in Freedom we'll live,
> Our purses are ready,
> Steady, Friends, Steady.
> Not as Slaves but as Freemen our money we'll give.

Some of the commentary was visual, as in Paul Revere's engraving illustrating the landing of British troops in Boston, published in Samuel Stearns's *Edes and Gill's North-American Almanack . . . for . . . 1770.* At least three New England almanacs for 1776 published accounts of the battles of Lexington and Concord.

As the political content in almanacs increased in the late eighteenth century, the space devoted to astrology seemed to diminish. To be sure, many compilers still included the traditional astrological calendars with the moon's phases, tide tables, and prognostications, but it was unclear whether readers were able any longer to decipher their meaning. Nathaniel Ames occasionally offered a remedial course for those readers he thought less well versed in how to use the astrological features. This subtle shift in the almanac's content may suggest a general decline in the public belief in the occult and a shift in the meaning of astrology. By the nineteenth century, astrology was no longer associated with mysticism and witchcraft but with a nature-centered, empirical universe promoted by a new belief in scientific agriculture. No one demonstrated this change better than Robert Bailey Thomas, the founder of the *Farmer's Almanac*. Instead of basing his weather predictions on astrological events such as the moon's phases, Thomas promoted folkloric weather wisdom and practical farming based on recurrent weather patterns. What Thomas never said in print was that these weather predictions, grounded, it would seem, in the new scientific agriculture, derived from the old astrological beliefs in lunar cycles.

THE *FARMER'S ALMANAC*

First published in 1792, Robert B. Thomas's *Farmer's Almanac* heralds the beginning of the end of the reign of the American almanac. Certainly, Thomas's almanacs, among many others, continued to record brisk sales up to the mid-nineteenth century. Yet the growth in the publishing industry and the competition from other kinds of publications may have been too much for the old, reliable almanac. The number of newspapers grew exponentially from a century earlier and focused more on local events and information. For entertainment, readers soon had much to choose from: novels, story papers, travelogues, adventure tales. Even as a daily record-keeper and timepiece, the almanac had new competition—the pocket diary. Introduced in the early nineteenth century by stationers and booksellers, the pocket diary combined features of the almanac, such as the astrological calendar, with a diary section for the recording of daily reminders. Thus, buyers didn't need to interleave their almanacs any longer to keep track of the weather or the days of the week. They could do it in new, more portable form.

The almanac remained popular throughout the nineteenth and into the twentieth century among at least one group of readers—farmers, who continued to rely on it for weather predictions. Indeed, *The Old Farmer's Almanac*, as it's now called, is still published annually and has not missed a year of publication since its founding. From their website at www.almanac.com, the compilers of *The Old Farmer's Almanac* reveal their trade secrets for accurate weather predictions, which are "based largely on cycles of the Sun and the Moon, with other variables mixed in." As far as the rest of the almanac's content, they vow to continue to adhere to Thomas's 1829 motto: "Our main endeavor is to be useful, but with a pleasant degree of humour." Ames might have found this formula familiar. And yet, while the survival of *The Old Farmer's Almanac* is commendable, its reputation today as folksy meteorologist clouds the almanac's rich history. The almanac was not meant for farmers alone, nor was it simply a tool for agriculture. Those were later roles. The early American almanac is hard to categorize simply because it played so many roles. It was a piece of literature, a book of facts, a calendar, a religious artifact, a diary. It taught as it entertained. And its multidimensional character and versatility attracted a widespread and diverse audience. It was truly a universal book.

See also **The Print Revolution; Rhetoric and Belles Lettres** *(volume 1);* **Periodicals** *(in this volume); and other articles in this section.*

BIBLIOGRAPHY

Books

Amory, Hugh, and David D. Hall. *A History of the Book in America: The Colonial Book in the Atlantic World.* Vol. 1. Cambridge, U.K., 1999.

Bailyn, Bernard. *The Ideological Origins of the American Revolution.* Enlarged Edition. Cambridge, Mass., 1992.

Capp, Bernard. *English Almanacs, 1500–1800: Astrology and the Popular Press.* Ithaca, N.Y., 1979.

Drake, Milton. *Almanacs of the United States.* New York, 1962.

Hall, David D. *Worlds of Wonder, Days of Judgment: Popular Religious Belief in Early New England.* Cambridge, Mass., 1989.

Kittredge, George Lyman. *The Old Farmer and His Almanack.* 1904. Reprint, Gansevoort, N.Y., 1974.

Perkins, Maureen. *Visions of the Future: Almanacs, Time, and Cultural Change, 1775–1870.* Oxford, U.K., 1996.

Sagendorph, Robb H. *America and Her Almanacs: Wit, Wisdom, and Weather, 1639–1970.* Dublin, N.H., 1970.

Stowell, Marion Barber. *Early American Almanacs: The Colonial Weekday Bible.* New York, 1977.

Tyler, Moses Coit. *A History of American Literature, 1607–1765.* 1878. Reprint, Ithaca, N.Y., 1966.

Warner, Michael. *The Letters of the Republic: Publication and the Public Sphere in Eighteenth-Century America.* Cambridge, Mass., 1995.

Wenrick, John Stanley. "For Education and Entertainment: Almanacs in the Early Republic, 1783–1815." Diss., Claremont Graduate School, 1974.

Articles

Eisenstadt, Peter. "Almanacs and the Disenchantment of Early America." *Pennsylvania History* 65 (1998): 143–169.

Pencak, William. "Nathaniel Ames, Sr., and the Political Culture of Provincial New England." *Historical Journal of Massachusetts* 22 (1994): 141–158.

———. "Politics and Ideology in 'Poor Richard's Almanack.'" *The Pennsylvania Magazine of History and Biography* 116 (April 1992): 183–211.

Raymond, Allan R. "To Reach Men's Minds: Almanacs and the American Revolution, 1760–1777." *New England Quarterly* 51 (1978): 370–395.

Ruffin, J. Rixey. "'Urania's Dusky Vails': Heliocentrism in Colonial Almanacs, 1700–1735." *New England Quarterly* 70 (1997): 306–313.

LIBRARIES

Kenneth E. Carpenter

At the beginning of the twenty-first century the term "library" covers many types of institutions of vastly different sizes and widely varying purposes. At one extreme is the Library of Congress in Washington, D.C., one of the largest libraries in the world, with holdings of all kinds of materials—all noncirculating—in numerous languages, open six days a week, and serving readers from around the world, both in person and increasingly through electronic access. At the other end of the spectrum is the New England village library, housed in a small, wooden building, to which citizens may come one or two afternoons a week, for a few hours, to return books and to select others to take home to read from the library's very small holdings. Even greater diversity exists, however, for there are college and university libraries, some open only to their students and faculty; state libraries; church libraries, medical libraries; libraries of bar associations, of symphony orchestras, of museums, of hospitals, of prisons, of horticultural societies, and of business firms, among others.

The term "library," as used in the past, also encompasses similar variety, and not just because some of the aforementioned types are very old, such as the college library, which goes back to Harvard University Library, founded in 1638, and the church library, which also extends back to the seventeenth century. Past diversity of institutional form and purpose was in some respects even greater in the nineteenth century than today. Now there is one predominant institutional form for providing reading materials to the general public, namely the municipally financed and freely accessible "public library."

Municipally financed libraries, which began in approximately 1850, did not for decades supplant the variety of libraries that Americans had earlier formed and financed in order to make reading materials more accessible. Some were open only to proprietors or subscribers, who at times constituted a specific group in the population. Other libraries were charitable, for example, those aimed at workingmen, as in the case of the apprentices' libraries, or those intended to advance religious views, as in the case of Sunday school libraries or Young Men's Christian Association libraries. Moreover, some states attempted to disseminate books, albeit selected ones, through forming school district libraries and then providing them with books.

EARLY LIBRARIES

The most common type of library in the eighteenth century was what was then often termed "a social library." The few surviving such libraries term themselves "membership libraries," because one obtained access by buying a share, or by paying an annual fee, or both. The first such library, one that still exists, is the Library Company of Philadelphia, which was established in 1731, when Benjamin Franklin brought together a few friends to share their books.

Similar libraries were established in other cities during the colonial era, among them the Redwood Library in Newport, Rhode Island (1747), the Charleston Library Society (1748), the Providence Library Company (1753), and the New York Society Library (1754). Boston was not among the cities with such a library, but many less important towns were, among them Hatborough, Pennsylvania (1755), Burlington, New Jersey (1757), Portsmouth, New Hampshire (1758), Lancaster, Pennsylvania (1759), Bridgetown, New Jersey (1768), and Chester, Pennsylvania (1769). The number of such libraries grew greatly in the 1790s after the establishment of the new government. These libraries began, much as did Benjamin Franklin's Library Company, out of a realization that it was possible to have at hand a good collection of books "without the Expence of procuring a Library Each Man for his own Private Use," as it was put in Portsmouth in 1758.

The main competition for the membership libraries were the commercial circulating libraries from which one could borrow books for a fee. During the period from 1765 to 1789, the median size of those circulating libraries for which catalogs exist was 1,500 volumes; in the following decade, the median was 3,000 volumes. By contrast, most social libraries were much smaller, as shown by their printed catalogs: the 1772 catalog of the library of Charleston, South Carolina, had 408 entries; the 1796 catalog of the library in Haverhill, Massachusetts, had 175 entries; the 1796 catalog of the library in Gloucester, Rhode Island, had 115 entries; the 1796 catalog of the library in Portsmouth, New Hampshire, had 220 entries; the 1797 Boston Library Society catalog had 500 entries; and the 1800 catalog of the library in Bristol, Rhode Island, had 225 entries. (Entries and volumes do not precisely correspond, since large numbers of entries were for multivolume works.) The circulating libraries also had a higher percentage of the most recent publications among their holdings. Thus, the New York Society Library, whose 1793 catalog had 2,100 entries, was dwarfed by the New York circulating library of Hocquet Caritat, who in 1800 claimed to have 30,000 volumes (Caritat was also a bookseller of current publications).

Commercial circulating libraries, which lasted into the twentieth century, did not, however, compete with the membership libraries solely over size or the quantity of recent publications. They also attracted customers by staying open for longer hours. Since the library's proprietor usually sold books or was in another retail trade, such as millinery, the library's hours corresponded with the duration of the opening of the shop. Membership libraries, in contrast, except for a very few of the largest, were essentially book depots, open only at limited times for members to get books to take home to read. They did not have the financial resources to pay someone to keep them open for extended hours. The circulating libraries, much more than the membership libraries, also stocked books to be read for pleasure, particularly fiction, whereas membership libraries so often owed their origin to a desire for improvement, so much so that at times a local clergyman was designated to choose the books that constituted the nucleus of the library. Moreover, the membership library's founders saw themselves as forming a permanent institution, which would naturally tend toward acquiring books perceived to be of permanent value, rather than the literature of the day.

Circulating libraries also competed with the membership libraries by welcoming women to a greater extent than did the membership libraries. They offered fiction and the "light" reading that it was assumed would be wanted primarily by women. They also specifically mentioned women in catalogs and other advertisements. To be sure, women could often be members of membership libraries—many referred specifically to "him and her" in their rules—but the appellation "widow" to a female name in a list of members shows that customarily women were officially members only when no man was present to assume that role.

Membership libraries had their advantages in the competition. To be among the founders or supporters of a library affirmed a degree of elevated status in the community, though membership was by no means restricted to the elite. Based on detailed information about Connecticut in 1820, it seems that in New England approximately one-fifth or one-quarter of the inhabitants of rural areas had access to a library, even though membership was often very small, thirty or fifty households, and even though the collections themselves were often only one hundred or so volumes. (Access to a library in the South and the Midwest was less common, though New Englanders migrating west founded libraries as soon as population density was sufficient. In the South, the population density of white Americans was low, while it was illegal to teach slaves to read.) Libraries also fostered sociability through meetings of officers or of the membership, sometimes held in a local tavern. And into the 1810s members of the Charleston Library Society had dinners.

Sociability was not, however, enough to give these libraries long life, for without the resources to make frequent additions the collections remained small, so small that it was possible to read through them. As members did so, a cycle of decline would set in, with the books gradually being dispersed. Perhaps decades later the remaining books would become part of the collection of a new library association, or perhaps be donated to a newly established public library, or to a library association founded to establish a public library.

In 1820 two new types of libraries began to be established in the cities, both to serve different populations of young men. One type, the apprentices' library, was an explicitly charitable venture. For example, in New York City the idea was first broached at a meeting of the Society for the Prevention of Pauperism and then transferred over to the General Society of Mechanics and Tradesmen. It was hoped that the library's beneficiaries, the young men who were migrating to the cities, would obtain useful information that would benefit their employment and that at the same time the library would be a morally sound alternative to less wholesome forms of entertainment available to young men. The first of these libraries was established in Boston, and other cities soon followed: New York City, Philadelphia, Portland, Maine, and Salem, Massachusetts (1820); Albany, New York, and Providence (1821); Baltimore, Maryland, and Burlington, New Jersey (1822); Brooklyn, New York, and Portsmouth, New Hampshire (1823); Charleston (1824); Washington, D.C. (1828); Lancaster, Pennsylvania (1829).

The other type of new library first established in 1820 was the mercantile library. Its clientele were merchant and law clerks. Though not avowedly charitable, the wealthy and powerful certainly helped them financially and otherwise. Thus, in Philadelphia, the mercantile library was founded at a meeting in the mayor's office. For their members, the mercantile libraries were a mode of professional advancement, through the learning that took place via reading and lectures as well as through the development of organizational skills, honed through contested elections for office and through managing an institution. The mercantile libraries also linked morality and success, at the very least by signifying to a prospective employer that the individual did not waste time in frivolous or immoral pursuits.

The connection between morality and reading was so close in the minds of contemporaries that Sunday schools and Sunday school libraries began to be established in the 1820s, amid great hopes for what could be accomplished. Thus, even in the infancy of this type of library, one enthusiast, writing in the *Sabbath School Visitant* in 1829, calculated that through Sunday school libraries 600,000 persons read, probably, 52 books each per year. "What a channel is this, thought I, for the dissemination of useful knowledge." He dreamed of more Sunday schools and more books read, and he concluded, "When I thought of this, my country seemed to rise in peace, waving in perennial greenness, and presenting to the world a scene of prophetic millennial glory."

The dream of books being available to everyone was certainly not fulfilled by libraries directed at particular categories of young men or by libraries available in Sunday schools. The gaps were partially filled when additional groups formed libraries for their members. Thus, the mechanics, a term that refers to manufacturers, created libraries. So too did members of the Typographical Union in New York City, which established a library in 1834. African Americans in the North also established libraries, such as the Philadelphia Library Company of Col-

ored Persons in 1833 and the Rush Library Company and Debating Society in 1836. Many cities had such libraries, and libraries were, at times, probably more often than is recorded, maintained by the numerous debating and literary societies, including those formed by African American women. They existed in the South as well as the North, for the free black members of the Clionian Debating Society in Charleston, which lasted from 1847 to at least 1851, paid monthly dues for supporting a library. The same applies, of course, to literary societies formed by white men and women, and to lyceums, which sometimes had libraries.

Libraries geared to particular groups in the population were primarily in the cities. Those in the countryside were not so limited, but that does not mean that they prospered. In fact, the membership libraries founded in the 1790s and the first two decades of the nineteenth century declined and failed to such an extent that there began to be concern about the absence of reading material and about what was being read. Educators in particular voiced the fear that students would learn to read and then, once out of school, have nothing available to read. There also arose anxiety about what was being read and the consequences of reading it. Changes in printing technology and in transportation in the first decades of the nineteenth century made it possible to print large editions and to distribute them; the material being sold throughout rural areas by peddlers and others at very low prices was frequently fiction or "lurid" accounts of murder or prostitution, or both. This material was seen as harmful to intellect on the grounds that the mind, if not stretched, would atrophy. Morality and intellectual development were, however, seen as related, for morality was as much an escape from vice as a positive acquisition, and the idleness that led to vice had its antidote in reading improving books. Thus, educators, including Horace Mann, who devoted to libraries his third report (1840) as the Massachusetts commissioner of education, felt libraries were essential to developing a "powerful and an exemplary people." The obvious solution was to place libraries in the schools.

In promoting school district libraries, Mann was following the lead of the state of New York, which in 1835 passed a law enabling school districts to tax themselves to provide libraries. Few did so, and it was a state allocation in 1838 of $55,000 from the United States Deposit Fund, created by the sale of western lands, that resulted in such libraries being ubiquitous in New York State. With state money also went state control over the content of such libraries, exerted primarily through working with publishers to commission and publish secular works that would disseminate useful information. These were then often distributed as a "library," packed in a box with dividers that served as a bookcase upon arrival. New York State was by far the greatest provider of school district libraries, there being in 1850 more than 8,000 such libraries, with 1,338,848 volumes. Massachusetts had the next largest number: 700 libraries with 91,539 volumes. School district libraries were not, however, confined to the Northeast. In 1850 Alabama and Mississippi had quantities similar to the other New England states, while Michigan had many more; and soon other Midwestern states would follow the school district library approach, notably Indiana, Ohio, and Wisconsin.

Historians cannot firmly determine the extent to which the books in these libraries were read, but the experience of Upper Canada is instructive in suggesting relatively little use. There, where the Council of Public Instruction made selected books available at low prices, but nonetheless at the expense of local communities, the applications for additional books fell off markedly after the first year. That new purchases were not made suggests that the books were not being read and valued by local communities.

Elites formed another type of institution in antebellum America, called athenaeums. Instead of existing for the purpose of supplying reading matter that could be taken home, athenaeums were initially primarily for on-site reading, particularly of newspapers and periodicals, exactly the kind of material most needed by those engaged in business and involved in public affairs. The first athenaeum in the United States was established in Boston in 1807, and others continued to be formed in the first decades of the nineteenth century, mainly throughout the Northeast, but to some extent also in the South and in such Midwestern communities as Zanesville, Ohio.

RESEARCH LIBRARIES

Since athenaeums, with their emphasis on current information, supplemented by the basic reference works, were in a sense research libraries, it is not surprising that the Boston Athenaeum did, in fact, seek to expand its holdings to offer in-depth research possibilities. In 1826 it joined with the newly established Scientific Association and sought to ob-

tain funds to buy sets of the transactions of the learned societies in London, Edinburgh, Dublin, Paris, St. Petersburg, Berlin, Turin, Göttingen, Stockholm, Copenhagen, Madrid, and Lisbon. Ultimately, despite gathering materials that continue to make it a scholarly resource in the twenty-first century, the Athenaeum, for lack of resources, failed to transform itself into a general research library with in-depth collections across the various fields of learning. That the need for research libraries was becoming widely recognized is also shown by the formation in 1831 of the Philadelphia Library of Foreign Literature and Science, though it was short-lived. Only slightly earlier, in 1818, John Thornton Kirkland, president of Harvard, had written that an "extensive library" was essential to learning, and in 1831 Francis Calley Gray, a Harvard spokesman, put forward the case for a large allotment of public money for Harvard's library. Gray's statement shows that learning in early nineteenth-century America was no longer seen as a personal attainment that would indirectly benefit society, in which case enough good books for one individual would have sufficed, but rather that learning was to be applied directly to the increase of knowledge for public benefit, in which case society gains from a library with all necessary books.

Changes in the world of learning fueled these early affirmations of the need for research libraries. One was the increased publication of scientific journals, which was accompanied by public consciousness of being in a period of scientific advance. Another was the new textual criticism of the Bible and the classics. Without access to this literature, which originated in Germany in the late eighteenth century and continued to be primarily German, a scholar in the United States could not be up-to-date. Historical studies also changed, as exemplified by Edward Gibbon's *Decline and Fall of the Roman Empire,* which moved scholarship away from sole emphasis on elite historical actors and heightened awareness that even anonymous and ephemeral material could cast unique light on an historical era.

These developments required that there be libraries of great depth as well as libraries of international scope, to which all of the important current publications were to be added on a regular basis. This was definitely not what a library such as Harvard's had been before. Despite being the largest library in the country in 1850, with 84,200 volumes in all of the libraries, including those maintained by students, its size primarily resulted from donations of material that private individuals no longer wanted, from occasional purchase of collections, and, in the 1840s, from spending a fund raised for library purchases—a fund that was exhausted by the early 1850s.

The creation of research libraries happened initially through the formation of new institutions, supported by private wealth, rather than through the transformation of existing libraries. The first was the Astor Library, provided for by a codicil dated 22 August 1839, to John Jacob Astor's will, which took effect upon his death in 1848. He bequeathed $400,000 for erecting a building and for endowing the library, which was merged with other libraries in 1895 to form the New York Public Library. In 1851 George Peabody, an American banker in London, conceived the idea of establishing in Baltimore a cultural institution whose central focus would be a research library. The founding letter for the Peabody Institute was dated 12 February 1857. In it Peabody promised $300,000, but by his death his gifts had amounted to $1.4 million. Not long after its opening in 1866, the first provost, N. H. Morison, claimed that Peabody "undoubtedly" had in mind as a model the British Museum and the National Library in Paris.

Astor was of German birth; Peabody lived abroad. In Boston, others with international connections also formed a research library. Although George Ticknor, the social arbiter of Boston society, advocated that the proposed new library in Boston, which was to be supported by the city government, should have a circulating collection that would contain the "pleasant literature of the day," he also urged that there should be established a "department for consultation only." Ticknor's hopes received a major boost when the banker-philanthropist Joshua Bates, who had grown up in Boston and was a senior partner in the financial firm Baring Brothers & Company, offered $50,000 to the city for the purchase of books, and three years later proposed to pay for "French, German and Italian books, and such English works as are most needed, the whole not to exceed $20,000 or $30,000." Ticknor set off for Europe to buy the books to go in the new building of the Boston Public Library.

In the meantime the Library of Congress began to become a research library; because 35,000 of its 55,000 volumes had been destroyed by fire in 1851, the task was basically to build a new library. Congress thereafter appropriated $75,000 for books and continued significant annual appropriations. By 1860 there were 75,000 volumes. In 1866 the Smithsonian Institution, after making the decision to de-

vote itself to scientific research rather than to library building, turned over its 44,000 volumes to the Library of Congress, thus making it the largest library in the United States, a position confirmed in 1867 by the first great purchase, the historical collection of the printer-archivist Peter Force, consisting of 60,000 titles.

The research library formation then going on stimulated Harvard to ever-greater consciousness of its library deficiency. Harvard presidents recognized in the 1850s that more and more scholarly literature was being produced and that Harvard faculty required access to it in the library. They made public appeals, and in 1859 the alumnus William Gray promised $5,000 a year for five years expressly for the purpose of purchasing new books. Ongoing growth could take place not only because of gifts for current use but also because of endowed funds. Charles William Eliot, who became president of Harvard University in 1869, advocated endowed funds, and private individuals established the funds that permitted ongoing, steady acquisitions.

Private individuals not only gave money but also formed collections that enriched established libraries or formed the initial foundation collection for new research libraries, such as the Newberry Library in Chicago, the Pierpont Morgan Library in New York City, the Huntington Library in San Marino, California, and the Folger Shakespeare Library in Washington, D.C., as well as research libraries within established institutions, notably the John Carter Brown Library at Brown University and the William Andrews Clark Memorial Library at the University of California at Los Angeles. The independent research libraries, including such long-established institutions as the American Antiquarian Society in Worcester, Massachusetts, and the Library Company of Philadelphia, constitute a group that, beginning in the late twentieth century, has helped to develop the resources of these institutions and foster ways of making them more widely accessible and useful in an era when scholarship is centered primarily around universities.

University libraries also profited in the second half of the nineteenth century and, even more so, in the twentieth by the private collecting of individuals who gave or bequeathed their collections, funded the purchase of collections, or created endowments for ongoing acquisitions. Individuals also gave buildings for the housing of rare books and manuscripts. The Houghton Library at Harvard University, in Cambridge, Massachusetts, which opened in 1942, was the first general rare-

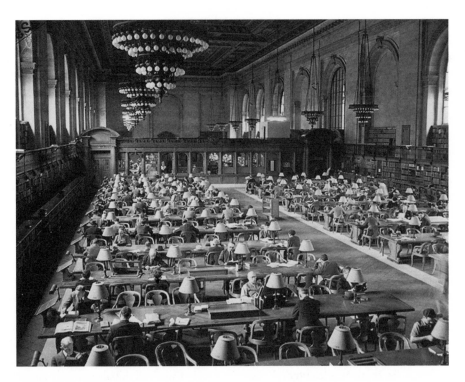

Main Reading Room of the New York Public Library (1950). Countless writers, scholars, and inventors have used the New York Public Library as a resource for their work.
© BETTMANN/CORBIS

book library in a university, but others followed, among them the Beinecke Library at Yale University in New Haven, Connecticut; the Lilly Library at Indiana University in Bloomington, Indiana; the Kenneth Spencer Research Library at the University of Kansas in Lawrence, Kansas; and the Bancroft Library at the University of California, Berkeley.

In the immediate post–World War II decades state legislatures also sought to turn their universities—and the libraries connected with them—into research institutions. Large appropriations made possible the Harry Ransom Humanities Research Center at the University of Texas at Austin and major en bloc purchases by numerous other university libraries. University libraries deepened their collections, for they began to collect manuscript materials, a type of source material that before had largely been left to historical societies. It was not, however, only rare and unique materials that libraries acquired. Just as expanded production of books and serials had stimulated the creation of research libraries in the middle of the nineteenth century, so did an ever-increasing output of scholarly materials make necessary expanded acquisitions by libraries in universities seeking to be research institutions. University libraries also sought to internationalize

their collections, and it became possible to find resources in depth, somewhere in a library in the United States, for the study of almost any part of the world or any subject whatsoever.

Statistics depict the rapid postwar growth. In 1940 American college and university libraries had 41,689,000 volumes. In 1961 the total had grown to 100,702,000, and in the following decade college and university libraries added nearly one and a half times the number present in 1940, the grand total in 1971 being 161,567,000. However, as the twentieth century came to an end, many librarians became concerned that the funds available for collection building, particularly of foreign-language materials, were no longer sufficient. Adoption of computer technology was rarely an add-on, and expenses for technology as well as rapidly rising serial prices, especially of scientific serials, meant declining acquisitions of monographs.

At the same time, though, the computerization of catalogs, the retrospective conversion of card catalogs, the on-line availability of those cataloging records, the production of periodical indexes and other kinds of reference tools in digital form, the creation of manuscript finding aids that are searchable on-line, the increasing digitization of the content of books and serials, and much more began to transform libraries and the research of scholars.

PUBLIC LIBRARIES

The initial period of research library formation and growth, which took place about the middle of the nineteenth century, coincided with the start of a new pattern for providing reading to Americans generally, namely the public library. Thus, in 1848 the Massachusetts legislature passed legislation that empowered the city of Boston to support a library from public funds, and it extended this legislation to all towns in 1851. Meanwhile, New Hampshire, in 1849, had passed such a bill. Other states followed, but slowly: Maine (1854); Vermont (1865); Ohio (1867); Colorado, Illinois, Wisconsin, and New York (1872); Indiana and Iowa (1873); Texas (1874); Connecticut and Rhode Island (1875); Michigan (1876); Nebraska (1877); California, Minnesota, and New Jersey (1879); Montana (1883); New Mexico (1884); Missouri (1885); Kansas and Wyoming (1886); North and South Dakota (1887); Pennsylvania (1887); Washington (1890); Mississippi (1892); Utah (1896); North Carolina and Tennessee (1897); Maryland and Georgia (1898); Delaware, Arizona, and Oklahoma (1899). Thus, in each state the development of libraries has been different, with the institution of the tax-supported public library by no means being immediately adopted.

One reason for the slow passage of enabling legislation by the states was citizen opposition to paying taxes for libraries, out of a general concern over new taxes, out of anxiety that public property, that is, the books, would be lost or damaged, and out of a fear that the library would be politically partisan or favor one set of religious views. Indeed, it was also argued that having many books available would divert from the reading of the Bible.

Existing library organizations, even without outright opposition to public library legislation, hindered public library formation through making it less clear that library service required public financing. In addition to the membership libraries formed earlier and the new ones that continued to be created, new types of libraries began after 1850. Widespread were Young Men's Christian Association libraries "sought after" by "most communities" in the 1870s and 1880s. Particularly in Michigan women formed numerous Ladies' Library Associations. Moreover, some states sought to control libraries centrally, as in the case of those with ex-tensive school district libraries, or, as in Michigan and Indiana township libraries whose books were supplied by the state.

Enabling legislation was not sufficient, in and of itself, for communities to form public libraries. More than a small tax was needed to start a library. Although in some cases the books of an existing membership library formed the nucleus of the new library's collection, substantial capital funds were often required to purchase a stock of books. Moreover, to house the books a building was required, for, unlike early in the nineteenth century, a library's collection was expected to number in the many hundreds or in the thousands, not merely a hundred or so. Even having space to store the books and deliver them over to readers was not enough; it came to be accepted that a library should also have a reading room.

In New England, in particular, and also New York, library buildings were often gifts, thanks to the industrialization that had concentrated private wealth in the hands of factory owners throughout those states, wealth that subsequently led to philanthropy, and thanks as well to the young men who had left the farms and towns for the big cities but felt continuing ties to their native communities. For these men or their heirs, library buildings were a form of philanthropy that earned them recognition and gratitude from the community.

The steel magnate and philanthropist Andrew Carnegie did for the rest of America what numerous individuals had done for New England and New York. As of 1896 the number of communities in other regions that had received Carnegie library buildings was 1,298, which far exceeded in number the 361 communities with non-Carnegie public libraries of 1,000 or more volumes; whereas in New England and New York, the ratios are reversed, with 114 Carnegie libraries in contrast to the 610 library buildings funded by other sources.

In communities that benefited from individual philanthropy, the offer of a building was sometimes the impetus behind the formation of a public library, but often it went the other way and was a culmination of a struggle, one that increasingly was led by women, especially women united in the clubs that became widespread. Community involvement became essential in obtaining a Carnegie grant, since Carnegie philanthropy required a commitment of ongoing support.

Although Andrew Carnegie's gifts, both personally and through the Carnegie Foundation, were crucial in spreading libraries, they coincided with an active role by state governments to spread libraries and to increase library services in rural areas. In 1889 Andrew Carnegie published an article entitled "The Best Fields for Philanthropy" in the *North American Review.* He argued that libraries were the best single field and that this was exemplified by the Enoch Pratt Free Library in Baltimore, where its founder Enoch Pratt "has poured his fertilizing stream upon soil that was ready to receive it and return a hundred-fold." Moreover, such gifts promised to end antagonism between classes and lead to the day when the "high and the low, the rich and the poor, shall . . . indeed be brothers."

The next year, in 1890, Massachusetts established a state library commission. New Hampshire followed in 1892, and by 1905 twenty-five states had established similar bodies. These aimed to provide library service to parts of the population that had not been served: communities hitherto without a library; people in rural areas; and immigrants, who needed to be provided with books in their native languages. Women lobbied state legislatures to create such bodies and to support them, and women also served on their boards. Commissions also employed librarians, mainly women, to travel to libraries to help organize them and to establish the procedures that librarians had been standardizing, above all since 1876, when the American Library Association (ALA) was founded.

Before 1876, librarians learned from each other through informal contacts, sometimes ones that were planned, as in the case of a tour of libraries. The annual conventions of the ALA provided opportunities for formal learning, as did the start in 1876 of the *Library Journal,* but the increasing number of small libraries meant an ever-growing need for instruction in how to run a library. Melvil Dewey, then librarian of Columbia College in New York City, opened a School of Library Economy in January 1887. The school's emphasis was on the practical aspects of librarianship, with authority to determine "best reading" left to others outside librarianship, a stance that accorded with Dewey's interests but was also, given cultural attitudes, particularly appropriate for a school whose students were primarily young women. Women had worked in libraries at least as early as 1857, but Dewey's establishment of a formal educational program helped to make librarianship a field in which women could rise to major positions. Although it has been argued that the feminization of librarianship is responsible for the low status of librarianship, it has also been argued that the high quality of American libraries is related to the large numbers of capable women who entered librarianship, thanks to the opportunities it offered for women to advance, as compared to other occupations.

A school preparing its students for a particular occupation necessarily also imparts an ethos, and that inculcated by Dewey's school was a commitment to serving as large a body of the population as possible. In this Dewey was certainly not alone. Librarians, as part of efforts to expand the usefulness of the library, had begun in the second half of the nineteenth century to try to reach more and more elements of the population. Libraries tried to attract workers through the provision of material that might be useful on the job. In the twentieth century, business branches were opened.

Various efforts have been made to serve children. One method in the nineteenth century was to place books in the hands of teachers. Another was to lower the age at which it was possible to get a library card. Yet another is, of course, the children's room, or even the children's library, with its story hours, its attractive space, its large quantity of books, and its various means to stimulate reading, including summer contests for the most books read.

Librarians have acted out of a missionary spirit (or "library spirit," as Dewey put it), but librarians have also wanted to demonstrate their utility to municipal officials and to the citizenry. As media other than print have come into being, librarians have expanded holdings of nonbook materials such as videotapes, audiotapes, and CD-ROMs, and libraries are providing access to on-line files. Librarians have also employed increasingly diverse ways to attract users, among them reading lists, exhibitions, book talks, newspaper publicity, and library newsletters. Libraries sponsor lectures, provide space for reading groups, mount art exhibitions, and thus seek to make public libraries into community centers as well as book depots.

Bringing books closer to readers has also been practiced. Branch libraries go back to the second half of the nineteenth century, and the placing of book "delivery stations"—that is, small, rapidly changing collections in stores—began in the 1890s. Bookmobiles were long a fixture of twentieth-century public librarianship.

The desire of librarians to get as many books or other materials as possible into the hands of borrowers inherently means taking the stance that the public should be supplied with what it wants. That implies no censorship, and, indeed, librarians have, through the Library Bill of Rights, a document officially approved by the ALA, taken a position opposed to censorship and in favor of maintaining the confidentiality of borrowing records. That position has evolved over time, for in the late nineteenth century librarians often consciously acted as censors; librarians attempted to keep fiction deemed to be harmful out of collections and out of the hands of readers. Indeed, fiction was seen by some to be inherently harmful, and some libraries had policies designed to limit the quantity of fiction that was borrowed. It is also obvious that in selecting materials for libraries librarians have more or less unconsciously often reflected majoritarian views. It is fair to say, though, that in the twentieth century librarians have sought to let the public be the judge of what it should borrow, that librarians have sought to keep personal views out of decision-making over the supply of material, and that librarians see themselves as willing to fight attempts at censorship.

Librarians have not, however, always been the prime movers in shaping libraries. Librarianship grows out of a past in which to be a librarian meant primarily to record loans and returns, to put in bookplates, and, generally, to keep the library functioning. The further evolution of the librarian's role—from policy advocate and then to policy maker—took place slowly in the nineteenth century and then only in the largest libraries, and, indeed, in many college libraries faculty members still control the allocation of funds and the selection of materials. Control of the library is still a contested area. Thus, for a variety of reasons—the position of librarians, the need for public support in order to maintain and increase funding, and the missionary ethos of librarianship—librarians have emphasized providing what the public wanted.

Providing what the public wants is arguably what librarianship should be in the United States. Once it is accepted that reading and access to information are desirable for the individual and that the community benefits through that individual's reading and self-improvement, then society has a stake in furthering that reading. Precisely what the benefit is varies from era to era and from group to group, with the emphasis being variously on forming a citizenry that will ensure continuation of democracy, on fostering morality, on elevating taste, on training the intellect, on advancing knowledge, on providing useful skills, on furthering access to information, or on encouraging harmless entertainment. As scholars study the history of reading, they are learning that the articulated goals of library supporters and librarians are but one part of the story, that individuals, in reading a book, take from it what they need at that particular moment, even that they create meanings that are personal to them. This has implications for society's view of the library institutions that have been created at various periods and of the function of libraries in the future.

See also **Education in Early America; The Print Revolution; Southern Intellectual Life; Urban Cultural Institutions** *(volume 1);* **The Culture of Self-Improvement; Popular Culture in the Public Arena** *(volume 2);* **Books; Periodicals** *(in this volume); and other articles in this section.*

BIBLIOGRAPHY

The classic works of American library history appeared shortly after World War II: Jesse H. Shera, *Foundations of the Public Library: A Social History of the Public Library Movement in New England, 1629 to 1855* (Chicago, 1949) and Sidney Ditzion, *Arsenals of a Democratic Culture: A Social History of the American Public Library Movement in New England and the Middle States from 1850 to 1900* (Chicago, 1947). Despite their focus, which is limited to the institutional basis of the public library and the spread of that form of library, no works of similarly broad scope have superseded them.

Many historical accounts of individual public libraries exist, but Deanna B. Marcum's *The Public Library as a Cultural Force in Hagerstown, Maryland, 1878–1920* (Westport, Conn., 1994) is rare in its effort to relate a small-town library to that community's cultural development. Phyllis Dain's *The New York Public Library: A History of Its Founding and Early Years* (New York, 1972) is a richly detailed account of our greatest public library. Michael H. Harris shattered the consensus over the nobility of the early public library "movement" with his revisionist stand over the motives behind early public library development; see his *The Role of the Public Library in American Life: A Speculative Essay* (Urbana, Ill., 1975). Dee Garrison's *Apostles of Culture: The Public Librarian and American Society, 1876–1920* (New York, 1979) began a debate on the ways that public libraries were shaped by the social origins of American library leaders in this crucial period as well as by the numerical predominance of women in librarianship. Wayne A. Wiegand took an internal view of librarianship in *The Politics of an Emerging Profession: The American Library Association, 1876–1917* (Westport, Conn., 1986). Abigail A. Van Slyck, *Free to All: Carnegie Libraries and American Culture, 1890–1920* (Chicago, 1995) is an account of the ubiquitous Carnegie library by an architectural historian. Major works on public libraries that move beyond the early decades of the twentieth century do not exist, though Jane Aikin Rosenberg's *The Nation's Great Library: Herbert Putnam and the Library of Congress, 1899–1939* (Urbana, Ill., 1993) does contribute to understanding more recent decades in public libraries because of the central role of the Library of Congress. On the Library of Congress, see also a number of works by John Y. Cole.

Only one general account of university libraries exists: Arthur T. Hamlin, *The University Library in the United States: Its Origins and Development* (Philadelphia, 1981); but, based on secondary literature, it reflects the gaps in that literature.

Much of the work on library history has appeared in the journal *Libraries and Culture,* formerly the *Journal of Library History.* It began in 1966 and is published by the University of Texas Press. A call for a new history of American libraries, which focuses on aspects of the nineteenth century, is Kenneth E. Carpenter, *Readers and Libraries: Toward a History of Libraries and Culture in America* (Washington, D.C., 1996), and a similar essay, which focuses on the twentieth century, is Wayne A. Wiegand, "Tunnel Vision and Blind Spots: What the Past Tells Us about the Present: Reflections on the Twentieth-Century History of American Librarianship," *Library Quarterly* 69 (January 1999).

MUSEUMS

Steven Conn

THE MUSEUM'S EARLY BEGINNINGS

In 1895, George Brown Goode concluded an essay on "The Principles of Museum Administration" with the following pronouncement: "The degree of civilization to which any nation, city or province has attained is best shown by the character of its public museums and the liberality with which they are maintained." If this statement seems a bit bombastic, consider Goode's position: as the assistant secretary of the Smithsonian Institution Goode took it as his job to champion American museums, and he wrote those words in the midst of an extraordinary period of museum building, as many of America's industrial giants helped found museums with their vast new fortunes.

Whether he realized it or not, Goode wrote his essay almost precisely one hundred years after America's first important museum opened to the public. In 1794 the Philadelphian painter Charles Willson Peale moved his collection of natural history specimens and portraits of Revolutionary War heroes from his home, where they had been on display for ten years, into the halls of Philadelphia's American Philosophical Society. After a few years there, Peale moved his growing museum into space in Independence Hall provided to Peale by the Commonwealth of Pennsylvania free of charge. Perhaps it was this kind of liberality Goode had in mind.

The museum as an institution, of course, traces its origins back through European royal collections, private cabinets of curiosities, medieval religious treasuries, and Roman and Greek temples dedicated to the muses. In the United States, however, museum history is almost exactly coterminous with the history of the nation itself and over those roughly two hundred years museums have been central fixtures in the nation's cultural and intellectual landscape. Beginning with Peale's museum, American museums number over five thousand of all kinds and are located everywhere—from the enormous Metropolitan Museum of Art in New York City to the more modest Mustard Museum in Mount Horeb, Wisconsin. Taken together, American museums annually attract visitors in the hundreds of millions.

The significance of Peale's museum lies not in the fact of its being first—indeed Charleston, South Carolina's small natural history museum opened in 1773—but rather in the founder's conception of what a museum could be. In many ways, Peale defined what would be distinctive about American museums. First and foremost, Peale organized his collection systematically, and he displayed his museum objects in an orderly, rational way. Here was the Enlightenment's Great Chain of Being in glass cases. Second, he envisioned his museum as an educational engine, at the forefront both of producing knowledge about the natural history of the new nation—for example, President Thomas Jefferson presented many of the specimens collected by the Lewis and Clark expedition to the museum—and of making that knowledge democratically accessible to a visiting public.

In 1799 Peale offered a course of public lectures to explain to the public why an understanding of the natural world should be pursued by all the elements of American society: "The farmer ought to know," Peale told his listeners, "that snakes feed on field mice and moles, which would otherwise destroy whole fields of corn. . . . To the merchant, the study of nature is scarcely less interesting, whose traffic lies altogether in material either raw from the stores of nature or wrought by the hand of ingenious art. . . . The mechanic ought to possess an accurate knowledge of many of the qualities of those materials with which his art is connected." Implicit in this lecture was Peale's vision that his museum too would be patronized by farmers, merchants, and mechanics (Brigham, p. 5).

Peale displayed fossils, animal specimens, portraits, and even innovative pieces of technology, like the ingenious physiognotrace, a device used to produce silhouettes; the museums that followed in his wake were not so comprehensive. The heart of Peale's museum had been its collection of natural history specimens, and museums devoted to this topic proliferated. Though these ranged in size from large, urban institutions like the Academy of Natural Sciences in Philadelphia, to teaching collections at small, relatively isolated colleges, natural history displays in the first half of the nineteenth century were organized along the same intellectual principles.

Natural history was to be studied through the careful collection, classification, and exhibition of specimens, and the goal of this study was to demonstrate that scientists could discern the patterns of God's creation. As the Unitarian Orville Dewey put it in 1830: "It is not enough to say, in the general, that God is wise, good, and merciful. . . . We want statements, specifications, facts, details, that will illustrate the wonderful perfection of the infinite creator." In the galleries of natural history museums, the natural facts about an ever-expanding nation—its mineral resources, its peculiar animals, the remains of its ancient life—were amassed, studied, and classified. In natural history museums, scientists could demonstrate intellectual dominion over a continent.

BEYOND THE NATURAL HISTORY MUSEUM

If natural history museums purported to carry Peale's mantle of both scientific rationality and public education, then at the same time a new kind of museum with very different aims arose in the jostling chaos of America's burgeoning cities. So-called dime museums occupied a central place in the new world of urban entertainment, appealing to a wide range of city dwellers. Unlike the natural history museums, which strove to present God's creation as orderly and rational, dime museums presented the public with the bizarre, the fantastic, the grotesque, and, as often as not, the fraudulent. These institutions can be epitomized in a single word: Barnum.

P. T. Barnum, one of the great showmen of the nineteenth century, bought John Scudder's American Museum in New York in 1841; four years later he acquired what was left of Peale's museum and established his own museum. There visitors could see not only collections of shells and minerals and animals both stuffed and live, but midgets and bearded ladies, a stuffed mermaid, and most spectacularly a set of waxworks scenes graphically illustrating the evils of drink.

While Americans could choose to be educated at a natural history museum or to be entertained at a dime museum, in the period before the Civil War they could not visit, unless they lived in Hartford, Connecticut, what we would recognize as an art museum. Several institutions, like Boston's Athenaeum, collected and exhibited paintings as a small part of larger missions, while others, like the Pennsylvania Academy of the Fine Arts in Philadelphia, kept paintings in order to train painters. Philadelphians had the chance, briefly, to see the artistic production of China when Nathan Dunn, a merchant in the China trade, opened his museum of "ten thousand Chinese things" in 1838. An extraordinary museum that claimed to reproduce "China in miniature," it did not last long on Ninth Street. Dunn packed his crates and moved his museum to London in the early 1840s. But Hartford's Wadsworth Athenaeum, founded in 1842, stands as the most significant museum founded in the antebellum period to serve primarily as an art gallery.

THE GOLDEN AGE OF MUSEUM BUILDING

Barnum's museum burned in 1865, an event that, along with the end of the Civil War, marks as conveniently as any the beginning of the golden age of American museum building. Though Barnum's own promise to rebuild his museum went unfulfilled, museums popped up at a remarkable rate in American cities between the end of the Civil War and the beginning of the Great Depression in 1929. Even a partial list is at once familiar and astonishing: the Museum of Fine Arts in Boston; the Metropolitan Museum of Art and the American Museum of Natural History in New York City; the Art Institute and Field Museum of Natural History in Chicago; the Detroit Institute of Arts; and the Philadelphia Museum of Art. As the Philadelphia paleontologist Edward Drinker Cope put it in 1876, "As the middle ages were the period of cathedrals, so the present age is one of colossal museums."

The museums of the postwar era distinguished themselves from their antebellum predecessors in several ways. First and most obviously was their number and scale. The museums that were rooted in the urban soil of Gilded Age America grew to be both larger than their predecessors and more numerous. By comparison, "colossal" seems the right word indeed. And there is no question that the size of these museums and their proliferation reflected the growing fortunes of America's industrial robber barons. The list of museums offered earlier might be matched by a list of industrial titans who involved themselves heavily in building museums: J. P. Morgan, Marshall Field, John Wanamaker, Andrew Carnegie, and a variety of Rockefellers. As a writer for *Science* put it in 1912, "The growth of our museums is largely parallel with the growth of our national wealth."

Beyond legitimating money sometimes dubiously made, however, the museums of the late Victorian age should also be seen as perhaps the most sparkling jewels among a collection of extraordinary public institutions built in this same period. The public sphere in American cities was redefined in this era to include public school systems, public parks, hospitals and universities, public libraries, and, of course, public museums. Museums may have been built by a wealthy elite, but they were an integral part of a larger middle-class urban culture.

Just as important, these new museums reached back beyond the dime museum spectacles to resurrect Peale's orderliness and rationality. The new museums wanted to be everything Barnum was not: scientific, respectable, educational. In the late nineteenth century, the English writer David Murray assured people of this distinction: "The museum of 1897 is far in advance of the museum of 1847."

Not merely storehouses of accumulation, these new museums were built upon an intellectual architecture of systematics and categorical knowledge. If the prewar museums had been, in the words of one critic, "mere miscellaneous lots of objects brought together with no purpose," then the new museums replaced the freakish with the ordinary, the "monstrosities, cheap theatricals, and legerdemain" with the representative. Rather than presenting a world turned upside down, they presented one in which everything had its place. Further, these museums presented a world with an essential design that could be revealed and understood through museum exhibits. The museum of the late nineteenth century strove to be, in the words of George Brown Goode in an 1888 lecture, a "house full of ideas, arranged with the strictest attention to system."

These museums were also founded with the belief that knowledge inhered in the objects that made up that category. Visitors could learn about a particular topic by carefully studying and observing the objects associated with that topic, provided museum curators had collected, classified, and arranged those objects properly. Edward Everett Ayer of Chicago's Field Museum described this epistemological faith in objects central to these museums

in 1894: "All museum material should speak for itself upon sight. It should be an open book which tells a better story than any description will do."

This faith in the ability of museum objects, displayed correctly, to tell stories may explain the characteristic form that museums took in the late nineteenth century. Typically museum objects were displayed in long glass cases located in even longer skylit galleries. Specimen after specimen, case after case—this arrangement of objects strikes most twenty-first-century Americans as mind-numbingly dull. But the glass case played a functional role in facilitating the kind of visual learning central to museums. The cases forced visitors to stare at and study objects and to consider them without too much visual distraction—first on their own terms and then in relation to categorically neighboring objects.

If individual objects were seen to tell stories when properly displayed and carefully studied, then a museum's entire collection usually told a grand narrative as well. All museums in the post–Civil War era had to wrestle in some way with the Darwinian revolution, and the result was museum exhibits that told an evolutionary tale. From the simplest to the most complex, from the lowest to the highest, museums presented the public with a version of the world in which progress and evolution were synonymous. In 1878 the Harvard University professor Charles Eliot Norton told a crowd that science "has proved that the development of the universe has been a progress from good to better ... a benign advance towards ever higher forms of life." He spoke those words at the opening of New York's American Museum of Natural History.

Goode sketched out the categories of knowledge that museums might exhibit in 1895. His schema included six: museums of art; historical museums; anthropological museums; natural history museums; technological museums; and commercial museums. For Goode, as for many historians in the late nineteenth century, these categories represented a way of organizing and displaying the world and the sum of knowledge that could be displayed in museums. If individual museums conceived of themselves as encyclopedias, where objects served as entries and the goal was to accumulate as many entries as possible, then Goode outlined a six-volume set. In this sense, the museums of the late nineteenth century represented a great encyclopedic project.

Most museums from this period attempted a version of encyclopedic completeness, differing to some extent over how the task would be defined (and differing in the amount of money available to complete the task). Only Philadelphia, however, attempted to build the whole set. By the end of the Civil War, Philadelphia's Academy of Natural Sciences, grown to over 200,000 specimens, had been open to the public for forty years. By the 1930s the Academy had been joined by the Philadelphia Museum of Art; the University of Pennsylvania's Museum of Anthropology; the Henry Mercer Museum, an American history museum named for its founder and builder; the Philadelphia Commercial Museum (the only one of its kind built in the United States); and the Franklin Institute Science Museum. Museums in other cities grew bigger, but no other place attempted to embody categorical knowledge in museum form as completely as Philadelphia. Fitting too, as Philadelphia had been the site of the nation's first important museum and in 1876 the city had played host to the nation's first large-scale exposition.

World's fairs and museums in this era were intimately linked. Often fairs spurred cities to build new museums, providing them with a core of objects around which to build a large collection. Philadelphia's art museum grew out of the 1876 Centennial Exposition and Chicago's Field Museum, which opened in 1894, was a lasting result of the otherwise temporary World's Columbian Exposition. In fact, the Field occupied one of the fair's buildings until the 1920s. The World's Columbian also provided the initial objects for Philadelphia's Commercial Museum which became, until 1926, the semiofficial repository for material from these spectacular events in an attempt to create a permanent home for the ephemeral fairs.

Encyclopedically assembled and systematically organized, museums were at the forefront of knowledge production in the last part of the nineteenth century. They stood as the institutional manifestation of an epistemology that relied on collection, classification, and arrangement, and in which objects were central. They were also conceived of as places that would both produce the very latest knowledge about the world and make that knowledge democratically accessible to a visiting public.

In these two ways, museums saw themselves as importantly different from America's colleges. By the end of the Civil War, these remained sleepy, moribund places, some still committed to theological training, others merely glorified finishing schools. In 1866 the philosopher John Fiske identified "the whole duty" of a university as having two parts. First, to train the "mental faculties" of students to pursue "varied and harmonious activity," and second to give them "the means of acquiring a thorough elementary knowledge of any given branch of science, art, or literature." Fiske's "whole duty" revolved around teaching, rather than original research, and seems a far cry from the mission of the contemporary university.

Museums, however, saw original research as central to their purpose. Edward Drinker Cope, who worked both at the Academy of Natural Sciences and at the University of Pennsylvania, described the difference succinctly when he wrote, "The bulk and amount of material necessary for investigation in the natural sciences is so great, that very few universities can supply it." The equation was simple: new knowledge comes from working with objects; museums, not universities, had those objects; new knowledge therefore would be produced at museums.

In addition, American museums, harkening back to Charles Willson Peale, congratulated themselves on their democratic impulses. They were open to anyone—though in truth not all were free of charge—as opposed to colleges, which remained bastions for a tiny elite. William Ruschenberger of the Academy of Natural Sciences summarized the differences between universities and museums in the late nineteenth century crisply, if a bit sardonically: "The purpose of the University is to teach what has been ascertained and is already known. . . . The purpose of the Academy is to ascertain what has been hitherto unknown, and freely give whatever new truth it may acquire to any person who may seek it." He went on, "But the Academy does not teach high-jumping, baseball or any form of athletics now recognized to be essential to the highest grade of intellectual cultivation and polish."

Distinguishing themselves from both the Barnumesque museums of the antebellum period, and from contemporary colleges and universities, museums in the Gilded Age stood as visual expressions of a way of organizing the world, based on the collection, classification, and display of objects. The systematics and categorical knowledge upon which these museums rested were central not merely to these institutions but to the way knowledge was produced during the period. In this sense, museums occupied center stage in the intellectual life of late-nineteenth-century America.

THE RELOCATION OF KNOWLEDGE: THE MUSEUM FACES THE UNIVERSITY

This golden age of museum building can be said to have ended with the Stock Market Crash of 1929. Institution building of all kinds slowed during the years of World War II and the Great Depression for obvious reasons. But, just as significantly, by the 1920s America's museums had lost their place at the center of knowledge production and had been replaced in that role by aggressive and expansive universities. The year 1876 marks the date of Philadelphia's Centennial Exposition and the beginning of the important relationship between fairs and museums, but it also marks the founding of the Johns Hopkins University, the first university in the country designed along largely German lines. Hopkins stressed graduate training, research seminars, and scientific labs and signaled a revolution in American higher education. By the early twentieth century Harvard, Chicago, Pennsylvania, and a host of other universities had followed its lead.

Universities, too, were committed to categorical knowledge, organized into different departments. These departments, and the rest of the research apparatus built at universities, proved more dynamic and effective producers of knowledge than the museums. At a very basic level, the encyclopedic conception of nineteenth-century museums implied that knowledge was finite. A complete understanding of the world only awaited the collection and classification of its objects. Universities, and their constituent departments, better envisioned a world where knowledge was conceived as infinite, and they both shaped and were more responsive to the ways the boundaries of knowledge shifted and changed. In the end, the stasis and completeness to which nineteenth-century museums aspired meant that they ceded their intellectual authority to universities.

The relocation of knowledge production from museums to universities represented more than an institutional transition. As universities won the struggle for intellectual authority, they took it away both from competing institutions and from objects themselves. By the first quarter of the twentieth century, objects had lost the capacity to tell stories the way they did in the late nineteenth century. More accurately, perhaps, Americans lost the capacity to hear them.

In addition, faculty in university departments, who also joined a host of disciplinary associations founded at the turn of the twentieth century, were committed to a level of professional training, credentialing, and specialization that was antithetical to the democratizing impulse of museums. To enter the world of knowledge production in the twentieth century meant first gaining access to a restricted and exclusive world of scholarly exchange. The golden age of American museums coincided with the last moment when American intellectual life was dominated by amateurs. The triumph of universities over museums for intellectual primacy also meant the disappearance of the amateur intellectual.

Finally, the rise of the university to dominance in American intellectual life had profound implications for the availability of knowledge to the general public. Universities, where the latest researches were now taking place, did not feel the same obligation to communicate with the public that museums did. Indeed, as knowledge production moved more and more squarely onto university campuses, the very language of scholarly discourse became increasingly opaque to most people. Even those on the same campus but in different departments had a difficult time understanding one another; for an amateur but interested public, the task proved frustrating to the point of impossibility.

THE MUSEUM ADAPTS TO A CHANGING CULTURE

Despite their challenges with the universities, museums continued to see education as central to their mission. But by the early years of the twentieth century, few believed that visitors could be educated unaided. Many museums hired staff or set up whole departments to do this. Especially in museums other than those of fine art, these efforts focused particularly on educating schoolchildren.

Museums acknowledged the disappearance of an epistemology rooted in objects in these years by changing their exhibitionary strategy. In natural history museums in particular, the glass cases were removed and replaced with more visually engaging dioramas. These dioramas—stuffed lions posed in their "natural habitat"—replaced a metonymic value for museum objects with a contextual one. Anthropological collections were displayed similarly: mannequins representing a particular people were arranged holding and using the objects associated with those people: the Zulu, for example, in their "natural habitat." By the 1960s, displaying so-called primitive peoples in this way had become politically unacceptable, not to mention anthropologically outdated. The end of colonialism brought with it a sense that people in Africa, Asia, and Central and South America were themselves political actors, and not merely objects of the West's anthropological scrutiny. As a result, beginning in the 1970s increasing numbers of fine art museums began exhibiting what had once been seen as anthropological artifacts as pieces of "fine art." International political circumstances forced certain objects to jump from one category to another, and from one kind of museum into another.

Art museums, too, created dioramas for their pieces and called them period rooms. Immensely popular beginning in the 1920s, these rooms strove to create a complete context for paintings, furniture, ceramics, and, in some cases, like the Philadelphia Museum of Art, installed in authentic pieces of period architecture. The Cloisters, the Metropolitan's museum of medieval art, opened in 1938 and built stone by stone from a series of medieval European buildings brought over by boat, stands in Fort Tryon Park as a period room on the grandest possible scale.

Professionalization came to the museums in the middle years of the twentieth century. Curatorship came to be seen as something that required specialized training and knowledge. In the 1920s, 1930s, and 1940s Harvard University's Fogg Art Museum offered a course to train museum professionals. The graduates of this program went on to constitute an entire generation of museum leaders. Most important, 1906 saw the founding of the American Association of Museums (AAM). Functioning in many ways like the professional academic associations, the AAM holds an annual conference, publishes a journal, and serves in part as a deliberative body to decide questions of museum policy on a national level. When the AAM authored a definition of what constitutes a museum in 1970, it underscored its commitment to the processes of professionalization by insisting that to be a museum in the first place meant employing "a professional staff."

The postwar years witnessed another attempt to create an encyclopedic set of museums, this time in the town where Goode spent his career. The Smithsonian Institution had been founded through a bequest by the Englishman James Smithson in 1846, and established a national museum with the money. It was not until after the mid-twentieth century, however, that the Smithsonian grew into its constellation of museums. Mirroring both the growth of the federal government and the sense that the United States needed a capital commensurate with its own sense of international prestige, the Smithsonian expanded beyond its natural history and anthropological collections to include American history, fine art, science, and technology. Goode's vision of a vast museum complex was achieved, making the Smithsonian the cultural heart of Washington.

At the same time, American museums attempted to embody two new categories of knowledge. One of these was the "modern" and the other was America itself. American historic sites had been the subject of preservation efforts since President George Washington's home at Mount Vernon was rescued from real estate developers in the 1850s, but in the 1930s work at Williamsburg, Virginia, began in earnest. Williamsburg stands as an enormous museum of a particular moment in American history, resuscitated through the careful work of archaeologists, architects, and historians. At this same moment, American art and craft was being discovered as a subject for museum collecting. The opening of the Whitney Museum of American Art in New York in 1930 signaled the arrival of American art as a category of museum display.

The Museum of Modern Art (MOMA) had been found just the year before, in 1929, though it would not move into its permanent home until 1939. European high modernism had met with a decidedly mixed reaction in the United States when it was exhibited for the first time on a large scale at the 1913 Armory Show. The MOMA, then, took on the task of making modernism legitimate by giving it a permanent institutional home. More than that, MOMA was instrumental in creating an art historical canon of modernism—the arrangement of its galleries looks remarkably similar to the arrangement of "modernism" in art history survey texts.

Putting the modern in a museum, however, creates an obvious definitional dilemma: when does the modern cease to be so? Gertrude Stein was reported to have quipped that a museum can either be a museum or it can be modern, but it can't be both. MOMA found itself facing this dilemma squarely in the late 1990s when it had to hand over one of its paintings to the Metropolitan Museum of Art. The original donor had stipulated that after fifty years the painting would no longer be "modern," and thus would no longer belong at MOMA.

Modernism found itself with another New York shrine with the establishment of the Guggenheim Museum in 1939, known then as the Museum of Non-Objective Painting. Though the Guggenheim differs in its collecting and exhibit focus from MOMA, the real difference between the two institutions came in 1959 when the Guggenheim's permanent home opened on Fifth Avenue. Designed by Frank Lloyd Wright—it was his last building and was completed, with some controversy, after he died—the Guggenheim Museum instantly became more famous for its architecture than for anything on display inside. Museums built in the late nine-

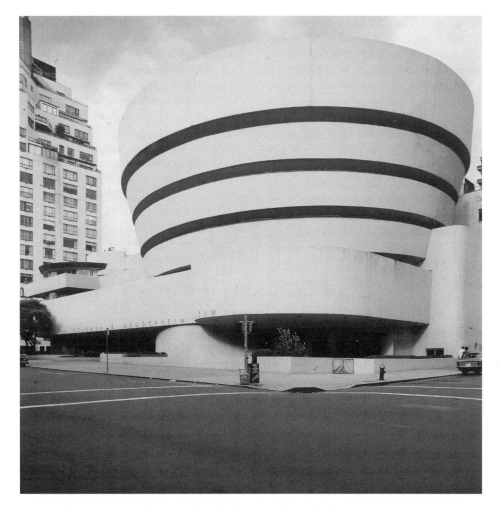

Solomon R. Guggenheim Museum, New York. Frank Lloyd Wright's novel design ushers visitors to the top of the museum via an elevator. The artwork is then viewed while walking down a spiral ramp that encircles an open rotunda. © ANGELO HORNAK/CORBIS

teenth and early twentieth centuries were usually grand, sometimes even pompous affairs, variations on the beaux arts, neoclassical themes made popular at the 1893 Chicago World's Fair. The Guggenheim, however, marked a shift in the architectural pretentions of the museum.

Museums in the postwar period often attempted to make dramatic architectural statements, and indeed several architects have made their reputations designing museum buildings. Perhaps among Louis I. Kahn's most successful American buildings are the three museums he designed: the Yale University Art Gallery and the Yale Center for British Art (both in New Haven, Connecticut) and the Kimbell Art Museum in Fort Worth, Texas. Postmodernist Robert Venturi has designed two remarkably successful museums, the Seattle Art Museum and the Sainsbury Wing of London's National Gallery. The most

dramatic is Frank Gehry's Guggenheim Museum in Bilbao, Spain (a branch of New York's Guggenheim). After the design of Spain's Guggenheim, a museum's collection became only part of its reputation: the building itself had to be a major work of art.

CONTEMPORARY CHALLENGES

At the turn of the twenty-first century, American museums found themselves challenged on several fronts. On the one hand, museums had never been so well attended, and they were without question central parts of the cultural life of the United States. On the other hand, many faced severe budgetary crises and could not rely on gate receipts alone to survive. In the absence of generous or reliable government funding art museums in particular had to rely increasingly on corporate underwriting and "blockbuster" exhibits to make ends meet. Science and natural history museums moved more in the direction of "infotainment" as they competed with a variety of high-tech distractions for the attention of the nation's children. Indeed, at the Center of Science and Industry in Columbus, Ohio, which opened in 1999, the use of the word "museum" was assiduously avoided altogether because museums were perceived, according to the market research, as too boring. Needless to say, these developments raised difficult questions about the intellectual autonomy and seriousness of purpose museums may have in the future.

Additionally, in the last quarter of the twentieth century, museums found themselves as the trenches over which vicious battles in the culture wars were fought. Shows as disparate as a retrospective of the life of the psychoanalyst Sigmund Freud and an exhibition featuring images of the West in art generated tremendous controversy. While it is surely true that museum exhibits had the capacity to shock and irritate in past centuries, the degree to which museums found themselves under attack in the 1980s and 1990s was unprecedented. In 1995, the Smithsonian's proposed exhibit marking the fiftieth anniversary of the dropping of the atomic bomb never came to fruition because of a well-orchestrated attack by veterans' groups, conservative congressmen, and others. In 1999, New York Mayor Rudolph Giuliani was in court threatening to evict the Brooklyn Museum from its city-owned building because of an exhibit he and others had deemed offensive. It was not at all clear what would happen if the mayor won, though some proposed an enormous flea market in Prospect Park. At the root of many of these controversies there seemed to be an assumption that museums, because they deal in objects, ought to present knowledge "objectively," and that any attempt to interpret through objects must represent a bastardization of a museum's purpose. This, of course, sounds remarkably like the faith nineteenth-century museum builders had that objects could simply tell simple stories.

See also **Urban Cultural Institutions** *(volume 1);* **Popular Culture in the Public Arena** *(volume 2);* **Painting; Sculpture; Myth and Symbol; History and the Study of the Past** *(in this volume); and other articles in this section.*

BIBLIOGRAPHY

Alexander, Edward P. *Museum Masters: Their Museums and Their Influence.* Nashville, Tenn., 1983.

Bennett, Tony. *The Birth of the Museum: History, Theory, Politics.* London, 1995.

Brigham, David R. *Public Culture in the Early Republic: Peale's Museum and Its Audience.* Washington, D.C., 1995.

Conn, Steven. *Museums and American Intellectual Life, 1876–1926.* Chicago, 1998.

Dennet, Andrea Stulman. *Weird and Wonderful: The Dime Museum in America.* New York, 1997.

Duncan, Carol. *Civilizing Rituals: Inside Public Art Museums.* London, 1995.

Hudson, Kenneth. *Museums of Influence.* Cambridge, Mass., 1987.

THE INTERNET AND ELECTRONIC COMMUNICATIONS

John Markoff

As its name indicates, the Internet is a global communications network that links, and surpasses, previously developed computer networks. On the edge of the twenty-first century millions of computer users around the world could make use of the Internet to send messages to each other and to obtain information from an increasingly wide variety of sources. By virtue of these connections, the computer had evolved from a tool for rapid computation into an entry into new forms of communication in which words, images (including moving images), and sounds could be sent almost instantly to distant locations. The variety of uses made of the new technology by governments (including militaries), police, criminals, artists, journalists, researchers, students, financiers, industrialists, political parties, children, sages, and crackpots; the novel, semianarchic organization of the Internet itself as a social system; the excitement of easy use by large numbers of people of what seemed a revolutionary technology hardly imagined even a quarter century earlier; the new forms of leisure that for some were becoming part of everyday life; the new threats to a social order that was so rapidly permeated by computer connection and therefore newly fragile in the face of new kinds of breakdown—all these had entered American culture (and beyond) by the end of the twentieth century. Hopes for scientific advance, for economic progress, for the widespread and democratic dissemination of knowledge, and for new leisure pleasures beckoned, but so did fears of new kinds of criminality, new forms of economic dislocation, new types of irrationality, new challenges to established cultures, and new mechanisms of impoverishment. And extravagant statements of hope or fear were challenged by skeptical counterclaims to the effect that the social impact of the new technology was being much overblown.

PREHISTORY: ORIGINS AND DEVELOPMENT OF THE COMPUTER

If the history of the Internet must begin with the modern, high-speed electronic computer, the computer itself may be seen as emerging from the originally separate histories of two different technologies: first, the development of rapid and reliable calculating machines, and, second, the development of means to externally control the sequence in which a machine performed its operations. There is much dispute about the early history of calculators, but by the late seventeenth century, machines carrying out arithmetic functions were known and the search was on for increasing their speed and the complexity of their computations. The question of external control arose in industrial processes: how to design a machine whose operations could be readily altered so that the advantages of speed, cost, and standardization of mechanization could be combined with flexibility. Here the pioneering locale was the eighteenth-century French silk-weaving industry, which saw a series of inventions in which punched tapes or punched cards could alter the operation of mechanical looms and thereby permit mechanized weaving of multiple patterns. The two technological streams were brought together by the English mathematician Charles Babbage, who in 1836 applied the punched-card technique to controlling the sequence of activities of a mechanical calculator. In the further development of such technology in the United States, the census of 1890 may be noted for its extensive use of punched-card technology. Inventor-entrepreneurs competing for work on the census went on to found rival firms to make computing equipment, including an ancestor of International Business Machines (IBM), which took on that name in 1924.

The search for technological advance, already impelled by commercial rivalry, took on new vigor as the exigencies of World War II led governments to invest enormous amounts in hopes of military advantage. Thus was born the electronic computer, the first of which, supported by the U.S. Army's Ballistic Research Laboratory, was ready in 1945. The drive for increased computational complexity and speed continued apace. The development of the internally stored program radically increased the power of the machines because the programs themselves could now be manipulated by other programs. The movement from vacuum tubes to transistors, integrated circuits, and microchips radically increased speed.

ORIGINS OF THE INTERNET: FROM CONTROL TO COMMUNICATION

In 1957, the Soviet Union succeeded in placing an artificial satellite, *Sputnik,* into orbit around the Earth. The United States responded with an increased commitment to developing advanced technology, and the Department of Defense established its Defense Advanced Research Projects Agency (DARPA), which became a major center for advances in computer science. At the same time academic researchers were working on some of the same technical problems. One powerful idea was to augment the capacity of individual computers by developing ways to link them to each other; another was the notion of interactive computing, in which users would be able to get the result of some commands to the computer quickly enough to be able to engage in a dialogue with the machine. Putting these two ideas together amounted to a vision of a whole group of computer users in interactive encounters with each other and having access to computing power far beyond their individual machines. It seems likely that the sense of community among the scientists working on these issues and their desire to improve their communications with each other provided a basis in their own social experience that was then followed up in technological breakthrough. In 1962 one DARPA scientist was calling the community of computer scientists the "Intergalactic Network." By 1965, the linking of a computer in California to one in Massachusetts over telephone lines amounted to the "first [however small] wide-area computer network ever built." By 1969, the Defense Department scientists had established the ARPANET. The first public presentation was in 1972, when the feasibility of electronic mail, or "e-mail," was demonstrated. (It is typical of this history that e-mail became much more common than anyone initially imagined, and began to create its own culture, on which more to come.)

Other communities of users were now developing their own networks with names like USENET and BITNET (from "bit," a unit of information as well as "because it's time"). Academic users were extremely important participants. As computer scientists developed the technology of connecting these networks to each other, the INTERNET came into existence. The continuing advances in miniaturizing computers now were making a reality of the small, personal computer of far less cost and far greater power than the large computers of but a few years earlier. Computer use, for computation, information storage and retrieval, recreation, and communication began to spread well beyond the narrow worlds of generals and professors. And networks of users proliferated. One estimate of the rapidity with which individual networks have been developed and then connected to the Internet suggests that in the late 1970s there were three such networks, by the early 1980s there were sixty, by the late 1980s there were nine hundred, and by the mid-1990s the number totaled 50 thousand. By the 1990s the Internet had become something quite different than its military and academic origins might have suggested: its span went well beyond the United States. Its mode of governance had more resemblance to the dreams of anarchists than the dreams of generals. It had spawned new cultures among its users. It provided instantaneous worldwide dissemination of information, misinformation, and disinformation. It had become an integral part of the United States and the global economy. It had become a factor in U.S. politics. And it had entered the realm of the imagination.

COMMUNICATIONS REVOLUTIONS

The development of new modes of communication has probably always been a significant context for politics, economics, and culture. The invention of writing may first and foremost have served purposes of central control in ancient empires (through making possible tax records, standardized laws, and administrative continuity). But writing eventually found many other uses as well: recording commercial activity; fixing religious traditions; expanding communication between persons separated by space, time, and social status; enlarging the possibilities for systematic abstract thought (including mathematics); and enhancing and shaping the individual imagination. Not the least such consequence, rising literacy in early modern Europe and North America, helped shaped the early history of modern social movements. By enabling people who were geographically distant from one another to coordinate their activities, it became easier to imagine organizing long-term campaigns directed at central governments. The very act of reading, moreover, probably helped create a sense of a community among those reading the same things, even if not simultaneously and not in sight of one another. This experience could be transferred to identifying with a social movement on behalf of ideas embodied in written form. Probably closely connected was the notion of a public that debates, judges government, and is potentially capable of action. So literacy began as a tool of government and has remained so, but it also became a vehicle of contention, challenge, and even of rebellion.

The nineteenth century brought new technology that began to radically alter the capacity of distant regions and distant people to enter into speedy contact. The telegraph, telephone, radio, motion picture, and television each played distinctive roles, each had social consequences beyond the purposes of their initial invention, and each brought people into new kinds of relationships with one another. Authoritarian states in eastern Europe after 1945 all had notoriously poor telephone systems, probably because their governments were uncomfortable about the ease with which telephones facilitate decentralized communication among potentially oppositional people. By the same token these governments were happy to make use of government-operated television stations to get their messages to their citizens. But many of the social consequences of new communications technology have been unplanned in any sense. One of the sources of the weakening of the political machines that used to be of such importance in urban politics in the United States was probably the post–World War II arrival of television in many American homes and the consequent decline of interest in a visit from the local boss, no longer a welcome source of conversation, but an interruption in a favorite television program.

In the long history of new communications technology, from writing to electronic media, no transformation seemed more rapid or more rich in unplanned consequences than the linkage of millions of computer users that had developed worldwide a mere three decades after that initial telephonic connection of East and West Coast computers. Many observers expected even more dramatic changes in the near future; as one put it in 1997, "The next quarter century will see the fast-

est technological change the world has ever known." But some scholars of the history of communications were apt to wonder whether the Internet was but the latest in a very long list of innovations that only cumulatively and not particularly rapidly provided the technological context for social change; in this mildly skeptical view, according to Brian Winston, the Internet was "the most important single development in the history of human communications since the invention of 'call waiting'" (*Media, Technology, and Society,* p. 336). Nonetheless, to many observers a society of "users," who communicated in "cyberspace," whose realities were sometimes "virtual," seemed, at the tail end of the twentieth century, to be coming into existence.

The significance of the new technology reached well beyond the immediate worlds of the individuals for whom the use of computers had become an important part of immediate daily existence. In the late 1990s some people were wondering what would happen if the next millennium commenced with widespread failure of computer systems due to the feared "millennium bug," no noxious insect but a "computer glitch"—that is, error—in the form of a general incapacity of the internal clocks of computers to distinguish the year 2000 from the year 1900 because of the two-digit system with which they had been designed. This was an indication of how profoundly many social institutions, government organizations to lay people, had become reorganized to take advantage of computers' capabilities, but also had become vulnerable to their frailties. This state of affairs is reflected in Hollywood films like *The Net* (1995), which depicts the ways in which a person's public identity becomes dependent on the information stored in intercommunicating computers: the villain nearly destroys the heroine's life by manipulating her electronic records and thereby eliminating her identity.

Beyond the Internet, by the turn of the twenty-first century there was an increasing richness and complexity of electronic communication emerging more generally, in at least three ways:

1. Technological advance in transmission of images and sounds were dissolving the distinctions that separated television, telephone, motion picture, publishing, and audio technologies.
2. The embedding of computer chips into all sorts of devices was beginning to make possible a rich exchange of information among such devices, suggesting not only the possibility of "smart" coffeepots turning them-

selves on when signaled by the household car that is fifteen minutes from home, but also of vast amounts of information embedded in passports, waiting to be scanned as travelers crossed national frontiers.

3. The development of a rich array of portable signaling and connecting devices, from small lightweight computers that could transmit via satellites, through cell phones and pagers, as indicated in many large urban settings by the new audioscapes of beeps, rings, and buzzes that were beginning to seem omnipresent.

ECONOMIC POTENTIALS AND VULNERABILITIES

The yoking of the capacity of computers for information storage, retrieval, and manipulation to near-instantaneous communication unimpeded by distance was remaking economic life in the late twentieth century. An enterprise could now keep precise track of inventories and send off instant orders to distant suppliers when necessary. Since less of virtually any material needed to be kept on hand, a new system of "just-in-time" delivery and reduced inventories encouraged "flexible specialization," in which distant firms were linked by their interchange of messages and goods, able to shift to new suppliers and new outlets. At the same time, the virtually worldwide organization of finance meant that investors could almost instantly shift their investments from one part of the globe to another in response to the latest news from a third locale.

While the movement of workers had not acquired the same ease and speed of movement as capital, the new immigrants moving into the economies of the wealthier countries, including the United States, could keep in instant contact with their points of origin to a degree unknown in previous waves of immigration. A group of Mexican workers in New Jersey, for example, with some access to faxes, phones, and e-mail could continue to participate in the life of a particular Mexican village, a process aided by the long-term decline of air travel costs.

These economic processes were producing a sense of "globalization," of the world as a single, shrunken space with, in turn, important cultural consequences. For example, in the United States, as in the older industrial democracies of western Europe, some political figures were seeking electoral victory through opposition to the fears aroused by this sense of change and challenge. National states,

virtually worldwide, seemed to be losing control of the transnational flow of capital, people, and symbols. There could be significant political advantage in opposing the transnational movements of capital that could seem to threaten national autonomy and local control of resources; in opposing unpalatable ideas whose point of origin might be anywhere on the globe but which were now on the home television or the even less isolatable computer screen; in opposing further cultural disorientation as foreign languages, religions, foods, and humor seemed everywhere; and in opposing immigrants from afar who carried foreign cultures, used our services, and took our jobs.

Of course, national political figures themselves made use of the new communications technology. In the late 1990s, Americans could learn from the television news, or from the Internet itself, of a variety of proposals, none successfully put into practice, aimed at insulating children from pornography on their home computers; in 1998, the U.S. Congress made available on the Internet a vast compilation of what were claimed to be intimate details of the sexual activity of the president of the United States. In the age of Internet, the president's laundry was washed in a very public place; such details were instantly known to anyone who wanted to know virtually worldwide, and Americans who wanted to know could learn something, almost equally instantaneously, of what people in France, or Japan, or (seemingly) anywhere, thought of these activities.

Economic restructuring brought other cultural consequences as well. With flexible specialization, middle-class expectations of structured careers seemed challenged, as firms could expand, contract, combine, relocate, or disassemble themselves with changing business opportunities and threats. Economic insecurity now began to seem not merely the age-old lot of the poor or of those who lived in times of crisis, but a routine element of ordinary life. If these were the micro-insecurities of the global economy, there were macro-insecurities as well. The tight economic linkages that tied producers, suppliers, and outlets together across cyberspace and across national borders meant that the economic problems of formerly distant places did not seem very distant. For scholars of such processes, at the beginning of the twenty-first century it was an unanswered question whether such transborder economic connections had become tighter to a degree unprecedented in world history, or whether the new communications technology had simply created an awareness of such connections. But many Americans were feeling themselves a part of a larger economic world as never before, and while some saw great opportunity, others found much to fear.

REDEFINING THE SOCIAL

Every channel of human communication encourages some kinds of relations among people, some kinds of messages, and some ways of experiencing oneself in communication. For example, written communication is far more prone than oral to encourage the construction of elaborate abstract systems (there are many traditions of oral poetry, but there is no oral mathematics). In the 1990s scholars were speculating about the quality of human relationships in which the connections of person to person were through the emerging electronic media. The distinctive characteristics of such communications were their mix of speed, ease of use, multidirectionality, and authorial control. At least when the systems were working properly, physical distance was virtually eliminated as a barrier; unlike television, one could respond instantly to one or many persons, and one could choose to respond at a convenient time. What was much in debate was the question, What sorts of social experience did such communication amount to? Was electronic communication a way for the bashful to open their hearts, shielded by the anonymity of a self-chosen "user name," or was it a step toward a new form of isolation? Did it open up the possibility of profound personal enrichment through the capacity to try on a variety of electronic personae, such as, for example, a new gender? Was the avoidance of the multifaceted complexity of face-to-face relations a new form of personal impoverishment? Was it a vehicle for new kinds of community, less bounded by territorial locality but self-organized around commonality of concern, or was it a vehicle for the erosion of any kind of community? Did the unusual features of computer-mediated social interaction constitute a profound experience for participants or a trivial one? Some sociologists thought the unusual features of electronic interactions called for new thinking about human interaction, and others were dubious.

Observers, including social scientists, offered much interesting speculation on the impact of computers on social relations, but the ratio of systematic evidence to speculation has remained low. One very important, and unanswered, question was, To what degree did participants use the new technology to enhance social relationships already established and interact in ways that improved upon, but were not radically different than, those already available via

letter (known as "snail mail") and telephone? Were Internet users establishing wholly new relationships, saying wholly new things, and having wholly new experiences?

By the 1990s new subcultures had developed around the new media, with their own rules of etiquette (for example, it is bad form to send e-mail to a whole network in order to get your message to a particular person; the overuse of capitalization is regarded somewhat like shouting in face-to-face communication), their own sense of identity (as in "wirehead"), and their own keepers of order and champions of rebellion (who figure prominently in the literary genre "cyberpunk"). For how many people such subcultures were an important part of their lives, for how many a minor one, and for how many, even among computer users, an insignificant one, is unknown.

The development of such electronic communication seemed to suggest some vital quality to face-to-face direct encounters with physically present others. Large American cities developed cyber cafes whose clientele seemed to take pleasure in hanging out side by side with other computer users, even as they sent their messages. The new reach of global financial networks, linked electronically, gave renewed vigor to so-called "global cities" like New York, where top managers found a need to cluster for face-to-face communication.

BRINGING UP THE NEXT GENERATION

Did the new media permit imaginative and enterprising students to find new connections as they chased down hypertext links, or did it threaten a breakdown of the intergenerational processes of cultural transmission by live teachers to physically present students? In the 1990s educators grappled with the implications of the new technology. For some it heralded a tremendous enhancement of learning resources open to students, as learners had a multiplicity of information sources readily available, well beyond school libraries; for others it held out the promise of reduced costs, with electronic classrooms and electronic student networks needing far fewer teachers; for still others, it heralded the possibility of teaching young people with complex, shifting, fascinating multimedia stimulation that might make learning fun. But the more skeptical worried about the quality of information available electronically and the potential diminution of older traditions of literacy still vital to real learning. Some educators had already been concerned about complex consequences of long hours devoted to television in competition for hours spent on reading and hours spent in social interaction with family or peers. Now many were wondering whether the more interactive style of dealing with computer-based communication was not the antidote to television, with reading words on the screen as a new variant on literacy. Still others wondered if the computer screen was not just a more fascinating version of the television screen, and hence even more of a threat to valued patterns of intellectual growth and social interaction.

But there was no question that computers had entered the educational scene, with early childhood programs in computer literacy, professors beginning to develop electronic journals for the dissemination of their own research, and university libraries, hard pressed by radically rising costs of books and periodicals, beginning to experiment with new modes of accessing information. As evidenced by the essays they published, scholars were reflecting on such topics as "Preparing Urban Teachers for the Technological Future," "Mapping the Cognitive Demands of Learning to Program," and "Young Children, Videos, and Computer Games."

DEMOCRACY

The widespread availability of personally owned, often readily portable communications devices, from camcorders to cell phones, and the expanding Internet that linked so many personal computers in a web that seemed beyond the control of established governments suggested to many observers—social scientists and citizens alike—many new democratic potentials generated by what some were calling the "virtual community." Among these potentials:

(1) Some saw the possibilities of citizens as active participants in electronic discussion, rather than as passive recipients of information, not merely because one could as readily send messages somewhere as get them but because the proliferation of web pages on which one could put whatever texts, images, and sounds one wished constituted a form of promulgation of ideas that did not have to pass through the gates that were carefully watched by the scrutiny of editors and were possibly beyond the regulatory capacities of states.

(2) It had suddenly become technologically feasible for citizens with personal computers to vote electronically on issues of the day, suggesting new potentials in the movement for a more direct democracy. Referenda on state and local issues have been well-established distinctive features of U.S. democracy (and citizen recall a virtually unique American institution); the new media created the technological potential for a radically greater weight to be assigned to the direct polling of citizens and a diminished role for legislators. As of the late 1990s, this was only a potential, with electronic voting in elections in one state constituting only the tiniest step in this direction, a step already derided by fearful critics for enhancing the power of those with too little interest to go to the conventional polling booth.

(3) In light of the strategic role that access to computer networks was beginning to play in economic organization, antidemocratic regimes in the 1990s were facing a difficult choice between (a) encouraging the proliferation of computer hardware and relevant computer skills and accepting a considerable loss in their capacity to control information flows; and (b) trying to keep at bay both threatening information and the establishment of autonomous social networks not under their control.

(4) A proliferation of new forms of antiestablishment activity abounded, ranging from the free distribution of software, the ease of access to pirated versions of everything from compact discs to computer programs, and the pranks of "hackers" who electronically penetrated the guarded recesses of secret files. For some, these were self-conscious acts of defying established authority, and they heralded new forms of social organization.

(5) Some suggested that electronic media constituted new resources for social movements, as activists in one country readily learned what their counterparts elsewhere had done; as participating in electronic communication shaped communities of participants and some of those communities developed forms of action; as activists in one country found it easier to mobilize support abroad; as the flow of information galvanized new conceptions of injustices; as diaspora communities kept in easier touch with homelands and used resources in their new locations to participate in politics back home.

But there were counterarguments to all the above.

(1) It was not obvious whether the bonds forged in electronic interaction would have the strength to sustain long-term or risky political commitments.

(2) Antidemocratic movements could use the new electronic media as readily as democratic ones. Under democratic auspices, including in the United

States, many observers noted that computer networks were ready sources of information for the technology of the small weapons, including concealable explosives, dear to insurrectionary groups. Websites of such insurrectionaries, and the activity of computer communication, were showing signs of facilitating new networks of violent resistance to democratic states and new foci for a sense of identity among those drawn to such activities.

(3) Just as literacy was as much an instrument of bureaucratic power as of social movement challenge, the new electronic technology seemed as likely to expand the toolkits of the powerful as to undermine them. With their vast potential for surveillance, information storage and retrieval, and intercommunication, the technical capacity of states to track people's movements; to have access to school, medical, financial, and police records; and even to take note of books borrowed from libraries or bought from stores was becoming radically enhanced.

(4) Access to the information superhighway was highly stratified. Personal computers were far more widely distributed in richer countries than in poorer countries. The English language predominated on the networks (although some observers thought that might change in time), the middle and upper classes were far more likely to have their own personal computers in addition to working for organizations that would provide such access, and so forth. So the information superhighway seemed as likely to enhance the differential power that accrued to wealth as to undermine it.

(5) The quantity of information of some sort so far outran the quality of electronic conversation that the electronic contribution to an informed citizenry made by the post-television electronic media seemed no greater in practice than that made by television. Rather than increase the capacity for autonomous citizens to engage in reasoned debate, some observers were wondering if the electronic media did not simply help blur any distinction between political life and entertainment, with political figures converted into "celebrities" like film actors, pop singers, or television wrestlers (and political figures might even be actors, singers, or wrestlers) whose scandalous doings might be more likely to be under discussion than their policies.

(6) Rather than enhance citizen participation in public life, the new media may provide merely another distraction from active engagement.

CONCLUSION

In considering the social impact of the new communications technology, it seems important to note that actual and potential uses of such technology can be radically distinct, as indicated by the long history of writing and literacy. Historians may recall the long period in which writing seemed to have primarily served the purposes of administrators before other uses flowered; historians may recall as well the times and places when writing has played far more of a role in stabilizing communal religious tradition than in facilitating individual intellectual innovation. So historians must not presume that any conceivable possible usage of the new technology will of course be realized, but they must also not presume that that the present insignificance of innovative usages negates such potentialities.

Some three and a half decades after the first long-distance computer communication, then, it was still not obvious whether the possibility of a more democratic world was enlarged or diminished as a result of advances in communications technology. In the United States, major political actors, political parties, lobbying organizations, organizers of violence, champions of human rights, racists, and journalists all were making extensive use of the new possibilities to get out their message, to perform research, and to talk to one another, but whether the position of any major participant was thereby significantly advanced or retarded, or whether important new participants were being created, was equally far from clear.

See also other articles in this section.

BIBLIOGRAPHY

Bailie, Mashoed, and Dwayne Winseck, eds. *Democratizing Communication?: Comparative Perspectives on Information and Power.* Creskill, N.J., 1997.

Brook, James, and Iain A. Boal, eds. *Resisting the Virtual Life: The Culture and Politics of Information.* San Francisco, 1995.

Cairncross, Frances. *The Death of Distance: How the Communications Revolution Will Change Our Lives.* Boston, 1997.

Calhoun, Craig. "Community without Propinquity Revisited: Communications Technology and the Transformation of the Urban Public Sphere." *Sociological Inquiry* 68 (1998): 373–397.

Castells, Manuel. *The Rise of the Network Society.* Cambridge, Mass., 1996.

Cerf, Vinton. "A Brief History of the Internet and Related Networks." Available on line at: http://www.isoc.org/internet-history/cerf.htn.

Cerulo, Karen A., Janet M. Ruane, and Mary Chayko. "Technological Ties that Bind: Media Generated Primary Groups." *Communication Research* 19 (1992): 109–129.

Cerulo, Karen A., ed. "Technologically Generated Communities." Special sections of *Sociological Inquiry* 67 (1997): 48–118; 68 (1998): 372–425.

Collins, Richard, and Cristina Murroni. *New Media, New Policies: Media and Communications: Strategies for the Future.* Cambridge, Mass., 1996.

Dery, Mark, ed. *Flame Wars. The Discourse of Cyberculture.* Durham, N.C., 1994.

Ferrarotti, Franco. *The End of Conversation: The Impact of Mass Media on Modern Society.* New York, 1988.

Fischer, Claude. "Technology and Community: Historical Complexities." *Sociological Inquiry* 67 (1997): 112–118.

Ganley, Gladys D. *The Exploding Political Power of Personal Media.* Norwood, N.J., 1992.

Goody, Jack. *The Logic of Writing and the Organization of Society.* Cambridge, Mass., 1987.

Graff, Harvey. *The Legacies of Literacy: Continuities and Contradictions in Western Culture and Society.* Bloomington, Ind., 1987.

Hauben, Michael. *History of ARPANET.* Available online at http://www.dei.isep.ipp.pt/docs/arpa.html.

Hobart, Michael E., and Zachary S. Schiffman. *Information Ages: Literacy, Numeracy and the Computer Revolution.* Baltimore, 1998.

Kurland, D. Midian, Catherine A. Clement, Ronald Mawby, and Roy D. Pea. "Mapping the Cognitive Demands of Learning to Program." In *Mirrors of Minds: Patterns of Experience in Educational Computing,* edited by Roy D. Pea and Karen Sheingold, 103–127. Norwood, N.J., 1987.

Leitner, Barry M., Vinton G. Cerf, David D. Clark, Robert E. Kahn, Leonard Kleinrock, Daniel C. Lynch, Jon Postel, Larry G. Roberts, and Stephen Wolf. *A Brief History of the Internet.* Version 3.1. 1998. Available online at: http://www.isoc.org/internet-history/brief.htn.

Markley, Robert. *Virtual Realities and Their Discontents.* Baltimore, 1996.

Markoff, John. "Some Effects of Literacy in Eighteenth Century France." *Journal of Interdisciplinary History* 17 (1986): 311–333.

Mitchell, William J. *City of Bits: Space, Place, and the Infobahn.* Cambridge, Mass., 1995.

Splichal, Slavko, Andrew Calabrese, and Colin Sparks, eds. *Information Society and Civil Society: Contemporary Perspectives on the Changing World Order.* West Lafayette, Ind., 1994.

De Sola Pool, Ithiel. *Politics in Wired Nations: Selected Writings of Ithiel de Sola Pool.* New Brunswick, N.J., 1998.

Portes, Alejandro. "Transnational Communities: Their Emergence and Significance in the Contemporary World-System." In *Latin America in the World-Economy,* edited by Roberto Patricio Korzeniewicz and William C. Smith, 151–158. Westport, Conn., 1996.

Rheingold, Howard. *The Virtual Community: Homesteading on the Electronic Frontier.* New York, 1993.

Robertson, Roland. *Globalization: Social Theory and Global Culture.* London, 1992.

Rosenberg, Richard S. *The Social Impact of Computers.* Boston, 1992.

Sanger, Jack, with Jane Wilson, Bryn Davies, and Roger Whitaker. *Young Children, Videos, and Computer Games: Issues for Teachers and Parents.* London, 1997.

Sassen, Saskia. *Globalization and its Discontents: Essays On the New Mobility of People and Money.* New York, 1998.

Sheingold, Karen, Laura M. W. Martin, and Mari E. Endreweit. "Preparing Urban Teachers for the Technological Future." In *Mirrors of Minds: Patterns of Experience in Educational Computing,* edited by Roy D. Pea and Karen Sheingold, 67–85. Norwood, N.J., 1987.

Turkle, Sherry. *The Second Self: Computers and the Human Spirit.* New York, 1984.

Virnoche, Mary E., and Gary T. Marx. "'Only Connect'—E. M. Forster in an Age of Electronic Communication: A Case Study of the Establishment of an Electronic Network." *Sociological Inquiry* 67 (1997): 85–100.

Walther, Joseph B. "Interpersonal Effects in Computer-Mediated Interaction: A Relational Perspective." *Communication Research* 19 (1992): 52–90.

Winston, Brian. *Media, Technology, and Society: A History; From the Telegraph to the Internet.* London, 1998.

JOURNALS OF OPINION

Robert S. Fogarty

Magazines have existed in the United States since Benjamin Franklin published his *American Magazine, or a Monthly View of the Political State of the British Colonies* in 1741, but they were few in number and influence in colonial America. During the antebellum period various periodicals emphasized literary and social issues (such as the *United States Magazine, Democratic Review,* and the *Dial*), others advocated particular causes (such as *DeBow's Review,* which urged secession), and yet others were general cultural magazines (*Godey's Lady's Book*) that attempted to reach a broad audience. Newspapers and pamphlets were the primary vehicles for political discourse; with the founding of the *Nation* in 1865, however, a new kind of publication was launched. What became known as the "journal of opinion" first took shape in New York City to aid the cause of freedmen.

THE NATION

The *Nation* is usually twinned with the *New Republic* when one thinks of contemporary political magazines because they both grew out of specific economic, social, and historical circumstances and were formed in response to a perceived crisis. The *Nation* was founded by the journalist E. L. Godkin (editor 1865–1881) to "discuss the topics of the day, and, above all, of legal, economical, and constitutional questions, with greater accuracy, and moderation than are now to be found in the daily press" (Prospectus for the *Nation,* 6 July 1868). The Civil War had stirred up emotions, divided the nation, and wrecked the southern economy.

The *Nation* hoped to heal the wounds of the war, protect the interests of the recently freed slaves, and offer vital and accurate information about the "condition of the laboring class at the South." Yet it professed that it would "not be the organ of any party, sect, or body. It will, on occasion, make an earnest effort to bring to the discussion of political and so-

cial questions a really critical spirit, and to wage war upon the vices of violence, exaggeration and misrepresentation." (ibid).

The *Nation* (as its title indicates) was to have a broader scope than political and economic commentary and promised to contain "sound and impartial criticism and works of art." The original financial backers of the *Nation* included the Boston abolitionist George Luther Stearns and James Miller McKim, one of the founders of the American Anti-Slavery Society and the Boston-based Loyal Publication Society, which distributed newspapers, pamphlets, and broadsides favorable to the Union cause free of charge to newspaper editors. Henry James Sr., the noted Swedenborgian philosopher, appeared in the first issues, as did his son, the famous writer Henry James. The latter found a regular place in the magazine's pages, appearing over two hundred times. His essay, "Saratoga," praised the spa's character and noted that women dressed "for everyone" and hence they dressed "for no one" (3 August 1870). His brother, the philosopher William James, wrote about French and German philosophy for the magazine.

Though the magazine was passionate about the cause of freedom for blacks, it had little sympathy for anarchists (Godkin called for the hanging of Chicago's Haymarket Square anarchists in 1887), opposed trade unions, and attacked socialists. It was, in short, a liberal magazine devoted to free trade ("John Stuart Mill was our prophet," Godkin wrote, "and Grote and Bentham our daily food"), civic reform, and moral values. During its early years it championed tariff reform, civil service reform, and proportional representation. From 1881 to 1914 it was part of the larger *New York Evening Post* and during the 1890s the magazine was a stalwart of anti-imperialist sentiment.

Under the guidance of Oswald Garrison Villard from 1918 to 1932, the *Nation* emerged as a distinctive, sharp-tongued journal. Villard was a pacifist, a founder of the Anti-Imperialist League and an advocate of civil rights for blacks. Under his stewardship the *Nation* supported the goals of the NAACP, denounced the Treaty of Versailles, and supported the American Civil Liberties Union, which Villard helped to found in 1920. H. L. Mencken joined the *Nation* in 1921 as a contributing editor. The publication also opened its pages to the black intellectual W. E. B. Du Bois, covered the Passaic, New Jersey, textile strikes in 1925, and in 1926 ran Langston Hughes's commentary on the Harlem Renaissance, "The Negro Artist and the Racial Mountain." Villard had a large hand in organizing the Citizens National Committee for Sacco and Vanzetti, and the magazine covered their trial closely.

Throughout the 1920s the *Nation*'s editor Freda Kirchwey (who would later become publisher) wrote about women's rights (particularly reproductive rights). During the 1930s Mary McCarthy contributed essays and in 1937 Margaret Marshall began her tenure as the literary editor, which lasted until 1953. James T. Farrell ("The Fall of Joe Louis," 1936), John Dos Passos ("Big Parade–1936 Model," 1936), and George S. Kaufman ("Einstein in Hollywood," 1938) wrote commentaries during the 1930s. By 1937 its circulation had grown to 43,000 and it had a regular, committed audience. Villard's pacifism and the events leading up to World War II split the editorial staff. In 1940 he stopped writing for the *Nation* and it became, under Freda Kirchwey's direction, an antifascist journal. The finances of the magazine were perilous in the 1940s and 1950s and discussions were held about a merger with the *New Republic,* but nothing came of them.

Kirchwey gave way to Carey McWilliams in 1955. Writing about the latter's tenure, his successor, Victor Navasky, wrote that

> McWilliams always insisted that he was not an innovator—that *The Nation* he ran from 1955 to 1975 was informed primarily by his study of Godkin's conception of a journal of opinion. . . . McWilliams also insisted *The Nation* was not a "news" magazine, that its destiny and strength had to do with ideas, with opinion journalism, with exploring the meaning of events rather than reporting them. (vanden Heuvel, 1990, p. 525)

During the late 1950s and early 1960s the *Nation* published Dalton Trumbo's essay on blacklisting and Fred Cook's investigations of the FBI and CIA. It was, early on, opposed to America's role in Vietnam. Some of the best and most scholarly pieces to come out of the antiwar movement appeared in the *Nation.*

Victor Navasky became editor in 1978 (when circulation was at 100,000) and continued the mag-

azine's emphasis on defending the First Amendment issues, promoting racial justice, and critically examining government intrusions into the political life of the nation. The *Nation* was among the few political magazines that promoted the cause of poetry after the 1920s, including an annual award for the best collection submitted by a young poet. W. S. Merwin was once poetry editor and Grace Schulman had long held the post by the end of the twentieth century. Writing 125 years after the founding of the magazine, the editor Katrina vanden Heuvel indicated that the magazine's commitments had been steadfast, including "passionate support for civil rights and civil liberties, opposition to racism in all its guises, and unrelenting struggle against militarism, imperialism, corruption, and abuse of power" (p. xv). From the early years of the twentieth century, the *Nation* was the quintessential liberal magazine, adding a pro-union stance, among changes, to Godkin's commitments. Two of its modern editors, McWilliams and Navasky, argued that what held the *Nation* together (despite its financial and editorial problems) could be found in its "moral view." On 18 June 1908 the magazine had editorialized that

> there is no force so potent in politics as a moral issue. Politicians may scorn it, ambitious men may despise it or fight shy of it, newspapers may caricature or misrepresent it; but it has a way of confounding the plans of those who pride themselves on their astuteness and rendering powerless the most formidable enginery of party or boss.

THE NEW REPUBLIC

When the editors of the *New Republic* published their twenty-fifth anniversary issue in 1939, they featured the work of sixteen distinguished intellectuals who had appeared in its pages since its founding. These included the critic Archibald MacLeish, the historian Charles A. Beard, the novelist Thomas Mann, the labor leader Sidney Hillman, and the politician Henry Wallace. This mix of literary and political figures represented the views of a journal founded in the pivotal year of 1914 as "A Journal of Opinion Which Seeks the Challenge of a New Time." Its opening editorial statement on 7 November 1914 had proclaimed:

> *The New Republic* is frankly an experiment. It is an attempt to find a national audience for a journal of interpretation and opinion. . . . When the plan of *The New Republic* was being discussed it received spontaneous welcome from people in all parts of the country. They differed in theories and programs;

but they agreed that if *The New Republic* could bring sufficient enlightenment to the problems of the nation and sufficient sympathy to its complexities, it would serve all who feel the challenge of the time. On the conviction that this is possible *The New Republic* is founded. . . . We set out with faith. (p. 1)

The term "journal of opinion" signified to its readers that it was going to have views (progressive in this case), and that it was going to make an impression (upon Washington, D.C., and upon policy-makers), and that it would articulate a new belief system (a liberal one) for new times.

The magazine had been formally launched at a dinner at the Players Club in New York City, with the notable figures in attendance including Willard Straight, its benefactor; Learned Hand, the distinguished jurist; and Walter Lippmann, the journalist. Also in attendance at the dinner was Herbert Croly, whose monumental work, *The Promise of American Life* (1909), was the intellectual bible of the magazine and who was the magazine's first editor. The *New Republic* was the "voice of Eastern, metropolitan progressivism. It was intellectual, stylish, urbane—remote in mood, if not in politics, from the evangelical progressives of La Follette in Wisconsin or Hiram Johnson in California" (in Lucas, p. 25), according to Arthur Schlesinger Jr. In the 1920s, with progressivism waning as a political force, the magazine attacked "Babbittry" and embraced the arts and an emerging critical culture. Cultural critic Edmund Wilson became an editor in 1925. Virginia Woolf's "Genius" appeared in 1926; T. S. Eliot's review of Julien Benda's *The Treason of the Intellectuals* (1928) two years later; and Robert Penn Warren's poem, "Kentucky Mountain Farm," in 1930.

Writing about Croly, the founding editor Felix Frankfurter said he "would frequently talk about the 'purging of personalities from opinion'" (in Conklin, p. 343). The *New Republic* showcased opinion rather than personalities even though there were powerful figures associated with the magazine. Fine writing was often featured, with Jonathan Mitchell's 1935 "Joe Louis Never Smiles" being one of the best essays of the decade. In November 1938 it ran an impassioned editorial concerned with refugees from Nazi, Germany, "Let the Jews Come In," that signaled its continuous concern about social questions in an international perspective. With the outbreak of World War II the magazine urged the country to unite in democratic solidarity against fascist power and aggression. Henry Wallace became its editor in 1947 and eulogized President Franklin Roosevelt for his emphasis on progressive values and action. In the post-1945 period the magazine focused on the growth of McCarthyism and championed Adlai Stevenson as the standard bearer of the Democratic Party in 1952 and 1956. It also began to devote more space to the arts and literature. Delmore Schwartz wrote about film and Malcolm Cowley about literature; in one issue (in 1964) it featured essays by the journalist Murray Kempton, the theater critic Robert Brustein, the historian Gertrude Himmelfarb, and the film critic Stanley Kauffmann.

During the 1960s the magazine supported John F. Kennedy over Stevenson for the Democratic presidential nomination and reemphasized the magazine's concerns about race, economics, and world affairs. However, with the rise of the so-called New Left, the *New Republic* began to separate itself from the emerging radical-liberal perspective. With the purchase of the magazine in 1974 by Martin Peretz, there was a concerted effort to return the magazine to certain liberal cultural and political values during a period when black nationalism and interest group politics had emerged as dominant forces. Under the direction of Michael Kinsley, Morton Kondracke, and Leon Wieseltier it moved rightward and critics complained that it had taken a conservative, anti-communist stance on foreign policy. Although critical of Ronald Reagan's domestic agenda it supported some of his other initiatives. For example, an editorial on 24 March 1986 stated: "We believe that preventing the establishment of a Leninist dictatorship in Nicaragua is a goal worthy of support" (in Wickenden, p. 502). Throughout this period (as Dorothy Wickenden reported) the *New Republic* criticized a tendency within the Democratic Party to substitute "interest group politics for ideological integrity, becoming nothing more than a mix of independent and heterogeneous principalities with interests so divided it can't be called a coalition."

DISSENT

Founded as a magazine of socialist opinion in 1954 by the critic Irving Howe at the suggestion of the sociologist Lewis Coser, *Dissent* was the outgrowth of sectarian disputes within the communist and socialist movements, serving primarily a vehicle for radicals in New York City disenchanted with Stalinist policies. There had been earlier magazines devoted to the socialist cause, including the famous *Appeal to Reason,* founded in 1895 and reaching a circulation of 750,000 in 1912, and magazines like the *New Masses* (1926) that had a literary and political agenda. *Dissent* was intent on forging a "new" socialist identity during the cold war that would address discrete social issues without having to resort to "blueprints, elaborate schemes." In the second number of the magazine, Coser and Howe wrote that "the aim of socialism is to create a society of cooperation, but not necessarily, or at least not universally, of harmony. Cooperation is compatible with conflict, is indeed inconceivable without conflict, while harmony implies a stasis." There were three "modern" questions the magazine expected to explore: bureaucracy ("bureaucratization signifies a deformation, though not necessarily a destruction, of democratic processes"); planning and centralization ("From what we can learn about Stalinist 'planning' we see that an economic plan does not work, it quickly breaks down, if arbitrarily imposed from above, and hedged in with regard to specifications which allow for none of the flexibility, none of the economic play, that a democratic society requires"); and work and leisure ("No Marxist concept has been more fruitful than that of 'alienation.'"; all of above in Mills, pp. 38, 40, 42).

Michael Harrington, the social critic and author of *The Other America* (1962), wrote that even though *Dissent* had been an heir to a European socialist tradition, it was eager to examine issues relevant to the American condition:

> When *Dissent* broke with failed world views and began to confront specific problems of socialism in crisis, there was a certain creative rediscovery of what was wrong with America. It was no longer possible, so to speak, to live off the European socialist inheritance. So it was that the magazine published a wide ranging series of analyses of the American power structure (including notable contributions by C. Wright Mills). (in Irving Howe, ed. *The Radical Imagination* [New York, 1955], p. 3)

The magazine was based in New York City and often ran articles of local interest, such as the failure of the public schools to educate, race relations in the city, and cultural events. Yet it paid more attention to events in Prague than in Queens or Omaha and that focus represented the interests of its urban, intellectual, socialist editorial board.

Dissent had an internationalist agenda and writers from Europe regularly appeared: Ignazio Silone in 1955 ("The Choice of Comrades"); Erazin Kohari in 1969 ("Requiem for Utopia"); Andrei Sinyavsky in 1984 ("Dissent as a Personal Experience"); and Günter Grass in 1993 ("On Loss: The Condition of Germany"). Despite the political emphasis of the magazine, Howe was able to publish some distinguished cultural criticism from writers as diverse as Norman Mailer ("The White Negro") in 1957, Paul

Goodman ("Growing Up Absurd") in 1960, and Todd Gitlin ("The Rise of 'Identity Politics'") in 1993.

Dissent also devoted many pages to discussion of the contentious issue of race. Martin Kilson's "The New Black Intellectuals" appeared in 1969, Henry Louis Gates Jr.'s "Blackness without Blood" in 1989, William Julius Wilson's "American Social Policy and the Ghetto Underclass" in 1988, and Cornel West's "Nihilism in Black America" in 1991.

The term "struggle" appeared with great regularity in *Dissent* pieces since a neo-Marxist dialectic informed all discussions. In 1993 Irving Howe (during the year of his death) noted in "Two Cheers For Utopia" that he was living in an "exhausted" age where there was a growing realization that the historical legacy of Communism had been disastrous, and where conservative forces were on the rise throughout the world, particularly in America. Socialism had become a pale imitation of its glorious past, but he still held out hope for the future: "We Dissenters, the handful of us, try to hold fast to a vision of social transformation. . . . You want to call us utopians? That's fine with me" (Mills, p. 461).

NATIONAL REVIEW

A conservative journal of opinion, the *National Review* was founded in 1955 by William F. Buckley Jr., a thirty-year-old graduate of Yale who had published in 1951 an attack on his alma mater in *God and Man at Yale: The Superstitions of Academic Freedom*. Buckley charged that Yale (and the other Ivy League schools) had a bias against religion and for socialism. Buckley hoped to make the magazine the centerpiece for all conservative thought (libertarian, anticommunist, traditionalist) and to fight back against what he saw as the overwhelming preponderance of liberalism's intellectual strength in journals of opinion. By his count the liberals had eight journals at their command while the conservatives had none. "They know the power of ideas, and it is largely for this reason," Buckley wrote, "that socialist-liberal forces have made such a great headway in the past thirty years."

Among the early contributors to the magazine were ex-communists and ex-Trotskyists (James Burnham, Max Eastman, Whittaker Chambers), libertarians (John Chamberlain, Frank Chodorov), and traditionalists (Russell Kirk, Donald Davidson). The opening editorial stated their opposition to Communism and big government and their support for the free market system and individual values. According to one historian, "Buckley proclaimed, in the first issue," that the *National Review* "stands athwart history yelling Stop," and by 1958 Buckley could proudly write that:

> National Review has entered the mainstream of American thought, and is now an institutional fact of American life. It is no longer a new and experimental magazine. It is no longer a flash fire by the Neanderthal Right. It is the voice of American conservatism, and more and more it is recognized as such. (in Nash, p. 148)

In the early years, disputes between the various factions of the conservative movement surfaced in

the magazine's letters column and in sharp reviews such as Whittaker Chambers's negative critique of Ayn Rand's *Atlas Shrugged* (1957) ("Big Sister Is Watching You"). John Chamberlain and Russell Kirk thought the book had merit, while Chambers deplored its godless character. The Eisenhower administration was too liberal for the *National Review* group, which tried to stiffen the backs of conservatives all over the country by opposing liberalizing and centralizing trends such as the growing power of the centralized state and the power of the liberal press. There was a distinct Catholic presence in the

Commonweal. Edited by laypeople, *Commonweal* operated independently of the U.S. Catholic hierarchy. © 1998 COMMONWEAL FOUNDATION, REPRINTED WITH PERMISSION

magazine, with Buckley and Frank Meyer, a convert, using classical Thomist arguments to bolster their political cases. Max Eastman left the magazine in 1958 because of its "religious" orientation. Libertarians charged that the *National Review,* because of its vigorous anticommunist stance at home and abroad, was "willing to squelch civil liberties at home . . . tended to be arrogant about its Christianity and willing to merge Church and State . . . [and] exalted the community over the individual . . ." (in Nash, *The Conservative,* p. 159).

The magazine maintained active contact with correspondents in Europe and featured Continental conservatives like Otto von Habsburg (heir to the Austro-Hungarian throne). The invasion of Hungary in 1956 by Soviet troops solidified the bond with Europe and strengthened the magazine's commitment to the eradication of Communism at home and abroad. While looking overseas for culture and tradition, the editors were sympathetic to "displaced" Americans like the Southern Agrarians. The *National Review* was critical of integrationist efforts by the federal government and the courts to impose their will on the states. Also, the civil rights demonstrations of the early 1960s were seen as misplaced liberal efforts to achieve integration. According to the *National Review* the way to emancipation was through hard work and discipline, not government handouts and programs. During the 1960 election the magazine declined to support either John F. Kennedy or Richard Nixon. Revolutionary forces in Africa in the 1960s (Angola, the Congo) were depicted as disorderly, Soviet-sponsored movements intent on dismantling an orderly structure. The United Nations' role in the Congo and nearly all other UN activities were roundly condemned. In 1961 the publication attacked the liberal papal encyclical of Pope John XXIII "Mater et Magistra" as a "venture in triviality" and issued a rhetorical rebuff: "Mater, si; Magistra, no." Barry Goldwater's 1964 campaign received enthusiastic support from the magazine, which also promoted the Young Americans for Freedom.

By 1970 the *National Review,* with 100,000 subscribers, felt that the tide was turning in its direction. With the landslide election of Ronald Reagan to the presidency in 1980, conservatives moved into the White House once again. The *National Review* had played a large part in raising conservative issues, keeping the conservative flame alive, and enlarging conservatism's sphere of influence.

Journals of opinion founded in the twentieth century appealed to religious groups (*Commonweal* for Catholics, the *Christian Century* for Protestants, *Commentary* for Jews, the *Rutherford Institute Report* for evangelicals) and others (for example, the *Crisis* for blacks, *Ms.* for women), but each publication mirrored the style and format of the *Nation,* the *New Republic, Dissent,* and the *National Review.* All spoke to contemporary issues and attempted to forge a link with a disaffected audience, turn the political dialogue in a new direction, and sway public and intellectual opinion. These journals of opinion were characterized by reportorial fact gathering, a polemical approach to public issues, and concern with matters of taste and literature.

See also **The Print Revolution; Rhetoric and Belles Lettres; Radical Alternatives** *(volume 1);* **The Struggle for the Academy** *(volume 2);* **Periodicals; Marxist Approaches** *(in this volume); and other articles in this section.*

BIBLIOGRAPHY

Bender, Thomas. *New York Intellect: A History of Intellectual Life in New York City, from 1750 to the Beginnings of Our Own Time.* New York, 1987.

Buckley, William F., Jr. *A Hymnal: The Controversial Arts.* New York, 1978.

Conklin, Groff, ed. *The New Republic Anthology, 1915–1935.* New York, 1936.

Cruse, Harold. *The Crisis of the Negro Intellectual.* New York, 1967.

Fleming, Donald, and Bernard Bailyn, eds. *The Intellectual Migration: Europe and America, 1930–1960.* Cambridge, Mass., 1968.

Gorman, Paul R. *Left Intellectuals and Popular Culture in Twentieth-Century America.* Chapel Hill, N.C., 1996.

Howe, Irving, ed. *The Radical Imagination. An Anthology from* Dissent *Magazine.* Introduction by Michael Harrington. New York, 1967.

Jacoby, Russell. *The Last Intellectuals: American Culture in the Age of Academe.* New York, 1987.

Jordan, Patrick, and Paul Baumann, eds. Commonweal *Confronts the Century: Liberal Convictions, Catholic Traditions.* New York, 1999.

Luce, Robert B., ed. *The Faces of Five Decades: Selections from Fifty Years of the* New Republic, *1914–1964.* New York, 1964.

Mills, Nicolaus, ed. *Legacy of Dissent: Forty Years of Writing from* Dissent *Magazine.* New York, 1994.

Mott, Frank Luther. *A History of American Magazines.* 5 vols. Cambridge, Mass., 1938–1968.

Nash, George H. *The Conservative Intellectual Movement in the United States, since 1945.* New York, 1976.

Pells, Richard. *The Liberal Mind in a Conservative Age: American Intellectuals in the 1940s and 1950s.* New York, 1985.

Peterson, Theodore. *Magazines in the Twentieth Century.* 2d ed. Urbana, Ill., 1964.

Phillips, William. *A Partisan View: Five Decades of the Literary Life.* New York, 1983.

Phillips, William, and Philip Rahv, eds. The Partisan Review *Anthology.* New York, 1962.

vanden Heuvel, Katrina, ed. The Nation, *1865–1990: Selections from the Independent Magazine of Politics and Change.* New York, 1990.

Wald, Alan. *The New York Intellectuals: The Rise and Decline of the Anti-Stalinist Left from the 1930s to the 1980s.* Chapel Hill, N.C. 1987.

Wickenden, Dorothy, ed. The New Republic *Reader.* New York, 1994.

Part 16

THE ARTS AND CULTURAL EXPRESSION

Part 16, *continued*

BOOKS

Paul Gutjahr

EARLY AMERICA

Americans have long been distinguished by their love of books. From the Bible's incalculable influence on almost every American institution to the 19 million copies of Dr. Spock's *Baby and Child Care* (1946; seventh edition, 1998), which proved central to twentieth-century American notions of child care, books have played a pivotal role in forming and framing almost every aspect of American society. It is remarkable that fewer than one hundred years after Johannes Gutenberg's invention of a printing press using movable type, the Italian printer Juan Pablos set up shop in Mexico City, producing his first book in 1539. There is some evidence that other books may have appeared as early as 1535 in Mexico City, but Pablos was the first printer to produce a large variety of books in the Northern Hemisphere, publishing thirty-seven different titles by the time he died in 1560. Not surprisingly, Pablos printed mostly religious books, which were Roman Catholic in their orientation. Both Catholics and Protestants were among the first to see the opportunities afforded by printing in the Americas, and while religious publishing in Mexico and the Southwest remained small in the decades that followed, the influx of Protestants in the American Northeast provided the cornerstone of the country's commitment to books and the printed word.

The history of books in colonial America cannot be separated from a history of literacy. Colonial literacy rates—particularly in the northeastern region—were among the highest in the world. Prior to 1700 the dense populations of English Puritan immigrants in the Northeast were responsible for literacy rates that ranged from 60 percent for white males to 40 percent for white females. Puritans had come to the American colonies to set up a new kind of theocratic commonwealth based on tenets found in the Bible. So important was the Bible to their way of life that Puritans believed that everyone should be able to read it, and as early as 1642 the colonists set up laws mandating literacy education for their young.

Although literacy rates were extremely high in the Northeast, colonial printing enterprises were still in a primitive state of development. Throughout the seventeenth and eighteenth centuries the majority of books found in the colonies were imported from Europe. Printing was an expensive business demanding good quality raw materials such as paper, type, and ink, resources not readily available in most American towns and villages. Book printing did commence in the colonies, however, in the seventeenth century, when the Reverend Josse Glover and Stephen Day brought the first printing press to Massachusetts in 1638. Glover had died on the voyage over to the colonies, but his widow, Day, and Day's sons set up the press and began printing material in 1639. The first extant book from this period is the *Whole Booke of Psalmes* (or the *Bay Psalm Book*), a quarto work comprising 148 leaves published in 1640.

While the American production of books and literacy rates steadily grew throughout the seventeenth century, it would be misleading to say that American reading led to wide-scale change in American ideology. Most of seventeenth-century American printed material was used to reinforce the religious standards and beliefs held by the community, not to introduce radical new ways of thinking. The reading of this period was of an intensive variety that had Americans reading a few texts— such as the Bible, prayer books, and religious sermons—over and over again. American magistrates and educators were also aware that print was a powerful medium that demanded careful monitoring. Printed material could be used to shape public opinion and public policy, and colonial governing officers demanded that everyone who owned a printing press have the local government's permission to operate it.

While seventeenth-century authorities took pains to regulate printing, there was not an abundance

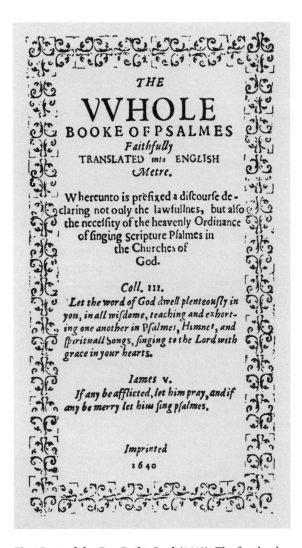

First Page of the *Bay Psalm Book* (1640). The first book printed and entirely written in the English colonies. The preface is generally attributed to Richard Mather, although a case has been made for John Cotton's authorship. AMERICAN ANTIQUARIAN SOCIETY

of such material being produced in the colonies. Throughout the seventeenth and eighteenth centuries, books remained scarce and precious commodities in America. Only a small percentage of Americans owned more than one or two books, and many Americans owned no books at all. As a consequence, books came to be more than simply a medium for the dissemination of information; they became cultural markers as well. Prior to the American Revolution ministers, large landowners, and lawyers were often the colonists who owned the greatest number of books. The possession and careful display of these books helped mark these men as learned, refined, and often wealthy members of their communities. Books could thus be "read" on

a number of levels in early American society, a fact that remains true today as people still swear on the Bible in American courtrooms and buy large sets of leather-bound "classics" to display in their homes. Americans have long read the outside as well as the inside of books, allowing books to take on roles of symbolic as well as informational importance.

THE EIGHTEENTH CENTURY

By the eighteenth century colonial book production had spread from the seventeenth-century center of Boston to Philadelphia and New York City and gradually to the remainder of the original thirteen colonies. The southern colonies were among the slowest to obtain significant printing enterprises, depending both on Europe and the North to supply most of their books. This trend in American publishing continued into the twenty-first century, with most major American publishers located in the northern portion of the country, the majority of these clustered in the Northeast. Exceptions are few, but there were publishing enterprises in New Orleans; Charleston, South Carolina; and Nashville, Tennessee.

Perhaps the most stunning publishing event of the eighteenth century was the publication in January 1776 of Thomas Paine's *Common Sense*, which burst like a lightning bolt on the publishing horizon. In an era where the common press run for books was often fewer than two thousand copies, *Common Sense* sold 120,000 copies in its first three months. Within a few years, one copy of this book circulated for every five inhabitants of the colonies. No political booklet in the colonies had ever experienced such popularity. *Common Sense* is important because it participated in an ever-growing political print culture that helped significantly reshape the political landscape in North America beginning in the 1770s.

Common Sense is also important because it stands as a vivid example of how American print culture was reaching beyond its predominantly religious heritage. This new print culture involved increasing and diversified types of printed material, which in turn led to patterns of more extensive reading. While Americans still read a few texts repeatedly, they increasingly read a wider variety of books, newspapers, almanacs, journals, and tracts as this material became available. The United States was undergoing a revolution in terms of printed material, which began with the American Revolution itself.

THE NINETEENTH CENTURY

The printing revolution that Paine did much to create in the late eighteenth century hit its stride in the 1820s, when a number of factors combined to help American publishing grow exponentially. Whereas printed material in the United States remained relatively scarce at the close of the eighteenth century, publishers congratulated themselves in 1853 with the news that the industry was growing at a pace ten times that of the general population. The factors that led to such incredible growth are diverse and include new papermaking technology, spearheaded by the Fourdrinier papermaking machine; the stereotyping process, which replaced the tedious and expensive method of setting type for each edition of a book; the introduction of power presses that greatly increased the number of pages that could be printed in an hour; a change from leather to cloth binding, which allowed publishers to produce books more quickly and at less cost; a substantial growth in the number of libraries and schools in the country; and the growth of the U.S. canal and railroad network, which opened new markets for the sale of books.

There were also important changes in literacy in the first half of the nineteenth century, which coincided with changes in the production and distribution of books. While literacy among white males in the North had hovered around 90 percent since the American Revolution, this high literacy rate was finally matched by northern white women by the time of the Civil War. A number of factors drove this increase in literacy rates, most notably the democratic ideology tied to the fact that the United States was still a young experiment in democracy, one that many thought would not survive unless its citizens were both virtuous and well informed.

Books were considered critical avenues to virtue and information. Religious reading remained strong throughout the antebellum period, causing the French writer and politician Alexis de Tocqueville to comment in 1835 of Americans in the 1830s that they did not turn to their business ledgers at the end of the day but to their Bibles. Information for these virtuous citizens came through a number of printed sources, including newspapers, tracts, and books. Americans placed great importance on educating their children, a sentiment captured in 1826 by Governor DeWitt Clinton of New York when he addressed his state's legislature: "A general diffusion of knowledge is the precursor and protector of republican institutions; and in it we must confide as the conservative power that will watch over our liberties" (quoted in Welter, *American Writings on Public Education*, p. 24).

Along with a belief in literacy as a means to a solid citizenry, Americans wanted to read for other reasons as well. The ability to read helped a person secure a better job in a society that was increasingly industrializing and was thus creating a new nonfarming class of nonmanual labor. Reading also allowed one to attain certain markers of refinement. Nineteenth-century college curriculums were replete with training in the Latin and Greek classics, and knowing such works was a widely recognized sign of elite social and educational status. As a self-identifying middle class was beginning to appear before the Civil War, being able to read and what one read became markers of being a member of this emerging class. It also should come as no surprise that reading became a means of recreation. Americans read voraciously in this regard, especially favoring history books, travel narratives, and novels. Novels were so popular, in fact, that titles such as *The Wide, Wide World* (1850) by Susan Warner, *The Lamplighter* (1854) by Maria Cummins, and *Uncle Tom's Cabin* (1852) by Harriet Beecher Stowe all sold more than 100,000 copies each.

It is worthy of note that while *Common Sense*, the work that rocked the political world of the late eighteenth century, was only forty-seven pages long, Stowe's *Uncle Tom's Cabin*, perhaps the most significant piece of political writing to take book form in the nineteenth century, was published in two volumes of more than six hundred pages. The physical differences between these two titles are important. While paper and other publishing resources were scarce at the time of the American Revolution, by the Civil War printing had changed to such a degree that large volumes could be mass produced and mass distributed in ways that reached an entire nation of readers—readers who were almost equal parts men and women. *Common Sense* was written by a man for men. *Uncle Tom's Cabin* was written by a woman, but it electrified the nation's political world by influencing readers of both sexes. *Uncle Tom's Cabin* clearly demonstrates that both the physical book and the audience for books had grown and changed significantly by the mid-nineteenth century.

With this antebellum print revolution, several of the country's great publishing houses emerged. First and foremost was the firm of Harper and Brothers, which was founded in 1817 and eventually eclipsed Carey, Lea, and Blanchard of Philadelphia as the premier book publisher in the nation. Other major houses to emerge in this period included John Wiley

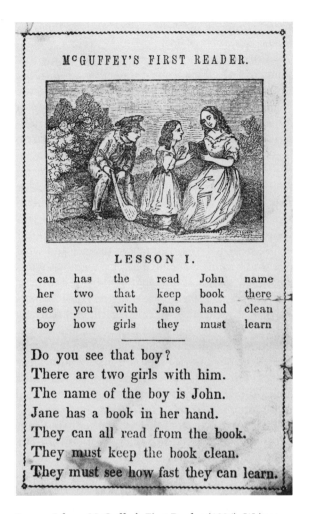

Lesson I from McGuffey's First Reader (1836). Written by William Holmes McGuffey for several different levels, the McGuffey Readers taught millions to read.
© BETTMANN/CORBIS

and Sons; Putnam; Appleton; Baker and Scribner; E. P. Dutton; J. B. Lippincott Company; Houghton Mifflin; Little, Brown; Ticknor and Fields; and G. and C. Merriam.

Not only were many of the country's major printing houses established during these years, but certain trends in publishing also were established. Alongside the tremendous growth in the American appetite for novels, two other trends in the antebellum years are worthy of notice. First, the largest portion of the book market during this period was the school textbook market, comprising about 40 percent of books sold. The McGuffey Readers alone sold 47 million copies between 1836 and 1870. The dominance of the school market was still true at the end of the twentieth century, comprising roughly three-quarters of the books published in the United States. Second, rather than religious literature re-

ceding in the ever-diversifying and growing American print marketplace, such literature multiplied at a pace comparable to its competition, so that throughout the early nineteenth century religious literature continued to comprise a large segment of books sold in the United States.

As American book production entered the second half of the nineteenth century, three developments had significant influence on the publishing industry. The first of these was subscription publishing. A method whereby publishers first enlisted subscribers for a certain edition of a book before they printed it to guarantee sales, subscription publishing dated back to the eighteenth century in the United States. While publishers had long used variations on subscription publishing to sell their books, the decade following the Civil War saw the massive multiplication of publishing enterprises bent on selling books by subscription only, bypassing the established book selling outlets of bookstores and book auctions. By the 1870s, fifty thousand door-to-door sales agents had flooded the United States, cutting out traditional publishing middlemen and penetrating areas of the country often unreached by more traditional book selling methods.

The second development was an integration between books and other media. By the 1870s many of the country's major publishers had entered the magazine field, publishing such magazines as *Scribner's Monthly* (1870), *Lippincott's Magazine* (1868), *Harper's Bazaar* (1867), *Harper's Weekly* (1857), *Appleton's Journal* (1869), and *Putnam's Monthly* (1853). Although many of these magazines were short-lived because the publishers simply did not have the resources to sustain such periodicals along with their other publishing endeavors, this diversification served as an initial foray into the field of integrated media endeavors. In much the same way of twentieth-century publishing, these magazines helped advertise the wares and interests of their parent publisher. Consequently, new authors, works, genres, and other products could be given initial or added exposure through a book publisher's magazine.

Another medium that significantly influenced publishing—and served as a vivid precedent for the interaction between books and motion pictures—was the theater. One of the best examples of the symbiotic relationship of book and theatrical play is found in how Lew Wallace's 1880 blockbuster *Ben-Hur* gave birth to a theatrical version in 1899, which was seen by millions of Americans in the next twenty-one years as it played an extended tour on

Broadway and then toured the country in multiple companies. The play and the book played off one another to their mutual benefit. People who were familiar with the book wanted to see the play, and seeing the play made people want to read, or reread, the book.

The third important postbellum print development took the form of cheap, paperback books known as dime novels. Although low-cost fiction was available in the United States as early as the 1840s, it was not until the rise of the dime novel, pioneered as a form in 1860 by Irwin P. Beadle and Company of New York, that American fiction became widely affordable in book form. These books often sold for five to twelve cents, when many hardbound books still sold for more than a dollar. This made hardbound books an extravagance for the average American, costing about a day's wage for a typical male worker and four days' wages for a woman. Largely adventure novels, cheap advice tracts, and travelogues, the American public voraciously consumed dime novels and similar cheap paperbacks, marking a pivotal moment when books other than inexpensive school texts and religious works had become so affordable that they were truly becoming a democratic medium.

THE TWENTIETH CENTURY

One of the most enduring legacies of American book publishing in the early twentieth century was a natural extension of the dime novel. In 1939 Robert De Graff founded Pocket Books, a company dedicated to providing quality literature to the masses by printing pocket-size, paperback editions. While it may be hard to imagine a book market without the pocket paperback, this initial foray into small book publishing was considered by many a foolhardy endeavor. Following the lead of Beadle and Company, De Graff gambled that there was a rich American market for cheap books. He was right. Assuring his readers they were getting unabridged texts for a quarter, the initial sales of Pocket Books were astounding. Sold in train stations, cigar stands, bookstores, and countless other locations, 100,000 Pocket Books flew off the shelves in the first three weeks of their release. A host of firms quickly rose up to compete with Pocket Books in this lucrative new market, including Bantam, Signet, Penguin, and New American Library. Popular literary genres such as the Western, mysteries, science fiction, and self-help books all blossomed in the pocket paperback format.

The paperback market was just one sign of growth in a publishing industry that would explode following World War II. So popular were books and reading in the late 1940s that in 1946 alone seventeen new book clubs and forty-three new publishing houses came into existence. The largest book clubs in operation, the Literary Guild and the Book-of-the-Month Club, which began about two decades before World War II, had a combined membership of three and a half million members by 1946.

The radical growth of American publishing beginning in the 1940s continued up to the 1980s, but these decades were also marked by a growing trend toward mergers between publishers, such as the notable joining of Harper and Row and J. B. Lippincott in 1980. While more than three hundred such publishing mergers took place in the 1960s, almost all of these publishers were merging with other publishers. The nature of these mergers would radically change by the late 1970s and early 1980s, when large corporations such as Viacom and Time Warner began acquiring publishing houses to add to their already diversified list of businesses. Only two large independent publishers would survive this wave of amalgamation, W. W. Norton and Houghton Mifflin. Other large publishing enterprises including HarperCollins, the Penguin Group, Simon and Schuster, and Random House would all be eventually subsumed by larger corporations.

The influence on American book publishing of such corporate acquisition was profound for two reasons. First, the old culture of publishing, which attracted and kept quality people because of their love of books, slowly changed as a more corporate model was instituted that concentrated on financial bottom lines over the quality and coherency of a publisher's list. Second, books were produced and advertised with a great deal more emphasis on their relationship to other media rather than strictly their content.

The celebrity status of authors such as the home and entertaining mogul Martha Stewart, the prominence of news events such as the O. J. Simpson trial, and the motion picture interests of many of these corporations all influenced publishers to produce books that stand in dialogue not so much with other forms of printed material as they do with current events or a corporation's other investments. For example, once the venerable old firm of Little, Brown (established in 1837) was acquired in 1968 by Time Warner, certain changes in their list became pronounced. Books that sell other Time Warner products began to be foregrounded. Biographies of the actress-singer Barbra Streisand and the rock star

BEST-SELLER LISTS IN THE UNITED STATES

In 1895 a small article appeared in the first issue of New York's *The Bookman* magazine entitled "Books in Demand." *The Bookman* collated information from booksellers in sixteen American cities to produce a list of the nation's most popular novels. The best-seller list was born. *The Bookman* added yearly summaries to this list, and eventually these computations took a weekly form. At the end of the twentieth century, the two great lists of best-sellers appeared in the *New York Times Book Review* and the magazine *Publishers Weekly*. Both lists were rather mysterious, however, because neither weekly released the exact methods by which they chose the posted titles. As a consequence, there were claims that these lists were as much promotional devices manipulated by publishers as they were indicators of the public's taste.

In the end, it is hard to know who actually controls the term "best-seller." Is it the publishers who advertise their books as best-sellers? Is it the owners and publishers of best-seller lists? Is it the American reading public that buys the book? "Best-seller" is a vexatious term because it lacks definition. Unlike gold and platinum records, no exact sales figure is needed in order to claim the title "best-seller" for a given book.

While best-seller lists may do little to give us an exact idea of what the term "best-seller" actually means, they can remind us of two important facts concerning American book publishing. First, books and their readers come in all shapes and sizes. This diversity is captured in the idea of a fractured publishing market. There is not a single American reading public but a fractured one. People like to read different kinds of books, and best-seller lists serve as vivid reminders of this diversity as they categorize books as fiction and nonfiction, hardcover and paperback, business, children's, advice, how-to, and miscellaneous.

Second, books become popular for a wide range of reasons. They may sell because they are tied to religious traditions like the Bible, the Book of Mormon, or the scientologist L. Ron Hubbard's *Dianetics* (1955). They may sell because they are linked to various institutions. For example, school curriculums kept students reading J. D. Salinger's *The Catcher in the Rye* (1951) for decades, making it a perennial best-seller. Endorsements can also sell books; a word from the talk show host Oprah Winfrey, and a book can almost instantaneously begin selling thousands of copies. The reputation of an author such as Stephen King or motion pictures such as the *Star Wars* series can also translate into strong book sales. Positive word-of-mouth among readers can also sell books, like the sleeper-hit *The Bridges of Madison County* (1992) by Robert J. Waller.

No matter what segment of the American market a popular book reaches, or how that popularity came about, a book's popularity can provide insights into certain aspects and strata of American culture. Preoccupations with deadly diseases, getting rich quick, mastering computer skills, or preparing for the end can all lead to certain genres of books selling well while telling us a great deal about the hearts and minds of various segments of America's reading population.

Kurt Cobain helped sell records, and novels centered on the character Batman and the *Star Wars* saga helped sell movie tickets.

It should be noted that within the dominance of large publishing firms, smaller houses continued to function and provide books that the larger publishers did not think lucrative enough to sponsor. Academic presses and smaller independent publishers continued to push in the areas of fiction and nonfiction, giving guidance and care to the development of authors and book projects that larger publishers simply did not have time for. Although consolidation among the biggest publishing houses continued in the 1990s, smaller American publishers still thrived as the industry continued to grow.

Aside from the emergence of the paperback market and the changing ownership of publishing's largest houses, another pivotal development in American book production came in the 1980s with the wide adoption of computer technology in printing. Computer technology and the resultant changes in the ways that books were designed, formatted, and typeset offered the first radical industry change in terms of printing technology since the early nineteenth century. The industry once again had to radically reshape itself as old ways of setting page layouts and completing editing were drastically reshaped by technologies that instantly indexed, cut and pasted material, collated information, calculated page formats, and allowed a multitude of design variations to be executed in a fraction of the time and cost of former methods.

Although the influence of these technological changes was seen everywhere in American book publishing, it was perhaps most clearly evident in the number of complex books and reference works that were sped to press. Books that formerly took years, sometimes decades, to complete were in the hands of readers in much less time. Dictionaries, Bibles with extensive commentaries, and reference books with complex sidebars and thousands of illustrations were all made with greater speed, layout diversity, complexity in indexing, and access to current information because of the use of computers in American book design and production.

As the twentieth century drew to a close, publishers continued to find new ways to reach the reading public in this century. Earlier in the century, the rise of book clubs became instrumental in serving both as arbiters of taste in modern American literature and a new way to get books to Americans. Later, the American independent bookseller increasingly was besieged as mall bookstores such as B. Dalton and Waldenbooks and then megastores like Barnes and Noble and Borders came to populate the American landscape, using their collective buying and distribution power to once again filter what Americans would read. Finally, the Internet, with firms like Amazon.com, once again shifted the shape of American bookselling so that independent stores comprised less than 20 percent of the bookstores in America, and buyers have millions of titles available to them.

THE FUTURE OF THE BOOK

As American publishing entered the twenty-first century, there was a great deal of discussion on whether the book would long survive in an age full of computer technology and electronic information. The times had indeed changed, as the sales of books fell to fourth place behind the sales of television sets, motion picture tickets, and computer games. Some argued that books, long the repositories of cultural memory in the United States, with the advent of computers and the World Wide Web, the traditional codex format (a book with bound paper enclosed by two covers) would go the way of the dinosaur.

It is notoriously hard to predict the future. Books have long been important for their ability to transfer information in a highly portable manner. No doubt the computer will change the role and importance of books, but the question is how much. Thus, it is likely that any move away from books will be a gradual process, which will almost certainly never be absolutely complete. There will always be books. They may simply be overtaken by other methods of recording, storing, and retrieving information.

The increasing presence of electronic pathways of information used in place of the traditional book raises some interesting issues, however. Many of these issues revolve around the influence such pathways will have on American reading practices. With the growing presence of visual pictures alongside written texts and computer formats that allow hypertext reading, there are some indications that changes in informational media will lead to certain changes in how Americans read and think. Although far too little empirical research has been done on this issue, scholars point to certain trends to watch, including shorter attention spans, a growing difficulty in thinking in abstract terms, and a diminishing ability to think and reason analytically.

Books have long been the repositories of information and cultural memory in the United States.

Whether such information will forever be held in the traditional codex format that has reigned supreme in the Western world for hundreds of years is impossible to say. Whatever the future might hold, it is essential to remember that the history of the United States is so intertwined with the presence of books that no one can fully appreciate the nation's character and development without first understanding the place of books in American culture.

See also **The Print Revolution; Rhetoric and Belles Lettres; American Romanticism; Realism in Art and Literature; The Popular Arts** *(volume 1);* **Education; Culture for Mass Audiences; Textbooks; Libraries; Biography; Hermeneutics and American Historiography; History and the Study of the Past** *(in this volume); and other articles in this section.*

BIBLIOGRAPHY

General

Davidson, Cathy N., ed. *Reading in America: Literature and Social History.* Baltimore, 1989.

Hart, James D. *The Popular Book: A History of America's Literary Taste.* New York, 1950.

Mott, Frank Luther. *Golden Multitudes: The Story of Best Sellers in the United States.* New York, 1947.

Tebbel, John William. *A History of Book Publishing in the United States.* 4 vols. New York, 1972.

Early America

Cremin, Lawrence A. *American Education: The Colonial Experience, 1607–1783.* New York, 1970.

Lockridge, Kenneth. *Literacy in Colonial New England: An Enquiry into the Social Context of Literacy in the Early Modern West.* New York, 1974.

Thomas, Isaiah. *The History of Printing in America.* Edited from the 2d ed. by Marcus McCorison. Barre, Mass., 1970.

Eighteenth Century

Brown, Richard D. *Knowledge Is Power: The Diffusion of Information in Early America, 1700–1865.* New York, 1989.

Hamilton, Milton W. *The Country Printer: New York State, 1785–1830.* New York, 1936.

Joyce, William L., et al., eds. *Printing and Society in Early America.* Worcester, Mass.: American Antiquarian Society, 1983.

Nineteenth Century

Charvat, William. *The Profession of Authorship in America, 1800–1870: The Papers of William Charvat.* Edited by Matthew Bruccoli. Columbus, Ohio, 1968.

Cmiel, Kenneth. *Democratic Eloquence: The Fight over Popular Speech in Nineteenth-Century America.* New York, 1990.

Cremin, Lawrence. *American Education: The National Experience, 1783–1876.* New York, 1980.

Davidson, Cathy N. *Revolution and the Word: The Rise of the Novel in America.* New York, 1986.

Denning, Michael. *Mechanic Accents: Dime Novels and Working-Class Culture in America.* New York, 1987.

Gutjahr, Paul C. *An American Bible: A History of the Good Book in the United States, 1777–1880.* Stanford, Calif., 1999.

Sheehan, Donald. *This Was Publishing: A Chronicle of the Book Trade in the Gilded Age.* Bloomington, Ind., 1952.

Soltow, Lee, and Edward Stevens. *The Rise of Literacy and the Common School in the United States: A Socioeconomic Analysis to 1870.* Chicago, 1981.

Tocqueville, Alexis de. *Democracy in America.* 2 vols. New York, 1990. Originally published in 1835.

Welter, Rush, ed. *American Writings on Popular Education: The Nineteenth Century.* Indianapolis, Ind., 1971.

Zboray, Ronald J. *A Fictive People: Antebellum Economic Development and the American Reading Public.* New York, 1993.

Twentieth Century

Cremin, Lawrence. *American Education: The Metropolitan Experience, 1876–1980.* New York, 1988.

Davis, Kenneth C. *Two-Bit Culture: The Paperbacking of America.* Boston, 1984.

Kaestle, Carl F. *Literacy in the United States: Readers and Reading since 1880.* New Haven, Conn., 1991.

The Nation. 80 (23 February 1905): 148–149.

The Future of the Book

Lanham, Richard A. *The Electronic Word: Democracy, Technology, and the Arts.* Chicago, 1993.

Nunberg, Geoffrey, ed. *The Future of the Book.* Berkeley, Calif., 1996.

JOURNALISM

John Nerone

The term "journalism" contains a family of related notions that are not always consistent. Journalism means simultaneously reporting the news and participating in political discourse; it refers to both public affairs and cultural or everyday matters; it implies sometimes an active news-gathering persona who intones in a distinctive voice and sometimes an effaced reporter; it is variously a practice of advocacy, revelation, neutrality, literary comment, and humor. Common to all these notions of journalism (and there are others) are two enduring elements: a notion of timeliness (the very word "journalism" is derived from the Latin for "day" and is related in meaning to the Greek-derived "ephemeral"), and a sometimes strong, sometimes weak relationship to a public that is conceived in some measure as free citizens of a polity. All modern journalism presents itself as somehow democratic, and in the United States the development of journalism has always been involved with shifting notions of self-rule. The story of U.S. journalism is, because of its many meanings, a very diverse one, but unifying it is the thread of the developing notion of the republic and citizenship.

Journalism in any guise is a matter of relations. Journalists, even in common parlance, relate things. But in a more abstract sense, journalism is a system of relationships, constructing and maintaining structured connections between various institutions of the state and civil society (the police, the New York Stock Exchange, major league baseball) and various constituencies in the public. These relationships are material inasmuch as journalism and its institutions transmit actual goods or information from one point to another. For example, on a typical sports page reporters transmit news of athletic contests to (mostly male) fans and at the same time assemble their readers into an audience that the newspaper can in turn sell to, say, tire retailers. Material relationships are often concealed by other "represented" relationships. On the sports page of a daily newspaper, for instance, baseball reporting is represented as a ritual shared by fans of the local baseball team. More to the point, in political (or public affairs) reporting, the represented relationship is always one of citizenship, although the material relationships might be quite different—and in some cases (like the Gulf War of 1991) may actually be better described as propaganda.

Journalism is therefore always historically constructed. As the media changed in terms of technology, ownership, work routines, and regulation, the shifting pocket of media content and personnel called journalism also changed. What is called journalism today will be displaced when new media formations arise.

ORIGINS

In England the earliest periodicals that we would call news media appeared in the seventeenth century during the Thirty Years' War (1618–1648). Always subject to official licensing or censorship, these periodicals presented themselves as bland, voiceless, and inoffensive, mere digests of otherwise available documents. Existing alongside these were news-books, nonperiodical occasional pamphlets that focused on sensational events like crimes or coronations. These media honored an implicit distinction between a relatively small political class and everyone else. Inasmuch as a newsbook was likely to be read by the larger public, it avoided content suggestive of the inner workings of governance—stuff that was universally agreed to be the province of the few and not the many, though which few was often a matter of debate. In seventeenth- and early-eighteenth-century England, through a series of intra-elite struggles, effective regulation of printing lapsed, and something like freedom of the press, and with it political journalism, appeared by accident.

English political history was the framework within which the American development of news media commenced. Colonial leaders communicated the news through letter writing and in occasional newsbooks. Most scholarship on these early media concentrates on New England, which featured both printing and a well-articulated ministerial letter writing network. In both cases, news transmission was heavily inflected by religious concerns and was understood as important to maintaining social stability and harmony. Eventually, the letter writing function was taken over by printed newsletters—the first colonial newspapers. The first of these, the *Boston News-Letter,* was established in 1704.

Colonial newspapers were composed by non-journalists, that is, men (and sometimes women) who primarily identified themselves as essayists, officials, or most commonly printers. Their newspapers contained very little original reporting and virtually no editorial commentary. For news, they copied items from other (usually London) newspapers and reproduced official documents verbatim. For commentary, they printed (usually for a fee) contributions from their readers, distancing themselves from the opinions expressed.

The uses of such newspapers seem obscure to modern readers, who look to their media for news about their immediate surroundings. What colonial printers intended was something embedded in a more particular sociology. They sought to provide a simulation of a merchant's coffeehouse browsing. They produced a digest of gleanings from a range of newspapers that approximated what would have been available to the reader were he (rarely she) physically present in a London coffeehouse; the printer selected the most likely items and arranged them in the order in which a coffeehouse reader would most likely have run across them.

The selection of items implied a highly informed reader. To make sense out of the matter, one would have to be well acquainted with the European world—know the major players in the politics and armies of all the relevant countries—and have a well-developed sense of how European affairs would play out in the colonies. One would have to know how to read between the lines of a governor's proclamation or any other verbatim pronouncement. One would have to be able to fill in the implications of pseudonymous contributions from local writers. In other words, colonial newspapers remained the instruments of an elite. As such, they assumed a responsibility to maintain the boundaries of political discussion and to contain the effects of political controversy. Despite their apparent publicness, they did not aim to include ordinary citizens in affairs of state.

JOURNALISM AND A NATIONAL PUBLIC SPHERE

The revolutionary controversy in the colonies transformed the newspaper. The practical demands of the movement and the theoretical implications of its arguments combined to create a need for instruments that would continually inform, represent, and elicit consent from ordinary citizens. Printers were recruited to use their newspapers to these ends. The result was a compelling fiction about a public sphere, a fiction that influenced actual newspaper development.

The American Revolution produced a generation of propaganda papers. At no point did the movement consider debate on its fundamental legitimacy an acceptable practice, and at no point did the revolutionaries countenance loyalist publications in territory they controlled. Tactics of subsidy and suppression were developed, justified on the grounds that it was necessary for the formation of a political community to represent a unanimous public actually consenting to its new government. British authorities and loyalist activists followed the same logic. They understood that if they could convincingly represent the colonial public as divided, they would undermine the legitimacy of any new government. Revolutionary printers and pamphleteers like Isaiah Thomas and Thomas Paine self-consciously played this game of representing the public.

Once the government was established and the Revolution effected, this sort of policing became superfluous. Instead of actively shaping a revolutionary public, newspapers were assigned a new mission, that of supporting a continual public deliberation. Because republican governments were understood in theory to require an active and vigilant citizenry, and because the new governments of the United States in practice needed to continually elicit allegiance from their subjects, newspapers were promoted as instruments of both public information and debate. The result was a vision of public communication best enunciated by Thomas Jefferson in a famous 1787 letter to Edward Carrington, in which he called for universal penetration of newspapers so that "public opinion" could stand "in the place of law." Given such a communications system, Jefferson could happily contemplate a society with newspapers but no government. Such a system would create a space for public reason to form and then provide it with mechanisms to steer policy, in harmony with a vision of the public sphere later elucidated by Jürgen Habermas (1989).

The Boston News-Letter.

Published by Authority.

From **Monday** May 8. to **Monday** May 15. 1704.

Westminster, November 11. 1703.

The Humble Address of the House of Commons, *Presented to Her Majesty in the following Expressions.*

Most Gracious Sovereign,

WE Your Majesties most Dutiful and Loyal Subjects, the Commons in Parliament Assembled, do humbly return Your Majesty our most hearty Thanks for Your Majesties most Gracious Speech from the Throne.

We are truly Sensible of Your Majesties earnest Endeavours to bring the War to a glorious and speedy Conclusion, of which Your Majesty has given us so fair a prospect, by Your Great Wisdom and Conduct in engaging the King of *Portugal* and Duke of *Savoy* in Your Alliance, for recovering the Monarchy of *Spain* from the House of *Bourbon*, and restoring it to the House of *Austria*.

We do most gratefully acknowledge Your Majesties singular care in the good management and application of the Publick Money, whereby Your Majesties Exchequer hath greater Credit, in this so expensive a War, than was ever known in the most flourishing times of Peace, and Your most signal and unparallel'd Grace and Goodness to Your People, in contributing out of Your own Revenue, towards the Publick Service, particularly Your Majesties most seasonable assistance to the Circle of *Suabia*. The many Blessings we enjoy under Your Majesties most auspicious Reign, and Your tender regard to the general Welfare & Happiness of Your Subjects, justly require our utmost returns of duty and gratitude. And Your Majesty may be assured, ... Commons will support Your Majesty in Your Alliance, and effectually enable Your Majesty to carry on the War with vigour: to which nothing can more contribute, than a firm Union among our selves: We therefore crave leave further to assure Your Majesty, that we will, according to Your Majesties desire, carefully avoid any heats or divisions that may give encouragement to the common Enemies of the Church & State.

To which Her Majesty return'd Her most Gracious Answer, in the following words.

I Am very well pleased with your Assurances of Supporting Me in the present War, and your kind acknowledgments of My endeavours to bring it to a happy Conclusion.

You may assure your selves, I shall always pursue the true Interest of the Kingdom and Omit nothing that may promote the general Welfare of My People.

Her Majesty of *England*'s Congratulatory Letter to the King of *Spain*, & the King of *Spain*'s Answer.

My Lord and Brother,

I Have heard with great Satisfaction, of Your being declar'd King of *Spain*, and do hearti

Congratulate You upon this Account, and with that the *Spanish* Crown, which is Your Right, may prove as Prosperous to You as it has been to Your Ancestors; and to give proof of My Friendship to the House of *Austria*, My esteem for Your Person and Merits, and My concern for Your Honour and Interest, I am resolved to employ all the strength of My Arms in Your favour. I have Ordered the Duke of *Marleborough*, Captain General of My Forces, to Assure Your Majesty, that I shall neglect no Opportunities, of giving You real proofs of the Sincerity with which I am,

My Lord and Brother, Your most
Affectionate Sister,
ANNA REGINA.

The King of *Spain*: Answer to Her Majesty.

My Lady and Sister,

I Am the more affected with the Assurances of Your Friendship, signified in the Letter deliver'd to Me by the Duke of Marleborough, *Your Embassador and Captain General of Your Forces; since thereby You have so generously, renew'd the Affection and Promises made to the House of* Austria, *in the beginning of Your Reign. If Our Arms be blest with Success according to Your Wishes, I assure Your Majesty, that they shall be only employ'd against Our Common Enemies, and for the advantage of Your Kingdoms, and the Preservation of the Liberties of Europe. I desire Your Majesty to Honour Me with Your Wise Counsels, which are a terror to Your Enemies, but the Support of Your Allies, and the happiness of Your Subjects: And I shall always follow them with respect and deference, as having manifestations of Your good and sincere aims. I look upon it as a Sign of Your most particular Esteem, that Your Majesty has made choice of the Duke of* Marleborough, *to be Witness of the regard I have for Your concerns, and of My admiration of the Merits of Your Person. And that I Wish nothing more earnestly, than to have Opportunities to shew with what Sincerity and Gratitude I am,*

Lady and Sister, Your most
Affectionate Brother,
CHARLES.

Advice from *Rome* and *Italy*,

The Pope's partiality in the Affair of the *Spanish* Succession discovers it self more and more, His dissimulation can no longer hold out against the force of his inclination: and considering his deportment within this little while, there is great reason to believe, that a very small thing would perswade him to declare openly for *France*. His Holiness call'd a Congregation of State, on purpose to consider, whether or no he should recal his Nuncio from *Vienna*, because the Arch-Duke had assum'd the Royal Title and for that the Emperour refused to give him audience. However the question being put, it was carry'd in the Negative by several voices. Some sort of proof that the Disciples have more wit than their master.

Yet in the midst of all his troubles and vexations

Boston News-Letter. The first serial newspaper in the colonies, the *Boston News-Letter* was published by John Campbell, postmaster of Boston, and printed by Bartholomew Green. First issued in 1704, it remained the only serial until 1719. COURTESY OF THE AMERICAN ANTIQUARIAN SOCIETY

This particular vision of public communication, dominated by the metaphor of the town meeting, called for a highly constricted yet decentralized journalism. Newspapers were to be passively conducted, transparent mechanisms for transmitting reliable information and neutral forums for citizen discussions. Because most newspapers remained printerly affairs, they accommodated the forms of this sort of public communication, particularly the official document and the pseudonymous contribution. Although their apparent passivity and neutrality often concealed substantive commitment to a political party, in an atmosphere of vigorous antipartisanism, newspapers fervently proclaimed their independence of factional loyalties.

But party activism in the 1790s produced a class of actively edited partisan journals. In Washington, D.C., truly national organs appeared—especially the Federalist newspapers of John Fenno and William Cobbett and the Democratic-Republican ones of Philip Freneau and Benjamin Franklin Bache. These featured a vigorous and often scathingly satirical political commentary, patterned on the partisan journalism of English writers like Jonathan Swift and Daniel Defoe. Essays from the party press were copied by equally partisan journals in the state capitals as well as by formally impartial printers throughout the country.

Partisan journalism remained ideologically suspect, however. Attempts to punish partisan excesses by passing laws against seditious libel, culminating in the Federal Sedition Act of 1798, attest to the common expectation that partisan energies endangered the Republic. Despite professions of belief in freedom of the press, the postrevolutionary generation clearly still distinguished liberty from licentiousness, thought that licentiousness was constitutionally unprotected, and considered partisan journalism licentious. Newspapers were meant to be neutral forums, not party organs.

It was that model of neutral newspapers that early postal regulation subsidized. The postal system was set up to support newspapers in two ways. One, cheap postage for mail delivery was a direct distribution subsidy, making it much easier for newspapers to reach subscribers. The other was an information subsidy. Franking privileges were extended to postmasters, congressmen, and other officeholders, and printers and editors were allowed to exchange newspapers among themselves for free. The exchange system that grew up through the mails became the main source of content for the newspapers. Most antebellum newspapers sent a full 10 percent of their print runs to other newspapers, receiving in return copies of all other important newspapers in their state and select ones from around the nation. This was a remarkably democratic news system. The postal system itself, in its insistence on low-cost universal service regardless of location, imposed the logic of the Republic on an unwilling geography and asserted distributive equality in the face of divisive and uneven terrain: it was a true attempt to obliterate space. Its special provisions for newspapers encouraged the establishment of newspapers in remote and obscure locations that would certainly have been bypassed by a more commercial communication system and helped to create a decentralized newspaper network in which every node was a potential point of entry to any other node. This "press-post" system worked by the distributive logic of politics (one person one vote) rather than that of the market (one dollar one vote).

This system produced tremendous growth in newspaper production and readership. Because of the various postal subsidies, along with other forms of patronage like government printing, newspapers were cheap to start and run. Ironically, the very abundance of newspapers made it possible for them to move away from their commitment to impartiality. With so many newspapers in operation, and any sizable community served by one, no single newspaper need bear responsibility for representing the entire populace. Although anti-party sentiment did not disappear overnight, journalism began to claim the right to advocate partisan interests in the courtroom of public opinion just as a new era of mass politics commenced.

THE EDITOR AS JOURNALIST

By the 1820s many of the ideological and structural barriers to partisan journalism had weakened. A full-fledged system of mass electoral politics was forming and with it the wherewithall to subsidize competing newspapers in every electoral center. Meanwhile, the position of editor separated from that of printer. Editors, often lawyers by profession, usually had not imbibed the traditions of print craft, and lacked the characteristic modesty of printer-editors. Called "hirelings" by their critics, editors owed their allegiance and their positions to the parties. Typically, they served on party committees and were important members of the policy elites within party organizations. The party editor, like all the partisans of the antebellum period, took the revolutionary movement as a model. Parties and their newspapers adopted the committee structure, propaganda techniques, rhetoric, and martial atmosphere of the Revolution, secularizing it to a system of permanent political contest.

In so doing, they took the intolerance toward dissent found in the Revolution and translated it to the party structure. Just as revolutionaries excluded loyalists and conferred social death on informers through tarring and feathering, party activists and editors policed their publics, exiling and silencing nonconformists of various sorts, but especially abolitionists. Because neither party could win nationally while appearing to the South to be "unsound" on the slavery issue, both parties warred rhetorically and with both real and symbolic violence against antislavery activists. Exiled from the party press, generations of reformers established their own newspapers, usually appealing to some version of the ideology of rational liberty that had come out of the Revolution.

Although they erected barriers against the heterodox, the party editors significantly expanded the appeal of the newspaper to the ordinary reader. In a time of rapidly growing electorates, editors self-consciously tried to put their arguments into terms that every reader could find appealing. To intellectuals and older generation politicos, this popularization of political debate was understood as debasement and declension; it generated a highbrow reaction against party politics that mirrored contemporary criticisms of other popular amusements.

THE COMMERCIALIZATION OF THE PRESS

Almost simultaneously with the politicization of newspapers came a wave of commercialization. As market relations grew and increasingly penetrated the everyday lives and politics of ordinary people, newspapers in general became more integrated into markets, carrying economic information and advertising, promoting internal improvements, and refashioning themselves and their contents as commodities. The leading edge of the process of commercialization were the New York penny papers of the 1830s, especially Benjamin Day's *Sun* and James Gordon Bennett's *Herald.*

Hostility to party journalists was inscribed onto the commercialization of the press. Highbrow critics despised penny journalism in the same terms as party journalism, and at the same time penny papers adopted the critique of partisanism as their own credo, declaring their independence from the "trammels" of party. Some scholars have taken these professions of political neutrality to signal a revolution in news. In fact, penny press editors developed a fairly routine partisanism of their own, and in short order the parties adopted the penny press format as well.

More fundamental changes in journalism were occurring at a deeper level. Specifically, new ways of owning and selling news, which also meant new ways of manufacturing news, were being developed, especially in competitive urban markets. Two particular innovations were the rise of reporting and the emergence of telegraphic news. Hiring writers to glean information and compose accounts of both local news and more remote affairs (for example, correspondence from Washington regarding congressional debates) allowed newspapers to own the copy that resulted, to label it as their own, and to add value to their papers. But other newspapers still copied it for free. The telegraph allowed newspapers to sell the news they owned and provided a means to separate the news from the newspaper and send it on ahead, thereby creating a market for news. Meanwhile, the railroad system (which was technologically closely allied with the telegraph) permitted metropolitan dailies to expand their area of circulation beyond the core city to broader environs.

A news system emerged that more closely matched the commercial structure of the emerging city system. New York City became the dominant news distribution center as well as the largest manufacturer of newspapers. Innovations in news gathering and design usually came from second-tier cities, like San Francisco, St. Louis, and Chattanooga (where the press barons William Randolph Hearst, Joseph Pulitzer, and Adolph Ochs started, respectively); they were imported to New York then reexported to the nation as a whole (with the exception of the South for most of the nineteenth century). The commercial newspaper sought new economies of scale, especially when available in the form of new printing technologies, like the steam press, the linotype, and stereotyping. Economies of scale, coupled with the homogenization of news content through the wire services, would eventually render the daily newspaper a natural monopoly.

The commercial system of newspapering worked by principles that were in tension with the Jeffersonian vision of public communication and the egalitarian tradition of partisan newspapering. It created new pockets of informational privilege and hierarchy and instituted occupations that prefigured modern reporting.

PRECURSORS OF MODERN REPORTING: CORRESPONDENT AND SCAVENGER

The partisan editor was more like a present-day network anchor than a reporter or even a city managing, or editorial page editor. He (sometimes she) was the public face of the newspaper, and not only opined but also selected and introduced the news items, often with a stock phrase like "We read in last week's Register." Editors worked typically at paragraphing—composing single paragraphs of comment and news. The brevity and wit of the paragraph was considered the hallmark of American journalism. Gradually, however, the distinction of U.S. newspapers shifted from editorial matter to news columns, and the characteristic figures shifted from editors to reporters. By the end of the nineteenth century, the heroes of journalism were not the thunderers—Horace Greeley, Charles Dana—but the entrepreneurs—Pulitzer, Hearst—and the reporters—Lincoln Steffens, Upton Sinclair, and David Graham Phillips.

The development of such reporting was gradual and intertwined with literary professionalism more generally. Before the rise of the commercial newspaper, news gathering, when it was not passive clipping, consisted of correspondence, that is, letter writing. The "correspondent" was at first an entirely amateur position. An acquaintance of the editor or proprietor, or perhaps a figure of some notoriety, would agree to write letters for publication. Sometimes these would describe a journey; sometimes they would provide an insider's glimpse of goings-on at a scene of power. Over time, the correspondent became more routinized as an occupation, but well into the 1880s correspondence remained in epistolary form. By midcentury political correspondence had become somewhat formalized, and newspapers began to distinguish themselves by the quality of their (often pseudonymous) letter writers. Correspondents still operated by principles that later reporters would find alarming. Among other things, they were opinionated, often duplicitous, and notoriously corrupt, trading coverage for favors of various sorts. But such practices simply underscore the fact that they saw themselves as actors in the political drama, not as mere observers. The habits of detachment later codified as objectivity came much later.

If the correspondent was the precursor of the reporter abroad, the counterpart at home was the scavenger. Beginning in the 1830s in the largest markets and spreading to other markets by the 1850s, local "intelligence" became an increasingly important selling point for newspapers. So, they hired "reporters" to glean interesting facts from the police courts and City Hall and the marketplaces. The scavenger's reporting was specifically news, not commentary, explanation, interpretation, or analysis. As the press commercialized, a particular sense of news as facts distinguished by timeliness and novelty modified an earlier sense that the stuff of a newspaper should be intelligence to assist self-government. Printers and editors had always included the bizarre or tragic—what came to be called "human interest" stories—in their original matter, because these were the sorts of universally appealing items that the hinterland could contribute to the exchange system in return for the accounts of public affairs emanating from the metropoles. Commercial dailies used reporter-scavengers to mass produce such content for local consumption.

The scavenger's authorial posture was also different. The correspondent always had a persona, a voice, even if concealed by a pseudonym, and the correspondent always depicted, opined, and interpreted. The reporter-scavenger was an information gatherer. As such, he (sometimes she) was not entitled to a persona and was subject to ruthless wage pressure. Especially in the 1870s and 1880s, when a new wave of popular newspapers appeared, economic pressures encouraged owners to cut costs by tying reporters' pay to space. Whereas correspondents worked in the fairly luxurious dimensions of the essay, scavengers were reduced to the meaner proportions of payment by the line. This put them in an adversarial relationship with the newly emerging occupation of copy editor, who cut reporters' incomes by cutting their copy. Reporters waged a battle to "regain" the status of correspondents—a status that only a few had ever merited—by professionalizing.

PROFESSIONALIZATION

The professionalization of journalism came from a variety of sources. One was the occupational struggles just described. But also in action were the defensive maneuvers of entrepreneurs, the broader social transformation of the middle class, and a pervasive crisis of cultural authority.

Entrepreneurs—the owners of newspapers—faced mounting public hostility through the years of industrialization. As the press became a big business and as economies of scale turned print shops into factories and proprietors into captains of industry, the power of the press seemed to grow and its control to become ever more irresponsible. Public distrust ironically increased as newspapers declared themselves independent of party.

Newspapers had always been advocates of one sort or another. The revolutionary newspaper had propagandized for the patriot cause; the impartial newspapers of the early Republic had been advocates of rational self-governance; partisan newspapers had advocated the interests of Jacksonians or Whigs; the reform press had promoted this or that cause. But the stance of advocacy always carried responsibility. Newspaper advocacy, unlike say commercial advocacy or advertising, always needed to justify itself as being in the highest public interest, a feat of varying difficulty for the different forms of journalism. It was relatively easy for revolutionary printers, who thought of themselves as simply patriots and so claimed to be advocates for all the people. It was more difficult for partisan editors, who had to work hard to achieve respectability and acceptance. By midcentury they had done so.

Partisanism, which seems like "bias" and therefore a source of distrust to present-day journalists, certified reliability to nineteenth-century readers, who were always on the alert for concealed partisanism in independent newspapers. No matter how much you hated a partisan like Dana, you knew how to read him. Common readers and elite critics both had to suspect the new industrial newspapers, although their suspicions took different forms. Common readers wondered whether "the interests" controlled the press (and especially the Associated Press, which was formed in 1848 to gather news for six New York City newspapers); sometimes elite critics did too, but more commonly they believed that the "sensational" press was debasing the political culture in the same fashion as the worst partisan journals. Both had plenty of ammunition. The Associated Press became a particular target of criticism for Republican bias and political machinations; shadow ownership of major newspapers by "robber barons" reached the point where federal legislation on truth in ownership was passed; and mounting appeals to public passions produced a widespread sense that the "yellow" journals could pressure the nation into rash action, even into war. And, as always in U.S. history, political leaders, moral guardians, and business interests found advantage in scapegoating the press.

Press owners responded with political savvy and effective publicity. They used their press associations to lobby the state legislatures to create journalism training programs in the new land grant universities, and they waged an informational campaign to instruct the public in the workings of the new industrial newspaper. The late nineteenth century saw an unprecedented barrage of magazine articles on newspapers, and by the twentieth century the public knew more about the internal workings of the newspaper than about any other industrial enterprise. There were more steelworkers than journalists, but the copy editor and the city editor were familiar figures and the puddler was not. Publishers also began their relentless championing of the First Amendment. A serious constitutional reeducation was necessary to convince people that the press had become the steward of the public's right to free speech; many argued that the press had simply stolen it. For all these reasons, publishers endorsed and in some ways invented a professional ethos for reporting.

Meanwhile, a general crisis of cultural authority swept the modern West. Traditional forms of authority (the Bible) had become intellectually suspect, and new scientific models of the world (from Marx, Darwin, and Freud) offered forms of expertise that seemingly lacked a moral dimension. Moreover, as authority became expertise, it lurched beyond the realm of public supervision. Science, after all, was science, no matter what people thought— the law of gravity had not been passed by Congress.

All of these currents came to a head in the period between the two world wars, a period framed by Walter Lippmann's *Public Opinion* (1922) and the Hutchins Commission's report *A Free and Responsible Press* (1947). The latter was issued by the Commision on the Freedom of the Press, a blue-ribbon panel of intellectuals funded by Henry Luce of the *Time-Life* media empire and chaired by Robert Maynard Hutchins, the youthful and charismatic president of the University of Chicago. Both these classic texts take on the problem of the people, the press, the truth, and democracy by stipulating that the press is industrialized and commercialized, the people are increasingly unable to understand complex affairs, the truth is both in flux and scientifically knowable, and, therefore, deliberative democracy can proceed only if experts are available to inform and shape it. Lippmann argued that the press was too enslaved by its commercial interests to provide the needed expertise. The Hutchins Commission, though admitting the challenge posed by the ownership and business structure of the media, nevertheless felt that the press could be both free and responsible. Its criticism of the press, and its insistence that responsible behavior was required despite First Amendment freedoms, provoked angry responses from journalists. But it issued a set of requirements that have since become common sense among professional journalists: a responsible press must provide "a truthful, comprehensive, and intelligent account of the day's events in a context which gives them meaning"; "a forum for the exchange of comment and criticism"; "the projection of a representative picture of the constituent groups in the society"; "the presentation and clarification of the goals and values of the society"; and "full access to the day's intelligence." Who could disagree with any of that?

Lippmann and the Hutchins Commission reasoned out the position that journalism had already groped its way into. The competing needs of critics, owners, and reporters were brokered by professionalization, so that owners achieved protection from government interference, critics won a new certification of reliability, and reporters gained some occupational autonomy along with added prestige and, not incidentally, income. But each also gave up something. Owners gave up their right to be irresponsible or purely commercial; critics gave up schemes for structural reform of the press; and journalists gave up their quest for the "manly independence" of the preprofessional correspondent—there would be no opining—as well as, for the most part, their identification as workers. Professionals in the twentieth century were not supposed to form unions—it would compromise their independence.

Professionalization devalued the scavenger. Professional journalists follow critics in drawing a bright line between news and sensationalism, which includes all the news that is of interest primarily because of its weirdness. So, the professional repressed the market-driven content that drove much of the popular journalism of the turn of the century, and this content instead turned up in marginal venues—urban and supermarket tabloids, syndicated television shows, and the World Wide Web—which constitute the unruly other against which "proper" journalism can identify itself, contrasting its interest in public affairs with trivial, everyday, and private concerns.

THE BIFURCATED PUBLIC SPHERE

The professionalization of journalism in the twentieth century presumed a bifurcated public sphere divided into active and passive realms. In the active part of the public sphere, political leaders, policy elites, the representatives of organized public opinion, lobbyists, and other opinion leaders engaged in various kinds of deliberation. Journalists were privy to these discussions and sometimes took part in them as active players, but they were also responsible to the passive public sphere. In this realm, the discussions of the enfranchised were represented to the great public of ordinary people, who were invited to participate through spectatorship primarily, and then by implication through various kinds of (devalued) feedback mechanisms—letters to their congressional representatives, public opinion polls, and, ultimately, voting. Journalism inhabited the threshold between the active and passive public spheres.

This liminal status left journalists with a divided soul. On the one hand, the real news was the play of elites, and journalists achieved high status by gaining access to the inside dope. The most revered journalists of the late twentieth century were those who achieved access to the most restricted circles, sometimes as insiders like James "Scotty" Reston, Washington bureau chief of the *New York Times,* who withheld news of the Bay of Pigs invasion during the Kennedy administration and relayed leaks from Henry Kissinger during the Nixon Administration, and Helen Thomas of the United Press International, for decades the senior correspondent at presidential press conferences, and sometimes as outsiders, like Seymour Hersh, whose report on the My Lai massacre still stands as a high point in investigative reporting, and I. F. Stone, whose independent weekly newsletter held scriptural status for political nonconformists. Journalists like these conferred as equals with policy elites and high elected officials.

On the other hand, the rationale of the power that journalism enjoyed was its service to the great public. Journalists claimed certain privileges from law and custom because they are supposed to be the eyes and ears of a dependent public. Thus, journalists must continually sweeten their sources through favorable reporting and yet resist "source capture," that is, becoming the unofficial public relations arm of the powerful. That this task is difficult—perhaps insurmountable—is demonstrated by the widespread belief that journalism is propaganda, either for the state and corporate interests or for an eastern liberal intelligentsia. Reporters have developed an arsenal of defensive postures to distance themselves from their sources, including balancing (always getting an opposing point of view) and insisting that remarks be "on the record"

Presidential Press Conference, 1963. President John F. Kennedy, with Assistant Press Secretaries Malcolm Kilduff and Andrew Hatcher, earns his reputation for charm under fire as he faces members of the press in a news conference at the State Department Auditorium. Televised press conferences at times resembled staged confrontations between a mob of reporters and a lone leader. COURTESY JOHN F. KENNEDY LIBRARY AR 811-C; PHOTO BY ABIE ROWE

with sources clearly identified, but will always be confronted with unattributable leaked information and will always face ethical dilemmas pitting the "public's right to know" against manipulation by sources.

The apparatus of professional journalism takes special form in the most highly valued news arenas—war, elections, and legislative struggles. In wartime, journalists are called upon to assist the war effort. Traditionally, the journalist will identify with the "man in uniform," taking special pains to not print information that will aid the enemy or cause undue distress to soldiers or civilians. During World War II, for example, war photography observed a code that forbade gore and recognizable faces on the dead—loved ones should not learn of a battle-field death through the impersonal channel of the

media. This role of the journalist as loyal patriot was attenuated by modern undeclared wars—Vietnam is the classic example—but the 1990s saw the U.S. military continually in combat without any declaration of war. Instead, the military deployed an increasingly sophisticated system of positive publicity. Reporters objected to being treated as either disloyal or as tools of the Pentagon, but the success of this strategy, coupled with the mythology that the press undermined the U.S. effort in Vietnam, augurs its permanence.

Elections are another special occasion. Journalists exercise their professional status during elections by being equally critical of all candidates and by assuming a position above the contest. Most election coverage follows what Thomas E. Patterson has called the "game schema." Because reporters want to abjure allegiance and yet retain some special authority, they lean toward reporting the strategies behind campaign events rather than the events themselves. When a candidate makes a policy speech, the "news" is not the speech but the intended effect of that speech on a particular voting or contributing constituency—organized labor, say, or sugar farmers. Again, access is golden, as journalists seek to be privy to the strategizing of especially presidential campaigns.

Similar strategies pervade other public affairs coverage. When a major legislative initiative is under consideration, journalism seeks to relate not the content of the arguments advanced but the strategies behind speeches or other events. In this, as in elections, public affairs journalism is accused of imitating sportswriting. The accusation of "horse-race" coverage is fair in one dimension but inaccurate also. Sportswriters are all fans of the game, whereas political reporters convey cynicism toward politics. Sportswriters are all fans of their teams, whereas political reporters must be above attachment to a party or candidate. Sportswriting always presumes that it is subsidiary to actually watching the athletes, while political reporting takes the place of observing the politicians and assumes that few readers or viewers will have actually done so. And sportswriting assumes an audience of spectators, whereas political reporting assumes an audience of citizen participants.

But the forms of professional reporting ultimately contradict the assumption of a participatory audience. The chief act of a report is to unveil something. In a legislative initiative the indispensable function of the journalist is to penetrate the represented action—the floor debates and so on—to show the people the action behind the show. The show itself is already available to citizens on C-SPAN or in the *Congressional Record*. Reporters take us behind the scenes to where the actors rehearse the spectacle the public will see. But far more citizens learn about legislative action through Associated Press stories than by actually watching or reading debates. And even those who do watch the debates will know through the reportage that it is all a show, that the real decision making is done backstage. The very form undermines not just the people's role in the deliberative process, but the role of deliberation in the legislative process, too. At the same time, it introduces a new urgency to attempts to rationalize action as officials become more alert to and sophisticated about the way things will play in reportage and especially on television.

THE FALL OF THE PROFESSIONAL JOURNALIST

The media structures that supported professional journalism began to erode at the end of the twentieth century. Professionalization is always premised on some level of monopolization—doctors monopolize medical practice through education and licensing, for instance. The monopolies or bottlenecks that allowed and necessitated professionalization in journalism came from conditions of "natural monopoly" in daily newspapers and the wire services and were strengthened by oligopolistic and federally regulated network broadcasting. The monopoly daily newspaper has a long life expectancy but began showing signs of age as new technologies lowered the fixed costs of publication and new media began to cherry pick at valued revenue streams like classified advertising and traditional content like financial and sports information. Broadcasting also saw inroads from cable and personal computers.

Four sorts of trends were visible. One was niche-oriented publication. As media marketing became more sophisticated, news organizations increasingly resembled consumer magazines, targeting desirable audience segments for more efficient resale to advertisers, a strategy that Mark Wilkes made notorious during his tenure as publisher at the *Los Angeles Times*. A second was deprofessionalization. The new porousness of barriers to entry to reporting allowed a return to tabloid content by web-based journalists like Matt Drudge and partisanship by talk-radio hosts like Rush Limbaugh. Together such figures represented a new populist frontier to the land of news. Third, the disentangling of information streams grew easier. From the age of industrialization on, the daily newspaper was the necessary stop for encountering public affairs, classified advertising, financial information, sports news, consumer advertising, and lifestyle commentary. But the newspaper itself assembled its content from outsourced producers—Dow Jones, the Associated Press, the National Basketball Association, and so forth. The newspaper itself was a reified portal. Because it was a necessary portal, however, it provided a home for journalism. In the electronic environment, this portal will become just a portal, and the difference between the *Cincinnati Enquirer* and Yahoo! will diminish. Fourth, news organizations were increasingly likely to be bought up by media conglomerates, which in turn became increasingly oligopolistic. Tamed news units like CBS, home of Edward R. Murrow and Walter Cronkite, perhaps the most trusted faces in the history of journalism, became subsidiaries of companies primarily dedicated to entertainment, further eroding the always compromised line between entertainment and news.

Who knows what will become of journalism? In any event, the period of the "high modernism" of journalism has certainly begun its decline.

See also **The Print Revolution; Rhetoric and Belles Lettres; Urban Cultural Institutions** *(volume 1);* **Authorship, Intellectual Property, and Copyright; Literary Reviews and "Little Magazines"; Almanacs and Ephemeral Literature; Journals of Opinion** *(in this volume); and other articles in this section.*

BIBLIOGRAPHY

Baldasty, Gerald J. *The Commercialization of News in the Nineteenth Century.* Madison, Wisc., 1992.

Barnhurst, Kevin G., and John Nerone. *The Forms of News.* New York, 2000.

Blondheim, Menahem. *News over the Wires: The Telegraph and the Flow of Public Information in America, 1844–1897.* Cambridge, Mass., 1994.

Botein, Stephen, "'Meer Mechanics' and an Open Press: The Business and Political Strategies of Colonial American Printers." *Perspectives in American History* 9 (1975): 130–211.

Carey, James W. *Communication as Culture: Essays on Media and Society.* Boston, 1988.

Clark, Charles E. *The Public Prints: The Newspaper in Anglo-American Culture, 1665–1740.* New York, 1994.

Commision on Freedom of the Press (Hutchins Commission). *A Free and Responsible Press: A General Report on Mass Communications.* Chicago, 1947.

Dicken Garcia, Hazel. *Journalistic Standards in Nineteenth-Century America.* Madison, Wisc., 1989.

Habermas, Jürgen. *Structural Transformation of the Public Sphere.* Cambridge, Mass., 1989.

Hallin, Daniel C. "The Passing of the High Modernism of American Journalism." In his *We Keep America on Top of the World: Television Journalism and the Public Sphere.* New York, 1994. Pp. 170–180.

Herman, Edward S., and Noam Chomsky. *Manufacturing Consent: The Political Economy of the Mass Media.* New York, 1988.

John, Richard R. *Spreading the News: The American Postal System from Franklin to Morse.* Cambridge, Mass., 1995.

Lawson, Linda. *Truth in Publishing: Federal Regulation of the Press's Business Practices, 1880–1920.* Carbondale, Ill., 1993.

Leab, Daniel J. *A Union of Individuals: The Formation of the American Newspaper Guild, 1933–1936.* New York, 1970.

Lippmann, Walter. *Public Opinion.* New York, 1922.

McIntyre, Sheila. "I Have Heard It So Variously Reported: News-Letters, Newspapers, and the Ministerial Network in New England, 1670–1730." *New England Quarterly* 71 (December 1998): 593–614.

Nerone, John. *Violence against the Press: Policing the Public Sphere in U.S. History.* New York, 1994.

Nord, David Paul. "Teleology and News: The Religious Roots of American Journalism, 1630–1730." *Journal of American History* 77 (June 1990): 9–38.

Osthaus, Carl R. *Partisans of the Southern Press: Editorial Spokesmen of the Nineteenth Century.* Lexington, Ky., 1994.

Patterson, Thomas E. *Out of Order.* New York, 1993.

Pred, Allan Richard. *Urban Growth and the Circulation of Information: The United States System of Cities, 1790–1840.* Cambridge, Mass., 1973.

Schiller, Dan. *Objectivity and the News: The Public and the Rise of Commercial Journalism.* Philadelphia, 1981.

Schudson, Michael. *Discovering the News: A Social History of American Newspapers.* New York, 1978.

Sellers, Charles Grier. *The Market Revolution: Jacksonian America, 1815–1846.* New York, 1991.

Siebert, Fred Seaton. *Freedom of the Press in England, 1476–1776: The Rise and Decline of Government Controls.* Urbana, Ill., 1952.

Sinclair, Upton. *The Brass Check: A Study of American Journalism.* Published by the author, 1919.

Sommerville, C. John. *The News Revolution in England: Cultural Dynamics of Daily Information.* New York, 1996.

Stephens, Mitchell. *A History of News: From the Drum to the Satellite.* New York, 1988.

Stewart, Donald Henderson. *The Opposition Press of the Federalist Period.* Albany, N.Y., 1969.

Summers, Mark W. *The Press Gang: Newspapers and Politics, 1865–1878.* Chapel Hill, N.C., 1994.

Warner, Michael. *The Letters of the Republic: Publication and the Public Sphere in Eighteenth-Century America.* Cambridge, Mass., 1990.

Wilson, Christopher P. *The Labor of Words: Literary Professionalism in the Progressive Era.* Athens, Ga., 1985.

PERIODICALS

Susan Belasco

"Periodicals" is a generic category that includes newspapers, magazines, journals, reviews, newsletters, weeklies, and monthlies—print publications that are issued at more or less regular intervals. The formal qualities of a periodical are difficult to define. In the eighteenth and nineteenth centuries, the distinctions between newspapers and magazines were considerably blurred. Additionally, historians differ about whether the term "periodical" refers to a single issue or number of a magazine or newspaper, a volume, or the complete publication run. Others define periodicals in terms of the capitalist economic system that produced them; printers, editors, writers, distributors, and advertisers all combine to make and sell a product. Because periodicals with their flexible bindings are typically inexpensive, disposable in nature, and usually carry responses from readers, they are often viewed as more democratic and less hierarchical than the closed form of books with their stiff covers and privileged status as artifacts. From the humble origin of crudely printed newsheets to the hypertext format of Internet magazines, periodicals have played an important role in the development of an urban industrial society and in the mass communication of news and ideas within the United States. As the most modern of print forms and the one most closely associated with the development of a literary marketplace, periodicals are deeply implicated in the construction of American cultural practice.

COLONIAL PRINTERS

The first periodicals published in the United States were newspapers and newsheets in the colonies; the forerunners of modern magazines and journals did not appear until the middle of the eighteenth century. The development of newspapers in colonial New England was prompted primarily by individual printers who wished to supplement their incomes from books and pamphlets and, often, to promote their own views. Broader cultural transformations also played a role: political upheavals in England and the colonies, the growing literate population, the desire for news of other places; the needs of businesses to advertise and sell their products and services; and the necessity for creating a public record of events. Eight of the first fifteen American newspapers were published in Boston, the largest town in the colonies with a population of 5,500 by 1700. Boston was an important center of business and had a system of shipping and postal services in place that created many advantages for the publication of newspapers. Benjamin Harris's *Publick Occurences, Both Forreign and Domestick,* the first newsheet published in British America, was printed in Boston in 1690 and immediately suppressed by the British government, because it presumably contained what the government considered offensive references to the French king and the Indian Wars. The second newspaper to be published in the colonies was the *Boston News-Letter* (1704–1776), founded and edited initially by John Campbell, the postmaster of Massachusetts. The weekly *News-Letter* presented information about deaths and crimes, announcements of the arrivals and departures of ships, summaries of foreign news, and notices of the activities of the colonial government, all presented without much commentary or analysis. An official with strong allegiance to the colonial government, Campbell printed the newspaper primarily to provide a chronological record of public events in Boston.

In the midst of growing antagonisms between the Anglicans in the colonial government and the predominantly Puritan colonists, the weekly *New England Courant* (1721–1728) was established by John Checkley and printed by James Franklin, the older brother of Benjamin Franklin. Unlike the earlier papers, the *Courant* mixed news items with commentary and essays. A fierce and acrimonious exchange, for example, was published between

Checkley, an ardent Anglican, and Cotton Mather, the powerful Puritan leader. While the *Courant* was largely viewed as the instrument of high Anglicanism, Benjamin Franklin published his secular "Silence Dogood" letters in the *Courant* before he abandoned his apprenticeship and went to Philadelphia. Like other colonial newspapers, the *Courant* made liberal use of news items and articles gleaned from other publications. In the age before copyright, information was shared freely and usually without acknowledgment. Sharing was a commonplace and a staple of every newspaper that appeared.

The number of newspapers grew slowly throughout the colonies. Newspapers were established in New York in 1725 and in Pennsylvania in 1719. By 1739 there were twelve weekly papers in the thirteen colonies, which then had a total population of roughly one million people. One successful paper was the *South-Carolina Gazette*, edited by Elizabeth Timothy from 1739, the year of her husband's death, until 1747, when she turned the profitable paper over to her son. But printing and publishing newspapers was a highly risky and uncertain business; although there clearly was a developing market for news and commentary, failures were more frequent than successes.

Since a few British magazines were imported and eagerly read by some in the colonies, enterprising American printers began to think of ways of attracting readers with periodicals that would provide more entertainment than the existing newspapers. Thinking that a market might exist for such periodicals (but having little hard evidence), Benjamin Franklin, while the editor of the *Pennsylvania Gazette*, planned a monthly magazine in 1740, the *General Magazine, and Historical Chronicle, for all the British Plantations in America*. It was not, however, the first magazine in the colonies. The *General Magazine* was first published on 16 February 1741, three days after Andrew Bradford initially published his *American Magazine, or a Monthly View of the Political State of the British Colonies*. These magazines, modeled closely on popular British publications like the *London Magazine*, included virtually no American materials and, instead, freely copied articles and essays from the British magazines. The seventy pages of the *General Magazine* included historical sketches, poetry, and articles on religion. The *American Magazine*, half the length of Franklin's magazine, published mostly articles on politics. The ventures of both Bradford and Franklin failed within a year. Their experiences were typical. Some forty-five magazines would be attempted during the next fifty years, but not until just before the Revolutionary War and in the period immediately afterward would magazines begin to capture and hold the attention of readers. For instance, the strongly patriotic *Royal American Magazine*, first edited by Isaiah Thomas, was published in 1774 and 1775 and included many illustrations and articles on literature, poems, notices of marriages and deaths, weather reports, geographical descriptions of the American colonies, and in one issue a series of engravings by Paul Revere.

THE REVOLUTION AND THE YOUNG REPUBLIC

In the meantime, newspaper circulation increased throughout the colonies. This, along with the news sharing and copying among newspapers that had been an unquestioned part of periodical publication from its origins in colonial America, had the effect of promoting colonial unity. As many colonists became increasingly restless under the restrictions of the British government, newspaper printers and editors began to shape and reflect public opinion for a wider audience that was increasingly eager for news. Concomitantly, the British government was looking for ways to pay its debts from years of fighting the French and Indians for control of the British colonies in America, and also was seeking money to pay for the further defense of the frontier after defeating its rivals. The resulting Stamp Act of 1765—which imposed a special tax on newspapers, books, and legal documents—was a galvanizing event for American printers and editors, who had a strong personal and economic stake in opposing the tax. The tax would mean the end of many newspapers and make it almost impossible to begin new ventures. Because of the informal system of sharing information, opposition to the Stamp Act quickly became a feature of virtually every paper. The colonial printers of the twenty-six newspapers in existence in 1765 were divided by geography, a limited transportation system, and political affiliation but united by the economic implications of the Stamp Act. The repeal of the act in 1766 demonstrated the power of the colonial press.

But the unity of the periodical press was short-lived. As the British government searched for alternative means to solve its budgetary problems, new taxes were levied on the colonies, and opposition to these and the British government generally increased. Opinion was deeply divided about the future of the colonies, however, and the newspapers were published from both the Tory and the Whig, or patriot, perspectives of their editors and audiences. During the Revolution, newspaper publishing was severely disrupted; nearly one-third of the papers in circulation at the beginning of the war did not survive. Many of these failed simply because they were unable to get paper and other basic supplies from their sources in Europe.

With the end of the war, however, periodical publication entered a new phase. The first daily newspaper in America, the *Philadelphia Evening Post,* began publication on 30 May 1783, and a second daily, the *New-York Daily Advertiser,* began in 1785. By 1800 there were 241 newspapers in the United States, 24 of them dailies. Magazines also enjoyed a revival, although their development was much slower than that of newspapers, and few survived for more than a year or two. The magazines that were published provided engravings of fashion and social life; short fiction; and articles on religion, politics, and morals. In 1787 John Trenchard, an engraver, started the *Columbian Magazine,* which attempted to provide a history of the Revolutionary War. Isaiah Thomas published the *Massachusetts Magazine* (1789–1796) and the *New-York Magazine* (1790–1797); although short-lived, they included original contributions by Charles Brockden Brown and Noah Webster. Webster's own publication, the *American Magazine* (1787–1788), lasted only a year.

THE GOLDEN AGE

For a variety of reasons, periodicals of all kinds developed quickly throughout the nineteenth century. By 1825 there were some one hundred magazines in circulation, most of them distributed through the mail. The Erie Canal, completed in 1825, created a link from New York City to Buffalo that eased travel westward and consequently drew the Northeast and the Midwest closer together both economically and politically. The election of the first populist president, Andrew Jackson, in 1828 marked important changes in the nature of the presidency as well as in government policies. It was an era of expansion, and the growth in the number and scope of periodicals reflected the mood of the country.

Important changes in technology also played a role in expanding the periodical press. In 1825 the *New-York Daily Advertiser* became the first newspaper to use the Hoe cylinder press, which speeded production to two thousand four-page papers per hour. By 1832 R. Hoe and Company had developed a double cylinder press that would print both sides

of a page at once and could also be operated by steam power instead of hand crank. The production level doubled to four thousand copies of a paper per hour. In addition, the development of stereotype printing and the availability of cheap, machine-made paper—developed by an American, Thomas Gilpin—further altered the course of periodical publication. Cheaper postal rates contributed to wider distribution and a larger potential audience for printed materials. In addition, railroads were connecting various parts of the country very quickly. By 1840 there were nine thousand miles of track; by the beginning of the Civil War, there were more than thirty thousand. Not only did the railroads provide more efficient transportation for goods and mail, they also provided opportunities for travel as well as a new outlet for selling portable reading materials. Periodical publication soared as demand increased. With the establishment of the *New York Sun* in 1833, the "penny" papers began. These were daily newspapers carrying a variety of local and national news, designed for the average person and costing a few cents a copy. The *New York Times* was founded in 1851, and within ten weeks of its start-up, it had a circulation of twenty thousand. By 1840 some 1,500 ongoing periodicals of various kinds existed in the country; as the editors of the *New-York Mirror* (1823–1843) proclaimed, "This is the golden age of periodicals!"

In addition to the publication of magazines that were meant to be of general interest, enterprising editors and printers began to develop periodicals designed to appeal to special interests and audiences. For example, the first religious newspaper in America, the *Boston Recorder,* was published beginning in 1816 by Nathaniel Willis. He was the father of Sara Payson Willis (Fanny Fern), the first weekly newspaper columnist in America, and of Nathaniel P. Willis, the successful editor of the *Home Journal,* founded in 1846 and surviving into the twenty-first century as the elegant magazine of high society, *Town and Country.* From 1827 to 1862 the elder Willis also edited *Youth's Companion* from the children's section of the *Recorder,* turning it into a religious newspaper designed to provide instruction as well as amusements specifically for children. Lydia Maria Child founded and edited the first children's magazine, the *Juvenile Miscellany,* from 1826 to 1834. In addition to religious periodicals and those designed for children, many editors targeted particular audiences for publications in medicine, agriculture, and the interests of middle-class women. Forty-five periodicals for women emerged between 1800 and 1830; more than sixty-five more appeared in the thirty years before the Civil War. Among the most popular of the early periodicals was *The Ladies Companion* (1834–1843), published by William W. Snowden, who printed contributions by a variety of well-known women writers, including Lydia Sigourney, Lydia Maria Child, Elizabeth Oakes Smith, and Catharine Sedgwick. The most popular women's magazine of the nineteenth century, however, was *Godey's Lady's Book* (founded in 1830), edited by Sarah Josepha Hale from 1837 to 1877. The highly visible and successful *Godey's* maintained a list of 70,000 subscribers by 1851 and reached 150,000 just before the Civil War. Interested in defining middle-class roles for women, Hale published poetry, light sketches of domestic life, engravings, and music, while steadfastly ignoring both the antislavery movement and even the Civil War. Although Hale envisioned a primarily female audience and actively promoted women writers in the pages of her magazine, her contributors also included Edgar Allan Poe, Nathaniel Hawthorne, Ralph Waldo Emerson, and Nathaniel P. Willis.

The African American periodical press began in 1827 with *Freedom's Journal*, published in New York City by Samuel Cornish and John B. Russwurm. This paper, like the others that followed, was conceived primarily for the 300,000 free black people living in the United States before the Civil War. Later New York City periodicals included the *Rights of All* (1829), the *Weekly Advocate* (1837), and the *Colored American* (1837–1842). Farther west, Martin Delany's *Mystery* was published in Pittsburgh from 1843 to 1847 and the *Alienated American* was published in Cleveland from 1852 to 1856. Frederick Douglass, the best-known black editor, published the *North Star* (1847–1850), *Frederick Douglass' Paper* (1850–1860), and *Douglass' Monthly* (1858–1863). Genteel and positive in tone, black periodicals before the Civil War generally tended to stress the importance of education and morality for blacks and tried to attract white readers by showcasing the abilities and successes of free blacks.

Almost simultaneous with the development of the black press was the development of periodicals for American Indians. The first of those newspapers was the four-page *Cherokee Phoenix*, first published in New Echota, Georgia, on 21 February 1828. Like the other Indian newspapers to follow, the *Phoenix* was a bilingual publication, printed partly in English and partly in Cherokee, using the alphabet developed by Sequoyah, a Cherokee silversmith. Shaped by the Cherokee tribal government, the primary purpose of the paper was educational: to assist Indians in reading, writing, and learning English so that they might better cope with the encroaching white civilization. At the same time, the paper sought to fight the removal of tribes further west and was clearly designed to show white readers that Native Americans had literate voices and could use them effectively. The prospectus of the *Phoenix* explained that the paper would carry laws and documents of the Cherokee nation, accounts of manners and customs, news of other tribes, and articles that would promote "Literature, Civilization and Religion among the Cherokees" (Murphy and Murphy, *Let My People Know*, p. 25). Regular lessons in spelling, grammar, and usage were also published.

Periodicals also served political purposes for disparate groups of people in the nineteenth century. William Lloyd Garrison established one of the first abolitionist newspapers, *The Liberator* (1831–1865), proclaiming that "The right to be free is a truth planted in the hearts of men." Although the paper never had a subscriber list of more than three thousand, it was an important influence on the developing antislavery sentiment in the United States. The *National Anti-Slavery Standard* (1840–1870) published, among other unconventional works, letters from Frances E. W. Harper, a free black woman, who was gaining a considerable reputation as a brilliant abolitionist orator. Another successful abolitionist newspaper was the *National Era* (1847–1860), edited by Gamaliel Bailey and the poet John Greenleaf Whittier. The most famous novel of the nineteenth century appeared first as a serial in the *Era*: Harriet Beecher Stowe's *Uncle Tom's Cabin; or, Life among the Lowly* (1852) ran from 5 June 1851 to 1 April 1852. Although the serialization of works of fiction was not new in periodicals, the success of *Uncle Tom's Cabin* in the *Era* spurred the serial publication of longer works of American fiction, a tradition continuing into the twenty-first century.

Periodicals developed steadily throughout the nineteenth century and quickly came to play a central role in general communication, information, and entertainment. In 1845 William Kirkland, a contemporary critic and reviewer for *Godey's*, observed that periodicals were rapidly becoming the pervasive reading material of the day:

> A large percentage of books published scarce find a publisher; numbers of those purchased are never read and many that *are* read, are read by one or two persons, while with periodicals the *un*-read are the exception. One has but to look into circulating libraries, reading-rooms and the like places to see that an extensive class of readers finds time or inclination for little else." (Price and Smith, p. 6)

The ubiquitousness of the periodical made it a natural forum for the dissemination of general education. Mary Abigail Dodge (Gail Hamilton), who wrote at various times for the *National Era,* the *Independent,* the *Congregationalist,* the *North American Review,* and *Harper's,* commented that there were many readers "who without the magazines would not only not read Bacon and Plato, but would not read anything." Similarly, Margaret Fuller, whose career was fundamentally shaped by her experiences as an editor of the literary magazine the *Dial* and as the literary editor for Horace Greeley's *New-York Tribune* (1841–1924), stressed the educational mission of the periodicals in her essay "American Literature": "The most important part of our literature, while the work of diffusion is still going on, lies in the journals, which monthly, weekly, daily, send their messages to every corner of this great land, and form, at present, the only efficient instrument for the general education of the people" (pp. 137–138).

THE PROFESSIONALIZATION OF AUTHORSHIP

Periodicals also played a formative role in the professionalization of authorship in the United States. On 29 December 1855 an arresting notice appeared on the front page of a popular weekly publication, the *New York Ledger,* a newspaper designed for family entertainment within the home. Accustomed to a steady supply of family-oriented short stories, serials, articles, and poems written by celebrated writers, readers would not have been surprised to learn about the latest *Ledger* acquisition: Fanny Fern. The announcement indicated that Robert Bonner, the innovative editor and owner of this flourishing family "story" paper, had successfully negotiated an unprecedented arrangement with this rising star, a journalist and author of the best-selling novel *Ruth Hall* (1855). Earlier in the year Bonner had, with considerable fanfare and advertising acumen, published Fern's *Fanny Ford,* a novella in ten parts, for which he had paid one hundred dollars for each installment, an unparalleled sum of money for newspaper writing in 1855. Following the success of this serial, Bonner contracted with Fern to write exclusively for the *Ledger,* inventing a new feature for newspapers: a signed weekly column. Under the terms of the agreement, Fanny Fern became the first women to write such a column in the United States and among the most highly paid writers in the country. Her spirited, witty articles of social criticism and commentary appeared weekly from 5 Jan-

uary 1856 until 12 October 1872, two days after her death from cancer at age sixty-one. In becoming a part of Bonner's enterprise, Fanny Fern joined an impressive group who wrote for the *Ledger,* one that would eventually include many of the major and influential writers of the day, such as Lydia Sigourney, E. D. E. N. Southworth, Sylvanus Cobb Jr., Henry Ward Beecher, John Greenleaf Whittier, Henry Wadsworth Longfellow, Edward Everett, Louisa May Alcott, James Parton, Harriet Beecher Stowe, George Bancroft, William Cullen Bryant, Alice and Phoebe Cary, Sara Jane Lippincott (Grace Greenwood), and even such British luminaries as Alfred, Lord Tennyson and Charles Dickens, to whom Bonner paid five thousand dollars for a three-part serial, "Hunted Down," published in 1859.

These writers were part of the larger literary establishment that wrote for the periodical press, including Herman Melville, Edgar Allan Poe, Nathaniel Hawthorne, Walt Whitman, Margaret Fuller, Frances E. W. Harper, Frederick Douglass, Lydia Maria Child, Ralph Waldo Emerson, Henry David Thoreau, and Elizabeth Barstow Stoddard, all of whom wrote poems, stories, serialized fiction, or articles and essays that appeared in papers like the abolitionist *Liberator,* the monthly *Godey's Lady's Book,* and Greeley's *New York Tribune.* They also wrote for the high-powered literary journals that began to emerge at midcentury, such as the *Atlantic Monthly* (1857–), *Harper's Weekly* (1857–1916), and *Harper's New Monthly Magazine,* established in 1850 and later called *Harper's Magazine.* Although the initial editors published mostly British writers, after the Civil War, *Harper's* began to publish American writers, and the work of artists like Winslow Homer, Frederic Remington, and John Singer Sargent also appeared regularly. By 1884 illustrations took up about 15 percent of the space in *Harper's* and other magazines like *Scribner's Monthly* (1870), which became the *Century Illustrated Magazine* in 1881. From that time on, illustrations were an important part of periodical publication.

During the Civil War the numbers of both magazines and newspapers declined. In the aftermath of the war, however, periodicals of all kinds were in heavy demand. New York City gradually replaced Boston and Philadelphia as the center of publishing, and the increased migration to the West created new markets and audiences for both newspapers and magazines of general and specialized interest. By 1880 the number of daily newspapers in the United States stood at 850; by the end of the

❦

THE ATLANTIC MONTHLY (1857–)

The *Atlantic Monthly: A Magazine of Literature, Art and Politics* was the inspiration of Free Soiler Francis Underwood and writers such as Ralph Waldo Emerson, Oliver Wendell Holmes, and James Russell Lowell. Founded as an elite monthly journal whose cultural mission was to guide the age in literature, politics, science, and the arts, the magazine was also firmly antislavery in political orientation. Under its first editor, James Russell Lowell, the *Atlantic* published essays and reviews, most of them by established American writers such as Ralph Waldo Emerson, Harriet Beecher Stowe, John Greenleaf Whittier, Thomas Wentworth Higginson, and Henry Wadsworth Longfellow. Despite its fairly narrow focus on New England, the *Atlantic* was acknowledged to be the best literary magazine of the day and within two years its circulation had reached thirty thousand. When it was purchased in 1859 by the successful publishing company of Ticknor and Fields, the *Atlantic* expanded and established a tradition of including diverse writers from geographic locations beyond New England, beginning with Rebecca Harding Davis and John W. DeForest. William Dean Howells, who edited the journal from 1871 to 1881, articulated his theory of realistic fiction both in his editorial columns and by publishing works like Mark Twain's autobiographical *Old Times on the Mississippi* (1876) in 1875 and much of Henry James's early fiction, including his first novels, *Watch and Ward* (1878; serialized in August–December 1871) and *Roderick Hudson* (1878; serialized in January–December 1875). Howells's successor, Thomas Bailey Aldrich, published Charles Chesnutt's "The Goophered Grapevine," thus offering the first national audience to a writer who would become the most influential African American fiction writer at the turn of the twentieth century. In 1900 the *Atlantic* published "Impressions of an Indian Childhood," "The School Days of an Indian Girl," and "An Indian Teacher Among Indians," the autobiographical account of Zitkala-Sa (Gertrude Bonnin), a Native American woman writer born to a Sioux mother and a white father.

Although the *Atlantic* continued to publish literature in the twentieth century, declining circulation prompted its editors to broaden its coverage and include more articles on politics and current events. Martin Luther King Jr.'s "Letter from Birmingham Jail" appeared first in the *Atlantic* in 1963; it also published essays about technology by Albert Einstein in the postwar years. At the same time, the *Atlantic* published the first fiction of Louise Erdrich and Sue Miller, as well as the poems of James Dickey. While other magazines used increasing numbers of illustrations and artwork to attract readers, the *Atlantic* refrained from doing so until the 1940s; the first pictorial cover appeared in 1947. At the end of the twentieth century, the *Atlantic* maintained its status as a serious magazine and with its eleventh editor, William Whitworth, covered an increasingly broad range of topics.

century, the number had reached 1,400. By 1900 some 3,500 magazines were in existence with an estimated readership of 65 million. Copyright laws, developing slowly through the nineteenth century, put an end to the unauthorized printing of stories and articles, effectively prompting more diversity and originality within periodicals. Inevitably, the distinctions between kinds of periodicals became more pronounced. Throughout the eighteenth and nineteenth century American periodicals were heterogeneous publications that combined news with literature.

THE TWENTIETH CENTURY

With the turn of the century, a new era in periodical production began. The character of the newspaper became firmly news oriented. Additionally, the development of competing national news bureaus, the concomitant emphasis on the marketing of news, and the expansion of large-city newspapers such as the *Louisville Courier-Journal,* the *Los Angeles Times,* and, of course, the *New York Times* (whose motto became "All the News That's Fit to Print" in 1896) tended to reduce and eventually eliminate the space that was previously devoted to fiction and poetry. By the end of the twentieth century, the mergers of newspapers into chains (such as Gannett and Knight-Ridder), the growing number of syndicated columnists, and the use of press association copy tended to standardize newspaper content.

As a result, periodicals in the form of magazines and journals came to serve as the primary vehicles for public expression of culture. The number and character of magazines published in the twentieth century reflected the diversity of the country itself. At the turn of the century, magazines like *McClure's, Munsey's,* and the *Saturday Evening Post* lowered prices, gained enormous circulations, and funded themselves not through subscriptions but primarily through advertisements. In particular, the *Saturday Evening Post* (1821), appealed directly to America's middle-class audiences. With Norman Rockwell covers that illustrated everyday scenes of American life, steady offerings of popular fiction writers, and informative news stories, the *Post* was the great popular success of the first third of the twentieth century. The *Colored American,* established in 1900 and edited in part by Pauline Hopkins, was designed as a general purpose magazine for black audiences and as an alternative to magazines such as *McClure's* and *Munsey's.* Other magazines, such as *The Ladies Home Journal,* established in 1883, were designed to appeal to upper-middle-class white women. Although this magazine and others, such as *Harper's Bazaar* (1867) and *Vogue* (1892), published fashion news and advertisements for women's clothing and accessories, they also included articles on medicine, politics, the arts, and housekeeping practices. Like the nineteenth-century magazines for women, these also published fiction by writers like Edith Wharton, Mary Austin, Ida Tarbell, and Mary Roberts Rinehart.

Between the world wars, magazines that offered condensations of books and summaries of the news came into vogue. *Reader's Digest* (1922), with its condensations of articles and fiction from other

BOOTH TARKINGTON · COREY FORD · PERCY MADEIRA

Saturday Evening Post, **11 July 1936.** First published as a newspaper, in 1898 the *Post* became a magazine emphasizing business, public affairs, and romance. Norman Rockwell's first cover was published in May 1916. The *Post* ceased publication in 1971. PRINTED BY PERMISSION OF THE ROCKWELL FAMILY TRUST © 1936 THE ROCKWELL FAMILY TRUST

magazines, its humorous jokes and stories, and its small, portable size, became very popular. News magazines established equally loyal followings. The first issue of *Time* appeared on 3 March 1923, and as the editors announced, the magazine was designed to provide condensed accounts of national and world news for the "busy man" who had little time for extensive commentary and analysis. *Newsweek,* established in 1933, was specifically conceived to compete with *Time* and advertised that it would sift and select the significant news of the week for its readers. During World War II the news magazines were the primary sources of information about the progress of the war; and photojournalism came into its own. Even with government censorship of war pictures, magazines like *Look* and *Life* (both established in the 1930s) printed hundreds of photographs of the war, bringing its realities into American homes. Photographers like Margaret Bourke-White at *Life* were as well known as the writers of the articles.

THE NEW MEDIA

The advent of television in the 1950s altered both the news and entertainment aspects of periodicals, but magazines responded with extensive coverage of television itself. After midcentury, specialized magazines became common and served almost every conceivable special interest in trade, commerce, medicine, agriculture, and education. At the same time, new kinds of publications for ethnic groups and both genders enjoyed a boom in the second half of the century. Magazines like *Ebony* (1945) reflected and shaped the Black Pride movement; *Sports Illustrated* (1954) capitalized on the increasing enthusiasm for sports at all levels; *Ms. Magazine* (1972) demonstrated the changing role of women in the United States; and *People* (1974) promoted the American obsession with celebrities. The increasing numbers of Hispanic peoples in the United States created an audience for magazines in Spanish, and in 1983 the De Armas Hispanic Magazine Network was established; it distributed Spanish versions of many well-known magazines, such as *Mechánica Popular.*

Also after World War II, sex became a significant trend in magazines. Often called "skin magazines," *Playboy, Penthouse,* and the more graphic *Hustler* attracted large, mostly male audiences, especially in the 1970s. Under heavy attack by women's groups and by fundamentalist religious organizations, the magazines, especially *Playboy,* gradually downplayed sexual content and included more articles on current politics and business. In 1985 *Playboy*'s circulation was 4.2 million, down from 7.2 million in 1972. Increasingly, cable television channels, pay-per-view outlets, and videotapes overtook the market for the sexually explicit materials of the earlier magazines. During this same time, magazines about individual cities found wide readerships. While the *New Yorker,* established in 1925 by Harold Ross, was the first, new versions such as *Dallas, Chicago,* and even *New York* magazine in the latter part of the twentieth century focused less on literary fare and more on articles for tourists and consumers. Entertainment features and guides, restaurant reviews,

and advice on where to shop comprised the bulk of these publications. At the end of the twentieth century, however, periodicals once more became risky ventures. The high costs of publication, increased postal rates, decreased readership, and the inroads of television on sources of advertising revenues have combined to cause even long-established magazines to falter and fold. Publication of the prestigious *Saturday Review* ceased in 1982 and *Life,* which for decades was a staple of middle-class American households, existed at the beginning of the twenty-first century only as an occasionally produced special issue.

As print culture began giving way to electronic culture, however, periodicals once more led the way. While books in electronic form were increasingly available on the Internet in the 1990s, far more popular among persons on-line were the increasing number of electronic periodicals. Some newspapers and magazines, like the *New York Times* and *Harper's Magazine,* provided much of the same text online as in print. Others, like the *Atlantic Monthly,* maintained two formats: one in print and one in electronic form. As the editors suggested, *Atlantic Unbound,* a website established in 1993, was an "experimental venture into a new medium." The site invited interactivity with readers by encouraging comments and e-mail responses, provided historical information about the magazine, maintained an electronic archive of reviews of important books, and offered search capabilities for the previous several issues of the magazine, none of which was immediately available in the printed forms, firmly bound on the shelves of libraries. Still other periodicals of the 1990s, like *Salon Magazine,* a daily Internet magazine of entertainment, literature, politics, and business founded in 1995, moved entirely beyond the limits of print and paper, existing only in electronic space. Readership figures (provided by the editors) indicated that there was an average of one million visits to the site each month. As periodicals were once the most modern of print forms, it seemed that they might soon prove to be the most modern of electronic forms.

See also **The Print Revolution; Rhetoric and Belles Lettres; Radical Alternatives** (*volume 1*); **Authorship, Intellectual Property, and Copyright; Elite vs. Popular Cultures; Culture for Mass Audiences; Learned Societies and Professional Associations; Literary Reviews and "Little Magazines"; Almanacs and Ephemeral Literature; Libraries; Journals of Opinion; Journalism; Marxist Approaches** (*in this volume*).

BIBLIOGRAPHY

Baldasty, Gerald J. *The Commercialization of News in the Nineteenth Century.* Madison, Wisc., 1992.

Beetham, Margaret. "Towards a Theory of the Periodical as a Publishing Genre." In *Investigating Victorian Journalism.* Edited by Laurel Brake, Aled Jones, and Lionell Madden. New York, 1990.

Chielens, Edward E. *American Literary Magazines: The Eighteenth and Nineteenth Centuries.* New York, 1986.

———. *American Literary Magazines: The Twentieth Century.* Westport, Conn., 1992.

Daniel, Walter C. *Black Journals of the United States.* Westport, Conn., 1982.

Fuller, Margaret. *Papers on Literature and Art.* New York, 1852.

Humphrey, Carol Sue. *The Press of the Young Republic: 1783–1833.* Westport, Conn., 1996.

Hutton, Frankie. *The Early Black Press in America, 1827 to 1860.* Westport, Conn., 1993.

Johanningsmeier, Charles A. *Fiction and the American Literary Marketplace: The Role of Newspaper Syndicates in America, 1860–1900.* New York, 1997.

Marzolf, Marion. *Up from the Footnote: A History of Women Journalists.* New York, 1977.

Murphy, James E., and Sharon M. Murphy. *Let My People Know: American Indian Journalism, 1828–1978.* Norman, Okla., 1981.

Okker, Patricia. *Our Sister Editors: Sarah J. Hale and the Tradition of Nineteenth-Century American Women Editors.* Athens, Ga., 1995.

Price, Kenneth M., and Susan Belasco Smith. *Periodical Literature in Nineteenth-Century America.* Charlottesville, Va., 1995.

Schwarzlose, Richard A. *Newspapers: A Reference Guide.* New York, 1987.

Sedgwick, Ellery. *The Atlantic Monthly, 1857–1909: Yankee Humanism at High Tide and Ebb.* Amherst, Mass., 1994.

Sloan, William David, and Julie Hedgepeth Williams. *The Early American Press, 1690–1783.* Westport, Conn., 1994.

Tebbel, John, and Mary Ellen Zuckerman. *The Magazine in America, 1741–1990.* New York, 1991.

Zboray, Ronald J. *A Fictive People: Antebellum Economic Development and the American Reading Public.* New York, 1993.

ARCHITECTURE

Paul E. Ivey

History is most significantly inscribed in its buildings, public as well as private. Architecture expresses the political and economic climates and cultural frameworks of a nation. Particularly, successful public architecture—found in capitol buildings, city halls, and other administrative structures, as well as banks, corporate buildings, museums, universities, transportation buildings, religious structures, and memorials—represents the power and permanence of American institutions. If architectural styles evoke cultural meanings in syntactic, metaphorical, and often didactic ways, then public buildings address their spectators with loud authority. Understanding American architecture as cultural expression involves tracing the evolution of the nation's cultural symbols, which are often embedded in architecture to promote local, regional, and national identities.

EARLY CIVIC AND RELIGIOUS MODELS

During the colonial seventeenth century, architectural antecedents were more closely aligned to medieval buildings than to official European structures. As newly emerging rural and urban populations began taking political and social control from royalty and the official church, they needed places to assemble and make laws. These buildings were larger than houses, topped by a bell to summon the populace, and often flanked with a market. As settlements grew, more elaborate needs concerning public law and welfare and the regulation of trade emerged and required larger buildings. During this period, colonists worked with what they had—natural forms made with local materials obviously taken from nature, such as rough hewn wood and baked brick.

The earliest colonial public buildings were usually built when needed, but were constructed following vernacular house models according to direct and logical designs. The exception was the impres-

sive architecture of New Spain in California and the American Southwest that expressed the imperial power of Spain with striking mission churches such as San Esteban Mission Church (c. 1629–1642) at Acoma Pueblo, New Mexico, and later the Mission San Xavier del Bac (1784–1797) near Tucson, Arizona. By contrast, early French, Dutch, and English settlers established their unique architectural presence in several distinct settlements in Eastern North America, such as New France, New Netherlands, and New England, many of which resembled medieval towns.

The most common public buildings in the colonies were churches and meetinghouses. Puritan New England, for example, employed simple architecture for both, sometimes crowning meetinghouses with pyramidal roofs and belfries that emphasized Puritan nonconformist beliefs. In Philadelphia's neat grid of streets (1682), Quaker meetinghouses were similar to Puritan ones and were used for both sacred and secular purposes. Public buildings in these places were not much different from people's homes and reflected simple, direct worship.

In contradistinction to the Puritan and Quaker suspicion of government and its trappings, Virginia was an elite Anglican culture that viewed church and state as mutually supporting. Churches followed a simple medieval church tradition, built of brick rather than stone, with square towers at the front, as in St. Luke's Episcopal Church (1632) in Smithfield, Virginia.

One of the first nonreligious public buildings to display an example of contemporary style from Europe was Christopher Wren's 1695 College of William and Mary, in the then-fashionable classical Georgian style. By the early eighteenth century, capitols were being built in some of the original colonies, such as the early Francis Nicholson Virginia Capitol at Williamsburg (1699–1737), also designed in the symmetrical elegance of the Georgian style. Religious architecture such as Samuel Cardy's St. Michael's Episcopal Church (1752–1761) at Charleston,

South Carolina, is a grand Georgian church with a tall steeple.

By the mid-eighteenth century colonial economies began to stabilize as did demographic patterns. With the rise of new cities, the wilderness was subdued into increasingly comfortable countryside, and new formal architecture was needed to express the stability and permanence of the colonies themselves. Much of this public architecture was close to the Wren tradition of Georgian architecture.

Wren's classical influence was also felt in a wide range of ecclesiastical architecture, such as Peter Harrison's 1749 Anglican King's Chapel in Boston, a stone and masonry church with a Corinthian porch. Harrison looked to Wren's English predecessor Inigo Jones, and to Jones's interest in Palladian motifs, for his Touro Synagogue (1762) in Newport, Rhode Island. Much of this eighteenth-century work challenged the more informal architecture of the seventeenth century, with its irregularities and emphasis on natural materials. New public buildings, with geometries, columnar orders, and classical decoration, revealed a growing sense of the colonists' interest in simple yet harmonious buildings that were designed with plans and decorations for specific social, religious, and cultural purposes. Important permutations of the classical style became popular in the eighteenth century, such as the Federal or Adam style, inspired by the Scottish architect Robert Adam and his brothers as a more softened and decorative approach to classicism. This style was particularly popular for large town houses. Increasingly, the Roman classical was accepted as the model style for public buildings, inspired primarily by the influence of Thomas Jefferson.

BIRTH OF A NATIONAL IMAGE OF UNION

The overwhelming classicism of the buildings and monuments dedicated to the public has become emblematic of American self-representation. In the Early Republic, Jefferson, well-versed in architectural theory, agreed with other eighteenth-century architects that properly articulated and proportioned structures could positively influence the behavior of American citizens. He supported a return to the architecture of ancient Rome and Greece because he believed neoclassical architecture would promote the ideals of Western civilization, at both the structural and symbolic levels. Public buildings would compel culture and democracy into the minds of the citizenry, and would continue to influence posterity. Through its historical reference to

the republic of Rome and the cradle of democracy, neoclassical architecture would not only represent culture but would also transmit republican values into society. Early examples of Jefferson's own neoclassical vision are his home, Monticello (1769–1809); the rotunda, campus buildings, and general layout of the University of Virginia at Charlottesville (1817–1826); and the Virginia State Capitol (1785–1792) in Richmond, the first truly Roman building in the United States, inspired by the Maison Carrée at Nîmes.

Decorative programs on buildings as well as monumental sculpture also contributed to the construction of the culture of America. The important transition from colonies to a union of states required grander buildings—showcases of national unity that were often decorated with symbols such as the flag, which still flies from official buildings. The American eagle and thirteen elements such as stars or arrows were most common. Like most Western nations, the United States often used allegorical figures as icons for the nation. Many of these appeared on public architecture throughout American history. In the seventeenth century, artists used the noble Indian princess as the emblem for America; by the last half of the eighteenth century she had become a Caucasian goddess of American Liberty or Columbia in Greek garb.

After the Revolution, George Washington became the most applauded and represented hero. In Jefferson's State Capitol of Virginia, Jean-Antoine Houdon's 1792 statue of the national hero suggests his place as a new Caesar, supported by the bundled fasces that were the insignia of Roman senators. Two later Presidents, Thomas Jefferson and Abraham Lincoln, were enshrined as American heroes within tremendous architectural settings: Henry Bacon's Lincoln Memorial (1922), John Russell Pope's Jefferson Memorial (1943), and later, more symbolically, Eero Saarinen's 1965 Jefferson National Expansion Memorial Arch in St. Louis. These memorials continue to communicate complex messages. The Lincoln Memorial includes inscriptions of Lincoln's own words, murals by Jules Guerin, and a large statue placed by Daniel Chester French in the position of a classical deity. But it also has become a site for historical public events, such as Martin Luther King Jr.'s famous "I Have a Dream" speech.

As the locus of political and cultural power, Washington, D.C., has always been the most conspicuous place for the production of public ceremonial architecture as a powerful expression of centralized government in the United States. As the

Virginia State Capitol (1785–1792). The design for the capitol was the result of a collaboration between Thomas Jefferson and the French architect Charles-Louis Clérisseau. Photograph, 1865. © MEDFORD HISTORICAL SOCIETY COLLECTION/CORBIS

ninth home of the legislature that had met briefly in New York, Pennsylvania, Maryland, and New Jersey, this new site was from its beginning conceived as a tremendous new space for the display of the political and cultural symbols of constitutional democracy. Its overall configuration, however, developed by the Frenchman Pierre Charles L'Enfant in 1790, more closely resembled the palatial baroque cities of Europe, with radiating streets and squares named after the original thirteen states, and statues and other memorials dedicated to revolutionary leaders. L'Enfant grouped the legislative and executive branches separately, following the organization of powers in the United States Constitution. The executive branch was to be centered in the President's House, not officially called the White House until 1902.

L'Enfant, Jefferson, and Washington all had ideas for the President's House. Jefferson suggested

a front much like Perrault's new facade for the Louvre in Paris. James Hoban won the competition and used the Palladian great houses of Ireland and England as models. Hoban worked on the commission between 1792 and 1802. Benjamin Latrobe, who had already successfully built the important and symbolic Bank of Pennsylvania Building in 1800, began work on the building with Jefferson between 1803 and 1832. After being burned down in 1814 by British troops (along with the new Capitol building), reconstruction began in 1815. Charles Bulfinch became involved in 1825 and completed the building in 1829. McKim, Mead, and White, riding the successful Beaux Arts wave produced by the success of the 1893 World's Columbian Exposition in Chicago, expanded both public and private quarters starting in 1902.

The Capitol of the United States was the most monumental building for the new Union and therefore had an important symbolic function as well as a practical one. To Thomas Jefferson, the Capitol represented national union as well as the balance of power set forth in the Constitution: this had to be visibly legible to the public. Also, the Capitol was for all Americans, therefore it should be unusually grand and welcome the interaction of the citizenry with civic space. It was both an iconic symbol of civic power and cultural legacy and a public place.

Jefferson felt that the neoclassical style was most appropriate to symbolize stability as had been the case in several important bank buildings, among them Samuel Blodgett Jr's. First Bank of the United States (1795–1797) and, later, William Strickland's Second Bank of the United States (1818–1824), a large Doric structure that was the first building in the United States to imitate the Parthenon. Jefferson's Virginia State Capitol was also an important model for the federal Capitol. Charles Bulfinch's much-applauded 1798 Massachusetts State House, with its high gilded dome and Corinthian porch, indicated that the column and dome were principal motifs and even symbolic of early American democracy. Most early statehouses included the columned portico, a dome over a centralized public space or rotunda, and two large meeting rooms opposite one another, usually in separate wings. Capitols built in the first thirty years of the nineteenth century, such as those in New York, Harrisburg, and New Haven, included combinations of these elements and revealed that a common approach to community architecture was emerging.

The Greek Revival style was embraced by many Americans in the second quarter of the nineteenth century, even for home designs. The 1821 Greek rebellion against Turkey must have reminded many Americans of their own revolution as well as that of the French. Greek democracy was represented in temple-fronted homes, as well as in public buildings in the North and the South. But the classical style was an unstable signifier, being associated with the destiny of the individual citizen in the North and with an aristocratic view of culture in the South.

The United States Capitol therefore took what was becoming a tradition in the new states and centered it in Washington, D.C. George Washington, Thomas Jefferson, Benjamin Latrobe, Stephen Hallet, William Thornton, James Hoban, Charles Bulfinch, and Thomas U. Walter all contributed to the final structure, built between 1793 and 1867. The iconography of the federal Capitol included monumental pediment sculptures with figurative emblems and symbols of European culture and American civilization spreading across the conti-

nent. Between 1859 and 1863 a new, much larger dome began to rise, derived from St. Peter's Basilica and based on Thomas Walter's successful Library of Congress dome from 1852.

The United States Capitol consolidated the use of classical revival architecture for state capitols, customhouses, courthouses, large post offices, and city halls. The increasing size of public buildings, not only libraries, museums, and government structures but also railway terminals and department stores, reveals that size and impressive styles were ends in themselves, and new state capitols and city halls led the way.

STATE CAPITOLS, CITY HALLS, POST OFFICES

American cities grew rapidly as people moved from the country to urban centers and through mass immigration from abroad. Civic problems and needs such as sanitation, police, education, and poverty emerged that required local organized government structures in each city. These were housed in increasingly more prominent buildings. One of the first major city halls was Joseph Mangin and John McComb Jr.'s New York City Hall (1802–1811) in the French Renaissance and Adam styles, with ceremonial spaces, a rotunda, council, and reception rooms. By the 1850s more city services, such as fire fighting, street cleaning, and other public health requirements were taken over by city governments, and even larger and more elaborate practical and symbolic structures were needed. Gamaliel King's Brooklyn Borough Hall (1845–1849) and James Gallier's New Orleans City Hall (1845–1850) inculcate the classical ideals represented in multiservice federal buildings. Even more impressive was the Second Empire–style Philadelphia City Hall (1871–1901) by John McArthur Jr. and Thomas U. Walter, with its grand tower designed to be a recognizable landmark for the citizens. Second Empire style became increasingly popular for incredibly elaborate state buildings such as the State, War, and Navy Building (1871–1888) in Washington, D.C., and the St. Louis Post Office and Customhouse (1873–1884), both by Alfred B. Mullet, supervising architect of the Treasury Department.

Robert Mills designed the General Post Office in Washington, D.C., in the late 1830s. However, most post offices were owned by local communities even though their purpose was to be a visible form representing the local presence of the federal government. Throughout the seventeenth and eighteenth centuries, town post offices were most likely found in taverns and coffeehouses and sometimes in print shops and churches. The Founding Fathers established a postal system, along with a free press, and the Postal Act of 1792 expanded the postal service and subsidized the press, ensuring cheap rates for increasingly important newspaper, magazine, and pamphlet publishers, as well as for the general letter-writing public.

After the Civil War, the Post Office Department introduced free delivery in cities; by the turn of the twentieth century it had expanded the service to villages and rural areas. In small towns, vernacular buildings designed by local builders were usually main street structures with simple classical elements and ornamentation. However, by the 1860s, post offices in growing cities were designed by the Treasury Department's Office of the Supervising Architect, who oversaw the design, construction, and maintenance of new government-owned buildings, including post offices, courthouses, and customhouses. Between the end of the Civil War and the turn of the twentieth century more than three hundred projects were undertaken. These were designed in classically inspired styles by Robert Mills, who preferred neoclassical or Greek designs in the 1830s; Ammi B. Young, who built Renaissance Revival buildings in the 1840s and 1850s; and Alfred B. Mullett, who utilized Second Empire styles in the 1860s and 1870s. As classicism waned in the 1870s, William A. Potter designed Victorian Gothic buildings, and Willoughby J. Edbrooke rode the wave of Henry Hobson Richardson's celebrity in the 1890s by utilizing the Romanesque style, demonstrated in the Washington, D.C., Post Office (1899) with its massive tower.

REPRESENTING RELIGION

After the Revolutionary War, a new period that emphasized public union and centrality was introduced, but one which nonetheless was based on freedom of religion. American church architecture was not tied to any one style, though it had often perpetuated traditional church architectures from worshippers' homelands. The rise of neoclassicism in government buildings also influenced church designs. The best known example is Benjamin Latrobe's magnificent Old Roman Catholic Cathedral in Baltimore (1806–1821), the first cathedral in the United States with a tremendous Roman dome fronted by an Ionic porch. Strickland's Masonic Temple (1837) in Philadelphia mixed Oriental and

Egyptian motifs with Norman and Greek elements. The Gothic Revival style, emblem of a larger Romantic movement that privileged nature and stylistic innovation, also rose to prominence by the mid nineteenth century, particularly felt in church commissions. This was due to the belief that the Gothic style was an architectural lesson in Christian doctrine. Groups such as the New York Ecclesiologists, inspired by the English Gothicist A. W. H. Pugin, wrote extensively on the importance of the historically correct Gothic styles as impelling Christian, albeit primarily Episcopal, values into the public sphere. Richard Upjohn, the most important architect of this group, built one of its most memorable examples in his Trinity Church (1846) in New York. James Renwick Jr. built another important example in his Grace Church (1846) in New York and finally his St. Patrick's Cathedral (1858–1879).

Catholics and Episcopalians built cathedrals in the United States throughout the twentieth century, often at great or even prohibitive expense, particularly those lavish examples designed as public symbols. For example, the National Cathedral, designed by George Bodley and Henry Vaughan, was begun in 1907 and completed in 1990. Far more impressive than Saint Patrick's, and revealing denominational rivalries, the Cathedral of Saint John the Divine, by La Farge and Heins and Ralph Adams Cram, was begun in 1893 and remains unfinished today.

CHALLENGES TO THE CLASSICAL MODEL

By 1871 Mullett's State, War, and Navy Building, the first major post–Civil War building, was erected in Washington, D.C. Built in the Second Empire style, it completely abandoned Greek and Roman precedents for mansard roofs, grouped columns, three-dimensional uneven variegated facades, and multiple transhistorical ornamentation, in what some architects were calling High Victorian style and others "picturesque eclecticism," after an appreciation for nature's asymmetries. The best examples were John McArthur Jr.'s City Hall of Philadelphia (1871–1881) and Frank Furness and George Hewitt's Pennsylvania Academy of the Fine Arts (1871–1876), also in Philadelphia. With these new eclectic styles, America pronounced that it had integrated all of European civilization into its architecture and declared a great confidence in its international expansion. The asymmetry and mixed motifs of the Victorian style were hybrid and new, not orderly and logical like the United States Capitol.

Old Roman Catholic Cathedral, Baltimore (1806–1821). The cathedral was designed by Benjamin Henry Latrobe, America's first professional architect. © Bettmann/corbis

State, War, and Navy Building, Washington, D.C. (1871–1888). The building, designed by Alfred B. Mullet, was almost demolished in 1957. It is now known as the Old Executive Office Building. © corbis

This impulse for original usage of historical styles had begun in the eighteenth century with Adamesque architecture, which used the conventions of classicism without historical accuracy. But in the rise of a smorgasbord of styles, an earlier preoccupation with notions of the beautiful and the cultured had begun in earnest with the landscape architect A. J. Downing's *Theory and Practice of Landscape Gardening*, from 1841. Downing agreed that public buildings could be Greek but he suggested a rural vernacular eclecticism for most other buildings. For Downing, architecture was still translated directly into cultural meanings. Gothic should be used for churches, Roman should be used for civic structures, Greek for courthouses, Egyptian for funerary architecture. An early example would be John Haviland's 1829 Eastern State Penitentiary in Philadelphia, which was designed as a medieval fortress with battlements. Downing and others, such as Alexander Jackson Davis, were at the forefront of debates concerning the art and meaning of historically derived styles versus the use of restrained and orderly classicism. Downing followed John Ruskin's precepts concerning the relationship of nature to architecture, suggesting that this relationship, properly understood, created social morality and unfolded as the individual improved his or her capacity to appreciate art. He was preoccupied with the moral function of the beautiful and picturesque.

This new Romanticism emerged with great aplomb with the creation of a number of parks in many American cities. Frederick Law Olmsted and Calvert Vaux, a Downing protégé, were commissioned to create, among other parks, the magnificent Central Park in New York City (1858–1878). Parks were also viewed as great democratizers, allowing all people to put off the strains of city life. Nature and its forms were viewed as healthful—therefore, an architecture which proceeded from nature was equally as beneficial. By the mid nineteenth century, many of the new courthouse squares were flanked with gardens.

The most impressive public expression inspired by the principles of Downing was the red sandstone castle built on the Mall in Washington, D.C., the Smithsonian Institution, designed by James Renwick and completed in 1855. Its dissimilar towers and combination of medieval elements were defended as equally as meaningful to the cultural well-being of the citizenry as Roman buildings. Debates continued to pit academic classicism against a nonconforming Romantic vision and the exotic symbolism of eclectic architecture. Defenders of the

The Smithsonian Institution, Washington, D.C. (1855). The original building, designed by James Renwick Jr., and popularly known as "the Castle," was constructed of red sandstone from Seneca Creek, Maryland. © PETER FINGER/ CORBIS

medieval and Gothic argued that these were drawn from the world of nature, not geometry. To many adherents, the landscape should determine cultural identity, not a pure, timeless form.

The Smithsonian Institution, created by the United States government from a generous bequest of James Smithson in 1835, reflects the Victorian romantic obsession with medieval, picturesque forms and resists the neoclassicism so apparent in the federal city. Renwick was already well known for his Gothic Grace Church in New York City. The final Renwick plan included Victorian asymmetry on a picturesque castellated building, with nine architecturally diverse towers designed to evoke the environment of a medieval English university.

By the 1870s the architect Henry Hobson Richardson designed buildings that struck a chord in the minds and souls of Americans enamored with both classical ideas and romantic ones in historically

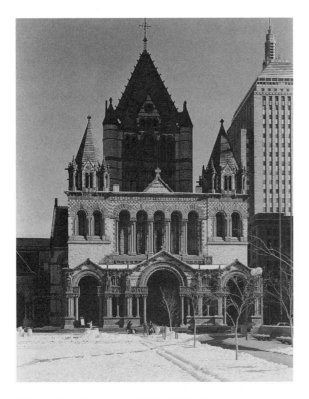

Trinity Church, Boston (1872–1877). The church was designed by Henry Hobson Richardson. The large central tower, visible from all sides, was inspired by the Cathedral of Salamanca, Spain. G. E. KIDDER SMITH/CORBIS

derived Romanesque style. His Trinity Church (1872–1877) in Boston combined large barrel arches at the entrance, checkerboard brickwork, and rough stonework crowned by a massive square tower. This unique structure inspired a number of public buildings throughout New England and beyond, including libraries, schools, railroad stations, and other civic buildings, such as his Albany City Hall (1881–1882) and Allegheny County Courthouse (1883–1888) in Pittsburgh, as well as commercial structures, such as his Marshall Field Warehouse (1887) in Chicago. The warehouse is considered his best-designed building; the weight and texture of the Romanesque style inspired the Chicago architect Louis Sullivan, who continued to develop his theories of architecture based on natural and organic forms, and also Frank Lloyd Wright, who was inspired by the romantic ideal of the truly American democratic individual.

Richardson's legacy was really a continuity of historical quotations, with many firms continuing to design academic reproductions from historical models. On the one hand, McKim, Mead, and White's Boston Public Library (1887–1895), Shep-

ley, Rutan, and Coolidge's classical revival Art Institute of Chicago (1893), and the Gothic University of Oklahoma (1910); as well as firms such as Cram and Goodhue and Carrére and Hastings, all followed Beaux Arts classical examples. On the other hand, more "progressive" architects followed the dictates of site specificity and were interested in modernized historical forms, rather than slavish academic copying. Examples include Louis Sullivan, who integrated classicism and organic decoration into commercial architecture, and whose rich decorative motifs are evident in his and George Elmslie's National Farmer's Bank (1906–1908) in Owatonna, Minnesota; Frank Lloyd Wright, known especially for his prairie style private residences and his Unitarian Unity Temple (1906) in Oak Park, Illinois; and Bernard Maybeck, best known for his Gothic-inspired First Church of Christ, Scientist (1910) in Berkeley, California. Irving Gill, in his First Church of Christ, Scientist (1920) in San Diego, California, modernized the California Mission style. These examples notwithstanding, the rise of the academic classical idiom as the public expression of American ideals continued to exert the most influence on architects of public buildings. This was particularly apparent in the many world's fairs held in American cities since the centennial of the United States. These fairs also consolidated the use of classical revival architecture as they explored America's expansive view of its culture and purpose on the world stage.

EXPOSITIONS AND NATIONAL CULTURAL IDENTITY

The great international expositions were very important venues for economic and cultural display, in impressive architectural settings, and were instrumental in defining American culture for the masses. Expositions gave Americans an idealized view of their world, away from depressions and social unrest at home and warfare abroad, and allowed them to become caught up in America's economic, political, and cultural imperial expansion. As such, the fairs encouraged a positive view of America's growing industrial power and emerging social and cultural institutions. They were visually stunning and their unusual grandness positioned the throngs of people who attended them as citizens of a great imperial power that was nonetheless governed by "the people." In their architecture, these fairs positioned America in terms of an imaginary past and a future of progress.

446

First Church of Christ, Scientist, Berkeley, California (1910). The church was designed by Bernard R. Maybeck. © G. E. KIDDER SMITH/CORBIS

The "moral influence" of the fairs was a most important component in their success. This influence was pervasive in the architecture and its ornaments, in cultural displays, and in monumental public sculpture. The gates of the 1876 Centennial Exhibition in Philadelphia's Fairmount Park were festooned with American flags, shields, and eagle motifs, which greeted the masses. Statuary representing religious liberty and American heroism dotted the park, including the torch from the yet unfinished Statue of Liberty. The five main exhibition buildings in commercial cast iron were clothed in a variety of styles. The colossal Main Building was similar to the architecture of Paxton's successful 1851 Crystal Palace. The Smithsonian exhibitions included ethnological displays designed to show the history of the vanishing American native cultures. These displays were counterpoised to the overarching message of the exposition that economic and cultural progress was rapidly unfolding with the introduction of new mechanical and industrial devices: the impressive Corliss engine could be viewed in the Machinery Hall and was the centerpiece of the entire fair. The Art Building, designed by the chief architect Herman Schwarzmann, was an openly Beaux Arts classical revival structure, which subsequently inspired architects in other major American cities to use this style for their large art galleries. Enjoyment of private art became public; the Boston Museum of Fine Arts, the Chicago Art Institute, and the New York Metropolitan Museum, as well as many symphony halls, were also built before the end of the nineteenth century.

The onward march of American material and cultural progress was celebrated in 1893 at the World's Columbian Exposition in Chicago. This fair, marking the four hundredth anniversary of Columbus's "discovery" of America, once again

World's Columbian Exposition, Chicago (1893). Richard M. Hunt's Administration Building exemplifies the Beaux Arts style, the exposition's main architectural theme. It served as the headquarters for the chief officers of the exposition. © CORBIS

reproduced Rome and provided a model for public buildings in its magnificent White City, a visionary stage-set urbanscape that consolidated the appeal of classicism as the official style for monumental building in the United States. Its restoration of classicism in a new Beaux Arts interpretation was the work of Daniel Burnham, together with Richard Morris Hunt, Solon Beman, George B. Post, Charles F. McKim, and Louis Sullivan, with grounds laid out by Frederick Law Olmsted. The Court of Honor displayed gleaming white buildings in classical uniformity, akin to Jefferson's vision of Washington, D.C. Replicas of Columbus's ships floated in the Grand Basin. The symbolic sculptural program in the monumental White City included Saint-Gaudens's statue of Columbus setting foot on land and a sixty-five-foot-tall gilded allegorical statue of a woman, crowned with laurel and holding symbols of Roman imperialism, entitled "The Republic," by Daniel Chester French, famed since 1875 for his *Minute-man* statue at Concord.

Louis Sullivan's Transportation Building was the exception to the fair's monumental classicism, but the superiority of the classical revival style was ob-

vious, and Sullivan denounced it as a contagion that would infect American architecture for fifty years. Architects continued to use classicism as the dominant mode of monumental architecture at other fairs, including the Omaha Trans-Mississippi Exposition of 1898, the Buffalo Pan-American Exposition of 1901, and the St. Louis Louisiana Purchase Exposition of 1904. The Tennessee Centennial Exposition in 1897 at Nashville featured an exact replica of the Parthenon from the Athenian Acropolis, providing a physical reminder of the restoration of democracy in the United States and particularly in the New South.

Prominent architects of public architecture such as McKim, Mead, and White, whose firm was founded in 1879, moved from Richardson's Romanesque into Hunt's broader historicism. After the Chicago's World's Fair, they continued to develop classical revival styles for prominent commissions such as the Rhode Island State Capitol (1895–1904) in Providence, the Morgan Library (1906), and the immense Pennsylvania Station (1906–1910), inspired by the baths of Caracalla in Rome.

448

CITY BEAUTIFUL AND BEYOND

The architect Daniel Burnham, in attempting to design new civic centers in several American cities as permanent architectures based on the fair, suggested that the ensemble of monumental buildings was the embodiment of civic life. The successful fair architecture became his model for a civilized American city. Public buildings stylistically unified and beautiful would constantly remind the urban citizenry of the benevolence and democratic roots of political and social power. The City Beautiful movement, based on the successful fair architecture, would bring uniformity and beauty to America's cities. The disciplined vision of the ideal American city also inspired the creation of national municipal leagues and other city beautification movements.

Burnham had already been involved in the evolution of the new office building, or commercial skyscraper, since the 1880s. After the fair, however, he turned his attention solely to the improvement of American urban spaces, even helping to complete L'Enfant's grand plan for Washington, D.C., as well as producing plans for Cleveland and San Francisco. These imperial centers were never fully realized, but the fair reinforced an interest in Beaux-Arts planning concepts, particularly in the rational principles of creating harmonious "ensembles" of public buildings.

The Beaux-Arts tradition, so well established at the world's fairs, continued to influence important civic architects such as John Russell Pope, architect of the National Gallery of Art (1941). Another proponent was Paul Cret, architect of the Pan American Union Building (1910), Indianapolis Public Library (1914–1917), Detroit Institute of Arts (1921), Folger Shakespeare Library (1928–1932), and, with Frederic W. Southworth, the 1940–1942 U.S. Naval Medical Center in Bethesda, Maryland, a skyscraper hospital with art deco elements.

DOMESTIC ARCHITECTURE: HISTORICISM, INDIVIDUALITY, AND CONFORMITY

Early American domestic architecture was generally utilitarian and not concerned with the cultural accoutrements of style. From the seventeenth-century New England saltbox clapboard houses and the brick structures of the middle colonies to the thick-walled adobe homes of the Southwest, these basically practical structures were built for survival, not comfort or culture, though the plain houses of New England have sometimes been said to reflect the austerity and anti-ornamentation prevalent in Puritan theology. From the early colonies, the home was not only the space of domestic femininity, but also the center of the Christian virtues of most Americans. Hence, in its earliest form, the house was practical, simple, and efficient. Early single-family models in the rural East were built around a central fireplace core, and city dwellings were often unornamented row houses.

By the mid-eighteenth century, houses built by successful landowners and merchants became public spectacles of new wealth and prestige. These triumphal models were often copied by builders from plates out of pattern books featuring elegant English homes, many of them Palladian in form. Showy mansions in the northern colonies also flourished, particularly surrounding Philadelphia, and were primarily built in the Georgian or Federal styles, quoting other popular European types. Town houses in cities such as Boston revealed a more elegant neoclassical reticence. In all examples, the classical style dominated.

By the early nineteenth century, many American architects, after returning from their grand tours of European architecture, were inspired by a number of architectural models, most significantly the Greek style that dominated both southern antebellum mansions and northern country houses. In the antebellum South, plantation houses and the villas of New Orleans and Natchez presented the public face of wealthy sugar and cotton magnates clothed in ever-dramatic historical styles that provided settings for ritual and pageantry.

However, Romantic architects such as Downing believed that Renaissance Italian villas (albeit more diminutive examples) were the most appropriate "cultural" models for Americans and produced a number of plans for builders to use. He and other picturesque architects also agreed that the country was the most prestigious place to live because rural living instilled not only health and vigor but allowed Americans to choose architectural styles that expressed their individuality. Architectural pattern books contained numerous examples of the many different stylistic possibilities, and manufacturers increasingly offered mail-order factory-produced building materials. Through the end of the nineteenth century, the wealthy built houses in a great assortment of exotic and picturesque styles, from Moorish to High Victorian Gothic. Examples include Calvert Vaux and Frederic Church's Olana (1870) at Hudson, New York, and Samuel and Joseph C. Newsom's William Carson House (1885) in Eureka, California. Newport, Rhode Island, contained the largest number of these mainly summer pleasure palaces by the turn of the twentieth century, including Richard Morris Hunt's impressive Italian villa The Breakers (1892–1895). Asymmetrical designs in Italianate, Gothic, Queen Anne, Romanesque, and many other revival styles competed with each other for cultural prominence. Eclecticism dominated. In contradistinction to this practice, spacious designs by Greene and Greene, such as their Gamble House (1908) in Pasadena, California, with its Arts and Crafts–inspired style but generous human-scaled open plan, as well as Irving Gill's concrete Walter Dodge House (1914–1916) in Los Angeles, with its simple geometries, reveal that American architects, particularly in California, were also interested in producing designs that were very original and certainly less grandiose that many of the elaborate turn-of-the-century, European-inspired examples of the East Coast.

As cities grew after the Civil War, the housing originally located in the central arena of the city was increasingly pushed to the perimeter, allowing for even grander homes to be built by the newly wealthy. This demographic change also eventually led to the construction of suburban single-family homes for the middle class, while city cores became dotted with multistory apartment hotels. After the Civil War the triumphal mansard roof of the Second Empire style held sway on New York's Fifth Avenue with the business elite.

The eclecticism of domestic housing, particularly in the most lavish examples, was responded to by architects in Chicago such as Louis Sullivan and Frank Lloyd Wright with a call for indigenous, site-specific architecture not based on historical style that took both the natural site for the building into account and used local building materials when practical. Inspired by the simplicity of Japanese designs, Wright's first homes were dubbed "prairie houses," because they seemed to integrate organically, a horizontal structure that articulated its relationship to the plains through long, low-massing, and sheltering cantilevered roofs. His Frederick C. Robie House (1910) in Chicago best expresses this emphasis on the horizontal aspect of the plains, and his open plan subsequently influenced many European modern architects.

By the middle of the nineteenth century, new residential areas were planned that were prototypes of the contemporary American suburb that became fully developed in the twentieth century. Llewellyn Park (1853) in New Jersey was fully residential but Riverside, Illinois (1869), is an early example of a fully planned autonomous village, made possible by new railroad lines. In these spaces, the status of a family could be said to be expressed in the exterior style of the facade of its house, from Carpenter Gothic and Queen Anne to Stick and Eastlake styles. More complex plans and more ornamentation, as well as important interior appointments and decorations, showed the cultural values and virtues of the inhabitants, particularly women, who were encouraged to be the ministers of their homes.

By the late nineteenth century, the newly emerging middle class, particularly women, were offered lots of advice concerning building and maintaining the American home. Magazines such as the *Ladies' Home Journal, House Beautiful,* and *House and Garden* positioned the home as the moral, cultural, and artistic statement of its occupants, reflecting status and fashion, from the elaborate Victorian house to the practical bungalow.

Simpler craftsman bungalows of the late nineteenth and early twentieth centuries became popular as the apartment block began to dominate the urban landscape. These single-family homes associated American families with nature through their exposed stone, brick, and wood construction, often set in small gardens. These homes were more simplified in their designs in order to maximize the efficiency of the duties of the housewife-turned-domestic engineer. After World War II, strict zoning agreements created increasingly race-restrictive and homogenous neighborhoods. Suburban tract homes, like those at Levittown, New York (1950), were more uniform, and while no longer clothed in historical styles, they were comfortable and convenient in their family-friendly plans and in their provision of new household appliances.

By the 1920s, modern architecture from Europe began to make inroads in America due to the influences of Raymond Schindler, Richard Neutra, and Eliel Saarinen, and later in the 1930s of Mies van der Rohe, Walter Gropius, and Le Corbusier. The so-called machine aesthetic rejected historical style for honest universal form based on the pure geometries of industrial design, many of them prefabricated. Often reminding viewers of a stripped-down industrial version of classicism, houses such as Richard Neutra's Lovell House (1927–1929) in Los Angeles reveal influences from the Viennese modernism of Adolph Loos; Mies's later Farnsworth House (1946–1951) in Plano, Illinois; Charles and Ray Eames's Eames House (1949) in Los Angeles; and Philip Johnson's Glass House (1948–1949) are all examples of modernist domestic architecture in America based on international style precedents.

More recently, postmodern architecture, with its references to historical architecture and pop commercial culture, began in the late 1960s and early 1970s as a reaction to modernist purity. The architect Robert Venturi's *Complexity and Contradiction in Architecture,* (1966) and, with Denise Scott Brown, *Learning from Las Vegas* (1972), had the effect of challenging the hegemony of the modern movement and advocated for architecture as "decorated shed" replete with historical pastiche, applied ornament, and lots of ambiguity. The Vanna Venturi House (1962) was the original contemporary example offered by Venturi, while Charles Moore, Michael Graves, Robert Stern, and the deconstructionist Frank Gehry represented different historicist and stylistic approaches to this broad late-twentieth-century architectural movement.

REGIONALISM TO THE INTERNATIONAL STYLE

The huge building boom of the 1930s and 1940s, with its emphasis on regional American building during the Great Depression, led to the erection of hundreds of new public buildings, particularly post offices, which often included beautiful murals by artists supported by the Works Progress Administration's Federal Art Project (1934–1943). These often represented nostalgic images of people at work in timeless epochal realism. Many of the buildings were designed in a stripped-down modernist classical style. Much of the building boom was standardized and economical.

With the continued interest in academic historical models, the Gothic reemerged as the architecture of spiritual and moral reform, supported primarily by Ralph Adams Cram and Bertram Grosvenor Goodhue, and was the accepted style for college buildings, additions, and chapels at the United States Military Academy at West Point (1903–1904). The style was also demonstrated in Horace Trumbauer's 1930–1932 chapel at Duke University in Durham, North Carolina, with its 210-foot tower.

The classical idiom continued to dominate public building projects, but by the mid 1920s a forward-looking regional architecture, based on the uniqueness of the American landscape and local history, began to rise, particularly during the depression, with its conservative, xenophobic spirit. This was also due, in part, to new government programs such as the Public Works Administration in the 1930s and the Works Projects Administration

(the renamed WPA) into the early 1940s, which officially validated architects' increasing preoccupation with defining a unique American style. Several important architects called for an authentic American architecture: Sullivan advocated an architecture that emerged gradually through the process of public cultural development, Wright called for an organic architecture that grew out of the American soil, and Elmer Grey called for a site-specific "new world" architecture. Another solution to "original" American architecture came in a renewed interest in the colonial style. Many architects believed colonial architecture was truly American and looked to the 1732 Independence Hall in Philadelphia, though much changed through its history, as the appropriate American model. An emblem of this "cult of the colonial" was Williamsburg, which was restored to its original splendor by the Rockefellers during the 1920s. But even up to the twenty-first century, many cities and states have continued to use regional styles as public architecture, including the territorial style of the New Mexico State Capitol (1965–1966) in Santa Fe, and the 1970 Taos County Courthouse, whose form echoes nearby Indian pueblos.

THE SKYSCRAPER AND AMERICAN COMMERCIAL ASPIRATIONS

Of original American architecture, the skyscraper is truly the American idiom. Up until 1930 its innovative steel technology was usually clothed in European styles; for example, Cass Gilbert's 1913 Woolworth building was a Gothic cathedral in the sky. New designs were sometimes based on American machine technology, from William Van Allen's 1928–1930 chrome, gargoyled Chrysler Building with its art deco style, to the undecorated McGraw-Hill Building (1930) by Raymond Hood. The international style also arrived at New York's Museum of Modern Art in the 1930s and announced that historicism, at least in skyscrapers and corporate structures, was on the wane. This new modern architecture of glass and steel found its pinnacle in Mies van der Rohe and Philip Johnson's Seagram Building of 1958 and was also chosen for the truly politically international United Nations complex.

These modern structures had their genesis in early American mills and factories with their regulated work forces, particularly those along the rivers of New England. These structures also led to the mail-order 1840s cast-iron storefronts and later to entire urban facades such as the warehouses of

Manhattan's SoHo. Technology was the key to the metal building's success in rapidly growing urban areas like Chicago and New York that built upward for more space. These large iron-and-masonry structures supported a growing capitalism that thrived on ideas of civilization and progress solidified in architectural form.

When the Otis elevator was introduced in 1853 at the New York Crystal Palace Exhibition, in a large greenhouse structure inspired by Paxton's in Britain (1851), architecture and land speculation would never be the same. The railroad trestle bridges and rails preceeded the steel skeleton, but the same casting processes now produced prefabricated interchangeable modular elements that could support structures that reached into the skies. Bogardus patented his cast-iron factory in 1848, and J. P. Gaynor and Daniel Badger's 1857 Haughwout Store in New York became the intersection where Otis elevators and the cast-iron structure coalesced into an image later greatly magnified by the skyscraping office building, viewed mainly as a Chicago invention.

William Le Baron Jenney's 1885 Home Insurance Building in Chicago, with its steel structure and ten floors, announced the new possibilities for commercially practical and symbolically progressive architecture, and Daniel Burnham's fourteen-story Reliance Building (1894–1895) in Chicago honestly articulated its steel structure through a thin metal and glass facade. Adler and Sullivan's 1895 Guaranty Building in Buffalo, New York, continued to evolve the aesthetics of the skyscraper through careful attention to the materials and proportions of the building, as opposed to quoting historical styles, though in the 1922 competition for the Tribune Tower in Chicago, Gropius's purified modernism lost to Howells and Hood's more richly referential Gothic structure, with the European-based International style only in its infancy.

Frank Lloyd Wright's office building with open atrium, the Larkin Building (1904) in Buffalo, offered a nonornamental and ahistorical response to the office building, as did his later 1951 Johnson Wax Research Center in Racine, Wisconsin. The grand stripped-down skyscrapers of the 1930s, with their stepped-back facades (mandated by setback

Chrysler Building (1928–1930). William Van Alen's (1883–1954) Chrysler Building, in New York City, has a stainless steel metal top and automobile-derived ornamental details, including radiator-cap gargoyles. It was briefly the tallest building in the world. © UNDERWOOD & UNDERWOOD/ CORBIS

laws from 1916), became important American models of corporate commerce. Examples include Rockefeller Center (1931–1939), by Reinhard and Hofmeister, Corbett, Morris, Harmon, and MacMurray, and Hood and Fouilhoux; the Empire State Building (1928–1931), by Shreve, Lamb, and Harmon; and Howells and Hood's 1930 New York Daily News Building, all in New York City; along with Howe and Lescaze's 1932 Philadelphia Savings Fund Society in Pennsylvania. Later, Mies van der Rohe's Chicago Lakeshore Apartments, and Skidmore, Owings, and Merrill's 1950–1952 Lever House introduced the universal possibilities of the glass curtain facade for a variety of building functions. The international style had arrived and the corporate skyscraper became an enduring symbol of America's economic prowess and aspirations, expressed in an especially intimidating form in Skidmore, Owings, and Merrill's 1976 Sears Tower in Chicago.

Today, some cities are turning to the broadly historicist postmodern pastiched style for both public and commercial architecture. The best known examples are Michael Graves's 1980–1982 Portland Public Service Building in Portland, Oregon, with its colorful facade, stylized garland motifs, and Raymond Kaskey's statue *Portlandia* peering over the entrance; and Philip Johnson and John Burgee's 1978 American Telephone and Telegraph Building in New York City.

After World War II there was a general movement to the suburbs and ensuing urban core decay with urban renewal through the 1970s. Most public buildings used corporate models based on the ideals of efficiency and truth to industrial materials. With the rebirth of downtowns, major public buildings were often important cultural symbols, such as I. M. Pei's Dallas City Hall (1972–1977) or were featured in large master plans, such as Pei's 1961 Boston Master Plan, with Kallmann, McKinnell, and Knowle's 1962–1968 Boston City Hall as its centerpiece. With the terrorist destruction of the Federal Building in Oklahoma City, a new memorial to the victims of the bombing was erected as a civic centerpiece, the Oklahoma City National Memorial (1998–2000) by Butzer Design Partners.

CONCLUSION

Departing from this brief discussion of American architecture leads us to consider other important public cultural buildings and monuments, including libraries, railroad stations, schoolhouses, war memorials, and even simpler vernacular structures, such as barns, firehouses, gas stations, diners, and drive-ins. Larger spaces such as airports, zoos, shopping malls, and Native American and utopian communal settlements also contribute to the built American cultural environment. Significant American buildings and landscapes located outside the United States, especially embassies and war memorials, are also important to understanding the political and cultural self-image the United States projects abroad. This discussion could also be extended to include nontraditional architectures such as grain elevators, dams, bridges, large urban warehouses, and industrial structures such as factories and mining buildings that have also served as symbols of American growth and economic strength. Certain practical forms of public buildings, often rooted in historical European architecture, have evolved over the history of the United States. These architectural forms and styles have become elaborate symbols of American culture and the aspiration to provide not only functional spaces for citizens, worshipers, and consumers but also spectacles of the power and prestige of American political, economic, cultural, social, and religious institutions.

See also **The Fine Arts in Colonial America; The Classical Vision; The Arts in the Republican Era** *(volume 1);* **The Culture and Critics of the Suburb and the Corporation; The Design of the Familiar; Postmodernism and the Arts; The City** *(volume 2);* **The Visual Arts** *(in this volume); and other articles in this section.*

BIBLIOGRAPHY

Primary Sources

Burnham, Daniel H., and Edward H. Bennett. *Plan of Chicago.* New York, 1970.

Gifford, Don, ed. *The Literature of Architecture: The Evolution of Architectural Theory and Practice in Nineteenth Century America.* New York, 1966.

Jefferson, Thomas. *Writings.* New York, 1984.

Wright, Frank Lloyd. *When Democracy Builds.* Chicago, 1945.

Secondary Sources

Alexander, Charles. *Here the Country Lies: Nationalism and the Arts in Twentieth-Century America.* Bloomington, Ind., 1980.

Badger, Reid. *The Great American Fair: The World's Columbian Exposition and American Culture.* Chicago, 1979.

Bradley, Betsy Hunter. *The Works: The Industrial Architecture of the United States.* New York, 1999.

Bruns, James H. *Great American Post Offices.* New York, 1998.

Condit, Carl. *The Chicago School of Architecture: A History of Commercial and Public Building in the Chicago Area, 1875–1925.* Chicago, 1964.

Field, Cynthia R., Richard E. Stamm, and Heather P. Ewing. *The Castle: An Illustrated History of the Smithsonian Building.* Washington, D.C., 1993.

Glazer, Nathan, and Mark Lilla, eds. *The Public Face of Architecture: Civic Culture and Public Spaces.* New York, 1987.

Goodsell, Charles T. *The Social Meaning of Civic Space: Studying Political Authority through Architecture.* Lawrence, Kans., 1988.

Gowans, Alan. *Images of American Living: Four Centuries of Architecture and Furniture as Cultural Expression.* New York, 1964.

Grossman, Elizabeth Greenwell. *The Civic Architecture of Paul Cret.* New York, 1996.

Handlin, David P. *The American Home: Architecture and Society, 1815–1915.* Boston, 1979.

Harris, Neil, Wim de Witt, James Gilbert, and Robert W. Rydell. *Grand Illusions: Chicago's World Fair of 1893.* Chicago, 1993.

Hitchcock, Henry Russell, and William Seale. *Temples of Democracy: The State Capitols of the USA.* New York, 1976.

Ivey, Paul E. *Prayers in Stone: Christian Science Architecture in the United States, 1894–1930.* Urbana, Ill., 1999.

Jordy, William H. *American Buildings: Progressive and Academic Ideals at the Turn of the Twentieth Century.* Garden City, N.Y., 1972.

Kostof, Spiro. *America by Design.* New York, 1987.

Lebovich, William L. *America's City Halls.* Washington, D.C., 1984.

Lee, Antoinette J. *Architects to the Nation: The Rise and Decline of the Supervising Architect's Office.* New York, 2000.

Loeffler, Jane C. *The Architecture of Diplomacy: Building America's Embassies.* New York, 1998.

Marty, Martin E. *A Nation of Behavers.* Chicago, 1976.

Randel, William Peirce. *The Evolution of American Taste.* New York, 1978.

Robin, Ron. *Enclaves of America: The Rhetoric of American Political Architecture Abroad, 1900–1965.* Princeton, N.J., 1992.

Ryan, William, and Desmond Guiness. *The White House: An Architectural History.* New York, 1980.

Rydell, Robert W. *All the World's a Fair, Visions of Empire at American International Expositions, 1876–1916.* Chicago, 1984.

Scott, Pamela. *Temple of Liberty: Building the Capitol for a New Nation.* New York, 1995.

Scully, Vincent. *American Architecture and Urbanism.* New York, 1969.

Stanton, Phoebe B. *The Gothic Revival and American Church Architecture.* Baltimore, 1968.

Taylor, Lisa, ed. *Housing, Symbol, Structure, Site.* New York, 1990.

Vale, Lawrence J. *Architecture, Power, and National Identity.* New Haven, Conn., 1992.

Van Slyck, Abigail A. *Free to All: Carnegie Libraries and American Culture, 1890–1920.* Chicago, 1995.

Williams, Peter. *Houses of God, Region, Religion, and Architecture in the United States.* Urbana, Ill., 1997.

Wilson, William H. *The City Beautiful Movement.* Baltimore, 1989.

Wright, Gwendolyn. *Building the American Dream: A Social History of Housing in America.* Cambridge, Mass., 1981.

Zelinsky, Wilbur. *Nation into State: The Shifting Symbolic Foundations of American Nationalism.* Chapel Hill, N.C., 1988.

FILM

Alan Nadel

The role of film in American culture emerged out of the tension between its commercial production and its ideological impact. If, in less than a century, film—and particularly Hollywood-style film—has become an inherent and multifarious component of everyday American life, it has assumed that role because of a relentlessly complex set of industrial conditions, working in response to (as well as often in conjunction with) elaborate mechanisms of censorship. Because these factors circumscribe so extensively film's role as art, when the anthropologist Hortense Powdermaker wrote in 1950 that movies were "the first art form of any kind, popular, folk, or fine, to become a trust," she accurately identified film's marriage of art and commerce, but her history was backward: film was a monopoly that became an art form.

Moving pictures developed out of the same technical interest in time and motion that produced the Ford Motor Company's assembly line. Fordism broke a manufacturing job into simple, easily repeatable motions and assigned discrete tasks to discrete workers, who could repeat their motion with optimal efficiency. The illusion of motion on a screen, similarly, requires breaking down motion into discrete still photographs and then running them past a viewer so rapidly that they appear to comprise a coherent whole.

Motivated initially by a desire to "illustrate" sound, Thomas A. Edison developed in the late nineteenth century a viewing machine called a "kinetoscope" used in peep shows. These peep shows were viewed individually, devoid of drama, narrative, and shared communal experience. With the advent of projection technology, the moving picture became a more widely dispersed novelty, appearing in amusement parks, tent shows, circuses, and on vaudeville bills. Audiences enjoyed short movies of boxing matches, local events, and war news. Early motion pictures, in fact, helped rally public support for the Spanish-American War in 1898.

Moving pictures had no inherent exhibition venue, however, until the period between 1905 and 1910, which saw the rise of the nickelodeon, an inexpensive, walk-in exhibition place, featuring a continuous run of short motion pictures. By 1910, ten thousand nickelodeons had sprung up in an array of easily accessible areas—business districts and working-class neighborhoods—providing a variety of news and fictional narratives.

FILM AS AN INDUSTRIAL PRACTICE

Even before World War I, moviegoing had become a practice of everyday American life, dependent on a regular flow of standardized products and prices and a reliable network of distribution, sales, and advertising. Much of film's development as an aspect of American culture derived from these industrial conditions. The manipulation of time and space endemic to cinematic narrative, for example, required complex codes that allowed for the integration of close-up and long shot, event and reaction, unfolding and recollection in a coherent and objective manner; the audience had to learn how to distinguish between sequential and simultaneous events and how to construct an imaginary three-dimensional space out of a series of two-dimensional projections. Between 1903 and 1916, Edwin S. Porter initiated and D. W. Griffith developed the uses of camera shots and editing sequences that were to become the lingua franca of motion pictures, analogous in their uniformity to the internal combustion engine and the crankshaft in the automotive industry. Just as any licensed driver could operate the standard auto, any competent viewer could understand film narrative because it conformed to uniform production practices.

An array of monopolistic activities expedited the codification of these practices. Edison, who always favored restraint of trade to protect the profits from his patents, in 1908 helped form the Motion

Pictures Patents Company, which sought to limit access to film production. While production at that time was too geographically and economically diversified for this kind of monopoly to succeed, it did unify the major film production corporations and helped establish Hollywood as the industry's center. Shortly thereafter, the nickelodeons started to face competition from elaborate entertainment chains. Just as the beginning of the twentieth century saw the growth of chain distribution of food (for example, A&P) and household items (for example, Sears Roebuck), the period after World War I gave rise to the movie chains such as the New York–based Loew's theaters. In order to ensure a flow of quality films, by the mid-1920s, these chains strongly invested in studio production. The Loew's theater chain, for example, purchased Metro Pictures in 1919 and Goldwyn Pictures in 1925 to form Metro-Goldwyn-Mayer. During the same period, Balaban and Katz, a Chicago-based chain, acquired Paramount Pictures, and Stanley, a Philadelphia chain, acquired Warner Brothers.

Along with two somewhat smaller production-distribution chains, RKO and Fox (later Twentieth Century–Fox), these studios by the mid-1920s dominated the production and distribution of American films in much the way that the major auto manufacturers controlled automobile sales and production. Independent theaters were coerced into block bookings so that only those films produced by one of the five major studios were guaranteed uniformly wide distribution. These monopolies also controlled the rate of distribution by releasing films through a sequence of runs, starting with high-priced first-run houses, often as few as one per city, moving to a slightly larger number of second-run houses with slightly lower prices, and all the way down to the local fourth- or fifth-run movie theaters. Thus, over as much as a two-year period a film could occupy several different roles in American culture, from an expensive and somewhat exclusive theatergoing experience to a very inexpensive and casual pastime.

To establish film as a reliable and recognizable experience, films, like autos or bacon, had to deliver a standard product that appealed to a predictable taste. To this end, genre films—particularly westerns, gangster movies, and salacious domestic melodramas—became a mainstay of the industry. These films, like most Hollywood films, were made in a uniform style that has come to be known as the "classical Hollywood style." The classical style worked to efface its conditions of production, employing editing techniques that create the illusion that the story is telling itself to a spectator who occupies a position of quasi-omniscience. The plots of the classical style, moreover, focused strongly on the goals of a few individuals who assumed privileged importance, and the resolutions left virtually no loose ends. Thus, in a typical adventure story, the hero's success in his adventure and with his "love interest" coincided completely. By 1920 audiences could predictably expect that films would perform a kind of cultural therapy; in ninety minutes, they could see resolved on a fantasy level many of the conflicts that found no resolution in their quotidian lives. Their ability to identify with that fantasy resolution was facilitated by a sophisticated combination of visual and narrative codes that encouraged their identification with a hierarchy in which a few people were always more worthy than all the others. Even when these principals were "ordinary" Americans, their desires were treated as extraordinary, and while the films thus seemed to transcend class distinctions, they did so by substituting cinematic caste for economic class.

Despite the predictability of the Hollywood style, each new film had to seem unique. To further this end, a star system developed after World War I that was to have a lasting impact on America's cultural dynamics. Even before films presented extended narratives, they capitalized on celebrity, allowing turn-of-the-century viewers to see such famous people as the boxer John L. Sullivan and President William McKinley in fully animated activities. If the moving image of political and sports celebrities fascinated early filmgoers, that fascination transferred easily to celebrities created by films themselves. In the pre–World War I period, studios kept the names of their stars secret, preferring to rely on the brand name of the manufacturer, especially since the studios had more control over their product than over their performers. The performers were simply "parts" in an elaborate contraption, and overvaluing specific components would drive up total production costs.

By 1910, however, the public was starting to identify its favorites, and the industry quickly capitalized on this cultural tendency. In 1910 Carl Laemmle, head of the Independent Motion Picture Company (IMP), contracted Florence Lawrence, formerly identified with Biograph Pictures. To announce her switch to IMP, Laemmle planted the rumor that Lawrence was dead and then squelched the rumor in a newspaper ad stating that she was alive and would continue to appear in IMP films. This, one of the earliest of the industry's publicity stunts, was followed by personal appearance tours, surrounded by a steady flow of press releases and photographs. In a short time most studios followed suit, many creating fan magazines to promote their stars. (Although initially these magazines covered only the stars of their respective studios, they eventually broadened their base to create the illusion of objective journalism.)

By the 1920s high-priced stars were among a studio's most valuable assets. As such, stars found that their contractual obligations extended beyond the parameters of their performances to include not only personal appearances but also control over and publicizing of any aspects of their personal lives that could affect public image. Just as public figures helped popularize the novelty of moving pictures, the popularity of moving pictures helped turn the image of a star, derived from fictional narratives, into a transcendent aspect of American culture. Film had become a ubiquitous source of powerful images, rendered with unprecedented verisimilitude and, in numerous ways, eliding the boundaries between life and performance, fiction and reality.

THE DANGERS OF FILM

Many sectors of the public were less than sanguine about the cultural implications of this potent medium. Complaints arose about the unhealthy atmosphere in which films were viewed. The early nickelodeons were congested places, often firetraps. As a gathering place for the lower classes, they also were viewed as breeding grounds for crime. Exaggerated accounts of theft and violence in the nickelodeons and of people imitating the antisocial behavior they saw on the screen fueled fears that films endangered the general public and encouraged youths to pursue criminal activity. Critics also pointed out that they provided youth unsatisfactory alternatives to constructive social interactions in fresh air.

Many felt, furthermore, that the content of the films was even more corrupting than the conditions of spectatorship. In 1909, when the majority of films were imported from Europe (silent films, of course, more easily garnered international audiences than those requiring subtitles or dubbing), films were subject to nativist worries about importing European morals, undress, vulgarity, and moral tone. The use of firearms in films and the exploitation of such lurid topics as white slave trade were also found objectionable. The popularity of nickelodeons thus focused popular fears about the lower class, regarded as a particularly impressionable and poten-

tially dangerous group. This resulted in legislation and litigation to control motion pictures. In 1915 the U.S. Supreme Court, basing its decision both on the idea that movies were "entertainment" not "speech" and that they had the capacity to promote evil, declared that films were not protected as free speech under the First Amendment. Furthermore, since Hollywood had invested heavily in blurring distinctions between a star's fictional roles and off-screen persona, scandals surrounding the reckless lifestyles of the Hollywood community created even more pressure on the industry to monitor its activities.

The Hays Office Most states by 1921 had some form of censorship board. In response, the following year the industry set up the Motion Pictures Producers and Distributors of America, known as the Hays Office, after its president, Will H. Hays, a socially and politically conservative midwesterner. Hays, being in the employ of the industry, was charged not with banning films, but with getting them distributed. Thus, despite his personal values, his untenable position rendered his office relatively ineffective in curbing what a boisterous minority found indecent. While maintaining the guise of morality dramas, films of the 1920s attracted vast audiences with a significant display of violence, nudity, and sexual promiscuity. With the growth of luxurious movie "palaces," located in middle-class neighborhoods—featuring ushers, comfortable seating, elaborate decor, the first use of public air conditioning, and even free child-care centers in the basement—the audiences for these formulaic fantasies shifted from working class to middle class, and moviegoing by the mid-1920s thus was a commonplace event in middle-class American life. As such, its potential for corrupting public morals seemed, to some, all the more potent.

Throughout the 1920s Hays was involved in elaborate negotiations to institute self-regulation procedures that would mollify the public, resulting, in the 1930 "production code," a set of industry guidelines, authored with strong input from conservative Roman Catholic interests and containing a peculiar admixture of broad philosophical positions and particular plot essentials. It was not until 1934, however, that the code was strictly enforced, as the result of several factors, including the widely published results of the Payne Foundation Studies, claiming to prove that films had deleterious effects on children. The sharp drop in movie attendance caused by the Great Depression of the 1930s, moreover, made the industry particularly sensitive to the

---

EXCERPTS FROM THE PRODUCTION CODE

"Wrong entertainment lowers the whole living condition and moral ideals of a race."

"No picture should lower the moral standards of those who see it."

"Law, natural or divine, must not be belittled [or] ridiculed."

"Comedies or farces *should not make fun* of good, innocence, morality, or justice."

"[Adultery] is *never* a fit subject for *comedy.*"

"The presentation of scenes . . . deliberately meant to excite . . . manifestations [of sex and passions] on the part of the audience is always wrong, is subversive to the interest of society, and a peril to the human race."

"The name of *Jesus Christ* should never be used except in reverence."

"Dances with movements of the breasts, excessive body movements while the feet remain stationary, the so-called 'belly dances'—these dances are immoral, obscene, and hence altogether wrong."

"[The use of bedrooms (as locations)] in comedy or farce . . . is wrong, because they suggest sex laxity and obscenity."

"Ministers of religion in their characters of ministers should not be used in comedy, as villains, or as unpleasant persons."

"Methods of smuggling should not be presented."

"MISCEGENATION . . . is forbidden."

Catholic Legion of Decency's opposition to films that did not conform to the code.

All the major studio heads met in 1933 with Dr. A. H. Giannini, a prominent lay Catholic, who was president of the Bank of America in Los Angeles. After Giannini threatened to withhold financing from motion pictures, Joseph Scott, an attorney who accompanied him, launched into an explicitly anti-Semitic tirade, accusing the Jewish studio heads of undermining the country and assuring them that many people in America were sympathetic to the actions being taken in Nazi Germany. In the face of this assault, virtually all studio heads begged for a chance to prove they were loyal Americans. Shortly thereafter, a Catholic boycott of films in Philadelphia resulted in a 40 percent drop in the city's box-office revenues. In 1934 the industry appointed the conservative Catholic Joseph I. Breen to the Hays Office, investing him with absolute power to enforce the code, a job he performed (aided by a staff) until 1954. Breen was involved with every aspect of film production, from early script approval to review of the final product. Virtually every studio release was

scrutinized and usually modified in some way to accommodate Breen. Countless projects were dropped completely (or never even considered) because of Breen.

Thus, the major studio releases from the 1930s to the 1950s reflected a very narrow range of topics, treatments, and plot structures as the result of specific social and cultural forces. The advent of the social practice of moviegoing—independent of the allure of specific films—raised serious concern, especially among religious groups, over the ideological impact of that practice. In response, the owners of the big studios, fearful of anti-Semitic backlash and shaken by the depression's fragile market, sought to present a noncontroversial, highly normative, and distinctly positive view of American life. In consequence, they produced covert and overt morality plays, implicitly based on an "essential" American character, one that was tough but sentimental, pragmatic but principled. Rewarded for being more romantic than libidinous, optimistic than conniving, active than introspective, this type—embodied by such stars as John Wayne, Jimmy Stewart,

Gary Cooper, and Humphrey Bogart—projected a persona uniquely and quintessentially "American" in the sense that that term represented a cinematic projection of America, rather than a dramatic reflection of it, or a critical investigation into its problems and contradictions.

Particularly in its representation of race, American film contributed greatly to perpetuating the tacit assumption that America was a white nation. Although approximately 30 percent of all actual cowboys were black and Mexican, and two of the cavalry divisions most active in Indian-fighting were all black, American Westerns—by far the most prolific film genre for the first sixty years of the century—were usually devoid of black faces. When blacks did appear in Westerns, they usually played the same servants and menials that they played in the general spectrum of film genres. The absence of blacks in Westerns is particularly significant, moreover, because of the privileged place the West has occupied in American mythology. In the nineteenth century, the "West" referred both to the edge of an expanding frontier and to the source of narratives defining an American character that seemed to emanate from that space. At just about the same time that the West ceased to be a physical frontier, narrative films first produced a new kind of imaginary space that could serve even more ably than the geographic West as a scaffold for American mythology. Film, in short, did not portray the West; it became it—that imaginary space where American character, history, and destiny merged in a white, male world.

This does not mean that there were no blacks in early films. Even before 1920, at the same time that most black film characters were played by whites in blackface, there were some independent black film companies, but they saw limited success because they were unable to attain wide distribution and because successful black actors were often signed by studios (that then relegated them to stereotypical roles). Two of the landmark motion pictures in the history of American film, *The Birth of a Nation* (1915) and *Gone with the Wind* (1939), moreover, valorized the values of the Old South, portraying—more benignly so in *Gone with the Wind*—black autonomy as a form of social blight. If Hattie McDaniel's Academy Award for the role of Mammy in *Gone with the Wind* marked an end to the period when black stereotypes would be played by blackface whites, it did little to move blacks into central dramatic roles, impel a complex representation of black American life, or confront racial problems. With a handful of exceptions, instead of confronting segregation, the Hollywood studios throughout their half-century of production and distribution dominance instituted their own version of it.

Un-American Activities   In that the industry labored from 1934 on under the guidance of Breen to reinforce consistently as part of a ritualized social practice that quintessence of imaginary Americanness, it is particularly ironic that the next major crisis in the industry came from congressional scrutiny for its potential involvement in "un-American" propaganda activities. Once again, the ideological potency of films impelled scrutiny, such that a 1941 Senate resolution empowered "complete investigation of any propaganda disseminated by motion pictures . . . to influence public sentiment in the direction of participation . . . in the present European war." This was the culmination of an assault on the industry by isolationist senators that had begun in the late 1930s. These senators were particularly fearful that the Jewish industry's anti-Nazi sentiments might compromise American neutrality.

The bombing of Pearl Harbor in December 1941 put an end to those accusations and turned film's propaganda potential into a virtue, such that the newly formed Office of War Information (OWI) was soon working closely with the industry to help the war effort. Although the office had no power to enforce censorship, like Breen it reviewed scripts prior to production. Setting the tone for the culture of communist containment that would follow World War II, the office viewed war propaganda as a multifarious enterprise, one that entailed not only supporting the military and demonizing the enemy but also representing the broad spectrum of American life as admirable and hence inherently superior.

This sensibility characterized the cold war effort even more accurately, but the enemies had changed and films, lauded during the war, were suspected by the late 1940s of being pro-communist rather than antifascist. In 1947 the House Committee on Un-American Activities (HUAC) initiated hearings to investigate communist influence in the movie industry. These hearings served as morality dramas invoking the image of film as ideological threat. Although for more than a decade they had been carefully laundered of material deemed detrimental by Breen, and throughout the war years further laundered by the OWI, films were still felt to be potentially subversive. No doubt the industry was scrutinized in part because the studios were headed by Jews and in part because Hollywood had a vocal left-wing community, especially among writers and directors. No level of prior censorship, the hearings

***Gone with the Wind* (1939).** Vivien Leigh's indomitable Southern belle and Butterfly McQueen's stereotypical house servant are among the enduring images of one of America's most popular films. © BETTMANN/CORBIS

implied, no degree of scrutiny during production could prevent "disloyal" filmmakers from slipping in subversive messages. The solution was to separate the "loyal" members of the industry from the disloyal. To this end, the committee heard from witnesses it deemed "friendly" and those it deemed "unfriendly," and the only way an "unfriendly" witness could prove his loyalty was to recant his political beliefs and supply the names of other "subversives." The first set of unfriendly witnesses—screenwriters who came to be known as the Hollywood Ten—refused to cooperate with the committee and were blacklisted. Although some writers were able subsequently to produce scripts under pseudonyms, in general the hearings started a rash of self-policing that aborted numerous Hollywood careers and put a huge number of those who retained their jobs into a state of paranoid self-restraint.

The hearings were an object lesson for the general public as well, because, as the committee accurately sensed, films had always provided larger-than-life sites of cultural identification that extended far beyond the fictional parameters of a specific film or the spatial and temporal constraints of the movie theater. The star system relied on films' generating a limitless chain of cultural associations impacting on everything from clothing styles and idioms of speech to an orchestrated fetishizing of the details of stars' personal lives. That the disciplining of the film industry was the disciplining of American culture was made clear when studio head Louis B. Mayer compared film stars to Britain's royal family; American democracy needed a similar object of worship, he argued, and thus anything that shook public loyalty was cause for grave alarm (and also bad for the box office, we might infer). Even if HUAC was unsuccessful in proving that any films

HUAC WITNESSES

THE HOLLYWOOD TEN

Alvah Bessie, writer

Herbert Biberman, director

Lester Cole, writer

Edward Dmytryk, director

Ring Lardner Jr., writer

John Howard Lawson, writer

Albert Maltz, writer

Sam Ornitz, writer

Robert Adrian Scott, writer-producer

Dalton Trumbo, writer

SOME "FRIENDLY" WITNESSES

Walt Disney, studio head

Sterling Hayden, actor

Elia Kazan, director

Clifford Odets, writer

Robert Rossen, writer-director

Budd Schulberg, writer

Artie Shaw, bandleader

Jerome Robbins, choreographer

Robert Taylor, actor

Jack Warner, studio head

were subversive, it did demonstrate the need for loyalty, manifest as compliance with the committee.

And by 1947 compliance was something at which the industry had become expert, even if some individuals working in it had not. At that point, moreover, the major studios still had enough economic and structural grip on film production to enforce its compliance. In 1951, at the height of McCarthyism, HUAC resumed its investigation of Hollywood, this time examining whether leftists in Hollywood were exploiting their wealth and prestige to assist communist causes. These hearings were very effective shows, garnering compliance from a great many movie stars and directors, who were well aware of the studios' power to destroy their careers.

THE END OF STUDIO CONTROL

The late 1940s and early 1950s, while being a period of heightened studio control over the political content of the films and the free speech of its employ-

ees, was also the period that marked the beginning of the end of the studio system. While films experienced peak years immediately after the war, the baby boom and the introduction of large-scale television programming in the late 1940s afforded baby-bound parents alternative entertainment that put a huge dent in movie attendance. The response of the movie industry—to develop an array of new moviegoing experiences, including 3-D, Aroma-rama, and widescreen formats such as Cinema-Scope, VistaVision, and Cinerama—demonstrated once again how much film figured as a pastime rather than the experience of discrete narratives.

The most significant change in the moviegoing experience during the 1950s was the rapid proliferation of drive-in movies, which increased to six thousand screens nationwide by 1963. The drive-in provided convenient, inexpensive entertainment for families with young children and a uniquely private dating experience for a new generation of teens. The theaters were also very accessible to the growing suburban population; just as the movie palaces of the 1920s attracted middle-class audiences by being located in residential urban areas near public transit, the drive-ins tapped the postwar suburban middle class that went everywhere by car. The drive-ins, which rarely provided the best selection of films or optimal sight and sound quality, eventually succumbed to competition from theaters located in shopping centers and malls. These theaters not only offered comfort and state-of-the-art presentation equipment but also a choice of high-quality, first-run films. (By the end of the twentieth century, relatively few theaters presented a single film, and multiplex theaters featured as many as twenty-four screens.)

The development of local first-run theaters was made possible by a 1948 Supreme Court decision ordering the breakup of Hollywood's vertical monopolies. This decision destroyed the industry's capacity to control bookings to ensure steady demand for a studio's output and allow the same film to maximize profits through separate runs. Faced with a more open market as well as competition from television, producers, now freer to finance independent productions, felt less constrained by the production code. In addition, a 1952 Supreme Court decision extending free speech protection to motion pictures liberated producers from fear of governmental censorship. In consequence, they were more willing to test Breen and the Legion of Decency. This led to a slow erosion of the code's effectiveness, so that by the second half of the 1960s the cultural lag between the representation of America mandated by the code and the experience of everyday American life—marked by an acute awareness of sex, drugs, and rock music—became huge. The code thus became a distribution impediment rather than an asset, and in 1968 the industry abandoned it in favor of a rating system. The system, which has undergone some modifications since its inception, in effect removed all restrictions on film content, although producers and directors have often voluntarily modified films in order to get the rating deemed most useful for marketing purposes.

In the mid-1970s, under the new rating system, a few hard-core pornographic films—most notably *Deep Throat*—found a large general audience, but by the 1980s the novelty of these films had worn off and virtually all films intended for mass distribution contained nothing more graphic than simulated sex. During this period verbal profanity also entered the acceptable range of popular film possibilities and, with the famous "blood ballet" shoot-out that concluded *The Wild Bunch* (1969), so did new heights of graphic violence.

One moderating force on the use of these elements, however, was television, because by the 1970s television had ceased to be a rival of film and became instead one of its distribution venues, as sales of films to television became very lucrative, although many popular films required reformatting to accommodate the visual parameters of the TV screen; the films also often required editing and overdubbing to meet the strict censorship regulations of broadcast television. The growth of cable television—especially premium channels such as HBO, Showtime, and Cinemax—obviated that restraint, as did video rentals and purchases. Films at the end of the twentieth century proliferated throughout American culture more extensively than ever before, as a variety of discrete experiences, typically theatrical first-runs (often simultaneously on as many as two thousand screens nationally), followed by broadcast on premium cable channels, then release for video sale or rental, and finally for general television broadcast.

FILM AS ART

In many ways, the same issues of censorship and commercial motivation that circumscribed Hollywood production also formed the matrix of criteria that would identify some Hollywood products as works of art. The French interest in "auteurism," which began in the 1950s, focused attention on a number of American directors who were able to

IMPORTANT EXAMPLES OF FILM NOIR

The Maltese Falcon (1941)
Double Indemnity (1944)
Mildred Pierce (1945)
The Postman Always Rings Twice (1946)
The Big Sleep (1946)
Body and Soul (1947)
Dark Passage (1947)
Dead Reckoning (1947)
Nightmare Alley (1947)
Force of Evil (1948)
The Asphalt Jungle (1950)
D.O.A. (1950)
The Big Heat (1953)

create distinctive bodies of work by fashioning the demands of Hollywood to their own unique vision. A serious look at such directors as Orson Welles, Alfred Hitchcock, Howard Hawks, and John Ford opened the door to a rich examination of American film. Of particular interest to auteur critics was the element of mise-en-scène—the creation of the scene and staging of the action—the aspect of production over which studio directors had significant control. Genre films also attracted attention. Instead of being regarded as formulaic products, they were seen as accomplishments in stylization. John Ford's West thus was the imaginative product of his unique vision, and all of his works became germane in understanding that vision. The French also identified a uniquely American group of films under the rubric "film noir." Although most of these films received code approval, they were anomalous in that they represented a dark, seamy, often amoral and pessimistic vision of American life, rather than the optimistic and morally enhancing vision proscribed by the code.

In the 1960s select theaters in urban areas and in college communities began to specialize in revivals and the film noir classics. The films of Charlie Chaplin, the Marx Brothers, and W. C. Fields; the acting of Humphrey Bogart, Katharine Hepburn, Carole Lombard, Marlon Brando, and James Dean; as well as the films of several American directors discovered a new audience that took for granted that they were seeing works of art, comparable or

Charlie Chaplin in *The Great Dictator* (1940). Chaplin played two characters in the film: the dictator Adenoid Hynkel and the downtrodden Jewish barber. These were his first speaking roles. © BETTMANN/CORBIS

even superior to the foreign films exhibited since the end of World War II in small urban theaters known as "art houses."

In the 1960s film also became the subject of academic study. Courses in the art of the film and graduate programs in film criticism and film production arose. From the early graduates of the production programs came a new generation of film directors, including Martin Scorsese, Steven Spielberg, Francis Ford Coppola, and George Lucas. These directors had an unprecedented knowledge of their medium's history and technique. Having been able, as their predecessors were not, to spend countless hours in film libraries, studying the cuts, framing, lighting, and camera movements that comprised their artistic heritage, they brought to American film a dazzling mastery of technique and a learned respect for the ways in which that technique created mass entertainment. This they substituted for any deep literary sense. Whereas their earliest predecessors, such as D. W. Griffith, were informed by Victorian novels, their chief knowledge base was other films, and their primary literary medium was script dialogue. This accounts for the self-conscious awareness of film history and genre that their films manifest. Films such as *The Godfather*

(Coppola), *Star Wars* (Lucas), and *Raiders of the Lost Ark* and *Saving Private Ryan* (Spielberg) are all profoundly shaped by their directors' understanding of the American film genre in which they were working. (Even Scorsese's early film *Mean Streets* manifests its debt to the Bowery Boys series.)

This self-consciousness has become in a newer generation of filmmakers such as Quentin Tarentino a form of pastiche, in which word, image, and music allude to multiple genres, disconcertingly juxtaposed. With the demise of studio production, Hollywood has seen a large influx of directors from such areas as advertising, music video, and independent filmmaking. While these influences have to some degree affected visual and editing styles, the increasing cost of film production and distribution has narrowed the range of film topics and genres, with the bulk of films intensely targeted at a peak audience. (Fourteen-year-old boys are the most lucrative of those target audiences.)

CINEMATIC IDENTITY

With a public exposed to a potentially limitless flow of cinematic narrative, film in the last decades of

465

the twentieth century had moved from an avid pastime to a ubiquitous consciousness, such that, it has been argued, in many ways Americans understand their lives as movies and interpret the full spectrum of their personal and civic experiences cinematically. If one legacy of the first half of the twentieth century was the erosion of boundaries between a star's persona and his or her roles, the legacy of the second half may be the erosion of the boundaries between the spectator's acts of identification and the constitution of his or her identity.

See also **The World According to Hollywood; Postmodernism and the Arts; Artistic, Intellectual, and Political Refugees** *(volume 2);* **The Visual Arts; Elite vs. Popular Cultures; Culture for Mass Audiences; Marxist Approaches** *(in this volume); and other articles in this section.*

BIBLIOGRAPHY

Belton, John. *American Cinema/American Culture.* New York, 1994.

Black, Gregory. *Hollywood Censored: Morality Codes, Catholics, and the Movies.* New York, 1994.

Bordwell, David, Janet Staiger, and Kristin Thompson. *The Classical Hollywood Cinema: Film Style and Mode of Production to 1960.* New York, 1985.

Ceplair, Larry, and Steven Englund. *The Inquisition in Hollywood: Politics in the Film Community 1930–1960.* Garden City, N.Y., 1980.

Crowdus, Gary, ed. *The Political Companion to American Film.* New York, 1994.

Custen, George F. *Bio/Pics: How Hollywood Constructed Public History.* New Brunswick, N.J., 1992.

Doherty, Thomas Patrick. *Projections of War: Hollywood, American Culture, and World War II.* New York, 1993.

Gabler, Neal. *An Empire of Their Own: How the Jews Invented Hollywood.* New York, 1988.

Gomery, Douglas. *Shared Pleasures: A History of Movie Presentation in the United States.* Madison, Wisc., 1992.

Grant, Barry Keith, ed. *Film Genre Reader II.* Austin, Tex., 1995.

Koppes, Clayton R., and Gregory D. Black. *Hollywood Goes to War: How Politics, Profits, and Propaganda Shaped World War II Movies.* New York, 1987.

Mast, Gerald, ed. *The Movies in Our Midst: Documents in the Cultural History of Film in America.* Chicago, 1982.

May, Lary. *Screening Out the Past: The Birth of Mass Culture and the Motion Picture Industry.* New York, 1983.

Nadel, Alan. *Flatlining on the Field of Dreams: Cultural Narratives in the Films of President Reagan's America.* New Brunswick, N.J., 1997.

Navasky, Victor S. *Naming Names.* New York, 1980.

Powdermaker, Hortense. *Hollywood, The Dream Factory: An Anthropologist Looks at the Moviemakers.* New York, 1950.

Reid, Mark A. *Redefining Black Film.* Berkeley, Calif., 1993.

Robinson, David. *From Peep Show to Palace: The Birth of American Film.* New York, 1996.

Schatz, Thomas. *Hollywood Genres: Formulas, Filmmaking, and the Studio System.* Philadelphia, 1981.

Shindler, Colin. *Hollywood Goes to War: Films and American Society, 1939–1952.* London, 1979.

Silver, Alain, and Elizabeth Ward, eds. *Film Noir: An Encyclopedic Reference to the American Style.* 3d ed. Woodstock, N.Y., 1992.

Sklar, Robert. *Movie-Made America: A Cultural History of American Movies.* Rev. ed. New York, 1994.

Vasey, Ruth. *The World According to Hollywood, 1918–1939.* Madison, Wisc., 1997.

PHOTOGRAPHY

Marjorie L. McLellan

Photography—as a commercial, popular, and artistic medium—has played a role in Americans' perception of their world; it has both expressed and channeled social change. In photographs, Americans discovered themselves in unpredictable and surprising ways, connected with different periods and social contexts as well as new technologies. Photography cannot be understood as a timeline of formal styles and schools; instead one must look at photography's multiple meanings in various social and cultural contexts over time. Photographs are read as contemporary or historical documents; on the other hand, they are regarded as works of creativity addressing aesthetic and philosophical problems. Between and around these notions of photography lie family snapshots, fashion photographs, propaganda, pornography, postcards, and photojournalism. Each photograph contains the evidence and imprint of both the photographic event (with its actors, setting, equipment, and interactions) and the visual event in which the image is viewed. While individual images have become symbols and icons of American culture and history, photography, like subsequent generations of film and video, mimics or captures what is before the lens, thereby emphasizing the documentary or truth-telling functions over the interpretive and symbolic dimensions of traditional arts such as painting and sculpture.

THE DEVELOPMENT OF PHOTOGRAPHY

An American, Samuel F. B. Morse, a painter and inventor of the telegraph, claimed to have produced a photographic image through a process similar to the paper calotype; however, when he saw that the image was a negative, he concluded that the process was a failure. The early developments in the photographic process occurred instead in England and France during the 1820s and 1830s and then spread to the United States.

Before images could be fixed on paper or glass, the camera obscura was used for popular entertainment and artistic pursuits. Light entering a darkened room through a small hole produces a faint, upside down image of the scene on a blank wall or canvas, where it can be traced. Mirrors and lenses refract, enlarge, and redirect the image. Wedgwood, an English pottery company, used the camera obscura to reproduce images of family mansions and estates on custom-made dinner services. Thomas Wedgwood attempted to make images on chemically treated material as early as 1800, but he failed to fix the results, which gradually disappeared. In the early nineteenth century, other inventors recognized the potential for capturing the camera obscura images with light-sensitive chemical compounds coated on either paper or a metal plate. These first images were called heliography, or sun pictures.

Learning from these first crude photographic attempts, artist and set designer Louis Daguerre in 1837 developed a process using silver-plated copper. The materials exposed to light were fixed on the surface, and the remaining light-sensitive materials were removed by bathing the plate. Early photographs were not prints from negatives but monoprints; the daguerreotype was the actual pale negative image on a sheet of silver-plated copper, which, because of its reflective qualities, appeared in certain light as a positive image. A detailed image initially required about a thirty-minute exposure (exposure times varied with the lighting conditions); this limited the range of subject matter and resulted in stiffly formal portraits. Daguerre's invention was hailed as a "mirror with a memory." Soon new lenses increased the aperture, making a brighter image, and new chemical processes strengthened the resulting image.

In England, Henry Fox Talbot had been pursuing a way to print the camera obscura image onto paper dipped in silver chloride. While the first image was a negative, he realized that it could be printed onto another sheet of paper, thus reversing the light and dark areas and creating a positive print. By waxing the paper into translucence, the original could be used as a negative to produce positive prints. Talbot rushed to publish his results when word of Daguerre's invention spread from Paris. The name "photography," or light drawing, was proposed for the British invention. While Daguerre produced a single positive image, Talbot used a two-step process to produce both a negative and subsequent positive prints. Talbot also discovered the latent image and the process of developing photographs. His process, patented in 1841, was called the calotype. Although the daguerreotype, which produced a sharper image than Talbot's calotype paper negative process, was more widely adopted by the public at the time, it was a technical dead end; Talbot's negative/positive process became the basis for future developments in photography.

EARLY AMERICAN PHOTOGRAPHY

In the 1840s, daguerreotype portrait studios were established in Europe and in America. The earliest portrait studios were windowed boxes constructed on the flat roof of a building. These "daguerreotype galleries," with sky-lit studios, traveled in wagons and even on flatboats. In the studio, on a bright day, the subject—with head held in position with a metal clamp and arms resting on the arms of the chair—would sit still, staring into the camera lens. When the subject was in place, the negative was placed in the camera for an exposure time between three to ten minutes. The long exposures dampened expression and spontaneity and limited the range of poses. Identity was conveyed by dress and lighting as well as studio backdrops and props. Studios also offered to hand color the "likeness."

Millions of daguerreotypes were produced; young couples, aging patriarchs, politicians, inventors, ministers, philosophers, and artists posed for portraits in the decades before the Civil War. Prospective miners paused for daguerreotypes before rushing off to California, and daguerreotypes of celebrities such as the Swedish singer Jenny Lind were sold as postcards. Daguerreotypists also captured the last images of loved ones, photographing the dead in what has been described as a uniquely American phenomena.

The next advance produced a transparent negative that offered the ability to make multiple prints, like the calotype, with the crisp detail of the daguerreotype. The wet-plate negative process involved coating a glass plate with a light-sensitive chemical solution suspended in a sticky binder substance. The substance, called collodion, was more effective than previous experiments with albumen. The photographer exposed the plate to capture a scene or image before the emulsion dried, then quickly fixed the negative image in a chemical bath. The collodion could be used as both a glass-plate negative and as a positive image on glass.

The wet-plate process dominated American photography for thirty years. Though the use of collodion and better lenses sped up the photographic process, it was still cumbersome and limited largely to professionals. With the wet-plate process, however, access to photography was no longer limited to the upper class, and interest in photography spread. Most people wanted photographs of their families, creating a visual genealogy, sometimes with props symbolizing occupation, status, or religious persuasion. Wet-plate photographs were also subject to manipulation; artistic photographs were created by combining figures or scenery from several photographs on a background print, then retouching and copying the image.

Lantern slides, evolved from the calotype process, were positives, contact printed on a glass plate coated with light-sensitive chemicals suspended in albumen. With a lantern focused to send light through the glass plate, the image could be projected onto a wall. The Phasmatrope, or the magic lantern projection mechanism, was the basis of an early motion picture device. Glass slides, arranged around the spokes of a wheel, rotated through a projector. The first motion picture sequences projected for the public included the inventor, Henry Heyl, and his wife waltzing to synchronized orchestral music as well as a dramatic exhortation by "Uncle Sam," then known as "Brother Jonathan."

In a process suggesting the close links between applied science and the art of photography, the collodion process was also used to produce stereoscopic images. Using a camera with two lenses set close together, two images could be exposed simultaneously, side by side on the glass plate. Prints made from these negatives were mounted on card stock and viewed through a double lens to mimic three-dimensional views. Itinerant and studio photographers sometimes produced stereoviews as well, making it possible for families to picture themselves along with commercially produced stereoscopic images. Although most consumers looked at stereoviews one at a time in a hand-held stereopticon, a bulky, box-shaped stereoscopic drum or parlor viewer could hold as many as three hundred scenes.

Rotated by hand, a parlor viewer could present a narrative, giving rise to such popular entertainment as Coleman Seller's Kinematoscope in 1861. Thomas A. Edison followed with his creation of the Kinetoscope, or cabinet viewer for early motion picture film, which he patented in 1863.

Into the Field: Mathew Brady's Civil War   Mathew Brady opened a daguerreotype portrait studio on Broadway in New York City in 1844. At mid-century, portraiture, Western expansion, and the natural environment were frequent subjects in American photography. Brady operated portraiture studios in both Washington and New York when, with the onset of the Civil War, he embarked on the first major American documentary project. Although credited as the creator of "Brady photographs," he took relatively few photographs himself due to poor eyesight; instead, Brady bought negatives from other photographers and employed several collodion photographers to record events. Mathew Brady and his teams traveled in closed wagons that functioned as darkrooms in the field. These photographs, exhibited in galleries during the war, revealed to Americans the details of camp life as well as the gruesome aftermath of battle.

Although Brady was himself bankrupted photographing the Civil War, his photographs provided historians not only with powerful evidence but with a means to visually represent their subject matter. By the turn of the century, scientists, sociologists, anthropologists, and folklorists turned to photography to gather data for their studies.

Amateur Photography   American photographers were introduced to dry-plate glass negatives at their national convention in 1880. The unwieldy wet-plate process was replaced with dry-plate technology using gelatin to bind the light-sensitive chemicals to glass. The photographer no longer prepared the negative; instead, the dry plate fueled the manufacture of plates that were more consistent and could be purchased either in a local shop or by mail order. Photographers in the field were no longer freighted with tents, chemicals, and wagons to transport gear. Factories produced a wide array of cameras, including the more portable view cameras, which were wooden boxes fitted with negative holders and a bellows lens set on a tripod, and boxy magazine cameras, which held a dozen dry plates, making it easier to take photographs on location. The simplified process encouraged experimentation and novelty, including a "spy" camera concealed in a hat. The new emulsions were far more light sensitive, creating the need for a mechanical shutter to replace the simple lens cap that was used to time exposures in the past. At the same time, at the new speeds, photographers could often work without a tripod in the field or could set up a copy stand to reproduce both old family photographs, such as cabinet views, and mass-produced photographs (including commercial pornography) at home. The mass production of gelatin-coated photographic paper simplified printing, and the faster paper emulsions paved the way for enlargers.

While a few affluent amateurs took up wet-plate photography, the dry plate democratized the picture making process—the matrons of the growing streetcar suburbs and the sons of hinterland farmers could take up the new hobby, making postcard size, direct contact prints in a closet, without an enlarger, from the $4'' \times 5''$ glass plates.

George Eastman, among the first to enter the dry-plate market, began manufacturing glass-plate negatives in 1880. Eastman saw everyone as a potential photographer and thus a potential customer; the problem was keeping costs low enough that consumers would buy mass-produced dry plates instead of producing their own, as they had with collodion or wet-plate negatives.

While photographs suggested truthful documentation, family photography came to document the ideal of family and domesticity. Photographs gave tangible form to the family's economic status or their interest in travel. As they produced visual evidence of family cohesion, material achievement, and even farm productivity, photographers and their subjects demonstrated their aesthetic sensibility, their technical expertise, and their participation in the mainstream of American life.

Photography made the most fundamental aspects of everyday life, such as gender roles, available for play and manipulation, as dressing up and even cross-dressing for the camera became a social activity among ordinary folk like Wisconsin farm families. People lay claim to the consumer-oriented, mass-produced hobby in ways that manufacturers could not have anticipated. Just as amateur photography offered Americans opportunities to see themselves as consumers, it also provided a medium through which they could visualize, critique, and transform the roles and social expectations that shaped their lives.

PHOTOGRAPHY AS MASS MEDIUM

Studio photographers—and amateurs as well—in rural communities and big cities often turned their

Mathew Brady and His Crew. Brady's Civil War images offered the first photographic documentation of a war. © BETTMANN/CORBIS

cameras on the local scene, photographing rural landscapes and the vestiges of earlier times, as well as new factories, department stores, streetcars, and urban centers. In New York, Alice Austen photographed street scenes, while James Van Der Zee documented the vitality of the Harlem Renaissance in studio portraits and photographs commissioned for churches and organizations like Marcus Garvey's Universal Negro Improvement Association, as well as in street photography.

Historian Frederick Jackson Turner's "Frontier Thesis," presented at the 1893 Chicago exposition, heightened awareness of the "vanishing" cultures of American Indians. Answering a variety of impulses, photographers turned their lenses on Indians. Americans already had a long-standing fascination with popular representations of American Indian life in Wild West shows, dioramas, reenactments, and archaeological displays at fairs and exhibitions, and the railroad opened access to, and popular interest in, the American Southwest. Photographers like Edward S. Curtis and Adam Clark Vroman demonstrate the range of imagery. While Vroman sought an unvarnished portrait of modern day life and practice, including the impact of cultural tourists like himself, Curtis actively romanticized an American Indian past, suppressing evidence of modernity and acculturation in his enormously popular studies.

Jacob Riis, Lewis Hine, Sigmund Krausz, and others documented the lives of the "other half," the working poor and destitute of America. Like the American Indians in Curtis's photographs, these immigrants—Italians, Jews, Chinese—represented the exotic "other." However, these photographs were produced to shock and discomfit Americans, and they inspired citizens to support both charitable projects and activist, reform-minded legislation.

The social awareness conveyed in these photographs reflected the Progressives' confidence in the rational fair-mindedness of Americans. The photographs, which presented the facts of urban squalor or of child labor, aimed to both document and persuade. Lewis Hine, working for the National Child Labor Committee, gathered evidence of children working long days in dangerous settings, and carefully laid out the dimensions of the problem, using statistics, photographs, and other evidence, in compelling essays. In photographic exhibits that warned of the dire social implication, he persuaded the public that the federal government should play an active role in promoting child welfare.

PHOTOGRAPHY AS ART

Early photographers produced artistic images conveying emotion, drama, and meaning, as well as visual qualities of line, volume, texture, shading, and contrast. The painters Thomas Eakins, Albert Bierstadt, and later Charles Sheeler took up, and were influenced by, photography. Bierstadt made stereoviews of western landscapes, which he used as reference for his paintings, but which he also published and sold to the public. Eadweard Muybridge produced crisp scenes of Yosemite's trees, mountains, and waterways in 1872. Even as they used photography as a tool, visual artists came to see the world around them through the distinctive photographic lens, which suggested new approaches to composition and framing.

Early efforts to assert the aesthetic qualities of photography moved, interestingly enough, away from the accurate representation of subject in order to convey more reflective, interior qualities through softly focused, artfully posed, and carefully lit images. In other words, photographers—as artists—sought to create a more profound representation by undermining the frank reality intrinsic to photography.

The New York Camera Club and other groups across the country popularized the activities of amateurs shooting "artistic views." Amateur photographers often identified themselves as artists and exhibited their work through local camera clubs. For their annual dues, camera club members had the use of a darkroom, a library of photographic publications, lectures by prominent photographers, technical demonstrations, opportunities to exhibit their work, an annual excursion to a locale rich in photographic opportunities, and a variety of social activities. Camera clubs even circulated and showed lantern slide sets produced by other clubs. Although some local camera clubs did not admit women members, women played an integral role in the development of art photography as well as family photography. By the turn of the century, American women engaged in photography as both a hobby and a profession. While a few owned studios and made their living from photography, many affluent women with training in the arts joined camera clubs, showed their work, and entered competitions.

To elevate photography to a high art, as defined by the genteel Victorian tastemakers, photographers looked to the style and themes of painting, which, in the mid-nineteenth century, emphasized both romantic imagery and accurately detailed representation. The popular tableaux vivantes had their artistic counterparts as photographers grouped costumed and sometimes nude subjects before painted backdrops to create biblical or literary scenes like Longfellow's *Evangeline.* Viewers read these images as moral stories, identifying the characters, setting, plot, and meaning in the carefully rendered figures. Although the undertaking was serious and challenging, the results were often clumsy, as the posed nude figures contrasted melodramatically with the Victorian moral message.

Alfred Stieglitz, influential editor of *American Amateur Photography* and the New York Camera Club's elegant *Camera Work,* with its high quality photogravure and halftone reproductions, elevated photography to an elite, artistic profession in America. Stieglitz challenged conventional forms of artistic photography in America. After studying engineering in Germany, he took up photography and was influenced by European interests in pictorialism, or photography in which aesthetic concerns with composition, lighting, and other artistic qualities took precedence over documentation. Pictorialists made creative decisions behind the camera or in the darkroom as they printed the images. Working in New York City at the same time as documentary photographers Jacob Riis and Lewis Hine, Stieglitz captured the character of weather, smoke, and light against street scenes, railroad stations, and skyscrapers in luminous, atmospheric images. Although Stieglitz's own work later took new, more symbolic directions, and he operated galleries until his death in 1946, the "Photo-Secession" movement he founded had run its course before World War I.

Photographers interacted with contemporary trends in the world of art including modernism, abstract expressionism, cubism, and surrealism, yet they defined photography as a separate medium with its own distinctive characteristics and potential. Rather than emulating painting, photographers sought to exploit photographic technique. Photographers turned their lenses on the human form as well as on plow blades, water tanks, vegetables, skyscrapers, bridge trusses, chrome headlights, and household furnishings with a renewed fascination in texture, composition, line, form, volume, and light. Having shed sentiment and pictorialism, they looked to exploit the full range of the medium in both abstract and realist photography. Dadaist Man Ray experimented with household objects and photographic paper, creating "photograms" or "rayographs" by exposing objects placed on photographic paper with a lightbulb. Surrealist photographs emphasized a dreamlike quality in which familiar objects were mixed together in jarring or incongruous ways or were barely recognizable as a result of distortion, focus, and framing.

On the other hand, technical quality was central to photographers like Paul Strand who adopted an intensified realism. Strand photographed stark geometric patterns and forms created in the interplay of light and shadow through close-ups that concealed or de-emphasized the overall identity of ordinary objects. In the 1930s, Charles Sheeler, Strand, Lewis Hine, and others photographed industrial scenes; they used bold composition and dramatic vantage points to convey the scope and social impact of mass production, the new landscapes of skyscrapers, and assembly-line manufacturing. Edward Weston conveyed both a rich tonality and sculptural form in monumental photographs of the veins of a cabbage leaf, the curves of a bell pepper, an enamel toilet, or a human form lit like a still life.

The conservationist and writer Ansel Adams combined an eye for evocative landscapes with the technical skill to control the entire photographic process—from behind the camera to the dark room and the printed page. Immogen Cunningham, who had worked for Edward W. Curtis's portrait and photographic firm in Seattle, took celebrity portraits while she experimented with abstract forms and multiple exposures. Some critics, who dismissed their "technical obsession" with realistic, sharply focused images, found their purism regressive and confining.

THE 1930s AND THE 1940s

In the 1930s, as the Great Depression cast a shadow across both American individualism and international capitalism, developments in photography reflected the political and social climate. Photographers sought to record the social realities of everyday life and the simple dignity of ordinary Americans, placing greater emphasis on the content of the image than on technical skill or artistry. Leftist political groups hired photographers to document the conditions and the collective efforts of industrial workers and tenant farmers. A small group of photographers, eventually including Walter Rosenblum, Lisette Model, Aaron Siskind, Jerome Liebling, and Consuelo Kanaga, among others, organized as the Photo League and embraced the message of social justice inherent in the work of Progressive reform photographers. Although claiming the work of French photographer Eugène Atget and Mathew Brady's Civil War endeavor as models, Walter Rosenblum and his work recalled the quiet presence of Lewis Hine within the Photo League, which took over the archives of Hine's prints and negatives when he died in 1940.

Franklin D. Roosevelt's New Deal seized upon this tradition in order to document social conditions, promote New Deal reforms, and record the work of government agencies. New Deal arts programs supported photography as well as music, sculpture, murals, dance, and theater. Photographers were hired to generate historical records and to catalog historic architecture and design. For example, Berenice Abbott, in her project "Changing New York," recorded street scenes, architectural details, residences, and public works.

The Farm Security Administration   Photography's greatest role as documentary was realized by the Historical Unit of the Farm Security Administration (FSA), a government office documenting the plight of farmers and the rural conditions addressed by the New Deal between 1935 and 1943. Directed by Roy Emerson Stryker, the agency produced over 270,000 images documenting the story of rural life in a simple, understated, yet empathetic style. FSA photographers captured revealing details: a gnarled homesteader's hands, sparse furnishings, family portraits, and children bent intently over their readers. Stryker distrusted artistry and looked for compassion and rapport in the photographers that he hired. The team that he assembled included, over the years, Walker Evans, Arthur Rothstein, Carl Mydans, Ben Shahn, Dorothea Lange, Russell Lee, Marion Post, John Collier Jr., John Vachon, Jack Delano, Gordon Parks, and a dozen others.

Dorothea Lange's "Migrant Mother, Nipoma, California, 1936" has taken on iconic significance as a testament to the human spirit in the face of the adversity of rural dislocation. Lange's photograph, like other dramatic FSA images, was the product of a collaboration in which the photographer posed and rearranged the subjects in a series of images. Although Stryker sought honest, direct images, FSA photographs were also intended to promote and persuade. They struck a balance between neutral information gathering and persuasive interpretation, at times sparking controversy between the Democratic administration and its Republican critics. The FSA photographs made up, as Stryker intended, a sweeping historical record of hard times and change in rural America and fostered public support for the New Deal.

"Migrant Mother, Nipoma, California, 1936." Dorothea Lange's first assignment for the FSA was in the Southwest. Among her stops was a pea-pickers' camp, where she photographed the families of migrant agricultural workers. These images become the most familiar representations of the Great Depression. © CORBIS

military operations, and combat employed thousands of photographers—those in the military as well as photojournalists and industrial photographers. The lines between government work and reporting blurred as *Life* provided training for military photographers while professional photographers carried their skills into military service during the war. Edward Steichen organized and led the Naval Aviation Unit, which produced recruitment and publicity photographs. Hungarian-born Robert Capa, who had photographed the Spanish Civil War in the 1930s, participated in the D-Day landing at Omaha Beach as a *Life* photographer. Margaret Bourke-White, Carl Mydans, W. Eugene Smith, and other noted photographers brought the war home between the covers of *Life* magazine. As they pushed to document the human experience of combat, the casualty rate for photographers rose to four times the rate for military personnel. On the other hand, both American military photographers and photojournalists aimed to move as well as to inform their audiences, and they have been criticized for staging and re-creating scenes for heightened drama. Photojournalists experienced conflicting pulls between supporting the cause and presenting the violence and ghastly consequences of combat. In later years, photographs of Korea and Vietnam brought home more starkly, in more personal terms and with less censorship, the nature and impact of war.

Life The great breakthrough in the influence of photojournalism came when Henry Luce began *Life* magazine in 1936. *Life* inverted the traditional relationship of news story and image: the photojournalist would interpret events in a sequence of images, or a photo-essay, supported and enhanced by the text. Reflecting the FSA style, photographers tempered artistic and technical accomplishment with social concern. *Life* was immediately successful and soon faced competition from *Look, See,* and other photomagazines bearing witness to the events of the day: fascism in Europe, civil war in Spain, depression, migration, athletic competition, massive public works projects, technological innovation, poverty, wealth, and the onset of World War II. *Life* published the work of Lange and Evans as well as Henri Cartier-Bresson, Berenice Abbot, László Moholy-Nagy, Lisette Model, Brassai, Alfred Eisenstadt, Gordon Parks, Margaret Bourke-White, W. Eugene Smith, and others.

War creates a variety of demands, and in World War II the need for photographs of war production,

PHOTOGRAPHY AFTER WORLD WAR II

While the New Deal and World War II had generated a demand for photographs in government programs, in later years the U.S. Information Service, engaged in a cold war for influence abroad, relied on photographs testifying to the high quality of life and industrial power of Americans as a tool of propaganda. In 1946, photojournalists organized a photographers' cooperative, Magnum Photos, to market and place their work in newspapers and magazines. After World War II, new careers opened up in industrial photography and scientific imaging. Industrial photography emphasized clarity and technical skill in documenting equipment, products, and processes, while scientific imaging relied on precision equipment to record both microscopic and satellite images, opening up new visual worlds in publications like *National Geographic.*

At the same time, prosperity and an increasingly youthful population spurred growth and transformation in fashion and advertising. Commercial photography emphasized a simple, uncluttered look. While air travel made it possible to shoot in natural settings on location around the world, studio photographers turned to simple backdrops, such as white paper, and crisp figures with unobtrusive rather than glamour lighting. Posters, record covers, and movie advertising created new avenues for photography.

In the 1930s, studio photographers and a small number of amateurs were shooting color photographs; however, processing was complex and color labs were rare. Kodak launched Kodachrome in the 1930s, but color film did not overtake black and white until the 1970s. Plastic molding techniques, developed for military applications during the war, led to inexpensive, compact consumer cameras. Following the Korean War, Japan produced cheap automatic cameras as well as 35-mm, single-lens reflex cameras for the U.S. market. Edwin Land's Polaroid Corporation produced instant color pictures beginning in 1963 (the black-and-white Polaroid process was introduced in 1947). The first Polaroids emerged from the camera as a negative and print sandwiched together; the single sheet Polaroid that ejects from the camera and develops as one watches was marketed in 1972. Polaroid technology—which offers a variety of view formats, the opportunity to manipulate color images as they develop, and rich color tones—fostered its own following among artists like William Wegman. The use of roll film took the emphasis away from the creation of individual images in amateur photography and paved the way for more spontaneous photographs. The symbolic use of objects declined as home photography moved toward sequences of photographs recording events and activities, rather than a few images mediating and condensing experience.

Combining commercial graphic design with a tradition of social activism, photography played an important role in protest movements, from nuclear disarmament and civil rights to environmental campaigns, the antiwar movement, and women's rights. When Emmett Till, a fourteen-year-old black boy from Chicago, was brutally murdered when visiting relatives in Mississippi in 1955, his mother, Mamie Till Bradley, brought the body home to Chicago for an open casket service and burial. Although newspapers covered the funeral, *Jet,* a black weekly magazine, carried photographs of Emmett's battered, unrecognizable face. Images from the pages of *Life* of the mushroom cloud and of the bombing of Hiroshima and Nagasaki became the symbols of the nuclear age. Photographs of Neil Armstrong on the moon in 1969 conveyed the high optimism of President John F. Kennedy's "New Frontier." The Eddie Adams photograph "General Loan Executing a Vietcong suspect, February 1, 1968" had a similar iconographic significance.

Photography reflected a turn inward: the search for personal meaning, with a new emphasis on introspection and subjectivity. Change and anonymity brought both a restless sense of placelessness or detachment and a new freedom to invent oneself. The city was often the locus for this vision of modern life and, although color has come to dominate amateur photographs, black and white remained an important medium for artists and photojournalists. The photographs of the 1950s, however, had a different quality from earlier social activist photography. Photographers in the 1950s produced images of poverty, yet sought an inner sensibility rather than a wider social awareness. These photographers eschewed the authoritative voice of the artist/creator and left interpretation or explanation to the viewer.

Street photography expressed a fascination with the haunting modern sense of physical and emotional isolation as well as the enterprise, grit, dislocation, angularity, energy, and freedom of urban life. These photographs often took on more spontaneous, blurred, grainy qualities. Robert Frank's introspective work in *The Americans,* first published in France in 1958, suggested a cultural shallowness, a vacuous American consumerism set in mindless landscapes. Weegee (Arthur Fellig) roamed the night to produce stark images of urban desolation and violence. Diane Arbus discovered bizarre, harsh, and troubling realities in mundane aspects of American life.

Keith F. Davis describes the expansion of interest in photography since 1970 as "the photography boom." Accepted as an art form, photography has become the focus of graduate programs, academic journals, criticism, major exhibitions, galleries, museum collections, and popular interest. Davis attributes this transformation to the rise of television, "Economics aside, the dominance of television in American life accelerated a dramatic shift in attitude toward the still image. . . . This utilitarian shift freed the earlier medium to be appreciated as art." Contemporary photographers have sometimes found models in schools or approaches that were eclipsed in the early twentieth century. At the same time, photographers have resurrected cumbersome old technologies while embracing the new, including digital images, electronic processes, and even toy cameras. With many more people approaching photography from diverse perspectives, in a multiplicity of regional networks, photography has developed many centers, bringing to the field what Davis calls "a radical pluralism." The tensions between science, art, commerce, and documentary as well as the engagement of both professionals and amateurs that have defined the history of photography are evident today. Digital media offer new tools for both imaging and manipulating images; at the same time, artists mine and innovate upon older technology large format daguerreotypes and Polaroids, for example and themes.

See also **The Popular Arts; The Artist and the Intellectual in the New Deal** *(volume 1);* **The World According to Hollywood; Popular Culture in the Public Arena; Postmodernism and the Arts** *(volume 2);* **The Visual Arts; Elite vs. Popular Cultures; Culture for Mass Audiences** *(in this volume); and other articles in this section.*

BIBLIOGRAPHY

Davidov, Judith Fryer. *Women's Camera Work: Self/Body/Other in American Visual Culture.* Durham, N.C., 1998.

Davis, Keith F. *An American Century of Photography from Dry-Plate to Digital: The Hallmark Photographic Collection.* New York, 1999.

Goldberg, Vicki. *The Power of Photography: How Photographs Changed Our Lives.* New York, 1991.

Harison, Jim. "Unimaginable Visions: A Salute to Photography." *Harvard Magazine,* November–December 1989: 21–30.

Szarkowski, John. *Photography until Now.* Boston, 1989.

Taft, Robert. *Photography and the American Scene: A Social History, 1839–1889.* 1938. Reprint, New York, 1964.

Welling, William. *Photography in America: The Formative Years, 1839–1900.* Albuquerque, N.M., 1987.

PAINTING

Angela Miller

In traveling from Europe to America, painting from the seventeenth century on made the journey from societies dominated by institutional patronage to one shaped by an emerging market economy. Painting in the British colonies and in the United States developed virtually without the support of state or other forms of official patronage until the federally sponsored decoration of the U.S. Congress beginning in the early nineteenth century. Public investment in the fine arts proceeded episodically over the next century and a half.

For much of its history, therefore, painting in the United States was the expression less of an established state culture shaping public and civic pronouncement than it was an arena of exchange between artists and their public audience. As the character of the audience for the fine arts changed, so too did the art. In a young democracy largely lacking official channels of expression the fine arts explored themes of nationhood, citizenship, and democratic polity. With the institutional entrenchment of a high culture of museums, didactic mural art, and private patronage in the later nineteenth century, the democratic mandate of the fine arts waned in favor of greater involvement by elites. The shifting relations of painting with its audience were further complicated by the rise of mass media, popular journalism, illustration, and advertising in the early twentieth century.

ORIGINS

In the colonies, the fine arts made their appearance a half century after the earliest English settlement. First brought over by the dissenting religious cultures of Anglo immigrants in the form of portraiture, painting was initially supported by wealth and served as an indicator of social status. *Mrs. Elizabeth Freake and Baby Mary* (1671 to 1674) is a provincial variant of an Elizabethan courtly style that by the seventeenth century was distinctly old-fashioned. It

found a new life in the English colonies, where it served a local gentry anxious to establish its material affluence, along with the spiritual approbation such wealth conveyed. Early colonial portraits were painted by anonymous artisans whose picture-making skills centered on the fine delineation of pattern and on jewel-like color. They relay a medieval indifference to spatial illusionism as achieved through chiaroscuro or perspective. The commemorative function of portraiture found ready acceptance in a young society where status had few material expressions. Protestant strictures against sensuous displays of form—driven by fears about the visual deceptions of Catholicism—continued to shape the character of the fine arts in the young republic.

The seventeenth-century anonymous limner was the ancestor of later itinerant and largely self-taught portraitists who served provincial elites from the early eighteenth century on. Provincial limners learned from European print sources, resulting in a continuing emphasis on linearity, along with a preference for abstract patterning, and for discrete color areas.

In the Southwest, colonized by settlers from Mexico City in the seventeenth century, an entirely different visual tradition developed around devotional images of the saints and the Christ figure. Painted or carved in wood, these images were the work of anonymous *santeros* who traveled throughout the small farming villages of northern New Mexico, furnishing images for use in family chapels or other domestic settings. Along with altarpieces for churches, these *santos* constituted the major artistic production of the Hispanic Southwest, an expression of a deeply pious Catholicism deriving from medieval Spain but shaped by frontier conditions. In the lapse of centralized church authority on the frontier of Spanish colonization in the New World, local expression flourished, keeping alive a form of religious iconography that had become archaic within the Catholic Church, and developing a

Mrs. Elizabeth Freake and Baby Mary. Anonymous painting, early seventeenth century. The work is one of a pair of portraits of a prosperous young Boston couple. Husband John Freake was a lawyer and merchant, a member of an emerging colonial property-owning elite. © BURSTEIN COLLECTION/CORBIS

Truchas Master (Pedro Antonio Fresquis), ***Our Lady of Guadalupe*** **(c. 1790–1840).** This version of the Blessed Virgin is specific to the New World, forming part of a popular religious cult throughout the Spanish Southwest. Its origins are traced to the miraculous appearance of the Virgin, speaking the Aztec language Nahuatl, to the newly converted Indian peasant Juan Diego in 1531. COLORADO SPRINGS FINE ARTS CENTER, TAYLOR MUSEUM

colorful style of flattened and highly conventional- ized forms distantly derived from a Baroque visual language. Distinct as well from the Protestant visual culture of the East Coast was the active role of im- ages in everyday life. *Santos* were venerated as in- tercessors on behalf of those who owned and prayed to them, in contrast to the iconophobic character of Protestant societies. Marginalized in the later nineteenth century by the flood of mass-produced printed images of the saints from Mexico and the United States, the *santero* tradition has been peri- odically revived, under the encouragement of the federal government during President Franklin D. Roosevelt's New Deal, and since the 1970s, when a new generation of Hispanic artisans took self- conscious pride in extending this rich regional tradition.

Painting in the South was largely limited to por- traiture through the Civil War; aspiring artists born in the South took up careers in New York City in order to pursue opportunities still unavailable in the largely agrarian section. An emerging southern na- tionalism before the war assumed forms distinctly different from the North, with its symbolic invest- ment in the landscape and in explorations of a dem- ocratic polity.

EUROPEAN INFLUENCE

The arrival in 1728 of John Smibert, a trained painter from London, offered aspiring colonial art- ists their first exposure to the grand tradition of European history painting and portraiture. Smibert brought with him his copies of the masters, along with a collection of engravings, inspiring a new level of both craft and theoretical knowledge. The tran- sition from a medieval artisanal to a Renaissance humanist artistic culture was as rapid as the colo- nies' own emergence into a transatlantic economy

480

trafficking in consumer goods, books, prints, and other sources of Anglo-American cultural ideals. Colonial talent such as Robert Feke and John Singleton Copley (both New Englanders) emerged in the following generation. Copley's portraiture brought a new physical presence and psychological immediacy to his subjects. Outgrowing the limitations of his provincial environment, he became the first of many American-born expatriate artists to win international celebrity as an artist when he took up a career in London.

Though frustrated by the absence of a market for the more elevated forms of history painting, Copley found avid patrons from Boston to New York, ranging from ostentatiously wealthy Anglophile merchants (*Nicolas Boylston,* 1767) to members of a proud, politically and socially self-conscious artisanal class (*Paul Revere,* 1768). For each, Copley's powers realized a stunning public projection of a sitter's preferred image and helped constitute an emerging sense of class identity in a socially fluid colonial society.

Despite the lack of private or public art collections, academies for training (the British Royal Academy itself was founded in 1768), or European artists of note, American artists fed their ambitions on engravings after Raphael and other masters, as well as on printed treatises that approached painting as a humanistic discipline (Charles-Alphonse du Fresnoy, Joshua Reynolds). Among those so inclined was Benjamin West, of Quaker parentage, who found tutelage first through local artists, then by going abroad. Sent to London through a subscription raised on his behalf by a wealthy Philadelphia merchant hoping to promote the fledging arts, West quickly rose to the heights of the British art world through a skillful deployment of his exotic image as a New World "savage" and his ability to rethink British academic traditions from within. Most notable was the "revolution" in British history painting he launched with his *Death of General Wolfe* (1770) in which—renouncing the convention of painting history subjects in ancient dress—he created a compelling image of a Christlike hero in modern military uniform. West's contribution to history painting was put to service by John Trumbull, aide-de-camp to George Washington, and a Harvard-educated member of an old New England family, in a series of virtuosic oil sketches of major episodes in the American Revolution. Trumbull used his art to put forward a model of heroic self-sacrifice in the name of an idealized aristocratic noblesse. Those sketches became the basis for a series of Revolutionary War scenes in the U.S. Capitol

John Singleton Copley, *Paul Revere* **(c. 1768).** Oil on canvas. Revere, an esteemed Boston silversmith, prepares to engrave a teapot in an act of contemplation that brings together head and hand. Copley may have traded the portrait for silver goods, although its precise origins are undocumented. © BETTMANN/CORBIS

rotunda, commissioned by Congress, yet preceded by years of fierce lobbying on Trumbull's part. Public history painting, as well as engravings and popular prints made after such works, thus played a role in collective remembering of pivotal moments in America's history. During the Civil War, such visual commemoration was largely the preserve of photography, and later, of sculptural memorials.

Well into the nineteenth century, American artists continued to form part of a transatlantic culture that imbued them with artistic aspirations difficult to realize under the conditions of a utilitarian, go-ahead market society with little time for self-cultivation. Some, like Samuel F. B. Morse, feeling that painting, "a smiling mistress to many," had been "a cruel jilt to me," took a more practical turn at invention, with well-known results. Others adopted the tactics of the market and turned to sensational subjects from the Bible and ancient history, touring massively scaled didactic and allegorical works such as Rembrandt Peale's *Court of Death* (1819–1820) throughout the Northeast on a fee-per-visit basis. Such a form of art production brought painting to the public rather than requiring the public to come to the privileged private and institutional venues for the fine arts that continued to dominate European painting. Despite the elitism of the fine arts, and their limited circulation, American painters—with notable exceptions—increasingly shaped their careers around the requirements of democratic patronage.

By their nature paintings did not circulate as widely through American culture as reproductive forms of image-making such as broadsheets, political cartoons, and lithographs. To gain a national reputation artists had to reproduce their paintings in print form, through such international print firms as Goupil or the New York–based American Art-Union (AA-U) and the Cosmopolitan Art Association. Paintings also won a wider public through exhibition at such venues as regional expositions, sanitary fairs during the Civil War, and, from 1876 on, World's Fairs (most notably in Chicago in 1893). The rise of an established gallery system awaited the later nineteenth century, and when it did appear, mostly featured works by European artists to the detriment of American art production. Countering this, however, were new forms of institutional patronage that encouraged artists to engage American subjects. Among the most noteworthy of these was the short-lived AA-U (1844–1851), which engraved works of "national value" for circulation to subscribers. The AA-U gave substance to the concept of an art of shared ideals that reconciled regional and national identities, and that drew forth collective lessons from local materials. The ideal of a national art was further embodied in the National Academy of Design, founded in New York City in 1826 as an artist-run institution dedicated to exhibiting works by American artists.

With the opening of the Erie Canal in 1825, New York City emerged as the center of artistic production in the new republic. Bringing artists together with an infrastructure of studios, private and commercial galleries, exhibition and training opportunities, major publishing houses, and journals dedicated to arts and letters, New York City processed raw artistic talent from around the country into the finished products of a national culture, while its position as leading metropolis assured artistic and literary work wide dissemination.

Boston and Philadelphia, however, retained their discrete identities as centers of learning, science, artistic, and literary production. Dominated by a conservative patrician elite with ties to Harvard University and to a reform Protestantism uneasy with mass democracy, the artistic culture of Boston nurtured such idiosyncratic personalities as Washington Allston, who transformed the tradition of grand manner history painting and biblical narra-

tive into an instrument of public prophecy with which to scourge a materialistic society (*Belshazzar's Feast,* 1817–1843). Allston embodied the English Romantic critique of utilitarianism and a belief in the transcendental powers of imagination. In a series of elegiac fancy pictures featuring lone female figures in a landscape, Allston explored a form of non-narrative associational or mood painting grounded in the synaesthetic properties of color. This work anticipated the later nineteenth century movement away from literary or didactic subject matter. Allston was the most likely source for the figure of the artist as frustrated visionary in Nathaniel Hawthorne's short story "The Artist of the Beautiful" (1844).

THE DEMOCRATIZATION OF ART: GENRE PAINTING AND LANDSCAPE

Following the War of 1812 and the resulting wave of cultural nationalism and Anglophobic sentiment, nationalist critics and patrons embraced the arts as a new arena within which to explore evolving concepts of national identity. First in genre painting, and then in landscape subjects, American artists in the Northeast and the burgeoning West eagerly addressed an expanding audience prepared to embrace artists who answered their needs for self-images of the new nation.

In the ensuing decades, John Lewis Krimmel, William Sidney Mount, and others turned to genre scenes featuring everyday life in the rural areas of the eastern United States. Looking to the example of the Scottish artist Sir David Wilkie, the satirical works of the eighteenth-century English artist William Hogarth, and Flemish and Dutch genre of the seventeenth century, American genre painters seized on rich opportunities for social commentary on their own emerging middle-class society. Anxieties over identity found expression in a carefully calibrated social typology. Mount, having imbibed the ideals of the grand tradition, found inspiration in a cast of characters drawn from theater and popular culture. In *The Painter's Triumph* (1838), the artist, flourishing his palette, stands back from his easel, as a well-dressed farmer, crop in hand, bends down with a look of dawning recognition on his face. The bare-bones studio suggests the absence of standard academic props except for a drawing of the head of the Apollo Belvedere, a well-known Hellenistic sculpture in the Vatican that represented the exalted aesthetic ideals of the classical tradition. A venerated work, the Apollo seems to turn away in disgust at such pandering to popular taste. Despite this satirical twist, Mount's sympathies seem firmly grounded in a democratic credo of open dialogue between the artist and his newly expanded public. Richard Caton Woodville was trained at the Dusseldorf Academy in Germany, the destination of many aspiring antebellum genre and history painters in the United States. Until his death in 1855, he turned his sardonic wit to narrative scenes that explored the complex process by which mid-century Americans negotiated their identities. In such works as *News of the Mexican War* (1848) he presented the gender and racial hierarchies operating within a democratic polity. *The Card Players* (1846) and *Politics in an Oyster House* (1848) feature the confidence men and partisan debaters of a new and socially amiguous urban milieu. In the Mississippi Valley, George Caleb Bingham transformed the unruly and heterogeneous society of the western frontier into reassuringly stable, serene compositions grounded in Renaissance formulae. His paintings of commerce on the river, the electoral process in the small towns of Missouri, and the social phases of frontier life, marshaled a narrative of development that gave structure to the open-ended future of the region, and encouraged the economic and spatial integration of frontier into nation. Lilly Martin Spencer is a rare example of a woman artist who achieved national fame in a period when few managed to throw off the burden of domestic responsibilities to pursue their own careers. She brought humor and energy to her portraits of the "separate sphere" of feminine domestic life. Such works as *Shake Hands?* (1854) endowed domestic labor and child nurture with republican associations of equality and the respect owed to women for their role in raising the next generation of citizens.

Along with genre painting, images of the American landscape formed a major part of art production from the 1820s through the Civil War. The earliest views of the American landscape—overmantel paintings, or backdrops to portrait images—originated in the eighteenth-century English topographical tradition. The beginnings of a more ambitious landscape mode coincided with the rise of American Romanticism a generation or so after its initial appearance in England. A cultural reaction to industrial capitalism and urbanization, Romanticism turned away from the settled landscape and embraced the indwelling spiritual power of nature and the organic imagination as a source of moral and artistic authority. The founding figure of the national landscape school was Thomas Cole, an English émigré. Encountering the wilds of the Ohio

Valley, and later the White Mountains and the Catskills, the young and largely self-taught artist brought to his earliest views of the 1820s a reverence for nature informed by the poetry of William Wordsworth and fueled by his first-hand witness to the ravages of the industrial revolution in his native region of Lancashire. Also significant in his development as an artist is his background in dissenting Protestantism, which brought with it a marked tendency to read nature in the typological terms of the Bible, as a drama of death and salvation. Aspiring to the higher forms of history painting, Cole developed a serial format that carried an explicit narrative dimension. In his five-part allegorical cycle *The Course of Empire* (1833–1836), Cole explored the popular theme of empire's rise and fall. Of a deeply conservative and pious temperament, Cole used his art to deliver "sermons in paint," as a later critic wrote about his work. Convinced that Americans were squandering their divine birthright—an Edenic New World republic that drew its virtue from intimacy with nature—Cole became increasingly disillusioned with the utilitarian and money-driven habits of his adopted country. Eventually he withdrew into private allegories of spiritual salvation such as his popular *Voyage of Life* (1840), engraved and widely circulated. During a career cut short by his early death in 1848, however, Cole combined elements of the place-specific topographical tradition with grand synthetic compositions that drew upon the painting of the old masters.

Cole's form of prophetic landscape art reached its fullest development in the following generation. During the 1850s, in the hands of such artists as Asher B. Durand (later president of the National Academy), and Frederic Church, perhaps the leading figure of midcentury American art, landscape served the complex expressive needs of a nation whose historic identity as a republic was challenged by sectionalism, industrial exploitation of the wilderness, and growing class difference. Church's *Twilight in the Wilderness* (1860), painted on the eve of the Civil War, uses the metaphor of sunset to explore a charged moment of historical transition, balanced between millennial promise and apocalypse. From the 1850s on, landscape painters turned to South America (Church, Martin Johnson Heade, and others), the Rocky Mountain West (Thomas Moran and Albert Bierstadt), and the stark coastal regions of New England (John Frederick Kensett and Fitz Hugh Lane), in an effort to revitalize outworn picturesque conventions through the encounter with startling new landscapes.

Richard Caton Woodville, *War News from Mexico* (1848). Posed beneath a sign labeled "American Hotel," a group of "sovereigns"—white male voters—suggest a range of social types in Woodville's emblematic genre scene. The figures of a woman and an African American man and child—excluded from citizenship—are pointedly situated outside the defining boundaries of the porch. © BETTMANN/CORBIS

Though there were later expressions of the prophetic tradition—notably Thomas Moran's *Mountain of the Holy Cross* (1875)—landscape moved into a more private, mood-filled, and intimist mode beginning in the 1880s. George Inness's tonalist landscapes preferred atmospheric effects and a muted palette, eschewing the didactic narrative symbolism of earlier landscape painting. Influenced by Swedenborgian mysticism, his art contained a spiritual content absent from others who pursued his aesthetic effects.

THE LATE NINETEENTH CENTURY: CULTURAL RETRENCHMENT AND COSMOPOLITAN TRENDS

In a different mode was the work of the American Impressionists, who adapted the high-keyed color, broken brushstrokes, and sparkling light effects associated with their French counterparts, while painting nostalgic views of New England village life and coastal and rural landscapes. In place of the French embrace of modern life was a refined aes-

Frederic Edwin Church, *Twilight in the Wilderness* **(1860).** Oil on canvas; 101.6 x 162.6 cm. © THE CLEVELAND MUSEUM OF ART, 2000, MR. AND MRS. WILLIAM H. MARLATT FUND, 1965.233

theticism associated with the highly evolved upper classes of Anglo heritage.

Leading artists of the later nineteenth century served an elite ideal of self-culture through the contemplation of beauty. The "genteel tradition," a term coined by the philosopher George Santayana in 1911, embodied a belief in the uplifting and socializing function of art, a dedication to abstract ideals—often given allegorical expression—and a distaste for realism, or anything that—in the words of one disgruntled editor—would "offend a virgin." Such was the hold of genteel ideals on American art that Thomas Eakins's powerful *Portrait of Doctor Gross (The Gross Clinic)* (1875) was consigned to the medical section of the Philadelphia Centennial, because it showed the famous surgeon with blood on his hands.

Repudiating what cultural historian T. J. Jackson Lears has termed the "evasive banality" of American elite culture, Eakins was largely ignored by critics nationally. Eakins drew on his Philadelphia heritage of empirically precise, sober realism, in tandem with French academic training, to produce—along with Copley—the greatest body of portraiture in American art. But if Copley furnished an amplified projection of the social ambitions of sitters, Eakins was known to age his sitters, presenting them as the thoughtful, physically worn embodiments of an age of waning confidence, diminished expectations, and skepticism concerning human and social achievements. Eakins's ability to express the dilemmas of modern selfhood won him the admiration of the first generation of modernists, as an example of a usable past that anchored their own emerging search for an art that was both modern and American.

With the post–Civil War expansion of transatlantic steam travel, growing wealth, and a reaction against the perceived provincial character of meticulously painted narrative or anecdotal art, the final quarter of the nineteenth century saw a turn toward more cosmopolitan identities. Paris and Munich replaced London in the late eighteenth century, Rome in the early nineteenth, and Dusseldorf in the mid-nineteenth century as centers of artistic training. Expatriation, having long been a characteristic of American art culture, became a prominent feature; indeed, two of the leading international figures of the art world in these years—James McNeill Whistler and John Singer Sargent—spent their entire careers in France and England, although American by birth. Mary Cassatt found greater freedom to pur-

Thomas Eakins, *The Thinker: Portrait of Louis N. Kenton*
(1900). Oil on canvas; 208.3 x 106.7 cm (82 x 42 in.).
METROPOLITAN MUSEUM OF ART. JOHN STEWART KENNEDY
FUND, 1917 (17.172)

sue her art as a woman by moving to Paris, where
she became an intimate of the Impressionist circle.

Most artists, however, returned from abroad to
make their careers at home, bringing with them a
French taste for exotic, premodern subject matter,
which they applied to a range of subjects, from Native American to Colonial Revival and other historical themes treated with antiquarian accuracy. A
sophisticated academicism looked to Renaissance
and other revival styles for archaeologically precise
renditions of the past. Large-scale allegory, employing the classically draped female figure, paid tribute
to the new importance of historical precedent and
to the nation's emerging imperial identity as "heir

of the ages." In this atmosphere of Europhilia, the
native realism of Winslow Homer appealed to
American nationalist critics, substituting a "virile"
grasp of homegrown subjects for what they felt was
the effete "art for art's sake" of much French-
influenced American painting. All the same, Homer
himself learned a great deal from other artists, amal-
gamating the attention to surface pattern he learned
from Japanese prints with other currents in European art in powerful compositions that tapped the
deepest themes of life and death in nature.

The so-called Ashcan artists around Robert
Henri represented the first full-fledged revolt
against the genteel tradition. Turning to the new
immigrant cultures of lower Manhattan, and to the
popular venues of urban modernity—parks, res-
taurants, movie houses, and street life—they employed a deliberately rough, journalistic style that
rejected careful composition and facture. Yet their
urban images remained indebted to the social typing and insurgent realism of French artists like
Honoré Daumier.

The reception of European modernism in the
United States occurred on several different fronts.
Alfred Stieglitz—a photographer and tireless promoter of new art forms—presented the work of
leading European modernists at his New York gallery "291" as well as publishing *Camera Work,* the
leading source for the writings of the French philosopher Henri-Louis Bergson, the Russian painter
Wassily Kandinsky, and other influential figures.
Stieglitz also supported a group of American artists
who came to be known as the Stieglitz circle.
Among them were Georgia O'Keeffe (later Stieglitz's
wife), and Arthur Dove, who explored organic abstraction, a native idiom rooted in the isolation, enlargement, and recontextualization of objects in nature. Dove's breakthrough into pure abstraction in
1910 placed him among the very earliest artists in
Europe or the United States to abandon figuration.
Marsden Hartley drew various native and European
sources together in a powerful if eclectic form of
personal expressionism that looked back to the
American symbolist Albert Pinkham Ryder. John
Marin produced dynamic images of the pulsatingly
alive modern city, and later of the energies of nature, which during his lifetime earned for him fame
as perhaps the leading American modernist before
Jackson Pollock.

Stieglitz's elitism, however, limited his influence
on the larger public; the so-called Armory Show,
held at the 69th Regiment Armory in New York City
in 1913, offered massive public exposure to new artistic currents. It surveyed the range of the Euro-

pean avant-garde, past and present, with some omissions, and included apprentice American modernists, in an exhibition that helped shape the emerging narrative of modern art as well as drawing clearly the battle lines between apologists for the new and the outraged defenders of the old.

The 1920s saw the domestication of European movements such as cubism and futurism in a distinctive American style and subject matter drawing upon a machine-age iconography of skyscrapers, factories, and new technology. The new visual environment of advertising, packaging, product design, and billboards also offered inspiration for such artists as Charles Demuth, Gerald Murphy, and Stuart Davis, who once wrote, "I do not belong to the human race but am a product made by the American Can Company and the New York *Evening Journal*."

American precisionism, dubbed "cubo-futurism" by contemporary critics, domesticated cubist spatial structures in the flattened planes and collapsed perspectives of the skyscraper city. Its hard-edged geometries expressed utopian longings for a world freed of organic accident, but also occasionally dystopian concerns about the inhuman potential of the new urban order. Charles Sheeler combined work in both photography and painting to develop a style calculatedly uninflected by emotion; often basing paintings on photographs, he turned to the new River Rouge plant of the Ford Motor Company in Dearborn, Michigan, as well as to the pristine surfaces of machinery to explore, often hauntingly, the brave new world of industry and technology.

At the same time, modernists like Sheeler also turned to the preindustrial past to ground the technological present in a functionalist and nonornamental aesthetic. Shaker design, patchwork quilts, tools, and utilitarian objects held forth an indigenous legacy for American modernism. A new rubric—folk art—linked the formal concerns of modernist art to the naively direct and anti-illusionistic devices of untrained limners. Sheeler produced a series of paintings and photographs exploring the formal geometries of barns in Bucks County, Pennsylvania; in addition he collected Shaker furniture, rag rugs, and preindustrial artifacts that inspired other work.

Modernism in the 1920s thus faced in two directions: exploring an idiomatic "homegrown" modernism that drew upon an array of commercial, vernacular, and regional landscapes, and investigating an indigenous aesthetic tradition by looking to native roots. Following World War I, many artists and writers formed colonies in such nonurban environments as Taos, New Mexico. The Taos school was an early expression of an emerging regionalist sensibility whose various expressions between the wars were unified by an antimodern reaction against standardization, vulgar commercialism, and the deadening mechanization of everyday life. Drawn to the ritual life of the Pueblo Indian and Hispanic Catholic societies of the region, a range of artists, from John Marin to Georgia O'Keeffe and Ernest Blumenschein, shared a longing for more intense communal connection to the spiritual dimension of human experience. A later generation of modernists, beginning with Adolph Gottlieb and Jackson Pollock, drew a different inspiration from tribal cultures: moving away from national pride in the native inheritance of American art, they looked to the transhistorical power of symbols as a means of reintegrating the fragmented modern personality.

By the late 1920s modernist aesthetics had filtered down to the level of the "middlebrow." A number of texts popularized modern art for an educated middle-class public by introducing readers to the language of formalist criticism. Dealers like Charles Daniel and Edith Halpert promoted American modernists. Others, like Katherine Dreier, tirelessly missionized the creed of modern art through such organizations as the Société Anonyme.

In the years between the wars, however, such critics as Thomas Craven and Royal Cortissoz also attacked "rootless" international modernism, often in anti-Semitic and xenophobic terms, and argued instead for a nonderivative American art. At a moment of popular exposure, then, modernism faced an often virulent backlash from critics, as well as artists such as Thomas Hart Benton, even as he fully assimilated its lessons into his own reinvented figurative language. Benton was grouped in the 1930s with two other artists—Grant Wood in Iowa and John Steuart Curry in Kansas—as the primary figures of regionalism. Marked by very different styles, the regionalists formed part of an international impulse, between the wars, to ground national identity in the soil; romanticizing the traditions of rural America, the regionalists gave visual expression to a "folk" culture of producers connected to the rhythms of nature and grounded in tradition. Their sometimes satirical work, such as Wood's *Parson Weems' Fable* (1938–1939), is characterized by robust faith in the power of myths to define communal life. In this self-conscious acknowledgement of the mythic structure of public memory they differed from the German painters of the Third Reich, with whom they were sometimes compared.

Charles Sheeler, *American Landscape* (1930). Oil on canvas; 24 x 31 in. Sheeler's painting shows the vertical integration of the Ford plant at River Rouge, including the transportation and processing of raw materials. Its taut formal equilibrium is broken only by the tiny moving figure of a workman, suggesting a point of rupture between the human and the technological. Pastoral and antipastoral elements are ambiguously opposed. THE MUSEUM OF MODERN ART, NEW YORK. GIFT OF ABBY ALDRICH ROCKEFELLER. PHOTOGRAPH © 2000 THE MUSEUM OF MODERN ART, NEW YORK.

A different reaction against what many felt was an introverted modernism obsessed with purely formal concerns came with the advent of social realism in easel and mural painting during the 1930s. During the years of the Great Depression, President Roosevelt's New Deal directed unprecedented levels of federal funding into the cultural sphere; artists in a variety of media received weekly wages for their work. New Deal programs eroded the boundaries between artmaking and other forms of labor, promoting a greater involvement with political and social themes. Unemployment, labor militancy, heroic work, and a sometimes satirical grasp of the class- and race-stratified social landscape of cities all formed major themes, painted in a range of figurative styles. New Deal art programs also invested in public murals, from post offices to state and federal buildings. Private patrons like John D. Rockefeller and the Detroit Institute of Art, underwritten by Edsel Ford, also commissioned Diego ("Hog of Walls") Rivera, the leading mural artist of the Mexican Revolution who completed a number of important projects in the United States between 1930 and 1933. Despite his Marxist beliefs, Rivera was by then a critical inspiration for mural artists in this decade with his massive Renaissance-inspired frescoes.

With the emergence of Harlem as a major social, commercial, and cultural center of black life in the 1920s, artists such as Aaron Douglas, Palmer Hayden, and William H. Johnson expressed issues of cultural nationalism and black heritage previously closed to a community that had been, with few exceptions, thoroughly marginalized from the fine arts tradition. Helping them to overcome historical disadvantages were such private foundations as the Harmon, which sponsored annual competitions. Over the next decades, black artists explored their relationship to the European art tradition and to an emerging modernism; they produced narratives of

Georgia O'Keeffe, *Jack-in-the-Pulpit* **(1930).** Oil on canvas; 40 x 30 in. *Jack-in-the-Pulpit* formed part of a series of six paintings focusing progressively upon the interior landscape of stamen and pistil. O'Keeffe's flower paintings exploited the ambiguity created by framing and radical enlargement of scale, transforming intimate passages of nature into landscapes that reference the topographies of the body. COURTESY NATIONAL GALLERY OF ART, WASHINGTON, ALFRED STIEGLITZ COLLECTION, BEQUEST OF GEORGIA O'KEEFFE

their history, from slave rebellion to the migration of the southern diaspora (Jacob Lawrence, *Migration* series, 1940–1941); and they created a rich and varied portrait of black urban life, sometimes in styles that evoked visual and improvisational traditions within black culture.

Despite the pronounced differences between the figurative art of the 1930s and the return to abstraction in the 1940s, they were connected by a shared interest in the integrative function of myth, both in national and in psychic terms. In the 1930s, the communal uses of myth were often characterized by an antifascist message about the virtues of American democracy; artists in the next generation, by contrast, turned to ancient Greek myths to explore a universal substructure of powerful emotion that was precultural. Informed by a construct known as "Modern Man," the mythmakers of the 1940s located the origins of social behavior in such ahistorical forces as instinct and the pull of the primordial

Thomas Hart Benton, *Persephone* **(1938).** Egg tempera and resin oil over casein on linen over plywood panel. © THE NELSON-ATKINS MUSEUM OF ART, KANSAS CITY, MISSOURI (PURCHASE: ACQUIRED THROUGH THE YELLOW FREIGHT FOUNDATION ART ACQUISITION FUND AND THE GENEROSITY OF MRS. HERBERT O. PEET, RICHARD J. STERN, THE DORIS JONES STEIN FOUNDATION, THE JACOB L. AND ELLA C. LOOSE FOUNDATION, MR. AND MRS. RICHARD M. LEVIN, AND MR. AND MRS. MARVIN RICH) F86-57 © T. H. BENTON AND R. P. BENTON TESTAMENTARY TRUSTS/ LICENSED BY VAGA, NEW YORK

Jacob Lawrence, "The Migration Gained in Momentum." Panel 18 from *The Migration Series* 1940–1941; text and title revised by the artist). Tempera on gesso on composition board, 18 x 12 in. The series consisted of sixty small panels that told the story of the great interwar migration of African Americans from South to North. Migration between worlds had been the defining experience for Americans throughout the nation's history. Here it serves as a parable of transformation from rural to urban, preindustrial to modern, fusing modernist form with mythic narrative. THE MUSEUM OF MODERN ART, NEW YORK. GIFT OF MRS. DAVID M. LEVY. PHOTOGRAPH © 2000 THE MUSEUM OF MODERN ART, NEW YORK

past. Redemption lay in the reintegration of conscious and unconscious energies through the agency of mythic narrative. Abstraction in the 1940s was still referential, however, evoking underwater, cellular, and biomorphic forms resonant with links to a landscape of the psyche (Mark Rothko, *Slow Swirl at the Edge of the Sea*, 1944).

Psychological projection, surreal juxtapositions, and dreamlike landscapes were the components of a "magic realist" mode largely overlooked in accounts of American painting in the 1940s and 1950s, a rubric that included a stylistically diverse range of artists. Figurative artists such as Jared French shared with better known abstract painters a fascination with Jungian archetypes. Connecting many of these works was a deep sense of psychic unease and alienation prompted by the wartime revelation of human savagery. Moving away from the overtly mythic iconography of 1940s abstrac-

tion, artists such as Jackson Pollock and Mark Rothko began exploring new techniques of artmaking that would liberate unconscious energies and achieve, through painting itself, new forms of experience. Pollock's figurational and later "drip" paintings drew upon automatist techniques of surrealism to create extended, densely woven scrims of paint that redefined the visual field and used the body of the artist to interrupt the autonomy of the art object. Across a range of styles, from the energetically gestural to the color-field approach taken by Rothko and by Barnett Newman, Abstract Ex-

Mark Rothko, *Slow Swirl at the Edge of the Sea* **(1944).** Oil on canvas; 6.28 x 7.75 feet. Rothko began his career in the 1930s as a figurative artist of social subject matter. By the 1940s, under the influence of European artistic exile, Rothko turned to abstractions that evoke aqueous and suggestively human forms conveyed in lyrical gesture and calling to mind the origins and cycles of life. THE MUSEUM OF MODERN ART, NEW YORK. BEQUEST OF MRS. MARK ROTHKO THROUGH THE MARK ROTHKO FOUNDATION, INC. PHOTOGRAPH © 2000 MUSEUM OF MODERN ART, NEW YORK

pressionism was a widely influential and internationally heralded movement centered in New York that combined abstraction of means with a subject-centered art. Despite differences among artists, it was unified by a common investment in the heroic subjectivity of the artist and the defining role of artistic process in the creation of meaning. Working within the context of Abstract Expressionism, Helen Frankenthaler, as early as 1952 (*Mountains and Sea*), created a lyrical new expressive language of diluted color applied to unprimed canvas. Her "stain paintings" influenced Morris Louis and Ken-

neth Noland, key figures in the color-field painting of the 1960s.

Artists of the next generation extended Pollock's restaging of the art act in new directions, using their bodies as paintbrush, extending their field of action out into the room and the world beyond the canvas. In a reaction against the emotionally heated and expressionist practice of Pollock and others was the cool, parodic stance of "pop art." Already in the early 1950s, Robert Rauschenberg was transforming the meaning of the gesture from a statement of existential presence into a playful and self-referential exploration of painting's boundaries. Pop artists such as Andy Warhol and Roy Lichtenstein turned to the banal imagery of advertising, comics, and mass-marketed commodities for their subject matter. Using commercial silkscreen techniques, reproducing the benday dots of mass circulation newspaper print, isolating and monumentalizing consumer objects, and presenting the oral fixations of Americans in images of food and cigarettes, pop art investigated the boundaries between life and art. Conceptual art, reacting against the commodification of high art and its institutionalization in the museum, has further eroded the privileged status of the easel painting, while the minimalist painting of Agnes Martin and others has explored the boundaries of perception. Such questioning has had the paradoxical effect of revitalizing and redefining the ongoing engagement of artists with painting. Though never a mode of fully democratic expres-

sion, the history of painting in the United States reveals consistent efforts to disseminate the benefits of artistic culture to a democratic audience. Alongside of this was a countertrend to buttress the received authority of the fine arts and to reinforce their privileged mode of address to the public. Painting has likewise served the opposing challenges of exploring collective ideas and myths, as well as private subjective worlds. It has simultaneously served the requirements for easily recognizable meanings and narrative readability, on the one hand, and the purposes of personal exploration that occasionally expanded and redefined the boundaries of cultural knowledge and understanding, on the other. Its history thus focuses on the dilemmas of private versus public meanings, and of an elitist versus a democratic construction of cultural authority, offering unique forms of evidence for the cultural historian.

See also **The Fine Arts in Colonial America; The Arts in the Republican Era; American Romanticism; Realism in Art and Literature; Radical Alternatives; The Artist and the Intellectual in the New Deal** *(volume 1);* **The Ideal of Spontaneity; Postmodernism and the Arts; Artistic, Intellectual, and Political Refugees** *(volume 2);* **The Visual Arts; Elite vs. Popular Cultures; Museums** *(in this volume); and other articles in this section.*

BIBLIOGRAPHY

Primary

McCoubrey, John W. *American Art, 1700–1960: Sources and Documents.* Englewood Cliffs, N.J., 1960.

Rose, Barbara. *Readings in American Art, 1900–1975.* New York, 1975.

Secondary: Colonial

Craven, Wayne. *Colonial American Portraiture: The Economic, Religious, Social . . . Foundations.* Cambridge, Mass., 1986.

Harris, Neil. *The Artist in American Society: The Formative Years, 1790–1860.* New York, 1966.

Rebora, Carrie, et al. *John Singleton Copley in America.* New York, 1995.

Wroth, William. "New Mexican Santos and the Preservation of Religious Traditions." In *Critical Issues in American Art: A Book of Readings,* edited by Mary Ann Calo. Boulder, Colo., 1998.

Nineteenth Century

Burns, Sarah. *Inventing the Modern Artist: Art and Culture in Gilded Age America.* New Haven, Conn., 1996.

Fryd, Vivien Green. *Art and Empire: The Politics of Ethnicity in the United States Capitol, 1815–1860.* New Haven, Conn., 1992.

Johns, Elizabeth. *American Genre Painting: The Politics of Everyday Life.* New Haven, Conn., 1991.

Lears, T. J. Jackson. *No Place of Grace: Antimodernism and the Transformation of American Culture, 1880–1920.* New York, 1981.

Lubin, David M. *Picturing a Nation: Art and Social Change in Nineteenth-Century America.* New Haven, Conn., 1994.

Miller, Angela L. *The Empire of the Eye: Landscape Representation and American Cultural Politics, 1825–1875.* Ithaca, N.Y., 1993.

Miller, Lillian B. *Patrons and Patriotism: The Encouragement of the Fine Arts in the United States, 1790–1860.* Chicago, 1966.

Pyne, Kathleen A. *Art and the Higher Life: Painting and Evolutionary Thought in Late Nineteenth-Century America.* Austin, Tex., 1996.

Weinberg, H. Barbara. *The Lure of Paris: Nineteenth-Century American Painters and Their French Teachers.* New York, 1991.

Wilmerding, John, ed. *Thomas Eakins.* Washington, D.C., 1993.

Twentieth Century

Davidson, Abraham A. *Early American Modernist Painting, 1910–1935.* New York, 1981.

Doss, Erika Lee. *Benton, Pollock, and the Politics of Modernism: From Regionalism to Abstract Expressionism.* Chicago, 1991.

Hurlburt, Laurance P. *The Mexican Muralists in the United States.* Albuquerque, N. Mex., 1989.

Joachimides, Christos M., and Norman Rosenthal, eds. *American Art in the 20th Century: Painting and Sculpture, 1913–1993.* London, 1993.

Leja, Michael. *Reframing Abstract Expressionism: Subjectivity and Painting in the 1940s.* New Haven, Conn., 1993.

Montclair Art Museum. *Precisionism in America, 1915–1941: Reordering Reality.* New York, 1994.

Park, Marlene, and Gerald E. Markowitz. *New Deal for Art: The Government Art Projects of the 1930s, with Examples from New York City and State.* Hamilton, N.Y., 1977.

Polcari, Stephen. *Abstract Expressionism and the Modern Experience.* New York, 1991.

Powell, Richard, and David A. Bailey. *Rhapsodies in Black: Art of the Harlem Renaissance.* Berkeley, Calif., 1997.

Sims, Lowery Stokes. *Stuart Davis: American Painter.* New York, 1991.

Shapiro, David, ed. *Social Realism: Art as a Weapon.* New York, 1973.

Turner, Elizabeth Hutton, ed. *Jacob Lawrence: The Migration Series.* Washington, D.C., 1993.

Weinberg, H. Barbara, Doreen Bolger, and David Park Curry. *American Impressionism and Realism: The Painting of Modern Life, 1885–1915.* New York, 1994.

Zurier, Rebecca, Robert W. Snyder, and Virginia M. Mecklenburg. *Metropolitan Lives: The Ashcan Artists and Their New York.* Washington, D.C., 1995.

SCULPTURE

Melissa Dabakis

SCULPTURE'S HUMBLE ORIGINS

Visual culture in the United States faced many difficulties during its early history. Art remained a luxury in the colonies, not central to notions of cultural identity as in the European centers of Paris and Rome. Ornamental and figural carving for ships' heads, weather vanes, furniture, and gravestones served as the most common forms of plastic expression. Accomplished woodworkers, such as the brothers John Skillin and Simeon Skillin Jr. and Samuel McIntyre, first attended to the figural form in their decorative furniture carving. Until the late eighteenth century, craftsmen rather than artists dominated visual production.

America's first native sculptor, William Rush, followed in his father's footsteps in Philadelphia as a ship's head carver before becoming professor of sculpture and founder (in 1805, with Charles Willson Peale) of the Pennsylvania Academy of the Fine Arts, the first art school established in the United States. Committed to a national mission for the arts and aware of international art styles, Rush established a formative identity for the American artist. In 1814, he created the first native, life-size portrait sculpture of *George Washington*. Having carved his figure in white pine, he painted it white to simulate marble, which was unavailable in the United States at the time. Revealing the influence of neoclassicism—an international art movement that evoked the style, subject matter, and political ideals of the ancient world—Rush depicted Washington leaning on a Doric column with classical drapery ornamenting his contemporary attire. This allusion to the antique world signaled to a contemporary audience America's allegiance to republican values.

After the American Revolution, sculpture assumed the important role of producing durable symbols of the young republic. National heroes, like George Washington, appeared regularly in sculptural form in an effort to establish a spirit of political unity. Not surprisingly, however, when the federal government commissioned official sculpture to ornament the newly built U.S. Capitol or the State of Virginia wished to create an homage to the first president, they turned to European sculptors who had been trained in an academic tradition. Luigi Persico and Enrico Causici, among other skilled Italian sculptors, carved the first monumental statuary for the Capitol. Jean-Antoine Houdon, the most famous sculptor in France, produced the statue of Washington to be housed in the magnificent new neoclassical State House in Richmond, Virginia, designed by Thomas Jefferson. In his marble sculpture *George Washington* signed in 1788, Houdon created a successful icon of American identity. He presented the image of Washington in great detail: his face had been modeled from life and his general's uniform reveals such detailed realism as a missing button. In this sculptural treatment, Washington no longer holds his command; his sword hangs suspended from a fasces (a bundle of thirteen rods representing the original states of the Union). Despite the statue's naturalism, Houdon carefully inserted classical allusions into his sculpture. The fasces, derived from Roman imagery, symbolizes political unity—the thirteen states were individually weak, but strong when united. Moreover, he compared the American general to the Roman soldier Cincinnatus, who had given up his command to return to the peaceful pursuit of farming—a political meaning made evident by the plow situated behind Washington. Thus, Houdon produced a naturalistic sculpture that would inspire American artistic ambitions.

THE PROFESSIONALIZATION OF AMERICAN SCULPTURE

The first professional school of American sculpture, led by Horatio Greenough, Hiram Powers, and Thomas Crawford, was centered in Italy between 1825 and 1875. Because few opportunities for sculp-

Horatio Greenough, *George Washington* (**1840**). Marble; 136 x 102 x 82.5 in. Greenough is as remembered for his aesthetic writings on the relation of form to function as for his sculpture. SMITHSONIAN AMERICAN ART MUSEUM, TRANSFER FROM THE U.S. CAPITOL 1910.10.3

tural training existed in the United States in the first quarter of the nineteenth century, Americans studied abroad. Italy, with its abundance of antique and Renaissance statuary, allowed sculptors firsthand opportunity to study great masterworks. Moreover, Italy produced the world's most beautiful marble at its Carrara quarries and was home to excellently trained carvers who were essential to the production of marble sculpture. When in Italy, American sculptors learned the art of marble carving. They conceived the idea for their sculptures and produced models first in clay, then in plaster; next, the skilled hands of the carvers translated their designs into marble, after which the artists adjusted details and put the finishing touches on their works. American and European patrons on the Grand Tour—travel by the upper classes to European sites and the Holy Land—visited the studios of American artists in Florence and Rome and readily commissioned sculptures as souvenirs of their travels. To be sure, American sculptors were now participants in an international artistic community in which neoclassicism dominated sculptural expression.

In 1832, Horatio Greenough became the first American sculptor to receive a government com-

mission, a project on which he worked in Florence from 1832 to 1841. In his monumental marble sculpture *George Washington,* based upon the famed image of Zeus by the classical Greek sculptor Phidias, Greenough depicted the first president as bare-chested, donning toga and sandals, with one arm raised in a rhetorical gesture and the other handing the sword of power to the people. Housed in the Capitol rotunda between 1841 and 1843 (and later on the Capitol grounds), the sculpture received both criticism and ridicule. Although Greenough had intended a democratic message, contemporary viewers understood the sculpture as a symbol of despotic authority which was anathema to American values. As a means of communicating political ideals, the neoclassical style—so popular in Europe—had failed in the United States. The language of naturalism—communicated so successfully by Houdon—became the official sculptural style of the United States. Henry Kirk Brown, among other artists who remained in the United States, championed what American artists considered a "truly American art" by maintaining an allegiance to this naturalistic style.

Outside of official circles, however, neoclassicism remained quite popular. Hiram Powers produced one of the most famous statues of the nineteenth century, the *Greek Slave,* in 1843. In response to the War of Greek Independence, Powers depicted a Greek maiden who had been captured by the Turks and put on the slave block. Among the first female nudes in American sculpture, the figure stands shackled—her chained wrists signifying captivity while concealing her sexuality. Chastely looking away from the viewer, she demonstrates feminine virtue and Christian modesty despite her pathetic and victimized demeanor. The support on which she leans holds a cross and locket, symbols of love and faith. To be sure, the sculpture's renown was grounded in its appeal to dominant middle-class gender values. Within the language of the ideal, this sculpture presents an image of proper mid-nineteenth-century femininity, a model of "true womanhood" that is virtuous, submissive, and pious.

By the 1850s, a second generation of American sculptors inhabited the cultural terrain of Italy. These include William Wetmore Story, Randolph Rogers, and a notable group of women artists such as Harriet Hosmer, Edmonia Lewis, and Vinnie Ream. Significantly, these female sculptors provide American art history with its first model of women's professional accomplishments, and their statuary allows a unique glimpse into women's experiences. Harriet Hosmer, for example, produced a searching

Hiram Powers, *The Greek Slave* **(1841–1843).** Marble; 66.5 x 21.38 x 18.38 in. Powers's sculpture was so well received that he produced six slightly different versions of it. © THE CORCORAN GALLERY OF ART/CORBIS

exploration of female power and vulnerability in her *Zenobia in Chains* of 1859. Having ruled Palmyra in Syria for six years after her husband's death, Zenobia was defeated by the Roman emperor Aurelian. Paraded through the streets of Rome in chains, she was forced to live out her life in exile. Rather than depict this queen as a symbol of acquiescence and defeat as had been common, Hosmer presented her historical subject with strength, courage, and pride. The sculptural figure's heavy drapery, while enhancing her physical stature, serves as an armature that shields her body from the prying gaze. Although depicted in a solemn walk with downcast eyes, *Zenobia* conveys both dignity and resilience, in stark contrast to the submissiveness and victimization embodied by the *Greek Slave.*

PUBLIC MONUMENTS IN AMERICAN CULTURE

After the trauma of the Civil War, the wounds of the once-divided nation required healing. Sculpture, once again, served a historic mission, providing a public means to mourn the dead—both the common soldier and the martyred president, and to commemorate the war's outcome—the preservation of the Union and the emancipation of the slaves. In 1869, Martin Milmore was among the first sculptors to produce a prototype for a monument that would adorn public squares throughout the North and South. Erected in 1871, his *Civil War Monument,* located in Keene, New Hampshire, depicts a Union soldier, leaning on his rifle and contemplating the graves of his fallen comrades. This single figure, often surmounting a shaft, served also as a model for Confederate loss, with only small changes in uniform, insignia, and inscription. Ubiquitous throughout the land, these public sculptures encouraged political unity by demonstrating that Union and Confederate soldiers were brothers who had fought valiantly for their respective causes.

Only a few days after the war's end, the assassination of President Abraham Lincoln shocked America. Congress acted quickly to ensure that the martyred President's image would be enshrined in the Capitol rotunda. In July 1866, Vinnie Ream, a nineteen-year-old sculptor who had apprenticed with Clark Mills in his Capitol studio and had modeled Lincoln's bust from life shortly before his assassination, received the prestigious commission for the life-size standing sculpture. After much controversy—Senator Charles Sumner of Massachusetts and others had argued vociferously for her lack of

Vinnie Ream (Hoxie), *Abraham Lincoln* **(1871).** Marble; 6.9 ft. The sculpture is in the rotunda of the U.S. Capitol; the painting in the background is John Trumbull's *Surrender of Lord Cornwallis at Yorktown* (1786–1787). Ream also created sculptures of Admiral David G. Farragut, explorer Albert Pike, Cherokee leader Sequoya, and others. © KELLY-MOONEY PHOTOGRAPHY/CORBIS

competence due to her age and sex—Congress approved the appointment, the first federal commission to be awarded to a woman. In 1871, after Ream had spent a year in Rome, the sculpture was installed with much fanfare in the Capitol rotunda. In what would become a standard format for standing Lincoln statues in the 1860s and 1870s, Ream represented the president with the Emancipation Proclamation in hand. She captured with detailed accuracy his slightly bowed head and face aged with worry. Moreover, with a brilliant rhetorical flourish, she depicted the president handing the scroll to an imagined freed slave, an identity all viewers assume before the sculpture.

Although statues of Lincoln proliferated, no public monument adequately commemorates the abolition of slavery. In 1867, Harriet Hosmer produced a design for the "Freedman's Memorial to Abraham Lincoln," a monument to emancipation to be located in the nation's capital and funded by freed slaves. Her complex proposal focused attention upon four African American men who represented the journey of slaves from disempowerment to manhood, thus foregrounding issues of black citizenship. With the cost of her monument in excess of the committee's funds, the commission fell to

Thomas Ball in 1868. In what has come to be known as the *Emancipation Group* of 1875, Ball translated the meaning of emancipation into manumission, upholding the power relations between master and slave when he depicted President Lincoln bestowing freedom upon a kneeling slave. Although representing the black man in public statuary for the first time, his design freezes the figure of the freed slave, Archer Alexander, within a posture of perpetual subservience. Signaling the end of Reconstruction—the collective failure of will to enfranchise the freed slave population—the monument commemorates the legacy of slavery rather than the political potential of freedom.

In 1897, Augustus Saint-Gaudens created a memorial that commemorates not only the heroic leadership of Robert Gould Shaw but also the courage of his African American troops when they attacked Fort Wagner on Charleston Harbor in 1863. Erected in Boston, the *Robert Gould Shaw Memorial,* a heroic bronze relief (sculpture that is developed from a back plane through low or high carving or modeling), depicts Shaw in an equestrian pose (astride his horse); his troops march behind him, each depicted with dignity in an individual portrait style. Trained in Paris, the new international art

498

Augustus Saint-Gaudens, *Colonel Robert Gould Shaw Monument* (Detail, 1884–1897). Bronze relief; 11 by 14 ft. Among Saint-Gaudens's other Civil War monuments were *Abraham Lincoln* ("The Standing Lincoln"; 1884–1887; Chicago), *General John A. Logan* (1894–1897; Chicago), and *General William Tecumseh Sherman* (1892–1903; New York City). © LEE SNIDER/ CORBIS

center at the end of the nineteenth century, Saint-Gaudens brought to this work an exquisite handling of the bronze medium and a lively naturalism. In a 1982 restoration, the names of the sixty-two African American soldiers who died at Fort Wagner were inscribed upon the monument.

REALISM, MODERNISM, AND THE AMERICAN ART MARKET

The National Sculpture Society (NSS), founded in 1893, promoted monumental sculptural production and encouraged the exhibition and sale of the plastic arts. The prestigious sculptor, John Quincy Adams Ward, served as its first president. The NSS supported such urban beautification projects as the *Lincoln Memorial* of 1922, with its architectural design by Henry Bacon and colossal marble image of Lincoln by Daniel Chester French. Erected on the National Mall, the memorial represents one of the last great projects of the American Renaissance in

which traditional civic statuary took as its purpose the expression of universal ideals and the advancement of public education to a broad public.

With the exception of the mass-marketing to bourgeois homes of small-scale plasters by John Rogers, such as *The Fugitive's Story* of 1869 or *Checkers up at the Farm* of 1877, American sculpture entered the market economy of the nineteenth century slowly. By the turn of the twentieth century, however, a new art market, based on personal taste rather than transcendent principles, informed sculptural production. Purchasing portable sculpture in marble and bronze, middle-class patrons supported a range of sculptural expression, from traditional ideal statuary and sculptural celebrations of the American West by Frederick Remington to genre sculpture (plastic depictions of everyday life) and abstract sculpture in an experimental modernist style.

Not surprisingly, art galleries assumed a prominence in this new market economy. The Macbeth Galleries of New York supported art that was com-

Alexander Calder, *Four at Forty-Five* **(1966).** Polychromed sheet metal; 5 x 18 ft. Hailing from a family with two generations of sculptors, Calder initially studied mechanical engineering and even attained a master's degree in the subject, before taking a serious interest in art. Nonetheless his body of work is immense. © STATE OF NEW YORK/CORBIS

mitted to documenting the new urban scene, including the genre sculpture of Mahonri Mackintosh Young and Abastenia St. Leger Eberle, for example. In her *Windy Doorstep* of 1910, Eberle represented a woman hard at work at her domestic chores. Her hair, covered by a babushka, serves as a sign of her immigrant status, and her body, thick and robust, signals her working-class identity. Eberle's sculptures illustrate women's urban experience with a socially conscious imagery and a realist style.

By contrast, Alfred Stieglitz supported modernist expression in his 291 Gallery in New York. Committed to personal expression in a highly experimental abstract style, the American sculptors Max Weber and John Storrs looked to European art movements such as cubism and futurism for inspiration while also paying homage to American technological prowess. Weber studied in Paris from 1905 to 1908 and brought back to New York some of the most radical innovations in artistic form. In his *Spiral Rhythm* of 1915, one of the earliest American sculptures to treat form nonobjectively, he distorted the human figure by fragmenting it into segmented planes that celebrate the machine and simulate the dynamic energy of modern life.

Artists responded in a variety of ways to this new modernist practice. Marcel Duchamp, a French artist working in New York in the years surrounding World War I, questioned the nature of the art with his "ready-made," and expanded the sculptural field to include any object (like a bottle rack, bicycle wheel, or urinal) selected by the artist. In his insistence upon the conceptual nature of art, he rejected craftsmanship in favor of the mass-produced commodity, a distinctly American contribution, he believed, to modern art. Alternately, direct carvers William Zorach and John B. Flannagan assumed a craftsmanlike status by working directly with stone or wood and celebrating the sculptural medium itself for its expressive power. Informed by surrealist and constructivist developments that he had encountered in Paris, Alexander Calder created a completely new sculptural form, "the mobile," in which motion, change, and space came to define the sculptural experience. In the place of the massive volumetric forms of wood or stone carving, the mobile interacted with the space around it through its random movement, producing a constantly changing set of formal relations within the work. Abstract and colorful, his "stabiles" were regularly commissioned

500

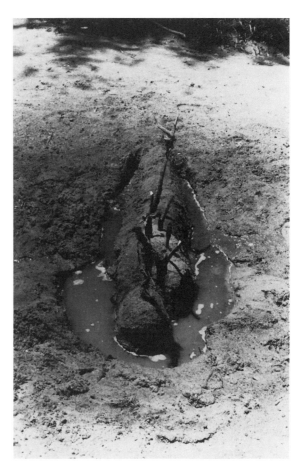

Ana Mendietta, *Untitled.* From the series *Fetish.*
Chromogenic color print mounted on paperboard, 20 x
13¼ in. Purchase, with funds from the Photography
Committee. Photograph Copyright © 1997 Whitney
Museum of Art, New York

David Smith, *Tank Totem IV* (1953). Steel; 92⅝ x 29 x 34
in. Smith was one of the twentieth century's most
influential sculptors. Collection Albright-Knox Art
Gallery, Buffalo, New York, Gift of Seymour H.
Knox Jr., 1957. © Estate of David Smith/Licensed by
VAGA, New York

as successful public sculpture in the United States.
The African American sculptor Augusta Savage engaged with aspects of European modernism as an
artist and teacher during the Harlem Renaissance.
She produced *The Harp* in painted plaster for the
1939 New York World's Fair. Inspired by James Weldon Johnson and Rosamond Johnson's song "Lift
Every Voice and Sing," this sculpture depicts the
hand of the creator supporting a choir and imaginatively conjoining the singing figures within the
structure of the harp in a simplified and abstracted
sculptural vocabulary.

CONTEMPORARY ISSUES IN
AMERICAN SCULPTURE

Sculpture provided one of the most dynamic areas
of artistic innovation in the years following World

War II. David Smith experimented with new forms and materials that revolutionized sculptural production. As a member of the New York school, he looked to the psychoanalyst Sigmund Freud and surrealism for sculptural inspiration. In his *Tank Totem* series of the mid-1950s, he produced anthropomorphic totems that were primitivist in spirit (showing an interest in the primal and universal characteristics of native cultures) and attentive to unconscious desire. No longer relying on the traditional sculptural media, he utilized found industrial materials that he welded together in a freeform manner.

By the 1960s, sculpture grew increasingly expansive in its use of space. George Segal and Edward Kienholz employed found materials of everyday life to create tableaus that featured the figural form. Haunting in their effect, these dramatic tableaus poetically re-created the lived world with a sense of nostalgia, alienation, and at times biting social criticism. Minimalism, in its focus upon the primary object, rejected the figural form and thus redefined the nature of sculpture. Donald Judd, Sol Lewitt, and Carl André, among others, produced sculptural forms of geometric simplicity, technological precision, and conceptual clarity that insist upon experiencing the object within its spatial environment. This infatuation with space culminated in the earth works of Michael Heizer and Robert Smithson who produced their sculptural work in uninhabited lands—far from the New York art market—where they carved and shaped the surface of the earth. Ana Mendietta used earth and mud to create the fragile and impermanent impression of her body against the natural landscape. Feminist artists, like Mendietta, helped reintroduce the body—both actual and metaphorical—into artistic practice, culminating in the performance pieces of such as artists as Carolee Schneemann and Adrian Piper. With the advent of installation art in the 1980s—as exemplified in the work of Anne Hamilton—sculpture no longer distinguished itself from a broader mixed-media experimentation with form and content.

In the last two decades of the twentieth century, Americans witnessed a resurgence of the public monument, radically transformed, however, from the figurative statues of great men that dominated the nineteenth century. When Maya Lin, a young art student at Yale University, produced the winning design for the *Vietnam Veteran's Memorial,* installed on the National Mall in 1982, she redefined the monument in terms of memory and experience. The reflective surface of the black granite wall both records the names of the war dead and reflects the beliefs and values of those participating in this process of commemoration. Reconfigured and ubiquitous, the public monument has regained its centrality to American culture, bearing once again the responsibility of mourning, commemorating, and healing.

See also **Fine Arts in Colonial America; The Arts in the Republican Era; American Romanticism; Realism in Art and Literature; The Artist and the Intellectual in the New Deal** *(volume 1);* **Postmodernism and the Arts** *(volume 2);* **The Visual Arts; Elite vs. Popular Cultures; Museums** *(in this volume); and other articles in this section.*

BIBLIOGRAPHY

Armstrong, Thomas, et. al. *200 Years of American Sculpture.* New York, 1976.

Bogart, Michele. *Public Sculpture and the Civic Ideal in New York City, 1890–1930.* Chicago, 1989.

Boime, Albert. *The Unveiling of the National Icons: A Plea for Patriotic Iconoclasm in a Nationalist Era.* New York, 1998.

Cikovsky, Nicolai, Jr., Marie H. Morrison, and Carol Ockman. *The White Marmorean Flock: Nineteenth-Century American Women Neoclassical Sculptors.* Poughkeepsie, N.Y., 1972.

Craven, Wayne. *Sculpture in America.* New York, 1968.

Dabakis, Melissa. *Visualizing Labor in American Sculpture: Monuments, Manliness and the Work Ethic, 1880–1935.* New York, 1999.

Fort, Ilene Susan. *The Figure in American Sculpture: A Question of Modernity.* Los Angeles, 1995.

Fryd, Vivien Green. *Art and Empire: The Politics of Ethnicity in the U.S. Capitol, 1815–1860.* New Haven, Conn., 1992.

Gerdts, William H., Jr. *American Neo-Classic Sculpture: The Marble Resurrection.* New York, 1973.

Kasson, Joy. *Marble Queens and Captives: Women in Nineteenth-Century American Sculpture.* New Haven, Conn., 1990.

Krauss, Rosalind. *Passages in Modern Sculpture.* New York, 1977.

Rubinstein, Charlotte Streifer. *American Women Sculptors: A History of Women Working in Three Dimensions.* Boston, 1990.

Savage, Kirk. *Standing Soldiers, Kneeling Slaves: Race, War and Monument in Nineteenth-Century America.* Princeton, N.J., 1997.

Taft, Lorado. *The History of American Sculpture.* 1903. Reprint, New York, 1969.

Tolles, Thayer, ed. *American Sculpture in the Metropolitan Museum of Art: Vol. 1, A Catalogue of Works by Artists Born before 1865.* New York, 1999.

TELEVISION

Lynn Spigel

More than any other communication medium, television has become synonymous with life itself. Its ability to transmit images simultaneously the world around and its intimate relation to our lives at home make it so fundamental to everyday experience that it is easy to forget that television as a means of mass communication dates back only to the 1940s. Like other communication technologies, television's rise as a cultural form is a product of human choices. Its industrial practices, its reception by audiences, its regulation, and its methods of storytelling and visual display are rooted in wider political, economic, social, and cultural struggles.

This essay traces the rise of television in its classical form: the three-network commercial broadcast system. This system evolved in the late 1940s from its roots in U.S. radio, solidified its industrial and cultural practices in the 1950s and 1960s, and dominated the American landscape until the late 1980s. The system was predicated on (1) network distribution; (2) production concentrated in the hands of a relatively small number of studios, usually in Hollywood and usually backed by networks; (3) private reception in the home; (4) commercial sponsorship; (5) government regulation of station allocation by the Federal Communications Commission (FCC); and (6) the designation of one channel as a noncommercial, public broadcast system.

TELEVISION IN THE INTERWAR YEARS

Although the idea of television and the process of technological invention leading to it date back to the late nineteenth century, it was not until the 1920s that organized efforts to develop it began. Engineered by the leading radio and electrical companies, television—and its rise as a communication medium—was controlled largely by big business and government policies.

No one person invented television; numerous people in different countries contributed to its development. Most notable in the United States were Philo T. Farnsworth and Vladmir Zworykin. Farnsworth invented the image dissector, a device that took pictures apart for signal transmission. Working independently of big business, Farnsworth found himself in patent wars with the corporate giant Radio Corporation of America (RCA), which eventually had to secure licenses from him to market its own system. Zworykin, a Russian émigré, worked as an engineer for Westinghouse. In 1923 he invented the iconoscope, the first electronic camera pickup tube suitable for studio use. By 1930 RCA had hired Zworykin to head its research team in Camden, New Jersey. The Camden team went on to develop a complete electronic television system that was adopted for the consumer market in the 1940s.

The fact that television was designed and controlled by big industry greatly affected the ways in which people imagined its potential social uses and effects. In the 1930s RCA tested television in factories, hoping to improve labor efficiency by monitoring workers on the job. During the Great Depression, as increasing numbers of workers found themselves unemployed, this "surveillance" plan for television was not always popular. In fact, this same period witnessed a growing public skepticism that manifested itself in tales of television out of control. Films like *Murder by Television* (1935) and *Modern Times* (1936) depicted television as the brainchild of evil industrialists who were using it as a means of social domination. For example, in *Modern Times* Charlie Chaplin portrayed an exploited assembly-line worker tortured by his tyrannical boss who spies on him via an enormous television screen.

Despite such cultural skepticism, there was also great optimism for television's possible future, especially on the part of the broadcast industry. Over the course of the 1930s, the Columbia Broadcasting System (CBS) and the National Broadcasting Company (NBC) developed various program formats that they broadcast over their experimental stations.

But these broadcasts were by no means conducted for a mass audience. Out of the price range of most Americans, TV sets were still only for the rich.

The first wide-scale public displays of television took place in the same period. In 1933 the Hudson-Essex corporation displayed television at the Century of Progress Exhibition in Chicago, and by 1939 RCA demonstrated its National Television System Committee (NTSC) television system in its radio-tube-shaped pavilion at the New York World's Fair. (Similar displays took place in England, while in Germany the Nazi government broadcast the 1936 Olympics with great public fanfare.) Despite the spectacular promotions, however, Gallup polls at the time revealed that most people did not believe that they would install a TV set in their own homes. That was a moot issue for a time, since a regulatory struggle over technical standards delayed RCA's marketing plans for several years. (It was not until 1941 that RCA's NTSC system was adopted as the official standard.) World War II further delayed industry attempts to place TV on the consumer market.

EARLY POSTWAR TELEVISION

In the booming postwar economy of the late 1940s, the era of television broadcasting began. Inundated with applications for licenses, the Federal Communications Commission (FCC) put a freeze on station allocation that lasted from 1948 to 1952. This meant that during television's formative period, many areas of the country had either just one or no station. With the most stations to choose from, people in the Northeast installed television sets sooner than the rest of the country. New York, Los Angeles, and to a lesser degree Chicago served as the largest production centers.

Despite the medium's initially regional nature, the major radio networks envisioned television as a national phenomenon. CBS, NBC, the American Broadcasting Company (ABC), and the short-lived DuMont network attempted to secure affiliate contracts and thereby re-create the oligopolistic control over national broadcasting that they still enjoyed in the radio business. By 1948 the networks were already offering a full schedule of prime-time shows and by the 1950s they were considering how to fill the daytime slots. Under the direction of programming vice president Sylvester "Pat" Weaver, NBC premiered the morning program *Today* in January 1952. The popular soap opera format (first engineered by soap advertisers in the 1930s) was transferred from radio to the TV medium.

By building a daily schedule, the networks were able to attract both affiliates and advertisers. Furthermore, since the FCC freeze made it virtually impossible for new players to enter the television broadcast market, the networks enjoyed an early competitive edge in all these endeavors. The FCC's 1952 *Sixth Report and Order*, which effectively ended the freeze, presented rules about color standards, UHF (ultrahigh frequency) stations, and the allocation of 242 channels for educational use. UHF stations, however, had notoriously poor reception, and so the networks contracts with VHF (very high frequency) stations gave them a great deal of power over the national broadcast market.

As the networks solidified industrial control, manufacturers began marketing television sets to the public. Advertisers promoted the new receivers, telling consumers that television would repair the war-torn lives of American families by creating a new electronic hearth around which mom, dad, and the kids could gather. The public response was unprecedented. While in 1948 approximately 2 percent of American households were equipped with a TV set, by 1960 almost 90 percent of households had at least one receiver and the average American watched TV for approximately five hours a day. This rapid penetration rate not only meant that television had become the dominant forum for entertainment and information, it also signaled an important shift in patterns of everyday life.

Television's incorporation into domestic space coincided with demographic shifts and ensuing changes in leisure-time expenditures. Faced with a severe housing shortage in major cities and aided by a GI Bill that granted veterans mortgage loans, increasing numbers of Americans moved from urban areas to new mass-produced suburbs. Television offered these new suburbanites a cheap and convenient kind of entertainment. Whereas a night at the movies often required baby-sitters, a commute into the city, and a search for parking, TV was brought into the home "free" by the sponsor. Given this, it is not surprising that box office figures at the movies fell with television's arrival in various regions of the country.

The change from public to private reception had important cultural ramifications. Social science studies conducted at the time found many people, especially women, testifying to television's impact on married and family life. For example, women complained that they went out less often and that their husbands ignored them in favor of watching the new TV. Perhaps anticipating these feelings of domestic isolation, the industry tried to convince the public that television viewing would be like a romantic night out on the town. In 1955 NBC advertised its evening lineup in women's magazines, telling women to "make a date to see the greatest theatre in the world" (Spigel, *Make Room for TV,* p. 126).

Although urban and rural populations obviously watched TV as well, television's cultural form was tailored to suit the new suburban environment. First and foremost, television and suburbia both catered to white middle-class publics, building a sense of community upon processes of exclusion. Building start and zoning policies of the Federal Housing Administration were predicated on practices of segregation that ensured that suburban communities consisted almost exclusively of white families of the middle to lower-middle class. Targeting this same demographic, television developed a parallel universe of households filled with privileged white nuclear families like the Nelsons (*The Adventures of Ozzie and Harriet,* ABC, 1952–1966) and the Cleavers (*Leave It to Beaver,* CBS, 1957–1958; ABC, 1958–1963).

Live TV   As an aesthetic form, television further blurred the boundaries between physical and electronic worlds by promoting a sense of "liveness." Producers, critics, and network executives placed special emphasis on television's capacity to convey a feeling of immediacy, spontaneity, and presence at the events unfolding on the screen. In so doing, television would ideally offer viewers the fantasy of participating in a vibrant public culture while allowing them to remain within the safe space of the home. As one production manual stated, television programs "owe their success . . . to the feeling they give the home viewer of having a front seat at a Broadway show. That's a good feeling to have in Hinterland, Iowa, or Suburbia, New Jersey."

Vaudeville and Broadway theater served as the models for live theatrical entertainment. The former spawned what the trade magazine *Variety* called the "vaudeo" trend, including shows like the *Texaco Star Theater* (NBC, 1948–1953), with comedian-host Milton Berle. These vaudeo programs capitalized on television's ability to make viewers feel as if they were at an exciting live performance by featuring nightclub entertainment, kinetic motion (with animal acts or tumblers), and studio audiences that provided an imaginary community of ordinary folks just like the viewers at home. While the vaudeo trend drew on Jewish ethnic humor and a populist sensibility, the "legitimate" Broadway stage inspired television's live anthology dramas, which featured teleplays on a weekly basis. Sponsored by major corporations, series such as *Goodyear TV Playhouse* (NBC, shot live from 1951–1957) and *Philco Television Playhouse* (NBC, 1948–1955) were produced in-house by advertising agencies. Despite their commercial origins, these series came to be valued as programs of a Golden Age of television. Writers, directors, and actors such as Paddy Chayefsky, Arthur Penn, John Cassavetes, James Dean, Paul Newman, and Julie Harris all went on from teleplays to the Hollywood film industry. The transition from television to film also worked in the opposite direction. Female film stars found that television offered them a chance to participate in creative and business endeavors that Hollywood movies had historically denied them. Lucille Ball, Loretta Young, Joan Davis, and Ida Lupino (who had previously made independent films) started their own TV production companies.

The Threat of Censorship   Although the networks showcased "legitimate" theater and attempted to validate television's cultural worth, TV became a target for censors. By the early 1950s social scientists, the clergy, the Parent-Teacher Association, citizen groups, and government officials had all expressed concerns about television's effects on the public, especially children. While the FCC was empowered to regulate broadcasting in "the public interest, convenience, and necessity," its mandate explicitly forbade government censorship of program content. Largely in order to quell the growing controversies over content and to stave off government regulation of any kind, the National Association of Broadcasters (NAB) created an industrywide censorship code that worked as a form of self-censorship. Instituted in 1952, the code worked largely like the radio code before it, and it remained in place with some revision until late 1982.

Despite these industry maneuvers, however, television continued to stir public controversies. Shortly after the code's creation, U.S. representative Ezekiel Gathings of Arkansas spearheaded a House investigation of radio and television programs, which presented testimony from citizens groups concerned with television's effects on children. By 1954 Tennessee Senator Estes Kefauver's subcommittee hearings on juvenile delinquency had begun investigating television's relationship to the perceived increase in youth crimes. From 1961 to 1964, Connecticut Senator Thomas J. Dodd's investigation of television violence attacked crime and adventure series for their depiction of violence and other transgressions of public taste. While none of these hearings resulted in government censorship per se, these congressional probes set out the terms for raging debates about the First Amendment's application to television (and later the Internet) that continued through the century.

Ethnic and Racial Stereotyping

Ethnic and Racial Stereotyping Although the 1952 code included a prohibition against racial stereotyping, the racism of early television went largely unchecked. A number of ethnic situation comedies, many adapted from radio, depicted the lives of second-generation European immigrants. Shows like the Jewish situation comedy (or "sitcom") *The Goldbergs* (CBS 1949–1951; NBC, 1952–1953; DuMont, 1954) and the Italian comedy *Life with Luigi* (CBS, 1953) presented nostalgic ideals of ethnic family life, yet they often poked fun at their heroes' and heroines' "old world" ways. Characters like Molly Goldberg spoke in malapropisms, while Luigi could not figure out how to buy on credit. These shows, then, presented the public with a mixed message about ethnicity. On the one hand, they romanticized the close-knit family structures of first-generation immigrants; on the other, they suggested that people should assimilate into the melting pot and adopt postwar consumer values.

Early television presented black characters through the cultural stereotypes already available from minstrel theater and film. Two black-cast situation comedies, *Amos 'n' Andy* (CBS, 1951–1953) and *Beulah* (ABC, 1950–1953), each deployed a litany of such stereotypes, from shifty, lazy black men to the happy mammy of the Old South. Having been a subject of protest among many African Americans since its radio broadcasts in the 1930s, the television version of *Amos 'n' Andy* raised especially heated debate. While some believed that the program provided opportunities for black actors to work on television, others focused on its degrading characterizations and plots. The National Association for the Advancement of Colored People (NAACP) protested the show throughout its series run, asking for its removal from the air. After two years, the sponsor pulled out of the program and production was cancelled. Nevertheless, the program remained on the air in rerun syndication. In fact, in 1954 it appeared on twice as many local stations as it had when it was aired over the networks. It was not until 1966 that CBS (faced with protests from the civil rights movement) finally pulled the show from syndication.

The racism of early television was not caused only by cultural prejudices; it was also a function of the structure of commercial network broadcasting itself. Because the networks had contracts with affiliate stations across the country, they attempted to present programming that would not offend the regional tastes of specific markets, and they were especially concerned not to offend southern affiliates. In addition, sponsors shied away from programs they feared would be unpopular with what they assumed were the tastes of their target audience: whites with buying power. For example, in the 1956–1957 season NBC presented singer Nat "King" Cole in his own variety show but could not secure a sponsor. While NBC initially featured it as a sustaining program, within a year the network took it off the air. Reflecting on the cancellation, Cole told *Ebony* magazine, "Madison Avenue, the center of the advertising industry, and their big clients didn't want their products associated with Negroes" (MacDonald, *Blacks and White TV*, p. 62).

The black actor Paul Robeson also experienced cancellation, but in his case for his political views. In 1950 Robeson was scheduled to appear on a talk show hosted by Eleanor Roosevelt. In advance of the show, NBC received hate mail protesting Robeson's scheduled appearance, not only because he was black, but also because he was outspokenly pro-Soviet. When NBC decided not to air the show, it received protest mail from African Americans and criticism from Robeson as well as the black press. One year later NBC developed a public relations campaign announcing a new corporate policy that it called "Integration without Identification." The policy called for the network to employ blacks in roles that were not necessarily designated for black characters. It was thereby intended to open up more jobs for blacks and at the same time do away with racist stereotypes by allowing blacks to appear in dramatic series in roles other than minstrels, mammies, and scoundrels. Despite its idealistic vision, NBC did little to implement its new policy.

Blacklisting

Blacklisting As the case of Robeson suggests, early television was especially vulnerable to the "red scare," a term used to describe the period's rampant fears that there were "Communists in our midst." In 1950 a book called *Red Channels* named 151 writers, performers, and other creative talent who supposedly had transmitted Communist sentiments over the airwaves. The purpose was to promote the blacklisting of those named, a tactic also promoted by Senator Joseph McCarthy of Wisconsin and by the House Un-American Activities Committee

(HUAC). Blacklisting had already devastated creative talent in the film industry; in the case of television, the blacklist was especially successful because the networks, producers, broadcast stations, and advertising agencies were all intimidated by the threat of potential sponsor boycotts should their shows be associated with the names that appeared in *Red Channels*.

Even the most distant association with anything labeled "red" could ruin one's career. For example, in 1950 the actress Jean Muir was hired to appear on *The Aldrich Family* (NBC, 1949–1953). Before the season's opening telecast, however, her sponsor, General Mills, suddenly cancelled her contract. Muir, it turned out, had been cited in *Red Channels* because she had signed a cable of congratulations to the Moscow Art Theater on its fiftieth anniversary. Despite the fact that General Mills claimed no disloyalty on her part, it nevertheless fired Muir, claiming the need to avoid "controversial" people on programs it sponsored.

But the very medium that was so vulnerable to blacklisting also helped to end it. Especially important here were the efforts of newscasters Edward R. Murrow and Fred Friendly, whose CBS program, *See It Now* (1952–1958), spoke out against McCarthyism in numerous episodes. The most famous of these was an episode concentrating on the "witch-hunt" nature of Senator McCarthy's anti-Communist crusade. Broadcast 9 March 1954, the program showed McCarthy at work, exposing the way he intimidated witnesses by accusing them with innuendo rather than evidence. Certainly, Murrow and Friendly took considerable risks in airing this and other anti-blacklisting episodes. In fact, even while McCarthy was already falling from public favor in 1954, CBS was so nervous about engaging in controversy that it refused to advertise the telecast in advance.

HOLLYWOOD TV AND THE "CLASSICAL" NETWORK SYSTEM

Although small, independent telefilm companies existed in the late 1940s, it was not until the mid-1950s that telefilm began to displace live production as the industry's medium of choice. One of the first studios to demonstrate the viability of filmed production was Lucille Ball and Desi Arnaz's company Desilu. Formed in 1950, Desilu worked independently with CBS and sponsor Philip Morris to produce its first show, the widely popular *I Love Lucy* (1951–1957). In order to retain the sense of spontaneity and immediacy of live TV, Desilu filmed the

I Love Lucy (1951–1957). Lucille Ball (*center*) is shown tied up while Desi Arnaz and Vivian Vance look on. © BETTMANN/CORBIS

sitcom before a studio audience. The studio refined the practice of multicamera shooting that was still used fifty years later for many episodic series.

Most important from the point of view of profits, Arnaz and Ball understood the ultimate economic value inherent in film. Unlike live TV, which could endure only through low-quality kinescopes (that is, films shot off the screen itself), telefilms could be reproduced, rerun, and remarketed endlessly. At the time, however, the networks did not understand that audiences would actually want to watch TV shows over again. CBS was so ignorant of the potential profits in the rerun syndication market that it agreed to allow Arnaz to retain the rights to his films in exchange for his own investment capital. By retaining the rights to *I Love Lucy*, Ball and Arnaz were able to build their own TV empire. More generally, by the end of the 1950s it was commonly understood that the key to profits in the television industry was the rerun market.

Hollywood and the Evolution of Television By 1953 the major Hollywood film studios, which had initially taken a wait-and-see attitude toward television, were increasingly eager to invest in the new medium. In 1954 the fledgling ABC network (which had seriously trailed behind CBS and NBC) entered into a deal with Disney, which was interested in using television to promote its film products and especially its new theme park in southern California. The 1954 television program *Disneyland* was the result, followed the next year by *The Mickey Mouse Club*. The Warner Bros. studio continued this practice, producing TV Westerns in the hopes of promoting its film products.

By the end of the 1950s and through the 1960s, the major Hollywood studios were less interested in using television to promote their films than they were in the lucrative markets that television itself offered. Now the common mode of program development entailed coproductions between networks and Hollywood studios (both the film studios like Columbia's Screen Gems and TV studios like Desilu), which in turn often contracted out to independents. Rather than sponsoring a single show, advertisers now bought time in the schedule, thereby spreading their investments across more diverse program offerings. The era of the classical network system was under way.

By the late 1950s these industrial transitions had a significant impact on American culture, and especially on reigning cultural attitudes toward television itself. Influential East Coast television critics, writing in such venues as the *New York Times,* began to mourn the passing of television's so-called Golden Age. Dismayed by programming trends that favored popular rather than elite tastes, they were especially upset by the cancellation of "prestige" programs like anthology dramas and the documentary series *See It Now* (whose termination in 1958 sparked a particularly heated debate). They protested the slew of formulaic genres, especially sitcoms, Westerns, and quiz shows. Some of these critics blamed the FCC for its failure to live up to its mission to regulate television in "the public interest." Others blamed the broadcast networks and the sponsors for their greed.

Scandals, Investigations, and Critiques This situation came to a head in the late 1950s with the advent of the quiz show scandals. Programs like *The $64,000 Question* (1955–1958) and *Twenty-One* (1956–1958) came under suspicion when it was charged that the sponsors and producers had fed answers to contestants in the hopes of heightening dramatic appeal. Charges to that effect were initially investigated by a New York grand jury in 1958; by late 1959 the quiz show scandals were a matter of national attention as a congressional committee and the FCC held hearings on the accusations. When the hearings revealed that contestants in *Twenty-One* had in fact been given answers, critics took it as final proof that sponsors, networks, producers, and regulators had failed the public trust. In the end, the industry managed to weather the scandals. Of the twenty-three persons indicted for perjury, all but one were contestants. Yet the quiz show scandals aroused a widespread disappointment with television that was expressed by critics, educators, the clergy, and other opinion leaders.

During 1959, in the midst of these controversies, the FCC announced an inquiry into network operations. Ultimately, however, rather than overhauling the commercial and monopolistic business practices of the networks, the regulators adopted a reform strategy that focused on program quality. In 1961 FCC commissioner Newton Minow delivered his famous "vast wasteland" speech before the National Association of Broadcasters. In that speech Minow blamed the networks for serving up a "steady diet of sitcoms, game shows, and Westerns" at the expense of delivering more culturally uplifting fare. While he was critical of the network's "concentration of power" and called for educational channels, his reform strategy did not attack the fundamental commercial structure of network television. However, in the wake of the scandals and the threat of FCC investigations into network practices, some important changes were made.

Minow's call for arts and education gave federal support to the already ongoing efforts of educational broadcasters. The formation of the Corporation for Public Broadcasting (CPB) in 1967 stemmed partly from Minow's vision. The CPB was set up as a corporation under the auspices of the Ford Foundation, but its maintenance required federal subsidies as well as donor support. In 1969 the Public Broadcasting Service emerged as the central channel through which education and the arts would be transmitted.

Meanwhile, the critical attacks on television and Minow's campaign increased the networks' desire to upgrade their image and prove their cultural worth. While Hollywood genres still dominated the schedule, all three networks lengthened their news formats from fifteen to thirty minutes, and featured new documentary programs that often dealt with serious issues of the day.

Documentaries and News Programs During the Kennedy and Johnson administrations, television's documentary and news programming covered national triumphs and tragedies. President Kennedy's assassination in 1963 and the moon landing of 1969 demonstrated television's function in the creation of media events. The Vietnam War, often called the first "living room war," was covered by remote news cameras that gave people a view of horrors never before seen by civilians on a daily basis in their homes.

News and documentary programming also featured coverage of the social and political movements of the time. In the early 1960s ABC's *Close-up, CBS Reports,* and *NBC White Papers* presented episodes about the civil rights movement. Civil rights leaders were also heard on network newscasts and talk shows. These shows favored moderate leaders like Martin Luther King Jr., while more radical leaders such as Malcolm X were depicted as threatening to whites. In 1958 the CBS news reporter and talk show host Mike Wallace presented a five-part series entitled "Negro Racism" that represented Black Muslims as "the hate that hate produced." Commenting on the series, Malcolm X claimed that it was a "kaleidoscope of 'shocker' images" designed to create a public panic about Black Muslims and black nationalism (MacDonald, *Blacks and White TV,* p. 86).

After the early 1960s, the number of network documentaries on African American life diminished. The remaining coverage tended to feature graphic images of urban rebellions rather than explorations of the social and political meanings of the civil rights movement. Viewers and city officials often blamed the networks for inciting riotous behavior with their news cameras. In the summer of 1968, however, the networks returned to a fuller examination of race issues, presenting at least twenty-two documentaries on African Americans. In part, this renewed interest was related to government pressure. In 1967, responding to the increased number of uprisings in major cities throughout the country, President Lyndon B. Johnson appointed a Commission on Civil Disorders to analyze the causes of the riots. One year later the Kerner Commission, as the panel was called, issued a report that blamed white racism for the riots, concluding that America was a nation headed toward apartheid. Government officials met with network executives, urging them to devote more time to black issues. The government plea, coupled with the assassination of Dr. Martin Luther King Jr. in 1968, created a climate in which the networks were more willing to present programming that focused on issues such as white racism, black history, and the media's own bias.

Social Issues and Trends Throughout the 1960s, entertainment programming responded to the changing social climate, even if in watered-down ways. Early in the decade, the networks aired dramas like the *Defenders* (CBS, 1961–1965) and *East Side/West Side* (CBS, 1963–1964), which dealt with social issues including welfare, housing, divorce, and racism. The creation of the independent producer David Susskind, *East Side/West Side* was among the first network series to feature a black actor (Cicely Tyson) as a recurring character in a dramatic series. *I Spy* (NBC, 1965–1968) became the first network series to feature an African American (Bill Cosby) as a lead character since the cancellation of *Amos 'n' Andy.* Diahann Carroll became the first black woman since Ethel Waters and Louise Beavers (both in *Beulah*) to star in the lead role in a network series. Her program, *Julia* (ABC, 1968–1971), featured a young working mother whose husband had been killed in Vietnam. Written and produced by whites for ABC, *Julia* was received with mixed sentiments. Many critics dubbed Julia a "white Negro" and claimed that the program did not deal sufficiently with issues of racism and inequality.

Certainly, television programs like *Julia* did not so much reflect an accurate picture of society in the 1960s so much as they responded to new network and advertiser agendas. Over the course of the 1960s, advertisers began to put more stock in demographics (market research that measured kinds of audiences) rather than aggregate ratings (market research that measured audience size). By the end of the decade, the networks knew that in order to sell program time to advertisers it was necessary to provide them with the kind of audiences that were most likely to purchase their products. Many advertisers especially wanted young, urban, upscale audiences and the new working woman market. Also, though to a lesser degree, they were interested in the growing black middle class.

Catering to these demographics, by the end of the 1960s networks revised the course of previous programming trends, ushering in a "turn toward relevance." ABC's *The Mod Squad* (1968–1973) was a youth-centered police drama featuring three "hippie" cops and plots that dealt with social issues of the day. In 1969 CBS president Robert D. Wood decided to revamp network programming in order to attract a younger, urban, upscale audience. His desire to rid CBS of its "bucolic" image was backed by the chairman of the board and founding executive, William S. Paley. Shows that were skewed toward rural audiences—*Green Acres* (1965–1971),

The Beverly Hillbillies (1962–1971), *Petticoat Junction* (1963–1970)—were dropped in favor of programs like *All in the Family* (1971–1983) and *M*A*S*H* (1972–1983), both of which dealt with social controversies and tried to give the sitcom genre a new sense of realism.

Responding to the feminist movement, "new woman" sitcoms like *The Mary Tyler Moore Show* (CBS, 1970–1977) and *Alice* (CBS, 1976–1985) showed women living on their own. While these followed in the path of previous "working girl" comedies, the new woman sitcoms often dealt with the central agendas of the liberal feminist movement. *Maude* (CBS, 1972–1978) became the first prime-time program to feature a divorced woman as its lead character. Maude was also the first prime-time heroine in a continuing series to have an abortion, a plot which raised considerable controversy for CBS.

Changes in Regulatory Policies Independent production companies—including Mary Tyler Moore and Grant Tinker's MTM and Norman Lear and Bud Yorkin's Tandem—created many of the new "relevant" sitcoms for CBS. In 1970 the FCC formulated rules (the Financial Interest Rule and Syndication Rules) that limited the networks' rights over ownership and distribution in the off-network (rerun) syndication market. These rules facilitated the growth of independent production houses and at the same time outraged the network executives who called the rules "a restraint of trade."

Competition with the three-network system was also initiated with cable deregulation. In 1977 the HBO case questioned the entire structure of the FCC's cable rules, and by 1980 the FCC dropped most of its cable regulation regarding signal carriage, and this in turn allowed cable to flourish. In 1984 Congress passed the Cable Communications Policy Act, which further deregulated the cable industry. In 1985 an appeals court struck down the "must carry" rules that had previously required each cable system to carry the signals of all "significantly viewed" television stations in the cable system's signal reach.

These decisions cumulatively represented the beginning of a new era for cable television. In addition, because cable had the effect of enhancing UHF signals, deregulation also facilitated the rise of the fourth broadcast network in 1985. Fox was now able to build a network by affiliating with UHF stations that were received loud and clear in homes with cable. Although the three original networks still were the dominant force, the classical network system was nevertheless facing a new set of industrial and political conditions that ultimately challenged its stronghold on television in the 1990s.

THE CHANGING TELEVISION LANDSCAPE

While many of its basic aesthetic and industrial practices were formed in its first two decades, American television subsequently underwent important changes. Many of them can be attributed to technological innovations: not only the growth of cable and satellite delivery systems in the 1980s, but also the sweeping changes that were being wrought at the end of the century by the convergence of television and computers.

As is obvious from the case of cable, these technological changes went hand in hand with deregulation policies formulated in the Reagan and Bush administrations. These policies were ostensibly meant to open up the existing three-network system to greater market competition. Deregulation, however, was a response to the changing nature of big business in the age of multinational capitalism and digital technologies. By loosening rules regarding ownership and the vertical integration of business practices, these new communication policies did not break up monopolistic practices; rather, they allowed global conglomerates to aggressively acquire increasing amounts of media properties.

In the 1980s all three networks were bought out by new parent corporations, and by the end of the 1990s mergers between media industries had become commonplace. The players ranged from international tabloid king Rupert Murdoch (whose News Corporation owned such properties as newspapers, magazines, and TV stations as well as the Fox movie studio and broadcast network), Disney (which owned ABC in addition to film and theme park holdings), Time-Warner (whose properties included CNN, HBO, Warner Bros. TV, theater chains, and Time-Life books), Viacom (a leading syndication company which owned cable networks and Paramount studios and then merged with CBS). In the new corporate structure, it is possible for a single company to own production, distribution, and exhibition outlets in both broadcast and cable venues to a degree never previously possible.

Deregulation also affected the degree to which broadcasters were held responsible to their publics. The FCC's revocation of the Fairness Doctrine in 1987 meant that broadcasters no longer, when editorializing about controversial issues, had to provide response time for community members. Revocation of "ascertainment rules" in 1984 meant that stations no longer had to abide by FCC rules for determining local program needs, although they were still required to operate in the "public interest" of their market. In 1985, guidelines (not rules) on the amount of advertising per hour were also dropped.

The rise of the Fox network, the growth of cable and digital technologies, the rapid diffusion of remote controls and VCRs, massive deregulation, globalization, and the many corporate mergers and buyouts of the late twentieth century gave television a new set of meanings in the lives of most Americans. These changes, as well as related changes in TV programming itself, ushered in a new wave of speculation about television's social effects.

Some critics argued that rather than providing more choice, the proliferation of television channels simply provided more outlets for a narrow set of commercial programs that ultimately looked the same. Critics also wondered whether the new practices of narrowcasting would result in audiences so divided in their niche markets that television would no longer create a national forum for communication. Still others wondered if the uneven distribution of new technologies across the population would widen the gulf between the information poor and the information rich.

Meanwhile, despite the proliferation of channels, many of the social and political struggles of the earlier decades continued at the turn of the twenty-first century. Although television in many ways responded to the society around it, the demands of mass broadcasting and commercial profits still limited the medium's ability to deal with the diversity of the population it supposedly represented and entertained. For example, while two cable networks targeted the Hispanic market, they had difficulties finding advertiser support. Meanwhile, in 1999 the NAACP protested that the networks had failed to produce pilots featuring black actors in lead roles. Certainly, the industry was still disproportionately white, and people of color were generally underrepresented both on screen and offscreen.

Indeed, despite many technological and industrial transitions, cultural change was often slow. While some critics derided television for its cautious response to social struggles and the needs of diverse populations, others concentrated on television's portrayals of sex and violence, arguing that TV had lost its sense of family values.

At the start of the twenty-first century, then, technological and industrial changes were accompanied by heated culture wars over television's social uses and effects. Whatever the outcome, broadcast history demonstrated that "the moment of any new technology is a moment of choice" (Williams, *The Year 2000,* p. 146). In this sense, even while television was often constrained by its commercial agenda, its past and current uses did not foreclose alternative possibilities for the future.

See also **Women and Family in the Suburban Age; Popular Culture in the Public Arena; Vietnam as a Cultural Crisis** *(volume 2);* **Technology; Consumerism; Elite vs. Popular Cultures; Culture for Mass Audiences; The Internet and Electronic Communications** *(in this volume); and other articles in this section.*

BIBLIOGRAPHY

Anderson, Christopher. *Hollywood TV: The Studio System in the Fifties.* Austin, Tex., 1994.

Barnouw, Erik. *The Tube of Plenty: The Evolution of American Television.* New York, 1990.

Boddy, William. *Fifties Television: The Industry and Its Critics.* Urbana, Ill., 1990.

Culbert, David. "Television's Nixon: The Politician and His Image." In *American History, American Television: Interpreting the Video Past.* Edited by John E. O'Connor. New York, 1983.

Ely, Melvin Patrick. *The Adventures of Amos 'n' Andy: A Social History of an American Phenomenon.* New York, 1991.

Gitlin, Todd. *Inside Prime Time.* New York, 1983.

Hawes, William. *American Television Drama: The Experimental Years.* N.p., 1986.

Jackson, Kenneth T. *Crabgrass Frontier: The Suburbanization of the United States.* New York, 1985.

Kerr, Paul. "The Making of (The) MTM (Show)." In *MTM: "Quality Television."* Edited by Jane Feuer, Paul Kerr, and Tise Vahimagi. London, 1984.

Lichty, Lawrence W., and Malachi C. Topping, comps. *American Broadcasting: A Source Book on the History of Radio and Television.* New York, 1975.

Lipsitz, George. *The Possessive Investment in Whiteness: How White People Benefit from Identity Politics.* Philadelphia, 1998.

MacDonald, J. Fred. *Blacks and White TV: Afro-Americans in Television since 1948.* Chicago, 1983.

Montgomery, Kathryn. *Target, Prime Time: Advocacy Groups and the Struggle over Entertainment Television.* New York, 1989.

Spigel, Lynn. *Make Room for TV: Television and the Family Ideal in Postwar America.* Chicago, 1992.

Spigel, Lynn, and Denise Mann, eds. *Private Screenings: Television and the Female Consumer.* Minneapolis, Minn., 1992.

Spigel, Lynn, and Michael Curtin, eds. *The Revolution Wasn't Televised: Sixties Television and Social Conflict.* New York, 1997.

Stasheff, Edward, and Rudy Bretz. *The Television Program: Its Writing, Direction, and Production.* New York, 1951.

Steinburg, Cobbett S. *TV Facts.* New York, 1980.

Susman, Warren I. *Culture as History: The Transformation of American Society in the Twentieth Century.* New York, 1984.

Williams, Raymond. *The Year 2000.* New York, 1983.

RADIO

Derek Vaillant

Radio evokes nostalgia among markedly different generations of Americans linked by their relationship to a technology they discovered in strikingly different social, cultural, and historical contexts. The vibrant subculture of collectors of old-time radio broadcasts and aficionados of music from rhythm and blues to punk rock share a particular linkage through their relationships to radio. Radio continues to win converts who discover the pleasures of exploring the bandwidth.

The history of broadcasting illuminates America's shifting and sometimes contested relations with leisure, technology, and commercial amusement culture. Radio emerged as a domestic, leisure technology in the 1920s and 1930s whose marketing challenged a trend toward leaving the domestic interior for public consumption of commercial amusements such as dancing, cinema, and sports. While millions of Americans listened to radios in stores, businesses, factories, and taverns, it nevertheless retained its primary identity as a home leisure device until after World War II. Television supplanted radio as a domestic totem in the postwar era. Radio responded by reinventing itself by the late 1950s. Buoyed by American consumption patterns, suburban development, and postwar American car and youth culture, radio enjoyed a renaissance as a portable accompaniment to life outside the home. Since it became an entertainment staple in the 1930s, Americans have repeatedly found ways to make room for radio in their daily lives by rediscovering its strengths: simplicity, affordability, and ease of use.

Commercial network broadcasting began in the late 1920s to entertain and inform a heterogeneous population of rural and urban Americans. The National Broadcasting Company (NBC), established in 1926, and the Columbia Broadcasting System (CBS), established in 1927, provided programs via their nationwide networks of stations. Operations were supported by direct advertisement. Radio promoted the culture of abundance and consumption that defined twentieth-century American society by impressing brand recognition on listener consciousness (most major programs had a single sponsor). The direct advertisement network model established a precedent for the postwar innovation of television.

National radio networks represented a movement toward literal and figurative connectivity that Americans welcomed on some fronts but resisted on others. Many yearned to be connected to the excitement of national entertainment acts, sporting events, national and world news, and new ideas. Yet radio listeners also desired programming representative of their local communities. Such programs shaped local and regional conceptions of public culture, influenced listeners' opinions of their standing in society at large, and permitted the audience to express and celebrate its differences. The tension between local and national control of radio represents a recurring theme in radio history that has animated important changes in its content and use over time.

Radio's cultural history is instructive for what it teaches about the roots of the multimedia conglomerates of the present. The nineteenth-century invention of wireless telegraphy spurred partnerships between stations and major merchandisers, city newspapers, electronics manufacturers, and the government. Federal regulators, including the U.S. Navy, the Department of Commerce, the Federal Radio Commission (FRC), and the Federal Communications Commission (FCC) proved indispensable in furthering corporate interests. Almost from the beginning, government and big business helped shape broadcasting's content, form, and to large extent, its identity. Elite concerns legally exploited a public medium for private gain, and used broadcasting to generate the concept of a national, white, middle-class community rooted in ritual consumption. The nation's less powerful social groups have found production access to broadcasting difficult and have struggled to counter distorted representations on the air. Despite popular appeal of radio, history reveals substantial economic, political, and cultural limitations of mainstream broadcasting to uniformly serve the public interest of all Americans.

Despite the constraints of the direct advertisement/network model, different subsets of the population built important group and individual relationships with radio as station operators, individual broadcasters, and listeners. From their first encounters with broadcasting in the 1920s, listeners managed to incorporate radio into their daily lives on their own terms. This diverse pool of listener publics included women, workers, and ethnic and racial minorities. Subcultures of radio producers and consumers flourished in the interstices of corporate dominance, making use of low-power AM stations, purchasing blocks of time on stations, obtaining access to the air via community, municipal, and not-for-profit FM stations, speaking up as callers on talk radio, or simply by consuming content differently.

Radio diffused ideas and information integral to individual and group identity formation in the twentieth century. Network and local programs circulated and helped legitimate representations of class, ethnicity, gender, race, and sexuality that contributed to understandings of American identity. Beginning in the 1930s, the "America" depicted in popular network comedy/dramas often bore only passing resemblance to the world inhabited by the millions listening. Caricatures and stereotypes as well as outright omissions of the lived experience of millions of Americans were commonplace, and remained so to a considerable extent. Beneath the veneer of escapism and fantasy surrounding radio program content lay themes of cultural contestation and social anxiety in twentieth-century history. Listening to radio became a ritual of participatory Americanism for first- and second-generation immigrants, migrants, and other groups. Knowing why and how this heterogeneous population took to radio and assessing the complex uses listener publics made of radio programming as it changed over time is vital to understanding processes of identity formation central to the cultural and intellectual history of the twentieth century.

Network radio promised a society strengthened and ennobled through simultaneous national connectivity. Radio broadcasts enabled large-scale "live" aural celebration of athletic, comedic, dramatic, and musical expression and events among listeners scattered across a room, a city, or a continent. Radio promoted and popularized America's sporting pastimes, such as baseball, football, and boxing. Radio news reportage linked millions together in times of economic hardship, tragedy, and war. The medium helped alter the American political tradition and the dynamics of election campaigns and statecraft, most notably by Franklin D. Roosevelt's fireside chats. On-air political appeals, talks and speeches, and spot advertising gave politicians a new means of campaigning through direct appeal to the electorate. Always within this web of shared behavior, however, lay complex and substantively different responses and reactions to listening. It is to these elusive and ephemeral responses that many cultural historians of American radio are drawn.

THE EARLY YEARS OF BROADCASTING

Approximately a half century of international experimentation with wireless telegraphy preceded the establishment of broadcasting. Experiments in wireless communication preceded Alexander Graham Bell's invention of the telephone in 1876. In 1864 James C. Maxwell, a Scottish physicist, theorized the existence of invisible electromagnetic energy waves. In 1888 German physicist Heinrich Hertz proved Maxwell's theory in a laboratory setting. By 1895 Italian inventor Guglielmo Marconi had built a transmitter and receiver capable of making wireless radio transmissions through the "ether" using pulses of energy. In 1906 Reginald A. Fessenden perfected continuous wave transmission, meaning that signals such as the human voice and music could be carried via radio. Lee De Forest patented the audion, a vacuum tube capable of amplifying radio signals for comfortable listening via headphones and loudspeakers, and the essential features of home radio listening were in place. "Tube" technology would dominate the radio electronics industry until the introduction of the transistor in the 1950s.

These inventors attempted with mixed success to translate their breakthroughs into viable businesses. In 1902 both Fessenden and De Forest established wireless companies to manufacture radio equipment. Fessenden's venture ended quickly in disappointment. De Forest fared better, and eventually sold patents to American Telephone and Telegraph (AT&T) in 1913. Marconi built and controlled an international chain of companies that dominated the first generation of the wireless telegraphy industry. The Marconi Wireless Company of America (American Marconi) made a triumphant demonstration of the new technology at the America's Cup yacht races in New York in 1899. In 1907 Marconi opened a transatlantic wireless news service charging a fraction of the cost per word of undersea cable operators. In 1919 British Marconi sold its American Marconi operations to General Electric (GE) to form the Radio Corporation of America (RCA). The deal produced the infamous "Radio Trust," a patent sharing scheme between AT&T, GE, and Westinghouse to dominant the radio parts, equipment, and broadcast business. While the trust ultimately crumbled under regulatory pressure, it produced the country's first network, the National Broadcasting Company (NBC).

Amateurs in the Pre-Network Era Prior to 1920, radio transmissions consisted largely of Morse code signals sent point-to-point by professional and amateur radiomen. Their efforts garnered publicity during floods, hurricanes, and other kinds of disasters when ordinary channels of communication were disrupted. After a highly publicized sea rescue in 1909, Congress passed the Wireless Ship Act of 1910 to standardize the practice of keeping wireless sets aboard large vessels. The government took additional regulatory steps two years later following the disastrous sinking of the *Titanic* in April 1912. Although radio distress signals brought the *Carpathia* to rescue survivors in lifeboats, amateurs so jammed the airwaves during the operation that rescue communications were hampered. The Radio Act of 1912 was the first legislative package to regulate broadcasting. The act empowered the Secretary of Commerce to issue broadcast licenses, regulate frequencies, and institute special procedures in the event of distress signals or other emergencies where public safety or national security appeared to be at stake. Much to their consternation, amateur wireless operators were banished to short wave frequencies of 200 meters and below. The federal government would hereafter retain a vested interest in controlling access to the airwaves.

At the time that the act was passed, an estimated 122 amateur wireless clubs catering to "ham" operators existed across the United States. Hams reveled at exchanging messages with others and "DXing," performing feats of long-distance communication with operators beyond the range of everyday point-to-point transmission. In 1914 the Amateur Radio Relay League (ARRL) formed to support the activities of thousands of such wireless buffs. Three years later, however, the U.S. Navy, one of the chief customers of wireless manufacturers, curtailed civilian experimentation. The Navy obtained exclusive rights to use various commercial

radio patents to build equipment and attempted to obtain a monopoly over the technology.

When Westinghouse's KDKA Pittsburgh took to the air on 11 November 1920, the absence of a national market for assembled radios forced enthusiasts to build their own wireless sets. In American high schools, on college campuses, and in the garage, male members of the white middle class constructed and tinkered with radio sets. Hundreds of clubs formed in the early 1920s as conduits for information. A raft of popular journals provided information on building sets and on the engineering of transmitters and receivers. Enterprising radio buffs used everyday materials including oatmeal containers, "Model T" ignition coils, telephone handsets, even discarded umbrella ribs. Early radio receivers required patient adjustment and perpetual tweaking, extending the impression of radio as a challenging sport.

Consumption of radio equipment and a proliferation of broadcast stations illustrate the rapidity with which Americans took to radio. The rate of household penetration of radio exceeded telephones. In 1922 only 30 standard broadcast stations operated across the county. By 1923 that number had leapt to 556. The number of radio sets commercially manufactured jumped fivefold in that same period, a number dwarfed by the hundreds of thousands of homemade sets assembled by hobbyists. By the mid-1920s, radio kits were widely available through hobby and electronics shops, and department stores were selling units designed to resemble furniture.

Popular sentiments expressed in print toward radio in the early to mid-1920s combined trepidation, bombast, idealism, and humor. Commentators debated radio's prospects as a tool, a toy, a device for education and culture, and a leisure and recreation device. Industry publications informed the public that radio could help stabilize a nation disrupted by rapid urbanization, industrialization, and immigration. Other early mentions of radio were lampoons, chortling at radio's obsessive "distance fiends," who paid no heed to the content of broadcasts, but were merely interested in their origination points.

Rural Cultures In 1920 a majority of the American population resided in urban environments. Rural America had witnessed a disturbing depopulation as opportunities beckoned in cities. A cultural preoccupation with the plight of farmers, spurred by Theodore Roosevelt's "Country Life" movement, influenced the early use of radio in rural

America to help the American farmer. On 15 December 1920, the U.S. Department of Agriculture (USDA) presented its first national broadcast to the nation's farmers. By the following June, the USDA provided regular market reports and forecasts from the U.S. Weather Bureaus. Farm families owned an estimated 100,000 radios in 1922; the number more than tripled by 1925.

In the Midwest, major land-grant agricultural colleges, such as Wisconsin and Ohio State, with support from their extension service departments, provided programming geared toward cultural uplift in rural and poorer areas of the nation. Many educational institutions sponsored radio "schools of the air" by the 1930s. By the early 1940s, tens of thousands of students listened to cultural and educational broadcasts in their classrooms. Radio had established itself as a promoter of civics and state-sanctioned entertainment.

Women and Radio   Gender played a defining cultural role in popular ideas about radio technology in the pre-broadcast era, since wireless enthusiasts were disproportionately men and boys. As radio broadcasting took hold, however, the identity of the medium and the social and cultural expectations among broadcasters, the nascent radio industry, and users shifted. Gender remained salient, as broadcasters and marketers now reached out to female listeners.

Women, girls, and the family constituted integral segments of the emerging radio audience of the mid-1920s. Radio combined practical features as an information tool (providing weather and market news) with those of a leisure device (music, lectures and public affairs, sports, and comedy). Manufacturers and vendors redesigned their marketing campaigns to include the female consumer as well as the male technophile. Advertising campaigns for radio receivers in popular magazines used domestic settings with family members present, burnishing the image of radio as a desirable accompaniment to American life at its happiest and most fulfilled. One of the earliest genres of radio programming indicative of radio's dualistic identity as information tool and leisure device were the farm and home shows directed to rural listening audiences, which catered to farmers with their early-morning reports but then segued into material directed toward homemakers. Home economics lectures, recipe exchanges, and health advice were among the topical areas these programs addressed. A study of radio customers classified by sex declared that by 1930 women shopping alone purchased over half of the nation's radio sets.

Urban Culture   In major cities of the 1920s, radio performed a decidedly different social and cultural function due to the higher concentration of licensees and a dramatically different economic, social, and cultural base. Scores of local radio stations busily shaped the vibrant and eclectic character of early broadcasting. Independent of national affiliations or chains, these modest, low-power stations brought program services representing specific ethnic, religious, and local cultural interests. In Chicago, for example, independent radio presented foreign-language broadcasts directed at German, Polish, Bohemian, Greek, Swedish, and other ethnic groups. Local stations broadcast ethnic music, religious services, and community service programs for circumscribed neighborhood audiences. In the new public medium of radio space, ethnic groups could control and experiment with self-representation.

Not all groups were so well served by radio. A sustained, self-directed African American presence on American radio emerged only sporadically prior to World War II. It took entrepreneurial African Americans to pressure white station owners into brokering time to get African American programs on the air. In 1928 Jack L. Cooper began producing the "Negro Hour" on WSBC in Chicago. Cooper managed his own staff of African American technicians, studio personnel, and talent to broadcast music, educational, and civic programs geared toward African American listeners, and African Americans won a crucial point of entry into the electronic public sphere of 1920s music radio.

Making Radio Pay   The need to sustain radio broadcasts, expand programming, and upgrade production standards put pressure on the diverse participatory base of early broadcasting. Broadcasters adopted various strategies to survive, from sustaining programs themselves in hopes of building good will in their local communities, to carrying sponsored programs, to broadcasting direct advertisements. Certain radio executives expressed leeriness about aggressive on-air pitches for fear of aggravating listeners. While broadcasters may have wished for alternatives, the exploding market for radio sets and growing demand among advertisers for access to American radio consumers established a powerful set of incentives that linked broadcasters, listeners, and capital together and helped determine the direct advertising model for radio that resulted.

While some independent stations sustained themselves through other means, by the mid- to late 1920s, sponsor-identified programs and direct advertisements were the norm on the nation's major stations. Listeners grew accustomed to hearing programs such as "The Palmolive Hour" and "The Wrigley Review." Radio orchestras and ensembles adopted the name of their sponsors, including Goodrich, Vicks, and Champion. One such ensemble, the Cliquot Club Orchestra, sponsored by the ginger ale producer, originated programs at New York station WEAF that were carried to about a dozen stations on the East Coast and in the Midwest.

NBC, the first network, arose from the recognition that a permanent chain might well offer the best combination of efficiency, economy of scale, and profitability that radio entrepreneurs desired. Chain broadcasts—short-term links among stations to carry feeds of major news, sporting events, dramas, and concerts—were increasingly commonplace. These sponsored broadcasts dramatically increased the percentage of Americans able to simultaneously consume special events, and generated major revenue as well.

The formative history of NBC illustrates the degree to which corporate interests had entrenched themselves in broadcasting by 1926. The founding of NBC occurred after years of negotiation between Owen Young and David Sarnoff, representatives of the so-called "Radio Group" (GE, RCA, Westinghouse), and the "Telephone Group" (AT&T and Western Electric). Both sides struggled to agree on how to divide station operation, radio equipment production, and the telephone functions of broadcasting. None of these corporate players wanted to provoke antitrust regulators who had punished the monopolistic Radio Trust. Talks to create NBC were conducted in secrecy.

In 1926 the parties reached an agreement in which AT&T agreed to leave the radio arena to concentrate exclusively on the telephone industry. This left Westinghouse, RCA, and GE as principal manufacturers of radio sets and operators of stations. The stations formerly affiliated with AT&T became the NBC Red network. Stations under RCA formed NBC Blue, a smaller network. These two networks were joined by CBS in 1927. Regulators supported the move until the early 1940s, when the Supreme Court upheld an FCC demand forcing NBC to sell one of its networks. NBC Blue changed hands to become the American Broadcasting Company (ABC) in 1945.

Radio and the Federal Government   The swift rise of NBC and CBS could not have occurred without strategic intervention in American broadcasting by federal regulators. In 1927 Congress, which had supported the laissez-faire directives of Commerce Secretary Herbert Hoover to allow free competition in radio, formed the Federal Radio Commission (FRC) to take control of the airwaves. Responding to network complaints about overcrowded airwaves, independent stations crowded onto frequencies, and a lack of a centralized authority to adjudicate station disputes, the FRC redefined the character of broadcasting by enforcing a definition of the "public interest, necessity, and convenience."

In a five-year span, regulators drove 20 percent of the nation's extant stations off the air, endorsing the logic that large, commercial stations were best equipped and financed to meet public programming needs. The landmark Communications Act of 1934 established the Federal Communications Commission (FCC), which supplanted the FRC.

Critics of the federal government's favorable treatment of commercial networks spurred a group of educators, nonprofit broadcasters, and civic groups to lead a defiant charge against the commercial radio lobby, but they made only minimal headway in Congress and had trouble overcoming the tremendous popular fascination with network serial programs. Not until 1945 would the government substantively review its policy toward independent broadcasters by setting aside FM bandwidth space for special use by educational and nonprofit broadcasters.

RADIO AS MASS CULTURE

The 1930s heralded an era of dominance for the major radio networks. Some 599 stations broadcast regularly across the country. Americans grew accustomed to listening to programs produced and packaged by advertisers and a handful of well-capitalized production companies. The network delivered these programs to affiliates who paid for the privilege, and on-air advertising supported operations at both ends.

By the 1930s, networks and advertisers routinely consulted with public relations firms and market research organizations, commissioning audience surveys to determine broadcast strategy. Research conducted by academics, as well as private sector studies by public relations and marketing concerns, influenced the form and content of network programs. Organizations such as the American Association of Advertising Agencies, headed by Daniel Starch, investigated the popularity of sponsored programs and helped convince corporations to advertise with certain programs.

The tradition of mass communications research produced alternative points of view on constructing mass audiences for commercial gain. Studies showed that although the wealthiest Americans were most likely to own radios, and the poorest least likely, the rate of listening was inversely proportional, with middle- and lower-income Americans consuming the most programming. Theodor W. Adorno, the Frankfurt school critical theorist, attacked America's "totalitarian radio" as an instrument of powerful corporate interests and commodified pleasures. Whatever powers of aesthetic and cultural uplift progressives might have hoped for had expired, Adorno seemed to suggest, once the airwaves became commodified.

Music in the Golden Age The 1930s are deservedly known as radio's "Golden Age" for a combination of memorable programs, popular audience affection, and network profitability. Radio played an extraordinary role in shaping the contours of American popular culture in the areas of music, comedy/drama, sports, and news. Radio circulated a broad and eclectic range of art and popular instrumental and song styles and showed itself to be an important outlet and promoter of African American jazz and the compositions of Tin Pan Alley. Because of radio, a few African American musicians, including Louis Armstrong and Duke Ellington, enjoyed tremendous celebrity and improved the image of African Americans generally in popular culture of the time.

The careers of Ellington and Armstrong marked an exception to a general tendency during an era in which African American musicians faced difficulty getting themselves on the air. A general trend in the network era, and in the popular entertainment industry reaching to the previous century, involved the appropriation of African American dance music by white performers for middle-class audiences. As it had when it transformed Southern "rags" into respectable parlor music, the popular music industry appropriated African American jazz idioms and styles and translated the "hot" syncopated music into "sweet" melodic ballroom music. When swing exploded as a popular dance style in the 1930s and 1940s, cults of radio fandom sprang up around white leaders Benny Goodman, Tommy Dorsey, and Fletcher Henderson, leaving most talented African American bandleaders consigned to nightclub and theater settings.

Even as networks popularized the music, Jim Crow customs in organized labor and the commer-

cial music industry pushed African American musical talent to the margins. Exclusions upheld by the American Federation of Musicians kept talented African American musicians out of lucrative studio orchestras and prevented announcers from obtaining radio jobs. The spontaneity of the live feed from a 1920s black-and-tan dance hall, which introduced many Americans to the distinctive improvisational style of jazz, increasingly gave way to the scripted precision of the big band and the network studio orchestra, which hired from musicians' unions respecting the color bar.

The 1930s also marked a turning point for the availability of classical music via radio. With millions flowing into network coffers, major market stations formed studio "orchestras" staffed by classically trained musicians capable of performing popular standards as well as light classical music. NBC made a dramatic commitment to classical music on the air in 1937 when it hired Arturo Toscanini to conduct the NBC Symphony. For eighteen seasons, Toscanini brought live symphonic music into the homes of millions of Americans on a regular basis, and promoted radio as a site of serious cultural programming.

Comedy/Drama in the Golden Age "Amos 'n' Andy," carried by NBC and sponsored by Pepsodent, ranked as one of the earliest and most successful network radio comedies in history. It starred Freeman Gosden and Charles Correll, white vaudevillians who "blacked up" their voices as stock minstrel characters. Since the antebellum period, consumers of commercial amusement culture had turned to the minstrel stage for ideas to bring to the popular mainstream. Despite its overt racism, the show won millions of listeners of all races. By the late 1930s, ratings slipped, as African Americans mobilized to express their disapproval of the show's corrosive depictions of African American life. They organized boycotts using the *Pittsburgh Courier* and the National Association for the Advancement of Colored People (NAACP). Their efforts could not stop the program from continuing, but negative publicity helped topple it from its ratings perch.

Comedy/dramas borrowing talent and routines from the urban, ethnic vaudeville stage became staples of network radio in the 1930s. Many stars were immigrants and ethnic Jews, among them Jack Benny (Benjamin Kubelsky), George Burns (Nathan Birnbaum), Al Jolson (Asa Yoelson), and Eddie Cantor (Edward Iskowitz). These acts derived their crackling pace and exquisite comedic timing from the ethnic stage and urban vaudeville halls, and per-

Amos 'n' Andy **Radio Show (1935).** Freeman Gosden (Amos) stands as he plays the part of the Kingfish, while Charles Correll bellows out the part of Andy. © BETTMANN/CORBIS

formed before live studio audiences, they translated perfectly to the invisible medium of radio.

The 1930s domestic comedy emerged as an enduring popular genre on network radio, suiting the domestic and family market that advertisers wished to reach. "Fibber McGee and Molly" ran on NBC from 1935 to 1961. The "George Burns and Gracie Allen Show" portrayed another lively and likeable couple whom the nation took to its heart.

Sports in the Golden Age Professional sports broadcasting represented another of radio's most enduring and loved contributions to American culture during the network era. Through chains in the 1920s, and later through networks, Americans were able to follow a full range of sports, both live and rebroadcast, including football, horse racing, and basketball.

Athletic achievement and the public character of sportsmen in the public eye aided groups, such as African Americans, who were otherwise marginalized in American society. Radio broadcasts of Joe Louis's prizefights in the 1930s helped create a folk hero among African Americans and whites alike. Radio fueled national sentiment across the divides of race when Louis competed against German boxer Max Schmeling in 1938. By the 1930s, some of the most recognizable voices in America were those of

a stable of sports announcers. Mel Allen, the voice of the Yankees; Red Barber, the first broadcaster to be elected to the Hall of Fame; Graham McNamee; and Gordon McLendon, artful recreator of the Game-of-the-Day on the Liberty Broadcasting System were pioneering radio personalities as well as technicians of sport announcing who ingrained their verbal styles and expressions into the consciousness and everyday speech of millions of listeners.

Franklin D. Roosevelt displayed a prescient understanding of the American public's special relationship with radio, which he used during the uncertainties of the Great Depression. Roosevelt instituted informal addresses to the nation about New Deal policies and national economic concerns through the "Fireside Chat" series, which began in March 1933. The informal populist tone set by these broadcasts transformed the relationship between the Executive Office and the news media. Despite enormous editorial resistance to the New Deal in the nation's press, Roosevelt spoke directly to his constituents without interruption or rebuttal. When Roosevelt invited listeners to "tell me your troubles," they responded by the hundreds of thousands in letters personally addressed to the president.

Radio and the War Beginning in the late 1930s, the major networks (NBC, CBS, and Mutual) invested significant funds to develop their news divisions and hire foreign correspondents to cover the turbulent political situation in Europe. Exposés of propaganda ruses during World War I using doctored photographs and biased news reporting had sensitized Americans to the fallibility of their news gatherers. Yet studies indicated that the integrity of sound and the human voice remained a trusted source of information for the majority of Americans. The networks entrusted a handful of individuals with supplying the nation with breaking news of the war and inaugurated a new era in America's relationship with its media institutions and individual broadcasters.

When war erupted, correspondents H. V. Kaltenborn, Edward R. Murrow, and William Shirer brought the association of radio with immediacy, heroism, and drama to a new level. In addition to regular dispatches from their familiar voices, Americans heard live broadcasts of Hitler's speeches, listened to the passionate declaration of war by Roosevelt the day after Japan's attack on Pearl Harbor, and aurally accompanied invading troops during the D-Day invasion of Normandy. Women correspondents reported via radio as well, including Marvin Breckinridge Patterson, CBS radio's first female staff broadcaster, Janet Flanner of NBC, and Katherine L. Clark, accredited by WCAU radio.

The federal government became an evermore active broadcaster during the war. Building on lessons learned during the New Deal, the Roosevelt administration supported programming initiatives designed to promote consensus and counteract social unrest at home. The Office of War Information (OWI) promoted the broadcast circulation of news and public affairs information concerning the activities of dozens of governmental agencies. The OWI promoted cooperation with the Armed Forces Radio Network to carry entertainment and information programs to servicemen abroad. In February 1942 the Voice of America began broadcasting governmentally controlled presentations outside the United States. It later became a vital tool of the State Department during the cold war, carrying a variety of programs in English and other languages. The VOA remains active, producing over two thousand hours of programs each week.

Surviving the Test of Television The heyday of network radio's comedy/drama and variety programs began to fade by the late 1940s and early 1950s as television appropriated radio program formats and siphoned off leading talents, including Jack Benny and Bob Hope. In 1951 CBS radio cut its advertising rates for the first time. Between 1950 and 1955, network radio revenues plummeted by almost half from $131.5 to $64.1 million dollars. By the end of the 1950s, television had supplanted radio as the dominant American leisure activity.

Radio managed to remain a profitable medium in the 1950s, even as the revenue-generating power of the major radio networks eroded. Recognizing a need to fend for themselves, local stations bolstered their bottom lines by building niche markets for themselves, developing new audiences, and seeking community advertising support. Light entertainment remained a staple, but experiments with news and documentary programs, public affairs shows, religious programs, and new music formats grew more common on the nation's airwaves.

The crisis gripping network radio proved salutary for African Americans in broadcasting. Announcers gained new opportunities in the experimental industry atmosphere of the late 1940s and 1950s. White-owned stations were willing to diversify their formats if they could be assured of audiences, and African American announcers and musicians were prepared to take advantage of this dynamic.

By the late 1940s, there were dozens of "black-appeal" experiments throughout the country in cities with significant black populations. In Chicago, "the Ole Swingmaster," Al Benson, held court over station WGES, speaking in a thick, southern drawl, as a member of the working-class African American population who consumed his programs. Similar personalities emerged in Memphis, Detroit, Philadelphia, Pittsburgh, and New York.

Radio Discovers Rock and Roll As historian William Barlow argues, the success of black-appeal radio prompted imitation among white disc jockeys (DJs) at stations in the South and elsewhere. According to Barlow, a "counterfeit rendering of black vernacular speech" became commonplace on stations not willing to hire African American announcers. Imitative white announcers represented yet another appropriation of African American culture. The love and theft of African American music and speech led directly to a new cultural formation that exploded in the 1950s: rock and roll.

Rock and roll music represented a hybrid of the rhythm and blues heard on black-appeal stations and country (formerly hillbilly) music. In 1951 Alan Freed launched "Moondog's Rock 'n' Roll Party" on Cleveland station WJW. The show, aimed at attracting interracial audiences, featured African American music exclusively. Freed jumped to WINS in New York where his "Rock 'n' Roll Party Time" program and concerts at Brooklyn's Paramount Theatre garnered legions of fans. The show promoted new hits from dozens of labels recording new acts in cities such as Memphis, Chicago, New York, and Los Angeles.

Historian Susan Douglas has observed that Freed and a cadre of national on-air personalities, including Bobby Smith ("Wolfman Jack"), George "Hound Dog" Lorenz, and Murray the K, cultivated an energetic, hip, airshift-as-nonstop-party approach that appropriated African American DJ styles. *Broadcasting* magazine declared the DJ to be "the big business factor in today's new concept of radio." Freed and other high profile DJs became the target of investigations by the music industry that revealed evidence of payola practices. Freed adamantly defended his promotional practices but could not salvage his career in radio.

Cultural historians argue that part of the backlash against rock and roll in the 1950s centered on social and cultural apprehensions over race and class relations in America. AM radio became a conduit for African American culture just as the civil rights movement gained national momentum. Race concerns articulated in the protest style of black and white DJs mattered in this equation, as did the rebellious posture of rhythm and blues and rock and roll representing a youthful generation's frustration at 1950s conformity.

Manufacturing the Top 40

An end result of the payola scandals is that it permitted radio conglomerates and the commercial music industry to standardize, package, and market rock and roll to consumers with extraordinary precision. The birth of the "Top 40," and its wholesale adoption by the late 1950s, marked a shift from the early DJ-driven rock programs to a regulated, self-perpetuating system of marketing pop music to American youth. Borrowing the insight that music lovers would respond to radio programs that served up familiar hits the way a jukebox did, programmers Todd Storz in Omaha and Gordon McLendon in Dallas independently instituted a revolutionary program strategy. They replaced the customary broad and eclectic playlist, covering the range of available popular music, with a tight, carefully-researched and tracked rotation of hits that was played over and over again. To a marked degree, the strategy of repetition surrounding advertising jingles in the 1920s and 1930s had simply been extended to the musical content. Reliability, repetition, and consistency of product defined Top 40 radio down to the personality of the DJs hired by stations as generically upbeat accompaniments to the endless loop of pre-programmed hits. Stations were decades away from relying on the computers of the 1970s and 1980s to organize playlists and operate stations, but the responsibility of the DJ to put a human face and facade of spontaneity on an increasingly prepackaged, market-driven cultural production took hold.

During the 1950s and into the 1960s, the purchasing power of Americans mushroomed to new heights. The emerging social and cultural rituals of suburban living—the dominant middle-class experience by the mid-1950s—had important consequences for radio's place. By 1960 the typical American family owned several radios that were used by different family members in a wide range of contexts. Radio had become a fixture in the everyday routines of Americans when they awoke, dressed, drove to work, worked, drove home. Television had conquered primetime in the evenings, but radio survived and flourished by diffusing into the interstices of an increasingly mobile, suburbanized society where multiple generations of one household controlled the radio. By the early 1960s, the majority of American automobiles contained radio. Clear-channel, high power signals made listening possible under more conditions than ever before. As a result of the affordability of battery-powered transistor units that replaced bulky tube units, Americans took radio out of the home. Beaches, parks, sports stadiums, and other public meeting grounds buzzed to the strains of Motown, pop, and rock standards produced with an eye to teenage consumers.

The Rise of FM Broadcasting

The invention of FM (frequency modulation) broadcasting occurred decades before the networks controlling broadcasting began supplying it to the public. Networks held FM licenses, but generally used them as duplicate carriers of their AM schedule. The situation changed in 1964 when the FCC, in an effort to stimulate diversity of programs, imposed a limited duplication rule prohibiting the use of FM as a secondary carrier for an AM station's programming. FM stations now needed to generate original programming. Within two years, "progressive rock" entered the American lexicon to describe programming experiments featuring longer song selections, fewer interruptions and advertisements, and a wider range of musical styles. Some stations opted for "beautiful music" consisting of instrumental arrangements of soft pop hits. Others explored the terrain of "freeform radio" in which DJs were given full artistic license to blend music, commentary, and other aural accompaniments to create a holistic listening experience. The format derived its inspiration from trends in youth counterculture in the 1960s and 1970s and marked a convergence of multimedia expression and experimentation involving music, poetry, theater, and politics, and was commonly heard on the nation's not-for-profit college and community stations and cities.

A growing market for high-fidelity audio equipment capable of playing stereophonic recordings converged with baby boomer incomes and a taste for rock and roll to sustain the strong growth of FM radio. Album Oriented Rock (AOR) became a popular format for middle-class white American youth, as did disco in the mid-1970s. Collectively, these formats drew listeners across class and race divides to FM such that by 1979, for the first time, more Americans were listening to FM than AM radio.

The late 1960s and 1970s marked attempts at supporting independent, not-for-profit programming on the public airwaves by federal regulators. The Public Broadcasting Act of 1967 led to the formation of the Corporation for Public Broadcasting (CPB). The CPB supported not-for-profit, educational radio initiatives. National Public Radio (NPR) organized a network of educational stations in 1971 and gradually became a successful news, information, and cultural programming source. The Pacifica Network, founded in 1949 at KPFA Berkeley, gained national attention as an outspoken voice of protest against the war in Vietnam and a supporter of women and minority voices and opinion on FM radio. Many nonprofit college and community stations asserted themselves in the 1960s and 1970s as supporters of New Left coalition politics and alternative cultural and musical programming.

Later Trends Telecommunications deregulation, begun in the 1980s and continuing through the 1990s, encouraged an explosion of FM licenses (4,392), permitted greater concentration of ownership, and drove up radio revenues, which more than doubled between 1982 and 1990 to almost $7 billion. Susan Douglas notes that by the late 1990s, four companies, Capstar Broadcasting, CBS, Clear Channel Communications, and Jacor, controlled 90 percent of national radio advertising revenue. Changing lifestyles altered the ways that Americans used radio at the end of the century. By the early 1990s, almost 60 percent of radio listening occurred outside the home, with about a third of all listening occurring in cars as Americans commuted longer and farther to work. Most Americans listen to FM

(and have done so since 1979). They can sample over a dozen major radio formats, from adult contemporary/soft rock to country to Christian to urban contemporary music, as well as specialty music, including Latin, Celtic, Afro-Caribbean, Middle Eastern, and other regional music.

Beginning in the 1970s, talk radio became a familiar on-air presence, as call-in programs expanded the interactive nature of radio listening. From politics to sports to sex, talk radio provided an electronic forum for Americans to air sentiments in a new public forum. By the 1980s and 1990s, syndicated radio personalities such as Larry King, "Dr. Ruth" Westheimer, Rush Limbaugh, "Dr. Laura" Schlessinger, and Don Imus commanded huge followings. Limbaugh and Imus drew considerable publicity in the early 1990s for their outspoken politics and alleged roles in influencing electoral opinion. In the twenty-first century, local and national talk radio continues to serve an array of listener needs from NPR's "Morning Edition" and morning "shock jocks," to call-in sports programs, health shows, and community affairs and political programs.

While deregulation and ownership concentration has undermined localism in one sense, there are signs that listener publics are getting what they want from radio through nationally based mininetworks. Satellite technology has enabled even small stations to join multiple networks for special concert and event feeds. While NBC dissolved its radio network, others such as Westwood One and the American Urban Radio Network have emerged as major players in radio. Public Radio International has demonstrated support for independent radio artists and personalities whose craft and production values, writing, and dramatic skills suggest that radio remains a realm of imaginative possibility. Moreover, the convergence of radio broadcasting with digitized transmission of audio via satellite, fiber-optic networks, and the Internet suggests a continuing reformulation of the meaning of networks as a means of promoting local, national, and transnational connectivity.

The ethos of localism remains a powerful basis of radio's continued support among the nation's immigrant and ethnic groups. AM radio continues to support listeners seeking talk and public affairs formats as well as foreign-language broadcasts. In recent years, commercial network service for the nation's growing Asian American and Latino population has increased substantially. There are major Spanish-language networks serving markets in cities such as Los Angeles, New York, and Miami.

See also **The Popular Arts** *(volume 1);* **Women and Family in the Suburban Age; Popular Culture in the Public Arena; Multiculturalism in Theory and Practice** *(volume 2);* **Technology; Consumerism; The Visual Arts; Education; Elite vs. Popular Cultures; Culture for Mass Audiences; The Internet and Electronic Communications** *(in this volume); and other articles in this section.*

BIBLIOGRAPHY

Baker, John Chester. *Farm Broadcasting: The First Sixty Years.* Ames, Iowa, 1981.

Barlow, William. *Voice Over: The Making of Black Radio.* Philadelphia, 1999.

Barnouw, Erik. *A Tower in Babel: A History of Broadcasting in the United States to 1933.* New York, 1966.

———. *The Golden Web: A History of Broadcasting in the United States, 1933–1953.* New York, 1968.

Butsch, Richard. "Crystal Sets and Scar-Pin Radios: Gender, Technology and the Construction of American Radio Listening in the 1920s." *Media, Culture and Society* 20 (1998): 557–572.

Ditingo, Vincent M. *The Remaking of Radio.* Boston, 1995.

Douglas, Susan J. *Inventing American Broadcasting, 1899–1922.* Baltimore, 1987.

———. *Listening In: Radio and the American Imagination.* New York, 1999.

Ely, Melvin Patrick. *The Adventures of Amos 'n' Andy: A Social History of an American Phenomenon.* New York, 1991.

Erenberg, Lewis A. *Swingin' the Dream: Big Band Jazz and the Rebirth of American Culture.* Chicago, 1998.

Godfrey, Donald G., and Frederic A. Leigh. *Historical Dictionary of American Radio.* Westport, Conn., 1998.

Hilmes, Michele. *Hollywood and Broadcasting: From Radio to Cable.* Urbana, Ill., 1990.

———. *Radio Voices: American Broadcasting, 1922–1952.* Minneapolis, 1997.

Lasar, Matthew. *Pacifica Radio: The Rise of an Alternative Network.* Philadelphia, 1998.

MacDonald, J. Fred. *Don't Touch That Dial! Radio Programming in American Life, 1920–1960.* Chicago, 1979.

McChesney, Robert W. *Telecommunications, Mass Media, and Democracy: The Battle for the Control of U.S. Broadcasting 1928–1935.* New York, 1993.

McFadden, Margaret. "America's Boyfriend Who Can't Get a Date: Gender, Race, and the Cultural Work of the Jack Benny Program, 1932–1946." *Journal of American History* 80, no. 1 (1993): 113–134

Nachman, Gerald. *Raised on Radio: In Quest of the Lone Ranger, Jack Benny. . . .* New York, 1998.

Nasaw, David. *Going Out: The Rise and Fall of Public Amusements.* New York, 1993.

Rosen, Philip T. *The Modern Stentors: Radio Broadcasters and the Federal Government, 1920–1934.* Westport, Conn., 1980.

Savage, Barbara Dianne. *Broadcasting Freedom: Radio, War, and the Politics of Race, 1938–1948.* Chapel Hill, N.C., 1999.

Smulyan, Susan. *Selling Radio: The Commercialization of American Broadcasting, 1920–1934.* Washington, D.C., 1994.

Susman, Warren. *Culture as History: The Transformation of American Society in the Twentieth Century.* New York, 1984.

Wik, Reynold. "The USDA and the Development of Radio." *Agricultural History* 62 (1988).

ADVERTISING

Susan Smulyan

DEFINITIONS

People in the advertising industry often write that their profession began in prehistoric times with cave paintings or proudly point to biblical references to their work. Such attempts at using history to give advertising legitimacy seem pretty strained. In the American colonies the *Boston News-Letter* published the first advertisements in May 1704, but two of the three notices concerned goods stolen from the advertisers. While advertising volume grew during the eighteenth century, the techniques remained the same as newspaper advertisements continued to be small and set in tiny type. The bulk of advertisements in the early and middle nineteenth century were announcements by tradesmen and promoters of new goods on hand. Advertising was primarily local and resembled today's classified notices in newspapers.

The change in advertising between about 1900 and what had come before was sharp, definite, and transforming. In 1897 *Harper's Weekly* described a new kind of ad that was beginning to appear: "Once we skipped [advertisements] unless some want compelled us to read, while we now read to find out what we really want" (in Pope, p. 5). Modern advertising, then, is about one hundred years old.

But the term "advertising" covers a lot of ground. In this essay, advertising refers to nationally marketed and branded product promotion. Such a definition usually includes marketing (deciding what products consumers want); distribution (getting the products to the consumers); and promotions (everything from free decoder rings to people spritzing you with perfume in department stores); rather than simply referring to print and broadcast messages sent by manufacturers to convince consumers to buy one product rather than another. This definition leaves out local advertising, classified advertising, direct-mail advertising, outdoor advertising, political advertising, and even the newest incarnation, Internet advertising.

More important than arguments over the definition of advertising are the controversies over how best or why it should be studied. Some scholars say advertising is the grease that makes capitalism work. Others contend that advertising is vaguely immoral because it influences folks to buy things they do not need or cannot afford. On the one hand, many writers claim that advertising reflects society. Historians, in this view, should and could use advertising as a tool to discover previously unrecoverable attitudes and ideas, to figure out what ordinary people thought. On the other hand, advertising influences society as an important socializing agent.

Arguments over whether advertising reflects or shapes culture, whether it is necessary or evil, leave out two important kinds of information that a study of advertising history can bring forward. In every era there have been people who objected to advertising, from the truth in advertising movement in the 1910s, the consumer movement of the 1930s, the unhappy advertising agents in the 1950s, the counterculture in the 1960s, the parents and broadcasting reformers who called television a "vast wasteland" in the 1970s, up to the activists of the 1990s who wrote books with titles like *Marketing Disease to Hispanics*. The opinions of all these people raise valid and important points about capitalism and advertising and tell us a lot about how hegemony struggles to respond to and contain dissident views. Often the critiques of advertising led to government action, and, without government support, advertising as a cultural institution would not exist.

Most important, advertising in the twentieth century became a way of seeing and knowing. A nineteenth-century "producer ethic," a value system based on work, sacrifice, and saving, evolved into a dominant twentieth-century "consumer culture" expressed in advertising. In many ways advertising is the language of American culture, rather than its shaper or reflector. Late-twentieth-century scholarship insisted that language and culture are

527

intimately connected. The content of what you can say and do is tied to the language you have at your command. If your language comes from the marketplace, that is going to affect what you want to talk about. Thus, advertising presents a crucial object of study for anyone who wants to understand twentieth-century America.

INDUSTRIALIZATION AND ADVERTISING

Advertising changed drastically between 1890 and 1920. In 1893 more than half of the top one hundred advertisements were for patent medicines. By 1920 the top categories of goods advertised looked much like they did at the end of the century. Among the ten biggest advertisers of 1998, Procter and Gamble, General Motors, Philip Morris, Chrysler, Sears Roebuck, and Ford Motor Company (or their predecessors or allied companies) also appeared on top-ten lists between 1900 and 1920. Among the leading categories of national advertisers there were far more changes in the twenty-five years before World War I than in the following one hundred years. By 1920 American advertising and ad agencies had more in common with their late-twentieth-century counterparts than with the advertising and agencies of the late nineteenth century.

The reasons for the growth of advertising can be found in the most important economic and social trends of the late nineteenth century in America: industrialization (the change from an agricultural economy to one based on manufacturing); urbanization; and new developments in transportation and communication. Given these changes, why did businesses decide to advertise?

Manufacturing after the Civil War changed in both quantity and quality. The scale of operations increased in manufacturing as new technologies created capital-intensive means of production, which meant there were substantial costs before production began and such costs called for bigger companies to cover the large initial investments. The need for a large investment in equipment (with accompanying debt service) proved to be a particular problem in industries with seasonal or inconsistent seasonal demand. A bottling plant sits empty in January if people drink soda only in the summer, but owners still have to pay interest on the loans taken to buy the equipment. Advertising could help match demand to the conditions of continuous production required and made possible by new technology.

If concentration and capital-intensive production provided motives for businessmen to advertise, the development of a communications and transportation network made the development of national advertising possible. Not many products were distributed nationally before the completion of the nation's railroad system. Once a national network of transportation and communication was in place, products could be sent nationwide and advertising could reach more people more easily and quickly.

The growth of cities also called forth more advertising, directly and indirectly. National advertisers found receptive customers for their goods and suitable media for their appeals in the new urban centers. In addition to having many people in one place and easy ways to reach them, cities also altered the types of goods and information about them that people wanted. For example, 10 percent of the bread eaten in 1850 was baked commercially, mostly specialty items for holidays; the rate rose to 25 percent in 1900 and to 60 percent in 1930. Some rural families bought new products, of course, and certain kinds of ads were aimed at rural folks, for example, Sears Roebuck's mail-order selling, but in the main advertising grew along with cities.

Advertising was the marketing policy of some businesses but not all. Many large national producers reacted defensively and hesitantly to changes in marketing environments. When the Campbell Soup Company awarded its first advertising appropriation in 1899, the company's secretary turned to the treasurer and remarked, "Well, we've kissed that money goodbye" (quoted in Pope, p. 61). Advertising was a business strategy adopted by different kinds of companies who decided to sell, make, and advertise brand-name consumer products.

The paths to national advertising of branded products were varied. Some manufacturers altered what they sold to reach national markets while others actively sought out products and markets that could be nationally advertised. All advertisers sought a unique product that they could name and "brand" so that customers asked for a specific good. National Biscuit Company's marketing of the Uneeda biscuit is an example of how products and marketing could be reshaped to take advantage of advertising. In 1898 National Biscuit Company, a large company formed by mergers, differentiated their new soda cracker by cutting off the corners to give the cracker an octagonal shape and worked with the N. W. Ayer and Son advertising agency to come up with a name for the new product. They rejected Taka Cracker, Usa Cracker, and Want a Cracker in favor of Uneeda biscuit as more dignified. A newly designed wax-lined cardboard box kept the crackers fresh. But a unique product, a catchy name, and clever packaging was not enough. A staff of salesmen and a network of branch sales offices soon followed to make sure customers got their crackers fresh and unbroken. An advertising campaign bolstered all of these changes. National Biscuit supposedly became the first company to appropriate one million dollars a year for advertising. So Uneeda biscuits and National Biscuit took an old product and differentiated it by giving it a new package, new distribution, and new advertising.

During industrialization, three things happened: companies in capital-intensive, mass-production industries needed to sell more goods and so needed to increase demand; manufacturers sought products that could be branded and made to seem unique; and customers came to accept advertising as a form of information. Advertising professionals, who invented their own jobs in the late nineteenth century, helped implement these changes.

ADVERTISING AGENCIES

The rise of national advertising for branded products gave advertising a new economic purpose and brought a change in advertising agency structure and practice. Advertising agencies of the nineteenth century owed their existence to the staggering problems of coordinating the needs of advertisers and media. By the 1890s about four thousand entrepreneurs wanted to advertise goods beyond their localities. Meanwhile, the number of daily newspapers grew from 254 in 1859 to 2,226 in 1900. Weeklies increased at a comparable pace, from 991 in 1838 to 13,513 in 1904. The complexity of matching advertisers with media was magnified by the absence of reliable information about either side. For advertisers, no trustworthy list of the nation's newspapers existed, and, until at least World War I, circulation information was unreliable. Publishers had no idea if national advertisers were creditworthy. What did you do if someone thousands of miles away refused to pay after an ad had been run?

Advertising agents began to take over some of the risks involved in national advertising in the 1840s. Volney B. Palmer, generally considered the first American advertising agent, began his agency in Philadelphia in 1843 as part of his real estate business. Palmer announced he would take over the placing of ads for companies, and by the end of the 1840s he operated offices in Boston, New York, Philadelphia, and Baltimore. Palmer seems to have made his money in the form of a commission paid to him by newspapers. Everything else about advertising agencies has changed, but despite controversy, the commission system survives.

New developments in the market for advertising space and a need for different kinds of services brought about another change. As national publishing grew to include magazines as well as newspapers, and as the publishers became more rational and businesslike in their dealings with advertisers, there seemed to be less for agencies to do. For example, mass circulation magazines maintained their stated roles and attracted advertiser attention without the intermediary work of advertising agents. New products and retailers needed advertising services that were different than those supplied by space brokers.

Early manufacturers wrote their own advertisements, often simply presenting the facts. Department stores were the first major advertisers that needed skilled assistance in preparing their advertisements. As they expanded their range of goods and as new urban streetcar lines widened their marketing territories, downtown retailers needed to induce customers to shop by letting them know what products were in the stores. At Wanamaker's in Philadelphia, John E. Powers, with his plainspoken essays describing merchandise, became the first copywriter and the first person to make a living writing advertisements. As the manufacturers of new branded consumer goods invested in distribution, persuasive advertising became a pressing need for them as well. Publicity was too important to be left to space brokers. Copy, layout, and artwork had to be carefully considered; advertisements had to fit a broad marketing strategy.

Early in the twentieth century, the job of preparing advertisements became a central responsibility of advertising agencies. Agencies hired armies of people to write, most of them trained in journalism. As copywriting became a craft, skilled illustration and layout became necessary to achieve continuity and strengthen selling appeals. Successfully assuming the job of preparing advertisements for national advertisers was a big step toward assuring the survival and well-being of advertising agencies.

National advertisers did not do their own advertising because large companies were becoming vertically integrated, bringing everything needed to make and sell products into one company. Yet between the 1890s and the 1920s independent agencies supplied advertising services to virtually all important national advertisers. The continuance of the commission system helped agencies maintain and solidify their positions. Periodicals publishers still paid agencies a commission for all the space bought through their agencies, and agencies kept the publishers from giving any other business the same commission.

At the same time advertising agents worked hard to gain respect to shore up their still somewhat tenuous position. The "truth in advertising" movement, part of the progressive reforms attempting to control big business, became an important vehicle. Truth in advertising, like many later movements, questioned the legitimacy of advertising. At the same time, the campaign definitely strengthened the advertising industry. The truth in advertising campaign gained momentum at a 1911 convention of the Associated Advertising Clubs of America. Convention oratory focused on the intertwined themes of the truthfulness of the advertisements themselves and the professional status of advertising agents. By 1913 a model statute making dishonest advertising (within very limited boundaries) illegal was introduced in about fifteen states and by 1921 had been passed in twenty-three. The laws defined "truth" quite narrowly, allowing a great deal of puffery to be excluded from potential prosecution.

While quite successful in its own terms, the truth in advertising movement remained fraught with ironies. Using moral language, the movement was shaped by self-interest. The achievements of the truth in advertising movement gave advertisers many ways to lie and still stay within the rules. Advertisements could strongly imply, and even sometimes directly state, that products made consumers popular, thinner, and happier, for instance, and not run afoul of government or industry regulations. In addition, the movement solidified the position of advertising agencies and advertising professionals as important players in the new, industrialized, consumption economy.

CHANGES IN THE ADS

Significant changes in advertisements themselves accompanied changes in manufacturing and in the structure of the advertising industry. In the nineteenth century advertisements focused on the product, gave rational information, and explained why people should buy the product. As industrialization brought more goods to market and advertising agencies professionalized and added more staff, the new ads focused on the consumer, appealed to emotions, and explained how the products would change consumers lives. Advertising professionals

sometimes claim that advertising at a particular moment features "reason why" or rationally based arguments, while older advertising was "emotional," but the general trend has been away from informational advertising. Because advertising constantly searches for some new approach, the industry does switch between rational and emotional appeals, but the so-called rational advertising never simply provides information. Such ads could be written and placed without the need of advertising professionals and so do not exist in the national market. The big change, early in the twentieth century, moved ads from a focus on the product to a focus on the consumer.

The historians Richard M. Ohmann and Roland Marchand examined thousands of magazine advertisements in two different time periods (1890–1910 by Ohmann and 1920–1940 by Marchand) to describe exactly how advertising professionals affected this change. Ohmann describes how the early advertising agents influenced people's needs and desires by creating a new language of brand names, slogans, and associations, coupled with a new form of design that featured bigger ads with an increased ratio of image to text. These new ads, which appeared between 1890 and 1910, used a personal form of address, often talked to consumers as "savvy neighbors," and invoked the privilege of the upper classes to sell goods to working- and middle-class consumers. The idea that using a particular product would help consumers be upwardly mobile became ever more important as the century progressed.

Discussing the advertising of the 1920s and 1930s, Marchand describes how advertising professionals drew consumers into the world constructed by advertising. He claims that advertising presented twentieth-century "parables," short, melodramatic vignettes that seem disinterested and could thus sell goods more readily. While Marchand notes differences in the advertising of the relatively affluent 1920s and that of the 1930s, the parables he names can be seen in contemporary advertising as well. For example, "The Parable of the Democracy of Goods" promises that no American is shut out of the good life. A particularly poignant example appeared in a 1933 issue of the *Saturday Evening Post*. In this ad, a working-class couple stops to look at a luxurious new sedan and the young man tells his girlfriend, "Anyway his tires are just like mine." Marchand writes that the ad "demonstrated how disappointed ambitions might be allayed by taking to heart the parable of the Democracy of Goods" (p. 294).

As Americans became used to and accepted the self-serving and emotional rhetoric of advertisers, two types of events challenged advertising's new success. The introduction of a new medium, radio, and the two world wars, each in their own ways, presented hurdles that advertising professionals needed to surmount.

BROADCAST ADVERTISING

When radio broadcasting began in 1920 no one knew how to make money from it. Manufacturers and the advertising industry wanted nothing to do with the new medium. How could one tell how many people were listening? Advertising expenditures, always difficult to justify, seemed to dissipate in the air with broadcast advertising. But radio professionals worked hard to convince the ad agencies that advertising over the radio could work.

Before radio could become part of the familiar advertising environment, it had to reach a national audience with a unified message. The push for advertising supported the development of network radio, which overcame technical problems by sending programs over telephone wires for rebroadcast by local affiliates. The first regional advertisers who hired anonymous recording stars in the 1920s to advertise their products by assuming their names—the Clicquot Club Eskimos, the Ipana Troubadours, the Gold Dust Twins—gave way to larger manufacturers seeking a national audience with well-known vaudevillians like Eddie Cantor, Ed Wynn, and Edgar Bergen. Rather than taking the name of their sponsors, each radio performer in the 1930s worked on a show wholly sponsored by one advertiser. To give them a financial stake in the new medium, broadcasters gave advertising agencies control over the production of the programs, and thus they and their clients had enormous influence over radio programming.

The advertisers and their agencies believed they knew the pattern over-the-air commercials should take. In order to accommodate the advertisements properly, the form of radio programs became inflexible. Some of the artists used the rigid form as a spur to creativity, like poets working within a strict sonnet form, but for most it cut off programming possibilities. Radio became a way to sell products. Programs filled the time between commercials and joined commercials in trying, sometimes successfully, sometimes not, to manipulate the audience, not to entertain, educate, or uplift, unless those actions would help sell a product. Despite its drawbacks, commercialized national radio did offer listeners some benefits. The vaudeville performers who flocked to radio in the 1930s brought the audience a high quality of entertainment, some variety, and a sense of belonging to a national audience, but listeners missed a sense of connection to the performers and had no control over programming.

In the 1950s television took over radio's commercialized form and its premier place as the advertising medium of choice for major national advertisers. In the beginning, one sponsor took responsibility for financing and producing each television show, just as they had in radio. Problems with sponsor interference and the growing importance of "impartial" news programming led television networks to take over program production from advertising agencies and move to a system of "spot" advertisements. Advertising agencies became, once again, experts at placing advertisements and added new client services, primarily in research and demographics, to make up for the loss of broadcast production. Through all these changes, the federal government, which regulated broadcasting in the "public interest," acquiesced in a commercialized, basically unregulated broadcasting system. Federal regulations did not extend to advertisements and thus supported the development of a fully commercialized system.

GOVERNMENT SUPPORT OF ADVERTISING

The federal government often acted to entrench advertising as crucial to American life. During the world wars the government provided important support to advertising, and its intervention saved and strengthened the advertising industry. Before both wars advertising faced important challenges, but with the federal government's help the advertising industry beat back any opposition. The advertising profession aimed both to help win the wars and help win the war for consumer acceptance of advertising.

When the United States entered World War I in 1917, advertising professionals worried that the public did not perceive them as professionals and that progressives hoped to dismantle the industry. At the same time President Woodrow Wilson needed to mobilize public opinion for a war that many found, given U.S. isolationist preferences, unnecessary. Wilson chose the progressive investigative journalist George Creel to head the Committee on Public Information. The CPI informed the public about the assistance the government needed to win the war. In his book *How We Advertised America*

Advertising Television. Extensive advertising campaigns accompanied the introduction of television. A Motorola advertisement illustrates not only the continued emphasis on the consumer, rather than the product, but also the way in which advertising positioned television as a central part of the family's activities. COURTESY MOTOROLA INC. AND HARTMAN CENTER FOR SALES, ADVERTISING, AND MARKETING HISTORY, DUKE UNIVERSITY

(1920), Creel wrote, "The work of the committee was so distinctively in the nature of an advertising campaign, though shot through and through with an evangelical quality, that we turned almost instinctively to the advertising profession for advice and assistance." Some advertising professionals felt that, as a mark of respect, the government should pay for their services. But the advertising industry ended up offering their services for free, and their work helped boost advertising's reputation. One of

their most memorable activities involved calling on commercial artists to design and execute propaganda posters in the style of prewar ads.

The war both strengthened and changed advertising. Creel, who early in the war had thought of advertising men as "plausible pirates," came to believe that his committee's use of advertising men gave advertising "the dignity of a profession." After the war advertising professionals moved even farther away from the view of consumers as rational and toward an even greater emphasis on persuasion and irrationality as advertising tactics.

Despite their success in World War I, most advertisers feared the approach of World War II. The consumer movement of the 1930s had attacked advertising because it raised prices and lied about products and had called on the government for help. War meant fewer goods to sell and valid reasons for not buying, and it seemingly brought a dissonance between a wartime spirit of self-denial and advertising's spirit of self-fulfillment.

In addition, government economic measures to extend wartime mobilization might have constrained the advertising industry. Companies wanted to put untaxed wartime profits into advertising aimed at postwar consumption, but an excess profits tax could cut all advertising. In addition, the government controlled the prices of most things during the war and could have disallowed advertising costs in computing maximum prices. But the government moved slowly and advertising soon established itself as important to the war effort. Things might have been very different if advertising had been banned during the war. Instead, the industry again emerged strengthened with profits poured into it with the government's blessings.

Companies making only war goods used wartime advertisements to keep their names in front of the public. Many such ads conflated war aims and consumption. One ad, paid for by an insurance company, asked: "Will you ever own another car? Another radio? Another gleaming refrigerator? Those who live under dictators merely dream of such possessions" (quoted in F. W. Fox, p. 27). According to the ads, war was fought to give people the freedom and opportunity to consume, and the ability to make all those consumer goods ensured an American victory. "Shouldn't it occur to you," the Westinghouse Company asked the Axis, "that a fellow can't win when he's fighting against a nation with the inventiveness and resources to produce weapons like this?" (Fox, p. 41). So the war bailed the advertising industry out of its difficulties with the American public, and advertising professionals again emerged convinced that the role of advertising was to "persuade" and to sell a way of life based on consumption.

It is ironic that during war, when advertising might seem at its most superfluous, that the U.S. government worked to support the advertising industry. The actions of the federal government during both world wars ensured that advertising became a permanent part of the American landscape. Advertising's seemingly natural, hegemonic posi-

tion was the result of careful work by the advertising industry with the aid of the government.

POSTWAR ADVERTISING

After World War II advertising agencies and advertising professionals came to stand, within American culture at large, for a conformist and consumerist impulse. "The man in the gray flannel suit" epitomized advertising's shortcomings as well as those of contemporary culture (despite the fact that in the novel of that title the "man" worked in public relations rather than advertising). Many advertising men, returning from wartime military service, found their old profession shallow. In the novel *The Hucksters* (1946), by Frederic Wakeman, an advertising executive tells the hero that veterans "don't seem able to readjust to this business. Object to irritating radio commercials, that sort of thing." Popular writers like Vance Packard, in his book *The Hidden Persuaders* (1957), joined with academics like the mass culture critics, influenced by the Frankfurt school of sociology, to complain that advertising was no better than propaganda.

Advertising agency professionals were, in many ways, the ultimate modern men, leading the consumption culture. Popular fiction took special notice of the double selling in which all advertising professionals engaged: they first sold their services to clients and then turned around and sold a product to consumers. In *The Hucksters*, one character explains:

> I hate this job. . . . A man cooks up some fat and presses it into a bar of soap. He perfumes it. Wraps it up fancy. Then he needs a barker to sell this miraculous combination of herbs, roots and berries. So he calls me in to bark for him. But not at him. God no, dear, not that. So all I gotta do is bark real good and if he starts needling me, I also gotta be careful to keep a civil tongue in his conference room. (pp. 42–43)

Admen lived uncertain lives and, according to the myth, spent every waking minute pitching. Their insecurity (clients could leave, consumers could refuse to buy), their need to ingratiate themselves with both clients and consumers, and their constant attempts to influence the behavior of others made advertising professionals metaphors for life in the 1950s.

Thirteen novels set in advertising agencies and published between 1946 and 1958 criticized the dishonesty of the advertising business; the conformity of behavior and background called for by the advertising industry; the emptiness of consumption; and the meaninglessness of the advertising profession. The main characters of these fictionalized accounts were disillusioned advertising guys who wanted to write a novel while all the authors were disillusioned advertising guys who did write a novel. Herman Wouk, whose first novel, *Aurora Dawn* (1947), was set in an ad agency, found advertising work boring and stupid. Of his hero, Wouk wrote:

> Andrew was in the sales department of the Republic Broadcasting Company, and his job was to see that cordiality was maintained between the sponsors who paid such large sums for radio time, the network which gave them its gargantuan technical facilities in return, and the advertising agencies which acted as middlemen. He was assigned the supervision of several programs and kept a watchful eye on the hothouse blossom of personal relations in each of them, moistening and fertilizing as necessary. The requirements of his task were nine parts likableness to one part intelligence; if a young man began to exceed the proposition in favor of intelligence he was on his way to dismissal or an executive post, depending on how well his superiors enjoyed his company. (p. 41)

In the 1960s advertising professionals found a way to turn these criticisms into successful advertising.

In *The Conquest of Cool: Business Culture, Counterculture, and the Rise of Hip Consumerism* (1997), Thomas Frank outlines how the advertising of the 1960s did not simply co-opt the counterculture, did not just use symbols available in the culture—hippies, flowers, revolution—to sell products. The story, he explains, involved changes under way in the advertising industry even before the cultural changes usually lumped under the rubric of "the sixties." Frank described the criticisms of business and advertising in the 1950s that came from within the industry as "a critique of their own industries, of over-organization and creative dullness, that had much in common with the critique of mass society which gave rise to the counterculture" (p. 9).

Within the advertising industry, new and smaller agencies that were organized differently came to the fore and emphasized the creative side of advertising. Bill Bernbach, the prototypical adman of the 1960s, saw advertising as an art, not a science, and complained about the previous decade's advertising professionals who proposed rules for successful advertising.

Whimsical advertisements often made fun of advertising and consumption while proposing "hip" consumerism as a proper response to a mass culture critique. The first and perhaps most famous example of this type of advertising was Doyle Dane Bernbach's "Think Small" campaign for Volkswagen in 1960. These ads seemingly broke all the rules of automobile advertising, using humor, "honesty," self-deprecation, and simple graphics to change the image of Volkswagens from Nazi cars to vehicles for alienated consumers.

The "cool" affected by advertising in the 1960s has not disappeared. People still distrust advertising and are attracted to ads that seem to share their distrust. Each succeeding generation of advertising agents rediscovers this formula first used in the 1960s. As it always has, advertising embraced and was embraced by the surrounding culture, whose cadences advertising adopted.

CONCLUSION

Advertising grew along with industrialization and then contributed to the change from a producer to a consumer culture. As consumer culture changes in a time of deindustrialization, for some and in some places, advertising adapts. Other factors that influenced advertising include the technology available for reaching consumers. Newspapers, magazines, radio, and then television became advertising-driven media, and the Internet seems poised to undergo the same transformation. At once the expression and the power behind an industrialized consumption economy, advertising remains a key site for understanding American history and culture.

See also **The Print Revolution** *(volume 1);* **Women and Family in the Suburban Age; The Design of the Familiar; The Culture of Self-Improvement; The World According to Hollywood; Popular Culture in the Public Arena** *(volume 2);* **Success; Consumerism; Individualism and the Self; Family; Culture for Mass Audiences; Almanacs and Ephemeral Literature; The Internet and Electronic Communications; Myth and Symbol** *(in this volume); and other articles in this section.*

BIBLIOGRAPHY

Books

Appel, Joseph. *The Business Biography of John Wanamaker.* New York, 1930.

Barnouw, Eric. *The Sponsor: Notes on a Modern Potentate.* New York, 1979.

Creel, George. *How We Advertised America.* New York, 1920.

Fox, Frank W. *Madison Avenue Goes to War: The Strange Military Career of American Advertising, 1941–1945.* Provo, Utah, 1975.

Fox, Stephen. *The Mirror Makers: A History of American Advertising and Its Creators.* New York, 1984.

Frank, Thomas. *The Conquest of Cool: Business Culture, Counterculture, and the Rise of Hip Consumerism.* Chicago, 1997.

Lears, Jackson. *Fables of Abundance: A Cultural History of Advertising in America.* New York, 1994.

Marchand, Roland. *Advertising the American Dream: Making Way for Modernity, 1920–1940.* Berkeley, Calif., 1985.

Maxwell, Bruce, and Michael Jacobson. *Marketing Disease to Hispanics.* Washington, D.C., 1989.

Ohmann, Richard M. *Selling Culture: Magazines, Markets, and Class at the Turn of the Century.* New York, 1996.

Pope, Daniel. *The Making of Modern Advertising.* New York, 1983.

Presbrey, Frank. *The History and Development of Advertising.* Garden City, N.Y., 1929.

Schudson, Michael. *Advertising, the Uneasy Persuasion: Its Dubious Impact on American Society.* New York, 1984.

Strasser, Susan. *Satisfaction Guaranteed: The Making of the American Mass Market.* New York, 1989.

Williams, Judith. *Decoding Advertisements: Ideology and Meaning in Advertising.* New York, 1978.

Critiques

Chase, Stuart, and F. J. Schlink. *Your Money's Worth: A Study in the Waste of the Consumer's Dollar.* New York, 1928.

Packard, Vance. *The Hidden Persuaders.* New York, 1957.

Rorty, James. *Our Master's Voice: Advertising.* New York, 1934.

Autobiographies

Calkins, Earnest Elmo. *The Advertising Man.* New York, 1922.

Della Femina, Jerry. *From Those Wonderful Folks Who Gave You Pearl Harbor: Front Line Dispatches from the Advertising War.* New York, 1970.

Fitz-Gibbon, Bernice. *Macy's, Gimbel's and Me: How to Earn $90,000 in Retail Advertising.* New York, 1967.

Hopkins, Claude C. *My Life in Advertising.* Lincolnwood, Ill., 1998.

Ogilvy, David. *Confessions of an Advertising Man.* Rev. ed. New York, 1988.

Reeves, Rosser. *Reality in Advertising.* New York, 1961.

Woodward, Helen Rosen. *It's An Art.* New York, 1938.

Novels

Green, Gerald. *The Last Angry Man.* New York, 1956.

Hodgins, Eric. *Mr. Blandings Builds His Dream House.* New York, 1946.

Kelly, James. *The Insider.* New York, 1958.

Morgan, Al. *The Great Man.* New York, 1955.

Wakeman, Frederic. *The Hucksters.* New York, 1946.

Wilson, Sloan. *The Man in the Gray Flannel Suit.* New York, 1955.

Wouk, Herman. *Aurora Dawn.* New York, 1947.

RHETORIC

Jill Swiencicki

Before the rise of print literacy in conveying public sentiment, the oral tradition of public, persuasive speech was the basis of civic and cultural expression in America. Since the eighteenth century, Euro-American students received formal training in the skills of public address, and used it for judicial, deliberative, and epideictic purposes: to argue in court, preach in the pulpit, represent individual or civic interests, and to commemorate an important person or event. Those who couldn't or didn't receive formal training in the persuasive arts read the elocution (speech and delivery) manuals that proliferated in the eighteenth and nineteenth centuries, and practiced their skills in the home, the tavern, the town hall, and at their voluntary associations. Originally the study and practice of rhetoric was limited to those who had access to the public sphere of rational debate: white, propertied men. But as the public began to diversify socially, politically, and economically in the antebellum period, those who were excluded from public participation—women, African Americans, and Native Americans, to name a few—demanded to be heard. In the process they created rich, new rhetorical practices and diversified the spaces in which rhetoric occurred.

The history of rhetoric in the United States betrays a tension between two purposes: using persuasive, public speech to unify citizens around issues of national importance, and using speech to express the needs of individuals or specific identity groups. Scholars have bemoaned the decline of the unified civic sphere that was transformed with the rise of a more diverse public, and with the rise of professional and mass media cultures that fragmented the civic body, hailing audiences as consumers, not citizens. Others argue that the desire for civic unity was a desire to use rhetoric to justify the exclusion of those who for so long did not qualify for citizen status and that this "ideal" actually silenced the interests and rights of those groups. But rather than seeing a decline in civic culture, still others believe that civic rhetoric found new avenues for expression in the twentieth century in emergent activist and visual rhetorics. Further, rhetoric as an intellectual pursuit has also been invigorated by the awareness that rhetoric does not just help express ideas, but actually creates knowledge. Rhetoric, more than creating eloquent speech, is the process through which people create meaning in language. A glance at some of the main genres within oratorical practice—religious, civic, professional, reform, and visual rhetorics—shows not just changing strategies for persuasion, but the changing values, beliefs, and knowledges of American culture.

RELIGIOUS RHETORICS

The Puritan Tradition Religious rhetorics offered a public forum for sharing the ideas and sentiment of a culture since the early settlements of North America by Euro-Americans. Religious, cultural, and political interests each came together forcefully in the Puritan rhetoric of the seventeenth century. The Puritan tradition is frequently left out of rhetorical histories because this English Protestant sect was notoriously hostile to the concept of purposeful strategies of persuading an audience. Puritans followed the well-accepted approach of the French philosopher Peter Ramus, who insisted that rhetoric was merely an ornament for speech that, in the wrong hands, could obscure truth. Ramus relegated rhetoric to the canon of style and elevated dialectic as the inventive art of disputation. This approach to rhetoric marginalized its role in European universities and scholarly circles throughout the period. Nonetheless, in their approach to public address, Puritans created fascinating and enduring rhetorical genres.

Puritan rhetoric explores events occurring in the community through biblical knowledge in order to locate the appropriate public response to them. In Puritan interpretations of political, religious, or national events, God is in control, the people are instruments of God's plan, and the people are encouraged to work, not for individual reward, but to strengthen the communal identity. As John Winthrop argued in his speech aboard the *Arbella* in 1630, "We must delight in each other, make others' conditions our own, rejoyce together, mourn together, labor and suffer together, always having before our eyes our community as members of the same body." This ethical appeal to communal values was perceived as being important for survival on earth. Later, in a 1741 sermon titled "Sinners in the Hands of an Angry God" in Enfield, Connecticut, Jonathan Edwards made a pathetic (or emotional) appeal that linked communal values and behavior to religious salvation. Edwards's vivid imagery of the sufferings of hell was aimed at the "unconverted" members of the audience:

> The use of this awful subject may be for awakening unconverted persons in this congregation. This that you have heard is the case of every one of you that are out of Christ—That world of misery, that lake of burning brimstone, is extended abroad under you. There is the dreadful pit of the glowing flames of the wrath of God; there is hell's wide gaping mouth open; and you have nothing to stand upon, nor any thing to take hold of; there is nothing between you and hell but the air; it is only the power and mere pleasure of God that holds you up.

One way that Puritans expressed this collective struggle is through the rhetoric of the "jeremiad," or lamenting religious prophecy. A jeremiad is a speech or text that accounts for the misfortunes of an era as a just penalty for great social and moral evils, but holds out hope for changes that will bring a happier future. Another rhetorical genre that was central to the Puritan culture is the record of the individual's quest for the experience of grace, or the "conversion narrative." Conversion narratives explore whether or not the individual has been accepted into the divine life, an acceptance signified by psychological changes which the autobiographer comes to recognize in his or her past experience. The jeremiad and the conversion narrative follow very clear rhetorical formulas and do the cultural work of making the incoherence of the New World, and internal, personal desires, coherent.

Religious Awakenings
The republican period was a time of the great spiritual revivals that transformed the culture and offered a fundamental challenge to the Puritan preaching system. These revivals prompted debate about the people's voice—its provenance and the scope and nature of its representativeness. The Great Awakening was a grassroots religious movement that democratized religion by shifting the balance of power between minister and congregation. It offered a direct challenge to clerical authority in stating that authority to preach depended on experiential knowledge. A new class of preachers emerged—women, people of color, and children—to preach the glories to the colonies of the promise of regeneration. Its dramatic, emotionally disruptive, colloquial, extemporaneous speech offered a religious rhetoric whose transformation carried into the political and intellectual realms. Such an experience was offered by the British evangelist George Whitefield, who attracted more than 20,000 to his 1740 Boston Common sermon. "The grand itinerant," Whitefield traveled through towns, rural outposts, and cities offering crowds a "new birth." This insistence that God was accessible to all intensified the revelatory aspects of religious experience. This rhetorical shift privileged personal experience and emotion over formal knowledge. Whitefield's extempore preaching aroused audiences who responded to expressive vernacular over orthodox scholasticism, and his speech was marked by "roarings, agonies, screamings, tremblings, dropping down, ravings." This enthusiasm—eliciting response from worshipers rather than silence—is part of a revolutionary ideology of participation.

If eighteenth-century Calvinists such as George Whitefield and Jonathan Edwards stressed the sinful nature of humans and their inability to overcome this nature without direct action from God, nineteenth-century evangelists like Lyman Beecher emphasized the sinfulness of humans but encouraged them to embrace moral action. By the 1820s evangelism had become one of the most dynamic and important cultural and rhetorical forces in American life. Ministers asked participants to prepare for the millennium and Jesus' Second Coming. Central to this rhetoric is the process of conversion: the ability to see God's power and mercy and receive the promise of salvation. Religious revivals were the vehicles for provoking conversions, eroding earlier notions of predestination with the hope for universal salvation. The remnants of this genre can be seen in contemporary mass religious revivals, the most obvious being the mass meetings of the evangelist Billy Graham. For decades Graham has filled churches, football stadiums, and convention centers, "work[ing] diligently in calling men and women to repent of their sins and receive the Lord Jesus Christ into their hearts by faith."

The "Middling" Style
In the nineteenth century, pulpit rhetoric combined high and low speech, in-

cluding elements of the Puritan plain style and the emotional, audience-oriented speech of evangelism. An exemplar of this "middling" style of oratory is Henry Ward Beecher. A brother to the writers Harriet Beecher Stowe and Catharine Beecher, Henry became a preacher and settled in what became the largest and most well-known parish in the Northeast, Plymouth Church of Brooklyn, New York. At Plymouth Church and on the lecture circuit, Beecher's sermons combined the refined with the spectacular and the crude, incorporating political, popular, and reform-minded issues into his sermons. For example, on several occasions between 1848 and 1860, he conducted well-publicized mock slave auctions at Plymouth Church where the congregation secured the freedom of the slaves. This rhetorical stunt was meant to demonstrate to the nation the barbarity of selling people who had been created, according to the Bible, "in the image of God." His *Yale Lectures on Preaching* (1872–1874) expresses an oratorical ideal that combines such rhetorical spectacle and immediacy with a reverence for the vocation:

> A preacher is in some degree a reproduction of the truth in personal form. The truth must exist in him as a living experience, a glowing enthusiasm, an intense reality. The word of God in the Book is a dead letter. It is paper, type, and ink. In the preacher the word becomes again as it was when first spoken by prophet, priest, or apostle. It springs up in him as if it were first kindled in his heart, and he were moved by the Holy Ghost to give it forth. He is so moved.

The debate between spoken versus written rhetoric has raged since ancient times, most notably in Plato's *Phaedrus,* with Socrates siding firmly with the spoken word. Here Beecher expresses a tension between spoken and written rhetoric that reflects the increasing influence of print culture on oratorical culture in this period. Beecher insists on the ability of speech to access truth in ways that "the dead letter," in his estimation, never can.

CIVIC AND PROFESSIONAL RHETORICS

The Citizen-Orator The rhetorical ideal of the revolutionary and republican periods was the citizen-orator: the man who rises up from the crowd to eloquently argue on behalf of the national interest. Ralph Waldo Emerson exalted this representative figure, whom he saw exemplified in such diverse orators as John Quincy Adams, Daniel Webster, and Patrick Henry. Twice in his 1858 essay, "Eloquence," for example, Emerson asked his audience to envi-

sion a packed town meeting, one where a solitary man rises from among the restless crowd and, through his eloquent oration, manages to win its sympathies and unite what was once a hopelessly fragmented group around an issue of civic importance. In these scenes, eloquence emerges within a civic occasion where the citizen-turned-orator takes the crisis as an opportunity to move the audience to his will. When this happens, when the orator persuades or, as Emerson said, "defeats" his audience, then "for the time, his exceeding life throws all other gifts into shade . . . and yet how every listener gladly consents to be nothing in his presence, and to share this surprising emanation, and be steeped and ennobled in the new wine of his eloquence." For Emerson the virtue of eloquence lay in this transfer of power: in the orator's ability to represent the civic body and unify its disparate interests.

This expression of the importance of the orator can be explained with a glance at the oratorical culture of the period, in which the hierarchical social relations that were dominant in the late eighteenth century began eroding in the nineteenth. Such relations were formed in three main social institutions: the family, the local community, and the church. All three were traditional, vertical institutions in which the lines of force radiated downward, from the father, the elected officials, and the minister, and the prevailing pattern of social relationships was authority and deference. To be an eloquent man at this time was to be an authority and that status was achieved depending on how close one was to the powerful centers of those institutions. From the early to mid-nineteenth century, as the population rapidly expanded, as the vote was extended to include all white men, as social institutions such as the church lost central authority, and as the economy shifted from an agricultural to a commercial base, concerns grew about how the diversity of economic and social interests would or could be unified. Social critics wondered if the division of labor in commercial cultures destroyed civic-mindedness, with "citizens" replaced by "experts." Leading figures of the oratorical culture like Emerson feared that ethos—the belief in the speaker's ethical strength and virtue—was disappearing in favor of playing different roles to meet the differing needs of one's audience and their interests.

Professional Culture By the mid-nineteenth century, sites of rhetorical expression began to shift from the space of political and civic concerns to

That man over there says that women need to be helped into carriages, and lifted over ditches, and to have the best place everywhere. Nobody helps me any best place. And ain't I a woman? Look at me! Look at my arm! I have plowed I have planted and I have gathered into barns. And no man could head me. And ain't I a woman? I could work as much, and eat as much as a man—when I could get it—and bear the lash as well. And ain't I a woman? I have borne children and seen most of them sold into slavery, and when I cried out with a mother's grief, none but Jesus heard me. And ain't I a woman?

Source: "Ain't I a Woman" speech delivered by Sojourner Truth at the Women's Rights Convention of 1851 in Akron, Ohio (Logan, *With Pen and Voice,* p. 24)

professional and individual ones. This transition is most evident in the rise of the lyceum movement, or public lecturing. In the 1830s public lectures on a variety of topics began to emerge, and by the 1840s a full-blown lecture system was in place throughout the Northeast and into the Midwest. Between 1840 and 1860 more than three thousand lectures were advertised in newspapers across the country on an encyclopedic range of topics, from astronomy to the art of conversation to "the true mission of women." As a public event, lectures were expected to incorporate information "useful to all and offensive to none," in a neutral or civic space. The lecturers were usually men of national status— clergymen, such as Henry Ward Beecher, college presidents or professors, journalists, reformers, public intellectuals such as Ralph Waldo Emerson, and businessmen, such as the famous showman P. T. Barnum.

The lecture movement promoted self-culture, a space where those who did not attend college or have social connections could get information they needed to get ahead in new business and commercial spheres. This was vital in a period in which the organization of trades and professions of the eighteenth century were dissolving and the bureaucratic professional structures of the last part of the nineteenth century were not yet in place. With no clear sense of how to achieve upward mobility or eco-

nomic stability, the useful knowledge of the lecture was broad and expansive enough to promise audiences the hold on life that their aspirations for "betterment" and "success" seemed to require. While usually frequented by young men from urban centers, lyceums attracted diverse audiences of women and men, from farmers to shopkeepers to professors. Knowledge was considered a public commodity to be consumed and made available to all, and the system could respond to demands for the newest kinds of knowledge available. Public lectures were public rituals that instructed and inspired, creating both local publics and the sense of belonging to a national public. This was the case when newspapers started to respond to the public's desire for press coverage of lectures, and speakers began to be publicized in newspapers, competing with the theater and concerts for audiences. In professional culture, rhetoric was moved from the bar, pulpit, senate, and university and into the lecture hall, theater, and mixed site of entertainment, edification, and professional development.

REFORM RHETORICS

Abolitionism Antebellum America was a period of cultural expression most vital in areas of political, social, and moral reform. Rhetoric was the main vehicle used in attempts by disenfranchised and oppressed people to assert their positions and gain social power. Nowhere was this more apparent than in efforts to abolish chattel slavery. Exemplary in this rhetoric was the work of the white abolitionist William Lloyd Garrison and his weekly paper, the *Liberator.* The antislavery movement of the 1830s, of which Garrison was a driving force, worked actively to win audiences to the sympathies of antislavery and promote legal, social, and economic change. Frederick Douglass describes Garrison speaking at an antislavery meeting in Nantucket:

It was an effort of unequal power, sweeping down, like a very tornado, every opposing barrier, whether sentiment or opinion. For a moment, he possessed that almost fabulous inspiration, often referred to but seldom attained, in which a public meeting is transformed, as it were, into a single individuality— the orator wielding a thousand heads and hearts at once, and by the simple majesty of his all controlling thought, converting his hearers into the express image of his own soul. That night there were at least one thousand Garrisonians, in Nantucket! (*My Bondage and My Freedom*, p. 358)

Garrison instituted a lecture tour that featured former slaves telling the stories of their experiences.

One of those lecture agents was the young Frederick Douglass. Douglass was encouraged by Garrison to show the "stripes" (or scars) on his back from the beatings he received in order to elicit the audience's pathos, or emotions, on the subject. In *My Bondage and My Freedom* (1855) Douglass stated his displeasure at this request. Interestingly, a few years later, at the 1851 Women's Rights Convention in Akron, Ohio, Sojourner Truth, a free black woman and one-time evangelist, purposefully used a rhetoric of embodiment to move her mostly white audience. These protests of unjust laws and affirmation of black experience found rich soil in the black church, and offered precursors for the nonviolent oratory of Martin Luther King Jr. and the diverse oratory of the civil rights movement, and the later Black Arts and Black Power movements, in which black culture, arts, and political aspirations were validated and expressed.

Women's Rights   Antislavery conventions and societies were originally segregated by sex, but they became a space for women activists and orators to do important cultural work for the cause: signing and circulating petitions, collecting donations, and even speaking publicly. This form of cultural expression was controversial. For example, in 1838 Pennsylvania Hall in Philadelphia was burned to the ground when an angry mob discovered that the first speeches on antislavery would be given by both African American and Euro-American women.

In their rhetoric, women often made the analogy between the condition of enslaved black persons and all women. This is obvious in the rhetoric of the Seneca Falls Convention of 1848 in Seneca Falls, New York, where Elizabeth Cady Stanton first presented her "Declaration of Sentiments": "The history of mankind is a history of repeated injuries and usurpations on the part of man toward woman, having in direct object the establishment of an absolute tyranny over her." Here Stanton rewrote the Declaration of Independence with more inclusive language, savvily understanding the ways that language creates and reflects social reality. Twentieth-century organizations such as the Feminist Majority and the National Organization for Women (NOW) have maintained and furthered such vigilant cultural critiques with rhetorics that connect rhetoric with action on behalf of women's rights.

American Indian Reform Rhetorics   The rhetorical work of Native Americans has flourished as cultural expression, survival tactics, and critiques of Euro-American power structures. With the rise of Indian boarding schools which enforced cultural assimilation through Western literacy practices, indigenous practices of textual and oral rhetoric postcontact have been both a colonialist affliction and a means of agency in the public sphere. An example of this rhetorical position is seen in the *Cherokee Phoenix,* the first newspaper published by American Indians. The paper was typeset in both the Roman alphabet and Cherokee syllabary and was distributed in the Cherokee Nation, the eastern United states, and in parts of Europe. It provided news of Cherokee progress in farming, education, and industry, and in one sense was a tool of propaganda to resist harassment from United States government officials and prevent further removals and encroachments upon their culture. Elias Boudinot was the paper's editor and a well-known, eloquent Cherokee speaker.

The Piute Indian Sarah Winnemucca Hopkins also occupied a dual role within white and Indian cultures, rhetorically positioning herself within both for the benefit of her people. In her autobiography, *Life among the Piutes: Their Wrongs and Claims* (1883), Hopkins detailed the rhetorical aims of mediating between her people and the white soldiers and government officials during military disputes, as well as arguing for her people before Congress. In the twentieth century the American Indian Movement (AIM) furthered such activist approaches in its rhetorical stances with the government, occupying government and state buildings, staging sit-ins and protests, and engaging debate. In the late twentieth century, native rhetorics took the form of direct legal debate and contest within the courts over struggles for sovereignty and land rights, health issues on reservations, and projects for economic agency and educational opportunities. A leading political and rhetorical figure in these struggles is Wilma Mankiller. As a Cherokee leader, Mankiller's rhetoric relies on ethical (ethos) and logical (logos) appeals to argue for native rights, as she did in an April 1993 speech at Sweet Briar College:

> If you look at history from a native perspective, and I know that's very difficult for you to do, the most powerful, or one of the most powerful countries in the world as a policy first tried to wipe us off the face of the earth. And then, failing that, instituted a number of policies to make sure that we didn't exist in 1993 as a culturally distinct group of people, and yet here we are. Not only do we exist, but we're thriving and we're growing, and we're learning now to trust our own thinking again and dig our way out. So it was that tenacity that I felt we could build on.

Temperance   The largest reform membership of the eighteenth, nineteenth, and early twentieth centuries belonged to temperance movements, which called for restraint from drinking, reform of drinkers, and at various points the prohibition of the manufacture and sale of alcohol. Temperance rhetoric often combined the pious with the profane, bringing rhetorical reform into line with or competing with the theater for audiences. This is especially true of the Washingtonian temperance movement of the 1840s, which aimed to pull young, urban men from the theaters and billiard houses and into the meetinghalls where "respectable" people went to associate among those who pledged to stay sober and aimed at "rising in the world." "Experience speeches"—or confessions of past intemperance in which speakers pledged to reform— became rhetorical centerpieces of meetings. The following is an excerpt from the experience speech of John Gough, the most popular temperance orator of the period:

> I related how I was once respectable and happy, and had a home; but that now I was a houseless, miserable, scathed, diseased, and blighted outcast from society. I said, scarce a hope remained to me of ever becoming that which I once was; but having promised to sign the pledge, I had determined not to break my word, and would now affix my name to it. I . . . signed the total abstinence pledge, and resolved to free myself from the inexorable tyrant— rum.

The rhetoric of the experiential meeting continues in present-day twelve-step programs such as Alcoholics Anonymous, in which groups compose safe spaces in which to share stories and gain emotional strength.

Mass Meetings The mass political meetings of Jacksonian America unnerved those longing for more genteel forms of civic participation. A fear of "mobocracy," or mob rule, emerged, suggesting that the power of the masses was less reliable than the wisdom of a solitary, eloquent orator. But the mass groups of men and women that united publicly for an issue created a democratic body that was able to have rhetorical impact through spectacle, size, and suggestive force. Mass visibility was useful in the labor movements of turn-of-the-century America, and in the late twentieth century this practice of mass meeting was revived by African Americans who took this rhetorical tack to represent themselves against the misrepresentations and abuses they endured from the government and its social policies. A series of "million"-person marches in various cities in the late 1990s—the Million Man March, the Million Woman March, and the Million Youth March—became statements of self-help, pride, and refusal to be represented as "unfit" parents, youths, and citizens. In spring 2000, the "million"-march theme was appropriated by the Million Mom March, a group of mostly middle- to upper-middle-class working mothers who were dissatisfied with the government's approach to gun safety laws and wanted their size and visibility to strike a powerful rhetorical note with politicians. The mass meeting, like most reform rhetorics, complicates the rhetorical concept of *kairos*, which means appropriate or timely speech—speech that fits the language to the subject and to the audience it is directed to at just the right time. Rhetorics that aim to end injustice are often accused of being inappropriate, unruly, or untimely. Martin Luther King Jr. powerfully addresses this point in his "Letter from Birmingham Jail":

> We know through painful experience that freedom is never voluntarily given by the oppressor; it must be demanded by the oppressed. Frankly, I have yet to engage in a direct-action campaign that was "well timed" in the view of those who have not suffered unduly from the disease of segregation. For years now I have heard the word "Wait!" It rings in the ear of every Negro with piercing familiarity. This "Wait" has almost always meant "Never." We must come to see, with one of our distinguished jurists, that "justice too long delayed is justice denied."

Reformist rhetorics create their own kairotic moment, interrupting the status quo and often creating radical change—and radical rhetorics—in the process.

VISUAL RHETORICS

Does a building have a rhetoric? What about a website? Can these entities have persuasive effects? In the twentieth century the focus of rhetorical practice and study had shifted from simply the spoken and written art of persuasion to any cultural artifact that shapes and determines meaning. Such approaches are less invested in re-creating the nineteenth-century civic tradition than inventing new kinds of rhetorical action based in an ever-expanding visual, technological, and media culture. These persuasive media have in common the predominance of the visual in creating and expressing knowledge. As the art and media critic John Berger argued:

> Seeing comes before words. The child looks and recognizes before it can speak. . . . It is seeing which establishes our place in the surrounding world; we explain that world with words, but words can never

undo the fact that we are surrounded by it. The relation between what we see and what we know is never settled.

New rhetorical genres have been created within a vast visual culture, requiring what scholars call visual literacy, or the ability to understand and make visual statements, sensitizing people to the world around them and to the relationships and systems of power of which subjects are a part. Such rhetorics often blend influences from popular culture, the mass media, and burgeoning computer technology. Some of these visual rhetorics have been taken up by social activist movements, such as those associated with feminism and gay and lesbian activism, producing powerful and effective reformist activism.

Activist Political Rhetoric   Activists in the late twentieth century were looking for what the AIDS activist Douglas Crimp called "engaged, activist aesthetic practices" and found them in a variety of visual rhetorical strategies aimed at promoting awareness and action. Some of the most groundbreaking of them include the rhetorics surrounding the outbreak of the HIV virus and the mobilization of action around breast cancer, as these groups enacted consciousness-raising through provocative visual imagery that could be consumed in public places: the subway, the billboard, the art museum.

In the twenty-first century, one such group is ACT UP, "a nonpartisan group of diverse individuals united in anger and committed to direct action to end the AIDS crisis." ACT UP is best known for its poster of a pink triangle with the caption "Silence = Death." The pink triangle, the symbol of homosexual persecution during the Nazi period and a positive symbol of gay identity since the 1960s, uses a rhetoric of historical comparison and aesthetic directness and simplicity to persuade viewers into action. The pink triangle references a past oppression and links it to a present crisis, creating historical links and associations that have powerful rhetorical resonance. This strategy of intertextuality—a text that refers to other texts to make an argument—creates a persuasive effect in a condensed, quick, almost unconscious way. Since "activist art involves questions not only of the nature of cultural production, but also of the location, or the means of distribution, of that production," rhetoric involving the ancient Greek philosopher Aristotle's appeals of ethos (ethics), pathos (emotion), and logos (logic) is taken out of the arena of the paid lecture, the university, and the pulpit, and into the streets and onto the Internet with the hope of saving lives.

RHETORIC FOR THE TWENTY-FIRST CENTURY

In "Eloquence," Ralph Waldo Emerson stated that "the conditions for eloquence always exist. It is always dying out of famous places and appearing in corners. Wherever the polarities meet, wherever the fresh moral sentiment, the instinct of freedom and duty, come in direct opposition to fossil conservatism and the thirst for gain, the spark will pass." Here Emerson suggested that rhetoric's role in cultural expression has always been complicated and ever-changing. When one form of expression of cultural sentiment seems to be wearing thin, another emerges to express more adequately a culture's beliefs, knowledge, and values and inform, persuade, or entertain audiences. Emerson was optimistic about how rhetoric will change in order to best express "freedom" and "duty."

But twenty-first-century conservative, liberal, and radical Americans alike have not been so optimistic. When discussing the speeches of America's politicians, the term "rhetoric" often takes on a pejorative cast: "It's all just rhetoric—he doesn't mean what he says." With politicians relying more heavily on private polling practices and public relations teams to make meaning, citizens wonder whether political rhetoric is self-interested, and more interested in the power of the politician than the truth or the representative needs of the people. The old questions about rhetoric as obscuring truth return throughout rhetoric's history. Those who study rhetoric and culture are also concerned about finding free and disinterested forums for effective argument. With the growth of global capitalism, the means of production and control of media sources are in the hands of a select few, creating what some fear is the impossibility of diverse voices from all sides of the issues getting heard.

But in *The Good Citizen* Michael Schudson argues "the rhetoric of decline should send up a red flag; for the socially concerned intellectual, it is as much an off-the-rack rhetoric as is a rhetoric of progress for the ebullient technocrat." If rhetoric is a reflection of the culture which produces it, America enjoys a diverse and vibrant public culture still. Americans may look for examples of rhetorical genres in "chat rooms" and on web pages, in 'zines and in alternative news productions, on cable access channels, and in multimedia formats that combine the visual and textual, producing new kinds of knowledge in the process, and reflecting new ways of communicating and provoking action and change.

See also **Popular Belief and Expression; Rhetoric and Belles Lettres** *(volume 1);* **Counter-cultural Visions; Intellectuals and Ideology in Government; Artistic, Intellectual, and Political Refugees** *(volume 2);* **The Role of the Intellectual; The Internet and Electronic Communications; Journals of Opinion** *(in this volume); and other articles in this section.*

BIBLIOGRAPHY

Introduction

Bizzell, Patricia, and Bruce Herzberg, eds. *The Rhetorical Tradition: Readings from Classical Times to the Present.* Boston, 1990.

Habermas, Jürgen. *The Structural Transformation of the Public Sphere: An Inquiry into a Category of Bourgeois Society.* Translated by Thomas Burger. Cambridge, Mass., 1991.

Religious Rhetorics

Beecher, Henry Ward. *Yale Lectures on Preaching.* New York, 1872.

Bercovitch, Sacvan. *American Jeremiad.* Madison, Wis., 1980.

Cmiel, Kenneth. *Democratic Eloquence: The Fight over Popular Speech in Nineteenth-Century America.* Berkeley, Calif., 1990.

Edwards, Jonathan. "Sinners in the Hands of an Angry God." 1741. In *Three Centuries of American Rhetorical Discourse,* edited by Ronald F. Reid, 66–78. Prospect Heights, Ill., 1988.

McLoughlin, William G. *The Meaning of Henry Ward Beecher: An Essay on the Shifting Values of Mid-Victorian America, 1840–1870.* New York, 1970.

Roberts-Miller, Patricia. *Voices in the Wilderness: Public Discourse and the Paradox of Puritan Rhetoric.* Tuscaloosa, Ala., 1999.

Shea, Daniel. *Spiritual Autobiography in Early America.* Madison, Wis., 1988.

Civic and Professional Rhetorics

Bledstein, Burton. *The Culture of Professionalism: The Middle Class and the Development of Higher Education in America.* New York, 1976.

Bode, Carl. *The American Lyceum: Town Meeting of the Mind.* New York, 1956.

Clark, Gregory, and S. Michael Halloran, eds. *Oratorical Culture in Nineteenth-Century America: Transformations in the Theory and Practice of Rhetoric.* Carbondale, Ill., 1993.

Emerson, Ralph Waldo. *The Collected Works of Ralph Waldo Emerson.* Edited by Alfred R. Ferguson, Jean Ferguson Carr, and Douglas E. Wilson. Cambridge, Mass., 1984.

———. "Eloquence." In *Society and Solitude,* 59–100. 1870. Reprint, New York, 1912.

Halttunen, Karen. *Confidence Men and Painted Women: A Study in Middle-Class Culture in America, 1830–1870.* New Haven, Conn., 1982.

Scott, Donald. "The Popular Lecture and the Creation of a Public in Mid-Nineteenth-Century America." *The Journal of American History* 66, no. 4 (March 1991): 791–809.

Sennett, Richard. *The Fall of Public Man.* New York, 1977.

Reform Rhetorics

Boudinot, Elias. *Cherokee Editor: The Writings of Elias Boudinot.* Edited by Thea Berdue. Athens, Ga., 1996.

Douglass, Frederick. *Oxford Frederick Douglass Reader.* Edited by William L. Andrews. New York, 1997.

Duffy, Bernard K., and Halford R. Ryan, eds. *American Orators of the Twentieth Century: Critical Studies and Sources.* Westport, Conn., 1987.

Faludi, Susan. "The Mom's Secret Weapon." *Newsweek.* (May 15, 2000): 30.

Gough, John Bartholomew. *An Autobiography.* Boston, 1845.

Hopkins, Sarah Winnemucca. *Life among the Piutes: Their Wrongs and Claims.* Reno, Nev., 1994.

King, Martin Luther, Jr. *Loving Your Enemies; Letter from Jail; Declaration of Independence from War in Viet Nam.* New York, 1981.

Logan, Shirley Wilson. *With Pen and Voice: A Critical Anthology of Nineteenth-Century African American Women.* Carbondale, Ill., 1995.

Mankiller, Wilma. "Rebuilding the Cherokee Nation." Address delivered at Sweet Briar College, April 2, 1993.

Matthews, Glenna. *The Rise of Public Woman: Women's Power and Women's Place in the United States, 1630–1970.* New York, 1992.

Mattingly, Carol. *Well-Tempered Women: Nineteenth-Century Temperance Rhetoric.* Carbondale, Ill., 1998.

Powers, Roger P., and William B. Vogele, eds. *Protest, Power, and Change: An Encyclopedia of Nonviolent Action from ACT-UP to Women's Suffrage.* New York, 1997.

Ryan, Mary P. *Women in Public: Between Banners and Ballots, 1825–1880.* Baltimore, 1990.

Visual Rhetorics

Angus, Ian, and Lenore Langsdorf, eds. *The Critical Turn: Rhetoric and Philosophy in Postmodern Discourse.* Carbondale, Ill., 1993.

Bender, John, and David E. Wellbery. *The Ends of Rhetoric: History, Theory, Practice.* Stanford, Calif., 1990.

Berger, John. *Ways of Seeing.* New York, 1977.

Bernard-Donals, Michael, and Richard R. Glejzer, eds. *Rhetoric in an Antifoundational World: Language, Culture, and Pedagogy.* New Haven, Conn., 1998.

Brummett, Barry. *Rhetorical Dimensions of Popular Culture.* Tuscaloosa, Ala., 1991.

Crimp, Douglas, ed. *AIDS: Cultural Analysis, Cultural Activism.* Cambridge, Mass., 1991.

Dondis, Donis A. *A Primer of Visual Literacy.* Cambridge, Mass., 1973.

Fairclough, Norman. *Discourse and Social Change.* Cambridge, U.K., 1992.

Jamieson, Kathleen Hall. *Eloquence in an Electronic Age: The Transformation of Political Speechmaking.* New York, 1988.

McLuhan, Marshall. *The Gutenberg Galaxy.* Toronto, 1999.

Mitchell, W. J. T. *Iconology: Image, Text, Ideology.* Chicago, 1987.

Welch, Kathleen E. *Electric Rhetoric: Classical Rhetoric, Oralism, and a New Literacy.* Cambridge, Mass., 1999.

Rhetoric for the Twenty-First Century

Schudson, Michael. *The Good Citizen: A History of American Civic Life.* New York, 1998.

PUBLIC MURALS

Diana L. Linden

When speaking of American public murals the word "public" can mean different things. While the word can refer to the use of public monies to commission art, both public and private funds have financed murals. In the late nineteenth century, "public" meant art located in easily accessible buildings. Yet the artist was far less accessible, having positioned himself apart from, and most often above, the public. Under the New Deal mural projects, artists were directed to be more responsive to the public and to create imagery relevant to the community's history, industry, and daily life. Since the 1960s, community-based muralists have removed the barriers that exist between artist and public by inviting members of the community to participate in the design and execution of their murals.

Public murals are an ambitious art form that strives for permanence, monumentality, and communication. Murals have often been associated with social movements and political ideologies, and therefore can lack a clear or established iconography since they draw from issues in the culture rather than from common texts. In the United States, there have been three primary periods of public mural patronage: the American Renaissance (1876–1917), the New Deal Mural Projects (1933–1943), and the Community Mural Movement (beginning in the mid-1960s).

THE AMERICAN RENAISSANCE

Because American artists lacked the necessary skills to create large-scale works, and because commissions were scarce, public murals were slow to start. By the later decades of the nineteenth century, more artists had trained at Paris's École des Beaux-Arts, enabling them to paint on a large scale and to work collaboratively with architects and sculptors who shared their training and sensibilities. In the United States, John La Farge's large-scale mural for Trinity

Church (1876) in Boston, Massachusetts, initiated the American Renaissance movement that spanned up through World War I. He created an eclectic and decorative mix drawing upon early and medieval Christian sources as well as Renaissance and Asian inspiration for his ecclesiastical mural. The architect H. H. Richardson, who like La Farge trained at the École des Beaux-Arts, had hired the painter to decorate the large wall and ceiling spaces of his Romanesque-inspired church. Both men were dedicated to the decorative unity of the arts, to the revival of historical styles, and the supremacy of craftsmanship. In 1902, the critic Pauline King credited La Farge with single-handedly elevating mural painting to an art form.

The latter part of the nineteenth century saw an unparalleled increase in America's wealth. With its victory in the Spanish American War in 1898, America became an imperial power, acquiring Cuba, Guam, Hawaii, the Philippines, and Puerto Rico. During this period of economic and political confidence, public art was designed to uplift and elevate society. In a style rooted in classical models, artists created murals that promoted civic ideals. As Richard Guy Wilson has written, this was an intensely nationalistic art and architecture.

Major mural commissions were done for the World's Columbian Exposition in Chicago (1893), the Walker Art Center at Bowdoin College (1894), the Boston Public Library (1894), the Criminal Courts Building (1895) and Appellate Courthouse (1899) in New York, the Library of Congress (1896), and the state capitols in St. Paul, Minnesota (1904) and Harrisburg, Pennsylvania (1902). Artists painted more than four hundred murals during this period and were supported by the formation of professional arts societies. In 1893, the Municipal Arts Society was created with its motto "To Make Us Love Our City, We Must Make Our City Lovely." Two years later, the National Society of Mural Painters was established. The proliferation of art journals and books, such as the *Craftsman, Bookman,* and *Architectural Record* chronicled and celebrated both the new buildings and their decorations.

In outdoor public statuary, figures of men dominated, whereas with murals mainly women were represented; this echoed the social stratification of gender with exterior space being the male domain, and women relegated to the interior. Furthermore, when men were painted in murals they were usually historical figures, in contrast to women who were allegorical representations. Such was the case with the Library of Congress, where muralist Edwin Howland Blashfield painted men in order "to convey that it was men on whose shoulders rested the intellectual advances of the west" (Van Hook, p. 118).

The World's Columbian Exposition

In 1893 America experienced a major economic depression, financial panic, and labor unrest. In the midst of this upheaval, the city of Chicago hosted the World's Columbian Exposition and welcomed over thirty million visitors. Dedicated to America's cultural, technological, and commercial achievements, the exposition marked the arrival of Columbus to the Americas. Directed by the architect Daniel H. Burnham, with Frank D. Millet in charge of the mural programs, this temporary city of some four hundred buildings was a tribute to beaux arts planning, training, and style. Ordered, symmetrical, balanced, the exposition's neoclassical buildings highlighted the unification of architecture, decorative, and applied arts, and the largest mural project to that date. Recalling the exposition several years later, Charles H. Caffin stated that this was the key event for the popularization of mural art across America.

Since the entire city was constructed to be temporary and made with ephemeral materials, many key murals have since been lost. Its nickname, the "White City," referred to the gleaming white structures; more recently the name suggests the strict racial hierarchies which ordered the exposition and that excluded equal participation, representation, and visitation by America's diverse populations.

Chicago's formidable Mrs. (Bertha) Potter Palmer oversaw the Board of Lady Managers, which insisted on a place for women at the exposition. Sophie Hayden, the first woman architect to graduate from the Massachusetts Institute of Technology, designed the Women's Building. According to Frances K. Pohl, the Board of Lady Managers was a select group of white middle- and upper-class women who "claimed to represent the interests (both industrial and artistic) of women of all races and classes. In actual fact, they did not" (Pohl, p. 290). Instead these women upheld an elite criteria that promoted European culture as the pinnacle of artistic, technological, and intellectual achievement, a hierarchical ordering that revealed both the racial and class-based biases of the board, the exposition, and the nation. However, as Pohl asserts, the Women's Building did successfully challenge the dominant cultural ideology that women were not capable of producing major art—namely, mural painting.

Among the artists who were awarded mural commissions were two expatriate Americans: Mary Cassatt and Mary Fairchild MacMonnies. Unfortunately, the location of their murals, if they still exist, remains unknown. Cassatt's and MacMonnies' murals were thematically linked to show women's progress. Cassatt selected "Modern Woman" as her theme, which Bertha Palmer lavishly praised: "I consider your panel to be the most beautiful thing that has been done for the Exposition." In her mural, employing a more colorful, forceful palette than many of her male contemporaries, Cassatt chronicled the advancement of modern women. The art historian Griselda Pollock has described Cassatt's lost panel as having shown "women together: as adolescents with expansive and unformed dreams of great achievement; as educated mothers, aunts, sisters, sharing the fruits of intellectual labor with the next generation; as creative artists and appreciative audiences for culture" (*Mary Cassatt*, p. 48). This intergenerational scene promoted the potential of women's achievements and modernity for middle-class women. In contrast to Cassatt's modern women shown in contemporary garb, for her "Primitive Women," MacMonnies created a classically inspired arcadian scene with women shown in Neo-Grecian flowing robes.

Although not employed at the World's Columbian Exposition, Violet Oakley was the only American woman to have a successful career as a muralist and was praised by the critic Caryl Coleman in the *Architectural Record* (1907) as among the foremost of American artists, evidencing an "innate genius." Inspired by theater and her own work as an illustrator, there was often a stagelike quality to her mural presentation. Perhaps her most famous commission was the murals for the Pennsylvania State Capitol Building in Harrisburg in 1902; she also received other commissions from the city of Harrisburg. Her mural in the capitol building represents William Penn's founding of the colony. In contrast to the majority of mural imagery from the American Renaissance, Oakley presented women as the

"THY GOD BRINGETH THEE INTO A GOOD LAND OF FOUNTAINS AND DEPTHS THAT SPRING OUT OF VALLEYS AND HILLS A LAND WHOSE STONES ARE IRON AND OUT OF WHOSE HILLS THOU MAYEST DIG BRASS"

Violet Oakley, *The Founding of the State of Liberty Spiritual* **(Detail).** Oakley's cycle, comprising eighteen murals in the Governor's Reception Room at the Pennsylvania State Capitol, Harrisburg, is based upon William Penn's founding of the Commonwealth. Oakley also painted murals in the Vassar College alumni house and the First Presbyterian Church in the Germantown section of Philadelphia. COURTESY OF THE CAPITOL PRESERVATION COMMITTEE, HARRISBURG

active agents of history, rather than simply as allegorical figures.

The Boston Public Library Boston selected the leading architectural firm of McKim, Mead, and White to design its public library in 1895, and in turn three artists were selected to paint mural cycles: Pierre-Cécile Puvis de Chavannes, one of the most influential muralists of the day; Edwin Austin Abbey, who created a medieval-inspired wall painting; and the expatriate artist John Singer Sargent. Abbey, a British artist, depicted the Holy Grail in a mural filled with historical details, which Henry James explained in its accompanying brochure. In contrast,

Puvis attempted a less literary and more symbolic presentation, writing that "I have sought to represent under a symbolic form and in a single view the intellectual treasures collected in this beautiful building." The French artist created murals that were filled with Neo-Grecian figures and costumes to pay homage to the arts of poetry and literature, history, and science. Yet the most original and unconventional contribution was done by Sargent.

Known for his society portraits both in Europe and the United States, the artist created one of his most innovative works, which would occupy him for nearly two decades (1890–1919). Writing in *Scribners* (1903), Frank Fowler noted the unusual

John Singer Sargent, "Judgment" from *The Triumph of Religion.* Sargent's murals in the Boston Public Library, painted between 1890 and 1919, depict seventeen scenes. The lunette shown above is from the center of the west wall, intermediate to the lunettes of "Heaven" and "Hell." Sargent also painted murals for the Museum of Fine Arts, Boston, and Harvard University's Widener Library. COURTESY OF THE BOSTON PUBLIC LIBRARY

nature of the mural's program, that Sargent had not created a picture, but rather a thought, or an idea. Sargent's *The Triumph of Religion* traces the development of religious thought—covering Greek and Roman myths, Judaism, and Christianity. By shifting styles within the mural to echo the individual historical eras and the complex ideas of religion, Sargent created a work that is more evocative than didactic. Sargent, according to Sally M. Promey, presented contemporary religion in terms of spirituality and subjective experience, rather than creed and dogma; for Sargent this was a sign of American and Western thought. William A. Coffin, a critic writing for *Century Magazine* in 1896, praised the mural, writing that "the work as a whole is like a casket of jewels," and reveals the artist's love of things "weird and mysterious."

The Library of Congress The Library of Congress was the first important government building to be decorated in accordance with an understanding of the unity of the arts. In 1895 nineteen artists were hired to paint 112 murals, which they saw as

both a patriotic gesture and a way to further promote the cause of mural art as a civic necessity. Surveying the busyness of artistic decoration at the Library of Congress, Coffin noted in 1897 that "the spirit of art and labor, must have been like this in Renaissance Florence or Venice."

The Library of Congress was a collaborative vision of neoclassical embellishments employing twenty-two sculptors and nineteen muralists; however, the library's dense architecture limited the muralists, and there were few major surfaces for large-scale murals. The architects dismissed mural competitions (which was the main way that commissions were awarded later in the New Deal), preferring to maintain control by directly appointing artists. The critic Royal Cortissoz at the time praised Edwin Howland Blashfield as the best muralist of the group. Blashfield created a series of twelve seated figures symbolic of nations and epochs of specific significance to the intellectual and cultural development of the world. Blashfield, the "dean" of American muralists, was awarded the crowning mural in the center of the reading room where he

Dome of Rotunda   THE EVOLUTION OF CIVILIZATION   E.H. Blashfield, Artist.

E. H. Blashfield, *The Evolution of Civilization* **(Detail).** Blashfield's mural in the Library of Congress includes a total of twelve figures, representing Greece (Philosophy), Rome (Administration), the Middle Ages (Modern Languages), Italy (Fine Arts), Germany (Printing), France (Emancipation), Islam (Physics), England (Literature), Spain (Discovery), and the three shown above. His murals grace the walls of the Massachusetts Institute of Technology (his alma mater) as well as state buildings in Wisconsin, Iowa, and Minnesota, among other places. LIBRARY OF CONGRESS

painted the *Evolution of Civilization,* linking America to great artistic centers and past civilizations while trumpeting the call of beauty, harmony, and decoration.

Many of the leading American Renaissance muralists would continue to be active into the 1930s, lecturing, writing, and receiving commissions. Although murals were sporadically painted during the 1910s up to the early 1930s, there would not be a comprehensive mural program in America until the creation of the New Deal in 1933. With the New Deal, instead of drawing inspiration from the ancient civilizations of Greece and Rome, and the Italian Renaissance, artists and administrators would look to contemporary Mexico.

MURAL PROJECTS OF THE 1930s

In 1933, the artist George Biddle, in a letter to his friend President Franklin D. Roosevelt, wrote:

> The Mexican artists have produced the greatest national school of mural painting since the Italian renaissance. Diego Rivera tells me that it was only possible because [President Álvaro] Obregón allowed Mexican artists to work for plumbers' wages in order to express on the walls of the government buildings the social ideas of the Mexican revolution.

> . . . The younger artists of America are conscious as they have never been of the social revolution our country and civilization are going through; and they would be eager to express these ideals in a permanent art form if they were given the government's cooperation.

Roosevelt agreed. It is very likely that were it not for the Mexican mural movement, the United States would not have created its New Deal art programs. Yet despite the central role of the Mexican example, the two national programs were vastly different.

The Mexican mural movement was born out of the Mexican Revolution, a bloody civil war that followed the 1910 overthrow of the dictator Porfirio Díaz, who had held power since 1876. The new president, Álvaro Obregón, dismantled Díaz's power base of European elites, the army, foreign landowners, and the church. José Vasconcelos, Obregón's secretary of state for education, began in 1921 to commission young Mexican artists to paint murals on the walls of prominent state buildings. According to Octavio Paz, Vasconcelos "imposed no dogmas, either aesthetic or ideological on the artists." The muralists sought to educate a largely illiterate population through murals that were realistic, narrative, figurative, and that called attention to social issues. Through positive imagery, the artists sought to redeem precontact history and ancient Mexican cultures, to address contemporary social, economic, and political problems, and to counter disdain for indigenous and nonwhite populations. In the words of Rivera, muralism "for the first time in the history of monumental painting ceased to use gods, kings, chiefs of state, heroic generals, etc., as central heroes. . . . For the first time in the history of Art, Mexican mural painting made the masses the hero of monumental art" (Rochfort, *Mexican Muralists,* p. 8). Several artists active in the Communist Party, including Diego Rivera and David Alfaro Siqueiros, helped organize the Syndicate of Technical Workers, Painters, and Sculptors, a radical trade union. It was the syndicate that published the manifesto announcing their social and artistic dedication:

> Our fundamental aesthetic goal must be to socialize artistic expression and wipe out bourgeois individualism. We *repudiate* so-called easel painting and every kind of art favored by ultra-intellectual circles, because it is aristocratic, and we praise monumental art in all its forms, because it is public property.

Mexican Muralists in the United States   During the early 1930s, the Mexican artists received commissions to create large-scale public murals in the United States. Critical acclaim, media coverage, and controversy followed Rivera, Siqueiros, and José Clemente Orozco.

The earliest mural was Orozco's *Prometheus* begun in April 1930 for California's Pomona College and which shows the mythic "creator-destroyer" in fiery red tones. Orozco, who trained at Mexico's Academy of San Carlos, maintained an academic interest in the nude, Greek mythology, and heroes (Zapata, Quetzalcoatl, Christ), while also creating works that called for a new world order. In 1932 Orozco was contracted to paint murals for Dartmouth College, due in large part to the efforts of Lewis Mumford and the financing of Abby Rockefeller. According to the artist, "these are the walls for my best mural, my epic of America." Orozco concerned himself with the history of North America, rather than that of a single nation, and depicted the intertwined European and Indian histories on the continent. The Aztec god Quetzalcoatl was central to Orozco's narrative, which was rather somber and pessimistic in tone in contrast to Rivera's characteristic celebration of modernity and technology in the United States. For the New School for Social Research in New York City, Orozco created frescoes that drew from the work of Mumford. His *A Call for Revolution and Brotherhood of Man* included portraits of Mohandas K. Gandhi and Mexico's Felipe Carrillo Puerto, along with representatives of various ethnic and racial groups, and incorporated themes portraying nationalism and communism. While working on his murals at the New School, Orozco met Thomas Hart Benton, who was working on his *America Today* murals.

Diego Rivera arrived in San Francisco in 1930 and painted *Making of a Fresco* and *Allegory of California* (1931), both optimistic works celebrating the region's farming and industrial culture without overt class criticism. Rivera then went to Detroit to create his most ambitious mural in the States, *Detroit Industry* (1932–1933), which had the auto industry as its main subject. Despite the workers' strikes and hunger strikes that plagued the city in the worst years of the Depression, Rivera created a complex, yet utopian image of organized technology in which man and machine work together harmoniously.

It is important to acknowledge that it was leading American capitalists—the Fords and the Rockefellers—who financed Rivera. Altruism alone does not adequately explain their artistic patronage, for these industrialists also had land, rubber, and oil interests in Mexico and Latin America, which they wanted to prevent from being nationalized. For this, Rivera came under criticism. Selected by the Rockefellers to paint at the newly constructed Rockefeller Center in New York City, Rivera proposed his *Man at the Crossroads Looking with Hope and High Vision to the Choosing of a New and Better Future* (1933). In comparison to his Detroit murals, Rivera's message was more politically strident, more critical of America, and more openly Marxist in orientation, perhaps to counter the charge that he had sold out politically. Working as assistants were the young artists Ben Shahn and Lucienne Bloch, both of whom would soon create murals under the New Deal patronage programs.

Among the many figures Rivera depicted in his ambitious work was Lenin, which Nelson Rockefeller asked Rivera to remove. The artist refused. Overnight, Rockefeller canceled the contract and had Rivera's mural destroyed. E. B. White satirically captured the affair in his poem: "I Paint What I See (A Ballad for Artistic Integrity)." Young artists in New York—such as Bloch and Shahn—already politicized, seized Rockefeller's actions as the rallying cry to protest the rise of censorship and fascism and to show support for the newly formed federal arts projects and the need for artists to unionize.

The New Deal Mural Programs   Shortly after his inauguration in 1933, President Franklin D. Roosevelt launched the New Deal arts projects. This

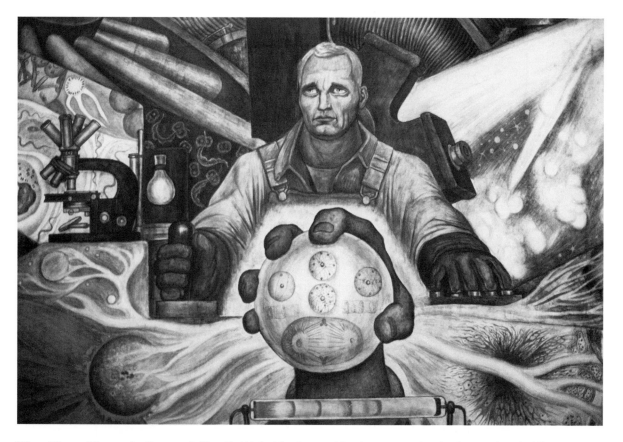

Diego Rivera, *Man at the Crossroads* (Detail; 1934). After he considered reconstructing the destroyed Rockefeller Center mural at the New Workers School on West 14th Street in New York City, Rivera instead decided to paint it for the Palace of Fine Arts in Mexico City. © DANNY LEHMAN/CORBIS

program included community arts centers, provisions to employ graphic artists as well as easel painters and sculptors, and an extensive mural program. The New Deal arts project (1933–1943) was actually funded through four separate agencies: the Public Works of Art Project (PWAP, 1933–1934), the Works Progress Administration's Federal Art Project (WPA/FAP, 1935–1943), the Treasury Relief Art Project (TRAP, 1935–1943), and the Treasury Section of Paintings and Sculpture (The Section, 1934–1943).

The immediacy of the economic crisis, as well as the 1930s shift of focus onto "the people" and "the common man," united these four projects. The New Deal arts program was the largest art program ever undertaken by the federal government and produced over four thousand murals. Through murals painted in schools, hospitals, community centers, and most famously, post offices, positive images of America's past and present were presented. Prior to the New Deal, few communities outside of big urban centers had any exposure to either living artists or the visual arts. By bringing

art and artists into communities, the New Deal sought to create a national culture, as well as to make the arts accessible to a greater number of citizens. No longer were artists separate from society; their labors were needed. No longer would the arts be the domain of the elite and monied few, as it had been during the American Renaissance.

Overall, the New Deal funded murals that were representational and figurative without abstraction or extreme distortion, positive rather than socially critical. In a time of severe economic crisis, the murals presented a stable vision of America in which workers are active, families are together, and the land is fertile. Optimism and hope pervaded. Among the most popular themes were the founding of the town, the local mail delivery, local industry, and work.

The contrasts between the mural programs in Mexico and the United States federal program are many. Overall, when the works in Mexico are compared with those of the New Deal artists, the United States murals are shown to be more politically restrained, of a smaller scale, and visually less complex

AFRICAN AMERICAN ARTISTS AND THE NEW DEAL

In 1936, Charles Alston was appointed to be the first African American artist to head a WPA/FAP project; Alston was to oversee a team of five other men and women, and their assistants, to design murals for New York's Harlem Hospital. Alston selected the theme of modern and primitive medicine for the entranceway to the women's wing. However, before Alston and the others could complete their designs as they wanted, they had to overcome the overt racism of the hospital administration. Officials tried to block the project on the basis that the works contained "too much Negro subject matter," and thus would not appeal to Harlem residents. Alston was inspired by Alain Locke, who encouraged artists to create from their ancestral heritage, and by Rivera, whom Alston had met when the Mexican was painting at Rockefeller Center. With perseverance, and organizing on the part of the artists, Alston and the others were able to complete their murals as intended.

Aaron Douglas created a mural cycle titled *Aspects of Negro Life* for the New York Public Library at its Harlem branch. In these four related works, Douglas depicted life in Africa, the experience of the Middle Passage, slavery, and Reconstruction. The murals were done in his innovative, signature style of compressed forms, silhouettes, and radiating circles of variegated tonalities. Douglas, like many artists and intellectuals during the 1930s, was Marxist. Originally, he had intended a fifth panel to show "the Negro's way out, the way outlined by Karl Marx in the unity of the black and white workers in the class struggle." Douglas, however, anticipated that officials would censor such a message, and so chose not to complete it.

Hale Woodruff received a grant to study with Rivera in Mexico, and later traveled to the Soviet Union. In 1938, Woodruff received a WPA/FAP commission to create murals for Talladega College in Alabama. For his subject matter Woodruff retrieved an important yet largely unacknowledged incident from African American history—the *Amistad* mutiny (1839) to inform and inspire his audiences.

and dynamic. Moreover, the majority of American murals were applied canvases rather than the more expensive and technically demanding art of fresco.

The New Deal program, however, was not without controversy. Objections ranged from the depiction of dairy cows nonspecific to the region to the racial content of murals in the South. Painting murals in the Bronx, Ben Shahn had to remove a quotation from Walt Whitman that local Catholic clergy deemed irreligious and offensive. Some artists anticipating objections to their mural's content or political orientation, selectively suppressed their ideas in order to obtain commissions. Others did not.

The legacy of compromise has in part contributed to disdain for the New Deal projects. Eclipsed by the rise of abstract expressionism after World War II, many New Deal murals were neglected and fell into disrepair. They were also ignored by scholars because the vast majority were populist and collaborative. Moreover, in the cold war period, social realism became associated with the Soviet Union. Later such art historians as Francis V. O'Connor, Karal Ann Marling, Belisario R. Contreras, Marlene Park, and Greta Berman reconsidered the New Deal art projects, writing important texts that remain central to the field. Because of these scholars and others, vital records were preserved, oral interviews with artists were conducted, and murals were conserved.

COMMUNITY MURAL MOVEMENT

After the New Deal program ended, there was a sharp decline in the production of public murals.

In the late 1960s, however, an interest in community-based, urban mural programs either tied to specific racial or ethnic groups or to urban renewal programs began. Although Chicago was the site of some of the first murals in the community mural movement, murals also appeared simultaneously in Los Angeles, Detroit, St. Louis, and Philadelphia. A number of artists disenchanted with the commercial nature of the art world turned to mural painting. For them, wall art, based in a community and dedicated to social communication, was a way toward artistic and political unity.

In the words of the art historian Lucy R. Lippard: "Murals are primarily for the community that lives with them, so it is important that the muralists live in or have some strong bond to the community, are not just parachuted in to Do Good for the supposedly artless Other" (Cockcroft, Weber, and Cockcroft, p. xi). The Chicago mural movement was a prime example of members of a community creating murals for their own community. In 1967, some black artists in Chicago formed the Organization for Black American Culture (OBAC) and created the *Wall of Respect*, which portrayed conditions within the community alongside portraits of African American leaders. Their work sent ripples across the nation, and soon African American muralists in other cities began to organize, claim, and paint the walls of their communities. "Walls of Respect," in fact, became a generic term for these community-based murals that began to appear.

Constructed in a time of social protest and unrest, these murals had several factors in common. They were located in urban, working class, and minority neighborhoods; they were initiated by the artists themselves; and they were more often than not created by several persons.

The Chicano Mural Movement The Chicano mural movement was intimately linked with the Chicano civil rights movement, led by Cesar Chavez and his Farm Workers Association (later the United Farm Workers [UFW]). Shifra M. Goldman identifies two 1968 works by Antonio Bernal on the UFW's Teatro Campesino Center, Del Rey, California, as the start of the mural movement.

As with the Mexican murals created by Rivera, Orozco, and Siqueiros, the Chicano murals of the 1960s used their works to question the existing power structure, to reclaim the pre-Columbian past by utilizing imagery and iconography from the ancient Mexican civilizations, and to celebrate their history. Some of the artists, such as Judith F. Baca, trained with Siqueiros, linking the Chicano movement with the Mexican muralists. Unlike the government-sponsored movement of postrevolutionary Mexico, however, the Chicano mural movement did not begin with government funds or on government walls; rather it was a grassroots movement.

From the late 1960s until the early 1970s, the majority of works of the Chicano mural movement were nationalist in theme and created solely by members of the Chicano communities. After that period, people of different racial and ethnic backgrounds became involved in the design and execution of murals.

In 1976 Judith F. Baca founded the Social and Public Arts Resource Center (SPARC) to ensure the documentation of the urban mural movement. Baca's *Great Wall of Los Angeles* (1976–1983) presented the history of California from the prehistoric up through the 1950s. Rather than a history from "the top down"—a history of leaders and battles—Baca created a social history of California that included the Zoot Suit riots, the impact of McCarthyism in the film industry, the United States closing its borders to Jewish refugees during the Holocaust, the Japanese internment camps, and the gay rights movement. More than two hundred teenagers painted the mural, at the time the longest in the world.

See also **Urban Cultural Institutions; Realism in Art and Literature; The Popular Arts; The Artist and the Intellectual in the New Deal** *(volume 1);* **Postmodernism and the Arts** *(volume 2);* **The Visual Arts; Culture for Mass Audiences; Museums** *(in this volume); and other articles in this section.*

BIBLIOGRAPHY

American Renaissance
PRIMARY SOURCES
Caffin, Charles H. "The Beginning and Growth of Mural Painting in America." *The Bookman* 28 (1908): 127–139.

Coffin, William A. "Decorations in the New Congressional Library." *Century Magazine* 53 no. 5 (March 1987): 694–711.

——. "Sargent and His Painting: With Specific Reference to his Decorations in the Boston Public Library." *Century Magazine* 52 no. 2 (June 1896): 163–178.

Coleman, Caryl. "An Appreciation: Mural Decorations, Harrisburg State Capitol." *The Architectural Record* 22 (1907): 457–465.

Cortissoz, Royal. "Painting and Sculpture in the New Congressional Library: Decorations of Mr. Edwin Howland Blashfield." *Harper's Weekly* 40 (11 January 1896): 35–37.

Fowler, Frank. "The Field of Art: Sargent's New Wall Paintings." *Scribner's Magazine* 34 (September 1903): 767–768.

King, Pauline. *American Mural Painting.* Boston, 1902.

SECONDARY SOURCES

Amico, Leonard N. *The Mural Decorations of Edwin Howland Blashfield (1848–1936).* Williamstown, Mass., 1978.

Carr, Carolyn Kinder, and Sally Webster. "Mary Cassatt and Mary Fairchild MacMonnies: The Search for their 1893 Murals." *American Art* 8 (1994): 52–69.

Likos, Patricia. "Violet Oakley (1874–1961)." *Philadelphia Museum of Art Bulletin* 75, no. 325 (June 1979): 2–32.

Murray, Richard. *Art for Architecture: Washington, D.C., 1895–1925.* Washington, D.C., 1975.

Pilgrim, Dianne, et al. *The American Renaissance: 1876–1917.* Exhibition catalog, Brooklyn Museum of Art. Brooklyn, N.Y., 1979.

Pohl, Frances K. "Historical Reality or Utopian Ideal? The Woman's Building at the World's Columbian Exposition, Chicago, 1893." *International Journal of Women's Studies* 5 (September/October 1982): 289–311.

Pollock, Griselda. *Mary Cassatt: Painter of Modern Women.* London, 1998.

Promey, Sally M. *Painting Religion in Public: John Singer Sargent's Triumph of Religion at the Boston Public Library.* Princeton, N.J., 1999.

Van Hook, Bailey. *Angels of Art: Women and Art in American Society, 1876–1914.* University Park, Penn., 1996.

Weinberg, H. Barbara. "John La Farge and the Decoration of Trinity Church, Boston." *Journal of the Society of Architectural Historians* 32 no. 4 (December 1974): 323–353.

West, Richard V. *The Walker Art Building Murals.* Brunswick, Maine, 1972.

Mexican Muralists

Anreus, Alejandro. *Orozco in Gringoland: The Years in New York.* Albuquerque, N. Mex., 2000.

Craven, David. *Diego Rivera as Epic Modernist.* New York, 1997.

Downs, Linda Bank. *Diego Rivera: The Detroit Industry Murals.* Detroit, 1999.

Hurlburt, Laurance P. *The Mexican Muralists in the United States.* Albuquerque, N. Mex., 1989.

Goldman, Shifra M. *Dimensions of the Americas: Art and Social Change in Latin America and the United States.* Chicago and London, 1994.

Lee, Anthony W. *Painting on the Left: Diego Rivera, Radical Politics, and San Francisco's Public Murals.* Berkeley, Calif., 1999.

LeFalle-Collins, Lizzetta, and Shifra M. Goldman. *In the Spirit of Resistance: African-American Modernists and the Mexican Muralist School.* New York, 1996.

O'Connor, Francis V. "The Influence of Diego Rivera on the Art of the United States during the 1930s and After." In *Diego Rivera: A Retrospective.* Exhibition catalog, Detroit Institute of Arts. Detroit, Mich., 1986.

Rochfort, Desmond. *Mexican Muralists: Orozco, Rivera, Siqueiros.* San Francisco, Calif., 1993.

New Deal Muralists

Berman, Greta. *The Lost Years: Mural Painting in New York City under the W.P.A./F.A.P., 1935–1943.* New York, 1978.

Contreras, Belisario R. *Tradition and Innovation in New Deal Art.* Cranbury, N.J., 1983.

Harris, Jonathan. *Federal Art and National Culture: The Politics of Identity in New Deal America.* New York, 1995.

Kendall, M. Sue. *Rethinking Regionalism: John Steuart Curry and the Kansas Mural Controversy.* Washington, D.C., 1986.

Linden, Diana L. "Ben Shahn's New Deal Murals: Jewish Identity in the American Scene." In *Common Man, Mythic Vision: The Paintings of Ben Shahn,* edited by Susan Chevlowe. New York and Princeton, N.J., 1998.

———. "Ben Shahn, the Four Freedoms, and the SSS *St. Louis.*" *American Jewish History* (December 1998): 420–440.

Marling, Karal Ann. *Wall-to-Wall America: A Cultural History of Post Office Murals in the Great Depression.* Minneapolis, Minn., 1982.

McKinzie, Richard. *The New Deal for Artists.* Princeton, N.J., 1973.

Melosh, Barbara. *Engendering Culture: Manhood and Womanhood in New Deal Public Art and Theater.* Washington, D.C., 1991.

Park, Marlene, and Gerald Markowitz. *Democratic Vistas: Post Offices and Public Art in the New Deal.* Philadelphia, 1984.

O'Connor, Francis V. *Art for the Millions.* Greenwich, Conn., 1973.

———. *Federal Support for the Visual Arts: The New Deal and Now.* 2nd ed. Greenwich, Conn., 1971.

O'Connor, Francis V., ed. *The New Deal Art Projects: An Anthology of Memoirs.* Washington, D.C., 1972.

Community Mural Program

Baca, Judith F. "Murals/Public Art." In *Chicano Expressions: A New View in American Art.* New York, 1987.

———. "Whose Monument Where? Public Art in a Many-Cultured Society." In *Mapping the Terrain: New Genre Public Art,* edited by Suzanne Lacy. Seattle, Wash., 1995.

Baca, Judith F., and Evagene H. Bond. "The Great Wall of Los Angeles: A Successful Art Product with a Social Impact." In *La Comunidad: Design, Development, and Self-Determination in Hispanic Communities,* edited by Evagene H. Bond. Washington, D.C., 1982.

Barnett, Alan W. *Community Murals: The People's Art.* Philadelphia, 1984.

Cockcroft, Eva, John Pitman Weber, and James Cockcroft. *Toward a People's Art: The Contemporary Mural Movement.* Albuquerque, N. Mex., 1998.

Cockcroft, Eva Sperling, and Holly Barnet-Sanchez, eds. *Signs from the Heart: California Chicano Murals.* Venice, Calif., 1990.

Doss, Erika. *Spirit Poles and Flying Pigs: Public Art and Cultural Democracy in American Communities.* Washington, D.C., 1995.

Dreschler, Tim, and Rupert Garcia. "Recent Raza Murals in the United States." *Radical America* 12, no. 2 (1978): 14–31.

Goldman, Shifra M. *Dimensions of the Americas: Art and Social Change in Latin America and the United States.* Chicago and London, 1994.

Griswold del Castillo, Richard, ed. *CARA: Chicano Art Resistance and Affirmation, 1965–1985.* Los Angeles, 1991.

Mexican Fine Arts Center Museum. *The Barrio Murals.* Exhibition catalog with essays by Victor Sorrell and Mark Ragovin. Chicago, 1987.

Pohl, Frances K. *Judith F. Baca: Site and Insights, 1974–1992.* Claremont, Calif., 1993.

MONUMENTS AND MEMORIALS

Edward T. Linenthal

John Quincy Adams, illustrating the early-nineteenth-century tension between a republican vision of an egalitarian future and a vision that looked to past social and political hierarchies as the model for the future, exclaimed, "Democracy has no monuments. It strikes no medals. It bears the head of no man on a coin." Were Adams to travel the United States in the twenty-first century, he would, no doubt, be astonished to find a landscape populated by monuments and other material memorial expression.

Like other peoples, Americans, even those suspicious of monuments as examples of elitism inappropriate in a democracy, do not wish to live in homogenous space. They have populated the land with a rich array of statues, obelisks, arches, cenotaphs, halls, cairns, and temples celebrating the "great men" who have been so often celebrated as the shapers of that which endures in the culture. Americans have flocked to natural monuments as tourists and pilgrims: Niagara Falls, Yellowstone, and Yosemite, for example. These were the American answer to the built grandeur of European cathedrals, and they were perceived as superior to any humanly constructed environment. In his poem "A Sabbath at Niagara," for example, Abraham Cole exclaims:

> If, in th' immensity of space,
> God makes one spot his special dwelling place,
> That spot is this.

The memorial landscape includes the natural sites of Native Americans, the San Francisco Peaks of Arizona, for example, that are often besieged sacred places, contaminated by tourism and development. It includes churches, mosques, temples, and meetinghouses. There are also regional monuments and memorials such as Stone Mountain, Georgia, with its huge carved figures of Jefferson Davis, Stonewall Jackson, and Robert E. Lee, and allegorical monuments on Civil War battlefields to justice, peace, and martial heroism honoring the Confederacy. A more flexible memorial form is *The Great Wall of Los Angeles,* a mile of painted panels in the Los Angeles river conduit illustrating California history, painted by 350 youths from the inner city, and Paul Bunyan and Babe, the Blue Ox, on the shore of Lake Bemidji, Minnesota, evidence, according to Karal Ann Marling, of the commemoration of the Bunyanesque virtues of "frontier savvy and the native grit of a nation" (*The Colossus of Roads,* p. 2).

There are representations of Justice and Liberty and the Pilgrim Mother (Plymouth, Massachusetts), as well as monuments to celebrities, including Tom Mix, Michael Jordan, Mickey Mantle, and Elvis Presley's pilgrimage center Graceland, in Memphis, Tennessee. There are also monuments to the Pony Express, to newspaper boys, to Hiawatha and Minnehaha, to wireless operators lost at sea, to dead firemen and policemen, to the mythological centaur, to rescue animals, and to the Jolly Green Giant. There is, however, a dearth of memorials to women and ethnic "outsiders." Likewise, there is a paucity of memorials to cultural figures. While there are house museums commemorating the lives of Nathaniel Hawthorne, Emily Dickinson, and Frederick Douglass, Wilbur Zelinsky observes that in spite of these "one must search long and hard across the land to track down monumental remembrances of such candidates for culture hero status as Francis Scott Key, Mark Twain, Whitman, Emerson, Ford, or Lindbergh" (*Nation into State,* p. 184).

American memorial expression reaches outside the geographical boundaries of the United States. American embassies, for example, were often intentionally designed to engender awe for American principles and power, and overseas military cemeteries recall the human cost of allegiance to principles of democracy.

Conspicuous in memorial expression is the patriotic landscape, radiating throughout the nation from the ceremonial center, Washington, D.C. The neoclassical architecture of the capital with its many monuments and memorials purposely express the grandeur of the American experiment. This landscape, however, extends far beyond the nation's capital. It comprises the site of primal origins, Plymouth Rock; the site of the political birthplace of the nation, Independence Hall, with the Liberty Bell; Old North Church; the birthplaces, homes, and grave sites of presidents; the Statue of Liberty; and the complex of buildings on Ellis Island that expresses the enduring power of the symbol "Promised Land." There are memorial sites transformed by cataclysmic public events: Ford's Theater, the site of the assassination of Abraham Lincoln, and the Petersen home across the street where he died; and the Texas School Book Depository—now a museum—the building from which Lee Harvey Oswald shot and killed President John F. Kennedy.

Other sites of violence that violated the nation's idealized image of itself are only slowly being transformed into memorial complexes: The Birmingham Civil Rights District, which includes Kelly Ingram Park, where police dogs attacked marchers in the 1960s; the Birmingham Civil Rights Institute, which commemorates through multimedia exhibitions the story of the Civil Rights Movement and other issues related to human rights; and the Sixteenth Street Baptist Church, the site of the 1963 bombing that killed four young girls.

The patriotic landscape includes many places that memorialize war: street names, memorial halls and highways, cemeteries, museums, and most significantly, battlefields. These are ceremonial centers where Americans come to compete for ownership of sacred national stories and to argue about the "meaning of war, the efficacy of martial sacrifice, and the significance of preserving the patriotic landscape of the nation" (Linenthal, *Sacred Ground*, p. 1).

Memorial space is often ritualized space, where various commemorative activities support or, less often, subvert cultural ideals or hierarchies. The ideology of memorial space and commemorative ritual does not simply emerge naturally but is produced, most often by elites who are culturally and politically empowered to claim ownership of the means of representation. Who gets mentioned in commemorative addresses, and what role are they assigned? Who gets to speak at commemorative events? Who sculpts a statue, and where is it placed? Who decides what or who is really worth remembering? What will be the story line in a museum exhibition? Who is forgotten or pushed to the periphery?

Memorials not only intentionally remember—commemorating people, events, or ideas—they also intentionally forget. The Lincoln Memorial remembers a transcendent Lincoln removed from history, a "great savior" but not the "emancipator." The text above Daniel Chester French's sculpture does not speak of slavery. Although the president of Tuskegee Institute was asked to speak at the dedication of the memorial in 1922, African Americans were seated separately from whites. As has been the case with so many memorials emerging from the Civil War and slavery, the issue of slavery was simply displaced by emptying Lincoln of historical relevance. The cultural energies expressed in activities of remembering and forgetting reveal that memorial spaces are dynamic sites. Whatever the intentions of those who constructed the Lincoln Memorial, African Americans have used it as a site of protest, a place to call the nation back to its ideals. On Easter Sunday in 1939 Marian Anderson—in response to her having been denied permission to sing in Constitution Hall by the Daughters of the American Revolution—gave a concert there, and on 28 August 1963 approximately 400,000 people gathered to hear Martin Luther King Jr. deliver his "I Have a Dream" speech.

In spite of the wishes of those who envision and build memorials and wish to emplace a particular memory in perpetuity, no memorial message is frozen in time. Some memorials, like Grant's Tomb in New York City, do not seem to be evocative for future generations at all, and decompose into graffiti-laden, vandalized ordinary places. (Only in 1997 was Grant's Tomb the site of preservation efforts, which still do not guarantee it a privileged place in the hierarchy of American memory.) Other memorial sites, however, are vibrant, contested sites. They function less as shrines or temples than as forums, where the act of remembering in public by different communities for various reasons may be the only activity that binds these communities together.

Sometimes acts of contestation are visible, argued out in public: Should, for example, Arthur Ashe's statue be located on Monument Avenue in Richmond, Virginia, a shrinelike space to Confederate heroes? Often, however, struggles for ownership of the means of representation or for ownership of the site itself are an invisible part of a memorial's history. It is through critical examination of the biography of memorial processes and memorial sites themselves that this hidden history becomes visible.

The Little Bighorn National Monument. The monument, near Crow Agency, Montana, commemorates the June 1876 battles between the Seventh Cavalry and the Lakota (Sioux), Cheyenne, and Arapaho. © KEVIN R. MORRIS/ CORBIS

TRANSFORMING MEMORY: THE LITTLE BIGHORN BATTLEFIELD NATIONAL MONUMENT

The news of the death of Lt. Col. George Armstrong Custer and approximately 225 men of the Seventh Cavalry at the hands of Sioux and Cheyenne warriors on 25 June 1876 electrified and horrified the nation. Immediately, the dominant interpretation of the battle was formed: Custer and his men died to open the west for white civilization. Their blood sacrifice was the price to be paid for Manifest Destiny. For a century, this interpretation was enacted in commemorative ceremonies. Native Americans were not forgotten, they were transformed into palatable figures in the dominant narrative, characterized as brave but barbaric enemies, who were to be subjected.

The ideology of sacrifice was supported by the ideology of place. The National Park Service built its visitor center near the cemetery—established shortly after the battle—and near Custer Hill, where the bodies of Custer and some of his command were found. The memorial gaze looked out at the broad valley of the Little Bighorn from the site of the drama of the "last stand," an event celebrated in poetry, art, literature, and film. Custer Hill was also the site of a 36,000-pound granite monument, which arrived at the battlefield in 1881. Under it were buried the men of the Seventh Cavalry, and on it were inscribed their names.

It was not until the rise of Native American activism in the 1970s that the dominant ideology of the Little Bighorn came under direct attack. In 1976, during the centennial anniversary, members of the American Indian Movement (AIM) danced around the memorial holding an American flag upside down as a sign of distress and sang "Custer Died for Your Sins." Cheyenne held a counter ceremony at a nearby reservation, "a spiritual gathering [that] will pay homage to our forefathers who fell a hundred years ago defending a way of life." The centennial protests made it dramatically clear to the custodians of the site, the National Park Service, that what had been a shrine to Custer and the men of the Seventh Cavalry would need to be transformed into a historic site, a place at which the public could learn and remember the stories of different American communities who had engaged each other violently at this place.

Processes of transformation are often highly contested. For those who maintained that the Little Bighorn should forever be a shrine, any proposed alteration registered as one of two forms of defilement: (1) desecration, which is the violation of a ritual order through which the purity of a sacred place is maintained; and (2) dispossession, in which symbolic ownership of a memorial message changes hands. For Custerphiles, the ritual order necessary to maintain the patriotic orthodoxy of the site had been disrupted by the alteration of museum exhibitions to give more attention to Plains Indian tribes and by revised brochures that spoke not only of the heroism of Custer and the Seventh, but of "the last armed efforts of the Northern Plains Indians to preserve their ancestral way of life." There was fierce objection to changing the name of the battlefield from "Custer Battlefield National Monument" to "Little Bighorn Battlefield National Monument," an act that occurred on 10 December 1991, and strong objection as well to an Indian memorial to be dedicated in the early years of the twenty-first century. Those who did not want an Indian memorial understood that a physical monument forever changes the physical as well as the ideological landscape, making it impossible for the site to appear ever again as an uncontested shrine to Custer and the Seventh Cavalry.

There had been occasional proposals for an Indian memorial at the Little Bighorn from both Native Americans and whites since the early part of the twentieth century, but it was not until 1988, on the occasion of the 112th anniversary of the battle, that Native Americans dramatically displayed their anger over the monument issue. Following a prayer service held on the battlefield in conjunction with American Indian International Peace Day, AIM spokesperson Russell Means led a group to the enlisted men's mass grave under the monument, dug up a square-yard of soil and laid a plaque that read: "In honor of our Indian Patriots who fought and defeated the U.S. Calvary [sic]. In order to save our women and children from mass-murder. In doing so, preserving rights to our Homelands, Treaties and sovereignty."

This group saw the Seventh Cavalry monument as an alien intrusion into their memorial space, an enduring symbol of violent conquest. They struck at a sacred site to call attention to their demand for an Indian Memorial at the Little Bighorn. And, by 1997, a formal design competition had taken place, and a design selected for the Indian Memorial, to be located across the road from the existing monument.

There is no more controversial memorial environment in the United States than the Little Bighorn. Custerphiles and Custerphobes strive to implant their felt-truths about the meaning of this place in many ways. The site continues to be a dynamic memorial site, whose message will continue to evolve as Americans gather there to recall clashing narratives about a volatile past.

LOCATING MEMORY: THE HOLOCAUST MEMORIAL MUSEUM

The placid visage of the Washington Mall appears to its visitors an unchanging repository of core national stories. The Mall, however, like other memorial environments, has a dynamic history. The original vision of Major Pierre Charles L'Enfant, hired by President George Washington to design the capital city in 1790, included the geographical expression of the separation of governmental powers represented by the White House and the Capitol, and a monumental environment, a "Grand Avenue, 400 feet in breadth." Before the Civil War, the area was swampy, commercial land, and slave pens appeared on the Mall until 1850. During the war, volunteers drilled and bivouacked on the Mall. The Smithsonian Castle, completed in 1855, and the Washington Monument, completed in 1876, helped transform the Mall from a series of fragmented gardens into a pedagogical and memorial space. The enduring influence of the McMillan Plan of 1901–1902—named after Senator James McMillan of Michigan— ensured a unified vision of the Mall as memorial space. As was the case with the Washington Monument, other memorial proposals including the Lincoln Memorial, the Jefferson Memorial, the Vietnam Veterans Memorial, the World War II Memorial, and the Franklin D. Roosevelt Memorial have engendered fierce debate over a memorial's location and appropriate representation of its subject. On 22 April 1993, the United States Holocaust Memorial Museum was dedicated after much controversy.

The recommendations from the President's Commission on the Holocaust, submitted to President Jimmy Carter on 27 September 1979, called for the establishment of a "living memorial," to be made up of an educational institute, museum and memorial space, and a committee on conscience, which would publicize ongoing instances of genocide. There were questions about the propriety of a national, that is, governmentally supported, Holocaust memorial in the United States. Would it be a memorial out of place? Since the Holocaust was a European event, should it not be memorialized in Berlin, Warsaw, even in Israel, but not in the United States? Those who argued in favor of a living memorial responded that many survivors made new lives in the United States. Their memories were part of the national story as were those memories of American troops who encountered and liberated the concentration camps. They held that a memorial would be an act of repentance for what they saw as America's role as a complicit bystander before the war, when the State Department refused entry to Jews.

When it became clear that some sort of memorial would be built, questions of location were paramount. In what city would the memorial be located? Some favored New York, with its huge Jewish population. Others argued that Washington, D.C., the nation's capital, was the appropriate place. Once Washington was chosen, questions arose concerning the site of the museum.

The location of a memorial gives a clue to the importance of the memory. In 1980 the United States Holocaust Memorial Council considered twelve locations in Washington, D.C., including the eventual site of the United States Holocaust Memorial Museum, a site adjacent to the Washington Mall. For Holocaust survivors and other supporters of the museum, the location was fortuitous. A location near the Mall declared that Holocaust memory was to be placed within the nation's core stories, since the museum-memorial would be built within the nation's memorial core.

Once issues of memorial location were addressed, issues of architecture arose. What kind of building could appropriately memorialize the Holocaust and house a museum, an archive, and an educational center? Originally, Elie Wiesel and other survivors were moved by old brick buildings on the site that reminded them of the brick barracks in the main camp at Auschwitz. Soon, however, it became clear that these building were in ill-repair and too small to serve as memorial and museum. Several building proposals failed to satisfy, and finally the distinguished architect James Ingo Freed designed the evocative building that stands on the site.

Freed believed that the building itself had to be expressive. It had to communicate something of the Holocaust to the visitor. It could not just be a neutral container, a site for a provocative museum exhibit. Freed's building contains the Hall of Remembrance, a hexagonal building, as well as the Hall of Witness, a three-story museum, library, and educational space.

The Hall of Witness is itself an eloquent architectural statement. Brick, steel, and glass work together to create a brooding and often cold building, evocative of the camps. Interestingly, while the location of the building adjacent the Washington Mall was significant, Freed's architecture wants to take visitors away from the Mall. His use of internal space is designed to communicate the feel of "inexorable, forced movement: disruption, alienation, constriction, observation, selection" (Linenthal, *Preserving Memory*, p. 88). Freed's windows do not allow museum visitors to be "saved" from their immersion in the world of the Holocaust by looking out clearly at the Mall. Their views are obstructed, narrow, removing them further from the United States.

The Hall of Remembrance, the distinct memorial space, was the subject of several substantive controversies. Freed had originally planned red brick windows, evocative of the ghettoes. Some members of the Fine Arts Commission, one of the regulatory groups charged with ruling on issues of aesthetic appropriateness in Washington buildings, were bothered by this, arguing that such gloomy windows would "contaminate" the Mall. Hence, Freed was pressured to change to limestone windows.

Another difficult issue concerned the question of inclusion. This was a national Holocaust Memorial Museum, and the issue of the portrayal of various victims in addition to Jews remained a sensitive one throughout the project. The guiding philosophy of the museum was that the Holocaust was a "unique" event, with Jews at its center, killed, in Elie Wiesel's aphoristic solution, because of who they were, not because of what they did. The pluralistic imperative of a national memorial museum, however, called for recognition of many other Holocaust victims. Some Jewish survivors argued that the Hall of Remembrance should be solely Jewish space, with "others" remembered elsewhere. After bitter arguments in the mid-1980s, the issue was resolved in favor of the pluralistic imperative, but the issue reveals the volatility of the construction of memorial space.

Several million people a year visit the United States Holocaust Memorial Museum. The use of distinct museum, memorial, and educational space became a conceptual model for another major project to memorialize the 19 April 1995 bombing of the Alfred P. Murrah Building in Oklahoma City that claimed 168 people, including 19 children.

CREATING MEMORY: THE OKLAHOMA CITY NATIONAL MEMORIAL

With the exception of sites associated with violent encounters between Native Americans and whites, Sand Creek, for example, the American memorial landscape does not contain many memorials to sites of mass murder. Cultural geographer Kenneth Foote observes that there is no societal "ritual of effacement," or ritual of purification to cleanse a community or a particular site from the shame and contamination of mass murder (*Shadowed Ground*, p. 179). Sites of mass murder are most often obliterated from the physical landscape in the hopes that they will be obliterated from memory. Edward Gein's farmstead in Wisconsin was burned down, Jeffrey Dahmer's Milwaukee apartment building was torn down, as was John Wayne Gacy's suburban Chicago home.

The response in Oklahoma City was remarkably different. The act was not only one of mass murder, but domestic terrorism, locating the story in a national context and removing many of the elements of shame that a community often feels when mass murder occurs in its midst. The iconic images of the jagged remains of the Murrah Building, the ongoing drama of the search for survivors and bodies of the dead, the horrific image of a baby's torn body—one-year-old Baylee Almon, cradled in the arms of fireman Chris Fields—moved many Americans, indeed many people around the world, to envision themselves part of a bereaved community that transcended geographical boundaries, and this led many to marshall the symbolic resources at their disposal and propose memorials within hours of the bombing.

These unsolicited proposals ranged from crayon drawings to sophisticated blueprints of parks, reflecting pools, fountains, statues, playgrounds, memorial halls, and a wide variety of monuments made out of the rubble of the Murrah Building. Many people specified certain kinds of memorial materials—stone, grasses, trees, or bushes that were appropriate to the state of Oklahoma and to the event.

In the meantime Ron Norick, mayor of Oklahoma City, appointed a 350-member task force—made up of family members of those killed, survivors of the bombing, rescue workers, and community leaders—whose job it was to recommend an appropriate memorial. This group undertook a mass solicitation of the public's ideas on what the memorial should express. It then composed a mission statement that included the themes that would have to be embodied in the memorial and created a design competition process.

One of the distinctive features of the creation of this memorial is the fact that the entire process has been self-consciously designed to be therapeutic for a bereaved community. Traditionally, at a dedication of a memorial, speeches will point to the healing elements of the memorial. In Oklahoma City, the very process of creating the memorial was public, sensitive to the fact that family members of those murdered and survivors of the bombing would not accept a memorial planned and executed only by artistic elites for them. In a clear example of the democratization of memorial processes, members of this bereaved community used a memorial process to engage their grief and create a memorial by consensus.

The task force eventually became the Oklahoma City National Memorial Foundation, and the formal design competition attracted over six hundred entries from all fifty states and twenty-three countries.

On 19 April 1997, the second anniversary of the bombing, the Oklahoma City Attorney Robert M. Johnson, chairman of the foundation, announced that the design of Hans and Torrey Butzer was chosen unanimously for the memorial, as it best embodied the guiding words of the mission statement: "We come here to remember those who were killed, those who survived and those changed forever. May all who leave here know the impact of violence. May this memorial offer comfort, strength, peace, hope, and serenity."

The Butzer's memorial removes visitors from urban space through "gates of time." An eastern gate is inscribed with the time "9:01," one minute before the bomb exploded, and the western gate is inscribed with "9:03." The grassy site of the Murrah Building, "sacred ground," according to the mission statement, is populated by 168 empty chairs, the heart of the memorial. The "Survivor Tree," which stands in what was a parking lot at the time of the bombing and was scarred by exploding cars, commemorates those who survived, and an orchard of fruit trees remembers rescuers. There is a special place for children, and a long reflecting pool near the empty chairs.

Like the Holocaust Memorial Museum, this is a memorial environment that includes an educational and exhibition center.

Another form of memorialization preceded the formal memorial processes initiated by the mayor's task force. In the early stages of the grim recovery work, search and rescue teams placed flags and flowers and wrote commemorative messages on the rubble, and people began bringing items to leave at fences set up several blocks from the Murrah Building that restricted entry to the site. After the implosion of the building in May 1995, a chain link fence was erected around the vacant Murrah site, and almost immediately this became a "people's memorial." A fence, designed to keep people off hallowed ground, to restrict entry, became something quite different. It became a complex memorial site that functioned for people in various ways.

There is a long tradition of pilgrims leaving devotional materials at sacred sites. In America, it has become increasingly popular to leave commemorative items at places of special concern, for example, at the site of John Lennon's death and at the site of the former McDonald's in San Ysidro, California, where on 18 July 1984 James Huberty shot and killed twenty-one people. The Vietnam Veterans Memorial in Washington, D.C., became much more than black walls of granite engraved with the names of American dead; it also became a people's

The Vietnam Veterans Memorial. Of the many memorials to Vietnam veterans across America, "The Wall" in Washington, D.C., designed by Maya Lin, is the most famous. © JAMES P. BLAIR/CORBIS

memorial through the tremendous expression of material commemoration. Indeed, the National Park Service now collects and catalogs items left at the wall.

As at the Vietnam Veterans Memorial, people in Oklahoma City made a simple chain link fence their own memorial through commemorative and devotional materials. Families brought personal items: a deceased's shoes or earrings, or a photograph, and placed them on the fence as well as letters to and about their loved ones and public letters that function as testimonial literature. Some people had birthday parties for their loved ones at the fence. It became a place to communicate with those who had died.

The fence became an intimate devotional space for family members and survivors as well as a public commemorative site for visitors. The fence became

so important to many family members and survivors that they were uncomfortable that the memorial design incorporated only several small sections. They felt larger portions of the fence should be a part of the memorial and available for continued memorial activity. On 26 October 1998, portions of the fence were moved and placed in the memorial environment.

Like the United States Holocaust Memorial Museum, the Oklahoma City National Memorial Foundation hoped its memorial would express the conviction "Never Again" to visitors. No matter how laudable the memorial message, however, memorials cannot do the remembering for people. It is in the interaction between memorial and visitor that memorials come alive or remain silent witnesses to the convictions of an earlier generation.

See also **The Classical Vision; The Arts in the Republican Era; American Romanticism; Realism in Art and Literature; The Artist and the Intellectual in the New Deal** *(volume 1);* **Postmodernism and the Arts** *(volume 2);* **Museums; Myth and Symbol; History and the Study of the Past** *(in this volume); and other articles in this section.*

BIBLIOGRAPHY

Bodnar, John. *Remaking America: Public Memory, Commemoration, and Patriotism in the Twentieth Century.* Princeton, N.J., 1992.

Chidester, David, and Edward T. Linenthal, eds. *American Sacred Space.* Bloomington, Ind., 1995.

Foote, Kenneth E. *Shadowed Ground: America's Landscapes of Violence and Tragedy.* Austin, Tex., 1997.

Hass, Kristin Ann. *Carried to The Wall: American Memory and the Vietnam Veterans Memorial.* Berkeley, Calif., 1998.

Kammen, Michael. *Mystic Chords of Memory: The Transformation of Tradition in American Culture.* New York, 1991.

Levinson, Sanford. *Written in Stone: Public Monuments in Changing Societies.* Durham, N.C., 1998.

Linenthal, Edward T. *Preserving Memory: The Struggle to Create America's Holocaust Museum.* New York, 1995.

———. *Sacred Ground: Americans and Their Battlefields.* 2d ed. Urbana, Ill., 1993.

Marling, Karal Ann. *The Colossus of Roads.* Minneapolis, Minn., 1984.

Marling, Karal Ann, and John Wetenhall. *Iwo Jima: Monuments, Memories, and the American Hero.* Cambridge, Mass., 1991.

Piehler, G. Kurt. *Remembering War the American Way.* Washington, D.C., 1995.

Rothman, Hal. *Preserving Different Pasts: The American National Monuments.* Urbana, Ill., 1989.

Savage, Kirk. *Standing Soldiers, Kneeling Slaves: Race, War, and Monument in Nineteenth-Century America.* Princeton, N.J., 1997.

Sears, John F. *Sacred Places: American Tourist Attractions in the Nineteenth Century.* New York, 1989.

Vale, Lawrence J. *Architecture, Power, and National Identity.* New Haven, Conn., 1992.

Williams, Peter W. *Houses of God: Region, Religion, and Architecture in the United States.* Urbana, Ill., 1997.

Wilson, Charles Reagan. *Baptized in Blood: The Religion of the Lost Cause, 1865–1920.* Athens, Ga., 1980.

Young, James E. *The Texture of Memory: Holocaust Memorials and Meaning.* New Haven, Conn., 1993.

Zelinsky, Wilbur. *Nation into State: The Shifting Symbolic Foundations of American Nationalism.* Chapel Hill, N.C., 1988.

MEMORY

David Thelen

The study of how individuals and groups remember the past exploded over the past two decades of the twentieth century from a peripheral concern in the human sciences to a central theme in topics stretching from personality to culture, from trauma to nationhood, from identity to power. "An astonishing variety of concerns are pulled in under that one heading: memory," the philosopher Ian Hacking commented in *Rewriting the Soul* (p. 3).

Observing that a "lack of clear focus" has led to definitional confusion in memory studies, Alan Confino and others have argued that perhaps the clearest approach to the topic is to explore changes, conflicts, and continuities over time in ways people have experienced and understood memory. A history of memory would explore intersections among concerns that have troubled people across centuries and particular challenges that gave a unique cast and special urgency to discussion of those concerns at particular moments. After introducing broad issues of technology, periodization, and recurring challenges, this essay illustrates the importance of time and place in shaping how people made sense of those challenges by focusing on two pivotal crises in Western understanding of memory: those of the early nineteenth and late twentieth centuries. The second of these crises propelled prominently to the center of historical debate two long-standing issues that receive separate attention at the end of the essay, the relation of individual to collective memory and more generally of memory to history.

HISTORY OF MEMORY

Four developments in forms of communications—oral, written, print, electronic—have framed a debate over the significance of media in shaping how individuals have recorded, retrieved, constructed, and transmitted memories. In an oral culture, for example, Patrick Hutton has argued, the past lives in memory through repetition and vanishes when it no longer serves a present need. By removing experiences from the flow of oral tradition and assigning them a specific time and place recorded in documents, writing encouraged people to distinguish now from then, the time of remembering from the time being remembered. While allowing them to reach further into the past and retrieve the past with greater confidence, print culture also introduced a new critical distance between past and present as people scrutinized before they reiterated accounts from the past. Other scholars have insisted that technological changes were not independent causes of change but rather embedded in larger conflicts of power. While the printing of large numbers of standardized versions of case reports made possible the emergence of the legal doctrine of precedent in early modern England, Richard Ross has argued, those printed reports of cases became the means for new lawyers to wrench power from local luminaries and judges and, more broadly, to shift the arena of judging behavior from the gossip and shaming by communities to trials managed by lawyers in courtrooms. Still others have argued that technologies have not changed how people use memories in their everyday relationships.

The explosion of attention to memory in the 1980s and 1990s has led scholars to try to identify other "memory crises" in the past. These were times when changes in the larger society interfered with the customary ease with which people drew on and transmitted their experiences. Memories became battlegrounds as new authorities invented new understandings and mechanisms for the transmission of memories and challenged the traditional competence and contents by which people remembered the past. These conflicts and ruptures in the ordinary transparency of memory made visible and urgent problems people experienced as they tried to use the past. Historians have identified unique features that connected and characterized different uses of memory in each period. In a brilliant study of "memory sites" that range from commemorative statues and stock market trades to forensic records and scientific research, Matt K. Matsuda identified a distinctive *Memory of the Modern* that set discussion of these issues in late-nineteenth-century France apart from debates about memory at other times.

RECURRING CHALLENGES TO MEMORY

The Greeks made their goddess of memory, Mnemosyne, also their goddess of wisdom, the mother of the muses, one of whom was Clio, the muse of history. From their memories people have long developed their awareness of what makes them like and unlike others. Even while noting the unique form memory takes at different times, Matt Matsuda observed that memory since antiquity has played recurring rhetorical roles of bearing witness, informing judgment, and giving voice. People have struggled with the painful knowledge that lessons and experiences will be forgotten, that the past can only be recalled imperfectly, and that memories of painful experiences cannot be controlled by an act of will.

Forgetting presents the first obstacle that people have grappled with as they have tried to insure that experiences and lessons will be remembered. Herodotus, considered by many the first historian, argued that history's purpose was "preserving from decay the remembrance of what men have done." Seeking to preserve their defining identity in the collective memory of their enslavement, deliverance, and redemption, Jews struggled against forgetting by embedding and re-enacting those defining experiences in rituals of Passover that at the family table insured that the vital past would be transmitted from one generation to the next. At every wedding Jews broke a glass to remember the destruction of the original temple. "Do this in memory of me," Jesus instructed his disciples at the Last Supper in launching a Christian ritual re-enacted at every subsequent mass or communion. In religious rituals or stained-glass windows or in strings tied around their fingers, people have struggled against forgetting.

The great creativity and difficulty of remembering resulted from a second challenge: people were driven by a vast range of present needs and contexts to reach into their pasts for guidance but knew, as Richard Terdiman wrote in *Present Past,* that the past "can never be brought back in tact" (p. 21). Instead of retrieving a full or accurate picture of what happened in the past, people expected memories to come as incomplete fragments of dubious accuracy, often the product of contests and shifting perspectives, constructed by them to meet present needs.

Since remembering was more about construction than retrieval, people had to face the difficulties of making those constructions in the present—clashing perspectives, fading fragments, blurring needs—that led them to revisit similar occasions in the past. They assessed how they felt in the present about what they had done and said in the past and whether in order to sustain or change their behavior they needed to take responsibility in the present for how they had acted in the past. The ancient origins of the words English speakers used to describe how they felt in the present about how they remembered earlier experiences are reflected in the Latin origins of the processes by which they recovered those experiences—re-present, re-live, re-enact, re-collect, re-trieve, and indeed re-member—the feelings those re-enactments triggered in the present—re-venge, re-gret, re-morse—and the actions they contemplated taking—re-tribution, re-pair, re-nig, rehabilitation, re-stitution, re-demption. The challenge of constructed memories introduced the rich range of choices in the present that challenged people as they remembered the past: pride and joy, guilt and shame, fear and hope, grief and mourning.

Observing that there were two kinds of memories—those that people could summon from their consciousness and those that rose, unsolicited and often unwanted, from the unconscious—Aristotle defined a third persistent challenge: how to put to rest the memory of suffering, pain and cruelty, indeed of dark and terrible things, both personal and cultural, that people have carried around and that returned unbidden as nightmares to haunt them. Religions provided sinners with rituals and beliefs that assisted them to move beyond things they had done and now wanted to forget. New theories and technologies of healing—psychoanalysis, for example—have emerged specifically to help people recover from and then move beyond unwanted traumas and memories.

MEMORY CRISIS OF THE EARLY NINETEENTH CENTURY

The memory crisis of the early nineteenth century grew from movements that profoundly challenged traditional uses of the past, giving memory, tradition, and history new visibility, authority, and uses, turning them from natural ways of retrieving the past into cutting edges of political and cultural conflicts. Before the nineteenth century, Pierre Nora has argued, memory was such an automatic part of everyday life that few people even commented on it. But political revolution, inspired by American (1776) and French (1789) examples, blurred into market and industrial revolution in the early nineteenth century. Champions of change sought to free individuals—their minds, souls, votes, enterprises, consciences, bodies—from traditional constraints and to create new agencies—nation-states, political parties, evangelical religious sects, popular newspapers—that could represent and fulfill their ambitions, dislodge privileged hierarchies, replace deference to tradition with a newfound faith in progress and development, and enshrine public opinion as the new arbiter of the desirability of claims to the authority of the past. To dislodge traditional rulers and their privileges they needed to dislodge the traditions that sustained them.

These interconnected movements—democracy, capitalism, nationalism, individualism, romanticism, progress—sought to legitimate their new order by presenting their new ways as the natural fulfillment of traditions. Indeed, they invented traditions and commemorations that they hoped could unite behind their causes, people who had in fact shared few memories. American nationalists fashioned a new civil religion grounded in veneration for how courageous individuals had fought to create a new nation founded in the defense of traditional English and European ideals of freedom whose fulfillment had been blocked in Europe. They created national heroes—George Washington, first and foremost—and placed their likenesses on statues, money, stamps, publications, parks, and street names to remind people of the great sacrifices that had gone into creating the new nation. They created a national holiday, the Fourth of July, to commemorate the nation's birth in a mission to fulfill traditional aspirations for freedom and equality.

The memory crisis came about because many Americans asserted memories and traditions to challenge the new nationalists. To resist competition and individualism nineteenth-century Americans created mutual aid societies around rituals they fashioned out of medieval pageantry—Knights of Pythias, Knights of Labor—that asserted that mutual aid, not competition, was the traditional way of life. Other Americans appealed to local memories to fuel movements to secede from the Union—most dramatically during the Civil War—for regional traditions continued throughout the nineteenth century, as Michael Kammen has argued, to

pose compelling alternatives to national narratives. And national traditions could be appealed to by people with radically different local values. Both abolitionists and slaveholders, Unionists and Confederates, quoted the Declaration of Independence as inspiration for their actions.

All over the West—in Italy, Germany, and Mexico, as in the United States—memories became battlegrounds as promoters of change faced popular resistance grounded in local traditions. Wars over memories widened into larger struggles over what had actually happened in the past, over what should be remembered and forgotten, over who had the authority and with what sources to arbitrate the conflicts and to provide the most authoritative narratives about change over time. The new discipline of history grew up alongside the new nation-states to record and champion their growing strength, to gather and disseminate the state's records, to impose national identities on earlier generations that had in fact not felt them, to provide the narratives that justified the new nation's claims to fulfill older aspirations. "To make themselves the masters of memory and forgetfulness is one of the great preoccupations of the classes, groups and individuals who have dominated and continue to dominate historical societies," Jacques Le Goff observed in *History and Memory* (p. 54). Developing a new "discipline" with critical methods for sorting through conflicting memories and documents to establish what had actually happened, the new historians argued that their new "science" made them the best people to be entrusted with remembering and to identify the continuities that should be passed on. In place of memories grounded in local traditions historians presented "national perspective," privileging wars, revolutions, changes in government bound together because they happened in the same country and justified the historians' faith in progress that culminated in the nation.

MEMORY CRISIS OF THE LATE TWENTIETH CENTURY

The central theme of the memory crisis at the end of the twentieth century was the emergence of "memory as an approach to so many of the problems of life, from child rearing to patriotism, from aging to anxiety," Ian Hacking wrote (p. 3). The development that centered this explosion of interest in memory (and its twin, forgetting) was the opposite of the cause of the early-nineteenth-century crisis: the collapse of faith in the nation-state as the consolidator of diverse experiences and of confidence in its narratives as organizing frameworks for individuals, groups, and the discipline of history. In place of national narratives and nineteenth-century faith in technology and progress, American and other cultures fragmented, with people finding new authenticity in personal and group instead of national memories.

With the rapid spread of global commerce and communications and growing charges—from the Left in the 1960s and the Right in the 1980s—that nation-states were incapable of governing, citizens of Western countries began to question their earlier faith that nation-states were necessary, desirable, or even inevitable. As Americans increasingly questioned whether the nation-state could deliver economic growth, justice, and order at home and abroad, the proportion of Americans who told Gallup's pollsters that they could "trust Washington to do what is right all or most of the time" plummeted from 78 percent in 1964 to 19 percent by 1994. This "retreat from transformative politics" and "loss of a future orientation, of progress toward civic enfranchisement and growing equality," in Charles Maier's words, led them to experience community mainly within the groups (p. 150).

The collapse of faith in a shared and just national future encouraged groups to profoundly reshape their uses of the past to fit new expectations for how the state should respond to injustices they experienced. At first, from the 1930s through the 1970s, labor, civil rights, antiwar, and feminist movements appealed to national ideals and demanded admission to the full benefits of American citizenship, benefits they also sought to expand. By the 1980s, with faith in national narratives declining, groups assembled and documented their experiences as a record of suffering and victimization that could be remedied not by inclusion in a national whole but by special recognition and compensation for their group. Groups presented their memories not as a future-oriented struggle for incorporation into a fairer and shared society but as a past-oriented attempt to document who had been a victim, entitled to compensation and apology, and who had been a perpetrator, entitled to censure and punishment. From the 1970s through the late 1990s seventeen nations established truth commissions to document and re-enact human rights violations from the past as they gave voice to the suffering and pain of victims and censured perpetrators. In 1973 Canada enacted a pioneering policy of "multiculturalism" that encouraged people to document, take pride in, and receive recognition and compensation for their distinctive cultural heritages. To compensate for suffering inflicted on 120,000 Japanese Americans through wartime relocation, Congress in the 1980s formally apologized and granted compensation to survivors. By the 1990s the movement for apologies and compensation broadened to include descendants of slaves, Indians, and others who had been victimized long in the past. Australians held formal Sorry Days in 2000 to apologize for their treatment of Aborigines.

Memories of the Holocaust and child abuse raised particularly troubling larger questions. As witnesses, survivors of the Holocaust brought firsthand knowledge to refute those who tried to deny or minimize the horrors of what had happened, and their accounts underscored limitations of historical scholarship in conveying deeper human meanings of experience. Many younger Germans faced difficulties reaching through written accounts to figure out their responsibility for what their grandparents' generation had done in administering the Holocaust. With the dying of witnesses came issues of how human meaning and memory would be passed on and at what point and in what ways the sins and traumas of the fathers should or could be visited upon, indeed shape, future generations.

The second group whose traumas drew special attention to issues of memory were psychiatric patients who in growing numbers told stories, often elicited by their therapists, of how they had been abused in childhood by their parents. Creating a False Memory Syndrome Foundation in 1992, many parents challenged therapists for instilling in their patients traumas that had never happened. The special urgency over how to remember and work through trauma, whether real or imagined, whether as victim or perpetrator, created controversies that centered on memory but also highlighted limitations as well as strengths of more conventional ways of recalling and recording the past.

The ebbing faith in a shared national past led individuals to place more trust in their own memories and experiences. In 1994–1995 Americans, when asked to choose, said they were more interested in the pasts of their families than the past of the United States. They trusted their grandparents more than books or television programs for information about the past and felt much closer to the past when they gathered with their families than when they studied history in school, Roy Rosenzweig and David Thelen reported from a national survey. The ebbing of faith in national progress by the 1970s and 1980s inspired movements to preserve the natural and built environment against change and to commemorate and reenact nostalgic moments. "Dissevered from any idea of national destiny," Raphael Samuel observed in *Theatres of Memory*, heritage "is free to wander at will . . . attaching itself to a promiscuous variety of objects" from Civil War re-enactments to Elvis Presley impersonators to baseball card collectors. "The past," Samuel observed, "is seen not as a prelude to the present but an alternative to it, 'another country'" (p. 221).

The routes by which scholars came to the subject of memory strikingly paralleled the larger decline of faith in the nation-state and the course followed by social movements. What began in the 1960s as a movement to create a new "history from the bottom up" that would present a more inclusive picture of the actors and activities and conflicts that together made up national history, as fuel for political movements to redistribute power, steadily retreated and turned inward along with the political movements that had spawned this new social history. Students of social groups increasingly envisioned themselves not as activists but as academic specialists. Gradually abandoning political activism, scholars developed increasingly sophisticated explanations for why the powerful were able to deflect movements for change in the past and why groups instead of fighting had turned inward to inhabit autonomous "separate spheres" on their own terms.

The new social history followed the broader cultural thrust toward "postmodernism," which encouraged scholars to abandon the faith that history followed grand narratives, its course defined by experts, and instead to champion the right and capacity of individuals and groups to make their own lives. Condemning totalitarianism and total wars, widening gulfs between haves and have-nots, scientific and technological nightmares as products and tolls of modernism, Jean-François Lyotard in his influential 1979 book, later published in English as *The Postmodern Condition*, defined the "*postmodern* as incredulity toward master narratives." Critics like Kerwin Klein characterized Lyotard's "postmodern reckonings of history as the marching black boot and of historical consciousness as an oppressive fiction" (p. 145). The study of memory—of the re-presentations people made of their living pasts—thus provided an approach for historians not to impose their narratives but instead to listen to people describe their own movement through time, construct their own histories.

Challenges to the nation-state and the capacity of history to represent what mattered from the past sparked "history wars" in the 1980s and 1990s. Pro-

fessional historians asserted that their special training made them uniquely competent to evaluate public presentations of history in school textbooks, museum exhibits, and television programs. A resurgent political Right in the 1980s and 1990s, victorious in politics, hoped to turn traditional patriotic narratives into weapons to dislodge the Left from the academic and cultural institutions it had captured with its new scholarship. While the academic Left and political Right fought over who had the right and competence to construct and interpret the past, both sides criticized Americans for "cultural amnesia" and a lack of "historical literacy," for the failure to remember what they needed to be citizens. In so doing they identified a central challenge in the late-twentieth-century memory crisis: individuals rarely conformed to collective or partisan visions of how they should use the past.

INDIVIDUAL AND COLLECTIVE MEMORY

Memory has remained a slippery topic because the same word describes a continuum from the personal and individual, where scholars have emphasized psychological issues of motivation and perception, to the collective and institutional, where scholars have emphasized anthropological and political issues about how cultures establish traditions. But scholars are coming to agree on how an individual connects with collective memory.

Individuals construct memories as acts of self-awareness. Individuals remember in order to become more autonomous people, to figure who they are and want to be, to frame choices for the future, to build competence and confidence as interpreters and participants in everyday relationships and the larger world. This work became harder at the turn of the twenty-first century precisely because individuals belong to multiplying numbers of groups and have access to proliferating traditions from which they construct their uses of the past.

But since they construct memories in relationships with others, individuals require other people to encourage and confirm their accounts, to help decide what to remember and how to interpret what they recalled. Indeed, this intimate making and sharing of memories is, as Fred Davis wrote, "in itself the very elixir of friendmaking" (*Yearning for Yesterday*, 1979, p. 43). They shape memories out of larger cultural and political conflicts out of which rivals present alternative narratives to define where the group comes from and is heading.

"How groups remember and contend in the marketplace of power and culture for hegemony is perhaps the central problem in the study of historical memory," David Blight wrote. Collective memory has become, as philosophers from Friedrich Nietzsche to Michel Foucault presented it, simply another arena for watching groups and cultures advance their interests. The fight for "collective memory is one of the great stakes of . . . dominated and dominating classes, all of them struggling for power or for life, for survival or for advancement," wrote Jacques Le Goff (pp. 97–98). For some, collective memories have been battlegrounds between groups, between newly freed slaves, Union and Confederate veterans for possession of memory of the Civil War, for example. For others collective memories have become more about documenting injustices and claiming power than guides to life, becoming battlegrounds between the nation-state or dominant culture and those who resist them, between "official" and "vernacular" memories, as John Bodnar has put it. The narrative of how workers and immigrants turned collective memories grounded in their workplace and ethnic cultures into nineteenth- and twentieth-century yardsticks for measuring and resisting changes imposed on them by employers and Americanizers has become a major theme of social history advanced by scholars like Herbert Gutman, David Montgomery, and George Lipsitz.

Since traditions instilled group identity with the authority of the past, groups sought to freeze and present their versions of the past in statues and memorials (to remember George Washington or war veterans), in commemorations and holidays (to remember the birth of Jesus Christ, Abraham Lincoln, or Martin Luther King Jr., or the struggles remembered on Labor, Armistice, or Independence Days), on names given to streets and parks, in photographs, in memoirs, and even in markings or uniforms they wore on their bodies. When their enemies came to power they destroyed statues (as Parisian Communards did in the 1870s to a towering monument to Napoleon and anti-Communists did in the 1980s to statues of Vladimir Lenin throughout Eastern Europe) and renamed streets. Groups gave memorials new meanings. The Lincoln Memorial was officially placed on the Mall in Washington in 1922 to commemorate Lincoln's victorious struggle to preserve the Union during the Civil War, but after the Park Service permitted the black singer Marian Anderson to use it for a 1939 concert after she was denied the right to sing in Constitution Hall, civil rights groups turned the Lincoln Memorial into a major site for civil rights struggles, the culminating point for many of the marches on Washington in the 1960s.

By the late twentieth century, a time when commemoration fragmented and individuals placed greatest faith in their own memories, many of the most popular commemorative activities combined the opportunity for individuals to honor and recognize other individuals, including those who viewed a memorial, with the larger group or cause they sought to commemorate. The Vietnam Veterans Memorial, placed on the Mall in Washington, quickly became the most popular memory site in Washington. Bearing the name of each veteran killed, reflecting off its black marble surface the face of individuals as they look at the memorial, inviting them to wonder what this event has to do with them, this memorial provided a stunning opportunity for individuals to bring their own memories to a commemorative site. In *To Heal a Nation*, Jan Scruggs, the veteran who led the campaign to create the memorial, insisted that "there was no such thing as 'the war in Vietnam.' There had been many wars. The people back home had fought about Vietnam while their soldiers fought in Vietnam. And the soldiers themselves had vastly differing opinions and experiences" (pp. 25, 70–71, 126). And individuals left at the memorial their personal memories as they left letters and mementos. "Dear Michael: Your name is here but you are not. I made of rubbing of it, thinking that if I rubbed hard enough, I would rub your name off the wall and you would come back to me. I miss you so." Or, wrote a mother: "So here I am again, left with empty arms and memories. But as my tears fall, I am thankful to God for having had you for 21 years and all the remembered love and happiness we shared. I will hold you in my memories and wait for another night when I dream of you again. Mom" (William Broyles, "A Ritual for Saying Goodbye," *U.S. News and World Report,* 10 November 1986, p. 9). Individuals brought and left items that linked them to individuals, but those artifacts, stuck into letters on the wall or left at its base, together contributed to making the memorial, in fact, a collective memorial to individuals who had fought and those individuals who had loved and remembered them as well as to those who wanted to remember their own struggles, from whatever perspective, over the Vietnam War.

This combining of vivid personal remembrances into a larger cultural and political statement took even more dramatic form in the AIDS Quilt. Individuals made visual reminders of loved ones who had died of AIDS on small patches of cloth, which were stitched together to make a huge quilt that turned hundreds of intimate relationships into a larger visual image of a culture suffering from a traumatic epidemic—giving collective and cultural meaning to the names and memories of individuals—a visual cry for help from a larger American culture whose hostility and indifference had contributed to the epidemic and thus to advocates' demands for compensation.

MEMORY AND HISTORY

The recent explosion of interest in memory has profoundly challenged historians to reconsider cherished assumptions. "The problem of memory's relationship to history has in the 1990s moved to the center of the historiographical stage. From the standpoint of the theory of history, the memory/history puzzle is conceivably today's most engaging topic," Patrick Hutton wrote in a 1994 article for *History and Theory* (vol. 33, 1994, p. 95).

Although the Greeks imagined Memory as the mother of History, historians over the past two centuries have generally presented them as opposing approaches to the past. They have portrayed history as the story of what happened in the past and memory as the story of what is remembered from what happened in the past. Originating in storytelling and oral traditions, transmitted in face-to-face relationships, memory is owned, revised, and passed on to meet needs of the relationship of a rememberer to the next person to receive the story. It travels in multiple fragments, among individuals, carried along by grief, pride, anger, sorrow, and loss as the living past blurs into and gets repeated in the present. History, by contrast, synthesizes and integrates individual experiences and fragments into a single larger narrative, a big picture, shaped by the historian. Where memory transmits the feeling of the moment, history is skeptical of all accounts and harnesses that skepticism to construct the most accurate possible account. Where memory transmits whatever is living at the moment of remembering, history emphasizes discontinuity with the past, a self-conscious act of looking at the past from a different time, the present. Heirs of a tradition reaching back at least to Friedrich Nietzsche, many historians have seen memory as the bearer of everything history existed to suppress, its opposite. "History is perpetually suspicious of memory," Pierre Nora wrote "and its true mission is to destroy it" (pp. 8–9, 22). The new prominence given to narratives presented by survivors and victims has further alarmed many historians by introducing unfamiliar psychological, spiritual, and religious perspectives on the past.

In the late twentieth century, however, many scholars sought to reconfigure relationships between memory and history. Constructing them as opposites imposed on each a coherence that each in fact lacks and makes it harder to choose among the many possibilities and traditions that have been carried by each. "The beauty of memory," Alan Confino wrote, "is that it is imprecise enough to be appropriated by unexpected hands, to connect apparently unrelated topics, to explain anew old problems" (p. 1403). Popular memory provides a meeting ground for academic and popular uses of the past. Long eager to present alternative voices for criticizing the mainstream developments they describe, historians have found in memory's concern with the intimate and authentic voice of lived experience a fertile source of just such alternatives, as Randolph Starn has argued. The accuracy of memories, some argued, should be challenged by history's skepticism, its quest for multiple and competing voices, because unexamined memories could be incomplete and inaccurate and could produce dysfunctional, paranoid, stupid, and even deadly use of the past—in violent forms of racist and anti-Semitic memories, for example. "A bit less memory and a bit more history would not be such a bad thing," Thomas Laquer observed, arguing for "the history of the political and moral failures, for example, that produced the Holocaust rather than the memory of its horrors" (p. 8). Sharing a postmodern uneasiness with both objectifying and totalizing practices inherited from the craft's past, eager to respect differences in ways people experienced their pasts, its intimacy and immediacy, others have looked for ways to incorporate the firsthand voices of survivors and witnesses into more conventional concerns of historians. Saul Friedlander has called for "the simultaneous acceptance" of both the "intense emotion" of survivors' memories and their wariness toward the "distancing or 'numbness'" of scholars' accounts and commentary to "disrupt the facile linear progression of the narration, introduce alternative interpretations, question any partial conclusion, withstand the need for closure" by "using any number of different vantage points" (pp. 131, 132). "Once history loses contact with memory, it tends to address dead issues," Dominick LaCapra has warned, but memory needs history both to adjudicate its claims to truth and to pass along critically tested memory (p. 20). Perhaps the most important breakthrough for historians in late-twentieth-century fascination with memory was the discovery that memory is "a process of engaging with the past rather than a means to call it up," Marita Sturken argued in *Tangled Memories*. "If memory is redefined as a social and individual practice that integrates elements of remembrance, fantasy, and invention, then it can shift the problematic role of standing for truth to a new role as an active, engaging practice of creating meaning" (p. 259).

But while late-twentieth-century approaches have emphasized memory's creative capacity for interpretation, Richard Terdiman reminds historians that "memory still incorporates a powerful intuition that the past is not just our own invention. The past still answers us and still constrains our own response to it" (p. 350) and that intuition is what sets both memory and history apart from other windows on culture.

See also **The Print Revolution** *(volume 1);* **Poststructuralism and Postmodernism; The Struggle for the Academy; Multiculturalism in Theory and Practice; Psychology, the Mind, and the Personality; Nationalism** *(volume 2);* **History and the Study of the Past** *(in this volume); and other articles in this section.*

BIBLIOGRAPHY

Anderson, Benedict. *Imagined Communities: Reflections on the Origin and Spread of Nationalism.* London, 1983.

Blight, David W. *Race and Reunion: The Civil War in American Memory.* Cambridge, Mass., 2000.

Bodnar, John. *Remaking America: Public Memory, Commemoration, and Patriotism in the Twentieth Century.* Princeton, N.J., 1992.

——. "Pierre Nora, National Memory, and Democracy: A Review." *Journal of American History* 87, no. 3 (December 2000).

Confino, Alan. "Collective Memory and Cultural History: Problems of Method." *American Historical Review* 102 (December 1997): 1386–1403.

Friedlander, Saul. *Memory, History, and the Extermination of the Jews of Europe.* Bloomington, Ind., 1993.

Gillis, John R., ed. *Commemorations: The Politics of National Identity.* Princeton, N.J., 1994.

——. *A World of Their Own Making: Myth, Ritual, and the Quest for Family Values.* New York, 1996.

Hacking, Ian. *Rewriting the Soul: Multiple Personality and the Sciences of Memory.* Princeton, N.J., 1995.

Halbwachs, Maurice. *The Collective Memory.* New York, 1950.

Hamilton, Paula. "The Knife Edge: Debates about Memory and History." In *Memory and History in the Twentieth-Century,* edited by Kate Darian-Smith and Paula Hamilton, pp. 9–32. Melbourne, Australia, 1994.

Hobsbawm, Eric, and Terrence Ranger, eds. *The Invention of Tradition.* Cambridge, Mass., 1983.

Hutton, Patrick K. *History as an Art of Memory.* Hanover, N.H., 1993.

Kammen, Michael. *Mystic Chords of Memory: The Transformation of Tradition in American Culture.* New York, 1991.

Klein, Kerwin Lee. "On the Emergence of *Memory* in Historical Discourse." *Representations* 69 (winter 2000): 127–150.

LaCapra, Dominick. *History and Memory after Auschwitz.* Ithaca, N.Y., 1998.

Laquer, Thomas. "Introduction." *Representations* 69 (winter 2000): 1–8.

Le Goff, Jacques. *History and Memory.* Translated by Steven Rendall and Elizabeth Claman. New York, 1992.

Linenthal, Edward T., and Tom Engelhardt, eds. *History Wars: The Enola Gay and Other Battles for the American Past.* New York, 1996.

——. *Preserving Memory: The Struggle to Create America's Holocaust Museum.* New York, 1995.

Lipsitz, George. *Time Passages: Collective Memory and American Popular Culture.* Minneapolis, Minn., 1990.

Maier, Charles S. "A Surfet of Memory: Reflections on History, Melancholy and Denial." *History and Memory* 5 (fall/winter 1993): 136–151.

Matsuda, Matt K. *The Memory of the Modern.* New York, 1996.

Nora, Pierre. "Between Memory and History: Les lieux de mémoire." *Representations* 26 (spring 1989): 7–25.

Ross, Richard J. "The Memorial Culture of Early Modern English Lawyers: Memory as Keyword, Shelter, and Identity, 1560–1640." *Yale Journal of Law and the Humanities* 10 (summer 1998): 229–326.

Rosenzweig, Roy, and David Thelen. *The Presence of the Past: Popular Uses of History in American Life.* New York, 1998.

Samuel, Raphael. *Theatres of Memory.* Vol. 1: *Past and Present in Contemporary Culture.* London, 1994.

Scruggs, Jan C., and Joel L. Swerdlow. *To Heal a Nation: The Vietnam Veterans Memorial.* New York, 1985.

Starn, Randolph. "Memory and Authenticity." *Studies in Twentieth Century Literature* 23 (winter 1999): 191–200.

Sturken, Marita. *Tangled Memories: The Vietnam War, the AIDS Epidemic, and the Politics of Remembering.* Berkeley, Calif., 1997.

Terdiman, Richard. *Present Past: Modernity and the Memory Crisis.* Ithaca, N.Y., 1993.

Thelen, David. "The Postmodern Challenge of Introducing Past to Present: Teaching About Memories and Monuments." *Perspectives in Education* 14 (winter 1993): 117–137.

Thelen, David, ed. *Memory and American History.* Bloomington, Ind., 1990.

Yerushalmi, Yosef Haim. *Zakhor: Jewish History and Jewish Memory.* Seattle, Wash., 1982.

DRAMA

Katie N. Johnson

CONTESTABLE BEGINNINGS

An examination of the American theater necessarily depends upon what we mean by "American" and by "theater." If "American" includes precontact native people, and "theater" encompasses a wide variety of performed actions, then this essay could very well begin with Native American storytelling and ritual performances. If "American" includes spaces outside national territories and "theater" describes performances in the European tradition, one might very well locate Marcos Farfan's *comedia,* written in Spanish and performed in what is now Texas in 1598, as yet another early American performance. Given these contestable beginnings and definitions, this essay will look at a larger context to reflect the rich diversity of theater.

If questions of identity have been important in theater history, they have also dominated representations on the colonial stage. From the early colonial period through the 1990s, there were intense struggles to negotiate questions of American identity through theatrical performance. In early colonial America, theater became a site where emerging national identity, increasingly understood as separate from Britain, was staged.

Puritanical Distrust One of the first ways early American identity became visible was in resistance to the theater, virtually all of which was British. The first European settlers in Jamestown in 1607 and Plymouth in 1620 put most of their energies toward survival and the worship of God, not entertainment. Like England, which closed its theaters from 1642 to 1664, colonial America, with its puritanical distrust of performative spectacle, was hostile to the theater. The first record of a dramatic performance in the colonies, *Ye Bare and ye Cubb,* by William Darby, created a scandal in 1665 when the cast and producers were arrested in Virginia for the "immoral activity" of presenting a play (though the thespians were eventually found not guilty). While

England recovered from theatrical censorship during the Restoration period, Americans continued to view the theater as "disreputable." Every colony except Virginia and Maryland had antitheater laws well into the eighteenth century.

Theatrical Imports Another likely explanation for the resistance to the theater was the colonists' growing desire to sever themselves from the British Empire. In spite of antitheater laws, permits were occasionally granted to theater troupes, most of which were British imports. The first acting company in America was headed by the British actors Walter Murray and Thomas Kean in 1749. Other British theater troupes—such as the Hallam Company and the Douglass Company, the latter being the leading acting troupe from 1758 until 1774—sometimes gained permission to perform by disguising their plays as "moral dialogues." Mounting anti-British sentiment caused Douglass's company to label itself American, although its repertoire was almost entirely English. In 1767 the first play written by an American colonist, the *Prince of Parthia* by Thomas Godfrey, was performed, but it was an inferior imitation of Shakespeare that ran for just one night. The struggle to develop native drama would weigh heavily on early writers and critics, and a profound sense of inferiority in regard to British drama would remain well into the twentieth century.

Theater Ban The nation's founders recognized the political power of the theater, as did the citizens, whose attitude toward theater grew increasingly hostile as the British and American conflict escalated. In October 1774, on the cusp of the Revolutionary War, the Continental Congress passed a resolution banning "all horseracing, and all kinds of gaming, cock-fighting, exhibitions of shews, plays, and other expensive diversions and entertainments" (Hewitt, *Theater U.S.A,* p. 30). The ban functioned to focus colonists' energies on the po-

577

litical conflict as well as to purge cultural ties to the mother country.

The ban did not, however, prevent colonists from staging their own political dramas. For example, propaganda plays sympathetic to the colonists' plight were published and performed, often by soldiers, including troupes performing for George Washington. Though some royalist plays appeared, the most popular were patriotic plays and political satires, such as those from the first female American playwright, Mercy Otis Warren.

POSTREVOLUTIONARY DRAMA: 1787–1830

First American Production   After the Revolution, the ban on theater was lifted and the stage became an important site for negotiating American and British identity. This tendency was perhaps most visible in Royall Tyler's comedy *The Contrast,* which emerged in 1787 as the first play written and produced by Americans. *The Contrast's* success can be attributed to its juxtaposition of American and British characters. Tyler introduced the first "stage Yankee," a homespun figure named Jonathan who was performed by one of the most famous American comedians of the time, Thomas Wignell. By contrasting the earthy Jonathan and his employer, the heroic Colonial Manly, with the pompous royalist character, Dimple, Tyler celebrated the triumph of American character.

The Quest for Native Drama   In the wake of *The Contrast,* many plays focused on nationalistic themes, though few with the success of Tyler's. As the American playwright James Nelson Barker put it in 1812, "a provincial sense of inferiority still lingers . . . with regard to the arts and refinements of society" (Wilson, p. 54). Among the first enduring native dramatists were John Howard Payne, best known for the song "Home Sweet Home" (1823), and William Dunlap, "the father of American drama," who wrote dozens of plays and the first historical account of American drama, the *History of the American Theatre* (1832).

With the growth of the western frontier, a certain kind of American identity, epitomized by rugged individualism and its quintessential "self-made man," found expression in native drama through elaborations of the Yankee figure. The Yankee was resurrected in countless plays like *The Forest Rose* (1825), featuring the character Jonathan Ploughboy, and *The Lion of the West* (1831), whose frontier Yankee was called Nimrod Wildfire.

The Yankee character celebrated white colonial masculinity, often against the backdrop of its counterpoint, the "Indian" figure. Theatrical representations of the "Indian" fit prevailing stereotypes about Native Americans as noble savages, drunkards, or Indian princesses. Such dramatizations both fueled and mirrored the colonial imagination, echoing the white expansionism evident in the Lewis and Clark expedition and the Monroe Doctrine of 1823. Staged as conquered curiosities (often against their will), Native Americans were exhibited as circus acts or in ethnographic displays as early as 1828; presented at government functions, like the farewell celebration for President James Monroe in 1822; and included in "Indian" ceremonies in theaters for white audiences. By the 1830s a surge of "Indian" plays by white authors—including George Washington Custis's *Indian Prophesy* (1827) and *Pocahontas* (1830) and John Augustus Stone's *Metamora* (1829)—revealed profound ambiguity toward native people by whites, who were fascinated yet repulsed by Native Americans.

Theater Riots   With the War of 1812 in recent memory, the lingering sense that American drama was inferior to British drama produced several explosive confrontations with touring British actors. Nowhere was this more evident than during the Kean riots in 1825. British star Edmund Kean had offended Boston audiences by refusing to perform there. When he later appeared in New York City, audiences, still outraged, refused to allow him to perform. Kean returned to Boston to apologize, but was met with a fierce mob, forcing him off the stage. He never returned to America.

Another register of British and American antagonism can be seen in the rivalry between the English tragedian William Macready and Edwin Forrest, the leading American actor at the Park Theater from 1829 to 1836. Forrest was an idol of the masses, in part because of his powerful physique, commanding voice, and dynamic acting style, which would come to emblematize heroic or "American" acting. Years of angry exchange between the two actors culminated during Macready's farewell tour of the United States in 1849. A mob of ten to fifteen thousand people, expressing anti-British sentiment, stoned New York City's Astor Place Opera House. A militia fired at the mob, killing twenty-two people. Macready fled not only the theater but the country, never to return. The Astor Place Riot is remembered as one of the most vivid, and deadly, theatrical expressions of national politics.

Astor Place Riot, 10 May 1849. After the Seventh Regiment fired into the unruly crowd, fingers of blame pointed in many directions. © BETTMANN/CORBIS

Early African American Theater   Most African American characters in early American drama were stereotypical figures played by whites in blackface. Though the earliest African American performances can be found in non-Western formats like African song, dance, and folk celebrations, the first instance of African American theater within the Western tradition was the formation of the African Company in New York City in 1821. Managed by William Henry Brown, the theater produced an all-African American *Richard III* in 1821 and Brown's own *The Drama of King Shotaway* (1823), the first drama by an African American. These auspicious beginnings were abruptly halted, however, when the theater was forced to close in 1823 by intolerant whites. Beyond occasional performances in minstrel shows, African Americans did not have a major presence in mainstream theaters until the Harlem Renaissance in the early twentieth century.

THE REIGN OF MELODRAMA: 1820–1870

From 1820 to 1870, melodrama, with its exaggerated moral conflicts, stock characters, and predictable format was the prevailing theatrical genre for audiences that were increasingly segregated by class. Although American theater had been directed at elite male patrons in upper-class theaters into the early nineteenth century, the rise of industrialism and immigration from 1835 to 1850 brought working-class audiences to urban theaters, most notably New York's Bowery and Chatham Theaters. Here, melodrama became popular entertainment for working-class women and for those falling under the designation "Bowery B'hoy," a rowdy "working-class dandy bristling with class and nativist antagonism" (McConachie, p. 132). Working-class audiences also turned to popular entertainments such as vaudeville, minstrelsy, burlesque, circus, museum-theaters, concert saloons, music halls, and immigrant theater, all of which redefined the nature of theater in the United States.

Critics, however, felt that melodrama's popularity thwarted the emergence of "good" American drama, a sentiment that was no doubt driven by class anxieties. Yet in spite of such critiques, melodrama became a powerful form of expression across class lines, as seen in the apocalyptic melodramatic spectacle *Mazeppa* (1833); Anna Cora Mowatt's *Fashion* (1834), a critique of New York's nouveaux riches; and the most popular antebellum melodrama, the dramatic adaptation of Harriet Beecher Stowe's novel, *Uncle Tom's Cabin* (1852). Melodramas by Dion Boucicault and Augustin Daly became the new theater of the business class from 1850 to

1870. Boucicault was the most enduring playwright of antebellum America, known especially for portraying urban poverty in *The Poor of New York* (1857) and mixed-race anxiety in *The Octoroon* (1859). Although all classes enjoyed melodrama, class division still made itself felt within the theater. The disruption of performances by the "Bowery B'hoys and G'alls" forced managers to create houses of respectability that would bring back bourgeois spectators who had fled to more exclusive theaters such as the Park. By the end of the nineteenth century, competing producers sought to establish respectable spaces for mixed-sex audiences. They created variety and vaudeville entertainment to contrast with the sultry music hall. For example, Tony Pastor cultivated a female audience by tidying up acts and sponsoring a "Ladies' Invitation Night." By the 1890s "refined vaudeville" attracted middle-class audiences.

Many playwrights patterned their melodramas after Boucicault, incorporating local material, as Edward Harrigan did with his portrayals of Irish immigrant family life on the Lower East Side in the *Mulligan Guard*. Defying the traditional moral world of melodrama, Daly's *Under the Gaslight* (1867) reversed dramaturgical logic by having the female heroine rescue a man tied to the railroad tracks. Yet while other art forms could claim American writers of note, the theater had yet to produce a native writer who was taken seriously by native or foreign critics. At the close of the Civil War, the most distinctly popular dramatic genre was melodrama.

THE RISE OF REALISM (1870–1914)

The period between the Civil War and World War I was one of immense prosperity for the legitimate theater, despite the continuing success of popular entertainments, especially vaudeville, in garnering audiences. The brutalities of the Civil War sobered American idealism, as did the emerging manifestations of modern society: innovations in technology, the rise of pseudosciences, and the struggle for women's suffrage, to name a few representative changes in the American social fabric. While the shock of the modern first found expression primarily in melodrama, increasingly the theater began to follow the documentary impulse of other modern arts and turned to realism.

Realistic Playwrights   James A. Herne is usually credited with launching American theatrical real-

ism—or what he called "Art for Truth's Sake" in his influential essay of that title—with *Margaret Fleming* (1891), his social drama about a husband's infidelity. However, in spite of Herne's contributions, some critics felt that American playwriting was still second-rate, and looked to European realism as a model. In 1904 William Dean Howells lamented that "few of the American plays will compare with the English, in dramatic art" (Downer, ed., p. 10).

Many of the nation's first "social problem" plays, modeled on Henrik Ibsen's and George Bernard Shaw's dramas, proved to be the most controversial, signaling ambiguous responses to societal "vices" and their representation on the stage. Clyde Fitch's sultry *Sapho* (1900), Shaw's American premiere in 1905 of *Mrs. Warren's Profession* (1902), and the "sex dramas" of the 1913 season incited famous obscenity trials. Some social problem plays satisfied police censors, however, by portraying views sanctioned by the dominant culture. These include Edward Sheldon's popular portrayal of a reformed prostitute in *Salvation Nell* (1908); Langdon Mitchell's satire on marriage and divorce in *The New York Idea* (1906), which earned him the title "the American Shaw"; and Rachel Crothers's insights on gender with *A Man's World* (1909), which established her as the leading commercial female playwright of her time.

Realistic Stage Technology   Other plays moved toward realism through more technical means. As early as 1880, the producer-director J. Steele MacKaye introduced the "elevator stage" to allow quick scene changes in under two minutes. William Young's *Ben-Hur* (1899) featured a spectacular chariot race with eight horses on a treadmill, moving scenery, and wind. One of the most charismatic promoters of realism was David Belasco, whose meticulous scenic realism and three-dimensional sets were epitomized in *The Easiest Way* (1909). Insisting upon authenticity, Belasco bought the interior of a New York flophouse and reassembled it onstage. Clyde Fitch, often labeled the best American dramatist of his era, was known especially for his obsession with realistic exactitude, which was called "Fitchian detail" (*The Revels History of Drama in English*, vol. 8, p. 210). This exactitude made him so popular that in 1901 four of his plays ran in New York City at the same time.

Theater Arts Programs and Theater Movements
Beyond experimentations with realistic drama, three significant changes occurred in the early

1900s. First, theater arts programs were established in American colleges. The first of these, pioneered by George Pierce Baker in 1904 at Harvard, nurtured the next wave of famous playwrights, including Edward Sheldon, Percy MacKaye, and Eugene O'Neill. Second, several independent theaters opened, forging the way for dramatic experimentation. The New Theater (1909) was New York's first "art theater," but it was too large, and its European repertoire was "woefully deficient," according to Walter Prichard Eaton, in American drama (*At the New Theater and Others*, p. 31). Beginning in 1915 the Provincetown Players fostered important experimentation by the emerging American playwrights Eugene O'Neill, Susan Glaspell, Djuna Barnes, and George Cram Cook. Third and finally, the Little Theater movement produced a groundswell of small and often amateur productions in local communities. These developments offered important alternatives to mainstream theater, which was itself beginning to emerge with newfound native authority.

Producers of Realism   Earlier in the nineteenth century, famous actor-managers—like Edwin Forrest and Laura Keene—had been the most powerful force in the theater. That power shifted, however, from the star actor to the director-producer in the mid-nineteenth century. In 1896, however, capitalistic control became more institutionally narrowed when individual producers were overpowered by the Theatrical Syndicate, a producing network that effectively controlled most theaters in several states. While members of the syndicate argued that it stabilized the theater, others, like the critic Walter Prichard Eaton, denounced the "artistic decay" resulting from the stifling of artistic experimentation (p. 3). The Shubert brothers broke the syndicate's monopoly in 1916, but developed their own powerful hold on the theater.

DRAMA BETWEEN THE WARS

Eugene O'Neill: America's First Preeminent Playwright   Four years after World War I ended, Stark Young echoed the repeated calls by critics to cut the dramaturgical "apron string" to England, to "find for ourselves in the art of the theater a real dialect" (Downer, ed., p. 76). That call was answered by the arrival of Eugene O'Neill. Many critics of the time expressed relief that America had a preeminent dramatist who matched the leading serious European-style drama while focusing on American themes and characters. O'Neill began with realistic dramaturgy, as in the portrayal of struggling farmers in his Pulitzer Prize–winning *Beyond the Horizon* (1920), but adopted expressionistic techniques in *The Emperor Jones* (1920) and *The Hairy Ape* (1922). O'Neill experimented also with modernist stream-of-consciousness dialogue in *Strange Interlude* (1928). His other Pulitzer Prize–winning plays explored social problems like prostitution in *Anna Christie* (1921) and alcoholism in *Long Day's Journey Into Night* (1939–1941). Much of O'Neill's work was autobiographical, and his later plays, like *The Iceman Cometh* (1939), returned to a realistic aesthetic. O'Neill set the benchmark for American dramatic excellence and at the turn of the twenty-first century remained for many critics one of the most important playwrights of the twentieth century.

Plays that Stage Identity   While many critics have upheld O'Neill as the first excellent American dramatist, other theater of the 1920s and 1930s was also impressive, marked by urgent questions of class, immigrant status, and racial identity. Those who were discontent with modern industrial culture turned to workers' theater, or political "agit-prop," which used propaganda to agitate worker resistance to capitalism. John Howard Lawson's *Processional* (1925) demonstrated how the theater could build class consciousness among striking workers.

Many Pulitzer Prize–winning plays from this period strayed from myths of homogenous national identity and portrayed diverse characters with regional or ethnic dialects. For example, Sidney Howard's *They Knew What They Wanted* (1924) featured an Italian American love story, Hatcher Hughes's *Hell-Bent fer Heaven* (1924) was set in rural Carolina, and Marc Connelly's *Green Pastures* (1930) and Paul Green's *In Abraham's Bosom* (1926) explored slavery and racism through southern black heroes. Immigrant tensions may have best been captured by Maxwell Anderson's two plays about the infamous Sacco and Vanzetti anarchy trial, *Gods of the Lighting* (1928) (with Harold Hickerson) and *Winterset* (1935).

While often overlooked by white audiences and shut out of prize competitions, many African American writers dramatized issues relevant to the black American experience during the Harlem Renaissance. Georgia Douglas Johnson's *Plumes* (1927) gained acclaim for its powerful portrayal of racism in medicine, Zora Neale Hurston investigated miscegenation in *Color Struck* (1925), and Langston

WOMEN PLAYWRIGHTS BETWEEN THE WARS

Too often the historical record has overlooked important female dramatists. Just one year after women secured the right to vote, Zona Gale was the first woman playwright to win the Pulitzer with *Miss Lulu Bett* (1921), an analysis of gender inequity. As some critics have noted, Susan Glaspell was second only to O'Neill in founding American modernism with *Trifles* (1916), *The Verge* (1921), and *Alison's House* (1930), for which she won the Pulitzer. Zoë Atkins is best remembered for *Déclassée* (1919) and her Pulitzer Prize–winning *The Old Maid* (1935). A leading playwright of her time, Lillian Hellman portrayed confrontational themes, like the crushing power of homophobia in *The Children's Hour* (1934) and the devastating effects of a destructive family in *The Little Foxes* (1939). Gertrude Stein's experimental plays were rarely produced in her own time, but scholars have recently celebrated her important contribution to modern American drama.

Hughes likewise explored mixed-race anxiety in *Mulatto* (1935).

Dramatic Experimentation after O'Neill   Other playwrights followed O'Neill's experimentation with more radical forms of modernist theater. Elmer Rice's *The Adding Machine* (1923) and Sophie Treadwell's *Machinal* (1928) were successful expressionist dramas portraying an alienating and dehumanized modern world. Thornton Wilder was another experimental force with *Our Town* (1938), which dispensed with realistic stage conventions by making the stage manager a character in the play.

Popular Entertainments   While most drama critics focused on the importance of what they called "serious" drama, commercial shows dominated theater seasons during the Roaring Twenties. Despite its ethnic stereotypes, the longest-running show of the 1920s was Anne Nichols's *Abie's Irish Rose* (1922), a farcical love story about an Irish girl and Jewish boy. Song and dance shows like *Ziegfeld Follies* and musicals like *Showboat* (1927) were widely popular, as were social comedies like Philip

Barry's *The Philadelphia Story* (1939) and S. N. Behrman's witty comedies of manners. Though the press lamented the scarcity of native playwrights, the 1927–1928 season tells otherwise: 280 new plays were produced on Broadway, the most new plays ever.

Producing Organizations   In the 1930s three theatrical organizations significantly influenced the course of American theater. From 1919 to 1930, the Theatre Guild produced important and ambitious works, such as Elmer Rice's expressionistic *The Adding Machine* (1923) and Eugene O'Neill's *Strange Interlude* (1928). William Saroyan, a leading avant-garde writer, was known for his witty *The Time of Your Life* (1939), which captured both the Pulitzer and Drama Critics' Circle Award for the first time.

Following the Theatre Guild, from 1931 to 1941 the Group Theatre produced American plays of social significance and artistic integrity. Founded by Harold Clurman, Lee Strasberg, and Cheryl Crawford, the Group produced groundbreaking works by Clifford Odets, William Saroyan, and others. As the leading Group playwright, Odets established himself with *Waiting for Lefty* (1935), a play that captured not only the problems of the working class, but also successfully incorporated the Group's new naturalistic acting style.

The other important producing organization, the Federal Theatre Project (FTP), was created in 1935 under the Depression's Works Progress Administration to employ theater artists. While other countries had long traditions of subsidized national theater, the FTP was the first, though brief, instance of such theater in the United States. Under Hallie Flanagan's dynamic leadership, the FTP developed original plays and Living Newspapers that dramatized current events. Because of its leftist politics, however, the FTP came under attack by conservatives, and Congress eventually eliminated funding for the project in 1939.

The Method   The distinctly American acting style that emerged during the 1930s and 1940s was known as psychological naturalism, which became known as the Method. Inspired by Konstantin Stanislavksy's acting theories, the Method was developed by actors of the Group Theatre, who experimented with inner psychological exercises to relate their personal experiences to the character being portrayed. Stella Adler's study with Stanislavsky later revealed that his theories had been misunderstood, but the Method's realism dominated American acting and remained the prevalent style at the end of the twentieth century.

REVISED REALISM: 1945–1960

During World War II, mainstream theater boomed. Musicals like the optimistic *Oklahoma!* (1943), fantasy comedies like *Harvey* (1944), and revivals of older plays offered an escape from the brutalities of war. After the war, dramas frequently focused on themes of reconstruction, within an increasingly realistic aesthetic. The two dominant playwrights of this period, Arthur Miller and Tennessee Williams, crafted important realistic works that elevated dramatic styles and themes.

One of the most significant American playwrights after O'Neill, Miller reinvigorated realism and captured the national desire to come to terms with the war with *All My Sons* (1947). Miller's first major triumph, however, was *Death of a Salesman* (1949), America's first tragedy of a common man, or "low man," Willy Loman. As Miller put it, "I believe that the common man is as apt a subject for tragedy in its highest sense as kings were" ("Tragedy and the Common Man," p. 143). *Salesman*'s set became famous for combining realism with expressionistic qualities.

Miller's realism investigated not only the common person's demise, but also the destructive capabilities of the red-baiting politics of the early 1950s. The depiction of the Salem witch trials in Miller's *The Crucible* (1953) suggested that the proceedings of the House Committee on Un-American Activities were a kind of witch-hunt of artists and activists. Miller's other works included tragedies, like *A View from the Bridge* (1955), about the crippling effects of incest, and *After the Fall* (1964), dealing with his troubled relationship with Marilyn Monroe. He also wrote numerous essays on the theater.

Like Miller, Tennessee Williams helped reshape realistic conventions in the American theater. In 1945 *The Glass Menagerie,* a chilling memory play, established Williams's lyric voice. But it was *A Streetcar Named Desire* (1947) that cemented Williams as a prominent writer of revitalized realism. His plays often explored frustrated heterosexual lovers, though these characters were likely stand-ins for homosexual desire that Williams dare not openly portray, as in *Summer and Smoke* in 1948 and *Cat on a Hot Tin Roof* in 1955. After *Night of the Iguana* (1961), the quality of Williams's plays declined, as did his health.

A Streetcar Named Desire. Marlon Brando as Stanley Kowalski and Jessica Tandy as Blanche DuBois in the Broadway premiere, 1947. © JOHN SPRINGER COLLECTION/ CORBIS

While for Miller and Williams the "individual" was assumed to be white, other dramatists used realistic dramaturgy to unpack white privilege. Carson McCullers's *The Member of the Wedding* (1950), Louis Peterson's *Take a Giant Step* (1953), Alice Childress's *Trouble in Mind* (1955), and Loften Mitchell's *A Land beyond the River* (1957) portrayed race problems with racially mixed casts. Pivotal was Lorraine Hansberry's award-winning portrayal of an African American family confronting individual and institutional racism in *A Raisin in the Sun* (1959).

THE END OF BROADWAY'S HEGEMONY: 1960s–1980s

Off-Broadway In the 1950s the enormous expense of producing theater on Broadway led to the development of smaller theaters outside Times Square, which were collectively referred to as Off-Broadway. A revival of Tennessee Williams's *Summer and Smoke,* performed in 1952 by the newly formed Circle in the Square Theatre, cemented Off-Broadway's success. Off-Broadway provided a challenge to conservative mainstream culture, opening the door for alternative theater.

Off-Off-Broadway As opposed to the "medicated generation" of the 1950s, the 1960s were typified by rebellion, including the fight for civil and women's rights. This rebellious and experimental climate gave birth to Off-Off-Broadway, alternative theater in small coffeehouses off the main theater row. This movement began with Joe Cino's Caffe Cino and Ellen Stewart's La Mama Group in 1961. Dozens of such coffeehouses boomed during the 1960s, and experimentation flourished. This movement was so large that by the 1966–1967 season, the number of Off-Off-Broadway productions was twice that of Broadway and Off-Broadway combined.

Experimental theater of the 1960s and 1970s rejected conventional theater in every sense: production values, hierarchy, space, acting style, and the audience's role. Many such experiments were unscripted "happenings," where performers allowed the performing environment, the audience, and improvisation to dictate what would happen. The first wave of alternative theater included theater collectives like the Living Theatre, the San Francisco Mime Troupe, and the Open Theatre. The second wave, inspired by the antiwar movement and other countercultural movements, included work by Richard Foreman, Robert Wilson, Meredith Monk, the Performance Group, and the Wooster Group. In contrast to the happenings and ritual theater of earlier alternative theater, these second-wave productions were more formally composed.

In the 1970s the number of shows produced on Broadway declined, while Off-Broadway and Off-Off-Broadway offered more plays. If the 1960s were characterized by revolution, then the experimental drama of the 1970s expressed the pessimism of a post-Watergate and post-Vietnam culture. While much of Broadway reinstated realism and the well-made play, experimental theater challenged them. Sam Shepard was one of the most important experimental playwrights of this period, though his work was not as commercially successful as that of mainstream playwrights. His *Curse of the Starving Class* (1978) and the Pulitzer Prize–winning *Buried Child* (1979) captured a sense of American disillusionment. His meditations on American myths, such as the cowboy or the failure of the American dream, appeared in later works. Lanford Wilson's work was more successful, but it too centered on bitter plots. His *Hot L Baltimore* (1973) is a bleak portrayal of a rundown hotel and its residents. The Pulitzer Prize–winning *Talley's Folly* (1978) portrays emotionally disabled characters. Maria Irene Fornes made important dramaturgical experiments with her deconstruction of linearity in *Fefu and Her Friends* (1977), among other plays.

Theater of Social Change The theater of social change, which blended experimental theater and politics, was another important force in alternative theater. Groups such as El Teatro Campesino and the Bread and Puppet Theatre, along with gay theater like Charles Ludlam's Theatre of the Ridiculous, challenged the dominant culture's assumptions about such things as the rights of migrant farm workers and society's demand for compulsory heterosexuality. No longer staging theater on a bourgeois stage, the theater of social change often took the theater to the streets.

Early Feminist Theater Feminist theater, drawing on a variety of feminist philosophies, was another important form of alternative theater. Feminist dramas frequently centered on social issues affecting women and subverted patriarchal plots and themes. For example, Spiderwoman Theater's *An Evening of Disgusting Songs and Pukey Images* (1978) was an irreverent send-up of the dominant culture's expectations for women. The earliest feminist groups included the New Feminist Theatre, It's All Right to Be Woman Theatre, and At the Foot of the Mountain. Other theaters, like the Wow Café and Split Britches, created venues for lesbian artists and continue into the twenty-first century.

African American Theater: 1960s and 1970s Alternative theater by African Americans had particular force in the 1960s and 1970s. The revolutionary theater of this era, the Black Theater movement, is epitomized by the award-winning angry play about black-white relations, *Dutchman* (1964), by Amiri Baraka (formerly LeRoi Jones). Other experimentation followed with Adrienne Kennedy's shattering of traditional mimetic form and African American identity in *Funnyhouse of a Negro* (1969). Charles Gordone's *No Place to Be Somebody* (1969) was the first work by a black playwright to receive a Pulitzer. Ntozake Shange's choreopoem *for colored girls who have considered suicide/when the rainbow is enuf* (1976) fused poetry with drama for a stirring piece about African American women's experiences.

Performance Art Performance art, a raw, subversive art form that drew from several disciplines,

Janet League and Ntozake Shange in *for colored girls who have considered suicide/when the rainbow is enuf* **at the Anspacher Public Theatre.** Shange's choreopoem was first produced in New York City at Studio Riobea in 1975, then at the Public Theatre and on Broadway in 1976. © BETTMANN/CORBIS

arose in the late twentieth century as another significant alternative to mainstream theater. Growing from the 1960s feminist and gay rights movements, performance art recognized the radical potential of autobiographical exploration and the subversion of tradition aesthetics. Examples near the century's end included Laurie Anderson's postmodern techno-music collages, Ron Athey's ritualized use of the body to portray the destruction of AIDS, Guillermo Gómez-Peña's multicharacter and multilingual explorations of Chicano-Anglo relations, and Karen Finley's edgy indictment of sexual violence toward women. Though performance art remained one of the most important forces in theater in the 1990s, it decidedly resided on the margins of dominant culture.

MAINSTREAM THEATER: 1960s–1980s

The revolutionary fervor of alternative theater permeated mainstream theater to some degree. One of the most important mainstream dramatists to emerge after Williams and Miller was Edward Al-

bee, whose earlier works, *The Zoo Story* (1958) and *The American Dream* (1960), reflected an absurdist impulse. Combining realism and surrealism, Albee achieved acclaim with his biting portrayals of destruction in *Who's Afraid of Virginia Woolf?* (1962) and *A Delicate Balance,* which won the Pulitzer in 1966. Albee's *Three Tall Women* (1992), which won the Pulitzer in 1994, reestablished Albee as an enduring, vital American playwright.

While Albee is often recognized as the most important playwright of the 1960s, Neil Simon was less experimental and more commercially successful. Early critics dismissed Simon's well-made plays as superficial, but his "Midas touch" was undeniable with comedies like *The Odd Couple* (1965) and his later tragicomedies, such as *The Sunshine Boys* (1972).

The neoconservatism of the Reagan era resonated with mainstream dramatists, many of whom returned to realism and focused on the individual. David Mamet, one of the most prolific writers for theater and film captured (some would say uncritically) self-interested masculinity in *Sexual Perversity in Chicago* (1974) and the Pulitzer Prize–winning

Glengarry Glen Ross (1984). Inspired by British playwright Harold Pinter, Mamet expressed the American vernacular in a highly formalized and spare, yet realistic, dialogue that became his trademark.

With the rise of identity politics in the 1980s, mainstream theater began to embrace what had once been considered marginal playwrights and topics, albeit with rather conventional, and often realistic, dramaturgy. Feminist plays like *Crimes of the Heart* (1981), by Beth Henley; *'night, Mother* (1983), by Marsha Norman; and *The Heidi Chronicles* (1988), by Wendy Wasserstein, all captured Pulitzers, bringing women's concerns center stage. African American drama also garnered mainstream attention with Charles Fuller's realistic portrayal of racism in the military, *A Soldier's Play* (1981) and August Wilson's focus on African American characters with his Pulitzer Prize–winning *Fences* (1985) and *The Piano Lesson* (1990). The late 1980s also featured David Henry Hwang, the first Asian American playwright to achieve mainstream success; his *M. Butterfly* stirringly portrayed interracial romance and gender confusion.

A NEW MILLENNIUM

The quest to represent American identity in drama over the centuries involved numerous voices and shifts in aesthetics. At the turn of the twenty-first century, the fabric of theater was likewise comprised of diverse threads. Two, however, were central. The first trend, in mainstream drama, reflected neoconservatism and a cultural nostalgia for yesteryear. Popular musicals for pure entertainment, epitomized by the long-running *Cats,* became enduring presences on Broadway. Disney's investment in Broadway during the 1990s, where it mounted musical extravaganzas based on cartoons, seemed largely determined by corporate profit. Broadway seasons in the late 1990s eschewed experimentation, relying upon realistic new plays, musical revivals, and remountings of classics by Miller, Williams, and O'Neill.

Still, there was a second trend found in regional theaters, new play festivals, and Off-Broadway theaters, where challenging new works about social issues were being developed. The AIDS epidemic was explored in plays like Terrence McNally's *Lips Together, Teeth Apart* (1991); Tony Kushner's epic "gay fantasia on national themes," *Angels in America* (1991–1992); and Jonathan Larson's rock opera, *Rent* (1996). The last two Pulitzers of the millennium were awarded to Paula Vogel's examination of a young girl's molestation in *How I Learned to Drive* (1998) and Margaret Edson's depiction of a clever ovarian cancer patient in *Wit* (1999).

Given these conflicting trends, any attempt to characterize American theater at the beginning of the twenty-first century as homogenous would overlook the cacophony of voices, both on and "Off" Broadway. One conclusion, however, is undeniable: American theater remained vital and diverse as a site of negotiating identity.

See also **Thought and Culture in the Free Black Community; American Romanticism; Urban Cultural Institutions; Realism in Art and Literature; Cultural Modernism; The Popular Arts** *(volume 1);* **The World According to Hollywood; Popular Culture in the Public Arena; Postmodernism and the Arts; Multiculturalism in Theory and Practice** *(volume 2);* **Elite vs. Popular Cultures; Culture for Mass Audiences** *(in this volume); and other articles in this section.*

BIBLIOGRAPHY

Bank, Rosemarie K. *Theatre Culture in America, 1825–1860.* Cambridge, U.K., 1997.

Bean, Annemarie, James V. Hatch, and Brooks McNamara, eds. *Inside the Minstrel Mask. Readings in Nineteenth-Century Blackface Minstrelsy.* Hanover, N.H., 1996.

Bogard, Travis, Richard Moody, and Walter J. Meserve, eds. *The Revels History of Drama in English.* Vol. 8, *American Drama.* London, 1977.

Brockett, Oscar G. *History of the Theatre.* Boston, 1968.

Canning, Charlotte. *Feminist Theaters in the U.S.A.* London, 1996.

Chinoy, Helen Krich, and Linda Walsh Jenkins, eds. *Women in American Theatre.* Rev. ed. New York, 1987.

Downer, Alan S., ed. *American Drama and Its Critics. A Collection of Critical Essays.* Chicago, 1965.

Drain, Richard, ed. *Twentieth-Century Theatre. A Sourcebook.* New York, 1995.

Eaton, Walter Prichard. *At the New Theatre and Others: The American Stage, Its Problems and Performances, 1908–1910.* Boston, 1910.

Hay, Samuel A. *African American Theatre. A Historical and Critical Analysis.* Cambridge, U.K., 1994.

Hewitt, Barnard. *Theatre U.S.A., 1668–1957.* New York, 1959.

King, Bruce, ed. *Contemporary American Theatre.* New York, 1991.

Lagner, Lawrence. *The Magic Curtain. The Story of a Life in Two Fields, Theatre and Invention by the Founder of the Theatre Guild.* New York, 1951.

McConachie, Bruce A. *Melodramatic Formations: American Theatre and Society, 1820–1870.* Iowa City, Iowa, 1992.

Miller, Arthur. "Tragedy and the Common Man." In *Arthur Miller: Death of a Salesman, Text and Criticism.* Edited by Gerald Weales. New York, 1967.

Mordden, Ethan. *The American Theatre.* New York, 1981.

Moses, Montrose J., ed. *The American Theatre as Seen by its Critics, 1752–1934.* New York, 1934.

O'Connor, John, and Lorraine Brown, eds. *Free, Adult, Uncensored: The Living History of the Federal Theatre Project.* Washington, D.C., 1980.

Peiss, Kathy. *Cheap Amusements: Working Women and Leisure in Turn-of-the-Century New York.* Philadelphia, 1986.

Quinn, Arthur Hobson. *A History of the American Drama from the Civil War to the Present Day.* New York, 1943.

Robinson, Marc. *The Other American Drama.* New York, 1994.

Roudané, Matthew C. *American Drama since 1960. A Critical History.* New York, 1996.

Sainer, Arthur. *The New Radical Theatre Notebook.* Rev. ed. New York, 1997.

Savran, David. *Breaking the Rules. The Wooster Group.* New York, 1988.

Shafer, Yvonne. *American Women Playwrights, 1900–1950.* New York, 1995.

Shank, Theodore. *American Alternative Theatre.* New York, 1982.

Wilmeth, Don B. *Staging the Nation. Plays from the American Theater, 1787–1909.* Boston, 1998.

Wilmeth, Don B., and Christopher Bigsby, eds. *The Cambridge History of American Theatre.* 2 vols. Cambridge, U.K., 1998–1999.

Wilson, Garff B. *Three Hundred Years of American Drama and Theatre. From* Ye Bare and ye Cubb *to* Hair. Englewood Cliffs, N.J., 1973.

Witham, Barry B., ed. *Theatre in the United States: A Documentary History.* Vol. 1. Cambridge, U.K., 1996.

FICTION

Dale M. Bauer

The American novel is considered to be the most democratic of forms, capable of accommodating the diverse voices in American culture. In search of a national literature and culture, American readers found in the novel a genre elastic enough to represent the changing demographics and ideologies of American life. In these novels, the revolutionary rhetoric is cast into an affirmation of United States culture—a version of what the scholar Sacvan Bercovitch has called the American jeremiad.

From the outset, American novelists stressed fiction's importance in the public sphere as part of the new national endeavor to make United States culture estimable both to itself and to foreign observers. With so much at stake, critics alternately praised unworthy contenders because of the politics they favored, or they abused books as insufficient to the great national goal of discovering exemplary American voices.

REVOLUTIONARY FICTION

The first American novelists had to contend, as did their English counterparts, with the moral arguments against novels. The case against fiction's undesirable tendencies was that much more intense in a country trying to establish itself as a state with sober, industrious people. On one side, American fiction intended to respond to the new forms of social and political life now being conducted; on the other, its foremost impetus was to achieve popularity. To this end, the seduction novel flourished. Religious arbiters often challenged works of the imagination, seeing in novels and stories nothing short of the devil's work, which, at best, encouraged an unregulated taste for amusement and, at worst, inflamed the imagination and emotions of young people, especially young women.

The first American novel, by William Hill Brown, was *The Power of Sympathy; or, The Triumph of Nature* (1789) and was "written to expose the dangerous Consequences of Seduction and to set forth the advantages of female Education." The author may have been a male, but, following the American Revolution, the vast preponderance of United States fiction was written by women. Their novels seemed to overtake the country, frequently issuing their own call for women's education and political influence. In this endeavor, these books were both creating and responding to an increase in female literacy rates, which increased from 58 percent in the late 1770s to the relatively stable rate of 85 percent in 1810.

While prerepublican traditions of female modesty and restrictions against women's public roles shaped life in the colonies, legions of women writers wanted to add to the fervor of political change and fulfill their duties as "republican mothers" by using fiction to serve political and social urgencies. Perhaps the two most famous, Susanna Rowson's *Charlotte Temple* (1791) and Hannah Foster's *The Coquette* (1797), may be said to establish the limits of allowable fiction: seduction novels wherein the transgressive heroines are punished and republican order is vigorously challenged but set aright. Interestingly, these novels often inveighed against novel-reading itself, claiming that the book in the reader's hand was the sole exception to the power of fiction to mislead impressionable readers. If the men would not "Remember the Ladies," as Abigail Adams admonished her husband, John Adams, to do in a letter on 31 March 1776, then the female novelists would remind the women of their own revolutionary potential.

Such changes inevitably led to the new moral role of fiction in America. Fiction such as Charles Brockden Brown's several gothic romances, including *Wieland* (1798), at the turn of the nineteenth century, transformed the conventional horror and melodrama of the genre into an argument about political and social identity. Arguably, one of the first literary efforts to gain a national audience,

Washington Irving's satirical *A History of New York . . . by Diedrich Knickerbocker* (1809), followed the same purpose of instructing Americans in the moral categories of citizenship. More popular than American fiction in the first quarter of the nineteenth century was British fiction, especially the novels of Sir Walter Scott. English writers, unprotected by United States copyright laws, could expect their books to be reprinted for Americans the moment they were published, a business that was nothing short of piracy since the authors did not collect royalties on these printings. This corrupt practice also exerted at least one deleterious effect on American fiction: it discouraged United States novelists in pursuit of artistic achievement. In order to contra-distinguish themselves from the British talent, American writers had to concentrate on primarily social, even domestic, subjects.

After 1810, novels became somewhat less didactic and more devoted to understanding the place of reason and passion in the new republic. Rebecca Rush's *Kelroy* (1812) illustrates the first appearance of the nouveaux riches and the working class in the American novel, and Rush was careful to show their assimilation into American society despite their comic status as "originals." Later, in the Jacksonian era, national and familial fiction such as Catherine Sedgwick's *The Linwoods* (1835) attempted to determine how United States culture might make the national and familial transition from revolution to republic. Either way, early or late, novelists debated what to make of American citizens and how to make them; that is, who would count as a citizen and what virtues would be associated with the "new" American. James Fenimore Cooper's novels—from *The Spy* (1821) through The Leatherstocking tales—fostered a nostalgia for the heroic citizen even as Cooper repeatedly showed the demise of the old American order of manly virtue and the rise of the new American enterprise of the market revolution. So successful were these books that Cooper was hailed as the American Scott: he developed out of native historical materials an animated fictional account of the nation's expansion, especially the cultural politics of Indian removal, which could be understood to reveal the rights of citizens by showing who they could, with impunity, expel or murder.

Washington Irving is reputed to be the first American writer to make his living from belles lettres. Surely his great contributions to United States fiction are his two volumes of short tales and sketches, *The Sketch Book* (1819) and *Tales of a Traveler* (1824). Although the latter concentrates on European traditions, the stories, imitating the highly popular travel accounts, were well received, though it was *The Sketch Book's* anecdotes of the Hudson Valley, like "Rip Van Winkle" and "The Legend of Sleepy Hollow," that galvanized the development of the American short story. On the opposite end of the spectrum, Hugh Henry Brackenridge's multi-volume epic novel, *Modern Chivalry* (1792–1815), satirizes relations between the sexes as well as the values of citizenship on a grand scale.

This is not to suggest that completely "separate spheres" developed in American fiction, despite the critical orthodoxy—overturned in the last generation—to read the highly gendered domains as distinct rather than mutually constitutive. For the prevailing call in the first half of the nineteenth century, and beyond, was for a national American literature, and it resounded from a host of places—the political and cultural group known as the Young Americans, the Fireside poets, Edgar Allan Poe, and Margaret Fuller. In order to break through a stifling allegiance to European, especially English, literature, such critics and writers challenged the country to live up to its "genius," or to create a literature that could explain the nation to itself. Once the burden of epic poetry—Walt Whitman's *Leaves of Grass* (1855) is conceived in this spirit—it now fell mainly to the novel to meet this demand. Much of the era's popular fiction writers were centrally concerned with the need to create this national mythography, whether it was portrayed in the Kentucky forests, as in Robert Montgomery Bird's *Nick of the Woods* (1837); in South Carolina, as in William Gilmore Simms's *The Yemassee* (1835); or in Vermont, as in Daniel Pierce Thompson's *Green Mountain Boys* (1839), which went through fifty printings in twenty years.

Nathaniel Hawthorne's first collection of stories, *Twice-Told Tales* (1837), can also be read in this light, insofar as so many of them treat his career-long interest in developing a cultural psychology or moral history of New England. His second collection, *Mosses from an Old Manse* (1846), makes this aspiration explicit. The other great founder of American short fiction, Edgar Allan Poe, wrote stories that resist easy national descriptions but instead base their appeal on the achievement of their formal artistry and psychological density, especially in the detective fiction, the genre he is said to have invented, like "The Purloined Letter" (1844) or "The Murders in the Rue Morgue" (1843). Still, even Hawthorne's final collection of stories, *The Snow-Image* (1851), is dedicated to the proposition of demonstrating the vitalizing presence of the national spirit and reprises some of the consciously nation-making tales, like his "Alice Doane's Appeal" (1835)—a tale about the legacy of Gallows Hill in Salem, Massachusetts.

As much as Hawthorne's tales immediately established him as the consummate artist for whom America had been searching, his longer fiction commanded even more respect. He called these works "romances," though few others at the time would have understood why, since they lack that genre's pervasive improbability, commitment to plot coincidence, or stereotypical characters. The first may be the most famous novel ever written by an American and, for many readers, a flawless book—*The Scarlet Letter* (1850), a tragic story of adulterous passion and psychological havoc played out in seventeenth-century Puritan New England. The minister's corrosive guilt and the liberating force of will in Hester Prynne's bid for fulfillment combine to suggest the twin engines of the American psyche. These, combined with the unruliness of the child as well as the husband's outraged desire for knowledge and revenge, suggest something of the complex destiny of being an American. Hawthorne followed this brilliant achievement with two other novels, one dedicated to explaining how the past weighs on and helps to shape the present for good and for ill, *The House of the Seven Gables* (1851), and *The Blithedale Romance* (1852), a tragedy of Hawthorne's contemporary culture and the failure of social reform.

Hawthorne's novels proved extremely influential, at least for two writers who represent various strains of his aesthetic—his contemporary, Herman Melville, and his legatee, Henry James. Both moved to surpass Hawthorne's lessons and did so by creating their own kind of fictions, which have, in turn, inspired many followers. Although *Moby-Dick* (1851) is dedicated to Hawthorne, its achievement is so vast that it is idle to speak of Hawthorne, or any other writer, at all in connection with it. Melville, a novelist whose first success was in fictional adventure stories, grew into a master of psychological allegory. Not only should *Moby-Dick,* his great novel about whale hunting, be understood in this light, but so too lesser novels, like *Pierre* (1852), his resounding failure at writing a best-seller, or *The Confidence-Man* (1857), a novel whose intricacies have taken over a century to unwind. After *Moby-Dick,* however, Melville's most enduring successes came in the series of magazine tales that include the elusive tale of Wall Street, "Bartleby, the Scrivener" (1853), and *Benito Cereno* (1856), Melville's haunting historical psychodrama about the effects of slavery. At his death, he left a manuscript that revealed his final effort in this form, *Billy Budd* (1891), which critics have read as Melville's lament of the violence inherent in American culture.

AMERICAN RENAISSANCE

The recent revolution in criticism has revised scholars' understanding of the fiction produced during the 1850s in New England and New York, that great burst of creative energy called the American Renaissance. This revision recovers the value of gothic and sentimental writing that the American Renaissance writers saw themselves as combatting.

For many years, the literary historians thought Hawthorne's and Melville's fictions typified the dominant tradition of American novels and stories, often at the expense of two kinds of other popular fictions. Writers working in the gothic and sentimental tradition, like George Lippard in his popular *The Quaker City; or, The Monks of Monk Hall* (1844) and T. S. Arthur in *Ten Nights in a Barroom and What I Saw There* (1854), gained an unprecedented following. The 1830s had inaugurated the cultural work of the domestic writers, whose novels were devoted to social causes as various as temperance, abolition, Native American removal policies, and religious polemics. (Walt Whitman's one novel, *Franklin Evans,* published in 1842, lent itself to the temperance crusade.) Even earlier, novels like Lydia Maria Child's *Hobomok* (1824) and Catharine Maria Sedgwick's *Hope Leslie* (1827), tell the story of the limits of American assimilation at the border between civilization and Native American westward frontiers.

Arguably Harriet Beecher Stowe is the model for the American sentimental tradition: her first novel, *Uncle Tom's Cabin* (1852), shattered the nation's complacency about slavery and became both a national and international phenomenon. Stowe's success was sustained in *Dred* (1856) and developed through her forty other books and hundreds of essays, until her last novel in 1878 (*Poganuc People*). She published New England novels, New York novels, a feminist defense of Lord Byron's half-sister, *Lady Byron Vindicated* (1870), and novels that stage her debate with American Calvinist doctrine, such as *The Minister's Wooing* (1859). Perhaps her lasting influence was due to a style designed to engage her readers in the symbolic witnessing of slavery's horror and to enlist them in a Protestant crusade to change the course of history. Moreover, Stowe's arguments about interpreting the Bible inaugurated a new wave of women's fiction that describe spiritual doctrine from women's perspectives.

A host of women writers followed in Stowe's famous wake: Maria Cummins, Susan Warner, Fanny Fern, E. D. E. N. Southworth, Ann Stephens, among many others still being recovered by literary critics and scholars, a group that Hawthorne denigrated in an infamous phrase as a "d----d mob of scribbling women," a general condemnation by which he meant to distinguish Fanny Fern's work as an exception.

Not every author followed in Stowe's liberal path. Anti-Catholic, anti-Mormon, anti-Masonic, and anti-Semitic novels persisted throughout nineteenth-century fiction, lending themselves to the political forces of the Know-Nothing Party and later the Ku Klux Klan. (In an effort to out-Stowe Stowe, Thomas Dixon would capitalize upon her sentimental strategies in order to turn his early twentieth-century novels—such as *The Leopard's Spots*, 1902—into best-sellers in favor of racist politics.) Like Stowe's novels, these critiques of other religions taking root in America (due largely to immigration) also provided a way to turn a harsh lens on Protestantism itself. Two of the most famous novels of the midcentury—Maria Monk's *Awful Disclosures of the Hotel Dieu Nunnery of Montreal* (1836) and Rebecca Theresa Reed's *Six Months in a Convent* (1835)—were wildly popular reports, first published as "facts"—about the sexual abuses of the Catholic church and its threat to American democracy, embodied in lecherous priests and pimping nuns. These sensational books were legion by the 1860s, and such formerly "domestic" writers, like Louisa May Alcott and Harriet Prescott Spofford adopted their strategies and themes.

"THE GREAT AMERICAN NOVEL"

Greater and greater psychological complexity and social realism characterized the postbellum novel. Indeed, the business of the novel through the second half of the century was primarily to entertain a rising middle-class readership in fantasies of individual fulfillment and to instruct this audience in the new morality of cultural expansion.

The years following the Civil War saw the rise of best-sellers and "dime novels," the widespread manufacture and distribution of books written for young, male, working-class readers, catering to their interest in sensationalism and adventure. Parallel to this development was the proliferation of genteel fiction, also aimed at boys, with tales of good boys triumphing over bad. This form of fiction reached its ascendancy in the works of Horatio Alger Jr.,

whose stories of "luck and pluck" and of being "bound to rise" also reveal the dream work of what would later be called the "Protestant Ethic," a culture moving closer to monopoly capitalism. Some of Mark Twain's earliest tales and sketches satirize such Sunday school morality, as in "The Story of a Bad Little Boy" (1865). Eventually novels featured "bad girls"—like Stephen Crane's *Maggie: A Girl of the Streets* (1893) and Charlotte Perkins Gilman's short story "The Yellow Wall-Paper" (1892), tales of wayward or misunderstood young women. The story of girls in search of their own fulfillment developed into New Woman novels, like Kate Chopin's *The Awakening* (1899) and Edith Wharton's *The House of Mirth* (1905), which, along with Theodore Dreiser's *Sister Carrie* (1900) and David Graham Phillips's *Susan Lenox, Her Fall and Rise* (1917), generally repudiated Victorian American ideals of womanhood in favor of more modern expectations.

Women writers after the Civil War created the new genre of social gospel fiction, and it largely effected the transition between the domestic fiction of the antebellum United States and the social imperatives of Reconstruction. These novels were part of the drive to cure American society and to establish incipient welfare states for the poor, destitute, and insane. For example, in Rebecca Harding Davis's "Life in the Iron Mills" (1861) and Elizabeth Stuart Phelps's *The Silent Partner* (1871), working-class women are irredeemably separated from middle-class reformers who are affecting melioration, if not revolution, in their working conditions. This protest literature, written by and for the middle-class readership, struck a nerve by pointing out the vast differences between American social classes.

AMERICAN REALISM AND NATURALISM

America's turn toward the middle class as the dominant readership of fiction came in post-Reconstruction America. This realism began, for William Dean Howells, as an attempt to establish the genteel values that would dominate the ascendancy of the American middle class. In the scholar Eric Sundquist's terms, realism became "the romance of money," a major endeavor to define the effects of capitalism, the Gilded Age, and the fantasies of mechanical and technological revolutions.

One real event, the completion of the transcontinental railroad in 1869, might stand as a metaphor for the postbellum novel's new enterprise of bringing the disparate parts of America into communication and commerce with each other. The primary urge of new realism was to record an America disillusioned after the terrible toll of death and grief that the Civil War dealt to the nation's spirit. To render the actual circumstances of ordinary people through the most direct forms of literary expression became the shared imperative, especially as realist writers followed the brilliant example of America's three foremost writers: Howells, the novelist and critic who did more than anyone to introduce European realism to American social life; Henry James, the artist par excellence who brought the realist creed to the examination of psychology; and Mark Twain, the popular favorite who may be said to have invented the vernacular language of American literature.

The decade of the 1880s was the heyday of American realism, realized in the publication of Howells's *The Rise of Silas Lapham* (1885), James's *The Portrait of a Lady* (1881), and Twain's *Adventures of Huckleberry Finn* (1885). These novels chart the moral development of a series of "representative" Americans: the entrepreneurial male, the gifted young woman, and the "good bad boy." From Howells's "economy of pain" to Twain's dilemma surrounding Jim's freedom, these realist morals exemplify how the average American cannot trust the public for morality but has to develop an individual ethics. These moral selves have to withstand the lures of money and luxury, as well as the "sivilising" and normalizing of capitalism.

At the same time, more and more writers were combing the interest of their particular regions to gratify the appetite of readers who wanted to know more about the country. Regionalism sought to delineate cultural differences apparent in each section of the country—sometimes in stark opposition to the democratic nationalism or union that the earlier novels sought to inculcate—but its complementary ideal is that, together, these cultural differences accumulate into a national entity. Although earlier regionalists, like Joseph Baldwin and William Gilmore Simms, performed a similar service, they did so to emphasize a certain native exoticism, especially about the South or what used to be called the Southwest (Alabama, Arkansas, Mississippi, and Missouri). From the 1880s through the new decades of the twentieth century, regionalists followed the example of Edward Eggleston (of Indiana), George Washington Cable (of Louisiana), Sarah Orne Jewett and Mary Wilkins Freeman (of New England), and Hamlin Garland (of the upper Midwest) and treated these places both for their particularity and, in doing so, sought to portray how the local might

stand for general propositions about the nation. Regional tales became the dominant fiction of magazines like the *Atlantic Monthly* and *Harper's* during the last quarter of the century.

Rejecting Howellsian realism as the "drama of a broken teacup, the tragedy of a walk down the lane," Frank Norris, like his contemporaries Jack London and Theodore Dreiser, reformulated the social directive of American fiction: Norris wanted fiction to be a surgical tool, a way of getting at the blood and bones of life or what he termed "nature red in tooth and claw." Traditionally, naturalism has been defined as the movement to demonstrate how luck, fate, heredity, and environment—forces beyond the inner resources whose cultivation realism meant to encourage—shape the human condition. Stephen Crane's *The Red Badge of Courage* (1895) broke new ground in portraying Henry Fleming, a Civil War deserter who flees from the bloody reality of the war. Rather than a conversion from romantic innocence to realistic awareness marking his fate, the novel creates an indifferent universe that projects no implicit framework—moral, spiritual, or social—for human decisions.

For Jack London, too, destiny is created by forces outside oneself, even in physical laws governing the cosmos. In the last decade of American literary scholarship, naturalism has come to be understood as a challenge to bourgeois conventions of verisimilitude. Norris's *McTeague* (1899) is one such example, focusing as it does on the career of an untutored dentist (before there were credentials for such professions), whose greed—like that of nearly every character in the novel—leads to his undoing. His end—handcuffed to his dead rival, dying of thirst in the desert while he carries his canary's birdcage—was the fittingly ludicrous end to a life blighted by misplaced ambition and unfulfilled desire. The naturalist whose career more fully created a bridge to modern fiction is Theodore Dreiser, especially his study of money, culture, and character, *An American Tragedy* (1925).

African American fiction developed alongside—less often in tandem with—American realism and regionalism. African Americans emerged as subjects in mainstream fiction in the postbellum years, in the works of the liberal novelist Albion Tourgée, and in reactionary ones, like Thomas Nelson Page, and in writers like George Washington Harris of "Uncle Remus" fame, who saw himself as liberal but who later generations perceived as racist. The first works by African American writers—like William Wells Brown's *Clotel* (1853), Harriet Wilson's *Our Nig* (1859), and Harriet Jacobs's *Incidents in the Life of a Slave Girl* (1861)—initiated a significant tradition in American fiction. Largely devoted to examining the practices and consequences of slavery, these books also demonstrate a resistance to and subversion of white and patriarchal literary traditions, namely the stereotypes promulgated about black male sexuality and black female lasciviousness. Both Wilson's and Jacobs's accounts of slavery especially challenge the notions that a black woman had power or "moral influence" over men, especially their lusts for power.

Regionalism gave rise to novels and stories about the folk practices as well as the contemporaneous mores of African Americans, most notably in the work of Charles Chesnutt, whose tales such as those collected in *The Conjure Woman* (1899) and whose novels, such as *The House Behind the Cedars* (1900) and *The Marrow of Tradition* (1901) brought a broader sense of African American reality. (His books did not sell, and Chesnutt had to give up his career as a writer.)

By the time Reconstruction had failed in the South, black authors such as Emma Kelley in *Megda* (1891) and Frances Harper in *Iola Leroy* (1892) returned to the challenge of showing how racial uplift was tied to undoing the stereotypes of African Americans as "vulgar," part of the lower orders of humanity, incapable of education or citizenship. Pauline Hopkins would add a crucial trio of novels to this agenda: *Contending Forces* (1900), *Hagar's Daughter* (1901–1902), and *Of One Blood* (1903). Her work alerted readers to the tragic legacy of the historical past and the potential embodied in the black women's "virtue," meaning for Hopkins a conscious choice, not a physical or sexual quality.

In all of these novels, one crucial strategy of African American fiction in undoing stereotypes can be found in the many novels of "passing," plots that turn on a light-skinned African American crossing the color line of a segregated America by moving into the world of whites, often with tragic consequences. James Weldon Johnson's *Autobiography of an Ex-Coloured Man* (1912) and Nella Larsen's *Passing* (1929) bring this story out of the nineteenth century and give it a modern application of estrangement, even alienation.

Not only did realism provide a rationale for the stories and novels about the world beyond New England, but it also described the reshaping of American demographics. Previous fiction about the Jews or Irish was written from an outsider's perspective, largely restricted—in the latter case—to virulent anti-Catholicism, but the new immigrant fiction sought to explore the terms of American identity.

Immigrant fiction was written from within, and about the experience of what America was making of new people, particularly Jews. It was in 1896, when Abraham Cahan published *Yekl*, a story about the effects of assimilation on newly arrived Jews, and a few years later *The Imported Bridegroom and Other Stories* (1898), that Jewish Americans could claim their first literary spokesman. Immigrant novels flourished over the next three decades, especially Cahan's *Rise of David Levinsky* (1917) and Anzia Yezierska's *Salome of the Tenements* (1922) and *The Bread Givers* (1925), along with Ole Rölvaag's *Giants in the Earth* (1927) and *Peder Victorious* (1929).

Perhaps the last significant development in early-twentieth-century realism is found in social protest literature: a type of fiction that was conceived as an antidote to a sickly mainstream literature, one that features Christian sentimentality, the glorification of rural values, or silly escapism, including visits to imaginary countries. Edward Bellamy's *Looking Backward, 2000–1887* (1888) introduced utopian writing into the American mainstream. The grandest achievement of protest writing was undeniably Upton Sinclair's *The Jungle* (1906), a celebrated exposé of the meat industry, one that so relentlessly unmasked business corruption that it led to an act of Congress and the establishing of the Food and Drug Administration. Sinclair enjoyed a fifty-year career as a novelist, and while he later won a Pulitzer Prize, the success of this book would never be superseded. Other notable protest writers include Henry B. Fuller, Charlotte Perkins Gilman, and Robert Herrick, all of whom wrote vigorous critiques of new social mores, especially the rise of professional culture.

AMERICAN MODERNISM

American modernism was riven by competing claims for literature as having a greater highbrow or mass-market appeal. At the time, modernism meant the "revolt from the village," a denunciation of American provinciality and an aspiration toward a more cosmopolitan vision, one more fully in accord with the upheavals in art and philosophy that found expression in Europe prior to and following the First World War. Modernism came to signify the belief that perception shapes reality, a new vision to be found in the rejection of the social agendas of realism and naturalism and perhaps in a misplaced faith in the higher truths and beauties of art. This revolt, on the one hand, was conducted in the

Portrait of Gertrude Stein (**Pablo Picasso, 1906**). Stein was one of the twentieth century's most influential authors.
© FRANCIS G. MAYER/CORBIS

United States by such social critiques as Sherwood Anderson's *Winesburg, Ohio* (1919) and Sinclair Lewis's *Main Street* (1920). Edith Wharton's *Age of Innocence* (1920) and Willa Cather's *The Professor's House* (1925) participate in this trend, though their perspective often entails an antimodernist anxiety over upheaval and social change. On the other, Gertrude Stein, in her experiments in prose such as *Three Lives* (1908), would inspire later modern artists, like Ernest Hemingway, especially in *The Sun Also Rises* (1926) and Djuna Barnes in *Nightwood* (1936), who looked to her for lessons in style as well as a new representation of consciousness.

In addition, the cultural embrace of the popular and the middlebrow marks this new modernist fiction: Anita Loos joined Wharton and Willa Cather in trying to accommodate modernity's complexity, even as Hemingway and F. Scott Fitzgerald tried to create an ever more accessible modern style. William Faulkner began the 1920s as a regionalist, committed to family stories, and while that label never ceases to apply, he also tried to give broader historical and philosophical scope to his frequently gothic tales of cultural terror by reimagining how fiction can represent time, especially sequentiality and history, as well as the workings of consciousness. His trio of modernist greats—*The Sound and the Fury* (1929), *Light in August* (1932), and *Absalom, Absalom!* (1936), along with *As I Lay Dying* (1930)—tower above his other novels, ones less committed to the kinds of experiments he otherwise would make. His short fiction too is somewhat divided: witness stories of classic unity and coherence, like "A Rose for Emily" (1930), written mainly for magazine circulation, and the modern masterpiece of "The Bear" (1942), incomprehensible in places yet perhaps more searching and brilliant than any story he ever told.

Fitzgerald emerged as the most celebrated of the era, a fame attributable to his phenomenally successful short stories, often published during the 1920s in the slick magazine *Saturday Evening Post,* rather than the novels, including *The Great Gatsby* (1925), on which his reputation later depended. Even though Hemingway became the most widely imitated writer of the time, his influence on both short fiction and the novel was not yet noticeable in the 1920s. In fact, the modernist movement was more of a rebellion undertaken by a small, if ever-growing cadre of writers than a full-scale change. The era's serious fiction was dominated by social observers, like Joseph Hergesheimer, James Branch Cabell—both forgotten now—and Booth Tarkington.

Throughout the 1920s, the Harlem Renaissance produced such important experimentalists as Jean Toomer (*Cane*, 1923), Claude McKay (*Home to Harlem*, 1928), and Wallace Thurman (*The Blacker the Berry*, 1929). Carl Van Vechten's *Nigger Heaven* (1926) was a novel by a white writer purporting to present an inside view of Harlem during the jazz age. Also influenced by the spirit of cultural, literary, and intellectual ferment were novelists like Jesse Fauset (*There Is Confusion,* 1924; *Plum Bun,* 1928) and, most notably, Zora Neale Hurston, whose novels are based on her anthropological studies and employ some of their methods, especially in her *Their Eyes Were Watching God* (1937); Hurston sought to expose both gender oppression and American racism at the same time that she celebrated the folk life of African Americans and African Caribbeans of the Bahamas.

Typifying the fiction of the 1930s are the regional and historical novels that proliferated during this decade. Novels upon novels were devoted to the local character—both historical and social—of nearly every corner of the United States. Moreover, novels about such events as the Revolutionary and Civil Wars often topped best-seller lists. Perhaps a more trenchant examination of the present could be found in the emerging modernist consciousness. The publication of the *U.S.A.* trilogy (1930–1936) by John Dos Passos, for example, inaugurated a fresh set of aesthetic concerns with the function of hyperrealism, while Nathanael West's *Miss Lonelyhearts* (1933) and *The Day of the Locust* (1939) exploited the popularity of mass culture, framing them within his critique of the superficiality of modern intimacy.

Protest fiction of the 1930s more generally drew on the authors' experiences in radical politics—particularly the Communist front—to advance the revolution of the working class. Novelists such as Albert Halper, Josephine Herbst, Meridel LeSueur, Michael Gold, Tillie Olsen, Tess Slesinger, and Fielding Burke created fictions that sought to "agitate" and awaken their readers to class consciousness. One stirring work, also in the ethnic tradition, is Pietro Di Donato's *Christ in Concrete* (1937). Protest fiction and social realism reached their popular and aesthetic fulfillment at the end of the decade in two critically acclaimed exemplars—John Steinbeck's *The Grapes of Wrath* (1939) and Richard Wright's *Native Son* (1940).

Throughout the 1930s, 1940s, and into the 1950s, fiction in the Howellsian tradition focused on the current circumstances of the bourgeoisie and gave rise to chroniclers like Dorothy Canfield, John Marquand, Ellen Glasgow, and James Gould Cozzens. Such books and stories, often devoted to the very immediate past, gratified readers' tastes for social analysis, without engaging in divisive class arguments. Throughout the 1940s, these novelists took up a variety of social issues (in much the same way as writers in the 1840s and 1850s were perceived to do) to help readers understand changes in the body social. Such books include Lillian Smith's study of racism, *Strange Fruit* (1944); Charles Jackson's portrait of an alcoholic, *The Lost Weekend* (1944); and Laura Z. Hobson's *Gentleman's Agreement* (1947), which explores American anti-Semitism. These books were occasionally commercial successes and were often greeted warmly by the public and respectfully by the critics. Much more popular were the epics and melodramas, novels that frequently followed the often sad descent of a heroine who struggles against gender mores of her time, published by novelists as diverse as Edna Ferber, Fannie Hurst, and Frank Yerby.

POSTMODERNISM AND MINIMALISM

Since 1945, the novel in America might be characterized as a compendium of all the experimental and ritual conventions preceding it. Following World War II, American fiction was dominated by the ever-present war novel and its correlative story of the GI's return. Literally hundreds of these stories were written, though only a handful, like James Jones's *From Here to Eternity* (1951) and Norman Mailer's *The Naked and the Dead* (1948), are remembered by twenty-first-century readers. The postwar era often stressed the literature of alienation, of protagonists profoundly distanced from their communities, families, and, ultimately, from themselves. Often the setting for these books is the new suburbia, a change in the American landscape, and include *The Man in the Gray Flannel Suit* (1956). James Baldwin's stories and novels, J. D. Salinger's *The Catcher in the Rye* (1951), Flannery O'Connor's haunting tales, Saul Bellow's *Seize the Day* (1956), Bernard Malamud's fiction, and Mary McCarthy's *The Group* (1963), along with John Cheever's stories as well as Shirley Jackson's, focus on the psychological results—especially the dark underside—of the Second World War and American exceptionalism. Out of this tradition came the two most enduring writers of the postwar era, John Updike and Philip Roth, both of whose careers have spanned five decades and continue, while Bellow has also enjoyed even greater longevity and, as a Nobel Prize winner, even greater acclaim. This fic-

tion also drew on the gothic tradition of estrangement published in the 1940s, like the work of Carson McCullers and Eudora Welty; Faulkner's work is a lingering example. Ralph Ellison's *Invisible Man* (1952) has proven to be both the enduring modernist example of this literature and arguably the profoundest meditation on American race relations.

This literature of alienation also gave rise to a revitalized period of experimentalism, developments loosely grouped under the rubric of the "postmodern." The attributes of the postmodern, beyond an absurdist perspective on the conduct of normal life, includes pastiche and parody—a general disparagement of the realist tradition, on the one hand, and a dissatisfaction with the modernist exploitation of inferiority on the other. Novels and stories by Donald Barthelme and John Barth in the 1950s and 1960s, along with the fiction of Robert Coover in the 1960s and 1970s, captured the imagination of critics, if not the public. Perhaps the best-selling work in this vein was Joseph Heller's black comedy of army life during World War II, *Catch-22* (1961).

CONTEMPORARY FICTION

Some critics see postmodernism as the end of the novel's devotion to or affirmation of democratic culture. One of the most prominent conjunctions of fiction and politics emerged in the 1960s, with the demand for civil rights, protest over the Vietnam War, and the second wave of feminism. Michael Herr's *Dispatches* (1977), one of the new fictions that verged on nonfiction, reported the war and its effects on the grunts who served in it. Marilyn French's *The Women's Room* (1977) became the American version of Virginia Woolf's directive for "a room of one's own." In their wake came Toni Morrison's novels, depicting what she termed the "African presence in American literature." Her works, from *The Bluest Eye* (1970) to *Beloved* (1987), have been celebrated as the new realism—replete with ideological and historical significance, but also utopian enough to satisfy an American demand for hope, for Ralph Waldo Emerson's optative mood.

Ethnic and regional writing developed a new audience in the works of such Native American fiction as N. Scott Momaday's *House Made of Dawn* (1968), Leslie Marmon Silko's *Ceremony* (1977), and Louise Erdrich's *Love Medicine* (1984), among many others. Although there had been earlier efforts by Asian

American and Chicano/a writers, a contemporary cadre of writers like Maxine Hong Kingston, Amy Tan, and Gish Jen among Asian Americans, as well as Sandra Cisneros among Mexican American story writers and novelists, has also flourished. A new literary movement—border literature—also emerged, one that capitalizes on the hybridity and liminality of experience in "la frontera," the places nominally of the United States but where Chicano culture thrives.

Perhaps the dominant mode of American fiction from the mid-1970s through the 1980s was a movement to be described as minimalism—minimal in its demands on mimetic art. This spare, attenuated fiction concentrates on surfaces and conversation, mining the interest of passing human connections, pursuing tokens rather than symbols, alert to the resonance of popular culture rather than the profundities of the Western philosophical tradition. Thomas Pynchon's works—from *The Crying of Lot 49* (1966) to *Gravity's Rainbow* (1973) and *Vineland* (1990)—are grand experiments in life in late capitalism. Frederick Barthelme's stories of shopping malls and apartment developments seem to typify the settings at this new soullessness. Its most famous practitioner was Raymond Carver, whose stories collected in *Cathedral* (1984) and *What We Talk About When We Talk About Love* (1981) have achieved the level of classic. Ann Beattie's and Lorrie Moore's stories have also proved vital in sustaining minimalism through the 1980s and 1990s.

American fiction of the twenty-first century still generates enthusiasm for its vitality and imagination, especially in the works of such authors as Russell Banks, E. L. Doctorow, Richard Ford, and Jane Smiley, but it is equally clear that the audience for this fiction has dwindled, with readership lost to new forms of media and discourse. In fact, the rise of the entertainment industry has always exerted a serious impact on American fiction. Before the rise of mass media, the novel was perhaps the principal way art and amusement could be conjoined. With the advent first of popular magazines (like *True Story* in 1919), radio, Hollywood films (especially talkies), and television, fiction needed to compete more forcefully. With each new elaboration of mass culture, fiction writers had to assimilate the changes wrought and set a new challenge, though ultimately nothing fiction writers could do would survive the immediacy of television. Instead, publishers developed the circulation of "blockbuster" fiction, a handful of titles that could be expected, each season, to thrill the marketplace, initially in the works of Herman Wouk, Harold Robbins, James Michener, and, later, in the novels of Jacqueline Susann and Danielle Steel and their many, many imitators. Techno-thrillers, such as the works of Dean Koontz, elaborate on the spy thrillers quite popular during the cold war era. John Grisham has made a lucrative career of creating novels that turn twists of legal cases into social dilemmas. Of lasting interest has been the career of Stephen King, who has merged such venerable forms as the detective novel with nineteenth-century sensational fiction and Hollywood horror films. Also of enduring appeal have been the mass-produced Harlequin novels as well as the historical sagas of Louis L'Amour. "Serious" fiction and popular fiction—categories once coincident or overlapping—seem to be at their greatest distance from each other in the emergence of the twenty-first century.

See also **The Classical Vision; The Arts in the Republican Era; American Romanticism; Realism in Art and Literature; The Popular Arts** *(volume 1);* **The Ideal of Spontaneity; The World According to Hollywood; Popular Culture in the Public Arena** *(volume 2);* **The Visual Arts; Authorship, Literary Property, and Copyright; Elite vs. Popular Cultures; Culture for Mass Audiences; Literary Reviews and "Little Magazines"; Myth and Symbol** *(in this volume); and other articles in this section.*

BIBLIOGRAPHY

Baker, Houston A., Jr. *Modernism and the Harlem Renaissance.* Chicago, 1987.

Baym, Nina. *Woman's Fiction: A Guide to Novels by and about Women in America, 1820–1870.* Ithaca, N.Y., 1978.

Brodhead, Richard H. *Cultures of Letters: Scenes of Reading and Writing in Nineteenth-Century America.* Chicago, 1993.

Carby, Hazel V. *Reconstructing Womanhood: The Emergence of the Afro-American Woman Novelist.* New York, 1987.

Cawelti, John G. *Adventure, Mystery, and Romance: Formula Stories as Art and Popular Culture.* Chicago, 1976.

Chase, Richard. *The American Novel and Its Tradition.* New York, 1957.

Davidson, Cathy N. *Revolution and the Word: The Rise of the Novel in America.* New York, 1987.

Douglas, Ann. *The "Feminization" of American Culture.* New York, 1977.

Elliott, Emory, ed. *The Columbia History of the American Novel.* New York, 1991.

Hoffman, Frederick J. *The Twenties: American Writing in the Postwar Decade.* New York, 1954.

Holland, Laurence B. *The Expense of Vision; Essays on the Craft of Henry James.* Princeton, N.J., 1964.

Kazin, Alfred. *On Native Grounds: An Interpretation of Modern American Prose Literature.* New York, 1942.

Lauter, Paul. *Canons and Contexts.* New York, 1991.

Matthiessen, F. O. *American Renaissance: Art and Expression in the Age of Emerson and Whitman.* New York, 1941.

Michaels, Walter Benn. *The Gold Standard and the Logic of Naturalism: American Literature at the Turn of the Century.* Berkeley, Calif., 1987.

Rideout, Walter B. *The Radical Novel in the United States, 1900–1954: Some Interrelations of Literature and Society.* Cambridge, Mass., 1956.

Samuels, Shirley. *The Romances of the Republic: Women, the Family, and Violence in the Literature of the Early American Nation.* New York, 1996.

Sundquist, Eric J., ed. *American Realism: New Essays.* Baltimore, 1982.

———. *To Wake the Nations: Race in the Making of American Literature.* Cambridge, Mass., 1993.

Tate, Claudia. *Domestic Allegories of Political Desire: The Black Heroine's Text at the Turn of the Century.* New York, 1992.

Tompkins, Jane. *Sensational Designs: The Cultural Work of American Fiction, 1790–1860.* New York, 1985.

POETRY

Lisa M. Steinman

There is debate over what constitutes "American literature," with critical surveys beginning anywhere from 1492, with Christopher Columbus, to 1837, the year of Ralph Waldo Emerson's "The American Scholar" (which calls for an American literature, a phrase that only began to appear in the 1830s). Moreover, at least since the 1990 *Heath Anthology of American Literature*, descriptions of American poetry in particular often insist on including popular works from oral and print culture as well as works by Native Americans, African Americans, Latinos, Asian Americans, women, and other often marginalized groups.

Until recently, studies of poetry in the colonial era most often singled out the poems of Anne Bradstreet and Edward Taylor—the former for her more intimate or domestic lyrics; the latter for his poems influenced by English metaphysical poets like John Donne and George Herbert—as exceptional, while finding Michael Wigglesworth's 1662 *The Day of Doom* more characteristic of the period's poetry. Wigglesworth's versified homiletics in ballad meter were purchased by one out of every twenty people in New England, making the "Doomsday verses" an early best-seller although the poetry is not generally attractive to more modern readers. Critics have pointed out that the Puritan resistance to imaginative writing and theologically based insistence on unadorned language seem to make Puritan poetics an oxymoron. John Cotton's 1640 preface to *The Bay Psalm Book* explicitly presented its New World translation of the psalms as avoiding "poetical license." Between 1940 and 1960, however, a wider range of poems, including love lyrics, hymns, and elegies by writers from various walks of life—John Saffin, Roger Williams, Sarah Kemble Knight, Jane Colman Turell, and Anna Hayden, to name a few— were discovered and published. Most of these poets did not circulate their work, but they help suggest poetry was a more common Puritan practice and less theologically suspect than previously thought. The revised view of Puritan poetics takes account of how biblical typology, especially the trope of marriage as a type of the soul's bond with God, underwrites some uses of metaphorical language. Plain language and unpolished metrics also could be purposeful, taken as marks of the soul's strenuous meditations and of the human inability to present ultimate truths. Finally, the most recent literary histories note that poetry of the colonial period is not limited to Puritan poetry. Newer anthologies include poetry from the Hispanic new world, like the work of Sor Juana Inés de la Cruz—whose learned, highly formal poems are often compared with those of her older English-speaking contemporary, Anne Bradstreet—as well as Native American oral poetry from Inuit to Aztec.

Here, to consider the public cultural expression of American poetry historically (emphasizing both a public sphere and a self-consciously nationalist identity) is to focus primarily on what was widely circulated within the nation. Much of the history of the United States from 1776 to the present involves a relatively narrow canon. Indeed, the notion of a national literature requires addressing the question of the often extraliterary forces that helped to craft conceptions of American poetry.

From the early days of the Republic, poetry occupied a special position within public print culture. Print and printers were associated with the construction of a public sphere and of a nationalist rhetoric in revolutionary America, not surprisingly for a nation that was founded by literary fiat with the Declaration of Independence. As the critics Michael Warner and Larzer Ziff have argued, the rhetoric of public discourse during the Revolution and Early Republic tried to ward off any appearance of privilege or exceptionalism by appealing to a common readership of ordinary citizens.

By the 1790s, there were many forms of public print in circulation, including political and religious tracts, almanacs, and newspapers. The decade saw more newspapers founded than had the previous century; novels too began to gain a larger readership. American novels by writers like Charles Brockden Brown and Hannah Webster Foster proposed the genre in which they worked as a new instrument for constructing the *idea* of a shared public sphere. Within fiction in particular, the public sphere was increasingly proposed as privatized or interiorized rather than active. While the republican rhetoric of print continued to link print to the public good, there was also a rising undercurrent of anxiety about the ignorance of plain citizens who might act in the public sphere (specifically a fear that revolutionary ideals might be re-imported from France). The 1790s introduced new concerns for writers, concerns about public and private roles and about the role of reading or writing in directing public action.

One might think that poetry would have benefited from a national celebration of citizens as readers and even from the growing insistence on private sensibility. Poetry in English, after all, had been increasingly associated with sensibility (although also with personal exceptionalism) since the middle of the eighteenth century. In America, however, poetry had difficulty competing with other public print forms. The rhetoric of citizenship was not always congruous with that of the poetic self. Poetry was seen as a class commodity, associated with British aristocratic tradition and with idle leisure. While the British "Country" or "Commonwealthman" rhetoric of poets such as John Milton and James Thomson echoes throughout early American political discourse—Thomas Paine's *Common Sense* assumes readers familiar with both British poets—political speeches used the rhetoric not as poetry per se, still less as a sign of cultured accomplishment, but for its perceived moral and political clout.

Americans with literary ambitions in the field of poetry early in the nation's history faced American audiences suspicious of their genre's link with inherited privilege, luxury, or decadence at the same time that they faced foreign skepticism (which one hears voiced at least up until the early twentieth century) about the ability of Americans to participate in civilized pursuits like poetry. The very props and rhetorical designs that marked writing as accomplished poetry could at home signal what was thought most dangerous publicly: imported hierarchy or decadent luxury. An African American poet like Phillis Wheatley could draw on the techniques of high poetry, using heroic couplets, for instance, without threatening to reestablish a European hierarchy; her poetic embodiment of eloquence made her point about the civilized accomplishments of her race. But for others, European and especially British poetic models sent mixed signals.

If the rhetoric of poetry was suspect, the rhetoric of public prose offered no clear alternative model for poets, especially given that the inherited voices of high poetry as constructed in seventeenth- and eighteenth-century Britain laid claim to personal exceptionalism. The elevated tone of high poetry was understood as either "un-American," or, later, as signifying irrational passions that seemed to foster public discord.

POETS OF THE EARLY REPUBLIC

One of the earliest national attempts at poetic epic, Joel Barlow's 1787 *Vision of Columbus*, revised as the *Columbiad* in 1807, presents a secularized version of providential history and progressive republicanism. Barlow draws on both Miltonic epic and Thomsonian georgics, while showing an acute self-consciousness about the difficulties of transplanting British traditions to America. As Barlow wrote, "Too much of Europe, here transplanted o'er, / Nursed feudal feelings on [America's] tented shore" (book 8, lines 383–386). Barlow's construction of a public voice tries to borrow its rhetorical stance from civic prose as well. Barlow, however, also felt the need to surround his poem with notes and a preface, in order to insist on his dedication to "rational liberty," against "deleterious passion," and to spell out the difficulties of reconciling his didactic purpose with, as he says, "a manner of treating it" that is "most poetical." Republican politics and poetic language did not rest easily together, and by all appearances Barlow did not trust his poetry to convey his intended message to readers without prose guidance.

Barlow's *Columbiad* also illustrates further problems facing poetry that attempted to assert its place in the public sphere. Although he insisted on two cheaper editions in order to reach "various levels of the public," Barlow first sought a Baltimore publisher because he thought (mistakenly, as it turned out) that the city would provide a market for a luxury edition; in Baltimore, he wrote, "the wealthy . . . may think libraries an ornamental species of furniture" (Charvat, *The Profession of Authorship*, pp. 8, 12). Boston, Philadelphia, and to a lesser extent New York, were far more active centers of American publishing in Barlow's day. He was considering demand (rather than supply); it is telling that this imagination of his readership is at odds with his own (and with earlier revolutionary or republican) politics. In attempting to circulate the poem, even the radical Barlow, who supported the French Revolution, like the conservative circle of poets who opposed it (the so-called Connecticut wits including Timothy Dwight and David Humphreys) from whom Barlow broke in 1788, positioned his poetry to circulate and sell as a mark of refinement, addressing not common readers but the privileged for whom books of poetry were commodities and marks of social status.

There is a related emblem of the perceived tension between the public sphere and poetry in attacks on John Quincy Adams during his presidential campaign. Adams's poetry stood out from that of most educated and publicly prominent verse-makers of the period. His work is collected in Emerson's 1874 *Parnassus* and remains in Edmund Clarence Stedman's 1900 *An American Anthology,* although Stedman's notes declare Adams's poetry "quaint." Only Oliver Wendell Holmes seems to have garnered a similar place in both public and poetic history. In Adams's own day, the pursuit of the muse was used to mark him as too rarefied, too elite, by his opponents, with the Republican General Committee of New York describing him, sarcastically, as "an elegant scholar, and a poet, too, forsooth."

Ironically, despite its perceived elite audience, poetry was at the same time not a lucrative endeavor for those who produced it. It appeared as filler in newspapers, which found a plentiful and thus inexpensive supply of verse for such purposes. As Benjamin Franklin's *Autobiography* reports his father saying, "Verse-makers were generally Beggars." Poetry seemed both unproductive idleness—a decadent luxury commodity—and unprofitable.

These and related difficulties facing those with aspirations for poetry's participation in national public discourse can also be traced in the career and poems of Barlow's contemporary, the poet Philip Freneau. Like Barlow, Freneau's collections of his poetry (1795 and 1809) indicate his conception of poetry's public role; his work was advertised in the *New York Journal* (6 July 1775) as blending "Ciceronian eloquence and patriotic fire." By the 1790s, as Dwight's attack on Freneau as an "incendiary" suggests, fire or passion deployed in the public arena was suspect in political (especially Federalist) rhetoric even as it continued to be a trope commonly used to depict poetic inspiration or genius. The problem was how recognizably to be a poet, to matter publicly or address larger audiences on mat-

ters of public concern, and yet not to seem to American ears either to claim the social high ground or to sound notes too divisive. Although he sent his poems to James Madison and Thomas Jefferson with the hope that his poetry would serve the public, Freneau, like Barlow, ultimately affected political events primarily because of his position as a newspaper editor.

These early poetic efforts might be said to fail, although interestingly, in their double-edged endeavors. The public status of poetry in America remained in question even while a growing chorus of local and foreign voices still deplored the absence of an authentically national literature.

POETRY IN THE ANTEBELLUM MARKET

After the War of 1812 ended in 1815, the rhetoric of public power shifted in all genres. The era also marks the true beginning of what has been called a market revolution. Although poetry did not at first fully participate in this revolution, that is, was not commodified because it was not lucrative and because audiences were not yet mass audiences, there was nonetheless a rise in magazine, newspaper, and gift book circulation among middle-class readers (and a rising culture of middle-class managed esteem) that affected poetry. Other influences on poetry were the increasingly internalized representations of the public sphere as well as literary imports, specifically British Graveyard and Romantic poetry.

The two most popular poems in America immediately following the end of the war were William Cullen Bryant's "Thanatopsis," first drafted in 1815, and Lydia Sigourney's "The Mother of Washington" (1815). While both poets were politically active in extraliterary ways and both were influential literary tastemakers as editors, their best-known poems also initiated (and participated in) a shift in poetic practice and taste. Both poems are elegiac and insist on personal sensibility while including internalized images of the nation. Sigourney's poem is on the death of George Washington's mother; Bryant's, on death, solitude, and an imagination of the North American continent as a republic of the dead. Both thus acknowledge the closing of the heroic revolutionary age of America and view poetry as able to monumentalize this now-closed past, but not as publicly effective in an active way.

Bryant and Sigourney represent views that Emerson, most prominently—as one of the strongest influences on nineteenth-century definitions of poetry—inherited and struggled with, as he did with the other inherited and often contradictory definitions of poetry as public and private, as high calling and decadent idleness, as elite and unprofitable.

With the shift to a market society, definitions of labor (and so of poetry's defenses against charges of luxury or idleness) also changed along with shifting definitions of a public sphere. Critics such as Michael Newbury point to newly developing ideologies and defenses of male, middle-class labor and to the ways in which authorship in particular became professionalized; within these larger cultural shifts, however, poetry again occupied a distinct position. Emerson's lectures and essays, for which he was (and is) best known, repeatedly use poetry as an image of the ideal of creative American intellectual work and yet consistently return to an acknowledged distinction between manual labor, public work, and imaginative work. His prose at least up through the late 1840s, from one perspective, is structured as a series of meditations on new versions of old problems would-be poets inherited from the turn of the century: how to understand private thought as public work; how to valorize intellectual work despite its apparent lack of practical or public efficacy (not to mention marketability); how to promote pastoral or meditative solitude without appearing to value promotion over substance or to be simply irrelevant.

Like many earlier prominent American poets, Emerson's influence did not stem primarily from his poems but in his case from his position as lyceum lecturer (which made him one of America's first professional intellectuals), as editor of the *Dial* until it folded in 1844, and as the American popularizer of Thomas Carlyle's work. His poems circulated in gift books and periodicals, but Emerson's 1846 volume of poetry did not sell as well as his prose or his lectures, although he, like Barlow, attended to the marketing of his book. Like Barlow, too, when it came to practical considerations, he conceived of poetry's audience as more genteel than that of prose, proposing to a prospective publisher a costly first edition of his *Poems,* which finally did appear as the only one of his books to be bound in white boards.

Whether marketing or writing poems, Emerson's practice was not identical with the theories his essays and lectures popularized. Although Emerson called for a literary revolution comparable to America's political declaration of independence, his poems themselves are even now not highly touted or widely studied as innovative. Yet his prose and his

anthology helped redefine American poetry for the Victorians.

GENTEEL POETRY IN POST–CIVIL WAR VICTORIAN AMERICA

Although the earliest anthology of exclusively American poems appeared as early as 1793, edited by Elihu Hubbard Smith, it is not until the 1840s–1850s that anthologies of or including American poetry began to define anything like a canon of American poetry. As Alan Golding's valuable history of anthologies suggests, Rufus Wilmot Griswold's 1842 *The Poets and Poetry of America* was a best-seller, but most late-eighteenth- and early-nineteenth-century poetry in America generally appeared in newspapers or magazines, and while there were increasing numbers of both, neither had long shelf lives. Nonetheless, in light of late-twentieth-century charges about the exclusivity of poetic canons, it is useful to note what was collected and included by the middle to late nineteenth century in the editions and surveys by Stedman or anthologies like *Parnassus*. These were the sources from which many aspiring poets received their ideas of (and their ears for) poetry, since American poets generally worked in isolation (America having a democratic if sometimes disconcerting lack of a literary center).

Despite some now conspicuous lacunae (Emerson omits Walt Whitman and Emily Dickinson), both *Parnassus* and Stedman's *An American Anthology,* are surprisingly inclusive: both include song (including, in 1900, a small section entitled "Negro Spirituals"). One finds as well regional poets (Joaquin Miller, Edwin Arlington Robinson, Madison Cawein, known as "the Keats of Kentucky") and a number of women, especially in Stedman's collection, which represents Sigourney, Margaret Fuller, and Lydia Maria Child. Stedman's anthology includes more poems by Lizette Woodworth Reese, Louise Imogen Guiney, and the African American poet Paul Laurence Dunbar than by William Ellery Channing or Herman Melville.

Looking at what was considered representative of American poetry and at the ways in which later nineteenth-century compilers categorize poetry reveals a concentration on sentimental or internalized lyric as opposed to the more publicly ambitious poetry of someone like Barlow. The twentieth century looked back to Whitman and Dickinson as the seminal American poets; mid-nineteenth-century American culture was more aware of the poetry of

Emily Dickinson. Undated miniature painting in the possession of the Dickinson family. Though Dickinson (1830–1886) published just seven poems in her lifetime, she wrote throughout her entire adult life, composing 1,775 poems and many stylish letters. Two years after her death *Poems by Emily Dickinson* began to establish her reputation. © BETTMANN/CORBIS

those history has dubbed Fireside Poets: Bryant, Holmes, James Russell Lowell, John Greenleaf Whittier, and Henry Wadsworth Longfellow, whom Stedman's anthology calls "America's untitled laureate."

Despite the appearance in some anthologies of Civil War poetry by Melville or Whitman, or of the public verse of Emma Lazarus or Julia Ward Howe (usually represented by the "Battle Hymn of the Republic"), little political and less epic poetry is included. Emerson's late Victorian collection devotes only one relatively short section (out of twelve) to poems labeled "Heroic," by which he means "Patriotic Historical Political."

Although to later readers the most widely circulated post–Civil War poetry seems of a piece, part of what George Santayana dubbed in 1911 the "genteel tradition," writers of the period differentiated among themselves, as the historian John Tomsich has detailed. There were ties between groups, but also arguments as the writers Santayana had in

mind when he spoke of genteel poetry (Thomas Bailey Aldrich, Richard Henry Stoddard, or Stedman himself, called the dean of American letters by the *New York Times* when he died in January 1908) saw themselves reacting against the New England Brahmins and especially Lowell. They also defended a late Emersonian view of poetry as high calling and refuge against tastemakers with a commitment to more realist literature. The obvious reference was to those like William Dean Howells, president of the American Academy of Arts and Letters and influential as an editor of quality magazines including *Atlantic Monthly* and *Cosmopolitan.*

On the one hand, as John Tomsich again suggests, the genteel poets, many of whom were associated with journalism or magazine editing in an age where both continued to be growth industries, mark the first generation of poets to make a living, albeit as "magazinists" not as poets per se. Many of the journals that featured poetry—*Harper's, Putnam's, Atlantic*—were founded in the 1850s and many, such as the *Atlantic* or the *Century,* had circulations over 100,000 by the late 1880s. On the other hand, the social construction of the poet's role in many ways remained that of someone not engaged in practical or public business, whose writing was a pastime or avocation—whether viewed positively, a sign of being above the quotidian world, or negatively, marking poets as bluestockings or producers of verse that was, to quote Santayana, "grandmotherly."

Such gendered descriptions of poetry, part of what is often called the "feminization of American culture," are common. Stedman's anthology described his era as the "woman's age." Victorian American poets and their readers shared a sense, not always welcome, that creative culture in general and poetry in particular were part of the feminine (and private) sphere. While associations between poetry and private feeling or between poetry and refinement were not new, the sense of poetry's readership as primarily female was. It is against such a sense that one also finds in the period attempts at more "manly" verse, like that of James Whitcomb Riley, who reached a large public readership in weekly journals such the *Saturday Evening Post* and whose books sold close to 3 million illustrated gift editions between 1893 and 1949.

Despite the high-mindedness of genteel poets or the popularity of poets like Riley, long-standing contractions facing poetry in America persisted. Poetry remained a mixed marker of status. "Poet" often appeared as an honorific title; for instance the *New York Times* called Albert Einstein a "poet in science" (3 April 1921). Yet poetry itself was not a viable profession, and to call oneself a poet was embarrassing for many nineteenth- and early-twentieth-century writers like William Carlos Williams or Wallace Stevens, because it allied them with what was considered unworldly or feminized.

AMERICAN MODERNISM

Robert and Helen Lynd's 1929 study of library readership in Muncie, Indiana, suggests that Americans were not much interested in any literary genre. Their book, *Middletown,* documents a rising popular interest (increasing sixty-two fold between 1903 and 1923) in what were called the "useful arts"—technology, salesmanship, and advertising. The library did not even bother to categorize poetry separately from fine arts and fiction, the readership for which as a whole grew less than half as much as that for more practical volumes. The most popular poetry was that of the British-born Edgar A. Guest (whose 1916 volume of sentimental verse, *A Heap O' Livin'*, was a best-seller), with Riley's poetry a close second. American modernist poets (most notably Stevens, Williams, Hart Crane, and Marianne Moore at home, and the expatriates T. S. Eliot and Ezra Pound) reacted against the folksy popular verse of Riley or Guest as well as the feminized and idealized image of genteel poetry and attempted to redefine poetry as a way to remarry creative intelligence with the everyday commercial and technological reality (and taste) of modern America, a project that would not have surprised Emerson although it dismayed his genteel heirs. Commercial, industrial America is both stylistically and thematically prominent in American modernist poetry. By contrast, genteel poetry, and even the best-selling Riley's, despite his use of dialect, generally retained traditional poetic structure and emphasized idealized or sentimentalized rural settings.

By the early twentieth century, America was admired for its business know-how, engineering, and technological ingenuity, although, as in the Early Republic, American art was not recognized abroad. Yet writers and visual artists abroad began to draw on a machine aesthetic—emphasizing clean lines, efficiency, and the effect of speed—to initiate a new movement in the arts, namely modernism, which deliberately positioned itself against traditional practices.

In 1913 the Armory Show (exhibited in New York and Chicago) brought postimpressionist art to relatively wide, although not uniformly enthusias-

JANUARY MORNING XV
(1917)

All this—
      was for you, old woman.
I wanted to write a poem
that you would understand.
For what good is it to me
if you can't understand it?
      But you got to try hard—

Source: William Carlos Williams, *Collected Poems,* 1: 103–104.

tic, public attention; the same year, Pound published an "Imagist Manifesto" in Harriet Monroe's newly founded magazine, *Poetry.* Poets like Williams, whose earliest verse is still most reminiscent of late-romantic gentility, saw in both Pound's instructions to write unornamented poetry using concrete images and the visual artists' new, experimental aesthetic a way to fulfill their desire to "be a mirror to . . . modernity." Many American poets between 1914 and 1918 (a period known as the "Little Renaissance") seized on new publications like *Poetry* and the press coverage of the new art as signs of a cultural revolution that defined an important, national community in which they might participate. As Pound wrote to Monroe, the "American Risorgimento" would make "the Italian Renaissance look like a tempest in a teapot!"

Although both in America and abroad, modernist manifestoes proposed a series of new movements within the literary and visual arts (futurism, imagism, surrealism, and objectivism, to name a few), there was considerable overlap between practices and practitioners and considerable interaction not only between the arts but—especially with an influx of French expatriates to New York in World War I—between Americans and Europeans. Ironically, although the new poetic experiments in both style (such as free verse that looked back to Whitman, imagism's short "clean" lines, or Moore's unobtrusively rhymed machinelike syllabics) and subject matter (such as Williams's celebrations of the aesthetic qualities of industrial urban landscapes) were aligned with the modernity of United States culture by Europeans, American audiences did not embrace modernism. Americans seemed rather to value commerce or modern business practice over impractical art, even while apparently preferring art untainted by the workaday world.

Facing skeptical audiences abroad and at home, modernist poets tried to place themselves within the larger modernist movement, claiming a style that could be seen as modern and indigenous and asserting poetry's importance despite the fact that few people liked or read modernist poetry. Yet there was not even a large popular appreciation of the regional concreteness of the work of the less obviously stylistically experimental generation of modern (but not modernist) poets such as the Midwesterners Carl Sandburg, Vachel Lindsay, and Edgar Lee Masters; the Southerner John Crowe Ransom; or the New Englander Robert Frost. *Poetry,* seeing the new poets it championed as the flowering of an American tradition, took its motto from Whitman, "To have great poets there must be great audiences too." The *Dial* also looked back to claim an American heritage, naming itself after the journal Emerson and Fuller had edited. The *Little Review's* motto was probably more to the point: "A Magazine of the Arts Making No Compromise with the Public Taste."

Widely circulated popular magazines continued to publish only genteel poetry. The magazines featuring more experimental work—*Soil, Broom, Others, The Blind Man*—most often were short-lived; even longer-lasting "little magazines" like *Poetry* had comparatively small circulations. Most American readers of poetry wanted poems as refuges from, not reminders of, commercialized industrial urban culture. The years 1921–1923 might be seen as the full blossoming of American modernism, with the appearance of Eliot's *The Waste Land,* and of books by Williams, Moore, and Stevens. Yet it was not until midcentury or later that many American readers recognized modernism as marking the coming-of-age of American poetry in the world's eyes.

CONTEMPORARY AND CURRENT PRACTICES

If ordinary American readers continued to prefer genteel poetry (reincarnated in Rod McKuen's commercially successful inspirational verse or parodied in the humorous verse of Ogden Nash, who had a large following up through at least the 1960s), many poets by midcentury already felt the need to distinguish themselves from the towering presences of the modernists by returning to more traditional verse forms. As Alan Golding notes, American poetic culture by 1960 is broadly characterized by the so-called anthology wars, between what Robert Lowell called "the cooked and the raw," the former collected in the 1957 *New Poets of England and America* edited by the poets Donald Hall, Robert Pack, and Louis Simpson. More "open form" poetry in what is often called open field composition or projectivist verse was promoted by Donald Allen's 1960 collection, *New American Poetry, 1945–1960,* which included the work of Charles Olson, Robert Creeley, and Denise Levertov, as well as of Beat poets (such as Allen Ginsberg) and of the West Coast, Zen-influenced Philip Whalen and Gary Snyder. Although the poems in the 1957 anthology more obviously differ from the previous generation's, the poets in Allen's volume considered themselves more radical aesthetically and politically.

The distinction between "cooked and raw," however, obscures both how rapidly many individual styles shifted after 1960 and the larger settings in which poetry after modernism took shape. Within two decades of the appearance of the neatly defined anthology camps, many of the poets who began writing more formal, often technically dazzling poetry (Josephine Miles, Elizabeth Bishop, Robert Lowell, John Berryman, among those born in 1910–1920; W. S. Merwin, Adrienne Rich, James Wright, among those born in the 1920s) radically changed their styles to more open, free verse, affected both by the reintroduction of a Whitman- and modernist-influenced South American poetry and by the social upheavals of the civil rights movement and the Vietnam War. The cooked became raw in style, subject, or both. Moreover, poetic practice and audiences for poetry were further affected by the introduction of modern American poetry into the curricula of American schools, as well as by the opening of American higher education that began after World War II.

Since midcentury, as well, poetry writing has become professionalized to some degree, with countless local writing workshops to train aspiring poets and over a tenfold growth in the number of programs that grant graduate degrees in writing. This has led some to complain about a homogenization of American poetic practice, with a turn toward what critics dub "the workshop poem," and what Charles Altieri has called the "scenic lyric," descriptive poems that become occasions for crafting intense emotionally charged scenes or that aim at the effect of intensity in an age where a rhetoric and subject matter of shared public concern (or a belief in essential or shared truths) seem difficult to come by.

The complaints about homogenization notwithstanding, pluralism might best characterize the state of later twentieth-century American poetry. The numbers of writing programs listed by professional organizations like the Associated Writing Programs or Poets & Writers, not to mention the existence of more than one such professional organization, mark one reason to characterize contemporary poetry as pluralistic. One can also list multiple poetic camps, both self-identified and formed by critical retrospect: the New York school of Frank O'Hara and John Ashbery; the Deep Image school of Robert Bly and W. S. Merwin; feminist poets; confessional poets; postmodernists or LANGUAGE poets; new formalists; poets of witness; and a variety of poets who identify their poetry with their ethnic heritage. Few poets, moreover, easily fit within one poetic identity since some of the above-mentioned schools or positions are constituted by subject matter or subject position; others, by style or even professional association. A. R. Ammons, whose Whitmanian lines and Emersonian poetics yield a modern nature poetry, nonetheless studied with Miles and claims Ashbery as his most significant contemporary. A poet like Yusef Komunyakaa is a lyricist, a poet self-conscious about his African American identity who looks to a jazz aesthetic, and could as well be claimed as a poet of witness (for his familial and his Vietnam War poems).

American poetry continues to reveal the existence of traditional tensions between the public and private status of poetry and between the apparently elite or impractical nature of the art and the populist aspirations of poets, although these tensions take different shapes in response to distinctive features of the contemporary American world, including mass audiences, advertising, and consumer culture. The distinction between mass and popular culture (the question of how to characterize genuinely populist forms of culture and of when culture is constructed or manipulated by the consumer culture industry for its own ends) was a subject for public debate by the 1930s, as reflected in poems by, for instance, Moore or Williams (who although critical of the marketing of poetry nevertheless participated in it). Almost 150 years earlier, Joel Barlow already saw a rift between the marketing and practice of poetry, although he presumably could not have envisioned the dilemma of poets in an age of television appearances, poetry slams, and a widespread devaluation of all public rhetoric. In short, the poet's contemporary dilemma—how to reach and be valued by a broad audience, when no clearly poetic rhetoric appropriate to such an audience is available—is a version of a problem one can trace back to the eighteenth century.

There are new difficulties, admittedly. Modernists could announce themselves as avant-garde because their educational backgrounds as well as the prevalence of genteel poetry made their manipulations and refusals of tradition meaningful. By definition the avant-garde is generally a privileged group, constituted of those who have so internalized the rules of cultural practice as to be able to break them meaningfully. Contemporary poets facing a more pluralist culture cannot take for granted that the diverse mass audience they increasingly imagine themselves addressing shares any common assumptions.

Nonetheless, many features of contemporary poetry's cultural position are familiar; few trade publishers or best-seller lists even attend to a genre that still commands a relatively small market share. Poetry continues as a status marker (often relying on the perceived status of the avant-garde); however, the appearance of poets and poetry in television commercials for fast food or athletic shoes does not fund the writers of poetry. Poetry writing continues to be relatively unlucrative despite an unprecedented number of (not usually well-paying) small poetry magazines, presses, and awards. American culture—as it has since Emerson's day—continues to use poetry to market everything except poems, which might be seen as a variation on earlier republican tensions between poetry as status marker and poetry's ultimate irrelevance to public culture.

By the early twentieth century, anthologies and publishing, as well as the establishment of the American Academy of Arts and Letters, served to institutionalize what counted as American poetry. Throughout the early 1900s, too, there were influential central institutions that marked and marketed poetic careers, not simply the appointment of poets to the Library of Congress or the Academy, but also, from 1919, the influential Yale Younger Poets competition, by which older established poets including Stephen Vincent Benét and W. H. Auden identified promising poets of the next generation. Almost a century later, however, with so many such venues, there is no obvious central avenue for legitimation. The numbers bespeak the continued production of poetry, but also suggest a new incarnation of the decentered nature of American poetic culture.

See also **The Classical Vision; American Romanticism; Realism in Art and Literature** *(volume 1);* **The Ideal of Spontaneity; Artistic, Intellectual, and Political Refugees** *(volume 2);* **Culture for Mass Audiences; Literary Reviews and "Little Magazines"; Almanacs and Ephemeral Literature; Myth and Symbol** *(in this volume); and other articles in this section.*

BIBLIOGRAPHY

Altieri, Charles. "Sensibility, Rhetoric, and Will: Some Tensions in Contemporary Poetry." *Contemporary Literature* 23, no. 4 (1982): 451–479.

Barlow, Joel. *The Works of Joel Barlow.* 2 vols. Edited by William K. Bottorff and Arthur L. Ford. Gainesville, Fla., 1970.

Baym, Nina, et al., eds. *The Norton Anthology of American Literature.* 4th ed. 2 vols. New York, 1979.

Charvat, William. *The Profession of Authorship in America, 1800–1870.* 1968. Reprint, New York, 1992.

Douglas, Ann. *The Feminization of American Culture.* New York, 1977.

Franklin, Benjamin. *Writings.* Edited by J. A. Leo Lemay. New York, 1987.

Freneau, Philip. *Poems of Freneau.* Edited by Harry Hayden Clark. 1929. Reprint, New York, 1968.

Emerson, Ralph Waldo. *Emerson: Collected Poems and Translations.* Edited by Harold Bloom and Paul Kane. New York, 1994.

——. *The Letters of Ralph Waldo Emerson.* 3 vols. Edited by Ralph L. Rusk. New York, 1939.

Emerson, Ralph Waldo, ed. *Parnassus.* 1874. Reprint, New York, 1970.

Golding, Alan C. "A History of American Poetry Anthologies." In *Canons,* edited by Robert von Hallberg. Chicago, 1984.

Lauter, Paul, ed. *The Heath Anthology of American Literature.* Lexington, Mass., 1990.

Lehman, David, ed. *Ecstatic Occasions, Expedient Forms.* 2d ed. Ann Arbor, Mich., 1996.

Lynd, Robert Staughton, and Helen Merrill. *Middletown: A Study in Contemporary American Culture.* New York, 1929.

McClatchy, J. D., ed. *The Vintage Book of Contemporary American Poetry.* New York, 1990.

Miles, Josephine. *Collected Poems, 1930–83.* Urbana, Ill., and Chicago, 1983.

Moore, Marianne. *The Complete Poems of Marianne Moore.* New York, 1967.

Newbury, Michael. "Healthful Employment: Hawthorne, Thoreau, and Middle-Class Fitness." *American Quarterly* 47 (December 1995): 681–714.

Perkins, David. *A History of Modern Poetry: From the 1890s to Pound, Eliot, and Yeats.* Cambridge, Mass., 1976.

Pound, Ezra. *The Literary Essays of Ezra Pound.* Norfolk, Conn., 1954.

——. *The Selected Letters of Ezra Pound, 1907–1944.* Edited by D. D. Paige. 1950. Reprint, New York, 1971.

Santayana, George. *The Genteel Tradition: Nine Essays by George Santayana.* Edited by Douglas L. Wilson. Cambridge, Mass., 1967.

Stedman, Edmund Clarence, ed. *An American Anthology, 1787–1900.* Boston and New York, 1900.

Steinman, Lisa M. *Made in America: Science, Technology, and American Modernist Poets.* New Haven, Conn., 1987.

——. *Masters of Repetiton: Poetry Culture and Work in Thomson, Wordsworth, Shelley, and Emerson.* New York, 1998.

Stevens, Wallace. *The Collected Poems of Wallace Stevens.* New York, 1954.

Tomisch, John. *A Genteel Endeavor: American Culture and Politics in the Gilded Age.* Stanford, Calif., 1971.

Walker, Cheryl, ed. *American Women Poets of the Nineteenth Century.* New Brunswick, N.J., 1992.

Warner, Michael. *The Letters of the Republic: Publication and the Public Sphere in Eighteenth-Century America.* Cambridge, Mass., 1990.

Weaver, Mike. *William Carlos Williams: The American Background.* Cambridge, U.K., 1971.

Williams, William Carlos. *The Collected Poems of William Carlos Williams.* Edited by A. Walton Litz and Christopher MacGowan. 2 vols. New York, 1986–1988.

Ziff, Larzer. *Writing in the New World: Prose, Print, and Politics in the Early United States.* New Haven, Conn., 1991.

MUSIC

Tammy L. Kernodle

America's musical history is an artistic reflection of the country's developing identity. For over two hundred years, American music has served as evidence of ethnicity, regionalism, economic status, and religious beliefs. Historians have attempted to explain these musical phenomena through terms such as "cultivated," "vernacular," "classical," and "popular." Such terminology, however, has failed to define concretely the eclectic nature of America's music.

MUSICAL PRACTICES IN THE COLONIES

Early musical practices in America remained tied to England long after governmental alliances were severed. This early American music consisted primarily of psalmody, based on existing hymn melodies, and broadsides, which were secular songs sung to well-known melodies. The immigration of various religious and ethnic groups would alter, over time, these traditions.

Initially, the musical focus of the colonists was sacred music. Musical practices were communal, with an emphasis on congregational singing. Tune books such as the *Bay Psalm Book* (Boston, 1640) and the *Ainsworth Psalter* (Amsterdam, 1612) defined the content and stylistic features of the tradition. The creation of the first singing school in Boston in 1722 suggests a desire to elevate the quality of colonial music. Promoting the development of musical skills, the singing school became the center of musical and social life, and its popularity spread beyond the New England colonies. By the late eighteenth century, singing schools were established in Maryland, New York, South Carolina, and Philadelphia.

The sacred music tradition continued to evolve as new forms were created. Dr. Isaac Watts contributed to these changing styles with his opposition to the strict, old-fashioned style of English psalmody. His compositions, primarily hymns and spiritual songs, reflected new developments in American religious life promoted by the Great Awakening in the 1740s. A significant religious revival movement headed by James Davenport, Jonathan Edwards, and George Whitefield, the Great Awakening revitalized religion in the colonies. Watt's hymnody consisted of paraphrased versions of psalms that were selected because of their feasibility for Christian worship. The compositional efforts of Watts, John Wesley, John Cennick, and John Newton resulted in a new form of American hymnody.

This hymnody tradition, over time, came to represent a vast and diverse tradition as more religious groups established themselves. Most notable were the Shakers, signified by their unique practice of dancing, shaking, running, and singing. The Shakers left some eight to ten thousand religious songs and dance tunes that were preserved in over eight hundred manuscripts and tune books. Their community cultivated a unique musical and religious experience that included singing in unknown tongues while gyrating violently. The German-speaking Moravians, however, were one of the first independent Protestant sects to compose and perform both sacred and secular music. Their focus was on not only congregational music but concert music as well. The principal Moravian music service, the Love Feast, was a nonsacramental meal that consisted of continuous music in the form of anthems, hymns, and solo songs. The music of the church consisted mainly of hymns accompanied by horns, trumpets, flutes, and violins. However, as the church expanded into other areas of the country (Nazareth and Lititz, Pennsylvania, and Salem, North Carolina) organs were built and orchestras (collegia musica) organized. These ensembles not only accompanied the choir but often performed European chamber music. With few exceptions, the music composed in the church was written for performance on specific occasions by amateur performers, and only a small amount was published before 1950. Sacred music retained a central role in the development of American music throughout the nineteenth century, but other factors soon overshadowed these existing traditions, and new forms emerged.

MUSICAL AND CULTURAL CHANGES

An influx of European immigrants, expansion beyond the coastal settlements of the colonies, and the Atlantic slave trade would provide the most significant cultural stimuli to music in America. The importation of African slaves, beginning in 1619, introduced a culture unlike that of America's European émigrés. The Africans brought a musical tradition that expanded beyond the boundaries of the European tonal system and that relied heavily on polyrhythms. Slaveholders, attempting to eradicate the slaves' cultural traditions, restricted African musical instruments as well as linguistic and religious practices. Despite these attempts, African cultural forms influenced other musical traditions. The banjo (*banjar, banjer, banshan*), an African instrument retained in the slave's music making, was later adopted into Euro-American musical practices, including minstrel shows and bluegrass and country music. Syncopation, the irregular accenting of beats, is one of the polyrhythmic elements of West African music that would later find its way into Tin Pan Alley songs, ragtime, and minstrel show tunes. Eventually, the acculturation of Africans in America and their changing sense of identity would be reflected in various forms of music: the African American interpretation of Christianity produced the spiritual; emancipation and life after the Civil War cultivated the blues; and these forms later developed into gospel, jazz, rhythm and blues, and hip-hop.

The British tradition, represented by two varying practices, developed as colonists no longer viewed themselves as displaced Europeans but as American citizens. These traditions are generally described as "cultivated" and "vernacular," or "classical" and "popular." Development of the cultivated, or classical, tradition began in the late eighteenth century as American music started to reflect culture and social status. The so-called gentlemen's culture encouraged the study of dancing, art, and music as an accompaniment to wealthy landowners' central role in national and regional politics. Benjamin Franklin, Francis Hopkinson, and Thomas Jefferson personify the "gentleman amateur," as they were well versed in the musical arts and contributed greatly to the cultivation of America's early concert tradition.

Musical societies, which increased the general public's access to concert music, became an important aspect of musical life in eighteenth-century America. The oldest was formed in 1762 in Charleston, South Carolina, and sponsored subscription concerts as well as other cultural events in the city for several years. Southern society cultivated a strong musical environment until shortly after the Revolutionary War. The focus of concert life then shifted to northern cities such as Boston, Philadelphia, and New York. In Boston, the Handel and Haydn Society, founded in 1815 by J. C. Gottlieb Graupner, was one of the more prominent organizations dedicated to the advancement of musical taste and practices.

America's concert environment grew as large numbers of professional European musicians and performers immigrated to America. America's concert taste, as a result, shifted; many resisted the music of American-born composers and instead embraced European performers and composers. English ballad operas and concerts of Germanic-based music dominated the musical scene. Increasingly, the British musical ideals of the past were replaced with the Germanic masterpieces of Bach, Haydn, and Mozart. The American composer and performer, juxtaposed between the gentleman amateur and the European professional, soon found that the opportunities for performing were waning.

The vernacular or "popular" tradition developed from a similar cultural foundation. The influx of immigrants from England, Ireland, and Scotland in the early eighteenth century contributed greatly to this tradition. Many of these immigrants were indentured servants who eventually migrated away from the urban areas. They resettled in the mountainous areas of the East and survived as farmers and laborers. Most were illiterate and their musical tradition, much like the Africans', was orally based. The ballad was the chief musical form, detailing the folklore, superstitions, and social mores of its performers. These songs included the so-called "Child Ballads," which were named after Francis James Child, who collected the older songs. Although the basis of the ballad tradition was European, the genre eventually reflected a new American context. The texts of traditional songs were appropriated for analysis of life in America, and melodies, generally pentatonic, were sung with a highly embellished nasal tone.

Commonly referred to as Appalachians, these individuals also developed a strong sacred tradition.

Their sacred music was initially based on an oral tradition—similar to the psalmody and hymnody traditions of the late seventeenth and early eighteenth centuries—known as "lining out." "Lining out" consisted of a leader singing the first line of a psalm or hymn and the congregation repeating it. This would continue until the song was completed. This method of singing flourished in the South and cross-culturally influenced black sacred traditions in the nineteenth century.

Toward the end of the eighteenth century (ca. 1795–1835), the Second Great Awakening began. Revivals held in small towns and larger cities gave birth to the camp meeting hymn. The focus of this movement was the increase of church membership, the winning of souls, and the advancement of moral reforms. In addition, the singing school tradition of the New England colonies had spread to the South and West, and the "lining out" practice was altered with the introduction of "shape-note" hymnody. Organized in the early nineteenth century, the shape-note tradition flourished among many whites and some blacks in the South and Midwest. Much of the music was written by late-eighteenth-century singing school composers of New England, and it was notated in a system that consisted of various shapes designating pitches. This practice, sustained by the publication of tune books and singing guides, allowed musically illiterate singers to participate without trepidation. Although many of these shape-note books retained the repertoire of New England tune books, their melodic structure and harmonization were very different. Shape-note singing grew in popularity and shape-note singing conventions (two-day festivals) developed throughout the South, Southwest, and Midwest.

In the nineteenth century, Americans continued to develop a diverse musical identity. Music making during this time seemed to affect every aspect of life in America: the rising middle class continued to cultivate a concert tradition; marching bands and dance music became increasingly important in amateur and professional music making; a music curriculum was added to the public education system; and women were being urged to pursue musical instruction.

A central figure in the early-nineteenth-century American music scene was Lowell Mason. Mason, with Thomas Hastings, advocated a strong concert tradition in America. However, their crusade did not champion the cause of American composers, but Germanic. Mason also opposed the shape-note tradition of the New England singing schools. As a composer, he concentrated on sacred music. His

Lowell Mason. As a musician, composer, and educator, Mason (1792–1872) was arguably the most important figure in nineteenth-century American music. ARCHIVE PHOTOS

most famous hymns are "My Faith Looks Up to Thee" and "Nearer My God to Thee." During his career, he published some twenty collections of Protestant church music that dominated American hymnody for over one hundred years. Mason is best known for his integration of music education in the public school curriculum. He convinced the Boston school system to institute music instruction and established the Boston Academy, which provided teacher training, classes in sacred music performance, and voice instruction. The efforts of Lowell Mason created a legacy of music education that significantly increased the number of people with musical training in nineteenth-century America. The expansion of music making opportunities and the introduction of the music curriculum into the educational system deepened the need for materials. The printing and publication of music in America increased throughout the nineteenth century, and music served as an important social stimulus.

MEDIA AND THE DISSEMINATION OF MUSIC

The publishing industry (and later, the broadcasting and sound recording industries) has had considerable influence in the advancement of both the cultivated and vernacular musical traditions. Music publishing in America was established with the printing of Yankee tune books and psalters in the seventeenth and eighteenth centuries. Sheet music publishing was a stable industry by the 1790s, with the repertoire centered on theater songs. In the late nineteenth century, the popularity of piano sheet music and vaudeville songs ignited the publishing industry. Both became important to Victorian family life in the 1890s, when technology made the piano more affordable and conducive to domestic use. New York City became the center of popular music as many publishing houses and instrument manufacturers relocated there in the late nineteenth and early twentieth centuries. Although there were successful publishers in other cities, New York publishers concentrated on popular music and significantly shaped the taste of the musical public. America's music industry grew between 1890 and 1930 as "Tin Pan Alley" (West 28th Street in New York) became the cradle of the American popular song. The compositions of Tin Pan Alley composers George Gershwin, Jerome Kern, Cole Porter, and others reflected the urbanization of the American song and appealed to the white urban middle class.

The invention of the first sound recording device by Thomas Edison in 1877 would change the manner in which Americans consumed music. Edison's invention, coupled with the contributions of Alexander Graham Bell (1886) and Émile Berliner (who received the patent for the disc phonograph in 1888), increased the possibilities of the reproduction of sound. Of the three inventors, Berliner was apparently the only one who envisioned sound recordings as entertainment. By the end of the nineteenth century, several companies were established to manufacture recordings and the equipment necessary for playback. Initially, recording involved sound-wave patterns being stored as lateral deviations from a basic spiral path on a rotating disc. Electronic amplification, introduced in 1925, furthered the capabilities of the industry. Electrical recording is similar to acoustic recording in that sound waves are converted by a transducer into electrical current. After the current is amplified, it is applied to another transducer that cuts the spiral groove into the disc. As sales of recordings grew and eventually displaced sheet music, the American public over time converted from active performer to passive listener. Tin Pan Alley, following public taste, turned its focus to recording and broadcasting.

The early twentieth century marked an important period in the recording industry. Before 1920, most of the recordings made were of sentimental songs, dance music, and operatic and symphonic works. After World War I, however, the recording industry took interest in many of the vernacular forms that had developed throughout the eighteenth and nineteenth centuries. Victor Recording Company in 1917 recorded the Original Dixieland Band, sparking an interest in jazz bands. In 1920 Okeh Records produced the first blues recording— "Crazy Blues" by a Cincinnati-based singer named Mamie Smith—which has been deemed the most significant recording of the period. Its success inspired the creation of a series of records that were marketed primarily to the black community. The "race record" series expanded the market for the blues, which previously had been heard only at live performances at tent shows, dance parties, and theaters. Several record companies, including Gennett, Paramount, Columbia, Blue Note, Vocalion, Brunswick, and Okeh, began to enlist black performers for their profitable race series. This marketing strategy peaked from 1927 to 1930 with approximately five hundred recordings issued annually. Record companies expanded their target areas beyond New York and Chicago and traveled to the Southeast, New Orleans, and the Mississippi Delta. White southern folk traditions were "discovered" and recorded in 1923 by Okeh Records. This recording of Fiddlin' John Carson ("The Little Old Log Cabin in the Lane") marked the beginning of the country music industry. By the end of the 1920s, recordings of fiddlers, banjo players, and singing groups were sold all over the United States. Country music, black vernacular forms, and immigrant music became important branches of the American recording industry. Before long, however, phonographs lessened in popularity. The Great Depression reduced the buying power of most Americans, who turned to a cheaper form of entertainment: radio. Then, World War II depleted sources of the shellac used to make phonographic discs.

Radio, by the end of the 1920s, had become widespread, and more Americans were buying units. The depression increased radio's popularity, and its influence on musical taste grew as it programmed everything from pop singers to dance bands to operas and concert music. This popularity led to the enactment of copyright laws and the establishment of organizations to protect the rights of composers and songwriters. The American Society of Composers, Authors, and Publishers (ASCAP) served as a collection agency for music royalties.

Louis "Satchmo" Armstrong. Armstrong's contribution to jazz is without rival; his contribution to American culture, inestimable. © BETTMANN/CORBIS

During the 1940s, when ASCAP and the National Association of Broadcasters disagreed on payment amounts, the networks banned the broadcast of music licensed by ASCAP. Since most composers and mainstream performers belonged to ASCAP, radio stations began to look to other forms of music for programming. Country (hillbilly), folk music, and black music forms (urban blues and rhythm and blues) not controlled by ASCAP filled programming voids. The result was the diversification of radio and popular music.

Radio eventually lost its promotional power with the arrival of television in the late 1940s. The promotional power of television was not fully recognized until the appearance of music shows such as Ed Sullivan's Sunday evening program, Dick Clark's "American Bandstand," and Don Cornelius's "Soul Train." These shows reinforced the musical style heard on radio and through recordings. Television became more important to music in the 1980s with the emergence of MTV, a cable music station, and the introduction of the music video. Initially, the impact of the music video was minimal, as only a few artists used the venue for promotional purposes. However, by the late 1980s, the

commercial power of short, two- to three-minute videos was realized. The music video propelled artists like Madonna into superstardom, and record companies poured money into short vignettes. Record sales increased during the late 1980s and early 1990s, though they later dropped considerably as the target age group changed and as more successful independent labels were bought by larger companies. By the 1990s, music videos had become modifiers of public taste and style.

In the late twentieth century, technology advanced with the creation of compact discs. These increased the quality of recorded material and the availability of music through Internet websites. The advent of MP3 files and rewriteable CDs has increased opportunities for listeners to customize their own recordings.

THE GENDER FACTOR IN MUSIC

Music scholarship has primarily focused on the contributions of male composers, performers, and entrepreneurs. Scholars have largely excluded women musicians from serious analysis, discussing primarily the roles of women in popular music. The contributions of women in popular music should in no way be ignored; however, this is a limited perspective. The gender factor in music has done much to define and shape Americans' conceptions of their sexual as well as national identity. However, despite having been limited to public performances of sacred music before the twentieth century, women have held important roles in music making in America.

As musical instruction and private performances became more important in identifying America's upper class, the trend to educate women musically increased. Female seminaries in the nineteenth century included instrument and vocal instruction in their domestic curriculums. Proficiency in "feminine" instruments such as the piano, harp, and guitar—which were well suited for domestic entertainment—symbolized status and culture. Some female seminaries educated their female students in "male-oriented" instruments (strings and brass instruments). This resulted in an increase in the number of female string and brass players and provided the stimulus for the creation of female professional orchestras during the early twentieth century. The proliferation and popularity of such organizations in cities such as New York, Chicago, and Boston provided an impetus for the female composer. Women as composers were initially rejected in musical circles and by the press. Critics asserted that because women's musical education focused primarily on performance and not on harmony and the principles of composition, they could not adequately compose music.

Despite such criticisms, there were many women composers who earned a place in American history. Amy Marcy Cheney Beach (Mrs. H. H. A. Beach) had a prominent role in the second New England school of composers during the late nineteenth century. She was not the first woman to compose music, but she was the first American woman to have a symphony performed by a major orchestra. The success of Beach's compositions opened the door for others, such as Mary Howe and Marion Bauer, whose compositional style embraced French impressionism; Ruth Crawford Seeger, whose radical approach to composition and activism yielded a style defined by short compositions with highly chromatic melodies, repeated patterns, and no key signature; Julie Smith and Radie Britain, who embraced the eclectic musical culture of the rural West and Southwest; and Florence Price, Undine Smith Moore, and Margaret Bonds, who combined European form with African American melodies. Yet for all of the advances women made in the field of art music, they have never equaled the status of women in popular music forms.

During the late nineteenth and early twentieth century, women participated in minstrel shows and vaudeville performances. Center stage, however, was not given to such performers until the arrival of the classic blues style of the 1920s. Ma Rainey (neé Gertrude Pridgett), "Mother of the Blues," virtually patented the classic blues. Her songs of lost loves and hardships struck a chord with poverty-stricken and disenfranchised blacks. The arrival of records, coupled with live performances on the Theater Owners Booking Association (TOBA), established the blues market. Bessie Smith, Maime Smith, Ethel Waters, Victoria Spivey, Alberta Hunter, and others would follow Rainey's successful path. However, by the mid-1930s, the classic blues could no longer compete with the emerging jazz style and faded into the unknown.

Although the primary focus of jazz is instrumental music, the female vocalist was an important part of the jazz tradition. One of the first influential and significant jazz singers was Billie Holiday. Most female vocalists of the time were hired for their physical assets and had limited musical talent. Holiday was different. After a short stint with Count Basie and Artie Shaw, she embarked on a successful solo career. Her career, however, was plagued by her addiction to drugs and alcohol, and she would never attain the acceptance of later singers such as Ella Fitzgerald and Sarah Vaughan. Nevertheless, she set the musical standard for female vocalists in the 1930s and 1940s.

Female vocalists were not the only successful women in music during the 1930s and 1940s; instrumentalists were working as well. Jazz women Lil Hardin (Lil Hardin Armstrong) and Mary Lou Williams infiltrated the fraternalistic ranks of the jazz world and were members of significant jazz bands. Their careers spanned several decades and their success inspired generations of female drummers, pianists, trumpeters, and bassists. The advent of World War II provided more opportunity for female jazz musicians. There were several all-female swing bands that performed throughout the 1940s. Ina Ray Hutton and the Melodears, a successful all-white female band, and the International Sweethearts of Rhythm, which at several times boasted an interracial personnel, recorded extensively and were featured in cameo appearances in various film shorts and movies. Their success, however, was short-lived: it ended with the return of male musicians from the war. The new roles women had taken on during the war effort had created a new sense of womanhood outside the domestic sphere. Popular culture, however, would try to eradicate such notions in the 1950s.

Domesticated femininity in the 1950s was personified in the films and pop songs of Doris Day, who presented an image of white women as chaste and glamorous without blatant sexuality ("the dream babe"). The music was light and satirical with some occasional adult themes. Black female performers, outside jazz, were perceived as the exotic "other," whose overt sexuality and tough exterior made her the antithesis of the "dream babe." Although these images lasted throughout the 1950s, by the end of the decade the focus had shifted to the doo-wop, rhythmically driven "girl group" sound. As empowering as the "girl group" image was for young American women, it was, as were these previous phenomena, a representation of male fantasy: black glamour with crossover appeal (the Supremes and Martha and the Vandellas), the tough, rebellious street-wise white girls (the Shangri-Las) and the exotic Puerto Ricans (the Rondells). These images both embraced and rebelled against the previous female personas of 1950s pop. Few, however, could have been prepared for the boisterous entrance of the women of rock in the 1960s.

Ma Rainey and Her Georgia Jazz Band, Chicago, 1923. Over her career, Rainey (1886–1939) made one hundred recordings, served as a model for Bessie Smith, and collaborated with Louis Armstrong, among others. FRANK DRIGGS/ ARCHIVE PHOTOS

Janis Joplin integrated women into the male-dominated field of rock music. Grace Slick, Cher, Pat Benatar, Joan Jett, and Tina Turner would follow Joplin and cultivate the image of the "rock chick." Cher and Turner would not only achieve superstardom after parting with their husbands/partners, but would show that women over twenty could be successful in a field governed by perceived beauty and sexuality. Loretta Lynn, Tammy Wynette, and Dolly Parton would bring to life the struggles of a background of poverty and unhappy relationships, establishing a major place for women in country music. By the year 2000 women's musical experiences reflected participation in various genres, from hip-hop to gospel to grunge to rock, country, and pop.

MUSIC IN THE NEW CENTURY

As America entered the twenty-first century, its musical tastes were as diverse and unique as its ethnic population. Music in twentieth-century America reflected the political, economic, and racial ideologies of its inhabitants. The classical tradition continued to develop, although much of the standard repertoire remains European-focused. The works of various American composers, including Charles Ives, William Grant Still, Gunther Schuller, George Gershwin, and others are programmed in concert halls throughout the country. This tradition has increased significantly, as performers such as Beverly Sills, Leontyne Price, Itzhak Perlman, Kathleen Battle, and others have achieved "star" status comparable to their colleagues in popular music forms. The increased popularity of musical theater performances such as *Rent, The Lion King, Bring in 'da Noise, Bring in 'da Funk,* and *Ragtime* have increased the number of Americans enjoying live music performances and have also ignited ticket sales for similar performances and adjoining record sales. Diversity among concert audiences has also increased as major symphonic and operatic organi-

Charles Ives. By day Ives (1874–1954) was an insurance executive, by night a composer. Though his music was rarely performed during his lifetime, its influence continues to resonate. © BETTMANN/CORBIS

zations and music conservatories have instituted community outreach initiatives. Despite such efforts, the classical tradition, for many, still remains a signifier of "high" culture and economic status.

Popular music in its various hybrid forms has come to mirror more realistically the everyday experiences of Americans. With the appearance of early rhythm and blues and rock and roll in the 1950s, the racial boundaries that had marginalized popular music performances were slowly being eradicated. The popularity of the two genres with both black and white audiences and the eventual desegregation of performance venues signaled gradual changes. In the 1960s and 1970s, black racial pride was ignited by the soul music recordings of James Brown ("I'm Black and I'm Proud") and Marvin Gaye ("What's Going On," "Inner City Blues"). Political messages advocating racial equality, gender equality, and the end of the Vietnam War also peppered the popular music scene of the 1960s, though they were later eclipsed by the British rock invasion of the Beatles and Rolling Stones. In the 1970s, disco music and the popularity of the discotheque provided a musical platform for all ethnicities and sexual orientations. The 1980s signaled a splintering of popular music styles into various genres such as hard rock, rap, pop, alternative, grunge, and rhythm and blues. It has also been deemed the decade of the "superstar," as performers such as Michael Jackson, Whitney Houston, Bruce Springsteen, and Madonna propelled the recording industry to its zenith and defined popular culture with their hairstyles and fashion. Musical tastes from the late 1980s to mid-1990s began to reflect more than ever geographic location in addition to racial and economic status: the grunge movement centered in the Northwest (Seattle, Washington) gave voice to the anguish of the white, pessimistic, twenty-something generation; hip-hop reflected the black and Latino urban experience in America; and rock music split into camps of heavy metal (a large West Coast contingence led by groups such as Poison and Motley Crüe) and alternative (Duran Duran and U2); and pop music continued to sustain its popularity through Madonna's changing sound and image, the advent of the male group sound (Backstreet Boys and N'Sync), and the sex kitten/bubble girl image of Britney Spears and the Spice Girls in the late 1990s. Popular music at the turn of the century came to reflect a generational attitude and its identity.

Although the racial identities of many groups are still rooted in specific genres and styles, music in America has come to reflect generational, economic, and political ideology, more than racial distinction. Hip-hop culture has expanded beyond the boundaries of the African American and Latino communities and can be heard on the car radios of suburban white teenagers as well. Salsa, samba, and Tejano music has increased in popularity among all Americans, as Latino populations have increased their numbers as well as their influence. The advent of the Madonna age has shaped the position of women in popular music; many have become sought-after producers (Lauryn Hill and Missy Elliot), have sponsored and sustained an all-women music festival (Sarah McLaughlin, the Lilith Fair), have dominated nominations for music industry awards, and have headed divisions and subsidiaries of major record companies (Madonna: Maverick Records; Tracey Edmonds: CEO of Yub Yum Records; Frances Preston: President of BMI). Whether it is the latest Andrew Lloyd Weber musical, Lauryn Hill rap, symphony, or rock tune, music in America is reflecting to the world its diverse cultural and artistic identity.

See also **Urban Cultural Institutions; The Popular Arts** *(volume 1);* **Popular Culture in the Public Arena; Postmodernism and the Arts** *(volume 2);* **Elite vs. Popular Cultures; Culture for Mass Audiences;** *(in this volume); and other articles in this section.*

BIBLIOGRAPHY

General History

Chase, Gilbert. *America's Music: From the Pilgrims to Present.* Rev. 3d ed. Urbana and Chicago, 1987.

Crawford, Richard. *The American Musical Landscape.* Berkeley, Calif., 1993.

Hamm, Charles. *Music in the New World.* New York, 1983.

Hitchcock, H. Wiley. *Music in the United States: A Historical Introduction.* 4th ed. Upper Saddle River, N.J., 2000.

Southern, Eileen. *The Music of Black Americans.* 3d ed. New York, 1996.

Struble, John Warthen. *The History of American Classical Music: MacDowell through Minimalism.* New York, 1995.

Ward, Brian. *Just My Soul Responding: Rhythm and Blues, Black Consciousness, and Race Relations.* Berkeley, Calif., 1998.

Women in American Music

Ammer, Christine. *UnSung: A History of Women in American Music.* Westport, Conn., 1980.

Bowers, Jane, and Judith Tick, eds. *Women Making Music: The Western Art Tradition, 1150–1950.* Urbana, Ill., 1986.

Bufwack, Mary A., and Robert K. Oermann. *Finding Her Voice: The Illustrated History of Women in Country Music.* New York, 1995.

Dahl, Linda. *Stormy Weather: The Music and Lives of a Century of Jazz Women.* New York, 1984.

Norton/Grove Dictionary of Women Composers. Edited by Julie Anne Sadie and Rhian Samuel. New York, 1994.

O'Brien, Lucy. *She Bop: The Definitive History of Women in Rock, Pop and Soul.* New York, 1996.

DANCE

Linda J. Tomko

What kind of dancing has animated American public cultural expression? What kinds of cultural meanings did dancing make for its practitioners, producers, purveyors, and consumers? These are questions that dance scholarship has addressed for selected time periods and groups of people, though not for the whole of United States history. Nor have dancing subjects themselves left equally accessible evidence from different places and eras. Thus, any account of dance as public cultural expression in the United States must be partial. Such an account must acknowledge large areas of movement practice that are known to have occurred but which are still partially or largely silent in historical analyses.

DANCE PRACTICES IN TRIRACIAL COLONIAL AMERICA

At least three different racial groups negotiated encounter and dominion in the seventeenth- and eighteenth-century American lands that came to comprise thirteen colonies of Britain. Aboriginal people (quickly reduced in number by diseases that immigrant Europeans transmitted) included dance among their cultural practices. Scholarship on these practices is still slender and draws together archaeological data, some period accounts, and insights from contemporary oral histories. Historians recognize that American Indians and colonists differed in their conceptions of being and knowledge, and they conceived quite differently the relationships between people and their communities. Researchers posit a continuity between the centrality of dance to present-day Native American lifeways and its salience for aboriginal people responding to colonial encounters. Thus, dance and movement practices are thought to have enacted sacred obligations, effected healing procedures, and acknowledged and harmonized relationships between Indian peoples and their sustaining physical environment. Dancing

could offer entertainment but also maintain collective memory. It nourished group identity and also supplied a medium for engaging with the changes that contact and conflict brought. Even these general statements should not collapse or obscure the great differences among Indian peoples, both within geographic regions and across great areal expanses.

African peoples, forcibly brought to the new lands as enslaved laborers, included dance among the practices with which they negotiated their new settings. The very act of transporting enslaved Africans across the Atlantic Ocean in the seventeenth and early eighteenth centuries brought dancing to the fore as a means by which transporters forced exercise upon the captives to preserve their health—which was fundamental to their commercial value. In the American colonies, purchasers sought slaves from African areas known for different modes of production. In South Carolina, for example, where rice was an important crop, purchasers sought African slaves skilled in rice cultivation. Dance practices among these peoples must be presumed to have differed. The research challenge of investigating and interpreting their differences is a great one, and it intersects earlier sociological debates about black culture in the United States. In the mid-twentieth century, sociologist E. Franklin Frazier argued that the trauma of the Middle Passage wiped cultural memory from the enslaved. Anthropologist Melville J. Herskovits made a compelling case for investigating African retentions in the practices of Caribbean and U.S. African Americans, and the syncretic combination of the old with the new. This strategy continues to bear fruit for research on dance conducted in the present, buttressed by continued study, as referents, of African people's movement practices in Africa.

The most extensively documented movement practices of colonial peoples were those of English and European immigrants. Among these groups, dancing was recognized as a mode of public sociability that had substantial European precedent, but the warrant for it was variously disputed or supported in the colonial contexts.

New England and the Middle Colonies

The situation was complex in seventeenth-century New England. Historian Percy Scholes in the 1930s dispelled the idea that the Puritans forbade dancing. Yet in 1628, William Bradford and John Endecott voiced one of the earliest negative pronouncements regarding dancing around a maypole at Merry Mount. This act provoked immediate associations with things pagan, which ran counter to the Puritan mission of establishing a new biblical commonwealth in America. Bradford and Endecott were also angry that the reveling dancers composed lyrics, some lascivious, and fixed these to the maypole, while others sold shot and powder to Indians. Here, dancing won denunciation for its connections with idolatry, sexual license, and risks to community security.

Dancing was approved by many New Englanders for the purpose of teaching manners, that is, for the schooling it provided in the etiquette of bowing to one's equals and superiors, of entering and departing company, and of carrying oneself well in social contacts. Dance historians generally accept that "English country dances," like those published in England by John Playford from 1651, were central to the repertoire of dances done for social purposes. In midcentury, round or circle formations were numerous, along with other, "longways" formations; in later years and into the eighteenth century, longways formations predominated. Such country dances arrayed men and women in same-sex, parallel lines that were oriented spatially from the top to the bottom of the dancing space. Men and women "figured" together. That is, they stepped geometrical and twining patterns in space, leaving their lines to join temporarily, coupling up only to disperse, linking arms only to let go. The "head" couple in the longways line progressively moved from the top to the bottom of the set of dancers, and others moved up to the top to take their places. In this way, the spatial referents continually changed even while the dance figures repeated over and over again. In England, such dance enacted the fluid and shifting dimensions of a social order in transition as it felt the impress of new consumption possibilities. The semiotics were arguably different in the quite hierarchical milieu of Puritan Massachusetts Bay Colony, and research remains to be done in this area.

Despite some ministerial objections, dancing continued as a form of social engagement in New England, and people of quality began to give balls at the turn of the century. Cotton Mather's undated *A Cloud of Witnesses,* updated but probably written around 1700, approved dancing as instruction for children. However, it inveighed against balls and argued that dancing incited participants to sexual liberties. Among arguments mounted were the objections to dancing with levity at a time of danger to the community and the time that preparations for balls—such as painting and patching the face—stole from daily religious devotions. Here, dancing is construed negatively at a time of perceived declension from the Puritan errand into the wilderness.

Dancing continued in eighteenth-century New England, and also in the middle colonies, stirring disapproval at points, figuring at other times in debates about education for "polish." The repertoire for middling and elite sociability included an expanding number of country dances, Scottish reels (weaving figures), allemandes (emphasis on interlaced arms), jigs (which historians attribute to Irish and African American sources), and also the minuet (emphasis on presenting and releasing hands). Extremely demanding of poise and rhythmical acuity, the minuet supplied a necessary opening venture in evening entertainments, and then gave way to group country dances requiring no less musical sensitivity but accommodating of much greater ranges of energy, control, and self-containment. Quadrilles gained favor from the 1770s on, danced in squares for four mixed couples, these alternated widely known, standard figures with novel choreographic patterns unique to given dances. Philadelphia in 1749 was the first colonial city to inaugurate a formal dancing assembly and a regular season for social dancing. With substantial subscription fees supplying barriers to entry by mechanics and the lower classes, and with a group of managers scrutinizing applicants, the conduct of the Philadelphia assembly enacted social distinction in the 1780s and 1790s. In this it gave dynamic form to an urban process that historians have discerned was at work in the prewar years and that helped make cities crucibles of revolution: the increasing concentration of urban wealth in the hands of an increasingly smaller proportion of the population. Colleges and universities in the middle and northern colonies struggled with the question of dancing as appropriate pursuit for students in ministerial training. At the same time, records document the persistence of itinerant dancing masters in providing instruction at the community level. After the Revolution, Washington's birthday began to be celebrated with annual balls, and the first president's inauguration sparked the first of the inaugural balls.

Southern Colonies   Itinerant dancing masters provided instruction for Euro-American people in the pre-Revolutionary southern colonies as well. But there, material and geographic situations differed substantially. Unlike the corporate community and urban organizations of colonies to the north, plantations supplied the principal form of land disposition and social organization in regions like the Tidewater Chesapeake, Virginia, and South Carolina. Single gentry families and their slave laborers supplied the social nucleus in large plantation holdings focused on cash crop production. Distances between plantations inhibited casual travel and limited the occasions for social mixing. Dancing masters spent time with a particular family or rotated among a set of families, and children from several plantations traveled to the great house where lessons and dancing events were held. Minuets, country dances, jigs, and quadrilles were staples. As in the north, fiddle music was a frequent accompaniment, here played by slaves or music masters.

Where southern practice differed so significantly from that to the north was in the positive recognition given dancing as part of an Anglican and elite culture, one that embraced conviviality and endorsed horse racing and gaming as part of a classed way of being in the world. Anglican gentry practice hewed to an English-based model of personal cultivation that may fairly be called "composing the self." George Washington, reared in Virginia, copied by hand some 110 rules of civility as part of the self-fashioning on which he embarked. That one could fashion one's postures, indeed one's reception by others, struck some readers as false, and indeed the English model of cultivation was not uniformly welcomed in the colonies. The rake and the fop were two negative stereotypes linked to aristocratic productions of the self, and republican ideology in the prewar years certainly distanced itself from courtly corruption. The religious revivalism of the Great Awakening made its way into Virginia, too, where New Light congregations resisted required participation in the Anglican establishment. The much-quoted example of the Reverend Deveraux Jarrett and his disapproval of dancing shows how the practice of dancing provided a potent arena in which New Light people could create—by declining to dance socially—religious and cultural distance from powerful gentry. Subscription to the patriot cause, as argued by historian Isaac Rhys, gave gentry leaders a way to reassert leadership in the region.

In southern colonies as in those more northward, dancing practices provided a means for ordinating leaders and followers, upper and lower classes, in colonial environments where questions of social order had to be met and met again, contested and retested.

DANCE PRACTICES IN THE NEW REPUBLIC AND EXPANDING NATION

As the United States moved from initial confederation to organization as a republic, dancing practices continued to be enmeshed with cultures in the circum-Atlantic world of commerce and connection. Westward landed expansion brought the movement practices of new people to the fore at the same time that it circulated customary practices in new domains. The United States in the nineteenth century did not see the articulation of a new national dance or the conversion of a prevailing movement practice. That would be undertaken by some in the twentieth century. What is remarkable in the new country was its vigorous production and marking of cultural "others" via dance and movement practices. This was the case for touring and emulated European ballet, for blackface minstrelsy, and, at the end of the century, for the exhibition of foreign peoples on World's Fair midways.

European Ballet in the United States   Theatrical ballet gained little foothold in America before the revolution; acting companies might insert *entr'acte* dances such as the solo hornpipe between the acts of a play, and they occasionally produced pantomimes that called for *commedia* figures skilled in movement. Emigrant Frenchman Alexandre Placide and collaborators changed the caliber of repertory available in the 1790s, presenting one-act ballets, pantomimes, and rope dancing. In 1792 they enjoyed successful seasons in New York and then Charleston, where Placide remained for the rest of his career. At this time, European ballet was making the transition from court-derived dances, of minimal physical contact and contained range of movement, to the increasingly gendered differentiation of male and female roles. Men began to partner women by supporting their balances, lifting them slightly from the floor, and framing them in adagio movements. By the 1830s, the option and requirement of dancing on the toes had been assigned to female performers. This pointe work was turned to libretti that featured supernatural characters, and wire technology for "flying" through space also assisted. The European repertoire that was performed in the mid-nineteenth century United States also placed emphasis on folk and national dances, which was understandable in light of the burgeoning nationalism and the revolutions of 1848 that swept Europe. These dances appealed aesthetically but lacked congruity with United States experiences. The same situation obtained in ballroom dancing. Middle- and upper-class Americans performed the ethnic-derived dances, like the waltz, polka, and mazurka, that characterized European salons.

Dancing, and Representations of Dancing, in Slave and Free African American Cultures

Dancing in African American slave culture also drew from circum-Atlantic circulation of people, goods, and cultural values. Traders frequently seasoned their human cargo in West Indies countries before transporting enslaved people to the mainland. As well, slave revolt in Haiti in the 1790s motivated a number of planters to move with their slaves to New Orleans and other areas of the United States. Knowing this, historians and ethnographers alike have scrutinized past records and current instances of Caribbean movement practices for insight into the dances that African Americans pursued in the United States.

Modern readers must realize that it was primarily white European male writers, occasionally females, who left accounts from the eighteenth and nineteenth centuries of the dancing by black and mixed-race Caribbean people. The race theories of the writers and the positions of power they occupied inescapably shaped these representations. Analyzing such accounts, historian Lynn Fauley Emery has identified three principal secular dances practiced in the historical West Indies: *calenda, chica,* and *juba. Calenda* involved a couple or couples, whose partners advanced and retreated from one another using shuffling steps and minimal play of limbs, with most movement originating in the hips. *Chica,* for one couple, emphasized rotation of the hips while the upper body was held still. It positioned the woman as coquette, pursued by the man; the woman held out her apron edges, and the man lunged and withdrew. Drumming was integral to both, and observers ringed *calenda* to sing and clap the rhythms of the dance. *Juba* was a competitive dance of skill, with a series of challenges between one individual and another. In addition to these secular types were distinctive Christmas-time, funeral, "crop-over" or harvest dances, and dances of the "people of color"—or encounter contexts for white males and mulatto females. Sacred dances drew from various African religions, and their rituals aimed at or facilitated "possession," or altered states of consciousness.

Connections can be drawn between Caribbean dance types and the movement practices of plantation and urban, slave and free African Americans in the United States. *Juba,* and other slave dances in the United States, had to do without drum accompaniment, by fiat of planters following failed slave revolts in the early eighteenth century. *Juba* continued as a competition dance aided by patting—the practitioners' stamping, clapping, and slapping of arms, chests, and thighs for rhythmic emphasis. In addition, the hybrid of "jigging" emerged. Thought to combine English clogging and Irish step dancing attributes, it fused with elements of *juba* and supplied the matrix of early tap dance. Named animal dances, like the buzzard lope and turkey trot, are credited to African Americans of the Georgia Sea Islands. Slaves removed to New Orleans after the Haitian revolution entered a milieu where social dance opportunities helped display the rankings of a complex caste system. Octoroon balls, for example, mobilized European-derived dances and provided grounds for contact between mixed-race women and white males, while dancing on Sundays at Congo Square—a public plaza—was reserved to African Americans in an effort to control the gatherings of enslaved people. Plantation slaves' recollections from the late antebellum period indicate that social dances of the white masters were performed there, too, including the European-modeled quadrilles, waltzes, and Virginia reels.

After the United States ceased external slave trade in 1808, American slave populations continued to reproduce themselves, carrying forward aspects of African traditions and also negotiating cultural practices. Among sacred dances, the ring shout notably had to accommodate southern white Protestant objection to dancing. This movement practice took the form of people shuffling together around a circle, feet barely leaving the floor, hands clapping, voices lifting, working toward a state of possession and exaltation.

The presence and continued subordinated status of African American people in the United States was negotiated in the white masters' world via production, and audience consumption, of racial stereotypes in nineteenth-century blackface minstrelsy. T. D. Rice is credited with creating the blackface Jim Crow characterization in movement and borrowed verse. By the 1840s, a group performance format had emerged for the blackface minstrel show. A "first part" arrayed a group of singer-instrumentalists in a semicircle, with "end men" respondents playing tambourine and bones, and an interlocutor seated in the center leading the comic verbal exchange. A processional walkaround preceded the olio, the second section for specialty song and dance acts. The latter could include jigs, clogs, and essence dances. The afterpiece presented sketches and eventually burlesques of contemporary theater fare, and it too concluded with a grand walkaround. Performed by white men only, until after the Civil War, minstrelsy exaggerated the face's orifices—and the connotations of primitive orality—by strategic use of burnt cork and white paint. It produced several distinct, negative stereotypes by means of costume and movement: the dandy zip coon, the "happy" plantation slave, and the shambling yet dexterous Jim Crow.

Minstrelsy as a commercial production type enabled the muting of class divisions among white Jacksonian Democrats in favor of a race-based sense of group solidarity. One of the most recent theoretical formulations argues that minstrelsy also allowed white classed audiences to take aspects of African American identity unto themselves. Counters to the minstrel production of racial stereotypes were hard to sustain. William Henry Lane, called Master Juba, performed such a counter-production in the 1840s and 1850s. An outstanding African American jig dancer of noted elegance, Lane bested white rival John Diamond in a three-part dance-off, garnered unnamed mention in Charles Dickens's *American Notes,* and performed profitably for noble and other audiences in England. Lane died in 1852, and the weight of minstrel stereotypes persisted in characterizing African American people as ridiculous or hapless beings.

Movement Practices and Westward Movements

The process of landed expansion brought movement practices to newly acquired locales, and it also required settlers and the government to reckon with movement practices of conquered peoples. Acknowledging the vast scale and great regional diversity in the United States by the end of the nineteenth century, two examples from the mining frontier offer illumination. Anne Ellis's book, *The Life of an Ordinary Woman* (1929), reports the temporary conversion of two destitute Colorado miners to the profession of dancing masters. To the European lancers and American square dances that English and American miners' families already enjoyed at Saturday night dances, the new teachers added waltzing, polkas, a schottische, even a varsovienne. They also taught bows, proper distance between

partners, and particulars of "round dance position." By the early nineteenth century, as ballet adopted men's physical support and partnering of women, so did social dancing reinforce normative heterosexuality with the close embrace by men of their female dancing partners still used in waltzing today. Style in this embrace varied by decade and supplied a potent site for surveillance by community standard keepers, even in poor mining towns.

Historian Susan Lee Johnson has noted that in the 1850s in some California gold rush towns, gender designations in dance were treated fluidly to address the shortage of white women. Some men took on the role of women at an evening's dance and signaled their new positionality by pinning a patch to their "inexpressibles." Johnson has also read with new insight the record of a Miwok Indian ceremony—the *pota* ritual—on the south fork of the Cosumnes River from the same period. It set Indian people dancing around a vertical, specially erected pole, attacking effigies that represented murderers or people held responsible for death in the community. White diarist Alfred Doten observed a U.S. flag attached to a *pota* pole in August 1855, a time when white-borne disease had killed a child. This ritual and its movement practice supplied Indians with interpretive mastery of the expansionist Euro-Americans. Some forty years later, and ignoring government bans on ceremonial dancing, the Sioux Ghost Dance religion and its movement practice provided a means for Indian people's renewal in the Plains arena of conflict over landed expansion. In these instances, Indian people enacted counter performances that enabled them to sustain distinct ways of being in the world, however fleetingly.

Recent scholarship has highlighted ways in which whites mobilized Indian imagery and identities for their own use. The incorporation of Indian "civilization" in culture epoch pedagogy and the construction of "Indian" dances in the amateur pageantry movement offer just two examples at the turn of the twentieth century. Dance scholarship has not yet analyzed historical movement practices of Chinese and, later, Japanese immigrants who were central to railroad construction, mining, and settlement of the Pacific West. The impact of Spanish and Californio people on western U.S. culture received attention in folk-dance scholarship of the 1940s and 1950s but needs renewed investigation.

The movement production of cultural others, sanctioned for educational, scientific, and civic reasons, reached one kind of zenith in the ethnological exhibition of "exotic" peoples in World's Fairs at the turn of the twentieth century. At the 1893 World's

Folk Dancing Festival in Central Park, 1912. The Girls' Branch of New York City's Public Schools Athletic League culminated each year's work learning folk dances with a "park fete" that drew thousands of girls together. FROM THE ELIZABETH BURCHENAL COLLECTION IN THE SPECIAL COLLECTIONS AT BOSTON UNIVERSITY

Columbian Exposition in Chicago, for example, the Midway Plaisance staged belly dancers on Cairo Street, a North American Indian display, and villages representing several Asian countries. At the 1904 St. Louis Fair, Indian people were put on view while engaged in arts and crafts tasks, or posed as feather-bonneted war chiefs. Such exhibition strategies capitalized on the power of movement and the staged performance of "everyday life" to instate racial rankings and to buttress the political rhetoric of progress and manifest destiny.

DANCE PRACTICES IN INDUSTRIAL AND LATE CAPITALIST AMERICA

The invocation of "incorporation" as a strategy for managing cultural and ethnic others in the United States became evident near the turn of the twentieth century. By the 1920s and 1930s, the impact of modernism as an aesthetic ideology further reinforced a notion of commonality and merged differences, identifying dance as a "universal language" understood by all people. At the end of the century, multiculturalism returned focus to the distinctive features of racial and ethnic groups, valorizing movement practices as sources that ensure cultural authenticity and continue tradition.

Dance and Movement Innovations in Industrializing America Native Americans continued to receive treatment as stereotypical others in dramatic, movement, and literary representations at

the end of the nineteenth century. African American people continued to be disfranchised and racially segregated. Their vital movement practices were adapted by white ragtime dance vogues, even while other kinds of race caricature persisted, as with blackface representations in the first "talking" film, *The Jazz Singer* (1927). The force of incorporative strategies was felt in substantial ways by major flows to the United States of people from Central and Southern Europe. These immigrants supplied a growing labor force for the industrializing American economy, and their settlement in major cities contributed to urbanization. Social settlement houses, the civic pageantry movement, and even newly minted after-school folk dance programs utilized movement practices to bridge and harmonize differences between new immigrants and longer-settled urban people. Settlements offered a wide variety of gymnastic, historical, and aesthetic dancing instruction to immigrant neighbors, and some pursued theatrical production. Civic pageants mobilized huge casts of local people to spatially choreograph and dramatically replay episodes of American history, aiming to produce thereby a commonly held narrative. New York City public schools fielded an after-school folk-dance program, in which games and dances from Western and Northern Europe provided immigrant children with an Anglicized movement heritage quite different from their familial roots.

Experiment with movement practices in these social welfare initiatives intersected the rise of physi-

Loie Fuller. Acting as her own choreographer and technical director, Fuller (1862–1928) mobilized yards of silk, carefully placed lights, and the motion of her body to create luminous images that suggested forms in nature. COURTESY NEW YORK PUBLIC LIBRARY FOR THE PERFORMING ARTS

cal education as a new profession and also the aesthetic innovations of pivotal women who constituted concert dance as aesthetically significant, commercial expression. Loie Fuller, Isadora Duncan, Ruth St. Denis, and the Canadian Maud Allan challenged the long-prevailing sexual division of labor in dance and claimed for themselves roles previously allocated to men: choreography, artistic direction, technical production, and company management. In so doing, they reinforced cultural perceptions of dance as female-gendered. Dance critical literature from nineteenth-century Romantic ballet had identified male presence on French ballet stages as a problem. Research currently underway is revealing debates about male dancers in England, for both their sexuality and their country of origin, more than a century earlier. While gay and lesbian people in dance professions remained mostly closeted for long stretches of the twentieth century, the impact of McCarthy-era politics in this regard is receiving serious scrutiny. Research on American dance in earlier and later periods has begun to probe the connection between sexualities, social constructions of the body, and the salience of dance and movement practices for confirming and contesting power structures and ideologies.

Modernist Aesthetics and Politics in Dance

The innovative practices of new female dance makers stimulated emergence in the 1920s of new cohorts who forged the distinctive genre of modern dance, laying claim to the universality of dance and the transparency of its meaning. The careers of leading figures Martha Graham, Charles Weidman, Doris Humphrey, Helen Tamiris, Hanya Holm, and—later—José Limón and Daniel Nagrin are well documented, illuminating their search for choreographic principles and theories, and also the angular lines and weighty shapes frequently demanded of performing bodies. Ted Shawn, who earlier partnered St. Denis in the Denishawn teaching and performing enterprise, formed a company of male dancers in the 1930s and staged muscular representations of masculinity for a seven-year stretch of touring. Recent scholarship has recovered the 1930s labors of leftist dancers and choreographers long written out of the record—probably in response to anticommunist politics—including Edith Segal, Sophie Maslow, Anna Sokolow, and Jane Dudley. Movement sympathy with or as working-class people provided another kind of solvent for difference in depression-era America.

Racial exclusion policies in American society shaped the exclusion of African Americans from any substantial participation in early white modern dance troupes, although a cohort of black people laid groundwork for a later flourishing of successful black concert dance in the 1940s and 1950s. Early endeavors by Helmsley Winfield, Edna Guy, Raymond Sawyer, Ollie Burgoyne, Charles Williams, and Asadata Dafora established models, developed training grounds, and explored viable repertory. Katherine Dunham and Pearl Primus mobilized Caribbean and African movement practices and their music for concert presentation and sustained tours. Lester Horton, white himself, formed in the 1940s the first multiracial dance company and drew choreographically on Caribbean and North American motifs. Alvin Ailey performed with Horton, worked briefly on Broadway, and created the powerful *Revelations* (1960) as one of the first works for his new company.

Dance was an important component of twentieth-century American musical theater and film. Until about the 1960s, however, the regnant modernist aesthetic valued the "art" concert dance forms of ballet and modern dance more highly than these "popular" forms. As historians in the late twentieth century began to specify the particular race, social, economic, and political situations that buttressed the modernist aesthetic, new scrutiny and revised valuation has turned to less frequently studied movement practices: tap, jazz dance, and social dance. Despite exclusion from white modern dance and ballet companies, for example, African Americans had created an important series of black musicals from the 1890s through the 1920s. Tap dance, an urban quotidian movement practice, was also deployed by African Americans in specialty acts for vaudeville and new cabaret venues. Fred Astaire and Gene Kelly were two very visible white performers who capitalized upon and extended tap performance in movie musicals from the 1930s to 1950s. The African American Nicholas Brothers, Harold and Fayard, positioned tap as a "class act" through their performance in movie vehicles, beginning in the 1930s. The status of tap dancing has been reordinated since the 1980s via a "renaissance" of jazz tap dancing. Important players in this resurgence have included Gregory Hines, Brenda Bufalino, Savion Glover, Fred Strickler, Lynn Dally, Camden Richman, and the Jazz Tap Ensemble and Manhattan Transfer troupes.

Ballet and Aesthetic Nationalism Vehicles for ballet production in the early-twentieth-century United States were few. Among them, the Metropolitan Opera since the 1880s had maintained a ballet troupe. Ballet Intime toured with its founder, émigré Russian dancer Adolph Bolm, in the 1920s. Former Diaghilev choreographer Michel Fokine settled in America in 1921 and formed a company. The troupes which made large and continuing impact were self-consciously inaugurated in the 1930s and 1940s. In this they paralleled motivations of modern dance choreographers, who aimed to speak to contemporary circumstances. Lincoln Kirstein mobilized resources to bring George Balanchine to the United States for the express purpose of creating an American ballet. The last choreographer of Diaghilev's Ballets Russes, Balanchine immediately started a school. His early-expressed interest in bringing white and black dancers together choreographically did not result in a racially mixed company. Weathering difficult depression-era years and different company configurations, the Balanchine-Kirstein collaboration issued in 1948 in the New York City Ballet. A vehicle for Balanchine's enormous creativity and extension of the academic canon, the company performed as well works by Jerome Robbins and some choreographers from within the dancer ranks. Ballet Theatre, later styled American Ballet Theatre, was initiated in the late 1930s by Lucia Chase and Richard Pleasant. Their plan was nationalist as well: to create distinct repertory wings for American, English, and classical choreography. It presented new work on American themes by Jerome Robbins, such as the sailors-on-the-town *Fancy Free,* before he transferred to New York City Ballet, and occasionally work by Agnes de Mille, including *Rodeo,* which adapted movement vocabulary from cowboy skills and hoe-down dances. It also provided a venue for Antony Tudor's "psychological" ballets.

Ballet companies built followings in major cities during the next decades. Lew and William Christensen formed companies in San Francisco and Salt Lake City, Utah. Ruth Page headed a troupe in Chicago, and Catherine Littlefield one in Philadelphia. By the 1950s, a strong civic ballet movement had emerged. Two of the earliest troupes formed in this way persist today as regional professional companies: the Atlanta and Dayton Ballet Companies. Founded in the late 1950s, the Joffrey Ballet established a then-unique position with reconstructions of earlier twentieth-century works, from Léonide Massine's *Parade* in the 1970s to Vaslav Nijinsky's *Le sacre du printemps* (*Rite of Spring*) in the 1980s. Arthur Mitchell, African American principal dancer with the New York City Ballet, established Dance Theatre of Harlem in 1969 to provide a platform for black performers in ballet and in response to the death of civil rights leader Martin Luther King Jr. Latter-day Ballets Russses companies continued to tour and circulate aspects of the Diaghilev repertory. Members of these companies who retired to teach in cities across the country trained a next generation of dancers. In the 1960s, Ford Foundation grants to students in regional dance companies and studios helped expand the geographic reach of ballet as a middle- and lower-class physical cultural practice. The nationalist goals that impelled individuals to form ballet companies in the 1930s found political issue in the tours abroad by ballet companies that the U.S. Information Agency sponsored in midcentury.

Interrogation as Choreographic Strategy The privileging of the concept of "genre" in dance may itself have been a modernist strategy, one still not completely dislodged. A sea change among new choreographers in the 1960s left mainstream concert dance practices in place while also seeding much of the "interrogatory" practice of late-twentieth-century dance. Taking a scrutinizing stance that has not abated at the end of the century, experimental choreographers continue to comment choreographically on the ways in which they work, and the politics of their work, as they work. One result has been the blurring of genres, or receding importance of categorization, for movement compositions that can combine spoken text with sonic resources, hip-hop dance with rope climbing and ballet techniques, and autobiography with radical repetition as sequencing strategies. Another result has been the dethroning of a *Gesamtkunstwerk* approach—collaborative synthesis of the arts—prevalent since the heyday of Diaghilev's Ballets Russes.

Merce Cunningham started to make work with John Cage before he left Martha Graham's company in the 1950s, and their collaboration challenged conventional audience-performer relationships, then-prevalent use of narrative frames and musical structures as scaffolding for dances, and the interdependence of creative people working on a single production. These initiatives, along with other explorations by people like Anna Halprin and Robert Ellis Dunn, enabled a 1960s cohort of dance makers to further rethink the production and consumption sides of dance composition and performance. Their work was described by some writers as "postmodernist," and the label has stuck. Many but not all of these dance makers presented work as the Judson Dance Theater in New York City in the early 1960s; individuals as well as collectives fashioned subsequent careers. Important figures included Carolee

Schneemann, James Waring, Trisha Brown, Steve Paxton, David Gordon, Yvonne Rainer, Kenneth King, Deborah Hay, Douglas Dunn, Barbara Lloyd, Rudy Perez, Meredith Monk, Lucinda Childs, Laura Dean, Viola Farber, and Jeff Slayton. Several kinds of factors underpinned the surge in new choreography and receptivity to it. Academic study of dance, which had entered U.S. universities via physical education programs in the Progressive Era, gained curricular status when dance faculties started to gain departmental status in the 1960s. At the same time, an expanding U.S. economy enabled increasing levels of college attendance for middle-class people. The federal government recognized dance via the National Endowment for the Arts in 1975, which launched a dance touring program that facilitated performance of dance across the country.

It is important to note that concert dance informed in whole or in part by modernist concerns continued and continues to circulate in U.S. culture in parallel with "postmodernist" innovation. Alwin Nikolais's magical light and sound environments situated dancers as one among equal elements in those stage milieus. West Coast choreographer Bella Lewitzky created dances that intensified viewers' perception of bodily shape and weight. Donald McKayle's well-crafted work included poignant pieces about African American struggles. Paul Taylor's musicality has informed forays into widely dispersed topics. Ze'eva Cohen challenged the single-choreographer model for company organization by touring a repertory program of modern dance choreographies. Alvin Ailey's company provided a proving ground for African American choreographers like Gary DeLoatch and Judith Jamison, the latter of whom assumed company leadership after Ailey's death. A number of other modern dance companies have experienced the death of their frequently long-lived founding choreographers, as have the New York City Ballet and Joffrey Ballet, and a second generation of leaders has taken the helm. Their positions as standard-bearers for a high or "art" culture has changed, however—by virtue of post-1960s challenges, but just as significantly by ascendance of a multicultural politics and aesthetics that prompts the recognition and articulation of dance practices that are traditional and distinctive to different peoples. At the same time, regard for retrospective periods and styles has issued in vogues for swing and tango as well as vintage styles of social dance. The modernist divide between participatory dance for pleasure and dance performance that distinguishes movers from viewers still obtains. It has been placed under pressure, however, in practices like contact improvisation, a 1970s innovation that challenged gendered giving and taking of bodily weight and fielded a "jam" presentation format that mediated performer/audience separation.

Post-1960s challenges to modernist dance aesthetics have extended to confrontation of normative heterosexuality in choreography and performance, as in work by Senta Driver, Mark Morris, Bill T. Jones, Arnie Zane, Ann Carlson, and David Rousseve. Dance makers have also refigured the presence and representation of African Americans in contemporary choreography. Jawolle Jo Willa Zohar with Urban Bush Women, Blondell Cummings, Dayton Contemporary Dance Theatre, Rousseve, Dianne McIntyre, Jones, and Ralph Lemon have been leading figures in this regard. Proceeding from another impetus, the advent of Native American powwows has constituted a new way of circulating Indian people's practices. These events are configured as nexuses for many tribes' dances. The touring presence of the professional American Indian Dance Theater has brought a related intertribal repertoire to the concert stage. At the turn of the twentieth century, the stance of movement practitioners who interrogate past conceptions and practices of dance makes for some of the most vital work to be seen, experienced, and contemplated. While genre distinctions may not have completely disappeared, fluidity characterizes a vibrant situation for dance as public cultural expression.

See also **Cultural Modernism; The Popular Arts** *(volume 1);* **Postmodernism and the Arts** *(volume 2);* **Elite vs. Popular Cultures; Culture for Mass Audiences** *(in this volume).*

BIBLIOGRAPHY

Aldrich, Elizabeth. *From the Ballroom to Hell: Grace and Folly in Nineteenth-Century Dance.* Evanston, Ill., 1991.

Banes, Sally. *Terpsichore in Sneakers: Post-modern Dance.* Middletown, Conn., 1987.

Brooks, Lynn. "The Philadelphia Dancing Assembly in the Eighteenth Century." *Dance Research Journal* 21, no. 1 (spring 1989): 1–6.

Ellis, Anne. *The Life of an Ordinary Woman.* 1929. Reprint, Lincoln, Nebr., 1980.

Emery, Lynne Fauley. *Black Dance in the United States from 1619 to 1970.* Princeton, N.J., 1988.

Graff, Ellen. *Stepping Left: Dance and Politics in New York City, 1928–1942.* Durham, N.C., 1997.

Heth, Charlotte. "Native American Aesthetics: Music and Dance." In *Encyclopedia of the North American Colonies.* Vol. 3, edited by Jacob Ernest Cooke. New York, 1993.

Heth, Charlotte, ed. *Native American Dance: Ceremonies and Social Traditions.* Washington, D.C., 1992. Includes cogent overview by Heth, excellent articles on dances of nine different Indian tribal groups.

Hill, Constance Valis. "Brotherhood in Rhythm: The Jazz Tap Dancing of the Nicholas Brothers." Ph.D diss., New York University, 1998.

Isaac, Rhys. *The Transformation of Virginia, 1740–1790.* Chapel Hill, N.C., 1982.

Johnson, Susan Lee. "Bulls, Bears, and Dancing Boys: Race, Gender, and Leisure in the California Gold Rush." *Radical History Review* 60 (1994): 4–37.

Keller, Kate van Winkle, and Charles Cyril Hendrickson. *George Washington: A Biography in Social Dance.* Sandy Hook, Conn., 1998.

Long, Richard A. *The Black Tradition in American Dance.* New York, 1989.

Lott, Eric. *Love and Theft: Blackface Minstrelsy and the American Working Class.* New York, 1993.

Magriel, Paul. *Chronicles of the American Dance: From the Shakers to Martha Graham.* 1948. Reprint, New York, 1978. Includes excellent articles on eighteenth- and nineteenth-century ballet (Lillian Moore, Marian Hannah Winter) and on *juba* and minstrelsy (Winter).

Marks, Joseph E., ed. *The Mathers on Dancing.* Brooklyn, N.Y., 1975.

Moore, Lillian. *Echoes of American Ballet.* Brooklyn, N.Y., 1976. A collection of seventeen articles by Moore spanning eighteenth- to twentieth-century ballet.

Perpener, John. O. "The Seminal Years of Black Concert Dance." Ph.D diss., New York University, 1992.

Rydell, Robert W. *All the World's a Fair: Visions of Empire at American International Expositions, 1876–1916.* Chicago, 1984.

St.-Mery, M. L. E. Moreau de. *Dance.* 1796. Translated by Lily and Baird Hastings, Brooklyn, N.Y., 1975.

Saxton, Alexander. "Blackface Minstrelsy and Jacksonian Ideology." *American Quarterly* 27, no. 1 (1975): 3–28.

Sweet, Jill Drayson. "Play, Role Reversal, and Humor: Symbolic Elements of a Tewa Pueblo Navaho Dance." *Dance Research Journal* 12, no. 1 (fall–winter 1979–1980): 3–12.

Tomko, Linda J. *Dancing Class: Gender, Ethnicity, and Social Divides in American Dance, 1890–1920.* Bloomington, Ind., 1999.

FASHION

Rob Schorman

Fashion, in a broad sense of the word, has always been part of American life. Before European contact, Native Americans on the North American continent produced wearing apparel with intent that went far beyond the merely utilitarian. Using a variety of decorative practices involving beads, quillwork, painting, dyes, feathers, and fringe, they produced garments that also served as a means of self-expression and adherence to cultural expectations (Paterek, *American Indian Costume*). A European concept of fashion—a stylish and changeable "mode" of dress that marked one's individual and social identity—arrived with the first colonists. Americans have long been concerned not only with fashion's form but also with its influence and cultural power. Debates about dress have frequently intertwined concerns over social and political issues. The cultural history of fashion in America is a history not only of garments but also of people's understanding of what those garments mean.

HISTORY AND FASHION

Seventeenth Century   Although rough work clothes were often a practical and economic necessity in colonial settlements, ample evidence exists in correspondence, diaries, wills, and portraiture that early colonists followed prevailing European fashion modes when they could. One scholar, looking over wills and estate inventories from seventeenth-century Virginia, reported that "many of the dresses worn must have been as handsome as the dresses of women of the same social class in England: there are numerous allusions to silk and flowered gowns, to bodices of blue linen or green satin, and to waistcoats trimmed with lace." He added, "The incongruity of shining apparel with the rude surroundings of new settlements in the wilderness does not seem to have jarred upon the perceptions of the population" (Bruce, *Economic History of Virginia*,

vol. 2, pp. 187, 193). Colonists imported the majority of their fabrics and fashion ideas as well as many completed garments from Europe. For men, the prevailing style would have included a shirt and doublet (a close-fitting outer garment, sometimes made without sleeves), knee-length breeches, and hose. Women's fashion dictated floor-length petticoats (often in several layers) and a fitted bodice, stiffened with boned stays for formal occasions.

The Massachusetts General Court passed its first sumptuary law (a law regulating the dress of citizens) in 1634, just a few years after its establishment as a colonial governing body in 1630. The law did not attempt to enforce a somber appearance—the notion that the Puritan colonists dressed only in black and gray is a misconception—but asserted that lavish apparel was displeasing to God. The temptations of fashionable dress apparently influenced even this pioneering, faith-based settlement, for the law explicitly expressed concern over "new and immodest fashions." Later laws attempted further to regulate clothing as a means of preserving social hierarchy. A 1651 ordinance prohibited gold and silver buttons, silk and tiffany hoods, and other new fashions—but only for the lower classes. Those with estates valued above £200 were allowed these extravagances (Trautman, pp. 9–21). Historians do not think these laws were particularly effective in limiting habits of dress. Their existence was nonetheless a testament to a continuing influence of and admiration for fashionable attire, even in a colonial society based largely on spiritual concerns, and even among its less wealthy and prestigious classes.

Eighteenth Century   In the eighteenth century, Americans emulated British cultural mores even more strongly, sometimes outdoing Londoners in their attempts to appear properly English. The many portraits of periwigged colonial notables from this era testify to the American willingness to follow the European mode, as powdered wigs were fashion necessities from the early 1700s until the time of the French Revolution. Their popularity was not the only fashion change. For men, the doublet faded and a coat and vest took its place. The cut of these garments, along with the knee breeches they accompanied, became more tight and formfitting as the century progressed. For women, hoops in petticoats and separate upper body garments of boned stays (ancestors of the corset) created a rigid form. Over these undergarments, a woman wore a loose gown that was left open at the front. Petticoats peeked through an inverted V-shaped gap in the lower front. A similar space in the upper front was filled with a stomacher, a sometimes ornate and usually stiffened triangular piece of fabric.

Historian T. H. Breen has argued that clothing became a principal means of constructing social identity in the colonies. Commenting on mid-eighteenth-century portraits, he wrote, "For provincial Americans the central element in these paintings may have been the sitter's clothes." In "The Meaning of 'Likeness': Portrait-Painting in an Eighteenth-Century Consumer Society" (1993), Breen observed that when early Americans were "called upon to describe another colonist they inevitably concentrated on the color and quality of the person's garments" (pp. 39, 46). Indeed, the surviving papers of George Washington reveal him ordering garments from England made up "according to the present taste" and resisting vigorously when out-of-fashion goods were substituted, as in this complaint to an English tradesman: "You may believe me that instead of getting things good and fashionable in their several kinds, we often have articles sent to us that could only have been used by our forefathers in days of yore" (quoted in McClellan, *History of American Costume*, vol. 1, p. 327).

The significance of clothing became a matter of political debate during the revolutionary era, when American patriots marked resistance to British rule and loyalty to the colonist cause in part by a willingness to substitute homespun cloth for imported British fabric. That colonists attached such importance to clothing as a means of expressing their social and ideological allegiances hints at why historians have begun to look more closely at fashion as a cultural form. Dress is a crucial means of self-presentation, existing on the literal border between the individual and the social world, and so plays a great role in making culture and ideology visible in everyday life. A polemicist for the revolutionary cause wrote, "Can he be a true lover of his country . . . who would sooner be seen strutting about the streets, clad in foreign fripperies, than to be nobly independent in russet grey?" Another put it even more bluntly: "The man who would not refuse himself a fine coat, to save his country, deserves to be hanged" (quoted in Breen, pp. 495, 500).

Nineteenth Century When the Revolution ended, the appeal of homespun clothing faded along with its political significance (at his second inauguration, Washington wore a black velvet suit with diamond knee buckles). The nineteenth century found Americans once again following the European mode. In fact, the growth of consumer culture, technological advances in textile production, the appearance of popular fashion magazines such as *Godey's Lady's Book* (founded in 1830), and the availability of paper dress patterns (brought to the mass market by Butterick in the 1860s) drew more people into the fashion orbit than ever before.

Stylistically, the most significant development might have been the phenomenon sometimes called "the Great Masculine Renunciation" (Flugel, *Psychology of Clothes,* p. 111). Although gendered differences had long been expressed in clothing, both men's and women's styles tended to involve similar degrees of bodily constriction and decorative flair through about the 1840s. Toward the middle of the century, however, men's clothing began more and more to feature the outline recognizable today in the modern business suit. A coat, vest, and trousers (which replaced breeches) were worn in drab colors with a relatively shapeless outline and very little ornamentation. Women's clothing, however, continued to stress an ostentatiously constructed, extremely elaborate, ornamented silhouette. The details of female fashion changed through the 1800s, but virtually all popular styles from midcentury on involved bodily restraint through some combination of hoops, corsets, bustles, pads, and the cut of the sleeve, placement of the armhole, or length of the skirt.

Fashion thenceforth came to been seen as the almost exclusive province of women, and gender depictions became ever more important as a cultural function of dress. When gender roles became the focus of political controversy or protest, "fashion" often became the subject of intense debate. The most famous nineteenth-century example occurred when a group of feminist thinkers sought to promote the Bloomer costume, an outfit involving a loose-fitting, shortened dress worn over baggy pantaloons, as a statement of women's rights and emancipation. The experiment was short-lived, and opposition probably flowed as much from the political significance of the clothes as from any aesthetic or practical objections. "Dress reform" continued to be an important social cause, however. Through the rest of the century, various individuals and groups promoted the use of more comfortable, healthful, or "natural" clothing for women. While these sartorial schemes often had a political edge, the condemnation of fashionable women's dress seemed just as likely to come from those with conservative principles as those with radical aims. Fashion was criticized from the left as a means of constraining and subjugating women; it was attacked from the right as encouraging promiscuity and unwomanly public display. Yet it was favored in the middle-class mainstream as a means of propriety, respectability, and self-expression. A popular etiquette book, *Sensible Etiquette of the Best Society* (1878), advised that "refinement of character is said never to be found with vulgarity of dress" and further noted that "the consciousness of being well-dressed confers upon a woman that peace of mind which even religion may fail to give" (Moore, pp. 248, 287).

One can glimpse the range of opinions evoked by the politics of fashion during the last part of the nineteenth century in magazine and newspaper articles titled "Fashion's Slaves" and "Tyranny of Fashion" on the one side and "Fashionable Dress Justified" and "The Beneficent Influence of Dress" on the other. The debate over the import of fashion spilled over into the academy, with leading historians, sociologists, economists, and psychologists undertaking the more serious examination of the cultural role of dress.

Twentieth Century Through the twentieth century, fashion for men continued to revolve around the business suit and changed only in details, although increasing informality and popularity of "sportswear" marked significant social changes. Even within these rather narrow limits, the cultural weight of fashion could take on serious dimensions, as demonstrated by the Zoot Suit riots of the 1940s. The zoot suit was a highly stylized version of the business suit that included a very long coat and pants worn high on the waist, cut wide at the knees, and tapered tightly at the ankles. Young men, especially Mexican Americans and African Americans, adopted the zoot suit to mark pride in their identity and refusal to acquiesce to mainstream expectations of subservience. In the summer of 1943, disturbances in several major cities involved violent clashes between off-duty servicemen and gangs of zoot-suiters. The military men, who were almost invariably white, might have been motivated by ra-

cial or ethnic bias against the zoot-suiters, but they were specifically provoked by the symbolic power of their clothing. In its extravagant cut, the zoot suit flouted wartime rationing regulations for clothing. Its wearers, usually young and male, appeared to be evading military service. *The Washington Post* reported that "police made no effort to halt auto loads of servicemen openly cruising in search of zoot-suiters," who, when found, were "snatched from bar rooms, pools halls and theaters and stripped of their attire" (quoted in Cosgrove, *History Workshop,* p. 90). The clashes prompted investigation by state and local un-American activities committees, who suggested that the zoot-suiters were being led by Nazi agitators.

For women, fashion went through radical stylistic changes after 1900 as the highly sculpted look of the nineteenth century gave way to more streamlined, less fitted fashions. Historians have sometimes equated the new styles, which were more revealing and less confining in many ways, with the increasing female emancipation that was evident in the more active and public role women achieved at this time. Yet the cylindrical fashion profile of the 1920s could as easily be interpreted as self-denying (erasing the feminine image) and emulative of a mannish body form, rather than an as assertion of female rights. Even though the corset was eliminated, heels remained high, and "obviously ornamental" hats were mandatory. Shorter skirts brought a new set of constraints, because sheer stockings required careful care and now women had to learn how to feel socially (and physically) comfortable while partially exposing their bodies. Many fashion trends of the century, including the squared shoulder pads of the 1930s, the miniskirt of the 1960s, and the dress-for-success business suit of the 1980s, have prompted similarly divergent analyses. To some they represent markers of female advance; to others they are symbols of female oppression. This ambiguity about fashion is the source of much of its fascination for cultural critics, who examine dress for evidence of complex social formations and change.

As the twentieth century drew to a close, fashion styles for women were more pluralistic and eclectic than ever, yet the cultural demand for gendered norms of appearance remained strong, and habits of dress continued to attract attention of social commentators. As in the previous century, some condemned fashion as oppressive, irrational, and materialistic, while others celebrated it as self-expressive and even subversive. Writing about sexual discrimination in the 1980s and 1990s, Susan

Faludi asserted that "in every backlash, the fashion industry has produced punitively restrictive clothing and the fashion press has demanded that women wear them" (*Backlash,* p. 173). But Elizabeth Wilson, no less committed to feminist principles, argued that fashion has been and continues to be a woman's means of self-expression, self-celebration, and opposition to dominant values. "To understand all 'uncomfortable' dress as merely one aspect of the oppression of women, is fatally to oversimplify" (*Adorned,* p. 244). The ubiquity of fashion and its evident social importance guarantee that there will be no shortage of commentary upon it. During the past one hundred years or so, writers have employed a wide range of approaches in attempting to plumb fashion's essential dynamic and meaning.

HISTORY AND THE UNDERSTANDING OF FASHION

Sociological, psychological, and aesthetic perspectives have provided the platforms for most attempts to understand the meaning and movement of fashion. The diversity of approaches multiplied during the latter part of the twentieth century, however, as the influence of postmodern theory and cultural history led scholars increasingly to value fashion as a form of cultural evidence and as a complex medium of cultural expression. The variety of approaches accords with the array of social meanings dress embodies. Fashion's multidimensional qualities are the very core of its cultural significance.

Sociological Interpretation   Through the early twentieth century, the most representative studies of fashion concentrated on careful documentation of stylistic details over time. Even the best of them, such as Elisabeth McClellan's *History of American Costume, 1607–1870* (1937; the first volume of which, entitled *Historic Dress in America, 1607–1800,* appeared in 1904), did not contain much cultural analysis. Two short articles published around the turn of the century signaled a new effort to dig deeper into the social significance of dress.

The first was written by Thorstein Veblen, an economist then teaching at the University of Chicago. Veblen published an article in 1894 called "The Economic Theory of Woman's Dress," which contained many ideas he would later expand in his book *The Theory of the Leisure Class* (1899). For Veblen, the key to understanding women's fashion was the realization that it functioned primarily to mark and maintain the border between social classes. Fashionable styles emphasized high status by their costliness and frequent turnover. Social position was also implicit in the uncomfortable and constraining details of women's clothing, which demonstrated that the wearer did not need to engage in physical labor. Veblen's examination of how women's dress revealed specific details about the imbalances of Victorian sexual politics presented an early example of gender as a useful category of historical analysis.

Veblen espoused a trickle-down theory of fashion that received more direct statement a few years later in the essay "Fashion" by German sociologist Georg Simmel. In Simmel's scenario, the upper classes adopt a style to express their distinctiveness, and the lower classes then imitate it out of desire to emulate their social superiors. Once the lower classes begin to achieve some success in imitating the current mode, the upper classes have to adopt a new style to maintain their elite status, and the cycle is repeated—hence, the constant movement of fashion.

The ideas of Veblen and Simmel continue to exert enormous influence on fashion commentary, although the trickle-down dynamic has been challenged from a number of directions. Some revisionists, such as Herbert Blumer ("Fashion: From Class Differentiation to Collective Selection," 1969), have presented evidence that fashion sometimes "trickles up" or "trickles across" as it gains popularity (in Roach-Higgins et al., *Dress and Identity,* pp. 378–392). Others have argued that the spread of ready-to-wear fashions, the mass-mediated circulation of fashionable images, and the development of a more pluralistic set of fashion standards have functioned more in the service of social equality than of class differentiation (Kidwell and Christman, *Suiting Everyone*). Still others have focused on the potential of clothing styles to express viewpoints that challenge rather than reinforce the dominant social structure (Hebdige, *Subculture*).

More recent sociological approaches to dress have increasingly acknowledged that social identity is not simply definable along one or two major fault lines but is achieved in terms of a shifting set of affiliations that combine and continually rearrange divisions based on class, ethnicity, gender, sexuality, and a host of other characteristics. A noteworthy attempt to synthesize the many attributes of fashion in a sociological framework is Fred Davis's *Fashion, Culture, and Identity* (1992), which stresses ambiguity and ambivalence as key to fashion's meaning.

Psychological Interpretation Studies that analyze dress in terms of basic psychological motives, especially sexual attraction, began to emerge around the turn of the century as well. Havelock Ellis's seven-volume *Studies in the Psychology of Sex,* which began to appear in 1900, contained several passages attempting to explain dress in terms of sexual drive. Ellis wrote, "The extreme importance of dress would disappear at once if the two sexes were to dress alike" (vol. 4, p. 209). The first sustained, modern treatment of clothing in psychological terms appeared in 1930 when J. C. Flugel published *The Psychology of Clothes,* in which he applied the theories of psychoanalysis to dress. Indeed, he declared that the fashion impulse is akin to a neurotic symptom and stated that "of all the motives for the wearing of clothes, those connected with the sexual life have an altogether predominant position" (pp. 25–27).

Flugel proposed a theory of fashion change that linked the steady pulse of stylistic innovation to a regular shift in the part of a woman's body deemed most attractive at a given historical moment. New fashions emerged to highlight these "shifting erogenous zones" (p. 160). The erogenous zones theory is vulnerable to a number of objections because it all but ignores men's clothing styles and is indifferent to many other factors—aesthetic, economic, and sociological—that bear on the development of dress style. Undoubtedly, however, clothing has important personal and psychological dimensions, and its psychoanalytic determinants have received increasingly subtle readings in more recent years in books such as Valerie Steele's *Fashion and Eroticism* (1985). The danger in such an approach is that it can become one-dimensional and even deterministic. Understanding fashion's richness and resilience as a social phenomenon requires steady attention to clothing's ability to convey many meanings at many levels simultaneously.

Aesthetic Interpretation Fashion is not only subject to social and psychological influences; it is also an art form. As such, it has to be understood at least in part in aesthetic terms, as a flow of design images, each of which modifies or rebels against what came before. Among the most provocative attempts to examine the aesthetics of dress is the work of Anne Hollander. Hollander has argued that prevailing pictorial conventions in art determine the look of fashion, and that in turn the look of fashion dictates what is considered normal for the human body. In other words, what is considered "natural" at a given time is derived from a sense of clothing styles, not

bodily form. Hollander makes a strong case against assigning intrinsic social meaning to a particular style or garment: "The tight-laced waist, the periwigged head, and the neck collared in a millstone ruff, along with the flattened breasts and blue-jeaned leg, have all been comfortable, beautiful, and natural in their time." Hollander saw fashion as a closed system with an "autonomous history," however, and tended to divorce the mode of dress almost entirely from the cultural moment, thus drastically understating fashion's role as social communication (*Seeing Through Clothes,* pp. xiii, 311).

Postmodern Interpretation In recent years, some writers have suggested that fashion can be best conceptualized in terms of postmodern theory, particularly those aspects that emphasize instability, surface effects, pastiche, recycling of past images, and blurring of boundaries between "high" and "low" art. They have suggested that fashion perfectly mirrors life in a postmodern age because it represents a completely untethered system of symbols "free to commute and permutate without limit" (Baudrillard, *Symbolic Exchange and Death,* p. 87). Such a position is as extreme as those which too simply tie fashion details to specific social meanings. Fashion's image over time is contingent and changeable but not completely random. Fashion is always about change, about the body, and about social interaction. It weaves tight but sometimes enigmatic linkages with prevailing notions of body politics and social structure. Its ambiguity and inexactness give fashion the capacity to promote both subservience and subversion, sometimes at the same time, and this ability symbolically to "manage" social and psychological contradictions is among its key cultural functions. Fashion's form is neither autonomous nor totally arbitrary. Rather, it responds to a continuously shifting convergence of influences from fashion's own visual traditions, current trends in the wider culture, and tendencies, including economic ones, of the fashion system itself.

Cultural Interpretation The latest attempts to synthesize insights into the history of dress might be labeled the "cultural approach" to fashion (Breward, *Culture of Fashion*). Scholars, under the influence of growing research in cultural studies and cultural history, have become more concerned with understanding expressive forms that had previously existed at the margins of historical inquiry. They are more likely to place issues of identity, gender, sexuality, and body politics at the core of a broad range of historical developments, more willing to embrace many-tiered, dynamic, and ambiguous realms of meaning. Clothing—omnipresent, inevitably linked to self-image and social interaction, almost inextricably intertwined with issues of gender—has consequently come under more and more scholarly scrutiny.

The cultural approach to fashion history has inspired a variety of studies that blur boundaries and represent interdisciplinary thinking. Two overviews are Malcolm Barnard's *Fashion as Communication* (1996) and Christopher Breward's *The Culture of Fashion* (1995). Barnard took a mainly theoretical approach to fashion as a cultural phenomenon, and his book touches on most of the major interpretative schools of fashion theory. Breward's book sur-

veys the broad sweep of fashion history from the medieval period, using a cultural approach.

Fashion undoubtedly will continue to attract scholarly interest. More than one hundred years ago, *Godey's Magazine* claimed that a person's clothes "betray, by evidences so plain that they cannot be misinterpreted, not only the pecuniary and social position, but the tastes, the temperament,—ay, even the emotions of the wearer" (June 1893, p. 784). The magazine's fashion editor captured in a single sentence the protean influences and vast symbolic potential of fashion, throwing out hints for any number of approaches to the subject. Scholars have increasingly come to agree that the influence of dress is pervasive and important, and they have taken increasingly imaginative and far-reaching means to investigate its cultural significance.

See also **Gender, Social Class, Race, and Material Life** *(volume 1);* **Women and Family in the Suburban Age; The World According to Hollywood; Women** *(volume 2);* **Consumerism; Individualism and the Self; Gentility and Manners** *(in this volume).*

BIBLIOGRAPHY

Barnard, Malcolm. *Fashion as Communication.* London and New York, 1996.

Baudrillard, Jean. *Symbolic Exchange and Death.* 1976. Translated by Iain Hamilton Grant. London, 1993.

Blumer, Herbert. "Fashion: From Class Differentiation to Collective Selection." In *Dress and Identity,* edited by Mary Ellen Roach-Higgins, Joanne B. Eicher, and Kim K. P. Johnson, pp. 378–392. New York, 1995.

Breen, T. H. "The Meaning of Likeness: Portrait-Painting in an Eighteenth-Century Consumer Society." In *The Portrait in Eighteenth-Century America,* edited by Ellen Miles, pp. 37–60. Newark, Del., 1993.

———. "Narrative of Commercial Life: Consumption, Ideology, and Community on the Eve of the American Revolution." *William and Mary Quarterly* 50, no. 3 (1993): 471–501.

Breward, Christopher. *The Culture of Fashion.* Manchester, U.K., 1995.

———. "Cultures, Identities, Histories: Fashioning a Cultural Approach to Dress." *Fashion Theory* 2, no. 4 (1998): 301–314.

Bruce, Philip. *Economic History of Virginia in the Seventeenth Century.* 2 vols. New York, 1896.

Cosgrove, Stuart. "The Zoot-Suit and Style Warfare." *History Workshop,* no. 18 (1984): 77–91.

Davis, Fred. *Fashion, Culture, and Identity.* Chicago, 1992.

Ellis, Havelock. *Studies in the Psychology of Sex.* 7 vols. Philadelphia, 1900–1928.

Faludi, Susan. *Backlash: The Undeclared War against Women.* New York, 1991.

Flugel, J. C. *The Psychology of Clothes.* London, 1930.

"Godey's Fashions." *Godey's Magazine* (June 1893): 783–800.

Hebdige, Dick. *Subculture: The Meaning of Style.* London, 1979.

Hollander, Anne. *Seeing Through Clothes.* Berkeley, Calif., 1993.

Kidwell, Claudia, and Margaret Christman. *Suiting Everyone: The Democratization of Clothing in America.* Washington, D.C., 1974.

McClellan, Elisabeth. *History of American Costume 1607–1870.* 2 vols., 1904. Reprint, New York, 1937.

Moore, Clara [Mrs. H. O. Ward]. *Sensible Etiquette of the Best Society.* Philadelphia, 1878.

Paterek, Josephine. *Encyclopedia of American Indian Costume.* Santa Barbara, Calif., 1994.

Simmel, Georg. "Fashion." In *On Individuality and Social Forms: Selected Writings,* edited by Donald N. Levine, pp. 294–323. Chicago, 1971. First published 1904.

Steele, Valerie. *Fashion and Eroticism: Ideals of Feminine Beauty from the Victorian Era to the Jazz Age.* New York, 1985.

Trautman, Patricia. "When Gentlemen Wore Lace: Sumptuary Legislation and Dress in 17th-Century New England." *Journal of Regional Cultures* 3, no. 2 (1983): 9–21.

Veblen, Thorstein. "The Economic Theory of Woman's Dress." *Popular Science Monthly* (November 1894): 198–205.

——. *The Theory of the Leisure Class.* 1899. Reprint, New York, 1994.

Wilson, Elizabeth. *Adorned in Dreams: Fashion and Modernity.* Berkeley, Calif., 1987.

Part 17

METHODS AND CONCEPTS

THE HISTORY OF IDEAS

James Hoopes

ORIGINS

Few contemporary historians or philosophers would describe themselves as historians of ideas, a term associated with such early-twentieth-century scholars as Arthur O. Lovejoy (1873–1962) and Perry Miller (1905–1963), who wrote of conflicts within and between large, imperious concepts that for a time dominated but ultimately failed to control a society's worldview. Lovejoy and Miller premised their studies not on human helplessness in the face of overarching worldviews but on the ironically self-defeating efforts of human beings to loyally sustain such worldviews. This ironic sensibility was scarcely unique to the early twentieth century; one can find it in the works of great nineteenth-century historians such as Henry Adams. Diminished contemporary interest in the history of ideas is due at least partly to methodological issues bedeviling the field since the 1960s and also to loss of interest in irony in favor of condemnation as the preferred style for understanding disturbing social and political change.

Study of conservative attempts to maintain inconsistent syntheses is the classic method of the history of ideas. According to this model of historical change, intellectual conservatives, ultimately failing to cover over the contradictions and conflicts within a system of ideas, succeed only in making it difficult to understand where the conflicts are, why the system is broken, and how new worldviews emerge. Historians of ideas such as Lovejoy and Miller saw their job as untangling the logical threads of the story, revealing its hidden drama and ironies, and morally chastening and humbling contemporary society for its own prideful confidence in its supposed self-knowledge.

Dramatic tension and irony characterize histories of ideas because individual thinkers, passionately committed to ideas and values on both sides of a flawed synthesis, trying to prevent its inevitable defeat, succeed only in delaying change, squeezing it into unexpected outlets and unrecognizable forms. Intellectual conservatives labor to prevent cracks from developing into fissures which in turn might become volcanoes. Yet ad hoc repairs to supposedly coherent bodies of thought only raise the pressure elsewhere, rupturing the system at new, unexpected places, which require still more intellectual patchwork till at last the original synthesis is changed beyond recognition. Despite and, ironically, because of conservative attempts to sustain revered systems of ideas, human societies unintentionally but ultimately create new worldviews. History is a work of the human mind but of no individual mind. History has a logic but not an easily detectable logic. Human societies move "crablike" toward the future, as Perry Miller put it in the second volume of his important study of early-American Puritanism, *The New England Mind: From Colony to Province* (1953). Recognizing logical direction within such seemingly mindless motion requires, he said, in a defiant preface to the book's paperback edition (1961), "a sensitivity to the nuances of ideas at least as delicate" as that with which "the best intellects of the period" had interpreted and, by interpreting, partly determined their experience.

The Great Chain of Being (1936), Lovejoy's best-known work, told the story of the idea of plenitude, the idea that God had created everything possible to create. In the chain stretching from highest to lowest creature, from angels down through humans, beasts, and plants, to the lowliest speck of dust, there was only the least possible difference between each being and its neighbors. Otherwise, as Lovejoy quotes Augustine, "the multiplicity of kinds of things of which the universe is constituted . . . would not exist" (p. 67). Interested in understanding the origins of his own evolutionary philosophy, Lovejoy looked back 2,500 years to learn why the long, enduring view of the universe as static and absolute gave way, abruptly, in the late nineteenth and early twentieth centuries, to a developmental and relativist cosmology.

According to Lovejoy's dynamic story of change, Plato and Plotinus had saddled Christianity with two conflicting ideas of God, only one of which could and did logically win out in the long course of Western thought. On the one hand God was absolutely self-sufficient, timeless, and otherworldly, needing nothing outside himself for completion or perfection. The other, conflicting idea was that God's generative essence and absolute goodness required the creation of everything that could possibly exist in time and space. Brilliantly, Lovejoy traced the tensions between these notions of God as they were manifest in ancient, medieval, and modern times along with the increasingly unsuccessful attempts of theologians and philosophers to cover over and patch up the problem. By the nineteenth century, for reasons both moral and scientific, the temporality of the world was so widely accepted that nature could not be accepted as complete once and for all. If nature reflected God's image, then God himself was a temporal being. The great chain of created beings moved not from highest to lowest but lowest to highest so that even God was an evolutionary process to be completed only in the fullness of time. The idea of God's timelessness was vanquished by the nineteenth-century fascination with history, which in itself was a manifestation of the ironic victory of the millennia-old notion of God's creativity over his self-sufficiency, his immanence over his otherworldliness.

Perry Miller, teaching American literature at Harvard, may have been influenced to write in the ironic mode when Lovejoy visited in the early 1930s to deliver the lectures that became *The Great Chain of Being.* Miller, the Great Depression decade's other great historian of ideas, wrote the genre's best book on an American subject, *The New England Mind: The Seventeenth Century* (1939). From Miller's *New England Mind,* much of the following half century's outpouring of work in American cultural and intellectual history was lineally descended, even if this work eventually became so cross-pollinated by radical political ideology and semiotic literary theory as to contain almost nothing of the classic, ironic method of the history of ideas.

Like Lovejoy, Miller told the story of the ironic decline of a seemingly coherent but actually self-contradictory body of thought. Unlike Lovejoy, Miller wrote of a small region in a short period of time—New England over the course of a mere century—and made up for the smallness of his canvas by the depth of his field. Richer than the story of a single idea, richer even than Lovejoy's account of so complex an idea as that of God, Miller's subject was the entire seventeenth-century Puritan worldview as revealed in New Englanders' thinking on theology, cosmology, physics, epistemology, psychology, sociology, logic, and rhetoric. In all these fields, according to Miller, they brought to bear what seemed to them a unified set of assumptions that were actually drawn from two different, contradictory sources. As people of the Renaissance, Puritans had an intellectual heritage that made them eager for new knowledge and enthusiastic about new methods of obtaining it. But they also were Augustinian pietists searching for regenerating grace through humility before God. Confident that what the deity had written in the book of nature would not contradict his word as revealed in Scripture, they came to New England attempting almost unwittingly to maintain their balance between their intellectual heritage and their pietist commitment.

Up to a point, the Puritan worldview "hung together as beautifully as any system has ever cohered within itself" (p. 190), but ultimately, Miller said, Puritans were mistaken in their hope that their intellectual heritage could be reconciled with their piety. Their synthesis of intellect and piety depended on their failure, useful in the short run, to distinguish between "reason" in the Aristotelian sense of a faculty for discovering truth in the external world and "reason" in the Platonic sense of an intuitive source of truth within human beings. Against Quakers, against Antinomians such as Anne Hutchinson, against all preachers of an inner light, Puritans invoked Aristotelian "reason" to insist that truth was found externally, whether in nature or Scripture. Against Episcopalians, Presbyterians, and other advocates of church unity Puritans defended congregational independence by insisting with Plato that intuitive "reason" could see wholeness even where there was no visible manifestation of it. But in the long run the awful God of Puritan piety lost mystery by making a world where humanity, with Aristotle, found only order. And the doctrine of innate depravity was difficult to reconcile with the Platonic celebration of innate human capacity. The intellectual heritage triumphed over piety not because of any intentional commitment to the one over the other but, ironically, because of the Puritan attempt to reconcile them. There was a logic or meaning to seventeenth-century New Englanders' movement toward the future, but it was a logic that frustrated rather than fulfilled their own intellectual ambitions.

In *The New England Mind: From Colony to Province,* Miller described the effect of the Puritans' flawed synthesis on the region's political history in

PERRY MILLER

If the earlier book [*The New England Mind: The Seventeenth Century*] has any merit it arises from the effort to comprehend, in the widest possible terms, the architecture of the intellect brought to America by the founders of New England. Hence that book was organized by topics, treating the entire expression of the period as a single body of writing and paying little or no attention to modifications forced upon the mind by domestic events. The method could be justified because throughout the century, and down to the first decades of the eighteenth, the official cosmology did remain more or less intact. Such developments as took place affected the lesser areas of church polity, political relations, or the contests of groups and interests. These could be, and indeed as I believe this narrative demonstrates often were, intense and shattering experiences without causing any alterations in the doctrinal frame of reference. Therefore *From Colony to Province* may be imagined as taking place, so to speak, inside *The Seventeenth Century.* While the massive structure of logic, psychology, theology stands apparently untouched, the furnishings of the palace are little by little changed, until a hundred years after the Great Migration the New England mind has become strangely altered, even though the process (which, all things considered, was rapid) was hardly perceptible to the actors themselves. A hundred years after the landings, they were forced to look upon themselves with amazement, hardly capable of understanding how they had come to be what they were.

Consequently the focus of the study is narrowed down to a merely provincial scene, and much is made of events which, in the perspective of American—not to say of world—history, seem so small as to be trivial. Frankly, did I regard this investigation as no more than an account of intellectual activity in colonial New England, I would long since have given it over as not worth the effort. But the fascination of this region, for the first two hundred or more years of its existence, is that it affords the historian an ideal laboratory. It was relatively isolated, the people were comparatively homogeneous, and the forces of history played upon it in ways that can more satisfactorily be traced than in more complex societies. Here is an opportunity, as nearly perfect as the student is apt to find, for extracting certain generalizations about the relation of thought or ideas to communal experience. I believe profoundly that the story herein recounted is chiefly valuable for its *representative* quality: it is a case history of the accommodation to the American landscape of an imported and highly articulate system of ideas. We have a chance to see exactly how this process, which began the moment the ships dropped anchor in Boston harbor, was driven by local influences, and yet was constantly diverted or stimulated by the influx of ideas from Europe. What I should most like to claim for this study is that it amounts to a sort of working model for American history.

Source: From "Foreword," *The New England Mind: From Colony to Province* (1953).

the seventeenth century. The foreword to this work summarized his method and goals with as much clarity and succinctness as he ever achieved. But his grandiose claim that the story has a "*representative quality*," that it is a "working model for American history," is a betrayal of the classic conception of the duty of the historian of ideas, who should question such models, not create them. On the highest level, historians of ideas, whose ironic model of history is as dubious as any other, always run the same risk of self-contradiction as their subjects. To claim that one specific story of irony is a model for later stories only compounds the risk.

DISCIPLES AND APOSTATES

That so formidable a scholar as Miller could not maintain his balance suggests the extraordinary difficulty of writing history of ideas, which may be one reason for lack of interest by historians. Miller taught in the English Department at Harvard and Lovejoy was a philosopher at Johns Hopkins. Also, history is not a good breeding ground for historians of ideas because the empirical bias of many historians implicitly suggests that little can have depended on past intellectuals' airy cobwebs and therefore little of importance is to be learned by untangling them. In the late twentieth century, an extreme reaction against empiricism in favor of the supposed impossibility of any historical objectivity at all damaged intellectual historians' confidence in the validity of their objectivist goals.

In the 1950s and 1960s, the history of ideas in America withered and, in one offshoot, became the American studies "myth and symbol" school. Many studies in this vein such as Henry Nash Smith's *Virgin Land: The American West as Symbol and Myth* (1950) and Leo Marx's *Machine in the Garden: Technology and the Pastoral Ideal in America* (1964) offered valuable readings of more or less canonical texts. But they also reflected the vanity into which the later Miller had fallen of claiming representative quality for themselves as studies of overarching "myths" explaining national character and history. It was not, as some subsequent critics claimed, that the field was elitist because representative claims were based on the writings of a few dead, white males. Rather, these studies used their few dead white males to represent too small an idea—the "meaning" of America instead of the more general problem of the risks run and rewards received when human beings interpret themselves and their situations. The only broad cultural "meaning" they represented, if any, was the brief midcentury confidence that the twentieth century was the American century. History of ideas in the American-studies vein became too much like the Puritan practice of theology as an act of justification instead of a study of the ironic effect of that justification. Oversimplified representationalism lingered on into the Vietnam era, condemnation having replaced justification, in such studies as Sacvan Bercovitch's *The Puritan Origins of the American Self* (1975).

A less self-conscious, less overreaching representationalism was at work in the 1950s and early 1960s in history departments. There, American intellectual history was written in a different vein, interested less in supposed myths and symbols than in the influence of one thinker or school of thought on another. Generic, high-quality examples are Morton White's *Social Thought in America: The Revolt against Formalism* (1949) and Henry May's *End of American Innocence: A Study of the First Years of Our Own Time, 1912–1917* (1959). Although the use of "America" in the titles of such studies left them open to later charges of mistaking the thoughts of the few for those of the many, such usage was conventional at the time, and the studies themselves dealt with well-defined issues and groups of thinkers. There was nothing of the American-studies mythical mystery tour in these books; their claim to representativeness owed mainly to the intellectually more innocent sins of knocking on doors that were partway open and supposing that more light in the already best-lit rooms would help illuminate the rest of the house. The influences and conflicts dealt with in such studies—the effect of pragmatism on social theory or the fortifications of genteel Americans against invasions of the European avant-garde—had been well recognized by the actors themselves. Gone were the unseen snares and dramatic ironies that had characterized the best histories of ideas a generation earlier. Gone, too, was the dramatic capacity to engage the imagination. Much as could be learned about the past from such books, they could not shock native sons and daughters into delighted recognition that they lived in a more complex world than they had imagined.

By the 1970s the uninspired, uninteresting solidity of mainstream intellectual history, along with the grandiose claims and oversimplifications of the American studies tradition, helped drive many younger scholars toward "the new social history," as it was called. Some of the more ardent proponents of this school argued that studies of intellectual elites were themselves elitist and that study of ordinary human beings who simply constituted past communities was the path to historical truth. It may be possible that intellectual activity has no large "meaning," but the implication of some 1970s social historians that societies are constituted without ideas is clearly mistaken. Based on statistical summaries of census, court, and church records, studies of small communities poured off the presses. Often lacking the large-scale explanatory power and dramatic irony of histories of ideas, the new social history sometimes seemed to have a static quality that ran the risk of appealing only to human interest rather than to the historian's traditional goal of understanding change over time.

When such local studies did strive for larger meaning it was not the ironic meaning of the history of ideas but a simple representationalism whereby community changes reflected the emerging force of some later intellectual construction such as capitalism or working-class consciousness. One of the finer examples of the genre was Paul Boyer and Stephen Nissenbaum's *Salem Possessed: The Social Origins of Witchcraft* (1974) which wonderfully reconstructed the social and economic circumstances surrounding the famous events of 1692. In the end, though, the individual human actors seemed only to represent the deeper market forces that explained the tragedy, so that study of the local community yielded less explanation or discovery than description or at most confirmation of a larger hypothesis. Not human activity or thought but changing social circumstances and conditions—resulting from who knew what?—became the subject of history. The new social history, with its disavowal of intellectual history, seemed ironically to prove, as Perry Miller contended in his preface to the paperback edition of *The New England Mind,* that in the absence of ideas, social history "cannot be made the central theme of a coherent narrative."

Nevertheless, the currents of academic politics and institutional power were running so strongly in the direction of social history that by the 1970s they were brave souls who identified themselves as historians of ideas. "Intellectual history" had long since become the preferred term, especially for the more overtly political studies of such earlier scholars as Vernon Louis Parrington, Ralph Henry Gabriel, and Merle Curti. Now, however, "intellectual history" took on a much narrower meaning. At the 1977 Wingspread conference in Racine, Wisconsin, the proceedings of which were published as *New Directions in American Intellectual History,* a scholar deeply influenced by social history suggested that historians should write what would come to be called the "social history of ideas," that is, ideas that could be grounded in well defined "social aggregates" (p. 21) so that when the rare generalization was made it would be "credible" by being "extremely hard earned" (p. 23).

Although this reductionism was answered at the same conference by hoary assertions of the reality of free will and national culture, the most influential response was more moderate. David Hollinger admitted that intellectual historians usually study elites but asserted that elite "discourse," if not democratically representative, nevertheless constituted a community among those participating in the discourse, even across several generations. Citing *The New England Mind* as an example of the study of discourse, Hollinger added that in Miller's recreation of Puritan discourse, "if anywhere . . . , is the life of the mind depicted as a *life* rather than as a set of discrete units of thought" (p. 47). The compatibility of intellectual history with "social aggregates," broadly conceived, was thus easily enough demonstrated, though the question of the relationship between elite discourse and broader social history was left in abeyance.

RESPONSES TO POSTMODERNISM

Far more difficult than the challenge posed by social history was the question of why, how, and even if such past intellectual discourse could be reconstructed. Intellectual historians had hardly dealt with the challenge of simplistic empiricism when a new challenge unexpectedly arose from the literary critics who had been erstwhile allies and even practitioners of the history of ideas. The trend toward deconstruction, poststructuralism, and postmodernism in English departments of the 1980s and 1990s challenged all representationalism, not just elite intellectuals' representativeness of society but surviving documents' representativeness of their authors' thoughts. The postmodern chestnut that words are free-floating signifiers, with no necessary relation to the objects signified, left texts open to entirely new meanings accorded them by their interpreters, not by their authors or their historical situations. According to postmodernists, who protested the idea of "presence," the supposed disconnect between signifier and signified meant that authors were "absent" from their writings. Liberating as literary theorists found it to be rid of authors, historians were consternated to be told that documents do not represent historical subjects.

There followed a flurry of methodological writings that the stoic reader can follow through the 1980s and 1990s in the pages of the *American Historical Review, History and Theory, Journal of the History of Ideas, Intellectual History Newsletter,* and other scholarly journals. Intellectual historians, led into philosophically treacherous water they were not always well prepared to navigate, sometimes cited Jacques Derrida or John Dewey as if invocation of these demigods could substitute for reasoned argument. Particularly challenging to the classic, ironic model of the history of ideas was the maverick, influential neo-pragmatism and anti-foundationalism propounded by the widely read philosopher Richard Rorty. Arguing against attempts at metaphysical foundations, he opposed the tradition of the great builders of architectonic systems from Plato to Hegel. Instead, Rorty wanted philosophers to be "liberal ironists" conversing about the rights and wrongs of modern society while accepting the fact that they could ground none of their ideas and judgments in some mythological foundation or substratum of reality. He thought this would mean that philosophers would be writing more like historians, which indicated that he had a very strange idea of what historians do, with their traditional, historicist goal of understanding the past in its own terms. Rorty's claim to be ironically self-aware that his own values were unfounded and subject only to the vicissitudes of conversation was of course the exact opposite of the irony in classic history of ideas, where the historian aims to untangle the threads by which human beings unintentionally ensnarl themselves in a new web of culture even as they insist on their loyalty to a past synthesis. When the history of the ideas of our own time is written, the question of whether the neo-pragmatists' consciously ironic stance is deliberately sustained or ironically defeated will make an interesting footnote.

Claiming that he wrote in the tradition of Dewey (who actually appealed for something more like a foundationalist naturalism than a free-floating conversation), Rorty helped touch off a wave of interest in American pragmatism. Among the rash of books celebrating the near centennial of the intellectual era when William James was at the height of his powers and Dewey's star beginning its ascent, probably the best was also one of the first, *Uncertain Victory: Social Democracy and Progressivism in European and American Thought, 1870–1920* (1986) by James Kloppenberg. Published during the second Reagan administration, *Uncertain Victory* located the philosophical origins of American liberalism and European social democracy in the Deweyesque notion of thought as an instrument for moving toward desired goals, subject always to further correction by experience, never certain. *Uncertain Victory* had a faintly *New England Mind*–like organization, with the first half devoted mainly to philosophers and the second to economists, political scientists, sociologists, and the like. But there was no intentionally ironic suggestion here that Deweyesque confidence in the social instrumentality of thought might by some not unusually bizarre twist of history have helped produce the Reagan presidency and the resurgence of atomistic individualism. Instead, Kloppenberg urged liberals to be of good cheer and recover whatever was salvageable— quite a lot, he seemed to suggest—from Dewey's generation of thinkers. In its political directness *Uncertain Victory* resembled many other, often lesser, more prescriptive, and even less ironic intellectual histories of recent years.

In defense of irony, John Patrick Diggins published *The Promise of Pragmatism: Modernism and the Crisis of Knowledge and Authority* (1994) which attempted to enlarge the vision of both neo- and traditional pragmatists by setting them against the great *fin-de-siècle* mugwump Henry Adams and the prominent Great Depression and cold war theologian Reinhold Niebuhr, whose *Irony of American History* (1952) owed much to the influence of Perry Miller. Unlike Rorty, Diggins dealt seriously not only with John Dewey and William James but also Charles Sanders Peirce, the latter being the original American pragmatist, who, partly because of his philosophical difficulty, is often ignored by intellectual historians. An interesting feature of Diggins's book was his use of the neo-pragmatists' conversational method to criticize their belief that human values can be based only on conversation. Diggins created a sort of counterfactual conversation by setting in opposition figures such as Dewey and Adams, who actually had not attended closely to each other's ideas, or at least not in writing. Judging the original pragmatists against the standard of the unpragmatic Adams and Niebuhr violated, as Diggins admitted, "the contextualist's commandments by ignoring . . . the historically conditioned character of texts" (p. 7). But, he added, "the history of ideas" may also aim at appreciating ideas "for their validity" (p. 7), an objective that differs not only from historical contextualism but also from Rorty's neo-pragmatic conversation. Interested as Rorty is in human values and social justice, he makes no claim for the validity of these concerns. Diggins in effect finds invalid or at least incomplete the ideas of the

CHARLES SANDERS PEIRCE

At any moment we are in possession of certain information, that is, of cognitions which have been logically derived by induction and hypothesis from previous cognitions which are less general, less distinct, and of which we have a less lively consciousness . . . back to the ideal first, which is quite singular, and quite out of consciousness. This ideal first is the particular thing-in-itself. It does not exist *as such.* That is, there is no thing which is in-itself in the sense of not being relative to the mind, though things which are relative to the mind doubtless are, apart from that relation. The cognitions which thus reach us by this infinite series of inductions and hypotheses . . . are of two kinds, the true and the untrue, or cognitions whose objects are *real* and those whose objects are *unreal.* And what do we mean by the real? It is a conception which we must first have had when we discovered that there was an unreal, an illusion; that is, when we first corrected ourselves. Now the distinction for which alone this fact logically called, was between an *ens* relative to private inward determinations, to the negations belonging to idiosyncracy, and an *ens* such as would stand in the long run. The real, then, is that which, sooner or later, information and reasoning would finally result in, and which is therefore independent of the vagaries of me and you. Thus, the very origin of the conception of reality shows that this conception essentially involves the notion of a *COMMUNITY,* without definite limits, and capable of an indefinite increase of knowledge. And so those two series of cognitions—the real and the unreal—consist of those which, at a time sufficiently future, the community will always continue to reaffirm; and of those which, under the same conditions, will ever after be denied. Now, a proposition whose falsity can never be discovered, and the error of which therefore is absolutely incognizable, contains, upon our principle, absolutely no error. Consequently, that which is thought in these cognitions is the real, as it really is. There is nothing, then, to prevent our knowing outward things as they really are, and it is most likely that we do thus know them in numberless cases, although we can never be absolutely certain of doing so in any special case.

Source: From "Some Consequences of Four Incapacities," in *Peirce on Signs* (1991), pp. 81–82.

neo-pragmatists and the original pragmatists; he finds them failing to deliver on their promise of incremental improvement in the management of the world through a process of inquiry with uncertain results. Their prideful certainty that uncertainty would deliver the goods might have been usefully tempered with a dose of Niebuhr's neo-Calvinist humility and Adams's neo-Catholic discouragement as to the ability of the human mind to impose unity on human experience.

In *Community Denied: The Wrong Turn of Pragmatic Liberalism* (1998) and other studies, the author of this essay reads Peirce as balanced between certainty and uncertainty in a way that suggests a different approach for the historian of ideas than Rorty's self-consciously ironic acceptance of ideas without foundations, different from but not inconsistent with Diggins's use of conversation over context to find ideas valid or invalid. Also not inconsistent with Hollinger's study of discourse or Kloppenberg's salvage operations, this approach does differ on the question of which pragmatist is most worth dredging up. James and Dewey, according to this account, misled later liberal social thinkers, including historians, by surrendering Peirce's rigorously logical commitment to truth as correspondence between a sign and the object it represents. (See the accompanying extract, which shows the philosopher reasoning his way toward certainty as to the possibility of truth even though it must always be uncertain that any particular idea is true.) James and Dewey, abandoning Peirce's logical precision, so emphasized the notion of uncertainty that some of their later adherents eventually interpreted pragmatism as a precursor of postmodernist theory, with its exhilarating but self-contradictory certainty that no knowledge is certain. Historians of ideas troubled by postmodernists' idea that historical objectivity is impossible may be interested to study the original pragmatism of Peirce, with its logical balance between certainty and uncertainty and its reasoned conclusion that objective truth is real even though we can never be sure in any particular instance that we have attained it. If Peirce is right, then the historian of ideas can not only aim at getting the story straight but at telling it in a way that captures whatever that story possesses of irony or any other dramatic quality that may improve humanity's ability to imagine the complexity of its situation.

See also **Cultural Modernism** *(volume 1);* **Poststructuralism and Postmodernism; The Struggle for the Academy; Constitutional Thought** *(volume 2);* **The Scientific Ideal; The Humanities; The Social Sciences;** *and other articles in this section.*

BIBLIOGRAPHY

Collins, Stephen A., and James Hoopes. "Anthony Giddens and Charles Sanders Peirce: History, Theory, and a Way Out of the Linguistic Cul-de-Sac." *Journal of the History of Ideas* 56 (October 1995): 625–650.

Diggins, John Patrick. *The Promise of Pragmatism: Modernism and the Crisis of Knowledge and Authority.* Chicago, 1994.

Higham, John, and Paul K. Conkin, eds. *New Directions in American Intellectual History.* Baltimore, 1979.

Hoopes, James. "Objectivity *and* Relativism Affirmed: Historical Knowledge and the Philosophy of Charles S. Peirce." *American Historical Review* 98 (December 1993): 1545–1555.

Kloppenberg, James. *Uncertain Victory: Social Democracy and Progressivism in European and American Thought, 1870–1920.* New York, 1986.

Lovejoy, Arthur O. *The Great Chain of Being: A Study of the History of an Idea.* 1936. Reprint, Cambridge, Mass., 1964.

Miller, Perry. *The New England Mind: The Seventeenth Century.* 1939. Reprint, Cambridge, Mass., 1954.

———. *The New England Mind: From Colony to Province.* 1953. Reprint, Boston, 1961.

Peirce, Charles Sanders. *Peirce on Signs: Writings on Semiotic.* Edited by James Hoopes. Chapel Hill, N.C., 1991.

Wilson, Daniel J. *Arthur O. Lovejoy and the Quest for Intelligibility.* Chapel Hill, N.C., 1980.

BIOGRAPHY

Scott E. Casper

Biography has existed since ancient times, long used to teach lessons in character and to inculcate political or religious ideas through the life story of a noteworthy individual. Historical biography developed as a distinct branch of the genre in the eighteenth century, when Voltaire's histories of Charles XII (1730) and Louis XIV (1751) and William Robertson's *History of the Reign of Emperor Charles V* (1769) made monarchs' lives into the organizing devices for historical epochs. More than the "life and times" model of historical biography, the "life and works" approach has characterized the biographies of intellectual and cultural figures, whose ideas and productions (writings, speeches, performances) loom larger than their political, military, or social actions. The relationship between life and works is a recurring problem for biographers. Some practice a form of biographical literary criticism, which employs the life story to comprehend the works. Others analyze the subject's works to offer insight, often psychological, on the life.

For intellectual and cultural historians, the challenge of biography has been the problem of the individual. Like other scholarly biographers, they strive to make sense of the particular subject, choosing which contexts matter most and deciding how to connect the subject's life and works to those contexts. Biographers' choices owe much to their own contexts, both within and beyond the historical profession and historiographical debate. Equally important, social and cultural historians since the 1960s have challenged the significance of the individual and the integrity of the self. The linguistic turn in cultural history, the expansion of historical study beyond "great men," and an emphasis on the lives of ordinary individuals have all forced intellectual and cultural historians to reassess the subjects, methods, and topics of biography.

ANTECEDENTS OF INTELLECTUAL AND CULTURAL BIOGRAPHY

Treating the Life and Works The English critic and lexicographer Samuel Johnson laid the foundations of literary and intellectual biography in his *Lives of the Poets* (1779–1781). Johnson added "valuative criticism of the works to the traditional components of characterization and chronology" and "cleared the way for biographical approaches to reading literary texts" (Cafarelli, p. 47). Johnson's biographies and the biographical principles expressed in his *Rambler* and *Idler* essays also suggested the imperative that biographers illuminate their subjects' individuality through those private habits and traits that distinguished one man from another. James Boswell's *Life of Johnson* (1791) exemplified this dictum, even if it revealed Johnson the man far more than it treated his literary works.

For much of the nineteenth century, Anglo-American intellectual and literary biography consisted largely of the compendious "lives and writings" of ministers and authors. Most religious biographies sought to commemorate the services of recently deceased ministers and the piety of ordinary Christians, and to inculcate religious principles and humility in the reader. These "memoirs" often included copious excerpts from their subjects' sermons, letters, or diaries, but little analysis of these writings. However, the biographies of earlier religious figures—especially of the Puritan divine Cotton Mather—became a staging ground for contemporary debates over America's intellectual and theological past and present. "Lives and letters" of authors came in several varieties. Some employed a thin biographical narrative to connect relatively undigested (though often bowdlerized) mountains of correspondence: these works were compiled more than composed, often by a relative or literary executor. Works such as John Gibson Lockhart's life of Walter Scott offered familiar glimpses into the lives of noted literati, à la Boswell. Another approach, exemplified by the novelist Elizabeth Gaskell's *Life of Charlotte Brontë* (1857), took biography as literary art and added a psychological dimension. In the United States, few literary biographies appeared before 1880: exceptions included Pierre M. Irving's *Life and Letters of Washington Irving* (1862–1864) in the compendious mode and William Hickling Prescott's 1834 *Life of Charles Brockden Brown* (in Jared Sparks's Library of American Biography series) in a literary-critical vein reminiscent of articles in the *North American Review*.

The last decades of the nineteenth century witnessed a new, more analytical form of literary biography. The English statesman and literary critic John Morley wrote lives of Burke, Voltaire, Rousseau, and Diderot that "marked the first firm welding of literary biography and intellectual history" by situating their subjects within the intellectual context of their times. In 1878, Morley launched the English Men of Letters series, "pocket-sized monographs" that treated the lives and works of individual authors analytically, without the masses of documents that critics argued had burdened the "lives and letters" approach (Altick, pp. 181–182). Morley's series inspired Houghton Mifflin's American Men of Letters series, begun in 1881 and edited by Charles Dudley Warner, in which the lives of authors comprised a literary history of the nation. Many of the biographers considered their subjects as representatives of broader literary milieus: Horace Scudder placed his Noah Webster into the context of early national literature, and Henry Beers presented Nathaniel Parker Willis as the exemplar of the antebellum world of sentimentalist writing. As a whole, the American Men of Letters series offered a critique of contemporary realist literature and championed an earlier romanticism, much derided by the 1880s. By the turn of the twentieth century, the biographical approach had become a significant means of explaining the works and ideas of intellectual and literary figures.

The Individual in Biography   Expressing the Romantic interest in extraordinary individuals, Thomas Carlyle and Ralph Waldo Emerson argued that biography ought to do more than narrate facts or compile documents. Carlyle's *On Heroes, Hero-Worship, and the Heroic in History* (1840) popularized the Hegelian idea that men of genius propelled human history. For Carlyle, the biographer needed to answer two central questions about his subject: "What and how produced was the effect of society on him? And what and how produced was his effect on society?" In *Representative Men* (1850), Emerson eschewed the "external biography" of families, domestic lives, and chronological facts in favor of the "interior" dimensions that made subjects unique and uniquely representative of the spirit of their times. By century's end, scholars influenced by theories of social and economic determinism questioned the Romantic preoccupation with the heroic individual in history. For instance, the subtitle of Justin Winsor's scholarly biography of Columbus (1891) contended that the explorer merely "received and imparted the spirit of discovery." The individual, in this formulation, became the product but not the shaper of his age.

Psychobiography explained the individual as the product of psychological factors, marking a change from both Romantic hero worship and the social-scientific approach. Sigmund Freud's *Leonardo da Vinci: A Study in Psychosexuality* (1910), the first major attempt at biography based on psychoanalysis, has been much criticized not just for its reliance on theories of neurotic regression to explain Leonardo's late turn toward science but also for its insufficient scholarship in history and art history. Through the first half of the twentieth century, popular biographies routinely drew on psychology, often to debunk rather than to understand their subjects. Erik Erikson moved psychohistory forward by asserting "that social influences on the individual are just as relevant as biological and familial ones and that the individual grows and develops rather than 'repeats'" (Arzt, p. 8). Nonetheless, psychobiography remains suspect to many historians, at least in part because many past subjects left far too little evidence for the biographer to draw persuasive psychological conclusions.

BIOGRAPHY AND INTELLECTUAL HISTORY

The History of Ideas Approach   The traditional approach to intellectual biography stems from the "history of ideas" method of intellectual history. In such biography, as Hannah Lavi Jaher and Frederic Cople Jaher have explained, "the hero's place in a chain of consciousness is located by the relationship of that thinker's ideas to those of predecessors, contemporaries, and successors" (p. 609). Personal background matters insofar as it affected the subject's thought and appears only or primarily in the first chapter. Intellectual biographies in the "history of ideas" mode generally proceed chronologically, registering change over time through the subject's writings. Explanation and explication of those writings are paramount. To the extent that the biographer considers the subject's milieu, it consists of other thinkers and their ideas, especially within the intellectual communities the subject inhabited. This mode of intellectual history rose to prominence in the 1940s and 1950s, as the earlier alliance between intellectual and social history—forged in their common challenge to "history as past politics"—collapsed (Darnton, p. 329). In his first volume of *The New England Mind* (1939), Perry Miller was among the leading intellectual historians who elevated ideas above and apart from their social context. In *American Renaissance* (1941), Miller's contemporary F. O. Matthiessen moved literary history in a similar direction. Matthiessen examined the work of five major mid-nineteenth-century writers by exploring their treatment of great ideas and their connections to each other and to the literary giants of the past, Shakespeare and Milton.

In "history of ideas" biographies of late-nineteenth- and twentieth-century intellectuals, the communities are the universities and professional disciplines in which they worked, and the principal context of these subjects' work is the history of philosophy. Thus Bruce Kuklick considered Josiah Royce's intellectual "connection to the tradition of philosophy at Harvard which extends from at least 1870 to the present" (p. 3). Here Harvard became a crucible of ideas more than a flesh-and-blood setting of social and professional activity or rivalry. These biographers, many of them philosophers by discipline, sought to rescue their subjects from a tendency in intellectual history and American studies that reached back to Vernon L. Parrington's *Main Currents in American Thought* (1927–1930) and similar works: the search for an "American mind." Particularly because that native intellectual trajectory emphasized pragmatism and enterprise (and made Benjamin Franklin its founding hero), it was susceptible to oversimplification. Writing in 1972, Kuklick noted that "intellectual historians . . . have generally been unconcerned with philosophy altogether," merely equating "pragmatism with the politics of Franklin Roosevelt's Brains Trust" or placing American figures into a story of the American mind. Although "sure that [Royce's] personal life influenced his writing" and that "thought must be understood within the social contexts in which it arises," Kuklick argued that "the major stimulus

to work in philosophy has always been previous or contemporary work in philosophy" and interpreted Royce's writings primarily in light of "the influence and writing of his fellow scholars" and of their place in a Kantian tradition (pp. 1–4). A variant of the "history of ideas" biography eschews chronological explication of the subject's works in favor of an opening chapter on the life and career and subsequent chapters that treat particular works or themes synchronically. The philosopher Gerald E. Myers employed this structure in *William James: His Life and Thought* (1986), as did the historian Joan Shelley Rubin in *Constance Rourke and American Culture* (1980). Rubin wrote that "this thematic structure, rather than a biographical approach, reflects the view that Rourke's contributions should be regarded as a whole, that she did not change very much once she began writing about American subjects" (p. xiv).

Social and Psychological Dimensions Many intellectual biographers widen the contextual frame. One recurring question is whether or how an individual was representative of the larger milieu, a version of the "American mind" issue. Moving beyond his early "history of ideas" work, Perry Miller in *Jonathan Edwards* (1949) argued that "no writer ever emerged more directly out of the passions, the feuds, and the anxieties of his society" (p. xxx), but that Edwards's relationship to that society was ironic, attempting to "protect himself" against the "clutch" of his surroundings. Consequently Edwards was misunderstood by his contemporaries as well as by twentieth-century historians such as Parrington, who made Edwards the Puritanical, pre-modern foil of Benjamin Franklin. In the depression years of the 1930s, "a generation responsive to the aesthetics of paradox and ambiguity as well as to the doctrines of original sin and the necessity of transforming grace" had rediscovered Edwards (Donald Weber, in Miller, p. xi). Like the neo-orthodox "critical realist" Reinhold Niebuhr in the 1930s, Miller's Edwards was a Jeremiah, an American thinker more modern than previous scholars had suggested—hence Miller's chapter epigraphs from Keynes, Kafka, T. S. Eliot, and other modern thinkers.

More commonly, intellectual biographers portray their subjects as representatives of larger intellectual milieus. In the mind of Frederick C. Dahlstrand's Amos Bronson Alcott "flowed every major intellectual current that shaped American ideas and culture": the clashes among Lockean sensationalism, transcendental idealism, and orthodox

Christianity; the "nineteenth-century synthesis of evangelical religion with Enlightenment rationalism" (pp. 11–12). What separates this work from "history of ideas" biography is Dahlstrand's emphasis on the rapid social and economic transformations that New England—and Alcott's own boyhood village of Wolcott, Connecticut—experienced in the Early Republic. New England's capitalist transformation is critical also to Mary Kupiec Cayton's 1989 biography of Emerson's first four decades. Cayton originally hoped to "foreground" that context and situate Emerson within it, but eventually she produced a different sort of work: "The central question . . . evolved over the years from 'How can we put social history and literary criticism together' to 'How much do intellectuals have the power to act as transformative agents within society, and how much are they inevitably shaped by the circumstances of the age?'" (p. ix–x). The latter question echoed Thomas Carlyle's fundamental questions of biography. But it also reflected the literary-critical new historicist movement of the 1980s, which examined how literature could at once overtly challenge and subtly reinforce the social order in which it was produced.

Like Cayton, Robert D. Richardson embarked upon an intellectual biography of Emerson only to change his focus. Richardson set out to write a study, like his earlier *Henry Thoreau: A Life of the Mind* (1986), of how Emerson's reading influenced his writing. Ultimately Richardson's *Emerson: The Mind on Fire* (1995) emphasized "personal and social life," including psychological dimensions. Beginning with a scene in which Emerson opens his wife's coffin fourteen months after her death, Richardson established the tone for his story of Emerson's "intellectual odyssey" (p. 3). Intellectual psychobiography also characterized work on William James by Cushing Strout, who argued that "the intellectual and the emotional urgencies that go into the complex making of *The Varieties of Religious Experience*" were "best understood in the light of his psychobiography as it relates concretely to his relationship with his father" ("Pluralistic Identity," p. 141). However, Strout also insisted on "the need to confront James as a philosopher with philosophical questions," for no "historical questioning," even psychohistorical, could replace the comprehension that "ideas have an autonomous rationality and integrity of their own" (Arzt, p. 21; Strout, "Ego Psychology," pp. 287–288).

Industrialization, America's rise to world power, and the professionalization of scholarly disciplines provide the social context for other intellectual biographies of twentieth-century subjects, such as Ellen Nore's *Charles A. Beard: An Intellectual Biography* (1983) and Robert B. Westbrook's *John Dewey and American Democracy* (1991). Westbrook was especially attentive to Dewey's multiple contexts. For example, Dewey's radical thought was nurtured in the 1890s by his presence in Chicago during the Pullman strike and other social ferment and by his association with Jane Addams, but he expressed it only circumspectly because the administration of his institution, the University of Chicago, had dismissed an economics professor for his radical views. The world wars, the Asian revolutions of the 1920s, and the socialist politics of the 1930s all entered into Westbrook's narrative, even as Dewey's intellectual journey remained in the foreground. In other biographies, notably Dorothy Ross's *G. Stanley Hall: The Psychologist as Prophet* (1972), subjects were the vehicles through which the histories of particular social theories and intellectual professions were told.

Widening the Scope of Intellectual Biography

Developments within the historical profession in the 1960s and 1970s helped change who became the subjects of intellectual biography and how such biographies were written. In the wake of challenges to consensus and "great man" history, numerous subdisciplines flourished: labor history, African American history, the history of women. Some of these had venerable traditions but were now redefined. The new labor and working-class history, for instance, owed much to E. P. Thompson's *The Making of the English Working Class* (1964) and other studies of the politics of cultural expression and the experience of rank-and-file workers. As James R. Barrett noted in 1984, this emphasis "has propelled the current generation of labor historians away from the individual and in the direction of the crowd," reflecting "an apparent methodological bias against biography as a way of understanding labor history." Bucking that trend, Nick Salvatore's *Eugene V. Debs: Citizen and Socialist* (1982) offered a portrait that was grounded in Debs's own community and in the larger labor battles of his time but that focused on how Debs's ideas symbolized "the clash between democratic republican values and the rising corporate capitalist political economy" (Barrett, p. 77). No less than Westbrook's Dewey, Salvatore's Debs was a social thinker worthy of intellectual biography, even if that biography required a social context. Similarly, Eric Foner's *Tom Paine and Revolutionary America* (1976) situated its subject within a Thompsonian frame: the social unrest and radical mass politics in the revolutionary capital became an essential context for the development of Paine's own radicalism (and an antecedent to the artisan republicanism that 1980s historians of nineteenth-century America identified).

The growth of African American history and women's history offered new subjects for intellectual biography. Waldo E. Martin's *The Mind of Frederick Douglass* (1984) sought to assess how, and how successfully, the most frequent African American biographical subject resolved "the dynamic tension between his identities as a Negro and as an American" (p. ix). Given that modern African American historical studies emerged in connection with the social movements of the 1960s, and that the historical experience of African American intellectuals was always intertwined with the "dilemma of being black in nineteenth-century America," a purely "history of ideas" approach to African American intellectual biography was impossible from the start (p. xi). Similar conditions applied to most intellectual biographies of American women, early exemplified by Kathryn Kish Sklar's *Catharine Beecher: A Study in American Domesticity* (1976). Beecher's "female identity constantly intruded into her consciousness and her career," excluding her from authority within the church and confining her "to a marginal social status when she sought a central one" (p. xiii). Perhaps because Beecher—unlike Douglass, Emerson, or the twentieth-century intellectual figures—had not had a previous modern biographer, Sklar's book performed several roles, situating Beecher's ideas within the narrative of her life and experiences as well as within the history of the domestic ideology that Beecher helped to shape.

Debs, Paine, Douglass, and Beecher were all known as thinkers and writers as well as activists in their own day, and all left numerous articles, books, pamphlets, and speeches. In terms of reputation and sources, therefore, they lent themselves to intellectual biography. Another trend within historical scholarship of the 1970s—the study of *mentalité*, or the intellectual dimensions of everyday life—raised the possibility that ordinary people could also receive intellectual biographies if some revealing source survived. The most prominent such work appeared in European history: Carlo Ginzburg's *The Cheese and the Worms* (1980), which reconstructed the worldview of a sixteenth-century Italian miller through confessional documents. Within American historiography, significant examples include Laurel Thatcher Ulrich's *A Midwife's Tale* (1990), a biography crafted from the diary of Martha Ballard of Maine, and Alfred F. Young's *The*

Shoemaker and the Tea Party: Memory and the American Revolution (1999), constructed from an elderly veteran's published memoirs. Both of these works also relied heavily on deep social-history research; both might be called social as well as (or perhaps more than) intellectual biographies.

BIOGRAPHY AND CULTURAL HISTORY

Defining "Cultural Biography" In *The Romance of Real Life*, his 1994 "cultural biography" of Charles Brockden Brown, Steven Watts defined this form by what it was not:

> It avoids the hoary "life and times" approach of the traditional historian, which assumes too much about each partner in this analytical construct. It also rejects the "intellectual biography" model, which frequently degenerates into a treatment of isolated, formal, and abstract ideas with little concern for their material and social connections. Finally, and rather obviously, such a study takes issue with the current postmodern dismissal of biography, in which the importance of the single life has disintegrated under an onslaught of epistemes, language codes, and intertextuality. With the postmodern linguistic invasion—here "words speak people rather than the other way around"—the author has become an inevitable casualty.

The three "principles" of Watts's study suggested what cultural biography was. First, Watts situated Brown's life and career within "struggles to 'construct' new meanings in social, political, and personal life" in the transformative years of the Early Republic. Second, he sought "to analyze Brown's writings in terms of an interplay of text, context, and self, with each factor recognized as mutually shaping the others." Finally, drawing on both the concept of cultural hegemony and the Frankfurt school, he was concerned "with political and cultural power and the way it is shaped, achieved, and internalized" (pp. xv–xvii).

The term "cultural biography" came into vogue in the 1990s, but most cultural biographers attempted only one of Watts's objectives. Hence Peter Conn explained the subtitle of *Pearl S. Buck: A Cultural Biography* (1996): "I have tried to situate Pearl Buck's career in the many contexts that are needed to understand her development and her significance. This has involved a continuous act of negotiation between her life and the social and political circumstances that surrounded her" (p. xviii). Although Conn discussed many of Buck's stories and novels, the book belonged primarily to the "life and times" category. Carolyn L. Karcher subtitled *The*

First Woman in the Republic "A Cultural Biography of Lydia Maria Child" (1994) to contrast it with "the traditional literary biography": "I have attempted to view nineteenth-century America through the window of Child's mind." Hoping "to furnish a potential model for analyzing the works of other neglected literary figures," Karcher examined many of Child's writings closely, making this a "life and works" biography within a framework of political and social debate, especially about race and gender (p. xv).

The best-known American "cultural biography" of the 1990s, David S. Reynolds's *Walt Whitman's America* (1995), retold Whitman's life and literary works within the context of New York's vibrant popular culture. Reminiscent of Reynolds's *Beneath the American Renaissance* (1998), which examined how canonical antebellum literature drew from contemporary popular, ephemeral genres, the heart of *Walt Whitman's America* lay in four central chapters on public performances, eroticism and gender, science and religion, and the visual arts.

Biographies of cultural figures—authors, artists, popular-culture heroes—abounded in the second half of the twentieth century, but most were not themselves works of cultural history. As cultural history and American studies developed after World War II their methods of treating individual subjects changed as well, with biography in cultural history reflecting different approaches to the larger field.

"Myth and Symbol" Biography and Its Successors

In the 1950s, the field of American studies was dominated by the "myth and symbol" school of analysis, which sought to identify how particular images—the frontier, the machine in the garden, the Brooklyn Bridge—had reflected larger national moods or values at particular moments. John William Ward applied this approach in *Andrew Jackson: Symbol for an Age* (1955), which argued that "the various concepts which give substance to the abstraction, nationalism"—defined here as Nature (the yeoman farmer), Providence (God's special concern for America), and Will (self-determination)—"were articulated in terms of Andrew Jackson, so that Andrew Jackson easily became a counter for the ideas themselves" (p. 6). Unlike earlier delineations of the American mind or "main currents," Ward's book examined images of Jackson created by others, rather than the subject's own speeches or writings. By the mid-1960s historians criticized "myth and symbol" scholarship for the abstraction of its arguments and particularly for its inattention to the power relations that ostensibly national images ex-

pressed or masked. Later variants of "myth and symbol" biography emphasized the political work of cultural imagery. For instance, echoing Richard Slotkin's trilogy about America's frontier myth, Garry Wills's *John Wayne's America: The Politics of Celebrity* (1997) argued that Wayne's screen persona offered "Manifest Destiny on the hoof" and "embodied . . . a politics of gender (masculine), ideology (patriotism), character (self-reliance), and responsibility" (pp. 17, 29).

"Man and image" biographies also date back to the 1950s, when Marcus Cunliffe's *George Washington: Man and Monument* sought to separate "myth and man" and explain how the Washington myth "of suffocating dullness" emerged in the first place (p. 3). Cunliffe concluded that "the real man and his legend have important elements in common," and that Washington's very demeanor—rooted in the classical codes of public behavior appropriate for eighteenth-century gentlemen—contributed to his marble image (p. 151). A. H. Saxon's *P. T. Barnum: The Legend and the Man* (1989) had a similar goal: to explore "the frequent antagonism between the Barnum of popular imagination, the wearer of 'horns & hoofs,' and Barnum as he really was or wished to be" (p. 3). In Barnum's case, the self-creation of legends occurred not in his demeanor but in his various autobiographies; Saxon aimed to get behind the public persona, partly by studying Barnum's previously unexamined private life.

Some "man and image" biographies, especially of twentieth-century subjects, explained how culture industries helped create public personae. For example, Charles J. Maland's *Chaplin and American Culture* (1989) argued that "a Chaplin *star image*, fashioned by Chaplin himself, by certain ideological and signifying practices within the film industry, by the press, and by representatives of other social institutions, was established and then evolved in American culture from World War I to the present" (p. xiv). Maland analyzed how "four kinds of media texts"—Chaplin's films, studio promotional materials, press publicity, and criticism and commentary—intertwined to shape the image. Although not a biography per se, *Chaplin and American Culture* employed a chronological narrative and discussed the interplay between events in Chaplin's life and their portrayal in the media. Wills's *John Wayne's America* offered a kindred examination of how the movie industry made "John Wayne" and how Wayne himself ultimately embraced the image that had been created for him. For an earlier period, Patricia Cline Cohen's *The Murder of Helen Jewett: The Life and Death of a Prostitute in Nineteenth-*

Century New York (1998) traced how the new penny press created Jewett's image after her death. Using the social historian's tools and sources as well as Jewett's own extant letters, Cohen revealed another Helen Jewett and placed both the image and Jewett's own self-fashioning into the context of emerging concepts of gender and sexuality.

Who Fashions the "Self"? Invoking the linguistic turn in cultural criticism, Marjorie Garber has asked, "If there is no 'self,' how can there be biography or autobiography?" (p. 175). In 1983, as historians were just beginning to consider the meaning of semiotic and poststructuralist theory for their discipline, David E. Nye used these theories to challenge biography directly. Traditional biographers and historians, Nye asserted in *The Invented Self: An Anti-Biography, from Documents of Thomas A. Edison,* serve "to assure modern people of the solidity of the individual and of the individual's unproblematic relation to an orderly flow of events. Their work embodies the myth that these individuals are (or were) not divided selves who remained essentially unknowable in their endless variations, but rather beings whose lives may be recovered" (p. 9). Nye thus rejected "the existence of" Edison and the attempt "to recapture him in language" (p. 16). Nor did Nye accept the underlying tenet of "man and image" biographies, that the biographer unmasks public images to reveal a private "reality" beneath, because the "private" self possesses no more inherent reality than the "false front which [biographers believe] must be penetrated" (p. 24–25). Instead, Nye focused on the documents—or "texts"—that historians might use to reconstruct Edison's existence: Edison's library, notebooks, and business records; the physical sites of his home and laboratory; discussions of him in the popular press. The chapters of *The Invented Self* did not reconcile these texts into a chronological narrative but treated categories of documents "as parts of discourses" in the broader culture: ideas about evolution, science, and alchemy, or discourses of gender and privacy. "If any of the documents are taken as 'signs of the self,'" Nye wrote, "other documents appear to be contrary 'signs' of that 'self.' Such oppositions are not accidental, but inhere in the very nature of signification. Taken seriously, they explode biogaphy" (pp. 21, 24).

The linguistic turn did not explode biography, but it did influence how some historians approached the genre. Most relevant for biographers, the concept of "self-fashioning" questions the notion of an essential self and considers the life itself as a text, not just written by the biographer but also constructed by the subject within specific cultural contexts. In *Sojourner Truth: A Life, a Symbol* (1996), Nell Irvin Painter showed how Truth created her own public image through *cartes-de-visite* and cabinet cards (souvenir cards with her photograph on them). "Truth's images may appear to be unmediated, the essence of her real self, but in fact they were carefully arranged" to convey "motherly womanliness," a bourgeois image associated with white women but unusual in visual presentations of African Americans (pp. 187, 196). Ormond Seavey's 1988 *Becoming Benjamin Franklin: The Autobiography and the Life* examined both Franklin's great literary achievement and his "creation of himself" as products of a larger "mode of consciousness," a "self-consistent assemblage of beliefs, attitudes, and mental reflexes, distinguishable from 'personality type' in that its style and signature reflect some engendering cultural situation" (pp. 5, 99). Seavey's book, conceived as "a contribution to a growing body of studies on the consciousness of the eighteenth century," attributed Franklin's self-fashioning to "Enlightenment ideas about the self" (pp. x–xi). Steven Watts—in *The Magic Kingdom: Walt Disney and the American Way of Life* (1997) as well as in his work on Charles Brockden Brown—has examined how the self is always historically contingent and constructed: in Disney's case, through cultivation of a small-town personal history at odds with his actual boyhood and with an increasingly urban America; in Brown's case, through the rise of "liberal," self-interested selfhood in the Early Republic. Watts's biographical sketches in *The Republic Reborn: War and the Making of Liberal America, 1790–1820* (1987), as well as many of the essays in *Through a Glass Darkly: Reflections on Personal Identity in Early America* (Ronald Hoffman et al., 1997), presented the emergence of new modes of selfhood—or the attempt to maintain older ones—as fraught with psychological and social tension.

COLLECTIVE AND COMPOSITE BIOGRAPHY

Cultural and intellectual historians have also employed collective and composite biography to limn a historical period or suggest the worldview of a larger group. Collective biography, in which different chapters generally treat different subjects, has more ancient roots than the biography of individuals. For cultural historians, it offers the opportunity to reveal multiple aspects of one period or group. Joseph J. Ellis's *After the Revolution: Profiles of Early American Culture* (1979) examined the lives and careers of the artist Charles Willson Peale, the novelist Hugh Henry Brackenridge, the dramatist William Dunlap, and the educator and linguist Noah Webster in order to reveal "how complicated and paradoxical the adjustment to modern institutions and values really was" (p. xiii). Watts's *The Republic Reborn* made a similar argument about this period: brief biographies of figures as wide-ranging as John Adams, the physician Benjamin Rush, and the enterprising moralist Mason Locke Weems demonstrated that the categories "republican" and "liberal," central to 1980s debates about early national political culture, were far less distinct in the minds of real Americans than in the writings of late-twentieth-century historians and political scientists. Daniel Walker Howe's *The Political Culture of the American Whigs* (1979) gave a multilayered face to the party long known only for its opposition to Andrew Jackson's Democrats. Through biographies of a dozen Whigs, Howe constructed an intellectual history of a party that included modernizers and evangelicals, businessmen and Burkean conservatives—categories that might provide a template for future studies of individual Whigs.

A different sort of collective biography traces change and continuity over time, through subjects who inhabit not the same few decades but a longer historical period. In Christopher Grasso's *A Speaking Aristocracy: Transforming Public Discourse in Eighteenth-Century Connecticut* (1999), six biographical treatments exemplified "the ways that learned men tried to shape the broader culture of eighteenth-century New England as the style, content, and social matrix of intellectual life and public communications evolved" (p. 2). Adding complexity to often simplistic frameworks such as "Puritan to Yankee," Grasso's biographies examined the place of individual learned men in a broader context of thought and its public expression—combining the approaches of cultural historian and the intellectual historian to discuss subjects once considered only the province of the latter.

Unlike collective biography, with its brief life studies of specific individuals, composite biography draws evidence from the lives of a variety of subjects in order to suggest the experience of a larger group. Composite biography is often associated with the social sciences and with quantitative social history, in which demographic data (for instance, about occupation, ethnicity, or age) help define the contours of collective experience. In cultural and intellectual history, composite biography employs the more humanistic artifacts of numerous subjects. Mary Kelley's *Private Woman, Public Stage: Literary Domesticity in Nineteenth-Century America* (1984) traced the experience of twelve popular women writers whose "female selves [were] unexpectedly transformed into public figures, economic providers, and creators of culture." Kelley's sources included her subjects' private papers *and* their published prose, which "inadvertently revealed to the public much of the woman's act in private" (pp. viii–ix). Chapters focused on specific aspects of the subjects' shared experience, such as their education and their ambivalence about fame, rather than on each individual writer.

What emerged was the intellectual biography of a group of women, whose experience was likely shared by other, less-renowned, women writers of their day. In *Victorian America and the Civil War* (1992), Anne C. Rose amassed "a set of substantially documented biographies brought together deliberately to explore the private dimensions of middle-class life." Rose chose seventy-five "white-collar" subjects, born between 1815 and 1837, who represented "diversity in terms of geographic region of residence, occupation (within the middle classes), and gender," who had left substantial writings, and most of whom had had biographies written about them (pp. 3–4). Like Kelley, Rose organized her study topically (religion, work, family, the Civil War); each chapter drew evidence from the lives of many subjects. Composite biographies offer insight into *mentalité*, not just quantifiable characteristics.

Many historians have denigrated biography for its focus on individual subjects at the expense of larger social developments, and for its traditional emphasis on anecdote at the expense of analysis. This critique, leveled a century ago with the decline of Romantic history, reemerged with the ascendancy of social history in the 1960s. For cultural and intellectual historians, however, biography invites new methods of narration and new approaches to analyzing sources—ever more so as the very categories of individual and self, life and works, text and context, have become problematic.

See also **Rhetoric and Belles Lettres** *(volume 1);* **Poststructuralism and Postmodernism** *(volume 2);* **Individualism and the Self; The Humanities; The Role of the Intellectual; Authorship, Intellectual Property, and Copyright; Books; Memory** *(in this volume); and other articles in this section.*

BIBLIOGRAPHY

Works about Biography as a Genre

Altick, Richard D. *Lives and Letters: A History of Literary Biography in England and America.* New York, 1969.

Amigoni, David. *Victorian Biography: Intellectuals and the Ordering of Discourse.* New York, 1993.

Cafarelli, Annette Wheeler. *Prose in the Age of Poets: Romanticism and Biographical Narrative from Johnson to De Quincey.* Philadelphia, 1990.

Casper, Scott E. *Constructing American Lives: Biography and Culture in Nineteenth-Century America.* Chapel Hill, N.C., 1999.

Cockshut, A. O. J. *Truth to Life: The Art of Biography in the Nineteenth Century.* New York, 1974.

Epstein, William H. *Recognizing Biography.* Philadelphia, 1987.

Epstein, William H., ed. *Contesting the Subject: Essays in the Postmodern Theory and Practice of Biography and Biographical Criticism.* West Lafayette, Ind., 1991.

Garber, Marjorie. "Postmodernism and the Possibility of Biography: Introduction." In *The Seductions of Biography,* edited by Mary Rhiel and David Suchoff. New York, 1996.

Garraty, John A. *The Nature of Biography.* New York, 1957.

Hoberman, Ruth. *Modernizing Lives: Experiments in English Biography, 1918–1939.* Carbondale, Ill., 1987.

O'Neill, Edward H. *A History of American Biography, 1800–1935.* Philadelphia, 1935.

Pachter, Marc, ed. *Telling Lives: The Biographer's Art.* Philadelphia, 1985.

See also the quarterly journal *Biography,* published by the Center for Biographical Research, University of Hawaii.

Biographies and Essays Quoted

Arzt, Donna. "Psychohistory and Its Discontents." *Biography* 1 (summer 1978): 1–36.

Barrett, James R. "American Socialism and Social Biography." *International Labor and Working-Class History,* no. 26 (fall 1984): 75–82.

Cayton, Mary Kupiec. *Emerson's Emergence: Self and Society in the Transformation of New England, 1800–1845.* Chapel Hill, N.C., 1989.

Conn, Peter. *Pearl S. Buck: A Cultural Biography.* Cambridge, U.K., 1996.

Cunliffe, Marcus. *George Washington: Man and Monument.* Rev. ed., New York, 1982.

Dahlstrand, Frederick C. *Amos Bronson Alcott: An Intellectual Biography.* Rutherford, N.J., 1982.

Darnton, Robert. "Intellectual and Cultural History." In *The Past before Us: Contemporary Historical Writing in the United States,* edited by Michael Kammen. Ithaca, N.Y., 1980.

Ellis, Joseph J. *After the Revolution: Profiles of Early American Culture.* New York, 1979.

Grasso, Christopher. *A Speaking Aristocracy: Transforming Public Discourse in Eighteenth-Century Connecticut.* Chapel Hill, N.C., 1999.

Jaher, Hannah Lavi, and Frederic Cople Jaher. "William James Resurrected and Revisited." *Reviews in American History* 15 (December 1987): 609–614.

Karcher, Carolyn L. *The First Woman in the Republic: A Cultural Biography of Lydia Maria Child*. Durham, N.C., 1994.

Kelley, Mary. *Private Woman, Public Stage: Literary Domesticity in Nineteenth-Century America*. New York, 1984.

Kuklick, Bruce. *Josiah Royce: An Intellectual Biography*. Indianapolis, Ind., 1972.

Maland, Charles J. *Chaplin and American Culture: The Evolution of a Star Image*. Princeton, N.J., 1989.

Martin, Waldo E., Jr. *The Mind of Frederick Douglass*. Chapel Hill, N.C., 1984.

Miller, Perry. *Jonathan Edwards*. 1949. Reprint, with an introduction by Donald Weber, Amherst, Mass., 1981.

Nye, David E. *The Invented Self: An Anti-Biography, from Documents of Thomas A. Edison*. Odense, Denmark, 1983.

Painter, Nell Irvin. *Sojourner Truth: A Life, A Symbol*. New York, 1996.

Richardson, Robert D., Jr. *Emerson: The Mind on Fire*. Berkeley, Calif., 1995.

Rose, Anne C. *Victorian America and the Civil War*. New York, 1992.

Rubin, Joan Shelley. *Constance Rourke and American Culture*. Chapel Hill, N.C., 1980.

Saxon, A. H. *P. T. Barnum: The Legend and the Man*. New York, 1989.

Seavey, Ormond. *Becoming Benjamin Franklin: The* Autobiography *and the Life*. University Park, Pa., 1988.

Sklar, Kathryn Kish. *Catharine Beecher: A Study in American Domesticity*. New York, 1976.

Strout, Cushing. "Ego Psychology and the Historian." *History and Theory* 7, no. 3 (1968): 281–297.

———. "The Pluralistic Identity of William James: A Psycho-historical Reading of *The Varieties of Religious Experience*." *American Quarterly* 23 (May 1971): 135–152.

Ward, John William. *Andrew Jackson: Symbol for an Age*. London, 1955.

Watts, Steven. *The Romance of Real Life: Charles Brockden Brown and the Origins of American Culture*. Baltimore, 1994.

Wills, Garry. *John Wayne's America: The Politics of Celebrity*. New York, 1997.

MYTH AND SYMBOL

David W. Noble

"Myth-symbol" is a term associated with a particular group of scholars who played an important role in establishing American studies as a new academic field between the 1930s and the 1960s. The myth-symbol school appeared, therefore, as a response to the crisis of national identity caused by American entry into World War II. The cultural nostalgia of the school was so appealing to members of English and history departments that the term "myth-symbol" seemed almost synonymous with the growing discipline of American Studies between 1950 and 1965. The term also designates the civil religion of this group of scholars, who attempted to define what was essentially American, to locate its sacred origins in the early nineteenth century, and to preserve it as an inspiriting myth for the United States during its revolutionary transition from nationalism to internationalism and from monoculturalism to multiculturalism.

American studies has its roots at Yale University, Harvard University, and the University of Pennsylvania, which established graduate programs in this new field in the 1930s, and Princeton University, Brown University, New York University, and the Universities of Maryland, Minnesota, and Texas, which established graduate programs in the 1940s. During this decade and the 1950s, many undergraduate programs were also established across the country. A journal, the *American Quarterly,* began publication at the University of Minnesota in 1949, with the purpose of making research in this new field available to scholars. A national American Studies Association soon followed (1951), which, at first, held meetings across the United States every two years and then moved to an annual meeting. The scholars who attended these first meetings were primarily teachers of American literature and American history.

However, the most groundbreaking work took place at Minnesota, where the American studies program was constructed in 1943 by professors from the English department. The leader of this group, Tremaine McDowell, became the first chair of the American studies program. He asked two of the first graduates of the Harvard program in the history of American civilization—Henry Nash Smith and Leo Marx—to join Minnesota's English department and provide scholarly leadership for the American studies graduate program. When Leo Marx wrote about the leaders of this new academic field at the end of the 1960s, he included himself and four other Harvard graduates—Smith, Daniel Aaron, R. W. B. Lewis, and Charles Sanford. He also included three graduates of the Minnesota program—Allen Guttmann, Alan Trachtenberg, and John William Ward—who had studied there with Marx and Smith. In the 1960s these were the men who were most strongly identified as leaders of the myth-symbol school of American studies and who would spend their careers carving out a niche in this arena.

The vision of an American culture that Smith and Marx were teaching their graduate students was one which they had learned from their teachers at Harvard, particularly F. O. Matthiessen. In 1941 he had published *American Renaissance,* a study of the great literary figures Ralph Waldo Emerson, Henry David Thoreau, Herman Melville, Nathaniel Hawthorne, and Walt Whitman. It was Matthiessen's argument that these men had given the fullest expression to the new national culture that had begun to emerge in the 1830s. It had taken this long since the American Revolution and the political beginning of the nation in 1789 for America to escape the influence of European culture in general and English culture in particular.

Matthiessen believed in a metaphor of two worlds, a European Old World and an American New World. For him, an American Renaissance expressed the moment in which an American national culture escaped from lifeless European cultural forms and was free to express itself. This expression was organic; it was a complete unity of the good, true, and beautiful. Matthiessen believed that European culture was filled with complexities and contradictions. His perspective was influenced by the views of the (St. Louis–born) British poet T. S. Eliot, who argued that there was an English Renaissance at the time of William Shakespeare in which, for a brief moment, there was an English national culture that had organic unity. But, for Eliot, this moment was fleeting, and England had quickly fallen back into contradictions. For Eliot and for Matthiessen, the moment of the Renaissance also was spiritual, in contrast to the materialism that preceded and followed it. Because the American Renaissance that began in the 1830s and found its most wonderful literary expression in the 1850s was disintegrating in the 1860s, Matthiessen agreed with the writer Mark Twain that the 1870s were a Gilded Age when materialism and fragmentation replaced spirituality and unity.

Matthiessen lauded an American civilization that had existed only for about thirty years. But he eventually came to qualify this narrative. The 1920s and 1930s were characterized by an intense resurgence of political and cultural nationalism. By the 1890s many painters, musicians, and architects had been attracted to the experiments in artistic abstraction taking place in France, Italy, and Germany. They frequently studied in Europe until some, like the painter Thomas Hart Benton or the composer Aaron Copland, left for the renaissance that was taking place in the United States. These men agreed with the most influential history book in the 1930s, Charles and Mary Beard's *The Rise of American Civilization,* which proposed that the exceptionally spiritual American nation must be segregated from the corruption and materialism of all other nations. So, too, did Matthiessen, whose hope of a second American Renaissance in the 1930s was crushed when the political leaders of the United States were successful in replacing a national identity of isolation with the new identity of internationalism. In such a world, there was no possibility of a national culture that had organic unity.

American Renaissance was published as the United States entered World War II. Matthiessen wanted his readers to remember America when the good, true, and beautiful had been one. Since the reality of 1830 to 1860 no longer existed, Matthiessen requested that Americans think of this memory as a living myth. Like the living reality of 1830 to 1860, the myth found symbolic expression in all aspects of national experience. Politics and economics, painting and literature, had been symbolic expressions of the unified national culture. Now the

varied aspects of that culture would continue to be symbolic expressions of the unified mythic culture that had lost its reality in the 1860s.

Henry Nash Smith, one of Matthiessen's students, published *Virgin Land* in 1950. Like Matthiessen, Charles and Mary Beard, and the Beards' predecessor, the historian Frederick Jackson Turner, Smith assumed the existence of an empty landscape. In this tradition it was the state of nature that made it possible for Europeans to step out of their Old World culture and assume their new identity as Americans. Americans were the children of nature; Europeans were the children of culture. This tradition, of course, suppressed the existence of American Indian cultures, which had interacted with the North and South American landscapes for thousands of years. When Smith, like Matthiessen, looked at the American born of the national landscape, he saw neither Indians nor African Americans nor Mexican Americans. The people born of that landscape were all Anglo-Protestants, and they were all men.

This concept of a national people was not exclusive to the leaders of the United States. As the political science educator Benedict Anderson demonstrated in his *Imagined Communities* (1983), the idea of the modern nation was invented during the period from 1770 to 1830 on both sides of the Atlantic. The European and Euro-American middle classes were imagining the nation as a space free from both international and local patterns. They were imagining a nation with a homogeneous culture. The "new man," the citizen, who was replacing the category of subject, was an adult male. The metaphors of two worlds had its origins in the middle-class rejection of an old world of internationalism and localism and Eurpoeans' anticipated arrival in a new world, where there would be only national homogeneity.

For all modern nationalists, the dream of cultural independence and isolation was threatened by what they saw as a transnational industrial revolution. Industrialism and the rapid urbanization it caused seemed to imply an international landscape that was fragmented, materialistic, and more powerful than the national landscape. Smith, like Matthiessen, was working within the framework of bourgeois nationalism described by Anderson. Europeans had escaped internationalism and localism to become part of a homogeneous national culture that was the gift of their national landscape. But then industrialism had crossed the Atlantic and destroyed this homogeneity.

The particular complexity feared by Matthiessen and Smith was that of class division. According to the model of bourgeois nationalism described by Anderson, a people was imagined as a classless fraternity. But industrialism brought class divisions. In Smith's story, this national landscape had made possible an economy of equality with many small farmers. This economic truth was politically good and also was beautiful as it was presented in the various arts. Because this economic truth and political virtue were lost after the Civil War, one could keep the beauty of this world alive as one wrote elegies for the lost reality. These elegies could preserve the vanished reality as a myth that could be passed from generation to generation. In the midst of the chaos of the new international world, one could remember when there had been an organic unity and express that unity in literary forms.

The major texts of the myth-symbol school, therefore, would look only at the period of the American Renaissance. Both Smith and Leo Marx wrote articles in which they argued the superiority of humanistic American studies methodology to that of the social sciences. Both argued that the social sciences looked only at parts, and that the methodology of American studies was holistic. Smith and Marx, however, could only imagine applying a holistic methodology to that brief moment in the first half of the nineteenth century when a unified culture had existed: a holistic methodology, for them, also was superior to that of the social sciences because it, unlike the social sciences, could evoke the deep values, the spiritual core of a culture. Again, however, they were limited to the era between 1789 and 1865 because colonial culture had been part of European materialism and lacked a spiritual core of values and this also was true of America after the Civil War.

Myth-symbol scholars were not interested in Euro-American cultures before 1789 because they saw the colonies as part of an international culture that had its center in Europe. And they did not focus on the United States after 1865 because they believed the nation was slipping back into an international capitalist economy. Matthiessen, therefore, in *American Renaissance* had found the essence of the new but brief national culture expressed by his five literary figures. He had argued that there had been a popular culture that expressed the ideal of bourgeois nationalism—liberty, equality, and fraternity. But, for Matthiessen, and as Smith argued in *Virgin Land*, popular culture had been corrupted by the materialism of industrial capitalism. This was a reason not only to ignore the essentially un-

American popular culture that existed after the Civil War but also to segregate the purity of that pre–Civil War democracy as it had been expressed in the works of the great literary artists.

To find the truth, beauty, and goodness of the democratic popular culture that supposedly existed between 1830 and 1860, one must look to a few spiritual texts. The myth-symbol scholars wanted to guard the boundaries of a literary canon and preserve the organic unity supposedly expressed in a few canonical texts against the possibility of literary miscegenation. For Matthiessen and his students in the myth-symbol school, organic unity was to be found most fully in the texts of the American Renaissance, written by Anglo-Protestant men from the Northeast. This organic unity available to study by the holistic method of American studies would be lost if one considered novels by Anglo-Protestant men from the South or by Anglo-Protestant women from the North or South. And, of course, myth-symbol scholars could not imagine polluting the essential American identity embodied in the literary canon with texts written by American Indians, African Americans, Mexican Americans, Asian Americans, or Catholic and Jewish immigrants from Europe.

The use of the metaphor of two worlds to segregate the myth of the pure America of 1830 to 1860 was an added reason for the myth-symbol scholars to reject the social sciences. Between the 1880s and World War I, many cultural leaders had imagined the end of national isolation. For them, American participation in World War I would bring the United States into an international environment. Because historical writing seemed to have developed in the nineteenth century as an art form that imagined autonomous nations, social sciences became more important on both sides of the Atlantic in the decades before World War I. The social sciences could discuss transnational patterns of industrialization and urbanization without rejecting them as abnormal, alien corruptions. The decades between World Wars I and II, however, were characterized by a resurgence of national history and a rejection of the international outlook of the social sciences. The American civilization programs created in the 1930s were part of that resurgence. Then the successful international revolution of World War II destroyed the legitimacy of the isolationism implied in the term "American civilization" and restored the legitimacy of the comparative and international logic of the social sciences. It is instructive, then, that although the terms "myth" and "symbol" were a standard part of the vocabulary of anthropologists, the American studies scholars of the myth-symbol school never associated their research and writing with the discipline of anthropology—primarily because anthropologists were concerned with comparing the mythic patterns of different cultures while the members of the myth-symbol school wanted to protect the uniqueness and purity of a mid-nineteenth-century America.

Following Smith's *Virgin Land,* the next major text of the myth-symbol school was R. W. B. Lewis's *The American Adam* (1955). Like Matthiessen and Smith, this Yale University professor, once a student of Matthiessen's, believed that the landscape of the United States had given rise to a sacred, exceptional nation. Like his predecessors, Lewis excluded everyone living in the United States from the term "American" except Anglo-Protestant males from the Northeast. Like them, he excluded all the other nations of North and South America from the term "American." Like them, he found what he called a "native American mythology" being created by the generation of Emerson, Thoreau, Melville, Hawthorne, and Whitman.

In this variation on *American Renaissance,* Lewis elaborated on the distinctions Matthiessen had drawn between Emerson, Thoreau, and Whitman on one side and Hawthorne and Melville on the other. For Matthiessen, Hawthorne and Melville had recognized and accepted the fleeting nature of the American Renaissance, and had self-consciously set out to preserve the brief moment of organic unity in their writings. But Matthiessen argued that Emerson, Thoreau, and Whitman had been reluctant to believe that political and economic life were becoming hopelessly fragmented. Lewis designated these groupings as the "Party of Irony" and the "Party of Hope."

The Party of Hope believed that this moment of escape from European culture to American nature, the escape from time to space, could endure forever. But Hawthorne and Melville, as the Party of Irony, understood the necessary fallout of an Edenic space into time. The American Adam also was expelled from the Garden. They, however, argued that the unity of truth, goodness, and beauty could be preserved in their writings as a redemptive memory. They were not foolish optimists like Whitman, who believed that a moment of political and economic unity lay in the future.

For Lewis it was important that Americans know they had been and still were different from Europeans because, unlike Europeans, they had the memory of escaping the corruption of time and embracing the purity of space. Implicit in *The American Adam* is Lewis's fear that the revolutionary transition from isolation to internationalism in the 1940s would lead Americans to forget the exceptional moment of the American Renaissance. In 1950 he found the major conflict in literature to be between the Party of Hope and the Party of Memory. The Party of Memory denied that Americans had ever escaped the contradictions and corruptions of European history. The members of this party now asked Americans to understand that World War II had ended the illusion of isolation and revealed the reality of American participation in Western civilization. For Lewis, however, the Party of Memory had a valid critique of the Party of Hope. But he wanted his readers to see that the position of the Party of Irony, which he shared, transcended the criticisms of the Party of Memory. The Party of Irony asserted that an America of space in contrast to a Europe of time had been achieved in the first half of the nineteenth century and then lost to European time in the second half of that century. If there was to be the study of American literature, it must focus on the ironic literature that celebrated the escape from time to space and then wanted to preserve the unity of that moment in works of literature. This literature, an American literature, would stand, therefore, as an eternal mythic alternative to the essentially un-American experience of most people in the United States. Once again, Lewis was justifying the role of literary critics as guardians of the sacred boundaries of the canon celebrated in Matthiessen's *American Renaissance.*

By 1965, just after Leo Marx's *The Machine in the Garden* and Alan Trachtenberg's *Brooklyn Bridge* were published, the myth-symbol school began losing its ability to persuade graduate students to dedicate their scholarly lives to the memory of the American past. The political leaders (themselves Anglo-Protestant men) of the United States had insisted during the 1940s that the American people was not a homogeneous body of Anglo-Protestant males, and that the children of Catholic and Jewish immigrants be considered equal citizens to Anglo-Protestants. By the end of the 1940s, the president of the United States ordered the desegregation of the armed forces as a statement that no longer would the national government officially define African Americans as second-class citizens. With World War II, middle-class elites on both sides of the Atlantic were replacing the sacred space of all bounded nations with an unbounded international marketplace as the most sacred space. And they were rejecting the idea of a homogeneous people as the product of that national space. These factors meant that America's national citizenship no longer had the sacred aura it had held between the 1830s and the 1930s. Women had been excluded from the sacred fraternity of modern citizenship, and symbolically excluded from the sacred public sphere. Now it was possible for women to speak in the public space of modern universities, which no longer had as their major responsibility the training of national citizens. Universities on both sides of the Atlantic began to teach students to imagine lives within the global economy.

By the mid-1960s, it was clear the myth-symbol scholars were faced with a much more pluralistic body of graduate students. It was difficult for graduate students who were women, Catholics, Jews, or African American, Mexican American, and Native American to imagine celebrating the organic unity of 1830 from which they had been excluded. Their scholarship would provide the beginning of multiculturalism within the field of American studies.

The first attack on the leadership of the myth-symbol school did not come from a female or ethnic group, however, but rather from white males who were attracted to the discipline of anthropology. The American studies department at the University of Pennsylvania did not express the synthesis of literary scholarship and the history of ideas that characterized the programs of Harvard, Yale, and Minnesota. For example, the Pennsylvania professor Murray Murphey published "American Civilization at Pennsylvania" in a 1970 issue of the *American Quarterly*, which defined the differences between the anthropology and literature-history approaches. Further, the *American Quarterly* had been moved from the University of Minnesota to the University of Pennsylvania. This was followed by the 1972 critique from another Pennsylvania faculty member, Bruce Kuklick, in his *American Quarterly* essay, "Myth and Symbol in American Studies." Murphey and Kuklick did not believe the claims of the myth-symbol scholars that a particular artist could represent a national culture.

Another major attack on the myth-symbol school came in the 1960s from scholars who could not believe that popular culture since the Civil War was not worth investigating. Of course, much of that popular culture expressed the pluralism feared by myth-symbol scholars because it threatened the value of an organic, homogeneous culture. When one talked about the urban-industrial nation that had become more important than an agricultural-pastoral nation, one was talking about a popular culture whose music was largely the creation of African Americans. One was talking about a popular

culture where vaudeville and then motion pictures were largely the creation of Catholic and Jewish immigrants. Accepting this popular culture as a meaningful experience within the United States, some scholars rebelled against the commitment of the *American Quarterly* to "high culture" and created alternative scholarly journals such as the *Journal of Popular Culture* (1967) and the *Journal of American Culture* (1978).

From the perspective of the first generation of women scholars in American studies and of African American and Chicano scholars, what Marx and Trachtenberg had to say was largely irrelevant. In *The Machine in the Garden* Marx had continued to define the term "America" as exclusive to the United States and the term "Americans" as exclusive to male Anglo-Protestants in the Northeast. He presented industrialism coming from Europe as a force that overpowered the national, pastoral landscape. He focused on symbols such as the railroad, which could be interpreted as penetrating the virgin land and implanting the seeds of an America that would no longer be exceptional but would be the child of the overpowering masculine European force. Like Matthiessen and Lewis, he celebrated writers such as Melville who accepted the inevitable replacement of the organic unity of the garden by the complexity and fragmentation of industrialism but who were committed to preserving the memory of the moment of unity in their scholarship. Like his colleagues, he was critical of figures such as Emerson who believed that the national, pastoral landscape was so powerful that it could envelop and define the industrialism coming from Europe.

It is significant that Trachtenberg's *Brooklyn Bridge*, usually defined by scholars as the last major work of the myth-symbol school, focused on the issue of the possible synthesis of the European machine with the American garden. In imagining that the bridge could be an artwork that had organic unity, one could imagine that the machine, like the pastoral landscape, had the ability to express the true, good, and beautiful. Trachtenberg concluded, however, that literary artists in the United States were not able to believe there was fundamental continuity between the two halves of the nineteenth century. They could not believe that there was an organic unity in technology that they could evoke in their art. Instead, the literary artists of the 1920s were a lost generation, isolated in an alien America.

But when other scholars in the 1960s began to look at the literary history of African Americans, it was difficult to relate that story to the male Anglo-Protestant sense of loss. For African Americans, the

665

The Brooklyn Bridge (**E. O. Hoppé, 1921**). The bridge, whose completion in 1883 led to the consolidation of Brooklyn and New York City, has served as a potent symbol for both poets, such as Hart Crane, and painters, including Guy Carleton Wiggins, Thomas Moran, Joseph Stella, and Georgia O'Keeffe. © E. O. Hoppé/Corbis

have porous boundaries. The governing hypothesis was that all cultures are always in the process of change, and these changes are influenced by other cultures as myths and symbols are borrowed and exchanged.

Applying this hypothesis to the history of the United States, one studied the symbolic interchanges of the colonial period taking place between the English invaders and the variety of American Indian cultures. One studied the symbolic interchanges between the English colonists, the slaves they brought from Africa, and the Native American cultures. The complexity of the hybridity increased as large numbers of Catholics and Jews came from Europe with myths and symbols dramatically different from the Protestantism of the English colonists. And, again, the complexity of the hybridity increased as one considered symbolic interchanges between various American Indian cultures and between them and varieties of African American cultures, themselves interacting, and the interaction within Mexican American cultures and Asian American cultures. In this new era of American studies, one did not identify static cultures with specific geographic spaces, but rather the constant interactions between cultures from all continents.

The last decade of the twentieth century spoke of moving from an old world of autonomous nations to a new world of globalism. But from the perspective that hybridity is always a part of cultural experience, there never were nations that were culturally autonomous, and there never were nations with homogeneous populations. What happened in American studies is that male Anglo-Protestants from the Northeast no longer had the aesthetic authority to monopolize the term "America" for the United States and the term "American" for themselves. Scholars and students alike could now clearly see the United States as a nation always engaged in cultural interchange with other groups in the Americas, Europe, Asia, and Africa, and the dominant male Anglo-Protestant culture of the Northeast as always engaged in cultural miscegenation with the variety of cultural groups within the political boundaries of the United States. In this way, the myth-symbol group lost its aesthetic control of the terms "myth" and "symbol" and American studies scholars focused on studying American cultures and their interrelationships with European, African, and Asian cultures.

1920s was the decade of the Harlem Renaissance. And women writers could not feel a sense of loss for the Edenic environment of American Adams. For new immigrants from Europe the urban-industrial landscape was the promised land, not the pastoral landscape of Emerson.

The history of American studies from the 1960s to the end of the twentieth century, therefore, was one of breaking boundaries and engaging in cultural miscegenation. The terms "myth" and "symbol" continued to be useful for late-twentieth-century American studies scholars, but within the context of anthropology. From this perspective, the scholar was taught not to be concerned with protecting the purity of any particular myth and its symbolic expression. As the boundaries of bourgeois nationalism lost their aesthetic authority, American studies scholars increasingly used the term "hybridity." By this they meant that all cultures

See also **Popular Belief and Expression; The Classical Vision; Prophetic Native American Movements; Thought and Culture in the Free Black Community; American Romanticism;**

Gender, Social Class, Race, and Material Life; Manhood; Realism in Art and Literature; The Athlete as Cultural Icon *(volume 1)*; Postmodernism and the Arts; Whites and the Construction of Whiteness; Pastoralism and the Rural Ideal; The Idea of the South; The Natural World *(volume 2);* The Scientific Ideal; Monuments and Memorials *(in this volume); and other articles in this section.*

BIBLIOGRAPHY

Primary Sources

Kuklick, Bruce. "Myth and Symbol in American Studies." *American Quarterly* 24, no. 4 (1972): 435–450.

Lewis, R. W. B. *The American Adam.* Chicago, 1955.

Marx, Leo. "American Studies: Defense of an Unscientific Method." *New Literary History* 1, no. 3 (1969): 75–80.

——. *The Machine in the Garden.* New York, 1964.

Matthiessen, F. O. *American Renaissance.* New York, 1941.

Murphey, Murray. "American Civilization at Pennsylvania." *American Quarterly* 22, no. 3 (1970): 495–510.

Smith, Henry Nash. "Can American Studies Develop a Method?" *American Quarterly* 9, no. 3 (1957): 197–208.

——. *Virgin Land: The American West as Symbol and Myth.* Cambridge, Mass., 1950.

Trachtenberg, Alan. *Brooklyn Bridge.* New York, 1965.

Secondary Sources

Anderson, Benedict. *Imagined Communities.* London, 1983.

Baym, Nina. "Melodramas of Beset Manhood: How Theories of American Fiction Exclude Women Authors." *American Quarterly* 33, no. 2 (1981): 123–139.

Bercovitch, Sacvan. "America as Canon and Context: Literary History in a Time of Dissensus." *American Literature* 58, no. 1 (1986): 99–108.

Cain, William. *F. O. Matthiessen and the Politics of Criticism.* Madison, Wis., 1988.

Carafial, Peter. *The American Ideal: Literary History as a Worldly Activity.* New York, 1991.

Gates, Henry Lewis, Jr. *Loose Canons: Notes on the Culture Wars.* New York, 1992.

Gilroy, Paul. *Black Atlantic: Modernity and Double Consciousness.* Cambridge, Mass., 1993.

Jay, Gregory. *American Literature and the Culture Wars.* Ithaca, N.Y., 1997.

Jay, Paul. *Contingency Blues: The Search for Foundations in American Literature.* Madison, Wis., 1997.

Kerber, Linda. "Diversity and the Transformation of American Studies." *American Quarterly* 41, no. 3 (1989): 415–431.

Kessler-Harris, Alice. "Cultural Locations: Positioning American Studies in the Great Debate." *American Quarterly* 44, no. 3 (1992): 299–312.

Kolodny, Annette. "The Integrity of Memory: Creating a New Literary History of the United States." *American Literature* 57, no. 2 (1985): 291–307.

Lowe, Lisa. *Immigrant Acts: On Asian-American Cultural Politics.* Durham, N.C., 1996.

Morrison, Toni. *Playing in the Dark: Whiteness and the Literary Imagination.* New York, 1992.

Noble, David W. *The End of American History.* Minneapolis, Minn., 1985.

———. "Revocation of the Anglo-Protestant Monopoly: Aesthetic Authority and the American Landscape." *Soundings* 79, no. 2 (1996): 1001–1020.

Owens, Louis. "The Song Is Very Short: Native American Literature and Literary Theory." *Weber Studies* 12, no. 3 (1995): 51–62.

Porter, Carolyn. "What We Know That We Don't Know: Remapping American Literary History." *American Literary History* 6, no. 3 (1994): 467–526.

Reising, Russell. *The Unusable Past: Theory and the Study of American Literature.* New York, 1986.

Saldívar, José David. *The Dialectics of Our America: Genealogy, Cultural Critique, and Literary History.* Durham, N.C., 1991.

Shumway, David. *Creating American Civilization: A Genealogy of American Literature as an Academic Discipline.* Minneapolis, Minn., 1994.

Tate, Cecil. *The Search for a Method in American Studies.* Minneapolis, Minn., 1973.

Wise, Gene. "Paradigm Dramas in American Studies: A Cultural and Institutional History of the Movement." *American Quarterly* 31 (1979): 293–337.

Wonham, Henry B., ed. *Criticism and the Color Line: Desegregating American Literary Studies.* New Brunswick, N.J., 1998.

HERMENEUTICS AND AMERICAN HISTORIOGRAPHY

Alan Sica

To what extent European theories of interpretative practices, known generally as hermeneutics, have affected American historiography is not easily determined, partly because the term remains as multivalent in the twenty-first century as it has for the last four hundred years of its existence. Additionally, American historians have been more reluctant than have their colleagues elsewhere to theorize along interpretative lines about how they create and evaluate their work and, accordingly, have been less inclined toward hermeneutic speculation. A few noted exceptions prove the rule. In 1933 Charles Beard delivered what became a famous presidential address to the American Historical Association, "Written History as an Act of Faith," wherein he revealed that his sources for the "subjective historical interpretation" he favored included the Italian philosopher Benedetto Croce and the German sociologist Karl Mannheim. Both these noted Europeans played important roles in the development of modern hermeneutic theories, yet were probably unknown then, and even now, to many American historians. By arguing that "perspectivalism," and not the "noble dream" of objectivity, should guide historians in their work, Beard ignited a debate which still continues, but has therefore cast hermeneutics in a suspicious light for many practicing historians.

Even though Beard himself admitted that objective truth was attainable in historiography, the seeds of doubt were sown. This complex and heated argument was finally documented by Peter Novick in *That Noble Dream* (1988), the foremost study in a small field of exceptions to the self-restraint typical of American historians when confronting what is known as "the objectivity question." If history cannot be told "objectively," if it cannot aspire to scientific standards of evidence and proof, it risks falling back into the Romantic histories of the nineteenth century, saturated by the charm of belles lettres, and thereby abandoning those very standards that gave rise to the American Historical Association (AHA) in 1884.

This has lately troubled Americans more than their philosophically jaded colleagues abroad. In fact, when historians in the United States use the word "hermeneutics," it is often with self-conscious reserve, or even hostility. For example, according to Thomas L. Haskell, "The pervasiveness of the political is commonly presented as a plain and palpable fact of the sort that only fools or knaves could deny, but in fact it is the predictable outcome of a hermeneutics of suspicion to which all of us resort in our most cynical moments, when we are eager to project our own aggression outward into the world" (*Objectivity Is Not Neutrality,* p. 211). Note the unsavory linking of cynicism with interpretative theorizing. In some ways concerns about either "objectivity" or "hermeneutics" could indeed be viewed as antithetical, even if most hermeneutic theorists would see the dichotomy as false. This also helps account for the widespread American academic ambivalence about hermeneutics as a field of inquiry or a method of discovery. After all, its roots lie in idealist philosophy, which brings with it a persistent questioning of source validity and a potentially fractious interpretation of texts.

It is ironic that Haskell could use the French philosopher-historian Paul Ricoeur's "hermeneutics of suspicion" (in part a response to the German historian Hans-Georg Gadamer's more trusting version of hermeneutic practice) in this corrosive way, since these very theories were primarily created to overcome disagreement rather than provoke it. Nevertheless, the belief that cynicism and hermeneutics are partners, that it is dangerous for historians to overinvolve themselves in disputes that arise from this ancient set of concerns, is almost an American intellectual birthright. The influence of hermeneutic practice, then, must be sought in American historiography at a level distinctly beneath the surface in many cases, where historians carry out hermeneutic labors without denoting them as much.

Considering this peculiar situation in American historiography when compared with other nations, it might be wise to begin here by defining what modern hermeneutics has come to mean over the nineteenth and twentieth centuries, and then to connect it with trends in American intellectual culture that, knowingly or otherwise, have partaken of its special analytic concerns.

MODERN HERMENEUTICS AND SOCIAL SCIENCE

Since World War I, intellectual change within the humanities and social sciences has embodied a slowly growing reflexivity, an awareness of the scholar's analytic process as itself a part of social life and therefore subject to shifting external pressures. This change in perspective is evidenced in works influenced by phenomenology, ethnomethodology, critical theory, and, more recently, poststructuralism and hermeneutic theory. What is interesting about this transformation from the methodological boldness of nineteenth-century positivism—which, judging from its programmatic statements, never felt threatened by the paralysis of self-analysis—is that it parallels developments in mutually remote fields. History, viewed either as *Geisteswissenschaft* (literally, "science of the spirit") or naturalistic science, has come to a point in its evolution that was reached by jurisprudence, theology, and philosophy in the eighteenth century, and, henceforth, it ignores or disparages hermeneutics at grave risk.

Theology gave birth to hermeneutics in the sixteenth century and exploded with interpretative schools and controversies between the Reformation and the early nineteenth century. Jurisprudence has enjoyed the company of careful, rigorous, and intellectually productive hermeneuticists for at least as long. It is, in fact, a hermeneutic discipline by definition, as is contemporary philosophy, ever since the German philosopher Martin Heidegger came to grips with hermeneutical problems textually and at the level of existential knowing. Those schools of philosophy, which have consciously minimized the importance to their projects of hermeneutical reflection, have now, it seems, been left in the wake of a consciousness that saturates continental thinking as well as significant centers of thought in Britain and the United States. Thus, in a movement which might have gladdened the English sociologist-philosopher Herbert Spencer, the human sciences which were last to spring up have also been last to come to hermeneutical understanding. In fact, in the United States, economics, political science, and psychology have yet to recognize fully the importance this "new" tack may hold for them.

But why is hermeneutics so crucial to the self-understanding of the social sciences? What are its claims upon historical thinking and research? Hermeneutics is of two types. The older and best known has played a central role in theological learning since the Middle Ages and also contributed to classical intellectual life in Greece, though with secular intentions. This strain of hermeneutics, still present in different guises, concerns itself exclusively with interpreting texts around which disagreements have sprung up, often of a doctrinal or canonical type. This hermeneutics is subdivided into "technical," "philological," or "grammatical" types, frequently dealing with texts in foreign languages. It is expected to supply rules which, if applied to a text in good faith, will render an "objective" (hence, doctrinally unproblematic) reading. Thus, hermeneutics within this tradition is clearly auxiliary in nature, a help to "larger" issues in the determination of meaning. The clearest example, of course, is the extensive mass of biblical hermeneutics that began in earnest with the Reformation, when Protestants identified themselves by means of unorthodox scriptural readings.

The other branch of contemporary hermeneutics bears little relation to its older, more easily understood counterpart. This version began with the German theologian and classical philologist Friedrich Schleiermacher (who also contributed to traditional hermeneutics) and was then broadened and deepened in scope by the German philosopher Wilhelm Dilthey. In the twenty-first century, it is best represented by philosophy influenced by Heidegger and the German philosopher Edmund Husserl, notably in the works of Hans-Georg Gadamer and Paul Ricoeur. The scheme of this "philosophical hermeneutics" might be roughly summarized as the phenomenological investigation of the "linguisticality of Being." The hermeneuticist is thus most interested in a text not for itself (the traditional view), nor in order to understand the mind of its author (aspects of Schleiermacher and Dilthey), but rather to illuminate the fundamental mental and ontological processes unique to human existence, which, it is argued, exist and are understandable only through language as phenomenologically understood. Texts, therefore, become "windows into Being" rather than merely the results of an author's inspired effort to communicate a particular view of the world.

There is also a third stream, or so some scholars believe, comprised of social scientists who, since the mid-1970s, have confronted Heideggerian hermeneutics, not in order to handle texts more felicitously, but in hopes of fortifying and enlarging their understanding and interpretation of social action, either at the level of collectivities or within the dyadic psychoanalytic setting. Important contributors to this "debate," as it is known in Germany, include Jürgen Habermas, Karl-Otto Apel, Albrecht Wellmer, Alfred Lorenzer, and Hans Jörg Sandkühler. This third version of hermeneutics is remote in scope and intention from the other two types. It is also distressing that the "Gadamer-Habermas debate"—arising largely from Habermas's attack upon Gadamer's explication of "tradition" and "prejudice"—has become widely known to concern hermeneutics in toto. For it could be shown that Habermas's appropriation of the term into his own theories does not adequately address what Gadamer's theory has to offer.

Aspects of traditional "grammatical" hermeneutics, as well as portions of philosophical hermeneutics, must begin informing historiography if it is to concern itself with its own tradition, its own "archaeology." As long as the classical tradition continues to speak to current scholarship, hermeneutics could become an essential tool for historical analysis, being, in a manner of speaking, the other side of the coin from cliometrics. In fact, for historians and other social scientists to begin reading each others' texts—those they own by legacy and those they create—with the sophistication long in evidence among philosophers, literary scholars, and others in the humanities, hermeneutics needs to become as much a part of historical methodology as are the other tools ritually forced upon apprentices in the field. This essay reviews how the field developed and why this claim is plausible.

Hermeneutics appears to have been first systematized by the ancient Greek philosopher Aristotle in his *Peri herméneias* (On interpretation), which mostly concerned rules for understanding "enunciation," a logical-grammatical procedure for assessing truth-claims. Thomas Aquinas's commentary exposed the broader sense of Aristotle's *Peri herméneia,* tied to a narrowly defined conception of knowing as a "primary operation of the intellect." Unfortunately for the history of hermeneutics, Aristotle's highly restricted application of *herméneia* slowed recognition of its potential as a general aid to understanding. Perhaps because of Aristotle's

overwhelming prestige before the Reformation, no systematic development of hermeneutics occurred until 1566, when the Lutheran reformer Matthias Flacius Illyricus composed his *Clavis scripturae sacrae* (Key to Sacred Scripture). Since then, the great names in the field have included Friedrich Ast, Friedrich Wolf, Schleiermacher, August Boeckh, Dilthey, Emilio Betti, and Eric D. Hirsch on one side, Heidegger and Gadamer on the other, with Ricoeur straddling both sides.

As is well known, Schleiermacher reconstructed the discipline along entirely new lines in his *Hermeneutik* (composed in rough form between 1805 and 1833), partly in response to his own struggles to translate the ancient Greek philosopher Plato into German for the first time. He concluded that misunderstanding, and not clear-eyed comprehension, is the *normal,* expected outcome when a reader confronts a text, particularly one composed in a foreign language at some remove in time. Though Dilthey names scores of hermeneuticists who preceded Schleiermacher, all of them (except on the one hand Aristotle, with Ast and Wolf on the other) desired to provide rules which textual interpreters could follow in producing adequate renderings of original meaning. This is the realm commonly called "grammatical" interpretation, and it is philological and technical in nature. Schleiermacher supplemented this with "psychological" interpretation, and by so doing began transforming hermeneutics singlehandedly from a guide to texts into a guide for life—a task completed by Dilthey and Heidegger. Without consciously meaning to do so (and he must have had reservations since he never published his hermeneutic manuscripts), he changed what had been pedantic discourse over words as precise meanings to be discovered into an entire philosophy of life. His belief, clearly stated in many works and especially his letters, is that life is dialogue and that understanding of that dialogue rests upon a "divinatory" penetration of the Other. In holding these beliefs, he set off the inexorable march of historicism within hermeneutics, which culminates in Gadamer's dictum that all interpretations are relative to the interpreter's existential-hermeneutical position, and, therefore, no interpretation is ever "final." If this sounds remarkably phenomenological, it is because Schleiermacher's decisive influence upon Dilthey and Heidegger has been neglected in late-twentieth-century accounts.

Schleiermacher believed that hermeneutics could promote in its student the capacity to experience an author's original cognitive and emotional state when the text under study was composed. It was a short step from this belief to Dilthey's claim that social science could not possibly emulate the natural sciences epistemologically, due to the requirements of "understanding" and "reexperiencing," which could never submit to the rules of naturalistic method. Although a thorough analysis of Schleiermacher's hermeneutics demands an entire study, the essential point for students of social science lies in the conviction that understanding the individual life is the ultimate goal of hermeneutics. Because consciousness escapes the bounds of language (Ricoeur's "surplus of meaning"), the task of hermeneutics is to discover the psyche behind the words: to root out inner consciousness as it struggles—always unsuccessfully—to reveal itself through language. This calls for a shift in hermeneutic practice from exclusive focus on the text as written (New Criticism) to the use of the text in pursuit of its author's Being: from language to psyche.

Thus, already in the early nineteenth century, hermeneutics construed as rules for textual critique was outmoded, at least for those following the later Schleiermacher. Needless to say, many interpreters have refused to follow him into the shadowy realm of "divinatory experience," but since the early 1800s the split in hermeneutics between strict textual critics and analysts of consciousness has widened at the expense of the former. For even if a text can be analyzed with some precision, even if the words on the page can be made comprehensible and their meaning utterly transmissible, the Schleiermachian question inevitably poses itself: what does this analysis tell us about the author, and about human life (through language) in general?

Before proceeding to later developments in hermeneutics, it might be useful to consider how students of the social sciences might profit from a text-centered (grammatical) hermeneutic of the kind Schleiermacher's superseded only with difficulty. Schleiermacher's inevitable drift toward what scholars identify as the Diltheyan problematic (the idea that texts are primarily windows into their author's personalities) was preceded by many years of conventional hermeneutic practice. In fact, his training in foreign languages, typical for an intellectual of his time, was broad and strenuous with particular attention to ancient tongues. This emphasis led him to his greatest intellectual triumph, a translation of Plato's dialogues into German with commentary. As noted, it was during this demanding exertion in traditional hermeneutics that he came upon many of his dicta regarding proper interpretative methods. Since these are not delivered in terms of *Verstehen, Nacherleben, Sprachlichkeit*

(understanding, reexperience, language) and other concepts that ever since Dilthey have obscured and complicated conventional hermeneutics as a method, some of Schleiermacher's suggestions can still benefit "close readings," especially those aimed at achieving relative objectivity in their results (as most recently proposed by Emilio Betti and Eric D. Hirsch).

The first point regarding the motivation behind Schleiermacher's comprehensive hermeneutical project is his anathema, Enlightenment faith in *vernünftige Gedanken* (rational ideas) as the key to understanding human speech and behavior. For him, also, the German priest Martin Luther's belief in the *sensus literalis* of the Bible—that its meanings are self-evident and beyond debate to the "right-thinking"—was at best naive, at worst deceitful. Johann Martin Chladenius shared Luther's confidence: "It is quite an exceptional thing for a passage to require interpretation." It is this very view, what might be called "hermeneutical naivety," that predominates among twenty-first-century social scientists, and consequently has become a major cause of so many discrepant, tendentious readings of classic texts. Ast, Wolf, and Schleiermacher, all at about the same time, came to realize that unless this blithe confidence in the likelihood of interpretative consensus, in the transparency of texts, could be deflated, no serious understanding of texts or their authors would take place. Considering this, contemporary scholars can charge many historians and social scientists with a pre-nineteenth-century perception of reading and a pretheoretical understanding of what it means to confront, and be confronted by, the alien presence of a text. For Schleiermacher, long before deconstruction existed, this viewpoint was meant not to mystify but rather to clarify meaning and precision.

Schleiermacher's transformation and elaboration of hermeneutics added a dimension of reflexivity by shifting from perceiving language and thought as being identical to regarding thought as always exceeding the limits of intersubjective display. In the late 1970s, this change was examined by Heinz Kimmerle, Gadamer's student, in an effort to rewrite Dilthey's rendering of Schleiermacher's theory. Dilthey wanted to highlight the psychologizing aspect of the latter's hermeneutics in order to legitimate his own method. The point was to see into the author's mind, to reexperience (*Nacherleben*) the creative act. One could then "understand an author better than he understood himself" (attributed to the German writer-critic Friedrich von Schlegel, Schleiermacher's associate). But Kimmerle saw instead, in Schleiermacher's earlier manuscripts, particularly within "grammatical" interpretation, an interest in language itself that transcends the subject, that is, the author. This interest, it is claimed, anticipates Heidegger and Gadamer, in a vision of the writer's "voice" as the expression of culture through linguistic restraints and opportunities, rather than the unique, self-generative fiction—the writer as creator—that stimulated Romantic arts and its hermeneutics. For Gadamer one must apply both language-centered interpretation and insight into the writer's consciousness, though in the final analysis, language (as Being) is preeminent. In addition, Kimmerle (following his teacher) accused Schleiermacher of ignoring the historical "conditionedness" of the exegete and of considering only the conditionedness of the text instead. The Gadamerian hermeneutic insists that neither the author of the text nor the interpreter be allowed to "step outside of history," nor beyond the perimeter of their own language limits. Both are subject to the historicality and linguisticality of Being, which is the guiding thread to successful interpretation. One "participates" in Being; one does not "eviscerate" it as revealed in texts.

In a short article it is impossible to review responsibly even the major ideas of the men whose names have already appeared. But a neglected aspect of hermeneutics, and one which is distinctly nonmetaphysical, direct, and sensible, is Schleiermacher's method of "grammatical" interpretation (remembering that the "psychological/technical" portion attends to the given author's psyche). Whereas one might reasonably debate Gadamer's claims for hermeneutic universality, Schleiermacher's less ambitious, pragmatically motivated rules can be considered more dispassionately and might well be joined to standard historiographical method more easily.

First of all, most texts do not require hermeneutics in any strict sense. For the text (script) of everyday talk, for instance—which, engendered in the child, is the root, according to Schleiermacher, of all later hermeneutical capabilities—it is fairly pointless to construct an elaborate apparatus of interpretation. Contemporary ethnomethodology and related schools of "ordinary language" analysis, built around Wittgenstein, Husserl, or Schutz, not Heidegger and Gadamer, would strenuously disagree with this idea, yet most social scientists would probably support Schleiermacher. What do require a systematized hermeneutic canon of rules are foreign, ancient, and contemporary texts, which (1) are by design not clear in themselves (James Joyce's *Fin-*

negans Wake, Heidegger's *Being and Time,* and symbolist poetry, for example) or (2) are so compressed and/or elaborate that the author's own conclusions omit a great deal (Max Weber's *Economy and Society,* George Simmel's *The Philosophy of Money,* and Karl Marx's *Grundrisse*). Schleiermacher came to believe even more fervently during his long exegetical career that the most successful hermeneutic was the result of "artistry," not mere technique. And yet, before reaching the level of art, exegesis first had to probe the grammatical, which worked in concert with the psychological/technical as part of the "hermeneutic circle." In retracing step by step the author's creative process, in pursuit of his or her "style" (the primary goal), the universal/objective (grammatical) nature of the text must be related dialectically to the particular/subjective (psychological). The "motion" of hermeneutics, then, is not mechanical, but craftlike, in moving between these poles and in producing what is now known as the "hermeneutic spiral," always upward toward absolute clarification. Gadamer has refined this image into three steps: the relation of part to whole within the language of the text; part to whole in the tradition within which the text falls; and part to whole within the writer's life and that moment which the text claims. Since one's own and the text's historicity ensure the "loss of immediate understanding," which is the normal condition of interaction, hermeneutics can be thought of as the attempt to recapture that lost immediacy, the robust dialogue in which the ancient Greek philosopher Socrates responds immediately, hiding nothing.

Schleiermacher wrote, "I do not understand anything that I cannot perceive and comprehend as necessary. In accordance with this . . . understanding is an unending task" (*Hermeneutics,* p. 41). Understanding must proceed by defining the "sphere of meaning" of key words. Words are used in a particular sense by an author but exist universally within their unique spheres of meaning. (Consider the term "rationalization" as used by the psychoanalyst Sigmund Freud, then by Weber, then in contemporary management writing.) Exegetes must make themselves familiar with as many meanings as possible and then determine which meaning(s) apply in each case at hand. Grammatical interpretation, then, begins with a determination of the "boundaries of meaning" embodied within each key term. And yet already one can foresee a substantial task. How might one reduce the sheer bulk of work confronting the hermeneuticist? Schleiermacher realized that his dicta are idealized, for they cannot be fulfilled perfectly by any single interpreter. He therefore insisted that where understanding must be not only reliable but also tractable, empirical analysis must be supplemented by "intuition," by artistic, speculative probing of the text and its author. The result is a *Kunstlehre* (doctrine of art), and not merely a *Technik* (skill). Whereas during his lifetime, this notion seemed obvious and inoffensive, in the twenty-first century it smacks of an aristocratic, hermetic definition of knowing. This is due mostly to the democratization of culture and with it the triumph of natural science methodology; hermeneutics has no defense against this accusation, if it is raised.

To the modern temperament it may seem that Schleiermacher's dicta regarding proper interpretive technique simply ask too much of even the most serious reader. Just as Schleiermacher admitted that one cannot hope to complete the hermeneutic circle viewed from the objective/universal or subjective/particular vantage points, twenty-first-century historians may well have to retreat before an idealized, thoroughgoing hermeneutic for no other reason than lack of multilingual training. Or, in his own words, "The success of the art of interpretation depends on one's linguistic competence and on one's ability for knowing people" (p. 101). Schleiermacher also stipulated that the avoidance of "eisegesis" (faulty interpretation due to ethnocentrism) cannot be guaranteed unless the reader enjoys familiarity with the author's personality, his intellectual setting, the use of language typical of that period, his peculiar innovations through language, and so on: "Historical interpretation . . . is the means for recreating the relationship between the speaker and the original audience, and interpretation cannot begin until that relationship has been established" (p. 104).

The modern scholar might be repelled by what seems the overweening claims of "proper" interpretation. And yet, what do scholars mean when they characterize a historical work as "capturing perfectly an epoch"? What is meant when a film or novel reveals a series of related experiences "perfectly"? Or, much more likely, when an aesthetic attempt fails to reach verisimilitude or misrepresents a human event? Scholars mean that the "divinatory" skill of the artist has not measured up to reality, or, better yet, has not yet gained enough strength to reshape reality in its own image, to give to its perceivers a redefinition of their own consciousness. Ideally, a proper hermeneutic, in Schleiermacher's estimation, could do just this for a text and its author: reveal qualities of both which would otherwise remain unknown to their creator and their audi-

ence. Or, if extended into Gadamer's orbit, bring to the surface the text's participation in Being, that is, of humanness. "Understanding" becomes not merely a tool, but rather the singular expression of Being itself as comprehensible to humankind. It is this search for a way to bring this being-as-language into view that makes philosophical hermeneutics so important, as well as unpalatable to "science."

Schleiermacher's final formulation of his theory was presented in "Two Academy Addresses of 1829" (1977: 175–214), in which the subjectivist, divinatory (Diltheyan) exegete was given most play. But in the "Compendium of 1819" (1977: 95–152), his major concern remained "grammatical" interpretation. Here he presented two major canons and explicated them exhaustively. The first canon: "A more precise determination of any point in a given text must be decided on the basis of the use of language common to the author and his original public" (p. 117). The next ten pages explain why this embraces more than meets the eye and how it applies to the New Testament. The second canon reads:

> The meaning of each work of a passage must be determined by the context in which it occurs. One moves from the first canon to the second. Each word has a determinate linguistic sphere. . . . Since the application of this canon, carried to its farthest extent, involves the entire theory of parallel passages, these two canons comprise the whole of grammatical interpretation. (pp. 127–128)

Before even covering "technical interpretation" Schleiermacher also discussed "formal" versus "material" elements of language and their relevance for "qualitative" and "quantitative" understanding; the nature of "organic connections"; the importance in dialectical texts of opposition, mediation, and mutual determination; identities and antitheses; primary and secondary thoughts; "pleonasms"; emphatic and imposed meanings; and so on.

The tradition of "grammatical" interpretation lives on in the works of Eric D. Hirsch (1965; 1967; 1972; 1976), who rigorously defends "objectivist" hermeneutics—the search for norms that guarantee accurate readings—and has attacked Gadamer for "relativizing" the discipline. His precursor and ally is Emilio Betti, whose landmark theory (1955) is closely tied to legal hermeneutics, not to aesthetics and philosophy as is Gadamer's, giving it a less ethereal tone. Betti's only work in English is an extreme condensation of his theory. Students of this debate (e.g., Hoy, 1978; Palmer, 1969; Mazzeo, 1978) seem to agree that Betti cannot overturn Gadamer's scepticism regarding even "relatively objective" interpretation, due principally to Betti's unwillingness to account for or refute what Gadamer calls a text's *Wirkungsgeschichte*—the history of the text's effects upon readers in different settings, which itself becomes part of the larger hermeneutical problem. An obvious example is Plato's *Dialogues,* whose *Wirkungsgeschichte* was crucial for Schleiermacher's exegesis, as it continued to be for Gadamer's, and helps account for their extreme difference. Betti insisted that we ought to be able to distinguish a "right" from a "wrong" interpretation (as one would expect from a jurist), but Gadamer's rejoinder might be that "understanding" is right or wrong differently over time, and that Schleiermacher's interpretation of Plato—except regarding technical details such as dating the *Dialogues*—is no less right than Gadamer's *Auslegung* (interpretation), only different.

What is the social scientist or humanist to make of this ambitious hermeneutic claim? Perhaps one way of addressing this without presenting a rule book, or "thirty theses on interpretation," is to hypothesize in gross outline how an ideal hermeneutic upon the work of a single historically significant writer might be carried out. The fact that such a hermeneutic will never be done perfectly does not lessen the value of conceptualizing it, just as the "ideal speech situation" in Habermas's work—requiring absolute honesty, equity, and rationality among participants—need not be attained in order to be useful theoretically.

The first precaution one must take is to avoid what has been called the "rape theory of interpretation." This manifests itself when, for example, intellectual historians are expected to provide usable "bits" for researchers to graft onto various "models." Thus, complex lifeworks of thought are reduced to easily digested propositional units for the purpose of instrumental test. This common practice seriously violates hermeneutic principles, for it forces upon that tiny portion of the text actually brought into contention preconceptions and predefinitions utterly foreign to it. The unspoken assumption is that twenty-first-century theoretical/empirical goals bear enough substantial contiguity with earlier thinking to justify facile "interbreeding." Historical texts are thus predefined by insisting that concerns of a previous era be "modernized" to fit with current discourse. Historicists have explained for decades the fallacy of this approach. Whether in Ast, Schleiermacher, Dilthey, or Gadamer, the hermeneutic circle or spiral is the central ingredient in successful interpretation, that special

movement endlessly seeking absolute clarification of meaning. As Gadamer explained:

> Thus the movement of understanding is constantly from the whole to the part and back to the whole. Our task is to extend in concentric circles the unity of understood meaning. The harmony of all the details with the whole is the criterion of correct understanding. The failure to achieve this harmony means that understanding has failed. (*Truth and Method,* p. 259)

How does this apply to historically pertinent texts? It applies differently to each of the three major loci Gadamer specified in renovating Schleiermacher's circle as an analytic tool. In order to win "harmony of all details," one must pursue three levels of hermeneutic analysis: (1) the single word must be contextualized within its sentence, and, more broadly, key terms must be isolated and their "spheres of meaning" determined in relation to the entire text; (2) each text must be located within the writer's total output and understood "objectively," but also must be seen as a feature of the writer's inner life, "subjectively"; and (3) the text must also be related to its place in the genre it represents, both at the time of composition and subsequently (which recalls Gadamer's central idea, "effective-history" or *Wirkungsgeschichte*). Gadamer actually truncated Schleiermacher's project considerably. The latter would in addition have the hermeneuticist probe, to whatever length possible, the author's personality, the nature of the author's intellectual setting, the use of language typical of the author's time, and whatever peculiar innovations the author introduced into language, hence thinking and Being. Again, this is an ideal program, the goal of which is to demystify as thoroughly as possible texts which by their nature refuse to reveal themselves spontaneously. And yet, with all this analytic machinery, the goal—particularly for Gadamer—remains to coax into view an author's meaning through a text and not to batter the writer or the product into submission to fit a preconceived framework. That sort of performance, common enough in the twenty-first century, is simply bad hermeneutics and therefore shoddy scholarship.

But how can one identify these "essentials" to an ideal hermeneutic, whether in the form of authors or concepts? This, perhaps, is where Schleiermacher's essentially aesthetic concept of "divination" can be brought to bear. Were scholars asked which single idea best represented (or least misrepresented) a given text or author, only a small number of terms or concepts would probably be mentioned repeatedly. One way the hermeneuticist can help reduce his or her work, through strategically premature "divination," is to guess which concept the author in question most likely believed to be most important—which of the entire range of possibilities might best form a "key" (recalling Flavius's notion of the *Clavis*) for unlocking a text's most ambiguous meanings.

HERMENEUTICS IN AMERICAN HISTORY

In American history, this approach has been taken a number of times, of course, sometimes setting off interpretative battles among scholars that lasted for generations. An obvious case is that of Perry Miller. Before his early book *The New England Mind: The Seventeenth Century* (1939), the notion that Puritanism should be understood, above all, as a series of linked theological and philosophical texts that gave rise to specific forms of behavior had not been seriously entertained. By performing a hermeneutic analysis of Puritan knowledge at a heroic level of depth and breadth, Miller made a case that remains fundamentally unshaken, despite decades of further research on the topic. Simply put, he took seriously the idea, foreign to a great deal of American historiography, that ideas matter at least as much if not more than more ordinary aspects of historical experience. With careful attention to Puritan writings, unprecedented in its thoroughness, Miller became a hermeneutic researcher of the first order, probably without any inkling of the work that Schleiermacher, Dilthey, and others had done prior to his own labors. And his reputation, hermeneutically created, seems solid enough: "The depth of Miller's analysis of ideas was unprecedented in any period of American thought ... scholars most sympathetic to his books sometimes go so far as to say that Miller's scholarship is so superior to the work of others that it defies comparison" (Skotheim, *American Intellectual Histories and Historians*, pp. 192, 309). This great esteem is a direct result of Miller's interpretative virtuosity, and therefore a model worth emulating.

Perhaps needless to say, Miller's practiced hermeneutic approach to Puritanism does not exhaust the record of late-twentieth-century historiography that explicitly links it to the interpretative tradition previously outlined. A later generation of historians, many trained in England but with professional affiliations and influence in the United States, has gone to extraordinary lengths ever since the 1960s to show how "proper" interpretation of historical documents might be carried out. Though often spe-

cializing in the history of ideas, these scholars put forth arguments that have handily made their way into a number of historical subfields. An early salvo for this regenerated hermeneutic stream is Quentin Skinner's 1969 article "Meaning and Understanding in the History of Ideas," among the most cited of such works. Though subtle and comprehensive in its arguments, the article's main point is that most modern readers impose anachronistic interpretations on texts from previous periods, and that what scholars need to do now is "recover the intentions" of authors who were in their time trying to solve particular problems unique to their settings. (This amounts to an updating and elaboration of Dilthey's hermeneutic theory.) This analysis requires detailed contextual knowledge surrounding the creation of a given discourse and has come to be known generally as the "historicist" rather than "presentist" way of carrying out research. The latter favors identifying those ideas of "lasting value" for all times and places, while the former emphasizes the truths peculiar to a stated period or thinker. Failure to acquire this preliminary contextual information almost always, so argued Skinner, leads to misinterpretations, such as modern misreadings of the Italian political philosopher Marsilius of Padua or the British jurist-politician Sir Edward Coke that turn on mere linguistic similarities or coincidences rather than substantive agreement with modern thought. Skinner has elaborated on this stream of thinking in a series of publications that have become canonical for students of interpretative theorizing, and his ideas have been analyzed by a range of scholars.

Closely allied with Skinner's ideas are those of J. G. A. Pocock, who dedicated to his colleague Skinner an important book treating these ideas, *Politics, Language, and Time* (1971). A densely argued essay, "Languages and Their Implications: The Transformation of the Study of Political Thought," opens the book, which during the last thirty years of the twentieth century was cited repeatedly whenever linguistically alert historians were invoked. Desiring to redirect his colleagues' attention away from material "reality," so-called, and toward linguistic aspects of political processes—which Pocock believed constitute what is genuinely "real" in the political world—he offered dicta toward invigorating a field that had become stultified:

> Men think by communicating language systems; these systems help constitute both their conceptual worlds and the authority-structures, or social words, related to these; the conceptual and social worlds may each be seen as a context to the other, so that

676

the picture gains in concreteness. The individual's thinking may now be viewed as a social event, an act of communication and of response within a paradigm-system, and as a historical event, a moment in a process of transformation of that system and of the interacting worlds which both system and act help to constitute and are constituted by. We have gained what we lacked before: the complexity of context which the historian needs.... Because factual and evaluation statements are inextricably combined in political speech, and because it is intended to reconcile and coordinate different groups pursuing different values, its inherent ambiguity and its cryptic content are invariably high . . . speech is a political operant . . . it invokes values, it summarizes information, it suppresses the inconvenient; it makes many kinds of statements and does so by means of formulations which can often convey several kinds of statement at once, while simultaneously diverting attention from others.... If the philosopher is concerned to keep statements of different orders distinct from one another, the historian is concerned with whether or not they were kept distinct, and with what happened as a result of either. (pp. 15, 17, 18, 21)

It is easy to see how this view of the historian's task ties in perfectly with similar dicta offered a century earlier by Schleiermacher and his disciple Dilthey. In a linked series of publications going back to 1960, Pocock investigated the role that language plays in historical change and the way that historians might best go about unraveling this complex relationship, both in the British and American contexts.

One piece in particular, "Virtue and Commerce in the Eighteenth Century," allows Pocock to deal directly with two other important American historians who worked within this language-sensitive scholarly tradition, Gordon S. Wood and Bernard Bailyn. Pocock claimed that Wood's *The Creation of the American Republic* (1969) forms "the latest statement in a process of re-evaluating the character and role of ideology in the American Revolution," the "central occurrence in this process remain[ing] the series of works published by Bailyn, in particular *The Ideological Origins of the American Revolution* [1967]. We are now living with the consequences of a major upheaval in historiography and attempting to assess a changed landscape" (p. 119). Though not overtly connected with the German tradition of hermeneutics, this new stream was so text based that comparison with that venerable set of practices is unavoidable. Pocock illustrated that this interpretative body of work "display[ed] the American Revolution less as the first political act of revolutionary enlightenment than as the last great act of the Renaissance. In a variety of ways, we are now to see the Founding Fathers as the culminating generation

of civic humanists and classical republicans.... Among the classicist characteristics which the Country ideology carried into the eighteenth century was a Renaissance pessimism concerning the direction and reversibility of social and historical change" (pp. 120–121).

It was Bailyn's innovation—he "flung a most refreshing challenge at the historians' orthodoxy which insists that ideologies and concepts are purely epiphenomenal to other social phenomena"—that gave later historians license to study texts and their purveyors with careful hermeneutic attention in a way that before had seemed unnecessary or even pernicious. Once begun in earnest, with Bailyn's early work, this new trend swept into its ken a range of works that fed off of and elaborated both Bailyn's and Wood's series of arguments about the role of ideas, language, and key texts in the creation of historical transformation. Hermeneutically inspired, this movement within American historiography shows no sign of flagging or giving up ground in its desire to produce narratives that do full historicist justice to those periods under analysis.

One final, somewhat technical observation: perhaps it is worth noting here that an interpreter who wishes to abide by the hermeneutic tradition, but who is more interested in pursuing a concept through the history of thought than in examining exhaustively one writer's work, can still apply Gadamer's rules. Less rigor will be feasible vis-à-vis a given author, but more stringent procedures are called for regarding the "life" of the concept itself. Whereas Dilthey, for one, would find this approach repellant, contemporary structuralist epistemology is sufficiently worked out to support the notion that a given framework or concept can indeed have a "life," without being explicitly tied to one writer. Therefore it is incorrect to charge that hermeneutics, as part of its Romantic legacy, is fatally "homocentric." It can be, of course, but good hermeneutic practice can just as well flow from a structuralist approach as it can from one based on Schleiermacher's principles. The risk of appearing "disembodied" is always there, however, which is why traditional hermeneuticists often find the structuralist approach dubious.

In sum, to utilize that ancient heritage kept alive by Gadamer, Betti, Ricoeur, and others, historians must accept the need to read even more carefully in-text materials pertinent to their interests than they might normally do, and in accordance with fundamental hermeneutic principles. It is no secret that writers of monumental stature are no longer alive. This is precisely why historians should appropriate their effort into the twentieth century, and by so doing elevate the level of scholarly discourse by applying as carefully as they can some of the hermeneutic principles described in this essay. If Schleiermacher was right—that *mis*understanding is the norm—historians really have no choice but to do so, or they risk forever rediscovering what was already known. They must either appropriate their legacy through hermeneutic practice or forgo the idea of intellectual progress entirely.

See also **Puritanism as a Cultural and Intellectual Force; The Rise of Biblical Criticism and Challenges to Religious Authority** *(volume 1);* **The Humanities; The Social Sciences** *(in this volume); and other articles in this section.*

BIBLIOGRAPHY

Bailyn, Bernard. "Political Experience and Enlightenment Ideas in Eighteenth Century America." *American Historical Review* 67, no. 2 (1962): 339–351.

——. *The Ideological Origins of the American Revolution.* 1967. Reprint, Cambridge, Mass., 1992.

——. "The Challenge of Modern Historiography." *American Historical Review* 87, no. 1 (1982): 1–24.

——. "Jefferson and the Ambiguities of Freedom. *Proceedings of the American Philosophical Society* 137, no. 4 (1993): 498–515.

——. *On the Teaching and Writing of History: Responses to a Series of Questions.* Hanover, N.H., 1994.

——. "Sometimes an Art, Never a Science, Always a Craft: A Conversation with Bernard Bailyn." *William and Mary Quarterly* 51, no. 4 (1994): 625–658.

Beard, Charles. "Written History as an Act of Faith." *American Historical Review* 34 (January 1934): 219–239.

Benson, John Edward. "Schleiermacher's Hermeneutics." Ph.D. diss., Columbia University, 1967.

Betti, Emilio. *Teoria Generale della Interpretazione.* 2 vols. Milan, 1955. Translated by the author into German as *Allgemeine Auslegungslehre als Methodik der Geisteswissenschaften.* Tübingen, Germany, 1967.

Bleicher, Josef. *Contemporary Hermeneutics: Hermeneutics as Method, Philosophy and Critique.* Boston, 1980.

Bruns, Gerald L. *Hermeneutics: Ancient and Modern.* New Haven, Conn., 1994.

Dilthey, Wilhelm. *Selected Writings.* Edited, translated, and introduced by H. P. Rickman. Cambridge, Mass., 1976.

——. *Introduction to the Human Sciences.* Edited by Rudolf Makkreel and Frithjof Rodi; multiple translators. Princeton, N.J., 1989.

——. *Hermeneutics and the Study of History.* Edited by Rudolf Makkreel and Frithjof Rodi. Princeton, N.J., 1996.

Frei, Hans W. *The Eclipse of Biblical Narrative: A Study of Eighteenth and Nineteenth Century Hermeneutics.* New Haven, Conn., 1974.

Gadamer, Hans-Georg. *Wahrheit und Method.* Tübingen, Germany, 1960.

——. "On the Scope and Function of Hermeneutical Reflection." In *Philosophical Hermeneutics,* edited and translated by David E. Linge. Berkeley, Calif., 1976.

——. "The Problem of Language in Schleiermacher's Hermeneutic." In *Schleiermacher as Contemporary,* edited by Robert W. Funk. Vol. 7 of *Journal for Theology and Church.* New York, 1970.

——. "The Continuity of History and the Existential Moment." *Philosophy Today* 16 (Fall 1972): 230–240.

——. *Truth and Method.* Translated by G. Barden and J. Cumming. New York, 1975.

——. *Dialogue and Dialectic. Eight Hermeneutical Studies on Plato.* New Haven, Conn., 1980.

Habermas, Jürgen. "A Review of Gadamer's Truth and Method." 1967. In *Understanding and Social Inquiry,* edited by Fred R. Dallmayr and Thomas A. McCarthey. Notre Dame, Ind., 1977. Pp. 334–363.

Haskell, Thomas L. *Objectivity Is Not Neutrality: Explanatory Schemes in History.* Baltimore, 1998.

Heidegger, Martin. *Being and Time.* Translated by J. Macquarrie and E. Robinson. New York, 1962.

Hirsch, Eric D., Jr. "Truth and Method of Interpretation." *Review of Metaphysics* 18, no. 3 (March 1965): 488–507.

——. *Validity in Interpretation.* New Haven, Conn., 1967.

——. "Three Dimensions of Hermeneutics." *New Literary History* 3, no. 2 (Winter 1972): 246–261.

——. *The Aims of Interpretation.* Chicago, 1976.

Hoy, David Couzens. *The Critical Circle: Literature, History, and Philosophical Hermeneutics.* Berkeley, Calif., 1978.

Kimmerle, Heinz. Introduction to *Hermeneutics: The Handwritten Manuscripts,* translated by F. D. E. Schleiermacher, J. Duke, and J. Forstman. Missoula, Mont., 1977.

Mazzeo, Joseph Anthony. *Varieties of Interpretation.* Notre Dame, Ind., 1978.

Novick, David. *That Noble Dream: The "Objectivity Question" and the American Historical Profession.* Cambridge, Mass., 1988.

Palmer, Richard E. *Hermeneutics: Interpretation Theory in Schleiermacher, Dilthey, Heidegger, and Gadamer.* Evanston, Ill., 1969.

Pocock, John Greville A. "Burke and the Ancient Constitution—A Problem in the History of Ideas." *Historical Journal* 3, no. 2 (1960): 125–143.

——. "The Origins of the Study of the Past: A Comparative Approach." *Comparative Studies in Society and History* 4, no. 2 (1962): 209–246.

——. "James Harrington and the Good Old Cause: A Study of the Ideological Content of His Writing." *Journal of British Studies* 10, no. 1 (1970): 30–48.

——. "Languages and Their Implications: The Transformation of the Study of Political Thought." In *Politics, Language and Time: Essays on Political Thought and History.* New York, 1971. Pp. 3–41.

——. "Virtue and Commerce in the Eighteenth Century." *Journal of Interdisciplinary History* 3, no. 1 (1972): 119–134.

——. *The Machiavellian Moment: Florentine Political Thought and the Atlantic Republican Tradition.* Princeton, N.J., 1975.

——. "Machiavelli in the Liberal Cosmos." *Political Theory* 13, no. 4 (1985): 559–574.

——. *Virtue, Commerce, and History: Essays on Political Thought and History, Chiefly in the Eighteenth Century.* Cambridge, U.K., 1985.

679

———. "Spinoza and Harrington: An Exercise in Comparison." *Bijdragen en Medelelingen betreffende de Geschiedenis der Nederlanden* (Netherlands) 102, no. 3 (1987): 435–449.

———. "States, Republics, and Empires: The American Founding in Early Modern Perspective. *Social Science Quarterly* 68, no. 4 (1987): 703–723.

———. "Machiavelli and the Rethinking of History." *Pensiero Politico* (Italy) 27, no. 2 (1994): 215–230.

Ricoeur, Paul. *Freud and Philosophy: An Essay on Interpretation.* Translated by Denis Savage. New Haven, Conn., 1970.

———. "The Model of the Text: Meaningful Action Considered as a Text." *Social Research* 38, (1971): 520–562.

———. "Ethics and Culture: Habermas and Gadamer in Dialogue." *Philosophy Today* 17 (1973): 153–165.

———. *The Conflict of Interpretations: Essays in Hermeneutics.* Edited by Don Ihde. Evanston, Ill., 1974.

———. *Interpretation Theory: Discourse and the Surplus of Meaning.* Fort Worth, Tex., 1976.

———. "Schleiermacher's Hermeneutics." *Monist* 60, no. 2 (April 1977): 181–197.

———. *From Text to Action.* Evanston, Ill, 1991.

Schleiermacher, Freidrich Ernst Daniel. *Schleiermacher's Introductions to the Dialogues of Plato.* 1836. Translated by William Dobson. Reprint, New York, 1973.

———. *The Life of Schleiermacher: As Unfolded in His Autobiography and Letters.* 2 vols. Translated by Frederica Rowan. London, 1860.

———. *Hermeneutics—The Handwritten Manuscripts.* Edited by Heinz Kimmerle. Translated by J. Duke and J. Forstman. Missoula, Mont., 1977.

———. *Hermeneutics and Criticism: And Other Writings.* Cambridge, Mass., 1998.

Shapiro, Gary, and Alan Sica, eds. *Hermeneutics: Questions and Prospects.* Amherst, Mass., 1988.

Skinner, Quentin. "Meaning and Understanding in the History of Ideas." *History and Theory* 8, no. 1 (1969): 3–53.

———. "The Limits of Historical Explanation." *Philosophy* 41, no. 157 (July 1996): 199–215.

———. *Reason and Rhetoric in the Philosophy of Hobbes.* Cambridge, U.K., 1996.

Skotheim, Robert Allen. *American Intellectual Histories and Historians.* Princeton, N.J., 1966.

Thomas Aquinas. *Aristotle: On Interpretation (Commentary by St. Thomas and Cajetan: Peri Hermēnias).* Translated by Jean T. Oesterle. Milwaukee, Wisc., 1962.

Tully, James, ed. *Meaning and Context: Quentin Skinner and His Critics.* Princeton, N.J., 1988.

Wood, Gordon S. "Rhetoric and Reality in the American Revolution." *William and Mary Quarterly,* 23, no. 1 (1966): 3–32.

———. *The Creation of the American Republic.* Chapel Hill, N.C., 1969.

———. "Conspiracy and the Paranoid Style: Causality and Deceit in the Eighteenth Century." *William and Mary Quarterly* 39, no. 3 (1982): 401–441.

———. "The Significance of the Early Republic." *Journal of the Early Republic,* 8, no. 1 (1988): 1–20.

———. "The Origins of the Bill of Rights." *Proceedings of the American Antiquarian Society* 101, no. 2 (1991): 255–274.

———. "Jefferson in His Time." *Wilson Quarterly* 17, no. 2 (1993): 38–51.

———. "Inventing American Capitalism." *New York Review of Books* (June 9, 1994): 44–49.

———. "A Century of Writing Early American History: Then and Now Compared, or How Henry Adams Got It Wrong." *American Historical Review* 100, no. 3 (1995): 678–696.

———. "The Enemy Is Us: Democratic Capitalism in the Early Republic." *Journal of the Early Republic* 16, no. 2 (1996): 293–308.

MARXIST APPROACHES

Paul Buhle

Revolutionary philosopher, economist, and political activist Karl Marx wrote relatively little on cultural subjects and treated intellectual history only in passing, mostly in a polemical manner directed against those writers that he disdained. But the identification of dissenting American intellectuals, including historians and cultural critics, with the social movements self-described as "Marxist" and the use of more general Marxist categories for analyzing American thought and culture have produced several distinct schools of interpretation and exerted wide influences.

In the broadest sense, then, Marxist influences have attached themselves successively to the largely immigrant, socialistic labor movements of the 1860s–1890s; the rather more Americanized and highly popular Socialist Party of 1900–1920; the intermittently insular and widely influential Communist Party of the 1920s–1940s, as well as small competitor movements (such as those following the lead of Russian intellectual Leon Trotsky); and the assorted radical movements of the 1950s onward, including the New Left, black power (also "red power" and Latino and Asian nationalist movements), Women's and Gay Liberation.

Marxists and those indirectly influenced by Marx or Marxism have opposed corporate capitalist control of the economy, the media, and U.S. foreign policy. In the place of such control, they have urged the collective power of ordinary people, workers, women, youth, and minorities. They have therefore often spoken not only for the dispossessed but also to the sentiments of the alienated intellectuals and avant-gardists seeking a dramatically different arrangement of cultural institutions, and of human relations, to the world of nature.

The application of Marxist influences in the study of intellectual and cultural history has often been so subtle that their significance has been underestimated and badly misunderstood. The history of these influences, like the history of the Marxist-influenced movements in the United States, has been continually interrupted, several times nearly eradicated or forgotten. But Marxist influences on scholarship have reappeared faithfully with signs of social crisis, and they have greatly strengthened during the last quarter of the twentieth century.

Broadly speaking, until the 1930s these influences were part of an eclectic socialist doctrine held widely by self-educated working-class constituencies adapted to American life (in a paradox more apparent than real) via dozens of non-English-language radical publications. The Great Depression signaled a shift of the intelligentsia toward Russian versions of Marxist doctrine more suited to economic determinism but practiced, nevertheless, chiefly as social, cultural, and intellectual interpretations of American life. Intermixed increasingly with Whitmanian strains of national traditions, this Marxism evoked the beginnings of a pluralistic, multicultural, democratic scholarship quashed by cold war moods and associated repressive measures. Its obverse, a demi-Marxism avidly supporting both high culture and the cold war, explored modernism mainly as literary history, while it attacked commercial popular culture. Most ironically, the later Marxist currents followed out the critique of form (often with scant economic content) while returning to an interpretation of popular culture enlightened now by the reborn multicultural political hopes of the vanished popular front. Along with the historical critique of imperial culture (highlighting its racial, gender, and consumerist elements) that nineteenth-century leftists had first observed, this rapidly accumulating body of scholarship spelled the latest Marxist interpretation of American life.

ORIGINS OF MARXIST INTERPRETATIONS

The founders of Marxism provided little in models for intellectual history, still less for cultural history. Apart from polemics against assorted nineteenth-century ideologues and economists, the literary tastes of Marx and Friedrich Engels themselves were classic and Shakespearean, but for nineteenth-century literature definitely eclectic—from the French writer Jean-Louis Guez de Balzac to ghost stories. Their tastes were definitely unrelated to the particular political beliefs of the writers they discussed. The tastes of Marxism's first mass followers, the working-class movements of the United States and Great Britain, were avowedly sentimental and romantic, embracing literary versions of the flags, costumes, ceremonial music, and parades that socialistic workers and their families experienced as the apotheosis of their millenarian expectations. William Morris, Britian's poet laureate and the most prominent cultural figure of nineteenth-century socialist movements, was viewed with increasing distrust by Engels after Marx's death in 1883, doubtless because the medievalism of the poet—viewing capitalism as a mere interruption in a more collective human history—was more in line with mass sentiments than with the materialism of strict Marxists.

The first generation of American socialists, overwhelmingly foreign born and until the 1890s largely emigrated from Germany, transformed this semi-Marxist understanding into their often influential agitation. German-language daily newspapers in New York, Chicago, Cincinnati, St. Louis, and elsewhere were often edited by sometime poets and playwrights, jack-of-all-trades intellectuals who delineated and exalted the legend of Wilhelm Tell, the Romantic writings of the *Vormärz* (pre-1848) poets, and the classics of German literature, from Johann Wolfgang von Goethe to Heinrich Heine, as a searchlight upon the human condition. The Marxist-anarchist journalist Robert Reitzel, whose widely read German American literary magazine *Der arme Teufel,* (The poor devil, published from 1882 to 1900) constituted a veritable encyclopedia of cultural commentary, typically treated a shared history of literature and culture as the revolutionary weapon against the "shoddy aristocracy" of the upstart American bourgeoisie. German American *Turnvereine,* benefit societies and language schools for children, meanwhile provided the institutional basis for ongoing education and community forums, treating historical and cultural traditions as the sacred legacy from earlier cultures to the modern, secular socialists.

Important new elements of this style of Marxism appeared with diffusion of socialism into the English-speaking population and the arrival of new immigrants from eastern and southern Europe. The earliest native writer of serious historical study, C.

Osborne Ward, published the massive two-volume cultural and intellectual history, *The Ancient Lowly* (1888) about the origins of the "slave religion" of Christianity, and how it finally became the ruling-class ideology of Rome-dominated Christendom. America's all-time best-selling socialist author, Edward Bellamy, rooted his social understanding in a close reading of American history—as seen in *The Duke of Stockbridge* (1879), a sympathetic treatment of Shays's Rebellion—and, after his famed *Looking Backward, 2000–1887* (1888), shaped his political testament in *Equality* (1897) in terms of women's rights, with wilderness conservation the most distinctive quality of American radicalism. Walt Whitman's literary executor and intimate, Horace Traubel, published from 1890 until his death in 1919 the *Conservator,* a tabloid weekly that was increasingly Marxist in its treatments of American (and international) literary and cultural traditions. Indeed, William English Walling's *Whitman and Traubel* (1916) can be described as the first full-length U.S. cultural and intellectual history written in Marxist (if decidedly eclectic socialist) terms.

The Jewish Diaspora, its intellectuals intensely engaged in Marxist ideas before arriving in the United States, added entirely new dimensions to the dialogue of values and tradition. Predominantly Yiddish in their daily language, Jewish intellectuals played a crucial role in the promotion of *Yiddishkeit* (literally, "Yiddishness"), contributing to the literary flowering of Yiddish in the period from 1890 to 1940. From the first days of the literary-journalistic popularity of socialism in American (predominantly New York) ethnic ghettos, a simultaneously materialist and millennial appeal to traditions of Jewishness and diasporic alienation thus played a key role in American socialist politics. Indeed, even for one or two generations following the immigrants, Yiddishness, a diminishing remnant within Jewishness, signified a special realm in which capitalist values were viewed with repugnance and socialism was seen as a natural expression of intelligent observation.

As in the dozen or so other ethnic groups important in the American Left, immigrant Jewish socialists denounced their own ethnic bourgeoisie as capitulators to cultural assimilation as well as junior exploiters supportive of American business. They, the Jewish socialists (similar claims were made by anarchists, labor Zionists, and, later, communists), claimed to constitute true Jewishness and Jewish Americanness, with a historical pedigree demonstrated in essays on historical, intellectual, and literary themes—precursors of the scholarly historical studies to follow.

Not surprisingly, the first American Marxist cultural journal appeared in Yiddish, *Di Naye Geist* (The new spirit), which lasted for only a few years after 1897; its true spirit, however, survived into the Yiddish popular press (including the *Jewish Daily Forward,* the most widely read Yiddish-language paper in the world), the heavily theoretical *Zukunft* (The future), and numerous small monthlies with similar agendas etched in Jewish tradition, secular uplift, and revolutionary anticipation. Morris Winchevsky, the *zeyde* ("grandfather") of Yiddish socialist journalism, contributed to many of these publications, meanwhile composing voluminous essays on literary and cultural traditions of Jewishness and labor. The communist litterateur Kalmon Marmor's careful biography of Winchevsky, appearing as the first volume of the poet-essayist's collected works in 1929, may well be described as the earliest full-length biographical treatment of an important American Marxist cultural figure.

Behind this ethnic literary expression stood multiple popular institutions devoted to a roughly Marxist vision of working-class self-education and self-cultivation. The *Arbeter Ring* (workmen's circle), launched in the early 1890s as a sickness-and-death benefit society, offered generations of working people and lower middle classes a secular setting for cultural discussions, common readings of Yiddish classics, current socialistic works, and translations of Marx or August Bebel. By the later 1910s, socialistic schools in Yiddish became the basis for a far-flung social movement of socialistic cultural retention. Union locals, heavily Jewish, developed their own educational apparatus. Even summer camps, which flourished by the 1920s, were substantially devoted to cultural messages, classes led by the poets and informal scholars of tradition. Immigrant Finns, Lithuanians, Slovenians, Hungarians, and others organized similarly and simultaneously for collective self-defense and cultural expression of socialistic ideas, widening the readership of Marxist notions while infusing them with diverse cultural traditions far beyond the narrow economism often attributed to socialist movements and their intellectuals. For working-class life but perhaps for popular Marxist understanding as well, these ethnic institutions proved superior to the cultural journals and university circles that succeeded them.

The heyday of American (English-language) socialism, the first twenty years of the twentieth century, brought little greater theoretical sophistica-tion, but a large degree of popular exploration of tradition, albeit more via journalism and fiction than in strict historical terms. The Anglophilic circle around the *Comrade* (1901–1905), including an elderly William Dean Howells, sought to infuse a Morrisian aesthetic into Marxism and to bring a specifically English tradition of avant-gardism and sentimentalism into the American movement. Its proper successor, the *Masses* (1911 to 1918, when it merged with the *Liberator*), not only revolutionized American art (popularizing Ashcan school artists) and the emancipation of women, but argued for modernism as a continuing of the emancipating moments of American (and international) culture. *Masses* editor Floyd Dell's *Intellectual Vagabondage: An Apology for the Intelligentsia* (1926) urgently sought to explain his generation in terms of its educational background and the history of its striving. Barely influenced by Marxism but deeply involved in the pursuit of traditions, the radical journal *Seven Arts* (1916 to 1917) spawned such intellectuals as Waldo Frank, Van Wyck Brooks, and Lewis Mumford, drawn toward Marxist perspectives in the decades ahead.

Parallel versions of the *Masses* in other languages and cultures broadened this sensibility. *Il Fuoco,* published by the Italian American hero of the Lawrence strike of 1912, Arturo Giovannitti, urged an immigrant modernism; a culturally reshaped Yiddish anarchist *Freie Arbeter Shtimme* opened its pages to the interpreters of Jewish poetic traditions, especially the anarcho-Marxist (and Zionist) B. Rivkin; most important, the African American *Messenger,* published by young A. Philip Randolph, urged a stylish view of Harlem culture as the outcome of a rise from slavery and folk culture into the heart of the modern avant-garde. W. E. B. Du Bois, influenced by Marxism (briefly a member of the Socialist Party) and shocked by World War I, took over the journal of the National Association for the Advancement of Colored People (NAACP), the *Crisis,* with a radical tone and deep historic sensibility as he matured into his own deeply cultural (and increasingly Pan-African) interpretation of United States history, *Black Reconstruction in America, 1860–1880* (1935).

The major phases of the studies of historic American cultures from the 1930s to the 1940s sputtered out with postwar trends. But it would be mistaken to disregard myriad other Marxist-influenced legacies, more frequently artistic than cerebral, from that era. Working under tight constraints, muralists for the Works Progress Administration, as well as an assortment of radical artists for the Federal Theater, had dealt widely with themes of cultural tradition. Among novelists, Josephine Herbst, Olive Tilford Dargan, Jack Conroy, William Attaway, Tom Bell, Robert Cantwell, and Meridel Le Sueur created characters (occasionally, caricatures) to carry forward historical class images. The John Reed clubs of the early 1930s, urging the establishment of a proletarian venue for literature, stressed a regional-historic sensibility and attention to class and race traditions.

Meanwhile, journals like the *Marxist Quarterly* and *Science and Society,* as well as the *Partisan Review,* carried literary studies and intellectual histories (especially of that favorite vanished giant, Thorstein Veblen). Even film reviews, in the *New Masses* especially, commented at length on the validity or (usually) patent falsity of cinematic portrayals of American history.

The formal Marxist scholarship that followed has a related origin. Communists, assuming charge of a much-diminished Left after 1920, devoted their energies within a sphere of splendid isolation until the early 1930s, producing several cultural journals (especially the *New Masses* and its Yiddish equivalent, *Der Hammer*) with vital discussions of literary traditions but little sustained intellectual work. An independent circle of intellectuals around the *Modern Quarterly,* launched in 1923 by the former Baltimore schoolteacher V. F. Calverton, proclaimed its "culturalism" as a badge of honor. Modernity demanded—after the organized Left had collapsed at any rate—scholarly attention to sex, gender, and race as well as social class. Anthropologists, sociologists, sexologists, and notably scholars of African American life would be central to this enterprise.

Calverton's own writing was exemplary of this effort, with all its inherent limitations. *The New Spirit* (1925), *Sex in Civilization* (1929), and *The Liberation of American Literature* (1932) offered a sweeping overview. Literature had evolved in three great stages of human culture: the pre-industrial culture dominated by the nobility; the bourgeois culture of the eighteenth and nineteenth centuries; and the proletarian culture from the last quarter of the nineteenth century onward. "Liberation" signified the final shedding of past restraints that had obscured the full realization of social literature. The process of shedding would leave behind the "colonial complex" of Anglophilia, the prudery of the Calvinist tradition, and the sentimentalism of Victorianism; joined with black folk culture and the freed sexual-social expression of women, it would prepare the great leap forward of society at large.

Critics complained that Calverton's method of reducing historical literatures to specific classes was unhelpful, but the vision and the comprehensive scope of *The Liberation of American Literature* could not be denied. Granville Hicks's *The Great Tradition* (1933), a text set upon a smaller canvas of major U.S. literary figures of roughly a century from the Concord circle to the 1920s, made the task more precise. The promise of radical transcendentalism, wiped out by the rampant sectionalism; the gentility of William Dean Howells's circle, unequal to the tasks of realism; and the uncertainties of the transitional generation of Hamlin Garland and Frank Norris yielded finally to the younger rebels like Theodore Dreiser and Sherwood Anderson, blocked again by war but bearing a promise evidently to be realized at last by the newest literary Left.

The milieu around Hicks and the *New Masses,* which he helped edit, grew from its hard-line pursuit of "proletarian literature" in the early 1930s to become something like a school of American Marxism. Joseph Freeman, Newton Arvin, Bernard Smith, and even the stiffly orthodox Mike Gold urged and practiced (usually in essays rather than monographic volumes) a coming-to-grips with American cultural traditions, including their own. American Writers Congress, a broader but closely related circle including Malcolm Cowley, Van Wyck Brooks, Theodore Dreiser, Lewis Mumford, Waldo Frank, and Kenneth Burke, assembled an agenda in the fight for American and democratic (also quietly Marxist) traditions against fascism, with the heavy emphasis upon the members' assorted contributions in widely read and admired contemporary writing. The disillusionment brought by the Hitler-Stalin Pact of 1939, and even more the fading of depression economics in the war boom, put an end to the popularity of the effort if not the effort itself.

The cultural currents coalescing in the group destined to be known as the New York Intellectuals took flight in specific opposition to these popular front trends. At first identifying with the Communist Party and then avidly against it, the *Partisan Review* spawned a cohort of intellectuals devoted to the autonomy of culture from economics and the centrality of nineteenth-century European literary-artistic traditions for American cultural life. While they expressed their ideas mainly in essays, a concentrated version of their early collective thought on the intellectual history of the United States can be found in Alfred Kazin's *On Native Grounds* (1942), the Jewish liberal's testament to successfully locating a space beyond the political demands and the millenarianism of the 1930s-style Left perspec-

V. F. CALVERTON

Born George Goetz in Baltimore at the turn of the twentieth century, the future literary impresario attended Johns Hopkins University, becoming in 1922 the editor of the *Modern Quarterly.* Renaming himself as he began a new life (he soon became a literary agent, and commuted between New York and Baltimore), Calverton staked out intellectual territory opened by the collapse of the pre-1920 Left. His journal offered an eclectic mix of history, anthropology, sociology, psychology, and literary criticism, nearly all of it shaded by an undogmatic Marxism. More than any previous Left journal in the United States or Europe, the *Quarterly* highlighted race issues and invited nonwhite contributors on a variety of subjects. As much as any up to that time, it urged the emancipation of women as the foremost lever of human progress at large. More than reinterpreting American cultural history, the *Quarterly* was itself cultural history in the making.

Calverton himself meanwhile turned out volumes at a breakneck pace, both monographs and anthologies, on literature and sexology. Achieving considerable popularity toward the end of the 1920s with sex subjects in particular, he sought to link "sex and the social struggle" in theoretical terms as the pre-1920 Greenwich Village radicals had linked them in art and aspiration. He thus explained the failure (or delay) of working class supremacy through "cultural compulsives," the psychological lag between social conditions and mass consciousness. As a scholar of intellectual and cultural history, he made his mark through a series of volumes culminating with *The Liberation of American Literature* (1932).

The problem of American intellectuals, by this sweeping (and often close textual) interpretation was the "colonial complex" of English literature, overlaid by the Puritanism of the first generations and the stuffy middle-class mentality of later nineteenth-century writers. "Liberation" would come with the maturation of realist, radical writers drawn (like himself) from sources close to the working class.

Modern Quarterly contributors like Samuel Schmalhausen, for a time Calverton's co-editor, also urged and themselves conducted the first sustained intellectual dialogue within the United States between Karl Marx and Sigmund Freud. If sexual relations could be analyzed in relation to social struggle (and women's advance), and if the vibrant qualities of African American culture could be understood in relation to modern working-class culture, then Marxism and Freudianism as intellectual systems could realize their joint potential. For the political mood of the 1920s, this was considerable advance, but sadly inadequate to the pressing economic and social questions posed by the Great Depression. Losing out to more focused journals like the *New Masses* and the *Partisan Review,* Calverton and his magazine became more directly political, to their considerable detriment.

The *Modern Quarterly* (monthly for a few years of the 1930s) did not survive Calverton, and the reputation of his work suffered badly in the decades following his death in 1940. At the close of his life, Calverton planned a series of volumes on American utopianism, of which only one (*Where Angels Dared to Tread,* 1941) actually appeared. Doubtless, Calverton was guilty of a mechanical correlation of economic conditions with ideas, but more so of a determined radicalism. Yet he (like his non-Marxist counterpart, V. L. Parrington) had formulated the basics of a materialist interpretation of American intellectual history. In gathering a lively circle of culturally oriented academic and nonacademic thinkers, Calverton had also formed the first version of "New York Intellectuals," superior in many ways, but above all politically, to their more prestigious but also fundamentally compromised successors around the *Partisan Review.*

tive, but in line with what he took to be the best socialistic-minded contributions to democracy. As Kazin's group moved sharply away from all sections of the Left, they swiftly threw off the Marxist mantle and treated American popular (or folk) cultures as anathema, radical traditions as irrational, and American intellectual traditions at large as unworthy and unimportant.

W. E. B. Du Bois's *Black Reconstruction* stood so far outside either popular front or anti–popular front aesthete positions that it might almost be declared sui generis and unrepeatable—except that it would become basic doctrine for Marxists in the last quarter of the twentieth century. Increasingly moving toward Marxist methodological positions during the 1920s and early 1930s, Du Bois pointed heretically (in Marxist terms) to the failure of American labor to support the black struggle of the late nineteenth century. That failure, alongside the renascent power of southern economic barons and American racism at large, had been a catastrophic loss to democracy (including a future proletarian democracy), not only for the United States but for the world at large. In cultural even more than economic terms, Du Bois had identified the "American Assumption"—that economic development and imperial destiny for white Americans would bring boons to all—the falseness of which lay at the heart of the society's failure. It was not a lesson, and not a historical interpretation, that either popular front Marxists or their aesthete opponents wanted to hear. Only the formally scholarly, Ph.D.-carrying generations to follow could put Du Bois's insights into monographic frameworks.

THE STUDIO AND THE UNIVERSITY

F. O. Matthiessen's *American Renaissance* (1941), the most widely read study of American literature until that time and for a generation after, was an apparently curious mixture of formalist (or semi-autonomous, nonreductive) aesthetics and popular front political sentiment. Here, as seen in the Concord circle, the tragedy that the West imposed upon itself, not by Philistinism and weakness toward communism (as in the *Partisan Review* perspective) but by its own triumphant individualism, might be surmounted by the reconciliation of native radical artistic and folk traditions with a Marxist worldview.

But Matthiessen's approach was less rare than later scholars seemed to appreciate. For the most part, the Marxist kernel was realized best in popular art, especially popular film. From the later 1930s to the artistic noir moment of American cinema at the close of the 1940s, Marxist screenwriters destined for the blacklist continually examined artistic and political traditions through setting, plot, and character, etching "American" types intimately identified with Katharine Hepburn, Humphrey Bogart, Alan Ladd, or John Garfield—the sentimental dirt farmer or child growing up on the frontier, the broken soldier from World War I, the brave African American and Native American, the silly bourgeois of virtually any American era, and so on. The nation's first serious film journal, *Hollywood Quarterly,* edited largely by Hollywood communists and near-communists, offered the intellectual culmination of this perspective for a few years (1946 to 1950) until purged of its political perspective.

One of its editors, the noir writer-director Abraham Polonsky, would be best remembered for his later historical drama, *Tell Them Willie Boy Is Here* (1969), neatly reversing the traditional stereotypes of the western saga. A handful of left-wing novelists, notably the later Marxist historian Alexander Saxton, also continued working historical veins with novels like *The Great Midland* (1948). The most orthodox of the Marxist screenwriters, John Howard Lawson, devoted his blacklisted years to a pair of expansive but unimaginative cultural histories: *The Hidden Heritage: A Rediscovery of the Ideas and Forces That Link the Thought of Our Time with the Culture of the Past* (1950) and *Film: The Creative Process* (1964). This tradition, going underground, provided the background for later media reconstructions of American history, from revisionist westerns like *Tell Them Willie Boy Is Here* to the revisionist war-setting film *MASH* (1970) and the ensuing all-time favorite television series that aired throughout the 1970s and early 1980s.

Contrary to this milieu but still on the leftward side, Dwight Macdonald's *Politics* magazine (from 1945 to 1949) offered another political perspective on American tradition, disliking most of it but in a more radical way than the disdainful New York Intellectuals. Like the intellectual activities of the Frankfurt school in exile, Macdonald's demi-Marxism added an important negative element, spurring not only the Marxist-anarchistic spirit of Macdonald's own voluminous writings on American culture and film, but also the eccentric interpretations of tradition by the social critic Paul Goodman and the continuing legacy of Thoreau-flavored radical sensibility in the *Liberation* magazine circle after 1956. Sidney Lens's influential intellectual history, *Radicalism in America* (1966), more Henry David Thoreau than Marx, nevertheless sought to reconcile the twin spirits.

A handful of intellectuals and cultural figures of the early to mid-1950s moved in roughly similar directions to *Politics* or the Frankfurt school—the homosexual Marxist-anarchist film critic and scholar Parker Tyler among the most creative. But the academy, as the coming center of intellectual production, went through a political shutdown similar to that in Hollywood. For some years, Marxist ideas (or at least their open and radical expression) were all but forbidden.

To the small group of Marxists firmly wedded to anticommunism, notably Irving Howe, this situation offered more opportunity than problem. With the decks seemingly cleared of competitors, Howe analyzed modernist strains in American literature with special fondness for Sherwood Anderson, insisting (as he would say in *Politics and the Novel,* 1957) that, historically, Americans had inevitably failed as writers and theorists to see beyond the personal to the social, had lacked, in effect, the kind of large-scale cultural understanding manifest in their European intellectual counterparts. As in the Zionist view of Jewish history, a "negative" had now to be resolved with a "positive"—in this case acceptance of European cultural traditions. By contrast, the gradually growing interest in popular culture, black or women's history, and colonialized subjects, seemed to Howe and his colleagues disruptive and unuseful. Other formerly Marxist literary scholars of the same milieu, notably Leslie A. Fiedler, carried over this burden of absence into purported American cultural failures of other kinds, such as a failure of heterosexual realization (in *Love and Death in the American Novel,* 1960), without shifting the essentially negative affect.

Former Marxists who had moved away from Marxism and from the avant-garde to the political middle carried this thought to its logical conclusion. Richard Hofstadter's *American Political Tradition and the Men Who Made It* (1948) and *The Age of Reform: From Bryan to F.D.R.* (1955) offered an influential intellectual history of perverse success: class-conscious milieus of heroic power ideologues in a society where possessive individualism ruled all. Like Louis Hartz's *The Liberal Tradition in America* (1955), Hofstadter's works take this reverse spin on Du Bois's American Assumption as a virtue, if one bearing significant limitations. He could do that because the perspective of Du Bois and others from nonwhite America was lost on these scholars (as on the remainder of the New York Intellectuals circle)

in the cold war, liberal frame of the 1950s and early 1960s.

This outlook, which turned the better parts of 1930s and 1940s Marxism upon its head, was in turn upended by the sentiments of early New Left scholars and their successors. The discovery or rediscovery of cultural resistance within lower-class groups in history became the driving urge of former youthful Marxists who had survived McCarthyism and come into the open as left-wing historians of the later 1960s and 1970s. Most of Herbert Gutman's work would properly be deemed social history, but his *Work, Culture, and Society* (1976) among other volumes had a rich cultural basis and methodological kernel in contemporary anthropological studies. George Rawick's studies of slave culture, *From Sundown to Sunup* (1972), and the accompanying forty-one published volumes of slave narratives collected by Works Progress Administration (WPA) fieldworkers, were more directly cultural history. Gutman, Rawick, Alfred Young, Jesse Lemisch, David Montgomery, and others ten or twenty years senior of the New Left sought to recreate the historical conditions of the era studied, but they frequently focused their search on cultural milieus and/or relied upon an intellectual history of the dissenters in an era to give their social history analysis a sharp articulation.

Journals of the New Left, with which such scholars had extensive contact, picked up this spirit in various ways. *Studies on the Left* (1959 to 1967), inspired by the work of the diplomatic historian William Appleman Williams, inclined toward analysis of the cultures of the rulers. *Radical America* (1967 to 1997), close in spirit to Rawick's own intellectual mentor, the Pan-African historian, sports scholar, and litterateur C. L. R. James, turned quickly to the hidden cultures of working people, women, and nonwhites. *Cultural Correspondence* (1975 to 1983), a child of *Radical America,* sought to extend the Marxist discussion into the realm of popular culture, as the locus of potentially radical dialogue between artist and mass. The *Minnesota Review* (in its Marxist phase, 1975 to present), has aimed at expressions in literature and criticism that include a recuperation of neglected traditions, offering an early version and continuing counterpart to those largely literary or cultural studies journals (*Social Text, Cultural Critique,* and a phase of the influential *South Atlantic Quarterly,* among others) with a decided Marxist orientation.

By the later 1970s, radical scholarship flourished but its Marxist and historical underpinnings wavered. Deconstruction, especially in its initial phases, pointed away from historical approaches as outdated and uninteresting. Yet some of the leading figures of the new critical movement were quite outspoken in their Marxist inclinations, however they carried out their critical work. Fredric Jameson, by all means the most influential literary theorist since F. O. Matthiessen, devoted himself to the study of form (best seen in his *Marxism and Form*, 1971) in which the "substructure" of Marxism bore a distant relation to the "superstructure" of the text, whether novel or architecture. Edward Said, one of the most controversial intellectual American figures in the last quarter of the twentieth century, made his mark with works that, like the later texts of the literary theorist Gayatri Chakravorty Spivak, chose to analyze the cultural sources as well as the outcome of colonialism. But in showing most concern for the West's myopia, it has been left to other scholars (such as the varied contributors to Amy Kaplan and Donald Pease's major anthology, *Cultures of United States Imperialism*, 1993) to concern themselves with United States subjects including forgotten counterimperial intellectual and cultural traditions.

Among the major scholars seeking to draw upon such traditions subsisting at the unrespected margins of American culture (and often deep within the popular culture), the former *Cultural Correspondence* editor George Lipsitz has been exemplary and widely influential. His *A Rainbow at Midnight: Class and Culture in Cold War America* (1980, 1994), for the most part a study of diverse blue-collar cultures during the 1940s and early 1950s, has guided younger scholars' attempts to reconnect political and cultural history. Lipsitz's *Time Passages: Collective Memory and American Popular Culture* (1990) extends the argument to cultures as apparently distant as television shows about European-American ethnic life and Chicano music of Los Angeles.

Michael Denning's *The Cultural Front: The Laboring of American Culture in the Twentieth Century* (1996) reads this history back, in a sense, to the 1930s to 1940s, where the artistry of the popular front era remains surprisingly little explored and where new meanings can be readily located in the intersection of left-wing cabaret, the filmmaker Orson Welles, labor union musicales, film animation, and the Marxist-influenced litterateurs who leaped across boundaries to take part in many of them. Cary Nelson, in *Repression and Recovery: Modern American Poetry and the Politics of Cultural Memory, 1910–1945* (1989), did much the same for the forgotten left-wing poetry of the 1920s to 1930s. Alan Wald, best known for his close intellectual history, *The New York Intellectuals* (1987), has filled out

much of the popular front–related territory through biographical and literary studies in various works, including his *Writing from the Left: New Essays on Radical Culture and Politics* (1994).

Mike Davis's highly prestigious *City of Quartz* (1990), drawing on similar Marxist traditions but coming to very different conclusions, looked backward at the intersections of race and class cultures in order to look forward into the nightmare that might have been Du Bois's final, pessimistic reading of America. For Davis, white skin privilege and "crowd control" have produced modern Los Angeles, the ultimate urban metaphor of planlessness and waste, as relentlessly as alternatives of all kinds have been avoided or suppressed.

The largest observable circle of historically minded scholars of the 1980s and 1990s influenced by Marxism has also sought to grasp the connections of organized labor and American society, but in earlier eras. The veteran Marxist Alexander Saxton prepared the way for this history in essays that made up his sweeping *Rise and Fall of the White Republic* (1990). Eric Lott (*Love and Theft: Blackface Minstrelsy and the American Working Class*, 1993), David R. Roediger (*The Wages of Whiteness: Race and the American Working Class*, 1991), and Noel Ignatiev (*How the Irish Became White*, 1995), most forcefully developed Saxton's argument that race privilege grants both material and psychological benefits.

Robin D. G. Kelley has carried this observation into the twentieth century and reversed its valence, arguing (with strong echoes of C. L. R. James) that such conditions have made African Americans politically volatile—frequently more than the American Left recognized. His massive social history of the southern black Left, *Hammer and Hoe: Alabama Communists during the Great Depression* (1990), contained a large measure of heretofore neglected intellectual and cultural history of the regional Left. Other works, such as his collection of essays, *Race Rebels: Culture, Politics, and the Black Working Class* (1994), extended the argument into the daily life of southern bus passengers, zoot suiters, and rap musicians. If LeRoi Jones/Amiri Baraka's historical-minded essays (best known in *Blues People*, 1963) had in some ways predicted the writer's shift from avant-garde to mechanistic Marxist, Kelley's later fluid Marxist view of culture set the tone for the historical-cultural race narratives of the end of the twentieth century.

A large handful of studies, including many biographies of American radicals, added to this determinedly optimistic perspective of locating prophetic and (in their time) heroic figures across the mostly hidden historical landscape. Among the new reference works compiled, the *Encyclopedia of the American Left* (2d ed., 1998) offered a comprehensive guide to Marxist intellectual and cultural subjects within a single volume. *The Political Companion to American Film* (1994), edited by the founder of the left-wing *Cineaste* magazine, provided a similarly Marxist-inclined interpretation from a rapidly growing area of cultural studies.

Claims for radical potential with U.S. experience were difficult for Marxists to make at the close of a bitterly disappointing century, even as (or because) a doggedly imperial America remained a prosperous island within a crisis-ridden planet. For that reason, a Marxist or post-Marxist discussion centered around the society of consumption, now figured in gender (and sometimes race) terms so as to explore the ambivalent impulses of a unique, if deeply divided, order.

An earlier elaboration of cultural history—most influentially in Great Britain by Stuart Hall and the younger scholars around the Center for Contemporary Cultural Studies in Birmingham, U.K.—rested its Marxist claims upon the Italian Communist Party founder Antonio Gramsci's theories of hegemony and the Frankfurt school's (almost uniformly hostile) interpretations of mass culture. American counterparts, usually at least one era removed from classic Marxist texts and working-class concerns as such, struggled to make a Gramscian interpretation work in terms of mass consumption and its rituals, and to argue that hints of collective self-consciousness remained to be discovered within such realms.

Warren Susman, in later years the television scholar David Marc, and George Lipsitz helpfully formulated this last point. The French Marxist-situationist text by Guy Debord, *Society of the Spectacle* (published originally in the United States as a 1970 issue of *Radical America*), articulated the "spectacular" theory of the all-expansive, all-encompassing postmodern and (for liberal intellectuals) post-Marxist process for American intellectuals. A handful of 1970s theorists filled out the theoretical perspectives, as texts like Richard Ohmann's *Selling Culture: Magazines, Markets and Class at the Turn of the Century* (1996) marshaled the evidence. Younger scholars continued to gather empirical data for the detailed work at hand at the close of the twentieth century.

Familiar and unresolved theoretical questions remained, however, behind every Marx-inflected mass cultural study of whether consumption was indeed a universal "modern" value or a wasteful and degrading phase of social self-destruction. No wonder a Marxist ecological view of connections between class, race, ethnicity, and the transformation of the landscape remained squarely on the scholarly-political agenda. Intellectuals involved with the journal *Capitalism, Nature, Socialism,* edited by the veteran Marxist economist James O'Connor, continued the dialogue popularized by its most widely received member, Mike Davis, in *City of Quartz.* Arguing that seemingly endless economic expansion had harbored a disguised contradiction all through class society's long history, O'Connor's landmark volume *Natural Causes: Essays in Ecological Marxism* (1998) indicates that the crisis-ridden economic, social, and cultural system has postponed (or suppressed the social symptoms of) disaster through heightened exploitation of the environment. Historically, culture reflected the crumbling of empires, the collapse of social systems, and the common destruction of contending classes, as intellectuals over the last century had only begun to grasp.

Such an overview of empire—close to the perspectives of William Appleman Williams, especially in his final volume, *Empire as a Way of Life* (1980)—proposes in cultural terms realizations that most American intellectuals have only slowly come to accept. Monumental revisionist histories of the West, such as Richard White's *"It's Your Misfortune and None of My Own"* (1991), bear the stamp of Williams's Marxist perspective indirectly, but many of those of more focused character, such as William G. Robbins's *Colony and Empire: The Capitalist Transformation of the American West* (1994), show Williams's influence still very much at work in recasting U.S. historiography at large.

This major late-twentieth-century historical argument within and around Marxist circles over the issue of "exceptionalism" takes up the very concept upon which liberal historians of the 1950s projected their views of a nearly classless society. Taking up the consequences of race and gender issues sturdily ignored by cold-war-era intellectuals, the newer Marxists turned the premises into something approaching their opposite. A major scholarly discussion of exceptionalism at University College in London in 1995, following by a decade another such discussion in the pages of the journal *International Labor and Working Class History,* came to the sobering conclusion that the purported exceptionalism of American political culture and intellectual life was an imperial formulation after all. Consensus within the standard intellectual histories had been reached by privileging specific elements of society (whites, middle and upper classes) over others and equally by ignoring the global costs. The theories and theorists themselves, far more than the society seen in a global or longer historical sense, had been "exceptional" and unrepresentative all along.

Marxist reinterpretations toward the end of the twentieth century took shape mostly under this sign. Some of the most notable volumes involved an issue of old contention, the decline of the Knights of Labor as an exhaustion of nineteenth-century reform movements, or their active suppression. By the mid-twentieth century, these questions were apparently resolved by a consensus history that stressed the impossibility of cultural,

economic, or political dissent surviving within a prosperous order; in the twenty-first century, the strength of the adversary, the amassed power of American corporations, seems to have been a far more likely cause. If so, the contribution of the cultural history is, in part, to point to the importance of economic and social studies. But it is also to pinpoint, as Timothy Messer-Kruse did in his *The Yankee International: Marxism and the American Reform Tradition 1848–1876* (1998), the ways in which American radicals had the strengths of their weaknesses, witnesses to empire but also actors against empire, creative strangers within an often strange land that they somehow managed to make their own.

See also **Patterns of Reform and Revolt; Racialism and Racial Uplift; The Popular Arts; Radical Alternatives** *(volume 1);* **World War and Cold War; Race, Rights, and Reform; Countercultural Visions; Multiculturalism in Theory and Practice; African Americans; German Speakers; Jews; Working Class; Social Reform; Socialism and Radical Thought** *(volume 2);* **Twentieth-Century Economic Thought; Race; Class; Journals of Opinion; Periodicals; Film** *(in this volume); and other articles in this section.*

BIBLIOGRAPHY

Early Marxist Histories, 1870–1950

Calverton, V. F. *The Liberation of American Literature.* New York, 1932.

DuBois, W. E. B. *Black Reconstruction in America, 1860–1880.* 1935. Reprint, New York, 1964.

Hicks, Granville. *The Great Tradition in American Literature.* New York, 1933.

Matthiessen, F. O. *American Renaissance.* London, 1941.

Smith, Bernard. *Forces in American Literature.* New York, 1939.

Walling, William English. *Whitman and Traubel.* New York, 1916.

Ward, C. Osborne. *The Ancient Lowly: A History of the Ancient Working People.* 2 vols. 1888. Reprint, New York, 1907.

Recent Radical Texts, 1950–Present

Abelove, Henry, et al., eds. *Visions of History.* New York, 1983.

Buhle, Mari Jo, Paul Buhle, and Dan Georgakas, eds. *Encyclopedia of the American Left.* New York, 1998.

Buhle, Paul. *Marxism in the United States.* London, 1987.

Buhle, Paul, ed. *History and the New Left, Madison, Wisconsin, 1950–1970.* Philadelphia, 1990.

Buhle, Paul, and Edmund Sullivan. *Images of American Radicalism.* Hanover, Mass., 1998.

Crowdus, Gary, ed. *The Political Companion to American Film.* Chicago, 1994.

Davis, Mike. *City of Quartz: Excavating the Future in Los Angeles.* New York, 1990.

Halpern, Rick, and Jonathan Morris, eds. *American Exceptionalism? U.S. Working-Class Formation in an International Context.* London, 1997.

Hofstadter, Richard. *The Age of Reform: From Bryan to F. D. R.* New York, 1955.

Kaplan, Amy, and Donald E. Pease, eds. *Cultures of United States Imperialism.* Durham, N.C., 1993.

Kuznick, Peter. *Beyond the Laboratory: Scientists as Political Activists in 1930s America.* Chicago, 1987.

Lawson, John Howard. *Film: The Creative Process.* New York, 1964.

Lipsitz, George. *A Rainbow at Midnight: Class and Culture in Cold War America.* Urbana, Ill., 1994.

McGilligan, Patrick, and Paul Buhle. *Tender Comrades: A Backstory of the Hollywood Blacklist.* New York, 1997.

Messer-Kruse, Timothy. *The Yankee International: Marxism and the American Reform Traditions 1848–1876.* Chapel Hill, N.C., 1998.

Montgomery, David. *Citizen Worker: The Experience of Workers in the United States with Democracy and the Free Market during the Nineteenth Century.* New York, 1993.

Nelson, Cary. *Repression and Recovery: Modern American Poetry and the Politics of Cultural Memory, 1910–1945.* Madison, Wis., 1989.

O'Connor, James. *Natural Causes: Essays in Ecological Marxism.* New York, 1998.

Phelps, Christopher. *Young Sidney Hook: Marxist and Pragmatist.* Ithaca, N.Y., 1997.

Robbins, William G. *Colony and Empire: The Capitalist Transformation of the American West.* Lawrence, Kans., 1994.

Voss, Kim. *The Making of American Exceptionalism: The Knights of Labor.* Ithaca, N.Y., 1997.

Weir, Robert. *Beyond Labor's Veil: The Culture of the Knights of Labor.* University Park, Pa., 1993.

Wald, Alan. *The New York Intellectuals: The Rise and Decline of the Anti-Stalinist Left from the 1930s to the 1980s.* Chapel Hill, N.C., 1987.

Williams, William Appleman. *Empire as a Way of Life.* New York, 1980.

GENDER

Nancy Isenberg

In 1987 Rosalind Rosenberg could write convincingly that scholars in the fields of women's history and intellectual history "have kept a discrete distance from one another over the years." Few women's historians at that time published what was considered intellectual history, and intellectual historians ignored women. Most of these historians did not see women as serious intellectuals worthy of study, nor did they consider women's issues as raising important philosophical or intellectual concerns. Yet American women's history changed dramatically in the decade following Rosenberg's diagnosis, primarily because of the "linguistic turn" and the influence of poststructuralism (such as discourse analysis, a blend of mainly Derridian, Foucauldian, French feminist, and Lacanian theory).

These influences gave rise to the "new cultural history," which revived interest in the study of language as a grounds of political contestation and social meaning. This shift can be attributed, in part, to the new focus on gender, and its more sophisticated and theoretical applications by feminist scholars and historians. At the same time, gender is no longer the sole province of women's historians. Its evolving meaning has ignited a new appreciation for understanding the construction of masculinity and the development of gay and lesbian identities. And gender analysis has furthered the growth of historical studies of sexuality, a new field which established its own journal, *The History of Sexuality,* in 1990.

Such changes become evident if one conducts a title search in any major research library database. A search at the University of Wisconsin at Madison found only eleven entries listed under "gender" that had publication dates prior to 1980. For 1980–1989, the number increased to 215 titles, but the real surge occurred between 1990 and 2000, with 973 entries. This means that out of a total of 1,199 titles, a significantly high percentage—81 percent—were published from 1990 to 2000. Further perusal suggested an astonishingly wide range of topics listed when gender was paired with virtually any other subject. Beginning with gender and anthropology, the topics included art and death, church and state, constructs, democracy, envy, fascism, genius, history, imperialism, Jim Crow, language, national identity, politics and MTV, power, science, sex, theory, the welfare state, and utopia in advertising, to name just a few.

Other developments were just as revealing, particularly the appearance of new book series introduced by prominent academic presses. In 1985 Columbia University Press began the Gender and Culture series, providing a new array of mostly literary and theoretical studies of gender. The University of North Carolina Press launched the Gender and American Culture series in 1988, primarily publishing books on historical topics. Also focusing on the history market, the Johns Hopkins University Press began a series in 1994 entitled Gender Relations in the American Experience. Although the University of Chicago Press featured the Women in Culture and Society series, inaugurated in 1984, this series, too, promotes books that use the word "gender" (in place of "women") in the title. Various scholarly journals also opt for "gender" in their names, such as *Gender and History,* which made its debut in 1989.

As feminist and poststructuralist theory gained ascendancy in literary, culture, and film studies, its arguments and insights migrated to history. An important turning point came with the publication of Joan Scott's article "Gender: A Useful Category of Historical Analysis" in 1986, which appeared in the flagship journal of the American Historical Association, the *American Historical Review.* Two years later, Scott's article was republished in her book *Gender and the Politics of History,* which became the first historical work to be included in Columbia University Press's Gender and Culture series. Scott's article served as a rallying cry for women's historians to adopt "theoretical formulations" that could "transform . . . dominant disciplinary concepts." Her critique centered on the failure of women's history to change how most historians explained the fundamental "truths" of history. Previous scholars had used gender mainly as a descriptive device. Scott believed that while women's historians had added many well-conceived case studies and sophisticated narratives of women's experiences, they had not altered the dominant paradigms used by historians, especially in the traditional fields of political, military, and intellectual history. Women's history will remain marginalized, she lamented, unless scholars begin to employ a more rigorous and theoretically informed definition of gender.

Scott offered two principles to guide historians in making gender into an analytical category. First, historians are meant to avoid the narrow view of gender as merely reflecting "perceived differences between the sexes," and instead recognize that gender can signify "relationships of power." Influenced by Michel Foucault's theory of discourse as "fields of force," Scott pointed out that gendered conventions and idioms (such as the use of sexual language in political controversies) can reveal a larger system of relationships that link together political ideologies and gender identity. Her argument rested on a crucial re-evaluation of gender as historically constructed through cultural "processes." That is, gender cannot be explained simply as a belief system rooted in a "single origin" of biological differences between the sexes. Breaking with the tradition that gender is tied to its origin in a particular capacity—usually sexual or reproductive roles—Scott suggested that gendered meanings are created, reproduced, and transformed in relation to other cultural and ideological practices. Simply put, gendered discourse often has nothing to do with actual biology, but rather is used as a proxy to define power relations in the state, law, church, or any larger political institution or social development. Gender, moreover, may work as the pivotal ideological matrix for structuring the rationale behind political decisions, for triggering some hidden source of cultural fears, or for contributing the dominant trope or symbolic referent in religious rituals.

Second, unlike the field of women's history at the time, Scott indicated that gender is never just about women—nor is gender a direct reflection of actual sexual practices. Indeed, Scott showed that what might be valued in society (for example, two-parent families, domesticity for women, heterosexuality) does not transparently reflect how society functions. Historians, she insisted, must learn to treat language and cultural practices with greater skepticism and scrutiny because self-evident words do not register a coherent reality. On the contrary,

past usages of language are unstable, meanings are contested, and words can distort, conceal, or construct meanings which ultimately contradict the lived experience of men and women.

Scott's essay synthesized several assumptions that allowed historians to situate gender in the center—rather than the margins—of historical scholarship. The move from women's history to gender history shifted the focus to *sexual difference,* or the premise that meaning is generated through differences, oppositions, and cultural tensions instead of the older preference for the search for unity. Thus, the category of "woman" only makes sense when compared with "man" and through a chain of deferred meaning, meaning that moves from place to place with no fixed frame of reference, sexual difference migrates to and informs other categories, such as race, class, religion, and nationality. In this way, gender discourse produces social knowledge in a random fashion that is often beyond the control of specific individuals, demonstrating how difference can transgress, if not disrupt, normative boundaries or the accepted ways of thinking about social order. For example, this perspective can be applied to biblical language, in which specific verses (such as the creation story) offer competing views of "woman"—and the meaning changes, depending on the different responses of readers or listeners. In fact, in the nineteenth century, three new religious movements—the Shakers, the Mormons, and the Oneida communal society—all developed very different views of sexual practices and reproduction by using the same biblical verse. Language, then, does not have a fixed center, words do not have a single meaning, and meaning may not follow a logical or clear trajectory because texts, in the words of French critic Roland Barthes, possess an "irreducible plurality."

Despite this interest in difference, scholars have used gender to uncover the "anonymous rules" that govern people's lives. The faith in individual autonomy and agency has been tempered, making historians more sensitive to the fact that identity is not just acquired but imposed. Gender scripts precondition and organize action before it happens, and certain rules, or doxa, are so fundamental and unquestioned that these guidelines are rarely if ever challenged. Similarly, if sexual arrangements fall into the category of social "givens," then the enforcement of such givens requires internalized discipline—or Foucault's notion that power is dispersed through desire (making people want to behave in certain ways) rather than through punishment alone. Power is exercised through knowledge, the privileging of scientific "truth" in modern society, which has led to the classification of normal and deviant behavior (setting apart the "other") and the encouragement of individuals to regulate themselves at the level of the body itself (through dress, posture, speech, emotional suppression, and bodily movement).

The recognition that knowledge is gendered has led to increased fascination with gendered metaphors, the word choices, analogies, and literary tropes found in discourses. Awareness of gendered language in writing and reading has also resulted in greater attention being paid to ways of seeing and hearing—that is, what is written down is not restricted to the text itself but is understood as a cultural performance. As literary critic Frederic Jameson has contended, "everything has become 'cultural' in some sense," which means that the "older stable reality of reference" (that a word reflects a self-evident truth) is no longer unproblematic. To understand how texts work, it is important to understand how they perform, reproduce, and replicate meaning, interpreting written documents in the same way a theater critic evaluates a play, seeing behind the words to uncover the process of creating cultural meaning. Historical action, then, has become more closely linked to language and the written word, which has opened the door for a new style of intellectual history that is not restricted to the "intellectual" or "thinking person" but also includes the cultural and gendered performer. How knowledge is organized, not just its literal meaning, is essential for understanding historical patterns of behavior, and the form of representing or enacting meaning is as valuable as the specific content.

RELIGION AND GENDERED SPEECH

One area where gender has changed intellectual history is in analyzing the "politics of speech." Jane Kamensky's *Governing the Tongue: The Politics of Speech in Early New England* (1997) demonstrates how men and women lived in communities where gender acutely shaped the rules of public speaking and silence. Returning to the favorite subject of intellectual historians—American Puritanism—Kamensky uncovers the previously overlooked religious and social conventions that regulated dissident speech. In the New World environment, everyday public speech—its form and content—became a source of avid contention. Speech also involved ritualized performances in which disorderly tongues faced punishment, silencing, ostracism, and called for the

verbally disobedient to make public apologies. In their own words, Puritans were "hearful," and women's dual roles as both ranter and the "silent" and pious follower created social tensions. Anne Hutchinson, the infamous antinomian dissident of the early seventeenth century, and Ann Hibbens, an elite woman forced to curb her acerbic tongue, are examples proving that outspoken women suffered different fates from men. Gender rules were not incidental, but were interwoven with issues of religious and social controversy.

Kamensky's study offers a new interpretation of witchcraft, as well, in which the women accused of consorting with the devil fit the model of deviant speakers. They were already viewed as scolds, gossips, or women likely to libel their neighbors and defy the expectations of godly womanliness. In *Damned Women: Sinners and Witches in Puritan New England* (1997), Elizabeth Reis focuses less on gender conflicts and more on the confessional narratives of women accused of witchcraft. While Kamensky concludes that witchly words were feminized, Reis notes that sin—or the susceptibility to sin—was a female-encoded trait. Puritans saw women's bodies as the more likely vessels for sin, and the sinful soul was feminized; more important, women themselves believed they were weaker, more easily seduced, as they effectively internalized Puritan theology and its gendered language. Puritan theology had a gendered register which was received and interpreted differently by men and women.

Reis's study puts gender at the heart of Puritan theology, offering a corrective to previous scholarship that assumed men and women understood and felt religion in the same way. Theological metaphors—the sexual language of seduction employed in describing sin or liaisons with the devil—combined to make the Puritan religious experience a deeply gendered affair for the average layperson. While Reis perceives that Puritan language reinforced gender expectations in private expressions of faith, Kamensky highlights how Puritan culture regulated the external forms of public speaking, in which the gender of the speaker mattered. Both scholars treat gender as a crucial variable in everyday exchanges and in highly structured and ritualized performances (such as the Salem witch trials of 1692). Differing from Foucault's notion of modern power, both Reis and Kamensky demonstrate that the seventeenth-century Puritan still believed in physical punishment and the law. Nevertheless, what each historian clearly underscores is the force of anonymous rules about speech—and the metaphorical power of theology—both of which serve as vital terrain for recasting Puritan culture upon a bedrock of gendered beliefs and practices.

SCIENCE AND GENDERED KNOWLEDGE

If religion defined gendered understandings of sin and selfhood in the premodern world, then science appropriated this practice once medicine, psychiatry, and the social sciences acquired cultural dominance in the late nineteenth and early twentieth centuries. Intellectual historians have long been enamored with the impact of professionalization on intellectual life, recognizing the ways academia, empiricism, and the striving for objective "truth" changed modern theories of knowledge. Feminist scholars such as Sandra Harding, Donna Haraway, and Evelyn Fox Keller have disputed scientific "objectivity" and shown how cultural, economic, and technological forces impinge on scientific models. Other historians have followed their lead by applying a gender analysis to understand and recover the formative years of various professional disciplines. Elizabeth Lunbeck's *The Psychiatric Persuasion: Knowledge, Gender, and Power in Modern America* (1994) is a microstudy of Boston Psychiatric Hospital, providing a careful reading of case histories and a detailed survey of the evolving treatments employed by psychiatrists and social workers. She claims that during the first three decades of the twentieth century psychiatrists expanded their cultural influence by shifting their focus from studying the insane to defining the "psychology of everyday life." By claiming the authority to set the parameters of what is "normal," in marriage, family, and sexuality, psychiatrists created a discourse for classifying and treating male and female patients through a regime of adjustment to "normal" womanhood and manhood.

Lunbeck closely adheres to Foucault's view of modern power, that knowledge is constructed, and she notes that psychiatry's imperial quest over knowledge rested in its changing conceptual apparatus. At the core of this epistemological shift was a preoccupation with sexual identity, especially female sexuality. Two classic female maladies, hypersexuality and hysteria, led to the invention of a new model of womanhood, both passionate and chaste, which placed female identity along a continuum in which sexual desire, fantasy, and fear configured the female psyche. Lunbeck also shows how psychiatry, despite its scientific pretensions to objectivity, mimicked cultural values: the female hypersexual, for instance, was vividly seen in everyday life as the flapper of the 1920s. Lunbeck further assesses the role of class and ethnicity in shaping diagnoses, and she observes how gender informed less obvious pathologies, such as the manic-depressive patient. Crucial to Lunbeck's study is her insight that knowledge of what is "normal" is fundamental to social power relations, and that gender is one of the most important categories for regulating social behavior.

Other scholars have examined the discourses, institutions, scientific apparatus, and power struggles between men and women. Helene Silverberg's collection of essays *Gender and American Social Science: The Formative Years* (1998) explores the academic disciplines of economics, political science, anthropology, and domestic science. Rejecting the old division between "professional" and "amateur" social scientists (which usually marginalized women's activities outside of academia), this collection returns social science to "the world" and demonstrates how ivory-tower academics have actively pursued their inquiries in reaction to contemporary issues. Gender has shaped the conceptual apparatus and professional ethos of the new disciplines. In the late nineteenth century, political scientists opposed woman suffrage in their scholarly works, and they readily depicted the city and its governing bodies as a male domain. This in fact contradicted the gendered landscape of urban politics, ignoring the increasing influence of women's clubs, settlement houses run by women, and the political visibility of the woman suffrage movement.

In the field of anthropology, which had been more accepting of female practitioners, Kamala Visweswaran's "'Wild West' Anthropology and the Discipline of Gender," included in Silverberg's collection, shows that the inclusion of professional women is not the only reason this discipline has invited studies of sex roles. By studying Native American life, female anthropologists have had to assume an unusual range of gender-coded performances: they had to do science "like a man," make deals with the government "like a man," and yet they also staked a claim to spread philanthropy as the special calling of a "woman." These shifting positions among female anthropologists reveal the impact of gender on fieldwork and how political negotiations with Native Americans and the government have involved gendered assumptions about professional performance. Visweswaran, moreover, suggests that female anthropologists have adopted different gender scripts for their negotiations, indicating that gender identity is not fixed or stable, but a more malleable condition.

RACE, CLASS, SEX: GENDERED BODIES, MARKETS, AND SPACES

Whereas historians of science are attuned to institutional practices and bodies of knowledge, cultural historians direct their analysis to public life—the rituals, popular expressions, and subcultures that define the world of "the people." Much of the new cultural history is built upon the ethnographic focus of social historians, albeit without the emphasis on cultural consensus when studying the daily lives of average Americans. For cultural historians, science moved beyond the halls of academia, or the walls of hospitals, generating a popular discourse for measuring social progress and articulating fears of the decline of civilization. Gail Bederman's *Manliness and Civilization: A Cultural History of Gender and Race in the United States, 1880–1917* (1995) covers this territory, re-evaluating the impact of popular evolutionary ideas on a new definition of "masculinity." Bederman argues that the Victorian ideal of "manliness," based on "sexual self-restraint, a powerful will, a strong character," was replaced by a code of masculine conduct now defined by "aggressiveness, physical force, and male sexuality."

By highlighting a series of prominent public intellectuals—the journalist Ida B. Wells, the psychologist G. Stanley Hall, the feminist and author Charlotte Perkins Gilman, and President Theodore Roosevelt—Bederman addresses the turn-of-the-twentieth-century preoccupation with the cultural trope of the white man as a symbol of "white supremacy, male dominance, and evolutionary advancement." She demonstrates that masculinity was repeatedly, explicitly marked by sexual prowess, physical strength, and creative mastery of the world, underscoring popular theories and debates about evolution and national progress. Roosevelt's fears of "race suicide," white reaction to the heavyweight boxing match between Jack Johnson and Jim Jeffries in 1910, and the racial ideology displayed at the 1893 Columbian World's Exposition enforced a racial, class, and gender hierarchy within the concept of "civilized manliness." Equally important, Bederman stresses the constructed role of anatomy in this process: white masculinity had to be elevated above the weakness associated with white femininity and had to be distinguished from the primitive, physically unevolved racial "other." When these cultural constructions were contested, as in Johnson's victory over the white Jeffries (one exemplar of white male virility), then controversy followed. Johnson became for whites the most despised black man in America, especially because he flaunted his wealth

and his sexual affairs with white women. His defiance, as Bederman notes, accentuated the inconsistencies that shaped this new standard of male identity. For example, G. Stanley Hall was troubled that the most highly evolved race, epitomized by the Anglo-Saxon middle class, was also more prone to debility or neurasthenia, which undercut its claim of unquestioned superiority. Yet such inconsistencies allowed opponents, like Ida B. Wells and Charlotte Perkins Gilman, to advance a critique of white male dominance, suggesting that resistance was a vital part of popular debates over race and gender at the turn of the century.

Bederman explores how bodies are racialized and engendered, filling in the absences in most historical scholarship, which assumed that "whiteness" and "masculinity" are invisible or neutral categories of analysis. While Bederman sidesteps ethnicity as a racial category, her work clearly shows the centrality of sexual difference in theories of evolution. Unlike Lunbeck's study of psychiatry, in which science delineates what is normal, the popular scientific discourse studied by Bederman was still informed by religious millennialism, and its advocates claimed the authority of moral absolutes. Thus, Bederman tells us that older discourses did not simply disappear but were accommodated to new cultural conditions; religion and science were reworked, and science did not displace American's faith in a higher authority or divine forces beyond human agency. Yet Bederman's study reveals the increasing emphasis on gendered bodies, the meaning invested in the visual, physical, and anatomical differences among races and between the sexes. In addition, Bederman demonstrates how evolutionary tropes served political goals by recasting human nature and American identity through a hegemonic or dominant vision of the white male body—a body encoded as sexually and physically aggressive, but civilized.

If Lunbeck's psychiatrists sexualized women's hidden feelings, Bederman's evolutionary proponents celebrated outward appearances that they believed were skin deep and sexually marked. Appearances were just as important to working-class women, according to Nan Enstad ("Fashioning Political Identities," *American Quarterly,* September 1998, pp. 745–782). Like Bederman, Enstad identifies the political significance of cultural practices. Rather than emphasize racial markings of the body, Enstad concentrates on the class implications of fashion, or the manipulation of appearances as a form of class resistance. She challenges the view of social historians who differentiate class politics and cultural expression by assuming that the desire for material goods and amusement, or the allure of the consumer culture, prevented working-class women from engaging in political action. Dress, Enstad concludes, engendered bodies in class terms. Working-class women did more than imitate bourgeois or upper-class ideals of style or taste; they wore exaggerated fashions both to declare their claims to "ladyhood" and to mock upper- and middle-class pretensions to an exclusive right to fashionable display. Working women gave expression to this critique in the political arena during the great Shirtwaist Strike of 1909–1910 in New York City.

Both Bederman and Enstad provide good examples of how cultural history has changed intellectual history, and vice versa. By paying attention to mass culture or popular beliefs, cultural historians have addressed the production of values, the ways in which the "culture industry" manufactured consumer markets. As Bederman persuasively shows, sources of amusement like the 1893 Chicago World's Fair in sporting events like boxing, and pulp fiction characters like Edgar Rice Burroughs's 1912 invention *Tarzan of the Apes* were all intended for mass audiences, combining scientific arguments and popular beliefs about gender and race. Cultural historians point out that intellectual activity was never restricted to "high culture" nor shaped only by public institutions (academia, the medical profession, the clergy); economic forces have informed cultural expression through commercial exchange, commodification, and spectorship.

Throughout the nineteenth century, sex became a commodity of mass culture. Americans and Europeans alike fetishized the female prostitute as an object of sale whose services—and whose body—could be purchased. Prostitution, however, represented only one of the gender discourses that fueled middle-class fears and sexual fantasies; the new cultural industry of murder and gothic mysteries was another, marketing lurid tales of sexual violence. As Karen Halttunen argues in *Murder Most Foul: The Killer and the American Gothic Imagination* (1998), popular accounts of murder contributed to a new literature that sexualized violence, a move that simultaneously gave readers a pornographic portrait of violence and a new type of criminal—the murderer as "moral monster." Readers experienced the vicarious pleasure of sexual voyeurism and the horror of human depravity, avidly responding to stories in which men assumed the role of vicious killers while women (wives, lovers, and daughters) were cast as innocent victims. Here again, women's bodies were marked even as corpses; mutilated, bloody, dismembered, the female corpse symbolized a new kind of sexual fantasy. This genre eroticized the once beautiful female murder victim, turning death into an aesthetic and sexual encounter, infusing women's bodies with gendered meaning even as corpses.

Reading provided an important means to the world of mass culture, but so did public spaces, social displays, and sexual encounters. Spaces, it seems, could be sexualized and engendered, a point convincingly made by George Chauncey in *Gay New York: Gender, Urban Culture, and the Making of the Gay Male World, 1890–1940* (1994). Chauncey argues that modern gay culture emerged in places like the Bowery, Greenwich Village, and Harlem, and permitted a highly visible world of gay sexuality where "fairies," "pansies," and "queens" openly sold their sexual wares beginning in the 1890s. Chauncey's study focuses on places of sexual pleasure, and he demonstrates how an individual man could see himself as masculine and normal but still participate in this gay world. This world allowed straight men to participate in sexual dalliances, as long as they played the masculine role. Chauncey shows that male homosexuality appropriated preexisting gender scripts; that is, fairies imitated the feminine role of passivity, or simulated the deviant acts of female prostitutes by engaging in fellatio, while straight men played the masculine role of sexual aggressor. He also contends that the city facilitated the construction of this gay world by attracting large numbers of single men who lived outside the control of the family. "Bachelor flats," lunch counters, baths, and "t-rooms" created a social environment in which homosexual activity could flourish and straight and gay men could freely meet and exchange sexual favors. It was not until the 1940s, Chauncey contends, that gay men were forced into the closet (another spatial term) as gender roles demanded greater discipline of sexual boundaries and more rigid standards of normalcy.

Significantly, Chauncey reveals the engendering of homosexual activity, the degree to which sexual practices had phallic meaning, and how certain sexual acts were coded as masculine/feminine, active/passive, dominant/submissive, and insertive/receptive. He does so while treating same-sex encounters as consensual. In light of Bederman's portrait of the new ethos of masculine aggressiveness and sexual prowess, Chauncey's emphasis on fluid boundaries between gay and straight men seems to gloss over the power relationship inherent in cross-class and cross-racial encounters. Chauncey nevertheless provides a compelling historical account of gay culture as a world constructed by erotic urban spaces, and by a gender system that marked gay men by anonymous rules and sexual scripts known to all men.

WAR, LAW, AND GENDER POLITICS

Beginning with Aristotle, political discourse had employed feminine weakness as a symbol of danger, seduction, and threat to the strength and endurance of empires and nation states. In "Sex and the Sectional Conflict" (in Gillespie and Clinton, *Taking Off the White Gloves*, 1998), Catherine Clinton notes that the rhetoric of feminine weakness was employed by antebellum northerners and southerners to engender political debates. Proslavery southerners mocked the threat of female abolitionists as unmanning the North, while abolitionists used the same charge of feminine stubbornness against southerners for refusing to end slavery. Even more dramatically, southerners portrayed John Brown's 1859 raid on the federal arsenal at Harpers Ferry as a "figurative rape" against a feminized South. Northern male abolitionists, moreover, used Brown's bold act to reaffirm the manly courage of all male reformers, anticipating the martial rhetoric soon to be employed during the impending crisis of the Civil War.

Similarly, in "The Feminized Civil War" (*Journal of American History*, March 1998, pp. 1461–1494), Alice Fahs argues that northerners remained captivated by a feminized literature that described a "woman's war" on the home front. It was not until the 1880s and 1890s that a masculinized culture of Civil War remembrance displaced the earlier preoccupation with white women's war experiences. Equally revealing, Fahs uncovers the figurative meaning of women's tears and "wounds," the emotional costs that women felt—wounds that symbolically paralleled men's physical injuries on the battlefield. If the purpose and economy of war center on the destruction of bodies, then female writers created a literary equivalent (drawn from the religious trope of wounds) that metaphorically placed women at the side of male soldiers, contriving to expiate the pain and suffering of the Union cause.

Citizenship in the antebellum era was marked by a masculine definition of political and legal rights, a condition that forced early women's rights advocates to expose its gendered construction. Nancy Isenberg's *Sex and Citizenship in Antebellum America* (1998) assesses the "imaginary" function of rights, shaped according to an idealized notion of the sovereign body of the male citizen, and not abstract principles alone. The law conceived a fictional version of the "rights-bearer," linked to the legal concept of capacity, which in turn determined standing. Whether they addressed married women's labor, property rights in the household, a mother's custody rights, a wife's right to self-defense against domestic violence, the legal right to serve on juries, or the political right to vote, jurists and politicians inevitably defined "rights" in relation to the superior capacities of the idealized male citizen. Consequently, women's rights advocates had to do more than cite the Declaration of Independence; they had to develop a coherent theory for restructuring gender notions of rights within the church, state, and family. Paulina Wright Davis, president of the 1850 Worcester, Massachusetts, women's rights convention, exposed the fraudulent logic underlying women's legal and political status by categorizing women as a "disabled caste." By calling for co-equal representation, activists expanded the meaning of equal protection and national citizenship, advancing a more inclusive script of civil identity.

Antebellum Americans used the myth of the social contract (as a parallel to the biblical creation story) to define political representation—a key concept in the practice of democracy. The social contract represents the moment when the state is created; it is an imaginary blueprint in which individuals agree to form a collective society, and they accept certain abstract principles, such as the rule of law. Critical to this idea of the social contract is that power comes from the "consent" of the people, those people who, in theory, participate in the creation of the original contract. Gender was at the heart of the political narrative; gender was used to circumscribe headship, political rank, and legal standing, causing early feminists to see the importance of offering their own versions of the creation story. Indeed, mythic stories of origins assumed a narrative function in preserving the memory of the women's rights movement itself. Historians have been remiss in not recognizing the political intent of such heralded narratives as the 1848 Seneca Falls women's rights convention—part myth and historical fact. The reconstituted memory of Seneca Falls has withheld recognition from prominent actors like Paulina Davis while elevating others (especially Elizabeth Cady Stanton) into the preeminent position among the "founders" of the women's movement. The singular story of origins thus obscures alternative accounts, narrowing our understanding of the diversity found in the women's movement.

701

In sum, gender has reconfigured intellectual history in two basic ways: by expanding the number of topics that are to be considered worthy of study, and by introducing radically different interpretations of traditional subjects. It has raised questions about the production of knowledge, it has redefined the boundaries that encompass intellectual disciplines, and it has forced scholars to consider not only ideas but also the process for narrating those ideas. Engendered physical bodies—and not merely bodies of abstract knowledge—form subjects of historical inquiry. The language of gender continually returns to the terrain of the human body, and to sexual practices: it is employed to uncover cultural meaning. Citizenship, rights, and the conduct of war—all defined in relation to ideals of masculinity—often turn on fundamental principles of political import that are then encoded through gendered concepts of human action. Through such understandings, gender has become crucial to the new intellectual history, revolutionizing the study of American history and recasting the terms of historical discourse for the twenty-first century.

See also **Conflicting Ideals of Colonial Womanhood; Women in the Public Sphere, 1838–1877; Gender, Social Class, Race, and Material Life; Gender and Political Activism; Manhood** *(volume 1);* **Women and Family in the Suburban Age; Second-Wave Feminism; Women** *(volume 2);* **Sexuality** *(in this volume); and other articles in this section.*

BIBLIOGRAPHY

Barthes, Roland. "From Work to Text." In *Textual Strategies: Perspectives in Post-Structural Criticism,* edited and with an introduction by Josue V. Harari. Ithaca, N.Y., 1979.

Bederman, Gail. *Manliness and Civilization: A Cultural History of Gender and Race in the United States, 1880–1917.* Chicago and London, 1995.

Biersack, Aletta. *The New Cultural History: Essays.* Berkeley, Calif., 1989.

Brown, Kathleen M. "Brave New Worlds: Women's and Gender History." *William and Mary Quarterly,* 3d ser., 50, no. 2 (April 1993): 311–328.

Chauncey, George. *Gay New York: Gender, Urban Culture, and the Making of the Gay Male World, 1890–1940.* New York, 1994.

Clinton, Catherine. "Sex and the Sectional Conflict." In *Taking Off the White Gloves: Southern Women and Women Historians,* edited by Michele Gillespie and Catherine Clinton. Columbia, Mo., 1998.

Enstad, Nan. "Fashioning Political Identities: Cultural Studies and the Historical Construction of Political Subjects." *American Quarterly* 50, no. 4 (September 1998): 745–782.

Fahs, Alice. "The Feminized Civil War: Gender, Northern Popular Literature, and the Memory of War, 1861–1900." *Journal of American History* 85, no. 4 (March 1998): 1461–1494.

Halttunen, Karen. *Murder Most Foul: The Killer and the American Gothic Imagination.* Cambridge, Mass., 1998.

Hutcheon, Linda. *The Politics of Postmodernism.* London and New York, 1989.

Isenberg, Nancy. "The Personal Is Political: Gender, Feminism, and the Politics of Discourse Theory." *American Quarterly* 44, no. 3 (September 1992): 449–458.

———. "Second Thoughts on Gender and Women's History." *American Studies* 36 (spring 1995): 93–104.

———. *Sex and Citizenship in Antebellum America.* Chapel Hill, N.C., 1998.

Jameson, Frederic. "Hans Haacke and the Cultural Logic of Postmodernism." In *Hans Haacke: Unfinished Business,* edited by Brian Wallis. Cambridge, Mass., 1986.

Kamensky, Jane. *Governing the Tongue: The Politics of Speech in Early New England.* New York, 1997.

Laslett, Barbara, Ruth-Ellen B. Joeres, Mary Jo Maynes, Evelyn Brooks Higginbothan, and Jeanne Barker-Nunn, eds. *History and Theory: Feminist Research, Debates, Contestations.* Chicago, 1997.

Lunbeck, Elizabeth. *The Psychiatric Persuasion: Knowledge, Gender, and Power in Modern America.* Princeton, N.J., 1994.

Reis, Elizabeth. *Damned Women: Sinners and Witches in Puritan New England.* Ithaca, N.Y., 1997.

Roberts, Mary Louise. "Gender, Consumption, and Commodity Culture." *American Historical Review* 103, no. 3 (June 1998): 817–844.

Rosenberg, Rosalind. "Twentieth-Century Intellectual History: Women and Gender." *Intellectual History Newsletter* 9 (April 1987): 22–28.

Ryan, Mary, Anne Norton, and George Shulman. "Conference Panel: On Political Identity." *Studies in American Political Development* 6, no. 1 (January 1992): 140–162.

Scott, Joan Wallach. *Feminism and History.* Oxford, U.K., and New York, 1996.

——. *Gender and the Politics of History.* New York, 1988.

——. "Gender: A Useful Category of Historical Analysis." *American Historical Review* 91, no. 5 (December 1986): 1053–1075.

Silverberg, Helene, ed. *Gender and American Social Science: The Formative Years.* Princeton, N.J., 1998.

Thurner, Manuela. "Subject to Change: Theories and Paradigms of U.S. Feminist History." *Journal of Women's History* 9, no. 2 (summer 1997): 122–146.

CULTURAL STUDIES

Mark Poster

In April 1990, the Unit for Criticism and Interpretive Theory at the University of Illinois at Urbana-Champaign hosted a conference entitled "Cultural Studies Now and in the Future." This event arguably is the best marker of the emergence of cultural studies as a major intellectual direction for the humanities and social sciences in the United States. The massive 800-page volume that appeared two years later, entitled simply *Cultural Studies,* including revisions of the talks and transcriptions of some of the discussions, bears eloquent witness to the variety of the field and the wide interest in it. The essay that follows is an intellectual history of the development of cultural studies in the United States and an attempt to outline its relation to the discipline of history.

A NEW "CULTURE"?

Defining the conceptual innovations of cultural studies is not an easy task, since a diversity of objects, methods, theories, and styles characterize this intellectual movement, if it has even that much coherence. Nonetheless some lines of emphasis are evident. Cultural studies, as the name suggests, proposes an intervention in our understanding of the term "culture." The word derives from Latin and refers to cultivation, or action upon nature: "culture" has generally been understood in opposition to "nature." Culture in the West, except for anthropologists, has long referred to what are regarded as the highest attainments of humanity. Hence Pierre Bourdieu's analysis of "cultural capital" in his book *Distinction* indicates how the attainment of culture itself operates as a social force elevating the status of the individual. While the term always implied an opposition of high and low culture, popular culture, in general academic parlance, had little standing or interest.

Cultural studies in the first instance expands the concept of culture to include the beliefs, values, and attitudes of all social groups. The spirit of the movement is to remove the taint of inferiority from lower-class culture, to acknowledge the importance of culture to the lower class, to erase somewhat the boundary between cultural levels, and to introduce political questions into the domain of culture, that is, to see how culture has been a resource for empowerment as well as a means of manipulation and accommodation. In this sense, "culture" now includes a vast range of practices—such as reading comic books and playing video games—not regarded as civilized in earlier definitions. If cultural studies refuses the distinction high-low with regard to culture, it also reflects the change within the domain of culture to mass culture, to the influence of print and electronic media in disseminating uniform cultural objects throughout society, to what many regard as postmodern culture. In addition cultural studies denies the tendency, widespread in the university, to privilege production over consumption. This discourse also heightens interest in the reception of cultural objects, in acts of consumption, and in the domain of advertising.

Increasingly the center of concern is the problem of the subject or identity. Cultural studies is animated by the investigation of the ways in which the subject is formed, is maintained, is transformed, is repressed, and is the source of resistance. To the extent that cultural studies simply expands the scope of culture to include the lower classes, it has been accused of romanticizing those groups, of elevating them in status by taking too seriously what some regard as their limited or petty or even degraded practices. At its best, however, cultural studies aims at more than this. It proposes the examination of the construction of the subject as well as the validation of identity as a site of contestation in its own terms.

Opening the question of the subject in this way leads to the most basic tension in cultural studies: a split between those primarily concerned with the hierarchical mechanisms or systems of domination through which identity is formed and those concerned primarily with studying identity as a resistant phenomenon. The former analyzes identity as it is constructed by power structures; the latter how such identities oppose those powers. A second area of contention derives from its interdisciplinarity. At one extreme among those associated with cultural studies are literary critics who approach the question of cultural identity in practices of textual interpretation. These scholars examine cultural objects in detail, be they textual, visual, or aural, carrying over their disciplinary training into the newly redefined domain. At the other extreme are scholars trained in methods of social science, especially in sociology, whose penchant is more for quantitative analysis, questionnaire studies, archival work, and interviewing. In between the two extremes are those who use ethnographic methods, those more theoretically inclined, and those from newer disciplines such as media studies whose methods are more eclectic. A third area of dispute within cultural studies, one that in part overlaps with the first, is the local-global divide. Scholars more concerned with processes of globalization, with colonialism and postcolonialism, with intercultural translation, and with transnationality, veer in directions different from those more focused on local conditions, on single groups or subgroups, and national conditions. While this divergence of initiatives need not result in contestation, in practice the two groups go in different directions. There are many other sources of tension among those who identify themselves with cultural studies. That this list should provide a sense of instability is the unity in the discourse.

Besides the tensions within cultural studies, the reception of the movement in the United States has been fraught with controversy. Practitioners of cultural studies have been accused of theoretical sloppiness, lacking historical depth, pandering to student interests with hip, mainly contemporary topics, and finally, a certain political correctness or knee-jerk leftism as in the shibboleth of "race, class, and gender." If we consider the spectacular success cultural studies has enjoyed in the United States, it is not surprising that there would be intense hostility to it. Such conflict is typical when new perspectives enter the arena of the humanities and social sciences. Such controversy certainly greeted the introduction of poststructuralist theory as well as the emergence of social history. Some of the objections clearly have merit, especially as they pertain to history, and will be discussed below.

THE BRITISH INFLUENCE

Cultural studies, it is generally agreed, originated in Britain with the publication of Richard Hoggart's *The Uses of Literacy* (1957), Raymond Williams's *Culture and Society* (1958), and E. P. Thompson's *The Making of the English Working Class* (1963). Hoggart's influence was especially marked on the study of literature, while Thompson's work in particular had enormous impact on the discipline of history, ironically in the direction of stimulating social, not cultural, history. These three works, however, all promoted new directions in the investigation of culture. But it was Williams's book that had the broadest appeal, treating the general question of culture in relation to Marxist paradigms. Williams convinced most of his readers that what rested in obscurity as the superstructure warranted attention in its own right, that the study of the working class ought not be limited to the outrages heaped upon it by the engine of the capitalist means of production but rightly concern as well the cultural creation of this benighted group.

The writings of Hoggart, Thompson, and Williams stimulated numerous investigations in Britain in the 1960s, 1970s, and 1980s. One thinks immediately of Dick Hebdige's *Subculture: The Meaning of Style* (1979), Paul Gilroy's *"There Ain't No Black in the Union Jack": The Cultural Politics of Race and Nation* (1987), and Angela McRobbie's *Postmodernism and Popular Culture* (1994) as undisputed classics of cultural studies. But cultural studies benefited too from its institutionalization as the Centre for Contemporary Cultural Studies, also known as the Birmingham school, founded by Hoggart in 1964 but then directed during its most productive years from 1969 to 1979 by Stuart Hall. By the time of the Urbana-Champaign conference in 1990, Stuart Hall was the leading figure of cultural studies. The key to understanding cultural studies rests firmly with Hall, his unique style of leadership, and his intellectual character.

A fine collection of Hall's work and that of younger members of the British cultural studies movement is *Stuart Hall: Critical Dialogues in Cultural Studies* (1996). Two salient and highly unusual characteristics typify Hall's work: his responsiveness to changes in the world and in intellectual life, and his promotion of collaboration in collective practices of research and study. One thinks back to the Frankfurt school for a comparable group of diverse scholars whose project changed with the times but maintained its rigor. In the case of Hall and the Birmingham school, the working paper becomes the model of intellectual work. Although Hall wrote quite a bit, he published few books until the mid-1990s. The model of the Birmingham School suggests an academic, degree-granting institution that also established a kind of intellectual public sphere. What was imported into the United States as cultural studies must then be understood as a changing intellectual configuration, unified by a few central concerns.

Perhaps the most significant and characteristic of Hall's intellectual moves may be seen in his response to Antonio Gramsci. The Italian Marxist (1891–1937) developed a theory of hegemony in which social hierarchies are politically stabilized through mechanisms of culture. Gramsci sought to explain how modern, civil society could contain class conflict without the systematic use of force that characterized other, mostly earlier, forms of social organization. Gramsci's notion of hegemony differs, for example, from Max Weber's understanding of legitimate authority in that the former highlights the political uniqueness of modern capitalism. With the notion of hegemony, Hall and the Birmingham School grasped a theory that located culture and the study of the working class in the center. Equally, the theory of hegemony draws attention to the political dimension of culture.

It might be noted that Gramsci was not alone in turning to culture as a pivot of Marxist theory and critique. The Frankfurt School emerged in Germany in the 1930s and spent the following decade in influential New York exile. Establishing itself to study the working class, the Frankfurt School pioneered the analysis of uniquely twentieth-century features of culture. "The Culture Industry: Enlightenment as Mass Deception," the classic chapter from *Dialectic of Enlightenment* (1944) by Max Horkheimer and Theodor Adorno, paved the way for research on the import of mass-mediated culture. In France, Roland Barthes's *Mythologies* (1957), Henri Lefebvre's *Everyday Life in the Modern World* (1958), and Michel de Certeau's *The Practice of Everyday Life* (1980) set the stage for a focus on the banal, the quotidian, the world of consumption, and the growth of media practices, doing this with an attention to language as a complex, constituting practice and to reception as resistance or at least as resignification. This important work had not made much impression in Britain, however, until the work of two immigrants changed everything.

In 1985 Ernesto Laclau and Chantal Mouffe published *Hegemony and Socialist Strategy,* altering significantly the Gramscian position by introducing the "linguistic turn" of poststructuralist thinkers such as Louis Althusser, Michel Foucault, Jacques Derrida, and Jacques Lacan. The appropriation of the Laclau-Mouffe revision of Gramsci by Hall would considerably deepen and complicate cultural studies. Chapter 3 of *Hegemony and Socialist Strategy* contained the heart of what would become known as "post-Marxism." It was entitled "Beyond the Positivity of the Social: Antagonisms and Hegemony." Laclau-Mouffe introduced into neo-Marxism the peculiar language theory of the French thinkers. One cannot grasp the impact of cultural studies without attending to this innovation.

Laclau-Mouffe explode the understanding of society as a set of fixed, "sutured" relations. They introduce the term "articulation" to signify the contingent nature of social phenomena. What we find in the social order are constituted relations of power, relations that are continuously reconstituted. Society is not a field of final facts but an eternal practice of making the real. In this sense social relations are like language: they are produced and reproduced, filled and refilled, continuously open to transformation like words (technically "signifiers"), which are reanimated in each use. With impressive rigor and systematicity, Laclau-Mouffe spelled out their post-Marxist theory redefining society as the continuous setting into play of articulations, resulting in the constitution of identities in these articulations. The character of the newly understood totality, one that is never final, they term "discourse."

The Birmingham School now had a social theory that remained, like Marxism, focused on hegemony, class contradictions, and antagonisms, but that understood these attributes of the social as a cultural process, that posited the political nature of the cultural process, and finally, that specified the question of identity as one of contingent construction. Rather than understanding stable characters in social relations ("working-class identity," "bourgeois identity"), scholars might now analyze the specific cultural processes through which group identities were constructed and reconstructed. Gone was the search for a working-class identity that might serve as an origin, a stable basis out of which revolutionary practice might emerge. Instead scholars might study gender systems, racial practices, and media techniques through which marginalized and oppressed groups were constituted, "discovered," appropriated, and refashioned. At a time when, in the United States, neo-Marxism and poststructuralism were for the most part seen in opposition, especially in history departments,

Stuart Hall and the Birmingham school were exploring the possibilities of a creative, synthetic, analytic reformulation of humanistic scholarship. Even in Great Britain they were an exception. Distinguished historians like E. P. Thompson and Eric Hobsbawm, and younger historians associated with London's History Workshop, such as Sheila Rowbotham and Gareth Stedman Jones, were initially skeptical of the turn to "high theory" in Laclau and Mouffe's book, and even more suspicious of its political implications. In his history of the cultural studies movement in Britain, Dennis Dworkin generously interprets this hostility as part of a learning process. The History Workshop, he writes, "often appearing to be motivated by a contempt for theory," was actually engaged in "a process of self-reflection whereby Workshop historians began to question their relation to the historical text and the basis of empiricist methodology." We shall see below the extent to which this entailed a substantial epistemological transformation when we discuss the debate over language in cultural history.

EARLY ADOPTERS

In the United States, Hall's brand of cultural studies found a ready acceptance in many quarters. Some scholars had already experimented with many of the same principles of analysis characteristic of the Birmingham School. *Writing Culture*, edited by James Clifford and George Marcus in 1986, revealed how far some anthropologists had gone in developing an understanding of culture that resonated with the work of Hall and his group. Janice Radaway's *Reading the Romance* of 1984 displayed how rich a gender critique of patriarchy could become when aimed at the "shallow" domain of pulp fiction. *Reading Television* by John Fiske and John Hartley in 1978 argued for the creative activity of reception in a medium generally regarded as an "idiot box." Gerunds of "write" and "read" in these titles indicate the opening of culture as a contested domain, a far cry from traditional, academic literary criticism. Language, politics, and culture were mixed in new ways by these writers.

All was not so smooth, however, with the importation of cultural studies. Right-wing intellectuals and political figures like Lynne Cheney and William Bennett responded aggressively, lumping cultural studies with a list of unsavory positions too long to reproduce here. In particular the blend of neo-Marxist and poststructuralist discursive gestures bothered scholars on both the right and the left. Cary Nelson, a leading figure of American cultural studies, nonetheless insists on the productive possibilities of the imbrication of cultural studies and poststructuralism:

> Conservative critics have claimed . . . that poststructuralism—and particularly its deconstructive incarnation—makes all moral argument empty. And indeed American deconstructive critics like Paul de Man were inclined to avoid larger moral issues. But Jacques Derrida, the founder of deconstruction, has for years regularly written cultural and political essays of clear moral urgency; he has written about apartheid, nuclear war, racism, and the politics of academia. (*Manifesto of a Tenured Radical*, p. 51)

In this way, a productive exchange opens between the reigning discourse of language-based critical theory and the newcomer, cultural studies.

A CAULDRON OF DISCOURSES

This early reception of cultural studies occurred at a time of great intellectual ferment. The 1970s and 1980s witnessed the emergence, exploration, and debate of a number of important theories and methodologies. Poststructuralism, deconstruction, feminism, postmodernism, postcolonialism, post-Marxism, multiculturalism, and transgender studies swept through the disciplines of the humanities, arts, and social sciences, stimulating considerations of basic epistemological tenets. In history, the leading figure promoting some of the new directions was Joan Wallach Scott. The fundamental issue raised by Scott and debated time and again with historians was the problem of language and cultural history. Although Scott focused on gender, it was the relation of language to culture in general—the salient theme of culture studies—that emerged as the heart of the matter. The reception of cultural studies by historians was foreshadowed in the Scott debates. To the extent that one accepted Scott's position on the relation of language and culture, one was predisposed to a cultural studies approach.

The debate began in 1983 with the publication of Gareth Stedman Jones's *Languages of Class*. Jones complained that E. P. Thompson's celebrated study of nineteenth-century workers was hampered in the understanding of culture by a notion of consciousness. Thompson understood working-class culture as this group's *consciousness* of their conditions. Jones argued that one must understand workers' culture through the mediation of language. Workers' "interests" were not "in" their consciousness but constructed in and through practices of language. In Jones's words, "it is the discursive structure of political language which conceives and defines interest in the first place. What we must therefore do is to study the production of interest . . . within political languages."

When Scott took up these issues, she applauded Jones's effort to theorize culture through language, but she found his book wanting in its actual exposition of working-class culture. In the chapter on the nineteenth-century English reform movement of Chartism, for instance, Jones returns to a conventional method of intellectual history which privileges consciousness and fails to understand language as producing identity and interest. Jones, she argued, interpreted the language of Chartism "thematically," as a "representation" of preexisting interests rather than as productive of those interests. According to Scott, many historians attempting to open cultural history to a new understanding of language have in practice retreated to older methods of intellectual history that configure language as instrumental, as an emanation of consciousness rather than studying the discursive processes through which identity is constructed. Many historians had difficulty with the paradigm shift enacted first in poststructuralism, in some feminist theory, and in postcolonial theory, then carried over into cultural studies.

CULTURAL STUDIES IN AND OUT OF THE DISCIPLINE OF HISTORY

Very little of the work of American cultural and intellectual historians qualifies as work of cultural studies. Unlike professors of literature, anthropology, sociology, film studies, media studies, communications, ethnic studies, education, women's studies, and interdisciplinary work in the humanities in general, historians by and large responded to the emergence of cultural studies with indifference, neglect, rejection, and hostility. One must look hard and long to find works by American historians of the United States that cite Stuart Hall, Dick Hebdige, Paul Gilroy, Lawrence Grossberg, or Cary Nelson and that are inspired by the concept of culture associated with these figures. Of the forty-one authors of *Cultural Studies* only one, James Clifford, received a Ph.D. in history, and he is generally regarded as an anthropologist.

Nevertheless, there was a form of cultural studies practiced by historians before "cultural studies" was imported into the United States. At the same time that the Birmingham School was emerging in Great Britain, several prominent American histo-

rians, inspired by the writings of Antonio Gramsci and to a lesser extent by the Frankfurt School, began working on a revision of cultural history: Eugene Genovese's *Roll, Jordan, Roll* (1974), Herbert Gutman's *The Black Family in Slavery and Freedom* (1976), and Christopher Lasch's *The Culture of Narcissism* (1978) contributed in varying ways to a renewal of the cultural study of U.S. history. Gramsci's understanding of culture as the broad set of meanings in a society and his appreciation of the political function of culture were both evident in these works, although Lasch's writing resonated more with the cultural pessimism of the Frankfurt School than with the activism of the Italian Marxist. In the 1980s, the Gramscian strain of American cultural history was extended most notably by Jackson Lears in such works as *The Culture of Consumption* (1983) and *Fables of Abundance* (1994).

The American historian who most assiduously followed the lessons of cultural studies was Warren Susman. His *Culture as History* (1984) brought the conceptual aspirations of the British movement most effectively into the history of the United States. Susman cited Raymond Williams as the one who defined the new direction for cultural history with *Keywords* (1976). Here Susman found an important turn to the everyday and the ordinary, to the media, to popular culture, and even to advertising, a phenomenon most historians of the time regarded as beneath the dignity of their craft. Above all Susman found an epistemological shift to language. In the following passage one finds what may be regarded as the first statement of cultural history by a U.S. historian in the mode of cultural studies. Susman proclaims:

> In the beginning are the words, all kinds of words from all kinds of places: words from philosophical treatises and tombstones, from government documents and fairy tales, from scientific papers, advertisements, dictionaries, and collections of jokes. There are, of course, other sources of information: images, sounds, objects of use and of enjoyment, ledgers of debits and of credits, gathered statistics— countless cultural artifacts, each of enormous value but analyzable only when translated into words. Thus the historian's world is always a world of words; they become his primary data; from them he fashions facts. He then can go on to create other words, propositions about the world that follow from his study of those data. (*Culture as History*, p. xi)

Susman here calls attention to the question of language: language as the object of the historian's study, as the tool used for analysis, as the medium of presentation.

The lesson of Warren Susman went unheeded by many American historians. Their resistance to facing the question of language derived from the historian's view that the past consisted of agents and their attitudes, their actions, and the forces that compelled them. These agents were complete unto themselves, using language as a tool of expression. Agents resisted or suffered. Agents had power or were subjected to it as from the outside. Agents were whole, complete, fully formed, albeit subject to external demands and internal urges. As long as the historical field was constituted by such an understanding of agents, the lesson of cultural studies could not be heeded.

For cultural studies the issue concerned precisely this: the position of individuals within language, their being constituted by it, and constituting it in turn. This is what is meant by culture. The salient project of cultural studies is the analysis of various forms of language and practice as these constitute subject positions while at the same time forming the context in which such subject positions react to their situations by appropriating popular culture and media. In Stuart Hall's formulation: "We have been trying to theorize identity as constituted, not outside but within representation; and hence of cinema, not as a second-order mirror held up to reflect what already exists, but as that form of representation which is able to constitute us as new kinds of subjects, and thereby enable us to discover places from which to speak." By contrast, those American historians who viewed language as instrumental were inclined to look with suspicion upon Susman's statement that he had become a literary critic, that attention to the medium of language as the historian's first and last resort led inexorably, they feared, to a blurred boundary between fact and fiction, history and literature. For the most part, then, historians resisted cultural studies as they had earlier resisted poststructuralism.

One interesting exception to the general reluctance of historians to consider the significance of language not only within the past but also within their own practice of writing and teaching history is Joyce Appleby's analysis of the role of historians' texts in constituting American identity as white, male, and middle class. In a chapter entitled "History Makes a Nation" she traces the two-hundred-year historiography in which historical texts *produce* a "nation" that is monocultural, masculine, and elitist. In 1776 a nation was born politically, but the cultural production of the nation, the process through which individuals identify themselves as Americans, also had to be constructed. Historians

played a major role in the formulation of narratives through which emerged one version of the meaning of being American. Without an understanding of the productive power of texts, historians "represented" the "truth" about history in an unconscious projection of their subject positions. By the mid-1990s some fault lines had appeared at the discipline's borders.

The fact remains that the work of writing history from a cultural studies vantage point was adopted primarily by scholars whose formal training was outside the discipline of history. We may take as a symptomatic text Michael Warner's fine *Letters of the Republic* (1990). In this study of colonial America, Warner, a literary critic by training, explores the medium of print in relation to the formation of a public sphere of political debate. Acknowledging debts to cultural studies, Warner demonstrates the specificity of the print medium in empowering some groups (white males from the North Atlantic states) and disadvantaging others (women, non-whites, slaves—all who lacked literacy or the status to use it as a position of enunciation). He also shows how in some contexts, such as Puritan congregations, print was employed but had little relation to the development of a public sphere. However, in those areas where the proper social conditions prevailed, print enabled the formation of a space beyond self-interest in which ordinary folk could speak for the emerging republic. The textual characteristics of print—stability of the sign, repeatability, broad dispersion of the same literature—open positions of speech in which a figure of the citizen could emerge. Warner's mixing of social context, communications medium, and textual analysis—a hallmark of cultural studies—leads to a provocative historical analysis of the birth of the public sphere.

Equally instructive of the adoption of cultural studies for historical analysis by scholars trained outside the discipline of history is Lynn Spigel's *Make Room for TV* (1992). Spigel, who teaches film studies, illuminates another side of the possible uses of cultural studies for historians. Her history of the introduction of television in the postwar United States combines several different methods of cultural analysis. Her interest in the question of gender leads her in one chapter to examine magazines for women, searching for their construction of an image of the home as compatible with television and with women's social position. In another chapter she looks at the space of television in the living room, much as an ethnographer might, investigating the physical presence of the tube in the context of the postwar family. In addition, Spigel uses her skills in the analysis of visual cultural objects to study characteristic television shows in relation to the family and gender positions. *Make Room for TV,* one of the more highly regarded works of cultural history, admirably displays its characteristic multiplicity of methodologies.

In addition to Warner and Spigel many other works of the 1980s and early 1990s could be discussed to prove the fecundity of cultural studies for historical work. Again, most of these are authored by scholars from other disciplines: literature (Thomas Richards, *The Commodity Culture of Victorian England,* 1990); sociology (Adrian Johns, *The Nature of the Book,* 1998); ethnic studies (George Lipsitz, *Rainbow at Midnight: Labor and Culture in the 1940s,* 1994); literature (Lisa Lowe, *Immigrant Acts,* 1996); and anthropology (Ann Laura Stoler, *Race and the Education of Desire,* 1995). Examples could be multiplied from gender studies, queer studies, science and technology studies, and so forth. A torrent of historical works of major importance had appeared by the end of the twentieth century which resort in each case to a considerable extent on cultural studies. Historians have an opportunity to benefit greatly from these pathbreaking explorations by building a new cultural history, one that will engage the work of colleagues in other fields and even in other countries.

See also **Race as a Cultural Category; Cultural Modernism; The Behavioral and Social Sciences** *(volume 1);* **The Culture and Critics of the Suburb and the Corporation; Analytic Philosophy; Poststructuralism and Postmodernism; Multiculturalism in Theory and Practice; Anthropology and Cultural Relativism** *(volume 2);* **The Humanities; The Social Sciences; Education; Disciplines and Their Institutionalization; The American University; Learned Societies and Professional Associations** *(in this volume); and other articles in this section.*

BIBLIOGRAPHY

The best introduction to the field of cultural studies is the volume *Cultural Studies* (New York, 1992) edited by Lawrence Grossberg, Cary Nelson, and Paula A. Treichler. It has been a resource of first resort for novices to the field. The forty essays, written by scholars primarily from Britain, the United States, Australia, and Canada, cover diverse aspects of popular and mass culture as well as theoretical and methodological issues. So divergent are the topics discussed that space prevents me from offering a detailed overview. Generally, however, the writers focus on areas that have become the central issues of the humanities and social sciences in the 1990s: medieval, sexuality, ethnicity, gender, intercultural exchanges, and the basic question of the subject of identity. The publication of the volume launched a movement within academia that had established itself by the end of the 1990s in programs, departments, and centers in cultural studies in the United States. Since then, numerous conferences have been held and important new journals have been launched such as *Cultural Studies* in 1996, *International Journal of Cultural Studies* in 1998, and *European Journal of Cultural Studies* in 1998. Countless disciplines and subdisciplines established journals in subject *X* and cultural studies. By the end of the decade, it was still unclear if cultural studies would become a discipline with full department status, remain an emphasis within disciplines, or continue as a general tendency between disciplines. The following is a list of other major, representative works in the field:

Appleby, Joyce, Lynn Hunt, and Margaret Jacob. *Telling the Truth about History.* New York, 1994.

Bourdieu, Pierre. *Distinction: A Social Critique of the Judgement of Taste.* Translated by Richard Nice. Cambridge, Mass., 1984.

Clifford, James, and George Marcus, eds. *Writing Culture: The Poetics and Politics of Ethnography.* Berkeley, Calif., 1986.

Dworkin, Dennis. *Cultural Marxism in Postwar Britain: History, the New Left and the Origins of Cultural Studies.* Durham, N.C., 1997.

711

Fox, Richard Wightman, and T. J. Jackson Lears. *The Culture of Consumption: Critical Essays in American History, 1880–1980.* New York, 1983.

Genovese, Eugene D. *Roll, Jordan, Roll: The World the Slaves Made.* New York, 1974.

Gutman, Herbert George. *The Black Family in Slavery and Freedom, 1750–1925.* New York, 1976.

Hall, Stuart. "Cultural Identity and Diaspora." In *Colonial Discourse and Post-Colonial Theory: A Reader,* edited by Patrick Williams and Laura Chrisman. New York, 1993.

Hunt, Lynn, ed. *The New Cultural History.* Berkeley, Calif., 1989.

Jenkins, Henry. *Textual Poachers: Television Fans and Participatory Culture.* New York, 1992.

Jones, Gareth Stedman. *Languages of Class: Studies in English Working Class History, 1832–1982.* New York, 1983.

Laclau, Ernesto, and Chantal Mouffe. *Hegemony and Socialist Strategy: Towards a Radical Democratic Politics.* Translated by Winston Moore and Paul Cammack. London, 1985.

Lasch, Christopher. *The Culture of Narcissism: American Life in an Age of Diminishing Expectations.* New York, 1978.

Lears, T. J. Jackson. *No Place of Grace: Antimodernism and the Transformation of American Culture, 1880–1920.* New York, 1981.

Marchand, Roland. *Advertising and the American Dream: Making Way for Modernity, 1920–1940.* Berkeley, Calif., 1985.

Morley, David, and Kuan-Hsing Chen, eds. *Stuart Hall: Critical Dialogues in Cultural Studies.* New York, 1996.

Nelson, Cary. *Manifesto of a Tenured Radical.* New York, 1997.

Rowe, John Carlos. *A Future for American Studies.* Minneapolis, Minn., forthcoming.

Scott, Joan Wallach. *Gender and the Politics of History.* New York, 1988.

———. "On Language, Gender, and Working-Class History." *International Labor and Working-Class History* 31 (1987): 1–13.

Spigel, Lynn. *Make Room for TV: Television and the Family Ideal in Postwar America.* Chicago, 1992.

Susman, Warren. *Culture as History: The Transformation of American Society in the Twentieth Century.* New York, 1984.

Warner, Michael. *The Letters of the Republic: Publication and the Public Sphere in Eighteenth-Century America.* Cambridge, Mass., 1990.

SOCIAL CONSTRUCTION OF REALITY

Martin J. Burke

That dimensions of social, cultural, and political life are socially constructed has become a commonplace, if not a cliché, in scholarship in the humanities and the social sciences. While the metaphor of social construction was first employed in the context of debates over sociological methods and theories in the 1960s and 1970s, from the 1980s onward it was appropriated by specialists in such disparate fields as the history of science, social psychology, and gender studies. To many of its advocates, the advent of social constructionism has been welcomed as part of a larger reorientation in the methodological practices and philosophical premises of the human sciences. For many of its critics, the popularity of constructionist studies has provided evidence of the debasement of the standards of rational inquiry. Though the long-term significance of social constructionism is unclear, by the close of the twentieth century it had emerged as a characteristic, and often contested, feature in many arenas of American academic discourse.

CONCEPTUAL ORIGINS

The sociologists Peter Berger and Thomas Luckmann introduced the concept of "social construction" in their 1966 volume *The Social Construction of Reality: A Treatise in the Sociology of Knowledge.* They wrote their text in order to lay the grounds for a new approach to the sociology of knowledge and to address one of the central issues in social theory, the relationship between the individual and society. In Berger and Luckmann's estimation the sociology of knowledge, which was developed by Max Scheler in the 1920s and was best exemplified by the work of Karl Mannheim, was in need of reorientation and renewal. They hoped to move the discipline from the margins to the center of sociological practice. The sociology of knowledge, they argued, had become too concerned with theoretical knowledge, with the social determinants of ideas, and with discovering the interested, ideological dimensions of all thought. They suggested, instead, that the sociology of knowledge should take for its subject all that passed for knowledge in a society regardless of its ultimate validity, and that it should seek to analyze how bodies of knowledge came to be socially established as reality. In particular, they were interested in the commonsense, stock knowledge shared by all members of a society, rather than the formal knowledge produced by intellectuals. Both Berger and Luckmann were students of Alfred Schutz, and it was from his writings on phenomenology that they derived their focus on the *Lebenswelt*—the world of everyday life—and on the processes of reification. In contrast to the phenomenology of Edmund Husserl, which sought among other things to explain how the transcendental ego was constituted in the empirical ego, Schutz's social phenomenology was concerned with explaining how people experienced the life-world. The *Lebenswelt* was the one that members of society encountered as a pre-existing, independent reality, although it was the product of human action. Though Berger and Luckmann adapted Schutz's emphasis on the socially constituted nature of the life-world, they also added the term "construction" as a descriptor. How actors constructed and were constrained by society was to be the central focus of the new sociology of knowledge. They hoped that a revived emphasis on human agency would contribute to the development of a more humanistic sociology that avoided the impersonal abstractions of structural-functionalism and the statistical methods of positivism.

Reality, which for Berger and Luckmann always referred to the social and not the natural world, was both objective and subjective, and was constructed dialectically. Society was the outcome of ongoing moments of externalization (the purposeful actions of humans in the world), objectivation (peoples' experiences of the facticity of institutions), and internalization (the appropriation by individuals of the objective social world into their subjective consciousness). Society became a human product through externalization, it became a reality through objectivation, and humans became social products through internalization. Social institutions were integrated and made meaningful for subsequent generations through the process of legitimation, while individuals were inducted into social life through the process of socialization. Language, Berger and Luckmann argued, was both the medium and the primary means for these interdependent social processes. Forms of knowledge were developed in the dialectic of social construction and were central to understanding the maintenance of social groups and individual identities. Knowledge was elemental in, not extraneous to, the construction of social reality.

In depicting the relationship between individuals and society in dialectical terms, Berger and Luckmann were indebted to Karl Marx, although they did not subscribe to the tenets of Marxist sociology. In developing their theories of primary and secondary socialization, of the roles played by significant others and social institutions, they relied heavily on the symbolic interactionist psychology of George Herbert Mead. When insisting upon the objective facticity of society, they followed the precepts of Emile Durkheim. When stressing the importance of subjective meanings for sociological analysis, they drew upon the work of Max Weber. Although *The Social Construction of Reality* was a theoretical, or meta-theoretical, treatise, and not an empirical investigation, in their examples Berger and Luckmann emphasized the contingency and the historicity of social institutions and forms of knowledge. Here, too, they were influenced by Weber. Sociology, they maintained, should have for its object of inquiry the making of society by man and the making of man by society in an ongoing historical process. In this sense, sociology was a humanistic discipline, which should be engaged in continuous conversations with history and philosophy.

Both Berger and Luckmann developed elements first introduced in *The Social Construction of Reality* in subsequent works: Berger in the sociologies of religion and intellectual life and Luckmann in social phenomenology. Although their theoretical recommendations for a dialectical sociology of knowledge and a broader humanistic sociology had limited appeal in their profession, their emphases on human agency, subjective meanings, and the importance of language as the medium and conversation as the site of social construction resonated more widely. Their text was one of a number of

works that appeared from the late 1950s onward that suggested alternative approaches to structural-functionalist theories and behaviorist methods in the social sciences. Among these were Erving Goffman's *The Presentation of Self in Everyday Life* (1959), Harold Garfinkel's *Studies in Ethnomethodology* (1967), and Aaron V. Cicourel's *Cognitive Sociology: Language and Meaning in Social Interaction* (1974). While there were significant differences in emphasis and methods in each of these texts, together they laid the basis for what would come to be known as interpretive sociology, an approach that drew together theoretical elements and research methods from symbolic interactionism, ethnomethodology, and social phenomenology. Symbolic interactionism investigates the common and reciprocal definitions used by actors in conducting ordinary life; ethnomethodology also examines how humans employ commonsense knowledge and shared understandings in creating social order; social phenomenology studies the ways in which people experience everyday life and imbue their activities with meaning. Interpretive sociologists were more interested in explaining the social world than in providing causal analyses along the lines of the natural sciences, or in making public-policy recommendations. Though their qualitative approach did not displace the dominant quantitative, positivist tradition in American social science, it made significant contributions to such areas as the sociology of everyday life, the sociology of social problems, social psychology, gender studies, and communications. In these and related fields, Berger and Luckmann's central claim that reality was socially constructed would become a point of departure for subsequent empirical research. In contemporary social construction studies, simple descriptions of everyday reality are problematized. Constructionists place an emphasis on humans as actors rather than as passive reactors to social forces and present multiple perspectives rather than the uniform, objective social reality posited by positivism. The degree to which Berger and Luckmann's meta-theoretical commitments inform such work is open to question. But the popularity of their central metaphor among many American social scientists at the beginning of the twenty-first century is not.

While Berger and Luckmann advocated a sociology that focused on the stock knowledge of everyday life, from the 1970s onward the term "social construction" was adopted by sociologists, philosophers, anthropologists, and historians more interested in formal knowledge, especially knowledge in the natural sciences and technology. Distinguishing between the purposes of sociology and philosophy, Berger and Luckmann deliberately avoided any discussions of the epistemological and ontological implications of arguing that forms of knowledge were socially constructed. However, many proponents of constructionism or "constructivism" readily engaged in philosophical critiques of realism, in particular scientific realism, and advocated variants of anti-realism and relativism. And though Berger and Luckmann's social phenomenological approach was concerned with understanding and explaining the world as it was—not with changing it—many subsequent proponents of constructionism celebrated it as a means for critiquing and transforming existing social arrangements. Within these larger scholarly and intellectual currents, "social construction" developed into an often controversial term, one whose meaning could vary greatly depending on how it was used, on the knowledge claims that its users made, and on the political positions they advocated.

SOCIAL CONSTRUCTIONISM AND THE SCIENCES

Uses of the term "social construction" and arguments about the historically contingent and culturally dependent nature of scientific and technical knowledge became hallmarks of a movement in the philosophy, history, and sociology of science often identified as the social studies of science, or science studies. The movement first emerged in the 1970s at the University of Edinburgh, under the aegis of the philosopher Barry Barnes and the sociologist David Bloor. In such texts as Barnes's *Interests and the Growth of Knowledge* (1977) and Bloor's *Knowledge and Social Imagery* (1976), members of the Edinburgh school proposed a "strong programme" for the sociology of scientific knowledge. They declined to differentiate between true and false scientific theories, and they assumed that knowledge was whatever groups of people took it to be. In contrast to Karl Mannheim, who deliberately exempted scientific knowledge from sociological analysis because of his concern about the implications of thoroughgoing relativism, Barnes and Bloor insisted that all knowledge was open to sociological investigation. Among their aims was the examination of the substance of scientific ideas and theories, and the demonstration of how, in specific social conditions, ideas and theories were invested with authority. They wished to provide social explanations for systems of belief. Advocates of the "strong

programme" sought to replace internal explanations of how scientists reached and maintained the conclusions they did—explanations that appealed to the quality of argument, the quantity of evidence, and the power of rational thought—with external explanations that appealed to such factors as the particular interests of scientists and the more general interests at work in a given society. Scientific knowledge, when viewed from the perspective of science studies, was not simply induced from observations of nature or deduced from predictive theories. Rather, it was produced by particular traditions, conventions, and social processes. In this sense scientific knowledge, like all knowledge, was socially determined.

Among other influential exponents of a social constructionist or social constructivist positions in science studies were Karin Knorr-Cetina, Bruno Latour, and Steve Woolgar. In *The Manufacture of Knowledge: An Essay on the Constructivist and Contextual Nature of Science* (1981), Knorr-Cetina argued that the results of science were contextually bound, contingent constructions. Scientific knowledge was manufactured in that it was primarily the outcome of the decisions made and operations carried out by scientists in laboratories, rather than the result of discoveries made in the world. In order to understand what scientists did, as opposed to what they claimed to be doing, Knorr-Cetina recommended an ethnographic approach to the generation and diffusion of scientific knowledge.

The most celebrated and controversial of these ethnographies was Bruno Latour and Steve Woolgar's *Laboratory Life: The Social Construction of Scientific Facts* (1979). They based their text on Latour's experience as a participant observer in an endocrinology laboratory at the Salk Institute in La Jolla, California. The purpose of the modern research laboratory, they maintained, was the generation of texts or "literary inscriptions"—figures, data, diagrams, grant requests, laboratory reports, learned papers—that would convince audiences that the claims in these texts referred to independently existing facts in nature. But facts in the natural sciences, they argued, were the outcomes of complex negotiations and were dependent on an array of social microprocesses. The endocrinologists did not discover entities: they constituted them through these inscriptions. Even though Latour and Woolgar acknowledged that the scientists at the Salk laboratory believed in the existence of objective scientific facts, their own statements about independently existing entities were inconsistent, if not contradictory. In the works of Knorr-Cetina, Latour,

715

and Woolgar, the lines separating scientific knowledge and the objects that such knowledge referred to became blurred. Science was a social practice, and scientific knowledge was a social construct.

Among historians of science and technology, constructivist science studies attracted a number of followers and generated new modes of accounting for scientific and technological change. In *Leviathan and the Air Pump: Hobbes, Boyle, and the Experimental Life* (1985), Steven Shapin and Simon Schaffer reinterpreted the emergence of organized science in early modern England from a constructivist perspective. They argued that Robert Boyle and his fellow founders of the Royal Society prevailed in their debates with Thomas Hobbes over the efficacy of the experimental method not because of the superior merits of their arguments but because of their superior ability in mobilizing material, literary, and social resources to their advantage. The processes by which the experimental scientific method came to be accepted as the best means for determining knowledge involved a complex set of social negotiations and personal linkages, not simply the triumph of truth over error. In *The Social Construction of Technological Systems: New Directions in the Sociology and History of Technology* (1987) Wiebe Bijker and his fellow contributors argued that technological change should not be depicted in terms of discoveries and innovations by heroic inventors but in terms of negotiated practices and situated knowledges. In these and similar studies, some historians of science and technology sought to demystify appeals to truth, reality, and progress, which to them were merely terms in the rhetoric of scientists. Immanent nature, they maintained, was not a repository of knowledge waiting to be discovered; rather, knowledge was the production of human actions. Economic, cultural, political, and social interests largely shaped the context and the content of past science. By extension, this was the case for contemporary science and technology as well.

The rise of constructivism in the history, philosophy, and sociology of science provoked rancorous debates, which moved from the laboratory and the university campus to the larger arenas of American public discourse and became enmeshed in broader public controversies over the perils or the promises of postmodernism. The battles over the social construction of science comprised, in the words of the philosopher and historian of science Ian Hacking, an episode in the culture wars, which raged in the last years of the twentieth century and beyond. Though the volume of this controversial literature was sizeable, the terms of the debate tended to proceed along a few standard lines. For many philosophers of science, such as Larry Laudan, constructivism raised once more the chronic dilemmas of relativism and skepticism. When appropriated by postmodernists, it encouraged forms of anti-realism and irrationalism. For many scientists and historians of science, the debunking, demystifying scholarship of social constructivists produced caricatures of the experimental method and failed to adequately account for the considerable explanatory and predictive powers of modern science. They rejected claims that scientific knowledge was merely the outcome of social practices: the existence of scientific facts did not depend on the circumstances of their discovery. And for critics of trends in American academe such as Alan Sokal, social constructionism was but one of a cluster of fashionable intellectual ills, including deconstruction and identity politics, responsible for the decline of the humanities, the dismissal of the natural sciences, and a destructive assault on truth.

CONSTRUCTIVISM IN POSTMODERN THOUGHT AND POLITICS

Many proponents of constructionism agreed that this approach did pose a threat: not a threat to science and rationality but to scientists' claims to objectivity and neutrality, or to the status quo in general. The discourse of scientists, they insisted, was just another form of discourse; it was not a privileged way of knowing the world. Expertise, in whatever guise, was always an exercise of power. Critics of gender, racial, and ethnic discrimination such as Donna Haraway embraced constructionism as a powerful tool for destabilizing social categories and for empowering excluded, marginalized, and oppressed groups. Discriminatory practices that appeared to be intrinsic to the natural order of things could be exposed as socially constructed. For literary critics and philosophers of a poststructuralist or postmodern bent, constructivist emphases on contingency and historicity supported their arguments about the crisis of representation in late modernity and the theory-dependent nature of all knowledge. Constructivist approaches were often described as complementary to the deconstructionist precepts of Jacques Derrida and the power/knowledge analyses of Michel Foucault, even though each possessed a distinct intellectual genealogy. While not everyone who employed the social-construction metaphor or endorsed constructionist methods was a postmodernist, invocations of the social construction of reality became one of the benchmarks of the postmodern persuasion.

Not all critiques of social construction have been polemical, however; a few are useful for assessing and clarifying the issues faced by scholars when employing the methods, and those faced by readers when evaluating the claims, of constructionism. In *The Social Construction of What?* (1999), Ian Hacking summarized the major positions taken in the constructionist debate, especially those pertaining to the natural sciences. From a wide range of scholarship in the social and natural sciences, Hacking abstracted a general set of constructionist propositions and suggested a gradation of constructionist arguments. Arguments that X was socially constructed were generally made about phenomena or practices which were taken for granted or seemed inevitable. Most constructionists, he observed, were critical of current social, cultural, political, or economic arrangements and tended to hold that for any X, X need not have existed or need not be as it was. X, or X as it was at present, was not determined by the nature of things; it was not inevitable. Many constructionists went farther and argued that X was quite as bad as it was, and that we would be much better off if X were done away with, or at least radically transformed. Hacking then graded constructionist arguments based upon the strength of their commitments to these three propositions. His gradation proceeded from "historical" to "ironic," through "reformist" and "unmasking," to "rebellious" and "revolutionary." Historical constructionists subscribed to the first proposition and argued that X had been constructed in the course of social processes, while reformist, rebellious, and revolutionary constructivists were committed to the second and third propositions as well. Much of the scholarship on the social construction of gender fell into the latter categories, Hacking argued. Similar arguments could be made for work on the construction of race and the construction of ethnicity.

When posing his central question to constructivist literature—What exactly was socially constructed?—Hacking found a good deal of confusion. While many texts purported to be about the social construction of phenomenon or practice X—be it literacy, lesbianism, mental illness, or anorexia—most were about classifications or categories or conceptions of X rather than about the phenomenon itself. Few, if any, constructivists consistently maintained that objects in the physical world were simply constructed by observers. Their assumptions about the theory-dependent nature of scientific knowledge did not always lead them to extreme forms of relativism or irrationalism, but these assumptions were often grounded in larger late-twentieth-century philosophical critiques of and reservations about realism. Constructivists tended to argue that scientific knowledge did not correspond to the way the world was. Rather, it was a convenient way of representing reality. Though constructivist studies of topics ranging from authorship to Zulu nationalism regularly suggested that processes of historical change were at work, these often did not explain in detail how or why such changes came about.

The premises and the problems of constructionist scholarship were also among the issues addressed by John Searle in *The Construction of Social Reality* (1995). In the course of accounting for the existence of social facts in terms of analytic philosophy, and connecting such facts to the brute facts in the natural world, Searle offered a robust defense of realism and provided a number of critical distinctions relevant to the constructionist controversy. He took exception to constructivist, poststructuralist, and anti-realist assertions that all reality was in some way a human creation and that all facts were dependent on the human mind. He granted that our knowledge of reality was the result of purposeful human interactions, that such knowledge was always relative to particular human interests, and that it was always situated within specific cultures. He allowed that categories and systems of classification were conventional and, to an extent, arbitrary. But it did not follow, Searle argued, that all reality was socially constructed, or that there were no facts in the world upon which to base truth claims about it. He maintained that there was an important difference between brute facts and social facts. Natural phenomena such as molecules and mountains existed regardless of our perceptions of or attitudes about them. Social phenomena such as money and marriage required the presence and participation of intending subjects. The former were not social constructs while the latter clearly were. Both natural and social phenomena were represented by means of language, yet only social practices and institutions were linguistically dependent. Searle granted no special privilege to science as a means of understanding reality, however. All reality was of a piece; only certain dimensions of it differed.

Among professional historians, social-construction metaphors and constructionist methods were employed by only a few scholars in the 1970s and 1980s. Berger and Luckmann's *Social Construction of Reality* was usually referred to or cited in these works, but otherwise there was little in the way of sustained engagement with interpretive sociology. Rather it was the positivist and behaviorist canons of American social science, from which Berger and Luckmann had dissented, that were the source of methods and models for an emergent "new" social history. But as quantitative social history gave way in turn to a "new" cultural history during the last decade of the twentieth century, social-construction approaches, sometimes along postmodern lines, became a more prominent feature in historical practice. Constructivist analyses of modes of knowledge as exercises of power, and emphases on the contingency and instability of such social categories as race, class, and gender, were attractive to historians who wished to situate their work within the larger currents of social criticism and cultural studies.

By the close of the twentieth century, the number of books and articles on "the social construction of" or "constructions of" or "constructing" was considerable. So, too, was the variety of subjects under consideration. Historical studies of social constructions appeared on such topics as brotherhood, the Jew in English literature and society, medieval sexuality, psychotherapy, race and ethnicity in the United States, and Russian culture in the age of revolution. It was clear that social construction and its variants were being applied in historical research, or at least in the titling of books and articles. Yet it was less clear precisely what historians meant when they used construction metaphors, or to what degree they were committed to the various projects of, and philosophical positions, in constructionism. In many studies, the "social construction of" seems simply to have replaced "changing conceptions" or "changing ideas" about phenomenon or practice *X* as a catchphrase without other notable differences in modes of analysis or empirical results. Only in a few texts, such as Peter Jackson and Jan Penrose's edited volume on *Constructions of Race, Place, and Nation* (1994), were there strong, programmatic endorsements of constructionist theory of a postmodern variety.

Nor was it always clear what the media or the mechanisms of social constructions were, or who the contractors or subcontractors might be. Ian Hacking's reservations about the lack of clarity and specificity in constructionist studies in the natural and social sciences were applicable to historical

scholarship as well. The turn to social construction by cultural historians also raises questions about the suitability of methods and the adequacy of evidence. Contemporary anthropological, sociological, and psychological constructionist studies utilize interviews, participant observations, survey data research, and evaluations of everyday conversations to establish the processes by which people describe and explain the world in which they live. With few exceptions, historians do not have access to extensive records of ordinary language use in the past. They must rely on manuscript and printed sources that may not be amenable to discourse analysis or appropriate for ethnomethodological interpretations. To the degree that social constructions of gender roles or class identities, for example, are matters of recipe phrases generated in the contexts of day-to-day conversations rather than fully developed statements, providing ample documentation of them can be quite problematic. Historical analyses of explicit claims and systematic theoretical knowledge are far less troublesome, and traditionally have been the province of intellectual history. But does a chronological compendium of statements made about race—or any other phenomena—in newspaper editorials, magazine articles, printed speeches, or public documents provide evidence of constructions of racial categories? How does one demonstrate that the terms of public discourse and the terms of ordinary language were the same, and that both informed the tacit and the stock knowledge of historical actors? Constructivist scholarship in the history of science and technology does provide models of external analyses of systematic knowledge, but how applicable these methods are to less formal cultural phenomena is also unclear.

Whether the claim that reality is socially constructed is merely a slogan, or whether it signifies a fundamental reorientation away from positivism and empiricism in the human sciences and realism in the natural sciences, remains a matter of considerable disagreement. So, too, do the consequences of social constructionism for the disciplines that have embraced it. Yet whatever the outcomes of these controversies, social constructionism has provided an interesting chapter in the often complicated intersections of history, philosophy, and the social sciences in late twentieth-century American intellectual life.

See also **The Behavioral and Social Sciences** *(volume 1);* **Analytic Philosophy; Poststructuralism and Postmodernism** *(volume 2);* **Technology; The Humanities; The Social Sciences** *(in this volume); and other articles in this section.*

BIBLIOGRAPHY

Andrews, George Reid, and Herrick Chapman, eds. *The Social Construction of Democracy, 1870–1990.* New York, 1995.

Barnes, Barry. *Interests and the Growth of Knowledge.* London, 1977.

Barnes, Barry, David Bloor, and John Henry. *Scientific Knowledge: A Sociological Analysis.* Chicago, 1996.

Berger, Peter L., and Thomas Luckmann. *The Social Construction of Reality: A Treatise in the Sociology of Knowledge.* Garden City, N.Y., 1966.

Bijker, Wiebe, Thomas P. Hughes, and Trevor Pinch, eds. *The Social Construction of Technological Systems: New Directions in the Sociology and History of Technology.* Cambridge, Mass., 1987.

Bloor, David. *Knowledge and Social Imagery.* London, 1976.

Cheyette, Bryan. *Constructions of the "Jew" in English Literature and Society: Racial Representations, 1875–1945.* Cambridge, U.K., and New York, 1993.

Cicourel, Aaron V. *Cognitive Sociology: Language and Meaning in Social Interaction.* New York, 1974.

Clawson, Mary Ann. *Constructing Brotherhood: Class, Gender, and Fraternalism.* Princeton, N.J., 1989.

Cook-Gumperz, Jenny, ed. *The Social Construction of Literacy.* Cambridge, U.K., 1986.

Coulter, Jeff. *The Social Construction of Mind: Studies in Ethnomethodology and Linguistic Philosophy.* London, 1979.

Cushman, Philip. *Constructing the Self, Constructing America: A Cultural History of Psychotherapy.* Boston, 1995.

Danzinger, Kurt. *Constructing the Subject: Historical Origins of Psychological Research.* Cambridge U.K., and New York, 1990.

Ferrente, Joan, and Prince Brown Jr., eds. *The Social Construction of Race and Ethnicity in the United States.* New York, 1998.

Garfinkel, Harold. *Studies in Ethnomethodology.* Englewood Cliffs, N.J., 1967.

Gates, E. Nathaniel, ed. *Critical Race Theory: Essays on the Social Construction and Reproduction of Race.* New York, 1996.

Gergen, Kenneth J. *Realities and Relationships: Soundings in Social Construction.* Cambridge, Mass., 1994.

Goffman, Erving. *The Presentation of the Self in Everyday Life.* Garden City, N.Y., 1959.

Hacking, Ian. *The Social Construction of What?* Cambridge, Mass., 1999.

Haraway, Donna J. "Class, Race, and Sex as Scientific Objects of Knowledge: A Marxist-Feminist Perspective on the Social Construction of Productive Nature and Some Political Consequences." *Das Argument* 24 (1984): 200–213.

Hollis, Martin, and Steven Lukes, eds. *Rationality and Relativism.* Cambridge, Mass., 1982.

Jackson, Peter, and Jan Penrose, eds. *Constructions of Race, Place, and Nation.* Minneapolis, Minn., 1994.

Kelly, Catriona, and David Shepherd, eds. *Constructing Russian Culture in the Age of Revolution, 1881–1940.* New York, 1998.

Knorr-Cetina, Karin. *The Manufacture of Knowledge: An Essay on the Constructivist and Contextual Nature of Science.* New York, 1981.

Latour, Bruno, and Steve Woolgar. *Laboratory Life: The Social Construction of Scientific Facts.* London, 1979.

Laudan, Larry. *Science and Relativism.* Chicago, 1990.

Lochrie, Karma, Peggy McCracken, and James A. Schultz, eds. *Constructing Medieval Sexuality.* Minneapolis, Minn., 1997.

Lorber, Judith, and Susan A. Farrell, eds. *The Social Construction of Gender.* Newbury Park, Calif., 1991.

Potter, Jonathan. *Representing Reality: Discourse, Rhetoric, and Social Construction.* London, 1996.

Samson, Colin, and Nigel South, eds. *The Social Construction of Social Policy.* New York, 1996.

Sarbin, Theodore J., and John I. Kitsuse, eds. *Constructing the Social.* London, 1994.

Searle, John R. *The Construction of Social Reality.* New York, 1995.

Shapin, Steven, and Simon Schaffer. *Leviathan and the Air Pump: Hobbes, Boyle, and the Experimental Life.* Princeton, N.J., 1985.

Simons, Herbert W., and Michael Billig, eds. *After Postmodernism: Reconstructing Ideology Critique.* London, 1994.

Sokal, Alan D., and Jean Bricmont. *Fashionable Nonsense: Postmodern Intellectuals' Abuse of Science.* London, 1997.

Velody, Irving, and Robin Williams, eds. *The Politics of Constructionism.* London, 1998.

HISTORY AND THE STUDY OF THE PAST

Mary Kupiec Cayton

From its ancient emergence until today, history as a scholarly endeavor has taken on the characteristics of whatever has been the dominant approach to knowledge at the time. History in colonial North America and in the United States has been no exception. In the Anglo-American tradition, which is dealt with in this essay, history in the colonial era relied mainly on a providential model of time and events. With the advent of Enlightenment rationalism, history was often viewed in a more cyclic fashion, and scholars looked to it to teach about the laws of nations and of men. A Romantic tradition saw history as an instrument through which to discover the essence and the genius of particular civilizations. By the end of the nineteenth century, historical scholarship became professionalized, and a newly systematized approach to history led to a kind of writing that looked something like the sciences—authoritative, based on rigorous empirical research, and often specialized beyond the reach of the common reader. By the late twentieth century, some historical writing had come to reflect skepticism about the authority and uses of knowledge in general. More notably, historians had begun constructing stories of the past with a self-consciousness often colored by political or social agendas.

Existing in tandem with historical scholarship, sometimes intersecting with it and sometimes not, has been a strain of popular historical consciousness that looks to history as a source of personal or group identity, entertainment, or pleasure. Americans at various times have utilized the past in ways that offered opportunities for escape, reflection, or communal bonding.

HISTORY IN EARLY AMERICA AND EARLY NATIONAL AMERICA

Native Americans preserved their history through myths and oral traditions; Europeans by the seventeenth century often did so through written histories. Though a number of chronicles and descriptions of the New World came from the pens of Europeans anxious to publicize both their discoveries and their exploits, the Calvinist settlers of New England produced both the most histories and the most distinctive. Writing in the providential tradition of history pioneered by St. Augustine's *City of God* centuries earlier, such historians as William Bradford (*Of Plimoth Plantation,* written 1630–1646), John Winthrop (*History of New England,* written 1630–1648), and Captain Edward Johnson (*The Wonder-Working Providence of Sion's Saviour in New England,* 1654) produced narratives showing the hand of God in the affairs of humans. Such writers saw human history within the context of divine history, and human affairs seen rightly were a working out of human salvation within a larger scheme of good and evil, fidelity to God or infidelity to him. A people or nation had the capacity to be rewarded or punished just as individuals did. God was active in human affairs, foreordaining events, working visible wonders, and sending as signs "special providences." Puritan settlers of New England comprised a New Israel whose behavior and exploits mattered in the larger schemes of salvation history. Although later historians, influenced by the Enlightenment, would turn elsewhere than the Bible for models, the notion of the United States as a chosen nation, a people set apart for great things, would endure well into the twentieth century in much of American historical scholarship.

The most notable of the Puritan histories, both in terms of ambition and volume, was Cotton Mather's *Magnalia Christi Americana; or, The Ecclesiastical History of New England* (1702), a mammoth undertaking produced by the man who was said to be the most learned in the colonies at that time. Mather did not stint in displaying his erudition, studding his descriptions of New England's affairs, both ecclesiastical and civil, with classical and Biblical comparisons, quotations in Latin, Greek, and

Hebrew, and numerous references accessible only to the learned. Much of Mather's work consisted of biographies of those he deemed to be New England's heroes—the contemporary counterparts of the lions of Israel. (For example, John Winthrop was the new Nehemiah.) Written in the wake of the Glorious Revolution and the revocation of Massachusetts's charter in 1688, Mather's "Biblia Americana" celebrated "the WONDERS of the CHRISTIAN RELIGION, flying from the deprivations of *Europe,* to the *American Strand.*"

Mather's use of biography as a basis of history was not unusual in seventeenth-century New England. New Englanders were exposed to history not only through immersion in the Bible and the histories of Protestant martyrs but also through sermons and eulogies rehearsing the lives of important men and women. Many Calvinist churches of the region also required a kind of autobiographical reconstruction of one's own life history in the conversion narrative. In order to provide others in the churches they wished to enter with presumptive evidence of election by God, would-be saints told the stories of their inner lives and their paths to conversion by God's grace.

Not all historians of early America were inspired by Biblical themes, of course, nor did they all employ scriptural tropes as ways of locating themselves in history. Captain John Smith, for example, provided two of the first histories of English North America—specifically, of England's Virginia colony there—using the discovery-chronicle-documentary genre popularized by the British geographer Richard Hakluyt. Such accounts were intended to spread the word about the new economic enterprise and to attract attention and investors. At the same time, they tended to glorify the author's exploits as explorer and adventurer. Works on Virginia by Robert Beverley (1705) and William Byrd (written 1728–1737) provided a chronicle-type record of a region as a way of naming it and putting it on readers' psychological maps.

By the mid-eighteenth century, much of Europe had come to be influenced by Enlightenment thought—an emphasis on rationalism and on the generation of knowledge based on human observation and induction only, not on revealed truth. Highly educated Americans had access to histories in which God was no longer so immanent as in Puritan culture, but rather discernible through the consistent laws of nature writ in the fabric of history. Works like Montesquieu's *Spirit of the Laws* (1748), William Robertson's very popular *History of the Reign of the Emperor Charles V* (1769), David

Hume's *History of England* (1754–1762), and Edward Gibbon's *History of the Decline and Fall of the Roman Empire* (1776–1788) provided models of time where superstition and authority warred with truth, the latter ultimately to triumph as human history progressed toward the rational happiness God had intended. Not that this progress was uninterrupted. Human time and events often exhibited a cyclic character, and civilizations tending toward democracy and freedom regularly brought themselves down as individuals yielded to ambition and avarice.

Even before the Revolution, historians such as the Loyalist governor of Massachusetts Thomas Hutchinson (*History of Massachusetts Bay,* 1764) took as their theme the laws and institutions of states. With the advent of the Revolution, however, the impulse to record, memorialize, analyze, interpret, and draw lessons from the events of the recent past gave rise to the genre of American national history. The first native historian of the American Revolution, David Ramsay, was a Pennsylvania-born physician who migrated to Charleston, South Carolina, and became a representative to the Continental Congress from that state. His *History of the American Revolution* (1789) shows the marks of providential history in the sense that he looked for the hand of God in human events. At the same time, his manner of using providence as a force in history shows marked differences from earlier Puritan themes: Ramsay wanted his readers to know that they could not know the will of God in human events ahead of time, but only after the fact as they reflected on the events that had befallen. In Massachusetts, Mercy Otis Warren, a member of Massachusetts Patriot aristocracy and a friend of many major Revolutionary figures, departed from her theatrical and satirical writing to pen her *History of the Rise, Progress, and Termination of the American Revolution* (1805). Like John Marshall's *Life of George Washington* (1804–1807), the best-selling history of the three, Warren's work affirmed the importance of seeing the disparate collection of former colonials as indeed one nation.

But the histories that followed the Revolution did not only take the new nation as their theme. An impressive variety of state and local histories appeared, as authors tried to give their readers and the regional and local communities to which they belonged a coherent and recognizable identity: Pennsylvania (Robert Proud, 1797–1798), Virginia (John Daly Burk, 1804–1816), North Carolina (Hugh Williamson, 1812), Connecticut (Benjamin Trumbull, 1818), Massachusetts (George Minot, 1798–

1803), and Maryland (John Leeds Bozman, 1811). These histories constructed for newly aware citizens political communities that were also cultural units with a shared past. In 1791, perhaps the most prominent of these regional historians, Jeremy Belknap (who had published his *History of New Hampshire* in 1784), founded the first American historical society, the Massachusetts Historical Society. By 1860, at least seventy-two local historical societies existed in cities and towns across the nation. Literary and social homes for men of letters, they promoted history and historical consciousness by publishing documents and reports, preserving antiquities, founding periodicals, and gathering together individuals of learning and social standing to discuss the past.

It would be a mistake to see history as the property only of the educated and the rich—although they certainly were producing the new output of scholarly and literary volumes that graced American libraries. For years, popular versions of history had been transmitted through printed ephemera, broadsides, and steady sellers that were readily and cheaply available. Religious literature and sermons provided accounts of lives of Protestant martyrs and worthies. Almanacs recounted either religious or civil stories important in establishing a common mythic identity. Broadsides published the exploits of criminals sentenced to death as warnings to others to avoid the path to evil.

The print revolution of the early eighteenth century made novels widely available, and though these fictionalized histories of individuals were sometimes seen to be a waste of time by those who recommended more serious material (such as history) to the young women and men who made them their reading matter of choice, these stories rapidly became suffused with historical detail and context. Sir Walter Scott, the best-selling author in the United States prior to 1860, brought historical novels into vogue and influenced the dozens of writers whose historically inspired fiction graced the pages of newly published periodicals. Writers such as James Fenimore Cooper, Lydia Maria Child, and Nathaniel Hawthorne chose historical themes as the basis of some of their most important works. In the area of biography, the peddler-bookseller and former minister Mason Locke Weems's portrait of George Washington (1800)—half truth, half larger-than-life myth—made history a source of inspiration and entertainment for thousands.

The trend toward valuing things historical in the early nineteenth century extended to the arts as well. Greek and Roman themes as well as depictions of more recent heroic battlefield scenes became staples of American art. Benjamin West and John Singleton Copley in painting, Benjamin Latrobe and Thomas Jefferson in architecture, and Hiram Powers and Horatio Greenough in sculpture, all drew on historical themes to provide depth and expressive resonance to their art. Ancient Roman and Greek buildings became patterns for important new American public spaces such as the state capitol building in Richmond, Virginia (Thomas Jefferson, 1788), and the national capitol building in Washington, D.C. (William Thornton, 1793), as well as the first cathedral in the United States in Baltimore (Benjamin Latrobe, 1809).

HISTORY IN THE AGE OF ROMANTIC EXPRESSION

German philosophers in the late eighteenth and early nineteenth centuries had begun to place history at the center of scholarly thought, and their historicist orientation spilled over to color the work of American romantic historians. Historicism provided a model of thinking in which tracing the genesis and development of cultures became the most important factor in understanding them. Cultures or civilizations had their own unique characters and geniuses. No longer was history a search for the universal laws of human nature written on the tablet of human experience. Instead, inspired by the work of such historians as Johann Gottfried von Herder, historians took as their task the delineation of the peculiar events and tendencies that made a people what they were and that determined their contribution to world progress.

George Bancroft, a Massachusetts Brahmin and the first German-trained American historian, put to use what he had learned abroad in his work, especially in his ten-volume *History of the United States* (1834–1874). Placing a democratic ethos at the center of American character, Bancroft traced the history of the United States as the carrier of progressive ideals of democratic equality. Other romantic historians such as John Lothrop Motley (*The Rise of the Dutch Republic*, 1856), Francis Parkman (*Montcalm and Wolfe*, 1884), and William Hickling Prescott (*History of the Conquest of Mexico*, 1843), although they did not take the United States as their subjects, wrote sweeping and panoramic histories that sang of heroes, exotic themes, and the working out of the ideal of progress in the lives of nations. This new breed of historians relied increasingly on primary source documents to tell their stories. If

Enlightenment-inflected history represented a mingling of philosophy, literary art, and politics, romantic history delved into questions of character, both of nations and of men, in self-consciously literary ways. The era produced a number of notable local and regional histories as well; and inspired in part by Thomas Carlyle's "great man" school of history, biographies also began to pour forth. Ralph Waldo Emerson's *Representative Men* (1850) embodied a romantic strain that suggested that all history was the history of significant individuals.

Those writing romantic histories by and large shared common socioeconomic and cultural backgrounds: highly educated, they came disproportionately from the Northeast. Often they were men of wealth and leisure, or if not that, then at least clergy or public officials able to carve out enough time in retirement to devote themselves to literary pursuits that carried moral and civic messages. The commonalities in their backgrounds in part led to histories of the United States that represented largely northeastern, Whiggish perspectives.

This is not to say that interest in history and the past flourished only among these people and in this location. Between 1800 and 1860, the United States saw a remarkable interest in the past, and in many different venues. According to George Callcott in *History in the United States, 1800–1860* (1970), of 248 best-selling books published in the United States between 1800 and 1860, over one-third contained historical themes (pp. 31–32). During this era as well, history was introduced into the curriculum of primary and secondary schools—colleges lagged behind—and textbooks and readers featured historical themes prominently. Historical topics were treated in periodicals, memoirs, and autobiographies; biographies asked people to consider the moral lessons conveyed in individual lives. Between 1834 and 1848, Jared Sparks edited a twenty-five volume Library of American Biography, containing portraits of forty prominent Americans. As the revolutionary generation died out and the events surrounding the founding of the nation became enshrined in memory, politicians and public figures celebrated past events and contested their meaning in speeches, debates, and public festivities.

Women participated in this making of history and this enshrinement of the past, particularly in the literary sphere. Because writing offered women the peculiar opportunity to appear before the public without really doing so physically, many women in the first half of the nineteenth century began to publish fiction, poetry, drama, moral tracts—and history. Though writers like Hannah Adams (the nation's first professional author) published specifically in the historical genre, an even larger number of women produced novels or sketches that incorporated backdrops and settings from the past (for example, Catharine Maria Sedgwick's *Hope Leslie*, 1827, and Lydia Maria Child's *Hobomok*, 1824). And between 1790 and 1860, at least twenty women published history textbooks for use in schools and homes. Educationally, young women were often encouraged to read histories instead of novels, since the former were presumably less frivolous and had a surer moral content. In addition, as women came to view themselves as moral teachers in the household, histories helped them to understand and inculcate the responsibilities of citizenship.

Although members of racial minorities could hardly celebrate the grand national and romantic themes that came more easily to members of the privileged majority culture, they also produced historical works in other modes that contributed to the period's emphasis on the past. Among African Americans in particular, the slave narrative—autobiographies or biographies of enslaved individuals—served the dual political purposes of making plain the cruelties of slavery and celebrating the ingenuity, the perseverance, and the goodness of individuals. These narratives were purposefully constructed so as to be both representative and individual. "What seems clear upon reading the earliest texts by black writers in English," Henry Louis Gates Jr. wrote in his introduction to *Pioneers of the Black Atlantic*, "is that the production of literature was taken to be the central arena in which persons of African descent could establish and redefine their status within the human community" (p. 2). Autobiographies by Olaudah Equiano (1789), Frederick Douglass (1845), and Harriet Jacobs (1861) provided chronicles of individual pasts that stood for collective ones. Among Native Americans as well, such personal narratives as William Apess's *A Son of the Forest* (1829) and George Copway's *The Life, History, and Travels of Kah-ge-ga-gah-bowh* (1847) countered the tendency of the majority culture to see Indians as romantic artifacts of the past. Utilizing many of the conventions of evangelical and slave narratives, these life stories provided portraits of real lives, although stylized in a way that appealed for justice and equality.

By the time of the Civil War, history as a way of reflecting upon the world and understanding the nature of individual and collective lives was firmly entrenched in American culture.

INVENTING SCIENTIFIC HISTORY

By the late nineteenth century the character of much of American historiography began to change. Germany produced the most enduring influence on American historical scholarship in the work of Leopold von Ranke. Often called "the father of scientific history," Ranke looked to empiricism as a method, conceiving of history as a craft to be practiced with precision and care. Ranke's emphasis on the use of written documents to reconstruct the past was not original; rather, his accomplishment was to provide a methodology of the past *wie es eigentlich gewesen* (as it really was) without recourse to preconceived notions of either metaphysics or theology. This method could be put to the positivistic ends of an age increasingly enamored of the scientific approach to knowledge. Although Ranke received his doctorate in 1817 from the University of Leipzig and produced solidly documented historical works until his death almost three-quarters of a century later, it was late-nineteenth-century practitioners who latched onto his principles with a vengeance to establish the new profession of history. Through seemingly value-neutral archival research designed to uncover the facts, historians now took as their charge the study without judgment of each age as it was in itself (or as Ranke put it, as "immediate to God"). Because the kinds of documents most accessible to researchers were state papers and the detritus of prominent statesmen, the first generation of scientific historians produced works dealing mainly with the development of the state, its laws, and its relations with other powers.

This Rankean notion of history spread through a system of doctoral training pioneered in Germany in the early nineteenth century. In the United States, institutions modeled on German research universities began to flourish by the late nineteenth century. The Johns Hopkins University, organized in Baltimore in 1876, was the first, followed by the University of Chicago (1891) and Stanford University (1891). These new centers of learning educated scholars in research methods designed to produce scientific, objective results. At the same time, professional organizations made methodological links between practitioners more formal and created communities of people who agreed on what counted as legitimate knowledge in a field and what did not. The forty years after the Civil War saw the founding of the American Social Science Association (1865), the American Philological Association (1869), the Modern Language Association (1883),

the American Historical Association (1884), the American Economic Association (1885), the American Society of Church History (1888), the American Psychological Association (1892), the American Philosophical Association (1901), the American Political Science Association (1903), and the American Sociological Association (1905). They had in common a tendency to restrict the making of knowledge in their respective fields to properly trained professionals well versed in the new research techniques. Amateurs were gradually excluded (or, preferring to operate under different standard assumptions and procedures, excluded themselves) as socially legitimate makers of knowledge. Not surprisingly, by the end of the first two decades of the twentieth century, the vast majority of the members of the new professional organizations were academically trained professionals.

This regularization of knowledge in departments and professional organizations led to a steady flow of empirically based research findings in the form of monographs. Gone were the sweeping narratives of Parkman and Bancroft. In their place, historians substituted smaller studies, accretions of truth, that taken together would provide an objective picture of the past. Gone too were the amateur gentlemen scholars of times past. In their place arose a cohort of professionally trained practitioners who supported themselves, though not altogether lavishly, with the positions they could find in colleges and in the new research universities.

PROGRESSIVE HISTORY AND THE SOCIAL SCIENCES

By about 1910, a liberal minority of historians began to express doubts that such unguided fact-finding as the Rankean approach sometimes produced was likely to lead anywhere useful: not only were the painstakingly detailed monographic studies virtually unreadable, they also lacked any general principle of investigation. Those who began to articulate alternatives to the conservative model included James Harvey Robinson, instructor of a popular course in European history at Columbia University and author of *The New History* (1912); Charles A. Beard, an Indiana-born historian of socialist inclinations, who co-authored with Robinson the innovative and broadly conceived *Development of Modern Europe* (1907); and Carl Becker, Robinson's student at Columbia, whose *The History of Political Parties in the Province of New York* (1909) saw the American Revolution to be as much a matter of social and economic conflict as political and institutional continuity. Styled alternatively the "New Historians" or "Progressive Historians," these individuals and their students began to look for alliances with the new social sciences. Robinson, perhaps its most self-conscious advocate, proclaimed history a conscious instrument "to meet our daily needs," in conjunction with its sister disciplines of anthropology, economics, psychology, and sociology (in Stern, *The Varieties of History*, p. 265). This new history would have a direct and pragmatic relation to contemporary life, illuminating its problems and preparing the way for effective interventions to solve them.

Scholarship produced by New Historians emphasized approaches to history that would open up new cultural and social areas of investigation. Intended to produce a "total history," or a history of all aspects of human life and not just the political and institutional ones, the New History existed in a relatively comfortable synergy with such disciplines as economics and sociology. Certainly not all American historians took this path, but enough influential ones did to establish a large role for the social sciences in American historical discourse.

It was at this time too that historians began to contend (as did practitioners within most other disciplines) with the question of whether objective knowledge was possible. Could determinate truths ever be discovered that would have validity entirely independent of the point of view of the observer? Controversies that began in the natural sciences in the 1920s by the 1930s reached key individuals within the historical profession. Progressives like Beard and Becker came to conclude that the project of the reconstruction of the past "as it really was" was a naive and impossible project: first, because historians must always bring their values to interpretation, like it or not; and second, because one could never recover all of the past, and the very act of selection introduced the element of bias or subjectivity into the process. Progressive historicism, with its emphasis on total history, had particularly opened itself up to the charge of subjectivity through selectivity: the social historian had no obvious limits on the documents or materials to be examined. Beard's presidential address, "Written History as an Act of Faith," delivered to the American Historical Association in 1933, underlined the ethical status of the historical endeavor by differentiating it sharply from the projects designed to produce absolute certainty. Becker's address, "Everyman His Own Historian" (1931), declared that

it should be a relief to us to renounce omniscience, to recognize that every generation, our own included, will, must inevitably, understand the past and anticipate the future in the light of its own restricted experience, must inevitably play on the dead whatever tricks it finds necessary for its own peace of mind. (p. 235)

But for some it was no relief. Historians and philosophers of history such as A. O. Lovejoy and Maurice Mandelbaum sought to minimize the selectivity involved in writing good historiography to the point of insignificance. Their point was that even if subjectivity influenced in some ways the writing of history, it need not play a large or decisive role in that work. Relativism, they believed, need not make a significant impact on the work of uncovering the past.

HISTORY AND THE STRUGGLE FOR CONSENSUS

Historians writing about the history of history in the 1940s and 1950s almost to a person note the disappearance of relativism as a live issue in the period surrounding World War II and after. Peter Novick saw epistemological concerns fading in the United States because of the ascendance of a politically charged vision of the world divided between free and totalitarian societies. Instead, many historians strove for a history that was consensus oriented—that is, a history that valued commonalities rather than conflict in national experience. This view sought such commonalities in models of analysis that identified fundamental agreements in a layer of reality below surface appearances. Models involving quantitative components promised to limit serendipity in the selection of sources and wide ranges of subjectivity in their interpretation. For example, Walt Rostow, the American economic historian who later in his career would become the author of the highly influential "take-off" theory of economic development, turned to numbers as a way of making sense of the past while he was a sophomore at Yale in 1934. Rostow adopted models taken from economics to "see what happened if the machinery of economic theory was brought to bear on modern economic history" (*American History and the Social Sciences*, p. 25–26).

Rostow was not the only one of his generation to turn to models generated by the social sciences, particularly quantificatory ones, as a way of providing clear focus to historical study. One could hope through them, according to the political historian (and quantifier) Lee Benson, "to work out a methodology which prevents bias from coloring historical research" (quoted in Novick, *That Noble Dream*, p. 385). The ultimate statement of the utility of social scientific models in historical investigation was produced in the Report from the Social Science Research Council's Committee on Historiography (1954). Reasserting the claim made by the committee eight years earlier that "schemes of reference influence all written and spoken history, and that historians by conscious clarification of thought and purpose should attempt to free themselves from the 'bondage' of the subconscious, the routine, and the surreptitious," the committee urged the self-conscious adoption of social scientific models as a means to that end (p. 10). During the 1950s political and economic history in particular bore the mark of this new concern with quantification.

In the United States, social science–oriented historians also began to speak about understanding social structures as a way of giving history more "complexity." Narrative history did insufficient justice to the complexity of human affairs. Only an analytic history that paid attention to complex factors such as those examined in sociology, anthropology, and psychology would provide adequate explanation. Many historians began to call for a move away from episodic history and toward the recognition of processes and structures that had "duration in time, recognizable patterns, and a high degree of continuity" (p. 97). The history of conscious action would be counterbalanced by the history of unconscious process.

The new emphasis on social scientific models raised the question of whether Clio's allegiances ought to lie primarily with those who produced humanistic narratives of the past, concerned with human motivation and agency, or with quasi-scientific analyses of processes beyond human control. A generation of intellectual historians whose work focused on the integrity and power of human ideas such as Perry Miller and Merle Curti contrasted with those of a more social scientific orientation in advancing a humanist agenda. Scholars in the American Studies movement such as Henry Nash Smith and John William Ward tried to walk a middle ground by chronicling in their myth/symbol work versions of a collective national mind that represented the life of the group while at the same time drawing on the human realm of conscious ideas.

HISTORY AS TRANSFORMATIVE AGENT: THE END OF THE TWENTIETH CENTURY

Consensus history was short-lived. Although the impulse to bolster the authority of historical knowledge by borrowing from quasi-scientific models remained a feature of historical discourse through the end of the twentieth century, these models did not produce agreement. Far from it. The keynote of historical scholarship from the late 1960s to the end of the century was a tendency to look at conflict within human culture rather than agreement, and at conflicts rooted in disparities of power.

Historians participated in the general questioning of authority that was a hallmark of social activism in the 1960s—not only in their overt political activity, but in their scholarship as well. One of the most significant trends in historiography, beginning in the 1960s, was "history from the bottom up." Attention in the United States to the experiences of "ordinary people" resulted from borrowings from and the convergence of a number of historiographical perspectives. The *Annales* school in France, for example, had for many years used quantification and social scientific models to look at long-term trends and issues in areas such as historical demographics and economy. Consideration of structural and "longue durée" features of historical experience, possible only through aggregate statistics or painstakingly detailed case studies of communities or groups of people, began to mark historiography in both Great Britain and the United States by the late 1960s. Experiences of those who were not necessarily famous or prominent seemed to be able to teach at least as much about the past as those of the notables who had been its primary subject before.

It was not just that new models and techniques enabled historians to fill in niches that had been relatively empty before. A significant and influential minority of those who entered the academy during these years began to see the transformation of inequalities and injustice in society as a major part of the historian's task. Social activism and a radical historiography that privileged attention to those marginalized by race, gender, or class went hand in hand. The work of this minority introduced Marxist and feminist models to mainstream historical practice and emphasized the degree to which power was constructed, exercised, and perpetuated in society. At the heart of such efforts often lay explicit attempts to challenge through historical scholarship the inevitability of structures of power and social arrangements that the scholars found immoral, unethical, or unjust. History during this era retained its Rankean facade of scientific validity, with its agreed-upon procedures for producing intersubjectively valid knowledge, while at the same time becoming in many instances a form of moral or political critique.

The first major movement to engage in such a critique was New Left, or Marxist, history. The inspiration of such American Marxists as Jesse Lemisch and Eugene Genovese came from both inside and outside the historical profession. From within, they drew on the models of British Marxists such as E. P. Thompson, whose examination of class and class consciousness in *The Making of the English Working Class* (1963) combined attention to the experiences of ordinary people with an analysis of their participation in and resistance to the power structures that helped to determine their experience. More than that, the American Marxists drew attention to the historical roots of the inequities within late capitalist culture and implicitly urged conscious opposition to its more degrading aspects. A widespread climate of social ferment in the United States from the early 1960s through the mid-1970s supported a general questioning of established institutions and structures of authority and power, and this tendency crystallized in Marxist or radical history.

The upheavals of the 1960s, particularly the civil rights movement, also gave the impetus to new work in African American history, particularly work by African Americans. Carter G. Woodson, a Harvard-educated scholar marginalized by the historical profession because of his race, had founded the Association for the Study of Negro Life and History in 1915 and its *Journal of Negro History* in 1916. There followed a host of monographs on African American history, though African American historians and history remained by and large on the edges of American historical scholarship until the late 1950s. And, even then, much of the new work on the interaction of blacks and whites was produced by whites like Kenneth Stampp, Leon Litwack, and C. Vann Woodward. In 1969, however, following the ferment of the civil rights and black power movements, San Francisco State University inaugurated the first program in black studies. Such programs, designed to involve more African American students in the educational process, provided institutional sites where scholarship by, for, and about African Americans was valued and encouraged. As more African Americans entered the historical profession, and in prestigious research institutions, the wealth of scholarship produced often reflected the historian's sense of responsibility to communities outside the profession. "Black scholars should attend to the pain, meaning pay attention to, not to avoid, the pain or to live lives complaining about it," wrote Vincent Harding, an African American historian of slavery, in 1986. "Their calling is always to seek for the meaning of the pain, to minister to the pain by pointing to its possible significance" (Hine, *The State of Afro-American History,* p. 280).

Black history and Marxist-influenced social and labor history were the first areas within professional historiography to begin to produce activist scholarship that transformed traditional historical narratives. There followed in subsequent decades scholarship in ethnic studies of various sorts and in gay and lesbian (or queer) studies, each of which produced historical scholarship that situated members of the group as participants in and shapers of historical experience. "I accept the notion that there may be a community of scholars," wrote the African American historian Clarence Walker in 1996, "but then they are driven by social and cultural biases. . . . The fact of a nation with a multi-ethnic body of thinkers seems to ensure competition among interests" (Banks, *Black Intellectuals,* p. 222). Scholars often found common ground at the end of the century not in their particular subject matter, which had become stunningly diverse, but in the types of issues most often addressed: identity and power.

Among the most visible advocates of transformation, both socially and academically, were feminist thinkers. The women's studies movement, like the black studies movement, was born of the political realities of its time and was the academic counterpart of the broader women's movement. Women's studies scholarship—including much of women's history—challenged implicit assumptions about the relations of women and men within society and saw itself as a potential change agent. "Women's history has a dual goal," the historian Joan Kelly wrote in 1976, "to restore women to history and to restore our history to women" (*Women, History, and Theory,* p. 1). In the wake of the feminist movement, women came into the academy in much larger numbers than before, with women comprising nearly half of all history Ph.D. recipients by the end of the century. Their presence in the historical profession and the wealth of scholarship produced on women and gender transformed scholarship, curricula, and professional organizations. In the 1990s, the annual Berkshire Conference of Women Historians had more participants and sessions than the American Historical Association.

The scholarship influenced by identity politics was buttressed and reinforced in many quarters by poststructuralist and postmodernist theory. Originating in Europe in the work of such scholars as Jacques Derrida and Michel Foucault, these approaches to knowledge questioned the very basis of the Enlightenment project. Objective and rational knowledge was an impossibility. All discourse (a word that increasingly replaced knowledge in postmodernist scholarship, indicating the tentativeness and provisionality of all utterance) was relative, reflecting the points of departure of those who made it and the power structures that it articulated, reinforced, and sustained. Derrida in particular treated all utterance as text. He emphasized the ultimate arbitrariness of discursive constructions that were fraught with contradictions, tensions, and *aporia* or perplexity. Foucault's major contribution was to apply the insights of poststructuralism to an analysis of the past and present structures of society. Knowledge was always a social construct and a technology of power, he maintained, and its effect was always to advance certain interests and to lend authority to certain practices at the expense of others.

Although poststructuralism and postmodernism had dramatic impacts in cognate fields such as literary studies, anthropology, and philosophy, their impact on historical practice was more subtle. History as a discipline continued to resist theorization and to be seen by its practitioners mainly as craft. Still, postmodernism did reinforce and solidify trends in the profession that had their origins elsewhere. Feminist history, history with a self-consciously multicultural cast, and history colored strongly by identity concerns drew on postmodernism as a theoretical rationale. The latter's emphasis on relativism, decentering, and challenges to the authority of existing knowledge often dovetailed with social change agendas that questioned the legitimacy and the authority of existing practices. The model became itself a device for lending authority to the effort to restructure narratives, placing those previously on the fringes of history at its center.

Yet a systematic and consistent postmodernist history never emerged and indeed almost seemed a contradiction in terms. History as a professional endeavor had always sought to establish authoritative knowledge about a past that was "real"—a past which, though always viewed perspectivally, always presumably existed apart from any individual version of it. The postmodern project meant to expose the arbitrariness of all versions of reality, opening the door for the construction of alternative versions of reality by individuals or groups. One could never *re*construct the past as it was, according to this scenario, since any history was always an arbitrary construction. This assertion was one that called the disciplinary practice of history into question. Despite the fears of many traditionalists, the specter of a postmodern strain of history had not materialized by the end of the century. The closest approaches

were imaginatively fictionalized reconstructions of the past by historians such as Simon Schama (*Dead Certainties*, 1991), or versions of the past where the author explicitly located him- or herself within the process of discovery (for example Jill Lepore's *The Name of War*, 1998, or Thomas Slaughter's *The Natures of John and William Bartram*, 1996).

This is not to say that postmodern philosophy did not have an impact on history as a professional endeavor. Even if it did not become a dominant model of practice, as was the case in literary studies, it did solidify attention within the profession to silences within traditional narratives, particularly those of race, gender, and class. It would be a mistake, however, to see the "linguistic turn" (as it came to be called in the late 1980s) as responsible for the heavy attention to such matters in professional historical discourse at the end of the century. A host of factors contributed. These included the changing demographics of the historical profession, with women, members of ethic minorities, and gay and lesbian historians often addressing problems, issues, persons, or events of significance to themselves and their particular identity groups. The late capitalist tendency within American culture to emphasize the rights, the self-esteem, and the satisfaction of individuals as the ultimate end of society also led to an enhanced historical attention to the lives of persons heroic for their resistance to depersonalizing culture, and members of formerly excluded groups often assumed this role. Poststructuralism and postmodernism did provide a legacy to history, even if they did not substantially transform the profession, in the form of a language and a vocabulary for talking about experiences and power. Knowledge and understandings of the world were "constructed"; relatively powerless persons within cultures "marginalized"; particular understandings of the world held by groups in power "authorized" or "privileged."

Ironically, the move toward histories of those formerly excluded from circles of power coincided with a specialization within the profession that opened up a wide gap between popular culture and professional history. Borrowings of sophisticated social or economic models, appropriation of language generated by professional philosophers in a European context, and the use of theoretical constructions often made topics designed to empower ordinary people impenetrable to them stylistically. Nevertheless, in many ways by the end of the century, history was more popular than ever as grist for popular culture. Ken Burns's historical documentary films on *The Civil War* (1990) and *Baseball*

(1994), for example, received wide acclaim. Historical topics remained the subject of films, popular novels, and television shows, with even an entire television channel devoted solely to the presentation of history. Museum visitation was at an all-time high, and living historical museums such as Colonial Williamsburg were popular family destinations. In 1994, the Disney Corporation even proposed an amusement park based on the American historical experience, a proposition that provoked a great deal of controversy and never materialized. Still, the point was clear: history provided people with good entertainment, and it had the potential for bringing in good money.

This despite the fact that history as a subject in primary and secondary schools languished, often taught only as part of an amorphous amalgam of subjects called "social studies." In the mid-1990s, 53 percent of those assigned to teach history in American schools had neither a college major nor a minor in history. In 1994, the standards for national history generated by the National Center for History in the Schools at the University of California, Los Angeles, and funded by the National Endowment for the Humanities, provided guidelines for history in the schools designed to remedy Americans' lack of knowledge about the past. They also aimed to incorporate into historical instruction the scholarship of everyday life and of marginalized groups produced since the 1960s. Though these standards were endorsed strongly by both the American Historical Association and the Organi-zation of American Historians, popular outcry against them was strong. Many conservatives in particular saw the major trends of the historical profession in the quarter century prior to the generation of the standards as negative, neglectful of common traditions, and cavalierly disregarding of American national heroes and culture. Though there seemed to be some agreement that a more systematic attention to history in the curriculum was important, systematic proposals by professional historians based on the most current scholarship did not generate widespread popular enthusiasm.

By the beginning of the twenty-first century, many historians had begun to experiment again with narrative, at least in part in the hopes of re-connecting with a general public. In the year 2000, however, the gap between professional history and public memory remained fairly substantial—a challenge to be dealt with in the new century if history as a meaningful discipline and subject of cultural contemplation is to survive in a recognizable form. "Recent American historiography," wrote Gerda Lerner, the prominent historian of women and former president of the American Historical Association, "has reflected the breakdown of commonly held values in the assertion by previously submerged and invisible groups of their right to be heard and to have their past recorded and interpreted" (*Why History Matters*, p. 122). What role history might play in restoring common values or in arbitrating among conflicting ones remains to be seen.

See also **The Classical Vision; Moral Philosophy; Cultural Modernism** *(volume 1);* **Analytic Philosophy; Poststructuralism and Postmodernism; The Struggle for the Academy** *(volume 2);* **The Social Sciences; Education; Disciplines and Their Institutionalization; The University; Learned Societies and Professional Associations; Textbooks; Libraries; Museums; Monuments and Memorials; Memory** *(in this volume); and other articles in this section.*

BIBLIOGRAPHY

Early America and the Early National Era

Callcott, George H. *History in the United States, 1800–1860: Its Practice and Purpose.* Baltimore, 1970.

Cohen, Lester H. *The Revolutionary Histories: Contemporary Narratives of the American Revolution.* Ithaca, N.Y., 1980.

Gay, Peter. *A Loss of Mastery: Puritan Historians in Colonial America.* Berkeley, Calif., 1966.

Jameson, J. Franklin. *The History of Historical Writing in America.* 1891. Reprint, New York, 1961.

Smith, William Raymond. *History as Argument: Three Patriot Historians of the American Revolution.* The Hague, Netherlands, 1966.

History in the Romantic Era

Baym, Nina. *American Women Writers and the Work of History, 1790–1860.* New Brunswick, N.J., 1995.

Gates, Henry Louis, Jr. Introduction to *Pioneers of the Black Atlantic: Five Slave Narratives from the Enlightenment, 1772–1815,* edited by Henry Louis Gates Jr. and William L. Andrews. Washington, D.C., 1998.

Levin, David. *History as Romantic Art: Bancroft, Prescott, Motley, and Parkman.* Stanford, Calif., 1959.

Peyer, Bernd C. *The Untutor'd Mind: Indian Missionary Writers in Antebellum America.* Amherst, Mass., 1997.

Scientific History, Progressive History, and Consensus History

Becker, Carl. "Everyman His Own Historian." *American Historical Review* 39 (1932): 219–231.

Higham, John. *History: Professional Scholarship in America.* Baltimore, 1965.

Novick, Peter. *That Noble Dream: The "Objectivity Question" and the American Historical Profession.* Cambridge, Mass., 1988.

Robinson, James Harvey. "The New History." In *The Varieties of History: From Voltaire to the Present,* edited by Fritz Stern, 258–266. New York, 1972.

Rostow, W. W. "Economics." In *American History and the Social Sciences,* edited by Edward Norman Saveth, 25–26. New York, 1964. First published in *Journal of Economic History* 17 (1957): 309–323.

Social Science Research Council, Committee on Historiography. *The Social Sciences in Historical Study: A Report.* New York, 1954.

History as Transformative Agent

Appleby, Joyce, Lynn Hunt, and Margaret Jacob. *Telling the Truth about History.* New York, 1994.

Banks, William M. *Black Intellectuals: Race and Responsibility in American Life.* New York, 1996.

Fox-Genovese, Elizabeth, and Elisabeth Lasch-Quinn, eds. *Reconstructing History: The Emergence of a New Historical Society.* New York, 1999.

Harding, Vincent. "Responsibilities of the Black Scholar to the Community." In *The State of Afro-American History: Past, Present, and Future,* edited by Darlene Clark Hine, 277–284. Baton Rouge, La., 1986.

Hine, Darlene Clark, ed. *The State of Afro-American History: Past, Present, and Future.* Baton Rouge, La., 1986.

Lerner, Gerda. *Why History Matters: Life and Thought.* New York, 1997.

Kelly, Joan. *Women, History, and Theory: The Essays of Joan Kelly.* Chicago, 1984.

Scott, Joan Wallach. *Gender and the Politics of History.* New York, 1988.

Wallace, Mike. *Mickey Mouse History, and Other Essays on American Memory.* Philadelphia, 1996.

Zinsser, Judith. *History and Feminism: A Glass Half Full.* New York, 1993.

WEBERIAN APPROACHES

Alan Sica

MAX WEBER'S INTELLECTUAL LEGACY

Since his death in 1920, the name of the German sociologist Max Weber has become virtually a synonym for unsurpassed creativity and breadth in social research and theorizing, especially in the United States and Europe. His scholarly influence in other parts of the world is extensive as well, principally because he made meticulous studies of social structures and social change concerning ancient Rome, medieval Italy and Spain, ancient Israel, India, China, colonial America, and other locales, thereby perfecting "comparative analysis" of the sort that is now routinely practiced by social scientists. He developed methodological tools for social and historical research, such as the "ideal-type," and illustrated their use in dozens of applied settings, from ancient Roman land use practices to workplace behavior in a German textile mill, which he studied in person. His importance to social and political theory, comparative religion, the sociology and philosophy of law, and the philosophy and method of the social sciences refuses to diminish. Each year scholarly studies and applications of his work appear in greater numbers than before, so that in English alone nearly 3,600 items now fill the largest bibliography of Weberian analysis. In the last several years of the twentieth century a dozen monographs exclusively about Weber were published in the Anglophone world alone, mimicked by similar rates of production in Asia and Latin America.

Additionally, it is now impossible to discuss American social science without quickly coming upon the terms "rationalization," "ideal-type," "unintended consequences of social action," "charismatic authority," "the iron cage of bureaucratic life," and "the Protestant Ethic," to name only a few of Weber's neologisms. All these terms were either of his own making or greatly augmented by his work, and when tied to his "nominalistic" and "value-free" approach to social research, go a long way toward defining what modern social science has

become. In short, if there has been a "Renaissance man" in modern historical and sociological scholarship, Weber comes as close to this polymathic ideal as anyone. His way of going about historical and social research has inspired countless studies in the past, and continues to exert widespread influence in the twenty-first century.

Though it is possible to separate Weber's life from his work in considering the latter, it is not advisable, for the same "tensions" (*Spannung*) which he constantly invoked in his writing, whether regarding ancient civilizations or his own, affected his private life profoundly. Born in 1864, Weber was the eldest son of a well-known nationalist political leader who operated comfortably within the harsh realm of realpolitik, and with whom Weber experienced constant, muted struggles, for approval and understanding. But he was much closer emotionally to his devout pietist mother, for whom every question in life revolved around pressing ethical and moral demands for propriety, issues that arose in letters they exchanged even when he was still quite young. It was this potentially explosive and classical dualism of character and motivation which led, in July 1897, to Weber's now famous break with his father, never reconciled before his father's sudden death six weeks later. A more classically perfect oedipal struggle could hardly be imagined. His father, Max Sr., with a heavy patriarchal hand, had pushed his wife and Weber's summer houseguest into an untenable ethical position regarding finances and domestic living arrangements. Weber Jr., violating the unwritten law of paternal authority, ordered his father to leave his home to protect his mother's autonomy, and the resulting rupture remained permanent. The impossibility of reconciliation occasioned by Max Sr.'s death in August led directly to his son's severe encounter with mental illness that lasted in full force for five years, but lingered in its life-changing impact until Weber's own death decades later. This event and its aftermath have occasioned several monographs and many articles, since it seems to encapsulate many of the positive and negative aspects of haute bourgeois existence at the fin de siécle, and Weber's special role within that constellation of cultural forces.

Weber wrote a self-analysis of this disoriented period of his life and consulted eminent psychiatrists (notably Karl Jaspers), but the documents were destroyed during the Nazi period by his wife, Marianne Weber, for fear they would be used by Hitler's government to discredit him. What historians do know is that he experienced insomnia, neurasthenia, hysterical paralysis, almost surely impotence, and perhaps worst of all given Weber's heroic dedication to academic labors, a nearly complete inability to read, write, or lecture for months at a time. That he survived this period without recourse to suicide (which had claimed some of his close relatives) is testimony to his iron will, even in the face of complete emotional and physical collapse. The argument has been made repeatedly by Weber scholars that it was largely in response to these overwhelming sensations of powerlessness, displacement, and pervasive meaninglessness, which he darkly believed saturated and characterized modern life for many modern sophisticates, that Weber began the single largest research task ever undertaken by a solo social scientist—and carried it remarkably far toward completion in his short professional life of about twenty years.

The influence of the German philosopher Friedrich Wilhelm Nietzsche is apparent in this general point of view, but Weber's response to cultural malaise followed entirely different lines than those of his fellow countryman. He sought to answer several large, interrelated questions, and found that only through rigorous comparative research could he attempt to offer plausible answers. Karl Marx's challenge to conventional historical methods posed itself to all social scientists and historians of Weber's generation, and forced him from the outset to consider the causal relation of ideas to societal change. Among the more dogmatic of Marx's followers, it was generally held that substructural forces ("the means of production") determined in more or less direct fashion the superstructural ideologies that guided human actions, and which supplied ethical, religious, and philosophical justifications for whatever historical events actually transpired. In short, for the intellectual Left, ideas held an epiphenomenal status vis-à-vis forces that churned along in the infrastructural (political-economic) sphere. Weber repeatedly stressed his agreements that, in the last instance, economic interests do guide "consciousness," and not vice versa. Yet his unrivaled historical knowledge and his accompanying sensitivity to the subtleties of historical explanation forced him to accede to the importance of the opposing, "idealist" view. This antinomy, which irreconcilably divided Marxist from "bourgeois" social science, Weber went further in mitigating than anyone before him, specifically through his studies in the "economic ethics of world religions." This gargantuan series eventually included *The Protestant Ethic and the Spirit of Capitalism* (1905), *The Religion of China* (1916), *The Religion of India* (1916–1917), and *Ancient Judaism* (1917), plus a study along similar lines regarding Islam which Weber did not live to finish. Each of these works has been judged a prescient masterpiece by generations of scholars who have learned from them, and they continue to be read and debated even in the twenty-first century. And it was in carrying out these works that he developed his most famous analytic, substantive, and methodological approaches to the problem of world history.

Yet he had begun much differently, and with more conventional, smaller aims. He had been excellently educated in history and languages prior to university training. One of the privileges attached to being his father's son was the opportunity to eavesdrop on conversations in his home among some of the leading political and intellectual leaders in Bismarck's Germany. Household visitors and friends included Wilhelm Dilthey, Theodor Mommsen, Heinrich von Treitschke, and many family members who were academics or clergymen. At a very early age, Weber wrote essays on "Reasons for the Decline of Rome" and similarly weighty topics, surely inspired in part by some of these houseguests. It was during this impressionable period of life that he also began to understand the definitive difference between actions based on political expediency versus knowledge acquired for its own sake, something which he codified and made famous in a set of paired speeches near the end of his life, "Science as a Vocation [*Beruf*]" (1917) and "Politics as a Vocation" (1919). This distinction not only grew from his witnessing of political strategy talks held between his father and his cronies, but also, and more importantly, it systematized a fault line which always existed between his parents' conflicting worldviews (*Weltanschauungen*). For his father the possession and exercise of political power was an end in itself, but for his religiously devout mother, only unblemished ethical ends should be energetically pursued for their own sake, and no quarter was given for the use of shabby means toward some "higher" end.

Weber's mature position on these issues, expressed in the two speeches, has become canonical, not only for the social sciences, but for all modern citizens wishing to understand political power on the one hand and undistorted truth on the other. He bluntly explained that an "ethic of responsibility" in political matters made it essential for political actors sometimes to make use of unsavory techniques in order to nurture their political agendas, whereas the scholar, committed in principle to an "ethic of absolute ends," could never allow himself (or herself) this luxury of "realism" or "instrumental rationality." He followed these dictates literally and thereby sometimes appeared to contemporaries as a genuinely Quixotic figure; for example, when he refused to appear at examinations of his own students by other professors as they tried to win beginning academic positions, since he did not want to prejudice the examiners "unfairly" with his prestige as a scholar.

Yet these developments came late in a hectic professional life. He had begun much differently, and with smaller aims. He had been excellently educated in history and languages prior to university training, and had written a number of phenomenally precocious essays on ancient history and political economy which already displayed both wide learning and remarkable analytic ability. After the obligatory law degree, he published a dissertation in 1889 on early global trading companies in Italy and Spain, for the writing of which he taught himself medieval Italian and Spanish (the tedium of which caused him to complain to his mother in letters home) in order to use the proper archival materials. Quickly he then composed an habilitation on Roman agrarian history and law (1891) using an entirely fresh set of data and methods, thereby winning for himself instant esteem among two entirely separate subfields within German historiography. The titan of Roman history, Theodor Mommsen, then seventy-four, was present at Weber's well-attended defense of the habilitation, spoken in Latin as by tradition, and when everyone else had finished, asked the young Weber a penetrating question which pitted Mommsen's own view against Weber's regarding *colonia* versus *municipium*. In characteristic fashion, Weber answered directly and honestly, after which Mommsen uttered the now famous line, "But when I have to go to my grave someday, there is no one to whom I would rather say, 'Son here is my spear; it is getting too heavy for my arm' than the highly esteemed Max Weber" (Marianne Weber, p. 114). There could not have been a more auspicious beginning than this to

an academic career as a humanist, and Weber had thereby qualified himself to teach and write in two separate areas of specialization.

This precocious recognition led to his being invited to oversee a vast empirical study of agrarian workers in Prussia. Though only twenty-eight years old when this nine-hundred-page report appeared, Weber had already adopted a style of conceptualization that stayed with him throughout his career. The specific concern of the sponsoring research organization was to learn what effect Slavic workers would have upon indigenous culture east of the Elbe. The sponsor feared that a mighty influx of uneducated agrarian laborers from what is now Poland and Russia would have deleterious effects on "the German character" and, more importantly, on the political economy of the region. But Weber, wishing always to bridge structure and process to identify the altering power of ideas within political-economic constraints, focused instead on the pull that urban "individualism" exercised on traditionally inert rural workers. He combined this social-psychological perspective with treatment of grosser issues concerning the transformation of the Prussian political economy due to revised circumstances and practices of the ruling (*Junker*) class in their new, "anti-traditional" pursuit of capitalist profit. As Junker private fortunes grew, their commitment to the commonwealth naturally declined. This reordering of priorities had long been in evidence among the bourgeoisie, who meanwhile "ennobled" themselves by purchasing landed titles. Taken together, these behavior patterns imperiled Prussian social structure, and hence the nascent German nation-state, whose military strength relied heavily on Prussian cultural practices. Weber took inordinate pains to work up the report, based on thousands of questionnaires submitted to local notables, doing the tabulations by hand himself, and filling the final report with dozens of tables, which at the time was still a new technique in social research. He thrived on just this sort of phenomena, since their explanation demanded the shrewd connecting of micro (psychological) with macro (structural) events and processes. Surely without being aware of it, Weber was helping to create a new mode of social research that brought together quantified survey data and high-level cultural and political theorizing, which, once he had illustrated it in practice, became his calling card throughout the rest of his work.

Even more importantly, though, his new mode of social research prompted Weber to reflect on the antinomic relation of ethics peculiar to precapitalist life and the totally different focus of action suited to capitalist social organization. Though published much later, after his death (as part of his chaotic masterpiece, *Economy and Society*), his typology of fundamental social action originated here, as he assessed the behavior of social actors, moving from one historical structure to the next. And with this structural transformation necessarily came rearrangements of personality. According to Weber's four fundamental types of social action—roughly translated as purpose-rationality, value-rationality, emotional, and traditional—it is most difficult to move from a traditional mode of behavior, characterized in almost pure form by the mindset of agrarian peasant life, to the purpose-rationality that typifies cost-benefit analysis within a capitalist environment. Weber understood as did few others at the time that each of these widely disparate *Weltanschauungen* offered strengths and weaknesses to the people who lived "within" them. And even though capitalist social organization was pushing relentlessly to extirpate traditional and emotional modes of social action, there still lay within these spheres a reservoir of resistance to the cold logic of profit-seeking which caught Weber's interest, and which he studied through a variety of topics, particularly religiously inspired economic behavior.

What Weber explained, at a level of thoroughness and complexity which surpassed everyone before him, was that as huge structural transformations began to take hold in Europe and the United States in the late nineteenth century, these necessarily demanded reconfigurations of individual character traits. What "worked" for laborers and entrepreneurs in early capitalist society no longer met the requirements of monopoly capital as practiced in the world's industrialized nations. The description of this type of linkage, between the micro environment of interpersonal life and the macro environment of large-scale, organizational interaction, could be viewed as Weber's major contribution to social theory and general social science. Yet it is also in some ways the most difficult to understand.

Many modern practitioners see Weber as principally a "structuralist," yet the quintessential Weberian analysis of the Protestant capitalist turns more upon social-psychological then organizational dynamics. (This could be said *tout court* for his theory of "charismatic domination.") For Weber the sociologist must attend not only to character types (the traditional mode of explanation), nor only to the frozen givenness of structure à la crude Marxism, but to a heuristically satisfying synthesis of both. This he did by dividing action into the famous typology of four types previously mentioned. The

subtleties of this arrangement cannot be pursued in this essay—entire monographs have been written elucidating them—but his overall intention seems clear. To the first two types (traditional and emotional forms of "social action") he ascribed prerational, precapitalist motivation and the resulting behavior which grew out of it. However, he circumspectly noted, as was his habit in everything he wrote, that none of these four "ideal-types" of action were ever to be found within social life in pure form, and that all four types (including purpose-rationality and value-rationality) played essential roles in modern existence. In fact, they could be seen working simultaneously within certain complex socioeconomic interactions, which was all the more reason to separate them for analytic purposes while analyzing social change.

That said, however, it became clear as he wrote about the origins of capitalism, in Europe and the United States, that *Homo oeconomicus* had "evolved" to become the core of the last type of action (*zweckrationalische*). To adopt "cold rationality" in economic *and* social calculations as the predominant organizing principle of life seemed to some economists of Weber's generation (and even in the twenty-first century) as the definitive indicator that a society's members had "modernized," throwing off the yoke of their traditional past. Weber understood this simplification to be nefarious in its distortion of historical data, as well as in its meaning for the future of industrialized societies. It is undoubtedly the case that purpose-rationality served not only as an empirical reference point for comparison with the other three types of action, but also became for many investigators, noticeably less subtle than Weber, a normative goal toward which contemporary social actors and the collectivities they constituted should aspire. This is important in understanding Weber's mature work and its remarkable staying power as a guide for social and historical research. It was as a rigorous, even ascetic proponent of rationality in all social arrangements, and especially in politics, that he most fully recognized the dimensions of the irrational or nonrationalizable aspects of societal existence. To argue that he became the Sigmund Freud of *collective* nonrationality is only a minor exaggeration (while choosing to ignore Gustave Le Bon, Vilfredo Pareto, and others who, though once central to this stream of thought, have fallen into eclipse).

Weber always pursued solutions to large questions through comparative research. When he wanted to disentangle the basic ingredients of the earliest capitalist social organization in Western Europe and the United States, he turned to Asia, rapidly producing masterful analyses of Hinduism, Confucianism, Buddhism, Judaism, and unfinished notes on Islam. Although these monographs reached in scope far beyond the central question which inspired them, the main purpose was to discover why sheer business acumen, even greed, had not produced within these cultures a capitalist form of behavior and organization of the type easily identified in northern Europe after the sixteenth century. Likewise, when assessing modern bureaucracies and their tendency toward ethical and practical "universalism" (of form and content)—that is, the systematic elimination of nonrationalizable categories of knowledge, advancement, and control—he studied bureaucracies in ancient Rome, China, India, and his own Prussia. Similarly, when he wanted to learn the prospects for democracy in his own country, he looked to Russia, and wrote a series of extraordinary studies, in 1905, of the penultimate revolution prior to Bolshevik hegemony in 1917. (To do this, incidentally, he learned to read Russian in about six weeks by hiring émigré tutors then in Heidelberg, so that he could follow news reports in Russian newspapers.)

One should not conclude, however, that because he studied the course of rationalization processes through history, noting their advances and retreats with equal care, that he embraced a rational model of action as an unequivocal good. He was not a crude Benthamite, or what in modern parlance would be a "rational choice theorist." But neither was he Hegelian or Romantic enough to overvalue the "organic" prerationality of social life prior to industrialism. There were aspects of the latter—personal honor and integrity, historical sensitivity, individual sacrifice for collective well-being—that he admired strongly. But he refused to join the massive chorus of protest against modernity and its values which could then be heard from many German intellectuals (perhaps most notably the poet Stefan George, with whom Weber had several unsatisfactory meetings). Though not an evolutionist, he recognized the irresistible power of rationality as it turned from one social institution to another—to use Hegelian imagery—creating sometimes irritating uniformity and predictability where before had been some measure of uniqueness and chance. The twenty-first century's celebration of the Other and "difference" were not welcome under the regimen of wholesale rationalization which Weber so carefully documented. The logic of modernization demanded predictability in mechanical as well as personal relations, in addition to consistency of approach, record keeping, and uniform action toward a specified goal. The fruits of this regimenting were obvious to all the celebrants of Victorian, imperialistic Europe, but Weber (along with Nietzsche and a few others) also saw the debilitating nature of profound rationalization, both for the individual and social organization at large. What had begun in the eighteenth century as a "light cloak" of social reorganization had resolutely evolved into an "iron cage," and in some of Weber's most famous lines, he warned: "No one knows who will live in this cage in the future. . . . For of the last stage of this cultural development, it might well be truly said: Specialists without spirit, sensualists without heart; this nullity imagines that it has attained a level of civilization never before achieved" (*The Protestant Ethic and the Spirit of Capitalism*, p. 182). One recalls Marx's prescient remark in his *Early Philosophic Manuscripts of 1844*: "An unobjective being is a *nullity*—an *unbeing*." For both theorists, the end result of massive rationalization for the affected individuals was a condition of nonbeing in its most fundamental sense.

Certain German scholars today argue that Weber was predominantly a moral and political philosopher and that his summary essays on the sociology of religion should be viewed as his Archimedean point. Yet whether one takes his theory of bureaucracy, his analyses of classical religious dogmas and their social structures, his work on Roman and modern law, or his abstract typologies of economic, political, and legal relations as the central achievement of the man, the reason he continues to lead social theorists and researchers into new paths is his moral vision and his courage in stating it boldly. What Nietzsche did for philosophy, Weber did for social science, but without the bravado and inaccuracy of long-dismissed authors like Oswald Spengler. He continued to believe that rationality, in creating the iron cage, at the same time proved its ability to soften the bars when applied wisely. What he could not find in 1920 was the social group skilled, lucky, powerful, or faithful enough to do it.

MAX WEBER AND AMERICAN HISTORIOGRAPHY

Applications of Weber's ideas within the context of American history are as various as his substantive and theoretical innovations were far-flung. The characteristic aversion most historians feel for the merely theoretical has not prevented them from plundering Weber's ideas when it suited them, though it is clear that many more could have strengthened their studies had they known more about his methods and ideas. The unusually high quality of Weber's theorizing probably reflects the fact that his theories always grew out of direct contact with historical data and reflects also his unswerving desire to solve substantive problems by means of theoretical innovation. Popular uses of his ideas among historians have included treatments of presidents and other leaders who either exhibited "charisma" (Abraham Lincoln, both Roosevelts, and John F. Kennedy) or lacked this mysterious power over their followers (most of the remaining ones). Weber borrowed the church historian Rudolf Sohm's notion of charisma ("gift of grace") from the latter's works in church history, then broadened it to include forms of political, military, or religious leadership that draw on "irrational" sources of attraction for inflamed followers. Hundreds of studies have put to use Weber's explanation of "charismatic domination" (the locus classicus for which is in his *Economy and Society*) including those by Charles Lindholm, Olin Spencer, James L. Peacock, and Arthur Schweitzer. No one has argued that this relatively small part of Weber's oeuvre can be viewed as an unassailable analytic device, yet its widespread use among historians and other social scientists, even in diluted form, suggests its fundamental strength as a way of interpreting mass movements.

Many more historians have put to extensive use, often with carefully documented caveats, Weber's perennially fascinating "Protestant ethic thesis," which has by now occasioned several thousand publications in the international scholarly press. Though tricky to summarize, the outline of Weber's complex argument can be laid out easily. Just emerging from his five-year emotional crisis in 1903, and on the heels of a pivotally important extensive tour of the United States in 1904, Weber turned to the question of why certain cultures seemed to promote capitalist accumulation in its earliest stages, while others either put roadblocks before its progress or were indifferent to the way it changed their social landscape.

In two landmark essays published in 1904–1905 in a specialty journal, Weber offered the world what has become one of the most frequently cited (if misunderstood) texts in the history of social analysis. He held that in northern Europe, Britain, and the United States, attitudes toward work, savings, and a prohibition against conspicuous consumption (to use the American economist Thorstein Veblen's term, coined in 1900) all conspired to establish fertile ground in which capitalism could flourish.

Southern European (hence, Catholic) countries, as well as those in Asia, did not inculcate in their citizens the requisite virtues of thrift, punctuality, rational accounting, and a fear of luxurious living necessarily attached to ideas of predestination that Weber identified as essential for capitalist processes and economic organization.

Weber did not argue that sharp business practices had never existed, say, in China, India, or Italy. Rather, capital accumulation and rational accounting procedures had never found so suitable an ideological basis as that provided by Reformation theology, much of which can be summarized in the unique German concept of *Beruf* (God-given work). This was well summarized by Thomas Chalkley, an American Quaker: "We not only have Liberty to labour in Moderation, but . . . it is our duty so to do. The Farmer, the Tradesman, and the Merchant do not understand by our Lord's doctrine, that they must neglect their Calling, or grow idle in their Business, but must certainly work, and be industrious in their Calling" (Tolles, p. 56). Weber's "data" for these conclusions were largely though not exclusively the published texts of important theological writers, from Martin Luther to John Calvin to John Wesley, augmented by his insightful analysis of religion and economic life in America which he saw first-hand (reported in his "The Protestant Sects and the Spirit of Capitalism," 1906), plus his personal knowledge of Protestant businessmen in Europe. Critics have argued that he would have done better to examine "hard" economic data rather than intellectual tracts, but Weber had already in his previous work done exactly this, and believed that the tracts were legitimate guides to the Protestant worldview.

Needless to say, his arguments about this issue, particularly because he used Benjamin's Franklin's *Autobiography*, Richard Baxter's devotional literature, and other familiar writings as hallmarks of "the Protestant Ethic," have been scrutinized in extraordinary detail. And not surprisingly, when particular cases have been considered (such as the merchants of seventeenth-century Boston), what is taken to be Weber's general prescription for capitalist growth has not always held. Part of this is the result of misinterpretation of what Weber actually claimed, and partly it's because even as good as he was in handling historical data, he could not possibly anticipate every anomalous case which researchers would subsequently be able to identify, for example, Kishichi Watanabe's "The Business Ideology of Benjamin Franklin and Japanese Values of the 18th Century."

James Henretta has examined Weber's thesis carefully in terms of the colonial American case and overall found considerable support for the argument, even if modifications must be made to accommodate peculiarities of place and time. First of all, it is child's play to find quotations from early Americans, especially in Quaker Philadelphia or Puritan Massachusetts, who wrote testaments of faith that clearly support Weber's portrait of the prototypical capitalist "mentality." As Weber put it, dedication to a calling originated in "rational planning of the whole of one's life in accordance with God's will" (*Protestant Ethic*, p. 153). Bernard Bailyn had already demonstrated the persuasiveness of Weber's view in an early work by quoting sources like Joshua Scottow of Boston, who, after moving to Maine, declared in 1691 that mercantile Boston had become "a lost Town . . . We must cry out" and admit "our Leanness, our Apostasy" (*New England Merchants*, pp. 122–123). Scottow knew that unbridled capitalist activity would spell the end of religious devotion, even as devout practices enlarged capitalist fortunes. Perry Miller and Frederick Tolles were early students of this phenomenon. They recognized that "the lives of such Puritans and Quakers were not easy, for this religious doctrine created a major tension in their lives" (Henretta, *Origins of American Capitalism*, p. 38). As Puritan and Quaker fortunes grew, the strain within their religiosity, and that of their children, naturally began to tell. Existential contradictions of this type were studied by later historians of the phenomenon, such as Stephen Foster and Larzer Ziff, and even though certain clarifications of Weber's claims had to be made, the edifice of his argument held.

The most important alteration sprang from the insight that independent entrepreneurial activity generated substantial friction when set opposite the needs of community, a problem that surfaced very early, as famously documented in Bernard Bailyn's *The Apologia of Robert Keayne* (1965). Keayne, a successful merchant, was punitively fined in 1639 for having practiced what merchants now call "price-gouging," but his windy self-defense celebrates the virtues of his business practices as part and parcel of his religious devoutness. Joyce Appleby, Jack P. Greene, Karl Hertz, Daniel Howe, Gary Nash, and Michael Walzer have elaborated this modification of the Weberian picture, highlighting the economic communalism that was practiced in early American society as opposed to ruthless capitalist practices of the ideal-type. Bruce Mann extended this stream of argument from the familiar case of Boston to a Connecticut village, with par-

ticular attention to the ways "community norms of equity" controlled profit-making. Yet even with all such qualifications duly registered, John Henretta summarized his survey with this observation: "The ambiguities of the 'Protestant ethic' carried to New England by John Hull, Joshua Scottow, and John Higginson had achieved a clear definition in the 'capitalist spirit' of the founders of Waltham and Lowell, their religious and biological descendants" (p. 70). Thus, considering early American history without utilizing Weber's ideas seems at this point in scholarly developments almost inconceivable.

A number of tangent scholarly streams can be connected to the Protestant Ethic debate. Dorothy Ross has shown that "another kind of new history emerged from efforts to use modernization theory as the narrative and analytical spine of American historiography. Modernization theory descends from ideas of liberal progress that have been powerful since the eighteenth century and from the sociological theories of Ferdinand Tönnies and Max Weber" (p. 93). She elaborates this argument by pointing out that modernization theory served broad American political interests during the cold war as an antidote to revolutionary Marxism, "casting economic development as the prime motor of progress, to which were linked changes in personality and politics . . . it tended to view modernization as an integrated, deterministic process but allowed for failure, particularly through the semi-autonomous sphere of politics." Although historians were "wary of it from the start," modernization theory had a strong impact on American foreign policy and theories of global economic life, much of which owes its fundamental notions to Weber's work in his magnum opus, *Economy and Society*. Just as an understanding of imperialism as an economic or political policy is impossible to understand with reference to Marx's work, so too modernization theory must necessarily be tied to Weber's conceptualization of the global market, and the violent struggles that typically occur when "traditional" societies are confronted by those committed to "rational action," particularly along economic lines. An important contribution to this neo-Weberian research is Robert H. Wiebe's *The Search for Order, 1877–1920* (Westport, Conn., 1967), in which "island communities" are shown over time to be unwillingly amalgamated into a nation-state built on capitalist foundations. Wiebe's version of what happened undercuts naive views of bureaucratization as being seamless, untroubled processes, for in fact, "separate bureaucracies, barely joined in some areas, openly in conflict elsewhere" were more the norm than the exception as the United States was being shaped into the mid-century powerhouse it later became (Ross, p. 300).

The range of historiography regarding U.S. culture, from its colonial beginnings to its postmodern incarnation, which has benefited from Weber's ideas is much too broad and deep to cover in this essay. But a sense of this extraordinary scope might be gained by mentioning a few other studies that typify the sort of work that has entered the Weberian canon. General statements that highlight Weber's use to historiographical method include studies by William Green and H. Stuart Hughes. In the 1920s Earl Hamilton used a Weberian perspective to show how riches plundered from the Americas buttressed capitalist development in Europe. In one of many such works, Ronen Shamir in the 1990s contrasts "formal" versus "substantive" rationalization in American legal history, two Weberian notions which are as central to the history of law as "charisma" has become to studies of leadership. There is also a body of work that connects Weber as a political actor or researcher with actual United States conditions during his lifetime, including Eileen Leonard's prescient dissertation, and Jonathan Imber's late-twentieth-century reflections. The history of political theory and practice in the United States can also be easily linked with Weber's work, such as in Stephen Kalberg's studies. And John King's *The Iron of Melancholy* (1983) illustrates how a more psychohistorical vantage point can be tied fruitfully to more old-fashioned concerns with conversion processes and religious activity. Such studies are the tip of an iceberg which has not yet been thoroughly analyzed, either by American historians or by Weber scholars.

That said, however, it remains the case that American historians have been less inclined than have their colleagues in the social sciences to incorporate in their work some of Weber's more famous theoretical innovations. Whereas "rationalization processes," "legitimation crises," "the typology of social action," and fine distinctions among "class, status, and party" have suffused a great many scholarly publications within U.S. historiography, it has been others of Weber's neologisms which have seen more use. In addition to issues of charisma and the Protestant Ethic, historians have been concerned at least since the days of Charles Beard with questions surrounding objectivity in the creation of historical knowledge. Weber wrote the seminal works in this regard, delivered as two speeches to large, unsympathetic audiences: "Science as a Vocation" and "Politics as a Vocation." He insisted that the scholar's job is to tell the truth, no matter what the social costs, and that the politician's is to further the goals of his or her platform, once duly elected. Thus, they cannot be one and the same person, and he who conflates the two roles risks destroying the efficacy of both. This highly contentious argument has been subjected, like so much of Weber's writing, to merciless critique, specifically by Thomas L. Haskell and Peter Novick. Yet in any analysis of the political uses to which social knowledge is put, Weber's essays form the bedrock of all subsequent discussion. And the same can be said—and has been with increasing frequency during the last thirty years—for nearly all of Weber's theoretical work in its relation to the most ambitious forms of historical writing and thinking now being carried out in the United States and abroad.

See also **Colonial Images of Europe and America** *(volume 1);* **Working Class** *(volume 2);* **Political Economy; Twentieth-Century Economic Thought; The Social Sciences** *(in this volume); and other articles in this section.*

BIBLIOGRAPHY

Selected Works by and about Max Weber

Bendix, Reinhard. *Max Weber: An Intellectual Portrait.* New York, 1960.

Käsler, Dirk. *Max Weber: An Introduction to His Life and Work.* Cambridge, U.K., 1988.

Mitzman, Arthur. *The Iron Cage: An Historical Interpretation of Max Weber.* New York, 1971.

Scaff, Lawrence. *Fleeing the Iron Cage: Culture, Politics, and Modernity in the Thought of Max Weber.* Berkeley, Calif., 1989.

Sica, Alan. *Weber, Irrationality, and Social Order.* Berkeley, Calif., 1988.

——. *Max Weber and the New Century.* Malden, Mass., 2001. Includes a 3,600-item comprehensive bibliography of works in English pertaining to Weber.

Weber, Marianne. *Max Weber: A Biography.* Translated by Harry Zohn. New York, 1975. Reprint, with a new introduction by Guenther Roth, New Brunswick, N.J., 1988.

Weber, Max. *General Economic History.* Translated by Frank Knight. London, 1927. Reprint, New Brunswick, N.J., 1981.

——. *The Protestant Ethic and the Spirit of Capitalism.* Translated by Talcott Parsons. London, 1930. Reprint, Los Angeles, 1995.

——. *From Max Weber: Essays in Sociology.* Translated, edited, and with an introduction by Hans H. Gerth and C. Wright Mills. New York, 1946.

——. *Religion of China: Confucianism and Taoism.* Translated and edited by Hans H. Gerth. Glencoe, Ill., 1951.

——. *Ancient Judaism.* Translated and edited by Hans G. Gerth and Don Martindale. Glencoe, Ill., 1952.

——. *Economy and Society: An Outline of Interpretive Sociology.* Edited by Guenther Roth and Claus Wittich. 3 vols. New York, 1968. Reprint, Berkeley, Calif., 1978.

——. *The Agrarian Sociology of Ancient Civilizations.* Translated by R. I. Frank. London, 1976.

——. *Weber: Political Writings.* Edited by Peter Lassman and Ronald Speirs. New York, 1994.

——. *The Russian Revolutions.* Translated by Gordon C. Wells and Peter Baehr. Oxford, 1995.

Works Using Weber's Ideas

Appleby, Joyce. "Value and Society." In *Colonial British America: Essays in the New History of the Early Modern Era,* edited by Jack P. Greene and J. R. Pole. Baltimore, 1984.

——. "New Cultural Heroes in the Early National Period." In *The Culture of the Market: Historical Essays,* edited by Thomas L. Haskell and Richard F. Teichgraeber III, pp. 163–188. Cambridge, U.K., 1993.

Axelrad, Allan M. "The Protagonist of the Protestant Ethic: Max Weber's Benjamin Franklin." *Rendezvous* 13, no. 2 (1978): 45–59.

Bailyn, Bernard. *The New England Merchants in the Seventeenth Century.* Cambridge, Mass., 1955.

——. *The Apologia of Robert Keayne: The Last Will and Testament of Me, Robert Keayne, All of It Written With My Own Hands and Began by Me, MO: 6: I: 1653, Commonly Called August.* New York, 1965.

Baltzell, E. Digby. *Puritan Boston and Quaker Philadelphia: Two Protestant Ethics and the Spirit of Class Authority and Leadership.* New York, 1979.

Bier, Jesse. "Weberism, Franklin, and the Transcendental Style." *New England Quarterly* 43, no. 2 (1970): 179–192.

Buck, Robert Enoch. "Protestantism and Industrialization: An Examination of Three Alternative Models of the Relationship between Religion and Capitalism." *Review of Religious Research* 34, no. 3 (1993): 210–224.

Burke, Peter. *History and Social Theory.* Ithaca, N.Y., 1992.

Burrell, Sidney A. "Calvinism, Capitalism, and the Middle Classes: Some Afterthoughts on an Old Problem." *Journal of Modern History* 32 (1960): 132ff.

Cooke, Timothy R. "Uncommon Earnestness and Earthly Toils: Moderate Puritan Richard Baxter's Devotional Writings." *Anglican and Episcopal History* 63, no. 1 (1994): 51–72.

Diggins, John Patrick. *Thorstein Veblen: Theorist of the Leisure Class.* Princeton, N.J., 1999. Originally published as *The Bard of Savagery: Thorstein Veblen and Modern Social Theory.* New York, 1978.

Falk, Gerhard. "Old Calvin Never Died: Puritanical Rhetoric by Four American Presidents Concerning Public Welfare." In *An American Historian: Essays to Honor Selig Adler,* edited by Milton Plesur, pp. 183–190. Buffalo, N.Y., 1980.

Foster, Stephen. *Their Solitary Way: The Puritan Social Ethic in the First Century of Settlement in New England.* New Haven, Conn., 1971.

Green, William A. *History, Historians, and the Dynamics of Change.* Westport, Conn., 1993.

Greene Jack P. *Pursuits of Happiness: The Social Development of Early Modern British Colonies and the Formation of American Culture.* Chapel Hill, N.C., 1988.

Hamilton, Earl J. "American Treasure and the Rise of Capitalism (1500–1700)." *Economica* 9, no. 27 (November 1929): 338–357.

Haskell, Thomas L. *Objectivity Is Not Neutrality: Explanatory Schemes in History.* Baltimore, 1998.

Henretta, John A. "The Weber Thesis Revisited: The Protestant Ethic and the Reality of Capitalism." In *The Origins of American Capitalism: Collected Essays,* edited by John A. Henretta, pp. 35–70. Boston, 1991.

Henretta, John A., and Gregory H. Nobles. *Evolution and Revolution: American Society, 1600–1820.* Lexington, Mass., 1973.

Hertz, Karl H. "Max Weber and American Puritanism." In *Max Weber: Critical Assessments 2,* edited by Peter Hamilton, pp. 86–102. London, 1991.

Howe, Daniel Walker. "The Decline of Calvinism: An Approach to Its Study." *Comparative Studies in Society and History* 14 (1972): 317ff.

Hudson, Winthrop S. "The Weber Thesis Reexamined." *Church History* 57 (Supplement 1988): 56–67.

Hughes. H. Stuart. "The Historian and the Social Scientist." *American Historical Review* 66, no. 1 (October 1960): 20–46.

Imber, Jonathan. " 'Incredible Goings-On': Max Weber in Pennsylvania." *American Sociologist* 27, no. 4 (Winter 1996): 3–6.

Jäger, Friedrich. "Culture or Society? The Significance of Max Weber's Thought for Modern Cultural History." *History and Memory* 2, no. 2 (1991): 115–140.

Johnson, Benton. "Max Weber and American Protestantism." *Sociological Quarterly* 12, no. 4 (Autumn 1971): 473–485.

Kalberg, Stephen. "Tocqueville and Weber on the Sociological Origins of Citizenship: The Political Culture of American Democracy." *Citizenship Studies* 1, no. 2 (1997): 199–222.

King, John Owen, III. *The Iron of Melancholy: Structures of Spiritual Conversion in America from the Puritan Conscience to Victorian Neurosis.* Middletown, Conn., 1983.

Kolbenschlag, Madonna Claire. "The Protestant Ethic and Evangelical Capitalism: The Weberian Thesis Revisited." *Southern Quarterly* 14, no. 4 (1975): 287–306.

Kolko, Gabriel. "Max Weber on America: Theory and Evidence." *History and Theory* 1, no. 3 (1961): 243–260.

Leonard, Eileen. "Max Weber and America: A Study in Elective Affinity." Ph.D. diss., Fordham University, 1975.

Lindholm, Charles. *Charisma.* Cambridge, Mass., 1990.

Lucas, Rex A. "A Specification of the Weber Thesis: Plymouth Colony." *History and Theory* 10, no. 3 (1971): 318–346.

Mann, Bruce H. "Rationality, Legal Change, and Community in Connecticut, 1690–1740." *Law and Society Review* 14 (1980): 196ff.

———. *Neighbors and Strangers: Law and Community in Early Connecticut.* Chapel Hill, N.C., 1987.

Miller, Perry. *The New England Mind: From Colony to Province.* Boston, 1953.

Nash, Gary. "Social Development." In *Colonial British America: Essays in the New History of the Early Modern Era,* edited by Jack P. Greene and J. R. Pole. Baltimore, 1984.

Niebuhr, H. Richard. *The Social Sources of Denominationalism.* New York, 1929.

Novick, Peter. *That Noble Dream: The "Objectivity Question" and the American Historical Profession.* Cambridge, U.K., 1988.

Peacock, James L. "Calvinism, Community, and Charisma: Ethnographic Notes." *Comparative Social Research* 11 (1989): 227–238.

Ross, Dorothy. "The New and Newer Histories." In *Imagined Histories: American Historians Interpret the Past,* edited by A. Molho and Gordon Wood. Princeton, N.J., 1998.

Schwartz, Barry. *George Washington: The Making of an American Symbol.* New York, 1987.

———. *Abraham Lincoln and the Forge of National Memory.* Chicago, 2000.

Shamir, Ronen. "Formal and Substantive Rationality in American Law: A Weberian Perspective." *Social and Legal Studies* 2 (1993): 45–72.

Spencer, Olin. "The Oneida Community and the Instability of Charismatic Authority." *Journal of American History* 67, no. 2 (1980): 285–300.

Tolles, Frederick B. *Meeting House and Counting House: The Quaker Merchants of Colonial Philadelphia, 1682–1763.* New York, 1948.

Walzer, Michael. "Puritanism as a Revolutionary Idea." *History and Theory* 3 (1963): 59–90.

Watanabe, Kishichi. "The Business Ideology of Benjamin Franklin and Japanese Values of the 18th Century." *Business and Economic History* 17 (1988): 79–90.

Ziff, Larzer. *Puritanism in America: New Culture in a New World.* New York, 1973.

CONTRIBUTORS

Jeremy du Quesnay Adams Professor of History at Southern Methodist University. He is the author of *Patterns of Medieval Society* (1969) and *The "Populus" of Augustine and Jerome* (1971). He publishes on the intellectual and cultural history of Louisiana as well as that of medieval Europe. NEW ORLEANS

Thomas G. Alexander Professor of History at Brigham Young University. He is the author of a number of books, including *A Clash of Interests: Interior Department and Mountain West, 1863–1896* (1977), *Mormonism in Transition: A History of the Latter-day Saints, 1890–1930* (1986; 2d ed., 1996); *Things in Heaven and Earth: The Life and Times of Wilford Woodruff, A Mormon Prophet* (1991; 2d ed., 1993), and *Utah, the Right Place: The Official Centennial History* (1995; 2d ed., 1996). UTAH AND MORMONISM

Patrick Allitt Professor of History at Emory University. He is the author of *Catholic Intellectuals and Conservative Politics in America: 1950–1985* (1993), *Catholic Converts: British and American Intellectuals Turn to Rome* (1997), and numerous articles and reviews. He is the editor of *Major Problems in American Religious History* (2000). ROMAN CATHOLICS; THE NATURAL WORLD

Douglas Ambrose Associate Professor of History at Hamilton College, where he teaches early American and Southern history. He is the author of *Henry Hughes and Proslavery Thought in the Old South* (1996), "Proslavery Christianity in Early National Virginia" in *Religion and the Antebellum Debate over Slavery* (1998), and "Statism in the Old South: A Reconsideration" in *Slavery, Secession, and Southern History* (2000). SOUTHERN INTELLECTUAL LIFE

Christopher Ames Charles A. Dana Professor of English at Agnes Scott College. He teaches twentieth-century literature and film. He is the author of *Movies about the Movies: Hollywood Reflected* (1997) and is currently at work on a study of the Hollywood novel. THE WORLD ACCORDING TO HOLLYWOOD

John A. Andrew III Professor of History at Franklin and Marshall College. He is the author of four books, including *The Other Side of the Sixties: Young Americans for Freedom and the Rise of Conservative Politics* (1997) and *Lyndon Johnson and the Great Society* (1998). RESURGENT CONSERVATISM

Michael W. Apple John Bascom Professor of Curriculum and Instruction and Educational Policy Studies at the University of Wisconsin–Madison. He is the author of *Ideology and Curriculum* (1979), *Teachers and Texts* (1986), *Official Knowledge: Democratic Education in a Conservative Age* (1993), *Education and Power* (1995), *Cultural Politics and Education* (1996), *Power, Meaning, and Identity* (1999), and *Educating the "Right" Way* (forthcoming). He is the series editor of Critical Social Thought. TEXTBOOKS

Robert Avila Doctoral candidate in History at the University of California, Berkeley. He is the associate editor of volume 1 of the Emma Goldman Papers (forthcoming). ANTI-STATISM

Dale M. Bauer Professor of English and Women's Studies at the University of Kentucky. He is the author of *Feminist Dialogics* (1988) and *Edith Wharton's Brave New Politics* (1994), and of articles about feminist theory and pedagogy, American women's writing, and American film. He is the editor of *The Yellow Wallpaper* by Charlotte Perkins Gilman (1998), and coeditor of *Bakhtin, Feminism, and the Dialogic* (1991), and *The Cambridge Companion to Nineteenth-Century American Women's Writing* (2000). FICTION

Mia Bay Associate Professor of History at Rutgers University. She specializes in the history of ideas about race in nineteenth- and twentieth-century America. Her most recent publication is *The White*

Image in the Black Mind: African-American Ideas about White People 1830–1925 (2000). RACE

Susan Belasco Professor of English at the University of Nebraska, Lincoln. The author of articles and reviews on nineteenth-century American women writers, she is the editor of Margaret Fuller's *Summer on the Lakes* and Fanny Fern's *Ruth Hall.* She is the coeditor of Fuller's *"These Sad but Glorious Days": Dispatches from Europe, 1846–1850* (1991), *Periodical Literature in Nineteenth-Century America* (1995), and *Approaches to Teaching* Uncle Tom's Cabin (2000). PERIODICALS

Daniel Belgrad Assistant Professor of Humanities and American Studies at the University of South Florida. He is the author of *The Culture of Spontaneity: Improvisation and the Arts in Postwar America* (1998) and articles on mid-twentieth-century American culture and society. THE IDEAL OF SPONTANEITY; THE SOUTHWEST

Casey Nelson Blake Professor of History and Director of the American Studies program at Columbia University. He is the author of *Beloved Community: The Cultural Criticism of Randolph Bourne, Van Wyck Brooks, Waldo Frank, and Lewis Mumford* (1990) as well as other studies in U.S. intellectual and cultural history. He is currently writing a book on the politics of contemporary public art. Among other editorial positions, Blake has been editor and coeditor of the Intellectual History Newsletter. OVERVIEW: FROM THE GREAT WAR THROUGH THE GREAT DEPRESSION

Stuart M. Blumin Professor of American History at Cornell University and Director of Cornell-in-Washington. He is the author or editor of five books on American social, cultural, and political history, including *The Emergence of the Middle Class* (1989), and coauthor of *Rude Republic: Americans and Their Politics in the Nineteenth Century* (2000). THE CITY

R. F. Bogardus Professor Emeritus of American Studies at the University of Alabama. He is the author of *Pictures and Texts: Henry James, A. L. Coburn, and New Ways of Seeing in Literary Culture* (1984) and numerous articles dealing with the arts and American culture. He is the coeditor of *Literature at the Barricades* (1982). THE VISUAL ARTS

Paul Boyer Merle Curti Professor of History at the University of Wisconsin–Madison. His books include *By the Bomb's Early Light: American Thought and Culture at the Dawn of the Atomic Age* (1985) and *Promises to Keep: The United States since World War II* (2d ed., 1999). He is the coauthor of *The Enduring Vision: A History of the American People* (4th ed., 2000) and editor in chief of *The Oxford Companion to United States History* (2001). WORLD WAR AND COLD WAR

Harold Brackman Consultant on Intergroup Relations for the Museum of Tolerance in Los Angeles. His recent publications include (with Stephen H. Norwood), "Going to Bat for Jackie Robinson: The Jewish Role in Breaking Baseball's Color Line" (*Journal of Sport History,* 1999) and "A Calamity Almost beyond Comprehension: Nazi Antisemitism and the Holocaust in the Thought of W. E. B. Du Bois" (*American Jewish History,* forthcoming). AFRICAN AMERICANS

David R. Brigham Curator of American art at the Worcester Art Museum. He has written on the early national cultural history of Philadelphia, including *Public Culture in the Early Republic: Peale's Museum and Its Audience* (1995) and coauthor of *Early American Paintings in the Worcester Art Museum* (2000), a book-length online catalog. PHILADELPHIA

Thomas J. Brown Assistant Professor of History at the University of South Carolina. He is the author of *Dorothea Dix, New England Reformer* (1998) and coeditor of *Hope and Glory: Essays on the Legacy of the 54th Massachusetts Regiment.* NEW ENGLAND

Dickson D. Bruce Jr. Professor of History at the University of California, Irvine. Among his books are *And They All Sang Hallelujah: Plain-Folk Camp-Meeting Religion, 1800–1845* (1974), *Black American Writing from the Nadir: The Evolution of a Literary Tradition, 1877–1915* (1989), and *The Origins of African American Literature, 1680–1865* (forthcoming). His research interests include the history of the American South and African American literary and intellectual history. SLAVE CULTURE AND CONSCIOUSNESS

Paul Buhle Lecturer in American Civilization at Brown University. He is author of *Marxism in the United States* (1991), coeditor of *Encyclopedia of the American Left* (1990), and founder of the Oral History of the American Left archive at Tamiment Library, New York University. MARXIST APPROACHES

Martin J. Burke Associate Professor of History at the City University of New York. His research interests include eighteenth- and nineteenth-century American intellectual and cultural history, the history of religion, and the history of the social sciences. He is the author of *The Conundrum of Class: Public Discourse on the Social Order in America* (1995) and of forthcoming studies on constructions of religious identities, and on the science of politics, in the nineteenth century. SOCIAL CONSTRUCTION OF REALITY

Colin Calloway Professor of History and Native American Studies, Chair of Native American Studies, and John Sloan Dickey Third Century Professor in the Social Sciences at Dartmouth College. His books include *The American Revolution in Indian Country* (1995), *New Worlds for All: Indians, Europeans, and the Remaking of Early America* (1997), and *First Peoples: A Documentary Survey of American Indian History* (1999). He has also edited several collections of essays and documents, including *The World Turned Upside Down: Indian Voices from Early America* (1994) and *After King Philip's War: Presence and Persistence in Indian New England* (1997). He is currently working on a history of the American West before Lewis and Clark. EUROPEAN AND INDIGENOUS ENCOUNTERS

Richard Cándida Smith Associate Professor of History at the University of Michigan. He is author of *Utopia and Dissent: Art, Poetry, and Politics in California* (1995) and *Mallarmé's Children: Symbolism and the Renewal of Experience* (1999). SOUTHERN CALIFORNIA

Kenneth E. Carpenter Assistant Director (retired) for Research Resources in the Harvard University Library. He has been editor of the Harvard Library Bulletin, and is the author of *The First 350 Years of the Harvard University Library* (1986) and *Readers and Libraries: Toward a History of Libraries and Culture in America* (1986). He is currently engaged, under the auspices of the Center for the Book at the Library of Congress, in producing a history of libraries in America. LIBRARIES

Barbara G. Carson Authority on American social history and the history of the decorative arts. She is the author of *The Governor's Palace at Williamsburg* (1987) and *Ambitious Appetites: Dining Behavior and Patterns of Consumption in Federal Washington* (1990). THE MATERIAL SHAPE OF EARLY AMERICAN LIFE; THE FINE ARTS IN COLONIAL AMERICA

Clayborne Carson Professor of History and Director of the King Papers Project at Stanford University. His publications include *In Struggle: SNCC and the Black Awakening of the 1960s: A Study of the Student Nonviolent Coordinating Committee* (1981) and *Malcolm X: The FBI File* (1991). He has coedited four volumes of *The Papers of Martin Luther King, Jr.* as well as *A Knock at Midnight: Inspiration from the Great Sermons of Reverend Martin Luther King, Jr.* (1998), *The Autobiography of Martin Luther King, Jr.* (1998), and *A Call to Conscience: The Landmark Speeches of Dr. Martin Luther King, Jr.* (2001). RACE, RIGHTS, AND REFORM

Scott E. Casper Associate Professor of History at the University of Nevada, Reno. He is the author of *Constructing American Lives: Biography and Culture in Nineteenth-Century America* (1999) and numerous articles on nineteenth-century American cultural history and the history of the book. BIOGRAPHY; AUTHORSHIP, INTELLECTUAL PROPERTY, AND COPYRIGHT

Andrew R. L. Cayton Distinguished Professor of History at Miami University in Oxford, Ohio. He is the author of *The Frontier Republic: Ideology and Politics in the Ohio Country, 1780–1825* (1986) and *Frontier Indiana* (1996); coauthor of *The Midwest and the Nation: Rethinking the History of an American Religion* (1990); and coeditor of *Contact Points: American Frontiers from the Mohawk Valley to the Mississippi* (1998) and *Writing Regionally: Essays on the History of the American Midwest*. OVERVIEW: THE REVOLUTIONARY ERA AND THE EARLY REPUBLIC; THE MIDDLE WEST

Mary Kupiec Cayton Professor of History and American Studies and Director of the University Honors Program at Miami University. She is the author of *Emerson's Emergence: Self and Society in the Transformation of New England, 1800–1845* (1989) and a coeditor of the *Encyclopedia of American Social History*. She is one of the editors of the Encyclopedia. HISTORY AND THE STUDY OF THE PAST

Naomi F. Collins Consultant to cultural and higher education organizations, writer, and scholar. She has served as Executive Director of the Maryland Humanities Council and of NAFSA: Association of International Educators. She has taught at the university level and published on intellectual and cultural history and higher education. THE HUMANITIES

Joseph Conforti Professor of American and New England Studies at the University of Southern Maine. He is a specialist on New England religious history. He has published two books and numerous essays on the cultural and theological history of religion in New England, focusing on the influence of Jonathan Edwards's thought and writings. THE NEW ENGLAND THEOLOGY FROM EDWARDS TO BUSHNELL

Steven Conn Assistant Professor at Ohio State University. He is the author of *Museums and American Intellectual Life, 1876–1926* (1998) in addition to a number of articles about American culture. He is currently at work on an anthology of American writings about architecture and on a book project entitled *Encounters with History: Native Americans and the Nineteenth Century Imagination.* URBAN CULTURAL INSTITUTIONS; MUSEUMS

Terry A. Cooney Professor of History and Academic Vice President at the University of Puget Sound. His work includes *The Rise of the New York Intellectuals* (1986) and *Balancing Acts: American Thought and Culture in the 1930s* (1995). THE ARTIST AND THE INTELLECTUAL IN THE NEW DEAL

George Cotkin Professor of History at California Polytechnic State University, San Luis Obispo. He is the author of two books, *William James, Public Philosopher* (1990) and *Reluctant Modernism: American Thought and Culture, 1880–1900* (1992). He has published articles on intellectuals in postwar American culture, the photographer Robert Frank, and hypertext and postmodernism. He is working on an intellectual and cultural history of existentialism in America. OVERVIEW: WORLD WAR II AND THE 1950S

Jefferson Cowie Professor at the School of Industrial and Labor Relations at Cornell University. He is the author of *Capital Moves: RCA's Seventy-Year Quest for Cheap Labor* (1999). His other articles and essays cover topics such as deindustrialization, borderlands development, global labor rights, and popular culture. WORKING CLASS

Hamilton Cravens Professor of History, Iowa State University. He is the author of *The Triumph of Evolution: The Heredity-Environment Controversy, 1900–1941* (1988), *Before Head Start: The Iowa Station and America's Children* (1993), and more than fifty articles, chapters in books, and other pieces. He is editor or coeditor of several other books, including *Health Care Policy in Contemporary America,* co-authored with Alan I. Marcus (1997). THE SOCIAL SCIENCES; THE BEHAVIORAL AND SOCIAL SCIENCES; INTELLIGENCE AND HUMAN DIFFERENCE

Donald T. Critchlow Professor of History at St. Louis University. He is the author and editor of *Intended Consequences: Birth Control, Abortion, and the Federal Government* (1999) and editor of *The Politics of Abortion and Birth Control in Historical Perspective* (1996) and *With Us Always: Private Charity and Public Welfare* (1998). He has also written monographs on the Brookings Institution and Studebaker Corporation. He is currently working on a new book, *Moral Populism: Phyllis Schlafly and the Grassroots Crusade against Liberal Culture.* He is the founding editor of the *Journal of Public Policy.* GOVERNMENT

Paul Jerome Croce Associate Professor and Chair of American Studies at Stetson University. He is the author of *Science and Religion in the Era of William James,* volume 1: *Eclipse of Certainty, 1820–1880* (1995), and of numerous articles on the history of science and religion, on nineteenth-century American cultural and intellectual history, and on William James and his circle. SCIENCE AND RELIGION

James P. Cullen Teaches in the Expository Writing Program at Harvard University. He is author of a number of essays and books, among them *The Civil War in Popular Culture: A Reusable Past* (1995) and *Born in the U.S.A.: Bruce Springsteen and the American Tradition* (1997), and is the editor of *Popular Culture in American History* (2000). He is currently completing a study tentatively titled *Restless in the Promised Land: Catholics and the American Dream* (forthcoming). THE POPULAR ARTS

Susan Curtis Professor of History and Director of American Studies at Purdue University. She is the author of *A Consuming Faith: The Social Gospel and Modern American Culture* (1991), *Dancing to a Black Man's Tune: A Life of Scott Joplin* (1994), and *The First Black Actors on the Great White Way* (1998). OVERVIEW: 1878–1912

Melissa Dabakis Associate Professor of Art History at Kenyon College. She is the author of *Visualizing Labor in American Sculpture: Monuments, Manliness, and the Work Ethic, 1880–1935* (1999). SCULPTURE

Jay P. Dolan Professor of History at the University of Notre Dame. He has written several books on the history of American Catholicism, including *The American Catholic Experience: A History from Colonial Times to the Present* (1985). He also has written books and essays related to the history of immigration. He has served as President of both the American Catholic Historical Association and the American Society of Church History. He was the founder of the Cushwa Center for the Study of American Catholicism at Notre Dame and served as its director from 1975 to 1993. IRISH AMERICANS

Ellen Dwyer Associate Professor in the Departments of Criminal Justice and History at Indiana University. She has a long-standing research and teaching interest in nineteenth-century American reform institutions, such as prisons and mental hospitals. Her book, *Homes for the Mad: Life inside Two Nineteenth-Century Asylums* (1988), offers a social history of New York State's first asylums. She is completing a history of epilepsy in the United States. REFORM INSTITUTIONS

Richard J. Ellis Mark O. Hatfield Professor of Politics at Willamette University. His research and teaching focuses on American political culture and political development, the American presidency, and the initiative and referendum. His books include *American Political Cultures* (1993), and *The Dark Side of the Left: Illiberal Egalitarianism in America* (1998). LIBERALISM

David C. Engerman Assistant Professor of History at Brandeis University. He teaches courses on the history of American thought, American foreign relations, and American radicalism. His research interests center on the role of Russia in American intellectual and political life. RADICAL ALTERNATIVES

Sara M. Evans Distinguished McKnight University Professor of History at the University of Minnesota. She is the author of several books including *Personal Politics: The Roots of Women's Liberation in the Civil Rights Movement and The New Left* (1979) and *Born for Liberty: A History of Women in America* (1989). SECOND-WAVE FEMINISM

Betsy Fahlman Professor of American art history at Arizona State University. She has published widely in the field on Charles Demuth, John Ferguson Weir, and Guy Pène du Bois. She is currently working on a book entitled *The Government Lens:*

New Deal Photography in Arizona. AMERICAN EXPATRIATE ARTISTS ABROAD

David Farber Professor of History at the University of New Mexico. His books include *Chicago '68* (1988), *The Sixties: From Memory to History* (1994), *The Age of Great Dreams: America in the 1960s* (1994), and *The Columbia Guide to America in the Sixties* (2001). VIETNAM AS A CULTURAL CRISIS

Andrew Feffer Associate Professor of History at Union College and Director of American Studies. He is the author of *The Chicago Pragmatists and American Progressivism* (1993) and various articles. INDUSTRIALISM AND ITS CRITICS

Thomas J. Ferraro Associate Professor of English at Duke University. He is the author of *Ethnic Passages: Literary Immigrants in Twentieth-Century America* (1993), "Ethnicity and the Literary Marketplace" in *The Columbia History of the American Novel* (1991), and "Catholic Ethnicity and the Modern American Arts" in *The Italian American Heritage* (1999). He is the editor of *Catholic Lives, Contemporary America* (1997). His current work deals with the media arts, Italian American structures of feeling, and what the discipline of cultural studies has to fear. ITALIAN AMERICANS

Peter S. Field Senior Lecturer at the University of Canterbury in Christchurch, New Zealand. He is the author of *The Crisis of the Standing Order: Clerical Intellectuals and Cultural Authority in Massachussetts, 1780–1833* (1998) and *Ralph Waldo Emerson: The Nation's First Democratic Intellectual.* He is the coauthor of *The Promise and Paradox of Freedom: A History of the United States.* DEMOCRACY

Paul Finkelman Chapman Distinguished Professor of Law at the University of Tulsa College of Law. He is the author or editor of more than a dozen books, including *His Soul Goes Marching On: Responses to John Brown and the Harpers Ferry Raid* (1995), *Slavery and the Founders: Race and Liberty in the Age of Jefferson* (1997), and *Dred Scott v. Sandford: A Brief History* (1997). He is the editor in chief of *Encyclopedia of the United States in the Nineteenth Century* (2001) and the coeditor of *Macmillan Encyclopedia of World Slavery* (1998). SLAVERY AND RACE

Winfried Fluck Professor and Chair of American Culture at the John F. Kennedy Institute for North American Studies of the Freie Universität Berlin. His books include *Ästhetische Theorie und literatur-*

749

wissenschaftliche Methode (1975), *Populäre Kultur* (1979), *Theorien amerikanischer Literatur* (1987), *Inszenierte Wirklichkeit: Der amerikanische Realismus, 1865–1900* (1992) and *Das kulturelle Imaginäre: Eine Funktionsgeschichte des amerikanischen Romans, 1770–1900* (1997). REALISM IN ART AND LITERATURE

Robert S. Fogarty Professor of History at Antioch College and editor of the *Antioch Review*. He is the author of *Dictionary of American Communal and Utopian History* (1980), *The Righteous Remnant: The House of David* (1981), *All Things New: Communal and Utopian Movements 1865–1914* (1990), and *Desire and Duty at Oneida* (2000), and editor of *Special Love/Special Sex: An Oneida Community Diary* (1994). His essays have appeared in the *Times Literary Supplement, The Nation, Manoa,* and *Missouri Review*. JOURNALS OF OPINION; LITERARY REVIEWS AND "LITTLE MAGAZINES"

Kathleen Franz Assistant Professor of History and Director of the Program in Museum Studies and Historic Preservation at the University of North Carolina at Greensboro. As a historian of technology, she is particularly interested in the cultural meanings of new machines and the practice of tinkering. TECHNOLOGY

Rachelle E. Friedman Middle and upper school teacher at the Fieldston School in New York City. She earned her Ph.D. in history at the University of California, Los Angeles; her dissertation is entitled, "Writing the Wonders: Puritan Historians in Colonial New England." She has also taught at Harvard University and Milton Academy. She is interested in early American religious and intellectual history, as well as American women's history. She is currently at work on a book-length culinary history of early America. PURITANISM AS A CULTURAL AND INTELLECTUAL FORCE

Robert C. Fuller Caterpillar Professor of Religious Studies at Bradley University. He is the author of eight books, including *Americans and the Unconscious* (1986), *Religion and the Life Cycle* (1988), *Alternative Medicine and American Religious Life* (1989), *Naming the Antichrist: The History of an American Obsession* (1995), and *Stairways to Heaven: Drugs and American Religion* (2000), PSYCHOLOGY, THE MIND, AND PERSONALITY; POPULAR INTELLECTUAL MOVEMENTS, 1833–1877

Roger L. Geiger Professor and Head of the Higher Education Program at Pennsylvania State University. He has written extensively on the history of American higher education and on issues affecting research universities and academic research, including two volumes on American research universities in the twentieth century: *To Advance Knowledge* (1986) and *Research and Relevant Knowledge* (1993). He is the editor of *The American College in the Nineteenth Century* (2000). He has edited *The History of Higher Education Annual* since 1993. THE AMERICAN UNIVERSITY

Anne Ruggles Gere Professor of English and Professor of Education at the University of Michigan, where she directs the Joint Ph.D. in English and Education. Her most recent book is *Intimate Practices: Literacy and Cultural Work in U.S. Women's Clubs 1880–1920* (1997). She is currently working on a study of nineteenth-century women teachers. She is president of the National Council of Teachers of English for 2000–2001 and a member of the Modern Language Association's Delegate Assembly 1998–2002. LEARNED SOCIETIES AND PROFESSIONAL ASSOCIATIONS

William E. Gienapp Professor of History at Harvard University. He has also taught at the University of California, Berkeley, and the University of Wyoming. He is a specialist in the Civil War era and mid-nineteenth-century American politics. His book, *The Origins of the Republican Party, 1852–1856* (1987), was co-winner of the Avery O. Craven Prize. OVERVIEW: THE ANTEBELLUM, CIVIL WAR, AND RECONSTRUCTION ERAS; JACKSONIAN IDEOLOGY

Nathan Glazer Professor of Sociology and Education emeritus at Harvard University. He is coeditor of *The Public Interest;* author of *Affirmative Discrimination: Ethnic Inequality and Public Policy* (1975), *Ethnic Dilemmas, 1964–1982* (1983), *The Limits of Social Policy* (1988), and *We Are All Multiculturalists Now* (1997); and coauthor of *Beyond the Melting Pot: The Negroes, Puerto Ricans, Jews, Italians, and Irish of New York City* (1963; 2d ed., 1970). MULTICULTURALISM IN THEORY AND PRACTICE

Michael Goldman Professor of Philosophy at Miami University. He is editor of the journal *Teaching Philosophy* and has published several articles in a variety of journals on subjects ranging from philosophical pedagogy and the philosophy of education to social and political philosophy, ethics, and the philosophy of science. ANALYTIC PHILOSOPHY

Amy S. Greenberg Assistant Professor of History at the Pennsylvania State University. She is author of *Cause for Alarm: The Volunteer Fire Department in the Nineteenth-Century City* (1998) and various articles on expansionism, manhood, and urbanization in the pre-Civil War era. MANHOOD

Robert A. Gross Forrest D. Murden Jr. Professor of History and American Studies at the College of William and Mary. He is the author of *Books and Libraries in Thoreau's Concord* (1988). He is book review editor of the *William and Mary Quarterly,* chair of the Board of Advisors for the American Antiquarian Society's Program in the History of the Book in American Culture, and coeditor of the newsletter *The Book.* THE PRINT REVOLUTION

Carl J. Guarneri Professor of History at Saint Mary's College of California. He has also taught at Bates College and the University of Paris VIII. He is the author of *The Utopian Alternative: Fourierism in Nineteenth-Century America* (1991), *America Compared: American History in International Perspective* (1997), and many articles and reviews on communitarianism, comparative history, and the American Civil War. COMMUNITARIANISM

Catherine Gudis Assistant Professor of American Studies and History at the University of Oklahoma, Norman. She has edited several books on contemporary art and is coediting an anthology on business culture entitled *From Babbitt to Rabbit.* Her forthcoming book is *The Road to Consumption: Outdoor Advertising and the American Cultural Landscape.* THE DESIGN OF THE FAMILIAR

Allen C. Guelzo Dean of the Templeton Honors College at Eastern College, St. Davids, Pennsylvania. He is the author of *Edwards on the Will: A Century of American Theological Debate* (1989), *For the Union of Evangelical Christendom: The Irony of the Reformed Episcopalians, 1870–1930* (1994), *The Crisis of the American Republic: A History of the Civil War and Reconstruction* (1995), and *Abraham Lincoln: Redeemer President* (2000). SECESSION, WAR, AND UNION; WHIG IDEOLOGY; MORAL PHILOSOPHY

Ramón A. Gutiérrez Professor of Ethnic Studies and History at the University of California, San Diego. He was the founding chair of the Ethnic Studies Department and director of the Center for the Study of Race and Ethnicity. He is the author of numerous articles and books on culture and ethnicity in the southwestern United States, including *When Jesus Came, the Corn Mothers Went Away: Marriage, Sexuality, and Power in New Mexico, 1500–1846* (1991), editor of *Home Altars of Mexico* (1997), and coeditor of *Contested Eden: California before the Gold Rush* (1998). BORDERLANDS

Paul Gutjahr Assistant Professor of English, American Studies, and Religious Studies at Indiana University. He has published extensively on American religious publishing and print culture studies. In addition to numerous articles, he has also written *An American Bible: A History of the Good Book in the United States, 1777–1880* (1999) and coedited *Illuminating Letters: Essays in Typography and Literary Interpretation* (2001). BOOKS

James R. Hackney Jr. Professor of Law at Northeastern University Law School. He has written several articles tracing the intellectual history of American legal theory. He is writing a book tentatively entitled *Under Cover of Science: American Legal Theory and the Quest for Objectivity.* LAW AND THE AMERICAN MIND

Sally E. Hadden Assistant Professor of History and Law at Florida State University. She is the author of *Slave Patrols: Law and Violence in Virginia and the Carolinas* (2001). Her specialty is colonial American legal history; her current research concerns legal cultures in colonial American cities. LAW (COLONIAL)

Mark Y. Hanley Associate Professor of History at Truman State University. A specialist in antebellum religion, he is the author of *Beyond a Christian Commonwealth: The Protestant Quarrel with the American Republic, 1830–1860* (1994). EVANGELICAL THOUGHT

D. G. Hart Academic Dean and Professor of Church History at Westminster Theological Seminary, Escondido, California. He is the author of *Defending the Faith: J. Gresham Machen and the Crisis of Conservative Protestantism in Modern America* (1994) and *New Directions in American Religious History* (1997), and coeditor of *The University Gets Religion: Religious Studies and American Higher Education* (1999) and *Evangelicals and Science in Historical Perspective* (1999). EVANGELICAL PROTESTANTS

Robert E. Hawkinson Adjunct Professor of Politics and Dean of College Life at Willamette University. His research and teaching has focused on political movements and organizations, American political thought and culture, and the politics of the Pacific Northwest. LIBERALISM

Carolyn Haynes Associate Professor of Interdisciplinary Studies and Interim Associate Director of the Honors Program at Miami University. She is author of *Divine Destiny: Gender and Race in Nineteenth-Century Protestantism* (1998) and *Innovations in Interdisciplinary Teaching* (2001). DOMESTICITY AND SENTIMENTALISM

Graham Russell Hodges Professor of History at Colgate University. Among his many books and articles are *New York City Cartmen, 1667–1850* (1986), *Slavery and Freedom in the Rural North: African Americans in Monmouth County, New Jersey, 1665–1865* (1997), and *Root and Branch: African Americans in New York and East Jersey, 1613–1863* (1999). NEW YORK CITY; THOUGHT AND CULTURE IN THE FREE BLACK COMMUNITY

J. David Hoeveler Professor of History at the University of Wisconsin–Milwaukee. He is the author of *The New Humanism: A Critique of Modern America, 1900–1940* (1977), *James McCosh and the Scottish Intellectual Tradition: From Glasgow to Princeton* (1981), *Watch on the Right: Conservative Intellectuals in the Reagan Era* (1991), and *The Postmodernist Turn: American Thought and Culture in the 1970s* (1996). His forthcoming book is *The American Colonial Colleges: Intellect and Politics.* CONSERVATISM

E. Brooks Holifield Charles Howard Candler Professor of American Church History at the Candler School of Theology and the Graduate Division of Religion of Emory University in Atlanta. He is the author of books on early American culture and thought, Puritan theology, religious thought in the Old South, health and medicine in American religion, and religion and psychology in America. GOD, NATURE, AND HUMAN NATURE

James Hoopes Professor of History at Babson College. He is the author of several books dealing with American intellectual history, including *Van Wyck Brooks: In Search of American Culture* (1977), *Consciousness in New England: From Puritanism and Ideas to Psychoanalysis and Semiotic* (1989), and *Community Denied: The Wrong Turn of Pragmatic Liberalism* (1998). THE HISTORY OF IDEAS

Joel D. Howell Professor of History and of Internal Medicine at the University of Michigan. He practices medicine and has written widely on the history of medicine, focusing on late-nineteenth- and twentieth-century use of medical technology in the United States and England. His most recent book is *Technology in the Hospital: Transforming Patient Care in the Early Twentieth Century* (1995). MEDICINE

Tracey E. Hucks Assistant Professor of Religion at Haverford College and author of several articles and other short pieces on the history of African-derived religions in the United States and the Caribbean. THE BLACK CHURCH: INVISIBLE AND VISIBLE

James Hudnut-Beumler Anne Potter Wilson Professor of American Religious History and Dean of the Divinity School at Vanderbilt University. He is the author of *Looking for God in the Suburbs: The Religion of the American Dream and Its Critics, 1945–1965* (1994) and *Generous Saints: Congregations Rethinking Money and Ethics* (1999). He is working on an economic history of American Protestantism from 1750 to the present. THE CULTURE AND CRITICS OF THE SUBURB AND THE CORPORATION

R. Douglas Hurt Professor and Director of the Graduate Program in Agricultural History and Rural Studies at Iowa State University. He is the author of *American Agriculture: A Brief History* (1994) and serves as editor of *Agricultural History.* AGRARIANISM AND THE AGRARIAN IDEAL IN EARLY AMERICA

George Hutchinson Tarkington Professor of Literary Studies at Indiana University, Bloomington. He is the author of *The Ecstatic Whitman* (1986) and *The Harlem Renaissance in Black and White* (1995). THE HARLEM RENAISSANCE

Noel Ignatiev Associate Professor of History and American Studies at the Massachusetts College of Art and a fellow of the W. E. B. Du Bois Institute for Afro-American Research, Harvard University. He is the author of *How the Irish Became White* (1995) and coeditor of *Race Traitor* (1996). WHITES AND THE CONSTRUCTION OF WHITENESS

Nancy Isenberg Co-Holder of the Mary Frances Barnard Chair in Nineteenth-Century American History at the University of Tulsa. She is the author of *Sex and Citizenship in Antebellum America* (1998) and of articles in the *Journal of American History,*

American Quarterly, American Studies, and the *Nation.* GENDER

William Issel Professor of History at San Francisco State University. He is the coauthor of *San Francisco, 1865–1932: Politics, Power, and Urban Development* (1986). His articles include "Business Power and Political Culture in San Francisco" (*Journal of Urban History,* 1989), "New Deal and World War II Origins of San Francisco's Postwar Political Culture" (in *The Way We Really Were: Everyday Life in California during World War II,* 1999), and "Politics, Environmentalism and the San Francisco Freeway Revolt" (*Pacific Historical Review,* 1999). He is currently at work on a study of religion, class, and race in San Francisco from the 1930s to the 1960s. THE SAN FRANCISCO BAY AREA

Paul E. Ivey Associate Professor of Art History at the University of Arizona in Tucson. He is author of *Prayers in Stone: Christian Science Architecture in the United States, 1894–1930* (1999). His current research considers the built environment of Eastern and esoteric religions in the United States as well as the relationship of religious architecture to alternative health regimens in nineteenth- and twentieth-century America. ARCHITECTURE

David Jaffee Associate Professor of History at the City College of New York. He is the author of *People of the Wachusett: Greater New England in History and Memory, 1630–1860* (1999). He has also written a series of essays on the role of artisans and artists in the industrial transformation of the United States and is currently working on a book entitled *Craftsmen and Consumer in Early America.* THE ARTS IN THE REPUBLICAN ERA

Julie Roy Jeffrey Professor of History at Goucher College. Her publications include *The Great Silent Army of Abolitionism: Ordinary Women in the Abolitionist Movement* (1998), *Converting the West: A Biography of Narcissa Whitman* (1992), and *Frontier Women: The Trans-Mississippi West, 1840–1880* (1979; rev. ed. 1998). ANTISLAVERY

Katie N. Johnson Assistant Professor of English at Miami University. Her work has appeared in such journals as *Theater Journal* and *American Drama,* as well as in an anthology entitled *Moral Performances: Women, Theater, and American Culture 1830–1930.* Her current book project, *Sisters in Sin,* examines how representations of prostitutes on the New York

stage intersect with antiprostitution reform at the turn of the century. DRAMA

Amelia Jones Professor of Art History at the University of California, Riverside. She has written *Postmodernism and the En-Gendering of Marcel Duchamp* (1994) and *Body Art/Performing the Subject* (1998), and coedited the anthology *Performing the Body/Performing the Text* (1999); she is the author of numerous articles. She has organized exhibitions, including *Sexual Politics: Judy Chicago's Dinner Party in Feminist Art History* (1996), for which she also edited a catalog. POSTMODERNISM AND THE ARTS

Neil Jumonville William Warren Rogers Professor of History at Florida State University, where he teaches American intellectual and cultural history. He is author of *Critical Crossings: The New York Intellectuals in Postwar America* (1991) and *Henry Steele Commager: Midcentury Liberalism and the History of the Present* (1999). THE ROLE OF THE INTELLECTUAL

Johanna C. Kardux Director of American Studies and Associate Professor of English at Leiden University, the Netherlands. She is the coauthor of *Newcomers in an Old City: The American Pilgrims in Leiden, 1609–1620* and coeditor of *Connecting Cultures: The Netherlands in Five Centuries of Cultural Exchange* (1994) and *The African American Century* (forthcoming). She is the author of various articles on American and African American literature and culture. OVERVIEW: FROM THE REAGAN ERA TO THE PRESENT

Rick Kennedy professor of History at Point Loma Nazarene University in San Diego, California. His primary areas of research have been logic, science, and mathematics education. PHILOSOPHY FROM PURITANISM TO THE ENLIGHTENMENT

Tammy L. Kernodle Assistant Professor of Music at Miami University. She is considered one of the leading scholars on William Grant Still's opera *Troubled Island* and produced ground-breaking work on the religious compositions and life of jazz pianist Mary Lou Williams. She has published in various journals, including *Musical Quarterly, The Arkansas Historical Review,* and the *Journal of Musicological Research.* She is currently working on a book on Mary Lou Williams. MUSIC

Joseph F. Kett Commonwealth Professor of History at the University of Virginia. He is the author of *The Formation of the American Medical Profession* (1968), *Rites of Passage: Adolescence in America, 1790–Present* (1977), and *The Pursuit of Knowledge under Difficulties: From Self-Improvement to Adult Education in America, 1750–1990* (1994). He is the coauthor of *The Dictionary of Cultural Literacy* (1989) and *The Enduring Vision* (1989). THE CULTURE OF SELF-IMPROVEMENT

Jeanne Halgren Kilde Visiting Assistant Professor of Religious Studies at Macalester College and Director of Curricular Activities for Macalester College's Lilly Project in Work, Ethics, and Vocation. She is the author of *Church Becomes Theatre: The Transformation of Evangelical Architecture and Worship in Nineteenth-Century America* (2001) and coeditor of *American Studies: A Transnational Reader* (2001). GENDER, SOCIAL CLASS, RACE, AND MATERIAL LIFE

Bruce A. Kimball Professor of Education at the University of Rochester. He is the author of *The True Professional Ideal in America* (1992, 1995) and *Orators and Philosophers: A History of the Idea of Liberal Education* (1986, 1995). He is writing a history of case-method teaching, with the support of a Senior Fellowship from the American Council of Learned Societies. THE PROFESSIONAL IDEAL

Claus-Dieter Krohn Professor of Modern History at the University of Lüneburg, Germany. He is the editor of the yearbook *Exilforschung*. He has published numerous studies on the social and cultural history of German and on the German intellectual immigration to the United States in the twentieth century. He is the author of *Intellectuals in Exile: Refugee Scholars and the New School for Social Research* (1993). ARTISTIC, INTELLECTUAL, AND POLITICAL REFUGEES

Bruce Kuklick Nichols Professor of American History at the University of Pennsylvania. His most recent work is *Philosophy in America: An Intellectual and Cultural History* (2001). THE TRANSFORMATION OF PHILOSOPHY

Pamela Walker Laird Adjunct Associate Professor of History at the University of Colorado at Denver. In addition to numerous articles on advertising history and consumer culture, she is the author of *Advertising Progress: American Business and the Rise of Consumer Marketing* (1998). Her work continues to analyze the practices and discourses of business within its historical and cultural contexts. CONSUMERISM

Ned C. Landsman Professor of History at the State University of New York at Stony Brook. He is the author of *Scotland and Its First American Colony, 1683–1765* (1985) and *From Colonials to Provincial: American Thought and Culture, 1680–1760* (1997). He is working on *The Evangelical Enlightenment: Religion and Moral Philosophy in the Atlantic Presbyterian Community*. OVERVIEW: EARLY AMERICA

Joshua Lane Curator of furniture at Historic Deerfield, Inc. He became interested in the politics and history of cultural identity as a graduate student in American material culture at Yale University. He has taught in the American Studies Department at Miami University. RACE AS A CULTURAL CATEGORY

Anita L. Larson Visiting Assistant Professor of History at Miami University. She received her degree in history from Miami University in 1999. Her dissertation on domestic violence and homicide reflects her research interests in women and gender. She is currently working on an article focusing on how domestic violence was framed in the popular press in the 1950s. WOMEN AND FAMILY IN THE SUBURBAN AGE

Elisabeth Lasch-Quinn Associate Professor of American Social and Cultural History at Syracuse University. She is the author of *Black Neighbors: Race and the Limits of Reform in the American Settlement House Movement, 1890–1945* (1993), editor of *Women and the Common Life: Love, Marriage, and Feminism* (1997), and coeditor of *Reconstructing History* (1999). She has published numerous articles and essays and writes frequently for the *New Republic* and the *Washington Times*. FAMILY

D. L. Le Mahieu Hotchkiss Presidential Professor of History and Chairperson of the Program in Communications at Lake Forest College. He is the author of *The Mind of William Paley: A Philosopher and His Age* (1976), and *A Culture for Democracy: Mass Communications and the Cultivated Mind in Britain between the Wars* (1988). CULTURE FOR MASS AUDIENCES

Eugene E. Leach Professor of History and American Studies at Trinity College, Hartford, Connecticut. He has published in the fields of American cultural and labor history. He is an associate editor of

Encyclopedia of the United States in the Nineteenth Century. He is currently working on a book entitled *Interpreting the American Dream.* PATTERNS OF RE-FORM AND REVOLT

Diana L. Linden Visiting Assistant Professor, Department of the History of Art, University of Michigan at Ann Arbor. She is a contributor to *Common Man, Mythic Vision: The Paintings of Ben Shahn* (1998). PUBLIC MURALS

Edward T. Linenthal Edward M. Penson Professor of Religion and American Culture at the University of Wisconsin–Oshkosh. He is the author of *Symbolic Defense: The Cultural Significance of the Strategic Defense Initiative* (1989), *Sacred Ground: Americans and Their Battlefields* (1991), and *Preserving Memory: The Struggle to Create America's Holocaust Museum* (1995). He is the coeditor of *American Sacred Space* (1995), and *History Wars: The Enola Gay and Other Battles for the American Past* (1996). MONUMENTS AND MEMORIALS

Charles H. Lippy LeRoy A. Martin Distinguished Professor of Religious Studies at the University of Tennessee–Chattanooga. He is the author or editor of more than a dozen books on American religious life, including *Pluralism Comes of Age* (2000). He was a coeditor of the *Encyclopedia of the American Religious Experience.* He is currently coediting a new edition of the *Encyclopedia of Religion in the South* and writing a book on male spirituality in American culture. RELIGIOUS LIBERALISM, FUNDAMENTALISM, AND NEO-ORTHODOXY; ANGLO-AMERICAN RELIGIOUS TRADITIONS; THE RISE OF BIBLICAL CRITICISM AND CHALLENGES TO RELIGIOUS AUTHORITY

Julia E. Liss Associate Professor of History at Scripps College. She is writing a book on Franz Boas, cosmopolitanism, and the development of anthropology in the United States. ANTHROPOLOGY AND CULTURAL RELATIVISM

Ann M. Little Assistant Professor in the Department of History at the University of Dayton. She has published articles on gender in colonial America and is at work on a book manuscript, *Abraham in Arms: Gender and Power on the New England Frontier, 1620–1760.* CONFLICTING IDEALS OF COLONIAL WOMANHOOD

Karen Lucic Associate Professor of Art at Vassar College. She is the author of *At Home in Manhattan: Modern Decorative Arts, 1925 to the Depression*

(1983), *Charles Sheeler and the Cult of the Machine* (1991), and *Charles Sheeler in Doylestown: American Modernism and the Pennsylvania Tradition* (1997). She has curated numerous exhibitions and published articles on Edward Hopper, Paul Strand, Winslow Homer, Navajo weaving, and other aspects of nineteenth- and early-twentieth-century American painting, photography, and design. ANTI-MODERN DISCONTENT BETWEEN THE WARS

Molly A. McCarthy Former journalist and doctoral candidate in the History of American Civilization Program at Brandeis University. She is tracing the evolution of the diary in America, from the interleaved almanac to the Palm Pilot. ALMANACS AND EPHEMERAL LITERATURE

Wilfred M. McClay SunTrust Bank Chair of Excellence in Humanities at the University of Tennessee at Chattanooga. He is the author of *The Masterless: Self and Society in Modern America* (1994) and has received fellowship awards from the Woodrow Wilson Center, the National Endowment for the Humanities, the National Academy of Education, the Howard Foundation, and the Danforth Foundation. INDIVIDUALISM AND THE SELF

Marjorie L. McLellan Director of the graduate program in Public History at Wright State University. She is the author of *Six Generations Here: A Farm Family Remembers* (1997), a study of family, memory, and photography. PHOTOGRAPHY

Michael D. McNally Assistant Professor of History at Eastern Michigan University. He is the author of *Ojibwe Singer: Hymns, Grief, and a Native Culture in Motion* (2000). PROPHETIC NATIVE AMERICAN MOVEMENTS

John Markoff Professor of Sociology, History, and Political Science at the University of Pittsburgh. His books include *Waves of Democracy* (1996) and *The Abolition of Feudalism: Peasants, Lords, and Legislators in the French Revolution* (1996), and is the coauthor of *Revolutionary Demands: A Content Analysis of the Cahiers de Doleances of 1789* (1998). THE INTERNET AND ELECTRONIC COMMUNICATIONS

Cathy Matson Member of the History Department at the University of Delaware. She directs the Program in Early American Economy and Society at the Library Company of Philadelphia. Her most recent book is *Merchants and Empire: Trading in Colonial New York* (1998). She has embarked on a comparative study of the Delaware River valley and Hudson River valley economic regions for the era 1750 to 1820 that will encompass the consuming and producing activities of merchants and farmers during a vital economic transformation. LIBERALISM AND REPUBLICANISM; MERCANTILISM

Glenna Matthews Independent scholar affiliated with the Institute for Urban and Regional Development at the University of California, Berkeley. Her publications include *The Rise of Public Woman: Woman's Power and Woman's Place in the United States, 1630–1970* (1992) and *American Women's History: A Student Companion* (2000), which was honored jointly by the Children's Book Council and the National Council for Social Studies. WOMEN IN THE PUBLIC SPHERE, 1838–1877

Kevin Mattson Associate Director of the Walt Whitman Center for the Culture and Politics of Democracy at Rutgers University and a faculty member of the Clemente Course in the Humanities at Bard College. He is the author of *Creating a Democratic Public: The Struggle for Urban Participatory Democracy during the Progressive Era* (1998). His writings in history and social criticism have appeared in numerous publications both academic and popular. SOCIAL REFORM

Ellen Messer-Davidow Associate Professor of English at the University of Minnesota Twin Cities. She teaches in the departments of English, American Studies, Cultural Studies, and Women's Studies. Her publications include four books, most recently *Disciplining Feminism: Episodes in the Discursive Production of Social Change* (2001), special issues of journals, and several articles, all on such topics as feminist studies, academic knowledge production, and social change. THE STRUGGLE FOR THE ACADEMY

Angela Miller Associate Professor of Art History at Washington University. She is the author of *Empire of the Eye: Landscape Representation and American Cultural Politics, 1825–1875* (1993) and numerous articles on the social and cultural history of American art. PAINTING

Gwendolyn Mink Writer and and commentor. Her work focuses on democracy in the U.S. and law and social policy affecting race/gender equality. She is author of *Old Labor and New Immigrants in American Political Development* (1986), *The Wages of Motherhood* (1995), *Welfare's End* (1998), and *Hos-*

tile Environment (2000). She is the editor of *Whose Welfare?* (1999) and coeditor of *The Reader's Companion to U.S. Women's History* (1998). She has written commentaries for the *New York Times, Newsday,* the Knight Ridder News Service, and the *San Jose Mercury.* WELFARE

Siobhan Moroney Associate Professor of Politics at Lake Forest College. Her writings on the history of educational thought have been published in the *Journal of Family History and History of Education Quarterly.* She continues to work on the educational thinking in the American Early Republic. EDUCATION IN EARLY AMERICA

Michael A. Morrison Associate Professor of History at Purdue University. He is the author of *Slavery and the American West: The Eclipse of Manifest Destiny and the Coming of the Civil War* (1997). He is the editor of *The Human Tradition in Antebellum America* (2000) and the coeditor of the *Journal of the Early Republic.* EXPANSION AND EMPIRE

Paul V. Murphy Assistant Professor of History at Grand Valley State University. He is the author of *The Rebuke of History: The Southern Agrarians and American Conservative Thought* (2001). THE IDEA OF THE SOUTH

Susan E. Myers-Shirk Associate Professor of History at Middle Tennessee State University. She has taught courses in gay and lesbian history and the history of sexuality. She was a 1997–1998 Faculty Fellow of the Pew Program in Religion and American History at Yale University. Her research interests include the history of gender and sexuality, U.S. intellectual and professional culture, and U.S. Protestantism. She is currently studying post–1945 U.S. Protestant attitudes toward homosexuality. SEXUALITY; GAYS AND LESBIANS

Alan Nadel Professor of Literature and Film at Rensselaer Polytechnic Institute. He is the author of many books and articles on American literature and culture, including *Invisible Criticism: Ralph Ellison and the American Canon* (1988), *Containment Culture: American Narratives, Postmodernism, and the Atomic Age* (1995), and *Flatlining on the Field of Dreams: Cultural Narratives in the Films of President Reagan's America* (1997). FILM

Daniel A. Nathan Visiting Assistant Professor of History and American Studies at Miami University. He is the author of essays in *Aethlon: The Journal*

of *Sport Literature, American Studies, Journal of Sport History,* and *Nine: A Journal of Baseball History and Social Policy Perspectives.* THE ATHLETE AS CULTURAL ICON

John Nerone Research Professor of Communications Research and Media Studies at the University of Illinois at Urbana-Champaign and author of four books and numerous articles on the history of the media, including *Violence against the Press: Policing the Public Sphere in U.S. History* (1994). He is the coauthor of *The Form of News: Visual Culture and Newspapers in U.S. History* (2001). He is coeditor of the History of Communications series for the University of Illinois Press. JOURNALISM

David W. Noble Professor of American Studies at the University of Minnesota. He has written extensively about parallels in the narratives that white male historians, novelists, and literary critics have used to structure their scholarship. His most recent books are *The End of American History* (1985) and *The Death of a National Landscape: Bourgeois Nationalism and the Crisis of American Cultures, 1890s–1990s* (forthcoming). MYTH AND SYMBOL

Ronald L. Numbers Hilldale and William Coleman Professor of the History of Science and Medicine at the University of Wisconsin–Madison and president of the History of Science Society. He has written or edited more than two dozen books, including, most recently, *Darwinism Comes to America* (1998) and *Disseminating Darwinism* (1999). He is writing a history of science in America and coediting the eight-volume *Cambridge History of Science.* THE SCIENTIFIC IDEAL

Kathryn J. Oberdeck Associate Professor of History at the University of Illinois at Urbana-Champaign. She is the author of *The Evangelist and the Impresario: Religion, Entertainment, and Cultural Politics in America, 1884–1914* (1999) and numerous articles and reviews in journals such as *American Quarterly, Radical History Review, Gender and History, Journal of American History, American Historical Review,* and *Journal of Urban History.* She is currently at work on a project on cultural conflicts over meanings of space and place in twentieth-century America. ELITE VS. POPULAR CULTURES

Eduardo Obregón Pagán Assistant Professor of History at Williams College. He teaches courses in U.S. Latino Studies. LATINAS AND LATINOS IN THE UNITED STATES

Cecilia Elizabeth O'Leary Associate Professor of History and Co-Director of the Oral History and Community Memory Institute at California State University, Monterey Bay. She is the author of *To Die For: The Paradox of American Patriotism* (1999). She is on the editorial board of *Social Justice* and consults with the National Museum of American History. NATIONALISM AND IMPERIALISM

Peter S. Onuf Thomas Jefferson Memorial Foundation Professor of History at the University of Virginia. He is the author of many works on the history of revolutionary America and the Early Republic, including *The Origins of the Federal Republic* (1983), *Statehood and Union* (1987), and *Jefferson's Empire* (2000), and coauthor of *A Union of Interests* (1990) and *Federal Union, Modern World* (1993). FEDERALISTS AND ANTIFEDERALISTS

John Opie Author of *Nature's Nation: An Environmental History of the United States* (1998) and *Ogallala: Water for a Dry Land* (1993; 2d ed., 2000). His publications include *Energy and American Values* (1981) and *The Law of the Land: Two Hundred Years of American Farmland Policy* (1987; 1994). He was the founding editor of the professional journal *Environmental History Review* and founding president of the American Society for Environmental History. He has consulted widely in government and industry, including the President's Council on Sustainable Development and the American Association of Engineering Societies. THE DISCOVERY OF THE ENVIRONMENT

Jane H. Pease and William H. Pease Professors Emeriti at the University of Maine and Associates in History at the College of Charleston. They are coauthors of *The Web of Progress: Private Values and Public Styles in Boston and Charleston, 1828–1843* (1985), *Ladies, Women, and Wenches: Choice and Constraint in Antebellum Charleston and Boston* (1990), *James Louis Petigru: Southern Conservative, Southern Dissenter* (1995), *A Family of Women: The Carolina Petigrus in Peace and War* (1999), and other books and articles. ANTEBELLUM CHARLESTON

William Pencak Professor of American History at Pennsylvania State University. He is the author of *War, Politics, and Revolution in Provincial Massachusetts* (1981), *America's Burke: The Mind of Thomas Hutchinson* (1982), *For God and Country: The American Legion* (1989), *History, Signing In: Studies in History and Semiotics* (1993), *The Conflict* *of Law and Justice in the Icelandic Sagas* (1996), and edited numerous books in semiotics and history. He also edits the journals *Pennsylvania History* and *Explorations in Early American Culture.* He served as President of the Semiotic Society of America in 1999–2000. POSTSTRUCTURALISM AND POSTMODERNISM

Fred Pfeil Professor of English at Trinity College, Hartford, Connecticut, where he teaches in the American Studies Program. His published work includes *White Guys* (1995), a critical study of gender, race, and class in contemporary American popular culture, and *What They Tell You to Forget* (1996), a collection of short fiction. COUNTERCULTURAL VISIONS; CLASS

Christopher Phelps Assistant Professor of History at Ohio State University. He is the author of *Young Sidney Hook: Marxist and Pragmatist* (1997) and has written for *American Quarterly, Journal of American History, New Politics, Monthly Review, Against the Current, In These Times,* and other publications. SOCIALISM AND RADICAL THOUGHT; PRAGMATISM AND ITS CRITICS

Mark Poster Director of the Film Studies Program and a member of the History Department at University of California, Irvine. He is a member of the Critical Theory Institute. His recent and forthcoming books are *The Mode of Information* (1990), *The Second Media Age* (1995), *Cultural History and Postmodernity* (1997), *What Is the Matter with the Internet: A Critical Theory of Cyberspace* (2001), and *The Information Subject* in the Critical Voices Series (2001). CULTURAL STUDIES

Jack N. Rakove Coe Professor of History and American Studies and Professor of Political Science at Stanford University. He is the author, among other books, of *Original Meanings: Politics and Ideas in the Making of the Constitution* (1996), which received the Pulitzer Prize in History, and the editor of *Interpreting the Constitution: The Debate over Original Intent* (1990). CONSTITUTIONAL THOUGHT

John Louis Recchiuti Associate Professor of History at Mount Union College. DEMOCRACY

William J. Reese Professor of Educational Policy Studies and Professor of History of European Studies at the University of Wisconsin–Madison. He is a former editor of the *History of Education Quarterly* and the author of *Power and the Promise of School*

Reform: Grassroots Movements during the Progressive Era (1986) and *The Origins of the American High School* (1995). He is the coeditor of *The Social History of American Education* (1988) and the editor of *Hoosier Schools: Past and Present* (1998). EDUCATION

Andrew Chamberlin Rieser Assistant Professor of History at St. Cloud State University. He is the coeditor of *H-Ideas,* an international forum and on-line resource for scholars in the history of ideas. He is the author of numerous articles and reviews dealing with American culture, ideas, and religion since 1880, including "Secularization Reconsidered: Chautauqua and the De-Christianization of Middle-Class Authority, 1880–1920," in *Middling Sorts: Essays in the History of the American Middle Class* (2000). LYCEUMS, CHAUTAUQUAS, AND INSTITUTES FOR USEFUL KNOWLEDGE

Jon H. Roberts Professor of History at the University of Wisconsin–Stevens Point. He is the author of a number of articles and *Darwinism and the Divine in America* (1988) and coauthor of *The Sacred and the Secular University* (2000). He is currently working on a manuscript on the interaction between Christian theology and psychology in the United States. THE STRUGGLE OVER EVOLUTION

David M. Robinson Member of the English Department at Oregon State University. He is the author of the chapter on the Transcendentalists in *American Literary Scholarship* and *The Unitarians and the Universalists* (1985), *Emerson and the Conduct of Life* (1993), and *World of Relations: The Achievement of Peter Taylor* (1998). He served as Fulbright Guest Professor at the University of Heidelberg (1984–1985) and President of the Ralph Waldo Emerson Society (1998–1999). TRANSCENDENTALISM; AMERICAN ROMANTICISM

Susan Sessions Rugh Assistant Professor of History at Brigham Young University. She is the author of *Our Common Country: Family Farming, Culture, and Community in the Nineteenth Century Midwest* (forthcoming). PASTORALISM AND THE RURAL IDEAL

Randolph Paul Runyon Professor of French at Miami University; he also teaches American Studies. He is the author of *Delia Webster and the Underground Railroad* (1996), *The Taciturn Text: The Fiction of Robert Penn Warren* (1990), *The Braided Dream: Robert Penn Warren's Late Poetry* (1990), *Reading Raymond Carver* (1992), and *In La Fon-*

taine's Labyrinth: A Thread through the Fables (2000). Franco-American Cultural Encounters and Exchanges

Vivien Sandlund Assistant Professor of History at Hiram College. She teaches American women's history, African American history, and twentieth-century American history. She has published several articles on the movement for gradual slave emancipation in the early nineteenth century. She is currently writing a biography of Daniel Coker, an African American Methodist minister and missionary who emigrated to Africa in 1820 on the first ship of colonists sent by the American Colonization Society. Gender and Political Activism

Rob Schorman He has published essays on fashion and advertising in journals including *American Studies, The Historian, Dress,* and the *Journal of American Culture*. His major research interest has focused on the relationships of gender roles, mass media, and consumer culture in the late nineteenth and early twentieth centuries, particularly as these relationships illuminate the interpenetration of American culture and the American marketplace. Fashion

Susan Schulten Assistant Professor of History at the University of Denver. He is the author of *The Geographical Imagination in America, 1880–1950* (2001). Success

Judith Sealander Professor of History at Bowling Green State University. She is the author of four books, including *Private Wealth and Public Life: Foundation Philanthropy and the Re-Shaping of American Social Policy from the Progressive Era to the New Deal* (1997). She is also the editor, coauthor, or contributor to fourteen other monographs or books of essays. She is completing a book titled *Re-Inventing Childhood: Twentieth Century American State Regulation of Children's Work, Education, Health, and Welfare*. Foundations and Philanthropy

Henry D. Shapiro Emeritus Professor of History at the University of Cincinnati. A specialist in American intellectual and cultural history, he is the author of *Appalachia on Our Mind* (1978), other books and articles, and the Appalachian entries in *The Encyclopedia of Southern History* (1979) and *The Encyclopedia of Southern Culture* (1989). Appalachia

David S. Shields Professor of English at The Citadel. He is author of *Oracles of Empire* (1990) and *Civil Tongues and Polite Letters in British America* (1997). He is a contributor to *The Cambridge History of American Literature* and *The History of the Book in America*. He is editor of *Early American Literature*. Colonial Images of Europe and America; Salons, Coffeehouses, Conventicles, and Taverns

David R. Shumway Professor of English and Literary and Cultural Studies, and Director of the Center for Cultural Analysis at Carnegie Mellon University. He is the author of *Michel Foucault* (1989), *Creating American Civilization: A Genealogy of American Literature as an Academic Discipline* (1994), and numerous scholarly articles on disciplines and disciplinarity. He is the coeditor of *Knowledges: Historical and Critical Studies in Disciplinarity* (1993) and *Disciplining English* (forthcoming). Disciplines and Their Institutionalization

Alan Sica Professor of Sociology and Director of the Social Thought Program at Pennsylvania State University. He is the former editor of the journal *Sociological Theory* and the former editor and publisher of *History of Sociology*. His books include *Hermeneutics* (1984); *Weber, Irrationality, and Social Order* (1988); *Ideologies and the Corruption of Thought* (1987); *What Is Social Theory?* (1998); and *The Unknown Max Weber* (2000). Weberian Approaches; Hermeneutics and American Historiography

Susan Smulyan Asociate Professor of American Civilization at Brown University. She is the author of *Selling Radio: The Commercialization of American Broadcasting, 1920–1934* (1994). She has worked on a curriculum project for middle and high school students that resulted in a website, "Whole Cloth" (http: // www.si.edu / lemelson / centerpieces / whole_cloth). Advertising

Werner Sollors Henry B. and Anne M. Cabot Professor of English Literature, Professor of Afro-American Studies, and chair of the American Civilization Program at Harvard University. He is the author of *Neither Black nor White Yet Both: Thematic Explorations of Interracial Literature* (1997) and *Beyond Ethnicity: Consent and Descent in American Culture* (1986) and editor of *The Invention of Ethnicity* (1989), *Theories of Ethnicity* (1996), *Multilingual America* (1998), *Interracialism* (2000), *The*

Life Stories of Undistinguished Americans (2000), and *The Multilingual Anthology of American Literature* (2000). ETHNICITY: EARLY THEORIES

Timothy Spears Associate Professor of American Literature and Civilization at Middlebury College. He is the author of *100 Years on the Road: The Traveling Salesman in American Culture* (1995) and has published articles in such journals as *American Quarterly, Chicago History, Journal of Urban History,* and *Prospects: An Annual Journal of American Cultural Studies.* CHICAGO

Mark David Spence Assistant Professor of History at Knox College. He is the author of *Dispossessing the Wilderness: Indian Removal and the Making of the National Parks* (1999) and coeditor of a forthcoming collection of essays on the Lewis and Clark bicentennial. THE FRONTIER AND THE WEST

Lynn Spigel Professor of Cinema and Television at the University of Southern California. She is the author of *Make Room for TV: Television and the Family Ideal in Postwar America* (1992) and *Welcome to the Dreamhouse: Popular Media and Postwar Suburbs* (2001). She has edited numerous anthologies on film and television. TELEVISION

James Spiller Assistant Professor of History at the State University of New York College at Brockport. He is currently working on a book examining the cultural politics of U.S. space and Antarctic exploration between the late 1950s and the end of the cold war. TECHNOLOGICAL ENCLAVES

David Steigerwald Associate Professor of American History at Ohio State University, Marion. His books include *Wilsonian Idealism in America* (1994) and *The Sixties and the End of Modern America* (1994). He is at work on a multivolume study of the rise of the idea of culture in the twentieth century, the first installment of which, *The Ruse of Diversity,* is forthcoming. INTELLECTUALS AND IDEOLOGY IN GOVERNMENT

Lisa M. Steinman Kenan Professor of English and Humanities at Reed College. She is the author of *Lost Poems* (1976), *Made in America: Science, Technology, and American Modernist Poetry* (1987), *All That Comes to Light* (1989), *A Book of Other Days* (1993), and *Masters of Repetition: Poetry, Culture, and Work in Thomson, Wordsworth, Shelley, and Emerson* (1998), and numerous articles on American and British poetry. POETRY

Louise L. Stevenson Professor of History and American Studies at Franklin and Marshall College. She has written extensively on nineteenth-century cultural and intellectual life and higher education. Her books include *Scholarly Means to Evangelical Ends* (1986) and *The Victorian Homefront* (1991). She soon will complete a history of American women's everyday intellectual lives. WOMEN

Catherine McNicol Stock Associate Professor of History and Chair of the American Studies program at Connecticut College. She specializes in the history of rural America. Her writings include *Rural Radicals: From Bacon's Rebellion to the Oklahoma City Bombing* (1997) and *Main Street in Crisis: The Great Depression and Old Middle Class on the Northern Plains* (1992). POPULISM

Mark Stoll Assistant Professor at Texas Tech University. He is the author of *Protestantism, Capitalism, and Nature in America* (1997), a chapter on the cold war and American religion in *The Cold War American West, 1945–1989* (1998), and a psychological analysis of John Muir's religious beliefs in *John Muir: Life and Work.* He is currently studying the influence of religion on ideas about nature. THE TRANSFORMATION OF AMERICAN RELIGION, 1776–1838

Shannon Sullivan Assistant Professor of Philosophy and Women's Studies at the Pennsylvania State University. She is the author of *Living across and through Skins: Transactional Bodies, Pragmatism, and Feminism* (2001) and articles on continental philosophy, feminist theory, and American pragmatism. She is the review editor of the *Journal of Speculative Philosophy* and a member of the editorial board of *Teaching Philosophy.* NEW PHILOSOPHICAL DIRECTIONS

Jill Swiencicki Assistant Professor of English at California State University, Chico. Among her writings are articles that appear in *Rhetoric, the Polis, and the Global Village* (1999), *Rhetorical Education in America* (2001), and *Multiple Literacies for the 21st Century* (2001). RHETORIC; RHETORIC AND BELLES LETTRES

David Sylvan Professor of International Relations at the Graduate Institute of International Studies in Geneva, Switzerland. He has done research on U.S. foreign policy, on the changing meaning of state sovereignty, and on the historical foundations of the international system. Among his publications are books on methodology and on disciplinarity. INTERNATIONAL RELATIONS AND CONNECTIONS

Dickran Tashjian Professor of Art History at the University of California, Irvine. He is the author of *Skyscraper Primitives: Dada and the American Avant-Garde* (1975), *William Carlos Williams and the American Scene* (1978), *Joseph Cornell: Gifts of Desire* (1992), *A Boatload of Madmen: Surrealism and the American Avant-Garde* (1995), and *Man Ray: Paris/L.A.* (1996), and coauthor of *Memorials for Children of Change* (1974) and *The Machine Age in America, 1918–1941* (1986). CULTURAL MODERNISM

David Thelen Professor of History at Indiana University, Bloomington. He has written several books that explore how Americans have experienced citizenship, including *Becoming Citizens in the Age of Television* (1996). He was the editor of *Memory and American History* (1990) and coauthor of *The Presence of the Past: Popular Uses of History in American Life* (1998). MEMORY

John K. Thornton Professor of History at Millersville University. He is the author of four books, including *Africa and Africans in the Making of the Atlantic World, 1400–1800* (1998) and *The Kongolese Saint Anthony* (1998) and numerous scholarly articles. His work focuses especially on the history of central Africa and the impact of Africans and African culture on early modern Atlantic society. AFRICA AND AMERICA

Daniel P. Thurs Doctoral candidate at the University of Wisconsin–Madison. His Ph.D. dissertation concerns the definitions of science in American popular culture during the nineteenth and twentieth centuries THE SCIENTIFIC IDEAL

Linda J. Tomko Associate Professor of Dance at the University of California, Riverside. She is President of the Society of Dance History Scholars, and Co-Director of the annual Stanford University Workshop in Baroque Dance and Its Music. She is the author of *Dancing Class: Gender, Ethnicity, and Social Divides in American Dance, 1890–1920* (1999). In 1997 she won the Gertrude Lippincott Prize, awarded by SDHS, for her article "Fete Accompli" published in *Corporealities* (1996). DANCE

Derek Vaillant Assistant Professor of Communication Studies at the University of Michigan in Ann Arbor. His research interests include the social and cultural history of broadcasting, as well as the role of music in shaping identity and civic culture during the Progressive era. RADIO

Eduard van de Bilt Associate Professor of History at the universities of Leiden and Amsterdam. He is the coauthor of *Newcomers in an Old City: The American Pilgrims in Leiden,* coeditor of *The U.S. Constitution after 200 Years,* and author of various articles on U.S. intellectual and cultural history. OVERVIEW: FROM THE REAGAN ERA TO THE PRESENT

Robert C. Vitz Professor of History at Northern Kentucky University. He is the author of *The Queen and the Arts: Cultural Life in Nineteenth Century Cincinnati* (1989) and has published articles in *New York History, American Music, The Old Northwest* and *Queen City Heritage.* CINCINNATI

Steve Waksman Assistant Professor of Ethnic Studies at Bowling Green State University. He is the author of *Instruments of Desire: The Electric Guitar and the Shaping of Musical Experience* (1999) and is on the editorial board of *Popular Music and Society.* POPULAR CULTURE IN THE PUBLIC ARENA

Robert Warrior Associate Professor of English at the University of Oklahoma. He is the author of *Tribal Secrets: Recovering American Indian Intellectual Traditions* (1995) and coauthor of *Like a Hurricane: The Indian Movement from Alcatraz to Wounded Knee* (1996). NATIVE AMERICANS

John Wenzler Independent historian, Berkeley, California. He is the author of articles about the history of American political economy and *Transcendental Economics: The Quest to Harmonize Economic and Moral Law in Nineteenth-Century American Social Thought* (forthcoming). TWENTIETH-CENTURY ECONOMIC THOUGHT; POLITICAL ECONOMY

Stephen J. Whitfield Max Richter Chair in American Civilization at Brandeis University. He has also served as a Fulbright visiting professor at the Hebrew University of Jerusalem and at the Catholic University of Leuven and Louvain-la-Neuve in Belgium, and has twice served as visiting professor of American Studies at the University of Paris IV (Sorbonne). His most recent book is *In Search of American Jewish Culture* (1999). JEWS

Daniel Wickberg Assistant Professor of the History of Ideas, University of Texas at Dallas. He is the author of *The Sense of Humor: Self and Laughter in Modern America* (1998) and is working on a cultural history of the idea of sympathy in eighteenth- and nineteenth-century America. HUMANITARIANISM; GENTILITY AND MANNERS

Carolyn Williams Associate Professor of History at the University of North Florida. RACIALISM AND RACIAL UPLIFT

Peter W. Williams Distinguished Professor of Comparative Religion and American Studies, Faculty Affiliate in History, and Director of the Program in American Studies Miami University. He has held visiting appointments at Bowdoin College and Stanford University, as well as three grants from the National Endowment for the Humanities. He is the author of *Popular Religion in America* (1980), *America's Religions: Traditions and Cultures* (1989, 2001), and *Houses of God: Region, Religion, and Architecture in the United States* (1997). He is the coeditor of *Encyclopedia of the American Religious Experience* (1988, with Charles H. Lippy) and of *Encyclopedia of American Social History* (1993, with Mary Kupiec Cayton and Elliott J. Gorn). He is editor of the series Studies in Anglican History, sponsored by the Historical Society of the Episcopal Church and *Perspectives on American Religion and Culture* (1999). He served as President of the American Society of Church History in 1998 and co-chairs the North American Religions section of the American Academy of Religion. His research interests focus on the built environment and landscape of religion in America and on religion and culture in the Progressive Era. He is one of the editors of the Encyclopedia. DETROIT

Susan Ford Wiltshire Chair of the Department of Classical Studies, Vanderbilt University. Among her books are *Public and Private in Virgil's* Aeneid (1989), *Greece, Rome, and the Bill of Rights* (1992), *Seasons of Grief and Grace: A Sister's Story of AIDS* (1994), and *Athena's Disguises: Mentors in Everyday Life* (1998). She is the coauthor of *Classical Nashville: Athens of the South* (1996). In 1996 she was appointed by President Bill Clinton to a six-year term on the National Council on the Humanities. THE CLASSICAL VISION

Douglas L. Winiarski Assistant Professor of Religion at the University of Richmond. He is the author of "'Pale Blewish Lights' and A Dead Man's Groan: Tales of the Supernatural from Eighteenth-Century Plymouth, Massachusetts" (*William and Mary Quarterly*, 1998). His current research focuses on popular religion in late colonial New England. POPULAR BELIEF AND EXPRESSION

Allan M. Winkler Distinguished Professor of History at Miami University. He has also taught at Yale University and the University of Oregon and the universities of Helsinki, Amsterdam, and Nairobi. He is author of numerous books, including *Life under a Cloud: American Anxiety about the Atom* (1993) and coauthor of textbooks at both the high school and college level. OVERVIEW: THE 1960S AND 1970S

Marianne S. Wokeck Associate Professor of History at Indiana University–Purdue University Indianapolis. Her interests include the history of the North Atlantic world from 1600 to 1800, immigration and ethnicity in early America, and the history of women. She is the author of *Trade in Strangers: The Beginnings of Mass Migration to North America* (1999) and editor of *The Papers of William Penn* (1986–1987), *Lawmaking and Legislators in Pennsylvania: A Biographical Dictionary* (1991), and *The Letters of George Santayana*. GERMAN SPEAKERS

Robert Wuthnow Gerhard R. Andlinger '52 Professor of Social Sciences and Director of the Center for the Study of Religion at Princeton University. His recent books include *Loose Connections: Joining Together in America's Fragmented Communities* (1998), *After Heaven: Spirituality in America since the 1950s* (1998), and *Growing Up Religious: Christians and Jews and Their Journeys of Faith* (1999). He is currently conducting research on religion and the arts and directing a collaborative project on the public role of mainline Protestantism. ORGANIZED RELIGION

Henry Yu Assistant Professor of History and member of the faculty of the Asian American Studies Center at University of California, Los Angeles. He is the author of *Thinking Orientals: Migration, Contact, and Exoticism in Modern America* (2001) and is working on a book entitled *How Tiger Woods Lost His Stripes*. ETHNICITY AND RACE; ASIAN AMERICANS

Wilbur Zelinsky Professor Emeritus of Geography at Pennsylvania State University. His research interests include the nature of America and the many meanings of being an American. Most of his publications have dealt with cultural, social, demographic, and landscape questions set in North

America. He is the author of *The Cultural Geography of the United States* (1973; rev. ed., 1992), *Exploring the Beloved Country: Geographic Forays into American Society and Culture* (1994), and *The Enigma of Ethnicity: Another American Dilemma* (2001). NATIONALISM; REGIONALISM

INDEX

Boldface page numbers refer to the main entry on the subject. *Italic* page numbers refer to illustrations. Museums are listed under "museums," titles of musicals appear under "musicals," orchestras are listed under "orchestras," titles of radio programs appear under "radio programs," and titles of television programs appear under "television programs." Individual books, films, and paintings appear under their own proper titles.

A

A bout de souffle (Godard), **2:**89
Aaron, Daniel, **3:**661
Abbey, Edward, **2:**537, 673
   Desert Solitaire, **2:**176
   Monkey Wrench Gang, The, **2:**178
Abbey, Edwin Austin, **2:**294, 298
   Boston Public Library mural, **3:**549
Abbott, Andrew D., **2:**61
Abbott, Berenice, **2:**300, 560; **3:**474, 475
   "Changing New York," **3:**474
Abbott, Edith, **3:**46
Abbott, Grace, **1:**623; **3:**46
Abbott, Lyman, **1:**592
   as Christian evolutionist, **2:**671
   Theology of an Evolutionist, **2:**683
Abie's Irish Rose (Nichols), **3:**582
Abingdon Bible Commentary, **1:**719
abolitionism, **1:**303, 318, 356
   belief in remaking society, **2:**794
   free blacks and, **1:**334
   and labor movement, **2:**803
   and literature, **1:**276
   New England as symbol of modernization, **2:**479
   political, **1:**362
   and racial stereotypes, **2:**702
   radical, **2:**802
   reactions to, **1:**355
   as reform liberalism, **2:**756
   rhetoric of, **3:**540–541
   women and, **1:**544
abortion
   Catholics and, **2:**412
   and women's liberation groups, **2:**164
Abraham Lincoln (French), **3:**177
Abraham Lincoln (Ream), **3:**498
Abraham Lincoln (Saint-Gaudens), **3:**499
Abrogation of the Seventh Commandment by the American Churches (Ruggles), **1:**337
Absalom, Absalom! (Faulkner), **2:**502; **3:**596
abstract expressionism, **2:**7–8, 561; **3:**182, 183
   and *Origin*, **3:**320
   in San Francisco, **2:**603

abstract impressionism, **3:**490–491
   French and, **2:**90
   in painting, **3:**489–490
Abstract of a Course of Lectures on Mental and Moral Philosophy (Mahan), **2:**710
Abu-Jamal, Mumia, **2:**139
Abu-Lughod, Lila, **2:**728
Abzug, Bella, **2:**162
academe
   controversy of humanities in, **3:**156
   professionalism in, **3:**291–292
academic disciplines, **3:**217–224
   establishment of, **3:**151
   rise of, **3:**271
   and specialized learning, **3:**290
Academic Revolution, The (Jencks and Riesman), **3:**273
academics
   opposed to Vietnam, **2:**185
   refugees, **2:**3, 304–305
   support of garment strikes, **1:**619
academies, **3:**165, 189
academy, struggle for, **2:**237–251
Academy of Natural Science (Philadelphia), **2:**579, 584
Academy of Pennsylvania, **1:**59
accident law, **3:**199
accommodationism, **1:**592–593
   of black churches, **1:**233
acculturation
   of Native Americans, **1:**601
Acheson-Lilienthal Report (1946), **2:**18
Achieving Our Country (Rorty), **1:**685; **2:**201–202
Achilles in Vietnam (Shay), **1:**244
Acosta, Ivan, **2:**394
Acosta, Oscar Zeta, **2:**393
acrylics, **2:**48
Actes and Monuments of these Latter and Perillous Dayes (Foxe), **1:**48
Action for Children's Television, **3:**39
activism
   political
      and gender, **1:**543–553
   of postwar conservatism, **2:**207
   women and, **1:**438–441
Actor's Studio, **2:**562
Acts of Trade and Navigation (England), **1:**120

ACT-UP (AIDS Coalition to Unleash Power), **2:**338, 339; **3:**543
Adair, James, **1:**16
Adamesque style, **3:**445
Adamic, Louis, **3:**113–114
Adams, Abigail, **1:**132; **3:**95, 348
Adams, Ansel, **2:**537; **3:**474
   in West, **1:**645
Adams, Charles Francis, **3:**35
Adams, Eddie, **3:**476
Adams, Fred, **2:**662
Adams, Hannah, **3:**724
   Summary History of New England, **2:**478
Adams, Henry, **3:**14, 15, 643
   on Chicago, **2:**565
   Democracy, **1:**566
   Education of Henry Adams, The, **1:**569, 638
Adams, Henry Carter, **1:**522
Adams, Herbert Baxter, **3:**356
Adams, Jasper, **2:**591
Adams, Jeremy du Quesnay, *as contributor*, **2:**629–639
Adams, John, **1:**91
   Defense of the Constitutions of Government of the United States of America, **1:**239
   and democracy, **2:**743
   Dissertation on the Canon and Feudal Law, **1:**41; **2:**476
   eulogy by Webster, **1:**243
   and Federalist conservatism, **2:**764
   on fine arts, **1:**107, 260
   on free press, **1:**271
   as lawyer, **1:**131–132
   on mansion of Nicholas Boylston, **1:**161, 258
   member of American Philosophical Society, **3:**289
   portrait by Benjamin Blyth, **1:***131*
   Watts on, **3:**658
Adams, John Quincy, **1:**188, 343
   and Boylston chair of rhetoric at Harvard, **1:**283
   on monuments, **3:**559
   as orator, **3:**539
   poetry of, **3:**603
   and rhetoric, **1:**281–282
   and strong central government, **3:**300

Life of an Ordinary Woman, The
(Ellis), **3:**625
Life of Charles Brockden Brown
(Prescott), **3:**652
Life of Charlotee Brontë (Gaskell), **3:**652
Life of George Washington (Marshall),
3:722
Life of Jesus Critically Examined
(Strauss), **1:**582
Life of Johnson (Boswell), **3:**651
Lifton, Robert Jay, **3:**68
"Ligeia" (Poe), **1:**404
Light and Truth (Lewis), **1:**338
Light in August (Faulkner), **3:**596
Lightning Field, The (De Maria), **3:**183
Like Lesser Gods (Tomasi), **2:**365–366
Lilly Endowment, **3:**286
Limbaugh, Rush, **2:**244; **3:**230, 426,
524
Limerick, Patricia Nelson, **2:**489, 494
Limited Nuclear Test Ban Treaty
(1963), **2:**23
Limits to Growth, The (Forester,
Meadows and Meadows), **2:**176
limners, **1:**108, 259; **3:**173
in colonial New York City, **2:**552
Limón, José, **2:**70; **3:**627
Lin, Maya, **3:**502
Lincoln, Abraham, **1:**305
and Civil War, **1:**457–458
Cooper Institute Address of 1860,
1:48
and creation of modern centralized
state, **1:**459
evangelical tone of second inaugural
address, **1:**384
on Henry Clay, **1:**202
and reconstruction, **1:**308
revival of Clay's American System,
1:203
in sculpture, **3:**497–498, 499
and slavery, **1:**318–319; **3:**29–30
Thanksgiving and, **3:**33
Lincoln Memorial, **1:**240; **3:**440, 499,
560, 562, 572
Lind, Jenny, **2:**592; **3:**248, 470
Lindeman, Eduard, **3:**358
Lindeman, Raymond, **2:**673
Linden, Diana L., *as contributor,*
3:547–558
Lindholm, Charles, **3:**738
Lindsay, Vachel, **3:**607
influence on Hughes, **1:**663
published in *Poetry,* **3:**317
Linenthal, Edward T., *as contributor,*
3:559–566
Linked Ring, **2:**299
Linnaeus, Carolus (Karl von Linne)
General System of Nature, **1:**149
and varieties of human beings,
3:125
Linton, Ralph, **2:**726
Linwoods, The (Sedgwick), **3:**590
Lion of the West, The (play), **3:**578

Lippard, George, **3:**242, 591
Lippard, Lucy R., **3:**555
Lippincott, J. Gordon, **2:**50
Lippincott's Magazine, **3:**410
Lippmann, Walter, **1:**520, 610, 624,
683
Bourne on, **2:**805
Drift and Mastery
and democracy, **2:**749
influence of Freud on, **1:**521
influence on Lindeman, **3:**358
and international relations, **2:**785
in the *Masses,* **1:**690
and the *New Republic,* **3:**399
Public Opinion, **3:**423–424
Lippy, Charles H., *as contributor,*
1:77–85, 581–588, 713–721
Lipsitz, George, **2:**437; **3:**572, 690, 691
Lipstick on Caterpillar Tracks
(Oldenburg), **3:**184
Lips Together, Teeth Apart (McNally),
3:586
Lipsyte, Robert, **1:**724
Lish, Gordon
published in *Antioch Review,* **3:**319
and *The Quarterly,* **3:**321
Liss, Julia E., *as contributor,*
2:721–731
*Listen Up: The Many Lives of Quincy
Jones* (film), **2:**289
literacy
among slaves, **1:**324
in antebellum South, **1:**474
in colonial era, **2:**552; **3:**187, 407
nineteenth century, **3:**409
Puritans and, **2:**474
Literary and Philosophical Society
(Charleston), **2:**588, 590
Literary and Philosophical Society
(New York City), **2:**553
literary criticism, Marxist, **1:**695
literary journals. *See* journals: literary
literary piracy, **1:**274–275
literary reviews, **3:317–322**
literary salons. *See* salons
literature. *See also* fiction; novels;
poetry
abolitionist, **1:**276
American influences on French
writers, **2:**85–86
in antebellum South, **1:**478
antislavery, **1:**405–406
Asian American, **2:**316
call for a national American
literature, **3:**590
Chicago and, **2:**569
Chicano, **2:**392–393
in Cincinnati, **2:**622
Cuban, **2:**394
dialect writers, **1:**499
ephemeral, **3:363–368**
French influence on American
writers, **2:**87–88
and frontier, **2:**492

Gilded Age, **1:**499
Harlem Renaissance, **1:**662–664;
2:282
impact of Vietnam war on, **2:**118
Knickerbocker school of writing,
2:553
Latinos, **2:**392–395
local color, **1:**499, 568; **2:**467
and the Middle West, **2:**526
Native American, **2:**403
naturalists, **1:**499
in New Orleans, **2:**631–633
French, **2:**631
as part of humanities, **3:**152
pastoralism and, **2:**454
postmodernism in, **2:**226
postwar fiction, **2:**7
proletarian movement, **1:**695
Puerto Rican, **2:**393–394
Puritan influence on, **1:**47–48
and racial relations, **2:**129
realism in, **1:565–572,** 566–570
regional movements
and pastoralism, **2:**455
in southern California, **2:**646
short stories, **3:**321, 590
of Fitzgerald, **3:**596
of southern renaissance, **2:**500, 501
spontaneity in, **2:**65
and the West, **2:**487
Literature and the American College
(Babbitt), **2:**765
lithographs, **1:**267
and western landscape, **2:**492
Little, Ann M., *as contributor,* **1:**137–
145
Little Bighorn Battlefield National
Monument, **3:**561–562, *561*
Little Big Man (film), **2:**116
Little Caesar (film), **1:**654
Littlefield, Catherine, **3:**628
Little Foxes, The (Hellman), **3:**582
Little Galleries of the Photo-Secession
(291), **1:**629
Little Renaissance, **3:**606
Little Review (magazine), **2:**300; **3:**317,
607
Little Richard, **2:**10, 11
Little Theater movement, **3:**581
Litwack, Leon, **2:**701
Litz, Katherine, **2:**70
Livermore, Mary A., **1:**437; **3:**354
Lives of the Poets (Johnson), **3:**651
Living Newspapers, **1:**708
"Living on a Lifeboat" (Hardin), **2:**176
Livingston, William, **2:**552; **3:**268, 351
Living Theatre, **2:**70, 72, 562; **3:**584
Living the Good Life (Nearing), **2:**457
Living Wage, A (Ryan), **2:**409
Llewellyn Park, New Jersey, **3:**450
Lloyd, Barbara, **3:**629
Lloyd, Henry Demarest, **2:**803; **3:**51
Wealth against Commonwealth,
1:498